CASES AND MATERIALS ON

CONSTITUTIONAL & ADMINISTRATIVE LAW

CASES AND MATERIALS ON

CONSTITUTIONAL & ADMINISTRATIVE LAW

Fourth Edition

Michael J Allen, LLB, LLM, Barrister

Brian Thompson, LLB, MLitt

BLACKSTONE PRESS LIMITED

First published in Great Britain 1990 by Blackstone Press Limited,
9–15 Aldine Street, London W12 8AW. Telephone 0181-740 2277

Second Edition 1992
Reprinted 1993
Third Edition 1994
Reprinted 1995
Fourth Edition 1996

ISBN: 1 85431 554 4

British Library Cataloguing in Publication Data
A CIP catalogue record for this book is available from the British Library

Typeset by Style Photosetting Ltd, Mayfield, East Sussex
Printed by Ashford Colour Press, Gosport, Hampshire

CONTENTS

PREFACE

This edition comes two years after the previous edition but despite the short space of time involved there has been a lot of activity in Parliament, the courts and elsewhere which is of significance. Most chapters have had new material added and several have been subject to major revisions. The chapter which has undergone the greatest change is Chapter Six, Parliamentary Government At Work. Some of its new extracts concern ministerial responsibility and accountablity, including material from the Scott Report on 'Arms to Iraq', and a new section on Standards in Public Life, which draws on both the Nolan Committee's recommendations and the response of the House of Commons. The chapter on Rule of Law features new material on judicial independence in the form of correspondence between Sir John Wood, former President of the Employment Appeal Tribunal and the Lord Chancellor, Lord Mackay of Clashfern and extensive extracts from the subsequent debate in the House of Lords which focused on this correspondence. Discussions on parliamentary supremacy and the rule of law by two distinguished judges writing extra-judicially, Sir John Laws and Lord Woolf of Barnes, are also included.

Some of the important cases from which extracts have been taken are *R* v *Horseferry Road Magistrates' Court, ex parte Bennett* in the House of Lords on the rule of law, *R* v *Central Independent Television plc* in the Court of Appeal and *Goodwin* v *United Kingdom* in the European Court of Human Rights on press freedom, and *R* v *Ministry of Defence, ex parte Smith* in the Divisional Court and Court of Appeal on *Wednesbury* review and human rights, *R* v *Secretary of State for the Home Department, ex parte Fire Brigade Union* in the House of Lords on prerogative, and *R* v *Ministry of Agriculture, Fisheries and Food, ex parte Hamble Fisheries* in the Divisional Court on substantive legitimate expectations.

As before we wish to thank the team at Blackstone Press for all their assistance and support.

Michael Allen
Brian Thompson

ACKNOWLEDGMENTS

The authors and publishers would like to thank and gratefully acknowledge the following for permission to reproduce copyright material:

T.R.S. Allan: 'The Limits of Parliamentary Sovereignty' [1985] *Public Law* 614.

R. Baldwin and J. Houghton: 'Circular Arguments — The Status and Legitimacy of Administrative Rules' [1986] *Public Law* 239.

E. Barendt: 'Dicey and Civil Liberties' [1985] *Public Law* 596.

Basil Blackwell Publisher Ltd: J. Lively, *Democracy* (1975).

D. Beetham: *The Legitimation of Power* (1991, Macmillan Press Ltd)

D. Beetham: 'Key Principles and Indices for a Democratic Audit' in Beetham (ed.), *Defining and Measuring Democracy* (1994, Sage Publications Ltd).

T.H. Bingham: 'The European Convention on Human Rights: Time to Incorporate.' (1993) 109 *Law Quarterly Review* 390.

Lord Browne-Wilkinson: 'The Infiltration of a Bill of Rights' [1992] *Public Law* 405.

Butterworth & Co. (Publishers) Ltd: C. Munro, *Studies in Constitutional Law* (1987), and cases reported in the *All England Law Reports* and the *New Law Journal.*

H. Calvert: *Constitutional Law in Northern Ireland* (1968, Stevens & Sons Ltd and Northern Ireland Legal Quarterly).

Cambridge University Press: Elster and Slagstad (eds.), *Constitutionalism and Democracy* (1988).

Canada Law Book Company: *Reference Re Amendment of the Constitution of Canada* (1982) 125 *Dominion Law Reports* (3d) 1.

Commission for Local Administration in England, for permission to reproduce extracts from annual reports.

Controller, Her Majesty's Stationery Office for permission to reproduce Crown and Parliamentary copyright material and extracts from *Legislation on Human Rights: A Discussion Document* (Home Office, 1976).

P. Craig: 'Dicey: Unitary, Self-correcting Democracy and Public Law' (1990) 106 *Law Quarterly Review* 105.

Dartmouth Publishing Co. Ltd: V. Bogdanor (ed), *Constitutions in Democratic Politics* (1988).

K.C. Davis: *Discretionary Justice* (1969, Louisiana State University Press).

C. Dewing and S. Watson: Sir Ivor Jennings, *The Law and the Constitution* (5th edn., University of London Press Ltd).

Mrs S.E. Finer: S.E. Finer, *Comparative Government* (1970, Allen Lane The Penguin Press).

C.J. Friedrich: *Limited Government: A Comparison* (1974, Prentice Hall Inc.).

W. Green & Son Ltd; extracts from *Scots Law Times*.

J.A.G. Griffith and M. Ryle: *Parliament: Functions, Practice and Procedures* (1989, Sweet and Maxwell).

Lord Hailsham of St. Marylebone: *The Dilemma of Democracy* (1978, Collins).

The Hansard Society for Parliamentary Government: *Making the Law* (1993).

C. Harlow and the Modern Law Review Ltd: C. Harlow 'Ombudsmen in Search of a Role' (1978) 41 *Modern Law Review* 446.

J.D. Hayhurst and P. Wallington: 'The Parliamentary Scrutiny of Delegated Legislation' [1988] *Public Law* 547.

K.H. Hendry 'The Tasks of Tribunals: Some Thoughts' (1982) 1 *Civil Justice Quarterly* 253.

R.F.V. Heuston: *Essays in Constitutional Law* (2nd edn., 1964, Stevens & Sons Ltd).

House of Commons Library: Factsheet No 30 (revised edition 1994) *Early Day Motions* © Parliamentary Copyright House of Commons. Reproduced by permission of the House of Commons Library.

The Incorporated Council for Law Reporting for England and Wales: extracts from the Law Reports and the Weekly Law Reports.

D. Judge: *The Parliamentary State* (1993, Sage Publications Ltd).

Sir John Laws: 'Is the High Court the Guardian of Fundamental Constitutional Rights?' [1993] *Public Law* 60, 'Law and Democracy' [1995] *Public Law* 81.

Lawyers Cooperative Publishing (a division of Thomson Information Services Inc.): extracts from *New York Times Co.* v *United States* 29 L Ed 2d 822.

Liberty: *A People's Charter* (1991, NCCL).

P. McAuslan and J. McEldowney, *Law, Legitimacy and the Constitution* (1985, Sweet & Maxwell Ltd).

C.H. McIlwain: *Constitutionalism: Ancient and Modern,* (1947, Revised Edition, Cornell University Press).

Macmillan Press Ltd: *Introduction to the Study of the Law of the Constitution* (10th ed.) by A.V. Dicey with an introduction by E.C.S. Wade.

G. Marshall and G. Moodie: *Some Problems of the Constitution* (5th edn., Hutchinson & Co. (Publishers) Ltd).

D.R. Miers and A.C. Page: *Legislation* (2nd ed., 1990, Sweet & Maxwell).

R. Miliband: *The State in Capitalist Society* (1969, Weidenfeld & Nicolson Ltd).

W.F. Murphy: 'Constitutions, Constitutionalism and Democracy' in D. Greenberg, S.N. Katz, M.B. Oliviero & S.C. Wheatley (eds) *Constitutionalism and Democracy* (1993, Oxford University Press Inc., USA).

P. Norton: *The Commons in Perspective* (1981) Martin Robertson; *Parliament in the 1980s* (1985, Basil Blackwell).

Oxford University Press for permission to reprint extracts from the following articles in *Parliamentary Affairs*:

A.Beith, 'Prayers Unanswered: A Jaundiced View of the Parlimentary Scrutiny of Statutory Instruments' vol. 34, No. 2, (1981).

C. Graham and J.A.W. Prosser, 'The Constitution and the New Conservatives' vol. 42, No. 3 (1989).

F.F. Ridley, 'There is no British Constitution: A Dangerous Case of the Emperor's Clothes' vol. 41, No. 3 (1988).

R. Rose, 'Law as a Resource of Public Policy' vol. 39, No. 3, (1986).

L. Wolf-Phillips, 'A Long Look at the British Constitution' vol. 37, No. 4 (1984).

D. Woodhouse, 'Ministerial Responsibility in the 1990's: When do Ministers Resign?' vol. 46, No. 3, (1993).

Oxford University Press for permission to reprint extracts from the following books:

R. Barker, *Political Legitimacy and the State* (1990).

J. Jowell and D. Oliver, The Changing Constitution (2nd edn, 1989).

H.L.A. Hart, *The Concept of Law* (1961).

C.B. Macpherson, *The Real World of Democracy* (1966).

G. Marshall, *Constitutional Theory* (1971).

G. Richardson and H. Genn, *Administrative Law and Government Action* (1994).

M.J.C. Vile, *Constitutionalism and the Separation of Powers* (1967).

K.C. Wheare, *Modern Constitutions* (2nd edn., 1966).

A. Page: 'MPs and the Redress of Grievances' [1985] *Public Law* 1.

H.F. Rawlings and Basil Blackwell Publisher; H. F. Rawlings, 'Judicial Review and the Control of Government' (1986) 64 *Public Administration* 134 © Royal Institute of Public Administration.

R. Rawlings: 'Parliamentary Redress of Grievance' in C. Harlow (ed.) *Public Law and Politics* (1986, Sweet and Maxwell).

J. Raz: 'The Rule of Law and its Virtue' (1977) 93 *Law Quarterly Review* 195.

Registrar of European Court of Human Rights, Press Releases, *Goodwin v United Kingdom* — judgment, 11–27 March 1996.

Routledge and N. Dorsen: N. Dorsen, 'Is there a right to stop offensive speech? The Case of the Nazis at Skokie' in Gostin (ed.) *Civil Liberties in Conflict* (1988).

A.T.H. Smith: 'Comment I on "Dicey and Civil Liberties" [1985] *Public Law* 608.

The Scottish Council of Law Reporting: extracts from Session Cases.

M.Sunkin and the Public Law Project, M. Sunkin, L. Bridges and G. Mészáros *Judicial Review in Perspective* (1993, Public Law Project).

Sweet & Maxwell Ltd: extracts from various articles in *Law Quarterly Review* and *Public Law;* and extracts from *Common Market Law Reports* and *European Court Reports*.

The Estate of C.F. Strong, M.G. Clarke and Sidgwick & Jackson Ltd: C.F. Strong, *Modern Political Constitutions* (8th edn., 1972).

The Rt. Hon. Lord Woolf of Barnes: 'Droit Public — English Style' [1995] *Public Law* 65

D. Yardley: 'The Functions of the Council on Tribunals' [1990] *Journal of Social Welfare Law* 265.

TABLE OF CASES

Cases reported in full are shown in heavy type. The page at which the report is printed is shown in heavy type.

TABLE OF STATUTES

Statutes, and sections thereof, which are set out in full or in part are shown in heavy type. The page at which the statute or section is printed is shown in heavy type.

TABLE OF EUROPEAN LEGISLATION

1 CONSTITUTIONAL LAW IN THE UNITED KINGDOM

(A) INTRODUCTION

Note

Constitutional law is the law relating to the constitution. While this statement may be true, it is not particularly helpful. To study constitutional law we need to discover what a constitution is. There are many competing definitions. While many clubs, organisations and other groupings have constitutions, our concern is with the constitutions of nation-states.

Thomas Paine, *Rights of Man* in *The Complete Works of Thomas Paine*, pp. 302–303

> A constitution is not the act of a government, but of a people constituting a government, and a government without a constitution is power without right. . . . A constitution is a thing antecedent to a government; and a government is only the creature of a constitution.

It was Paine's belief that England lacked a constitution, as he stated at p. 370 that 'the continual use of the word "constitution" in the English parliament shows there is none and the whole is merely a form of government without a constitution, and constituting itself with what power it pleases'. Paine admired, by contrast, the recent American Constitution.

C. H. McIlwain, *Constitutionalism Ancient and Modern* (1947), pp. 8 – 10

. . . [T]he analysis Paine made of the early American constitution was remarkably acute. The significant points in that analysis are these:

That there is a fundamental difference between a people's government and that people's constitution, whether the government happens to be entrusted to a king or to a representative assembly.

That this constitution is 'antecedent' to the government.

That it defines the authority which the people commits to its government, and in so doing thereby limits it.

That any exercise of authority beyond these limits by any government is an exercise of 'power without right.'

That in any state in which the distinction is not actually observed between the constitution and the government there is in reality no constitution, because the will of the government has no check upon it, and that state is in fact a despotism.

One thing alone Paine fails to make fully clear. If a government exercises some 'power without right,' it seems to be necessarily implied that the people have a corresponding right to resist. But is this a legal or is it only a political right? Is such resistance a legalized rebellion or merely an extralegal revolution? Or, further, is it possible to incorporate in the framework of the state itself some provision or institution by which a governmental act or command *ultra vires* may be declared to be such, and subjects therefore exempted from its operation and released from any legal obligation to observe or obey it? In short, can government be limited legally and effectively by any method short of force? To these questions Paine gives no clear answer. It might be assumed that forcible resistance to power without right must itself be legal and not revolutionary; but in every case there seems no recourse except to force of some kind.

The one conspicuous element lacking in Paine's construction therefore seems to be the element of judicial review. Writing when he did, and as he did, to justify an actual rebellion, it is perhaps not strange that he was thinking primarily of politics rather than of law, that the 'rights' he had in mind were the rights of man rather than the rights of the citizen, or that the sanction for these rights should be extralegal action rather than any constitutional check. Paine, like many idealists in a hurry, was probably impatient of the slowness of legal remedies for existing abuses. But others, who were more constitutionally minded than he, had begun to feel that any such remedies, to be truly effective, must ultimately have the sanction of law. Years before, Lord Camden had insisted that the principles of the law of nature must be incorporated in the British Constitution if they were to be observed, and that they actually were so incorporated. The necessary inference from such a principle as his is that the interpreters of law should be the ones to define the rights of individuals and to trace the bounds of legitimate government over them. The protection of rights became for him, and for all who thought as he did, the enforcement of 'constitutional limitations.'

Question

What did Paine mean by 'antecedent'? Did he mean that the constitution must exist prior in time to the government or that the principles of the constitution should be superior in character, and binding in authority, to the actions of government? If the former is correct, does the United Kingdom have a constitution? (See the discussion which follows.) If the latter is correct, could the United Kingdom ever have constitutional government? (See chapter 2.)

Note

Paine expressed a concept of constitutions which involved 'the conscious formulation by a people of its fundamental law' (McIlwain, *op. cit.*, p. 3).

This would find expression in a written document or documents. The alternative view sees constitutions not as a conscious creation but rather as an evolutionary consequence made up of 'substantive principles to be deduced from a nation's actual institutions and their development' (McIlwain, *ibid.*). This could include an unwritten or uncodified constitution. This view was expressed by Bolingbroke.

Bolingbroke, *A Dissertation upon Parties* (1733 – 34) in *The Works of Lord Bolingbroke* (1841), II, p. 88

By constitution we mean, whenever we speak with propriety and exactness, that assemblage of laws, institutions and customs, derived from certain fixed principles of reason, directed to certain fixed objects of public good, that compose the general system according to which the community hath agreed to be governed. . . . We call this a good government, when . . . the whole administration of public affairs is wisely pursued, and with a strict conformity to the principles and objects of the constitution.

Question

When Paine stated that a governmental act contrary to the constitution is an act of 'power without right', did he thereby imply that such an act would be unconstitutional? In Bolingbroke's terms such an act would warrant the conclusion that the government is not a good one; is this the same thing?

Note

It can be argued that, according to Bolingbroke's definition, the United Kingdom has a constitution, as there are laws, institutions and customs which combine to create a system of government to which the community agrees, or at least, from which it does not appear to dissent. This is the traditional view of most constitutional lawyers. Constitutional theorists have further refined their analysis of constitutions, creating other points of comparison. For example, K C Wheare, *Modern Constitutions* (1966), Chapter 2, proposed six classifications of constitutions: (1) written and unwritten; (2) rigid and flexible; (3) supreme and subordinate; (4) federal and unitary; (5) separated powers and fused powers; (6) republican and monarchical. If Wheare's definitions are applied to the United Kingdom, it may be said that there is an unwritten constitution in the sense that it is uncodified. There is no supreme or fundamental constitutional law, and the processes for changing the constitution are flexible. The state is a unitary, monarchical one where powers are fused, there being a parliamentary executive as opposed to a presidential executive.

While most writers on the constitution are satisfied that, by comparison with the various definitions, the United Kingdom does have a constitution, some writers insist that there is no constitution.

F. F. Ridley, 'There is no British Constitution: A Dangerous Case of the Emperor's Clothes' 41 *Parliamentary Affairs* (1988) pp. 340 – 343, 359 – 360

Having a constitution seems to be a matter of self-respect: no state is properly dressed without. Every democracy except Britain, New Zealand and (with qualifications)

Israel seems to have a written constitution, plainly labelled. Not to be left out of the world of constitutional democracies, British writers define constitution in a way which appears to give us one too, even though there is no document to prove it. The argument is that a constitution need not be embodied in a single document or, indeed, wholly written. We say instead that a country's constitution is a body of rules – some laws, some conventions – which regulate its system of government. Such a definition does not, however, bridge the gap between Britain and the rest of the world by providing us with a substitute for a documentary constitution: it simply shifts the ground, by using the word in an entirely different way.

We see this ambiguity in K C Wheare's now classic book on constitutions.

> The word constitution is commonly used in at least two senses in ordinary discussion of political affairs. First of all, it is used to describe the whole system of government, the collection of rules which establish and regulate it. These rules are partly legal and partly non-legal. When we speak of the British constitution that is the normal, if not the only possible meaning the word has. Everywhere else it is used in the sense of legal rules embodied in one document.

But that is not the real distinction. Foreign usage is not particularly concerned with the documentary character of a constitution. It appears in that form, but that is not its essential. Everywhere save Britain the constitution is defined as a special category of law. British usage dissolves the distinction between constitutional law and other laws because British courts recognise no such distinction. British political scientists, for their part, dissolve the distinction between law and other rules of behaviour because they are not much interested in law: for them, the constitution is practice.

Books of an old-fashioned sort with British Constitution in their title describe significant laws, conventions and institutions. This approach is now dismissed as formalistic by political scientists who regard such accounts as incomplete, if not misleading. They are right if their aim is to describe a system of government. In no country are all the important laws that shape the system of government embodied in a constitutional document. Nor can the operation of constitutional law be understood without reference to the practice of politics. Such arguments, however, miss the essential character of constitutions altogether. The wide focus of political scientists is right if their aim is to describe a system of government. Equating it with a study of the constitution, however, may owe less to a desire for realism than to a lack of concern about legal matters. This is often justified on the grounds that law is not a distinct and important element in understanding systems of government, but there are professional reasons too. Political studies did not originate in law faculties, as in continental Europe, and never subsequently developed any real interest in law. As a result, we get books called The British System of Government or, more fashionably, The British Political System, where politics is added to institutions. What such books include when they claim to describe the British 'constitution' depends on what their authors consider important to the framework of the system: what the 'constitution' consists of thus emerges from a survey of the system and is not determined by an independent, non-political definition that precedes it.

Much the same applies to books by lawyers. Works entitled Constitutional Law cover a selection of laws that appear important to the author, together with important conventions and often a reduced version of the topics treated by institutionally-oriented political scientists. Since there appear to be no consequences in judicial practice if the label constitutional is applied to a particular law, it is in the end no more than a convenient way for textbook writers to organise their material, just as they produce books on industrial law or commercial law. That emerges clearly from one textbook definition of the study of constitutional law as 'that body of knowledge dealing with the law of the constitution in a broader sense . . . matters pertaining to the organisation of government and its relation to citizens'. That may cover almost anything, indeed F W Maitland said that 'there is hardly any department of law which does not, at one time or another, become of constitutional importance.'

Though there is broad agreement on the contents of such books on constitutional law, in the last resort it depends on what academic lawyers consider relevant – and a quick survey of standard textbooks will show that at the margins there are significant variations in what is brought into the orbit of the British 'constitution'. In the absence of legal criteria that distinguish constitutional law from other laws, the definition becomes so broad that it defines nothing at all. In the context of the British legal system, the term constitutional law is thus literally meaningless. Borrowing from political science for their definition of the British constitution, however, academic lawyers hardly even really address the question whether in legal, or indeed logical, terms Britain has a constitution at all.

Such accounts of the British 'constitution' are only superficially the result of the absence of a constitutional document. Because we feel uneasy about our difference from other democracies which do have labelled constitution, we turn to what is now a peculiarly British usage of the word to prove that we are not really different at all. One purpose of this article is to show that Britain *is* different, and different in ways that are important politically as well as in law. It is to show that Britain does not really have a constitution at all, merely a system of government, even if some parts of it are more important to our democratic order than others or are treated (perhaps: were treated until Mrs Thatcher's time) with greater veneration. It may be embarrassing to explain that, as in the nursery tale, the Emperor has no clothes after all, that the constitutional attire his courtiers claim to see is empty words, but that is the essential of this article. Unless we face up to that fact, moreover, any discussion of how we can safeguard certain democratic arrangements that we regarded as part of the British 'constitution' in the past (e.g. the independence of local government) or entrench others (e.g. a Bill of Rights) against an 'elective dictatorship' will run into the sand.

Constitutions and their Characteristics

Use of the word constitution as the manner in which a polity is organised, the main characteristic of its governmental system, is undoubtedly the historic one. By the end of the eighteenth century, however, the word came to have another meaning. The American War of Independence and the French Revolution marked a turning point after which the new meaning became universal, Britain excepted. It applied to a special form of law embodied as a matter of convenience in a single document. As used elsewhere, it is now a term of law not politics. Constitutions there have certain essential characteristics, none of them found in Britain. Without these characteristics, it is impossible to distinguish a constitution from a description of the system of government in a way that is analytically precise. Without them, it is impossible to say that a country has a constitution in the current international sense of the word. More important, lest this be thought a linguistic quibble, without them a system of government lacks the legitimacy a constitution gives and a political system the protection it offers.

The characteristics of a constitution are as follows.

(1) It establishes, or constitutes, the system of government. Thus it is prior to the system of government, not part of it, and its rules can not be derived from that system.

(2) It therefore involves an authority outside and above the order it establishes. This is the notion of the constituent power ('pouvoir constituant' – because we do not think along these lines, the English translation sounds strange). In democracies that power is attributed to the people, on whose ratification the legitimacy of a constitution depends and, with it, the legitimacy of the governmental system.
(3) It is a form of law superior to other laws – because (i) it originates in an authority higher than the legislature which makes ordinary law and (ii) the authority of the legislature derives from it and is thus bound by it. The principle of hierarchy of law generally (but not always) leads to the possibility of judicial review of ordinary legislation.
(4) It is entrenched – (i) because its purpose is generally to limit the powers of government, but also (ii) again because of its origins in a higher authority outside the system. It can thus only be changed by special procedures, generally (and certainly for major change) requiring reference back to the constituent power.

James Bryce made all these points at the turn of the century. Defining a constitution as a framework of political society organised through law, he distinguished between 'statutory' and 'common law' types of constitutions. Of the former, he wrote: 'The instrument in which a constitution is embodied proceeds from a source different from that whence spring other laws, is regulated in a different way, and exerts a sovereign force. It is enacted not by the ordinary legislative authority but by some higher and specially empowered body. When any of its provisions conflict with a provision of the ordinary law, it prevails and the ordinary law must give way.' Bryce's alternative, the idea of a common-law constitution, is perhaps another way of saying that the British 'constitution' just grew, as the common law itself. His definition of a statutory constitution does, however, allow us to distinguish constitutional law from other law by clear criteria, thus giving the term not just a specific meaning, but a meaning with consequences. Though he, too, declared the distinction between written and unwritten constitutions old-fashioned, it is a pity that his summary has not served as a starting point for subsequent commentaries on the British 'constitution'.

. . . [T]he term British constitution is near meaningless even as used by British writers. It is impossible to isolate parts of the system of government to which the label may authoritatively be attached. There is no test to discriminate between constitutional and less than constitutional elements since labelling has no defined consequence, unlike countries where constitutions are a higher form of law. If used descriptively, as Wheare and others suggest, it is simply a fancy-dress way of saying the British system of government and at best redundant. More dangerous, those who talk of a British constitution may mislead themselves into thinking that there are parts of the system to which a special sanctity attaches. But in that normative sense the term is equally meaningless. When significant parts of the system are reformed, we have no test to tell us whether the outcome is an improper breach of the constitutional order, a proper amendment, or whether the reformed institutions were not part of the 'constitution' at all. I may be told that this is an academic quibble since our democratic politicians know what is of constitutional significance in our way of government, approach such matters differently from other reforms, and are politically if not legally constrained. That, however, is not the case. Our system of government is being changed, with increasing disregard for tradition, the only unwritten rules to which one might appeal as 'constitutional' principles.

There is cause for concern about the muddled way we think about the British 'constitution'; there is even greater cause for concern about the political consequences of its nature. It is sometimes said that our 'constitution' is now under stress as major changes occur far more rapidly than before in its written and unwritten parts. Is this due to changing ideas about how the British system of government should be organised, widely held, or is it simply that the government of the day is using its power to change the system in the pursuit of its own political goals? Is the constitutional order evolving or is it under attack? We have moved from consensus to conflict in politics: have we moved in that direction, too, as regards our constitutional order, taking that to mean the broad principles underlying the way government is organised and power exercised? Many old principles no longer command universal agreement and there are well-supported demands for new principles. We have had debates on the entrenchment of rights; on federalism or regional devolution as against the unitary state; on the case for consensus rather than majority as a basis for government, on the relative weight of national versus local mandates and the independence of local government; on the duty of civil servants; on electoral reform with all its implications for the operations of government; on who should define the national interest; on open government and official secrecy; on complementing representative democracy by referenda and other forms of participation – and much else. Political disagreement and disagreement on the proper constitutional order are linked. An ideologically-committed government, determind to implement its policies, will support different constitutional principles from those who want consensus policy-making; those concerned primarily with individual freedom and the rights of the public will support different principles from those who want strong government – and so on. Since opinion is now deeply divided on so many issues, one can probably no longer talk of the constitutional order as if it were a reflection of public opinion.

There are no grounds for complacency about British democracy.

Questions

1. Is there any truth in the following statement by Sidney Low, in *The Governance of England* (1904), p. 12: 'British government is based upon a system of tacit understandings. But the understandings are not always understood'?

2. Is there some inherent virtue in a system of government derived from a constitution, which is lacking in a country which does not have such a codified constitution? Indeed, why are constitutions enacted? See Wheare below.

K. C. Wheare, *Modern Constitutions* (1966), pp. 4 – 8

[W]hat a Constitution says is one thing, and what actually happens in practice may be quite another. We must take account of this possible difference in considering the form and worth of Constitutions. What is more, we must be ready to admit that although almost all countries in the world have a Constitution, in many of them the Constitution is treated with neglect or contempt. Indeed in the middle of the twentieth century it can be said that the majority of the world's population lives under systems of government where the government itself and particularly the executive government are of more importance and are treated with more respect or fear than the Constitution. It is only in the states of Western Europe, in the countries of the British Commonwealth, in the United States of America, and in a few Latin-American states that government is carried on with due regard to the limitations imposed by a Constitution; it is only in these states that truly 'constitutional government' can be said to exist. . . .

Since the Constitution of a country is only a part of that country's whole system of government, does it make any difference whether a country has a Constitution or not? The short answer is that in many countries the fact that there is a Constitution does make a difference. This brings to light a characteristic which most Constitutions exhibit. They are usually endowed with a higher status, in some degree, as a matter of law, than other legal rules in the system of government. At the least it is usually laid down that the amendment of the Constitution can take place only through a special process different from that by which the ordinary law is altered. . . .

It is natural to ask . . . why it is that countries have Constitutions, why most of them make the Constitution superior to the ordinary law, and, further, why Britain, at any rate, has no Constitution, in this sense, at all.

If we investigate the origins of modern Constitutions, we find that, practically without exception, they were drawn up and adopted because people wished to make a fresh start, so far as the statement of their system of government was concerned. The desire or need for a fresh start arose either because, as in the United States, some neighbouring communities wished to unite together under a new government; or because, as in Austria or Hungary or Czechoslovakia after 1918, communities had been released from an Empire as the result of a war and were now free to govern themselves; or because, as in France in 1789 or the U.S.S.R. in 1917, a revolution had made a break with the past and a new form of government on new principles was desired; or because, as in Germany after 1918 or in France in 1875 or in 1946, defeat in war had broken the continuity of government and a fresh start was needed after the war. The circumstances in which a break with the past and the need for a fresh start come about vary from country to country, but in almost every case in modern times, countries have a Constitution for the very simple and elementary reason that they wanted, for some reason, to begin again and so they put down in writing the main outline, at least, of their proposed system of government. This has been the practice certainly since 1787 when the American Constitution was drafted, and as the years passed no doubt imitation and the force of example have led all countries to think it necessary to have a Constitution.

This does not explain, however, why many countries think it necessary to give the Constitution a higher status in law than other rules of law. The short explanation of this phenomenon is that in many countries a Constitution is thought of as an instrument by which government can be controlled. Constitutions spring from a belief in limited government. Countries differ however in the extent to which they wish to impose limitations. Sometimes the Constitution limits the executive or subordinate local bodies; sometimes it limits the legislature also, but only so far as amendment of the Constitution itself is concerned; and sometimes it imposes restrictions upon the legislature which go far beyond this point and forbid it to make laws upon certain subjects or in a certain way or with certain effects. Whatever the nature and extent of the restrictions, however, they are based upon a common belief in limited government and in the use of a Constitution to impose these limitations.

The nature of the limitations to be imposed on a government, and therefore the degree to which a Constitution will be supreme over a government, depends upon the objects which the framers of the Constitution wish to safeguard. In the first place they may want to do no more than ensure that the Constitution is not altered casually or carelessly or by subterfuge or implication; they may want to secure that this important document is not lightly tampered with, but solemnly, with due notice and deliberation, consciously amended. In that case it is legitimate to require some special process of constitutional amendment – say that the legislature may amend the Constitution only by a two-thirds majority or after a general election or perhaps upon three months' notice.

The framers of Constitutions often have more than this in mind. They may feel that a certain kind of relationship between the legislature and the executive is important; or that the judicature should have a certain guaranteed degree of independence of the legislature and executive. They may feel that there are certain rights which citizens have and which the legislature or the executive must not invade or remove. They may feel that certain laws should not be made at all. . . .

In some countries only one of the considerations mentioned above may operate, in others some, and in some, all. Thus, in the Irish Constitution, the framers were anxious that amendment should be a deliberate process, that the rights of citizens should be safeguarded, and that certain types of laws should not be passed at all, and therefore they made the Constitution supreme and imposed restrictions upon the legislature to achieve these ends. The framers of the American Constitution also had these objects in mind, but on top of that they had to provide for the desire of the thirteen colonies to be united for some purposes only and to remain independent for others. This was an additional reason for giving supremacy to the Constitution and for introducing certain extra safeguards into it.

Note

As Ridley recognises the framers of a constitution may have particular aims in mind. Constitutions may serve different functions in different countries or even within the same country at different times.

W. F. Murphy, 'Constitutions, Constitutionalism and Democracy' in *Constitutionalism and Democracy*, D. Greenberg, S. N. Katz, M. B. Oliviero and S. C. Wheatley, (eds) (1993), pp. 8–10

What Are the Functions of a Constitution?

A Constitution as Sham, Cosmetic, or Reality. The principal function of a sham constitutional test is to deceive. Lest US citizens revel in righteousness, they might recall that Charles A. Beard charged the framers of the US text with hypocrisy, and the Conference of Critical Legal Studies still so accuses the entire American legal system. Whether Beard and the Critics have told the full story, they have reminded us that a constitutional document's representation of itself, its people, their values, and decisional processes is imperfect. Thus, even reasonably authoritative texts play a cosmetic role, allowing a nation to hide its failures behind idealistic rhetoric. But, insofar as a text is authoritative, its rhetoric also pushes a people to renew their better selves.

A Constitution as a Charter for Government. At minimum, an authoritative constitutional text must sketch the fundamental modes of legitimate governmental operations: who its officials are, how they are chosen, what their terms of office are, how authority is divided among them, what processes they must follow, and what rights, if any, are reserved to citizens. Such a text need not proclaim any substantive values, beyond obedience to itself; if it does proclaim values, they might be those of Naziism or Stalinism, anathema to constitutional democracy.

A Constitution as Guardian of Fundamental Rights. Thus the question immediately arises about the extent to which a constitutional text relies on or incorporates democratic and/or constitutional theories. Insofar as a text is authoritative and embodies democratic theory, it must protect rights to political participation. Insofar as it is authoritative and embodies constitutionalism, it must protect substantive rights by limiting the power of the people's freely chosen representatives.

The Constitution as Covenant, Symbol, and Aspiration. Insofar as a constitution is a covenant by which a group of people agree to (re)transform themselves into a nation, it may function for the founding generation like a marriage consummated through the pledging partners' positive, active consent to remain a nation for better or worse, through prosperity and poverty, in peace and war.

For later generations, a constitution may operate more as an arranged marriage in which consent is passive, for the degree of choice is then typically limited. Even where expatriation is a recognized right, exit from a society offers few citizens a viable alternative. Revolution becomes a legal right only if it succeeds and transforms revolutionaries into founders. And deeply reaching reform from within a constitutional framework tends to become progressively more difficult, for a system usually endures only by binding many groups to its terms.

The myth of a people's forming themselves into a nation presents a problem not unlike that between chicken and egg. To agree in their collective name to a political covenant, individuals must have already had some meaningful corporate identity *as a people*. Thus the notion of constitution as covenant must mean it formalizes or solidifies rather than invents an entity: it solemnizes a previous alliance into a more perfect union.

A constitution's formative force varies from country to country and time to time. The French, one can plausibly argue, have been the French under monarchies, military dictatorships, and assorted republics. It is also plausible, however, to contend that Germans have been a different people under the Kaiser, the Weimar Republic, the Third Reich, and the Federal Republic. In polyglotted societies such as Canada, India, and the United States or those riven by religious divisions and bleeding memories of civil war such as Ireland, 'there may be no other basis for uniting a nation of so many disparate groups.' A constitution may thus function as a uniting force, 'the only principle of order', for there may be 'no [other] shared moral or social vision that might bind together a nation.' [Sanford Levinson, *Constitutional Faith* (1988) p. 73.] It is difficult to imagine what has united the supposedly United States more than the political ideas of the Declaration of Independence and the text of 1787.

Reverence for the constitution may transform it into a holy symbol of the people themselves. The creature they created can become their own mythical creator. This symbolism might turn a constitutional text into a semisacred covenant, serving 'the unifying function of a civil religion.' [T. Grey, 'The Constitution as Scripture' (1984) 37 *Stanford Law Review* 1, 18.] In America, 'The Bible of verbal inspiration begat the constitution of unquestioned authority.'

Religious allusions remind us, however, that this symbolic role may also have a dark side. Long histories of bitter and often murderous struggles among Christians and among Muslims demonstrate that a sacred text may foster division rather than cohesion, conflict rather than harmony. The 'potential of a written constitution to serve as the source of fragmentation and disintegration' [Levinson] is nowhere more savagely illustrated than in the carnage of the US Civil War. For, ultimately, that fratricidal struggle was over two visions of one constitutional document. The result was a gory war that wiped out more than 600,000 lives. Complicating analysis is the fact that when the blood of battle dried, the document of 1787, duly amended, resumed its unifying role.

In a related fashion, a constitution may serve as a binding statement of a people's aspirations for themselves as a nation. A text may silhouette the sort of community its authors/subjects are or would like to become: not only their governmental structures, procedures, and basic rights, but also their goals, ideals, and the moral standards by which they want others, including their own posterity, to judge the community. In short, a constitutional text may guide as well as express a people's hopes for themselves as a society. The ideals the words enshrine, the processes they describe, and the actions they legitimize must either help to change the citizenry or at least reflect their current values. If a constitutional text is not 'congruent with' ideals that form or will reform its people and so express the political character they have or are willing to try to put on, it will quickly fade.

Note

While endless argument could be engaged upon on the question whether or not the United Kingdom has a constitution, perhaps a more profitable issue for consideration is whether the system of government in the United Kingdom displays congruence with certain values, principles and concepts associated with constitutional government in a liberal democratic state. Wheare's remarks above should be noted, namely, that in many countries the constitution is 'treated with neglect or contempt'. Thus the existence of a constitution of itself may not be a guarantee against repressive or totalitarian governments which disregard individual liberty and abrogate human rights.

V. Bogdanor (ed.), Introduction to *Constitutions in Democratic Politics* (1988), pp. 3 – 7

Constitutions are not, of course, confined to democratic states. Indeed, the vast majority of the 159 member states comprising the United Nations possess codified constitutions, although less than a third of these can fairly claim democratic credentials. The latter can, declares S E Finer with pardonable exaggeration, be counted on one's fingers and toes. Conversely, three countries which are indubitably democracies – Britain, Israel and New Zealand – lack . . . codified constitutions.

In the modern world, constitutions are almost ubiquitous and they are indeed part of the tribute which vice pays to virtue. For there *is* a conceptual connection, not so much between the constitution as a document and democracy, but between modern constitutionalism and the idea of a liberal democracy. Whether a country has a codified constitution is hardly something of great importance to the political scientist. Whether it achieves the aims which constitutions are intended to help achieve, is a matter of far greater moment. For codified constitutions are, after all, valued as a means to the end of limiting governmental power; and, in a democracy, limiting also the power of the people to whom government is responsible. The Founding Fathers in drawing up the American Constitution had, after all, two aims, not one. The first was to draw up a structure of government which could serve to protect the people from government, from the danger of a tyranny of the majority in the legislature; but the second aim was to protect the people from themselves.

Thus, the relationship between constitutionalism and liberalism . . . is by no means a simple or straightforward one. To live under an effectively working constitution is not the same as living under a regime of moral *laissez-faire.* Constitutional government presupposes a certain set of virtues amongst the ruled; and these virtues must include self-restraint, a willingness not to push the pursuit of one's aims beyond a certain point. In the 1930s, Mr Justice Stone declared that the United States Supreme Court ought not to see itself as the sole guardian of the constitution. While the other branches of the Constitution were limited by institutional restraints, by checks and balances, the only restraint which limited the Court was its sense of self-restraint. By analogy, one might argue that in a democracy in which the people are, in effect, sovereign, the only effective restraint in the last resort is likely to be that of the people over themselves. Constitutions thus both liberate and bind; they provide for a framework of ordered freedom within a set of rules which prevents both majorities and their elected representatives from doing what they might otherwise wish to do.

The term 'constitution', as S E Finer shows, is to be understood in positivistic terms as a code of rules which aspire to regulate the allocation of functions, powers and duties among the various agencies and officers of government, and defines the relationships between these and the public. Yet, even defined in these terms, the existence of a constitution, in so far as it is observed, serves to limit power. For, to allocate functions, powers and duties is also, *ipso facto,* to limit power. There must be some gain to the citizen, however minimal, in living under a constitution which regularises the way in which power is exercised; even where government is authoritarian, it matters that it is not arbitrary.

Yet, a number of democratic constitutions today contain more than a mere organisation chart of functions and powers; they contain Bills of Rights, which may also include a charter of social and economic rights, something characteristic of constitutions of the twentieth century, although generally honoured more in the breach than in the observance.

. . . [I]n the case of Britain and Israel, two countries without codified constitutions, such pressure as exists to adopt one is based less on the desire to possess a clear-cut organisational chart delimiting the institutions of government than on a feeling that rights would be better protected under a codified constitution than they are at present.

The concept of a constitution is closely bound up with the notion of the limitation of government by law, a source of authority higher than government and beyond its reach. An enacted constitution is a means – although, as the examples of Britain, Israel and New Zealand show, not an essential means – of securing this end. The law, it is suggested, is logically prior to government, and therefore constitutes a standard by which the actions of government are to be evaluated. It is . . . this 'appeal to a pre-existing law' which 'is the essence of constitutionalism'.

Yet analysis of constitutions cannot be restricted simply to the document called 'the Constitution', or to constitutional law. For a working constitution in a democracy implies reference to certain norms and standards which lie beyond and outside the document itself, and which cannot easily be inferred from it by someone who is not steeped in the history and culture of the country concerned. When conduct on the part of a government or some other public body is dubbed 'unconstitutional', what is often meant is not necessarily that the law has been broken, but rather that the action is out of keeping with the style or, more broadly, the 'way of life' of a country. . . .

This kind of appeal – to constitutional conventions – can, of course, also be raised in countries without codified constitutions. When, in Britain, it is suggested that the policies of the Conservative Government towards local authorities since 1979 raise constitutional questions, what is meant is not that these policies are in any sense illegal, but rather . . . that they breach hitherto accepted understandings, albeit tacit, as to how relationships between central government and local authorities should be ordered. These tacit understandings, which, in Sidney Low's graphic phrase, are so often misunderstood, may not be written down; yet they exert a normative influence upon those concerned with central/local relations comparable to, and perhaps greater than, the influence exerted by a constitutional document. What makes Britain together with Israel and New Zealand, constitutional democracies, despite the absence of codified constitutions, is this very fact that their governments in general feel under pressure to conform to such norms; when accused of unconstitutional action their defence is not that the term 'unconstitutional' is without meaning, but that their actions can, despite appearances, be defended in constitutional terms.

Thus, in addition to the basic meaning of 'constitution' – a document containing, at the very least, a code of rules setting out the allocation of functions, powers and duties among the various agencies and officers of government – there is a wider meaning of constitution, according to which every democratic state has a constitution. This wider meaning comprehends the normative attitudes held by the people towards government, their conception of how power ought to be regulated, of what it is proper to do and not to do. There are, as it were, pre-constitutional norms regulating government, and it is upon these that the health and viability of democratic systems will depend.

(B) CONSTITUTIONALISM

Governments wield considerable power. Constitutions, while they may create the institutions of government and allocate power to these institutions, also generally seek to control or restrain the exercise of power. The principle of constitutionalism rests on this idea of restraining the government in its exercise of power. Constitutionalism, therefore, is to be set in contradistinction to arbitrary power.

M. J. C. Vile, *Constitutionalism and the Separation of Powers* (1967), p. 1

Western institutional theorists have concerned themselves with the problem of ensuring that the exercise of governmental power, which is essential to the realization of the values of their societies, should be controlled in order that it should not itself be destructive of the values it was intended to promote. The great theme of the advocates of constitutionalism, in contrast either to the theorists of utopianism, or of absolutism, of the right or of the left, has been the frank acknowledgment of the role of government in society, linked with the determination to bring that government under control and to place limits on the exercise of its power.

C. J. Friedrich, *Limited Government: A Comparison* (1974), pp. 13 – 14

Constitutionalism by dividing power provides a system of effective restraints upon governmental action. In studying it, one has to explore the methods and techniques by which such restraints are established and maintained. Putting it another, more familiar, but less exact way, it is a body of rules ensuring fair play, thus rendering the government 'responsible.' There exist a considerable number of such techniques or methods.

The question confronts us: how did the idea of restraints arise? And who provided the support that made the idea victorious in many countries? There are two important roots to the idea of restraints. One is the medieval heritage of natural-law doctrine. For while the royal bureaucrats gained the upper hand in fact, the other classes in the community who had upheld the medieval constitutionalism – the barons and the free towns, and above all the church – developed secularized versions of natural law. At the same time, they clung to residual institutions, such as the *parlements* in France. After the task of unification had been accomplished, and the despotic methods of absolutism could no longer be justified, these elements came foward with the idea of a separation of power. Both the English and the French revolutions served to dramatize these events.

The other root of the idea of restraints is shared by medieval and modern constitutionalism and is peculiar to some extent to Western culture. It is Christianity, and more specifically the Christian doctrine of personality. The insistence upon the individual as the final value, the emphasis upon the transcendental importance of each man's soul, creates an insoluble conflict with any sort of absolutism. Here lies the core of the objection to all political conceptions derived from Aristotelian and other Greek sources. Since there exists a vital need for government just the same, this faith in the worth of each human being is bound to seek a balance of the two needs in some system of restraints which protects the individual, or at least minorities, against any despotic exercise of political authority. It is quite in keeping with this conflict that the apologists of unrestrained power have, in all ages of Western civilization, felt the necessity of *justifying* the exercise of such power, a necessity which was not felt elsewhere.

Nor was it felt by all in the West. Bacon and Hobbes, Bodin and Spinoza, and even Machiavelli insisted that some sort of inanimate force, such as reason, natural law, or enlightened self-interest would bring about a self-restraint. But a deep-seated distrust of power was part of the tradition that taught that 'my Kingdom is not of this world,' and that states are usually just 'great robber bands,' since they lack justice. Hence self-restraint of the ruler must be reinforced by effective institutions: restraints upon the arbitrary exercise of governmental power.

Modern constitutionalism then has always been linked with the problem of power, in theory as well as in practice. Historically, it constitutes a reaction against the concentration of power that accompanied the consolidation of modern states, dynastic and national. Its theorists have insisted on the importance of limiting and defining the power acquired by monarchs. Whilst Hobbes described the rational structure of such a concentration of power and developed it into a veritable philosophy of power, Locke, taking up the challenge, demanded that the exercise of this power, although it was derived from the ultimate and unified source of all power – the people – remain divided by virtue of a fundamental decision.

Questions

1. Which of the ideas of self-restraint or institutional restraint is the dominant one in the British system of government?

2. In the United Kingdom there is no codified constitution expressly imposing limits on governmental power. Is governmental power limited in other ways?

Note

In the United Kingdom, where Parliament is supreme and may enact, amend or repeal any law it chooses, there is no distinction between 'ordinary' laws and 'constitutional' laws. Laws of constitutional significance are not accredited 'fundamental' status – they have no special sanctity. No special procedures are required for amending or repealing such laws. Indeed, in the absence of a codified constitution, it is arguable that it is impossible to state what laws are of constitutional significance without reference to constitutions elsewhere to see what kinds of matters are dealt with therein. A further consequence is, as Bogdanor states in 'Britain: the Political Constitution' in Bogdanor, *Constitutions in Democratic Politics,* p. 56, that 'the term "unconstitutional" cannot in Britain mean contrary to law; instead it means contrary to convention, contrary to some understanding of what it is appropriate to do. But, unfortunately, there is by no means universal agreement on what the standards of appropriateness are or ought to be.' Should this be a matter of concern? Is it not sufficient to entrust Parliament with the task of ensuring that constitutionalism is respected in the United Kingdom?

J. Elster, 'Introduction' in *Constitutionalism and Democracy* (Elster and Slagstad, eds, 1988), pp. 8 – 9

Why would a political assembly want to abdicate from the full sovereignty which in principle it possesses, and set limits on its own future actions? In an intergenerational perspective, the question is what right one generation has to limit the freedom of action of its successors, and why the latter should feel bound by constraints laid down by their ancestors. A natural (although possibly misleading) point of departure is to consider individual analogies. Why, for instance, would two individuals want to form a legal marriage instead of simply cohabiting? What possible advantages could they derive from limiting their future freedom of action and by making it more difficult to separate should they form the wish to do so? One obvious answer is that they want to protect themselves against their own tendency to act rashly, in the heat of passion. By raising the costs of separation and imposing legal delays, marriage makes it less likely that the spouses will give way to strong but temporary impulses to separate. By increasing the expected duration of the relationship, legal marriage also enhances the incentive to have children, to invest in housing and make other long-term decisions. These decisions, in turn create bonds between the spouses and reinforce the marriage.

These answers have partial analogues in the constitutional domain. It is a truism that constitutional constraints make it more difficult for the assembly or the society to change its mind on important questions. Groups no less than individuals (although not in quite the same sense as individuals) are subject to fits of passion, self-deception and hysteria which may create a temporary majority for decisions which will later be regretted. But then, one may ask, why could the members of the assembly not simply undo the decisions if and when they come to regret them? The presumption must be, after all, that the assembly knows what it is doing, not that it needs to be protected against itself.

Part of the answer to this question is suggested by the marriage analogy. The expected stability and duration of political institutions is an important value in itself, since they allow for long-term planning. Conversely, if all institutions are up for grabs all the time, individuals in power will be tempted to milk their positions for private purposes, and those outside power will hesitate to form projects which take time to bear fruit. Moreover, if nothing could ever be taken for granted, there would be large deadweight losses arising from bargaining and factionalism.

Another part of the answer is that not all unwise decisions can be undone. Imagine that a majority untrammeled by constitutional constraints decides that an external or internal threat justifies a suspension of civil liberties, or that retroactive legislation should be enacted against 'enemies of the people.' In the first place, such measures have victims whom one cannot always compensate at later times. Examples abound: the internment of the American Japanese during the Second World War, the excesses during the Chinese Cultural Revolution, the *Berufsverbot* against Communists in several countries. When society again comes to its senses, the victims may be dead or their lives destroyed. In the second place, the temporary suspension of rights easily leads to the permanent abolition of majority rule itself and to its replacement by dictatorship. It suffices to cite the years 1794 and 1933. This is possibly the central argument for constitutional constraints on democracy: without such constraints democracy itself becomes weaker, not stronger.

Question
If Elster's analogy is not false, does it mean that the United Kingdom system of government lacks legitimacy?

(C) LEGITIMACY

Why, following a revolution, does a government which has effective power backed up with military force, seek to make a constitution? Friedrich, in *Limited Government: A Comparison,* p. 118, states that such a response is 'motivated by the belief that such a constitution, if popularly approved, would give them the right to rule, over and above the mere power to do so'. If a government has the right to rule it is regarded as legitimate, and this, in turn, provides it with authority. Legitimacy, therefore, is a quality which is valuable to government.

S. E. Finer, *Comparative Government* (1970), pp. 30 – 31

The stable and effective exercise of a government's power is that which derives from its authority. By this I mean that the commands to do or to abstain proceed from persons who – no matter whether this is logical or reasonable or justifiable by any objective criterion – are *believed* to be persons who have the moral right to issue them: so that, correlatively, those to whom the commands are addressed feel a moral *duty* to *obey* them. Authority represents a two-way process: a claim to be obeyed, and a recognition that this claim is morally right. No public recognition of a claim means no authority.

Where a population recognizes a moral duty to obey, there is no need for the government to reason with it, persuade it, bribe it or threaten it, though all these exercises of power may be necessary for the marginal recalcitrants. The mere recognition of a duty to obey achieves for the government what an overwhelming application of violence would not satisfactorily achieve. As Rousseau said: 'The strongest is never strong enough unless he succeeds in turning might into right and obedience into duty.' As human nature goes, fear is certainly the father of power, but authority is its mother. To inculcate the population with the belief that their rulers have the right to demand obedience and they the corresponding duty to give it is the principal art of government.

Question
What, then, is legitimacy, and how is it acquired?

D. Beetham, *The Legitimation of Power* (1991), pp. 11–12, 15–20, 25–27 and 34–36

The different dimensions of legitimacy

The key to understanding the concept of legitimacy lies in the recognition that it is multi-dimensional in character. It embodies three distinct elements or levels, which are qualitatively different from one another. Power can be said to be legitimate to the extent that:

(i) it conforms to established rules
(ii) the rules can be justified by reference to beliefs shared by both dominant and subordinate, and
(iii) there is evidence of consent by the subordinate to the particular power relation. . . .

(i) The first and most basic level of legitimacy is that of rules . . . Power can be said to be legitimate in the first instance if it is acquired and exercised in accordance with established rules. For convenience I shall call the rules governing the acquisition and exercise of power the 'rules of power'. These rules may be unwritten, as informal conventions, or they may be formalised in legal codes or judgments. . . .

The opposite of legitimacy according to the rules is, simply, *illegitimacy*; power is illegitimate where it is either acquired in contravention of the rules (expropriation, usurpation, coup d'état), or exercised in a manner that contravenes or exceeds them. The illegal acquisition of power usually has more profound, because more all-pervasive, consequences for legitimacy than some breach or contravention in its exercise, though that depends upon the seriousness of the breach, and whether it is repeated. Where the rules of power are continually broken, we could speak of a condition of chronic illegitimacy.

(ii) On its own, legal validity is insufficient to secure legitimacy, since the rules through which power is acquired and exercised themselves stand in need of justification. This is the second level of legitimacy: power is legitimate to the extent that the rules of power can be justified in terms of beliefs shared by both dominant and subordinate. What kinds of justification and what kinds of belief are needed? To be justified, power has to be derived from a valid source of authority (this is particularly true of political power); the rules must provide that those who come to hold power have the qualities appropriate to its exercise; and the structure of power must be seen to serve a recognisably general interest, rather than simply the interests of the powerful. These justifications in turn depend upon beliefs current in a given society about what is the rightful source of authority; about what qualities are appropriate to the exercise of power and how individuals come to possess them; and some conception of a common interest, reciprocal benefit, or societal need that the system of power satisfies.

No society is characterised by a complete uniformity of beliefs. Indeed, one of the distinctive features of power relations is the difference of circumstances, opportunities and values between dominant and subordinate groups. Yet without a minimum of the appropriate beliefs defined above being shared between the dominant and the subordinate, and indeed among the subordinate themselves, there can be no basis on which justifications for the rules of power can find a purchase. Naturally what counts as an adequate or sufficient justification will be more open to dispute than what is legally valid, and there is no ultimate authority to settle such questions; nevertheless clear limits are set by logic and the beliefs of a given society to what justifications are plausible or credible within it.

This second level or dimension of legitimacy has its corresponding negative or opposite. Rules of power will lack legitimacy to the extent that they cannot be justified in terms of shared beliefs: either because no basis of shared belief exists in the first place (e.g. slavery, 'artificial' or divided communities); or because changes in belief have deprived the rules of their supporting basis (e.g. hereditary rule or male power, in face of a declining belief in the superior qualities supposedly ascribed by birth or sex); or because changing circumstances have made existing justifications for the rules implausible, despite beliefs remaining constant. [For example] it is argued that the British electoral system, with its first-past-the-post rules determining who shall be elected in each constituency, is losing its legitimacy, and to an extent therefore also weakening that of the governments elected under it. This is not because of any shift in people's beliefs, but because the rules have increasingly delivered results that diverge, both regionally and nationally, from the proportion of votes cast, and hence from accepted notions about the representative purpose of elections in a democracy. It is the increasingly unrepresentative character of the electoral system, and its consequent vulnerability to attack in a society that believes in representation, that is the basis for the weakening legitimacy of governments appointed under it. The vulnerability was there before it was exploited, and the weakening of legitimacy took place before people publicly acknowledged it. It may have taken the poll-tax legislation to bring the issue to the forefront of public attention. But the potential for doing so was already present in the growing discrepancy between the rules and the beliefs or values underpinning them. . . .

These different situations clearly have widely differing significance, but they can all be described as examples, not so much of illegitimacy, as of *legitimacy deficit* or weakness.

(iii) The third level of legitimacy involves the demonstrable expression of consent on the part of the subordinate to the particular power relation in which they are involved, through actions which provide evidence of consent. . . . [T]he importance of actions such as concluding agreements with a superior, swearing allegiance, or taking part in an election, is the contribution they make *to* legitimacy. They do this in two ways. The first is that they have a subjectively binding force for those who have taken part in them, regardless of the motives for which they have done so. Actions expressive of consent, even if undertaken purely out of self-interest, will introduce a moral component into a relationship, and create a normative commitment on the part of those engaging in them. Secondly, such actions have a publicly symbolic or declaratory force, in that they constitute an express acknowledgement on the part of the subordinate of the position of the powerful, which the latter are able to use as confirmation of their legitimacy to third parties not involved in the relationship, or those who have not taken part in any expressions of consent. They are thus often associated with impressive forms of ceremonial. . . .

What is common to legitimate power everywhere . . . is the need to 'bind in' . . . the subordinate, through actions or ceremonies publicly expressive of consent, so as to establish or reinforce their obligation to a superior authority, and to demonstrate to a wider audience the legitimacy of the powerful.

It is in the sense of the public actions of the subordinate, expressive of consent, that we can properly talk about the 'legitimation' of power, not the propaganda or public relations campaigns, the 'legitimations' generated by the powerful themselves. And if the public expression of consent contributes to the legitimacy of the powerful, then the withdrawal or refusal of consent will by the same token detract from it. Actions ranging from non-cooperation and passive resistance to open disobedience and militant opposition on the part of those qualified to give consent will in different measure erode legitimacy, and the larger the numbers involved, the greater this erosion will be. At this level, the opposite or negative of legitimacy can be called *delegitimation.*

For power to be fully legitimate, then, three conditions are required: its conformity to established rules; the justifiability of the rules by reference to shared beliefs; the express consent of the subordinate, or of the most significant among them, to the particular relations of power. All three components contribute to legitimacy, though the extent to which they are realised in a given context will be a matter of degree. Legitimacy is not an all-or-nothing affair. . . . Every power relation knows its breaches of the rules or conventions; in any society there will be some people who do not accept the norms underpinning the rules of power, and some who refuse to express their consent, or who do so only under manifest duress. What matters is how widespread these deviations are, and how substantial in relation to the underlying norms and conventions that determine the legitimacy of power in a given context. Legitimacy may be eroded, contested or incomplete; and judgements about it are usually judgements of degree, rather than all-or-nothing.

Above all, the analysis I have given above demonstrates that legitimacy is not a single quality that systems of power possess or not, but a set of distinct criteria, or multiple dimensions, operating at different levels, each of which provides moral grounds for compliance or cooperation on the part of those subordinate to a given power relation. By the same token, power can be non-legitimate in very different ways, which I have signalled by the different terms: illegitimacy, legitimacy deficit and delegitimation. The erosion of justificatory norms, slavery, conquest, dictatorship, coup d'état, separatist agitation, revolutionary mobilisation — all are examples where power lacks some element of legitimacy, but does so in very different ways. The accompanying diagram summarises in tabular form the different dimensions of legitimate and non-legitimate power that I have distinguished, to reinforce the argument of the text.

Table 1.1 The three dimensions of legitimacy

Criteria of Legitimacy	Form of Non-legitimate Power
i conformity to rules (legal validity)	illegitimacy (breach of rules)
ii justifiability of rules in terms of shared beliefs	legitimacy deficit (discrepancy between rules and supporting beliefs, absence of shared beliefs)
iii legitimation through expressed consent	delegitimation (withdrawal of consent)

The significance of legitimacy

Legitimacy, as we have seen, comprises the moral or normative aspect of power relationships; or, more correctly, the sum of these aspects. . . .

To consider first the behaviour of those subordinate within a power relationship; its legitimacy provides them with moral grounds for cooperation and obedience. Legitimate power or authority has the right to expect obedience from subordinates, even where they may disagree with the content of a particular law or instruction; and subordinates have a corresponding obligation to obey. This obligation is not absolute — hence the dilemmas that occur when people are required by a legitimate superior to do things that are morally objectionable to them, as opposed to inconvenient or merely stupid. But it is the right that legitimacy gives those in authority to require obedience in principle, regardless of the content of any particular law or instruction, that makes it so important to the coordination of people's behaviour in all spheres of social life.

The legitimacy or rightfulness of power, then, provides an explanation for obedience through the obligation it imposes on people to obey, and through the *grounds or reasons* it gives for their obedience.

However, normative grounds or reasons are not the only reasons people have for obedience. . . .

[P]ower relations are almost always constituted by a framework of incentives and sanctions, implicit if not always explicit, which align the behaviour of the subordinate with the wishes of the powerful. They do so by giving people good reasons of a different kind, those of self-interest or prudence, for not stepping out of line. Obedience is therefore to be explained by a complex of reasons, moral as well as prudential, normative as well as self-interested, that legitimate power provides for those who are subject to it. This complexity may make it difficult to determine the precise balance of reasons in any one situation; but it is important to distinguish them analytically, since each makes a very different kind of contribution to obedience. . . .

[What are the consequences of legitimacy for the behaviour of the dominant within a power relationship?]

If legitimacy, as I have argued, enhances the order, stability and effectiveness of a system of power, then we should expect that the powerful will seek to secure and maintain the legitimacy of their power, in view of its advantages to them. Here again, however, we must be careful to avoid drawing the wrong conclusions from a mistaken definition of legitimacy. If we reduce it to people's 'belief in legitimacy', then we are likely to conclude that the way in which the powerful maintain their legitimacy is primarily by means of ideological work, and through the influence they have over the beliefs and ideas of the subordinate. . . .

I do not wish to discount altogether the role of ideological work, particularly in reinforcing the basic norms that underpin a given system of power, though I shall want to argue later that the processes involved are complex ones, and have been oversimplified in much of the relevant literature. What I would emphasise at this point, however, is that we need to look quite elsewhere for the effect of legitimacy on the behaviour of the powerful. If legitimate power is, as I have argued, power that is valid according to rules, and where the rules themselves are justifiable by and in conformity with underlying norms and beliefs, then the main way in which the powerful will maintain their legitimacy is by respecting the intrinsic limits set to their power by the rules and the underlying principles on which they are grounded. Legitimate power, that is to say, is limited power; and one of the ways in which it loses legitimacy is when the powerful fail to observe its inherent limits.

What are these limits? I would draw attention to two different kinds. One kind of limit is set by the rules which determine what the powers of the powerful are, and what they can rightly expect those subordinate to them to do — which specify, in other words, the respective duties and obligations of those involved in a power relationship. These rules may be largely conventional, or they may be legally defined. A feature of the modern world is the increasingly precise legal specification of the respective powers, or 'sphere of competence', of each powerholder. Even today, however, there is still considerable room left for 'custom and practice', for conventional understandings built up over time through processes of struggle and compromise, which govern the expectations of the powerful and the subordinate about what is, and is not, required of them; what can, and cannot, legitimately be demanded.

For the powerful to breach these rules in a substantial way, say by imposing some new or additional obligation on subordinates without warning or consultation, is either to invite action for legal redress, or, where the law is silent, to provoke informal protests which may develop into a more widespread crisis of legitimacy for the system of power. Unless they are arrogant or stupid, powerholders will only take such action when it is essential to some important purpose, or if they are driven to it by a serious predicament of their own. The fact that mostly they do not do so, and that they mostly respect the rules and conventions governing their relations with those subordinate to them, makes it easy to overlook an essential feature of legitimacy: that it sets limits to the behaviour of the powerful as well as imposing obligations on the subordinate. Because we more readily notice what the powerful do than what they refrain from doing, this essential feature of legitimacy tends to go unremarked.

The other kind of constraint which their need to maintain legitimacy imposes on the powerful is a more fundamental one: to respect the basic principles that underpin the rules or system of power, and to protect them from challenge. Rulers who derive their legitimacy from a divine source must respect religious traditions and defer to religious authorities; they will regard any threat to religion or religious belief as among the most serious they face. Those who derive their authority from the people will ignore at their peril any insistent and widespread popular current of opinion; to be seen to favour foreign interests at the expense of national ones will do more damage to their standing than almost anything else. Those who claim a monopoly of representation of the working class by virtue of a privileged knowledge of their interests cannot afford to allow independent sources of working-class opinion to find expression, or alternative institutions of representation to develop, which might challenge their monopoly. The legitimating ideas and justificatory principles that underpin the given institutions of power define which challenges the ruler has to take most seriously, because they strike at the basis of the system of rule itself.

Question

If a government, using its majority in Parliament, passes appropriate laws empowering it to do specified acts, are its activities thereby rendered legitimate because they are done in accordance with the law, regardless of how oppressive or repugnant those laws might be? See chapter 4 and also the extract which follows.

P. McAuslan and J. F. McEldowney, 'Legitimacy and the Constitution: the Dissonance between Theory and Practice' in *Law, Legitimacy and the Constitution* (1985) pp. 11 – 14

Legitimacy . . . does not deal so much with whether activities of government are lawful as whether they accord with what are generally perceived to be or what have for long been held up to be, the fundamental principles of the constitution according to which government is or ought to be conducted. Lawfulness is clearly an issue in so far as one of the fundamental principles of the British, no less than most other constitutions, is that government action should take place under the authority of, and in accordance with law – the narrow literal meaning of the rule of law – so that repeated unlawful actions or a perceived casualness towards the duty to comply with the law would in itself begin to raise doubts about the legitimacy of governmental action. The rule of law is generally thought to have a broader 'political' meaning which covers the same ground as, if it is not quite synonymous with, the concept of limited government. This meaning embraces such matters as fair and equitable administrative practices; recognition of the rights of political opposition and dissent; complying with constitutional conventions; adequate means of redress of grievances about governmental action affecting one. Thus a government which while adhering to the rule of law narrowly defined, flouted all or most of the practices generally thought to be covered by the rule of law broadly defined would also give rise to doubts about its legitimacy. One of the clearest and best examples of a government on the whole scrupulous to comply with the rule of law narrowly defined yet consistently flouting it, as to the majority of its citizens, when broadly defined is the government of the Republic of South Africa, in relation to its non-white citizens.

What makes the issue of the legitimacy of our constitutional arrangements so problematic is the general open–endedness of those arrangements; that is, the difficulty of knowing whether a practice or non-practice is or is not constitutional.

Even where practices may not differ over time, or place, there may be an inconsistency about them or a lack of knowledge about them, or a long-standing dispute about them, which could make it equally difficult to argue that following or not following a practice was or was not constitutional or legitimate. Probably the best example of this is the use of the royal prerogative, and the extent to which the courts may pass judgment on any particular use. Notwithstanding that the royal prerogative as a source of power for the government antedates Acts of Parliament, has been at the root of a civil war and a revolution in England and has been litigated about on countless major occasions in respect of its use both at home and overseas, its scope is still unclear as is the role of the courts in relation thereto. The use by the Prime Minister of powers under the royal prerogative to ban trade unions at the Government Communication Headquarters at Cheltenham in 1983 was contested both for its lawfulness – that is whether such powers could be used and if so whether they were used correctly – and also for its legitimacy – that is whether, even if the constitutional power existed, this was a proper and fair use of the power. It can be seen that questions of lawfulness and legitimacy shade into one another here though the answers do not: the lawfulness of the action taken, confirmed by the House of Lords in 1984 (*Council of Civil Service Unions* v *Minister for the Civil Service* [1984] 3 All ER 935) did not and does not dispose of its legitimacy.

The G.C.H.Q. case is valuable for another point. We have pointed out that lawfulness is not to be confused with legitimacy. No more is constitutionality. What the Prime Minister did was not merely lawful; she exercised the constitutional powers of her office in the way in which those powers had always been exercised. That is, the use of the royal prerogative as the legal backing for the management of the public service, the principle that a civil servant is a servant of the Crown and holds office at the pleasure of the Crown is one of the best known principles of constitutional law, hallowed by usage and sanctioned by the courts. What is in issue from the perspective of legitimacy is whether the particular use made of that undoubted constitutional power, the manner of its use, and the justification both for the use and manner of use – that considerations of national security required both a banning of trade unions and no consultation with affected officers before the ban was announced – was a fair and reasonable use of power? Did it accord with legitimate expectations of fair and reasonable persons or was it a high-handed exercise of power of a kind more to be expected of an authoritarian government than one guided by and subscribing to principles of limited government?

In considering the issue of legitimacy in relation to our constitutional arrangements and the exercise of governmental power, what has to be done is to examine a range of practices, decisions, actions (and non-practices, -decisions and -actions) statements and policies which between them can amount to a portrait of power, so that we can form a judgment or an assessment of that power set against the principles of limited government outlined and discussed so far. It is not every failure to comply with law or every constitutional and non-constitutional short cut which adds up to an approach to powers which give rise to questions of legitimacy. If that were so, there would scarcely be a government in the last 100 years which could be regarded as legitimate, but it is those uses of power and law which seem to betray or which can only be reasonably explained by a contempt for or at least an impatience with the principles of limited government and a belief that the rightness of the policies to be executed excuse or justify the methods whereby they are executed. If, as we believe to be the case, powers are being so exercised, then the issue of constitutional legitimacy which arises is quite simple: what is the value or use of a constitution based on and designed to ensure the maintenance of a system of limited government if it can, quite lawfully and even constitutionally, be set on one side? Have we not in such circumstances arrived at that 'elective dictatorship' of which Lord Hailsham gave warning in 1977:

> It is only now that men and women are beginning to realize that representative institutions are not necessarily guardians of freedom but can themselves become engines of tyranny. They can be manipulated by minorities, taken over by extremists, motivated by the self-interest of organised millions.

Occasionally the people from whom legitimacy ultimately derives, pass judgment on government.

McAuslan and McEldowney, *ibid.*, p. 1

Mr Clive Ponting's acquittal by a jury in February 1985, after he had admitted to passing official Government papers to a person not authorised to receive them, the very essence of section 2 of the Official Secrets Act 1911, and despite the most explicit summing up by the trial judge that they should convict, raises the question of what motivated the jury. It would suggest that when faced with a choice between a case which rests on constitutional theories about limited government derived from a 'higher law' which controlled what government could legitimately do, and a case which rested on actual practices of government bolstered by actual law, the jury preferred the theory of what the constitution ought to be to the practice of what it is. Little wonder that, as one newspaper put it, Ministers were aghast at the verdict. The *Concise Oxford Dictionary* defines 'aghast' as meaning terrified. This essay will seek to show Ministers would indeed have good reason to be terrified if ordinary people began preferring constitutional theory to government practice and acted on their preferences in their judgment of politicians. More particularly the jury's verdict in the Ponting trial may be seen then as the response of ordinary people to trends in government practices which seem to them to be, in perhaps indefinable ways, wrong.

Questions

1. In this case it was a jury of 12 which, by its verdict, appeared to be commenting on the legitimacy of governmental action in attempting to mislead the Foreign Affairs Select Committee about the circumstances surrounding the sinking of the *General Belgrano,* an Argentinian warship, during the Falklands Campaign in 1982. These 12 jurors may, or may not,

have been representative of the views of the public. Are there more representative ways in which public sentiments regarding governmental action may be expressed?
2. Is majority rule under a system of parliamentary democracy a sufficient guarantee of legitimacy? What does majority rule mean in the context of the United Kingdom?

(D) DEMOCRACY

In the opening sentences of *Le Contrat Social* (1762) Rousseau stated:

> Man is born free and everywhere he is in chains. One thinks himself the master of others, and still remains the greater slave than they. How did this change come about? I do not know. What can make it legitimate? That question I think I can answer.

The answer he gave was that the only ground of legitimacy is to be found in the general will of the people, as only the people can say who has the right to rule them. Thus it is the people who give legitimacy to a constitution – sovereignty resides with the people and, in turn, where the constitution sets up a system of elected representative government, that government acquires its authority both from the constitution and the people who elect it.

Does the constitution in the United Kingdom (if there is one) have a democratic basis? Is the system of government democratic? A starting point is to examine what a liberal-democracy is.

C. B. Macpherson, *The Real World of Democracy* (1966), pp. 4 – 11

[O]ur liberal-democracy, like any other system, is a system of power; that it is, indeed, again like any other, a double system of power. It is a system by which people can be *governed,* that is, made to do things they would not otherwise do, and made to refrain from doing things they otherwise might do. Democracy as a system of government is, then, a system by which power is exerted by the state over individuals and groups within it. But more than that, a democratic government, like any other, exists to uphold and enforce a certain kind of society, a certain set of relations between individuals, a certain set of rights and claims that people have on each other both directly, and indirectly through their rights to property. These relations themselves are relations of power – they give different people, in different capacities, power over others. . . .

[L]iberal-democracy and capitalism go together. Liberal-democracy is found only in countries whose economic system is wholly or predominantly that of capitalist enterprise. And, with few and mostly temporary exceptions, every capitalist country has a liberal-democratic political system. . . .

The claims of democracy would never have been admitted in the present liberal-democracies had those countries not got a solid basis of liberalism first. The liberal democracies that we know were liberal first and democratic later. To put this in another way, before democracy came in the Western world there came the society and the politics of choice, the society and politics of competition, the society and politics of the market. This was the liberal society and state. It will be obvious that I am using liberal here in a very broad sense. I use it in what I take to be its essential sense, to mean that both the society as a whole and the system of government were oganized on a principle of freedom of choice. . . .

To make this society work, or to allow it to operate, a non-arbitrary, or responsible, system of government was needed. And this was provided, by revolutionary action in England in the seventeenth century, in America in the eighteenth, in France in the eighteenth and nineteenth, and by a variety of methods in most other Western countries sometime within those centuries. What was established was a system whereby the government was put in a sort of market situation. The government was treated as the supplier of certain political goods – not just the political good of law and order in general, but the specific political goods demanded by those who had the upper hand in running that particular kind of society. What was needed was the kind of laws and regulations, and tax structure, that would make the market society work, or allow it to work, and the kind of state services – defence, and even military expansion, education, sanitation, and various sorts of assistance to industry, such as tariffs and grants for railway development – that were thought necessary to make the system run efficiently and profitably. These were the kinds of political goods that were wanted. But how was the demand to call forth the supply? How to make government responsive to the choices of those it was expected to cater to? The way was of course to put governmental power into the hands of men who were made subject to periodic elections at which there was a choice of candidates and parties. The electorate did not need to be a democratic one, and as a general rule was not; all that was needed was an electorate consisting of the men of substance, so that the government would be responsive to their choices.

To make this political choice an effective one, there had to be certain other liberties. There had to be freedom of associaton – that is, freedom to form political parties, and freedom to form the kind of associations we now know as pressure groups, whose purpose is to bring to bear on parties and on governments the combined pressure of the interests they represent. And there had to be freedom of speech and publication, for without these the freedom of association is of no use. These freedoms could not very well be limited to men of the directing classes. They had to be demanded in principle for everybody. The risk that the others would use them to get a political voice was a risk that had to be taken.

So came what I am calling the liberal state. Its essence was the system of alternate or multiple parties whereby governments could be held responsible to different sections of the class or classes that had a political voice. There was nothing necessarily democratic about the responsible party system. In the country of its origin, England, it was well established, and working well, half a century or a century before the franchise became at all democratic. This is not surprising, for the job of the liberal state was to maintain and promote the liberal society, which was not essentially a democratic or an equal society. The job of the competitive party system was to uphold the competitive market society, by keeping the government responsive to the shifting majority interests of those who were running the market society.

However, the market society did produce, after a time, a pressure for democracy which became irresistible. . . .

So finally the democratic franchise was introduced into the liberal state. It did not come easily or quickly. In most of the present liberal-democratic countries it required many decades of agitation and organization, and in few countries was anything like it achieved until late in the nineteenth century. The female half of the population had to wait even longer for an equal political voice: not until substantial numbers of women had moved out from the shelter of the home to take an independent place in the labour market was women's claim to a voice in the political market allowed.

So democracy came as a late addition to the competitive market society and the liberal state. The point of recalling this is, of course, to emphasize that democracy came as an adjunct to the competitive liberal society and state. It is not simply that democracy came later. It is also that democracy in these societies, was demanded, and was admitted, on competitive liberal grounds. Democracy was demanded, and admitted, on the ground that it was unfair not to have it in a competitive society. It was something the competitive society logically needed. . . .

What the addition of democracy to the liberal state did was simply to provide constitutional channels for popular pressures, pressures to which governments would have had to yield in about the same measure anyway, merely to maintain public order and avoid revolution. By admitting the mass of the people into the competitive party system, the liberal state did not abandon its fundamental nature; it simply opened the competitive political system to all the individuals who had been created by the competitive market society. The liberal state fulfilled its own logic. In so doing, it neither destroyed nor weakened itself; it strengthened both itself and the market society. It liberalized democracy while democratizing liberalism.

Question

If this view is correct, did, or does, the 'constitution' in the United Kingdom have a democratic basis, i.e. was, or is, its legitimacy to be found in the general will of the people? See Ridley below.

F. F. Ridley, 'There is no British Constitution: A Dangerous Case of the Emperor's Clothes', 41 *Parliamentary Affairs* (1988), pp. 340, 343 – 345

The first characteristic of a constitution . . . is that it constitutes – or reconstitutes – a system of government. . . . [I]n constitutional theory a governmental order derives its legitimacy from the constituent act which establishes it. . . .

Democratic constitutions universally state the principle of popular sovereignty and their legitimacy now rests on popular enactment. This follows the American tradition: 'We the people of the United States . . . do ordain and establish this constitution'. Similar words are found almost everywhere. Some may invoke a higher sanctity for parts of the constitution than the will of the people. Thus the American Bill of Rights is founded on the Declaration of Independence's self-evident truths that all men are endowed by their Creator with certain inalienable rights, but that does not alter the source of the constitution's authority. . . .

The people are generally called on to elect a special constituent assembly mandated to draft a constitution, though this may not always be the case – as in General de Gaulle's constitution for the Fifth Republic. Although the American constitution was ratified by state legislatures, in more recent times the people are almost universally called on to ratify it in a referendum. . . .

Britain never developed this idea of popular sovereignty in constitutional terms, even if we sometimes talk of the sovereignty of the electorate in political terms. Even if the latter were true, it would merely allow the people to choose their government: it does not base the governmental order, the British 'constitution', on their authority and thus only gives them only half their right. (Moreover, since a parliamentary majority can change that order, prolong its own life, alter the franchise or reform the electoral system, even the political rights of the electorate depend on Parliament.) What we have, instead, is the sovereignty of Parliament. Parliament determines – and alters – the country's system of government. If we ask where that power comes from, the answer is broadly that Parliament claimed it and the courts recognised it. The people never came into the picture. The liberal (middle-class) democracies established in Europe had, despite their generally limited franchise, to base their constitutions on the principle that ultimate authority was vested in the people. Britain seems to be the sole exception to this democratic path.

Question

If, as it is argued, the 'constitution' of the United Kingdom had no democratic basis, is the system of government nevertheless democratic? See Finer below.

S. E. Finer, *Comparative Government* (1970), pp. 63 – 66

(1) The primary meaning of democracy is government which is derived from public opinion and is accountable to it. As to *accountability;* this implies that it is not sufficient for a government to justify its existence because at some time in the past it was representative of popular opinion; for the two may have diverged since then. 'Accountability' entails that a government must continuously test its representativeness, that is to say whether its claim that it is 'derived from public opinion' is still valid.
(2) This public opinion, it must therefore be presumed, is overtly and freely expressed. For if it is not, how can anybody *know* that the government is still 'derived from public opinion', i.e. is still representative? But 'overtly and freely to express opinion' implies some opportunity and machinery for making that opinion known, and therefore implies some kind of a suffrage, some kind of a voice or vote. . . .
(3) In matters of contention between sections of public opinion it is the majority opinion that prevails.

These three characteristics must, it seems, form part of any definition of democracy. . . .

Thus the first assumption of liberal-democracy is that it is a democracy in the sense expressed above. But liberal-democracy is a *qualified* democracy. In this type of government there are other presuppositions or assumptions beyond the one which we have already stated.

The first of these is that government is *limited.* This implies that the government is operating in a world of autonomous, spontaneously self-creating, voluntary associations. In such conditions the government operates only at the margin of social activity. That it ought to interfere and regulate or even suppress these autonomous, self-creating, voluntary associations is a matter for it to prove: it is not assumed. . . . The authority of government therefore is limited; and this can be expressed by saying that certain rights of the individual and of the private association are safeguarded. A kind of ring fence is drawn around them and the onus lies on the government to show whether, why and to what extent this ought to be breached.

The second qualification to democracy in this particular 'liberal' form is that society is recognized as being *pluralistic.* . . . To recognize society as being pluralistic, therefore, carries the additional assumption that the government sets out to rule, not in the interest of any one group or alliance of groups, but in the common interest of all. . . .

This highlights the third qualification: the liberal-democratic type of government is one in which *it is denied that there is any objective science of society or of morals.* On the contrary, it is assumed that in the last resort truth is a matter of individual consciences where all consciences are held, by an act of faith, to be equal either in the sight of God or in the sight of man. Two working conclusions follow from this, namely, toleration and the qualification of majority rule.

Why toleration? Because if there is no objective science of society and morals, then clearly no group, not even the government, has any moral justification for imposing any creed, philosophy, religion or ideology upon the rest of society. Again, since it is assumed by this act of faith that all individuals are equal in the sight of God, man or both, then dissent must be tolerated and each has the right to put his own point of view. Again, since truth is held to be individual and also fallible, rulership will be both conditional and also temporary; because clearly the views as to what is true and therefore proper for government to act upon will change from time to time as opinion fluctuates amongst the body of the people. So, this qualified form of democracy entails that the government is representative of and responsive to public opinion; and that where this opinion is not unanimous it is representative of and responsive to the majority. But these majorities will usually be constantly changing. . . .

But even majority rule is seriously qualified in the liberal-democracy. . . . But being a liberal-democracy also implies that the minorities must be given a chance to become a majority; and that means, therefore, that they must be given a chance status and a means to convert the majority. In order to make this possible, certain guarantees and machinery would have to be established.

Note

Where there is a permanent majority, however, representative democracy may fail to provide legitimation either of a government or of the system of government. See Barker, below.

R. Barker, *Political Legitimacy and the State* (1990), pp. 141 – 143

It is difficult to determine in any precise way the contribution of elections to the maintenance of legitimacy. By comparing the history of Northern Ireland with that of the rest of the United Kingdom it is clear that the mere fact of elections is not sufficient. If the result is never in any doubt, so that it is not 'the people' but always and only a section and that the same section of them which confers consent on government, then those who feel themselves permanently excluded will also feel no great obligations to the regime. No legitimacy without representation. . . .

On the other hand, so long as the electoral system appears to give due weight to most parties, the fact that individual votes may often have little effect does not deter them from being cast. Voters turn out in large numbers in safe seats where their individual support or opposition to the sitting candidate can make no difference whatsoever to the result. Voting has a ritual aspect, whereby citizens formally and publicly show their preferences for one party over others, and hence their willingness to accept the result of the contest, and their legitimation of that result. It enables people to identify with those who lead or govern them, to see politicians and rulers as both special and, at the same time, exemplifying the character of their followers. . . .

Thus two broad sanctioning functions can be identified in voting. First of the policies of particular governments, second of the governing system in general, of the state. These may of course in practice be confused or entangled with each other, as they are in Northern Ireland, or as they are in any state where the elections are largely or wholly a political ritual or a way of mobilizing mass support or approval for a regime in which party and state are indistinguishable, and electoral choice between contestants for office non-existent. Once this occurs the democratic process can have an important function in *failing* to legitimize the state, and in providing justification for a rejection by groups of subjects not only of particular governments, but of more general constitutional arrangements. The predictable ineffectiveness of the nationalist vote in Northern Ireland can be used to justify rejection not just of a particular government but of the whole constitutional structure which maintains the inclusion of Northern Ireland in the United Kingdom rather than in a new all-Ireland state. In a smaller way after 1987 the emergence of a Scottish electorate overwhelmingly hostile to a Conservative government in power on the basis of English electoral success can sustain nationalist arguments for the general illegitimacy of the constitutional arrangements of the United Kingdom.

Note

The theory of limited government appears to demand more than simple majority rule. It is important to examine whether the system of government in the United Kingdom has advanced beyond this idea of the 'rightness' of the majority. This involves an examination of how elections operate, how governments acquire power, and how they use that power. Do they claim authority simply on the basis of electoral victory to do as they please, including changing the constitutional framework, or do they find themselves restrained from so acting by certain fundamental principles?

Endeavouring to answer such questions has, in the past, involved largely value judgements. Political scientists are now attempting to develop indices to assist in informing such judgements. The extract which follows outlines some of the issues involved.

David Beetham, 'Key Principles and Indices for a Democratic Audit' in *Defining and Measuring Democracy* Beetham, D. ed, 1994, pp. 25 – 30

First, it is necessary to explain the idea of a 'democratic audit' itself. This is the simple but ambitious project of assessing the state of democracy in a single country. Like other Western countries, the UK calls itself a democracy, and claims to provide a model for others to follow. Yet how democratic is it actually? And how does it measure up to the standards that it uses to assess others, including the countries of the Third World? Such questions are not accidental, but are provoked by a widespread sense of disquiet within the UK at the state of its political institutions – a disquiet which runs deeper than the mere fact that a single party has been in power for so long. . .

The project of a democratic audit, then, not only requires a clear specification of what exactly is to be audited. It also requires a robust and defensible conception of democracy, from which can be derived specific criteria and standards of assessment. An account of this conception and these criteria is provided in the following section.

Principles and indices of democracy

. . . Democracy is a *political* concept, concerning the collectively binding decisions about the rules and policies of a group, association or society. It claims that such decision-making should be, and it is realized to the extent that such decision-making actually is, subject to the control of all members of the collectivity considered as equals. That is to say, democracy embraces the related principles of *popular control* and *political equality.* In small-scale and simple associations, people can control collective decision-making directly, through equal rights to vote on law and policy in person. In large and complex associations, they typically do so indirectly, for example through appointing representatives to act for them. Here popular control usually takes the form of control over decision-*makers*, rather than over decision-making itself; and typically it requires a complex set of institutions and practices to make the principle effective. Similarly political equality, rather than being realized in an equal say in decision-making directly, is realized to the extent that there exists an equality of votes between electors, an equal right to stand for public office, an equality in the conditions for making one's voice heard and in treatment at the hands of legislators, and so on.

These two principles, of popular control and political equality, form the guiding thread of a democratic audit. They are the principles which inform those institutions and practices of Western countries that are characteristically democratic; and they also provide a standard against which their level of democracy can be assessed. As they stand, however, they are too general. Like the indices developed by other political scientists, they need to be broken down into specific, and where possible, measurable, criteria for the purpose of assessment or audit.

To do this we have separated the process of popular control over government into four distinct, albeit overlapping, dimensions. First and most basic is the popular election of the parliament or legislature and the head of government. The degree or extent of popular control is here to be assessed by such criteria as: the *reach* of the electoral process (that is, which public offices are open to election, and what powers they have over non-elected officials); its *inclusiveness* (what exclusions apply, both formally and informally, to parties, candidates and voters, whether in respect of registration or voting itself); its *fairness* as between parties, candidates and voters, and the range of effective choice it offers the latter; its *independence* from the government of the day; and so on. These criteria can be summed up in the familiar phrase 'free and fair elections', though this phrase does not fully capture all the aspects needed for effective popular control.

The second dimension for analysis concerns what is known as 'open and accountable government'. Popular control requires, besides elections, the continuous accountability of government: directly, to the electorate, through the public justification for its policies; indirectly, to agents acting on the people's behalf. In respect of the latter, we can distinguish between the *political* accountability of government to the legislature or parliament for the content and execution of its policies; its *legal* accountability to the courts for ensuring that all state personnel, elected and non-elected, act within the laws and powers approved by the legislature; its *financial* accountability to both the legislature and the courts. Accountability in turn depends upon public knowledge of what government is up to, from sources that are independent of its own public relations machine. In all these aspects, a democratic audit will need to assess the respective powers and independence, both legal and actual, of different bodies: of the legislature and judiciary in relation to the executive; of the investigative capacity of the media; of an independent public statistical service; of the powers of individual citizens to seek redress in the event of maladministration or injustice.

Underpinning both the first two dimensions of popular control over government is a third: guaranteed civil and political rights or liberties. The freedoms of speech, association, assembly and movement, the right to due legal process, and so on, are not something specific to a particular *form* of democracy called 'liberal democracy'; they are essential to democracy as such, since without them no effective popular control over government is possible . . . These rights or liberties are necessary if citizens are to communicate and associate with one another independently of government; if they are to express dissent from government or to influence it on an ongoing basis; if electoral choice and accountability is to be at all meaningful. A democratic audit will need to assess not only the legally prescribed content of these citizens' rights, but also the effectiveness of the institutions and procedures whereby they are guaranteed in practice.

A fourth dimension of popular control concerns the arena of what is called 'civil society': the nexus of associations through which people organize independently to manage their own affairs, and which can also act as a channel of influence upon government and a check on its powers. This is a more contestable dimension of democracy, not only because the criteria for its assessment are much less well formed than for the other three areas, but also because there is room for disagreement as to whether it should be seen as a necessary *condition for* democracy, or as an essential *part of* it. Our view is that a democratic society is a part of democracy, and goes beyond the concept of 'civil society', with its stress on the *independence* of societal self-organization, to include such features as: the representativeness of the media and their accessibility to different social groups and points of view; the public accountability and internal democracy of powerful private corporations; the degree of political awareness of the citizen body and the extent of its public participation; the democratic character of the political culture and of the education system.

The criteria or indices of popular control can thus be divided into four interrelated segments, which go to make up the major dimensions of democracy for contemporary societies. . . A complete democratic audit should examine each segment in turn, to assess not only the effectiveness of popular control in practice, but also the degree of political equality in each area: under free and fair elections, how far each vote is of equal value, and how far there is equality of opportunity to stand for public office, regardless of which section of society a person comes from; under open and accountable government, whether any individuals or groups are systematically excluded from access to, or influence upon, government, or redress from it; under civil and political rights or liberties, whether these are effectively guaranteed to all sections of society; under democratic society, the degree of equal opportunity for self-organization, access to the media, redress from powerful corporations, and so on.

(E) LIMITED GOVERNMENT

The concept of limited government comprises two ideals, that of accountability of government for the exercise of its powers, and that of limits placed on the exercise of those powers. What, then, are the conditions for accountable or, as it is often termed, responsible government?

Jack Lively, *Democracy* (1975), pp. 43 – 44

What then are the conditions necessary for the existence of responsible government? What is needed to ensure that some popular control can be exerted over political leadership, some governmental accountability can be enforced? Two main conditions can be suggested, that governments should be removable by electoral decisions and that some alternative can be substituted by electoral decision. The alternative, it should be stressed, must be more than an alternative governing group. It must comprehend alternatives in policy, since it is only if an electoral decision can alter the actions of government that popular control can be said to be established. . . . To borrow the economic analogy, competition is meaningless, or at any rate cannot create consumer sovereignty, unless there is some product differentiation.

In detail there might be a great deal of discussion about the institutional arrangements necessary to responsible government, but in general some are obvious. There must be free elections, in which neither the incumbent government nor any other group can determine the electoral result by means other than indications of how they will act if returned to power. Fraud, intimidation and bribery are thus incompatible with responsible government. . . . Another part of the institutional frame necessary to responsible government is freedom of association. Unless groups wishing to compete for leadership have the freedom to organize and formulate alternative programmes, the presentation of alternatives would be impossible. Lastly, freedom of speech is necessary since silent alternatives can never be effective alternatives. In considering such arrangements, we cannot stick at simple legal considerations; we must move from questions of 'freedom from' to questions of 'ability to'. The absence of any legal bar to association will not, for example, create the ability to associate if there are heavy costs involved which only some groups can bear. Nor will the legal guarantee of freedom of speech be of much use if access to the mass media is severely restricted.

This could be summed up by saying that responsible government depends largely upon the existence of, and free competiton between, political parties.

Whether the British system of government creates the conditions for responsible government is doubted in some quarters. Lord Hailsham spoke of elective dictatorship.

Lord Hailsham, *The Dilemma of Democracy* (1978), pp. 21 – 22

The old party structure, which for so long guaranteed the evolutionary character of our society, seems to me to have broken down. . . .

[I]t seems to me that we are moving more and more in the direction of an elective dictatorship, not the less objectionable in principle because it is inefficient in practice, and not the less tyrannical in its nature because the opposed parties, becoming more and more polarized in their attitudes, seek with some prospects of success to seize the new levers of power and use them alternately to reverse the direction taken by their immediate predecessors. All the more unfortunate does this become in the presence of narrow majorities, each representing a minority of the electorate, sometimes a small minority, and when at least one of the parties believes that the prerogatives and rights conferred by electoral victory, however narrow, not merely entitle but compel it to impose on the helpless but unorganized majority irreversible changes for which it never consciously voted and to which most of its members are opposed.

It seems to me that this is a situation the reverse of liberal and even the reverse of democratic, in the sense in which the word has hitherto been understood. Fundamental and irreversible changes ought only to be imposed, if at all, in the light of an unmistakable national consensus. It follows that, if I am right, the overriding need of the moment is to pursue policies and enact legislation to ensure that a like situation to the present is never allowed to recur. It is true that the present nature of the threat can be seen to come from the left. But this need not necessarily be so, and almost certainly it will not always be so. . . .

My thesis is that our institutions must be so structurally altered that, so far as regards permanent legislation, the will of the majority will always prevail against that of the party composing the executive for the time being, and that, whoever may form the government of the day will be compelled to follow procedures and policies compatible with the nature of Parliamentary democracy and the rule of freedom under law.

Questions

1. Lord Hailsham wrote in 1978; has anything changed since then to contradict his thesis, or have subsequent events confirmed his worst fears? See also Leslie Wolf-Phillips below.

2. N. Johnson, 'Constitutional Reform: Some Dilemmas for a Conservative Philosophy' in *Conservative Party Politics* (Layton-Henry, ed., 1980), at p. 139, stated: 'A relative majority in the House of Commons may rest on a minority position in the country. Government on these terms is tolerable if the party in power recognises that there are limits to what it is entitled to do.' Is there any evidence that such limits have been recognised in the last 17 years?

Leslie Wolf-Phillips, 'A Long Look at the British Constitution' 37 *Parliamentary Affairs* (1984), pp. 385, 398 – 401

The idealised view of the British system is that, under a head of State insulated from politics, generally admired, and with long and varied experience, the government of the day is led by a Prime Minister whose party has been given a parliamentary majority by a mature electorate which has participated in free and open elections. Parliament debates the great issues of the day, controls national expenditure and taxation, criticises government policy as an aid to its improvement, scrutinises the work of the central administration, and ensures the redress of collective and individual grievances. The Prime Minister heads a government composed of a Cabinet of her senior ministers and about eighty non-Cabinet ministers all bound to a policy implicitly approved by the electorate; the Prime Minister and all her colleagues must justify their actions and their policies before parliament, and if parliament withdraws its confidence, they must resign and face the stern judgment of the electorate upon their stewardship. Each minister has departmental responsibility and can be called to account for the working of his department before parliament; if incompetence or maladministration be proved then the minister will be called upon to resign either by the Prime Minister or by the direct action of parliament. The Queen as Head of State gives overall stability to the political system and the Prime Minister as Head of Government is one who has served a long apprenticeship in parliament in high office of state and who is the elected leader of a party which has the confidence of the nation. The 'Unwritten Constitution' has the virtue of flexibility and permits the wide use of constitutional conventions, both permitting and facilitating evolutionary consensual change. Finally, the House of Lords provides a forum removed from party ties and considerations, where the experienced and distinguished perform functions of assistance, advice, continuity and, when needed, a measure of restraint on the popularly-elected transient majority in the House of Commons.

What is the reality? The extension of the franchise, the growth of national mass parties and the development of the mass media have changed the nature of general elections, which have become largely personalised into a contest between party leaders. The majority of the electorate are only marginally politically conscious, and the personalisation of political issues and allegiances reflect this marginality. The voting pattern for the parties is so uniform throughout the country that the influence on a constituency of a particular candidate is insignificant; candidates without the support of a major party can expect to fail and minor or ad hoc or single-interest parties can expect to be swept aside. . . . Elections cannot be, and should not be regarded as, a means for approving the details of comprehensive manifestoes and the electors often seem to vote against a party rather than for the winning party. . . .

The only mandate that most electors consider they have given to newly-elected Members of Parliament is to support the party and its leader; certainly, the Prime Minister expects, and usually gets, the support of the mass of the parliamentary majority party and the entire hundred or so members of the Government that is formed.

The supremacy of the Prime Minister is further enhanced by the authority to obtain (or threaten to obtain) a dissolution of parliament, the possibility of rebel Members being disowned and replaced by their constituency parties, the feelings of loyalty to one's party and the fear of giving aid and comfort to the opposition parties. Whatever the formal constitutional conventions and party rules, the Prime Minister is normally in effective control. Not only does he or she have the authority to appoint and dismiss or advance or relegate ministers, but there is also access to the patronage system for honours, awards and selection of candidates for high public office. The appointments and preferments policies of the present Prime Minister has shown the influence that can be borne in these matters. The former belief that the Prime Minister was primus inter pares (first among equals) has given way to the realisation that the office-holder is primum mobile (the first mover). The Prime Minister dominates the cabinet, its members wait upon a summons; there is control and prior approval of the agenda from the Prime Minister; the skilful exploitation of collective responsibility by the Prime Minister can neutralise and isolate a recalcitrant cabinet minority which has no choice but to 'shut up or get out'; the Prime Minister has wide access to a network of policy-making cabinet committees, and 'deals' can be made in inter-departmental committees, cabinet committees, or between the Prime Minister and individual ministers. Business laid before the full cabinet has often been the subject of previous informal agreement between the Prime Minister and certain colleagues in order that opposition may be outmanoeuvred. . . .

In brief, the actual Westminster model is that of authoritarian single-party governments in a House of Commons dominated by the Prime Minister and composed largely of disciplined parties with most votes in the House of Commons being highly predictable; every three or four years there is a general election held under a crude simple majority electoral system with minimal participation by the electorate in the choice of who shall be their candidate, though they do have the choice between the candidates who are selected by the party activists; between 20% and 30% of the electorate do not vote at all. Governments rarely fall as a result of a vote in the House of Commons and resignations under ministerial responsibility are almost as rare. The vast majority of legislation proposed by the government of the day is passed; it is rare, indeed it is well-nigh impossible, for legislation to be passed of which the government does not approve. Orthodox constitutional theory bestows on individual members the right of independent action and does not regard them as the representative of the party without which they would not have been elected; over-solicitude for the wishes of their constituents would probably lead them into conflict with the party in parliament. The parties at large are not seen as the formers of policy for the government; that is a task reserved for the parliamentary members of the governing party.

Note

In what other ways may the powers of government be limited? At the outset it must be recognised that there are three institutions of government, each with specific functions. The legislature has the function of making new law or amending or repealing existing law. The executive has the administrative function of conducting government in accordance with the law. The judiciary has the function of interpreting the law and applying it to specific cases. In 1690 John Locke identified a danger arising from the possession of more than one power. In his *Second Treatise of Civil Government,* Chapter XII, para. 143, Locke stated:

> It may be too great a temptation to human frailty, apt to grasp at power, for the same persons who have the power of making laws, to have also in their hands the power to execute them, whereby they may exempt themselves from obedience to the laws they make, and suit the law, both in its making and execution, to their own private advantage.

This idea was developed further by Montesquieu, the French philosopher, who expressed the view that it was the separation of powers of government which ensured the liberty of the English. He expressed the doctrine in *L'Esprit des Lois,* Book XI, Chapter VI (2nd edn, vol. 1, p. 220) as follows:

> When the Legislative Power is united with the Executive Power in the same person or body of magistrates, there is no liberty because it is to be feared that the same Monarch or the same Senate will make tyrannical laws in order to execute them tyrannically. There is no liberty if the Judicial Power is not separated from the Legislative Power and from the Executive Power. If it were joined with the Legislative Power, the power over the life and liberty of citizens would be arbitrary, because the Judge would be Legislator. If it were joined to the Executive Power, the Judge would have the strength of an oppressor. All would be lost if the same man, or the same body of chief citizens, or the nobility, or the people, exercised these three powers, that of making laws, that of executing public decisions, and that of judging the crimes or the disputes of private persons.

This was a somewhat idealised view which did not truly reflect the political reality in England at the time. Montesquieu's views, however, were particularly influential in the eighteenth century as a reading of the Constitution of the United States of America reveals.

C. F. Strong, *Modern Political Constitutions* (1972), pp. 211 – 212

Now, in no constitutional state is it true that the legislative and executive functions are in precisely the same hands, for . . . the executive must always be a smaller body than the legislature. But it is not to this distinction that the theory of the separation of powers points. The application of the theory means not only that the executive shall not be the same body as the legislature but that these two bodies shall be isolated from each other, so that the one shall not control the other. Any state which has adopted and maintained this doctrine in practice in its full force has an executive beyond the control of the legislature. Such an executive we call non-parliamentary or fixed. This type of executive still exists in the United States, whose Constitution has not been altered in this particular since its inception. But France, which, as we have said, applied the doctrine in its first constitutions born of the Revolution, later adopted the British executive system, and this feature appeared in the Constitutions of the Third and Fourth Republics, and again, though greatly modified, in that of the Fifth Republic. The system is one in which a cabinet of ministers is dependent for its existence on the legislature of which it is a part, the members of the executive being also members of the legislature.

This system, generally known as the Cabinet system, has been, in its broad features, adopted by most European constitutional states, and it matters not at all whether they are called monarchies or republics. It is also characteristic of the governments of British Commonwealth countries, old and new. The non-parliamentary system, on the other hand, is peculiar to the United States and those Latin American Republics which have founded their constitutions upon that of their great neighbour.

Note

There is, accordingly, no separation of powers in the United Kingdom as Montesquieu expressed the doctrine. The government is made up of members of the legislature; ministers may have both legislative and adjudicatory functions; while Parliament may dismiss a government through a vote of no confidence, government, to a large extent, controls the legislative work of Parliament. However, in one area, separation appears to exist.

G. Marshall, *Constitutional Theory* (1971), pp. 103 – 104

A separation between the judicial and the legislative and executive branches obviously exists in both Britain and the United States in the sense that in practice the judges are secure in their offices and have an independent status. But whether the separation of powers doctrine implies the existence of that degree of checking or controlling which has come to be known as judicial review in the American sense is not easy to decide. The right to invalidate legislation obviously in one sense invades the principle that each department has an independent sphere of action and a right to take its own view on matters of constitutionality. On the other hand, the controlling or checking functions of the judicial branch can only consist in impartial application of the law, and where constitutional law places restrictions on legislative power, a duty to declare the law seems to imply a duty to declare when such restrictions have been violated, whether by the legislature or by anyone else.

Note

In the United States the Supreme Court in *Marbury* v *Madison* (1803) 1 Cranch 137, decided that it had the power to declare both the acts of Congress and of the President to be unconstitutional. In the United Kingdom courts have refused to adjudicate upon the validity of Acts of Parliament, but they have developed the doctrine of judicial review by which the exercise of power by other authorities may be reviewed in the courts.

R v *London Transport Executive, ex parte Greater London Council*
[1983] QB 484
Court of Appeal

KERR LJ: . . . Authorities invested with discretionary powers by an Act of Parliament can only exercise such powers within the limits of the particular statute. So long as they do not transgress their statutory powers, their decisions are entirely a matter for them, and – in the case of local authorities – for the majority of the elected representatives; subject, however, to one important proviso. This is – again to put it broadly – that they must not exercise their powers arbitrarily or so unreasonably that the exercise of the discretion is clearly unjustifiable. This is an imperfect and generalised paraphrase of the well-known statement of Lord Greene MR in *Associated Picture Houses Ltd* v *Wednesbury Corporation* [1948] 1 KB 223, 229, which has come to be known as the *Wednesbury* principle and applied in countless cases.

If an authority misdirects itself in law, or acts arbitrarily on the basis of considerations which lie outside its statutory powers, or so unreasonably that its decisions cannot be justified by any objective standard of reasonableness, then it is the duty and function of the courts to pronounce that such decisions are invalid when these are challenged by anyone aggrieved by them and who has the necessary locus standi to do so.

The role of the courts in the constitution was further elucidated in the following cases.

Duport Steels Ltd v *Sirs*
[1980] 1 WLR 142
House of Lords

Private steel companies sought injunctions against the Iron and Steel Trades Confederation who were calling on workers in the private sector of the steel industry to come out on strike to support workers in the public sector who were striking over pay. The correct interpretation of s. 13(1) of the Trade Union and Labour Relations Act 1974 (as amended in 1976) was central to the case. Section 13(1) conferred immunity from liability in tort for an act done by a person 'in contemplation or furtherance of a trade dispute'. The Court of Appeal reversed the judge's decision to refuse the injunctions sought.

LORD DIPLOCK: . . . My Lords, at a time when more and more cases involve the application of legislation which gives effect to policies that are the subject of bitter public and parliamentary controversy, it cannot be too strongly emphasised that the British constitution, though largely unwritten, is firmly based upon the separation of powers; Parliament makes the laws, the judiciary interpret them. When Parliament legislates to remedy what the majority of its members at the time perceive to be a defect or a lacuna in the existing law (whether it be the written law enacted by existing statutes or the unwritten common law as it has been expounded by the judges in decided cases), the role of the judiciary is confined to ascertaining from the words that Parliament has approved as expressing its intention what that intention was, and to giving effect to it. Where the meaning of the statutory words is plain and unambiguous it is not for the judges to invent fancied ambiguities as an excuse for failing to give effect to its plain meaning because they themselves consider that the consequences of doing so would be inexpedient, or even unjust or immoral. In controversial matters such as are involved in industrial relations there is room for difference of opinion as to what is expedient, what is just and what is morally justifiable. Under our constitution it is Parliament's opinion on these matters that is paramount.

A statute passed to remedy what is perceived by Parliament to be a defect in the existing law may in actual operation turn out to have injurious consequences that Parliament did not anticipate at the time the statute was passed; if it had, it would have made some provision in the Act in order to prevent them. It is at least possible that Parliament when the Acts of 1974 and 1976 were passed did not anticipate that so widespread and crippling use as has in fact occurred would be made of sympathetic withdrawals of labour and of secondary blacking and picketing in support of sectional interests able to exercise 'industrial muscle.' But if this be the case it is for Parliament, not for the judiciary, to decide whether any changes should be made to the law as stated in the Acts, and, if so, what are the precise limits that ought to be imposed upon the immunity from liability for torts committed in the course of taking industrial action. These are matters on which there is a wide legislative choice the exercise of which is likely to be influenced by the political complexion of the government and the state of public opinion at the time amending legislation is under consideration.

It endangers continued public confidence in the political impartiality of the judiciary, which is essential to the continuance of the rule of law, if judges, under the guise of interpretation, provide their own preferred amendments to statutes which experience of their operation has shown to have had consequences that members of the court before whom the matter comes consider to be injurious to the public interest. The frequency with which controversial legislation is amended by Parliament itself (as witness the Act of 1974 which was amended in 1975 as well as in 1976) indicates that legislation, after it has come into operation, may fail to have the beneficial effects which Parliament expected or may produce injurious results that Parliament did not anticipate. But, except by private or hybrid Bills, Parliament does not legislate for individual cases. Public Acts of Parliament are general in their application; they govern all cases falling within categories of which the definitions are to be found in the wording of the statute. So in relation to section 13(1) of the Acts of 1974 and 1976, for a judge (who is always dealing with an individual case) to pose himself the question: 'Can Parliament really have intended that the acts that were done in this particular case should have the benefit of the immunity?' is to risk straying beyond his constitutional role as interpreter of the enacted law and assuming a power to decide at his own discretion whether or not to apply the general law to a particular case. The legitimate questions for a judge in his role as interpreter of the enacted law are: 'How has Parliament, by the words that it has used in the statute to express its intentions, defined the category of acts that are entitled to the immunity? Do the acts done in this particular case fall within that description?'

LORD SCARMAN: . . . My basic criticism of all three judgments in the Court of Appeal is that in their desire to do justice the court failed to do justice according to law. When one is considering law in the hands of the judges, law means the body of rules and guidelines within which society requires its judges to administer justice. Legal systems differ in the width of the discretionary power granted to judges: but in developed societies limits are invariably set, beyond which the judges may not go. Justice in such societies is not left to the unguided, even if experienced, sage sitting under the spreading oak tree.

In our society the judges have in some aspects of their work a discretionary power to do justice so wide that they may be regarded as law-makers. The common law and equity, both of them in essence systems of private law, are fields where, subject to the increasing intrusion of statute law, society has been content to allow the judges to formulate and develop the law. The judges, even in this, their very own field of creative endeavour, have accepted, in the interests of certainty, the self-denying ordinance of 'stare decisis,' the doctrine of binding precedent: and no doubt this judicially imposed limitation on judicial law-making has helped to maintain confidence in the certainty and evenhandedness of the law.

But in the field of statute law the judge must be obedient to the will of Parliament as expressed in its enactments. In this field Parliament makes, and un-makes, the law: the judge's duty is to interpret and to apply the law, not to change it to meet the judge's idea of what justice requires. Interpretation does, of course, imply in the interpreter a power of choice where differing constructions are possible. But our law requires the judge to choose the construction which in his judgment best meets the legislative purpose of the enactment. If the result be unjust but inevitable, the judge may say so and invite Parliament to reconsider its provision. But he must not deny the statute. Unpalatable statute law may not be disregarded or rejected, merely because it is unpalatable. Only if a just result can be achieved without violating the legislative purpose of the statute may the judge select the construction which best suits his idea of what justice requires. Further, in our system the rule 'stare decisis' applies as firmly to statute law as it does to the formulation of common law and equitable principles. And the keystone of 'stare decisis' is loyalty throughout the system to the decisions of the Court of Appeal and this House. The Court of Appeal may not overrule a House of Lords decision: and only in the exceptional circumstances set out in the Practice Statement of July 1, 1966 (*Practice Statement (Judicial Precedent)* [1966] 1 WLR 1234), will this House refuse to follow its own previous decisions.

Within these limits, which cannot be said in a free society possessing elective legislative institutions to be narrow or constrained, judges, as the remarkable judicial career of Lord Denning himself shows, have a genuine creative role. Great judges are in their different ways judicial activists. But the constitution's separation of powers, or more accurately functions, must be observed if judicial independence is not to be put at risk. For, if people and Parliament come to think that the judicial power is to be confined by nothing other than the judge's sense of what is right (or, as Selden put it, by the length of the Chancellor's foot), confidence in the judicial system will be replaced by fear of it becoming uncertain and arbitrary in its application. Society will then be ready for Parliament to cut the power of the judges. Their power to do justice will become more restricted by law than it need be, or is today.

Appeal allowed

R* v *Her Majesty's Treasury, ex parte Smedley

[1985] 1 QB 657
Court of Appeal

SIR JOHN DONALDSON MR: . . . I think that I should say a word about the respective roles of Parliament and the courts. Although the United Kingdom has no written constitution, it is a constitutional convention of the highest importance that the legislature and the judicature are separate and independent of one another, subject to certain ultimate rights of Parliament over the judicature which are immaterial for present purposes. It therefore behoves the courts to be ever sensitive to the paramount need to refrain from trespassing upon the province of Parliament or, so far as this can be avoided, even appearing to do so. Although it is not a matter for me, I would hope and expect that Parliament would be similarly sensitive to the need to refrain from trespassing upon the province of the courts.

Note

While the courts are chary of 'trespassing upon the province of Parliament', because of the doctrine of the supremacy of Parliament, it appears that Parliament is not so willing to accord to the courts a rightful province upon which Parliament should not trespass. There are signs that government, by means of the legislation it is pushing through Parliament, is doing its utmost to prevent judicial review of governmental action.

C. Graham and J. A. W. Prosser, 'The Constitution and the New Conservatives' 42 *Parliamentary Affairs* (1989), pp. 330, 337

[I]t has become increasingly clear that judicial decisions unfavourable to government will face swift statutory reversal, sometimes with retrospective effect. This has always been a feature of political life, but has assumed new prominence since 1979. It has often occurred in the fields of social security and local government, in which the few local authority victories in the courts have proved extremely shortlived. A special mention should be made of the use of novel forms of clauses designed to exclude any possibility of judicial review. A striking use of such clauses is in the Local Government Finance Act 1987. Section 4(1) provides in relation to rate support grant: 'Anything done by the Secretary of State before the passing of this Act for the purposes of the relevant provisions in relation to any of the initial years or intermediate years shall be deemed to have been done in compliance with those provisions.' Section 4(6) provides: 'Subsection (1) above shall have effect notwithstanding any decision of a court (whether before or after the passing of this Act) purporting to have a contrary effect.' Sections 6(1) and 6(6) have similar effect in relation to the validation of the Secretary of State's past acts in relation to ratecapping. So much for limited government under the law!

Question

If separation of powers as expressed by Montesquieu does not exist, is there nevertheless sufficient separation of functions and a sufficient incidence of checks and balances to guarantee the maintenance of liberty?

(F) THE STATE

The last idea to consider in this chapter is the state. Wade and Bradley in *Constitutional and Administrative Law* (1985), p. 3, state that 'constitutional law concerns the relationship between the individual and the state, seen from a particular viewpoint, namely the notion of law. . . . Law is not merely a matter of the rules which govern relations between private individuals. . . . Law concerns the structure and powers of the state.' If we are to examine the ambit of constitutional law in the United Kingdom, we need to have some notion of what the state is.

C. F. Strong, *Modern Political Constitutions* (1972), pp. 4 – 5

[T]he state is something more than a mere collection of families, or an agglomeration of occupational organisation, or a referee holding the ring between the conflicting interests of the voluntary associations which it permits to exist. In a properly organized political community the state exists for society and not society for the state; yet, however socially advanced a people may be, the society which it constitutes – made up of families, clubs, churches, trade unions, etc. – is not to be trusted to maintain itself without the ultimate arbitrament of force.

All associations make rules and regulations for their conduct, and when men are associated politically these rules and regulations are called laws, the power to make these being the prerogative of the state and of no other association. Thus, in the words of R M MacIver, a 'state is the fundamental association for the maintenance and development of social order, and to this end its central institution is endowed with the united power of the community.' But this definition might conceivably cover a pastoral or nomadic society which, indeed, found a bond of union in the patriarch or head of the family who, in some sort, discharged the powers of government. Such a society, however, lacks territoriality, an indispensable condition of true political organization, a condition emphasized by H J W Hetherington when he says: 'The state is the institution or set of institutions which, in order to secure certain elementary common purposes and conditions of life, unites under a single authority the inhabitants of a clearly-marked territorial area.' But what is this 'united power of the community' in the first, this 'single authority' in the second definition? It is the power or authority to make law. So we come to the definition given by Woodrow Wilson: 'A state is a people organized for law within a definite territory.'

S. E. Finer, *Comparative Government* (1970), p. 24

The defining characteristics of a state . . . are: (1) It is a territorially defined association. (2) It embraces, compulsorily, all the persons in that territory. (3) It possesses the monopoly of violence throughout this area, by virtue of which it has the capacity, even if not the moral authority, to guarantee the finality of its decision in political disputes arising from the conflict of individuals or groups within its territory. (4) As a necessary accompaniment of all this, it has a body of persons who exercise this monopoly of violence in its name, namely, the common government.

R. Miliband, *The State in Capitalist Society* (1969), pp. 49 – 54

There is one preliminary problem about the state which is very seldom considered, yet which requires attention if the discussion of its nature and role is to be properly focused. This is the fact that 'the state' is not a thing, that it does not, as such, exist. What 'the state' stands for is a number of particular institutions which, together, constitute its reality, and which interact as parts of what may be called the state system.

The point is by no means academic. For the treatment of one part of the state – usually the government – as the state itself introduces a major element of confusion in the discussion of the nature and incidence of state *power*; and that confusion can have large political consequences. Thus, if it is believed that the government is in fact the state, it may also be believed that the assumption of governmental power is equivalent to the acquisition of state power. Such a belief, resting as it does on vast assumptions about the nature of state power, is fraught with great risks and disappointments. To understand the nature of state power, it is necessary first of all to distinguish, and then to relate, the various elements which make up the state system.

It is not very surprising that government and state should often appear as synonymous for it is the government which speaks on the state's behalf. It was the state to which Weber was referring when he said, in a famous phrase, that, in order to be, it must 'successfully claim the monopoly of the legitimate use of physical force within a given territory'. But 'the state' cannot claim anything: only the government of the day, or its duly empowered agents, can. Men, it is often said, give their allegiance not to the government of the day but to the state. But the state, from this point of view, is a nebulous entity; and while men may choose to give their allegiance to it, it is to the government that they are required to give their obedience. A defiance of its orders is a defiance of the state, in whose name the government alone may speak and for whose actions it must assume ultimate responsibility. . . .

A second element of the state system which requires investigation is the administrative one, which now extends far beyond the traditional bureaucracy of the state, and which encompasses a large variety of bodies, often related to particular ministerial departments, or enjoying a greater or lesser degree of autonomy – public corporations, central banks, regulatory commissions, etc. – and concerned with the management of the economic, social, cultural and other activities in which the state is now directly or indirectly involved. The extraordinary growth of this administrative and bureaucratic element in all societies, including advanced capitalist ones, is of course one of the most obvious features of contemporary life; and the relation of its leading members to the government and to society is also crucial to the determination of the role of the state.

Formally, officialdom is at the service of the political executive, its obedient instrument, the tool of its will. In actual fact it is nothing of the kind. Everywhere and inevitably the administrative process is also part of the political process; administration is always political as well as executive, at least at the levels where policy-making is relevant, that is to say in the upper layers of administrative life. . . . Officials and administrators cannot divest themselves of all ideological clothing in the advice which they tender to their political masters, or in the independent decisions which they are in a position to take. The power which top civil servants and other state administrators possesss no doubt varies from country to country, from department to department, and from individual to individual. But nowhere do these men *not* contribute directly and appreciably to the exercise of state power. . . .

Some of these considerations apply to all other elements of the state system. They apply for instance to a third such element, namely the military, to which may, for present purposes, be added the para-military, security and police forces of the state, and which together form that branch of it mainly concerned with the 'management of violence'.

In most capitalist countries, this coercive apparatus constitutes a vast, sprawling and resourceful establishment, whose professional leaders are men of high status and great influence, inside the state system and in society. . . .

Whatever may be the case in practice, the formal constitutional position of the administrative and coercive elements is to serve the state by serving the government of the day. In contrast, it is not at all the formal constitutional duty of judges, at least in Western-type political systems, to serve the purposes of their governments. They are constitutionally independent of the political executive and protected from it by security of tenure and other guarantees. Indeed, the concept of judicial independence is deemed to entail not merely the freedom of judges from responsibility to the political executive, but their active duty to protect the citizen *against* the political executive or its agents, and to act, in the state's encounter with members of society, as the defenders of the latter's rights and liberties. . . . But in any case, the judiciary is an integral part of the state system, which affects, often profoundly, the exercise of state power.

So too, to a greater or lesser degree, does a fifth element of the state system, namely the various units of sub-central government. In one of its aspects, sub-central government constitutes an extension of central government and administration, the latter's antennae or tentacles. In some political systems it has indeed practically no other function. In the countries of advanced capitalism, on the other hand, sub-central government is rather more than an administrative device. In addition to being agents of the state these units of government have also traditionally performed another function. They have not only been the channels of communication and administration from the centre to the periphery, but also the voice of the periphery, or of particular interests at the periphery; they have been a means of overcoming local particularities, but also platforms for their expression, instruments of central control and obstacles to it. For all the centralisation of power, which is a major feature of government in these countries, sub-central organs of government . . . have remained power structures in their own right, and therefore able to affect very markedly the lives of the populations they have governed.

Much the same point may be made about the representative assemblies of advanced capitalism. Now more than ever their life revolves around the government; and even where, as in the United States, they are formally independent organs of constitutional and political power, their relationship with the political executive cannot be a purely critical or obstructive one. That relationship is one of conflict *and* cooperation.

Nor is this a matter of division between a pro-government side and an anti-government one. *Both* sides reflect this duality. For opposition parties cannot be wholly uncooperative. Merely by taking part in the work of the legislature, they help the government's business.

As for government parties, they are seldom if ever single-minded in their support of the political executive and altogether subservient to it. They include people who, by virtue of their position and influence must be persuaded, cajoled, threatened or bought off.

It is in the constitutionally-sanctioned performance of this cooperative and critical function that legislative assemblies have a share in the exercise of state power. That share is rather less extensive and exalted than is often claimed for these bodies. But. . . it is not, even in an epoch of executive dominance, an unimportant one.

Question

Is the government the state, or is it an institution or servant of the state? See the cases which follow.

D v *National Society for the Prevention of Cruelty to Children*

[1978] AC 171

House of Lords

The mother of a child (alleged by an informant to be the victim of ill-treatment) brought an action against the NSPCC for damages for nervous shock alleged to be the result of the society's investigation pursuant to the informant's complaint. The mother sought discovery of the identity of the informant. The NSPCC, an independent body incorporated by royal charter, claimed 'public interest immunity' as justifying its refusal to disclose the identity of its informants. The mother argued that the society could not rely on this defence as it was not part of the state.

LORD SIMON OF GLAISDALE: . . . '[T]he state' cannot on any sensible political theory be restricted to the Crown and the departments of central government (which are, indeed, part of the Crown in constitutional law). The state is the whole organisation of the body politic for supreme civil rule and government – the whole political organisation which is the basis of civil government. As such it certainly extends to local – and, as I think, also statutory – bodies in so far as they are exercising autonomous rule.

Chandler v *Director of Public Prosecutions*

[1964] AC 763

House of Lords

The appellants, in seeking to further the aims of the Campaign for Nuclear Disarmament, entered and sought to immobilise an airfield. The airfield was a 'prohibited place' under s. 3 of the Official Secrets Act 1911. The appellants were charged with conspiracy to commit a breach of s. 1 of the Act, whereby it is an offence to enter any prohibited place 'for any purpose prejudicial to the safety or interests of the State'. The appellants argued that their actions were not prejudicial to the safety or interests of the state, but rather it was their belief that their actions would be beneficial to the state. They further argued that 'State' means the numerical collection of inhabitants in the geographical area and not the government or organs of government through which the state expresses its intentions.

LORD REID: . . . Next comes the question of what is meant by the safety or interests of the State. 'State' is not an easy word. It does not mean the Government or the Executive. 'L'Etat c'est moi' was a shrewd remark, but can hardly have been intended as a definition even in the France of the time. And I do not think that it means, as counsel argued, the individuals who inhabit these islands. The statute cannot be referring to the interests of all those individuals because they may differ and the interests of the majority are not necessarily the same as the interests of the State. Again we have seen only too clearly in some other countries what can happen if you personify and almost deify the State. Perhaps the country or the realm are as good synonyms as one can find and I would be prepared to accept the organised community as coming as near to a definition as one can get.

LORD DEVLIN: . . . What is meant by 'the State'? Is it the same thing as what I have just called 'the country'? Mr Foster, for the appellants, submits that it means the inhabitants of a particular geographical area. I doubt if it ever has as wide a meaning as that. I agree that in an appropriate context the safety and interests of the State might mean simply the public or national safety and interests. But the more precise use of the word 'State,' the use to be expected in a legal context, and the one which I am quite satisfied . . . was intended in this statute, is to denote the organs of government of a national community. In the United Kingdom, in relation at any rate to the armed forces and to the defence of the realm, that organ is the Crown. So long as the Crown maintains armed forces for the defence of the realm, it cannot be in its interest that any part of them should be immobilised.

LORD PEARCE: . . . I cannot accept the argument that the words 'the interests of the State' in this context mean the interests of the amorphous populace, without regard to the guiding policies of those in authority, and that proof of possible ultimate benefit to the populace may for the purposes of the Act justify an act of spying or sabotage. The protection covers certain specified places which are obviously vital to defence and other places to which the Secretary of State sees fit to extend the protection. . . . Parliament clearly intended to give stringent protection to such places. It is hard to believe that it intended to withhold that protection in all cases where a jury might think that the place in question was not necessary or desirable or where the authorities could not by evidence justify their policies to a jury's satisfaction. Questions of defence policy are vast, complicated, confidential, and wholly unsuited for ventilation before a jury. In such a context the interests of the State must in my judgment mean the interests of the State according to the policies laid down for it by its recognised organs of government and authority, the policies of the State as they are, not as they ought, in the opinion of a jury, to be. Anything which prejudices those policies is within the meaning of the Act 'prejudicial to the interests of the State.'

Questions

1. In the trial of Clive Ponting the judge directed the jury that the phrase 'in the interests of the state' in s. 2 of the Official Secrets Act 1911 means 'in the interests of the Government of the day'. This view was supported by the Attorney-General, Sir Michael Havers, in a speech in the House of Commons, but was contested by Lord Denning in a speech in the House of Lords. Who was correct? See Barker, below.

2. If the 'government' is synonymous with the 'state', does this have any consequences for ideas such as constitutionalism and limited government? See Barker, below.

3. If the government determines the interests of the state, does this harbour any threat to individual liberty?

R. Barker, *Political Legitimacy and the State* (1990) pp. 183 – 184

The Ponting case also illustrates the ways in which the legitimacy of the state may be threatened if any of its various temporary governors act in a way which breaks down the distinction between state and government, and by wrapping the acts of particular governments in the flag of the state, make it impossible to attack one without assaulting the other. A distinction between the state, as the institution which carries on the function of government, and the government as the politicians currently in office, makes it possible to oppose policies without denying legitimacy, or even to challenge the legitimacy of particular ministerial procedures, without confronting the constitution as a whole. When that distinction is eroded, so is the possibility of loyal opposition. Thus a state whose institutions appear to be newly absorbed or influenced by the partisan considerations of government is likely to suffer erosion of legitimacy whenever it is challenged on a particular point. But so long as the distinction remains, disaffection in so far as it appeals to existing principles of legitimacy, can be both conservative and loyal. Vivienne Hart has pointed out how many actions, of which she takes populism as her example, which have been presented as subversive of government, are in fact defensive of the constitution in general against the constitutionally subversive, or supposed constitutionally subversive actions of particular governments and politicians.

The view that states imperil their own legitimacy when they offend their own subjects' conservative conceptions of constitutionality is found more amongst other academic students of politics than amongst political scientists themselves. Patrick McAuslan and John McEldowney write of the contribution to disaffection throughout western Europe of what they term the gap 'between on the one hand the rhetoric of democracy, of even-handed administration, and of equal opportunities for all, and on the other the increasing centralization and insensitivity of public administration'. Resistance to government can rest on support for the constitution. It is both 'the response of ordinary people to trends in government practices which seem to them to be, in perhaps indefinable ways, wrong' and a preference for 'the theory of what the constitution ought to be to the practice of what it is'. Much that appears as rejection of the legitimacy of the state is in fact quite the reverse. Moreover because the forms and principles of legitimacy present at any one time are likely to be varied, it is not simply a case of appealing to principles against practices, but can also be a matter of appealing against practices justified by one form of legitimacy to alternative practices justified by other principles.

Note

The issues considered in this chapter have been, to a certain extent, theoretical. They are, however, issues of continuing relevance to any study of the constitution of the United Kingdom. Questions which it is worth keeping in mind when reading the remaining chapters in this book would be the following:

(a) To what extent is the doctrine of constitutionalism respected in the United Kingdom?

(b) To what extent does the principle of legitimacy inform constitutional debate?

(c) Is the principle of limited government respected? To what extent is government made accountable by (i) Parliament, (ii) the electorate, and (iii) the courts?

(d) Is the 'majoritarian principle' an adequate substitute for fundamental rights?

(e) Does the absence of a clear concept of the state, separate and distinguishable from government, prejudice individual rights?

2 THE LEGISLATIVE SUPREMACY OF PARLIAMENT

Note

The doctrine of the legislative supremacy of Parliament is often referred to as 'Parliamentary Sovereignty'. 'Sovereignty' is a word open to misunderstanding and one that is used in the sphere of international law (for example, the dispute with Argentina over the sovereignty of the Falkland Islands), and also in the political arena (for example, in the debates on the United Kingdom's membership of the European Community and on subsequent issues such as the Single European Act 1986 and European Monetary Union, there was considerable rhetoric on sovereignty). To avoid confusion with these ideas the terms 'legislative supremacy of Parliament' or 'Parliamentary supremacy' will be used. These terms have the virtue that they express clearly the central legal concept of the doctrine, that is, that under our constitutional arrangements Parliament is legislatively supreme. In the extracts from cases and other materials which follow, where the term 'sovereignty' is used, the judges or writers are using it in the sense of supremacy.

(A) THE LEGISLATIVE SUPREMACY OF PARLIAMENT AS A 'RULE OF RECOGNITION'

Part of the function of Parliament is to make laws, which it does by enacting statutes. These laws impose obligations on citizens, and obedience to these obligations is enforced by the courts. Why is a particular statute regarded as valid? Why do courts apply the law as declared in statutes and enforce their provisions? Whence does Parliament derive this power to make law?

H. L. A. Hart, *The Concept of Law* (1961), pp. 89 – 107

The Elements of Law

It is, of course, possible to imagine a society without a legislature, courts or officials of any kind. Indeed, there are many studies of primitive communities which not only claim that this possibility is realized but depict in detail the life of a society where the only means of social control is that general attitude of the group towards its own standard modes of behaviour in terms of which we have characterized rules of obligation. . . .[W]e shall refer to such a social structure as one of primary rules of obligation. If a society is to live by such primary rules alone, there are certain conditions which, granted a few of the most obvious truisms about human nature and the world we live in, must clearly be satisfied. The first of these conditions is that the rules must contain in some form restrictions on the free use of violence, theft, and deception to which human beings are tempted but which they must, in general, repress, if they are to coexist in close proximity to each other. . . . Secondly, though such a society may exhibit the tension, already described, between those who accept the rules and those who reject the rules except where fear of social pressure induces them to conform, it is plain that the latter cannot be more than a minority, if so loosely organized a society of persons, approximately equal in physical strength, is to endure: for otherwise those who reject the rules would have too little social pressure to fear. . . .

It is plain that only a small community closely knit by ties of kinship, common sentiment, and belief, and placed in a stable environment, could live successfully by such a régime of unofficial rules. In any other conditions such a simple form of social control must prove defective and will require supplementation in different ways. In the first place, the rules by which the group lives will not form a system, but will simply be a set of separate standards, without any identifying or common mark, except of course that they are the rules which a particular group of human beings accepts. They will in this respect resemble our own rules of etiquette. Hence if doubts arise as to what the rules are or as to the precise scope of some given rule, there will be no procedure for settling this doubt, either by reference to an authoritative text or to an official whose declarations on this point are authoritative. For, plainly, such a procedure and the acknowledgement of either authoritative text or persons involve the existence of rules of a type different from the rules of obligation or duty which *ex hypothesi* are all that the group has. This defect in the simple social structure of primary rules we may call its *uncertainty*.

A second defect is the *static* character of the rules. The only mode of change in the rules known to such a society will be the slow process of growth, whereby courses of conduct once thought optional become first habitual or usual, and then obligatory, and the converse process of decay, when deviations, once severely dealt with, are first tolerated and then pass unnoticed. There will be no means, in such a society, of deliberately adapting the rules to changing circumstances, either by eliminating old rules or introducing new ones: for, again, the possibility of doing this presupposes the existence of rules of a different type from the primary rules of obligation by which alone the society lives. . . .

The third defect of this simple form of social life is the *inefficiency* of the diffuse social pressure by which the rules are maintained. Disputes as to whether an admitted rule has or has not been violated will always occur and will, in any but the smallest societies, continue interminably, if there is no agency specially empowered to ascertain finally, and authoritatively, the fact of violation. . . .

The remedy for each of these three main defects in this simplest form of social structure consists in supplementing the *primary* rules of obligation with *secondary* rules which are rules of a different kind. The introduction of the remedy for each defect might, in itself, be considered a step from the pre-legal into the legal world; since each remedy brings with it many elements that permeate law: certainly all three remedies together are enough to convert the régime of primary rules into what is indisputably a legal system. . . .

The simplest form of remedy for the *uncertainty* of the régime of primary rules is the introduction of what we shall call a 'rule of recognition'. This will specify some feature or features possession of which by a suggested rule is taken as a conclusive affirmative indication that it is a rule of the group to be supported by the social pressure it exerts. The existence of such a rule of recognition may take any of a huge variety of forms, simple or complex. It may, as in the early law of many societies, be no more than that an authoritative list or text of the rules is to be found in a written document or carved on some public monument. . . .

In a developed legal system the rules of recognition are of course more complex; instead of identifying rules exclusively by reference to a text or list they do so by reference to some general characteristic possessed by the primary rules. This may be the fact of their having been enacted by a specific body, or their long customary practice, or their relation to judicial decisions. Moreover, where more than one of such general characteristics are treated as identifying criteria, provision may be made for their possible conflict by their arrangement in an order of superiority, as by the common subordination of custom or precedent to statute, the latter being a 'superior source' of law. . . . [E]ven in this simplest form, such a rule brings with it many elements distinctive of law. By providing an authoritative mark it introduces, although in embryonic form, the idea of a legal system: for the rules are now not just a discrete unconnected set but are, in a simple way, unified. Further, in the simple operation of identifying a given rule as possessing the required feature of being an item on an authoritative list of rules we have the germ of the idea of legal validity.

The remedy for the *static* quality of the régime of primary rules consists in the introduction of what we shall call 'rules of change'. The simplest form of such a rule is that which empowers an individual or body of persons to introduce new primary rules for the conduct of the life of the group, or of some class within it, and to eliminate old rules. . . . [I]t is in terms of such a rule, and not in terms of orders backed by threats, that the ideas of legislative enactment and repeal are to be understood. Such rules of change may be very simple or very complex: the powers conferred may be unrestricted or limited in various ways: and the rules may, besides specifying the persons who are to legislate, define in more or less rigid terms the procedure to be followed in legislation. Plainly, there will be a very close connexion between the rules of change and the rules of recognition: for where the former exists the latter will necessarily incorporate a reference to legislation as an identifying feature of the rules, though it need not refer to all the details of prcocedure involved in legislation. Usually some official certificate or official copy will, under the rules of recognition, be taken as a sufficient proof of due enactment. Of course if there is a social structure so simple that the only 'source of law' is legislation, the rule of recognition will simply specify enactment as the unique identifying mark or criterion of validity of the rules. . . .

The third supplement to the simple régime of primary rules, intended to remedy the *inefficiency* of its diffused social pressure, consists of secondary rules empowering individuals to make authoritative determinations of the question whether, on a particular occasion, a primary rule has been broken. The minimal form of adjudication consists in such determinations, and we shall call the secondary rules which confer the power to make them 'rules of adjudication'. Besides identifying the individuals who are to adjudicate, such rules will also define the procedure to be followed. Like the other secondary rules these are on a different level from the primary rules: though they may be reinforced by further rules imposing duties on judges to adjudicate, they do not impose duties but confer judicial powers and a special status on judicial declarations about the breach of obligations. Again these rules, like the other secondary rules, define a group of important legal concepts: in this case the concepts of judge or court, jurisdiction and judgment. Besides these resemblances to the other secondary rules, rules of adjudication have intimate connexions with them. Indeed, a system which has rules of adjudication is necessarily also committed to a rule of recognition of an elementary and imperfect sort. This is so because, if courts are empowered to make authoritative determinations of the fact that a rule has been broken, these cannot avoid being taken as authoritative determinations of what the rules are. So the rule which confers jurisdiction will also be a rule of recognition, identifying the primary rules through the judgments of the courts and these judgments will become a 'source' of law. . . .

If we stand back and consider the structure which has resulted from the combination of primary rules of obligation with the secondary rules of recognition, change and adjudication, it is plain that we have here not only the heart of a legal system, but a most powerful tool for the analysis of much that has puzzled both the jurist and the political theorist. . . .

Rule of Recognition and Legal Validity

In a modern legal system where there are a variety of 'sources' of law, the rule of recognition is . . . complex: the criteria for identifying the law are multiple and commonly include a written constitution, enactment by a lesiglature, and judicial precedents. In most cases, provision is made for possible conflict by ranking these criteria in an order of relative subordination and primacy. It is in this way that in our system 'common law' is subordinate to 'statute'. . . .

In the day-to-day life of a legal system its rule of recognition is very seldom expressly formulated as a rule; though occasionally, courts in England may announce in general terms the relative place of one criterion of law in relation to another, as when they assert the supremacy of Acts of Parliament over other sources or suggested sources of law. For the most part the rule of recognition is not stated, but its existence is *shown* in the way in which particular rules are identified, either by courts or other officials or private persons or their advisers. . . .

The use of unstated rules of recognition, by courts and others, in identifying particular rules of the system is characteristic of the internal point of view. Those who use them in this way thereby manifest their own acceptance of them as guiding rules and with this attitude there goes a characteristic vocabulary different from the natural expressions of the external point of view. Perhaps the simplest of these is the expression, 'It is the law that . . .', which we may find on the lips not only of judges, but of ordinary men living under a legal system, when they identify a given rule of the system. . . . This attitude of shared acceptance of rules is to be contrasted with that of an observer who records *ab extra* the fact that a social group accepts such rules but does not himself accept them. The natural expression of this external point of view is not 'It is the law that . . .' but 'In England they recognize as law . . . whatever the Queen in Parliament enacts. . . .' To say that a given rule is valid is to recognize it as passing all the tests provided by the rule of recognition and so as a rule of the system. We can indeed simply say that the statement that a particular rule is valid means that it satisfies all the criteria provided by the rule of recognition. . . .

The rule of recognition providing the criteria by which the validity of other rules of the system is assessed is in an important sense, which we shall try to clarify, an *ultimate* rule: and where, as is usual, there are several criteria ranked in order of relative subordination and primacy one of them is *supreme*. . . .

Of these two ideas, supreme criterion and ultimate rule, the first is the easiest to define. We may say that a criterion of legal validity or source of law is supreme if rules identified by reference to it are still recognized as rules of the system, even if they conflict with rules identified by reference to the other criteria, whereas rules identified by reference to the latter are not so recognized if they conflict with the rules identified by reference to the supreme criterion. A similar explanation in comparative terms can be given of the notions of 'superior' and 'subordinate' criteria which we have already used. It is plain that the notions of a superior and a supreme criterion merely refer to a *relative* place on a scale and do not import any notion of legally *unlimited* legislative power. Yet 'supreme' and 'unlimited' are easy to confuse – at least in legal theory. One reason for this is that in the simpler forms of legal system the ideas of ultimate rule of recognition, supreme criterion, and legally unlimited legislature seem to converge. For where there is a legislature subject to no constitutional limitations and competent by its enactment to deprive all other rules of law emanating from other sources of their status as law, it is part of the rule of recognition in such a system that enactment by that legislature is the supreme criterion of validity. This is, according to constitutional theory, the position in the United Kingdom. But even systems like that of the United States in which there is no such legally unlimited legislature may perfectly well contain an ultimate rule of recognition which provides a set of criteria of validity, one of which is supreme. This will be so, where the legislative competence of the ordinary legislature is limited by a constitution which contains no amending power, or places some classes outside the scope of that power. Here there is no legally unlimited legislature, even in the widest interpretation of 'legislature'; but the system of course contains an ultimate rule of recognition and, in the clauses of its constitution, a supreme criterion of validity. . . .

Some writers, who have emphasized the legal ultimacy of the rule of recognition, have expressed this by saying that, whereas the legal validity of other rules of the system can be demonstrated by reference to it, its own validity cannot be demonstrated but is 'assumed' or 'postulated' or is a 'hypothesis'. This may, however, be seriously misleading. Statements of legal validity made about particular rules in the day-to-day life of a legal system whether by judges, lawyers, or ordinary citizens do indeed carry with them certain presuppositions. They are internal statements of law expressing the point of view of those who accept the rule of recognition of the system and, as such, leave unstated much that could be stated in external statements of fact about the system. What is thus left unstated forms the normal background or context of statements of legal validity and is thus said to be 'presupposed' by them. But it is important to see precisely what these presupposed matters are, and not to obscure their character. They consist of two things. First, a person who seriously asserts the validity of some given rule of law, say a particular statute, himself makes use of a rule of recognition which he accepts as appropriate for identifying the law. Secondly, it is the case that this rule of recognition, in terms of which he assesses the validity of a particular statute, is not only accepted by him but is the rule of recognition actually accepted and employed in the general operation of the system. If the truth of this presupposition were doubted, it could be established by reference to actual practice: to the way in which courts identify what is to count as law, and to the general acceptance of or acquiescence in these identifications. . . .

Where . . . as in a mature legal system, we have a system of rules which includes a rule of recognition so that the status of a rule as a member of the system now depends on whether it satisfies certain criteria provided by the rule of recognition, this brings with it a new application of the word 'exist'. The statement that a rule exists may now no longer be what it was in the simple case of customary rules – an external statement of the *fact* that a certain mode of behaviour was generally accepted as a standard in practice. It may now be an internal statement applying an accepted but unstated rule of recognition and meaning (roughly) no more than 'valid given the systems criteria of validity'. In this respect, however, as in others a rule of recognition is unlike other rules of the system. The assertion that it exists can only be an external statement of fact. For whereas a subordinate rule of a system may be valid and in that sense 'exist' even if it is generally disregarded, the rule of recognition exists only as a complex, but normally concordant, practice of the courts, officials, and private persons in identifying the law by reference to certain criteria. Its existence is a matter of fact.

Question

What is the Rule of Recognition in the United Kingdom?

Dicey, *The Law of the Constitution* (10th edn 1965), pp. 39 – 40

The principle of Parliamentary sovereignty means neither more nor less than this, namely, that Parliament thus defined has, under the English constitution, the right to make or unmake any law whatever; and, further, that no person or body is recognised by the law of England as having a right to override or set aside the legislation of Parliament.

A law may, for our present purpose, be defined as 'any rule which will be enforced by the courts.' The principle then of Parliamentary sovereignty may, looked at from its positive side, be thus described: Any Act of Parliament, or any part of an Act of Parliament, which makes a new law, or repeals or modifies an existing law, will be obeyed by the courts. The same principle, looked at from its negative side, may be thus stated: There is no person or body of persons who can, under the English constitution, make rules which override or derogate from an Act of Parliament, or which (to express the same thing in other words) will be enforced by the courts in contravention of an Act of Parliament.

Note

Parliament is the supreme law-maker, but what is Parliament? The words of enactment at the beginning of every statute are as follows:

> Be it enacted by the Queen's most Excellent Majesty, by and with the advice and consent of the Lords Spiritual and Temporal, and Commons, in this present Parliament assembled, and by the authority of the same, as follows:-

Thus it is the Queen in Parliament which enacts legislation. A measure having received the approval of a majority in both Houses and the Royal

Assent is recognised by the common law as an Act of Parliament. This position has been modified, however, by the Parliament Acts 1911 and 1949, under which a Bill may be presented for the Royal Assent provided it has been passed by the House of Commons and other procedural requirements complied with, although it has not been passed by the House of Lords. If a Bill does not obtain the approval of a majority in each House, or if the Parliament Acts are not complied with, or if the Royal Assent is withheld, the product should not be regarded as an authentic Act of Parliament.

The courts, therefore, recognise as law and accord primacy to those measures which Parliament passes as Acts.

Why is Parliament legislatively supreme, and why are its enactments accorded primacy?

(B) THE POLITICAL CONTEXT

A common view is that the legal concept of the legislative supremacy of Parliament can, and indeed must, be distinguished from the political concept of sovereignty. This view, however, has been challenged. T R S Allan suggests that political concepts should inform judicial decisions about the precise meaning of supremacy.

T. R. S. Allan, 'The limits of Parliamentary Sovereignty' [1985] *Public Law* 614

No greater testimony exists to the power and resilience of positivism in modern legal thought than the debate between constitutional laywers about the nature of parliamentary sovereignty. At the root of almost all analyses of the nature and scope of the doctrine lies an unquestioned separation of legal from political principle. The political notion of the ultimate sovereignty of the electorate must be distinguished from the legal doctrine of legislative supremacy: the courts owe their allegiance to the latter and recognise no 'trust' between Parliament and people. Dicey was clear on the point, observing that

> 'the courts will take no notice of the will of the electors. The judges know nothing about any will of the people except in so far as that will is expressed by an Act of Parliament, and would never suffer the validity of a statute to be questioned on the ground of its having been passed or kept alive in opposition to the wishes of the electors.'

The extent of judicial loyalty to statute enjoined by the doctrine of parliamentary sovereignty therefore depends on the correct interpretation of the legal principle alone. It is a matter of accurately formulating the fundamental rule of the legal order. Its *existence* may be conceded to be a matter of political fact, but its normative content is a matter of law: the courts are required to enforce the terms of the most recent statement of Parliament's will, expressed in the usual form. . . .

In short, the fundamental rule that accords legal validity to Acts of Parliament is not itself the foundation of the legal order, beyond which the lawyer is forbidden to look. The fundamental rule, however it should properly be characterised, derives its legal authority from the underlying moral or political theory of which it forms a part. The sterility and inconclusiveness of modern debate about the nature of sovereignty stems from Dicey's attempt to divorce legal doctrine from political principle. Legal questions which challenge the nature of our constitutional order can only be answered in terms of the political morality on which that order is based. . . .

The legal doctrine of legislative supremacy articulates the courts' commitment to the current British scheme of parliamentary democracy. It ensures the effective expression of the political will of the electorate through the medium of its parliamentary representatives. If some conception of the nature and dimensions of the relevant political community provides the framework for the operation of the doctrine, equally some conception of democracy must provide its substantive political content. In other words, the courts' continuing adherence to the legal doctrine of sovereignty must entail commitment to some irreducible, minimum concept of the democratic principle. That political commitment will naturally demand respect for the legislative measures adopted by Parliament as the representative assembly, a respect for which the legal doctrine is in almost all likely circumstances a suitable expression. That respect cannot, however, be a limitless one. A parliamentary enactment whose effect would be the destruction of any recognisable form of democracy (for example, a measure purporting to deprive a substantial section of the population of the vote on the grounds of their hostility to Government policies) could not consistently be applied by the courts as law. Judicial obedience to the statute in such (extreme and unlikely) circumstances could not coherently be justified in terms of the doctrine of parliamentary sovereignty since the statute would plainly undermine the fundamental political principle which the doctrine serves to protect. The practice of judicial obedience to statute cannot itself be based on the authority of statute: it can only reflect a judicial choice based on an understanding of what (in contemporary conditions) political morality demands. The limits of that practice of obedience must therefore be constituted by the boundaries of that political morality. An enactment which threatened the essential elements of any plausible conception of democratic government would lie beyond those boundaries. It would forfeit, by the same token, any claim to be recognised as law.

Although, therefore, Dicey's sharp distinction between the application and interpretation of statute suffices for most practical purposes, it ultimately breaks down in the face of changing views of the contours of the political community or of serious threats to the central tenets of liberal democracy. Presumptions of legislative intent, which draw their strength from judicial perceptions of widely held notions of justice and fairness, cannot in normal circumstances override the explicit terms of an Act of Parliament. This is because a commitment to representative government and loyalty to democratic institutions are themselves fundamental constituents of our collective political morality. Judicial notions of justice must generally give way to those expressed by Parliament where they are inconsistent. The legal authority of statute depends in the final analysis, however, on its compatibility with the central core of that shared political morality. If Parliament ceased to be a representative assembly, in any plausible sense of the idea, or if it proceeded to enact legislation undermining the democratic basis of our institutions, political morality might direct judicial resistance rather than obedience. No neat distinction between legal doctrine and political principle can be sustained at this level of adjudication. Questions about the scope and limits of the doctrine of sovereignty are necessarily questions about the proper relations between the courts and Parliament. Such questions cannot be settled by resort to competing formulations of some supposed pre-existing legal rule: it is the scope and content of that rule which is itself in issue. Answers can only be supplied as a matter of political morality – and in terms of the values which the judges accept as fundamental to our constitutional order.

Dicey's insistence on distinguishing legal from political sovereignty entails an equivalent separation of law and convention. Neither distinction can be sustained when the courts are required to determine the limits of parliamentary sovereignty. The nature and limits of parliamentary sovereignty are constituted, in the same way that conventions are constituted, by the political morality which underlies the legal order. In this sense, the legal doctrine of sovereignty is the most fundamental of our constitutional conventions. I have argued that the limits of sovereignty are contained in the courts' central commitment to representative democracy: a purported statute which attempted to subvert democracy could derive no legal authority from the doctrine. Paradoxically, Dicey gives implicit support for this view when he considers the distinction between legal and political sovereignty in the context of conventions. He observes that, 'if Parliament be in the eye of the law a supreme legislature, the essence of representative government is, that the legislature should represent or give effect to the will of the political sovereign, *i.e.* of the electoral body, or of the nation.' His examination of a number of important constitutional conventions leads him to the conclusion that they are united in character by the possession of a single purpose – to secure that Parliament and government are ultimately subject to the wishes of the electorate. The right to demand a dissolution is the most striking example, since it represents an appeal from the legal to the political sovereign. 'The conventions of the constitution now consist of customs which (whatever their historical origin) are at the present day maintained for the sake of ensuring the supremacy of the House of Commons, and ultimately, through the elective House of Commons, of the nation. Our modern code of constitutional morality secures, though in a roundabout way, what is called abroad the 'sovereignty of the people'. Dicey presents conventions as a means of harmonising legal and political sovereignty, which remain conceptually distinct. A view of legal sovereignty as a component of political morality, however, locates its authority in the source from which the 'validity of constitutional maxims' is derived: it is equally 'subordinate and subservient to the fundamental principle of popular sovereignty.'

A residual judicial commitment to preserving the essentials of democracy does not provide the only constraint on parliamentary supremacy. The political morality which underlies the legal order is not exhausted by our attachment to democratic government. It consists also in attitudes about what justice and fairness require in the relations between government and governed, and some of these must be fundamental. If these attitudes authorise a restrictive approach to the interpretation of statutes which, more broadly construed, would threaten fundamental values, they might equally justify rejection of statutes whose infringement of such values was sufficiently grave. If an ambiguous penal provision should, as a matter of principle, be narrowly construed in the interests of liberty and fairness, a criminal statute which lacked all precision – authorising the punishment of whatever conduct officials deemed it expedient to punish – should, on the same principle, be denied any application at all. It would be sufficient for the court to deny its application to the particular circumstances of the case before it: there would in practice be no need to make a declaration of invalidity. The result, however, would be the same: the strength of the principle of interpretation, in effect denying the statute any application at all, would reflect the scale of the affront to the moral and political values we accept as fundamental. . . .

The limits of sovereignty clearly cannot be stated with any precision. The scope of the legal doctrine, and its implications for constitutional change, cannot be settled except by analysis of the political morality which gives it its authority. The boundaries of sovereignty must be determined in the light of the prevailing moral and political climate when difficult questions of constitutional authority arise. No single characterisation or particular formulation of the rule enjoining judicial obedience to statute can supply answers in advance. . . .

Questions

1. Allan states that a 'parliamentary enactment whose effect would be destruction of any recognisable form of democracy . . . could not consistently be applied by the courts as law.' This begs a question as to what is democracy? For example, what would the courts do if Party A obtaining 40 per cent of the vote gained 60 per cent of the seats in the legislature because the remaining 60 per cent of the vote was split between three other parties, and then it embarked on a legislative programme which was discriminatory, anti-libertarian and anti-democratic? What would political morality demand? How would the judges discover this political morality? Would it make any difference if Party A fought the election campaign on a manifesto which openly outlined its policies, as opposed to the adoption of these policies after winning the election? If the judges refused to enforce the offensive legislation and an election was held with the same result followed by a reintroduction of the legislation, what would judges then do?

2. Is the 'shared political morality' of majoritarianism an adequate substitute for constitutionalism? Does Allan suggest that it is? What do you think he means when he states:

> The political morality which underlies the legal order is not exhausted by our attachment to democratic government. It consists also in attitudes about what justice and fairness require in the relations between government and the governed, and some of these must be fundamental.

Who decides what justice and fairness require?

Note

What Allan is perhaps attempting to identify is a higher order of law which places a limit on the supremacy of Parliament. But this is, perhaps, to misstate the issue; the problem is not so much the supremacy of Parliament but the appropriation of that supremacy by the Executive which to all intents and purposes exercises a stranglehold over Parliament. Recent judicial appointees are showing a greater preparedness to challenge the Diceyan orthodoxy and to recognise the imperative of democracy – to recognise values more fundamental than a majority in Parliament (see further Lord Woolf, 'Droit Public — English Style' [1995] *Public Law* 57, *post* p. 237)

The Hon. Sir John Laws, 'Law and Democracy' [1995] *Public Law* 74

. . .

Democracy and fundamental rights

As a matter of fundamental principle, it is my opinion that the survival and flourishing of a democracy in which basic rights (of which freedom of expression may be taken as a paradigm) are not only respected but enshrined requires that those who exercise democratic, political power must have limits set to what they may do: limits which they are not allowed to overstep. If this is right, it is a function of democratic power itself that it be not absolute. . .

The government's constituency is the whole body of such citizens; and a democratic government can have no remit but to act in what it perceives to be their best interests. It may get it wrong, and let the people down. But it cannot *knowingly* do so, for that would be to act in bad faith; and no government can justify its own bad faith by pointing to the fact that it was elected by the people. That would be to assert that the electorate endorsed in advance the government's right deliberately to act against its interests, which is an impossible proposition.

Thus the free will of every citizen is a premise of all the government's dealings with the people, and so conditions its duty to act in good faith towards them. It cannot fulfil its duty without recognising this; but such a recognition entails the need to accord fundamental rights, high among them the right of freedom of expression. . .

Any but the crudest society will be ordered, will have, in whatever form, a government. Its citizens will make judgments about the government. The government can no more deny their right to do so, without also denying their nature as free and rational beings, than it can deny their right to make judgments upon each other. But more than this, the government cannot be *neutral* about free speech. If it is not to be denied, it must be permitted; there is no room for what the logicians would call an undisturbed middle; and if it must be permitted, it must be entrenched and protected, since its vindication is not a matter of legitimate political choice but an axiom of any community of free human beings. In the end the government's duty to good faith requires it to accord this fundamental freedom to the people.

The imperative of higher-order law

Now it is only by means of compulsory law that effective rights can be accorded, so that the medium of rights is not persuasion, but the power of rule: the very power which, if misused, could be deployed to subvert rights. We therefore arrive at this position: the constitution must guarantee by positive law such rights as that of freedom of expression, since otherwise its credentials as a medium of honest rule are fatally undermined. But this requires for its achievement what I may call a higher-order law: a law which cannot be abrogated as other laws can, by the passage of a statute promoted by a government with the necessary majority in Parliament. Otherwise the right is not in the keeping of the constitution at all; it is not a guaranteed right; it exists, in point of law at least, only because the government chooses to let it exist, whereas in truth no such choice should be open to any government.

The democratic credentials of an elected government cannot justify its enjoyment of a right to abolish fundamental freedoms. If its power in the state is in the last resort absolute, such fundamental rights as free expression are only privileges; no less so if the absolute power rests in an elected body. The byword of every tyrant is 'My word is law'; a democratic assembly having sovereign power beyond the reach of curtailment or review may make just such an assertion, and its elective base cannot immunise it from playing the tyrant's role. . .

Since in the last resort the government rules by consent, the source of public power is not the strong arm of the ruler, but the people themselves.

Even so, the fundamental sinews of the constitution, the cornerstones of democracy and of inalienable rights, ought not by law to be in the keeping of the government, because the only means by which these principles may be enshrined in the state is by their possessing a status which no government has the right to destroy. I have already argued this position in relation to fundamental individual rights; now I assert it also as regards democracy itself. It is a condition of democracy's preservation that the power of a democratically elected government – or Parliament – be not absolute. The institution of free and regular elections, like fundamental individual rights, has to be vindicated by a higher-order law: very obviously, no government can tamper with it, if it is to avoid the mantle of tyranny; no government, therefore, must be allowed to do so. . .

The thrust of this reasoning is that the doctrine of Parliamentary sovereignty cannot be vouched by Parliamentary legislation; a higher-order law confers it, and must of necessity limit it. Thus it is not, and cannot be, established by the measures which set in place the constitutional reforms of the late seventeenth century; nor by any legislation. Indeed Lord Browne-Wilkinson's construction of Article 9 of the Bill of Rights 1688, to which I have already referred, means only that no impediment may be placed on Parliamentary processes, such as, for instance, by a claim against an MP for defamation; it is no more nor less than a rule of absolute legal privilege. It has nothing to do with the question whether statutes in proper form are by law beyond challenge. Its effect is that no constraint of any kind is to be imposed on the freedom of Parliament to debate whatever it likes. That is of course a vital principle, and the courts have been at pains to respect what they regard as Parliament's rights. But it says nothing about the legal supremacy of legislation; the existence of a power in the courts to strike down a statute as inconsistent with a fundamental right or, were it to happen, with democracy itself, does not in any sense touch the freedom of members of either House, uninhibited by any law, to say whatever they choose during a Bill's passage.

So the rules which establish and vindicate a government's power are in a different category from laws which assume the existence of the framework, and are made under it, because they prescribe the framework itself. In states with written constitutions the rules are of course to be found in the text of the constitution, which, typically, will also contain provisions as to how they may be changed. Generally the mechanisms under which the framework may be changed are different from those by which ordinary laws, not part of the framework, may be repealed or amended; and the mechanisms will be stricter than those in place for the alteration of ordinary law.

But in Britain the rules establishing the framework possess, on the face of it, no different character from any other statute law. The requirement of elections at least every five years may in theory be altered by amending legislation almost as readily – though the 'almost' is important – as a provision defining dangerous dogs. The conventions under which cabinet government is carried on could in theory be changed with no special rules at all, as could any of the norms by which the government possesses the authority to govern. The rules by which the power of a government is conferred are in effect the same as the rules by which the government may legislate upon other matters after it has gained power. In the end the sanction for the maintenance of democracy is in point of law no greater than the sanction for the maintenance of the dangerous dogs definition. . .

Conclusion

We may now come full circle, and after this long discussion I can identify what seems to me to be the essence of the difference between judicial and elective power. The latter consists in the authority to make decisions of policy within the remit given by the electorate; this is a great power, with which neither the judges nor anyone else have any business to interfere. This is the place held by democracy in our constitution. It is the place of government. Within it, Parliament, even given its present unsatisfactory relationship with the Executive, is truly and totally supreme. It possesses what we may indeed call a political sovereignty. It is a sovereignty which cannot be objected to, save at the price of assaulting democracy itself. But it is not a constitutional sovereignty; it does not have the status of what earlier I called a sovereign text, of the kind found in states with written constitutions. Ultimate sovereignty rests, in every civilised constitution, not with those who wield governmental power, but in the conditions under which they are permitted to do so. The constitution, not the Parliament, is in this sense sovereign. In Britain these conditions should now be recognised as consisting in a framework of fundamental principles which include the imperative of democracy itself and those other rights, prime among them freedom of thought and expression, which cannot be denied save by a plea of guilty to totalitarianism.

For its part judicial power in the last resort rests in the guarantee that this framework will be vindicated. It consists in the assurance that, however great the democratic margin of appreciation (to use Strasbourg's language) that must be accorded to the elected arm of the state, the bedrock of pluralism will be maintained. We have no other choice. The dynamic settlement between the powers of the state requires, in the absence of a constitutional scripture, just such a distribution of authority. The judges are rightly and necessarily constrained not only by a prohibition against intrusion into what is Parliament's proper sphere, but by the requirement, and the truth, that they have in their duty no party political bias. Their interest and obligation in the context of this discussion is to protect values which no democratic politician could honestly contest: values which, therefore, may be described as apolitical, since they stand together above the rancorous but vital dissensions of party politicians. The judges are constrained also, and rightly, by the fact that their role is reactive; they cannot initiate; all they can do is to apply principle to what is brought before them by others. Nothing could be more distinct from the duty of political creativity owed to us by Members of Parliament.

Though our constitution is unwritten, it can and must be articulated. Though it changes, the principles by which it goes can and must be elaborated. They are not silent; they represent the aspirations of a free people. They must be spoken and explained and, indeed, argued over. Politicians, lawyers, scholars, and many others have to do this. Constitutional theory has, perhaps, occupied too modest a place here in Britain, so that the colour and reach of public power has not been exposed to a glare that is fierce enough. But the importance of these matters is so great that, whatever the merits or demerits of what I have had to say, we cannot turn our backs on the arguments. We cannot risk the future growth without challenge of new, perhaps darker, philosophies. We cannot fail to give principled answers to those who ask of the nature of state power by what legal alchemy, in any situation critical to the protection of our freedoms, the constitution measures the claims of the ruler and the ruled. The imperatives of democracy and fundamental rights do not only demand acceptance; they demand a vindication that survives any test of intellectual rigour.

Question

Has Sir John Laws successfully identified fundamental values arising from the notion of democracy which will be adequate to deal effectively with the worst excesses of naked majoritarianism? Is it the role of a judge to identify such values and exalt them to a position superior to an Act of Parliament?

Note

What would happen if there was a revolution and the monarchy was overthrown, Parliament dissolved and all its members imprisoned, and new elections held to a Constitutional Convention which draws up a new constitution with a presidential system of government and a single chamber assembly? If this new order is accepted by the people and the courts, the currently accepted doctrine of the legislative supremacy of Parliament would become redundant (cf. *Madzimbamuto* v *Lardner-Burke* [1969] 1 AC 645, *post* p. 83). It is power and politics which operate in such a situation, not legal theory. Under the old order the new regime would be regarded as illegal, but it will acquire its own legitimacy from the obedience shown to it. Sovereignty, as a political concept, ultimately resides in the people; if the people accept the new legal order they will thereby give to it validity and legitimacy. For example, while the Declaration of Independence in 1776 and the enactment of the United States Constitution in 1787 were illegal under the old legal order, they were validated by, and received their legitimacy and authority from, the People of the United States, who accepted them and agreed to abide by the new constitution.

Our constitutional order has evolved from the position where an absolute monarch was supreme, to the current position where Parliament is legislatively supreme. The biggest jump in this evolutionary process occurred in the seventeenth century with the Glorious Revolution of 1688, which led to the establishment of the doctrine of the legislative supremacy of Parliament. The ultimate authority for the doctrine stems from the acceptance by the people of William III as the new monarch, and the acceptance by the courts of the new legal order founded on this doctrine as expressed legally in the common law.

(C) THE NATURE OF THE LEGISLATIVE SUPREMACY OF PARLIAMENT

What are the implications of the legislative supremacy of Parliament? Dicey's statement of the doctrine (*ante* p. 52) may be converted into three propositions which will be examined in more detail. They are:

(i) Parliament is the supreme law-making authority.
(ii) The legislative powers of Parliament are unlimited.
(iii) No other body has authority to rule on the validity of its enactments.

Each of these propositions will be examined separately.

(i) Parliament – the supreme law-making authority

In the fourteenth century Parliament emerged as an effective, if not supreme, law-making body. In the seventeenth century James I, by insisting on his right to rule by prerogative, created the conditions in which the battle between the Monarch and Parliament for supremacy was fought in the courts.

The Case of Proclamations
(1611) 12 Co Rep 74; 77 ER 1352

The King sought to check the overgrowth of the capital by issuing a proclamation to prohibit the building of new homes in London. He also sought to preserve wheat for human consumption and issued a proclamation prohibiting the manufacture of starch from wheat. The Commons complained that this was an abuse of proclamations, and the King sought the opinion of Chief Justice Coke who consulted with his fellow judges.

In the same term it was resolved by the two Chief Justices, Chief Baron, and Baron Altham, upon conference betwixt the Lords of the Privy Council and them, that the King by his proclamation cannot create any offence which was not an offence before, for then he may alter the law of the land by his proclamation in a high point; for if he may create an offence where none is, upon that ensues fine and imprisonment: also the law of England is divided into three parts, common law, statute law, and custom; but the King's proclamation is none of them: also *malum aut est malum in se, aut prohibitum,* that which is against common law is *malum in se, malum prohibitum* is such an offence as is prohibited by Act of Parliament, and not by proclamation.

Also, it was resolved, that the King hath no prerogative, but that which the law of the land allows him.

But the King for prevention of offences may by proclamation admonish his subjects that they keep the laws, and do not offend them; upon punishment to be inflicted by the law, &c.

Lastly, if the offence be not punishable in the Star-Chamber, the prohibition of it by proclamation cannot make it punishable there: and after this resolution, no proclamation imposing fine and imprisonment was afterwards made, &c.

Note

The Stuart kings also claimed to have other prerogative powers of considerable importance, namely a *suspending* power,which could be used to postpone the operation of a statute for an indefinite period, and a *dispensing* power, which could be used to relieve offenders from the statutory penalties they had incurred. It was James II's use of the suspending power in respect of penal laws relating to religion in the Declarations of Indulgence 1687 and 1688 which led to the revolution of 1688.

In the area of taxation it had been established by the time of Edward I that direct taxes could only be levied with the consent of Parliament. However, the Stuarts claimed they could raise money by means of the prerogative. First, the prerogative relating to foreign affairs was used to regulate trade by the imposition of duties (see *The Case of Impositions (Bate's Case)* (1606) 2 St Tr 371). Secondly, the prerogative power to defend the realm in face of an emergency was used to raise money for the navy. The King was found to be the sole judge of whether an emergency existed (see *The Case of Shipmoney (R* v *Hampden)* (1637) 3 St Tr 825).

The claims by the Stuart kings to rule by prerogative were resolved by the Bill of Rights 1689.

The Bill of Rights 1689

I Will & Mary Sess 2 ch 2

Whereas the late King James the second, by the Assistance of divers Evil Counsellors, Judges, and Ministers, imployed by him did endeavour to Subvert and extirpate the Protestant Religion, and the Lawes and Liberties of this Kingdome. . . .

And whereas the said late King James the second having abdicated the Government and the throne being thereby vacant.

His Highnesse the Prince of Orange (whom it hath pleased Almighty God to make the glorious Instrument of delivering this Kingdom from Popery and Arbitrary Power) Did (by the advice of the Lords Spirituall and Temporall and divers principall persons of the Commons) Cause Letters to be written to the Lords Spirituall and Temporall being Protestants and other Letters to the several Countyes Citties Universities Burroughs and Cinqe Ports for the chuseing of such persons to represent them as were of right to be sent to Parliament to meet and sitt at Westminster upon the two and twentieth day of January in this Year 1688 in order to such an establishment as that their Religion Lawes and Libertyes might not againe be in danger of being subverted.

Upon which Letters Elections haveing been accordingly made.

And thereupon the said Lords Spirituall and Temporall and Commons pursuant to their respective letters and Elections being now assembled in a full and free representative of this nation taking into their most serious consideration the best meanes for atteyneing the ends aforesaid Doe in the first place (as their Ancestors in like Case have usually done) for the vindicating and asserting their antient rights and Liberties, Declare.

[1.] That the pretended power of suspending of Lawes or the execution of Lawes by Regall Authority without Consent of Parliament is illegall.

[2.] That the pretended power of dispensing with lawes or the Execution of lawes by regall authority as it has been assumed and exercised of late is illegall.

[3.] That the Commission for erecting the late Courte of Commissioners for Ecclesiasticall Causes and all other Commissions and Courts of like nature are illegall and pernicious.

[4.] That levying of money for or to the use of the Crowne by pretence of Prerogative without Grant of Parliament for longer time or in other manner, than the same is or shall be granted is illegall.

[5.] That it is the right of the Subjects to petition the King and all Committments and prosecutions for such petitioning are illegall.

[6.] That the raiseing or keeping a Standing Army within the Kingdom in time of Peace unlesse it be with consent of Parliament is against Law.

[7.] That the Subjects which are Protestants may have Armes for their defence Suitable to their Condition and as allowed by Law.

[8.] That Elections of Members of Parliament ought to be free.

[9.] That the freedome of Speech and debates or proceedings in Parliament ought not to be impeached or questioned in any Courte or place out of Parliament.

[10.] That excessive Bayle ought not to be required nor excessive fynes imposed nor cruel and unusuall Punishments inflicted.

[11.] That Jurors ought to be duely impannelled and returned and Jurors which passe upon men in tryalls for high Treason ought to be freeholders.

[12.] That all Grants and promises of fynes and forfeitures of particular persons before conviction are illegall and void.

[13.] And that for redress of all greivances and for the amending, strengthening and preserving of the Lawes, Parliaments ought to be held frequently.

And they do claime demand and insist upon all and singular the premises as their undoubted Rights and Liberties and that noe Declarations Judgements Doeings or proceedings to the prejudice of the People in any of the said premisses ought in any wise to bee drawne hereafter into Consequence or Example.

To which demand of their rights they are particularly Encouraged by the declaration of his Highnesse the Prince of Orange as being the only Meanes for obteyning a full redress and remedy therein.

Haveing therefore an intire Confidence that his said Highnesse the Prince of Orange will perfect the deliverance soe farr advanced by him and will still preserve them from the violation of their rights which they have here asserted and from all other attempts upon their Religion Rights and Liberties.

The said Lords Spirituall and Temporall and Commons Assembled at Westminster doe Resolve.

That William and Mary Prince and Princesse of Orange bee and bee declared, King and Queen of England France and Ireland and the Dominions thereunto belonging to hold the Crowne and Royall Dignity of the said Kingdom's and Dominions to them the said Prince and Princesss during their lives and the life of the Survivor of them and that the Sole and full exercise of the Regall Power be only in and executed by the said Prince of Orange in the Names of the said Prince and Princesse during their Joynt lives And after their deceases the said Crowne and Royall Dignity of the said Kingdoms and Dominions to be to the heires of the body of the said Princesse: And for default of such Issue to the Princesse Anne of Denmarke and the heires of her body. And for default of such Issue to the heires of the body of the said Prince of Orange.

And the said Lords Spirituall and Temporall and Commons doe pray the said Prince and Princesse of Orange to accept the same accordingly. . . .

Upon which their said Majestyes did accept the crowne and royall dignitie of the kingdoms of England France and Ireland and the dominions thereunto belonging . . . And thereupon their Majestyes were pleased that the said lords spirituall and temporall and commons being the two Houses of Parlyament should continue to sitt and with their Majesty's royall concurrence make effectuall provision for the settlement of the religion lawes and liberties of this kingdome soe that the same for the future might not be in danger againe of being subverted, to which the said lords spirituall and temporall and commons did agree and proceede to act accordingly. Now in pursuance of the premisses the said lords spirituall and temporall and commons in Parlyament assembled for the ratifying confirming and establishing the said declaration and the articles clauses matters and things therein contained by the force of a law made in due forme by authority of Parlyament doe pray that it may be declared and enacted that all and singular the rights and liberties asserted and claimed in the said declaration are the true auntient and indubitable rights and liberties of the people of this kingdome and soe shall be esteemed allowed adjudged deemed and taken to be and that all and every the particulars aforesaid shall be firmly and strictly holden and observed as they are expressed in the said declaration. And all officers and ministers whatsoever shall serve their Majestyes and their successors according to the same in all times to come. . . .

D. Judge, *The Parliamentary State* (1993), p.20

The Constitutional Settlement of 1689 and the Rise of the Liberal State

The potency of the Constitutional Settlement of 1689 stems from its implicit principle of the supremacy of parliament in law. The acceptance by William and Mary of the gift of the crown was conditional upon the terms set by parliament. Henceforth, monarchical power was dependent upon parliament rather than *vice versa.* After 1689, as Munro points out:

> Parliament was to be its own master and free from interference . . . Parliaments were to be held frequently, and the election of their members was to be free. The Crown's power to levy taxes was made subject to parliamentary consent, its power to keep a standing army made subject to statute, and powers of suspending or dispensing with laws . . . were declared illegal. (1987: 80)

In other words, what was asserted and accepted in 1689 was the principle of *parliamentary sovereignty*, whereby parliament secured legal supremacy amongst the institutions of the state. Thus, not only was the monarchy subordinated to parliament, but, also, the last vestiges of the claim of the courts that parliament could not legislate in derogation of the principles of the common law were removed. Constitutional theory was at last reconciled to the legal practice that had been developing for nearly a century.

Above all, therefore, the Bill of Rights was a restraint upon arbitrary behaviour. Its passage confirmed the distinctiveness of English state development from its continental European counterparts. The concentration of power in the hands of the monarch and the exclusion of parliament from policy making — the political hallmarks of absolutism — were outlawed in England in 1689. The authority of statute was conferred upon the pre-existing principles — of consent and representation — so confirming the differences between the state-form in England and those in the absolutist regimes in France and Prussia for example . . ..

(ii) The unlimited legislative powers of Parliament

Several cases have arisen where this idea has been tested.

There is a presumption used by the courts when construing statutes that Parliament does not intend to legislate contrary to the principles of international law, and, as far as possible, a statute will be interpreted in a way which avoids conflict. What do the courts do, however, when there is a clear conflict between a statute of the United Kingdom Parliament and the principles of international law? The answer is given in the following case.

Mortensen* v *Peters
(1906) 14 SLT 227
High Court of Justiciary

> Mortensen was the captain of a Norwegian trawler charged with illegal trawl fishing in waters within the Moray Firth contrary to a bye-law made by the Fishery Board for Scotland under s. 7 of the Herring Fishery (Scotland) Act 1889. The Act defined the area for which bye-laws could be made, that is, all of the Moray Firth, although much of it comprised international waters. The trawler had been fishing five miles off the coast in international waters but within the prohibited area. Mortensen was convicted by the Sheriff's Court and appealed.

THE LORD JUSTICE GENERAL: My Lords, I apprehend that the question is one of construction and of construction only. In this Court we have nothing to do with the question of whether the legislature has or has not done what foreign powers may consider a usurpation in a question with them. Neither are we a tribunal sitting to decide whether an act of the legislature is *ultra vires* as in contravention of generally acknowledged principles of international law. For us an Act of Parliament duly passed by Lords and Commons and assented to by the King, is supreme, and we are bound to give effect to its terms. . . .

It is said by the appellant . . . that International Law has firmly fixed that a locus such as this is beyond the limits of territorial sovereignty; and that consequently it is not to be thought that in such a place the legislature could seek to affect any but the King's subjects.

It is a trite observation that there is no such thing as a standard of International Law, extraneous to the domestic law of a kingdom, to which appeal may be made. International Law, so far as this Court is concerned, is the body of doctrine regarding the international rights and duties of States which has been adopted and made part of the Law of Scotland. Now can it be said to be clear by the law of Scotland that the locus here is beyond what the legislature may assert right to affect by legislation against all whomsoever for the purpose of regulating methods of fishing?

I do not think I need say anything about what is known as the three-mile limit. It may be assumed that within the three miles the territorial sovereignty would be sufficient to cover any such legislation as the present. It is enough to say that that is not a proof of the counter proposition that outside the three miles no such result could be looked for. The locus, although outside the three-mile limit, is within the bay known as the Moray Firth, and the Moray Firth, says the respondent, is *intra fauces terræ*. Now, I cannot say that there is any definition of what *fauces terræ* exactly are. But there are at least three points which go far to shew that this spot might be considered as lying therein.

1st. The dicta of the Scottish Institutional Writers seem to show that it would be no usurpation, according to the law of Scotland, so to consider it.

Thus, Stair, II i. 5: 'The vast ocean is common to all mankind as to navigation and fishing, which are the only uses thereof, because it is not capable of bounds; but when the sea is inclosed in bays, creeks, *or otherwise is capable of any bounds or meiths as within the points of such lands,* or within the view of such shores, then it may become proper, but with the reservation of passage for commerce as in the land.' And Bell, Pr. S 639: 'The Sovereign . . . is proprietor of the narrow seas within cannon shot of the land, and the *firths,* gulfs, and bays around the Kingdom.'

2nd. The same statute puts forward claims to what are at least analogous places. If attention is paid to the Schedule appended to section 6, many places will be found far beyond the three-mile limit – *e.g.,* the Firth of Clyde near its mouth. I am not ignoring that it may be said that this in one sense is proving *idem per idem,* but none the less I do not think the fact can be ignored.

3rd. There are many instances to be found in decided cases where the right of a nation to legislate for waters more or less landlocked or landembraced, although beyond the three-mile limit, has been admitted.

They will be found collected in the case of the *Direct United States Cable Company* v *Anglo-American Telegraph Company,* L R 2 App Cas 394, the bay there in question being Conception Bay, which has a width at the mouth of rather more than 20 miles.

It seems to me therefore, without laying down the proposition that the Moray Firth is for every purpose within the territorial sovereignty, it can at least be clearly said that the appellant cannot make out his proposition that it is inconceivable that the British legislature should attempt for fishery regulation to legislate against all and sundry in such a place. And if that is so, then I revert to the considerations already stated which as a matter of construction make me think that it did so legislate.

LORD KYLLACHY: . . . A legislature may quite conceivably, by oversight or even design, exceed what an international tribunal (if such existed) might hold to be its international rights. Still, there is always a presumption against its intending to do so. I think that is acknowledged. But then it is only a presumption; and, as such, it must always give way to the language used if it is clear, and also to all counter presumptions which may legitimately be had in view in determining, on ordinary principles, the true meaning and intent of the legislation. Express words will, of course, be conclusive; and so also will plain implication.

Now it must, I think, be conceded that the language of the enactment here in question is fairly express – express, that is to say, to the effect of making an unlimited and unqualified prohibition, applying to the whole area specified, and affecting everybody – whether British subjects or foreigners.

LORD JOHNSTON: [delivered a concurring judgment]

Appeal dismissed

Note

In *Cheney* v *Conn* [1968] 1 All ER 779, a taxpayer challenged an assessment of income tax made under the Finance Act 1964 on the ground that part of the money raised would be used for the manufacture of nuclear weapons contrary to a treaty, the Geneva Convention, to which the United Kingdom was party. Ungoed-Thomas J stated:

> What the statute itself enacts cannot be unlawful, because what the statute says and provides is itself the law, and the highest form of law that is known to this country. It is the law which prevails over every other form of law, and it is not for the court to say that a parliamentary enactment, the highest law in this country, is illegal.

See also *R* v *Secretary for the Home Department, ex parte Thakrar* [1974] QB 684.

If international law can place no limitation on Parliament's powers, can time do so?

In *Burmah Oil Co.* v *Lord Advocate* [1965] AC 75, HL, the company was successful in its claim for compensation against the Crown for the destruction of its installations in Burma during the Second World War, the destruction having been ordered by the commander of British forces to prevent the installations falling into the hands of the advancing Japanese forces. In response to this decision Parliament hastily passed the War Damage Act 1965 with retrospective effect to deny entitlement to compensation for damage for acts lawfully done by the Crown during a war in which the Sovereign was engaged.

(iii) Ruling on the validity of Parliament's enactments

The statement of Dicey above also suggests that no person or body has authority to rule on the validity of Parliament's enactments. Is it possible to challenge the validity of an Act of Parliament in the courts? In countries with a written constitution the ordinary courts or a constitutional court will have jurisdiction to determine whether the acts of the legislature are constitutional. In the United States the Supreme Court, in *Marbury* v *Madison* (1803) 1 Cranch 137, declared that it had power to decide whether or not the Acts of Congress conformed with the Constitution. In the United Kingdom the doctrine of legislative supremacy dictates that Parliament has power to legislate on constitutional matters. Thus Parliament may change the constitution by Act of Parliament. This being so, is it possible to challenge an Act on the ground that it is unconstitutional? Chief Justice Coke was of opinion that the courts could intervene if Parliament enacted outrageous legislation. He stated in *Dr Bonham's Case* (1610) 8 Co Rep 114, at p. 118:

> In many cases, the common law will control Acts of Parliament, and sometimes adjudge them to be utterly void: for when an Act of Parliament is against common right and reason, or repugnant, or impossible to be performed, the common law will control it, and adjudge such an Act to be void.

However, this statement precedes the Glorious Revolution of 1688, since when the doctrine of the supremacy of Parliament has developed its modern meaning. In *Ex p. Canon Selwyn* (1872) 36 JP 54 a question arose regarding the validity of the Irish Church Act 1869. Cockburn CJ stated:

> [T]here is no judicial body in the country by which the validity of an act of parliament could be questioned. An act of the legislature is superior in authority to any court of law. We have only to administer the law as we find it, and no court could pronounce a judgment as to the validity of an act of Parliament.

In *Pickin* v *British Railways Board* [1974] AC 765, Lord Reid stated:

> In earlier times many learned lawyers seem to have believed that an Act of Parliament could be disregarded in so far as it was contrary to the law of God or the law of nature or natural justice, but since the supremacy of Parliament was finally demonstrated by the Revolution of 1688 any such idea has become obsolete.

In *Manuel* v *Attorney-General* [1983] Ch 77, Sir Robert Megarry VC stated, at p. 86:

> [T]he duty of the court is to obey and apply every Act of Parliament, and . . . the court cannot hold any such Act to be ultra vires. Of course there may be questions about what the Act means, and of course there is power to hold statutory instruments and other subordinate legislation ultra vires. But once an instrument is recognised as being an Act of Parliament, no English court can refuse to obey it or question its validity.

But what happens if there are two Acts on the statute books which conflict with one another? See the case which follows.

Ellen Street Estates Limited v *Minister of Health*
[1934] 1 KB 590
Court of Appeal

The Acquisition of Land (Assessment of Compensation) Act 1919 provided by s. 2 for the assessment of compensation in respect of land acquired compulsorily for public purposes according to certain rules. Section 7(1) stated 'The provisions of the Act or order by which the land is authorised to be acquired, or of any Act incorporated therewith, shall in relation to the matters dealt with in this Act, have effect subject to this Act, and so far as inconsistent with this Act those provisions shall cease to have or shall not have effect. . . .' The Housing Act 1925, s. 46 provided for the assessment of compensation for land acquired compulsorily under an improvement or reconstruction scheme made under that Act in a manner differing in certain respects from that prescribed by the Act of 1919. Section 7(1) could be construed as applying to previous enactments, but it was argued that it applied also to subsequent enactments. If this was so, inconsistent provisions in the 1925 Act would be of no effect.

SCRUTTON LJ: . . . Such a contention involves this proposition, that no subsequent Parliament by enacting a provision inconsistent with the Act of 1919 can give any effect to the words it uses. Sect. 46, sub-s. 1, of the Housing Act, 1925, says this: 'Where land included in any improvement or reconstruction scheme . . . is acquired compulsorily,' certain provisions as to compensation shall apply. These are inconsistent with those contained in the Acquisition of Land (Assessment of Compensation) Act, 1919, and then s. 46, sub-s. 2, of the Act of 1925 provides: 'Subject as aforesaid, the compensation to be paid for such land shall be assessed in accordance with the Acquisition of Land (Assessment of Compensation) Act, 1919.' I asked Mr Hill [for the appellants] what these last quoted words mean, and he replied they mean nothing. That is absolutely contrary to the constitutional position that Parliament can alter an Act previously passed, and it can do so by repealing in terms the previous Act – Mr Hill agrees that it may do so – and it can do it also in another way – namely, by enacting a provision which is clearly inconsistent with the previous Act.

MAUGHAM LJ: . . . The Legislature cannot, according to our constitution, bind itself as to the form of subsequent legislation, and it is impossible for Parliament to enact that in a subsequent statute dealing with the same subject-matter there can be no implied repeal. If in a subsequent Act Parliament chooses to make it plain that the earlier statute is being to some extent repealed, effect must be given to that intention just because it is the will of the Legislature.

Appeal dismissed

Questions

1. Was this case concerned with the *content* of the legislation or the *form* of the legislation?

2. When Maugham LJ stated that Parliament cannot bind itself as to the form of subsequent legislation, was this *obiter* or *ratio*?.

Note

While there may be a reluctance on the part of the courts to rule on the validity of Acts of Parliament, a related issue which has arisen is whether they may adjudicate upon the question whether something purporting to be an Act of Parliament actually is such. It is the Queen in Parliament which enacts legislation. Under the common law, for a Bill to become law it must be approved by the Lords and Commons and receive the Royal Assent. If an Act is challenged on the basis that there have been procedural defects during its passage through Parliament, will the courts look behind the formal words of enactment and inquire whether the requirements of the common law have been satisfied?

Pickin v *British Railways Board*
[1974] AC 765
House of Lords

Pickin was a railway enthusiast who, in 1969, purchased from the owner of a piece of land adjoining a disused railway line, all his estate and interest in the railway land and track. By s. 259 of a private Act of Parliament of 1836 setting up the railway line, it was provided that, if a line should be abandoned, the lands acquired for the track should vest in the owners for the time being of the adjoining lands. Pickin brought an action against the Board, claiming that by virtue of s. 259 he was the owner of that land to mid-track. The Board claimed that it owned the land by virtue of a private Act of Parliament, the British Railways Act 1968. Pickin claimed that the relevant provision (s. 18) of the 1968 Act was invalid and ineffective to deprive him of his title, as Parliament had been misled by the Board to obtain the passage of the Act. In particular the Bill was presented as being unopposed, but notice had not been given to affected landowners as required by Standing Orders. In addition, the preamble to the Bill contained a false recital that plans of the lands and a book of reference to such plans containing the names of the owners, lessees and occupiers of the said land were duly deposited with the clerk of the county council. The Board sought to have these claims struck out as frivolous, vexatious and an abuse of the process of the court.

LORD REID: . . . The idea that a court is entitled to disregard a provision in an Act of Parliament on any ground must seem strange and startling to anyone with any knowledge of the history and law of our constitution, but a detailed argument has been submitted to your Lordships and I must deal with it.

I must make it plain that there has been no attempt to question the general supremacy of Parliament. In earlier times many learned lawyers seem to have believed that an Act of Parliament could be disregarded in so far as it was contrary to the law of God or the law of nature or natural justice, but since the supremacy of Parliament was finally demonstrated by the Revolution of 1688 any such idea has become obsolete.

The respondent's contention is that there is a difference between a public and a private Act. There are of course great differences between the methods and procedures followed in dealing with public and private Bills, and there may be some differences in the methods of construing their provisions. But the respondent argues for a much more fundamental difference. There is little in modern authority that he can rely on. The mainstay of his argument is a decision of this House, *Mackenzie* v *Stewart* in 1754.

[In the Court of Appeal Pickin successfully argued that this case was authority for the House of Lords refusing to give effect to a private Act obtained by fraud.]

. . . It appears to me that far the most probable explanation of the decision is that it was a decision as to the true construction of the Act. . . . [I]t seems to me much more likely that Lord Hardwicke LC adopted [the construction argued for by Mackenzie] than that he laid down some new constitutional principle that the court had the power to give relief against the provision of a statute.

If the decision was only as to the construction of a statutory provision that would explain why the case has received little attention in later cases. . . .

In my judgment the law is correctly stated by Lord Campbell in *Edinburgh and Dalkeith Railway Co.* v *Wauchope* (1842) 8 Cl & F 710; 1 Bell 252. Mr Wauchope claimed certain wayleaves. The matter was dealt with in a private Act. He appears to have maintained in the Court of Session that the provisions of that Act should not be applied because it had been passed without his having had notice as required by Standing Orders. . . . Lord Campbell [stated]:

> I must express some surprise that such a notion should have prevailed. It seems to me there is no foundation for it whatever; all that a court of justice can look to is the parliamentary roll; they see that an Act has passed both Houses of Parliament, and that it has received the royal assent, and no court of justice can inquire into the manner in which it was introduced into Parliament, what was done previously to its being introduced, or what passed in Parliament during the various stages of its progress through both Houses of Parliament. I therefore trust that no such inquiry will hereafter be entered into in Scotland, and that due effect will be given to every Act of Parliament, both private as well as public, upon the just construction which appears to arise upon it.

No doubt this was obiter but, so far as I am aware, no one since 1842 has doubted that it is a correct statement of the constitutional position.

The function of the court is to construe and apply the enactments of Parliament. The court has no concern with the manner in which Parliament or its officers carrying out its Standing Orders perform these functions. Any attempt to prove that they were misled by fraud or otherwise would necessarily involve an inquiry into the manner in which they had performed their functions in dealing with the Bill which became the British Railways Act 1968.

In whatever form the respondent's case is pleaded he must prove not only that the appellants acted fraudulently but also that their fraud caused damage to him by causing the enactment of section 18. He could not prove that without an examination of the manner in which the officers of Parliament dealt with the matter. So the court would, or at least might, have to adjudicate upon that.

For a century or more both Parliament and the courts have been careful not to act so as to cause conflict between them. Any such investigations as the respondent seeks could easily lead to such a conflict, and I would only support it if compelled to do so by clear authority. But it appears to me that the whole trend of authority for over a century is clearly against permitting any such investigation.

The respondent is entitled to argue that section 18 should be construed in a way favourable to him and for that reason I have refrained from pronouncing on that matter. But he is not entitled to go behind the Act to show that section 18 should not be enforced. Nor is he entitled to examine proceedings in Parliament in order to show that the appellants by fraudulently misleading Parliament caused him loss. I am therefore clearly of opinion that this appeal should be allowed. . . .

LORD MORRIS OF BORTH-Y-GEST: . . . The question of fundamental importance which arises is whether the court should entertain the proposition that an Act of Parliament can so be assailed in the courts that matters should proceed as though the Act or some part of it had never been passed. I consider that such doctrine would be dangerous and impermissible. It is the function of the courts to administer the laws which Parliament has enacted. In the processes of Parliament there will be much consideration whether a Bill should or should not in one form or another become an enactment. When an enactment is passed there is finality unless and until it is amended or repealed by Parliament. In the courts there may be argument as to the correct interpretation of the enactment: there must be none as to whether it should be on the Statute Book at all.

. . . The conclusion which I have reached results, in my view, not only from a settled and sustained line of authority which I see no reason to question and which I think should be endorsed but also from the view that any other conclusion would be constitutionally undesirable and impracticable. It must surely be for Parliament to lay down the procedures which are to be followed before a Bill can become an Act. It must be for Parliament to decide whether its decreed procedures have in fact been followed. It must be for Parliament to lay down and to construe its Standing Orders and further to decide whether they have been obeyed: it must be for Parliament to decide whether in any particular case to dispense with compliance with such orders. It must be for Parliament to decide whether it is satisfied that an Act should be passed in the form and with the wording set out in the Act. It must be for Parliament to decide what documentary material or testimony it requires and the extent to which Parliamentary privilege should attach. It would be impracticable and undesirable for the High Court of Justice to embark upon an inquiry concerning the effect or the effectiveness of the internal procedures in the High Court of Parliament or an inquiry whether in any particular case those procedures were effectively followed.

[His Lordship referred to *Edinburgh and Dalkeith Railway Co.* v *Wauchope* and several other cases and continued.]

Of equal clarity was the passage in the judgment of Willes J in 1871 when in *Lee* v *Bude and Torrington Junction Railway Co.* (1871) LR 6 CP 576 (in which case it was alleged that Parliament had been induced to pass an Act by fraudulent recitals) he said, at p. 582:

> 'Are we to act as regents over what is done by Parliament with the consent of the Queen, Lords, and Commons? I deny that any such authority exists. If an Act of Parliament has been obtained improperly, it is for the legislature to correct it by repealing it: but, so long as it exists as law, the courts are bound to obey it. The proceedings here are judicial, not autocratic, which they would be if we could make laws instead of administering them.'

. . . In the result I have not been persuaded that any doubt has been cast upon principles which are soundly directed as being both desirable and reasonable and which furthermore have for long been firmly established by authority.

I would allow the appeal. . . .

Appeal allowed

Questions

1. Are Standing Orders of the House of Commons the equivalent of statute law?

2. Does this case overrule the authority of *The Prince's Case* (1606) 8 Co Rep 1a, where it was stated that an enactment, even though entered on the parliamentary roll, would not be an Act of Parliament if assented to by the King and the Lords, or the King and the Commons, as the assent of all three is necessary?

3. When Lord Morris stated 'It must surely be for Parliament to lay down the procedures which are to be followed before a Bill can become an Act. It must be for Parliament to decide whether its decreed procedures have in fact been followed', was he referring to procedures laid down in Standing Orders or in Acts of Parliament?

(D) CAN PARLIAMENT LIMIT THE POWERS OF ITS SUCCESSORS?

The answer to this question depends upon the nature of parliamentary supremacy. There are differing theories. Hart recognised that there could be uncertainty regarding the nature of the rule of recognition.

H. L. A. Hart, *The Concept of Law* (1961) pp. 145 – 146

In the overwhelming majority of cases the formula 'Whatever the Queen in Parliament enacts is law' is an adequate expression of the rule as to the legal competence of Parliament, and is accepted as an ultimate criterion for the identification of law, however open the rules thus identified may be at their periphery. But doubts can arise as to its meaning or scope; we can ask what is meant by 'enacted by Parliament' and when doubts arise they may be settled by the courts. What inference is to be drawn as to the place of courts within a legal system from the fact that the ultimate rule of a legal system may thus be in doubt and that courts may resolve the doubt. Does it require some qualification of the thesis that the foundation of a legal system is an accepted rule of recognition specifying the criteria of legal validity?

To answer these questions we shall consider here some aspects of the English doctrine of the sovereignty of Parliament, though, of course, similar doubts can arise in relation to ultimate criteria of legal validity in any system. Under the influence of the Austinian doctrine that law is essentially the product of a legally untrammelled will, older constitutional theorists wrote as if it was a logical necessity that there should be a legislature which was sovereign, in the sense that it is free, at every moment of its existence as a continuing body, not only from legal limitations imposed *ab extra,* but also from its own prior legislation. That Parliament is sovereign in this sense may now be regarded as established, and the principle that no earlier Parliament can preclude its 'successors' from repealing its legislation constitutes part of the ultimate rule of recognition used by the courts in identifying valid rules of law. It is, however, important to see that no necessity of logic, still less of nature, dictates that there should be such a Parliament; it is only one arrangement among others, equally conceivable, which has come to be accepted with us as the criterion of legal validity. Among these others is another principle which might equally well, perhaps better, deserve the name of 'sovereignty'. This is the principle that Parliament should *not* be incapable of limiting irrevocably the legislative competence of its successors but, on the contrary, should have this wider self-limiting power. Parliament would then at least once in its history be capable of exercising an even larger sphere of legislative competence than the accepted established doctrine allows to it. The requirement that at every moment of its existence Parliament should be free from legal limitations including even those imposed by itself is, after all, only one interpretation of the ambiguous idea of legal omnipotence. It in effect makes a choice between a *continuing* omnipotence in all matters not affecting the legislative competence of successive parliaments, and an unrestricted *self-embracing* omnipotence the exercise of which can only be enjoyed once. These two conceptions of omnipotence have their parallel in two conceptions of an omnipotent God: on the one hand, a God who at every moment of His existence enjoys the same powers and so is incapable of cutting down those powers, and, on the other, a God whose powers include the power to destroy for the future his omnipotence. Which form of omnipotence – continuing or self-embracing – our Parliament enjoys is an empirical question concerning the form of rule which is accepted as the ultimate criterion in identifying the law. Though it is a question about a rule lying at the base of a legal system, it is still a question of fact to which at any given moment of time, on some points at least, there may be a quite determinate answer. Thus it is clear that the presently accepted rule is one of continuing sovereignty, so that Parliament cannot protect its statutes from repeal.

Note

Dicey was a proponent of the 'continuing' theory of parliamentary supremacy, usually referred to as the 'traditional' theory. Others have tended towards the 'self-embracing' theory, or a variant of it. Proponents of this 'new' view would argue that Parliament may change the procedures governing law-making. The two extracts which follow summarise this view and point to its consequences.

R. F. V. Heuston, *Essays in Constitutional Law* (2nd edn, 1964), Ch. 1, pp. 6 – 8

Summary of New View

It is suggested that the new view can be summarised thus:

(1) Sovereignty is a legal concept: the rules which identify the sovereign and prescribe its composition and functions are logically prior to it.

(2) There is a distinction between rules which govern, on the one hand, (a) the composition, and (b) the procedure, and, on the other hand, (c) the area of power, of a sovereign legislature.

(3) The courts have jurisdiction to question the validity of an alleged Act of Parliament on grounds 2 (a) and 2 (b), but not on ground 2 (c).

(4) This jurisdiction is exercisable either before or after the Royal Assent has been signified – in the former case by way of injunction, in the latter by way of declaratory judgment.

G. Marshall, *Constitutional Theory* (1971), p. 42 – 43

Dicey simply implied, without examining, the proposition that authority in a 'sovereign' Parliament must be exercised at all times by a simple majority of legislators, who, since they are unrestricted in their powers, can always repeal any constitutional protections or restrictions on power enacted into law by their predecessors. To do Dicey justice, the Sovereign described in the *Law of the Constitution* is the British Parliament (though he did sometimes speak in terms of sovereigns in general). But even in relation to the British Parliament he did not fully examine the possibility that Parliament as at present constituted might conceivably bind the future or circumscribe the freedom of future legislators, not by laying down blanket prohibitions or attempting to enact a fundamental Bill of Rights, but by using their authority to provide different forms and procedures for legislation. A referendum or a joint sitting, for example, might be prescribed before certain things could be done. Or a two-thirds majority. Or a seventy-five per cent or eighty per cent majority. If it is also provided that any repeal of such provisions should not be by simple majority, the courts may be able to protect the arrangements laid down by declaring in suitable proceedings that any purported repeal by simple majority of a protected provision is *ultra vires* as being not, in the sense required by law, an 'Act of Parliament'. In this finding they would not be in any way derogating from parliamentary sovereignty but protecting Parliament's authority from usurpation by those not entitled for the purpose in hand to exercise it. Thus, for the English lawyer or political theorist, sovereignty may be purged of its dangerous absolutism. He can believe both in an ultimate Sovereign and in the possibility of restraint imposed by law upon the way in which legal power is used. He can believe in the possibility even of a modified Bill of Fundamental Rights grafted into the British constitution – or, to be more accurate, in a relatively fundamental set of provisions in which selected civil liberties are protected from attack in the future by, so to speak, taking out legislative insurance in the present, in the shape of requirements of special procedures or majorities. This would be to do rather more than is done in Canada's Bill of Rights, which declares certain rights and freedoms to be fundamental, but leaves them open to attack by any future legislation which specifically declares itself to apply, notwithstanding the Bill of Rights.

For the views of a proponent of the continuing theory of supremacy, see H. W. R. Wade, 'The Basis of Legal Sovereignty' [1955] CLJ 172.

(i) The problem of entrenchment

The Parliament Acts 1911 – 49 provide that in certain circumstances a Bill may become an Act in the absence of approval by the Lords. The 1911 Act, which removed the power of the House of Lords to veto legislation, replacing it with a two-year delaying power, was enacted in accordance with the then existing law which required majorities in both Houses approving the Bill before it received the Royal Assent. The 1949 Act, which reduced the delaying power to one year, was likewise enacted in accordance with the then existing law as laid down in the 1911 Act. These Acts made alterations in the procedures for enacting legislation by dispensing, in certain circumstances, with the requirement that the Lords assent to legislation. If Parliament can make the passage of legislation easier in certain circumstances, could it impose procedural requirements to make the passage of legislation more difficult, for example, a requirement that a majority of voters vote in a referendum in favour of the proposed legislation, or a requirement of an enhanced majority in the Commons such as two-thirds instead of a simple majority? This issue has arisen in several Commonwealth cases.

Attorney-General for New South Wales v *Trethowan and Others*
[1932] AC 526
Privy Council

Under s. 5 of the Colonial Laws Validity Act 1865, the legislature of New South Wales had full power to legislate for its own constitution, powers and procedure, provided that these laws were passed in 'the manner and form' required by the law in force at the time, whether it be imperial or colonial. In 1929 the Constitution (Legislative Council) Amendment Act was passed, which inserted a new s. 7A in the Constitution Act 1902, providing that no Bill for abolishing the Legislative Council should be presented to the Governor for His Majesty's assent until it had been approved by a majority of electors voting in a referendum and, further, that any Bill to repeal this referendum requirement must also be approved at a referendum. In 1930, following a change in government, both houses of the legislature passed two Bills, one to repeal s. 7A and the other to abolish the Legislative Council, both of which the government intended to present for the Royal Assent without referenda being held. The plaintiffs were members of the Legislative Council and sought a declaration that the two Bills could not be presented for Royal Assent until approved by the electors in accordance with s. 7A, and injunctions restraining the presentation of the Bills.

LORD SANKEY LC: . . . [T]he point involved in the case, . . . is really a short one – namely, whether the legislature of the State of New South Wales has power to abolish the Legislative Council of the said State, or to repeal s. 7A of the Constitution Act, 1902, except in the manner provided by the said s. 7A. It will be sufficient for this Board to decide any other question if, and when, it arises.

[Section 5 of the Colonial Laws Validity Act 1865 provides:

Section 5. – Every colonial legislature shall have and be deemed at all times to have had full power within its jurisdiction to establish Courts of Judicature, and to abolish and reconstitute the same, and to alter the constitution thereof, and to make provision for the administration of justice therein; and every representative legislature shall, in respect to the colony under its jurisdiction, have, and be deemed at all times to have had, full power to make laws respecting the constitution, power, and procedure of such legislature; provided that such laws shall have been passed in such manner and form as may from time to time be required by any Act of parliament, letters patent, Order in Council, or colonial law, for the time being in force in the said colony.]

. . . In their Lordships' opinion the legislature of New South Wales had power under s. 5 of the Act of 1865 to enact the Constitution (Legislative Council) Amendment Act, 1929, and thereby to introduce s. 7A into the Constitution Act, 1902. In other words, the legislature had power to alter the constitution of New South Wales by enacting that Bills relating to specified kind or kinds of legislation (e.g., abolishing the Legislative Council or altering its constitution or powers, or repealing or amending that enactment) should not be presented for the Royal assent until approved by the electors in a prescribed manner. There is here no question of repugnancy. The enactment of the Act of 1929 was simply an exercise by the legislature of New South Wales of its power (adopting the words of s. 5 of the Act of 1865) to make laws respecting the constitution, powers and procedure of the authority competent to make the laws for New South Wales.

The whole of s. 7A was competently enacted. It was intra vires s. 5 of the Act of 1865, and was (again adopting the words of s. 5) a colonial law for the time being in force when the Bill to repeal s. 7A was introduced in the Legislative Council.

The question then arises, could *that* Bill, a repealing Bill, after its passage through both chambers, be lawfully presented for the Royal assent without having first received the approval of the electors in the prescribed manner? In their Lordships' opinion, the Bill could not lawfully be so presented. The proviso in the second sentence of s. 5 of the Act of 1865 states a condition which must be fulfilled before the legislature can validly exercise its power to make the kind of laws which are referred to in that sentence. In order that s. 7A may be repealed (in other words, in order that *that* particular law 'respecting the constitution, powers and procedure' of the legislature may be validly made) the law for that purpose must have been passed in the manner required by s. 7A, a colonial law for the time being in force in New South Wales. An attempt was made to draw some distinction between a Bill to repeal a statute and a Bill for other purposes and between 'making' laws and the word in the proviso, 'passed.' Their Lordships feel unable to draw any such distinctions. As to the proviso they agree with the views expressed by Rich J [in the High Court of Australia] in the following words: 'I take the word "passed" to be equivalent to "enacted." The proviso is not dealing with narrow questions of parliamentary procedure'; and later in his judgment: 'In my opinion the proviso to s. 5 relates to the entire process of turning a proposed law into a legislative enactment, and was intended to enjoin fulfilment of every condition and compliance with every requirement which existing legislation imposed upon the process of law making.'

Again, no question of repugnancy here arises. It is only a question whether the proposed enactment is intra vires or ultra vires s. 5. A Bill, within the scope of sub – s. 6 of s. 7A, which received the Royal assent without having been approved by the electors in accordance with that section, would not be a valid Act of the legislature. It would be ultra vires s. 5 of the Act of 1865. Indeed, the presentation of the Bill to the Governor without such approval would be the commission of an unlawful act.

In the result, their Lordships are of opinion that s. 7A of the Constitution Act, 1902, was valid and was in force when the two Bills under consideration were passed through the Legislative Council and the Legislative Assembly. Therefore these Bills could not be presented to the Governor for His Majesty's assent unless and until a majority of the electors voting had approved them.

For these reasons, their Lordships are of opinion that the judgment of the High Court dismissing the appeal from the decree of the Supreme Court of New South Wales was right. . . .

Appeal dismissed

Question

If the United Kingdom Parliament enacted a provision to the same effect as s. 7A, designed to protect the position of the House of Lords, would a subsequent Bill abolishing this provision and the House of Lords become an Act on receiving the Royal Assent, or would the referenda requirements be regarded by the courts as necessary prerequisites to the Bill becoming an Act?

Note

There is a division of view among constitutional theorists as to the relevance of the *Trethowan* case to the United Kingdom. Those who adhere to the traditional theory of supremacy argue that the decision is of no relevance as the New South Wales legislature was a subordinate legislature (see e.g. Wade, 'The Basis of Legal Sovereignty' [1955] CLJ 172; Munro, *Studies in Constitutional Law,* Chapter 5). The proponents of this view rely on *Ellen St Estates Ltd* v *Minister of Health* (*supra*). Opponents of this view argue that the decision is applicable on the basis that at common law there is a rule that legislation may be enacted only in such manner and form as is prescribed by the law (see e.g. Heuston, *Essays in Constitutional Law,* Chapter 1; Fazal, 'Entrenched Rights and Parliamentary Sovereignty' (1974) PL 295). If an Act lays down a specific procedure to be followed before it may be repealed, this is the law, and a measure passed in the normal way ignoring this procedure has not been passed in the manner and form prescribed by the law and therefore is not an Act of Parliament. Support for this view is found in *Harris* v *Minister of the Interior* 1952 (2) SA 428, and *Bribery Commissioner* v *Ranasinghe* [1965] AC 172. In the latter case the Privy Council held that the procedural requirement of the constitution of Ceylon regarding judicial appointments of a two-thirds majority of the legislature, was binding on the sovereign Parliament of Ceylon, which could not, therefore, set up the Bribery Commission by an ordinary Act of Parliament. The Privy Council held that the official copy of the statute was not conclusive of its validity if it appeared that the correct procedures had not been followed. Lord Pearce stated, at p. 197:

> [A] legislature has no power to ignore the conditions of law-making that are imposed by the instrument which itself regulates its power to make law. This restriction exists independently of the question whether the legislature is sovereign. . . .

This statement would appear to lend support to Heuston and Fazal. However, the traditional theorists argue that *Harris* and *Ranasinghe* are not relevant to the United Kingdom because the legislatures of South Africa and Ceylon were subject to constitutent instruments, whereas the United Kingdom has no written constitution. Latham in *The Law and the Commonwealth* (1949), p. 523, states:

> When the purported sovereign is anyone but a single actual person, the designation of him must include the statement of the rules for ascertainment of his will, and these rules, since their observance is a condition of the validity of his legislation are Rules of Law logically prior to him.

Is it crucial that these rules should be contained in a formal written constitution? Heuston believes not; he states (*supra* p. 26):

> It cannot make any difference whether the rules which identify the sovereign come entirely from the common law (as they did before 1911 in the United Kingdom) or entirely from statute (as they do in Ireland, New South Wales and South Africa) or partly from the common law and partly from statute (as they do in the United Kingdom since 1911). It is hard to see why those who argue thus should attach so much importance to the formal source of the complex set of rules identifying the location and composition of the sovereign. . . . The point here is the simple one that until these rules (whatever their source) have been changed in accordance with the manner which they themselves prescribe they must be obeyed.

Questions

1. Is it a necessary concomitant of supremacy that Parliament's powers to legislate be not subject to any procedural restraint?

2. Is Dixon misguided in stating, in 'The Law and the Constitution' (1935) 51 LQR 590, at p. 604, that the *Trethowan* case was:

> a modern reconciliation of the supremacy of the law and the supremacy of Parliament. For it is a demarcation of the limits of the operation of the two principles. The law existing for the time being is supreme when it prescribes the conditions which must be fulfilled to make a law. But on the question what may be done by a law so made, Parliament is supreme over the law?

(ii) The Acts of Union

So far it has been assumed that Parliament is not subject to any constituent instrument. However, in 1707 the Parliaments of England and Scotland passed Acts of Union ratifying the Treaty of Union and creating the new Parliament of Great Britain. In 1800 a similar union took place between Great Britain and Ireland, creating the United Kingdom of Great Britain and Ireland. As these Acts of Union were antecedent to the new Parliaments they created, it is arguable that they were constituent Acts bringing into being a new state and a new Parliament (see Mitchell, *Constitutional Law* (2nd edn, 1968), pp. 69 – 74; Calvert, *Constitutional Law in Northern Ireland* (1968), Chapter 1; for a contrary view see Munro, *Studies in Constitutional Law* (1987), Chapter 4).

Certain provisions of the Treaties were declared to be fundamental and unalterable. The subsequent history reveals, however, that such provisions have been amended or repealed (see e.g. the Universities (Scotland) Act 1853 and the Irish Church Act 1869); indeed the Union with Ireland was dissolved in 1922 when most of Ireland was given independence, with only Northern Ireland remaining in the United Kingdom. The issue of the nature of the Acts of Union has been argued in several Scottish cases but was not finally adjudicated upon.

MacCormick v *Lord Advocate*

1953 SC 396
Court of Session, Inner House

Two members of the Scottish public petitioned the Court of Session for a declaration that a proclamation describing the Queen as 'Elizabeth the Second of the United Kingdom of Great Britain' was illegal, as being contrary to Article I of the Treaty and Acts of Union. The Lord Advocate argued that there was no conflict with Article I and that the number 'II' was authorised by the Royal Titles Act 1953. *Held*: The petition was dismissed, and the petitioners' appeal to the First Division of the Inner House was likewise dismissed on the grounds that there was nothing in Article I which forbade the use of the numeral, the petitioners had no title to sue, and the Royal Titles Act 1953 was irrelevant as it was enacted after the designation 'Elizabeth the Second' had been adopted and used. The President then went on to express his opinion on the Union legislation.

THE LORD PRESIDENT (COOPER): . . . The principle of the unlimited sovereignty of Parliament is a distinctively English principle which has no counterpart in Scottish constitutional law. . . . Considering that the Union legislation extinguished the Parliaments of Scotland and England and replaced them by a new Parliament, I have difficulty in seeing why it should have been supposed that the new Parliament of Great Britain must inherit all the peculiar characteristics of the English Parliament but none of the Scottish Parliament, as if all that happened in 1707 was that Scottish representatives were admitted to the Parliament of England. That is not what was done. Further, the Treaty and the associated legislation, by which the Parliament of Great Britain was brought into being as the successor of the separate Parliaments of Scotland and England, contain some clauses which expressly reserve to the Parliament of Great Britain powers of subsequent modification, and other clauses which either contain no such power or emphatically exclude subsequent alteration by declarations that the provision shall be fundamental and unalterable in all time coming, or declarations of a like effect. I have never been able to understand how it is possible to reconcile with elementary canons of construction the adoption by the English constitutional theorists of the same attitude to these markedly different types of provisions.

The Lord Advocate conceded this point by admitting that the Parliament of Great Britain 'could not' repeal or alter such 'fundamental and essential' conditions. . . . I have not found in the Union legislation any provision that the Parliament of Great Britain should be 'absolutely sovereign' in the sense that that Parliament should be free to alter the Treaty at will. . . .

But the petitioners have still a grave difficulty to overcome on this branch of their argument. Accepting it that there are provisions in the Treaty of Union and associated legislation which are 'fundamental law,' and assuming for the moment that something is alleged to have been done – it matters not whether with legislative authority or not – in breach of that fundamental law, the question remains whether such a question is determinable as a justiciable issue in the Courts of either Scotland or England, in the same fashion as an issue of constitutional *vires* would be cognisable by the Supreme Courts of the United States, or of South Africa or Australia. I reserve my opinion with regard to the provisions relating expressly to this Court and to the laws 'which concern private right' which are administered here. This is not such a question, but a matter of 'public right' (articles 18 and 19). To put the matter in another way, it is of little avail to ask whether the Parliament of Great Britain 'can' do this thing or that, without going on to inquire who can stop them if they do. Any person 'can' repudiate his solemn engagement but he cannot normally do so with impunity. Only two answers have been suggested to this corollary to the main question. The first is the exceedingly cynical answer implied by Dicey (Law of the Constitution, (9th ed.) p. 82) in the statement that 'it would be rash of the Imperial Parliament to abolish the Scotch law courts, and assimilate the Law of Scotland to that of England. But no one can feel sure at what point Scottish resistance to such a change would become serious.' The other answer was that nowadays there may be room for the invocation of an 'advisory opinion' from the International Court of Justice. On these matters I express no view. This at least is plain, that there is neither precedent nor authority of any kind for the view that the domestic Courts of either Scotland or England have jurisdiction to determine whether a governmental act of the type here in controversy is or is not conform to the provisions of a Treaty, least of all when that Treaty is one under which both Scotland and England ceased to be independent states and merged their identity in an incorporating union. From the standpoint both of constitutional law and of international law the position appears to me to be unique, and I am constrained to hold that the action as laid is incompetent in respect that it has not been shown that the Court of Session has authority to entertain the issue sought to be raised. . . .

Note

In *Gibson* v *Lord Advocate* 1975 SLT 134, a Scottish fisherman challenged an EEC Regulation which had become law by virtue of the European Communities Act 1972. The Regulation gave member states equal access to fishing grounds. Gibson argued that this was invalid, being in breach of Article XVIII which forbade 'alteration . . . in the laws which concern private right except for the evident utility of the subjects within Scotland'. Lord Keith held that the control of fishing in territorial waters was not a matter of private right but of public law, and thus was not protected by Article XVIII. However, he went on to state *obiter:*

> Like Lord President Cooper, I prefer to reserve my opinion on what the question would be if the United Kingdom Parliament passed an Act purporting to abolish the Court of Session or the Church of Scotland or to substitute English law for the whole body of Scots private law. I am, however, of opinion that the question whether a particular Act of the United Kingdom Parliament altering a particular aspect of Scots private law is or is not 'for the evident utility' of the subjects within Scotland is not a justiciable issue in this court. The making of decisions upon what must essentially be a political matter is no part of the function of the court, and it is highly undesirable that it should be.

By contrast, in *Stewart* v *Henry* 1989 SLT (SH Ct) 34, Sheriff Stewart went so far as to say that he saw 'no absolute bar to a court's considering the question whether a particular change in the law is for the evident utility of the subjects in Scotland'. In the most recent case of *Pringle* 1991 SLT 330, which, like *Stewart* v *Henry*, concerned the legislation which introduced the community charge in Scotland one year earlier than in England and Wales, it was argued that this contravened Art. IV of the Scots Act of Union which it was claimed required that there should be no difference in the rights, privileges and advantages enjoyed by citizens in Great Britain unless expressly provided for in the treaty. The petitioner did not seek to have the relevant statute (the Abolition of Domestic Rates Etc. (Scotland) Act 1987) declared invalid but rather sought relief from his own liability under the Act to pay the charge because of its alleged contravention of Art. IV. The First Division of the Inner House dismissed the petition on the basis that it did not have jurisdiction to grant the exceptional remedy sought. While this was sufficient to decide the case Lord Hope, the Lord President declined to accept the respondent registration officer's submission that the petitioner's arguments that the 1987 Act breached Art. IV raised a non-justiciable issue. Lord Hope stated (at p. 333):

> The fact that the methods of raising finance for local government in the two parts of the United Kingdom were different for the year in question would not be sufficient to persuade me, without a much more detailed inquiry into the overall effects of these differences, that there was a failure to do what this part of Art. IV intended should be done.

The inference to be drawn is that Lord Hope believed there might be circumstances in which a court could consider whether legislation was inconsistent with union legislation. The question of the constitutional effect of the Scots Articles of Union continues to remain unresolved.

In *Ex p. Canon Selwyn* (1872) 36 JP 54, the issue of the validity of the Irish Church Act 1869 was raised. This Act disestablished and disendowed the Episcopal Church in Ireland which Article 5 of the Treaty of Union had established for ever. Mandamus was sought against the Lord President of the Council, commanding him to present to the Queen a petition asking her to refer for adjudication the question whether her assent to the Irish Church Act 1869 was contrary to the Coronation Oath and the Act of Settlement 1700. The application was refused by Cockburn CJ on the ground that 'there is no judicial body in the country by which the validity of an act of parliament could be questioned. An act of the legislature is superior in authority to any court of law.' Calvert takes issue with Cockburn CJ.

H. Calvert, *Constitutional Law in Northern Ireland* (1968), p. 21

These are strong words. But whilst the Coronation Oath did contain a solemn pledge to maintain the unified and established Church of England and Ireland, it is not here suggested that an Act can be challenged on this ground, or on grounds of contravention of the Act of Settlement. What it is suggested could have been, and what, surprisingly, was not argued in *Ex parte Canon Selwyn,* is that the severance and disestablishment of the Church of Ireland was a legal act power to effect which was withheld from the Parliament of the United Kingdom by its constituent Acts. It is all very well to speak of applying 'the law as we find it.' That begs the question of what we find. A judge appointed before 1800 and continuing in office after 1800 would find himself in a considerable dilemma. Sworn to uphold the laws of parliament, he would find two conflicting laws of two different parliaments, one purporting to disestablish the Irish Church and the other, which constituted the parliament enacting the first, having imposed upon it a statutory prohibition from disestablishing. It is, again, all very well to speak of 'an act of the legislature' being 'superior in authority to any court of law.' No doubt it is – but that is not the question. The question may be viewed as being whether 'an act of the legislature' is 'superior in authority' to a prior constituent Act of a predecessor parliament. There is a difference, which has been overlooked but which may well be crucial, between a parliament repealing its own Acts, and a parliament purporting to repeal the Acts of its constituent predecessor. English courts have never been faced, four square, with this question and English law has therefore never finally made up its mind – *a fortiori* Irish law.

Questions

1. Is Cockburn CJ's dictum reconcilable with the *obiter dicta* in *MacCormick* and *Gibson*?

2. Middleton, 'New Thoughts on the Union' 1954 JR 37, at p. 49, states that 'the fact that Parliament has done something cannot prove that it was entitled to do it'. Do the amendments to, and breaches and repeals of, provisions of the Acts of Union reveal that Parliament is supreme and unconstrained in its powers, or is it the case that Parliament is limited but there is no authority competent to rule on the validity of its Acts, that is, the amendments and repeals are invalid in legal theory but in political reality they exist and are acted upon?

3. Jennings, in *The Law and the Constitution* (5th edn, 1959), p. 170, argues that as the Acts of Union were passed to ratify two treaties, the amendments to these treaties were carried out in accordance with the maxim *nebus sic stantibus,* that is, it is a tacit condition attaching to all treaties that they shall cease to be obligatory so soon as the state of facts and conditions upon which they were founded has substantially changed. Is this a satisfactory explanation for the subsequent amendments to these treaties? If the conditions have not substantially changed in respect of a particular provision, would legislation in respect of it be illegal? If so, could or would any court declare it invalid?

(iii) Independence

One of the problems which constitutional lawyers have had to deal with this century is the granting of independence to many Commonwealth countries. This usually followed a two-stage process, with the colony being granted first Dominion status and subsequently being granted full independence. Section 4 of the Statute of Westminster provides:

> No Act of Parliament of the United Kingdom passed after the commencement of this Act shall extend, or be deemed to extend, to a Dominion as part of the law of

> that Dominion unless it is expressly declared in that Act that that Dominion has requested and consented to, the enactment thereof.

This gives rise to the question whether Parliament could ignore this provision and legislate directly for a Dominion without its request or consent? In *British Coal Corporation* v *The King* [1935] AC 500, at p. 520, Lord Sankey stated, regarding the application of s. 4 to Canada:

> It is doubtless true that the power of the Imperial Parliament to pass on its own initiative any legislation that it thought fit extending to Canada remains in theory unimpaired: indeed, the Imperial Parliament could, as a matter of abstract law, repeal or disregard s. 4 of the Statute. . . . But that is theory and has no relation to realities.

In *Blackburn* v *Attorney-General* [1971] 1 WLR 137, at p. 1040, Lord Denning stated:

> We have all been brought up to believe that, in legal theory, one Parliament cannot bind another and that no Act is irreversible. But legal theory does not always march alongside political reality. Take the Statute of Westminster 1931, which takes away the power of Parliament to legislate for the Dominions. Can anyone imagine that Parliament could or would reverse that Statute? Take the Acts which have granted independence to the Dominions and territories overseas. Can anyone imagine that Parliament could or would reverse those laws and take away their independence? Most clearly not. Freedom once given cannot be taken away. Legal theory must give way to practical politics.

However, legal theory still dominates judicial reasoning. In 1965 when Rhodesia declared UDI, the Southern Rhodesia Act 1965 was rushed through Parliament. In terms of practical politics the Act had no effect in Rhodesia, where it was ignored. However, in *Madzimbamuto* v *Lardner-Burke* [1969] 1 AC 645, Lord Reid recited legal theory:

> It is often said that it would be unconstitutional for the United Kingdom Parliament to do certain things, meaning that the moral, political and other reasons against doing them are so strong that most people would regard it as highly improper if Parliament did these things. But that does not mean that it is beyond the power of Parliament to do these things. If Parliament chose to do any of them, the courts could not hold the Act of Parliament invalid.

Is it therefore impossible for Parliament to divest itself of the power to legislate for independent territories? Dicey's solution to the problem was the idea of abdication. He stated (*supra*, p. 66):

> The impossibility of placing a limit on the exercise of sovereignty does not in any way prohibit either logically, or in matter of fact, the abdication of sovereignty. This is worth observation, because a strange dogma is sometimes put forward that a sovereign power, such as the Parliament of the United Kingdom, can never by its own act divest itself of sovereignty. This position is, however, clearly untenable.

Question

In 1982 the United Kingdom Parliament enacted a new constitution for Canada by the Canada Act, and terminated its own legislative competence for Canada. Section 2 provides:

> No Act of the Parliament of the United Kingdom passed after the Constitution Act 1982 comes into force shall extend to Canada as part of its law.

If Parliament subsequently legislated for Canada would this legislation be *ultra vires*? Would a United Kingdom court be acting unconstitutionally in light of Dicey's doctrine of abdication, if it did not declare the offending statute invalid?

Note

The confusion which reigns in this area is evident in the following case.

Manuel v *Attorney-General*
[1983] Ch 77
Chancery Division

> The Canada Act 1982 was enacted following the request of the Senate and House of Commons of Canada, and with the agreement of nine of the ten provincial governments. The plaintiffs were Indian Chiefs and sought declarations to the effect that the United Kingdom parliament had no power to amend the constitution of Canada so as to prejudice the Indian nations without their consent, and that the Canada Act 1982 was *ultra vires*. The basis of their claim was that the enactment of the Canada Act 1982 was inconsistent with and a derogation from the constitutional safeguards provided for the Indian peoples by the Statute of Westminster 1931 and the British North America Acts. The plaintiffs' contention was that the consent of all the provincial legislatures, the Indian nations of Canada and the federal Parliament were necessary before amendments to the Canadian Constitution (contained in the British North America Acts) could be enacted. The Attorney-General moved that the statement of claim be struck out as showing no reasonable cause of action.

MEGARRY VC: . . . On the face of it, a contention that an Act of Parliament is ultra vires is bold in the extreme. It is contrary to one of the fundamentals of the British Constitution. . . .

As was said by Lord Morris of Borth-y-Gest, at p. 789, it is not for the courts to proceed 'as though the Act or some part of it had never been passed'; there may be argument on the interpretation of the Act, but 'there must be none as to whether it should be on the Statute Book at all.' Any complaint on such matters is for Parliament to deal with and not the courts. . . .

Mr Macdonald [counsel for the plaintiffs] was, of course, concerned to restrict the ambit of the decision in *Pickin* v *British Railways Board.* He accepted that it was a binding decision for domestic legislation, but he said that it did not apply in relation to the Statute of Westminster 1931 or to the other countries of the Commonwealth. He also contended that it decided no more than that the courts would not inquire into what occurred in the course of the passage of a bill through Parliament, relying on what Lord Reid said at p. 787. This latter point is, I think, plainly wrong, since it ignores the words 'what was done previously to its being introduced' which Lord Reid cited with approval on that page. The wider point, however, is founded upon the theory that Parliament may surrender its sovereign power over some territory or area of land to another person or body. . . . After such a surrender, any legislation which Parliament purports to enact for that territory is not merely ineffective there, but is totally void, in this country as elsewhere, since Parliament has surrendered the power to legislate; and the English courts have jurisdiction to declare such legislation ultra vires and void. . . .

[The plaintiffs argued that the United Kingdom Parliament had, by the Statute of Westminster 1931, transferred sovereignty to Canada and had deprived itself of all power to legislate for Canada subject only to s. 7 of that Act. Section 7 reserved to Parliament the power to repeal, amend or alter the British North America Acts. The plaintiffs further argued that the true meaning of s. 4 of the 1931 Act dictated that these residuary legislative powers could only be exercised pursuant to the actual request and consent of the Dominion. For these purposes 'Dominion' meant not merely the Parliament of Canada but all the constituent constitutional factions of the Dominion, namely, Parliament, the provincial legislatures and the Indian nations. As no such general consent had been given it was argued that the United Kingdom Parliament could not legislate for Canada. Megarry VC continued.] I am bound to say that from first to last I have heard nothing in this case to make me doubt the simple rule that the duty of the court is to obey and apply every Act of Parliament, and that the court cannot hold any such Act to be ultra vires. Of course there may be questions about what the Act means, and of course there is power to hold statutory instruments and other subordinate legislation ultra vires. But once an instrument is recognised as being an Act of Parliament, no English court can refuse to obey it or question its validity.

In the present case I have before me a copy of the Canada Act 1982 purporting to be published by Her Majesty's Stationery Office. After reciting the request and consent of Canada and the submission of an address to Her Majesty by the Senate and House of Commons of Canada, there are the words of enactment:

> 'Be it therefore enacted by the Queen's Most Excellent Majesty, by and with the advice and consent of the Lords Spiritual and Temporal, and Commons, in this present Parliament assembled, and by the authority of the same, as follows: . . .'

There has been no suggestion that the copy before me is not a true copy of the Act itself, or that it was not passed by the House of Commons and the House of Lords, or did not receive the Royal Assent. . . . The Canada Act 1982 is an Act of Parliament, and sitting as a judge in an English court I owe full and dutiful obedience to that Act.

I do not think that, as a matter of law, it makes any difference if the Act in question purports to apply outside the United Kingdom. I speak not merely of statutes such as the Continental Shelf Act 1964 but also of statutes purporting to apply to other countries. If that other country is a colony, the English courts will apply the Act even if the colony is in a state of revolt against the Crown and direct enforcement of the decision may be impossible: see *Madzimbamuto* v *Lardner-Burke* [1969] 1 AC 645. It matters not if a convention had grown up that the United Kingdom Parliament would not legislate for that colony without the consent of the colony. Such a convention would not limit the powers of Parliament, and if Parliament legislated in breach of the convention, 'the courts could not hold the Act of Parliament invalid': see p. 723. Similarly if the other country is a foreign state which has never been British, I do not think that any English court would or could declare the Act ultra vires and void. No doubt the Act would normally be ignored by the foreign state and would not be enforced by it, but that would not invalidate the Act in this country. Those who infringed it could not claim that it was void if proceedings within the jurisdiction were taken against them. Legal validity is one thing, enforceability is another. Thus a marriage in Nevada may constitute statutory bigamy punishable in England (*Trial of Earl Russell* [1901] AC 446), just as acts in Germany may be punishable here as statutory treason: *Joyce* v *Director of Public Prosecutions* [1946] AC 347. Parliament in fact legislates only for British subjects in this way; but if it also legislated for others, I do not see how the English courts could hold the statute void, however impossible it was to enforce it, and no matter how strong the diplomatic protests.

I do not think that countries which were once colonies but have since been granted independence are in any different position. Plainly once statute has granted independence to a country, the repeal of the statute will not make the country dependent once more; what is done is done, and is not undone by revoking the authority do to it. Heligoland did not in 1953 again become British. But if Parliament then passes an Act applying to such a country, I cannot see why that Act should not be in the same position as an Act applying to what has always been a foreign country, namely, an Act which the English courts will recognise and apply but one which the other country will in all probability ignore. . . .

For the reasons that I have given, I have come to the conclusion that the statement of claim in the Manuel action discloses no reasonable cause of action, and that, despite the persuasions of Mr Macdonald, this is plain and obvious enough to justify striking out the statement of claim. . . .

Perhaps I may add this. I have grave doubts about the theory of the transfer of sovereignty as affecting the competence of Parliament. In my view, it is a fundamental of the English constitution that Parliament is supreme. As a matter of law the courts of England recognise Parliament as being omnipotent in all save the power to destroy its own omnipotence. Under the authority of Parliament the courts of a territory may be released from their legal duty to obey Parliament, but that does not trench on the acceptance by the English courts of all that Parliament does. Nor must validity in law be confused with practical enforceability.

The plaintiffs appealed

Court of Appeal

SLADE LJ: Mr Macdonald's argument will be seen to depend on a number of propositions, each one of which would be essential to its success at the trial of the action. Included among these essential propositions, though they are by no means the only ones, are the following three, each one of which must be established as arguable, if the plaintiffs are to succeed on this appeal: (1) that Parliament can effectively tie the hands of its successors, if it passes a statute which provides that any future legislation on a specified subject shall be enacted only with certain specified consents; (2) that section 7 (1) of the Statute of 1931 did not absolve the United Kingdom Parliament from the need to comply with the conditions of section 4 of the Statute of 1931 in enacting the Canada Act 1982, if the latter Act was to extend to Canada as an effective

Act; (3) that the conditions of section 4 of the Statute of 1931 have not in fact been complied with in relation to the Canada Act 1982.

At least at first sight, the first of these propositions conflicts with the general statement of the law made by Maugham LJ in *Ellen Street Estates Ltd* v *Minister of Health* [1934] 1 KB 590, 597 [*supra* p. 60] . . . For the purposes of this judgment we are content to assume in favour of the plaintiffs that the first of the three propositions to which we have referred is correct, though we would emphasise that we are not purporting to decide it. . . .

As regards the second of them, Mr Macdonald submitted that the Canada Act 1982 does not fall within the exempting provisions of section 7 (1) of the Statute of 1931, on the grounds that its provisions go beyond a mere 'repeal, amendment or alteration of the British North America Acts.' We do not think it has been or could be disputed that at least a substantial part of the contents of the Constitution Act 1982, if regarded in isolation, would amount to no more than a mere 'repeal, amendment or alteration of the British North America Acts,' within those exempting provisions. Mr Macdonald, however, has submitted that at least some others of its contents (for example, the Charter of Rights and Freedoms) fall outside such exemption and accordingly make it necessary that the conditions of section 4 of the Statute of 1931 should be complied with in relation to the whole of the Canada Act 1982.

By far the greater part of the plaintiffs' argument on this appeal has been devoted to an attempt to show that the conditions of section 4 have not been complied with in this context.

In the circumstances we will proceed to consider the third of the propositions referred to above which relates to section 4 of the Statute of 1931. We will revert briefly to the second of them and to section 7 at the end of this judgment.

For the time being, therefore, let it be supposed that Parliament, in enacting the Canada Act 1982, had precisely to comply with the conditions of section 4 of the Statute of 1931, if that new Act was to be valid and effective. What then are the conditions which section 4 imposes? It is significant that, while the Preamble to the Statute of 1931 recites that

> it is in accord with the established constitutional position that no law hereafter made by the Parliament of the United Kingdom shall extend to any of the said Dominions as part of the law of that Dominion otherwise than at the request and with the consent of that Dominion: . . .

Section 4 itself does *not* provide that no Act of the United Kingdom Parliament shall extend to a Dominion as part of the law of that Dominion unless the Dominion has *in fact* requested and consented to the enactment thereof. The condition that must be satisfied is a quite different one, namely, that it must be 'expressly declared in that Act that that Dominion has requested, and consented to, the enactment thereof.' Though Mr Macdonald, as we have said, submitted that section 4 requires not only a declaration but a true declaration of a real request and consent, we are unable to read the section in that way. There is no ambiguity in the relevant words and the court would not in our opinion be justified in supplying additional words by a process of implication; it must construe and apply the words as they stand: see *Maxwell on Interpretation of Statutes,* 12th ed. (1969), p. 33 and the cases there cited. If an Act of Parliament contains an express declaration in the precise form required by section 4, such declaration is in our opinion conclusive so far as section 4 is concerned.

There was, we think, nothing unreasonable or illogical in this simple approach to the matter on the part of the legislature, in reserving to itself the sole function of deciding whether the requisite request and consent have been made and given. The present case itself provides a good illustration of the practical consequences that would have ensued, if section 4 had made an actual request and consent on the part of a Dominion a condition precedent to the validity of the relevant legislation, in such manner that the courts or anyone else would have had to look behind the relevant declaration in order to ascertain whether a statute of the United Kingdom Parliament, expressed to extend to that Dominion, was valid. There is obviously room for argument as to the identity of the representatives of the Dominion of Canada appropriate to express the relevant request and consent. Mr Macdonald, while firm in his submission that all legislatures of the Provinces of Canada had to join the Federal Parliament in expressing them, seemed less firm in his submission that all the Indian Nations had likewise to join. This is a point which might well involve difficult questions of Canadian constitutional law. Moreover, if all the Indian Nations did have to join, further questions might arise as to the manner in which the consents of these numerous persons and bodies had to be expressed and as to whether all of them had in fact been given. As we read the wording of section 4, it was designed to obviate the need for any further inquiries of this nature, once a statute, containing the requisite declaration, had been duly enacted by the United Kingdom Parliament. Parliament, having satisfied itself as to the request and consent, would make the declaration and that would be that.

Mr Macdonald submitted in the alternative that, even if section 4 on its proper construction does not itself bear the construction which he attributed to it, nevertheless, in view of the convention referred to in the third paragraph of the preamble, the actual request and consent of the Dominion is necessary before a law made by the United Kingdom Parliament can extend to that Dominion as part of its law. Whether or not an argument on these lines might find favour in the courts of a Dominion, it is in our opinion quite unsustainable in the courts of this country. The sole condition precedent which has to be satisfied if a law made by the United Kingdom Parliament is to extend to a Dominion as part of its law is to be found stated in the body of the Statute of 1931 itself (section 4). This court would run counter to all principles of statutory interpretation if it were to purport to vary or supplement the terms of this stated condition precedent by reference to some supposed convention, which, though referred to in the preamble, is not incorporated in the body of the Statute.

In the present instance, therefore, the only remaining question is whether it is arguable that the condition precedent specified in section 4 of the Statute of 1931 has not been complied with in relation to the Canada Act 1982. Is it arguable that it has not been 'expressly declared in that Act that that Dominion has requested, and consented to, the enactment thereof'? In our judgment this proposition is not arguable, inasmuch as the preamble to the Canada Act 1982 begins with the words 'Whereas Canada has requested and consented to the enactment of an Act of the Parliament of the United Kingdom to give effect to the provisions hereinafter set forth . . .'

. . . [W]e conclude that, if and so far as the conditions of section 4 of the Statute of 1931 had to be complied with in relation to the Canada Act 1982, they were duly complied with by the declaration contained in the preamble to that Act.

Consequently, it is unnecessary to consider further the second of the three propositions referred to earlier in this judgment. It is unnecessary to consider whether the Constitution Act 1982 contains provisions which go beyond 'the repeal, amendment or alteration of the British North America Acts' so as to fall outside the exempting provisions of section 7 (1) of the Statute of 1931 and thus within section 4 of that Act. If it does contain such provisions, the express declaration of a request and consent required by section 4 is duly contained in the Canada Act 1982. If it contains no such provisions (as we understood Mr Mummery would have sought to submit on behalf of the Attorney-General, though we did not think it necessary to call on him), no declaration of request and consent was necessary.

Questions

1. Did the Court of Appeal decide whether Parliament can give up its sovereignty over a particular territory?

2. Did the Court of Appeal decide whether the validity of an Act of Parliament could be dependent upon the presence or absence of the consent of some other body?

3. How would Megarry VC answer the two questions above?

4. One of the fears of the proponents of the traditional theory of supremacy is that if Parliament could bind itself it could create a legislative vacuum. In cases of granting independence, a power to legislate is given to another body so there is no risk of a vacuum being created. The problem with the fully self-embracing theory of supremacy is that it does give rise to the possibility of Parliament binding its successors not to legislate on certain matters without transferring power to another body. In light of this and the above analysis, is it possible to argue that supremacy is a divisible concept: continuing with regard to the subject-matter of legislation; self-embracing with regard to territorial competence; and partly self-embracing with regard to the procedures to be followed and the manner and form in which legislation must be enacted?

3 THE EUROPEAN UNION

Notes

1. The Treaty on European Union (TEU) was signed at Maastricht on 7 February 1992 but the European Union it established only came into existence on 1 November 1993. This delay was caused by difficulties in the ratification of the treaty in some of the member states. In Denmark adjustments and clarifications were needed in order for the rejection of the treaty in one referendum to be overturned in a second one. In the UK the Parliamentary ratification process was complicated because the government's small majority in the House of Commons was in danger of being eroded by the coming together of the opposition parties who were in favour of the TEU apart from the UK's opt-out on the Protocol on Social Policy and government back-bench MPs who were opposed to the TEU. The complexity of the passage of the European Communities (Amendment) Bill culminated in a defeat for the government on a vote required by what became the European Communities (Amendment) Act 1993, s. 7, which stipulated that the Act would:

> . . . come into force only when each House of Parliament has come to a Resolution on a motion tabled by a Minister of the Crown considering the question of adopting the Protocol on Social Policy.

This defeat was reversed by the tactic of detaching the government's back-bench rebel MPs from the opposition parties by incorporating the resolution on the Protocol on Social Policy in a vote of confidence in the government.

Once the Bill had been approved by Parliament there was a delay before it received the royal assent and then the ratification of the TEU under the royal prerogative. This was caused by an unsuccessful application for judicial review challenging the government's actions: *R* v *Secretary of State for Foreign and Commonwealth Affairs, ex parte Rees-Mogg* [1994] 1 All ER 457.

Germany was the last country to ratify the TEU and this was done after the decision of the *Bundesverfassungsgericht* (Federal Constitutional Court) that the TEU was compatible with the *Grundgesetz* (Basic Law or constitution): see *Brunner* v *The European Union Treaty* [1994] 1 CMLR 57.

2. The structure of the European Union has been likened to the facade of a Greek temple and, in particular, to its pillars. There are three separate pillars in the Union. The most important of these is the one based upon the European Communities. The other two pillars deal with arrangements for (a) a Common Foreign and Security Policy; and (b) inter-governmental co-operation in justice and home affairs.

The European Communities are comprised of the European Coal and Steel Community (ECSC), the European Community (EC), which was originally named as the European Econonic Community (EEC), and the European Atomic Energy Community (EURATOM). The three Communities together create a new legal order which has a constitution provided by treaties. The ECSC was established in 1952 by Belgium, France, Germany, Italy, Luxembourg and the Netherlands. In 1957 they established the EEC and EURATOM. Subsequently other countries joined these Communities — Denmark, Ireland and the UK in 1973, Greece in 1982, Portugal and Spain in 1986, Austria, Finland, and Sweden in 1995. Norway has on two occasions rejected joining in referendums, however, along with Iceland and Liechtenstein, it is linked to the 15 member states in the European Economic Area.

3. The EC is the most important of the three Communities. It seeks to establish a single market in which there are (a) no barriers to trade amongst the member states, and (b) freedom of movement of capital and of people, both as workers and as providers of services. This project is more than one of economic cooperation as it involves a degree of economic and political integration. This is demonstrated by the framework and practice of the EC by which member states have agreed policies, the implementation of which is shared between Community institutions and themselves; and (b) the increasing scope of their partnership. Economic integration has been advanced by the Single European Act 1986 (SEA) and the TEU. Both of these treaties amended the founding treaties of the Communities. The SEA not only set a time-table for the completion of the single market, but also amended the decision-making process in respect of matters relating to the single market, while the TEU set out a timetable and process for a common currency and further revised the Community's decision-making processes. Integration in political matters is not as advanced as in the economic sphere. The SEA introduced European Political Cooperation and the TEU elaborated upon this second pillar by replacing it with the Common Foreign and Security Policy, and adding a third pillar dealing with cooperation in home affairs and justice. These two pillars are outside the special legal order of the European Communities' pillar.

(A) THE FRAMEWORK OF THE UNION AND THE EC

In the following extracts from the TEU and the Treaty of Rome as amended, the framework for the Union and EC is laid out with more detail given for the

EC. The treaties list objectives and create institutions which are to carry out specified tasks.

Treaty on European Union

His Majesty the King of the Belgians,
Her Majesty the Queen of Denmark,
The President of the Federal Republic of Germany,
The President of the Hellenic Republic,
His Majesty the King of Spain,
The President of the French Republic,
The President of Ireland,
The President of the Italian Republic,
His Royal Highness the Grand Duke of Luxembourg,
Her Majesty the Queen of the Netherlands,
The President of the Portuguese Republic,
Her Majesty the Queen of the United Kingdom of Great Britain and Northern Ireland,

RESOLVED to mark a new stage in the process of European integration undertaken with the establishment of the European Communities,

RECALLING the historic importance of the ending of the division of the European Continent and the need to create firm bases for the construction of the future Europe,

CONFIRMING their attachment to the principles of liberty, democracy and respect for human rights and fundamental freedoms and of the rule of law,

DESIRING to deepen the solidarity between their peoples while respecting their history, their culture and their traditions,

DESIRING to enhance further the democractic and efficient functioning of the institutions so as to enable them better to carry out, within a single institutional framework, the tasks entrusted to them,

RESOLVED to achieve the strengthening and the convergence of their economies and to establish an economic and monetary union including, in accordance with the provisions of this Treaty, a single and stable currency,

DETERMINED to promote economic and social progress for their peoples, within the context of the accomplishment of the internal market and of reinforced cohesion and environmental protection, and to implement policies ensuring that advances in economic integration are accompanied by parallel progress in other fields,

RESOLVED to establish a citizenship common to nationals of the countries,

RESOLVED to implement a common foreign and security policy including the eventual framing of a common defence policy, which might in time lead to a common defence, thereby reinforcing the European identity and its independence in order to promote peace, security and progress in Europe and in the world,

REAFFIRMING their objective to facilitate the free movement of persons, while ensuring the safety and security of their peoples, by including provisions on justice and home affairs in this Treaty,

RESOLVED to continue the process of creating an ever closer union among the peoples of Europe, in which decisions are taken as closely as possible to the citizen in ccordance with the principle of subsidiarity,

VIEW of further steps to be taken in order to advance European integration,

DECIDED to establish a European Union . . .

TITLE I COMMON PROVISIONS

Article A
By this Treaty, the High Contracting Parties establish among themselves a European Union, hereinafter called 'the Union'.

This Treaty marks a new stage in the process of creating an ever closer union among the people of Europe, in which decisions are taken as closely as possible to the citizen.

The Union shall be founded on the European Communities, supplemented by the policies and forms of cooperation established by this Treaty. Its task shall be to organise, in a manner demonstrating consistency and solidarity, relations between the Member States and between their peoples.

Article B
The Union shall set itself the following objectives:

— to promote economic and social progress which is balanced and sustainable, in particular through the creation of an area without internal frontiers, through the strengthening of economic and social cohesion and through the establishment of economic and monetary union, ultimately including a single currency in accordance with the provisions of this Treaty;

— to assert its identity on the international scene, in particular through the implementation of a common foreign and security policy including the eventual framing of a common defence policy, which might in time lead to a common defence;

— to strengthen the protection of the rights and interests of the nationals of its Member States through the introduction of a citzenship of the Union;

— to develop close cooperation on justice and home affairs;

— to maintain in full the 'aquis communautaire' and build on it with a view to considering, through the procedure referred to in Article N(2), to what extent the policies and forms of cooperation introduced by this Treaty may need to be revised with the aim of ensuring the effectiveness of the mechanisms and the institutions of the Community.

The objectives of the Union shall be achieved as provided in this Treaty and in accordance with the conditions and the timetable set out therein while respecting the principle of subsidiarity as defined in Article 3b of the Treaty establishing the European Community.

Article C
The Union shall be served by a single institutional framework which shall ensure the consistency and the continuity of the activities carried out in order to attain its objectives while respecting and building upon the 'acquis communautaire'.

The Union shall in particular ensure the consistency of its external activities as a whole in the context of its external relations, security, economic and development policies. The Council and the Commission shall be responsible for ensuring such consistency. They shall ensure the implementation of these policies, each in accordance with its respective powers.

Article D
The European Council shall provide the Union with the necessary impetus for its development and shall define the general political guidelines thereof.

The European Council shall bring together the Heads of State or of Government of the Member States and the President of the Commission. They shall be assisted by the Ministers for Foreign Affairs of the Member States and by a Member of the Commission. The European Council shall meet at least twice a year, under the chairmanship of the Head of State or of Government of the Member State which holds the Presidency of the Council.

The European Council shall submit to the European Parliament a report after each of its meetings and a yearly written report on the progress achieved by the Union.

Article E

The European Parliament, the Council, the Commission and the Court of Justice shall exercise their powers under the conditions and for the purpose provided for, on the one hand, by the provisions of the Treaties establishing the European Communities and of the subsequent Treaties and Acts modifying and supplementing them and, on the other hand, by the other provisions of this Treaty.

Article F

1. The Union shall respect the national identities of its Member States, whose systems of government are founded on the principles of democracy.
2. The Union shall respect fundamental rights, as guaranteed by the European Convention for the Protection of Human Rights and Fundamental Freedom signed in Rome on 4 November 1950 and as they result from the constitutional traditions common to the Member States, as general principles of Community law.
3. The Union shall provide itself with the means necessary to attain its objectives and carry though its policies.

TITLE II TREATY ESTABLISHING THE EUROPEAN COMMUNITY

His Majesty the King of the Belgians,
The President of the Federal Republic of Germany,
The President of the French Republic,
The President of the Italian Republic,
His Royal Highness the Grand Duke of Luxembourg,
Her Majesty the Queen of the Netherlands,

DETERMINED to lay the foundations of an ever closer union among the peoples of Europe,

RESOLVED to ensure the economic and social progress of their countries by common action to eliminate the barriers which divide Europe,

AFFIRMING as the essential objective of their efforts the constant improvement of the living and working conditions of their peoples,

RECOGNISING that the removal of existing obstacles calls for concerted action in order to guarantee steady expansion, balanced trade and fair competition,

ANXIOUS to strengthen the unity of their economies and to ensure their harmonious development by reducing the differences existing between the various regions and the backwardness of the less favoured regions,

DESIRING to contribute, by means of a common commercial policy, to the progressive abolition of restrictions on international trade,

INTENDING to confirm the solidarity which binds Europe and the overseas countries and desiring to ensure the development of their prosperity, in accordance with the principles of the Charter of the United Nations,

RESOLVED by thus pooling their resources to preserve and strengthen peace and liberty, and calling upon the other peoples of Europe who share their ideal to join in their efforts,

HAVE DECIDED to create a European Community . . .

PART ONE PRINCIPLES

Article 1
By this Treaty, the High Contracting Parties establish among themselves a European Community.

Article 2
The Community shall have as its task, by establishing a common market and an economic and monetary union and by implementing the common policies of activities referred to in Articles 3 and 3a, to promote throughout the Community a harmonious and balanced development of economic activities, sustainable and non-inflationary growth respecting the environment, a high degree of convergence of economic performance, a high level of employment and of social protection, the raising of the standard of living and quality of life, and economic and social cohesion and solidarity among Member States.

Article 3
For the purposes set out in Article 2, the activities of the Community shall include, as provided in this Treaty and in accordance with the timetable set out therein:

(a) the elimination, as between Member States, of customs duties and quantitative restrictions on the import and export of goods, and of all other measures having equivalent effect;
(b) a common commercial policy;
(c) an internal market characterised by the abolition, as between Member States, of obstacles to the free movement of goods, persons, services and capital;
(d) measures concerning the entry and movement of persons in the internal market as provided for in Article 100c;
(e) a common policy in the sphere of agriculture and fisheries;
(f) a common policy in the sphere of transport;
(g) a system ensuring that competition in the internal market is not distorted;
(h) the approximation of the laws of Member States to the extent required for the functioning of the common market;
(i) a policy in the social sphere comprising a European Social Fund;
(j) the strengthening of economic and social cohesion;
(k) a policy in the sphere of the environment;
(l) the strengthening of the competitiveness of Community industry;
(m) the promotion of research and technological development;
(n) encouragement for the establishment and development of trans-European networks;
(o) a contribution to the attainment of a high level of health protection;
(p) a contribution to education and training of quality and to the flowering of the cultures of the Member States;
(q) a policy in the sphere of development cooperation;
(r) the association of the overseas countries and territories in order to increase trade and promote jointly economic and social development;
(s) a contribution to the strengthening of consumer protection;
(t) measures in the spheres of energy, civil protection and tourism.

Article 3a
1. For the purposes set out in Article 2, the activities of the Member States and the Community shall include, as provided in this Treaty and in accordance with the timetable set out therein, the adoption of an economic policy which is based on the

close coordination of Member States' economic policies, on the internal market and on the definition of common objectives, and conducted in accordance with the principle of an open market economy with free competition.

2. Concurrently with the foregoing, and as provided in this Treaty and in accordance with the timetable and the procedures set out therein, these activities shall include the irrevocable fixing of exchange rates leading to the introduction of a single currency, the ECU, and the definition and conduct of a single monetary policy and exchange rate policy the primary objective of both of which shall be to maintain price stability and, without prejudice to this objective, to support the general economic policies in the Community, in accordance with the principle of an open market economy with free competition.

3. These activities of the Member States and the Community shall entail compliance with the following guiding principles; stable prices, sound public finances and monetary conditions and a sustainable balance of payments.

Article 3b

The Community shall act within the limits of the powers conferred upon it by this Treaty and of the objectives assigned to it therein.

In areas which do not fall within its exclusive competence, the Community shall take action, in accordance with the principle of subsidiarity, only if and in so far as the objectives of the proposed action cannot be sufficiently achieved by the Member States and can therefore, by reason of the scale of effects of the proposed action, be better achieved by the Community.

Any action by the Community shall not go beyond what is necessary to achieve the objectives of this Treaty.

Article 4

1. The tasks entrusted to the Community shall be carried out by the following institutions:

— a European Parliament,
— a Council,
— a Commission,
— a Court of Justice,
— a Court of Auditors.

Each institution shall act within the limits of the powers conferred upon it by this Treaty.

2. The Council and the Commission shall be assisted by an Economic and Social Committee and a Committee of the Regions acting in an advisory capacity.

Article 4a

A European System of Central Banks (hereinafter referred to as 'ESCB') and a European Central Bank (hereinafter referred to as 'ECB') shall be established in accordance with the procedures laid down in this Treaty; they shall act within the limits of the powers conferred upon them by this Treaty and by the Statute of the ESCB and of the ECB (hereinafter referred to as 'Statute of the ESCB') annexed thereto.

Article 4b

A European Investment Bank is hereby established, which shall act within the limits of the powers conferred upon it by this Treaty and the Statute annexed thereto.

Article 5

Member States shall take all appropriate measures, whether general or particular, to ensure fulfilment of the obligations arising out of this Treaty or resulting from action taken by the institutions of the Community. They shall facilitate the achievement of the Community's tasks.

They shall abstain from any measure which could jeopardise the attainment of the objectives of this Treaty.

Article 6

Within the scope of application of this Treaty, and without prejudice to any special provisions contained therein, any discrimination on grounds of nationality shall be prohibited.

The Council, acting in accordance with the procedure referred to in Article 189c, may adopt rules designed to prohibit such discrimination.

Article 7

1. The common market shall be progressively established during a transitional period of twelve years.

This transitional period shall be divided into three stages of four years each; the length of each stage may be altered in accordance with the provisions set out below.

2. To each stage there shall be assigned a set of actions to be initiated and carried through concurrently.

3. Transition from the first to the second stage shall be conditional upon a finding that the objectives specifically laid down in this Treaty for the first stage have in fact been attained in substance and that, subject to the exceptions and procedures provided for in this Treaty, the obligations have been fulfilled.

The finding shall be made at the end of the fourth year by the Council, acting unanimously on a report from the Commission. A Member State may not, however, prevent unanimity by relying upon the non-fulfilment of its own obligations. Failing unanimity, the first stage shall automatically be extended for one year.

At the end of the fifth year, the Council shall make its finding under the same conditions. Failing unanimity, the first stage shall automatically be extended for a further year.

At the end of the sixth year, the Council shall make its finding, acting by a qualified majority on a report from the Commission.

4. Within one month of the last-mentioned vote any Member State which voted with the minority or, if the required majority was not obtained, any Member State shall be entitled to call upon the Council to appoint an arbitration board whose decision shall be binding upon all Member States and upon the institutions of the Community. The arbitration board shall consist of three members appointed by the Council acting unanimously on a proposal from the Commission.

If the Council has not appointed the members of the arbitration board within one month of being called upon to do so, they shall be appointed by the Court of Justice within a further period of one month.

The arbitration board shall elect its own Chairman.

The board shall make its award within six months of the date of the Council vote referred to in the last subparagraph of paragraph 3.

5. The second and third stages may not be extended or curtailed except by a decision of the Council, acting unanimously on a proposal from the Commission.

6. Nothing in the preceding paragraphs shall cause the transitional period to last more than fifteen years after the entry into force of this Treaty.

7. Save for the exceptions or derogations provided for in this Treaty, the expiry of the transitional period shall constitute the latest date by which all the rules laid down must enter into force and all the measures required for establishing the common market must be implemented.

Article 7a

The Community shall adopt measures with the aim of progressively establishing the internal market over a period expiring on 31 December 1992, in accordance with the provisions of this Article and of Articles 7b, 7c, 28, 57(2), 59, 70(1), 84, 99, 100a and 100b and without prejudice to the other provisions of this Treaty.

The internal market shall comprise an area without internal frontiers in which the free movement of goods, persons, services and capital is ensured in accordance with the provisions of this Treaty.

Article 7b

The Commission shall report to the Council before 31 December 1988 and again before 31 December 1990 on the progress made towards achieving the internal market within the time limit fixed in Article 7a.

The Council, acting by a qualified majority on a proposal from the Commission, shall determine the guidelines and conditions necessary to ensure balanced progress in all the sectors concerned.

Article 7c

When drawing up its proposals with a view to achieving the objectives set out in Article 7a, the Commission shall take into account the extent of the effort that certain economies showing differences in development will have to sustain during the period of establishment of the internal market and it may propose appropriate provisions.

If these provisions take the form of derogations, they must be of a temporary nature and must cause the least possible disturbance to the functioning of the common market.

PART TWO CITIZENSHIP OF THE UNION

Article 8

1. Citizenship of the Union is hereby established.

Every person holding the nationality of a Member State shall be a citizen of the Union.

2. Citizens of the Union shall enjoy the rights conferred by this Treaty and shall be subject to the duties imposed thereby.

Article 8a

1. Every citizen of the Union shall have the right to move and reside freely within the territory of the Member States, subject to the limitations and conditions laid down in this Treaty and by the measures adopted to give it effect.

2. The Council may adopt provisions with a view to facilitating the exercise of the rights referred to in paragraph 1; save as otherwise provided in this Treaty, the Council shall act unanimously on a proposal from the Commission and after obtaining the assent of the European Parliament.

Article 8b

1. Every citizen of the Union residing in a Member State of which he is not a national shall have the right to vote and to stand as a candidate at municipal elections in the Member State in which he resides, under the same conditions as nationals of that State. This right shall be exercised subject to detailed arrangements to be adopted

before 31 December 1994 by the Council, acting unanimously on a proposal from the Commission and after consulting the European Parliament; these arrangements may provide for derogations where warranted by problems specific to a Member State.

2. Without prejudice to Article 138(3) and to the provisions adopted for its implementation, every citizen of the Union residing in a Member State of which he is not a national shall have the right to vote and to stand as a candidate in elections to the European Parliament in the Member State in which he resides, under the same conditions as nationals of that State. This right shall be exercised subject to detailed arrangements to be adopted before 31 December 1993 by the Council, acting unanimously on a proposal from the Commission and after consulting the European Parliament; these arrangements may provide for derogations where warranted by problems specific to a Member State.

Article 8c

Every citizen of the Union shall, in the territory of a third country in which the Member State of which he is a national is not represented, be entitled to protection by the diplomatic or consular authorities of any Member State, on the same conditions as the nationals of that State. Before 31 December 1993, Member States shall establish the necessary rules among themselves and start the international negotiations required to secure this protection.

Article 8d

Every citizen of the Union shall have the right to petition the European Parliament in accordance with Article 138d.

Every citizen of the Union may apply to the Ombudsman established in accordance with Article 138e.

Article 8e

The Commission shall report to the European Parliament, to the Council and to the Economic and Social Committee before 31 December 1993 and then every three years on the application of the provisions of this Part. This report shall take account of the development of the Union.

On this basis, and without prejudice to the other provisions of this Treaty, the Council, acting unanimously on a proposal from the Commission and after consulting the European Parliament, may adopt provisions to strengthen or to add to the rights laid down in this Part, which it shall recommend to the Member States for adoption in accordance with their respective constitutional requirements.

PART THREE COMMUNITY POLICIES

TITLE I FREE MOVEMENT OF GOODS

Article 9

1. The Community shall be based upon a customs union which shall cover all trade in goods and which shall involve the prohibition between Member States of customs duties on imports and exports and of all charges having equivalent effect, and the adoption of a common customs tariff in their relations with third countries.

2. The provisions of Chapter 1, Section 1, and of Chapter 2 of this Title shall apply to products originating in Member States and to products coming from third countries which are in free circulation in Member States.

Article 10

1. Products coming from a third country shall be considered to be in free circulation in a Member State if the import formalities have been complied with and

any customs duties or charges having equivalent effect which are payable have been levied in that Member State, and if they have not benefited from a total or partial drawback of such duties or charges.

2. The Commission shall, before the end of the first year after the entry into force of this Treaty, determine the methods of administrative cooperation to be adopted for the purpose of applying Article 9(2), taking into account the need to reduce as much as possible formalities imposed on trade.

Before the end of the first year after the entry into force of this Treaty, the Commission shall lay down the provisions applicable, as regards trade between Member States, to goods originating in another Member State in whose manufacture products have been used on which the exporting Member State has not levied the appropriate customs duties or charges having equivalent effect, or which have benefited from a total or partial drawback of such duties or charges.

In adopting these provisions, the Commission shall take into account the rules for the elimination of customs duties within the Community and for the progressive application of the common customs tariff.

Article 11

Member States shall take all appropriate measures to enable Governments to carry out, within the periods of time laid down, the obligations with regard to customs duties which devolve upon them pursuant to this Treaty.

CHAPTER 1 THE CUSTOMS UNION

SECTION 1 ELIMINATION OF CUSTOMS DUTIES BETWEEN MEMBER STATES

Article 12

Member States shall refrain from introducing between themselves any new customs duties on imports or exports or any charges having equivalent effect, and from increasing those which they already apply in their trade with each other.

Article 13

1. Customs duties on imports in force between Member States shall be progressively abolished by them during the transitional period in accordance with Articles 14 and 15.

2. Charges having an effect equivalent to customs duties on imports, in force between Member States, shall be progressively abolished by them during the transitional period. The Commission shall determine by means of directives the timetable for such abolition. It shall be guided by the rules contained in Article 14(2) and (3) and by the directives issued by the Council pursuant to Article 14(2) . . .

CHAPTER 2 ELIMINATION OF QUANTITATIVE RESTRICTIONS BETWEEN MEMBER STATES

Article 30

Quantitative restrictions on imports and all measures having equivalent effect shall, without prejudice to the following provisions, be prohibited between Member States . . .

Article 34

1. Quantitative restrictions on exports, and all measures having equivalent effect, shall be prohibited between Member States . . .

CHAPTER 3 APPROXIMATION OF LAWS

Article 100

The Council shall, acting unanimously on a proposal from the Commission and after consulting the European Parliament and the Economic and Social Committee, issue directives for the approximation of such laws, regulations or administrative provisions of the Member States as directly affect the establishment or functioning of the common market.

Article 100a

1. By way of derogation from Article 100 and save where otherwise provided in this Treaty, the following provisons shall apply for the achievement of the objectives set out in Article 7a. The Council shall, acting in accordance with the procedure referred to in Article 189b and after consulting the Economic and Social Committee adopt the measures for the approximation of the provisions laid down by law, regulation or administrative action in Member States which have as their object the establishment and functioning of the internal market.

2. Paragraph 1 shall not apply to fiscal provisions, to those relating to the free movement of persons nor to those relating to the rights and interests of employed persons.

3. The Commission, in its proposals envisaged in paragraph 1 concerning health, safety, environmental protection and consumer protection, will take as a base a high level of protection.

4. If, after the adoption of a harmonisation measure by the Council acting by a qualified majority, a Member State deems it necessary to apply national provisions on grounds of major needs referred to in Article 36, or relating to protection of the environment or the working environment, it shall notify the Commission of these provisions.

The Commission shall confirm the provisions involved after having verified that they are not a means of arbitrary discrimination or a disguised restriction on trade between Member States.

By way of derogation from the procedure laid down in Articles 169 and 170, the Commission or any Member State may bring the matter directly before the Court of Justice if it considers that another Member State is making improper use of the powers provided for in this Article.

5. The harmonisation measures referred to above shall, in appropriate cases, include a safeguard clause authorising the Member States to take, for one or more of the non-economic reasons referred to in Article 36, provisional measures subject to a Community control procedure.

Article 100b

1. During 1992, the Commission shall, together with each Member State draw up an inventory of national laws, regulations and administrative provisions which fall under Article 100a and which have not been harmonised pursuant to that Article.

The Council, acting in accordance with the provisions of Article 100a, may decide that the provisions in force in a Member State must be recognised as being equivalent to those applied by another Member State.

2. The provisions of Article 100a(4) shall apply by analogy.

3. The Commission shall draw up the inventory referred to in the first subparagraph of paragraph 1 and shall submit appropriate proposals in good time to allow the Council to act before the end of 1992.

Article 100c

1. The Council, acting unanimously on a proposal from the Commission and after consulting the European Parliament, shall determine the third countries whose nationals must be in possession of a visa when crossing the external borders of the Member States.

2. However, in the event of an emergency situation in a third country posing a threat of a sudden inflow of nationals from that country into the Community, the Council, acting by a qualified majority on a recommendation from the Commission, may introduce, for a period not exceeding six months, a visa requirement for nationals from the country in question. The visa requirements established under this paragraph may be extended in accordance with the procedure referred to in paragraph 1.

3. From 1 January 1996, the Council shall adopt the decisions referred to in paragraph 1 by a qualified majority. The Council shall, before that date, acting by a qualified majority on a proposal from the Commission and after consulting the European Parliament, adopt measures relating to a uniform format for visas.

4. In the areas referred to in this Article, the Commission shall examine any request made by a Member State that it submit a proposal to the Council.

5. This Article shall be without prejudice to the exercise of the responsibilities incumbent upon the Member States with regard to the maintenance of law and order and the safeguarding of internal security.

6. This Article shall apply to other areas if so decided pursuant to Article K.9 of the provisions of the Treaty on European Union which relate to cooperation in the fields of justice and home affairs, subject to the voting conditions determined at the same time.

7. The provisions of the conventions in force between the Member States governing areas covered by this Article shall remain in force until their content has been replaced by directives or measures adopted pursuant to this Article.

Article 100d

The Coordinating Committee consisting of senior officials set up by Article K.4 of the Treaty on European Union shall contribute, without prejudice to the provisions of Article 151, to the peparation of the proceedings of the Council in the fields referred to in Article 100c . . .

PART FIVE INSTITUTIONS OF THE COMMUNITY
TITLE I PROVISIONS GOVERNING THE INSTITUTIONS
CHAPTER 1 THE INSTITUTIONS
SECTION 1 THE EUROPEAN PARLIAMENT

Article 137

The European Parliament, which shall consist of representatives of the peoples of the States brought together in the Community, shall exercise the powers conferred upon it by this Treaty.

Article 138

[As amended by the Act concerning the election of the representatives of the European Parliament.]. . .

2. The number of representatives elected in each Member State is as follows:

Austria	21
Belgium	25
Denmark	16
Germany	99

Greece	25
Finland	16
France	87
Ireland	15
Italy	87
Luxembourg	6
Netherlands	31
Portugal	25
Spain	64
Sweden	22
United Kingdom	87

3. The European Parliament shall draw up proposals for elections by direct universal suffrage in accordance with a uniform procedure in all Member States.

The Council shall, acting unanimously after obtaining the assent of the European Parliament, which shall act by a majority of its component members, lay down the appropriate provisions, which it shall recommend to Member States for adoption in accordance with their respective constitutional requirements.

Article 138a

Political parties at European level are important as a factor for integration within the Union. They contribute to forming a European awareness and to expressing the political will of the citizens of the Union.

Article 138b

In so far as provided in this Treaty, the European Parliament shall participate in the process leading up to the adoption of Community acts by exercising its powers under the procedures laid down in Articles 189b and 189c and by giving its assent or delivering advisory opinions.

The European Parliament may, acting by a majority of its members, request the Commission to submit any appropriate proposal on matters on which it considers that a Community act is required for the purpose of implementing this Treaty.

Article 138c

In the course of its duties, the European Parliament may, at the request of a quarter of its members, set up a temporary Committee of Inquiry to investigate, without prejudice to the powers conferred by this Treaty on other institutions or bodies, alleged contraventions or maladministration in the implementation of Community law, except where the alleged facts are being examined before a court and while the case is still subject to legal proceedings.

The temporary Committee of Inquiry shall cease to exist on the submission of its report.

The detailed provisions governing the exercise of the right of inquiry shall be determined by common accord of the European Parliament, the Council and the Commission.

Article 138d

Any citizen of the Union, and any natural or legal person residing or having its registered office in a Member State, shall have the right to address, individually or in association with other citizens or persons, a petition to the European Parliament on a matter which comes within the Community's fields of activity and which affect him, her or it directly.

Article 138e

1. The European Parliament shall appoint an Ombudsman empowered to receive complaints from any citizen of the Union or any natural or legal person residing or having its registered office in a Member State concerning instances of maladministration in the activities of the Community institutions or bodies, with the exception of the Court of Justice and the Court of First Instance acting in their judicial role.

In accordance with his duties, the Ombudsman shall conduct inquiries for which he finds grounds, either on his own initiative or on the basis of complaints submitted to him direct or through a member of the European Parliament, except where the alleged facts are or have been the subject of legal proceedings. Where the Ombudsman establishes an instance of maladministration, he shall refer the matter to the institution concerned, which shall have a period of three months in which to inform him of its views. The Ombudsman shall then forward a report to the European Parliament and the institution concerned. The person lodging the complaint shall be informed of the outcome of such inquiries.

The Ombudsman shall submit an annual report to the European Parliament on the outcome of his inquiries.

2. The Ombudsman shall be appointed after each election of the European Parliament for the duration of its term of office. The Ombudsman shall be eligible for reappointment.

The Ombudsman may be dismissed by the Court of Justice at the request of the European Parliament if he no longer fulfils the conditions required for the performance of his duties or if he is guilty of serious misconduct.

3. The Ombudsman shall be completely independent in the performance of his duties. In the performance of those duties he shall neither seek nor take instructions from any body. The Ombudsman may not, during his term of office, engage in any other occupation, whether gainful or not.

4. The European Parliament shall, after seeking an opinion from the Commission and with the approval of the Council acting by a qualified majority, lay down the regulations and general conditions governing the performance of the Ombudsman's duties.

Article 139

The European Parliament shall hold an annual session. It shall meet, without requiring to be convened, on the second Tuesday in March.

The European Parliament may meet in extraordinary session at the request of a majority of its members or at the request of the Council or of the Commission.

Article 140

The European Parliament shall elect its President and its officers from among its members.

Members of the Commission may attend all meetings and shall, at their request, be heard on behalf of the Commission.

The Commission shall reply orally or in writing to questions put to it by the European Parliament or by its members.

The Council shall be heard by the European Parliament in accordance with the conditions laid down by the Council in its rules of procedure.

Article 141

Save as otherwise provided in this Treaty, the European Parliament shall act by an absolute majority of the votes cast.

The rules of procedure shall determine the quorum.

Article 142
The European Parliament shall adopt its rules of procedure, acting by a majority of its members.

The proceedings of the European Parliament shall be published in the manner laid down in its rules of procedure.

Article 143
The European Parliament shall discuss in open session the annual general report submitted to it by the Commission.

Article 144
If a motion of censure on the activities of the Commission is tabled before it, the European Parliament shall not vote thereon until at least three days after the motion has been tabled and only by open vote.

If the motion of censure is carried by a two-third majority of the votes cast, representing a majority of the members of the European Parliament, the members of the Commission shall resign as a body. They shall continue to deal with current business until they are replaced in accordance with Article 158. In this case, the term of office of the members of the Commission appointed to replace them shall expire on the date on which the term of office of the members of the Commission obliged to resign as a body would have expired.

SECTION 2 THE COUNCIL

Article 145
To ensure that the objectives set out in this Treaty are attained, the Council shall, in accordance with the provisions of this Treaty:

— ensure coordination of the general economic policies of the Member States;
— have power to take decisions;
— confer on the Commission, in the acts which the Council adopts, powers for the implementation of the rules which the Council lays down. The Council may impose certain requirements in respect of the exercise of these powers. The Council may also reserve the right, in specific cases, to exercise directly implementing powers itself. The procedures referred to above must be consonant with principles and rules to be laid down in advance by the Council, acting unanimously on a proposal from the Commission and after obtaining the Opinion of the European Parliament.

Article 146
The Council shall consist of a representative of each Member State at ministerial level, authorised to commit the government of that Member State.

The office of President shall be held in turn by each Member State in the Council for a term of six months, in the following order of Member States:

— for a first cycle of six years: Belgium, Denmark, Germany, Greece, Spain, France, Ireland, Italy, Luxembourg, Netherlands, Portugal, United Kingdom;
— for the following cycle of six years: Denmark, Belgium, Greece, Germany, France, Spain, Italy, Ireland, Netherlands, Luxembourg, United Kingdom, Portugal.

Article 147
The Council shall meet when convened by its President on his own initiative or at the request of one of its members or of the Commission.

Article 148
1. Save as otherwise provided in this Treaty, the Council shall act by a majority of its members.

2. Where the Council is required to act by a qualified majority, the votes of its members shall be weighted as follows:

Austria	4
Belgium	5
Denmark	3
Germany	10
Greece	5
Finland	3
France	10
Ireland	3
Italy	10
Luxembourg	2
Netherlands	5
Portugal	5
Spain	8
Sweden	4
United Kingdom	10

For their adoption, acts of the Council shall require at least:

— sixty-two votes in favour where this Treaty requires them to be adopted on a proposal from the Commission,

— sixty-two votes in favour, cast by at least ten members, in other cases.

3. Abstentions by members present in person or represented shall not prevent the adoption by the Council of acts which required unanimity.

Article 149
(repealed)

Article 150
Where a vote is taken, any member of the Council may also act on behalf of not more than one other member.

Article 151
1. A committee consisting of the Permanent Representatives of the Member States shall be responsible for preparing the work of the Council and for carrying out the tasks assigned to it by the Council.

2. The Council shall be assisted by a General Secretariat, under the direction of a Secretary-General. The Secretary-General shall be appointed by the Council acting unanimously.

The Council shall decide on the organisation of the General Secretariat.

3. The Council shall adopt its rules of procedure.

Article 152
The Council may request the Commission to undertake any studies the Council considers desirable for the attainment of the common objectives, and to submit to it any appropriate proposals.

Article 153
The Council shall, after receiving an opinion from the Commission, determine the rules governing the committees provided for in this Treaty.

Article 154
The Council shall, acting by a qualified majority, determine the salaries, allowances and pensions of the President and members of the Commission, and of the President, Judges, Advocates-General and Registrar of the Court of Justice. It shall also, again by a qualified majority, determine any payment to be made instead of remuneration.

SECTION 3 THE COMMISSION

Article 155
In order to ensure the proper functioning and development of the common market, the Commission shall:

— ensure that the provisions of this Treaty and the measures taken by the institutions pursuant thereto are applied;
— formulate recommendations or deliver opinions on matters dealt with in this Treaty, if it expressly so provides or if the Commission considers it necessary;
— have its own power of decision and participate in the shaping of measures taken by the Council and by the European Parliament in the manner provided for in this Treaty;
— exercise the powers conferred on it by the Council for the implementation of the rules laid down by the latter.

Article 156
The Commission shall publish annually, not later than one month before the opening of the session of the European Parliament, a general report on the activities of the Community.

Article 157
1. The Commission shall consist of twenty members, who shall be chosen on the grounds of their general competence and whose independence is beyond doubt.

The number of members of the Commission may be altered by the Council, acting unanimously.

Only nationals of Member States may be members of the Commission.

The Commission must include at least one national of each of the Member States, but may not include more than two members having the nationality of the same State.

2. The members of the Commission shall, in the general interest of the Community, be completely independent in the performance of their duties.

In the performance of these duties, they shall neither seek nor take instructions from any government or from any other body. They shall refrain from any action incompatible with their duties. Each Member State undertakes to respect this principle and not to seek to influence the members of the Commission in the performance of their tasks.

The members of the Commission may not, during their term of office, engage in any other occupation, whether gainful or not. When entering upon their duties they shall give a solemn undertaking that, both during and after their term of office, they will respect the obligations arising therefrom and in particular their duty to behave with integrity and discretion as regards the acceptance, after they have ceased to hold office, of certain appointments or benefits. In the event of any breach of these obligations, the Court of Justice may, on application by the Council or the Commission, rule that the member concerned be, according to the circumstances, either compulsorily retired in accordance with Article 160 or deprived of his right to a pension or other benefits in its stead.

Article 158

1. The members of the Commission shall be appointed, in accordance with the procedure referred to in paragraph 2, for a period of five years, subject, if need be, to Article 144.

Their term of office shall be renewable.

2. The governments of the Member States shall nominate by common accord, after consulting the European Parliament, the person they intend to appoint as President of the Commission.

The governments of the Member States shall, in consultation with the nominee for President, nominate the other persons whom they intend to appoint as members of the Commission.

The President and the other members of the Commission thus nominated shall be subject as a body to a vote of approval by the European Parliament. After approval by the European Parliament, the President and the other members of the Commission shall be appointed by common accord of the government of the Member States.

3. Paragraphs 1 and 2 shall be applied for the first time to the President and the other members of the Commission whose term of office begins on 7 January 1995.

The President and the other members of the Commission whose term of office begins on 7 January 1993 shall be appointed by common accord of the governments of the Member States. Their term of office shall expire on 6 January 1995.

Article 159

Apart from normal replacement, or death, the duties of a member of the Commission shall end when he resigns or is compulsorily retired.

The vacancy thus caused shall be filled for the remainder of the member's term of office by a new member appointed by common accord of the governments of the Member States. The Council may, acting unanimously, decide that such a vacancy need not be filled.

In the event of resignation, compulsory retirement or death, the President shall be replaced for the remainder of his term of office. The procedure laid down in Article 158(2) shall be applicable for the replacement of the President.

Save in the case of compulsory retirement under Article 160, members of the Commission shall remain in office until they have been replaced.

Article 160

If any member of the Commission no longer fulfils the conditions required for the performance of his duties or if he has been guilty of serious misconduct, the Court of Justice may, on application by the Council or the Commission, compulsorily retire him.

Article 161

The Commission may appoint a Vice-President or two Vice-Presidents from among its members.

Article 162

1. The Council and the Commission shall consult each other and shall settle by common accord their methods of cooperation.

2. The Commission shall adopt its rules of procedure so as to ensure that both it and its departments operate in accordance with the provisions of this Treaty. It shall ensure that these rules are published.

Article 163

The Commission shall act by a majority of the number of members provided for in Article 157.

A meeting of the Commission shall be valid only if the number of members laid down in its rules of procedure is present.

SECTION 4 THE COURT OF JUSTICE

Article 164
The Court of Justice shall ensure that in the interpretation and application of this Treaty the law is observed.

Article 165
The Court of Justice shall consist of fifteen Judges.

The Court of Justice shall sit in plenary session. It may, however, form chambers, each consisting of three or five judges, either to undertake certain preparatory inquiries or to adjudicate on particular categories of cases in accordance with rules laid down for these purposes.

The Court of Justice shall sit in plenary session when a Member State or a Community institution that is a party to the proceedings so requests.

Should the Court of Justice so request, the Council may, acting unanimously, increase the number of judges and make the necessary adjustments to the second and third paragraphs of this Article and to the second paragraph of Article 167.

Article 166
The Court of Justice shall be assisted by eight Advocates-General. However, a ninth Advocate-General shall be appointed as from the date of accession [of Austria, Finland and Sweden] until 6 October 2000.

It shall be the duty of the Advocate-General, acting with complete impartiality and independence, to make, in open court, reasoned submissions on cases brought before the Court of Justice, in order to assist the Court in the performance of the task assigned to it in Article 164.

Should the Court of Justice so request, the Council may, acting unanimously, increase the number of Advocates-General and make the necessary adjustments to the third paragraph of Article 167.

Article 167
The Judges and Advocates-General shall be chosen from persons whose independence is beyond doubt and who possess the qualifications required for appointment to the highest judicial offices in their respective countries or who are jurisconsults of recognised competence; they shall be appointed by common accord of the Governments of the Member States for a term of six years.

Every three years there shall be a partial replacement of the Judges. Eight and seven Judges shall be replaced alternatively.

Every three years there shall be a partial replacement of the Advocates-General. Four Advocates-General shall be replaced on each occasion.

Retiring Judges and Advocates-General shall be eligible for reappointment.

The Judges shall elect the President of the Court of Justice from among their number for a term of three years. He may be re-elected.

Article 168
The Court of Justice shall appoint its Registrar and lay down the rules governing his service.

Article 168a
1. A Court of First Instance shall be attached to the Court of Justice with jurisdiction to hear and determine at first instance, subject to a right of appeal to the

Court of Justice on points of law only and in accordance with the conditions laid down by the Statute, certain classes of action or proceeding defined in accordance with the conditions laid down in paragraph 2. The Court of First Instance shall not be competent to hear and determine questions referred for a preliminary ruling under Article 177.

2. At the request of the Court of Justice and after consulting the European Parliament and the Commission, the Council, acting unanimously, shall determine the classes of action or proceeding referred to in paragraph 1 and the composition of the Court of First Instance and shall adopt the necessary adjustments and additional provisions to the Statute of the Court of Justice. Unless the Council decides otherwise, the provisions of this Treaty relating to the Court of Justice, in particular the provisions of the Protocol on the Statute of the Court of Justice, shall apply to the Court of First Instance.

3. The members of the Court of First Instance shall be chosen from persons whose independence is beyond doubt and who possess the ability required for appointment to judicial office; they shall be appointed by common accord of the governments of the Member States for a term of six years. The membership shall be partially renewed every three years. Retiring members shall be eligible for reappointment.

4. The Court of First Instance shall establish its rules of procedure in agreement with the Court of Justice. Those rules shall require the unanimous approval of the Council.

Article 169

If the Commission considers that a Member State has failed to fulfil an obligation under this Treaty, it shall deliver a reasoned opinion on the matter after giving the State concerned the opportunity to submit its observations.

If the State concerned does not comply with the opinion within the period laid down by the Commission, the latter may bring the matter before the Court of Justice.

Article 170

A Member State which considers that another Member State has failed to fulfil an obligation under this Treaty may bring the matter before the Court of Justice.

Before a Member State brings an action against another Member State for an alleged infringement of an obligation under this Treaty, it shall bring the matter before the Commission.

The Commission shall deliver a reasoned opinion after each of the States concerned has been given the opportunity to submit its own case and its observations on the other party's case both orally and in writing.

If the Commission has not delivered an opinion within three months of the date on which the matter was brought before it, the absence of such opinion shall not prevent the matter from being brought before the Court of Justice.

Article 171

1. If the Court of Justice finds that a Member State has failed to fulfil an obligation under this Treaty, the State shall be required to take the necessary measures to comply with the judgment of the Court of Justice.

2. If the Commission considers that the Member State concerned has not taken such measures it shall, after giving that State the opportunity to submit its observations, issue a reasoned opinion specifying the points on which the Member State concerned has not complied with the judgment of the Court of Justice.

If the Member State concerned fails to take the necessary measures to comply with the Court's judgment within the time-limit laid down by the Commission, the latter may bring the case before the Court of Justice. In so doing it shall specify the amount of the lump sum or penalty payment to be paid by the Member State concerned which it considers appropriate in the circumstances.

If the Court of Justice finds that the Member State concerned has not complied with its judgment it may impose a lump sum or penalty payment on it.

This procedure shall be without prejudice to Article 170.

Article 172
Regulations adopted jointly by the European Parliament and the Council, and by the Council, pursuant to the provisions of this Treaty, may give the Court of Justice unlimited jurisdiction with regard to the penalties provided for in such regulations.

Article 173
The Court of Justice shall review the legality of acts adopted jointly by the European Parliament and the Council, of acts of the Council, of the Commission and of the ECB, other than recommendations and opinions, and of acts of the European Parliament intended to produce legal effects vis-à-vis third parties.

It shall for this purpose have jurisdiction in actions brought by a Member State, the Council or the Commission on grounds of lack of competence, infringement of an essential procedural requirement, infringement of this Treaty or of any rule of law relating to its application, or misuse of powers.

The Court shall have jurisdiction under the same conditions in actions brought by the European Parliament and by the ECB for the purpose of protecting their prerogatives.

Any natural or legal person may, under the same conditions, institute proceedings against a decision addressed to that person or against a decision which, although in the form of a regulation or a decision addressed to another person, is of direct and individual concern to the former.

The proceedings provided for in this Article shall be instituted within two months of the publication of the measure, or of its notification to the plaintiff, or, in the absence thereof, of the day on which it came to the knowledge of the latter, as the case may be.

Article 174
If the action is well founded, the Court of Justice shall declare the act concerned to be void.

In the case of a regulation, however, the Court of Justice shall, if it considers this necessary, state which of the effects of the regulation which it has declared void shall be considered as definitive.

Article 175
Should the European Parliament, the Council or the Commission, in infringement of this Treaty, fail to act, the Member States and the other institutions of the Community may bring an action before the Court of Justice to have the infringement established.

The action shall be admissible only if the institution concerned has first been called upon to act. If, within two months of being so called upon, the institution concerned has not defined its position, the action may be brought within a further period of two months.

Any natural or legal person may, under the conditions laid down in the preceding paragraphs, complain to the Court of Justice that an institution of the Community has failed to address to that person any act other than a recommendation or an opinion.

The Court of Justice shall have jurisdiction, under the same conditions, in actions or proceedings brought by the ECB in the areas falling within the latter's field of competence and in actions or proceedings brought against the latter.

Article 176

The institution or institutions whose act has been declared void or whose failure to act has been declared contrary to this Treaty shall be required to take the necessary measures to comply with the judgment of the Court of Justice.

The obligation shall not affect any obligation which may result from the application of the second paragraph of Article 215.

This Article shall also apply to the ECB.

Article 177

The Court of Justice shall have jurisdiction to give preliminary rulings concerning:

(a) the interpretation of this Treaty;

(b) the validity and interpretation of acts of the institutions of the Community and of the ECB;

(c) the interpretation of the statutes of bodies established by an act of the Council, where those statutes so provide.

Where such a question is raised before any court or tribunal of a Member State, that court or tribunal may, if it considers that a decision on the question is necessary to enable it to give judgment, request the Court of Justice to give a ruling thereon.

Where any such question is raised in a case pending before a court or tribunal of a Member State against whose decisions there is no judicial remedy under national law, that court or tribunal shall bring the matter before the Court of Justice.

Article 178

The Court of Justice shall have jurisdiction in disputes relating to compensation for damage provided for in the second paragraph of Article 215.

Article 179

The Court of Justice shall have jurisdiction in any dispute between the Community and its servants within the limits and under the conditions laid down in the Staff Regulations or the Conditions of Employment.

Article 180

The Court of Justice shall, within the limits hereinafter laid down, have jurisdiction in disputes concerning:

(a) the fulfilment by Member States of obligations under the Statute of the European Investment Bank. In this connection, the Board of Directors of the Bank shall enjoy the powers conferred upon the Commission by Article 169;

(b) measures adopted by the Board of Governors of the European Investment Bank. In this connection, any Member State, the Commission or the Board of Directors of the Bank may institute proceedings under the conditions laid down in Article 173;

(c) measures adopted by the Board of Directors of the European Investment Bank. Proceedings against such measures may be instituted only by Member States or by the Commission, under the conditions laid down in Article 173, and solely on the grounds of non-compliance with the procedure provided for in Article 21(2), (5), (6) and (7) of the Statute of the Bank;

(d) the fulfilment by national central banks of obligations under this Treaty and the Statute of the ESCB. In this connection the powers of the Council of the ECB in respect of national central banks shall be the same as those conferred upon the Commission in respect of Member States by Article 169. If the Court of Justice finds that a national central bank has failed to fulfil an obligation under this Treaty, that bank shall be required to take the necessary measures to comply with the judgment of the Court of Justice.

Article 181
The Court of Justice shall have jurisdiction to give judgment pursuant to any arbitration clause contained in a contract concluded by or on behalf of the Community, whether that contract be governed by public or private law.

Article 182
The Court of Justice shall have jurisdiction in any dispute between Member States which relates to the subject matter of this Treaty if the dispute is submitted to it under a special agreement between the parties.

Article 183
Save where jurisdiction is conferred on the Court of Justice by this Treaty, disputes to which the Community is a party shall not on that ground be excluded from the Jurisdiction of the courts or tribunals of the Member States.

Article 184
Notwithstanding the expiry of the period laid down in the fifth paragraph of Article 173, any party may, in proceedings in which a regulation adopted jointly by the European Parliament and the Council, or a regulation of the Council, of the Commission, or of the ECB is at issue, plead the grounds specified in the second paragraph of Article 173 in order to invoke before the Court of Justice the inapplicability of that regulation.

Article 185
Actions brought before the Court of Justice shall not have suspensory effect. The Court of Justice may, however, if it considers that circumstances so require, order that application of the contested act be suspended.

Article 186
The Court of Justice may in any cases before it prescribe any necessary interim measures.

Article 187
The judgments of the Court of Justice shall be enforceable under the conditions laid down in Article 192.

Article 188
The Statute of the Court of Justice is laid down in a separate Protocol.

The Council may, acting unanimously at the request of the Court of Justice and after consulting the Commission and the European Parliament, amend the provisions of Title III of the Statute.

The Court of Justice shall adopt its rules of procedure. These shall require the unanimous approval of the Council.

SECTION 5 THE COURT OF AUDITORS

Article 188a
The Court of Auditors shall carry out the audit.

Article 188b
1. The Court of Auditors shall consist of fifteen members.

2. The members of the Court of Auditors shall be chosen from among persons who belong or have belonged in their respective countries to external audit bodies or who are especially qualified for this office. Their independence must be beyond doubt.

3. The members of the Court of Auditors shall be appointed for a term of six years by the Council, acting unanimously after consulting the European Parliament.

However, when the first appointments are made, four members of the Court of Auditors, chosen by lot, shall be appointed for a term of office of four years only.

The members of the Court of Auditors shall be eligible for reappointment.

They shall elect the President of the Court of Auditors from among their number for a term of three years. The President may be re-elected.

4. The members of the Court of Auditors shall, in the general interest of the Community, be completely independent in the performance of their duties.

In the performance of these duties, they shall neither seek nor take instructions from any government or from any other body. They shall refrain from any action incompatible with their duties.

5. The members of the Court of Auditors may not, during their term of office, engage in any other occupation, whether gainful or not. When entering upon their duties they shall give a solemn undertaking that, both during and after their term of office, they will respect the obligations arising therefrom and in particular their duty to behave with integrity and discretion as regards the acceptance, after they have ceased to hold office, of certain appointments or benefits.

6. Apart from normal replacement, or death, the duties of a member of the Court of Auditors shall end when he resigns, or is compulsorily retired by a ruling of the Court of Justice pursuant to paragraph 7.

The vacancy thus caused shall be filled for the remainder of the member's term of office.

Save in the case of compulsory retirement, members of the Court of Auditors shall remain in office until they have been replaced.

7. A member of the Court of Auditors may be deprived of his office or of his right to a pension or other benefits in its stead only if the Court of Justice, at the request of the Court of Auditors, finds that he no longer fulfils the requisite conditions or meets the obligations arising from his office.

8. The Council, acting by a qualified majority, shall determine the conditions of employment of the President and the members of the Court of Auditors and in particular their salaries, allowances and pensions. It shall also, by the same majority, determine any payment to be made instead of remuneration.

9. The provisions of the Protocol on the Privileges and Immunities of the European Communities applicable to the Judges of the Court of Justice shall also apply to the members of the Court of Auditors.

Article 188c

1. The Court of Auditors shall examine the accounts of all revenue and expenditure of the Community. It shall also examine the accounts of all revenue and expenditure of all bodies set up by the Community is so far as the relvant constituent instrument does not preclude such examination.

The Court of Auditors shall provide the European Parliament and the Council with a statement of assurance as to the reliability of the accounts and the legality and regularity of the underlying transactions.

2. The Court of Auditors shall examine whether all revenue has been received and all expenditure incurred in a lawful and regular manner and whether the financial management has been sound.

The audit of revenue shall be carried out on the basis both of the amounts established as due and the amounts actually paid to the Community.

The audit of expenditure shall be carried out on the basis both of commitments undertaken and payments made.

These audits may be carried out before the closure of accounts for the financial year in question.

3. The audit shall be based on records and, if necessary, performed on the spot in the other institutions of the Community and in the Member States. In the Member States the audit shall be carried out in liaison with the national audit bodies or, if these do not have the necessary powers, with the competent national departments. These bodies or departments shall inform the Court of Auditors whether they intend to take part in the audit.

The other institutions of the Community and the national audit bodies or, if these do not have the necessary powers, the competent national departments, shall forward to the Court of Auditors, at its request, any document or information necessary to carry out its task.

4. The Court of Auditors shall draw up an annual report after the close of each financial year. It shall be forwarded to the other institutions of the Community and shall be published, together with the replies of these institutions to the observations of the Court of Auditors, in the Official Journal of the European Communities.

The Court of Auditors may also, at any time, submit observations, particularly in the form of special reports, on specific questions and deliver opinions at the request of one of the other institutions of the Community.

It shall adopt its annual reports, special reports or opinions by a majority of its members.

It shall assist the European Parliament and the Council in exercising their powers of control over the implementation of the budget.

CHAPTER 2 PROVISIONS COMMON TO SEVERAL INSTITUTIONS

Article 189

In order to carry out their task and in accordance with the provisions of this Treaty, the European Parliament acting jointly with the Council, the Council and the Commission shall make regulations and issue directives, take decisions, make recommendations or deliver opinions.

A regulation shall have general application. It shall be binding in its entirety and directly applicable in all Member States.

A directive shall be binding, as to the result to be achieved, upon each Member State to which it is addressed, but shall leave to the national authorities the choice of form and methods.

A decision shall be binding in its entirety upon those to whom it is addressed.

Recommendations and opinions shall have no binding force.

Article 189a

1. Where, in pursuance of this Treaty, the Council acts on a proposal from the Commission, unanimity shall be required for an act constituting an amendment to that proposal, subject to Article 189b(4) and (5).

2. As long as the Council has not acted, the Commission may alter its proposal at any time during the procedures leading to the adoption of a Community act.

Article 189b

1. Where reference is made in this Treaty to this Article for the adoption of an act, the following procedure shall apply.

2. The Commission shall submit a proposal to the European Parliament and the Council.

The Council, acting by a qualified majority after obtaining the opinion of the European Parliament, shall adopt a common position. The common position shall be communicated to the European Parliament. The Council shall inform the European Parliament fully of the reasons which led it to adopt its common position. The Commission shall inform the European Parliament fully of its position.

If within three months of such communication, the European Parliament:

(a) approves the common position, the Council shall definitively adopt the act in question in accordance with that common position;

(b) has not taken a decision, the Council shall adopt the act in question in accordance with its common position;

(c) indicates, by an absolute majority of its component members, that it intends to reject the common position, it shall immediately inform the Council. The Council may convene a meeting of the Conciliation Committee referred to in paragraph 4 to explain further its position. The European Parliament shall thereafter either confirm, by an absolute majority of its component members, its rejection of the common position, in which event the proposed act shall be deemed not to have been adopted, or propose amendments in accordance with subparagraph (d) of this paragraph;

(d) propose amendments to the common position by an absolute majority of its component members, the amended text shall be forwarded to the Council and to the Commission, which shall deliver an opinion on those amendments.

3. If, within three months of the matter being referred to it, the Council, acting by a qualified majority, approves all the amendments of the European Parliament, it shall amend its common position accordingly and adopt the act in question; however, the Council shall act unanimously on the amendments on which the Commission has delivered a negative opinion. If the Council does not approve the act in question, the President of the Council, in agreement with the President of the European Parliament, shall forthwith convene a meeting of the Conciliation Committee.

4. The Conciliation Committee, which shall be composed of the members of the Council or their representatives and an equal number of representatives of the European Parliament, shall have the task of reaching agreement on a joint text, by a qualified majority of the members of the Council or their representatives and by a majority of the representatives of the European Parliament. The Commission shall take part in the Conciliation Committee's proceedings and shall take all the necessary initiatives with a view to reconciling the positions of the European Parliament and the Council.

5. If, within six weeks of its being convened, the Conciliation Committee approves a joint text, the European Parliament, acting by an absolute majority of the votes cast, and the Council, acting by a qualified majority, shall have a period of six weeks from that approval in which to adopt the act in question in accordance with the joint text. If one of the two institutions fails to approve the proposed act, it shall be deemed not to have been adopted.

6. Where the Conciliation Committee does not approve a joint text, the proposed act shall be deemed not to have been adopted unless the Council, acting by a qualified majority within six weeks of expiry of the period granted to the Conciliation

Committee, confirms the common position to which it agreed before the conciliation procedure was initiated, possibly with amendments proposed by the European Parliament. In this case, the act in question shall be finally adopted unless the European Parliament, within six weeks of the date of confirmation by the Council, rejects the text by an absolute majority of its component members, in which case the proposed act shall be deemed not to have been adopted.

7. The periods of three months and six weeks referred to in this Article may be extended by a maximum of one months and two weeks respectively by common accord of the European Parliament and the Council. The period of three months referred to in paragraph 2 shall be automatically extended by two months where paragraph 2(c) applies.

8. The scope of the procedure under this Article may be widened, in accordance with the procedure provided for in Article N(2) of the Treaty on European Union, on the basis of a report to be submitted to the Council by the Commission by 1996 at the latest.

Article 189c

Where reference is made in this Treaty to this Article for the adoption of an act, the following procedure shall apply:

(a) The Council, acting by a qualified majority on a proposal from the Commission and after obtaining the opinion of the European Parliament, shall adopt a common position.

(b) The Council's common position shall be communicated to the European Parliament. The Council and the Commission shall inform the European Parliament fully of the reasons which led the Council to adopt its common position and also of the Commission's position.

If, within three months of such communication, the European Parliament approves this common position or has not taken a decision within that period, the Council shall definitively adopt the act in question in accordance with the common position.

(c) The European Parliament may, within the period of three months, referred to in point (b), by an absolute majority of its component members, propose amendments to the Council's common position. The European Parliament may also, by the same majority, reject the Council's common position. The result of the proceedings shall be transmitted to the Council and the Commission.

If the European Parliament has rejected the Council's common position, unanimity shall be required for the Council to act on a second reading.

(d) The Commission shall, within a period of one month, re-examine the proposal on the basis of which the Council adopted its common position, by taking into account the amendments proposed by the European Parliament.

The Commission shall forward to the Council, at the same time as its re-examined proposal, the amendments of the European Parliament which it has not accepted, and shall express its opinion on them. The Council may adopt these amendments unanimously.

(e) The Council, acting by a qualified majority, shall adopt the proposal as re-examined by the Commission.

Unanimity shall be required for the Council to amend the proposal as re-examined by the Commission.

(f) In the cases referred to in points (c), (d) and (e), the Council shall be required to act within a period of three months. If no decision is taken within this period, the Commission proposal shall be deemed not to have been adopted.

(g) The periods referred to in points (b) and (f) may be extended by a maximum of one month by common accord between the Council and the European Parliament.

Article 190

Regulations, directives and decisions adopted jointly by the European Parliament and the Council, and such acts adopted by the Council or the Commission, shall state the reasons on which they are based and shall refer to any proposals or opinions which were required to be obtained pursuant to this Treaty.

Article 191

1. Regulations, directives and decisions adopted in accordance with the procedure referred to in Article 189b shall be signed by the President of the European Parliament and by the President of the Council and published in the Official Journal of the Community. They shall enter into force on the date specified in them or, in the absence thereof, on the twentieth day following that of their publication.

2. Regulations of the Council and of the Commission, as well as directives of those institutions which are addressed to all Member States, shall be published in the Official Journal of the Community. They shall enter into force on the date specified in them or, in the absence thereof, on the twentieth day following that of their publication.

3. Other directives, and decisions, shall be notified to those to whom they are addressed and shall take effect upon such notification.

Article 192

Decisions of the Council or of the Commission which impose a pecuniary obligation on persons other than States, shall be enforceable.

Enforcement shall be governed by the rules of civil procedure in force in the State in the territory of which it is carried out. The order for its enforcement shall be appended to the decision, without other formality than verification of the authenticity of the decision, by the national authority which the Government of each Member State shall designate for this purpose and shall make known to the Commission and to the Court of Justice.

When these formalities have been completed on application by the party concerned, the latter may proceed to enforcement in accordance with the national law, by bringing the matter directly before the competent authority.

Enforcement may be suspended only by a decision of the Court of Justice. However, the courts of the country concerned shall have jurisdiction over complaints that enforcement is being carried out in an irregular manner.

CHAPTER 3 THE ECONOMIC AND SOCIAL COMMITTEE

Article 193

An Economic and Social Committee is hereby established. It shall have advisory status.

The Committee shall consist of representatives of the various categories of economic and social activity, in particular, representatives of producers, farmers, carriers, workers, dealers, craftsmen, professional occupations and representatives of the general public.

Article 194

The number of members of the Economic and Social Committee shall be as follows:

Austria	12
Belgium	12

Denmark	9
Germany	24
Greece	12
Finland	9
France	24
Ireland	9
Italy	24
Luxembourg	6
Netherlands	12
Portugal	12
Spain	21
Sweden	12
United Kingdom	24

The members of the committee shall be appointed by the Council, acting unanimously, for four years. Their appointments shall be renewable.

The members of the Committee may not be bound by any mandatory instructions. They shall be completely independent in the performance of their duties, in the general interest of the Community.

The Council acting by a qualified majority, shall determine the allowances of members of the Committee.

Article 195

1. For the appointment of the members of the Committee, each Member State shall provide the Council with a list containing twice as many candidates as there are seats allotted to its nationals.

The composition of the Committee shall take account of the need to ensure adequate representation of the various categories of economic and social activity.

2. The Council shall consult the Commission. It may obtain the opinion of European bodies which are representative of the various economic and social sectors to which the activities of the Community are of concern.

Article 196

The Committee shall elect its chairman and officers from among its members for a term of two years.

It shall adopt its rules of procedure.

The Committee shall be convened by its chairman at the request of the Councillor of the Commission. It may also meet on its own initiative.

Article 197

The Committee shall include specialised sections for the principal fields covered by this Treaty.

In particular, it shall contain an agricultural section and a transport section, which are the subject of special provisions in the Titles relating to agriculture and transport.

These specialised sections shall operate within the general terms of reference of the Committee. They may not be consulted independently of the Committee.

Sub-committees may also be established within the Committee to prepare on specific questions or in specific fields, draft opinions to be submitted to the Committee for its consideration.

The Rules of procedure shall lay down the methods of composition and the terms of reference of the specialised sections and of the sub-committees.

Article 198

The Committee must be consulted by the Council or by the Commission where this Treaty so provides. The Committee may be consulted by these institutions in all cases in which they consider it appropriate. It may issue an opinion on its own initiative in cases in which it considers such action appropriate.

The Council or the Commission shall, if it considers it necessary, set the Committee, for the submission of its opinion, a time-limit which may not be less than one month from the date on which the chairman receives notification to this effect. Upon expiry of the time-limit, the absence of an opinion shall not prevent further action.

The opinion of the Committee and that of the specialised section, together with a record of the proceedings, shall be forwarded to the Council and to the Commission.

CHAPTER 4 THE COMMITTEE OF THE REGIONS

Article 198a

A Committee consisting of representatives of regional and local bodies, hereinafter referred to as 'the Committee of the Regions', is hereby established with advisory status.

The number of members of the Committee of the Regions shall be as follows:

Austria	12
Belgium	12
Denmark	9
Germany	24
Greece	12
Finland	9
France	24
Ireland	9
Italy	24
Luxembourg	6
Netherlands	12
Portugal	12
Spain	21
Sweden	12
United Kingdom	24

The members of the Committee and an equal number of alternate members shall be appointed for four years by the Council acting unanimously on proposals from the respective Member States. Their term of office shall be renewable.

The member of the Committee may not be bound by any mandatory instructions. They shall be completely independent in the performance of their duties, in the general interests of the Community.

Article 198b

The Committee of the Regions shall elect its chairman and officers from among its members for a term of two years.

It shall adopt its rules of procedure and shall submit them for approval to the Council, acting unanimously.

The Committee shall be convened by its chairman at the request of the Council or of the Commission. It may also meet on its own initiative.

Article 198c

The Committee of the Regions shall be consulted by the Council or by the Commission where this Treaty so provides and in all other cases in which one of these two institutions considers it appropriate.

The Council or the Commission shall, if it considers it necessary, set the Committee, for the submission of its opinion, a time-limit which may not be less than one month from the date on which the chairman receives notification to this effect. Upon expiry of the time-limit, the absence of an opinion shall not prevent further action.

Where the Economic and Social Committee is consulted pursuant to Article 198, the Committee of the Regions shall be informed by the Council or the Commission of the request for an opinion. Where it considers that specific regional interests are involved, the Committee of the Regions may issue an opinion on the matter.

It may issue an opinion on its own initiative in cases in which it considers such action appropriate.

The opinion of the Committee, together with a record of the proceedings, shall be forwarded to the Council and to the Commission.

Notes

1. Subsidiarity is a principle which seeks to devolve powers. Its application to the EC is set out in Art. 3b. Some member states are concerned about the powers which may be exercised at the Community level rather than at national level. For academic discussion of Art. 3b see Emiliou 'Subsidiarity: An Effective Barrier against "the Enterprises of Ambition"?' (1992) 17 EL Rev 383; Toth 'The Principle of Subsidiarity in the Maastricht Treaty' (1992) CML Rev 1079; Cass 'The Word That Saves Maastricht? The Principle of Subsidiarity and the Division of Powers within the European Community' (1992) CML Rev 1107; Hartley 'Constitutional and Institutional Aspects of the Maastricht Agreement' (1993) 42 ICLQ 213, at 214–18; Wyatt, Dashwood et al. *Wyatt and Dashwood's European Community Law* (1993) at 658–9 and Weatherill and Beaumont *EC Law* (1995) at 13–15. Opinion is divided on the justiciability of the principle of subsidiarity, but it may be that the political effect of the provision is such to ensure that there will be agreement between the Community institutions and the member states, thereby obviating a challenge mounted on this principle before the European Court of Justice (ECJ).

2. The balance amongst the Community's institutions is quite different from that of organs of government in European states. The Commission is a permanent body and has important powers of proposal and supervision. It is required to act in the interests of the Community.

The Council will usually have the determinative say in the legislative processes and it represents the views of the member states. Within the Council legislation can be made acting by qualified majority voting (QMV) and by unanimity. Before the SEA, despite provision for QMV, unanimity was the rule. It was agreed that the completion of the single market was both important and unlikely to be achieved through unanimity, so it was agreed that QMV was to apply to single market measures. The range of measures to which QMV can be applied has been increased by the TEU.

The UK was concerned about the impact of the accession of the new member states upon the number of votes which could constitute a blocking minority under QMV. Whilst it is stipulated to be 27 by Art. 148, a compromise was agreed at Ioannina in March 1994, whereby if three member states have a total of 23 to 25 votes opposing the adoption of a proposal then the Council will do all that it can within a reasonable time, which respects treaty deadlines, to reach a satisfactory solution which would be supported by at least 65 votes.

The European Parliament (EP) has very limited powers. It is mainly a consultative body and its ability to hold the Commission to account by censure (Art. 144) is too blunt to be useful. The EP tends to take a Community view. The EP has been given greater powers under Art. 189b. If it is minded to, the EP could veto an act, whereas under Art. 189c the Council can override the EP's views if it acts unanimously.

The ECJ is of great importance and not just to lawyers. The ECJ as the final interpreter of the treaties and Community legislation has played a significant role in the development of the Communities and shaped a new legal order with distinctive legal doctrines. Two of these are explored in Section B.

3. The TEU amended Art. 171 so that there is now provision for the imposition of a financial sanction where a member state has not taken the necessary measures to comply with a judgment by the ECJ that the member state has failed to fulfil a Community obligation.

Treaty on European Union

TITLE V PROVISIONS ON A COMMON FOREIGN AND SECURITY POLICY

Article J

A common foreign and security policy is hereby established which shall be governed by the following provisions.

Article J.1

1. The Union and its Member States shall define and implement a common foreign and security policy, governed by the provisions of this Title and covering all areas of foreign and security policy.

2. The objectives of the common foreign and security policy shall be:

— to safeguard the common values, fundamental interests and independence of the Union;

— to strengthen the security of the Union and its Member States in all ways;

— to preserve peace and strengthen international security, in accordance with the principles of the United Nations Charter as well as the principles of the Helsinki Final Act and the objectives of the Paris Charter;

— to promote international cooperation;

— to develop and consolidate democracy and the rule of law, and respect for human rights and fundamental freedoms.

3. The Union shall pursue these objectives:

— by establishing systematic cooperation between Member States in the conduct of policy, in accordance with Article J.2;

— by gradually implementing, in accordance with Article J.3, joint action in the areas in which the Member States have important interests in common.

4. The Member States shall support the Union's external and security policy actively and unreservedly in a spirit of loyalty and mutual solidarity. They shall refrain

from any action which is contrary to the interests of the Union or likely to impair its effectiveness as a cohesive force in international relations. The Council shall ensure that these principles are complied with.

Article J.2

1. Member States shall inform and consult one another within the Council on any matter of foreign and security policy of general interest in order to ensure that their combined influence is exerted as effectively as possible by means of concerted and convergent action.

2. Whenever it deems it necessary, the Council shall define a common position.

Member States shall ensure that their national policies conform to the common positions.

3. Member States shall coordinate their action in international organisations and at international conferences. They shall uphold the common positions in such fora.

In international organisations and at international conferences where not all the Member States participate, those which do take part shall uphold the common positions.

Article J.3

The procedure for adopting joint action in matters covered by the foreign and security policy shall be the following:

1. The Council shall decide, on the basis of general guidelines from the European Council, that a matter should be the subject of joint action.

Whenever the Council decides on the principle of joint action, it shall lay down the specific scope, the Union's general and specific objectives in carrying out such action, if necessary its duration, and the means, procedures and conditions for its implementation.

2. The Council shall, when adopting the joint action and at any stage during its development, define those matters on which decisions are to be taken by a qualified majority.

Where the Council is required to act by a qualified majority pursuant to the preceding subparagraph, the votes of its members shall be weighted in accordance with Article 148(2) of the Treaty establishing the European Community, and for their adoption, acts of the Council shall require at least fifty-four votes in favour, cast by at least eight members.

3. If there is a change in circumstances having a substantial effect on a question subject to joint action, the Council shall review the principles and objectives of that action and take the necessary decisions. As long as the Council has not acted, the joint action shall stand.

4. Joint actions shall commit the Member States in the positions they adopt and in the conduct of their activity.

5. Whenever there is any plan to adopt a national position or take national action pursuant to a joint action, information shall be provided in time to allow, if necessary, for prior consultations within the Council. The obligation to provide prior information shall not apply to measures which are merely a national transposition of Council decisions.

6. In cases of imperative need arising from changes in the situation and failing a Council decision, Member States may take the necessary measures as a matter of urgency having regard to the general objectives of the joint action. The Member State concerned shall inform the Council immediately of any such measures.

7. Should there be any major difficulties in implementing a joint action, a Member State shall refer them to the Council which shall discuss them and seek appropriate

solutions. Such solutions shall not run counter to the objectives of the joint action or impair its effectiveness.

Article J.4

1. The common foreign and security policy shall include all questions related to the security of the Union, including the eventual framing of a common defence policy, which might in time lead to a common defence.

2. The Union requests the Western European Union (WEU), which is an integral part of the development of the Union, to elaborate and implement decisions and actions of the Union which have defence implications. The Council shall, in agreement with the institutions of the WEU, adopt the necessary practical arrangements.

3. Issues having defence implications dealt with under this Article shall not be subject to the procedures set out in Article J.3.

4. The policy of the Union in accordance with this Article shall not prejudice the specific character of the security and defence policy of certain Member States and shall respect the obligations of certain Member States under the North Atlantic Treaty and be compatible with the common security and defence policy established within that framework.

5. The provisions of this Article shall not prevent the development of closer cooperation between two or more Member States on a bilateral level, in the framework of the WEU and the Atlantic Alliance, provided such cooperation does not run counter to or impede that provided for in this Title.

6. With a view to furthering the objective of this Treaty, and having in view the date of 1998 in the context of Article XII of the Brussels Treaty, the provisions of this Article may be revised as provided for in Article N(2) on the basis of a report to be presented in 1996 by the Council to the European Council, which shall include an evaluation of the progress made and the experience gained until then.

Article J.5

1. The Presidency shall represent the Union in matters coming within the common foreign and security policy.

2. The Presidency shall be responsible for the implementation of common measures; in that capacity it shall in principle express the position of the Union in international organisations and international conferences.

3. In the tasks referred to in paragraphs 1 and 2, the Presidency shall be assisted if need be by the previous and next Member States to hold the Presidency. The Commission shall be fully associated in these tasks.

4. Without prejudice to Article J.2(3) and Article J.3(4), Member States represented in international organisations or international conferences where not all the Member States participate shall keep the latter informed of any matter of common interest.

Member States which are also members of the United Nations Security Council will concert and keep the other Member States fully informed. Member States which are permanent members of the Security Council will, in the execution of their functions, ensure the defence of the positions and the interests of the Union, without prejudice to their responsibilities under the provisions of the United Nations Charter.

Article J.6

The diplomatic and consular missions of the Member States and the Commission Delegations in third countries and international conferences, and their representations to international organisations, shall cooperate in ensuring that the common positions and common measures adopted by the Council are complied with and implemented.

They shall step up cooperation by exchanging information, carrying out joint assessments and contributing to the implementation of the provisions referred to in Article 8c of the Treaty establishing the European Community.

Article J.7

The Presidency shall consult the European Parliament on the main aspects and the basic choices of the common foreign and security policy and shall ensure that the views of the European Parliament are duly taken into consideration. The European Parliament shall be kept regularly informed by the Presidency and the Commission of the development of the Union's foreign and security policy.

The European Parliament may ask questions of the Council or make recommendations to it. It shall hold an annual debate on progress in implementing the common foreign and security policy.

Article J.8

1. The European Council shall define the principles of and general guidelines for the common foreign and security policy.

2. The Council shall take the decisions necessary for defining and implementing the common foreign and security policy on the basis of the general guidelines adopted by the European Council. It shall ensure the unity, consistency and effectiveness of action by the Union.

The Council shall act unanimously, except for procedural questions and in the case referred to in Article J.3(2).

3. Any Member State or the Commission may refer to the Council any question relating to the common foreign and security policy and may submit proposals to the Council.

4. In cases requiring a rapid decision, the Presidency, of its own motion, or at the request of the Commission or a Member State, shall convene an extraordinary Council meeting within forty-eight hours or, in an emergency, within a shorter period.

5. Without prejudice to Article 151 of the Treaty establishing the European Community, a Political Committee consisting of Political Directors shall monitor the international situation in the areas covered by common foreign and security policy and contribute to the definition of policies by delivering opinions to the Council at the request of the Council or on its own initiative. It shall also monitor the implementation of agreed policies, without prejudice to the responsibility of the Presidency and the Commission.

Article J.9

The Commission shall be fully associated with the work carried out in the common foreign and security policy field.

Article J.10

On the occasion of any review of the security provisions under Article J.4, the Conference which is convened to that effect shall also examine whether any other amendments need to be made to provisions relating to the common foreign and security policy.

Article J.11

1. The provisions referred to in Articles 137, 138, 139 to 142, 146, 147, 150 to 153, 157 to 163 and 217 of the Treaty establishing the European Community shall apply to the provisions relating to the areas referred to in this Title.

2. Administrative expenditure which the provisions relating to the areas referred to in this Title entail for the institutions shall be charged to the budget of the European Communities.

The Council may also:

— either decide unanimously that operational expenditure to which the implementation of those provisions gives rise is to be charged to the budget of the European Communities; in that event, the budgetary procedure laid down in the Treaty establishing the European Community shall be applicable;

— or determine that such expenditue shall be charged to the Member States, where appropriate in accordance with a scale to be decided.

TITLE VI PROVISIONS ON COOPERATION IN THE FIELDS OF JUSTICE AND HOME AFFAIRS

Article K

Cooperation in the fields of justice and home affairs shall be governed by the following provisions.

Article K.1

For the purposes of achieving the objectives of the Union, in particular the free movement of persons, and without prejudice to the powers of the European Community, Member States shall regard the following areas as matters of common interest:

1. asylum policy;
2. rules governing the crossing by persons of the external borders of the Member States and the exercise of controls thereon;
3. immigration policy and policy regarding nationals of third countries:

(a) conditions of entry and movement by nationals of third countries on the territory of Member States;

(b) conditions of residence by nationals of third countries on the territory of Member States, including family reunion and access to employment;

(c) combating unauthorised immigration, residence and work by nationals of third countries on the territory of Member States;

4. combating drug addiction in so far as this is not covered by 7 to 9;
5. combating fraud on an international scale in so far as this is not covered by 7 to 9;
6. judicial cooperation in civil matters;
7. judicial cooperation in criminal matters;
8. customs cooperation;
9. police cooperation for the purposes of preventing and combating terrorism, unlawful drug trafficking and other serious forms of international crime, including if necessary certain aspects of customs cooperation, in connection with the organisation of a Union-wide system for exchanging information within a European Police Office (Europol).

Article K.2

1. The matters referred to in Article K.1 shall be dealt with in compliance with the European Convention for the Protection of Human Rights and Fundamental Freedoms of 4 November 1950 and the Convention relating to the Status of Refugees of 28 July 1951 and having regard to the protection afforded by Member States to persons persecuted on political grounds.

2. This Title shall not affect the exercise of the responsibilities incumbent upon Member States with regard to the maintenance of law and order and the safeguarding of internal security.

Article K.3

1. In the areas referred to in Article K.1, Member States shall inform and consult one another within the Council with a view to coordinating their action. To that end, they shall establish collaboration between the relevant departments of their administrations.

2. The Council may:

— on the initiative of any Member State or of the Commission, in the areas referred to in Article K.1(1) to (6);

— on the initiative of any Member State, in the areas referred to in Article K.1(7) to (9):

(a) adopt joint positions and promote, using the appropriate form and procedures, any cooperation contributing to the pursuit of the objectives of the Union;

(b) adopt joint action in so far as the objectives of the Union can be attained better by joint action that by the Member State acting individually on account of the scale or effects of the action envisaged; it may decide that measures implementing joint action are to be adopted by a qualified majority;

(c) without prejudice to Article 220 of the Treaty establishing the European Community, draw up conventions which it shall recommend to the Member States for adoption in accordance with their respective constitutional requirements.

Unless otherwise provided by such conventions, measures implementing them shall be adopted within the Council by a majority of two-thirds of the High Contracting Parties.

Such conventions may stipulate that the Court of Justice shall have jurisdiction to interpret their provisions and to rule on any disputes regarding their application, in accordance with such arrangements as they may lay down.

Article K.4

1. A Coordinating Committee shall be set up consisting of senior officials. In addition to its coordinating role, it shall be the task of the Committee to:

— give opinions for the attention of the Council, either at the Council's request or on its own initiative;

— contribute, without prejudice to Article 151 of the Treaty establishing the European Community, to the preparation of the Council's discussions in the areas referred to in Article K.1 and, in accordance with the conditions laid down in Article 100d of the Treaty establishing the European Community, in the areas referred to in Article 100c of that Treaty.

2. The Commission shall be fully associated with the work in the areas referred to in this Title.

3. The Council shall act unanimously, except on matters of procedure and in cases where Article K.3 expressly provides for other voting rules.

Where the Council is required to act by a qualified majority, the votes of its members shall be weighted as laid down in Article 148(2) of the Treaty establishing the European Community, and for their adoption, acts of the Council shall require at least fifty-four votes in favour, cast by at least eight members.

Article K.5

Within international organisations and at international conferences in which they take part, Member States shall defend the common positions adopted under the provisions of this Title.

Article K.6

The Presidency and the Commission shall regularly inform the European Parliament of discussions in the areas covered by this Title.

The Presidency shall consult the European Parliament on the principal aspects of activities in the areas referred to in this Title and shall ensure that the views of the European Parliament are duly taken into consideration.

The European Parliament may ask questions of the Council or make recommendations to it. Each year, it shall hold a debate on the progress made in implementation of the areas referred to in this Title.

Article K.7

The provisions of this Title shall not prevent the establishment or development of closer cooperation between two or more Member States in so far as such cooperation does not conflict with, or impede, that provided for in this Title.

Article K.8

1. The provisions referred to in Articles 137, 138, 139 to 142, 146, 147, 150 to 153, 157 to 163 and 217 of the Treaty establishing the European Community shall apply to the provisons relating to the areas referred to in this Title.

2. Administrative expenditure which the provisions relating to the areas referred to in this Title entail for the institutions shall be charged to the budget of the European Communities.

The Council may also:

— either decide unanimously that operational expenditure to which the implementation of those provisions gives rise is to be charged to the budget of the European Communities; in that event, the budgetary procedure laid down in the Treaty establishing the European Community shall be applicable;

— or determine that such expenditure shall be charged to the Member States, where appropriate in accordance with a scale to be decided.

Article K.9

The Council, acting unanimously on the initiative of the Commission or a Member State, may decide to apply Article 100c of the Treaty establishing the European Community to action in areas referred to in Article K.1(1) to (6), and at the same time determine the relevant voting conditions relating to it. It shall recommend the Member States to adopt the decision in accordance with their respective constitutional requirements.

TITLE VII FINAL PROVISIONS

Article L

The provisions of the Treaty establishing the European Community, the Treaty establishing the European Coal and Steel Community and the Treaty establishing the European Atomic Energy Community concerning the powers of the Court of Justice of the European Communities and the exercise of those powers shall apply only to the following provisions of this Treaty:

(a) provisions amending the Treaty establishing the European Economic Community with a view to establishing the European Community, the Treaty establishing the European Coal and Steel Community and the Treaty establishing the European Atomic Energy Community;

(b) the third subparagraph of Article K.3(2)(c);

(c) Articles L to S.

Article M

Subject to the provisions amending the Treaty establishing the European Economic Community with a view to establishing the European Community, the Treaty establishing the European Coal and Steel Community and the Treaty establishing the European Atomic Energy Community, and to these final provisions, nothing in this Treaty shall affect the Treaties establishing the European Communities or the subsequent Treaties and Acts modifying or supplementing them.

Article N

1. The Government of any Member State or the Commission may submit to the Council proposals for the Amendment of the Treaties on which the Union is founded.

If the Council, after consulting the European Parliament, and, where appropriate, the Commission, delivers an opinion in favour of calling a conference of representatives of the governments of the Member States, the conference shall be convened by the President of the Council for the purpose of determining by common accord the amendments to be made to those Treaties. The European Central Bank shall also be consulted in the case of institutional changes in the monetary area.

The amendments shall enter into force after being ratified by all the Member States in accordance with their respective constitutional requirements.

2. A conference of representatives of the governments of the Member States shall be convened in 1996 to examine those provisions of this Treaty for which revision is provided, in accordance with the objectives set out in Articles A and B.

Article O

Any European State may apply to become a Member of the Union. It shall address its application to the Council, which shall act unanimously after consulting the Commission and after receiving the assent of the European Parliament, which shall act by an absolute majority of its component members.

The conditions of admission and the adjustments to the Treaties on which the Union is founded which such admission entails shall be the subject of an agreement between the Member States and the applicant State. This agreement shall be submitted for ratification by all the Contracting States in accordance with their respective constitutional requirements.

PROTOCOL ON THE TRANSITION TO THE THIRD STAGE OF ECONOMIC AND MONETARY UNION

THE HIGH CONTRACTING PARTIES,

Declare the irreversible character of the Community's movement to the third stage of Economic and Monetary Union by signing the new Treaty provisions on Economic and Monetary Union.

Therefore all Member States shall, whether they fulfil the necessary conditions for the adoption of a single currency or not, respect the will for the Community to enter swiftly into the third stage, and therefore no Member State shall prevent the entering into the third stage.

If by the end of 1997 the date of the beginning of the third stage has not been set, the Member States concerned, the Community institutions and other bodies involved shall expedite all preparatory work during 1998, in order to enable the Community to enter the third stage irrevocably on 1 January 1999 and to enable the ECB and the ESCB to start their full functioning from this date on.

This Protocol shall be annexed to the Treaty establishing the European Community.

PROTOCOL ON CERTAIN PROVISIONS RELATING TO THE UNITED KINGDOM OF GREAT BRITAIN AND NORTHERN IRELAND

THE HIGH CONTRACTING PARTIES,

RECOGNISING that the United Kingdom shall not be obliged or committed to move to the third stage of Economic and Monetary Union without a separate decision to do so by its government and Parliament,

NOTING the practice of the government of the United Kingdom to fund its borrowing requirement by the sale of debt to the private sector,

HAVE AGREED the following provisions, which shall be annexed to the Treaty establishing the European Community:

1. The United Kingdom shall notify the Council whether it intends to move to the third stage before the Council makes its assessment under Article 109j(2) of this Treaty.

Unless the United Kingdom notifies the Council that it intends to move to the third stage, it shall be under no obligation to do so.

If no date is set for the beginning of the third stage under Article 109j(3) of this Treaty, the United Kingdom may notify its intention to move to the third stage before 1 January 1998. . . .

PROTOCOL ON CERTAIN PROVISIONS RELATING TO DENMARK

THE HIGH CONTRACTING PARTIES,

DESIRING to settle, in accordance with the general objectives of the Treaty establishing the European Community, certain particular problems existing at the present time,

TAKING INTO ACCOUNT that the Danish Constitution contains provisions which may imply a referendum in Denmark prior to Danish participation in the third stage of Economic and Monetary Union.

HAVE AGREED on the following provisions, which shall be annexed to the Treaty establishing the European Community:

1. The Danish Government shall notify the Council of its position concerning participation in the third stage before the Council makes its assessment under Article 109j(2) of this Treaty.

2. In the event of a notification that Denmark will not participate in the third stage, Denmark shall have an exemption. The effect of the exemption shall be that all Articles and provisions of this Treaty and the Statute of the ESCB referring to a derogation shall be applicable to Denmark. . . .

PROTOCOL ON SOCIAL POLICY

THE HIGH CONTRACTING PARTIES,

NOTING that eleven Member States, that is to say the Kingdom of Belgium, the Kingdom of Denmark, the Federal Republic of Germany, the Hellenic Republic, the Kingdom of Spain, the French Republic, Ireland, the Italian Republic, the Grand Duchy of Luxembourg, the Kingdom of the Netherlands, the Portuguese Republic, wish to continue along the path laid down in the 1989 Social Charter; that they have adopted among themselves an Agreement to this end; that this Agreement is annexed to this Protocol; that this Protocol and the said Agreement are without prejudice to the provisions of this Treaty, particularly those which relate to social policy which constitute an integral part of the 'acquis communautaire'.

1. Agree to authorise those eleven Member States to have recourse to the institutions, procedures and mechanisms of the Treaty for the purposes of taking among themselves and applying as far as they are concerned the acts and decisions required for giving effect to the above-mentioned Agreement.

2. The United Kingdom of Great Britain and Northern Ireland shall not take part in the deliberations and the adoption by the Council of Commission proposals made on the basis of this Protocol and the above-mentioned Agreement.

By way of derogation from Article 148(2) of the Treaty, acts of the Council which are made pursuant to this Protocol and which must be adopted by a qualified majority shall be deemed to be so adopted if they have received at least forty-four votes in favour. The unanimity of the members of the Council, with the exception of the United Kingdom of Great Britain and Northern Ireland, shall be necessary for acts of the Council which must be adopted unanimously and for those amending the Commission proposal.

Acts adopted by the Council and any financial consequences other than administrative costs entailed for the institutions shall not be applicable to the United Kingdom of Great Britain and Northern Ireland.

3. This Protocol shall be annexed to the Treaty establishing the European Community.

Notes

1. The provisions dealing with the common foreign and security policy and cooperation in justice and home affairs indicate that the member states are here acting inter-governmentally and outside the scope and framework of the Communities. The institutional focus of these areas is the Council. The ECJ has no jurisdiction apart from Art. K.3(2)(c), and the Commission and EP are to consulted and kept informed. Decision-making by the Council will normally be on the basis of unanimity, although majority voting may be adopted for decisions on some areas, but such a decision must be unanimous (Arts. J.8, J.3(2), K.4(3), K.3).

2. A major feature of the TEU is the provision for a member state to opt-out of its provisions. The UK and Denmark have opted out of some of the provisions. One of the aims of the EC is the establishment of economic and monetary union (EMU) in which there would be a common currency. Both the UK and Denmark have opted out of the EMU timetable. Whilst the UK has declared that it will only move to the third stage of EMU following a decision to do so by the government and Parliament, Denmark has made it clear that it will not move to the third stage. This was done in the aftermath of the 1992 referendum which rejected ratification of the TEU when measures were taken to try to reassure the Danish people about the TEU but without renegotiating it. At the Edinburgh Summit in December 1992 there were (a) a Decision of the Heads of State or Government, and (b) Declarations by the European Council (not reproduced). Denmark's decision not to move to the third stage of EMU was incorporated in the Edinburgh Decision. Defence was another area which concerned the Danes and so the Edinburgh Decision notes that Denmark would not participate in the elaboration and implementation of decisions and actions with defence implications, and in the Declarations it was made clear that Denmark would not hold the Presidency of the European Union in matters having defence implications.

The UK also opted out of the Agreement on Social Policy which, for all of the other member states, is part of the EC.

Question
How much sovereignty have the member states given up in the fields of foreign and security policy, justice and home affairs with the coming into force of the TEU?

(B) THE RELATIONSHIP BETWEEN COMMUNITY LAW AND UK LAW

The treaties have created a new legal order in which measures made by the Community institutions become part of the law of the member states. Some measures, regulations, are directly applicable, i.e. they become part of the domestic law of the member states without any implementing action being taken, whereas the member states implement directives. In these circumstances it is possible that there could be confusion over, or conflict between, Community law and the domestic law of the member states. Accordingly, the European Court of Justice (ECJ), has been given the jurisdiction of the final interpreter of Community law. Under Article 177, national courts may seek preliminary rulings by asking questions on matters of Community law which are relevant points in cases before them. The decisions of the ECJ under this procedure have played an important part in the development of Community law.

(i) Supremacy of Community law
One of the most important doctrines of Community law developed by the ECJ is that of supremacy.

(1) The European Court of Justice's view

***Van Gend en Loos* v *Nederlandse Administratie der Belastingen* Case 26/62**
[1963] ECR 1
European Court of Justice

Article 12 of the European Economic Community (EEC) Treaty required member states not to introduce new customs duties or charges having equivalent effect, nor to increase existing duties on trade between member states. The plaintiff imported aminoplasts from West Germany into the Netherlands. Before the EEC Treaty came into force the duty was 3 per cent. Subsequently it was increased to 8 per cent under an international agreement. The plaintiff challenged this increase in the Dutch revenue courts. The Amsterdam *Tariefcommissie* sought a preliminary ruling on the interpretation of Art. 12 from the ECJ.

II – The first question

A – *Jurisdiction of the Court*

The Government of the Netherlands and the Belgian Government challenge the jurisdiction of the Court on the ground that the reference relates not to the interpretation but to the application of the Treaty in the context of the constitutional law of the Netherlands, and that in particular the Court has no jurisdiction to decide, should the occasion arise, whether the provisions of the EEC Treaty prevail over Netherlands legislation or over other agreements entered into by the Netherlands and incorporated into Dutch national law. The solution of such a problem, it is claimed, falls within the exclusive jurisdiction of the national courts, subject to an application in accordance with the provisions laid down by Articles 169 and 170 of the Treaty.

However in this case the Court is not asked to adjudicate upon the application of the Treaty according to the principles of the national law of the Netherlands, which remains the concern of the national courts, but is asked, in conformity with subparagraph (a) of the first paragraph of Article 177 of the Treaty, only to interpret the scope of Article 12 of the said Treaty within the context of Community law and with reference to its effect on individuals. This argument has therefore no legal foundation.

The Belgian Government further argues that the Court has no jurisdiction on the ground that no answer which the Court could give to the first question of the Tariefcommissie would have any bearing on the result of the proceedings brought in that court.

However, in order to confer jurisdiction on the Court in the present case it is necessary only that the question raised should clearly be concerned with the interpretation of the Treaty. The considerations which may have led a national court or tribunal to its choice of questions as well as the relevance which it attributes to such questions in the context of a case before it are excluded from review by the Court of Justice.

It appears from the wording of the questions referred that they relate to the interpretation of the Treaty. The Court therefore has the jurisdiction to answer them.

This argument, too, is therefore unfounded.

B – *On the substance of the Case*

The first question of the Tariefcommissie is whether Article 12 of the Treaty has direct application in national law in the sense that nationals of Member States may on the basis of this Article lay claim to rights which the national court must protect.

To ascertain whether the provisions of an international treaty extend so far in their effects it is necessary to consider the spirit, the general scheme and the wording of those provisions.

The objective of the EEC Treaty, which is to establish a Common Market, the functioning of which is of direct concern to interested parties in the Community, implies that this Treaty is more than an agreement which merely creates mutual obligations between the contracting states. This view is confirmed by the preamble to the Treaty which refers not only to governments but to peoples. It is also confirmed more specifically by the establishment of institutions endowed with sovereign rights, the exercise of which affects Member States and also their citizens. Furthermore, it must be noted that the nationals of the states brought together in the Community are called upon to cooperate in the functioning of this Community through the intermediary of the European Parliament and the Economic and Social Committee.

In addition the task assigned to the Court of Justice under Article 177, the object of which is to secure uniform interpretation of the Treaty by national courts and tribunals, confirms that the states have acknowledged that Community law has an authority which can be invoked by their nationals before those courts and tribunals.

The conclusion to be drawn from this is that the Community constitutes a new legal order of international law for the benefit of which the states have limited their sovereign rights, albeit within limited fields, and the subjects of which comprise not only Member States but also their nationals. Independently of the legislation of Member States, Community law therefore not only imposes obligations on individuals but is also intended to confer upon them rights which become part of their legal heritage. These rights arise not only where they are expressly granted by the Treaty, but also by reason of obligations which the Treaty imposes in a clearly defined way upon individuals as well as upon the Member States and upon the institutions of the Community.

With regard to the general scheme of the Treaty as it relates to customs duties and charges having equivalent effect it must be emphasized that Article 9, which bases the Community upon a customs union, includes as an essential provision the prohibition of these customs duties and charges. This provision is found at the beginning of the part of the Treaty which defines the 'Foundations of the Community'. It is applied and explained by Article 12.

The wording of Article 12 contains a clear and unconditional prohibition which is not a positive but a negative obligation. This obligation, moreover, is not qualified by any reservation on the part of states which would make its implementation conditional upon a positive legislative measure enacted under national law. The very nature of this prohibition makes it ideally adapted to produce direct effects in the legal relationship between Member States and their subjects.

The implementation of Article 12 does not require any legislative intervention on the part of the states. The fact that under this Article it is the Member States who are made the subject of the negative obligation does not imply that their nationals cannot benefit from this obligation.

In addition the argument based on Articles 169 and 170 of the Treaty put forward by the three Governments which have submitted observations to the Court in their statements of case is misconceived. The fact that these Articles of the Treaty enable the Commission and the Member States to bring before the Court a State which has not fulfilled its obligations does not mean that individuals cannot plead these obligations, should the occasion arise, before a national court, any more than the fact that the Treaty places at the disposal of the Commission ways of ensuring that obligations imposed upon those subject to the Treaty are observed, precludes the possibility, in actions between individuals before a national court, of pleading infringements of these obligations.

A restriction of the guarantees against an infringement of Article 12 by Member States to the procedures under Articles 169 and 170 would remove all direct legal protection of the individual rights of their nationals. There is the risk that recourse to the procedure under these Articles would be ineffective if it were to occur after the implementation of a national decision taken contrary to the provisions of the Treaty.

The vigilance of individuals concerned to protect their rights amounts to an effective supervision in addition to the supervision entrusted by Articles 169 and 170 to the diligence of the Commission and of the Member States.

It follows from the foregoing considerations that, according to the spirit, the general scheme and the wording of the Treaty, Article 12 must be interpreted as producing direct effects and creating individual rights which national courts must protect.

The ECJ ruled that Art. 12 produced direct effects and created rights which national courts must protect and left it to the Tariefcommissie to determine if Art. 12 had been breached by the Dutch revenue authorities.

Note

The style of judgment of the ECJ is somewhat different from a common law court. The ECJ uses consequentialist or purposive reasoning. The policy behind the creation of a Common Market is to remove trade barriers, and this will affect individuals. It would be counter to this policy to allow member states to determine EC matters. The ECJ concludes that there is a new legal order created by the Treaties, and they provide that the ECJ is to be the final authority on the interpretation of the Treaties and EC law.

The case also makes clear that provisions of the Treaties which do not make explicit reference to individuals can, nevertheless, produce direct effects, that is create rights for individuals which national courts are to protect. The governments which filed briefs before the ECJ argued unsuccessfully that only the Commission and member states could take legal action, under Arts 169–170 of the EEC Treaty, against any member state which was not honouring its EC obligations.

The nature of the new legal order was further developed in the following case.

Costa v ENEL Case 6/64
[1964] ECR 585
European Court of Justice

Mr Costa refused to pay an electricity bill. He was opposed to the nationalisation of the Italian electricity industry which had occurred after the EEC Treaty had come into force. In defending his non-payment Mr Costa argued that the nationalisation legislation breached Arts 102, 93, 53, and 37 of the EEC Treaty. The magistrate, the *Giudice Conciliatore,* sought a preliminary ruling from the ECJ.

The complaint is made that the Milan court has requested an interpretation of the Treaty which was not necessary for the solution of the dispute before it.

Since, however, Article 177 is based upon a clear separation of functions between national courts and the Court of Justice, it cannot empower the latter either to investigate the facts of the case or to criticize the grounds and purpose of the request for interpretation.

On the submission that the court was obliged to apply the national law

The Italian Government submits that the request of the Giudice Conciliatore is 'absolutely inadmissible', inasmuch as a national court which is obliged to apply a national law cannot avail itself of Article 177.

By contrast with ordinary international treaties, the EEC Treaty has created its own legal system which, on the entry into force of the Treaty, became an integral part of the legal systems of the Member States and which their courts are bound to apply.

By creating a Community of unlimited duration, having its own institutions, its own personality, its own legal capacity and capacity of representation on the international plane and, more particularly, real powers stemming from a limitation of sovereignty or a transfer of powers from the States to the Community, the Member States have limited their sovereign rights, albeit within limited fields, and have thus created a body of law which binds both their nationals and themselves.

The integration into the laws of each Member State of provisions which derive from the Community, and more generally the terms and the spirit of the Treaty, make it impossible for the States, as a corollary, to accord precedence to a unilateral and subsequent measure over a legal system accepted by them on a basis of reciprocity. Such a measure cannot therefore be inconsistent with that legal system. The executive force of Community law cannot vary from one State to another in deference to subsequent domestic laws, without jeopardizing the attainment of the objectives of the Treaty set out in Article 5(2) and giving rise to the discrimination prohibited by Article 7.

The obligations undertaken under the Treaty establishing the Community would not be unconditional, but merely contingent, if they could be called in question by subsequent legislative acts of the signatories. Wherever the Treaty grants the States the right to act unilaterally, it does this by clear and precise provisions (for example Articles 15, 93(3), 223, 224 and 225). Applications, by Member States for authority to derogate from the Treaty are subject to a special authorization procedure (for example Articles 8(4), 17(4), 25, 26, 73, the third subparagraph of Article 93(2), and 226) which would lose their purpose if the Member States could renounce their obligations by means of an ordinary law.

The precedence of Community law is confirmed by Article 189, whereby a regulation 'shall be binding' and 'directly applicable in all Member States'. This provision, which is subject to no reservation, would be quite meaningless if a State could unilaterally nullify its effects by means of a legislative measure which could prevail over Community law.

It follows from all these observations that the law stemming from the Treaty, an independent source of law, could not, because of its special and original nature, be overridden by domestic legal provisions, however framed, without being deprived of its character as Community law and without the legal basis of the Community itself being called into question.

The transfer by the States from their domestic legal system to the Community legal system of the rights and obligations arising under the Treaty carries with it a permanent limitation of their sovereign rights, against which a subsequent unilateral act incompatible with the concept of the Community cannot prevail. Consequently Article 177 is to be applied regardless of any domestic law, whenever questions relating to the interpretation of the Treaty arise.

The ECJ ruled that subsequent national measures cannot take precedence over EC law and that, whilst Arts 53 and 37 (2) produced direct effects creating rights for individuals which national courts must protect, this was not so for Arts 102 and 93.

Note

The ECJ again showed that EC provisions which do not specifically mention individuals may still create rights for them. The ECJ also developed its views about the new legal order, and stated that the logic of EC law gives it supremacy over the municipal law of the member states.

The full extent of this supremacy of EC law is revealed in the following case.

Internationale Handelsgesellschaft GmbH v *Einfuhr – und Vorratsstelle fur Getreide und Futtermittel* Case 11/70 [1970] ECR 1125 European Court of Justice

The plaintiff, a German company, had to obtain a licence to export cornflour. The EC provisions required a performance deposit, that is, if a licensee failed to export the full amount permitted in the licence then the deposit would be forfeit. The plaintiff failed to export the full amount specified in the licence and so forfeited the deposit. The plaintiff challenged this in the administrative court, the *verwaltungsgericht*. The German court sought a preliminary ruling on the EC provisions, as the court thought that they were in conflict with the basic rights guaranteed in the West German constitution.

[2] . . . It appears from the grounds of the order referring the matter that the Verwaltungsgericht has until now refused to accept the validity of the provisions in question and that for this reason it considers it to be essential to put an end to the existing legal uncertainty. According to the evaluation of the Verwaltungsgericht, the system of deposits is contrary to certain structural principles of national constitutional law which must be protected within the framework of Community law, with the result that the primacy of supranational law must yield before the principles of the German Basic Law. More particularly, the system of deposits runs counter to the principles of freedom of action and of disposition, of economic liberty and of proportionality arising in particular from Articles 2 (1) and 14 of the Basic Law. The obligation to import or export resulting from the issue of the licences, together with the deposit attaching thereto, constitutes an excessive intervention in the freedom of disposition in trade, as the objective of the regulations could have been attained by methods of intervention having less serious consequences.

The protection of fundamental rights in the Community legal system

[3] Recourse to the legal rules or concepts of national law in order to judge the validity of measures adopted by the institutions of the Community would have an adverse effect on the uniformity and efficacy of Community law. The validity of such measures can only be judged in the light of Community law. In fact, the law stemming from the Treaty, an independent source of law, cannot because of its very nature be overridden by rules of national law, however framed, without being deprived of its character as Community law and without the legal basis of the Community itself being called in question. Therefore the validity of a Community measure or its effect within a Member State cannot be affected by allegations that it runs counter to either fundamental rights as formulated by the constitution of the State or the principles of a national constitutional structure.

[4] However, an examination should be made as to whether or not any analogous guarantee inherent in Community law has been disregarded. In fact, respect for fundamental rights forms an integral part of the general principles of law protected by the Court of Justice. The protection of such rights, whilst inspired by the constitutional traditions common to the Member States, must be ensured within the framework of the structure and objectives of the Community. It must therefore be ascertained, in the light of the doubts expressed by the Verwaltungsgericht, whether

the system of deposits has infringed rights of a fundamental nature, respect for which must be ensured in the Community legal system.

The ECJ upheld the provisions creating the system of performance deposits.

Notes

1. So far we have looked at conflicts between the municipal law of member states and EC law where the ECJ, in its rulings, has affirmed the supremacy of the latter. The ECJ has taken this view further by declaring that EC law prevails over any conflicting provisions of Bills of Rights in member states' constitutions. Again, this followed on from the logic of the Treaties that EC law applies uniformly throughout the member states. The ECJ stated that it will protect fundamental rights. In *Nold* v *Commission* (Case 4/73) [1974] ECR 491 the ECJ reaffirmed that fundamental rights form part of the general principles of law protected by the court. It was also stated that the court would draw inspiration from the constitutional traditions common to the member states and from international treaties for the protection of human rights which member states may have collaborated on or ratified.

2. The declaration of the supremacy of EC law by the ECJ creates a problem for national courts: they are supposed to protect the rights conferred by EC law even where they conflict with the law of member states. How can this be done if a national court cannot strike down a municipal statute, as where, for example, only the member state's Constitutional Court can carry out such action? Advice was offered in the following case.

Amministrazione delle Finanze dello Stato v *Simmenthal SpA* Case 106/77
[1978] ECR 629
European Court of Justice

Simmenthal imported beef into Italy. In an earlier case, *Simmenthal SpA* v *Italian Minister of Finance* (case 35/76) [1976] ECR 1871, the ECJ had ruled that the Italian law requiring importers to pay for public health and veterinarian checks at the border was contrary to Arts 30 and 12 of the EEC Treaty. The Italian court ordered the refund of these fees paid by Simmenthal, and the Ministry argued that until the Constitutional Court set aside the legislation they had a good defence. The Italian court sought a preliminary ruling.

[13] The main purpose of the first question is to ascertain what consequences flow from the direct applicability of a provision of Community law in the event of incompatibility with a subsequent legislative provision of a Member State.

[14] Direct applicability in such circumstances means that rules of Community law must be fully and uniformly applied in all the Member States from the date of their entry into force and for so long as they continue in force.

[15] These provisions are therefore a direct source of rights and duties for all those affected thereby, whether Member States or individuals, who are parties to legal relationships under Community law.

[16] This consequence also concerns any national court whose task it is as an organ of a Member State to protect, in a case within its jurisdiction, the rights conferred upon individuals by Community law.

[17] Furthermore, in accordance with the principle of the precedence of Community law, the relationship between provisions of the Treaty and directly applicable measures of the institutions on the one hand and the national law of the Member States on the other is such that those provisions and measures not only by their entry into force render automatically inapplicable any conflicting provision of current national law but – in so far as they are an integral part of, and take precedence in, the legal order applicable in the territory of each of the Member States – also preclude the valid adoption of new national legislative measures to the extent to which they would be incompatible with Community provisions.

[18] Indeed any recognition that national legislative measures which encroach upon the field within which the Community exercises its legislative power or which are otherwise incompatible with the provisions of Community law had any legal effect would amount to a corresponding denial of the effectiveness of obligations undertaken unconditionally and irrevocably by Member States pursuant to the Treaty and would thus imperil the very foundations of the Community.

[19] The same conclusion emerges from the structure of Article 177 of the Treaty which provides that any court or tribunal of a Member State is entitled to make a reference to the Court whenever it considers that a preliminary ruling on a question of interpretation or validity relating to Community law is necessary to enable it to give judgment.

[20] The effectiveness of that provision would be impaired if the national court were prevented from forthwith applying Community law in accordance with the decision or the case-law of the Court.

[21] It follows from the foregoing that every national court must, in a case within its jurisdiction, apply Community law in its entirety and protect rights which the latter confers on individuals and must accordingly set aside any provision of national law which may conflict with it, whether prior or subsequent to the Community rule.

[22] Accordingly any provision of a national legal system and any legislative, administrative, or judicial practice which might impair the effectiveness of Community law by withholding from the national court having jurisdiction to apply such law the power to do everything necessary at the moment of its application to set aside national legislative provisions which might prevent Community rules from having full force and effect are incompatible with those requirements which are the very essence of Community law.

[23] This would be the case in the event of a conflict between a provision of Community law and a subsequent national law if the solution of the conflict were to be reserved for an authority with a discretion of its own, other than the court called upon to apply Community law, even if such an impediment to the full effectiveness of Community law were only temporary.

[24] The first question should therefore be answered to the effect that a national court which is called upon, within the limits of its jurisdiction, to apply provisions of Community law is under a duty to give full effect to those provisions, if necessary refusing of its own motion to apply any conflicting provision of national legislation,

even if adopted subsequently, and it is not necessary for the court to request or await the prior setting aside of such provision by legislation or other constitutional means.

The ECJ ruled:

> *A national court which is called upon, within the limits of its jurisdiction, to apply provisions of Community law is under a duty to give full effect to those provisions, if necessary refusing of its own motion to apply any conflicting provisions of national legislation, even if adopted subsequently, and it is not necessary for the court to request or await the prior setting aside of such provisions by legislation or other constitutional means.*

Note

While the ECJ states that any national court may set aside municipal legislation, this does not mean that such legislation is entirely void. It is only of no effect where there is a conflict between it and EC law.

Questions

1. The ECJ has declared that the treaties have created a new legal order. Within this new legal order, what is the hierarchy of ranking amongst EC law, constitutional law and ordinary municipal law?
2. What is the relationship between the ECJ and the national courts in this legal order?

(2) The United Kingdom courts' view

The traditional view of legislative supremacy explored in chapter 2 would appear to conflict with the ECJ's rulings on the supremacy of Community law.

In order for Community law to become part of the UK's domestic law, it had to be incorporated by legislation. This was done by the following provisions.

The European Communities Act 1972

2.—(1) All such rights, powers, liabilities, obligations and restrictions from time to time created or arising by or under the Treaties, and all such remedies and procedures from time to time provided for by or under the Treaties, as in accordance with the Treaties are without further enactment to be given legal effect or used in the United Kingdom shall be recognised and available in law, and be enforced, allowed and followed accordingly; and the expression 'enforceable Community right' and similar expressions shall be read as referring to one to which this subsection applies.

(2) Subject to Schedule 2 of this Act, at any time after its passing Her Majesty may by Order in Council, and any designated Minister or department may by regulations, make provision—

(a) for the purpose of implementing any Community obligation of the United Kingdom, or enabling any such obligation to be implemented, or of enabling any rights enjoyed or to be enjoyed by the United Kingdom under or by virtue of the Treaties to be exercised; or

(b) for the purpose of dealing with matters arising out of or related to any such obligation or rights or the coming into force, or the operation from time to time, of subsection (1) above;

and in the exercise of any statutory power or duty, including any power to give directions or to legislate by means of orders, rules, regulations or other subordinate instrument, the person entrusted with the power or duty may have regard to the objects of the Communities and to any such obligation or rights as aforesaid.

In this subsection 'designated Minister or department' means such Minister of the Crown or government department as may from time to time be designated by Order in Council in relation to any matter or for any purpose, but subject to such restrictions or conditions (if any) as may be specified by the Order in Council.

(4) The provision that may be made under subsection (2) above includes, subject to Schedule 2 to this Act, any such provision (of any such extent) as might be made by Act of Parliament, and any enactment passed or to be passed, other than one contained in this Part of this Act, shall be construed and have effect subject to the foregoing provisions of this section; but, except as may be provided by any Act passed after this Act, Schedule 2 shall have effect in connection with the powers conferred by this and the following sections of this Act to make Orders in Council and regulations.

3.—(1) For the purposes of all legal proceedings any question as to the meaning or effect of any of the Treaties, or as to the validity, meaning or effect of any Community instrument, shall be treated as a question of law (and, if not referred to the European Court, be for determination as such in accordance with the principles laid down by and any relevant decision of the European Court).

(2) Judicial notice shall be taken of the Treaties, of the Official Journal of the Communities and of any decision of, or expression of opinion by, the European Court on any such question as aforesaid; and the Official Journal shall be admissible as evidence of any instrument or other act thereby communicated of any of the Communities or of any Community institution.

Note

Section 2 (1) incorporates *some* EC law into UK law. This EC law is known as directly applicable EC law. Such law comes into effect in the UK without any further legislative action being taken by Parliament.

Section 2 (2) provides for the making of delegated legislation in order to implement EC obligations. Schedule 2 specifies the limitations upon such legislative action, and some of these include the inability to increase taxation, or to introduce retrospective measures, or to create new criminal offences.

Section 2 (4) provides that subsequent legislation is to be construed and to have effect subject to sections 2 (1) and (2). Does this resolve any problems of conflict between EC and UK law subsequent to the passage of the European Communities Act 1972?

The courts have taken time to accustom themselves to Community law. There has been a variety of approaches taken on the issue of the supremacy of Community law. One approach is that of implied repeal which is illustrated by a dictum from Lord Denning MR in *Felixstowe Dock and Railway Co* v *British Transport Docks Board* [1976] CMLR 655. In this case the British Transport Docks Board (the Board) wished to take over the Felixstowe Dock and Railway Company (the Company). Terms were agreed between the parties but the Board, as a statutory body with limited powers, needed parliamentary approval for this action. In an unsuccessful challenge to the agreement by the Company, the ownership of which had changed, it was argued, *inter alia,* that the agreement was contrary to EEC competition law and Art. 86 of the EEC Treaty in particular. Lord Denning MR said, at pp. 644–5:

> It seems to me that once the Bill is passed by Parliament and becomes a Statute that will dispose of all discussion about the Treaty. These courts will have to abide by the Statute without regard to the Treaty at all.

Another approach would give priority to Community law over inconsistent UK law, unless the domestic legislation expressly repudiates Community obligations. This approach can also be illustrated by dicta from Lord Denning MR, on this occasion from *Macarthys* v *Smith* [1979] ICR 785. This case involved a claim of unlawful discrimination on grounds of sex in relation to equal pay. Mrs Smith's contract of employment contained some minor differences from the contract of her male predecessor in the post. She received a smaller weekly wage than her male predecessor. The company's defence was that provisions of the Equal Pay Act 1970, as amended by the Sex Discrimination Act 1975, meant that Mrs Smith was only entitled to compare her pay with that of a male employee engaged in 'like work' at the same time as her. Mrs Smith argued that Art. 119 of the EEC Treaty permitted her to base a claim on a comparison with her male predecessor. In the Court of Appeal Lord Denning MR said, at p. 789:

> In construing our statute, we are entitled to look to the Treaty as an aid to its construction, and even more, not only as an aid but as an overriding force. If on close investigation it should appear that our legislation is deficient – or is inconsistent with Community law – by some oversight of our draftsmen – then it is our bounden duty to give priority to Community law. Such is the result of section 2 (1) and (4) of the European Communities Act 1972.
>
> I pause here, however, to make one observation on a constitutional point. Thus far I have assumed that our Parliament, whenever it passes legislation, intends to fulfil its obligations under the Treaty. If the time should come when our Parliament deliberately passes an Act – with the intention of repudiating the Treaty or any provision in it – or intentionally of acting inconsistently with it – and says so in express terms – then I should have thought that it would be the duty of our courts to follow the statute of our Parliament. I do not however envisage any such situation. As I said in *Blackburn* v *Attorney-General* [1971] WLR 137, 1040: 'But, if Parliament should do so, then I say we will consider that event when it happens.' Unless there is such an intentional and express repudiation of the Treaty, it is our duty to give priority to the Treaty. In the present case I assume that the United Kingdom intended to fulfil its obligations under article 119.

The House of Lords appears to have accepted that membership of the Communities and the European Communities Act 1972 have altered the rules on legislative supremacy where there is inconsistency between Community law and domestic law.

R* v *Secretary of State for Transport, ex parte Factortame Ltd and others
[1990] 2 AC 85
House of Lords

The applicants were companies which owned fishing vessels, the majority of which had first been registered as Spanish before being re-registered as British vessels. The UK government was concerned that the operation of quotas under the Common Fisheries Policy would adversely affect the British fishing industry by the inclusion in the UK quotas of vessels fishing for the Spanish market. Parliament passed the Merchant Shipping Act 1988 and the Merchant Shipping (Registration of Fishing Vessels) Regulations 1988 (SI 1988 No. 1926) which would have the effect of ending the applicants' registration under the Merchant Shipping Act 1894 and precluding them from registration under the new regulations. The applicants claimed that the legislation was contrary to those provisions of EC law which (i) prohibited discrimination on grounds of nationality between member states, (ii) prohibited restrictions on exports between member states, (iii) created a common market in agricultural products, (iv) provided for the freedom of movement of workers and the freedom of establishment of companies, (v) required that nationals of member states are to be treated equally with respect to participation in the capital of companies established in the EC. The Divisional Court decided to seek a preliminary ruling from the ECJ and decided to order as interim relief that, pending the ECJ's preliminary ruling on the compatibility of the UK law with EC law, Part II of the 1988 Act and the 1988 regulations be disapplied, and that the Secretary of State be restrained from applying them in respect of the applicants so as to enable the applicants' vessels to continue to be registered as British. On appeal the Court of Appeal reversed the decision on the granting of interim relief which involved the overriding of the UK legislation. This was appealed to the House of Lords. The relationship between domestic law and Community law was explained in a preliminary passage before dealing with the point about interim relief.

LORD BRIDGE: . . . By virtue of section 2 (4) of the Act of 1972 Part II of the Act of 1988 is to be construed and take effect subject to directly enforceable Community rights and those rights are, by section 2 (1) of the Act of 1972, to be 'recognised and available in law, and . . . enforced, allowed and followed accordingly; . . .' This has precisely the same effect as if a section were incorporated in Part II of the Act of 1988 which in terms enacted that the provisions with respect to registration of British fishing vessels were to be without prejudice to the directly enforceable Community rights of nationals of any member state of the EEC. Thus it is common ground that, in so far as the applicants succeed before the ECJ in obtaining a ruling in support of the Community rights which they claim, those rights will prevail over the restrictions imposed on registration of British fishing vessels by Part II of the Act of 1988 and the Divisional Court will, in the final determination of the application for judicial review, be obliged to make appropriate declarations to give effect to those rights.

Notes

1. Both the Court of Appeal and the House of Lords were of the view that domestic law did not allow, as interim relief, the disapplying of a statute where it had not been established that the statute was in breach of Community law. The House of Lords sought a preliminary ruling on this point from the ECJ which ruled that 'a national court which in a case before it concerning Community law considers itself that the sole obstacle which precludes it from granting interim relief is a rule of national law must set aside that rule' (*R* v *Secretary of State for Transport ex parte Factortame Ltd* [1989] 3 CMLR 1). Subsequently the House of Lords considered the application for interim relief and decided to grant it (*R* v *Secretary of State for Transport ex parte Factortame Ltd (No. 2)* [1991] 1 AC 603). The ECJ ruled on the Divisional Court's questions about the compatibility of the Merchant Shipping Act 1988 with Community law and ruled that Art. 52 had been infringed because of the local national and residence requirements for registration of owners of fishing vessels (*R* v *Secretary of State for Transport ex parte Factortame Ltd (No. 3)* Case C-221/89 [1991] 3 CMLR 589).

Before the ECJ gave its rulings on the questions referred to it by the High Court and House of Lords, the European Commission brought a successful action for interim relief in an action under Art. 169 against the UK, requiring that the nationality requirement of s. 14 of the Merchant Shipping Act 1988 be suspended (*Re Nationality of Fishermen: EC Commission* v *UK* Case C-248/89R [1989] 3 CMLR 601). This was implemented by the Merchant Shipping Act (Amendment) Order 1989 (SI 1989 No. 2006). Finally the ECJ upheld the Commission's challenge under Art. 169 that the nationality requirements breached Arts 7, 52 and 221 of the EEC Treaty (*Re Nationality of Fishermen: EC Commission* v *UK* Case C-248/89 [1991] 3 CMLR 706).

2. See also *R* v *Secretary of State for Employment, ex parte Equal Opportunities Commission* [1994] 2 WLR 409, at p. 399 *post*.

Questions

1. Does the experience of UK membership of the EC support Bradley's suggestion in his essay 'The Sovereignty of Parliament – in Perpetuity?', in Jowell and Oliver *The Changing Constitution* (3rd edn, 1994), that the orthodox doctrine of the supremacy of Parliament is not an immutable part of British constitutional law?

2. If the doctrine of the supremacy of Parliament can no longer be regarded as an immutable part of British constitutional law, is it possible to argue that Parliament could find a method of entrenching a Bill of Rights against subsequent amendment? Do the cases discussed in this section suggest a method or methods which could be used for this purpose?

(ii) Direct effect and directives

(1) Early development

In *Van Gend en Loos* (*ante* p. 132), the ECJ ruled that Community law can confer rights upon individuals which national courts must protect. Thus Community law may have a direct effect in member states' domestic law. In that case it was held that Art. 12 of the Treaty of Rome had direct effect. Could a directive do this? A directive sets an objective which member states are to implement, and in doing this they have a certain degree of discretion. The test for direct effect in *Van Gend en Loos* focused upon the unconditional nature of the prohibition in Art. 12.

Van Duyn v _Home Office_ Case 41/47
[1974] ECR 1337
European Court of Justice

Van Duyn, a Dutch woman, wished to take up employment with the Church of Scientology in the UK but was refused leave to enter by the Home Office. She sought to show that she could benefit from Community law on the freedom of movement of workers, particularly Art. 48 and Directive 64/221/EEC. The Home Office contended that the public policy exemption to the freedom of movement of workers applied here as they claimed that the Church was socially undesirable. The High Court made an Art. 177 reference, and one of the questions asked of the ECJ concerned the direct effect of directives.

[9] The second question asks the Court to say whether Council Directive No. 64/221 of 25 February 1984 on the coordination of special measures concerning the movement and residence of foreign nationals which are justified on grounds of public policy, public security or public health is directly applicable so as to confer on individuals rights enforceable by them in the courts of a Member State.

[10] It emerges from the order making the reference that the only provision of the Directive which is relevant is that contained in Article 3 (1) which provides that 'measures taken on grounds of public policy or public security shall be based exclusively on the personal conduct of the individual concerned.'

[11] The United Kingdom observes that, since Article 189 of the Treaty distinguishes between the effect ascribed to regulations, directives and decisions, it must therefore be presumed that the Council, in issuing a directive rather than making a regulation, must have intended that the directive should have an effect other than that of a regulation and accordingly that the former should not be directly applicable.

[12] If, however, by virtue of the provisions of Article 189 regulations are directly applicable and, consequently, may by their very nature have direct effects, it does not follow from this that other categories of acts mentioned in that Article can never have similar effects. It would be incompatible with the binding effect attributed to a directive by Article 189 to exclude, in principle, the possibility that the obligation which it imposes may be invoked by those concerned. In particular, where the Community authorities have, by directive, imposed on Member States the obligation

to pursue a particular course of conduct, the useful effect of such an act would be weakened if individuals were prevented from relying on it before their national courts and if the later were prevented from taking it into consideration as an element of Community law. Article 177, which empowers national courts to refer to the Court questions concerning the validity and interpretation of all acts of the Community institutions, without distinction, implies furthermore that these acts may be invoked by individuals in the national courts. It is necessary to examine, in every case, whether the nature, general scheme and wording of the provision in question are capable of having direct effects on the relations between Member States and individuals.

[13] By providing that measures taken on grounds of public policy shall be based exclusively on the personal conduct of the individual concerned, Article 3 (1) of Directive No. 64/221 is intended to limit the discretionary power which national laws generally confer on the authorities responsible for the entry and expulsion of foreign nationals. First, the provision lays down an obligation which is not subject to any exception or condition and which, by its very nature, does not require the intervention of any act on the part either of the institutions of the Community or of Member States. Secondly, because Member States are thereby obliged, in implementing a clause which derogates from one of the fundamental principles of the Treaty in favour of individuals, not to take account of factors extraneous to personal conduct, legal certainty for the persons concerned requires that they should be able to rely on this obligation even though it has been laid down in a legislative act which has no automatic direct effect in its entirety.

[14] If the meaning and exact scope of the provision raise questions of interpretation, these questions can be resolved by the courts, taking into account also the procedure under Article 177 of the Treaty.

[15] Accordingly, in reply to the second question, Article 3 (1) of Council Directive No. 64/221 of 25 February 1964 confers on individuals rights which are enforceable by them in the courts of a Member State and which the national courts must protect.

Note

In para. 12 the ECJ partially bases the direct effect of a directive on the weakening of the useful effect of the measure if individuals could not rely upon it in their national courts.

Compare the requirement of unconditionality in *Van Gend en Loos* with the treatment of the member state's discretion in implementing the directive in para. 13.

***Pubblico Ministerio* v *Ratti* Case 148/78**
[1979] ECR 1629
European Court of Justice

Ratti was charged with breaching certain Italian provisions although he had acted in conformity with Community law measures. These measures were directives made by the Council on the approximation of laws relating to the classification, packaging and labelling of (a) solvents (No. 73/173/EEC), and (b) paints, varnishes, printing inks, adhesives and similar products (No. 77/728/EEC). The period within which Directive 73/173/EEC should have been implemented had expired. If it had been implemented then the relevant Italian provisions should have been repealed. The period for the implementation of Directive 77/728/EEC had not yet expired. When implemented it would also have the effect of repealing the relevant Italian provisions. The *Pretura Penale* made an Art. 177 reference.

[18] This question raises the general problem of the legal nature of the provisions of a directive adopted under Article 189 of the Treaty.

[19] In this regard the settled case-law of the Court, last reaffirmed by the judgment of 1 February 1977 in Case 51/76 *Nederlandse Ondernemingen* [1977] 1 ECR 126, lays down that, whilst under Article 189 regulations are directly applicable and consequently, by their nature capable of producing direct effects, that does not mean that other categories of acts covered by that article can never produce similar effects.

[20] It would be incompatible with the binding effect which Article 189 ascribes to directives to exclude on principle the possibility of the obligations imposed by them being relied on by persons concerned.

[21] Particularly in cases in which the Community authorities have, by means of directive, placed Member States under a duty to adopt a certain course of action, the effectiveness of such an act would be weakened if persons were prevented from relying on it in legal proceedings and national courts prevented from taking it into consideration as an element of Community law.

[22] Consequently a Member State which has not adopted the implementing measures required by the directive in the prescribed periods may not rely, as against individuals, on its own failure to perform the obligation which the directive entails.

[23] It follows that a national court requested by a person who has complied with the provisions of a directive not to apply a national provision incompatible with the directive not incorporated into the internal legal order of a defaulting Member State, must uphold that request if the obligation in question is unconditional and sufficiently precise.

[24] Therefore the answer to the first question must be that after the expiration of the period fixed for the implementation of a directive a Member State may not apply its internal law – even if it is provided with penal sanctions – which has not yet been adapted in compliance with the directive, to a person who has complied with the requirements of the directive. . . .

[39] In a fifth question the national court asks whether Council Directive No. 77/728 of 7 November 1977, in particular Article 9 thereof, is immediately and directly applicable with regard to the obligations imposed on Member States to refrain from action as from the date of notification of that directive in a case where a person, acting upon a legitimate expectation, has complied with the provisions of that directive before the expiry of the period within which the Member State must comply with the said directive.

[40] The objective of that directive is analogous to that of Directive No. 73/173 in that it lays down similar rules for preparations intended to be used as paints, varnishes, printing inks, adhesives and similar products, and containing dangerous substances.

[41] Article 12 of that directive provides that Member States must implement it within 24 months of its notification, which took place on 9 November 1977.

[42] That period has not yet expired and the States to which the directive was addressed have until 9 November 1979 to incorporate the provisions of Directive No. 77/728 into their internal legal orders.

[43] It follows that, for the reasons expounded in the grounds of the answer to the national court's first question, it is only at the end of the prescribed period and in the event of the Member State's default that the directive – and in particular Article 9 thereof – will be able to have the effects described in the answer to the first question.

Note
If directives are to have direct effect they must be precise and unconditional and the period for their implementation must have expired.

Question
How does the ECJ justify holding that directives may have direct effect given the wording of Art. 189 (*ante* p. 115)?

(2) *Horizontal and vertical effect*

***Marshall* v *Southampton and South West Hampshire Area Health Authority (Teaching)* Case 152/84**
[1986] ECR 723
European Court of Justice

Marshall was dismissed by her employer when she reached the age of 62. She claimed that this was discrimination on grounds of sex as a male employee would not have been forced to retire at this age. Under the Sex Discrimination Act 1975 matters relating to retirement were excluded from the scope of sex discrimination. It was argued that the Equal Treatment Directive 76/207/EEC gave her a remedy for this situation; however, this directive had not been implemented in the UK although the period for implementation had expired. The Court of Appeal made an Art. 177 reference. The ECJ first found that this situation constituted sex discrimination.

[39] Since the first question has been answered in the affirmative, it is necessary to consider whether Article 5 (1) of Directive No. 76/207 may be relied upon by an individual before national courts and tribunals.

[40] The appellant and the Commission consider that the question must be answered in the affirmative. They contend in particular, with regard to Articles 2 (1) and 5 (1) of Directive No. 76/207, that those provisions are sufficiently clear to enable national courts to apply them without legislative intervention by the Member States, at least so far as overt discrimination is concerned.

[41] In support of that view, the appellant points out that directives are capable of conferring rights on individuals which may be relied upon directly before the courts of the Member States; national courts are obliged by virtue of the binding nature of a directive, in conjunction with Article 5 of the EEC Treaty, to give effect to the provisions of directives where possible, in particular when construing or applying

relevant provisions of national law (judgment of 10 April 1984 in Case 14/83 *von Colson and Kamann* v *Land Nordrhein-Westfalen* [1984] ECR 1891). Where there is any inconsistency between national law and Community law which cannot be removed by means of such a construction, the appellant submits that a national court is obliged to declare that the provision of national law which is inconsistent with the directive is inapplicable.

[42] The Commission is of the opinion that the provisions of Article 5 (1) of Directive No. 76/207 are sufficiently clear and unconditional to be relied upon before a national court. They may therefore be set up against section 6 (4) of the Sex Discrimination Act, which, according to the decisions of the Court of Appeal, has been extended to the question of compulsory retirement and has therefore become ineffective to prevent dismissals based upon the difference in retirement ages for men and for women.

[43] The respondent and the United Kingdom propose, conversely, that the second question should be answered in the negative. They admit that a directive may, in certain specific circumstances, have direct effect as against a Member State in so far as the latter may not rely on its failure to perform its obligations under the directive. However, they maintain that a directive can never impose obligations directly on individuals and that it can only have direct effect against a Member State *qua* public authority and not against a Member State *qua* employer. As an employer a State is no different from a private employer. It would not therefore be proper to put persons employed by the State in a better position than those who are employed by a private employer.

[44] With regard to the legal position of the respondent's employees the United Kingdom states that they are in the same position as the employees of a private employer. Although according to United Kingdom constitutional law the health authorities, created by the National Health Service Act 1977, as amended by the Health Services Act 1980 and other legislation, are Crown bodies and their employees are Crown servants, nevertheless the administration of the National Health Service by the health authorities is regarded as being separate from the Government's central administration and its employees are not regarded as civil servants.

[45] Finally, both the respondent and the United Kingdom take the view that the provisions of Directive No. 76/207 are neither unconditional nor sufficiently clear and precise to give rise to direct effect. The directive provides for a number of possible exceptions, the details of which are to be laid down by the Member States. Furthermore, the wording of Article 5 is quite imprecise and requires the adoption of measures for its implementation.

[46] It is necessary to recall that, according to a long line of decisions of the Court (in particular its judgment of 19 January 1982 in Case 8/81 *Becker* v *Finanzamt Münster-Innenstadt* [1982] ECR 53), wherever the provisions of a directive appear, as far as their subject-matter is concerned, to be unconditional and sufficiently precise, those provisions may be relied upon by an individual against the State where that State fails to implement the directive in national law by the end of the period prescribed or where it fails to implement the directive correctly.

[47] That view is based on the consideration that it would be incompatible with the binding nature which Article 189 confers on the directive to hold as a matter of principle that the obligation imposed thereby cannot be relied on by those concerned.

From that the Court deduced that a Member State which has not adopted the implementing measures required by the directive within the prescribed period may not plead, as against individuals, its own failure to perform the obligations which the directive entails.

[48] With regard to the argument that a directive may not be relied upon against an individual, it must be emphasized that according to Article 189 of the EEC Treaty the binding nature of a directive, which constitutes the basis for the possibility of relying on the directive before a national court, exists only in relation to 'each Member State to which it is addressed'. It follows that a directive may not of itself impose obligations on an individual and that a provision of a directive may not be relied upon as such against such a person. It must therefore be examined whether, in this case, the respondent must be regarded as having acted as an individual.

[49] In that respect it must be pointed out that where a person involved in legal proceedings is able to rely on a directive as against the State he may do so regardless of the capacity in which the latter is acting, whether employer or public authority. In either case it is necessary to prevent the State from taking advantage of its own failure to comply with Community law.

[50] It is for the national court to apply those considerations to the circumstances of each case; the Court of Appeal has, however, stated in the order for reference that the respondent, Southampton and South West Hampshire Area Health Authority (Teaching), is a public authority.

[51] The argument submitted by the United Kingdom that the possibility of relying on provisions of the directive against the respondent *qua* organ of the State would give rise to an arbitrary and unfair distinction between the rights of State employees and those of private employees does not justify any other conclusion. Such a distinction may easily be avoided if the Member State concerned has correctly implemented the directive in national law.

[52] Finally, with regard to the question whether the provision contained in Article 5 (1) of Directive No. 76/207, which implements the principle of equality of treatment set out in Article 2 (1) of the directive, may be considered, as far as its contents are concerned, to be unconditional and sufficiently precise to be relied upon by an individual as against the State, it must be stated that the provision, taken by itself, prohibits any discrimination on grounds of sex with regard to working conditions, including the conditions governing dismissal, in a general manner and in unequivocal terms. The provision is therefore sufficiently precise to be relied on by an individual and to be applied by the national courts.

[53] It is necessary to consider next whether the prohibition of discrimination laid down by the directive may be regarded as unconditional, in the light of the exceptions contained therein and of the fact that according to Article 5 (2) thereof the Member States are to take the measures necessary to ensure the application of the principle of equality of treatment in the context of national law.

[54] With regard, in the first place, to the reservation contained in Article 1 (2) of Directive No. 76/207 concerning the application of the principle of equality of treatment in matters of social security, it must be observed that, although the reservation limits the scope of the directive *ratione materiae*, it does not lay down any condition on the application of that principle in its field of operation and in particular

in relation to Article 5 of the directive. Similarly, the exceptions to Directive No. 76/207 provided for in Article 2 thereof are not relevant to this case.

[55] It follows that Article 5 of Directive No. 76/207 does not confer on the Member States the right to limit the application of the principle of equality of treatment in its field of operation or to subjct it to conditions and that that provision is sufficiently precise and unconditional to be capable of being relied upon by an individual before a national court in order to avoid the application of any national provision which does not conform to Article 5 (1).

[56] Consequently, the answer to the second question must be that Article 5 (1) of Council Directive No. 76/207 of 9 February 1976, which prohibits any discrimination on grounds of sex with regard to working conditions, including the conditions governing dismissal, may be relied upon against a State authority acting in its capacity as employer, in order to avoid the application of any national provision which does not conform to Article 5 (1).

Notes

1. The ECJ has limited the direct effect of directives to vertical effect, i.e. where an individual is seeking enforcement of rights against a state body. Enforcement of rights against another private individual, or horizontal effect, is not possible where a directive is the source of the rights.

2. It has been suggested that a reason for the ECJ changing the basis for giving direct effect to directives from 'useful effect' (*Van Gend en Loos*) to estoppel (*Ratti* and *Marshall*) was that it restricted the operation of direct effect, and this might lessen the opposition of national courts to the impact of Community law upon the legal systems of member states.

(3) The scope of vertical effect

In order to benefit from vertical effect of directives an individual must be seeking enforcement against a state body. Guidance on what constitutes the state was given in the following case.

***Foster* v *British Gas* Case C-188/89**
[1990] ECR I-3313
European Court of Justice

The applicant had been made to retire earlier than her male colleagues. She wished to rely upon the Equal Treatment Directive No. 76/207/EEC. The employer was the British Gas Corporation (BGC). The BGC was a statutory corporation and under the Gas Act 1972 it was responsible for developing and maintaining a system of gas supply in Great Britain and had a monopoly of the supply of gas. The Secretary of State appointed the members of the BGC and could issue directions on matters affecting the national interest. The BGC was required to submit reports to the Secretary of State and to run a balanced budget over two successive financial years. The House of Lords made an Art. 177 reference.

[13] Before considering the question referred by the House of Lords, it must first be observed as a preliminary point that the United Kingdom has submitted that it is not a matter for the Court of Justice but for the national courts to determine, in the context of the national legal system, whether the provisions of a directive may be relied upon against a body such as the BGC.

[14] The question what effects measures adopted by Community institutions have and in particular whether those measures may be relied on against certain categories of persons necessarily involves interpretation of the articles of the Treaty concerning measures adopted by the institutions and the Community measure in issue.

[15] It follows that the Court of Justice has jurisdiction in proceedings for a preliminary ruling to determine the categories of persons against whom the provisions of a directive may be relied on. It is for the national courts, on the other hand, to decide whether a party to proceeding before them falls within one of the categories so defined.

Reliance on the provisions of the directive against a body such as the BGC

[16] As the Court has consistently held (see the judgment in Case 8/81 *Becker* v *Finanzamt Münster-Innenstadt* [1982] ECR 53, paragraphs 23 to 25), where the Community authorities have, by means of a directive, placed Member States under a duty to adopt a certain course of action, the effectiveness of such a measure would be diminished if persons were prevented from relying upon it in proceedings before a court and national courts were prevented from taking it into consideration as an element of Community law. Consequently, a Member State which has not adopted the implementing measures required by the directive within the prescribed period may not plead, as against individuals, its own failure to perform the obligations which the directive entails. Thus, wherever the provisions of a directive appear, as far as their subject-matter is concerned, to be unconditional and sufficiently precise, those provisions may, in the absence of implementing measures adopted within the prescribed period, be relied upon as against any national provision which is incompatible with the directive or in so far as the provisions define rights which individuals are able to assert against the State.

[17] The Court further held in its judgment in Case 152/84 *Marshall*, paragraph 49, that where a person is able to rely on a directive as against the State he may do so regardless of the capacity in which the latter is acting, whether as employer or as public authority. In either case it is necessary to prevent the State from taking advantage of its own failure to comply with Community law.

[18] On the basis of those considerations, the Court has held in a series of cases that unconditional and sufficiently precise provisions of a directive could be relied on against organizations or bodies which were subject to the authority or control of the State or had special powers beyond those which result from the normal rules applicable to relations between individuals.

[19] The Court has accordingly held that provisions of a directive could be relied on against tax authorities (the judgments in Case 8/81 *Becker*, cited above, and in Case C-221/88 *ECSC* v *Acciaierie e Ferriere Busseni (in liquidation)* [1990] ECR I-495), local or regional authorities (judgment in Case 103/88 *Fratelli Costanzo* v *Comune di Milano* [1989] ECR 1839), constitutionally independent authorities responsible for the maintenance of public order and safety (judgment in Case 222/84 *Johnston* v *Chief Constable of the Royal Ulster Constabulary* [1986] ECR 1651), and public authorities providing public health services (judgment in Case 152/84 *Marshall*, cited above).

[20] It follows from the foregoing that a body, whatever its legal form, which has been made responsible, pursuant to a measure adopted by the State, for providing a public service under the control of the State and has for that purpose special powers beyond those which result from the normal rules applicable in relations between individuals is included in any event among the bodies against which the provisions of a directive capable of having direct effect may be relied upon.

[21] With regard to Article 5 (1) of Directive 76/207 it should be observed that in the judgment in Case 152/84 *Marshall*, cited above, paragraph 52, the Court held that that provision was unconditional and sufficiently precise to be relied on by an individual and to be applied by the national courts.

[22] The answer to the question referred by the House of Lords must therefore be that Article 5 (1) of Council Directive 76/207 of 9 February 1976 may be relied upon in a claim for damages against a body, whatever its legal form, which has been made responsible, pursuant to a measure adopted by the State, for providing a public service under the control of the State and has for that purpose special powers beyond those which result from the normal rules applicable in relations between individuals.

Note
In Case 103/88 *Fratelli Constanzo* v *Comune di Milano* [1989] ECR 1839 the ECJ held that the state included local authorities.

Question
Was the Court of Appeal wrong in *Doughty* v *Rolls Royce* [1992] 1 CMLR 1045 in holding that ownership by the State of an organisation was insufficient for vertical direct effect?

(4) Indirect effect

It does seem unfair that direct effect of directives depends upon whether one is in conflict with a state body. A possible method of circumventing the vertical/horizontal distinction has been claimed as a result of the reasoning in the next case.

Von Colson and Kamann **v** ***Land Nordrhein-Westfalen*** **Case 14/83**
[1984] ECR 1891
European Court of Justice

The applicants had been rejected for jobs on the grounds of sex. The Hamm *arbeitsgericht* held that there had been discrimination on grounds of sex but that the only remedy available under German law was the reimbursement of their travel expenses. Von Colson argued that this was contrary to Art. 6 of the Equal Treatment Directive 76/207/EEC. Under this directive member states are to introduce into their legal systems measures to enable victims of sex discrimination to pursue their claims by judicial process. Measures could include requiring employers to offer victims posts, or to receive adequate compensation. The directive left it to the discretion of member states to choose the remedy which met the objectives of the directive. An Art. 177 reference was made.

[22] It is impossible to establish real equality of opportunity without an appropriate system of sanctions. That follows not only from the actual purpose of the directive but more specifically from Article 6 thereof which, by granting applicants for a post who have been discriminated against recourse to the courts, acknowledges that those candidates have rights of which they may avail themselves before the courts.

[23] Although, as has been stated in the reply to Question 1, full implementation of the directive does not require any specific form of sanction for unlawful discrimination, it does entail that that sanction be such as to guarantee real and effective judicial protection. Moreover it must also have a real deterrent effect on the employer. It follows that where a Member State chooses to penalize the breach of the prohibition of discrimination by the award of compensation, that compensation must in any event be adequate in relation to the damage sustained.

[24] In consequence it appears that national provisions limiting the right to compensation of persons who have been discriminated against as regards access to employment to a purely nominal amount, such as, for example, the reimbursement of expenses incurred by them in submitting their application, would not satisfy the requirements of an effective transposition of the directive.

[25] The nature of the sanctions provided for in the Federal Republic of Germany in respect of discrimination regarding access to employment and in particular the question whether the rule in Paragraph 611a (2) of the Bürgerliches Gesetzbuch excludes the possibility of compensation on the basis of the general rules of law were the subject of lengthy discussion before the Court. The German Government maintained in the oral procedure that that provision did not necessarily exclude the application of the general rules of law regarding compensation. It is for the national court alone to rule on that question concerning the interpretation of its national law.

[26] However, the Member States' obligation arising from a directive to achieve the result envisaged by the directive and their duty under Article 5 of the Treaty to take all appropriate measures, whether general or particular, to ensure the fulfilment of that obligation, is binding on all the authorities of Member States including, for matters within their jurisdiction, the courts. It follows that, in applying the national law and in particular the provisions of a national law specifically introduced in order to implement Directive No. 76/207, national courts are required to interpret their national law in the light of the wording and the purpose of the directive in order to achieve the result referred to in the third paragraph of Article 189.

[27] On the other hand, as the above considerations show, the directive does not include any unconditional and sufficiently precise obligation as regards sanctions for discrimination which, in the absence of implementing measures adopted in good time may be relied on by individuals in order to obtain specific compensation under the directive, where that is not provided for or permitted under national law.

[28] It should, however, be pointed out to the national court that although Directive No. 76/207/EEC, for the purpose of imposing a sanction for the breach of the prohibition of discrimination, leaves the Member States free to choose between the different solutions suitable for achieving its objective, it nevertheless requires that if a Member States chooses to penalize breaches of that prohibition by the award of compensation, then in order to ensure that it is effective and that it has a deterrent effect, that compensation must in any event be adequate in relation to the damage sustained and must therefore amount to more than purely nominal compensation such

as, for example, the reimbursement only of the expenses incurred in connection with the application. It is for the national court to interpret and apply the legislation adopted for the implementation of the directive in conformity with the requirements of Community law, in so far as it is given discretion to do so under national law.

The Court ruled, in answer to the questions referred:

(1) Directive No. 76/207/EEC does not require discrimination on grounds of sex regarding access to employment to be made the subject of a sanction by way of an obligation imposed on the employer who is the author of the discrimination to conclude a contract of employment with the candidate discriminated against.

(2) As regards sanctions for any discrimination which may occur, the directive does not include any unconditional and sufficiently precise obligation which, in the absence of implementing measures adopted within the prescribed time-limits, may be relied on by an individual in order to obtain specific compensation under the directive, where that is not provided for or permitted under national law.

(3) Although Directive No. 76/207/EEC, for the purpose of imposing a sanction for the breach of the prohibition of discrimination, leaves the member states free to choose between the different solutions suitable for achieving its objective, it nevertheless requires that if a member state chooses to penalise breaches of that prohibition by the award of compensation, then in order to ensure that it is effective and that it has a deterrent effect, that compensation must in any event be adequate in relation to the damage sustained and must therefore amount to more than purely nominal compensation such as, for example, the reimbursement only of the expenses incurred in connection with the application. It is for the national court to interpret and apply the legislation adopted for the implementation of the directive in conformity with the requirements of Community law, in so far as it is given discretion to do so under national law.

Note

This approach is quite different from that used for direct effect. Using Art. 5 (see *ante* p. 97), the ECJ states that national courts must fulfil Community law obligations.

The ECJ has not settled the boundaries of this doctrine of 'indirect effect'. Compare the following two cases.

Marleasing SA v _La Commercial Internacional de Alimentacion SA_
Case C-106/89
[1990] ECR I-4135
European Court of Justice

Marleasing wished to have the company, La Commercial, declared a nullity on the basis of Spanish law. Article 11 of Directive 68/151/EEC lists the exclusive grounds on which nullity may be ordered, and this did not include the ground sought by Marleasing. This directive had not been implemented by Spain and the deadline had expired. The *Juzgado de Primera Instancia e Instrucción* made an Art. 177 reference on the status of the directive.

[6] With regard to the question whether an individual may rely on the directive against a national law, it should be observed that, as the Court has consistently held, a directive may not of itself impose obligations on an individual and, consequently, a provision of a directive may not be relied upon as such against such a person (judgment in Case 152/84 *Marshall* v *Southampton and South-West Hampshire Health Authority* [1986] ECR 723).

[7] However, it is apparent from the documents before the Court that the national court seeks in substance to ascertain whether a national court hearing a case which falls within the scope of Directive 68/151 is required to interpret it's national law in the light of the wording and the purpose of that directive in order to preclude a declaration of nullity of a public limited company on a ground other than those listed in Article 11 of the directive.

[8] In order to reply to that queseion, it should be observed that, as the Court pointed out in its judgment in Case 14/83 *Von Colson and Kamann* v *Land Nordrhein-Westfalen* [1984] ECR 1891, paragraph 26, the Member States' obligation arising from a directive to achieve the result envisaged by the directive and their duty under Article 5 of the Treaty to take all appropriate measures, whether general or particular, to ensure the fulfilment of that obligation, is binding on all the authorities of Member States including, for matters within their jurisdiction, the courts. It follows that, in applying national law, whether the provisions in question were adopted before or after the directive, the national court called upon to interpret it is required to do so, as far as possible, in the light of the wording and the purpose of the directive in order to achieve the result pursued by the latter and thereby comply with the third paragraph of Article 189 of the Treaty.

[9] It follows that the requirement that national law must be interpreted in conformity with Article 11 of Directive 68/151 precludes the interpretation of provisions of national law relating to public limited companies in such a manner that the nullity of a public limited company may be ordered on grounds other than those exhaustively listed in Article 11 of the directive in question.

[10] With regard to the interpretation to be given to Article 11 of the directive, in particular Article 11 (2) (b), it should be observed that that provision prohibits the laws of the Member States from providing for a judicial declaration of nullity on grounds other than those exhaustively listed in the directive, amongst which is the ground that the objects of the company are unlawful or contrary to public policy.

[11] According to the Commission, the expression 'objects of the company' must be interpreted as referring exclusively to the objects of the company as described in the instrument of incorporation or the articles of association. It follows, in the Commission's view, that a declaration of nullity of a company cannot be made on the basis of the activity actually pursued by it, for instance defrauding the founders' creditors.

[12] That argument must be upheld. As is clear from the preamble to Directive 69/151, its purpose was to limit the cases in which nullity can arise and the retroactive effect of a declaration of nullity in order to ensure 'certainty in the law as regards

relations between the company and third parties, and also between members' (sixth recital). Furthermore, the protection of third parties 'must be ensured by provisions which restrict to the greatest possible extent the grounds on which obligations entered into in the name of the company are not valid'. It follows, therefore, that each ground of nullity provided for in Article 11 of the directive must be interpreted strictly. In those circumstances the words 'objects of the company' must be understood as referring to the objects of the company as described in the instrument of incorporation or the articles of association.

[13] The answer to the question submitted must therefore be that a national court hearing a case which falls within the scope of Directive 68/151 is required to interpret its national law in the light of the wording and the purpose of that directive in order to preclude a declaration of nullity of a public limited company on a ground other than those listed in Article 11 of the directive.

***Officier van Justitie* v *Kolpinghuis Nijmegen* Case 80/86**
[1987] ECR 3969
European Court of Justice

A cafe owner was prosecuted for stocking for sale and delivery mineral water which was, in fact, tap water with added carbon dioxide. As part of the prosecution's case reliance was placed on Directive 80/777/EEC, which, at the time of the alleged offence, had not been incorporated into Dutch law even though the implementation deadline had expired. The *Arrondismentsrechtbank* made an Art. 177 reference.

[6] The first two questions concern the possibility whether the provisions of a directive which has not yet been implemented in national law in the Member State in question may be applied as such.

[7] In this regard it should be recalled that, according to the established case-law of the Court (in particular its judgment of 19 January 1982 in Case 8/81 *Becker* v *Finanzamt Münster-Innenstadt* [1982] ECR 53), wherever the provisions of a directive appear, as far as their subject-matter is concerned, to be unconditional and sufficiently precise, those provisions may be relied upon by an individual against the State where that State fails to implement the directive in national law by the end of the period prescribed or where it fails to implement the directive correctly.

[8] That view is based on the consideration that it would be incompatible with the binding nature which Article 189 confers on the directive to hold as a matter of principle that the obligaton imposed thereby cannot be relied on by those concerned. From that the Court deduced that a Member State which has not adopted the implementing measures required by the directive within the prescribed period may not plead, as against individuals, its own failure to perform the obligations which the directive entails.

[9] In its judgment of 26 February 1986 in Case 152/84 *Marshall* v *Southampton and South-West Hampshire Area Health Authority* [1986] ECR 723, the Court emphasized, however, that according to Article 189 of the EEC Treaty the binding nature of a directive, which constitutes the basis for the possibility of relying on the directive before a national court, exists only in relation to 'each Member State to which it is addressed'. It follows that a directive may not of itself impose obligations on an

individual and that a provision of a directive may not be relied upon as such against such a person before a national court.

[10] The answer to the first two questions should therefore be that a national authority may not rely, as against an individual, upon a provision of a directive whose necessary implementation in national law has not yet taken place.

The third question

[11] The third question is designed to ascertain how far the national court may or must take account of a directive as an aid to the interpretation of a rule of national law.

[12] As the Court stated in its judgment of 10 April 1984 in Case 14/83 *Von Colson and Kamann* v *Land Nordrhein-Westfalen* [1984] ECR 1891, the Member States' obligation arising from a directive to achieve the result envisaged by the directive and their duty under Article 5 of the Treaty to take all appropriate measures, whether general or particular, to ensure the fulfilment of that obligation, is binding on all the authorities of Member States including, for matters within their jurisdiction, the courts. It follows that, in applying the national law and in particular the provisions of a national law specifically introduced in order to implement the directive, national courts are required to interpet their national law in the light of the wording and the purpose of the directive in order to achieve the result referred to in the third paragraph of Article 189 of the Treaty.

[13] However, that obligation on the national court to refer to the content of the directive when interpreting the relevant rules of its national law is limited by the general principles of law which form part of Community law and in particular the principles of legal certainty and non-retroactivity. Thus the Court rules in its judgment of 11 June 1987 in Case 14/86 *Pretore di Salò* v *X* [1987] ECR 2545 that a directive cannot, of itself and independently of a national law adopted by a Member State for its implementation, have the effect of determining or aggravating the liability in criminal law of persons who act in contravention of the provisions of that directive.

[14] The answer to the third question should therefore be that in applying its national legislation a court of a Member State is required to interpret that legislation in the light of the wording and the purpose of the directive in order to achieve the result referred to in the third paragraph of Article 189 of the Treaty, but a directive cannot, of itself and independently of a law adopted for its implementation, have the effect of determining or aggravating the liability in criminal law of persons who act in contravention of the provisions of that directive.

The fourth question

[15] The question whether the provisions of a directive may be relied upon as such before a national court arises only if the Member State concerned has not implemented the directive in national law within the prescribed period or has implemented the directive incorrectly. The first two questions were answered in the negative. However, it makes no difference to those answers if on the material date the period which the Member State had in which to adopt national law had not yet expired. As regards the third question concerning the limits which Community law might impose on the obligation or power of the national court to interpret the rules of its national law in the light of the directive, it makes no difference whether or not the period prescribed for implementation has expired.

[16] The answer to the fourth question must therefore be that it makes no difference to the answers set out above if on the material date the period which the Member State had in which to adapt national law had not yet expired.

Note

Marleasing seems to be very wide, covering national law made both before and after the directive (para. 8). Should it, like *Kolpinghuis Nijmegen*, be understood as subject to the general principles of Community law, including, for example, legal certainty and non-retroactivity?

(5) Damages for failure to implement a directive

***Francovich* v *Italian Republic* Joined Cases C–6/90 and C–9/90**
[1991] ECR I–5357
European Court of Justice

Directive 80/987 was intended to guarantee employees a minimum level of protection under Community law in the event of the insolvency of their employer. Italy had not implemented the Directive before the period for doing so had expired. Employees who had not been paid by reason of their employers' insolvency sought the Directive's guarantee directly from the Italian state or, in the alternative, compensation. On Art. 177 references the ECJ was asked if an individual who had been adversely affected by a member state's failure to implement Directive 80/987 could directly invoke the legislation against that member state to obtain the guarantees which the state should have provided. The ECJ held on the first part of the question that, even though the Directive's provisions relating to the content of the guarantee were sufficiently unconditional and precise, the Directive did not identify the person liable to provide the guarantee and the state could not be considered liable to pay those guarantees solely on the ground that it had failed to implement the directive. On the second part of the question:

Liability of the State for loss and damage resulting from breach of its obligations under Community law

[28] In the second part of the first question the national court seeks to determine whether a Member State is obliged to make good loss and damage suffered by individuals as a result of the failure to transpose Directive 80/987.

[29] The national court thus raises the issue of the existence and scope of a State's liability for loss and damage resulting from breach of its obligations under Community law.

[30] That issue must be considered in the light of the general system of the Treaty and its fundamental principles.

(a) The existence of State liability as a matter of principle

[31] It should be borne in mind at the outset that the EEC Treaty has created its own legal system, which is integrated into the legal systems of the Member States and which their courts are bound to apply. The subjects of that legal system are not only the Member States but also their nationals. Just as it imposes burdens on individuals, Community law is also intended to give rise to rights which become part of their legal

patrimony. Those rights arise not only where they are expressly granted by the Treaty but also by virtue of obligations which the Treaty imposes in a clearly defined manner both on individuals and on the Member States and the Community institutions (see the judgments in Case 26/62 *Van Gend en Loos* [1963] ECR 1 and Case 6/64 *Costa* v *ENEL* [1964] ECR 585).

[32] Furthermore, it has been consistently held that the national courts whose task it is to apply the provisions of Community law in areas within their jurisdiction must ensure that those rules take full effect and must protect the rights which they confer on individuals (see in particular the judgments in Case 106/77 *Amministrazione delle Finanze dello Stato* v *Simmenthal* [1978] ECR 629, paragraph 16, and Case C–213/89 *Factortame* [1990] ECR I–2433, paragraph 19.

[33] The full effectiveness of Community rules would be impaired and the protection of the rights which they grant would be weakened if individuals were unable to obtain redress when their rights are infringed by a breach of Community law for which a Member State can be held responsible.

[34] The possibility of obtaining redress from the Member State is particularly indispensable where, as in this case, the full effectiveness of Community rules is subject to prior action on the part of the State and where, consequently, in the absence of such action, individuals cannot enforce before the national courts the rights conferred upon them by Community law.

[35] It follows that the principle whereby a State must be liable for loss and damage caused to individuals as a result of breaches of Community law for which the State can be held responsible is inherent in the system of the Treaty.

[36] A further basis for the obligation of Member States to make good such loss and damage is to be found in Article 5 of the Treaty, under which the Member States are required to take all appropriate measures, whether general or particular, to ensure fulfilment of their obligations under Community law. Among these is the obligation to nullify the unlawful consequences of a breach of Community law (see, in relation to the analogous provision of Article 86 of the ECSC Treaty, the judgment in Case 6/60 *Humblet* v *Belgium* [1960] ECR 559).

[37] It follows from all the foregoing that it is a principle of Community law that the Member States are obliged to make good loss and damage caused to individuals by breaches of Community law for which they can be held responsible.

(b) The conditions for State liability

[38] Although State liability is thus required by Community law, the conditions under which that liability gives rise to a right to reparation depend on the nature of the breach of Community law giving rise to the loss and damage.

[39] Where, as in this case, a Member State fails to fulfil its obligation under the third paragraph of Article 189 of the Treaty to take all the measures necessary to achieve the result prescribed by a directive, the full effectiveness of that rule of Community law requires that there should be a right to reparation provided that three conditions are fulfilled.

[40] The first of those conditions is that the result prescribed by the directive should entail the grant of rights to individuals. The second condition is that it should be possible to identify the content of those rights on the basis of the provisions of the directive. Finally, the third condition is the existence of a causal link between the breach of the State's obligation and the loss and damage suffered by the injured parties.

[41] Those conditions are sufficient to give rise to a right on the part of individuals to obtain reparation, a right founded directly on Community law.

[42] Subject to that reservation, it is on the basis of the rules of national law on liability that the State must make reparation for the consequences of the loss and damage caused. In the absence of Community legislation, it is for the internal legal order of each Member State to designate the competent courts and lay down the detailed procedural rules for legal proceedings intended fully to safeguard the rights which individuals derive from Community law (see the judgments in Case 60/75 *Russo* v *AIMA* [1976] ECR 45, Case 33/76 *Rewe* v *Landwirstschaftskammer Saarland* [1976] ECR 1989 and Case 158/80 *Rewe* v *Hauptzollamt Kiel* [1981] ECR 1805).
[43] Further, the substantive and procedural conditions for reparation of loss and damage laid down by the national law of the Member States must not be less favourable than those relating to similar domestic claims and must not be so framed as to make it virtually impossible or excessively difficult to obtain reparation (see, in relation to the analogous issue of the repayment of taxes levied in breach of Community law, *inter alia* the judgment in Case 199/82 *Amministrazione delle Finanze dello Stato* v *San Giorgio* [1983] ECR 3595).
[44] In this case, the breach of Community law by a Member State by virtue of its failure to transpose Directive 80/987 within the prescribed period has been confirmed by a judgment of the Court. The result required by that directive entails the grant to employees of a right to a guarantee of payment of their unpaid wage claims. As is clear from the examination of the first part of the first question, the content of that right can be identified on the basis of the provisions of the directive.
[45] Consequently, the national court must, in accordance with the national rules on liability, uphold the right of employees to obtain reparation of loss and damage caused to them as a result of failure to transpose the directive.
[46] The answer to be given to the national court must therefore be that a Member State is required to make good loss and damage caused to individuals by failure to transpose Directive 80/987.

Notes

1. It seems that this liability on member states includes failures to fulfil Community obligations other than a failure to implement a Directive within the specified period. See Ross 'Beyond *Francovich*' (1993) 56 MLR 55; Steiner 'From Direct Effect to *Francovich*: Shifting Means of Enforcement of Community Law' (1993) 18 EL Rev 3.

2. See the development by the ECJ of compensation for loss from infringements of EC law in *Brasserie du Pêcheur SA* v *Federal Republic of Germany*, *R* v *Secretary of State for Transport, ex parte Factortame (No. 4)* [1996] 2 WLR 506.

(6) The United Kingdom's courts' views on directives

The interpretation of directives by the House of Lords is somewhat confusing. Compare the following cases.

Duke v _GEC Reliance Ltd_
[1988] AC 618
House of Lords

The complainant had been dismissed in accordance with the employer's policy on different retirement ages for male and female employees. Whilst

Marshall held that this constituted sex discrimination, it also held that directives did not have horizontal effect. The complainant argued that the Sex Discrimination Act 1975 ought to have been interpreted according to the guidance in *Von Colson* so that it conformed to Community law. An appeal was made to the House of Lords.

LORD TEMPLEMAN: . . . [I]t is now submitted that the appellant is entitled to damages from the respondent because Community law requires the Equal Pay Act enacted on 29 May 1970 and the Sex Discrimination Act enacted on 12 November 1975 to be construed in a manner which gives effect to the Equal Treatment Directive dated 9 February 1976 as construed by the European Court of Justice in *Marshall's* case published on 20 February 1986. Of course a British court will always be willing and anxious to conclude that United Kingdom law is consistent with Community law. Where an Act is passed for the purpose of giving effect to an obligation imposed by a directive or other instrument a British court will seldom encounter difficulty in concluding that the language of the Act is effective for the intended purpose. But the construction of a British Act of Parliament is a matter of judgment to be determined by British courts and to be derived from the language of the legislation considered in the light of the circumstances prevailing at the date of enactment. The circumstances in which the Equal Pay Act 1970 and the Sex Discrimination Act 1975 were enacted are set forth in the 1974 White Paper, in the judgment of Phillips J in *Roberts* v *Cleveland Area Health Authority* [1978] ICR 370, in the judgment of Browne-Wilkinson J in *Roberts* v *Tate & Lyle Food and Distribution Ltd* [1983] ICR 521 and in the submission of the United Kingdom Government in *Marshall's* case [1986] QB 401. The Acts were not passed to give effect to the Equal Treatment Directive and were intended to preserve discriminatory retirement ages. Proposals for the Equal Treatment Directive dated 9 Febuary 1976 were in circulation when the Bill for the Sex Discrimination Act 1975 was under discussion but it does not appear that these proposals were understood by the British Government or the Parliament of the United Kingdom to involve the prohibition of differential retirement ages linked to differential pensionable ages.

The appellant relied on the speech of Lord Diplock in *Garland* v *British Rail Engineering Ltd* [1983] 2 AC 751, 770–771. Lord Diplock expressed the view that section 6(4) of the Sex Discrimination Act 1975 could and should be construed in the manner consistent with article 119 of the EEC Treaty, the Equal Pay Directive and the Equal Treatment Directive. In *Garland's* case, following a reference to the European Court of Justice it was established that there had been discrimination contrary to article 119 which has direct effect between individuals. It was thus unnecessary to consider the effect of the Equal Treatment Directive. Lord Diplock observed, at p. 771, that:

> even if the obligation to observe the provisions of article 119 were an obligation assumed by the United Kingdom under an ordinary international treaty or convention and there was no question of the Treaty obligation being directly applicable as part of the law to be applied by the courts in this country without need for any further enactment, it is a principle of construction of United Kingdom statutes, now too well established to call for citation of authority, that the words of a statute passed after the Treaty has been signed and dealing with the subject matter of the international obligation of the United Kingdom, are to be construed, if they are reasonably capable of bearing such a meaning, as intended to carry out the obligation, and not to be inconsistent with it. . . . The instant appeal does not

> present an appropriate occasion to consider whether, having regard to the express direction as to the construction of enactments 'to be passed' which is contained in section 2 (4) anything short of an express positive statement in an Act of Parliament passed after 1 January 1973, that a particular provision is intended to be made in breach of an obligation assumed by the United Kingdom under a Community treaty, would justify an English court in construing that provision in a manner inconsistent with a Community treaty obligation of the United Kingdom, however wide a departure from the prima facie meaning of the language of the provision might be needed in order to achieve consistency.

On the hearing of this appeal, your Lordships have had the advantage, not available to Lord Diplock, of full argument which has satisfied me that the Sex Discrimination Act 1975 was not intended to give effect to the Equal Treatment Directive as subsequently construed in the *Marshall* case [1986] QB 401 and that the words of section 6 (4) are not reasonably capable of being limited to the meaning ascribed to them by the appellant. Section 2 (4) of the European Communities Act 1972 does not in my opinion enable or constrain a British court to distort the meaning of a British statute in order to enforce against an individual a Community directive which has no direct effect between individuals. Section 2 (4) applies and only applies where Community provisions are directly applicable.

The jurisdiction, composition and powers of the European Court of Justice are contained in articles 164 to 188 of the EEC Treaty. Those sections include the following:

> 164. The Court of Justice shall ensure that in the interpretation and application of this Treaty the law is observed. . . .
> 177. The Court of Justice shall have jurisdiction to give preliminary rulings concerning: (a) the interpretation of this Treaty; (b) the validity and interpretation of Act of the institutions of the Community; (c) the interpretation of the statutes of bodies established by an act of the council, where those statutes so provide.

The submission that the Sex Discrimination Act 1975 must be construed in a manner which gives effect to the Equal Treatment Directive as construed by the European Court of Justice in *Marshall's* case is said to be derived from the decision of the European Court of Justice in *von Colson and Kamann* v *Land Nordrhein-Westfalen* (Case 14/83) [1984] ECR 1891, delivered on 10 April 1984. In the *von Colson* case the European Court of Justice ruled that the provisions of the Equal Treatment Directive which require equal treatment for men and women in access to employment do not require a member state to legislate so as to compel an employer to conclude a contract of employment with a woman who has been refused employment on the grounds of sex. The Directive does not specify the nature of the remedies which the member states must afford to a victim of discrimination. But the court also ruled, at p. 1910:

> 3. Although [the Equal Treatment Directive] 76/207/EEC for the purpose of imposing a sanction for the breach of discrimination, leaves the member states free to choose between the different solution suitable for achieving its object, it nevertheless requires that if a member state chooses to penalise breaches of that prohibition by the award of compensation, then in order to ensure that it is effective and that it has a deterrent effect, that compensation must in any event be adequate in relation to the damage sustained and must therefore amount to more than purely nominal compensation such as, for example, the reimbursement only of the expenses incurred in connection with the application. It is for the national court to

> interpret and apply the legislation adopted for the implementation of the Directive in conformity with the requirements of Community law, in so far as it is given discretion to do so under national law.

In the *von Colson* case the German court which submitted the case for a ruling asked whether it was acceptable that a woman who applied for a job and was refused because she was a woman, contrary to the intent of the Equal Treatment Directive, was only entitled under the German domestic law prohibiting such discrimination to the recovery of her expenses (if any) of her application. The German Government in making representations to the European Court expressed the view that under German law compensation for discrimination could include general damages for the loss of the job or of the opportunity to take up the job. The ruling of the European Court of Justice did not constrain the national court to construe German law in accordance with Community law but ruled that if under German law the German court possessed the power to award damages which were adequate and which fulfilled the objective of the Equal Treatment Directive then it was the duty of the German court to act accordingly. The *von Colson* case is no authority for the proposition that the German court was bound to invent a German law of adequate compensation if no such law existed and no authority for the proposition that a court of a member state must distort the meaning of a domestic statute so as to conform with Community law which is not directly applicable. If, following the *von Colson* case, the German court adhered to the view that under German law it possessed no discretion to award adequate compensation, it would have been the duty of the German Government in fulfilment of its obligations under the Treaty of Rome to introduce legislation or evolve some other method which would enable adequate compensation to be obtained, just as the United Kingdom Government became bound to introduce legislation to amend the Equal Pay Act 1970 and the Sex Discrimination Act 1975 in the light of *Marshall's* case. Mrs Advocate-General Rozès in her opinion, delivered on 31 January 1984 in the *von Colson* case, said, at p. 1919:

> In proceedings under article 177 it is not for me to express a view on questions which fall exclusively within the jurisdiction of the national courts inasmuch as they concern the application of national law.

The EEC Treaty does not interfere and the European Court of Justice in the *von Colson* case did not assert power to interfere with the method or result of the interpretation of national legislation by national courts.

It would be most unfair to the respondent to distort the construction of the 1975 Sex Discrimination Act in order to accommodate the 1976 Equal Treatment Directive as construed by the European Court of Justice in the 1986 *Marshall* case. As between the appellant and the respondent the Equal Treatment Directive did not have direct effect and the respondent could not reasonably be expected to reduce to precision the opaque language which constitutes both the strength and the difficulty of some Community legislation. The respondent could not reasonably be expected to appreciate the logic of Community legislators in permitting differential retirement pension ages but prohibiting differential retirement ages. The respondent is not liable to the appellant under Community law. I decline to hold that liability under British law attaches to the respondent or any other private employer to pay damages based on wages which women over 60 and under 65 did not earn before the amending Sex Discrimination Act 1986 for the first time and without retrospective effect introduced the statutory tort of operating differential retirement ages. I would dismiss this appeal.

Appeal dismissed.

Pickstone v *Freemans plc*
[1989] AC 66
House of Lords

The ECJ had ruled in *Commission of the European Communities* v *United Kingdom* Case 61/81 [1982] ICR 578, that UK law did not meet Community law requirements on the principle that men and women should receive equal pay for work of equal value. Following this decision the Equal Pay Act 1970 was amended. Women who were employed as warehouse operatives were paid less than a man who was employed as a checker warehouse operative. The women contended that as the work of the two jobs was of equal value, then, under the amended Equal Pay Act 1970, s. 1 (2) (c), they were entitled to the higher rate of pay. The Industrial Tribunal rejected the claim on the basis that their case came within s. 1 (2) (a) of the 1970 Act as there was a man who was employed at the same rate as the women in the post of warehouse operative. The Court of Appeal allowed the women's appeal on the basis of conformity with Art. 119 of the EEC Treaty. The employers appealed to the House of Lords.

LORD TEMPLEMAN: . . . Section 1 (2) (a) of the Act of 1970 as amended in 1975, was not further amended by the Regulations of 1983. Paragraph (a) enables any woman to claim equal pay with a man in the same employment engaged on like work. By section 1 (4) like work is work of the same or a broadly similar nature where the differences in work are not of practical importance. The issue of 'like work' is decided by the industrial tribunal.

Section 1 (2) (b) of the Act of 1970 as amended in 1975, was also not further amended by the Regulations of 1983. Paragraph (b) enables a woman to claim equal pay for work rated as equivalent to that of a man by a job evaluation study. By section 1 (5) the issue of 'equivalent work' is decided by the job evaluation study. Such a study can only be carried out with the consent and cooperation of the employer.

In compliance with the ruling of the European Court of Justice in *Commission of the European Communities* v *United Kingdom of Great Britain and Northern Ireland* (Case 61/81) [1982] ICR 578, the Regulations of 1983 introduced into the Act of 1970 as amended in 1975, a provision which enables a woman to claim equal pay for work of equal value where the employer refuses to consent to a job evaluation study. The Regulations introduced into the Act section 1 (2) (c) which modifies any term in a woman's contract which is less favourable than a term of a similar kind in the contract of a man

> (c) where a woman is employed on work which, not being work in relation to which paragraph (a) or (b) above applies, is, in terms of the demands made on her (for instance under such headings as effort, skill and decision), of equal value to that of a man in the same employment.

. . .

According to the employers in the present appeal, the Regulations of 1983 had the additional effect of depriving some women of the right to pursue their claims by judicial process or otherwise although they considered themselves wronged by failure to apply the principle of equal pay. The respondents may have a valid complaint in that they are not receiving equal pay with Mr Phillips for work of equal value. But if the respondents seek to remedy that discrimination under section 1 (2) (c) of the Act of 1970 as amended by the Regulations, they will be debarred because they are employed on 'work in relation to which paragraph (a) or (b) above applies.' It is said that paragraph (a) operates, not because the respondents are employed on like work with Mr Phillips but because the respondents are employed on like work with some other man. Since paragraph (c) is expressed to apply only when a woman is employed on work which is not 'work in relation to which paragraph (a) or (b) above applies,' it follows, so it is said, that where a woman is employed on like work with any man or where a woman is employed on work rated as equivalent with any man, no claim can be made under paragraph (c) in respect of some other man who is engaged on work of equal value. In my opinion paragraph (a) or (b) only debars a claim under paragraph (c) where paragraph (a) or (b) applies to the man who is the subject of the complaint made by the woman. If the tribunal decide that the respondents are engaged 'on like work' with Mr Phillips then paragraph (a) applies and the respondents are not entitled to proceed under paragraph (c) and to obtain the report of an Acas expert. If there is a job evaluation study which covers the work of the respondents and the work of Mr Phillips then the respondents are debarred from proceeding under paragraph (c) unless the job evaluation study itself was discriminatory.

Whenever there is a claim for equal pay, the complainant, or the complainant's trade union representative supporting the claimant, may wish to obtain a report from an Acas expert under paragraph (c) to use for the purpose of general pay bargaining and in the hope of finding ammunition which will lead to a general increase in wage levels irrespective of discrimination. For this purpose the more Acas reports there are the better. It may be significant that in the present case a claim is made under paragraph (c) and not under paragraph (a) as well, or, in the alternative, although it is obvious that work of equal value in terms of the demands made on a woman under such headings as effort, skill and decision which may amount to discrimination under paragraph (c) may also be work of a broadly similar nature with differences of no practical importance which found a complaint under paragraph (a). If there is discrimination in pay the industrial tribunal must be able to grant a remedy. But the remedy available under paragraph (c) is not to be applied if the complainant has a remedy in respect of the male employee with whom she demands parity under paragraph (a) or if paragraph (b) applies to the woman and to that male employee. To prevent exploitation of paragraph (c) the tribunal must decide in the first instance whether the complainant and the man with whom she seeks parity are engaged on 'like work' under paragraph (a). If paragraph (a) applies, no Acas report is required. If paragraph (a) does not apply, then the tribunal considers whether paragraph (b) applies to the complainant and the man with whom she seeks parity; if so, the tribunal can only proceed under paragraph (c) if the job evaluation study obtained for the purposes of paragraph (b) is itself discriminatory. If paragraph (b) applies then, again, no Acas report is necessary. If paragraphs (a) and (b) do not apply, the tribunal must next consider whether there are reasonable grounds for determining that the work of the complainant and the work of the man with whom she seeks parity is of equal value. If the tribunal are not so satisfied, then no Acas report is required. The words in paragraph (c) on which the employers rely were not intended to create a new form of permitted discrimination. Paragraph (c) enables a claim to equal pay as against a specified man to be made without injustice to an employer. When a woman claims equal pay for work of equal value, she specifies the man with whom she demands parity. If the work of the woman is work in relation to which paragraph (a) or (b) applies in relation to that man, then the woman cannot proceed under paragraph (c) and cannot obtain a report from an Acas expert. In my opinion there must be implied in paragraph (c) after the word 'applies' the words 'as between the woman and the man with whom she claims equality.' This construction is consistent with Community law. The employers' construction is inconsistent with Community law and creates a permitted form of discrimination without rhyme or reason.

Under Community law, a woman is entitled to equal pay for work of equal value to that of a man in the same employment. That right is not dependent on there being no man who is employed on the same work as the woman. Under British law, namely the Equal Pay Act 1970 as amended in 1975, a woman was entitled to equal pay for work rated as equivalent with that of a man in the same employment. That right was not dependent on there being no man who was employed on the same work as the woman. Under the ruling of the European Court of Justice in *Commission of the European Communities* v *United Kingdom of Great Britain and Northern Ireland* (Case 61/81) [1982] ICR 578, the Equal Pay Act 1970 as amended in 1975 was held to be defective because the Act did not entitle every woman to claim before a competent authority that her work had the same value as other work, but only allowed a claim by a woman who succeeded in persuading her employer to consent to a job evaluation scheme. The Regulations of 1983 were intended to give full effect to Community law and to the ruling of the European Court of Justice which directed the United Kingdom Government to introduce legislation entitling any woman to equal pay with any man for work of equal value if the difference in pay is due to the difference in sex and is therefore discriminatory. I am of the opinion that the Regulations of 1983, upon their true construction, achieve the required result of affording a remedy to any woman who is not in receipt of equal pay for work equal in value to the work of a man in the same employment.

In *Murphy* v *Bord Telecom Eireann* (Case 157/86) [1988] ICR 445, 29 women were employed as factory workers engaged in such tasks as dismantling, cleaning, oiling and reassembling telephones and other equipment; they claimed the right to be paid at the same rate as a specified male worker employed in the same factory as a stores labourer engaged in cleaning, collecting and delivering equipment and components and in lending general assistance as required. The European Court of Justice in their judgment, at p. 449, paragraph 9, said that the principle of equal pay for men and women

> forbids workers of one sex engaged in work of equal value to that of workers of the opposite sex to be paid a lower wage than the latter on grounds of sex, it a fortiori prohibits such a difference in pay where the lower-paid category of workers is engaged in work of higher value.

I cannot think that in Community law or in British law the result would be any different if instead of there being 29 women working on telephone maintenance and one male stores labourer, there were 28 women and one man working on telephone maintenance and one male stores labourer.

The draft of the Regulations of 1983 was not subject to any process of amendment by Parliament. In these circumstances the explanations of the Government and the criticisms voiced by Members of Parliament in the debates which led to approval of the draft Regulations provide some indications of the intentions of Parliament. The debate on the draft Regulations in the House of Commons which led to their approval by Resolution was initiated by the Under Secretary of State for Employment who, in the reports of the House of Commons for 20 July 1983 *Hansard*, column 479 et seq. said:

> The Equal Pay Act allows a woman to claim equal pay with a man . . . if she is doing the same or broadly similar work, or if her job and his have been rated equal

> through job evaluation in effort, skill and decision. However, if a woman is doing different work from a comparable man, or if the jobs are not covered by a job evaluation study, the woman has at present no right to make a claim for equal pay. This is the gap identified by the European Court, which we are closing. . . .

In the course of his speech at column 485, the Minister outlined the procedure which will apply if a claim is made under paragraph (c) in the following words:

> Under the amending Regulations which are the subject of this debate, an employee will be able to bring a claim for equal pay with an employee of the opposite sex working in the same employment on the ground that the work is of equal value. When this happens, conciliation will first be attempted, as in all equal pay claims. If conciliation is unsuccessful, the industrial tribunal will take the following steps. First, it will check that the work is not in fact so similar that the case can be heard under the current Act. Secondly, it will consider whether the jobs have already been covered by a job evaluation scheme and judged not to be of equal value. If this is the case, the claim may proceed only if the original job evaluation scheme is shown to have been sexually discriminatory. Having decided that the case should proceed, the tribunal will first invite the parties to see if they can settle the claim voluntarily. If not, the tribunal will consider whether to commission an independent expert to report on the value of the jobs. It will not commission an expert's report if it feels that it is unreasonable to determine the question of value – for example, if the two jobs are quite obviously of unequal value. Nor . . . will it commission an expert's report if the employer shows at this stage that inequality in pay is due to material factors other than sex discrimination. . . .

Thus it is clear that the construction which I have placed upon the Regulations corresponds to the intentions of the Government in introducing the Regulations. In the course of the debate in the House of Commons, and in the corresponding debate in the House of Lords, no one suggested that a claim for equal pay for equal work might be defeated under the Regulations by an employer who proved that a man who was not the subject of the complaint was employed on the same or on similar work with the complainant. The Minister took the view, and Parliament accepted the view, that paragraph (c) will only apply if paragraphs (a) and (b) are first held by the tribunal not to apply in respect of the work of the woman and the work of the man with whom she seeks parity of pay. This is also the only view consistent with Community law.

In *von Colson and Kamann* v *Land Nordrhein-Westfalen* (Case 14/83) [1984] ECR 1891, 1910-1911, the European Court of Justice advised that in dealing with national legislation designed to give effect to a Directive:

> 3. . . . It is for the national court to interpret and apply the legislation adopted for the implementation of the Directive in conformity with the requirements of Community law, in so far as it is given discretion to do so under national law.

In *Duke* v *GEC Reliance Systems Ltd* [1988] AC 618 this House declined to distort the construction of an Act of Parliament which was not drafted to give effect to a Directive and which was not capable of complying with the Directive as subsequently construed by the European Court of Justice. In the present case I can see no difficulty in construing the Regulations of 1983 in a way which gives effect to the declared intention of the Government of the United Kingdom responsible for drafting the Regulations and is consistent with the objects of the EEC Treaty, the provisions of the

Equal Pay Directive and the rulings of the European Court of Justice. I would dismiss the appeal.

Appeal dismissed.

Note

In *Pickstone* their lordships referred to *Hansard* to determine the intention of Parliament in passing the amendments to the 1970 statute.

Questions

1. Why was it distortion in *Duke* to interpret the legislation as being in conformity with Community law but permissible in *Pickstone*?

2. If the interpretation of *Von Colson* in *Duke* is incompatible with *Marleasing*, is it in accordance with *Kolpinghuis Nijmegen*?

Litster v *Forth Dry Dock & Engineering Co. Ltd*
[1990] 1 AC 546
House of Lords

A company had become insolvent and gone into receivership. An hour before the receiver transferred the business assets to a new owner, the employees were made redundant. Directive 77/187/EEC provides safeguards for employees where a business is transferred from one owner to another. Article 4 (1) of the directive stops a new owner from evading the safeguards by prohibiting dismissal of employees by the old owner. The directive was implemented by the Transfer of Undertakings (Protection of Employment) Regulations 1981. Regulation 5 (1) allows employees of the old owner to pursue claims against the new owner, but according to reg. 5 (3), the employee must have been in employment immediately before the transfer. The employees succeeded in claims before the Industrial Tribunal and the Employment Appeal Tribunal. The appeal to the Court of Session was allowed on the basis that the employees were not employed immediately before the transfer. On appeal to the House of Lords.

LORD KEITH: . . . In *Pickstone* v *Freemans Plc* [1989] AC 66 there had been laid before Parliament under paragraph 2 (2) of Schedule 2 to the European Communities Act 1972 the draft of certain Regulations designed, and presented by the responsible ministers as designed, to fill a lacuna in the equal pay legislation of the United Kingdom which had been identified by a decision of the European Court of Justice. On a literal reading the regulation particularly relevant did not succeed in completely filling the lacuna. Your Lordships' House, however, held that in order that the manifest purpose of the Regulations might be achieved and effect given to the clear but inadequately expressed intention of Parliament certain words must be read in by necessary implication.

In the present case the Transfer of Undertakings (Protection of Employment) Regulations 1981 were similarly laid before Parliament in draft and approved by resolutions of both Houses. They were so laid as designed to give effect to Council Directive (77/187/EEC) dated 14 February 1977. It is plain that if the words in regulation 5 (3) of the Regulations of 1981 'a person so employed immediately before the transfer' are read literally, as contended for by the second respondents, Forth Estuary Engineering Ltd, the provisions of regulation 5 (1) will be capable of ready evasion through the transferee arranging with the transferor for the latter to dismiss its employees a short time before the transfer becomes operative. In the event that the transferor is insolvent, a situation commonly forming the occasion for the transfer of an undertaking, the employees would be left with worthless claims for unfair dismissal against the transferor. In any event, whether or not the transferor is insolvent, the employees would be deprived of the remedy of reinstatement or re-engagement. The transferee would be under no liability towards the employees and a coach and four would have been driven through the provisions of regulation 5 (1).

A number of decisions of the European Court, in particular *P. Bork International A/S* v *Foreningen af Arbejdsledere i Danmark* (Case 101/87) [1989] IRLR 41 have had the result that where employees have been dismissed by the transferor for a reason connected with the transfer, at a time before the transfer takes effect, then for purposes of article 3 (1) of Council Directive (77/187/EEC) (which corresponds to regulation 5 (1)) the employees are to be treated as still employed by the undertaking at the time of the transfer.

In these circumstances it is the duty of the court to give to regulation 5 a construction which accords with the decisions of the European Court upon the corresponding provisions of the Directive to which the regulation was intended by Parliament to give effect. The precedent established by *Pickstone* v *Freemans Plc* indicates that this is to be done by implying the words necessary to achieve that result. So there must be implied in regulation 5 (3) words indicating that where a person has been unfairly dismissed in the circumstances described in regulation 8 (1) he is to be deemed to have been employed in the undertaking immediately before the transfer or any of a series of transactions whereby it was effected.

My Lords, I would allow the appeal.

LORD TEMPLEMAN: . . . Thus, it is said, since the workforce of Forth Dry Dock were dismissed at 3.30 p.m., they were not employed 'immediately before the transfer' at 4.30 p.m. and therefore regulation 5 (1) did not transfer any liability for the workforce from Forth Dry Dock to Forth Estuary. The argument is inconsistent with the Directive. In *P. Bork International A/S* v *Foreningen af Arbejdsledere i Danmark* (Case 101/87 [1989] IRLR 41, 44 the European Court of Justice ruled that:

> the only workers who may invoke Directive [(77/187/EEC)] are those who have current employment relations or a contract of employment at the date of the transfer. The question whether or not a contract of employment or employment relationship exists at that date must be assessed under national law, subject, however, to the observance of the mandatory rules of the Directive concerning the protection of workers against dismissal by reason of the transfer. It follows that the workers employed by the undertaking whose contract of employment or employment relationship has been terminated with effect on a date before that of the transfer, in breach of article 4 (1) of the Directive, must be considered as still employed by the undertaking on the date of the transfer with the consequence, in particular, that the obligations of an employer towards them are fully transferred from the transferor to the transferee in accordance with article 3 (1) of the Directive.

In *von Colson and Kamann* v *Land Nordrhein-Westfalen* (Case 14/83) [1984] ECR 1891, 1909 the European Court of Justice dealing with Council Directive

(76/207/EEC), forbidding discrimination on grounds of sex regarding access to employment, ruled that:

> the member states' obligation arising from a Directive to achieve the result envisaged by the Directive and their duty under article 5 of the Treaty to take all appropriate measures, whether general or particular, to ensure the fulfilment of that obligation, is binding on all the authorities of member states including, for matters within their jurisdiction, the courts. It follows that, in applying the national law and in particular the provisions of a national law specifically introduced in order to implement Directive [(76/207/EEC)] national courts are required to interpret their national law in the light of the wording and the purpose of the Directive in order to achieve the result referred to in the third paragraph of article 189.

Thus the courts of the United Kingdom are under a duty to follow the practice of the European Court of Justice by giving a purposive construction to Directives and to Regulations issued for the purpose of complying with Directives. In *Pickstone* v *Freemans Plc* [1989] AC 66, this House implied words in a regulation designed to give effect to Council Directive (75/117/EEC) dealing with equal pay for women doing work of equal value. If this House had not been able to make the necessary implication, the Equal Pay (Amendment) Regulations 1983 (SI 1983 No. 1794) would have failed their object and the United Kingdom would have been in breach of its treaty obligations to give effect to Directives. In the present case, in the light of Council Directive (77/187/EEC) and in the light of the ruling of the European Court of Justice in *Bork's* case [1989] IRLR 41, it seems to me, following the suggestion of my noble and learned friend, Lord Keith of Kinkel, that paragraph 5 (3) of the Regulations of 1981 was not intended and ought not to be construed so as to limit the operation of regulation 5 to persons employed immediately before the transfer in point of time. Regulation 5 (3) must be construed on the footing that it applies to a person employed immediately before the transfer or who would have been so employed if he had not been unfairly dismissed before the transfer for a reason connected with the transfer. . . .

LORD OLIVER: . . . The critical question, it seems to me, is whether, even allowing for the greater latitude in construction permissible in the case of legislation introduced to give effect to this country's Community obligations, it is possible to attribute to regulation 8 (1) when read in conjunction with regulation 5, the same result as that attributed to article 4 in the *Bork* case [1989] IRLR 41. Purely as a matter of language, it clearly is not. Regulation 8 (1) does not follow literally the wording of article 4 (1). It provides only that if the reason for the dismissal of the employee is the transfer of the business, he has to be treated 'for the purposes of Part V of the 1978 Act' as unfairly dismissed so as to confer on him the remedies provided by sections 69 to 79 of the Act (including, where it is considered appropriate, an order for reinstatement or re-engagement). If this provision fell to be construed by reference to the ordinary rules of construction applicable to a purely domestic statute and without reference to Treaty obligations, it would, I think, be quite impermissible to regard it as having the same prohibitory effect as that attributed by the European Court to article 4 of the Directive. But it has always to be borne in mind that the purpose of the Directive and of the Regulations was and is to 'safeguard' the rights of employees on a transfer and that there is a mandatory obligation to provide remedies which are effective and not merely symbolic to which the Regulations were intended to give effect. The remedies provided by the Act of 1978 in the case of an insolvent transferor are largely illusory unless they can be exerted against the transferee as the Directive contemplates and I do not find it conceivable that, in framing Regulations intending to give effect to the Directive, the Secretary of State could have envisaged that its purpose should be capable of being avoided by the transparent device to which resort was had in the instant case. *Pickstone* v *Freemans Plc* [1989] AC 66, has established that the greater flexibility available to the court in applying a purposive construction to legislation designed to give effect to the United Kingdom's Treaty obligations to the Community enables the court, where necessary, to supply by implication words appropriate to comply with those obligations: see particularly the speech of Lord Templeman, at pp. 120–121. Having regard to the manifest purpose of the Regulations, I do not, for my part, feel inhibited from making such an implication in the instant case. The provision in regulation 8 (1) that a dismissal by reason of a transfer is to be treated as an unfair dismissal, is merely a different way of saying that the transfer is not to 'constitute a ground for dismissal' as contemplated by article 4 of the Directive and there is no good reason for denying to it the same effect as that attributed to that article. In effect this involves reading regulation 5 (3) as if there were inserted after the words 'immediately before the transfer' the words 'or would have been so employed if he had not been unfairly dismissed in the circumstances described in regulation 8(1).' For my part, I would make such an implication which is entirely consistent with the general scheme of the Regulations and which is necessary if they are effectively to fulfil the purpose for which they were made of giving effect to the provisions of the Directive.

Appeal dismissed.

Finnegan v *Clowney Youth Training Program Ltd*
[1990] 2 AC 407
House of Lords

The facts of this case are similar to *Duke* (see p. 161) – the employer operated different retirement ages for male and female employees. The difference between the two cases lies in the fact that the parties to this case came from Northern Ireland where the relevant legislation was the Sex Discrimination (Northern Ireland) Order 1976 which had been made after the Equal Treatment Directive 76/207/EEC. The relevant provisions of the 1976 Order were the same as those in the Sex Discrimination Act 1975. The employee was successful in arguing sex discrimination before the Industrial Tribunal, but the Court of Appeal of Northern Ireland held that Parliament intended the 1976 Order to have the same effect in Northern Ireland as the 1975 Act did in England. On appeal to the House of Lords.

LORD BRIDGE: . . . [T]he relevant legislation by Order in Council applicable to Northern Ireland has been designed to reproduce precisely the substance of the legislation enacted by the Westminster Parliament. Thus, on turning to the Sex Discrimination (Northern Ireland) Order 1976, we find that article 8 reproduces precisely the provisions of section 6 of the English Act of 1975 and in the Equal Pay Act (Northern Ireland) 1970, set out in Schedule 1 to the Order of 1976 as amended by that Order, section 6 (1A) reproduces precisely the provisions of section 6 (1A) of the English Act of 1970. Similarly, following the *Marshall* case [1987] QB 401, appropriate amendments to the Order of 1976 were made by the Sex Discrimination (Northern Ireland) Order 1988 which precisely reproduced in article 4 the provisions of section 2 of the English Act of 1986.

On the face of it, therefore, the enactment applicable to the circumstances of the present employee's claim is indistinguishable from the enactment which fell to be applied in *Duke* v *GEC Reliance Systems Ltd* [1988] AC 618 and would appear, therefore, to dictate the inevitable result that the appeal must fail. This was the view of the Court of Appeal in Northern Ireland. Counsel for the employee submits, however, that a crucial distinction is to be derived from the chronology, in that the English Act of 1975 was passed before the Council of the European Communities adopted the Equal Treatment Directive, on 9 February 1976, whereas the Order of 1976 was not made until July of that year. He referred us to a familiar line of authority for the proposition that the national legislation of a member state of the European Community which is enacted for the purpose of implementing a European Council Directive must be construed in the light of the Directive and must, if at all possible, be applied in a sense which will effect the purpose of the Directive: see *von Colson and Kamann* v *Land Nordrhein-Westfalen* (Case 14/83) [1984] ECR 1891; *Pickstone* v *Freemans Plc* [1989] AC 66; *Litster* v *Forth Dry Dock and Engineering Co. Ltd* [1990] 1 AC 546.

I entirely accept the validity of the proposition, but I do not accept that it has any application here. Before the decision in the *Marshall* case [1986] QB, 401 it is apparent from the history I have recounted that neither the United Kingdom Parliament nor the United Kingdom Government perceived any conflict between the provisions of section 6 (4) of the Sex Discrimination Act 1975 and section 6 (1A) of the Equal Pay Act 1970 on the one hand and the provisions of the European Equal Treatment Directive on the other hand, such as to call for amendment of the English statutes after the adoption of the Directive. Accordingly, it would appear to me to be wholly artificial to treat the Order of 1976 enacting identical provisions for Northern Ireland, because it was made after the Directive, as having been made with the purpose of implementing Community law in the same sense as the Regulations which fell to be construed in the *Pickstone* and *Lister* cases. The reality is that article 8 (4) of the Order of 1976 being in identical terms and in an identical context to section 6 (4) of the English Act of 1975, must have been intended to have the identical effect. To hold otherwise would be, as in *Duke* v *GEC Reliance Systems Ltd* [1988] AC 618, most unfair to the employers in that it would be giving retrospective operation to the amending Order of 1988 and effectively eliminating the distinction between Community law which is of direct effect between citizens of member states and Community law which only affects citizens of member states when it is implemented by national legislation.

Alternatively counsel for the employee invited us to depart from *Duke* v *GEC Reliance Systems Ltd* in pursuance of *Practice Statement (Judicial Precedent)* [1966] 1 WLR 1234. I need only say that, so far from being persuaded that the decision in that case was wrong, I entertain no doubt that it was right for the reasons so clearly set out in the speech of Lord Templeman.

We were further invited to make a reference to the European Court of Justice under article 177 of the EEC Treaty. In my opinion, however, the determination of the appeal does not depend on any question of Community law. The interpretation of the Order of 1976 is for the United Kingdom courts and it is not suggested that the Equal Treatment Directive is of direct effect between citizens.

I would dismiss the appeal.

Appeal dismissed.

Questions

1. Has the House of Lords in these four cases simply been consistent in seeking to ascertain if the domestic legislation was intended to implement Community law?

2. Lord Bridge is correct in *Finnegan,* in that there was no question of horizontal effect, but should their lordships not have asked the ECJ for advice on the application of *Von Colson,* given that the Northern Irish legislation was passed after the directive?

Note

See Szyszczak (1990) 15 EL Rev 480 for a critical review of these four cases.

Webb* v *EMO Air Cargo (UK) Ltd (No. 2)
[1995] 1 WLR 1454
House of Lords

> The applicant was engaged by the employers with a view initially to her replacing, after a probationary period, a pregnant employee during the latter's maternity leave. Shortly after her appointment the applicant discovered that she too was pregnant and the employers dismissed her. Her claim that her dismissal was discrimination contrary to the Sex Discrimination Act 1975, s. 1, was rejected by an industrial tribunal, who held that the reason for her dismissal was her anticipated inability to carry out the primary task of covering for the absent employee. Appeals to the Employment Appeal Tribunal and the Court of Appeal were dismissed. On appeal to the House of Lords their Lordships sought a preliminary ruling from the ECJ on the implementation of the principle of the Equal Treatment Directive (76/207/EEC). The ECJ ruled that Art. 2(1) when read with Art. 5(1) of the directive precluded dismissal of an employee who had been recruited for an unlimited term with a view to replacing another employee during the latter's maternity leave and who could not do so because shortly after her recruitment, she had herself been found to be pregnant.

LORD KEITH OF KINKEL: . . . The provisions of the Act of 1975 which your Lordships must endeavour to construe, so as to accord if at all possible with the ruling of the European Court, are section 1(1)(a) and section 5(3).

Section 1(1)(a) provides:

> A person discriminates against a woman in any circumstances relevant for the purposes of any provision of this act if – (a) on the ground of her sex he treats her less favourably than he treats or would treat a man . . .

Section 5(3) provides:

> A comparison of the cases of persons of different sex or marital status under section 1(1) or 3(1) must be such that the relevant circumstances in the one case are the same, or not materially different, in the other.

The reasoning in my speech in the earlier proceedings [1993] 1 WLR 49, 53–55 was to the effect that the relevant circumstances which existed in the present case and which should be taken to be present in the case of the hypothetical man was unavailability for work at the time when the worker was particularly required, and that the reason for the unavailability was not a relevant circumstance. So it was not relevant that the reason for the woman's unavailability was pregnancy, a condition which could not be present in a man.

The ruling of the European Court proceeds on an interpretation of the broad principles dealt with in articles 2(1) and 5(1) of Council Directive (76/207/EEC). Sections 1(1)(a) and 5(3) of the Act of 1975 set out a more precise test of unlawful discrimination, and the problem is how to fit the terms of that test into the ruling. It seems to me that the only way of doing so is to hold that, in a case where a woman is engaged for an indefinite period, the fact that the reason why she will be temporarily unavailable for work at a time when to her knowledge her services will be particularly required is pregnancy is a circumstance relevant to her case, being a circumstance which could not be present in the case of the hypothetical man. It does not necessarily follow that pregnancy would be a relevant circumstance in the situation where the woman is denied employment for a fixed period in the future during the whole of which her pregnancy would make her unavailable for work, nor in the situation where after engagement for a such a period the discovery of her pregnancy leads to cancellation of the engagement.

Appeal allowed

Question

Did their Lordships here distort the construction of the Sex Discrimination Act 1975 so as to make it conform to the Equal Treatment Directive as interpreted by the ECJ?

4 THE RULE OF LAW

Note

The rule of law is considered to be one of the fundamental doctrines of the Constitution of the United Kingdom. The constitution is said to be founded on the idea of the rule of law, and this is a concept favoured by politicians and lawyers being imported into many debates. Despite its currency in political and constitutional discussion its meaning is far from precise, and it may mean different things to different people at different times.

Governments wield considerable power. Constitutions are concerned with the allocation of power and the control of its exercise. The doctrine of the rule of law is concerned with the latter. Aristotle stated that 'the rule of law is preferable to the rule of any individual'. This sentiment was echoed centuries later by English jurists.

Report of the Committee on Ministers' Powers Cmd. 4060, 1932, pp. 71 – 72

The supremacy or rule of law – Its history and meaning

1. The supremacy or rule of the law of the Land is a recognised principle of the English Constitution. The origin of the principle must be sought in the theory, universally held in the Middle Ages, that law of some kind – the law either of God or man – ought to rule the world. Bracton, in his famous book on English law, which was written in the first half of the thirteenth century, held this theory, and deduced from it the proposition that the king and other rulers were subject to law. He laid it down that the law bound all members of the state, whether rulers or subjects; and that justice according to law was due both to ruler and subject. This view was accepted by the common lawyers of the fourteenth and fifteenth centuries and is stated in the Year Books. In 1441, in the Year Book 19 Henry VI Pasch. pl. 1, it is said: 'the law is the highest inheritance which the king has; for by the law he and all his subjects are ruled, and if there was no law there would be no king and no inheritance.'

The rise of the power of Parliament in the fourteenth and fifteenth centuries both emphasized and modified this theory of the supremacy of the law. That the rise of the power of Parliament emphasized the theory is shown by the practical application given to it by Chief Justice Fortescue in Henry VI's reign. He used it as the premise, by means of which he justified the control which Parliament had gained over legislation and taxation. That the rise of the power of Parliament modified the theory is shown by the manner in which the theory of the supremacy of the law was combined with the doctrine of the supremacy of Parliament. The law was supreme, but Parliament could change and modify it. . .

The only period when this conception of the rule of law was seriously questioned was in the Stuart period. The Stuart Kings considered that the Royal prerogative was the sovereign power in the State, and so could override the law whenever they saw fit. Chief Justice Coke was dismissed from the bench because he asserted the supremacy of the law. But his views as to the supremacy of the law were accepted by Parliament when it passed the Petition of Right in 1628, and when it abolished the Court of the Star Chamber and the jurisdiction of the Privy Council in England in 1641. Those views finally triumphed as the result of the Great Rebellion, and the Revolution of 1688. In this, as in other matters, Coke's writings passed on the views of the medieval English lawyers into modern English law. But these views were passed on with one important addition, which was the result of the rise, in the sixteenth century, of the modern territorial state. The law which was thus supreme was the law of England; and this included the law, written and unwritten, administered by the Courts of Common Law, by the Courts of Equity, by the Court of Admiralty, and by the Ecclesiastical Courts. Thus the modern doctrine of the rule of law has come, as the result of this long historical development, to mean the supremacy of all parts of the law of England, both enacted and unenacted.

Note

Chief Justice Coke's assertion of the supremacy of law was stated clearly in the case which follows.

Prohibitions del Roy
(1607) 12 Co Rep 63; 77 ER 1342

Note, upon Sunday the 10th of November in this same term, the King, upon complaint made to him by Bancroft, Archbishop of Canterbury, concerning prohibitions, the King was informed, that when the question was made of what matters the Ecclesiastical judges have cognizance, either upon the exposition of the statutes concerning tithes, or any other thing ecclesiastical, or upon the statute 1 El. concerning the high commission or in any other case in which there is not express authority in law, the King himself may decide it in his Royal person; and that the Judges are but the delegates of the King, and that the King may take what causes he shall please to determine, from the determination of the Judges, and may determine them himself. And the Archbishop said, that this was clear in divinity, that such authority belongs to the King by the word of God in the Scripture. To which it was answered by me, in the presence, and with the clear consent of all the Judges of England, and Barons of the Exchequer, that the King in his own person cannot adjudge any case, either criminal, as treason, felony, &c. or betwixt party and party, concerning his inheritance, chattels, or goods, &c. but this ought to be determined and adjudged in some Court of Justice. . . . And the Judges informed the King, that no

King after the Conquest assumed to himself to give any judgment in any cause whatsoever, which concerned the administration of justice within this realm, but these were solely determined in the Courts of Justice.

[T]hen the King said, that he thought the law was founded upon reason, and that he and others had reason, as well as the Judges: to which it was answered by me, that true it was, that God had endowed His Majesty with excellent science, and great endowments of nature; but His Majesty was not learned in the laws of his realm of England, and causes which concern the life, or inheritance, or goods, or fortunes of his subjects, are not to be decided by natural reason but by the artificial reason and judgment of law, which law is an act which requires long study and experience, before that a man can attain to the cognizance of it: that the law was the golden met-wand and measure to try the causes of the subjects; and which protected His Majesty in safety and peace: with which the King was greatly offended, and said, that then he should be under the law, which was treason to affirm, as he said; to which I said, that Bracton saith, *quod Rex non debet esse sub homine, sed sub Deo et lege.*

Note

The law to which the Crown was subject was the common law as changed from time to time by Parliament. It is worth noting that at this time Parliament was not as active in legislating as it is now; the common law was the main source of law and legislation was very much a subsidiary source.

(A) GOVERNMENT ACCORDING TO THE LAW

Government according to the law means that the executive or any civil authority or government official cannot exercise a power unless such exercise of it is authorised by some specific rule of law.

Entick v *Carrington*
(1765) 19 St Tr 1030
Court of Common Pleas

Two King's messengers, under the authority of a warrant issued by the Secretary of State, broke and entered Entick's house and took away his papers. Entick was alleged to be the author of seditious writings. When the messengers were sued by Entick for trespass to his house and goods, it was argued that the warrant was legal as the power to issue such warrants was essential to government as 'the only means of quieting clamours and sedition'.

LORD CAMDEN CJ: . . . This power, so claimed by the Secretary of State, is not supported by one single citation from any law book extant. It is claimed by no other magistrate in this kingdom but himself. . . .

Before I state the question, it will be necessary to describe the power claimed by this warrant in its full extent. If honestly exerted, it is a power to seize that man's papers, who is charged upon oath to be the author or publisher of a seditious libel; if oppressively, it acts against every man, who is so described in the warrant, though he be innocent. . . .

Such is the power, and therefore one should naturally expect that the law to warrant it should be clear in proportion as the power is exorbitant.

If it is law, it will be found in our books. If it is not to be found there, it is not law.

The great end, for which men entered into society, was to secure their property. That right is preserved sacred and incommunicable in all instances, where it has not been taken away or abridged by some public law for the good of the whole. The cases where this right of property is set aside by positive law, are various. Distresses, executions, forfeitures, taxes, etc. are all of this description; wherein every man by common consent gives up that right, for the sake of justice and the general good.

By the laws of England, every invasion of private property, be it ever so minute, is a trespass. No man can set his foot upon my ground without my licence, but he is liable to an action, though the damage be nothing . . . . If he admits the fact, he is bound to shew by way of justification, that some positive law has empowered or excused him. The justification is submitted to the judges, who are to look into the books; and see if such a justification can be maintained by the text of the statute law, or by the principles of common law. If no such excuse can be found or produced, the silence of the books is an authority against the defendant, and the plaintiff must have judgment.

According to this reasoning, it is now incumbent upon the defendants to shew the law, by which this seizure is warranted. If that cannot be done, it is a trespass.

Papers are the owner's goods and chattels: they are his dearest property; and are so far from enduring a seizure that they will hardly bear an inspection; and though the eye cannot by the laws of England be guilty of a trespass, yet where private papers are removed and carried away, the secret nature of those goods will be an aggravation of the trespass, and demand more considerable damages in that respect. Where is the written law that gives any magistrate such a power? I can safely answer, there is none, and therefore it is too much for us without such authority to pronounce a practice legal, which would be subversive of all the comforts of society. . . .

I come now to the practice since the Revolution, which has been strongly urged, with this emphatical addition, that an usage tolerated from the area of liberty, and continued downwards to this time through the best ages of the constitution, must necessarily have a legal commencement. Now, though that pretence can have no place in the question made by this plea, because no such practice is there alleged; yet I will permit the defendant for the present to borrow a fact from the special verdict, for the sake of giving it an answer.

If the practice began then, it began too late to be law now. If it was more ancient, the Revolution is not to answer for it; and I could have wished, that upon this occasion the Revolution had not been considered as the only basis of our liberty. . .

With respect to the practice itself, if it goes no higher, every lawyer will tell you, it is much too modern to be evidence of the common law . . . .

This is the first instance I have met with, where the ancient immemorable law of the land, in a public matter, was attempted to be proved by the practice of a private office. The names and rights of public magistrates, their power and forms of proceeding as they are settled by law, have been long since written, and are to be found in books and records. Private customs indeed are still to be sought from private tradition. But who ever conceived a notion, that any part of the public law could be buried in the obscure practice of a particular person?

To search, seize, and carry away all the papers of the subject upon the first warrant: that such a right should have existed from the time whereof the memory of man runneth not to the contrary, and never yet have found a place in any book of law; is incredible. But if so strange a thing could be supposed, I do not see, how we could declare the law upon such evidence.

But still it is insisted, that there has been a general submission, and no action brought to try the right.

I answer, there has been a submission of guilt and poverty to power and the terror of punishment. But it would be strange doctrine to assert that all the people of this land are bound to acknowledge that to be universal law, which a few criminal booksellers have been afraid to dispute. . . .

It is then said, that it is necessary for the ends of government to lodge such a power with a state officer; and that it is better to prevent the publication before than to punish the offender afterwards. . . . [W]ith respect to the argument of State necessity, or a distinction that has been aimed at between State offences and others, the common law does not understand that kind of reasoning, nor do our books take notice of any such distinctions. . . .

If the king himself has no power to declare when the law ought to be violated for reason of State, I am sure we his judges have no such prerogative.

Lastly, it is urged as an argument of utility, that such a search is a means of detecting offenders by discovering evidence. . . .

In the criminal law such a proceeding was never heard of; and yet there are some crimes, such for instance as murder, rape, robbery, and house-breaking, to say nothing of forgery and perjury, that are more atrocious than libelling. But our law has provided no paper-search in these cases to help forward the conviction. . . .

If, however, a right of search for the sake of discovering evidence ought in any case to be allowed, this crime above all others ought to be excepted, as wanting such a discovery less than any other. It is committed in open day-light, and in the face of the world; every act of publication makes new proof; and the solicitor of the treasury, if he pleases, may be the witness himself. . . .

I have now taken notice of everything that has been urged upon the present point; and upon the whole we are all of opinion, that the warrant to seize and carry away the party's papers in the case of a seditious libel, is illegal and void.

Question

Lord Camden CJ stated that 'by the laws of England every invasion of private property, be it ever so minute, is a trespass.' Is this still true? See, for example, s. 8 of the Police and Criminal Evidence Act 1984; s. 26 (1) of the Theft Act 1968, s. 6 (1) of the Criminal Damage Act 1971; ss. 7 and 24 of the Forgery and Counterfeiting Act 1981; s. 46 of the Firearms Act 1968; s. 23 (3) of the Misuse of Drugs Act 1971; and s. 3 of the Obscene Publications Act 1959.

Note

Views on the legality of official action, however, may differ. Lord Camden revealed an enthusiasm for liberty which he declared in a sweeping declaration when he stated:

> The great end for which men entered into society, was to secure their property. That right is preserved sacred and incommunicable in all instances, where it has not been taken away or abridged by some public law for the good of the whole.

In the extracts from the case which follows, echoes of Lord Camden's approach may be discerned in the judgment of Lord Denning in the Court of Appeal; whereas a much more restrictive approach was adopted in the House of Lords, having important consequences for the rights of the citizen, the power of Government, and the effectiveness of the rule of law in controlling the official exercise of power.

R* v *Inland Revenue Commissioners, ex parte Rossminster Ltd
[1980] AC 952
Court of Appeal

Section 20C of the Taxes Management Act 1970, as amended, provides:

> '(1) If the appropriate judicial authority' – and he is defined as the circuit judge – 'is satisfied on information on oath given by an officer of the board that – (a) there is reasonable ground for suspecting that an offence involving any form of fraud in connection with, or in relation to, tax has been committed and that evidence of it is to be found on premises specified in the information; and (b) in applying under this section, the officer acts with the approval of the board given in relation to the particular case, the authority may issue a warrant in writing authorising an officer of the board to enter the premises, if necessary by force, at any time within 14 days from the time of issue of the warrant, and search them. . . . (3) On entering the premises with a warrant under this section, the officer may seize and remove any things whatsoever found there which he has reasonable cause to believe may be required as evidence for the purposes of proceedings in respect of such an offence as is mentioned in subsection (1) above. . . .'

Suspecting that some unspecified tax fraud had been committed by Rossminster Ltd, officers of the Inland Revenue obtained warrants to search Rossminster's premises. The officers seized anything which they believed might be required as evidence of a tax fraud, but they did not inform Rossminster Ltd of the offences suspected or of the persons suspected of having committed them. The warrants simply followed the wording in s. 20C without specifying what particular offences were suspected. The Court of Appeal, reversing the decision of the Divisional Court, granted, *inter alia*, an order of certiorari to quash the warrants.

LORD DENNING: . . . Beyond all doubt this search and seizure was unlawful unless it was authorised by Parliament. . . . The trouble is that the legislation is drawn so widely that in some hands it might be an instrument of oppression. It may be said that 'honest people need not fear: that it will never be used against them: that tax inspectors can be trusted, only to use it in the case of the big, bad frauds.' This is an attractive argument, but I would reject it. Once great power is granted, there is a danger of it being abused. Rather than risk such abuse, it is, as I see it, the duty of the courts so to construe the statute as to see that it encroaches as little as possible upon the liberties of the people of England. . . .

The warrant is challenged on the ground that it does not specify any particular offence. . . . The justification is: 'We do not wish to tell more to those we suspect because we do not want them to know too much about what we intend to do. Otherwise they will be on their guard.'

Is this a just excuse? The words 'an offence involving any form of fraud in connection with, or in relation to, tax' are very wide words. We were taken by Mr

Davenport through a number of offences which might be comprised in them. There is no specific section in the Act itself. But there are a number of other offences which involve fraud. . . . It seems to me that these words 'fraud . . . in relation to . . . tax' are so vague and so general that it must be exceedingly difficult for the officers of the Inland Revenue themselves to know what papers they can take or what they cannot take. . . . The vice of a general warrant of this kind – which does not specify any particular offence – is two-fold. It gives no help to the officers when they have to exercise it. It means also that they can roam wide and large, seizing and taking pretty well all a man's documents and papers.

There is some assistance to be found in the cases. I refer to the law about arrest – when a man is arrested under a warrant for an offence. It is then established by a decision of the House of Lords that the warrant has to specify the particular offence with which the man is charged: see *Christie* v *Leachinsky* [1947] AC 573. I will read what Viscount Simon said, at p. 585:

> If the arrest was authorised by magisterial warrant, or if proceedings were instituted by the issue of a summons, it is clear law that the warrant or summons must specify the offence . . . it is a principle involved in our ancient jurisprudence. Moreover, the warrant must be founded on information in writing and on oath and, except where a particular statute provides otherwise, the information and the warrant must particularise the offence charged.

Lord Simmonds put it more graphically when he said, at p. 592:

> Arrested with or without a warrant the subject is entitled to know why he is deprived of his freedom, if only in order that he may, without a moment's delay, take such steps as will enable him to regain it.

So here. When the officers of the Inland Revenue come armed with a warrant to search a man's home or his office, it seems to me that he is entitled to say: 'Of what offence do you suspect me? You are claiming to enter my house and to seize my papers.' And when they look at the papers and seize them, he should be able to say: 'Why are you seizing these papers? Of what offence do you suspect me? What have these to do with your case?' Unless he knows the particular offence charged, he cannot take steps to secure himself or his property. So it seems to me, as a matter of construction of the statute and therefore of the warrant – in pursuance of our traditional role to protect the liberty of the individual – it is our duty to say that the warrant must particularise the specific offence which is charged as being fraud on the revenue.

If this be right, it follows necessarily that this warrant is bad. It should have specified the particular offence of which the man is suspected. On this ground I would hold that certiorari should go to quash the warrant.

House of Lords

LORD WILBERFORCE: . . . The integrity and privacy of a man's home, and of his place of business, an important human right has, since the second world war, been eroded by a number of statutes passed by Parliament in the belief, presumably, that his right of privacy ought in some cases to be over-ridden by the interest which the public has in preventing evasions of the law. Some of these powers of search are reflections of dirigisme and of heavy taxation, others of changes in mores. . . . A formidable number of officials now have powers to enter people's premises, and to take property away, and these powers are frequently exercised, sometimes on a large scale. Many people, as well as the respondents, think that this process has gone too far; that is an issue to be debated in Parliament and in the press.

The courts have the duty to supervise, I would say critically, even jealously, the legality of any purported exercise of these powers. They are the guardians of the citizens' right to privacy. But they must do this in the context of the times, i.e. of increasing Parliamentary intervention, and of the modern power of judicial review. In my respectful opinion appeals to 18th century precedents of arbitrary action by Secretaries of State and references to general warrants do nothing to throw light on the issue. Furthermore, while the courts may look critically at legislation which impairs the rights of citizens and should resolve any doubt in interpretation in their favour, it is no part of their duty, or power, to restrict or impede the working of legislation, even of unpopular legislation; to do so would be to weaken rather than to advance the democratic process. . . .

[On the question of the validity of the warrants his Lordship went on to state] I can understand very well the perplexity, and indeed indignation, of those present on the premises, when they were searched. Beyond knowing, as appears in the warrant, that the search is in connection with a 'tax fraud,' they were not told what the precise nature of the fraud was, when it was committed, or by whom it was committed. In the case of a concern with numerous clients, for example, a bank, without this knowledge the occupier of the premises is totally unable to protect his customers' confidential information from investigation and seizure. I cannot believe that this does not call for a fresh look by Parliament. But, on the plain words of the enactment, the officers are entitled if they can persuade the board and the judge, to enter and search *premises* regardless of whom they belong to: a warrant which confers this power is strictly and exactly within the parliamentary authority, and the occupier has no answer to it. I accept that some information as regards the person(s) who are alleged to have committed an offence and possibly as to the approximate dates of the offences must almost certainly have been laid before the board and the judge. But the occupier has no right to be told of this at this stage, nor has he the right to be informed of the 'reasonable grounds' of which the judge was satisfied. . . .

The Court of Appeal took the view that the warrants were invalid because they did not sufficiently particularise the alleged offence(s). The court did not make clear exactly what particulars should have been given – and indeed I think that this cannot be done. The warrant followed the wording of the statute 'fraud in connection with or in relation to tax': a portmanteau description which covers a number of common law (cheating) and statutory offences (under the Theft Act 1968 et al.). To require specification at this investigatory stage would be impracticable given the complexity of 'tax frauds' and the different persons who may be involved (companies, officers of companies, accountants, tax consultants, taxpayers, wives of taxpayers etc.). Moreover, particularisation, if required, would no doubt take the form of a listing of one offence and/or another or others and so would be of little help to those concerned. Finally, there would clearly be power, on principles well accepted in the common law, after entry had been made in connection with one particular offence, to seize material bearing upon other offences within the portmanteau. So, particularisation, even if practicable, would not help the occupier.

I am unable, therefore, to escape the conclusion, that adherence to the statutory formula is sufficient.

LORD SCARMAN: . . . My Lords, I agree that these appeals should be allowed and add some observations only because of the importance of the issues raised, and because I share the anxieties felt by the Court of Appeal. If power exists for officers of the Board of Inland Revenue to enter premises, if necessary by force, at any time of the day or night and then seize and remove any things whatsoever found there which they have reasonable cause to believe may be required as evidence for the purposes of proceedings in respect of any offence or offences involving any form of fraud in connection with, or in relation to, tax, it is the duty of the courts to see that it is not abused: for it is a breath-taking inroad upon the individual's right of privacy and right of property. Important as is the public interest in the detection and punishment of tax frauds, it is not to be compared with the public interest in the right of men and women to be secure in the privacy of their homes, their offices, and their papers. Yet if the law is that no particulars of the offence or offences suspected, other than that they are offences of tax fraud, need be given, how can the householder, or occupier of premises, hope to obtain an effective judicial review of the entry, search and seizure at the time of the events or shortly thereafter? And telling the victim that long after the event he may go to law and recover damages if he can prove the revenue acted unlawfully is cold comfort – even if he can afford it.

It is therefore with regret that I have to accept that, if the requirements of section 20C of the Taxes Management Act 1970, a section which entered the law as an amendment introduced by section 57 of the Finance Act 1976, are met, the power exists to enter, and search premises, and seize and remove things there found and that the prospect of an immediate judicial review of the exercise of the power is dim. Nevertheless, what Lord Camden CJ said in *Entick* v *Carrington* (1765) 19 State Tr 1029, 1066, remains good law today:

> No man can set his foot upon my ground without my licence, but he is liable to an action, though the damage be nothing . . . If he admits the fact, he is bound to show by way of justification, that some positive law has empowered or excused him.

The positive law relied on in this case is the statute. If the requirements of the statute have been met, there is justification: but, if they have not, there is none. . . .

Appeals allowed.

Note

Lord Camden CJ's approach in *Entick* v *Carrington* sought to offer protection to the citizen from harsh and arbitrary treatment at the hands of government. Two hundred years later, however, this principle was still not fully understood or accepted. In Northern Ireland in 1971, powers granted under the Civil Authorities (Special Powers) Act (N.I.) 1922 were exercised by the Northern Ireland government to intern persons suspected of having acted or being about to act in a manner prejudicial to the preservation of peace or the maintenance of order. Some of those interned were interrogated by the security forces. The Crompton Report (Cmnd. 4823, 1971) detailed the interrogation procedures as including keeping the detainees' heads covered with hoods; subjecting them to continuous monotonous noise; deprivation of sleep; deprivation of food and water, apart from meagre rations of bread and water at six-hourly intervals; and making the detainees stand facing a wall with legs apart and hands raised. Three Privy Counsellors (Lord Parker of Waddington, a former Lord Chief Justice, J. A. Carpenter, a former Cabinet Minister, and Lord Gardiner, a former Lord Chancellor) were given the task of examining these procedures. They failed to agree and produced two conflicting reports.

Report of the Committee of Privy Counsellors appointed to consider authorised procedures for the interrogation of persons suspected of terrorism

Chairman: Lord Parker of Waddington
Cmnd. 4901, 1972

The Majority in their Report noted that the information obtained from interrogating suspects was responsible for saving lives. While not accepting that the end justified the means, they considered that the measure of whether the means were morally acceptable had to take account of the prevailing conditions. Thus expressions such as 'humane', 'inhuman', 'humiliating' and 'degrading' would acquire different meanings under different conditions. In light of the conditions prevailing, the Majority considered that the interrogation techniques would be acceptable provided there were proper safeguards 'limiting the occasion on which and the degree to which they can be applied'. Thus the techniques should only be used 'in cases where it is considered vitally necessary to obtain information', and then they should be applied in conformity with the Directive on Military Interrogation. There should be guidelines to assist the interrogator 'as to the degree to which in any particular circumstances the techniques can be applied', breach of which should result in a report to his superior officer. The techniques should only be used under the express authority of a UK minister, who should lay down guidelines on their use which should remain secret. The Majority considered that the Minister should be advised by a small and experienced Committee appointed by the Prime Minister in consultation with the Leader of the Opposition. If the techniques used involved criminal assaults or gave rise to civil liability, the Majority recommended that the Minister should take legal advice and 'if need be steps to ensure protection for those taking part in the operation'. There should be a senior officer in overall control at the interrogation centre and a panel of skilled interrogators. Further, a doctor with some psychiatric training should be present to observe interrogations and to warn the controller if interrogation was being pressed too far. Finally there should be a procedure for the investigation of complaints.

LORD GARDINER'S REPORT: . . .

Were they authorised?

8. We have found this a point of some difficulty because our terms of reference appear to assume that the procedures were or are authorised. The only evidence before us on this point was that it could not be said that UK Ministers had ever approved them specifically, as opposed to agreeing the general principles set out in the Directive on Military Interrogation. If any document or Minister had purported to authorise them, it would have been invalid because the procedures were and are illegal by the domestic law and may also have been illegal by international law. I regard this point as so important that I must develop it.

9. I agree with my colleagues that the only relevant document is the Directive. This lays down two requirements:

(a) Those concerned are to acquaint themselves with the laws of the country concerned, and are not to act unlawfully under any circumstances whatever.

(b) They are to follow the principles laid down in Article 3 of The Geneva Convention Relative to the Treatment of Prisoners of War (1949) and these include the prohibition of 'outrages upon personal dignity, in particular, humiliating and degrading treatment'.

10. *Domestic law*

(a) By our own domestic law the powers of police and prison officers are well known. Where a man is in lawful custody it is lawful to do anything which is reasonably necessary to keep him in custody but it does not further or otherwise make lawful an assault. Forcibly to hood a man's head and keep him hooded against his will and handcuff him if he tries to remove it, as in one of the cases in question, is an assault and both a tort and a crime. So is wall-standing of the kind referred to. Deprivation of diet is also illegal unless duly awarded as a punishment under prison rules. So is enforced deprivation of sleep.

(b) In Northern Ireland in normal times the powers of the police and prison officers in relation to those in custody are substantially the same except for an immaterial difference in their Judges' Rules. Of the Regulations scheduled to the Civil Authorities (Special Powers) Act (Northern Ireland) 1922, Regulation 10 provides that 'Any officer of the Royal Ulster Constabulary, for the preservation of the peace and maintenance of order, may authorise the arrest without warrant and detention for a period of not more than 48 hours of any person for the purpose of interrogation'. This Regulation does not in any way extend the ordinary police powers as to the permissible methods or limits of interrogation. Regulation 11 provides a limited power of detention and a limited right to photograph and finger-print and Regulation 12 a limited right of internment. . . .

(c) We have received both written and oral representations from many legal bodies and individual lawyers from both England and Northern Ireland. There has been no dissent from the view that the procedures are illegal alike by the law of England and the law of Northern Ireland. . . .

(d) This being so, no Army Directive and no Minister could lawfully or validly have authorised the use of the procedures. Only Parliament can alter the law. The procedures were and are illegal. . . .

20. I am not in favour of making such a recommendation for each of the following five reasons:

(1) I do not believe that, whether in peace time for the purpose of obtaining information relating to men like the Richardson gang or the Kray gang, or in emergency terrorist conditions, or even in war against a ruthless enemy, such procedures are morally justifiable against those suspected of having information of importance to the police or army, even in the light of any marginal advantages which may thereby be obtained.

(2) If it is to be made legal to employ methods not now legal against a man whom the police believe to have, but who may not have, information which the police desire to obtain, I, like many of our witnesses, have searched for, but been unable to find, either in logic or in morals, any limit to the degree of ill-treatment to be legalised. The only logical limit to the degree of ill-treatment to be legalised would appear to be whatever degree of ill-treatment proves to be necessary to get the information out of him, which would include, if necessary, extreme torture. I cannot think that Parliament should, or would, so legislate.

(3) Our witnesses have felt great difficulty in even suggesting any fixed limits for noise threshold or any time limits for noise, wall-standing, hooding, or deprivation of diet or sleep.

All our medical witnesses agreed that the variations in what people can stand in relation to both physical exhaustion and mental disorientation are very great and believe that to fix any such limits is quite impracticable. . . .

(4) It appears to me that the recommendations made by my colleagues in the concluding part of their Report necessarily envisage one of two courses.

One is that Parliament should enact legislation enabling a Minister, in a time of civil emergency but not, as I understand it, in time of war, to fix the limits of permissible degrees of ill-treatment to be employed when interrogating suspects and that such limits should then be kept secret.

I should respectfully object to this, first, because the Minister would have just as much difficulty as Parliament would have in fixing the limits of ill-treatment and, secondly, because I view with abhorence any proposal that a Minister should in effect be empowered to make secret laws: it would mean that United Kingdom citizens would have no right to know what the law was about police powers of interrogation.

The other course is that a Minister should fix such secret limits without the authority of Parliament, that is to say illegally, and then, if found out, ask Parliament for an Act of Indemnity.

I should respectfully object even more to this because it would in my view be a flagrant breach of the whole basis of the Rule of Law and of the principles of democratic government.

(5) Lastly, I do not think that any decision ought to be arrived at without considering the effect on the reputation of our own country.

For many years men and women and a number of international organisations have been engaged in trying patiently to raise international moral standards, particularly in the field of human rights. The results are to be found in the Universal Declaration of Human Rights, the four Geneva Conventions, which 129 countries have signed and ratified, the International Covenant on Civil and Political Rights and The European Convention on Human Rights. . . . And this is not all. The World Conference on Religion and Peace, representative of all the world's religions, held in October 1970 declared

> The torture and ill-treatment of prisoners which is carried out with the authority of some Governments constitute not only a crime against humanity, but also a crime against the moral law

while the subsequent Consultation of all the Christian Churches declared

> There is today a growing concern at the frequency with which some authorities resort to the torture or inhuman treatment of political opponents or prisoners held by them. . . . There exists at the present time, in certain regions of the world, regimes using systematic methods of torture carried out in the most refined way. Torture itself becomes contagious. . . . The expediency of the moment should never silence the voice of the Church Authorities when condemnation of inhuman treatment is called for.

There have been, and no doubt will continue to be, some countries which act in this way whatever Conventions they have signed and ratified. We have not in general been one of these. If, by a new Act of Parliament, we now depart from world standards which we have helped to create, I believe that we should both gravely damage our own reputation and deal a severe blow to the whole world movement to improve Human Rights.

Note

Lord Gardiner's view was eventually adopted by the Government and the interrogation procedures were discontinued. The issue of the interrogation of internees eventually reached the European Court of Human Rights on a reference from the government of Ireland alleging that the interrogation procedures breached Art. 3 of the European Convention on Human Rights. In *Ireland* v *United Kingdom* (1978) EHRR 25, the European Court of Human Rights held that the procedures amounted to inhuman and degrading treatment contrary to Art. 3 but did not amount to torture.

Questions

If the Government in response to the majority report had introduced legislation to authorise the interrogation procedures complained of, would the doctrine of the rule of law have provided any further protection to citizens interned and subjected to these procedures? Is the rule of law to be equated simply with the idea of legality, or does it impose some moral constraints on Government?

Note

If the rule of law is to have any meaning in a democratic society, it must mean at least that those who enforce the law abide by the law; there must be no room for an 'ends justifies the means' mentality. This is confirmed by the following case.

R v *Horseferry Road Magistrates' Court, ex parte Bennett*
[1994] AC 42
House of Lords

Bennett, a New Zealand citizen, was wanted by United Kingdom police for a series of offences allegedly committed by him. He was arrested in South Africa but there was no extradition treaty between South Africa and the United Kingdom. The South African police, however, placed him on an aircraft bound for London where he was arrested by English police officers. The magistrates committed Bennett to the Crown Court for trial. He applied for judicial review of their decision alleging that he had been returned to the jurisdiction against his will as a result of kidnapping or quasi-extradition. He further alleged that this had occurred at the request of the English police and that the South African police had placed him on the plane on the pretext of deporting him to New Zealand via London thereby enabling English police to arrest him. Bennett contended that in these circumstances it would be an abuse of the process of the court to permit the prosecution to proceed. The Divisional Court dismissed his application for judicial review of the magistrates' decision on the basis that even if he had been kidnapped and illegally removed from South Africa with the collusion of English police officers, the court had no jurisdiction to inquire into these matters and prevent a prosecution as these were not relevant to the issue of whether he would have a fair trial. The House of Lords (Lord Oliver dissenting) reversed the decision of the Divisional Court.

LORD GRIFFITHS: . . . Your Lordships have been urged by the respondents to uphold the decision of the Divisional Court and the nub of its submission is that the role of the judge is confined to the forensic process. The judge, it is said, is concerned to see that the accused has a fair trial and that the process of the court is not manipulated to his disadvantage so that the trial itself is unfair; but the wider issues of the rule of law and the behaviour of those charged with its enforcement, be they police or prosecuting authority, are not the concern of the judiciary unless they impinge directly on the trial process. In support of this submission your Lordships have been referred to *R* v *Sang* [1979] 2 All ER 1222 esp at 1230, 1245–1246, [1980] AC 402 esp at 436–437, 454–455 where Lord Diplock and Lord Scarman emphasise that the role of the judge is confined to the forensic process and that it is no part of the judge's function to exercise disciplinary powers over the police or the prosecution. . . .

[After examining the cases on abuse of process his Lordship continued:]

Your Lordships are now invited to extend the concept of abuse of process a stage further. In the present case there is no suggestion that the appellant cannot have a fair trial, nor could it be suggested that it would have been unfair to try him if he had been returned to this country through extradition procedures. If the court is to have the power to interfere with the prosecution in the present circumstances it must be because the judiciary accept a responsibility for the maintenance of the rule of law that embraces a willingness to oversee executive action and to refuse to countenance behaviour that threatens either basic human rights or the rule of law.

My Lords, I have no doubt that the judiciary should accept this responsibility in the field of criminal law. The great growth of administrative law during the latter half of this century has occurred because of the recognition by the judiciary and Parliament alike that it is the function of the High Court to ensure that executive action is exercised responsibly and as Parliament intended. So also should it be in the field of criminal law and if it comes to the attention of the court that there has been a serious abuse of power it should, in my view, express its disapproval by refusing to act upon it. . . .

The courts, of course, have no power to apply direct discipline to the police or the prosecuting authorities, but they can refuse to allow them to take advantage of abuse of power by regarding their behaviour as an abuse of process and thus preventing a prosecution.

LORD BRIDGE OF HARWICH: . . . There is, I think, no principle more basic to any proper system of law than the maintenance of the rule of law itself. When it is shown that the law enforcement agency responsible for bringing a prosecution has only been enabled to do so by participating in violations of international law and of the laws of another state in order to secure the presence of the accused within the territorial jurisdiction of the court, I think that respect for the rule of law demands that the court take cognisance of that circumstance. To hold that the court may turn a blind eye to executive lawlessness beyond the frontiers of its own jurisdiction is, to my mind, an insular and unacceptable view. Having then taken cognisance of the lawlessness it would again appear to be a wholly inadequate response for the court to hold that the only remedy lies in civil proceedings at the suit of the defendant or in disciplinary or criminal proceedings against the individual officers of the law enforcement agency who were concerned in the illegal action taken. Since the prosecution could never have been brought if the defendant had not been illegally abducted, the whole proceeding is tainted. If a resident in another country is properly extradited here, the time when the prosecution commences is the time when the authorities here set the extradition process in motion. By parity of reasoning, if the authorities, instead of proceeding by way of extradition, have resorted to abduction, that is the effective commencement of the prosecution process and is the illegal foundation on which it rests. . . .

Appeal allowed. Case remitted to Divisional Court for further consideration.

Note

The idea of government according to law has been illustrated in a range of decisions by the courts developing the principles of *ultra vires* (*post* chapter 8) and natural justice (*post* chapter 8) which are the central doctrines in administrative law. By development of these doctrines the courts have sought to control the ways in which authorities exercise their powers and the procedures they adopt. Thus the exercise of a power by an authority will be struck down as *ultra vires* where the authority acts in excess of the power (see e.g. *Laker Airways Ltd* v *Department of Trade* [1977] QB 643), or it abuses the power by exercising it ignoring relevant considerations or taking irrelevant considerations into account (see e.g. *Associated Provincial Picture Houses Ltd* v *Wednesbury Corporation* [1948] 1 KB 223), or where it exercises the power for an improper purpose (see e.g. *Roberts* v *Hopwood* [1925] AC 578), or it exercises the power unreasonably (*Wednesbury, ante*). Where powers are exercised courts may also impose procedural requirements upon the authority exercising the power to ensure that the decision to exercise the power was taken in accordance with the rules of natural justice or, more recently, that the decision respected the requirements of fairness. Thus the decision-maker should be unbiased and the subject of the decision should have had a fair hearing. What is fair may vary with the circumstances, but matters which will be taken into account are whether the subject received adequate notice of the hearing and the charges, was allowed to present his case in a written or oral form and call witnesses, and whether he was allowed legal representation.

While these developments may help protect the citizen from the arbitrary exercise of power, do they have any effect on the legislature in controlling the laws it may pass and, therefore, the powers it may bestow upon government and other official agencies?

(B) THE RULE OF LAW AS A BROAD POLITICAL DOCTRINE

Bradley and Ewing, *Constitutional and Administrative Law*, (11th edn, 1993), p. 106, state:

> If the law is not to be merely a means of achieving whatever ends a particular government may favour, the rule of law must go beyond the principle of legality. The inherited experience and values of the legal system are relevant not only to the question, 'What legal authority *does* the government have for its acts?' but also to the question, 'What legal powers *ought* the government to have?'

Several other writers have sought to specify certain minimum standards which laws should attain.

J. Raz, 'The Rule of Law and its Virtue' (1977) 93 *LQR*, pp. 195 – 202

. . . The rule of law is a political ideal which a legal system may lack or may possess to a greater or lesser degree. That much is common ground. It is also to be insisted that the rule of law is just one of the virtues which a legal system may possess and by which it is to be judged. It is not to be confused with democracy, justice, equality (before the law or otherwise), human rights of any kind or respect for persons or for the dignity of man. A non-democratic legal system, based on the denial of human rights, on extensive poverty, on racial segregation, sexual inequalities and religious persecution may, in principle, conform to the requirements of the rule of law better than any of the legal systems of the more enlightened western democracies. This does not mean that it will be better than those western democracies. It will be an immeasurably worse legal system, but it will excel in one respect: in its conformity to the rule of law. . . .

1. The Basic Idea

'The rule of law' means literally what it says: The rule of the law. Taken in its broadest sense this means that people should obey the law and be ruled by it. But in political and legal theory it has come to be read in a narrower sense, that the government shall be ruled by the law and subject to it. The ideal of the rule of law in this sense is often expressed by the phrase 'government by law and not by men.' No sooner does one use these formulae than their obscurity becomes evident. Surely government must be both by law and by men. It is said that the rule of law means that all government action must have foundation in law, must be authorised by law. But is not that a tautology? Actions not authorised by law cannot be the actions of the government as a government. They would be without legal effect and often unlawful. . . . There is more to the rule of law than the law and order interpretation allows. It means more even than law and order applied to the government. I shall proceed on the assumption that we are concerned with government in the legal sense and with the conception of the rule of law which applies to government and to law and is no mere application of the law and order conception.

The problem is that now we are back with our initial puzzle. If the government is, by definition, government authorised by law the rule of law seems to amount to an empty tautology, not a political ideal.

The solution to this riddle is in the difference between the professional and the lay sense of law. For the lawyer anything is the law if it meets the conditions of validity laid down in the system's rules of recognition or in other rules of the system. This includes the constitution, parliamentary legislation, ministerial regulations, policeman's orders, the regulations of limited companies, conditions imposed in trading licences, etc. To the layman the law consists only of a subclass of these. To him the law is essentially a set of open, general and relatively stable laws. Government by law and not by men is not a tautology if 'law' means general, open and relatively stable law. In fact the danger of this interpretation is that the rule of law might set too strict a requirement, one which no legal system can meet and which embodies very little virtue. It is humanly inconceivable that law can consist only of general rules and it is very undesirable that it should. Just as we need government both by laws and by men, so we need both general and particular laws to carry out the jobs for which we need the law.

The doctrine of the rule of law does not deny that every legal system should consist of both general, open and stable rules (the popular conception of law) and particular laws (legal orders), an essential tool in the hands of the executive and the judiciary alike. As we shall see, what the doctrine requires is the subjection of particular laws to general, open and stable ones. It is one of the important principles of the doctrine that *the making of particular laws should be guided by open and relatively stable general rules.*

This principle shows how the slogan of the rule of law and not of men can be read as a meaningful political ideal. The principle does not, however, exhaust the meaning of the rule of law and does not by itself illuminate the reasons for its alleged importance. Let us, therefore, return to the literal sense of the 'rule of law.' It has two aspects: (1) that people should be ruled by the law and obey it, and (2) that the law should be such that people will be able to be guided by it. As was noted above, it is with the second aspect that we are concerned: the law must be capable of being obeyed. A person conforms with the law to the extent that he does not break the law. But he obeys the law only if part of his reason for conforming is his knowledge of the law. Therefore, if the law is to be obeyed *it must be capable of guiding the behaviour of its subjects.* It must be such that they can find out what it is and act on it.

This is the basic intuition from which the doctrine of the rule of law derives: the law must be capable of guiding the behaviour of its subjects. It is evident that this conception of the rule of law is a formal one. It says nothing about how the law is to be made: by tyrants, democratic majorities or any other way. It says nothing about fundamental rights, about equality or justice. It may even be thought that this version of the doctrine is formal to the extent that it is almost devoid of content. This is far from the truth. Most of the requirements which were associated with the rule of law before it came to signify all the virtues of the state can be derived from this one basic idea.

2. Some Principles

Many of the principles which can be derived from the basic idea of the rule of law depend for their validity or importance on the particular circumstances of different societies. There is little point in trying to enumerate them all, but some of the more important ones might be mentioned:

(1) *All laws should be prospective, open and clear.* One cannot be guided by a retroactive law. It does not exist at the time of action. Sometimes it is then known for certain that a retroactive law will be enacted. When this happens retroactivity does not conflict with the rule of law (though it may be objected to on other grounds). The law must be open and adequately publicised. If it is to guide people they must be able to find out what it is. For the same reason its meaning must be clear. An ambiguous, vague, obscure or imprecise law is likely to mislead or confuse at least some of those who desire to be guided by it.

(2) *Laws should be relatively stable.* They should not be changed too often. If they are frequently changed people will find it difficult to find out what the law is at any given moment and will be constantly in fear that the law has been changed since they last learnt what it is. But more important still is the fact that people need to know the law not only for short-term decisions (where to park one's car, how much alcohol is allowed in duty free, etc.) but also for long-term planning. Knowledge of at least the general outlines and sometimes even of details of tax law and company law are often important for business plans which will bear fruit only years later. Stability is essential if people are to be guided by law in their long-term decisions. . . .

(3) *The making of particular laws (particular legal orders) should be guided by open, stable, clear and general rules.* It is sometimes assumed that the requirement of generality is of the essence of the rule of law. This notion derives (as noted above)

from the literal interpretation of 'the rule of law' when 'law' is read in its lay connotations as being restricted to general, stable and open law. It is also reinforced by a belief that the rule of law is particularly relevant to the protection of equality and that equality is related to the generality of law. The last belief is, as has been often noted before, mistaken. Racial, religious and all manner of discrimination is not only compatible but often institutionalised by general rules.

The formal conception of the rule of law which I am defending does not object to particular legal orders as long as they are stable, clear, etc. But of course particular legal orders are mostly used by government agencies to introduce flexibility into the law. A police constable regulating traffic, a licensing authority granting a licence under certain conditions, all these and their like are among the more ephemeral parts of the law. As such they run counter to the basic idea of the rule of law. They make it difficult for people to plan ahead on the basis of their knowledge of the law. This difficulty is overcome to a large extent if particular laws of an ephemeral status are enacted only within a framework set by general laws which are more durable and which impose limits on the unpredictability introduced by the particular orders.

Two kinds of general rules create the framework for the enactment of particular laws: Those which confer the necessary powers for making valid orders and those which impose duties instructing the power-holders how to exercise their powers. Both have equal importance in creating a stable framework for the creation of particular legal orders.

Clearly, similar considerations apply to general legal regulations which do not meet the requirement of stability. They too should be circumscribed to conform to a stable framework. Hence the requirement that much of the subordinate administrative law-making should be made to conform to detailed ground rules laid down in framework laws. It is essential, however, not to confuse this argument with democratic arguments for the close supervision of popularly-elected bodies over law-making by non-elected ones. These further arguments may be valid but have nothing to do with the rule of law, and though sometimes they reinforce rule of law type arguments, on other occasions they support different and even conflicting conclusions.

(4) *The independence of the judiciary must be guaranteed.* It is of the essence of municipal legal systems that they institute judicial bodies charged, among other things, with the duty of applying the law to cases brought before them and whose judgments and conclusions as to the legal merits of those cases are final. Since just about any matter arising under any law can be subject to a conclusive court judgment it is obvious that it is futile to guide one's action on the basis of the law if when the matter comes to adjudication the courts will not apply the law and will act for some other reasons. The point can be put even more strongly. Since the court's judgment establishes conclusively what is the law in the case before it, the litigants can be guided by law only if the judges apply the law correctly. Otherwise people will only be able to be guided by their guesses as to what the courts are likely to do – but these guesses will not be based on the law but on other considerations.

The rules concerning the independence of the judiciary – the method of appointing judges, their security of tenure, the way of fixing their salaries and other conditions of service – are designed to guarantee that they will be free from extraneous pressures and independent of all authority save that of the law. They are, therefore, essential for the preservation of the rule of law.

(5) *The principles of natural justice must be observed.* Open and fair hearing, absence of bias and the like are obviously essential for the correct application of the law and thus, through the very same considerations mentioned above, to its ability to guide action.

(6) *The courts should have review powers over the implementation of the other principles.* This includes review of both subordinate and parliamentary legislation and of administrative action, but in itself it is a very limited review – merely to ensure conformity to the rule of law.

(7) *The courts should be easily accessible.* Given the central position of the courts in ensuring the rule of law (see principles 4 and 6) it is obvious that their accessibility is of paramount importance. Long delays, excessive costs, etc., may effectively turn the most enlightened law to a dead letter and frustrate one's ability effectively to guide oneself by the law.

(8) *The discretion of the crime preventing agencies should not be allowed to pervert the law.* Not only the courts but also the actions of the police and the prosecuting authorities can subvert the law. The prosecution should not be allowed, e.g. to decide not to prosecute for commission of certain crimes, or for crimes committed by certain classes of offenders. The police should not be allowed to allocate its resources so as to avoid all effort to prevent and detect certain crimes or prosecute certain classes of criminals.

This list is very incomplete. Other principles could be mentioned and those which have been mentioned need further elaboration and further justification (why – as required by my sixth principle – should the courts and not some other body be in charge of reviewing conformity to the rule of law? etc.). My purpose in listing them was merely to illustrate the power and fruitfulness of the formal conception of the rule of law. It should, however, be remembered that in the final analysis the doctrine rests on its basic idea that the law should be capable of providing effective guidance. The principles do not stand on their own. They must be constantly interpreted in light of the basic idea.

The eight principles listed fall into two groups. Principles 1 to 3 require that the law should conform to standards designed to enable it effectively to guide action. Principles 4 to 8 are designed to ensure that the legal machinery of enforcing the law should not deprive it of its ability to guide through distorted enforcement and that it shall be capable of supervising conformity to the rule of law and provide effective remedies in cases of deviation from it. All the principles directly concern the system and method of government in matters directly relevant to the rule of law. Needlesss to say many other aspects in the life of a community may, in more indirect ways, either strengthen or weaken the rule of law. A free press run by people anxious to defend the rule of law is of great assistance in preserving it, just as a gagged press or one run by people wishing to undermine the rule of law is a threat to it. But we need not be concerned here with these more indirect influences.

See also Lon. L. Fuller, *The Morality of Law* (2nd edn, 1969).

Some of the principles identified by Raz are given judicial expression in the cases which follow.

(i) *Laws should be clear*

Merkur Island Shipping Corp. v *Laughton and Others*
[1983] 2 AC 570
Court of Appeal

In an action arising from a trade dispute between the owners and crew of a ship, members of the International Transport Workers' Federation were sued for damages for losses arising from secondary industrial action in which they had been involved. In deciding whether a trade union was immune from tortious liability, the court had to construe three statutes: The Trade Union and Labour Relations Act 1974, the Trade Union and Labour Relations (Amendment) Act 1976, and the Employment Act 1980.

LORD DONALDSON MR: . . . At the beginning of this judgment I said that whilst I had reached the conclusion that the law was tolerably clear, the same could not be said of the way in which it was expressed. The efficacy and maintenance of the rule of law, which is the foundation of any parliamentary democracy, has at least two pre-requisites. First, people must understand that it is in their interests, as well as in that of the community as a whole, that they should live their lives in accordance with the rules and all the rules. Second, they must know what those rules are. Both are equally important and it is the second aspect of the rule of law which has caused me concern in the present case, the ITF having disavowed any intention to break the law.

In industrial relations it is of vital importance that the worker on the shop floor, the shop steward, the local union official, the district officer and the equivalent levels in management should know what is and what is not 'offside.' And they must be able to find this out for themselves by reading plain and simple words of guidance. The judges of this court are all skilled lawyers of very considerable experience, yet it has taken us hours to ascertain what is and what is not 'offside,' even with the assistance of highly experienced counsel. This cannot be right.

We have had to look at three Acts of Parliament, none intelligible without the other. We have had to consider section 17 of the Act of 1980, which adopts the 'flow' method of Parliamentary draftsmanship, without the benefit of a flow diagram. We have furthermore been faced with the additional complication that subsection (6) of section 17 contains definitions which distort the natural meaning of the words in the operative subsections. It was not always like this. If you doubt me, look at the comparative simplicity and clarity of Sir Mackenzie Chalmers's Sale of Goods Act 1893, his Bills of Exchange Act 1882, and his Marine Insurance Act 1906. But I do not criticise the draftsman. His instructions may well have left him no option. My plea is that Parliament, when legislating in respect of circumstances which directly affect the 'man or woman in the street' or the 'man or woman on the shop floor' should give as high a priority to clarity and simplicity of expression as to refinements of policy. Where possible, statutes, or complete parts of statutes, should not be amended but re-enacted in an amended form so that those concerned can read the rules in a single document. When formulating policy, ministers, of whatever political persuasion, should at all times be asking themselves and asking parliamentary counsel: 'Is this concept too refined to be capable of expression in basic English? If so, is there some way in which we can modify the policy so that it can be so expressed?' Having to ask such questions would no doubt be frustrating for ministers and the legislature generally, but in my judgment this is part of the price which has to be paid if the rule of law is to be maintained.

These sentiments were echoed by Lord Diplock in the House of Lords, at p. 612:

LORD DIPLOCK: . . . I see no reason for doubting that those upon whom the responsibility for deciding whether and if so what industrial action shall be taken in any given circumstances wish to obey the law, even though it be a law which they themselves dislike and hope will be changed through the operation of this country's constitutional system of parliamentary democracy. But what the law is, particularly in the field of industrial relations, ought to be plain. It should be expressed in terms that can be easily understood by those who have to apply it even at shop floor level. I echo everything that the Master of the Rolls has said in the last three paragraphs of his judgment in this case. Absence of clarity is destructive of the rule of law; it is unfair to those who wish to preserve the rule of law; it encourages those who wish to undermine it. The statutory provisions which it became necessary to piece together into a coherent whole in order to decide the stage 3 point are drafted in a manner which, having regard to their subject matter and the persons who will be called upon to apply them, can, in my view, only be characterised as most regrettably lacking in the requisite degree of clarity.

(ii) *Laws should be prospective*

Phillips v _Eyre_
(1870) LR 6 QB 1
Exchequer Chamber

The legislature of Jamaica had passed an Indemnity Act following the suppression of a rebellion in the colony. If the Act was valid it would prevent the plaintiff suing for assault and false imprisonment.

WILLES J: . . . Retrospective laws are, no doubt, prima facie of questionable policy, and contrary to the general principle that legislation by which the conduct of mankind is to be regulated ought, when introduced for the first time, to deal with future acts, and ought not to change the character of past transactions carried on upon the faith of the then existing law. . . . Accordingly, the Court will not ascribe retrospective force to new laws affecting rights, unless by express words or necessary implication it appears that such was the intention of the legislature. . . .

In fine, allowing the general inexpediency of retrospective legislation, it cannot be pronounced naturally or necessarily unjust. There may be occasions and circumstances involving the safety of the state, or even the conduct of individual subjects, the justice of which, prospective laws made for ordinary occasions and the usual exigencies of society for want of prevision fails to meet, and in which the execution of the law as it stood at the time may involve practical public inconvenience and wrong, summum jus summa injuria. Whether the circumstances of the particular case are such as to call for special and exceptional remedy is a question which must in each case involve matter of policy and discretion fit for debate and decision in the parliament which would have had jurisdiction to deal with the subject-matter by preliminary legislation, and as to which a court of ordinary municipal law is not commissioned to inquire or adjudicate.

Questions

1. Can the doctrine of the rule of law prevent Parliament enacting retrospective laws? (See War Damage Act 1965, enacted pursuant to *Burmah Oil* v *Lord Advocate* [1965] AC 75, *ante* p. 66.)

2. Is Lord Reid's confidence misplaced when he states in *Waddington* v *Miah* [1974] 2 All ER 377, at p. 379, that 'it is hardly credible that any government department would promote or that Parliament would pass retrospective criminal lesiglation'? See s. 1 of the War Crimes Act 1991, which provides:

1. Jurisdiction over certain war crimes

(1) Subject to the provisions of this section, proceedings for murder, manslaughter or culpable homicide may be brought against a person in the United Kingdom irrespective of his nationality at the time of the alleged offence if that offence—

(a) was committed during the period beginning with 1st September 1939 and ending with 5th June 1945 in a place which at the time was part of Germany or under German occupation; and

(b) constituted a violation of the laws and customs of war.

(2) No proceedings shall by virtue of this section be brought against any person unless he was on 8th March 1990, or has subsequently become, a British citizen or resident in the United Kingdom, the Isle of Man or any of the Channel Islands.

(Retrospective penal legislation contravenes Art. 7 of the European Convention on Human Rights.)

(iii) *The independence of the judiciary must be guaranteed*

The maintenance of the independence of the judiciary is essential if the rule of law is to be respected. In his presidential address to the Holdsworth Club in 1950, Lord Justice Denning, as he then was, stated:

> No member of the Government, no Member of Parliament and no official of any government department has any right whatever to direct or influence or to interfere with the decisions of any of the judges. It is the sure knowledge of this that gives the people their confidence in judges . . . The critical test which they must pass if they are to receive the confidence of the people is that they must be independent of the executive.

Independence requires that judges must be free to interpret and apply the law as they see fit subject only to correction on appeal to a higher court. A crucial role is played by the Lord Chancellor in protecting the independence of the judiciary. In the Twelfth Francis Mann Lecture delivered by Lord Hailsham (see 'The Office of Lord Chancellor and the Separation of Powers' (1989) 8 *Civil Justice Quarterly* 308), he described this duty as follows:

> . . . the essential function of the Lord Chancellor in the working of the constitution remains the same. He is in the business of defending and preserving the independence and integrity of the judiciary. If he does it well, then he is a good Lord Chancellor whatever his other defects. If he does it ill, whatever his other qualities, he is not.

The current Lord Chancellor, Lord Mackay, expressed similar views in the House of Lords in the debate 'The Judiciary: Independence' (see HL Deb vol 554, cols 751–804, 27 April 1994) where he stated (at col 791):

> I personally believe very strongly and fundamentally in the independence of the judiciary. I also believe that it is vitally important for the Lord Chancellor to do all he can to preserve the independence of the judiciary.

This debate, however, was initiated by the Shadow Lord Chancellor, Lord Irvine of Lairg, following concerns that Lord Mackay had sought to interfere with the way in which the President of the Employment Appeal Tribunal, Mr Justice Wood, implemented procedures for dealing with notices of appeal to the Tribunal. The EAT may only deal with appeals from decisions of Industrial Tribunals which disclose a point of law. The procedure to be followed is laid down in the Employment Appeal Tribunal Rules 1980 (SI 1980 No. 2035) which were made by the Lord Chancellor under the Employment Protection (Consolidation) Act 1978, s. 35 and Schedule 11. Rule 3(2) provided:

> Where it appears to the Registrar that the grounds of appeal stated in the notice of appeal do not give the Appeal Tribunal jurisdiction to entertain the appeal, he shall notify the appellant accordingly informing him of the reasons for the opinion and, subject to paragraph . . . (5) of this rule, no further action shall be taken on the appeal.

By 1990 there was a serious backlog of cases and the Lord Chancellor and Treasury made it clear that it was unlikely that additional High Court judges would be appointed. On 1 May 1992 following written proposals which were discussed at the AGM of the Tribunal in April, Mr Justice Wood introduced a new form of procedure which involved the possibility of a preliminary oral hearing before a judge if he considered that justice required it, to assist in determining whether the notice of appeal contained a point of law. The Lord Chancellor considered that this did not comply with the rules and that it was slowing down the processing of appeals. In December 1992 he commenced correspondence with Mr Justice Wood.

Letter dated December 18, 1992 from Lord Mackay to Mr Justice Wood

> As you know, over the last year and more, I have been concerned at the growing backlog of cases at the EAT. . . . I wish to ensure that public money is not wasted on preliminary hearings in cases where there is no point of law shown in the Notice of Appeal. I am disappointed to note that you are still making little use of the power which Rule 3 gives you to reject notices which in your opinion show no point of law to give the tribunal jurisdiction to register the appeal.
>
> I need hardly remind you that the backlog of cases in England and Wales started the year at an unacceptably high level and has continued to rise rapidly. I cannot sit by and watch the state of affairs get worse. Equally, I am unwilling to commit more expensive resources in the way of judges to sit extra courts while procedural rules which allow for cheap and efficient disposal of clearly unmeritorious cases might be used to much greater effect.

A meeting took place between Mr Justice Wood and Lord Mackay on 1 February 1993 followed by a further exchange of letters in which Lord Mackay encouraged Mr Justice Wood to use Rule 3 in full to dismiss 'unmeritorious' or 'hopeless' appeals. Mr Justice Wood responded on 5 March 1993, by indicating that preliminary hearings were not used in the case of 'unmeritorious' or 'hopeless' appeals but only in the case of ambiguous notices stating:

> In these ambiguous cases my predecessors have clearly thought it expeditious, economical and conducive to justice to resolve the ambiguity by fixing an early oral hearing. I share their view, and cannot see any alternative way of fairly resolving the problem . . .

Letter dated 19 March 1993 from Lord Mackay to Mr Justice Wood

> I did not seek further discussion of Rule 3 but had sought to make it clear to you that I was not prepared to accept preliminary hearings being held where Rule 3 provides a cheap and expeditious procedure for final disposal of a purported appeal.
>
> I ask you again for your immediate assurance that Rule 3 is henceforth to be applied in full and that preliminary hearings are not being used where no jurisdiction is shown in a notice of appeal.
>
> If you do not feel you can give me that assurance, I must ask you to consider your position.

This letter was widely viewed as a demand for Mr Justice Wood to cease using preliminary hearings or resign although Lord Mackay denied this subsequently (see HL Deb vol 553, col 498, 21 March 1994).

Letter dated 23 April 1993 from Mr Justice Wood to Lord Mackay

> In your letter of March 19 you express disappointment with my letter of the 5th and say that you do not wish further discussion of Rule 3. Both that letter and this are, of course, my own, but they have been written after consultation with many others on the Bench. The statement of the law in that letter is, in our view, correct.
>
> Your letter also puts your criticisms in rather a different form. You refer specifically to Preliminary Hearing Procedures and demand, in effect, that they be phased out, save for use as the equivalent of a hearing for directions.

[Mr Justice Wood repeated the arguments he had made previously justifying the use of preliminary hearings and concluded the letter:]

> I have, of course, given the most serious considertion to my position as you required of me. You have demanded that I exercise my judicial function in a way which you regard as best suited to your Executive purposes, but I have to say that in all the circumstances that present themselves to me and in the light of the existing law, I cannot regard compliance with your demand as conducive to justice.
>
> You express disappointment. I express profound regret that it has ever been the uncomfortable duty of a judge in this country in compliance with his Judicial Oath,

to write to a Lord Chancellor refusing a demand such as the one which you have made of me.

The Lord Chancellor's Private Secretary formally acknowledged receipt of this letter on 5 May 1993 stating that the Lord Chancellor would reply shortly; he never did. In March and April 1994 the *Observer* ran stories about this dispute between Mr Justice Wood and Lord Mackay. The issues were fully aired in the debate in the House of Lords on 27 April 1994.

The Judiciary: Independence
House of Lords, HL Deb vol 554, col 751–804 April 27, 1994

Lord Irvine of Lairg rose to ask Her Majesty's Government whether, given the documents placed by the Lord Chancellor in the Library of the House concerning the differences arising during the period 1991 to 1993 between him and the then President of the Employment Appeal Tribunal, Mr Justice Wood, on the proper procedures for dealing with notices of appeal to that Tribunal, they are satisfied that the independence of the judiciary has been upheld.

The noble Lord said: My Lords, this debate is not of narrow interest to lawyers and judges alone. It is about the fundamental principle, vital for all, that the courts are wholly independent of the Executive. Our constitution, largely unwritten, is firmly based on the separation of powers. Parliament makes laws; the judiciary interprets and applies them. Thus, the fundamental principle is that the courts must be wholly independent of the Executive. I am confident that the noble and learned Lord would be the first to affirm that fundamental principal. . . . For myself, I would be disposed to accept – others may disagree – that a Lord Chancellor is entitled to satisfy himself that any court is having regard to all its powers and duties for the efficient disposal of its business and is applying and fulfilling them in accordance with its own judicial interpretation of them. However, what a Lord Chancellor is not entitled to do is to demand that a judge or court substitute for its own judicial view of the extent of its powers and duties the extra-judicial views of the Lord Chancellor. I invite the noble and learned Lord the Lord Chancellor to say whether he agrees with those propositions; and to make clear the powers he conceives that he has – and had, in relation to Sir John Wood – and how those powers arise.

LORD DONALDSON OF LYMINGTON: . . . The third issue concerns the perception of the noble and learned Lord the Lord Chancellor of his dual role as a judge and as a Minister. When in 1971 the NIRC [National Industrial Relations Court] was established, the noble Lord, Lord Carr of Hadley, was the Secretary of State for Employment. I well remember his asking me on a social occasion whether, as president, I was responsible to the Lord Chancellor or to the Lord Chief Justice. I replied that I was responsible to neither. I was responsible solely to the law and to my own conscience. I have no doubt that I was right. That is what the independence of the judiciary is all about. The judiciary as a whole is independent of the Executive. But it must never be forgotten that every judge is independent of every other judge.

The position was, in some ways to my regret, no different 11 years later when I was appointed Master of the Rolls. I could invite; I could advise; I could seek to persuade; I could, if you will, exercise leadership. But I could never require a Lord Justice to do or to refrain from doing anything, and I never sought to do so.

The Lord Chancellor in his capacity as head of the judiciary is in no different a position. He could and did seek to persuade Sir John Wood that Sir John was not making full and proper use of the Rule 3 procedure as required by the law. But if that failed – as it did – there was nothing further that he could do in his judicial capacity. No judge can ask another judge for an undertaking – still less an undertaking in writing which casts doubt upon the validity of an oral undertaking given by the judge – that he will act contrary to the law as that judge sees it. Still less can he be asked to 'consider his position' if he refuses.

In his capacity as a Minister, the Lord Chancellor is responsible to Parliament for the administration of justice. That responsibility is not, however, unlimited. It extends only to the extent that Parliament has given him authority to supply or withhold resources or give directions. If Sir John Wood's view of the true scope of the Rule 3 procedure was unacceptable to the Lord Chancellor in his capacity as a Minister, his only remedy was to secure an amendment of Rule 3 putting his interpretation beyond doubt. Had he done so, I am absolutely certain that Sir John would have given effect to the rule as amended.

This apparent lack of accountability on the part of the judiciary may well seem an odd situation, particularly in this day and age when we hear so much about accountability. Our freedom under the law depends upon it, and I have to say that it has stood the test of time. That it can produce what has been described as constructive friction between the judiciary on the one hand and the Lord Chancellor and his department on the other is not open to doubt. However, given the necessary degree of sensitivity on both sides, the emphasis is usually upon the word 'constructive' rather than upon the word 'friction'.

LORD OLIVER OF AYLMERTON: . . . We have no written constitution, but the concept of judicial independence, which goes back to the Act of Settlement, is one with which we have all grown up. It is a concept of no very certain content and there is concern both in the judiciary and in the legal profession now that in recent years, under pressure from government, from civil servants and particularly from the Treasury, it is being more and more narrowly construed with an eye more to what is boasted to be 'value for money' than to fairness and impartiality in our system of justice. . . .

[His Lordship referred to Lord Denning's presidential address to the Holdsworth Club in 1950 (*ante* p. 197).]

I would have hoped that what my noble and learned friend Lord Denning said was so well entrenched in our constitution that it could not be challenged. Recent pronouncements in this House have seemed to indicate that the noble and learned Lord the Lord Chancellor and his department interpret the principle of judicial independence in a very much more restricted sense and as meaning simply this: that judicial independence is infringed only if an attempt is made to indicate or influence the decision in a particular individual case. I hope very much that I am wrong about that because one has only to think about it to see where the logical train then leads. On that analysis, a direction in the 1930s by the German Ministry of Justice that judges were not to decide disputes in favour of members of the Jewish faith or against party members would have been no infringement of their judicial independence – and that, of course, is palpably absurd. . .

Was the constitutional principle of judicial independence infringed by what occurred in this case? The noble and learned Lord the Lord Chancellor did not, I feel quite sure, have any intention whatever to overstep the bounds of his constitutional authority, but I am bound to say that it seems to me that on any analysis at all the pressure which was applied in this case, for whatever reason, constituted an attempt by the Executive – no doubt in the praiseworthy interests of economy and expedition – to overbear the conscience of a judge in the way in which he was to exercise his judicial duty and his judicial discretion – not, it is true, in an individual case but in the case generally of those individuals who are not sufficiently articulate to make it clear beyond any doubt that they are within the jurisdiction which they seek to invoke. And in the case of a court many of whose clientele are without legal aid, without legal assistance, some of them ill-educated perhaps and some perhaps belonging to ethnic minorities without a full command of the English language, that is a matter of very grave public concern.

I recognise that there are a lot of people – I dare say that there are perhaps some noble Lords among them – who regard Her Majesty's judges as unduly sensitive about their independence from Executive interference, equiperating that with a claim to be immune from control and from any criticism. I do not, for my part, think that that is true or fair – but then I would say that, wouldn't I? But we are not talking about criticism. We are talking about interference with the judicial function – about dictation. I would remind the House that whatever failings there may be perceived to be in the judiciary, it is the judge alone who stands between the power of the state and the freedom of the individual under the law.

I also recognise – indeed, we must all recognise – the very real difficulties which confront the noble and learned Lord the Lord Chancellor in fulfilling his responsibilities for overseeing the administration of justice and in steering a course dictated by the multiplicity of hats which his office compels him to wear. Judges are, after all, human beings and they are susceptible to ordinary human fraility. If the noble and learned Lord forms the opinion that a judge is not doing his job properly – if, for instance, he spends more time on the golf course than in court, or if he does *The Times* crossword on the Bench, or brings discredit on his office by his private life – then it is, of course, his duty to take him to task, even, if necessary, to the extent of urging him to resign his office.

So we must all recognise the noble and learned Lord's difficulties and accept that he is right to be concerned with the proper deployment of judicial resources. It is he who has to answer for the perceived shortcomings in the administration of the courts and it is his right and his duty to counsel, to persuade and, if necessary, to criticise. But the question, as always, is: Where do you draw the line?

Advice, counsel, persuasion, criticism and, if need be, yes, protest fall on one side of the line. But Parliament has established an appellate hierarchy to correct judicial errors of law; and direct Executive interference or attempted interference in the way in which a judge conscientiously seeks to comply with his judicial oath is a different matter altogether. I have to say – and I say it with regret and with the utmost deference to the noble and learned Lord – that it is, I think, very difficult for anyone who has read this correspondence to accept that it did not fall on the wrong side of the line. It cannot be construed otherwise – and I know that the learned judge did so construe it – than as an attempt to coerce a judge to carry out his judicial function and exercise his judicial discretion in a manner contrary to the reasoned dictates of his own conscience.

THE LORD CHANCELLOR (LORD MACKAY OF CLASHFERN): . . .I personally believe very strongly and fundamentally in the independence of the judiciary. I also believe that it is vitally important for the Lord Chancellor to do all that he can to preserve the independence of the judiciary.

Judicial independence does not mean that judges are above the law. The rule of law applies to them and to their work. When Pariament in a statute provides rules to which a tribunal is subject, the judges who are members of that tribunal are, in my view, bound to apply those rules. . . .

What I asked Mr Justice Wood, then president of the EAT, in my letter of 19th March 1993, to do was to assure me that he would apply one of these rules as laid down for the EAT. This rule had been made, as the noble Lord, Lord Mishcon, said, as long ago as 1976, was modified in 1980 and was still in force in the form then modified in 1991, 1992 and 1993 – that is, in the whole period to which the correspondence referred to in the question of the noble Lord, Lord Irvine of Lairg, relates. I did not ask Mr Justice Wood to adopt my reading of the rule. Contrary to what has been suggested, I had no quarrel with his reading of the rule, as given in his lengthy letter, which preceded the letter of 19th March. . . .

My situation is that all through this correspondence I was concerned to ensure that the rules laid down by Parliament were being operated by Mr Justice Wood and the Employment Appeal Tribunal as a whole. I was not substituting my reading of the rules for his reading or anything of that kind. I was anxious that he should apply the rules as he understood them.

EARL RUSSELL: My Lords, I am grateful to the noble and learned Lord for giving way, but could he say whether Mr Justice Wood ever failed to observe the rules as he, Mr Justice Wood, understood them?

THE LORD CHANCELLOR: My Lords, it is as clear as a pikestaff. I thought that I had made it clear; but obviously I have failed. I shall try to make it clear now. Mr Justice Wood was not applying the rule at all at the beginning of this correspondence. He made it perfectly plain, as I understand it, that he did not think that that rule was suitable for use in England and Wales. That is the passage that I read from the very first document. I do not know whether the noble Earl has the document. I regard this as extremely important because it is fundamental to my whole approach to the situation, and I should not like the noble Earl to be in any difficulty about it. On page 5 of the first document he states:

> 'There are remarkably few cases which are clearly frivolous on the face of the documentation. This is really a case of *de minimis*. In Scotland an HEO (unqualified) sends an appeal back to the appellant as disclosing no point of law if he so thinks. There is an appeal from him to the Judge. Having considered this rather different procedure I do not consider it desirable here in England and Wales nor do I like it particularly.'

The procedure to which he refers is Rule 3 of the employment appeal rules—

EARL RUSSELL: My Lords, I am sorry to intervene again, but can the noble and learned Lord show us that Mr Justice Wood was contravening Rule 3(2) as he understood it?

THE LORD CHANCELLOR: My Lords, he was not applying it at all. There is no question of a difficulty of interpretation: he was just not applying the rule at all. He thought it was unsuitable. He did not consider the procedure under the rule,

> 'desirable here in England and Wales nor do I like it particularly.'

He was declining to apply it altogether. It was not a question of the rule as he understood it; he was not applying it at all. That is a much more fundamental point. I hope that I have made it clear now.

That was the position that I encountered. It has been said more than once that I was seeking to rule out the use of the procedures of preliminary hearings in cases that were doubtful. That is not my position and never has been. What I asked from Mr Justice

Wood in the ultimate letter was, as I said, an assurance that he was fully applying the rule. If he was not prepared to give me that assurance, he should consider his position. . . . I have never suggested that it is not appropriate to use preliminary hearings in a doubtful case. What I have suggested, and what I think Mr Justice Wood agreed, was that it was not appropriate for preliminary hearings to be used in a case in which it was clear that there was no jurisdiction in the tribunal. . . .

I was asking him to give me the assurance that he was applying the rule which Parliament had laid down to regulate the affairs of the Employment Appeal Tribunal. I see that my noble and learned friend wishes to intervene. I give way.

LORD ACKNER: My Lords, I am much obliged. Can my noble and learned friend tell the House exactly what are his criticisms of the letter from Mr Justice Wood of 5th March 1993?

THE LORD CHANCELLOR: My lords, I have no particular criticism of the letter. I am saying that the letter sets out Mr Justice Wood's understanding of the rule. I have no quarrel with that. However, what I did find absent from the letter was an undertaking by Mr Justice Wood that he would apply the rule. That is an important difference – that he would apply the rule. Your Lordships may think that the distinction is not important, but I believe that I will be able to show the House that it is.

LORD CALLAGHAN OF CARDIFF: My Lords, I am struggling to try to get to the truth of the matter. I just do not understand – and I apologise to all the other distinguished Members here who do – the status of such rules of Parliament. Is the Lord Chancellor the final arbiter of their meaning? Alternatively, is there some other body which is able to determine how the rules should be applied if there is a difference between a judge and the Lord Chancellor? For example, is there any appeal available?

THE LORD CHANCELLOR: My Lords, if there is a question of the meaning of the rule between myself and somebody else, I could have that determined in the court, if it were necessary. But this was not a question of the meaning of the rule. He was setting out the meaning of the rule at great length but I had not asked for that. What I had asked him for was an assurance that he was applying the rule, because your Lordships will remember that this correspondence started with an analysis by Mr Justice Wood in which he said this rule was not appropriate for England and Wales for reasons which he gave.

Parliament, or at least the Lord Chancellor under the authority of Parliament, had enacted the rule for England and Wales and had done so, in its form then in operation, in 1980. Therefore the opinion of Mr Justice Wood as to whether or not it was a good rule was of absolutely no consequence. So far as I was concerned, there was no dispute whatever between me and Mr Justice Wood about the meaning of the rule. What I wanted to know was whether he was applying the rule, and if he was applying the rule there was no problem about him saying so. He could give me that undertaking perfectly well. But he was not applying the rule, why not – not or else. Why not? 'What is your position? You are a statutory tribunal operating statutory rules. If you are not able to give me an assurance that you are applying the rules applicable to the tribunal, what is your explanation? What is your position? Consider it very carefully', because it must be quite wrong for a judge, subject to rules laid down by Parliament, not to apply them. That is the crux of this matter.

The response from Mr Justice Wood to my letter makes no reference whatever to terminating his position either as the President of the Employment Appeal Tribunal or as a judge. None whatever. I am not directing this correspondence to anyone except Mr Justice Wood; and he certainly did not in this letter of reply make any reference whatsoever to his entitlement to office as a judge, or as the President of Appeal Tribunal. What he says, in effect, is 'I am not giving this undertaking because it is contrary to my judicial oath'. I summarise as your Lordships have heard the whole letter. The point I make about that is that the judicial oath is that, 'I would write to all manner of persons according to the laws and usages of this realm'. So far as this is concerned, one of these laws was Rule 3 of the Employment Appeal Tribunal rules. I still do not understand why that undertaking was not given, but there was hope in his letter of 23rd April 1993 which states at the foot of page 1:

> 'In May 1992, in anticipation of the vast increase in the number of appeals, we introduced a new system under Rule 3'.

That is when he began to move from his original position as stated at the beginning of the document to the operation of Rule 3. The letter continues:

> 'We would not claim that it is perfect, and with experience it is being refined'.

So Mr Justice Wood was telling me that procedures in his EAT were moving, and I was delighted with that and anxious to see that that would happen. That is the reason I gave no further response to Mr Justice Wood, because I had seen before that he reacted quite strongly in his paper that went round the EAT to pressure being put on him to apply the rules as Parliament had enacted them. But then after a while, in May 1992, he did in fact make a move. I had hoped that the corresponding thing would happen after April 1993 and that he would fully apply the rule.

Many noble Lords have said that this has been a most unhappy debate. Your Lordships will understand that it has been a most unhappy matter for me ever since this matter arose. I certainly very greatly regret that this arose between me and Mr Justice Wood; and certainly looking back on it now with hindsight I wish that I had expressed myself more plaintly. But I am absolutely satisfied that the basic matter that I was seeking is a matter to which I was well entitled under the law of this land and was in no way prejudicial to the proper judicial independence of the judge. I am a strong believer in the independence of the judiciary individually and as a whole; and so long as I have the privilege of holding the office which I do, I shall do everything in my power to uphold that. But it is part of the principle that that independence is exercised according to and under the rule of law and I have responsibility for that also.

Some wider matters have been raised in the debate, going beyond what was mentioned in the Question. The office of the Lord Chancellor is a difficult one: I can attest to that. However, I do not think that it is easy to work out, against the background of our system, a good alternative that would protect, as this office does, the independence of the judiciary. I believe that it is important that in this country the Supply for the Crown is voted by the House of Commons. Therefore, it is necessary that there be some person accountable to Parliament who has responsibility for the courts. I believe that the arrangement under which the Lord Chancellor, as head of the judiciary, is also responsible to Parliament for the administration of the courts is probably as good an arrangement as we can achieve. I am open to detailed suggestions as to how this might be done. I know that some of my noble and learned friends in previous incarnations have been asked to provide me with some detail of their thoughts on these matters. However, I know that it is so difficult that the thoughts in writing are still awaited.

As I said at the outset, I am extremely grateful to the noble Lord, Lord Irvine of Lairg, for raising the matter, and also for the manner in which he raised it. It was put forward in a fair manner, giving me an opportunity to explain the matter fully. I greatly regret that I have taken much longer in doing so then I should normally have liked to, but I regard the matter as of fundamental importance, as your Lordships have done. It is important that your Lordships should understand that I was not telling this judge how to do his work. All I was telling him was that I wished him to give me the assurance that he was applying the rules which had been enacted under the authority of Parliament by my predecessors as Lord Chancellor.

I utterly repudiate any suggestion that I have wrongfully interfered with the independence of the judiciary or that I have in any way misled your Lordships at any time in the answers that I have given. I thoroughly believe that my answer was as truthful and as full as I could possibly give in the circumstances of an oral Question.

I also take the view that these are matters of importance about which we need continually to be on our guard. I am extremely sorry if I have caused any offence whatever to Mr Justice Wood. If I could have thought of better language, with hindsight I would have used it. But I was thinking entirely of the position which he had as a judge in a statutory tribunal with statutory rules. That is what I had in mind, nothing else. The letter was directed to him and not to anyone else.

I am grateful to your Lordships for your patience in listening to this, I do not wish to trespass on that patience any longer. . .

Questions

1. Was the Lord Chancellor guilty of unwarranted Executive interference in judicial affairs?

2. Should financial considerations take priority over the demands of justice? Is it for the judiciary or the Executive to determine what the 'demands of justice' are?

3. Is there a need to reconsider the office of Lord Chancellor as suggested by Lord Lester of Herne Hill in the above debate:

> I recognise that the Lord Chancellor has a duty to ensure that the legal system is efficiently administered and that it is financially accountable. I share the view of the noble Lord, Lord Irvine of Lairg, about that. Judicial independence does not mean that judges should be immune from being disciplined when they fail to perform their duties properly; or that the budget for the legal system is to be determined by the judges rather than by Parliament. But what it does mean, I suggest, is that the old system has become, in the office of Lord Chancellor, too institutionally schizophrenic to be able to reconcile the divergent, and to some extent inconsistent, requirements of public accountability, judicial independence and efficiency in the administration of justice. We surely need some new institution, some kind of judicial and legal services commission to protect the independence of the judges and of the legal profession from the pressures which the Lord Chancellor, as a politically active and administratively vigorous Minister of Justice, and his officials are driven to exert.

Note

For further discussion of judicial independence see: Purchas, 'The constitution in the market place' (1993) 143 *NLJ* 1604, 'Lord Mackay and the judiciary' (1994) 144 *NLJ* 527, 'What is happening to judicial independence?' (1994) 144 *NLJ* 1306; Oliver, 'The Lord Chancellor's Department and the judges' [1994] *Public Law* 157; McGarvie, 'Judicial responsibility for the operation of the court system' (1989) 63 *ALJ* 79; Kirby, 'Malaysia – the Judiciary and the Rule of Law' (1988) 41 *ICJR* 40.

(C) DICEY AND THE RULE OF LAW

Dicey's views on the rule of law cannot be ignored because of the lasting influence he has had. His influence is all the more remarkable in light of the widespread criticisms which have been levelled against his views. Dicey's views derived from his understanding of the nature of representative democracy in the UK as 'unitary [and] self-correcting . . . in which the will of the electors was expressed through Parliament, and in which Parliament controlled the government' (P. Craig, *Public Law and Democracy in the United Kingdom and the United States of America* (1990)). In *An Introduction to the Study of the Law of the Constitution* Dicey devoted a large part of the book to his exposition of the rule of law, to which he attributed three meanings. The views of Dicey's critics will be stated after each.

(i) *The rule of law and discretionary powers*

A. V. Dicey, *An Introduction to the Study of the Law of the Constitution* (10th edn, 1965), pp. 188 and 202

We mean, in the first place, that no man is punishable or can be lawfully made to suffer in body or goods except for a distinct breach of law established in the ordinary legal manner before the ordinary courts of the land. In this sense the rule of law is contrasted with every system of government based on the exercise by persons in authority of wide, arbitrary, or discretionary powers of constraint. . . . It means . . . the absolute supremacy or predominance of regular law as opposed to the influence of arbitrary power, and excludes the existence of arbitrariness, of prerogative, or even of wide discretionary authority on the part of the government. Englishmen are ruled by the law, and by the law alone; a man may with us be punished for a breach of the law, but he can be punished for nothing else.

Sir Ivor Jennings, *The Law and the Constitution* (5th edn, 1959), pp. 54 – 58

Dicey and the Rule of Law
The particular principle of the individualist or *laissez-faire* school was that any substantial discretionary power was a danger to liberty. The fact that he held such a principle was not explicitly avowed by Dicey, because he assumed that he was analysing not his own subjective notions (shared, of course, by many of his contemporaries), but the firm and unalterable principles of English constitutional law. . . . We need only contest the idea that the rule of law and discretionary powers are contradictory.

If we look around us we cannot fail to be aware that public authorities do in fact possess wide discretionary powers. Many of them formed part of the law even when Dicey wrote in 1885. Any court can punish me for contempt of court by imprisoning me for an indefinite period. If I am convicted of manslaughter, I may be released at once or imprisoned for life. If I am an alien, my naturalisation is entirely within the discretion of the Home Secretary. If the Queen declares war against the rest of the world, I am prohibited from having dealings abroad. If the country is in danger, my property can be taken, perhaps without compensation. If a public health authority wants to flood my land in order to build a reservoir, it can take it from me compulsorily. I can be compelled to leave my work for a month or more, in order to serve on a jury. All these powers, and many more, were possessed by public authorities in 1885, and can still be exercised.

Dicey did not mention all these, because nowhere in his book did he consider the *powers* of authorities. He seemed to think that the British Constitution was concerned almost entirely with the *rights of individuals.* He was imagining a constitution dominated by the doctrine of *laissez-faire.* The function of government, as he unconsciously assumed, was to protect the individual against internal and external aggression. Given such protection, each individual was allowed to live his life almost as he pleased, so long as he did not interfere with the similar liberty of others. He regarded this as desirable, and therefore tended to minimise the extent to which public authorities could interfere with private action. . . .

Nevertheless, the argument need not be placed entirely on this narrow ground. For the main discretionary power is placed in England not in the executive but in Parliament. Parliament, as has already been emphasised, can pass what legislation it pleases. It is not limited by any written constitution. Its powers are not only wide, but unlimited. In most countries, not only the administrative authorities but also the legislature have powers limited by the constitution. This, one would think, is the most effective rule of law. In England, the administration has powers limited by legislation, but the powers of the legislature are not limited at all. There is still, it may be argued, a rule of law, but the law is that the law may at any moment be changed.

Dicey attempts to meet this argument in two ways. 'The commands of Parliament,' he said, 'can be uttered only through the combined action of its three constituent parts, and must, therefore, always take the shape of formal and deliberate legislation.' Formal it may be; it may not be deliberate. We saw – Dicey saw before he died in 1922 – how the Defence of the Realm Act was passed in 1914. The Cabinet decided that it wanted drastic powers. The majority which it commanded in the House of Commons supported its motion to suspend the Standing Orders. The Bill was passed through at one sitting. The House of Lords did the same. Thus at one stroke, without any long deliberation, the Cabinet acquired the powers it needed. The 'gold standard' was similarly swept away in 1931. The Cabinet ordered the Bank of England not to exchange notes into gold. The next day Parliament met and the necessary legislation was passed through not only to make paper currency inconvertible, but also to ratify the illegal acts of the Cabinet and of the Bank before the Act was passed. Here was arbitrary power indeed, but it was by no means as arbitrary as the powers exercised by Parliament in 1939 and 1940.

R. F. V. Heuston, 'The Rule of Law' in *Essays in Constitutional Law* (2nd edn, 1964) pp. 40 – 42

The Rule of Law and Discretionary Powers

Two criticisms have, however, been made of this aspect of Dicey's definition. First, it is said that it is difficult to distinguish between regular law and arbitrary power. If the law gives the power, how can it be arbitrary or irregular? It may be very undesirable for such a power to have been given, but if it has been given, and validly given according to the legislative forms of that particular society, how, it is said, can it be criticised as being contrary to the Rule of Law? . . . What is authorised by the law cannot indeed be illegal within the framework of that particular system, but it may very well be contrary to the Rule of Law as a principle of constitutional government. The difficulty no doubt arises from the fact that Dicey described his doctrine as 'the Rule of Law,' thereby giving the impression that it was in some way a legal principle, whereas it is in truth only a constitutional principle based upon the practice of liberal democracies of the Western world. In this sense, the doctrine is still perfectly true today. Everyone, high or low, must be prepared to justify his acts by a reference to some statutory or common law power which authorises him to act precisely in the way in which he claims he can act. Superior orders or state necessity are no defence to an action otherwise illegal.

Secondly, it has been said that Dicey erred in saying that the doctrine of the Rule of Law 'excludes the existence even of wide discretionary authority on the part of the government.' This is certainly not true today. Modern government, as is well known, cannot be carried on at all without a host of wide discretionary powers, which are granted to the executive by the large number of statutes annually passed by Parliament. But it must be remembered, first of all, the kind of man Dicey was, and secondly, the times in which he wrote. First, Dicey was in politics an old-fashioned Whig. He was also a very typical example of the common lawyer who does not seriously believe in the existence of the Statute Book. To the true common lawyer the law is to be found in the law reports and books of authority. There are indeed statutes, but they can always be looked up if the opportunity arises. The judges, as has been well said, have never entered into the spirit of the Benthamite game and have always treated the statute as an interloper upon the rounded majesty of the common law. Secondly, it must be recalled that Dicey's great work was written in the early 1880s, a period when the *laissez-faire* state of the Victorians was only just beginning to give way to the welfare state of the modern world. Dicey was an acute, a marvellously acute, judge of public opinion and of the impact upon public opinion of legislative power, but even he hardly foresaw the extent to which statutory powers of government would change the nature of English constitutional law. Today the fundamental problem is that of the control of discretionary powers, and it is indeed a serious criticism of Dicey's doctrine that he suggests that discretionary powers are in some way undesirable or unnecessary.

Kenneth Culp Davis, *Discretionary Justice* (1971), pp. 17 and 42

Even when rules can be written, discretion is often better. Rules without discretion cannot fully take into account the need for tailoring results to unique facts and circumstances of particular cases. The justification for discretion is often the need for individualized justice. This is so in the judicial process as well as in the administrative process.

Every governmental and legal system in world history has involved both rules and discretion. No government has ever been a government of laws and not of men in the sense of eliminating all discretionary power. Every government has always been *a government of laws and of men.* A close look at the meaning of Aristotle, the first user of the phrase 'government of laws and not of men,' shows quite clearly that he did not mean that governments could exist without discretionary power. . . .

Elimination of all discretionary power is both impossible and undesirable. The sensible goal is development of a proper balance between rule and discretion. Some circumstances call for rules, some for discretion, some for mixtures of one proportion, and some for mixtures of another proportion. In today's American legal system, the special need is to eliminate *unnecessary* discretionary power, and to discover more successful ways to confine, to structure, and to check necessary discretionary power.

Note

Compare Heuston's first point with the contrasting views expressed in the Court of Appeal and the House of Lords in the *Rossminster* case above, p. 181. Heuston asserted that no one had sought to criticise Dicey's views as they related to the criminal law. Since Heuston wrote, these views have also been subjected to criticism.

A. T. H. Smith, 'Comment' [1985] *Public Law* 608

. . . Whilst constitutional lawyers and jurists talk in terms of Diceyan rhetoric – that 'no man is punishable or can be made lawfully to suffer in body or goods except for a distinct breach of law established in the ordinary legal manner before the ordinary courts of the land. In this sense the rule of law is contrasted with every system of government based on the exercise by persons in authority of wide, arbitrary, or discretionary powers of constraint,' the reality within the criminal process is rather different. My thesis is that (1) English criminal law is inherently offensive to the principle of legality – being a common law system, it is in places highly uncertain, and one that is therefore necessarily retrospective in character when the law is judicially developed; (2) that the judges (by whom I mean principally the House of Lords) in administering it are not currently sufficiently concerned with the protection of civil liberties; and (3) that the enactment of a criminal code would provide a fixed and objective starting point for delineating the permissible restrictions on the right to personal freedom, even if it could not solve all the problems of certainty inherent in a government by laws and men.

The Diceyan model was that the judges constituted a bulwark between the citizen and the State in the protection of the citizen's civil liberties. He illustrated this by reference to freedoms of the person, speech, and assembly, and argued that the law had been developed by the judges to support and bolster these values. It is commonly supposed by constitutional theorists and jurists that this protective pattern repeats itself throughout the criminal process, and that the rule of law infiltrates and permeates the criminal justice system through the application of *nulla poena* principles, with concomitant rules enjoining the strict interpretation of criminal statutes and narrowing where possible the ambit of the criminal law. Criminal lawyers think otherwise. Glanville Williams, for example, observes: '. . . in criminal cases, the courts are anxious to facilitate the conviction of villains, and they interpret the law wherever possible to secure this.' There seems to be, then, a gap between rhetoric and practice in the application and moulding of the scope of the substantive criminal law, and one that should be recognised and if possible accommodated by constitutional theorists.

Dicey's principal concern was with encroachment by the Executive (including the police) on civil liberties. He would, I think, warmly applaud the activities of the judges in the area that we now call administrative law. When a man's property and livelihood or his reputation are at stake in civil proceedings, the judges exhibit an admirable concern to protect the citizen against an encroaching State; they have fashioned what Professor Wade says amounts to a constitution. Furthermore, when they are supervising the agency of the State at the sharp end of the criminal law, the police, they frequently act in the way that Dicey suggests that they do and should.

There are other times, however, when civil libertarians will see their supervision as less commendable, instancing perhaps *Sang* [1980] AC 402, *Wills* v *Bowley* [1983] 1 AC 57 and *Mohammed-Holgate* v *Duke* [1984] AC 437. My assertion is that the checks and balances system that obtains as between the police and the courts, even if it is sometimes out of kilter, is not available at all as a fetter in the administration by the judges of the substantive criminal law, and that when the courts behave as an integral part of an institution whose principal purpose is the prevention of crime through the use of the criminal law, civil liberties are at risk. Against this possibly unwitting combination of police and courts, there is very little protective covering for the individual who has, in all probability, been up to some socially distasteful activity. One does not wish to exaggerate the threat that this poses. After all, the process is for the most part highly visible, the defendant has counsel to argue his corner and there is rarely any public expression of concern about the judges' manipulation of the substantive criminal law in a country where such criticism is liberally permitted. But the aims of the criminal justice system should include provision for the best safeguards of civil liberties as are compatible with maximum social protection, and a starting point for this should be the enactment of a criminal code. Decisions as to the mental element of the law of murder or rape, for example, upon which the liberty of the subject vitally depends, should be treated as legislative ones, and not be left at large for determination by the judiciary as at present.

My criticism of the present system of criminal law adjudication is arguably less apt now than it was in Dicey's time. Since then, the judges have formally foresworn their claim to be able to create new crimes. But I find it strange that Dicey did not see that the state of the substantive criminal law, with the discretion that it accorded to the judges themselves, was at odds with the principles he espoused. Even as Dicey was handing in his manuscript to his publishers in 1884, that other great Victorian jurist, Sir James Stephen, was deciding in his judicial capacity in *Price* that it was not for the judges to create new crimes in such a way as to outlaw cremation. Stephen's view was that the criminal law could best reflect the principles of legality if reduced to a criminal code. But his efforts in that direction had only two years previously finally foundered on the hostility of his judicial brethren to the prospect of having their discretionary powers and authority reduced.

Note

Article 7 of the European Convention on Human Rights (*post* p. 463) prohibits the retrospective imposition of criminal liability. Thus the creation by statute of offences with retrospective effect or the recognition by the courts of new common law offences with retrospective effect is offensive to the Convention (see *X Ltd and Y* v *UK No. 8710/79*, 28 DR 77 (1982)). A more frequent problem, however, is that of courts increasing the ambit of a particular offence either through the medium of statutory interpretation or the development of the common law definition of the offence to meet a new situation. In such a situation there is no breach of the Convention if such an interpretation or development was reasonably foreseeable at the time the act was performed or the omission occurred and was consistent with the essence of the offence (see *X Ltd and Y* v *UK* at p. 81 and *SW* v *UK* Case No. 47/1994/494/576 and *CR* v *UK* Case No. 48/1994/495/577, *The Times* December 5, 1995).

(ii) *The rule of law and equality*

A. V. Dicey, *An Introduction to the Study of the Law of the Constitution* pp. 202 – 203

It means . . . equality before the law, or the equal subjection of all classes to the ordinary law of the land administered by the ordinary law courts; the 'rule of law' in this sense excludes the idea of any exemption of officials or others from the duty of obedience to the law which governs other citizens or from the jurisdiction of the ordinary tribunals; there can be with us nothing really corresponding to the 'administrative law' (*droit administratif*) or the 'administrative tribunals' (*tribunaux administratifs*) of France. The notion which lies at the bottom of the 'administrative law' known to foreign countries is, that affairs or disputes in which the government or its servants are concerned are beyond the sphere of the civil courts and must be dealt with by special and more or less official bodies. This idea is utterly unknown to the law of England, and indeed is fundamentally inconsistent with our traditions and customs.

R. F. V. Heuston, 'The Rule of Law' in *Essays in Constitutional Law* (2nd edn, 1964), pp. 44 – 48

. . . This exposition is still perfectly true in the sense that the social or political or economic status of an individual is by itself no answer to legal proceedings, civil or criminal. Everyone, whatever his position, must be ready to justify his actions by reference to some specific legal rule and be ready so to justify them in the ordinary courts. . . .

This aspect of Dicey's doctrine has been criticised by Sir Ivor Jennings on the ground that it seems to suggest that officials have the same rights and duties as citizens. If Dicey did indeed mean that, then he was obviously wrong, for modern statutes have conferred wide powers on officials which the ordinary citizen has not got. Gas Board officials may enter my premises to collect the money from the meter, but my neighbours cannot. Officials of the Ministry of Supply can enter my rooms to see if I am conducting researches into nuclear fission, but the college porter cannot. Conversely, the Oxford City Council, as the local education authority, is under a duty to educate my children free although my employers, the University of Oxford and Pembroke College, are not. Many other examples could be produced. There is something in this criticism. We have already seen that Dicey was perhaps a little reluctant to read the Statute Book, and that if he had done so more regularly he might perhaps have altered some of his phrases. Nevertheless, I do not think that Sir Ivor Jennings' criticism touches the heart of the matter. This has been very well put by Lord Wright: 'all are equally subject to the law, though the law as to which some are subject may be different from the law to which others are subject.' In other words, however great the powers or the duties conferred upon the executive, all are equally responsible before the ordinary courts for the exercise of their powers, rights and duties. As was said in *R* v *Brixton Prison Governor, ex p. Soblen* [1963] 2 QB 243 at p. 273, *per* Stephenson J:

> I have no doubt that one of the court's most important duties is to see so far as possible that the great officers of State and those who act under their orders, no less than public bodies and private individuals, act lawfully in the exercise of their powers; and the greater the power which is exercised, and the higher the authority exercising it, the more important is the discharge by the court of this duty, and the more difficult.

A second criticism is much more serious. It arises from Dicey's assertion that the Rule of Law precludes anything corresponding to the administrative law (*droit administratif*) of France. This belief dominated English thinking for so long that not many years ago a Lord Chief Justice could refer to the phrase 'administrative law' as 'Continental jargon.' It is only within the last decade that it has become a respectable phrase. It is clear to us today that Dicey misunderstood the nature and functions of French administrative law, and especially the function of the *conseil d'état*, the chief court in the administrative hierarchy. This is not the time to go into detail; it is enough to say here that although the *conseil d'état* is not composed of professional judges, there are no grounds for supposing that it is in any way biased in favour of the administration. Indeed, there seems to be good reason to think that the liberties of the citizen are in many ways better protected by the *conseil d'état* than by the High Court of Justice. The mere fact that French officials are exempt from process in the ordinary civil courts does not necessarily mean that they are legally irresponsible. To Dicey, however, who had to the full the common lawyer's belief that it is the duty of the Queen's courts to control and supervise the activities of all other tribunals and persons within the realm, the notion that officials might be subject to a special system of rules administered in a special system of courts, was necessarily a very curious one.

Note

While it is accepted that, if the rule of law is to be adhered to, it is necessary that citizens be given legal protection against unlawful conduct on the part of officials, Dicey regarded it as necessary that such protection be afforded by the ordinary courts. He did not consider it possible to maintain the rule of law if there was a separate system of public law administered by separate courts, as occurred in France and many other continental countries. Dicey believed that this system was biased in favour of officials and that English law provided better protection. Dicey's influence was such that this view affected the development of administrative law for many years. It is only within the last 30 to 40 years that administrative law has come to be recognised as a separate branch of law, although the United Kingdom still lacks a separate system of administrative courts. There are, however, many tribunals dealing with administrative matters. In whatever way it is to be administered, the essential issue, if the rule of law is to be respected, is simply whether officials are subject to, and controlled by, the law.

Equality before the law should mean that no one is above the law. As with all rules, however, there are exceptions: for example, foreign sovereigns and diplomats, their staffs and families are immune from criminal prosecution or civil action; members of Parliament enjoy certain privileges; and judges enjoy the privilege of being immune from civil liability for anything said or done in the course of their office. These exceptions are limited and, in the case of judges and MP's, are designed to further the rule of law by giving protection to the institutions upon which a liberal democracy is founded, namely, an independent judiciary and an elected legislature.

In explaining his second proposition, Dicey stated that 'every man, whatever be his rank or condition, is subject to the ordinary law of the realm and amenable to the jurisdiction of the ordinary tribunals' (at p. 193). The accuracy of this statement came under challenge in the following case.

In re M
[1993] 3 WLR 433
House of Lords

M, a citizen of Zaire, arrived in the UK seeking political asylum. The Home Office rejected his application and ordered his removal from the UK, which was to take place by 6.30 pm on 1 May 1991. At 5.20 pm (after the Court of Appeal had refused an application for leave to apply for judicial review of the decision) a fresh application for leave to move for judicial review, alleging new grounds, was made to Garland J in chambers. Garland J indicated at about 5.30 pm that he wished M's departure to be postponed pending consideration of the application, and he understood from counsel for the Home Office that an undertaking to that effect had been given. (Counsel understood that he had only undertaken to *endeavour* to prevent M's removal.) Due to bungling and breakdown in lines of communication, M's departure was not prevented nor was he removed from the onward flight to Zaire during a stopover at Paris. At 11.20 pm Garland J, being informed of M's removal from the jurisdiction, made an *ex parte* order requiring the Home Secretary to procure the return of M to the jurisdiction and granting the Home Secretary liberty to apply for variation or discharge of the order on the morning of 2 May. Home Office officials then made arrangements for M's return. On the afternoon of 2 May, the Home Secretary, having taken advice from his officials and Treasury Counsel, concluded that the underlying asylum decision had been correct and that Garland J's *ex parte* order, being a mandatory interim injunction against a minister of the Crown, had been made without jurisdiction. Thereupon he cancelled the arrangements for M's return. On 3 May he applied to Garland J to set aside the order of 1 May, which Garland J did. Proceedings were then brought on behalf of M against the Home Office and the Home Secretary alleging contempt of court in respect of the breach of the undertaking and the *ex parte* order requiring M's return. Simon Brown J dismissed this motion on the basis that since the Crown's immunity from injunction was preserved by s. 21 of the Crown Proceedings Act 1947, neither it nor its departments, ministers and officials acting in the course of their duties could be impleaded for contempt of court. The applicant appealed.

The Court of Appeal held that the original order by Garland J. should not have been made as injunctions could not be issued against the Crown. However, as the order was binding until set aside, failure to comply with it was a contempt. Further, while the Crown and Government Departments are not subject to the contempt jurisdiction of the High Court because they are 'non-persons', Mr Baker, the Home Secretary, was, however, personally guilty of contempt.

The Secretary of State appealed and the applicant cross-appealed in respect of his original application against the Home Office. The House of Lords considered two issues of constitutional import: firstly, could injunctions be issued against a government minister or department, and, secondly, could a government minister or department be found to be in contempt of court for failure to comply with an order of the court.

LORD TEMPLEMAN: My Lords, Parliament makes the law, the executive carry the law into effect and the judiciary enforce the law. The expression 'the Crown' has two meanings; namely the monarch and the executive. In the 17th century Parliament established its supremacy over the Crown as monarch, over the executive and over the judiciary. Parliamentary supremacy over the Crown as monarch stems from the fact that the monarch must accept the advice of a Prime Minister who is supported by a majority of Parliament. Parliamentary supremacy over the Crown as executive stems from the fact that Parliament maintains in office the Prime Minister who appoints the ministers in charge of the executive. Parliamentary supremacy over the judiciary is only exercisable by statute. The judiciary enforce the law against individuals, against institutions and against the executive. The judges cannot enforce the law against the Crown as monarch because the Crown as monarch can do no wrong but judges enforce the law against the Crown as executive and against the individuals who from time to time represent the Crown. A litigant complaining of a breach of the law by the executive can sue the Crown as executive bringing his action against the minister who is responsible for the department of state involved, in the present case the Secretary of State for Home Affairs. To enforce the law the courts have power to grant remedies including injunctions against a minister in his official capacity. If the minister has personally broken the law, the litigant can sue the minister, in this case Mr. Kenneth Baker, in his personal capacity. For the purpose of enforcing the law against all persons and institutions, including ministers in their official capacity and in their personal capacity, the courts are armed with coercive powers exercisable in proceedings for contempt of court.

In the present case, counsel for the Secretary of State argued that the judge could not enforce the law by injunction or contempt proceedings against the minister in his official capacity. Counsel also argued that in his personal capacity Mr. Kenneth Baker the Secretary of State for Home Affairs had not been guilty of contempt.

My Lords, the argument that there is no power to enforce the law by injunction or contempt proceedings against a minister in his official capacity would, if upheld, establish the proposition that the executive obey the law as a matter of grace and not as a matter of necessity, a proposition which would reverse the result of the Civil War. For the reasons given by my noble and learned friend, Lord Woolf, and on principle, I am satisfied that injunctions and contempt proceedings may be brought against the minister in his official capacity and that in the present case the Home Office for which the Secretary of State was responsible was in contempt. I am also satisfied that Mr. Baker was throughout acting in his official capacity, on advice which he was entitled to accept and under a mistaken view as to the law. In these circumstances I do not consider that Mr. Baker personally was guilty of contempt. I would therefore dismiss this appeal substituting the Secretary of State for Home Affairs as being the person against whom the finding of contempt was made.

LORD WOOLF: . . . Mr. Richards submits on behalf of the Home Office and on behalf of Mr. Baker that neither the Crown in general, nor a department of state, nor a minister of the Crown, acting in his capacity as such, are amenable to proceedings in contempt. It is a necessary part of that submission that the courts also have no power to grant injunctions directed to such bodies and that the order which was made by Garland J., which it was held by Simon Brown J. as well as the Court of Appeal that Mr. Baker had contravened, was made without jurisdiction.

When advancing these submissions Mr. Richards stressed that it was no part of his case that the Crown or ministers are above the law or that ministers are able to rely on their office so as to evade liability for wrongdoing. He argued that this was not a consequence of his submissions and he accepted that the Crown has a duty to obey the law as declared by the courts. He accepted that if a minister acted in disregard of the law as declared by the courts, or otherwise was engaged in wrongdoing, he would be acting outside his authority as a minister and so would expose himself to a personal liability for his wrongdoing.

The fact that these issues have only now arisen for decision by the courts is confirmation that in ordinary circumstances ministers of the Crown and government departments invariably scrupulously observe decisions of the courts. Because of this, it is normally unneccessary for the courts to make an executory order against a minister or a government department since they will comply with any declaratory judgment made by the courts and pending the decision of the courts will not take any precipitous action. . . .

[His Lordship recounted the facts of the case.] What does appear to me to be clear from the events which occurred on 1 and 2 May 1991 is that, if there is no power in a court to make an order to prevent the Home Office moving a person in any circumstances, this would be a highly unsatisfactory situation. The facts of this case illustrate that circumstances can occur where it is in the interests both of a person who is subject to the powers of government and of the government itself that the courts should be in a position to make an order which clearly sets out either what should or what should not be done by the government. If there had been no confusion in this case as to the extent of the court's power, I have little doubt that Mr. Baker would not find himself in his present position where he has been found guilty of contempt. . . .

Injunctions and the Crown

Mr. Kentridge [for the applicant M] placed at the forefront of his argument the issue as to whether the courts have jurisdiction to make coercive orders against the Crown or ministers of the Crown. It was appropriate for him to do so for at least two reasons. First, and more importantly, because whether the courts have or do not have such a coercive jurisdiction would be a strong indicator as to whether the courts had the jurisdiction to make a finding of contempt. If there were no power to make coercive orders, then the need to rely on the law of contempt for the purpose of enforcing the orders would rarely arise. The second reason is that, on the facts of this case, the issue is highly significant in determining the status of the order which Garland J. made and which it is alleged Mr. Baker breached. If that order was made without jurisdiction, then Mr. Richards would rely on this in support of his contention that Mr. Baker should not have been found guilty of contempt. As Mr. Richards admitted, the issue is of constitutional importance since it goes to the heart of the relationship between the executive and the courts. Is the relationship based, as he submits, on trust and cooperation or ultimately on coercion?

Mr. Richards submits that the answer to this question is provided by the decision of *R* v *Secretary for State for Transport, Ex parte Factortame Ltd* [1990] 2 AC 85 and in particular by the reasoning of Lord Bridge of Harwich who made the only speech in that case. This speech was highly influential in causing Simon Brown J. and McCowan L.J. to take a different view from the majority of the Court of Appeal as to the outcome of the present proceedings. That case was not, however, primarily concerned with the question as to whether injunctive relief was available against the Crown or its officers. It involved the allegedly discriminatory effect of the requirement of British ownership and the other requirements of Part II of the Merchant Shipping Act 1988 and the associated regulations, which prevented fishing vessels which were owned by Spanish nationals or managed in Spain being registered under the legislation. This it was said contravened Community law. It was an issue of difficulty which had accordingly been referred to the European Court under article 177 of the EEC Treaty (Cmnd. 5179–II). The question then arose as to whether the applicants were entitled to interim relief pending the outcome of the reference. The primary contention of the applicants was that it was in the circumstances a requirement of Community law that interim relief should be available. This was an additional point as to which Community law was unclear so your Lordships' House decided that that issue should also not be determined until after a reference under article 177. This meant that pending the outcome of the second reference your Lordships had to determine whether interim relief should be granted under domestic law.

In deciding whether under domestic law interim relief should be granted Lord Bridge initially examined the position without reference to the involvement of a minister. He concluded that no relief could be granted since English law unassisted by Community law treated legislation as fully effective until it was set aside. . . .

However, Lord Bridge went on to give a second reason for his decision which is directly relevant to the present appeal. The second reason is that injunctive relief is not available against the Crown or an officer of the Crown, when acting as such, in judicial review proceedings. . . . Since the decision in *Factortame* there has also been the important development that the European Court has determined the second reference against the Crown so that the unhappy situation now exists that while a citizen is entitled to obtain injunctive relief (including interim relief) against the Crown or an officer of the Crown to protect his interests under Community law he cannot do so in respect of his other interests which may be just as important.

Before examining the second reason that Lord Bridge gave for his conclusion I should point out that I was a party to the judgment of the majority in the *Smith Kline* case. In my judgment in that case I indicated that injunctive relief was available in judicial review proceedings not only against an officer of the Crown but also against the Crown. Although in reality the distinction between the Crown and an officer of the Crown is of no practical significance in judicial review proceedings, in the theory which clouds this subject the distinction is of the greatest importance. My judgment in the earlier case may have caused some confusion in *Factortame* by obscuring the important fact that, as was the position prior to the introduction of judicial review, while prerogative orders are made regularly against ministers in their official capacity, they are never made against the Crown.

Lord Bridge in determining the second issue acknowledged the importance of the relevant history in determining this issue and it is necessary for me to set out my understanding of that history.

[His Lordship, starting from the premise that 'the fact that the Sovereign could do no wrong did not mean that a servant of the Crown could no no wrong', considered the history of civil proceedings aginst the Crown and the Crown Proceedings Act 1947, and the history of prerogative orders against Ministers of the Crown culminating in the introduction of judicial review in 1977 by RCS, Ord. 53 (*post* p. 600) which was followed by primary legislation in s. 31 of the Supreme Court Act 1981 (*post* p. 599). His Lordship considered in detail the speech of Lord Bridge in *Factortame* who, following the judgment of Upjohn J in *Merricks* v *Heathcoat-Amory* [1955] Ch. 567, held that injunctions could not be issued against a Minister of the Crown in judicial review proceedings. His Lordship, while agreeing with the decision in the latter case, considered that the reasoning was mistaken. His Lordship further concluded that Lord Bridge had misunderstood the issue in *Factortame* due in part to the fact that the matter had not been fully argued before their Lordships.]

I am, therefore, of the opinion that, the language of section 31 being unqualified in its terms, there is no warrant for restricting its application so that in respect of ministers and other officers of the Crown alone the remedy of an injunction, including an interim injunction, is not available. In my view the history of prerogative proceedings against officers of the Crown supports such a conclusion. So far as interim relief is concerned, which is the practical change which has been made, there is no justification for adopting a different approach to officers of the Crown from that adopted in relation to other respondents in the absence of clear language such as that contained in section 21(2) of the Act of 1947. The fact that in any event a stay could be granted against the Crown under Ord. 53. r. 3(10) emphasises the limits of the change in the situation which is involved. It would be most regrettable if an approach which is inconsistent with that which exists in Community law should be allowed to persist if this is not strictly necessary. The restriction provided for in section 21(2) of the Act of 1947 does, however, remain in relation to civil proceedings.

The fact that, in my view, the court should be regarded as having jurisdiction to grant interim and final injunctions against officers of the Crown does not mean that that jurisdiction should be exercised except in the most limited circumstances. In the majority of situations so far as final relief is concerned, a declaration will continue to be the appropriate remedy on an application for judicial review involving officers of the Crown. As has been the position in the past, the Crown can be relied upon to co-operate fully with such declarations. To avoid having to grant interim injunctions against officers of the Crown, I can see advantages in the courts being able to grant interim declarations. However, it is obviously not desirable to deal with this topic, if it is not necessary to do so, until the views of the Law Commission are known.

The validity of the injunction granted by Garland J.

What has been said so far does not mean that Garland J. was necessarily in order in granting the injunction. The injunction was granted before he had given the applicant leave to apply for judicial review. However, in a case of real urgency, which this was, the fact that leave had not been granted is a mere technicality. It would be undesirable if, in the situation with which Garland J. was faced, he had been compelled to grant leave because he regarded the case as an appropriate one for an interim injunction. In the case of civil proceedings, there is recognition of the jurisdiction of the court to grant interim injunctions before the issue of a writ, etc. (see Ord. 29, r. 1(3)) and in an appropriate case there should be taken to be a similar jurisdiction to grant interim injunctions now under Order 53. The position is accurately set out in note 53/1–14/24 to *The Supreme Court Practice 1993* where it is stated that:

> Where the case is so urgent as to justify it, [the judge] could grant an interlocutory injunction or other interim relief pending the hearing of the application for leave to move for judicial review. But, if the judge has refused leave to move for judicial review he is functus officio and has no jurisdiction to grant any form of interim relief. The application for an interlocutory injunction or other interim relief could, however, be renewed before the Court of Appeal along with the renewal of the application for leave to move for judicial review.

There having been jurisdiction for Garland J. to make the order which he did, it cannot be suggested that it was inappropriate for him to have made the order. On the view of the law which I now take, Garland J. was therefore not required to set aside the order though his decision to do so was inevitable having regard to the state of the authorities at that time.

The effect of the advice received by Mr. Baker
Having come to the conclusion that Garland J.'s order was properly made, the next question which has to be considered is the effect of the advice which was understandably given to Mr. Baker that the order was made without jurisdiction. Here there are two important considerations. The first is that the order was made by the High Court and therefore has to be treated as a perfectly valid order and one which has to be obeyed until it is set aside: see the speeches of Lord Diplock in *In re A Company* [1981] AC 374, 384 and *Isaacs* v *Robertson* [1985] AC 97, 102. The second consideration is that it is undesirable to talk in the terms of technical contempt. The courts only make a finding of contempt if there is conduct by the person or body concerned which can, with justification, be categorised as contempt. If, therefore, there is a situation in which the view is properly taken (and usually this will only be possible when the action is taken in accordance with legal advice) that it is reasonable to defer complying with an order of the court until application is made to the court for further guidance then it will not be contempt to defer complying with the order until an application has been made to the court to discharge the order. However, this course can only be justified if the application is made at the first practicable opportunity and in the meantime all appropriate steps have been taken to ensure that the person in whose favour the order was made will not be disadvantaged pending the hearing of the application.

Mr. Baker's difficulties in this case are that, while it was understandable that there should be delay before he could give the matter personal attention, Garland J. was not kept informed of what was happening and totally inadequate steps were taken to protect the position of M, pending the application to the court. In addition Mr. Baker has the problem that this House will not normally interfere with the assessment of the facts which was made by the Court of Appeal unless it can be shown that the assessment is flawed by some error of law.

Jurisdiction to make a finding of contempt
The Court of Appeal were of the opinion that a finding of contempt could not be made against the Crown, a government department or a minister of the Crown in his official capacity. Although it is to be expected that it will be rare indeed that the circumstances will exist in which such a finding would be justified, I do not believe there is any impediment to a court making such a finding, when it is appropriate to do so, not against the Crown directly, but against a government department or a minister of the Crown in his official capacity. Lord Donaldson of Lymington M.R. considered that a problem was created in making a finding of contempt because the Crown lacked a legal personality. However, at least for some purposes, the Crown has a legal

personality. It can be appropriately described as a corporation sole or a corporation aggregate: *per* Lord Diplock and Lord Simon of Glaisdale respectively in *Town Investments Ltd* v *Department of the Environment* [1978] AC 359. The Crown can hold property and enter into contracts. On the other hand, even after the Act of 1947, it cannot conduct litigation except in the name of an authorised government department or, in the case of judicial review, in the name of a minister. In any event it is not in relation to the Crown that I differ from the Master of the Rolls, but as to a government department or a minister.

Nolan L.J., at p. 311, considered that the fact that proceedings for contempt are 'essentially personal and punitive' meant that it was not open to a court, as a matter of law, to make a finding of contempt against the Home Office or the Home Secretary. While contempt proceedings usually have these characteristics and contempt proceedings against a government department or a minister in an official capacity would not be either personal or punitive (it would clearly not be appropriate to fine or sequest the assets of the Crown or a government department or an officer of the Crown acting in his official capacity), this does not mean that a finding of contempt against a government department or minister would be pointless. The very fact of making such a finding would vindicate the requirements of justice. In addition an order for costs could be made to underline the significance of a contempt. A purpose of the courts' powers to make findings of contempt is to ensure that the orders of the court are obeyed. This jurisdiction is required to be coextensive with the courts' jurisdiction to make the orders which need the protection which the jurisdiction to make findings of contempt provides. In civil proceedings the court can now make orders (other than injunctions or for specific performance) against authorised government departments or the Attorney-General. On applications for judicial review orders can be made against ministers. In consequence of the developments identified already such orders must be taken not to offend the theory that the Crown can supposedly do no wrong. Equally, if such orders are made and not obeyed, the body against whom the orders were made can be found guilty of contempt without offending that theory, which would be the only justifiable impediment against making a finding of contempt.

In cases not involving a government department or a minister the ability to *punish* for contempt may be necessary. However, as is reflected in the restrictions on execution against the Crown, the Crown's relationship with the courts does not depend on coercion and in the exceptional situation when a government department's conduct justifies this, a finding of contempt should suffice. In that exceptional situation, the ability of the court to make a finding of contempt is of great importance. It would demonstrate that a government department has interfered with the administration of justice. It will then be for Parliament to determine what should be the consequences of that finding. In accord with tradition the finding should not be made against the 'Crown' by name but in the name of the authorised department (or the Attorney-General) or the minister so as to accord with the body against whom the order was made. If the order was made in civil proceedings against an authorised department, the department will be held to be in contempt. On judicial review the order will be against the minister and so normally should be any finding of contempt in respect of the order.

However, the finding under appeal is one made against Mr. Baker personally in respect of an injunction addressed to him in his official capacity as the Secretary of State for the Home Department. It was appropriate to direct the injunction to the Secretary of State in his official capacity since, as previously indicated, remedies on an application for judicial review which involve the Crown are made against the appropriate officer in his official capacity. This does not mean that it cannot be appropriate to make a finding of contempt against a minister personally rather than against him in his official capacity provided that the contempt relates to his own default. Normally it will be more appropriate to make the order against the office which a minister holds where the order which has been breached has been made against that office since members of the department concerned will almost certainly be involved and investigation as to the part played by individuals is likely to be at least extremely difficult, if not impossible, unless privilege is waived (as commendably happened in this case). In addition the object of the exercise is not so much to punish an individual as to vindicate the rule of law by a finding of contempt. This can be achieved equally by a declaratory finding of the court as to the contempt against the minister as representing the department. By making the finding against the minister in his official capacity the court will be indicating that it is the department for which the minister is responsible which has been guilty of contempt. The minister himself may or may not have been personally guilty of contempt. The position so far as he is personally concerned would be the equivalent of that which needs to exist for the court to give relief against the minister in proceedings for judicial review. There would need to be default by the department for which the minister is responsible.

In addition Mr. Richards argued that for a finding of contempt against Mr. Baker personally it would not suffice to establish contempt to show that Mr. Baker was aware of the order and had not complied with it. It would also be necessary to show an intention to interfere with or impede the administration of justice. If such an intent was shown to exist, then Mr. Richards conceded that the conduct of the minister would fall outside his authority as a minister; it would be a personal act not the act of the Crown; and it would expose him to a personal liability for contempt. In support of the distinction which he relied upon, Mr. Richards referred to the speech of Lord Oliver of Aylmerton in *Attorney-General* v *Times Newspapers Ltd* [1992] 1 AC 191, 217–218, where Lord Oliver stated:

> A distinction (which has been variously described as 'unhelpful' or 'largely meaningless') is sometimes drawn between what is described as 'civil contempt,' that is to say, contempt by a party to proceedings in a matter of procedure, and 'criminal contempt.' One particular form of contempt by a party to proceedings is that constituted by an intentional act which is in breach of the order of a competent court. Where this occurs as a result of the act of a party who is bound by the order or of others acting at his direction or on his instigation, it constitutes a civil contempt by him which is punishable by the court at the instance of the party for whose benefit the order was made and which can be waived by him. The intention with which the act was done will, of course, be of the highest relevance in the determination of the penalty (if any) to be imposed by the court, but the liability here is a strict one in the sense that all that requires to be proved is service of the order and the subsequent doing by the party bound of that which is prohibited. When, however, the prohibited act is done not by the party bound himself but by a third party, a stranger to the litigation, that person may also be liable for contempt. There is, however, this essential distinction that his liability is for criminal contempt and arises not because the contemnor is himself affected by the prohibition contained in the order but because his act constitutes a wilful interference with the administration of justice by the court in the proceedings in which the order was made. Here the liability is not strict in the sense referred to, for there has to be shown not only knowledge of the order but an intention to interfere with or impede the administration of justice – an intention which can of course be inferred from the circumstances.

I happily adopt the approach of Lord Oliver. It reflects the distinction which I have drawn between the finding of contempt and the punishment of the contempt. I also accept the distinction which Lord Oliver draws between the position of a person who is subject to an order and a third party. I also recognise the force of Mr. Richards' submission that if Mr. Baker was not under a strict liability to comply with the order it would not be possible to establish that he had the necessary intention to interfere with or impede the administration of justice to make him guilty of contempt as a third party. However, although the injunction was granted by Garland J. against Mr. Baker in his official capacity this does not mean that he is in the same position as a third party. To draw a distinction between his two personalities would be unduly technical. While he was Home Secretary the order was one binding upon him personally and one for the compliance with which he as the head of the department was personally responsible. He was, therefore, under a strict liability to comply with the order. However, on the facts of this case I have little doubt that if the Court of Appeal had appreciated that they could make a finding against Mr. Baker in his official capacity this is what the court would have done. The conduct complained of in this case which justified the bringing of contempt proceedings was not that of Mr. Baker alone and he was acting on advice. His error was understandable and I accept that there is an element of unfairness in the finding against him personally.

In addition, there are technical differences between the two findings because of the provisions of RSC, Ord. 77, r. 1 which define an 'order against the Crown' in a broad sense to include an order against the government department or against an officer of the Crown as such. Unlike the definition of 'civil proceedings by the Crown,' this definition expressly applies to proceedings 'on the Crown side of the Queen's Bench Division.' This means that the provisions of Orders 45 to 52 (which deal with execution and satisfaction of orders of the court) would not apply to an order against the Home Secretary while they would do so in the case of an order against Mr. Baker personally.

It is for these reasons that I would dismiss this appeal and cross-appeal save for substituting the Secretary of State for Home Affairs as being the person against whom the finding of contempt was made. This was the alternative decision which was the subject of the cross-appeal, except that there the order was sought against the Home Office rather than the Home Secretary.

Order of Court of Appeal affirmed save for substitution of designation 'Secretary of State for Home Affairs' as proper object of finding of contempt.

Appeal and cross-appeal dismissed with costs.

Questions

1. Is the effect of this decision to give teeth to Dicey's second proposition regarding the rule of law?

2. Is it desirable that courts should seek to compel the government to comply with their orders rather than leaving it to the electorate to condemn them in a future election for their failure to comply?

3. Bagehot in *The English Constitution* (1867) drew a distinction between what he referred to as the 'dignified' parts of the constitution and the 'efficient' parts. The former he claimed 'excite and preserve the reverence of the population'. One of the dignified institutions is the monarchy, i.e. the Crown, to whom loyalty is felt or allegiance is owed. The institutions of government are the efficient parts of the constitution wherein real power is vested. In the United Kingdom government is conducted in the name of the Crown; thus it is referred to as Her Majesty's Government. When Lords Templeman and Woolf distinguished between the Crown as Monarch and the Crown as Executive, were they thereby adopting this distinction drawn by Bagehot?

Note

The position of members of the Security Service in relation to their criminal liability has given rise to some heated discussion in recent years. In *Francome and another* v *Mirror Group Newspapers Ltd and others* [1984] 2 All ER 408, at p. 412, Lord Donaldson MR stated:

> Parliamentary democracy as we know it is based on the rule of law. That requires all citizens to obey the law, unless and until it can be changed by due process. There are no privileged classes to whom it does not apply. [If one person] can assert [a] right to act on the basis that the public interest, as he sees it, justifies breaches of the criminal law, so can any other citizen. This has only to be stated for it to be obvious that the result would be anarchy. . . . The right to break the law . . . is not obtainable at all in a parliamentary democracy, although different considerations arise under a totalitarian regime.

In one of the cases arising from the *Spycatcher* affair, *Attorney-General* v *Guardian Newspapers Ltd and others (No. 2) and related appeals* [1988] 2 WLR 805, at p. 879, Lord Donaldson MR appeared to retreat somewhat from this position.

Thus far I have not considered what is 'wrongdoing.' Again there is a problem. Lord Denning in his report into the Profumo affair ((1963) Cmnd. 2152) stressed, at p. 91, paragraph 273 that:

> The members of the service are, in the eye of the law, ordinary citizens with no powers greater than anyone else. They have no special powers of arrest such as the police have. No special powers of search are given to them. They cannot enter premises without the consent of the householder, even though they may suspect a spy is there.

He went on to say that this deficiency of powers was made up for by close co-operation with the police forces.

It would be a sad day for democracy and the rule of law if the service were ever to be considered to be above or exempt from the law of the land. And it is not. At any time any member of the service who breaks the law is liable to be prosecuted. But there is a need for some discretion and common sense. Let us suppose that the service has information which suggests that a spy may be operating from particular premises. It needs to have confirmation. It may well consider that, if he proves to be a spy, the interests of the nation are better served by letting him continue with his activities under surveillance and in ignorance that he has been detected rather than by arresting him. What is the service expected to do? A secret search of the premises is the obvious answer. Is this really 'wrongdoing?'

Let us test it in a mundane context known to us all. Prior to the passing of section 79 of the Road Traffic Regulation Act 1967, fire engines and ambulances, unlike police vehicles, had no exemption from the speed limits. Their drivers hurrying to an emergency broke the law. So far as I am aware that is still the position in relation to crossing traffic lights which are showing red and driving on the wrong side of the road to bypass a traffic jam. The responsible authorities in a very proper exercise of discretion simply do not prosecute them.

Even in the context of the work of the Security Service which, I must stress, is the defence of the realm, there must be stringent limits to what breaches of the law can be considered excusable. Thus I cannot conceive of physical violence ever coming within this category. Or physical restraint, other than in the powers of arrest enjoyed by every citizen or under the authority of a lawful warrant of arrest. But covert invasions of privacy, which I think is what Mr Wright means by 'burglary,' may in some circumstances be a different matter.

It may be that the time has come when Parliament should regularise the position of the service. It is certainly a tenable view. The alternative view, which is equally tenable, is that the public interest is better served by leaving the members of the service liable to prosecution for any breach of the law at the instance of a private individual or of a public prosecuting authority, but may expect that prosecuting authorities will exercise a wise discretion and that in an appropriate case the Attorney-General would enter a nolle prosequi, justifying his action to Parliament if necessary. In so acting, the Attorney-General is not acting as a political minister or as a colleague of ministers. He acts personally and in a quasi-judicial capacity as representing the Crown (see article entitled 'How the security services are bound by the rule of law' by Lord Hailsham in *The Independent*, 3 February 1988). It is not for me to form or express any view on which is the most appropriate course to adopt in the interests of the security of the nation and the maintenance of the rule of law. However that problem is resolved, it is absurd to contend that *any* breach of the law, whatever its character, will constitute such 'wrongdoing' as to deprive the service of the secrecy without which it cannot possibly operate.

Questions

1. Would the rule of law be supported or undermined by criminal activity by members of the Security Service?

2. Does the following provision from the Security Service Act 1989 reaffirm the rule of law, or is it simply a shifting of 'the goalposts' by use of the legality principle? Who is left to decide what action is 'necessary'?

3. To what extent is it true to say that '[t]he section amounts to statutory authorisation of ministerial general warrants for reasons of state necessity of the kind which the common law disapproved in the celebrated case of *Entick* v *Carrington*' (I. Leigh and L. Lustgarten, 'The Security Service Act 1989' (1989) 52 *Modern Law Review* 801, at p. 825)?

SECURITY SERVICE ACT 1989

3.—(1) No entry on or interference with property shall be unlawful if it is authorised by a warrant issued by the Secretary of State under this section.

(2) The Secretary of State may on an application made by the Service issue a warrant under this section authorising the taking of such action as is specified in the warrant in respect of any property so specified if the Secretary of State—

(a) thinks it necessary for the action to be taken in order to obtain information which—

(i) is likely to be of substantial value in assisting the Service to discharge any of its functions; and

(ii) cannot reasonably be obtained by other means; and

(b) is satisfied that satisfactory arrangements are in force under section 2(2)(a) above with respect to the disclosure of information obtained by virtue of this section and that the information obtained under the warrant will be subject to those arrangements. . . .

(iii) *The rule of law and individual rights*

A. V. Dicey, *An Introduction to the Study of the Law of the Constitution* pp. 195, 203

We may say that the constitution is pervaded by the rule of law on the ground that the general principles of the constitution (as for example the right to personal liberty, or the right of public meeting) are with us the result of judicial decisions determining the rights of private persons in particular cases brought before the courts; whereas under many foreign constitutions the security (such as it is) given to the rights of individuals results, or appears to result, from the general principles of the constitution. . . . in short, the principles of private law have with us been by the action of the courts and Parliament so extended as to determine the position of the Crown and of its servants; thus the constitution is the result of the ordinary law of the land.

R. F. V. Heuston, 'The Rule of Law' in *Essays in Constitutional Law* (2nd edn, 1964), pp. 49–50

To [Dicey] such general principles of the constitution as the rights of free speech and public meeting are derived simply from the decisions of the courts in ordinary private law questions. There are no general guarantees contained in a formal written constitution. Dicey was thinking of the basic common law freedoms of liberty, speech and property, and as *Entick* v *Carrington* well shows, our law deals with these matters as governed by the ordinary principles of private law and not by any special system of public law. This particular aspect of the Rule of Law has been accepted by everyone without question; the only comment which has been made upon it, again by the acute Sir Ivor Jennings, is that it does not include the statutory rights to pensions, sickness benefit, free education, the right to vote and so on. Yet many would think that the statutory rights conferred on the citizen by the welfare state are as important as the common law principles which Dicey had in mind.

E. Barendt, 'Dicey and Civil Liberties' [1985] *Public Law* 596

Dicey's treatment of civil liberties and fundamental freedoms . . . has understandably received less attention than his formulation of the doctrine of Parliamentary Sovereignty and his analysis of constitutional conventions. He himself subsumed individual rights to personal freedom and freedom of discussion under 'The Rule of Law,' the lengthiest part of the *Introduction of the Study of the Law of the Constitution.* Criticism has, therefore, concentrated on the general coherence of 'the rule of law' principles and the contrast drawn by Dicey between the general absence of arbitrary discretionary power in England and what he (at the time) considered to be its daily employment under *droit administratif* in France. But what he wrote about individual rights and freedoms remains important, not so much because it is still a tolerably accurate account of the basic constitutional position of these liberties, but rather because his outlook – a paean of praise to the wisdom of the common law – continues to influence modern thinking on these matters. . . .

[T]he ambivalent character of Dicey's pronouncements in the *Law of the Constitution*, partly a matter of legal analysis, partly reflecting the author's Whig politics, has, I think, been responsible for their lasting influence. They have something to offer both lawyers and (most) politicians. In *Duncan* v *Jones*, Lord Hewart CJ cited Dicey as authority for the impeccable proposition that in English law the 'right of assembly . . . is nothing more than a view taken by the court of the individual liberty of the subject'; further, there is no special right to hold public meetings for political or other purposes. Most legislators find this conclusion attractive, for any 'right' to hold such meetings – if taken seriously – would curtail their law-making powers, as well as the discretion of the police and the courts. Dicey's arguments are put so persuasively that it is difficult sometimes to resist the conclusion that they are inevitably right, and that, therefore, in this context civil liberties can only be those recognised by the courts as common law. But this is not true, nor these days is that position desirable. . . . The English Constitution, a concept which arguably contains two erroneous assumptions, is for him judge-made law with all the good and bad characteristics of the common law.

We then, however, read of nothing but the benefits of judge-made law as the foundation of constitutional rules, in particular of fundamental personal freedoms. Because they are devised by courts, rights are integrally connected with remedies for their enforcement, for instance, the prerogative writ of habeas corpus, and common law freedoms may not so easily be suspended as the comparable rights guaranteed in a written constitution, at least 'without a thorough revolution in the institutions and manners of the nation.' Dicey does admit that some countries with constitutional declarations of rights, such as the United States, may as effectively provide remedies for invasion of these freedoms, as England does, and also that in practice at a particular time liberty may be as much respected in, say, Belgium as it is here, but for the most part the comparisons are designed to show that freedom is less securely protected in States with written constitutional guarantees. Such guarantees are often of more theoretical than practical worth, while common law freedoms necessarily reflect the traditions of a people. This last point is given some substance when Dicey observes that freedom of discussion is really the liberty to publish what twelve shopkeepers think it appropriate to be said or written. Clive Ponting at any rate might find something of value in that.

The principal implication of all this, as Sir Ivor Jennings pointed out, is that Englishmen are free simply to do whatever the law does not prohibit. In other words, civil liberties are residual. There are no special laws protecting them, though there may be particular remedies fashioned by the judges or provided by statutes, as with the Habeas Corpus Acts. So, there is personal freedom from arbitrary arrest or invasion of property rights because the courts have not recognised the existence of those wide powers which would effectively curtail the freedoms. Here, of course, the third tenet of Dicey's 'rule of law' only has substance because one or other, or both, of the other two principles are applicable. . . . *Entick* v *Carrington* . . . shows perhaps all three principles of the rule of law: the courts' hostility to arbitrary powers, the subjection of everyone including government officials to the common law, and the formulation of freedoms through concrete litigation. It also evinces a judicial enthusiasm for general principles, markedly lacking in most English judges today. Would modern English judgments contain a sentiment such as: 'The great end, for which men entered into society, was to secure their property. That right is preserved sacred and incommunicable in all instances, where it has not been taken away or abridged by some public law for the good of the whole.' Never mind the substance of this opinion: this type of approach would not now be adopted in a case involving freedom of speech, religion or any other fundamental right. . . .

[J]udged from a contemporary perspective, the thesis – and in particular this third tenet of the rule of law – seems peculiar. The contrast drawn between the formulation of rights in a written constitution or Bill of Rights and judge-made or common law is surely overstated. At the least it needs refinement. Constitutions have to be interpreted and applied by the courts, so that in a sense freedom of speech and personal freedom are as much judge-made law, say, in the United States as they are in Britain. Indeed, in the present day, when the role of the judiciary here is so much constrained by tightly-drawn statutes, judge-made law is much more significant in the USA, Germany and all other jurisdictions where the courts construe a constitution or Bill of Rights. . . .

Both judge-made law and statute are in various places in his constitutional writing contrasted with the broad declarations of principle found in written constitutions and Bills of Rights. Constitutional constraints on legislation are criticised for weakening the role of public opinion in developing the law, an attitude which is shared these days by populist Conservatives and (most) Socialists. Dicey then might well have identified the protection of individual freedoms by concrete common law *and legislative* rules as one feature of the rule of law in England, a formulation which would incidentally have been perfectly compatible with the other tenets of the doctrine. Arthur Goodhart has pointed out that Anglo–American concepts of the rule of law usually exaggerate the judicial process. As a desirable constitutional principle, its maintenance is also the responsibility of the legislative and executive branches of government. Moreover, Dicey would not have had so much difficulty in reconciling Parliamentary Sovereignty and the rule of law – surely one of the least happy chapters of his book – had he seen the latter as a legislative principle as well as a statement about the judicial role.

Is there any explanation for this aspect of Dicey's rule of law doctrine? I suspect the correct answer is rather dull and obvious. Even in the *Relation between Law and Public Opinion*, Dicey made no attempt to disguise his preference for the 'judicial legislation' of the common law and equity. It is more concerned than statute law with the general symmetry of the law, with the requirements of certainty and consistency and generally with the requirements of justice. Acts of Parliament are frequently the work of 'legislators who are much influenced by the immediate opinion of the moment, who make laws with little regard either to general principles or to logical consistency, and who are deficient in the skill and knowledge of experts.' Moreover, the areas of civil liberties chosen by Dicey for discussion in the earlier work were at that time more or less entirely governed by common law decisions, as will shortly be seen in the context of freedom of speech and freedom to hold meetings. The Habeas Corpus Acts discussed at some length in the chapter on 'The Right to Personal Freedom' were regarded as meeting the deficiencies of the common law writ rather than establishing new principles. The thesis that the general principles of the Constitution rested on judicial decisions was, as Sir Ivor Jennings has said, a partial presentation of the true position; but it was then much more accurate than it would be now, and in the case of the most important political freedoms, it was extremely plausible. . . .

Dicey's account of these rights was and remains accurate as a statement of the law, but its tone trivialises the issues which ought to be discussed: should there be positive rights to hold public meetings? Should there at least be equal rights of access for all political parties and groups to use public premises for meetings? What powers should the police enjoy to prevent outbreaks of violence at such gatherings? The rule of law does not provide an adequate framework for tackling these problems. But the same is true of civil liberties generally. I shall now explain why Dicey's account of this subject is so defective for the present day.

. . . The press . . . was in Dicey's view governed simply by the ordinary law of the land, and for him that meant the common law of criminal and civil libel. Statutory restrictions on speech and the exercise of other liberties were barely discussed, largely because they were then of relatively little significance. The absence of arbitrary power made so much of in *The Law of the Constitution* was an absence of autonomous executive or prerogative power; what we are more concerned with nowadays is the risk of governments abusing their powers through their *de facto* control of the legislature. Dicey appreciated that governments would from time to time need to acquire wider discretionary powers under Acts of Parliament, but he did not foresee that some of these, for example, the Official Secrets legislation and the Incitement to Disaffection Act, would remain permanent features of the statute book. And in the last page of his chapter dealing with the relation between the rule of law and sovereignty, he seems to have exaggerated the extent to which the courts are prepared to limit the scope of legislation by the application of liberal common law principles.

The rule of law is a quite valueless doctrine these days unless it is accepted as a rule which binds the legislature, either as a matter of constitutional law or at least as a general political principle or convention. There is little evidence for its general acceptance by modern British legislators. Might may not be right, but a parliamentary majority is. This is shown by the ease with which governments have secured the passage of such legislation as the Immigration Acts, and the rules made under them, which to some extent have retrospective effects; other rules have recently been held by the European Court of Human Rights to discriminate against women. Moreover, governments of recent decades have proved reluctant to clarify or reform civil liberties law until there has been an adverse ruling of the European Court, as shown by the telephone tapping saga discussed a little later. Where there has been no such impetus from abroad, British administrations prefer to remain idle. Thus, despite the conclusion of the Williams Committee that the present obscenity laws in so far as they may outlaw certain written publications are incompatible with freedom of expression, the discredited 1959 Act remains on the statute book.

If Dicey more or less ignored the role of Parliament in safeguarding the values implicit in the rule of law, he surely exaggerated the willingness and ability of the judiciary to perform this task. Although one or two judges have been keen to protect fundamental freedoms, wherever possible, and to shape the common law accordingly, many more give them inadequate weight or refuse to recognise the presence of a civil liberties question. I have already noted Lord Hewart CJ's adoption in *Duncan* v *Jones* of the Diceyan position on the right of assembly; the ruling of the Divisional Court to the effect that it constituted an obstruction of a police officer to refuse to disperse a meeting on his instructions completely outflanked earlier law on the right of public meetings, which the court thought wholly irrelevant to the case. Major cases on the scope of contempt of court have paid little or no regard to free speech implications. And in some recent decisions, the courts have extended police powers of arrest and of seizure of property, before the Police and Criminal Evidence Act 1984 rendered further judicial innovation on this subject unnecessary. Of course, this is only a partial picture of judge-made law in the civil liberties field, but it is perhaps enough to show that Dicey's reliance on the judiciary fully to protect these freedoms was excessive.

Moreover, there is an inevitable drawback to the conclusion that in England freedoms are residual, in that everyone is free to do whatever the law does not prohibit. For this proposition is as true for the Government and other public authorities as it is for the ordinary citizen, an equality required by the rule of law itself. In *Malone* v *Metropolitan Police Commissioner* [[1979] Ch 344], the plaintiff claimed an injunction to restrain telephone tapping by the Post Office under the warrant of the Home Secretary and on behalf of the police who suspected that Malone had handled some stolen property. Sir Robert Megarry VC refused to grant the remedy because the Post Office had committed no wrong; there was no trespass and English law does not recognise a cause of action for invasion of privacy. 'If the tapping of telephones by the Post Office at the request of the police can be carried out without any breach of the law, it does not require any statutory or common law power to justify it: it can lawfully be done simply because there is nothing to make it unlawful.' The same principles applied incidentally to prevent the common law developing any rules against discrimination; an employer, for example, was free to discriminate against blacks because this did not amount to any tort or wrong before the introduction of the Race Relations legislation.

Had the judge been a bold eighteenth century innovator, it is conceivable that he might have formulated a new tort of invasion of privacy, at least in this context, for it was clear that there was an injustice in the case which needed correction. But it is apparently no longer appropriate for the judiciary in England to create new rights; they and the citizen must wait for Parliament – or more likely, the European Court of Human Rights. This surely shows the advantage of a positive statement of fundamental freedoms and rights in some constitutional document or other. In the absence of such a statement and of a well-recognised cause of action (for trespass or assault, for instance), the courts cannot protect interstitial residual freedoms. Dicey's obsession with remedies made him oblivious to the importance of rights.

These paragraphs are not designed to prove that the constitutional guarantee of rights is everything. There are many rights which are better protected by detailed and specific legislation, providing remedies for their infringement. An obvious example is the right not to be discriminated against on the ground of race, colour or sex, etc., which both in Britain and in the United States (in addition to the Equal Protection Clause of the Fourteenth Amendment) is protected by legislative measures. The same may hold for claim-rights to, say, housing or education, where the State (or other public authorities) are required to do certain things to satisfy the citizen's needs. There are in any case some good arguments for not guaranteeing these freedoms in constitutions, for they are not easily susceptible to judicial enforcement and – to be controversial – they are not sufficiently fundamental to demand insulation from legislative regulation.

On the other hand, there are situations where the constitutional statement of a right is valuable because it enables courts in appropriate contexts to formulate some claim-right to the exercise of the particular freedom. For example, there is now some debate in Western democracies whether free speech requires the recognition of rights of access to the media and a right of reply to hostile or inaccurate articles in the press. In the United States, of course, the issue has become a constitutional one. There are powerful arguments against the judicial imposition of duties on the part of the media to afford rights of access or of reply, and for the conclusion that these rights are best left to development by administrative bodies or extra-legal provision. The point, however, is that a residual freedom can never found a claim-right, even if it is appropriate for the judiciary to prod the legislature (or some administrative agency) into action by upholding such a right in principle. In contrast, it is open for the European Court to recognise some positive claim-right of reply, or a right of access of a mother (or natural parents) to children under Article 8 of the Convention. In British law, the right to marry is residual or interstitial; it is what is left after the Government (or Parliament) have regulated the hours when people may marry, the prohibited degrees, age of marital capacity and so on. Only a statement of the freedom in a text would enable the courts restrictively to construe (or perhaps strike down) regulations which reduce the scope of the freedom to vanishing-point.

Dicey's treatment of civil liberties, therefore, seems inadequate now, first, because it leaves out of account the serious erosion that may be made on the exercise of the freedoms through legislation enacted in disregard of the rule of law principles, secondly, in view of the change in character of the judiciary and their attitude to development of the common law, and thirdly and perhaps most importantly, because residual freedoms can never provide a firm support for judicial innovation. The criticism is not made to belittle Dicey's analysis of English law at the time he wrote. The pity is that he has been taken too seriously by commentators who have often found his thesis attractive to wear with their own (and to some extent, it should be said, his) political creed.

Questions

1. Lord Scarman, *English Law – The New Dimension* (1974), p. 15, stated:

> It is the helplessness of the law in face of the legislative sovereignty of Parliament which makes it difficult for the legal system to accommodate the concept of fundamental and inviolable human rights.

Do you agree?

2. Lord Scarman went on to state:

> So long as English law is unable in any circumstances to challenge a statute, it is, in dangerous and difficult times, at the mercy of the oppressive and discriminatory statute.

Is the citizen defenceless against the power of the state at such times?

Note

Dicey's views on sovereignty and the rule of law derived from his understanding of representative democracy and the way in which it operated in the United Kingdom. In 'Dicey: Unitary, Self-correcting Democracy and Public Law', (1990) 106 LQR 105, Paul Craig challenges Dicey's views. If Craig is correct, the whole foundation of Dicey's writings is undermined. Craig argues that Dicey's views were premised upon certain assumptions concerning representative democracy which were misconceived and which failed to take account of important political developments occuring at the time he was writing. In Dicey's view, while the electorate was the political sovereign, it was Parliament which was the legal sovereign; Parliament was the body with the omnicompetent power of law-making. The exercise of legal sovereignty by

Parliament, however, would, he believed, always reflect the will of the political sovereign, *viz.* the electorate. The essence of Craig's critique is contained in the extracts which follow. (For a contrasting perspective, see T. R. S. Allan, 'Legislative Supremacy and the Rule of Law: Democracy and Constitutionalism' [1985] *Cambridge Law Journal* 111.)

P. Craig, 'Dicey: Unitary, Self-correcting Democracy and Public Law' (1990) 106 *LQR* 105

2 SOVEREIGNTY: LEGISLATIVE OMNICOMPETENCE AND CONSTITUTIONAL LAW

. . . For Dicey the external limit [upon legal sovereignty] was the need to secure the support of at least a portion of the population; the internal limit was indicative of the fact that a legal sovereign would perforce be moulded by his social environment and that this would condition the type of legislation which he sought to enact. In a despotism the external and internal limits might not coincide. In a representative democracy things were otherwise.

> Where a Parliament truly represents the people, the divergence between the external and the internal limit to the exercise of sovereign power can hardly arise, or if it arises, must soon disappear. Speaking roughly, the permanent wishes of the representative portion of Parliament can hardly in the long run differ from the wishes of the English people, or at any rate of the electors; that which the majority of the House of Commons command, the majority of the English people usually desire. To prevent the divergence between the wishes of the sovereign and the wishes of subjects is in short the effect, and the only certain effect of bona fide representative government. [Dicey, *An Introduction to the Study of the Law of the Constitution* (10th edn., 1959), p. 83.]

The absence of constitutional review and the Diceyan conception of sovereignty are therefore firmly embedded within a conception of self-correcting majoritarian democracy. Representative government would necessarily produce a coincidence between the external and internal limits of sovereign power in much the same way that the invisible hand of the market ensured a correspondence of supply and demand. A Parliament duly elected on the extended franchise represented the most authoritative expression of the will of the nation, and the exercise of public power was channelled through such a Parliament. This Parliament duly controlled the executive and therefore the affairs of the nation should be entrusted to those approved by a majority of the House. For Dicey, 'black letter' precedent and political principle formed a perfect union. All was well in the Garden of Eden. This beatific vision of legal and political harmony was to prove short-lived, and may never in reality have existed at all. . . . The force of this vision was however indirectly reinforced by Dicey's views on the rule of law and on conventions.

It was Dicey's third limb of the rule of law which added 'empirical' weight to the conclusions of principle which he had arrived at concerning sovereignty. The third sense of the rule of law was that in England civil liberties were the result of ordinary common law decisions, whereas under many foreign constitutions these interests were protected by, or resulted from, general principles of the constitution. Now while Dicey admits that constitutionally guaranteed rights, backed up with adequate remedies, can be as efficacious as the common law, he nonetheless evinces a marked preference for the latter over the former. . . . The common law in general furnished better protection for individual rights because constitutionally enshrined rights were often without adequate remedies and could be easily suspended. Common law protections could not be destroyed without a thorough-going revolution in the 'institutions and manners of the nation.'

Thus while the twin concepts of sovereignty and the rule of law could be at odds, they could also reinforce each other. The existence of representative government ensured that the wishes of the people would coincide with those of the sovereign Parliament. There should therefore be no serious problems concerning civil liberties. Insofar as such problems did occur the third limb of the rule of law, the common law protection of individual rights, was at hand, which was a more constitutionally enshrined declaration of rights. . . .

A similar thematic connection can be seen between Dicey's discussion of sovereignty and conventions. For Dicey the main purpose of such conventions was to ensure that Parliament or the Cabinet, which 'is indirectly appointed by Parliament,' should in the long run give effect to the will of the electorate. Conventions, seen as a 'modern code of constitutional morality,' indirectly secured the sovereignty of the people. For Dicey, the advance of democracy entailed the transference of supreme power from a single person, or a privileged or limited class, to the majority of the male citizens. The process of representation as it actually operated was 'nothing else than a mode by which the will of the representative body or House of Commons is made to coincide with the will of the nation.'. . .

4. THE TRADITIONAL VISION OF CONSTITUTIONAL LAW: APPEARANCE AND REALITY

. . .

(b) *The internal coherence of Dicey's argument*

First, even if we accept the accuracy of this picture of the constitution, the conclusions concerning the lack of need for constitutional review do not, in fact, follow as self-evidently as Dicey might have us believe. The argument appears to be simple. Our system of democracy is founded upon a channel of authority flowing from the bottom upwards. The electorate choose representatives. The MPs who are elected articulate the views of those who have chosen them, and they control the executive. Legislation which might be constitutionally questionable would, therefore, not be passed, or would be repealed expeditiously.

The ambiguity in this formulation becomes apparent upon further reflection, and is indeed embedded within the quotation cited above concerning the external and internal limits on sovereignty. Thus, we are told that the permanent wishes of the representative portion of Parliament can hardly differ from the wishes of the English people; that which the majority of the Commons command, the majority of the English people usually desire. The gap between these two formulations, which are juxtaposed in Dicey's text, is significant. Under the latter, it would be possible for the wishes of the majority to be faithfully translated into legislation by their elected representatives, and for this legislation to be constitutionally deleterious to the wishes of a minority. Dicey switches back and forth between these two formulations without readily appreciating the difference between them.

It is not apparent how Dicey would prevent or forestall this danger of majority oppression. A possible argument would be that the 'internal limit' placed upon the parliamentary rulers would serve to ensure that the despotism of the majority did not occur. The argument would be as follows. Dicey tells us that any ruler exercises power subject to an internal limit, in the sense that he or she would be moulded by the society in which the person lived. In a parliamentary system the majority representatives, although holding a particular view on a specific subject, would not attempt to pass legislation which would be constitutionally disadvantageous to a minority. The internal limits of that society would serve to preclude the exercise of such power. A majority might well, for example, believe fervently in Protestantism, but the pervasive spirit of toleration which constituted one facet of the internal limit within which the rulers ruled would mitigate against religious legislation which was discriminatory.

A distinctive, albeit complementary, theme can be found in Dicey's discussion of counter and cross-currents of opinion. Whether Dicey was correct in regarding legislation as the product of 'public opinion' is not our prime concern. What is of relevance is the light which Dicey's discussion sheds upon the prospect of majority oppression. One of the themes which Dicey stresses is that 'the reigning legislative opinion has never, at any rate during the nineteenth century, exerted absolute or despotic authority.' Its power is always diminished by counter-currents which are more or less directly opposed to the dominant opinion of a particular era. Such counter-currents impose a check upon the legislative action which results from those who hold the dominant faith. Thus Dicey argues that from 1830 to 1850 Benthamite liberalism was held in check by the 'restraining power' of the older toryism, and that ecclesiastical reform could not be properly understood without paying due attention to the varying counter and cross-currents which affected its passage. Religious legislation could only be properly comprehended by appreciating that such statutes were affected by a liberalism which aimed at the establishment of religious equality, and by cross-currents of ecclesiastical opinion which desired to maintain the rights or privileges of the Established Church.

Majority tyranny could therefore be forestalled by a combination of internal limits, coupled with counter and cross-currents of opinion, which together would preclude legislation which was constitutionally deleterious to a particular minority. This reasoning has some plausibitity. It is, however, difficult to accept that it would operate successfully in all or even the majority of instances in which minority oppression might occur. Legislation which is constitutionally suspect might well be passed because the majority perceives the 'internal limits' differently from the minority. They might view the specific boundaries which flow from the internal limitations distinctively from the minority who are being oppressed. Statutes may be enacted which are constitutionally questionable without the actual legislators sensing that they are controverting some societal norm which should be sacrosanct. Moreover, while the existence of counter and cross-currents of opinion may well be undeniable, their impact upon the problem at hand is more questionable. The existence of such strains within legislative opinion might well be of impact in reducing the pace or severity of statutory change. There is, however, no particular reason to conclude that they would prevent legislation which could be constitutionally harmful to minority interests. . . .

An alternative line of argument which might be pursued is to return to the connection between sovereignty and the third limb of the rule of law which was considered earlier. The common law, as noted, was perceived as the best protector of individual rights. The existence of representative government served to ensure that the wishes of the people would coincide with those of the sovereign Parliament. Serious problems concerning civil liberties should therefore be rare. If such problems did arise, the common law was at hand to protect the harassed citizen.

This 'corrective' is too simplistic and is, upon closer examination, not borne out by Dicey's own analysis. The matter may best be approached as follows. Let us imagine that the majority within Parliament has enacted legislation which could be deemed constitutionally harmful to a minority. The internal limitation upon the exercise of sovereign power has not proved successful, and certain fundamental minority rights have been curtailed. How will the common law protection avail these citizens, given Dicey's own doctrine of parliamentary omnicompetence? Dicey provides two responses, one of which is general in nature, the other of which is both more detailed and more particular.

The *general response* is that where civil liberties are deduced from a constitutional document they can be readily suspended; where, however, such rights emerged from the common law, they cannot be destroyed 'without a thorough revolution in the institutions and manners of the nation.' Now it may well be the case that Dicey had reason to be sceptical of continental experience with Declarations of Rights. The ephemeral quality of such documents would clearly warrant caution concerning their efficacy. The possibility of a wholesale restriction of rights, which occupies Dicey initially, is important, but does not serve to answer the conundrum posed above. A majority within Parliament may have no desire to restrict individual rights generally, either over time or over subject matter. There may be no intent to effect any revolution in the manners or institutions of the nation. Nor need this be the effect of legislation which curtails the rights of individuals within a particular area. Dicey himself admits that specific legislation could be, and had been passed, without producing the dramatic social consequences adumbrated above.

The more *particular response* provided by Dicey is to be found in his detailed examination of individual freedoms which have been secured and developed by the common law. The limitations of the common law become readily apparent by reflecting upon this detailed analysis. Dicey's argument within these chapters demonstrates the success which the common law can and did have in controlling the exercise of *executive* or *discretionary* power which could interfere with individual liberty. Arrest had to be founded upon statutory authority; executive fiat would not suffice. Freedom of discussion entailed the absence of any prior executive constraint; the individual could only be punished for a consequential wrong, such as libel.

Nothing within this analysis touches the situation in which authority does exist, the effect of which is to curtail individual liberty. Thus, Dicey admits that the government can and has secured the 'statutory suspension of habeas corpus' for limited periods and for limited classes of offence. The analysis of freedom of speech is equally revealing. Dicey juxtaposes the position of the Press at the time he wrote to that which had prevailed hitherto. The Press in the nineteenth century was not subject to prior censorship, but was governed by the ordinary law of defamation. He contrasts this with the position which had existed in the seventeenth century, where the Press was controlled by a special tribunal and was subject to regulation. The discretionary system of licensing, 'which was censorship under another name,' was given a statutory foundation in 1662, and remained in force until 1695. Dicey comments that,

> The passing, however, of the statute, though not a triumph of toleration, was a triumph of legality. The power of licensing depended henceforward, not on any idea of inherent executive authority, but on the statute law. The right of licensing was left in the hands of the government, but this power was regulated by the words of a statute; and, what was of more consequence, breaches of the Act could be punished only by proceedings in the ordinary courts. [*The Law of the Constitution*, p. 268]

This quotation aptly exemplifies Dicey's detailed analysis of specific individual rights. The common law could help to limit the exercise of broad executive discretionary power which threatened such rights. The first two limbs of the rule of law would be advanced by the transformation of discretionary power into statutory form. Once the power existed in statutory form, it was sacrosanct. A statute which curtailed civil liberties was beyond the reach of the common law, except perhaps insofar as the judiciary could construe such a statute restrictively should they choose. The minority rights in the example postulated above would be equally outside the ambit of common law protection. This result is to be expected given the centrality which Dicey accords to parliamentary omnicompetence. If the majority within Parliament does enact legislation which is detrimental to minority interests, no sanctuary can be expected from the common law. When representative democracy proves incapable of aligning the interests of the elected representatives with the nation as a whole, so that some are constitutionally disadvantaged, the oppressed can but hope for a shift in their political fortune. Dicey's claim that constitutional protection within the United Kingdom was not only historically unfounded, but also unnecessary, is therefore suspect even if our democracy did operate in the manner which he postulated.

(c) *The reality of constitutional power*

The second reason why Dicey's conclusions can be contested is that this image of the working constitution was in fact flawed. Put shortly, the nineteenth century model of representative democracy contained the seeds of its own destruction. The more closely it approached perfection, the more fragile did it become. The explanation for this apparent paradox is not hard to find. Three factors were of central importance.

The expansion of the franchise was of particular significance. This had increased the legitimacy of Parliament and provided substantive justification for regarding it as the authoritative expression of the will of the nation. The very need to appeal to an expanded electorate was, however, a key factor in the emergence of a more developed party system. Votes had to be won. Buying them was no longer practicable. Party organisation had to be improved in order to mobilise the expanded electorate into voting for a particular party. Central organisation and direction from the 'top' increased, thereby placing more power in the hands of the executive.

This tendency was furthered by the changing conception of the role of government. The idea that the government was responsible for preserving the peace, raising revenue, foreign relations and little else was undergoing a transformation. The picture of the nineteenth century as an era of laissez-faire was always misleading. A range of social legislation was passed during this period dealing with the poor, health, factories, and the like. The transformation which occurred was concerned, in part at least, with the role of government in the legislation which emanated from Parliament. Expansion of the suffrage necessitated not just the development of party organisation to mobilise the expanded electorate. It also required promises of legislation which would be beneficial to those accorded the vote. If at least some of these promises made to the electorate were to be carried out, the legislative process required alteration. This, in fact, occurred. The change was not sudden or immediate, but very real nonetheless.

The legislative process was both nationalised and centralised into the hands of the executive. Standing committees became increasing common. Fear that increased use of such committees would transform the Commons into a legislative machine did not ultimately deter the executive from instituting procedural changes designed to facilitate the passage of legislation. Cabinet committees became more common, adding impetus to the centralisation of the legislative initiative with the executive. Delegated legislation led to the same end by a different route: the legislature would accede to the passage of legislation which ultimately left a considerable residue of discretion to the executive to make further rules. Changes in the legislative process were attended by the increase in importance of the party system within Parliament. The party became the conduit for the transfer of power from the legislature to the executive. Discipline had to be tightened to ensure the passage of an enlarged governmental programme. Policy formulation became increasingly concentrated in the executive. Rarely could backbench MPs effectively stop a measure which had executive backing.

While these factors contributed to the flow of power from the Commons to the executive, the third was the growing realisation of centres of power outside of Parliament which nonetheless exercised a formative influence on the content of government policy. The development of pluralist thought in the United Kingdom was complex. Suffice it to say for the present that the recognition of the pluralist nature of society challenged the idea that Parliament wielded a monopoly of public power. . . .

The implications of the constitutional developments which have been just considered were not, therefore, to destroy Dicey's picture of sovereignty. It did, however, place the conceptual justification for the absence of review under strain. The possibility of some form of constitutional adjudication could no longer so easily be dismissed as unnecessary as well as lacking any foundation in 'precedent.' The growth of executive power, and the realisation that there were centres of power outside of Parliament, challenged the Diceyan view of representative democracy as a self-correcting mechanism. It became apparent that there might be a greater disjunction between Dicey's external and internal limits on sovereign power than had previously been perceived. If representative democracy had in fact become oligarchic, by concentrating authority in the executive and other powerful but non-representative institutions, then it became increasingly possible that the wishes of this small group might diverge considerably from those of the majority of the electorate. This potential was augmented by a voting system which worked against minority interests and which could not infrequently return a government supported by a minority of the population.

Dicey's union between historical precedent and constitutional principle was, therefore, rendered less secure than hitherto. The conception of self-correcting representative democracy was explicitly based upon a channel of authority flowing from the bottom upwards. The MPs who were elected articulated the views of those who had chosen them, and they controlled the executive. Legislation which might be constitutionally questionable, or detrimental to significant sections of the population, would therefore not be passed, or would be quickly repealed.

The structural development explored above rendered the neat, linear pattern of this reasoning suspect. Parliament's legitimacy continued to be derived from the electorate. In this formal sense, authority could still be perceived as flowing from the bottom upwards. In substance, our constitutional system became one dominated by the top, by the executive and the party hierarchy. The people voted, the government governed, and the system began to look increasingly Schumpeterian well before that classic, skeletal vision of democracy was produced. [Schumpeter, in *Capitalism, Socialism and Democracy* (1943), at p. 269, defined the democratic method as the institutional arrangement for arriving at political decisions in which individuals acquire the power to decide by means of competitive struggle for the people's vote.] This tendency was itself exacerbated by the growing control wielded by the organised parties over the electoral agenda and the electoral process.

The legislation which emerged from the 'top down' system could no longer be certain to reflect the electorate's wishes in the simplistic self-correcting sense postulated by Dicey. The concentration of authority and power within the party hierarchy and the executive increased the likelihood that legislation could emanate from Parliament, and remain on the statute books for a considerable period of time, even though it might be contrary to the desires of many within the electorate.

At base these structural changes weakened the very contrast which Dicey drew concerning the degree of coincidence between the external and internal limits on sovereign power which could be expected to operate within a monarchy and a representative democracy. In a monarchy, the sovereign, although subject to certain internal limits, might well be able to force upon his subjects legislation which they disliked. The only constraint upon such action was that the sovereign should be wary lest he transgress the external limits to his sovereign authority and provoke open resistance. A monarchical system left, however, considerable latitude to the sovereign to effectuate his personal goals which, although contrary to the desires of the people, were not sufficient to rouse them to revolt. It was this disjunction between the internal and external limits to sovereign power which the advent of representative democracy was, as we have seen, intended to cure. However, if representative democracy had become oligarchic in the manner described above, then such a disjunction became increasingly possible. The dominant group could impose its own goals, which might be contrary to the wishes of many, and yet not sufficient to produce actual resistance. Representative democracy as it actually operated could, therefore, not in fact be guaranteed to prevent a divergence between the external and internal limits of sovereignty. Power wielded by an elective oligarchy, in conjunction with other powerful but non-representative institutions, might be subject to no greater constraint than that exercised by the hereditary monarch.

Questions

1. If, as Craig asserts, 'the absence of constitutional review and the Diceyan conception of sovereignty are . . . firmly embedded within a conception of self-correcting majoritarian democracy', what protection is there for the rights of the minority?

2. Would the means of counteracting the danger of 'majority oppression' which Dicey identified be effective in the latter part of the twentieth century?

3. To what extent was W. S. McKechnie correct when he asserted that the self-correcting majoritarian democracy places 'the liberty and property, lives and honour of one half of the community absolutely and legally at the mercy of the other half' (W. S. McKechnie, *The New Democracy and the Constitution* (1912; repr. 1971), p. 164)?

4. Dicey believed that the common law was effective 'in controlling the exercise of executive or discretionary power which could interfere with individual liberty', but how effective is it when the curtailment of individual liberty is authorised by statute?

5. To what extent is Craig correct when he states that 'the legislative process was both nationalised and centralised into the hands of the executive'? Has representative democracy become oligarchic, leading to disjunction between the internal and external limits to sovereign power?

6. Does the extract which follows lend support to the view that the modern judiciary are more inclined to question the Diceyan orthodoxy? (See also Sir John Laws, 'Law and Democracy' [1995] *Public Law* 74, *ante* p. 56.)

The Rt. Hon. Lord Woolf of Barnes, 'Droit Public — English Style'
[1995] *Public Law* 57

. . . But what happens if a party with a large majority in Parliament uses that majority to abolish the courts' entire power of judicial review in express terms? It is administratively expensive, absorbs far too large a proportion of the legal aid fund and results in the judiciary having misconceived notions of grandeur. Do the courts then accept that the legislation means what it says? I am sure this is in practice unthinkable. It will never happen. But if it did, for reasons I will now summarise, my own personal view is that they do not. . . . Our parliamentary democracy is based on the rule of law. One of the twin principles upon which the rule of law depends is the supremacy of the Parliament in its legislative capacity. The other principle is that the courts are the final arbiters as to the interpretation and application of the law. As both Parliament and the courts derive their authority from the rule of law so both are subject to it and can not act in manner which involves its repudiation. The respective roles do not give rise to conflict because the courts and Parliament each respects the role of the other. For example, Parliament is meticulous in upholding the *sub judice* rule so as to avoid interfering with the role of the courts. Equally the courts always respect the privileges of Parliament and will not become involved with the internal workings of Parliament. In addition the courts will seek to give effect wherever possible to both primary and subordinate legislation. The courts will for example where there is a conflict between Community and domestic legislation uphold the domestic legislation as far as possible. The courts will also readily accept legislation which controls how it exercises its jurisdiction or which confers or modifies its existing statutory jurisdiction. I however, see a distinction between such legislative action and that which seeks to undermine in a fundamental way the rule of law on which our unwritten constitution depends by removing or substantially impairing the entire reviewing role of the High Court on judicial review, a role which in its origin is as ancient as the common law, predates our present form of parliamentary democracy and the Bill of Rights.

My approach . . . does involve dispensing with fairy tales once and for all, but I would suggest this is healthy. It involves a proper recognition of both the pillars of the rule of law and the equal responsibility that Parliament and the courts are under to respect the other's burdens and to play their proper part in upholding the rule of law. I see the courts and Parliament as being partners both engaged in a common enterprise involving the upholding of the rule of law. It is reflected in the way that frequently the House of Lords in its judicial capacity will stress the desirability of legislation when faced with the new problems that contemporary society can create rather than creating a solution itself.

There are however situations where already, in upholding the rule of law, the courts have had to take a stand. The example that springs to mind is the *Anisminic* case [1969] 2 AC 147. In that case even the statement in an Act of Parliament that the Commission's decision 'shall not be called in question in any court of law' did not succeed in excluding the jurisdiction of the court. Since that case Parliament has not again mounted such a challenge to the reviewing power of the High Court. There has been, and I am confident there will continue to be, mutual respect for each other's roles.

However, if Parliament did the unthinkable, then I would say that the courts would also be required to act in a manner which would be without precedent. Some judges might chose to do so by saying that it was an unrebuttable presumption that Parliament could never intend such a result. I myself would consider there were advantages in making it clear that ultimately there are even limits on the supremacy of Parliament which it is the courts' inalienable responsibility to identify and uphold. They are limits of the most modest dimensions which I believe any democrat would accept. They are no more than are necessary to enable the rule of law to be preserved.

5 CONSTITUTIONAL CONVENTIONS

(A) SOURCES OF THE CONSTITUTION

As the United Kingdom does not have a written constitution, the sources of our constitutional arrangements must be sought elsewhere. Most textbooks contain sections outlining the sources of the constitution. In these sections they highlight legislation and judicial precedent as the source of the legal rules of the constitution. The source of the non-legal rules is provided by conventions.

A. V. Dicey, *An Introduction to the Study of The Law of the Constitution* (10th edn, 1965), pp. 23 – 24

[T]he rules which make up constitutional law, as the term is used in England, include two sets of principles or maxims of a totally distinct character.

The one set of rules are in the strictest sense 'laws,' since they are rules which (whether written or unwritten, whether enacted by statute or derived from the mass of custom, tradition, or judge-made maxims known as the common law) are enforced by the courts; these rules constitute 'constitutional law' in the proper sense of that term, and may for the sake of distinction be called collectively 'the law of the constitution.'

The other set of rules consist of conventions, understandings, habits, or practices which, though they may regulate the conduct of the several members of the sovereign power, of the Ministry, or of other officials, are not in reality laws at all since they are not enforced by the courts. This portion of constitutional law may, for the sake of distinction, be termed the 'conventions of the constitution,' or constitutional morality.

To put the same thing in a somewhat different shape, 'constitutional law,' as the expression is used in England, both by the public and by authoritative writers, consists of two elements. The one element, here called the 'law of the constitution,' is a body of undoubted law; the other element, here called the 'conventions of the constitution,' consists of maxims or practices which, though they regulate the ordinary conduct of the Crown, of Ministers, and of other persons under the constitution, are not in strictness laws at all.

E. C. S. Wade, 'Introduction' in Dicey, *An Introduction to the Study of The Law of the Constitution* (10th edn, 1965) pp. cli – clvii

The Widened Sphere of Constitutional Conventions. – It is largely through the influence of Dicey that the term, convention, has been accepted to describe a constitutional obligation, obedience to which is secured despite the absence of the ordinary means of enforcing the obligation in a court of law. Dicey defined conventions as 'rules for determining the mode in which the discretionary powers of the Crown (or of the Ministers as servants of the Crown) ought to be exercised.' He was concerned to establish that conventions were 'intended to secure the ultimate supremacy of the electorate as the true political sovereign of the State.'

In discussing conventions as a source of constitutional law it must be noted that the obligation does not necessarily, or indeed usually, derive from express agreement. It is more likely to take its origin from custom or from practice arising out of sheer expediency. . . .

Dicey discusses mainly the rules governing the exercise of the royal prerogative by Ministers of the Crown and that part of the 'law and custom' of Parliament which rests upon custom alone. In both these cases the rules are based on custom or expediency rather than as a result of formal agreement. Conventions, however, have a wider application and have, during the present century, played an important part in building up the political relationship between the various member States of the British Commonwealth. Some of these conventions, in particular the rules governing the full competence of Commonwealth Parliaments to legislate, were made statutory by the Statute of Westminster, 1931, and later enactments. But much of the relationship is still conventional and has been based on agreement reached by Prime Ministers at Imperial Conferences. Constitutional matters no longer figure prominently on the agenda of the periodic meetings of Prime Ministers or other Ministers of Commonwealth Governments which are less formal than the earlier Imperial Conferences. But this is because constitutional issues have now been settled and in no way minimises the important part which conventions have in the past played in this sphere of constitutional development.

Dicey concentrated attention upon the conventional rules which precedent showed were fundamental to the working of the Cabinet. . . .

It is the prerogative of the Sovereign to appoint the Prime Minister. Convention limits the range of choice to that of a party leader who can command a majority in the House of Commons. This convention to some extent lacks the binding force which conventions in other fields possess. This does not mean that the rules can normally be disregarded, but that unforeseen circumstances may deprive them of their force on a particular occasion; any departure from the normal would have to conform to recognising the supremacy of the electorate and not to serve autocratic ends. Some writers would not include a practice or usage which is not regarded as obligatory, though none the less usually followed, in the category of constitutional conventions. It is, however, very difficult to draw the line between an obligatory and a non-obligatory practice. The characteristic of conventions, namely, that they supplement the laws which are enforced by the courts, would seem to preclude their precise definition. On the whole it seems preferable to regard the political practices of Sovereigns in choice of Prime Ministers as within the category of conventional rules, even though those rules are still somewhat inconclusive and therefore sufficiently flexible to meet unforeseen circumstances. For they are clearly rules of conduct referable to the requirements of constitutional government and are aimed at reflecting the supremacy of the electorate. The same is true of the practices and precepts which surround the prerogative of dissolution of Parliament. But in this case there is the fundamental understanding that the power may only be exercised on the advice of Ministers. That advice may not be available to the Sovereign in the choice of a Prime Minister, where his predecessor has been removed by death or his own resignation.

Perhaps the relationship between law and convention is best illustrated by contrasting the legal and conventional position of Ministers. They, like civil servants and members of the armed forces, are in law the servants of the Crown. By convention they, unlike all other servants of the Crown, are responsible directly to Parliament both for their own activities and those of civil servants, their subordinates, who by custom are never referred to by name in Parliament. This responsibility of Ministers is designed to make them answerable through Parliament to the electorate. To rely solely on their legal responsibility to their master, the Sovereign, would entirely fail to secure their responsibility to the public in general and indeed might make them the agents of a Sovereign who disregarded the public will, as in the days before the prerogative powers were restricted by Parliament.

Conventions relating to internal government go much further than the examples which were chosen by Dicey from the exercise of the royal prerogative and the relationship between the two Houses of Parliament. They nowadays provide for the working of the whole complicated governmental machine. A Cabinet in deciding upon policy will require to know whether it already has the power in law to take the action which it proposes. It is certainly not limited to exercising those prerogative powers of the Sovereign which are entrusted to it by convention. Through its command of a majority in the Houe of Commons it is normally in a position to take legal powers if they do not already exist. Moreover it is the responsibility of the Cabinet to ensure unity in the constitutional system and in particular to avoid or, if need be, to settle conflicts of policy and of action by the various departments. In all these activities rules and practices develop in order to secure the desired end. The growth of the committee system within the Cabinet organisation is an extra-legal development which has introduced important changes in Cabinet government since Dicey formulated his views on the place of conventions in the working of the constitution. One can properly describe this development as conventional. It is in no sense an obligation imposed by law upon Ministers that they should consult an elaborate system of committees. Yet no one supposes that a modern government could be conducted without some such machinery. So we have the position that the Cabinet itself is to all intents and purposes the creation of convention designed to secure political harmony between the Crown and its subjects. From this conventional institution there have grown up in the present century such devices as formal committees, like the Defence Committee, and *ad hoc* committees, appointed for a particular purpose but often remaining in being after their original purpose has been fulfilled. . . . In addition there are royal commissions, select committees of either House of Parliament, committees appointed by departmental Ministers, all of which play an important part in the formulation of policy. For none of these is there any legal requirement. But no appreciation of the working of the governmental machine would be complete without their inclusion. And since their purpose is to focus public opinion on a particular problem, they are designed to secure that harmony between the Ministers of the Crown and the public which is the principal justification for supplementing the law of the constitution with conventions.

Question
What are the various ways in which conventions may arise?

(B) WHAT ARE CONVENTIONS?

Conventions represent important rules of political behaviour which are necessary for the smooth running of the constitution. It is not only in the constitutional arrangements of the United Kingdom that conventions are important; K. C. Wheare, in *Modern Constitutions* (1966), p. 122, states that 'in all countries usage and convention are important and . . . in many countries which have Constitutions usage and convention play as important a part as they do in England.' Conventions facilitate evolution and change within the constitution while the legal form remains unchanged.

G. Marshall and G. C. Moodie, *Some Problems of the Constitution* (5th edn, 1971), pp. 23 – 25

What then are the conventions of the British Constitution? One way of answering the question is to point to particular examples. Thus, among them are such rules as that the Monarch should normally on the resignation of a government, ask the Leader of the Opposition to form the new one; or (before 1911) that the House of Lords should not oppose a money bill duly passed by the House of Commons; or (to quote from the Preamble to the Statute of Westminster of 1931) 'that any alteration in the law touching the Succession to the Throne or the Royal Style and Titles shall hereafter require the assent as well of the Parliaments of all the Dominions as of the Parliament of the United Kingdom'. An alternative approach is to put forward a formal definition. By the conventions of the Constitution, then, we mean certain rules of constitutional behaviour which are considered to be binding by and upon those who operate the Constitution, but which are not enforced by the law courts (although the courts may recognise their existence), nor by the presiding officers in the Houses of Parliament. Not all writers would agree to the inclusion of this last phrase. But it seems best to exclude from the category of convention 'the law and custom of Parliament' which define much of its procedure, and which are applied and interpreted by, for example, the Speaker of the House of Commons. On the other hand, certain important rules of procedure – for example, resort to the usual channels through which, among other things, important decisions about the agenda of the House of Commons are reached – are 'unkown' both to the courts and to the Speaker and must clearly be counted as conventions.

Such conventions are to be found in all established constitutions, and soon develop even in the newest. One reason for this is that no general rule of law is self-applying, but must be applied according to the terms of additional rules. These additional rules may be concerned with the interpretation of the general rule, or with the exact circumstances in which it should apply, about either of which uncertainty may exist, and the greater the generality the greater will the uncertainty tend to be. Many constitutions include a large number of additional legal rules to clarify the meaning and application of their main provisions, but in a changing world it is rarely possible to eradicate or prevent all doubts on these points by enactment or even by adjudication. The result often is to leave a significant degree of discretion to those exercising the rights or wielding the powers legally conferred, defined, or permitted. As Dicey pointed out, it is to regulate the use of such discretionary power that conventions develop. Thus the rules prescribing the procedure to be followed by the Monarch in the selection of a Prime Minister regulate the way in which she should exercise her prerogative power to appoint advisers. The legal prerogative remains intact, and appointments to the office of Prime Minister (itself a conventional position) can still be made only by the Monarch. Similarly, it remains true that no bill can become a statute until it receives the Royal Assent; but the Monarch's discretion in deciding whether or not to assent is governed by a rule that she should always assent to a bill which has duly passed both Houses. In this case the royal discretion is so limited as virtually to have been abolished. But the legal position remains untouched and thus, it is sometimes argued, may still be exercised under certain circumstances.

The definition of 'conventions' may thus be amplified by saying that their purpose is to define the use of constitutional discretion. To put this in slightly different words, it may be said that conventions are non-legal rules regulating the way in which legal rules shall be applied. Sometimes, of course, they do so only indirectly, in that they relate primarily to already existing conventions. Not all discretionary powers are so limited, but the most important ones usually are in some degree. In Britain it has been the growth of conventional limitations of the royal prerogative, in conjunction with changes in the legal rules contained in such statutes as the Act of Settlement and the various Acts extending the suffrage (as well as those changes brought about by judicial interpretation), which has largely created our modern system of government. As Sir Kenneth Wheare has said, it is 'the association of law with convention within the constitutional structure which is the essential characteristic'. This is why it is impossible to settle constitutional disputes merely by reference to the state of the law.

(C) LAWS AND CONVENTIONS

In the passage by Dicey (*ante* p. 239), he distinguished between laws and conventions, stating that laws are enforced by the courts whereas conventions are not. Sir Ivor Jennings in *The Law and the Constitution*, (5th edn, 1959), at pp. 103 – 36, takes issue with Dicey. Much of the argument is semantic, being centred on the issue whether all laws are enforced by the courts. Jennings chose to interpret this to mean that Dicey was suggesting that courts would apply sanctions for the breach of any and every law. Many laws are not enforced by the application of sanctions; but they are given effect to by the courts in that they are adhered to and applied. In this sense they are enforced, whereas conventions are treated differently. Other contrasts between laws and conventions have been noted by Munro.

C. R. Munro, *Studies in Constitutional Law* (1987), pp. 46 – 47

For example, instead of being concerned with the practical effects of breaches of rules, we might consider how the rules come into being. In a legal system, a certain number of sources are recognised as law-constitutive. So there are rules specifying what counts as law (or what, by implication, does not). In England, for instance, the courts accept as law only legislation made or authorised by Parliament and the body of rules evolved by the courts called common law. There are formal signs, such as the words of enactment used for Acts of Parliament, denoting that rules have passed a test for being laws. The point here is not merely to reiterate that conventions fall outside the categories recognised as law (which it has been the object of this section so far to show). Rather, what is significant is that conventions do not share the same qualities as laws. They do not come from a 'certain' number of sources: their origins are amorphous, and there are any number of dramatis personae whose behaviour may later be taken as evidence for the existence of a constitutional rule or practice. No body has the function of deciding whether conventions exist. There is no formal sign of their entitlement to be so regarded, as there are no agreed rules for deciding.

These points are related to a larger contrast which may be drawn. Rules of law form parts of a system. Included in the system are rules about the rules: there are provisions about entry to, and exit from, the system, and procedures for the determination and application of the rules. We cannot conceive of a single legal rule, in isolation from a system. However, conventions do not form a system. There is no unifying feature which they possess, and no apparatus of secondary rules. They merely evolve in isolation from each other.

Here, incidentally, lies the answer to Jenning's specious argument that laws and conventions are the same because both 'rest essentially upon general acquiescence'. That is quite misleading. Conventions rest entirely on acquiescence, but individually. If a supposed convention is not accepted as binding by those to whom it would apply, then there could not be said to be a convention, and this is a test on which each must be separately assessed. Laws do not depend upon acquiescense. Individual laws may be unpopular or widely disobeyed, but it does not mean that they are not laws. No doubt the system as a whole must possess some measure of de facto effectiveness for us to recognise it as valid, although it might be stretching language to describe the citizens of any country occupied by enemy forces . . . as 'acquiescing' in the laws which govern them. In any event, it is obvious that the comparison is inapt.

When 'acquiescence' is properly analysed, another means of distinguishing emerges. Breaches of a legal rule do not bring into question the existence or validity of the rule; for example, however frequently motorists might exceed the speed limits, the road traffic laws are no less laws for that. However, according to a generally accepted definition, conventions are supposed to be 'rules of political practice which are regarded as binding by those to whom they apply.' If such rules are broken, it becomes appropriate to ask whether they are still 'regarded as binding', and if they are broken often, surely one cannot say that any obligatory rule exists? In other words, the breach of a convention carries a destructive effect, which is absent with laws. The reason for this is that 'feeling obliged' is a necessary condition for the existence of a convention, whereas it is neither a necessary nor a sufficient condition for the existence of laws.

Question

If the courts do not apply sanctions for failure to observe a convention, why are conventions observed?

(D) THE NATURE OF CONVENTIONS

The nature of conventions received considerable attention in a Canadian case *Reference Re Amendment of the Constitution of Canada* (1982) 125

DLR (3d) 1. This case arose because of a special procedure in Canada whereby an issue may be referred to court for an advisory opinion; there is no such procedure in the United Kingdom.

The Dominion of Canada was created by the British North America Act 1867 which divided legislative and executive powers between the federal and provincial legislatures. As the 1867 Act was a Westminster statute, further amendment of it could only be carried out through legislation passed at Westminster. The British North America (No. 2) Act 1949 transferred powers of amendment of the constitution to the Canadian Federal Parliament, with the exception of amendments affecting the distribution of powers between the provincial and federal governments. Conventions developed in relation to the procedure for amendment. These were stated as four principles in a White Paper issued by the Canadian Government in 1965, entitled 'The Amendment of the Constitution of Canada'. The four principles were agreed by all the Provinces before the White Paper was published.

The Amendment of the Constitution of Canada (1965), p. 15

The first general principle that emerges in the foregoing resumé is that although an enactment by the United Kingdom is necessary to amend the British North America Act, such action is taken only upon formal request from Canada. No Act of the United Kingdom Parliament affecting Canada is therefore passed unless it is requested and consented to by Canada. Conversely, every amendment requested by Canada in the past has been enacted.

The second general principle is that the sanction of Parliament is required for a request to the British Parliament for an amendment to the British North America Act. This principle was established early in the history of Canada's constitutional amendments, and has not been violated since 1895. The procedure invariably is to seek amendments by a joint Address of the Canadian House of Commons and Senate to the Crown.

The third general principle is that no amendment to Canada's Constitution will be made by the British Parliament merely upon the request of a Canadian province. A number of attempts to secure such amendments have been made, but none has been successful. The first such attempt was made as early as 1868, by a province which was at that time dissatisfied with the terms of Confederation. This was followed by other attempts in 1869, 1874 and 1887. The British Government refused in all cases to act on provincial government representations on the grounds that it should not intervene in the affairs of Canada except at the request of the federal government representing all of Canada.

The fourth general principle is that the Canadian Parliament will not request an amendment directly affecting federal-provincial relationships without prior consultation and agreement with the provinces. This principle did not emerge as early as others but since 1907, and particularly since 1930, has gained increasing recognition and acceptance. The nature and the degree of provincial participation in the amending process, however, have not lent themselves to easy definition.

In 1980, after numerous attempts by the Federal Government to reach agreement with the provinces on constitutional reform, the federal government decided to press ahead with a scheme which would patriate the Canadian Constitution by ending the link with Westminster and establish a new procedure for constitutional amendment, and create a new Charter of Rights which would be binding on both federal and provincial legislatures. Eight of the ten provinces opposed the scheme. The question arose whether the federal authorities were entitled to request Westminster to enact the proposed scheme in the absence of unanimous approval from the provinces. The issue ended up in the Canadian Supreme Court when Manitoba, Newfoundland and Quebec (three of the dissenting provinces) instituted proceedings to obtain a ruling on the constitutionality of the action being taken by the federal government. Several important questions arose for determination. Was there a convention that the federal parliament would not request an amendment to the constitution affecting federal-provincial relationships without prior consultation and agreement with the provinces? Could the federal government *legally* request such amendment despite the absence of such agreement (in other words, could the convention, if it existed, be enforced by the courts)? Another question related to whether a convention could crystallise into law. The case is important because of the examination of the nature of conventions and how they may be recognised.

Reference Re Amendment of the Constitution of Canada
(1982) 125 DLR (3d) 1
Supreme Court of Canada

The essential questions for determination, and the answers of the majority, were as follows:

ON THE APPEAL FROM THE MANITOBA AND NEWFOUNDLAND COURTS OF APPEAL

1. If the amendments to the Constitution of Canada sought in the 'Proposed Resolution for a Joint Address to Her Majesty the Queen respecting the Constitution of Canada', or any of them, were enacted, would federal-provincial relationships or the powers, rights or privileges granted or secured by the Constitution of Canada to the provinces, their legislatures or governments be affected and if so, in what respect or respects?

Answer by all members of the Court: Yes.

2. Is it a constitutional convention that the House of Commons and Senate of Canada will not request Her Majesty the Queen to lay before the Parliament of the United Kingdom . . . a measure to amend the Constitution of Canada affecting federal-provincial relationships or the powers, rights or privileges granted or secured by the Constitution of Canada to the provinces, their legislatures or governments without first obtaining the agreement of the provinces?

Answer by the majority: Yes.

3. Is the agreement of the provinces of Canada constitutionally required for amendment to the Constitution of Canada where such amendment affects federal-

provincial relationships or alters the powers, rights or privileges granted or secured by the Constitution of Canada to the provinces, their legislatures or governments?

Answer by the majority: No.

ON THE APPEAL FROM THE QUEBEC COURT OF APPEAL

A. If the Canada Act and the Constitution Act 1981 should come into force and if they should be valid in all respects in Canada would they affect:

(i) the legislative competence of the provincial legislatures in virtue of the Canadian Constitution?

(ii) the status or role of the provincial legislatures or governments within the Canadian Federation?

Answer by all members of the Court: Yes.

B. Does the Canadian Constitution empower, whether by statute, convention or otherwise, the Senate and the House of Commons of Canada to cause the Canadian Constitution to be amended without the consent of the provinces and in spite of the objection of several of them, in such a manner as to affect:

(i) the legislative competence of the provincial legislatures in virtue of the Canadian Constitution?

(ii) the status or role of the provincial legislatures or governments within the Canadian Federation?

Answer by the majority: As a matter of law, Yes. As a matter of convention, No.

THE MAJORITY – The Law: . . . The proposition was advanced on behalf of the Attorney-General of Manitoba that a convention may crystallize into law and that the requirement of provincial consent to the kind of Resolution that we have here, although in origin political, has become a rule of law. . . .

In our view, this is not so. No instance of an explicit recognition of a convention as having matured into a rule of law was produced. The very nature of a convention, as political in inception and as depending on a consistent course of political recognition by those for whose benefit and to whose detriment (if any) the convention developed over a considerable period of time is inconsistent with its legal enforcement.

The attempted assimilation of the growth of a convention to the growth of the common law is misconceived. The latter is the product of judicial effort, based on justiciable issues which have attained legal formulation and are subject to modification and even reversal by the Courts which gave them birth when acting within their role in the State in obedience to statutes or constitutional directives. No such parental role is played by the Courts with respect to conventions.

It was urged before us that a host of cases have given legal force to conventions. This is an overdrawn proposition. One case in which direct recognition and enforcement of a convention was sought is *Madzimbamuto* v *Lardner-Burke et al.*, [1969] 1 AC 645. There the Privy Council rejected the assertion that a convention formally recognized by the United Kingdom as established, namely, that it would not legislate for Southern Rhodesia on matters within the competence of the latter's Legislature without its Government's consent, could not be overridden by British legislation made applicable to Southern Rhodesia after the unilateral declaration of independence by the latter's Government. Speaking for the Privy Council, Lord Reid pointed out that although the convention was a very important one, 'it had no legal effect in limiting the legal power of Parliament' (at p. 723). And, again (at the same page):

> It is often said that it would be unconstitutional for the United Kingdom Parliament to do certain things, meaning that the moral, political and other reasons against doing them are so strong that most people would regard it as highly improper if Parliament did these things. But that does not mean that it is beyond the power of Parliament to do such things. If Parliament chose to do any of them the courts could not hold the Act of Parliament invalid. It may be that it would be unconstitutional to disregard this convention. But it may also be that the unilateral Declaration of Independence released the United Kingdom from any obligation to observe the convention. Their Lordships in declaring the law are not concerned with these matters. They are only concerned with the legal powers of Parliament.

Counsel for Manitoba sought to distinguish this case on the ground that the *Statute of Westminster, 1931* did not embrace Southern Rhodesia, a point to which the Privy Council adverted. The *Statute of Westminster* . . . if it had been in force in Southern Rhodesia it would be only under its terms and not through any conventional rule *per se* that the Parliament of the United Kingdom would have desisted from legislating for Southern Rhodesia.

[Having examined various Canadian, United Kingdom and Commonwealth cases without finding any support for the crystallization argument, the Majority continued . . .]

We were invited to consider academic writings on the matter under discussion. There is no consensus among the author-scholars, but the better and prevailing view is that expressed in an article by Munro, 'Laws and Conventions Distinguished', 91 Law Q Rev 218 (1975), where he says (at p. 228):

> The validity of conventions cannot be the subject of proceedings in a court of law. Reparation for breach of such rules will not be effected by any legal sanction. There are no cases which contradict these propositions. In fact, the idea of a court enforcing a mere convention is so strange that the question hardly arises.

Another passage from this article deserves mention, as follows (at p. 224):

> If in fact laws and conventions are different in kind, as is my argument, then an accurate and meaningful picture of the constitution may only be obtained if this distinction is made. If the distinction is blurred, analysis of the constitution is less complete; this is not only dangerous for the lawyer, but less than helpful to the political scientist.

There is no difference in approach whether the issue arises in a unitary State or in a federal State: see Hogg, *Constitutional Law of Canada* (1977), at pp. 7–11.

A contrary view relied on by the provincial appellants is that expressed by Professor W. R. Lederman in two published articles, one entitled 'Process of Constitutional Amendment in Canada', 12 McGill LJ 371 (1967), and the second entitled 'Constitutional Amendment and Canadian Unity', Law Soc UC Lectures 17 (1978). As a respected scholar, Professor Lederman's views deserve more than cursory consideration. He himself recognizes that there are contrary views, including those of an equally distinguished scholar, Professor F. R. Scott: see Scott, *Essays on the Constitution* (1977), pp. 144, 169, 204–5, 245, 370–1, 402. There is also the contrary view of Professor Hogg, already cited.

Professor Lederman relies in part on a line of cases that has already been considered, especially the reasons of Sir Lyman P. Duff in the *Labour Conventions* case. The leap from convention to law is explained almost as if there was a common law of constitutional law, but originating in political practice. That is simply not so. What is desirable as a political limitation does not translate into a legal limitation, without expression in imperative constitutional text or statute. The position advocated is all the more unacceptable when substantial provincial compliance or consent is by him said to be sufficient. Although Professor Lederman would not give a veto to Prince Edward Island, he would to Ontario or Quebec or British Columbia or Alberta. This is an impossible position for a Court to manage.

Turning now to the authority or power of the two federal Houses to proceed by Resolution to forward the address and appended draft statutes to Her Majesty the Queen for enactment by the Parliament of the United Kingdom. There is no limit anywhere in law, either in Canada or in the United Kingdom . . . to the power of the Houses to pass resolutions. Under s. 18 of the *British North America Act, 1867*, the federal Parliament may by statute define those privileges, immunities and powers, so long as they do not exceed those held and enjoyed by the British House of Commons at the time of the passing of the federal statute. . . .

It is said, however, that where the Resolution touches provincial powers, as the one in question here does, there is a limitation on federal authority to pass it on to Her Majesty the Queen unless there is provincial consent. If there is such a limitation, it arises not from any limitation on the power to adopt Resolutions but from an external limitation based on other considerations. . . . [I]t is relevant to point out that even in those cases where an amendment to the *British North America Act, 1867* was founded on a Resolution of the federal Houses after having received provincial consent, there is no instance, save in the *British North America Act, 1930* where such consent was recited in the Resolution. The matter remained, in short, a conventional one within Canada, without effect on the validity of the Resolution in respect of United Kingdom action. . . .

This Court is being asked, in effect, to enshrine as a legal imperative a principle of unanimity for constitutional amendment to overcome the anomaly – more of an anomaly today than it was in 1867 – that the *British North America Act, 1867* contained no provision for effecting amendments by Canadian action alone. . . .

The stark legal question is whether this Court can enact by what would be judicial legislation a formula of unanimity to initiate the amending process which would be binding not only in Canada but also on the Parliament of the United Kingdom with which amending authority would still remain. It would be anomalous indeed, overshadowing the anomaly of a Constitution which contains no provision for its amendment, for this Court to say retroactively that in law we have had an amending formula all along, even if we have not hitherto known it; or, to say, that we have had in law one amending formula, say from 1867 to 1931, and a second amending formula that has emerged after 1931. No one can gainsay the desirability of federal-provincial accord of acceptable compromise. That does not, however, go to legality. . . .

The provincial contentions asserted a legal incapacity in the federal Houses to proceed with the Resolution which is the subject of the References and of the appeals here. Joined to this assertion was a claim that the United Kingdom Parliament had, in effect, relinquished its legal power to act on a Resolution such as the one before this Court, and that it could only act in relation to Canada if a request was made by 'the proper authorities'. The federal Houses would be such authorities if provincial powers or interests would not be affected; if they would be, then the proper authorities would include the Provinces. It is not that the Provinces must be joined in the federal address to Her Majesty the Queen; that was not argued. Rather their consent (or, as in the Saskatchewan submission, substantial provincial compliance or approval) was required as a condition of the validity of the process by address and Resolution and, equally, as a condition of valid action thereon by the United Kingdom Parliament. . . .

[T]he *Statute of Westminster, 1931* . . . is put forward not only as signifying an equality of status as between the Dominion and the Provinces vis-à-vis the United Kingdom Parliament, but also as attenuating the theretofore untrammelled legislative authority of that Parliament in relation to Canada where provincial interests are involved. . . . What s. 7(1), reinforced by s. 7(3), appeared to do was to maintain the *status quo ante*; that is, to leave any changes in the *British North America Act, 1867* (that is, such changes which, under its terms, could not be carried out by legislation of the Provinces or of the Dominion) to the prevailing situation, namely, with the legislative authority of the United Kingdom Parliament being left untouched. As Sir William Jowitt put it . . . 'the old machinery' remained in place as a result of the *Statute of Westminster, 1931*. No other conclusion is supportable on any fair reading of the terms of the *Statute of Westminster, 1931*. . . .

It was argued that the 'request and consent' which must be declared in a British statute to make it applicable to Canada, is the request and consent of the Dominion and the Provinces if the statute is one affecting provincial interests or powers, for example, an amendment of the *British North America Act, 1867* as envisaged by the Resolution herein. The word 'Dominion' in s. 4, it is said, must be read in what may be called a conjoint or collective sense as including both the Dominion and the Provinces; otherwise, it is submitted, the purpose of the *Statute of Westminster, 1931* would be defeated. . . .

Nothing in the language of the *Statute of Westminster, 1931* supports the provincial position yet it is on this interpretation that it is contended that the Parliament of the United Kingdom has relinquished or yielded its previous omnipotent legal authority in relation to the *British North America Act, 1867,* one of its own statutes. As an argument . . . it asserts a legal diminution of United Kingdom legislative supremacy. The short answer to this ramified submission is that it distorts both history and ordinary principles of statutory or constitutional interpretation. The plain fact is that s. 7(1) was enacted to obviate any inference of direct unilateral federal power to amend the *British North America Act, 1867*. . . .

[T]he challenge to the competency in law of the federal Houses to seek enactment by the Parliament of the United Kingdom of the statutes embodied in the Resolution is based on the recognized supremacy of provincial Legislatures in relation to the powers conferred upon them under the *British North America Act, 1867,* a supremacy vis-à-vis the federal Parliament. Reinforcement, or perhaps the foundation of this supremacy is said to lie in the nature or character of Canadian federalism.

The supremacy position, taken alone, needs no further justification than that found in the respective formulations of the powers of Parliament and the provincial Legislatures in ss. 91 and 92 of the *British North America Act, 1867*. Federal paramountcy is, however, the general rule in the actual exercise of these powers. This notwithstanding, the exclusiveness of the provincial powers (another way of expressing supremacy and more consonant with the terms of the *British North America Act, 1867*) cannot be gainsaid. . . .

What is put forward by the Provinces which oppose the forwarding of the address without provincial consent is that external relations with Great Britain in this respect must take account of the nature and character of Canadian federalism. It is contended that a legal underpinning of their position is to be found in the Canadian federal system as reflected in historical antecedents, in the pronouncements of leading political figures and in the preamble to the *British North America Act, 1867*.

The arguments from history do not lead to any consistent view or any single view of the nature of the *British North America Act, 1867*. . . . History cannot alter the fact that in law there is a British statute to construe and apply in relation to a matter, fundamental as it is, that is not provided for by the statute. . . .

So too, with pronouncements by political figures or persons in other branches of public life. There is little profit in parading them.

Support for a legal requirement of provincial consent to the Resolution that is before this Court, consent which is also alleged to condition United Kingdom response to the Resolution, is, finally, asserted to lie in the preamble of the *British North America Act, 1867* itself, and in the reflection, in the substantive terms of the Act, of what are said to be fundamental presuppositions in the preamble as to the nature of Canadian federalism. The preamble recites (and the whole of it is reproduced) the following:

> Whereas the Provinces of Canada, Nova Scotia, and New Brunswick have expressed their Desire to be federally united into One Dominion under the Crown of the United Kingdom of Great Britain and Ireland, with a Constitution similar in Principle to that of the United Kingdom:
>
> And whereas such a Union would conduce to the Welfare of the Provinces and promote the Interests of the British Empire:
>
> And whereas on the Establishment of the Union by Authority of Parliament it is expedient, not only that the Constitution of the Legislative Authority in the Dominion be provided for, but also that the Nature of the Executive Government therein be declared:
>
> And whereas it is expedient that Provision be made for the eventual Admission into the Union of other Parts of the British North America: . . .

What is stressed is the desire of the named Provinces 'to be federally united . . . with a Constitution similar in principle to that of the United Kingdom'. The preamble speaks also of union into 'one Dominion' and of the establishment of the Union 'by authority of Parliament', that is the United Kingdom Parliament. What, then, is to be drawn from the preamble as a matter of law? A preamble, needless to say, has no enacting force but, certainly, it can be called in aid to illuminate provisions of the statute in which it appears. Federal union 'with a constitution similar in principle to that of the United Kingdom' may well embrace responsible government and some common law aspects of the United Kingdom's unitary constitutionalism, such as the rule of law and Crown prerogatives and immunities.... There is also an internal contradiction in speaking of federalism in the light of the invariable principle of British parliamentary supremacy. Of course, the resolution of this contradiction lies in the scheme of distribution of legislative power, but this owes nothing to the preamble, resting rather on its own exposition in the substantive terms of the *British North America Act, 1867*. . . .

[I]t is the allocation of legislative power as between the central Parliament and the provincial Legislatures that the Provinces rely on as precluding unilateral federal action to seek amendments to the *British North America Act, 1867* that affect, whether by limitation or extension, provincial legislative authority. The AttorneyGeneral of Canada was pushed to the extreme by being forced to answer affirmatively the theoretical question whether in law the federal Government could procure an amendment to the *British North America Act, 1867* that would turn Canada into a unitary State. That is not what the present Resolution envisages because the essential federal character of the country is preserved under the enactments proposed by the Resolution.

That, it is argued, is no reason for conceding unilateral federal authority to accomplish, through invocation of legislation by the United Kingdom Parliament, the purposes of the Resolution. There is here, however, an unprecedented situation in which the one constant since the enactment of the *British North America Act* in 1867 has been the legal authority of the United Kingdom Parliament to amend it. The law knows nothing of any requirement of provincial consent, either to a resolution of the federal Houses or as a condition of the exercise of United Kingdom legislative power.

THE MAJORITY – Convention: . . . [M]any Canadians would perhaps be surprised to learn that important parts of the Constitution of Canada, with which they are the most familiar because they are directly involved when they exercise their right to vote at federal and provincial elections, are nowhere to be found in the law of the Constitution. For instance it is a fundamental requirement of the Constitution that if the Opposition obtains the majority at the polls, the Government must tender its resignation forthwith. But fundamental as it is, this requirement of the Constitution does not form part of the law of the Constitution.

It is also a constitutional requirement that the person who is appointed Prime Minister or Premier by the Crown and who is the effective head of the Government should have the support of the elected branch of the Legislature; in practice this means in most cases the leader of the political party which has won a majority of seats at a general election. Other ministers are appointed by the Crown on the advice of the Prime Minister or Premier when he forms or reshuffles his cabinet. Ministers must continuously have the confidence of the elected branch of the Legislature, individually and collectively. Should they lose it, they must either resign or ask the Crown for a dissolution of the Legislature and the holding of a general election. Most of the powers of the Crown under the prerogative are exercised only upon the advice of the Prime Minister or the Cabinet which means that they are effectively exercised by the latter, together with the innumerable statutory powers delegated to the Crown in council.

Yet none of these essential rules of the Constitution can be said to be a law of the Constitution. It was apparently Dicey who, in the first edition of his *Law of the Constitution*, in 1885, called them 'the conventions of the constitution' (W. S. Holdsworth, 'The Conventions of the Eighteenth Century Constitution, 17 Iowa Law Rev 161 (1932)), an expression which quickly became current. What Dicey described under these terms are the principles and rules of responsible government, several of which are stated above and which regulate the relations between the Crown, the Prime Minister, the Cabinet and the two Houses of Parliament. These rules developed in Great Britain by way of custom and precedent during the nineteenth century and were exported to such British colonies as were granted self-government.

Dicey first gave the impression that constitutional conventions are a peculiarly British and modern phenomenon. But he recognized in later editions that different conventions are found in other constitutions. As Sir William Holdsworth wrote (W. S. Holdsworth, *op. cit.*, p. 162):

> In fact conventions must grow up at all times and in all places where the powers of government are vested in different persons or bodies – where in other words there is a mixed constitution. 'The constitutent parts of a state,' said Burje, [French Revolution, 28] 'are we obliged to hold their public faith with each other, and with all those who derive any serious interest under their engagements, as much as the whole state is bound to keep its faith with separate communities.' Necessarily conventional rules spring up to regulate the working of the various parts of the constitution, their relations to one another, and to the subject.

Within the British Empire, powers of government were vested in different bodies which provided a fertile ground for the growth of new constitutional conventions unknown to Dicey whereby self-governing colonies acquired equal and independent status within the Commonwealth. Many of these culminated in the *Statute of Westminster,* 1931, 22 Geo. V, c. 4 (U.K.). . . .

The main purpose of constitutional conventions is to ensure that the legal framework of the Constitution will be operated in accordance with the prevailing constitutional values or principles of the period. For example, the constitutional value which is the pivot of the conventions stated above and relating to responsible government is the democratic principle: the powers of the State must be exercised in accordance with the wishes of the electorate; and the constitutional value or principle which anchors the conventions regulating the relationship between the members of the Commonwealth is the independence of the former British colonies.

Being based on custom and precedent, constitutional conventions are usually unwritten rules. Some of them, however, may be reduced to writing and expressed in the proceedings and documents of Imperial conferences, or in the preamble of statutes such as the *Statute of Westminster, 1931,* or in the proceedings and documents of federal-provincial conferences. They are often referred to and recognized in statements made by members of governments.

The conventional rules of the Constitution present one striking peculiarity. In contradistinction to the laws of the Constitution, they are not enforced by the Courts. One reason for this situation is that, unlike common law rules, conventions are not judge-made rules. They are not based on judicial precedents but on precedents established by the institutions of government themselves. Nor are they in the nature of statutory commands which it is the function and duty of the Courts to obey and enforce. Furthermore, to enforce them would mean to administer some formal sanction when they are breached. But the legal system from which they are distinct does not contemplate formal sanctions for their breach.

Perhaps the main reason why conventional rules cannot be enforced by the Courts is that they are generally in conflict with the legal rules which they postulate and the Courts are bound to enforce the legal rules. The conflict is not of a type which would entail the commission of any illegality. It results from the fact that legal rules create wide powers, discretions and rights which conventions prescribe should be exercised only in a certain limited manner, if at all.

[An] example will illustrate this point.

As a matter of law, the Queen, or the Governor General or the LieutenantGovernor could refuse assent to every bill passed by both Houses of Parliament or by a Lesiglative Assembly as the case may be. But by convention they cannot of their own motion refuse to assent to any such bill on any ground, for instance because they disapprove of the policy of the bill. We have here a conflict between a legal rule which creates a complete discretion and a conventional rule which completely neutralizes it. But conventions, like laws, are sometimes violated. And if this particular convention were violated and assent were improperly withheld, the Courts would be bound to enforce the law, not the convention. They would refuse to recognize the validity of a vetoed bill. This is what happened in *Gallant* v *The King,* [1949] 2 DLR 425 . . . a case in keeping with the classic case of *Stockdale* v *Hansard* (1839), 9 Ad & E 1, 112 ER 1112, where the English Court of Queen's Bench held that only the Queen and both Houses of Parliament could make or unmake laws. The Lieutenant-Governor who had withheld assent in *Gallant* apparently did so towards the end of his term of office. Had it been otherwise, it is not inconceivable that his withholding of assent might have produced a political crisis leading to his removal from office which shows that if the remedy for a breach of a convention does not lie with the Courts, still the breach is not necessarily without a remedy. The remedy lies with some other institutions of Government; furthermore, it is not a formal remedy and it may be administered with less certainty or regularity than it would be by a Court.

This conflict between convention and law which prevents the Courts from enforcing conventions also prevents conventions from crystallizing into laws, unless it be by statutory adoption.

It is because the sanctions of convention rest with institutions of government other than Courts, such as the Governor General or the Lieutenant-Governor, or the Houses of Parliament, or with public opinion and ultimately, with the electorate that it is generally said that they are political. . . .

It should be borne in mind, however, that, while they are not laws, some conventions may be more important than some laws. Their importance depends on that of the value or principle which they are meant to safeguard. Also they form an integral part of the Constitution and of the constitutional system. . . .

That is why it is perfectly appropriate to say that to violate a convention is to do something which is unconstitutional although it entails no direct legal consequence. But the words 'constitutional' and 'unconstitutional' may also be used in a strict legal sense, for instance with respect to a statute which is found *ultra vires* or unconstitutional. The foregoing may perhaps be summarized in an equation: constitutional conventions plus constitutional law equal the total Constitution of the country.

[The Majority next addressed the issue whether a particular convention exists or not is purely a political question or one upon which a court may adjudicate. They concluded that this was a constitutional question which it is proper for a court to decide and they cited various cases in which courts had recognised the existence of conventions.]

In so recognizing conventional rules, the Courts have described them, sometimes commented upon them and given them such precision as is derived from the written form of a judgment. They did not shrink from doing so on account of the political aspects of conventions, nor because of their supposed vagueness, uncertainty or flexibility.

In our view, we should not, in a constitutional reference, decline to accomplish a type of exercise that Courts have been doing of their own motion for years . . . .

The requirements for establishing a convention bear some resemblance with those which apply to customary law. Precedents and usage are necessary but do not suffice. They must be normative. We adopt the following passage of Sir W. Ivor Jennings in *The Law and the Constitution*, 5th edn. (1959), p. 136:

> We have to ask ourselves three questions: first, what are the precedents; secondly, did the actors in the precedents believe that they were bound by a rule; and thirdly, is there a reason for the rule? A single precedent with a good reason may be enough to establish the rule. A whole string of precedents without such a reason will be of no avail, unless it is perfectly certain that the persons concerned regarded them as bound by it.

(i) *The precedents*

An account of the statutes enacted by the Parliament of Westminster to modify the Constitution of Canada is found in a White Paper published in 1965 under the authority of the Honourable Guy Favreau, then Minister of Justice for Canada, under the title of 'The Amendment of the Constitution of Canada' (the White Paper). . . . [The Majority listed the 22 amendments noting that five of these directly affected federal-provincial relationships in the sense of changing provincial legislative powers.]

Every one of these five amendments was agreed upon by each Province whose legislative authority was affected.

In negative terms, no amendment changing provincial legislative powers has been made since Confederation when agreement of a Province whose legislative powers would have been changed was withheld.

There are no exceptions.

Furthermore, in even more telling negative terms, in 1951, an amendment was proposed to give the Provinces a limited power of indirect taxation. Ontario and Quebec did not agree and the amendment was not proceeded with. . . .

The accumulation of these precedents, positive and negative, concurrent and without exception, does not of itself suffice in establishing the existence of the convention; but it unmistakedly points in its direction. Indeed, if the precedents stood alone, it might be argued that unanimity is required. . . .

Finally, it was noted in the course of argument that in the case of four of the five amendments mentioned above where provincial consent effectively had been obtained, the statutes enacted by the Parliament of Westminster did not refer to this consent. This does not alter the fact that consent was obtained.

(ii) *The actors treating the rule as binding*

[The Majority referred next to the White Paper of 1965 and the four principles it stated (*ante* p. 245).]

The text which precedes the four general principles makes it clear that it deals with conventions. It refers to the laws and conventions by which a country is governed and to constitutional rules which are not binding in any strict sense (that is in a legal sense) but which have come to be recognized and accepted in practice as part of the amendment process in Canada. The first three general principles are statements of well-known constitutional conventions governing the relationships between Canada and the United Kingdom with respect to constitutional amendments.

In our view, the fourth general principle equally and unmistakedly states and recognizes as a rule of the Canadian Constitution the convention referred to in the second question of the Manitoba and Newfoundland References as well as in Question B of the Quebec Reference, namely, that there is a requirement for provincial agreement to amendments which change provincial legislative powers. . . . It seems clear that while the precedents taken alone point at unanimity, the unanimity principle cannot be said to have been accepted by all the actors in the precedents. . . . [The Majority quoted statements of former Prime Ministers in various Commons Debates.]

In 1965, the White Paper had stated that: 'The nature and the degree of provincial participation in the amending process . . . have not lent themselves to easy definition.'

Nothing has occurred since then which would permit us to conclude in a more precise manner.

Nor can it be said that this lack of precision is such as to prevent the principle from acquiring the constitutional *status* of a conventional rule. If a consensus had emerged on the measure of provincial agreement, an amending formula would quickly have been enacted and we would no longer be in the realm of conventions. To demand as much precision as if this were the case and as if the rule were a legal one is tantamount to denying that this area of the Canadian Constitution is capable of being governed by conventional rules.

Furthermore, the Government of Canada and the Governments of the Provinces have attempted to reach a consensus on a constitutional amending formula in the course of ten federal-provincial conferences held in 1927, 1931, 1935, 1950, 1960, 1964, 1971, 1978, 1979 and 1980. (Gérald A. Beaudoin, *op. cit.,* at p. 346.) A major issue at these conferences was the quantification of provincial consent. No consensus was reached on this issue. But the discussion of this very issue for more than fifty years postulates a clear recognition by all the Governments concerned of the principle that a substantial degree of provincial consent is required.

It would not be appropriate for the Court to devise in the abstract a specific formula which would indicate in positive terms what measure of provincial agreement is required for the convention to be complied with. Conventions by their nature develop in the political field and it will be for the political actors, not this Court, to determine the degree of provincial consent required.

It is sufficient for the Court to decide that at least a substantial measure of provincial consent is required and to decide further whether the situation before the Court meets with this requirement. The situation is one where Ontario and New Brunswick agree with the proposed amendments whereas the eight other Provinces oppose it. By no conceivable standard could this situation be thought to pass muster. It clearly does not disclose a sufficient measure of provincial agreement. Nothing more should be said about this.

(iii) *A reason for the rule*

The reason for the rule is the federal principle. Canada is a federal union. The preamble of the *BNA Act* states that 'the Provinces of Canada, Nova Scotia, and New Brunswick have expressed their Desire to be federally united . . .'.

The federal character of the Canadian Constitution was recognized in innumerable judicial pronouncements. We will quote only one, that of Lord Watson in *Liquidators of Maritime Bank* v *Receiver-General of New Brunswick* [1982] AC 437] at pp. 441–2:

> The object of the Act was neither to weld the provinces into one, nor to subordinate provincial governments to a central authority, but to create a federal government in which they should all be represented, entrusted with the exclusive administration of affairs in which they had a common interest, each province retaining its independence and autonomy.

The federal principle cannot be reconciled with a state of affairs where the modification of provincial legislative powers could be obtained by the unilateral action of the federal authorities. It would indeed offend the federal principle that 'a radical change to [the] constitution [be] taken at the request of a bare majority of the members of the Canadian House of Commons and Senate'. (Report of Dominion-Provincial Conference, 1931, p. 3.) . . .

Furthermore, as was stated in the fourth general principle of the White Paper, the requirement of provincial consent did not emerge as easily as other principles, but it has gained increasing recognition and acceptance since 1907 and particularly since 1930. This is clearly demonstrated by the proceedings of the Dominion-Provincial Conference of 1931.

Then followed the positive precedents of 1940, 1951 and 1964 as well as the abortive ones of 1951, 1960 and 1964, all discussed above. By 1965, the rule had become recognized as a binding constitutional one formulated in the fourth general principle of the White Paper already quoted reading in part as follows:

> *The fourth general principle* is that the Canadian Parliament will not request an amendment directly affecting federal-provincial relationships without prior consultation and agreement with the provinces.

The purpose of this conventional rule is to protect the federal character of the Canadian Constitution and prevent the anomaly that the House of Commons and Senate could obtain by simple resolutions what they could not validly accomplish by statute. . . .

We have reached the conclusion that the agreement of the Provinces of Canada, no views being expressed as to its quantification, is constitutionally required for the passing of the 'Proposed Resolution for a joint Address to Her Majesty respecting the Constitution of Canada' and that the passing of this Resolution without such agreement would be unconstitutional in the conventional sense.

Questions

1. If conventions will not be enforced by the courts, what is the sanction for failure to observe a convention?

2. Is it possible to state and define conventions with precision?

3. Is Jenning's test for recognising conventions, approved by the Supreme Court, a satisfactory and precise test?

4. Should the courts in the United Kingdom be asked to give advisory opinions on the constitution?

Note

What would have happened if the federal government had pressed ahead with the request in the absence of a 'substantial degree of provincial consent'? Would Westminster have passed the necessary legislation? Was it a convention that any amendment requested by Canada be automatically enacted by Westminster, regardless of the degree of support in Canada for the requested amendment? Certainly there was no example of such a request being refused in the past; but was this sufficient to establish a convention? This matter was examined by the House of Commons Select Committee on Foreign Affairs which reported before the Supreme Court's decision.

First Report of the Foreign Affairs Committee (Kershaw Report)
HC 42 of 1980–81

The purpose of our inquiry

4. The Canadian Government have been vigorously arguing, since the beginning of October 1980, that

> the British Parliament or government *may not look behind any federal request* for amendment, including a request for patriation of the Canadian constitution. Whatever role the Canadian provinces might play in constitutional amendments is a matter *of no consequence as far as the UK Government and Parliament are concerned.*

But the same Canadian Government document, in the preceding sentence, also said: 'The British Parliament is bound to act in accordance with a *proper* request from the federal government . . .'. So our first question was, and remains: Under what conditions is a request from the Canadian Government a proper request?

5. At the same time, our attention was directed by the FCO to a series of Ministerial statements in the UK Parliament. These have, as their common thread, the formula:

> If a request to effect such a change were to be received from the Parliament of Canada it would be *in accordance with precedent* for the United Kingdom Government to introduce in Parliament, and for Parliament to enact, appropriate legislation in compliance with the request.

So we were led to ask: What are the precedents, in relation to requests from Canada? Is there a significant difference between the UK Ministers' references to requests from the Canadian *Parliament* and the Canadian Government's references to requests from the Canadian *Government*? If there is a significant difference, does it reflect a convention, requiring that requests, to be 'proper', must have the support of the Parliament (Senate as well as House of Commons) of Canada? If that is a convention recognised by the UK Government, are there other conventions defining what counts as a proper request from Canada? How and when did such conventions arise? If a convention or principle is created, or becomes recognised, by action and opinion in Canada, is it to be taken into account by the UK Government and Parliament? And, even if it is to be taken into account in the UK, does such a principle of the Canadian constitution *determine* the responsibilities of (or 'bind') the UK Parliament?

6. The fundamental question we had to consider is the subject of Chapter VI of this Report: Is the UK Parliament bound, by convention or principle, to act automatically on any request from the Canadian Parliament for amendment or patriation of the BNA Acts? In view of the weight of evidence against an affirmative answer to that question, it became necessary to consider the further question, discussed in Chapter VII: Is it correct to say that the UK Parliament, when requested to enact constitutional changes which would directly affect Canadian Federal–Provincial relations, should not accede to the request unless it is concurred in by all the Provinces directly affected? . . .

A requirement of automatic action?

56. In this Chapter, we consider the question whether there is a rule, principle or convention that the UK Parliament, when requested by the Canadian Government and Parliament to amend (or patriate) the BNA Acts, should accede to the request 'automatically', ie regardless of the way that amendment would affect Federal-Provincial relations and of the concurrence or lack of concurrence of the Provinces in an amendment directly affecting the powers or rights of the Provincial legislatures or governments.

Proper requests should be enacted without delay

57. There can be no doubt that if a request by the Canadian Government and Parliament is a proper request, it is the responsibility of the UK Government and Parliament to secure the enactment of the request with all the urgency or priority which the Canadian Government may reasonably desire. That, indeed, is the practice of the UK Parliament, and it should be adhered to. But it is one thing to treat all proper requests as matters of priority, and quite another to consider oneself bound to regard all requests as proper requests. . . .

UK practice since 1931

68. There is nothing in UK *practice* (as distinct from Ministerial statements. . .) that should be regarded as creating a convention of automatic action in the sense specified in para 56 above. For the Canadian Government and Parliament, from 1931 to this day, have been careful not to make any request for UK action, in any matter clearly and 'directly affecting federal-provincial relations' in the sense of the 'fourth general principle' set out and explained by the 1965 White Paper . . . except with the concurrence of all the Provinces. The amendments of 1940, 1951, 1960 and 1964 directly affected the powers or rights of Provincial authorities as such. All these were requested only with the agreement of all Provinces. The amendments of 1943, 1946 and 1949 (twice), which were requested without Provincial concurrence, did not affect the powers or rights of Provincial authorities as such. . . .

The central issue of principle: Canada's federal character

82. Canada's constitutional system is federal. This federal character is stressed again and again in the authoritative Canadian judicial and political pronouncements which we analysed in paras 32–37 and 47–55 above. Those pronouncements have all underlined the way in which the federal nature of Canada's constitutional system affects the law, convention and practice relating to amendment of that system.

83. All the evidence and advice which we received from UK constitutional lawyers and UK academic authorities learned in Commonwealth constitutions was to the same effect: *it would be in accord with the established constitutional position for the UK Government and Parliament* – particularly Parliament – *to take account of the federal nature of Canada's constitutional system,* when considering how to respond to a request by the Canadian Government and Parliament for amendment and/or patriation of the BNA Acts. For when it acts or declines to act, on such a request, the UK Parliament is exercising its powers and responsibilities as . . . 'part of the process of Canadian constitutional amendment'. It would *not* be in accord with the established constitutional position for the UK Parliament to regard itself as in any way the subject of a rule, principle or convention that it should accede to such requests automatically, ie regardless of whether the request was made in a manner contrary to the principles of Canada's federal system and/or to the conventions regulating the making of such requests. If the UK Parliament were to proceed on the basis that it ought to accede to such requests automatically (subject only to the requirements of correct legislative form), it would be treating itself as for all relevant purposes the agent of the Canadian Government and Parliament. It would thus be treating the Canadian Government and Parliament as having, in constitutional reality, a substantially unilateral power of amending or abolishing Canada's federal system. For any one Government and Parliament to have such a unilateral power is inconsistent with the federal character of that system; nor is it in accord with the 'rules and principles relating to amendment procedures' which have 'emerged from the practices and procedures employed in securing various amendments to the British North American Act since 1867'.

84. Such is the gist of all the evidence and advice from UK experts. . . . We accept it as an accurate delineation of the role and responsibility of the UK Parliament in relation to the amendment and/or patriation of the BNA Acts. The precedents, consisting of actions by the UK Government and Parliament and statements in Parliament by UK Ministers, seem to us not to involve any acknowledgement of a requirement of automatic action. Those precedents all relate to requests made by the Canadian Government and Parliament in apparent conformity with the established Canadian constitutional position regarding the making of requests. They leave the UK Government and Parliament *constitutionally (not merely legally or technically) free to decide that the making of a request is so out of line with the established constitutional position that the UK Government can rightly decline to act on that request.* There is *no precedent* for the UK Government and Parliament receiving and acting upon a request, the making of which was clearly and substantially not in accord with the established Canadian constitutional position. . . .

Conclusions

111. The considerations set out in this Chapter, taken with the preceding Chapter, lead us to the conclusion that the UK Parliament is not bound, even conventionally, either by the supposed requirement of automatic action on Federal requests, or by the supposed requirement of unanimous Provincial consent to amendments altering Provincial powers. Instead the UK Parliament retains the role of deciding whether or not a request for amendment or patriation of the BNA Acts

conveys the clearly expressed wish of Canada as a whole, bearing in mind the federal nature of that community's constitutional system. In all ordinary circumstances, the request of the Canadian Government and Parliament will suffice to convey that wish. But where the requested amendment or patriation directly affects the *federal* structure of Canada, and the opposition of Provincial governments and legislatures is officially represented to the UK authorities, something more is required.

112. We recognise that that conclusion involves an unpalatable and thankless role for the UK Government and Parliament. . . .

113. The role involves a responsibility in relation to Canada as a federally structured whole. It is not a *general* responsibility for the welfare of Canada or of its Provinces and peoples. It is simply the responsibility of exercising the UK Parliament's residual powers in a manner consistent with the federal character of Canada's constitutional system, *inasmuch as that federal character affects the way in which the wishes of Canada, on the subject of constitutional change, are to be expressed. It would be quite improper for the UK Parliament to deliberate about the suitability of requested amendments or methods of patriation,* or about the effects of those amendments on the welfare of Canada or any of its communities or peoples.

114. Is there any available criterion for measuring whether a request accords with the wishes of the Canadian people as a federally structured community? We do not think the UK Parliament should invent a criterion of its own; what is needed is a criterion with a basis in the constitutional history and politics of Canada. Such a criterion seems to us to be available. We think that it would not be inappropriate for the UK Parliament to expect that a request for patriation by an enactment significantly affecting the federal structure of Canada should be conveyed to it with *at least that degree of Provincial concurrence* (expressed by governments, legislatures or referendum majorities) *which would be required for a post-patriation amendment* affecting the federal structure in a similar way. For example a federal request that had the support of the two largest Provinces and of Provinces containing 50 per cent of the Western and 50 per cent of the Atlantic populations would be one that could be said to correspond to the wishes of the Canadian peoples on a whole. This criterion has roots in the historic structure of Canadian federalism as reflected in the Divisions of Canada for the purposes of the Provincial representation in the Senate of Canada; and it broadly accords both with the last (if not the only) clear consensus of Canadian Federal and Provincial governments (at Victoria in 1971) and with the present proposals . . . of the Canadian Government in relation to post-patriation amendment.

115. Some forms or modes of patriation would affect the federal structure of Canada less than would some amendments of the BNA Acts. So one further possibility arises for consideration. The UK Government and Parliament might receive from the Canadian Government and Parliament, without the concurrence of the Provinces, a request for patriation/amendment involving *only* (i) termination of the UK's legislative powers and (ii) a post-patriation amendment formula providing for amendment only with at least such a degree of provincial support as is required to initiate an amendment procedure in Part IV of the proposed 'Canada Constitution Act, 1980'. It might well be proper for the UK Parliament to accede to such a request. For such action by the UK Parliament, while arguably not strictly pursuant to the clearly expressed wishes of Canada as a federally structured whole, would give effect, for the future, to those constitutional changes, and only those changes, which corresponded with such wishes. Since the UK Parliament's action would involve no other substantial constitutional change, it would not substantially affect the federal character of Canada's constitutional system and would not be out of accord with the UK's role in the established constitutional position as we have tried to explain it.

Note

The decision of the Supreme Court that the convention required a substantial degree of provincial consent was in line with the view expressed by the Kershaw Committee. The convention was designed to protect the federal character of the Canadian Constitution and prevent the federal parliament achieving by means of a resolution addressed to Westminster what it could not achieve domestically by means of legislation.

Question

In a Memorandum to the Kershaw Committee, Professor H. W. R. Wade stated:

> Conventions are the rules of the game of politics, and it may be necessary to correct one infringement by another. If for example a British government were to refuse to resign after being defeated on a motion of no confidence, the Queen would be justified in dismissing the ministers against their will. The fact that the UK Parliament does not in practice look behind amendments requested by Canada is entirely dependent upon those requests being in conformity with Canadian conventions. If those conventions are infringed, the duty of the UK Parliament is to take corrective action.

Is it desirable that the sanction for breach of one convention is the breach of another – a principle of constitutional tit for tat?

Note

In response to the Supreme Court's decision the federal government decided not to press on with the request to Westminster to enact legislation. Further discussions were held with the provinces and concessions were offered. In response, nine provinces agreed to the revised proposals. A new request was made, and the Canada Act 1982 was duly enacted at Westminster following a recommendation from the Kershaw Committee that consent from nine out of ten provinces constituted a substantial measure of support for the proposals.

First Report of the Foreign Affairs Committee (Kershaw Report)
HC 128 of 1981–82

6. The criteria suggested in our First Report for assessing the appropriate level of Provincial support were put forward, not as minima required by any existing constitutional rule or convention, but rather as indications of what 'Parliament would be justified in regarding as sufficient' or of what 'it would not be inappropriate for the UK Parliament to expect'. Since then, the Supreme Court of Canada has determined that what is constitutionally required is 'at least a substantial measure of Provincial consent'. The Court decided that unanimity is not required, but did not define or quantify 'a substantial measure'. The Government of Quebec have, we understand, commenced litigation to establish whether their concurrence is constitutionally required. So it is important to observe that the Supreme Court has stated, 'It will be for

the political actors, not this Court, to determine the degree of provincial consent required'. The Federal-Provincial Agreement of 5 November 1981, made in the wake of the Supreme Court's judgement and accepted by nine of the ten Provinces, appears to us to amount to a determination by the political actors in Canada that the concurrence of nine Provinces is constitutionally sufficient, albeit the dissenting Province be Quebec.

7. In this situation, what we said in our First Report seems applicable: 'the UK Parliament is bound to exercise its best judgement in deciding whether the request, in all the circumstances, conveys the clearly expressed wishes of Canada as a federally structured whole'. In our view, the present request does this.

(E) CAN CONVENTIONS CRYSTALLISE INTO LAW?

This question was answered in the negative by the Supreme Court in *Reference Re Amendment of the Constitution of Canada* (*ante* p. 246). It also arose before a United Kingdom court in *Manuel* v *Attorney-General* [1983] 1 Ch 77. The suggestion in this case was that the convention that Westminster would not enact legislation for a dominion except at its request and with its consent, had crystallised into law so that actual consent had to be established. The action had been brought by Indian chiefs seeking a declaration that the Canada Act 1982 was *ultra vires* as the consent of the Indian people did not exist. Section 4 of the Statute of Westminster 1931 provides:

> No Act of Parliament of the United Kingdom passed after the commencement of this Act shall extend, or be deemed to extend, to a Dominion as part of the law of that Dominion, unless it is expressly declared in that Act that that Dominion has requested, and consented to, the enactment thereof.

This section did not enact the convention but incorporated it in a modified form. The issues involved are clearly stated in the judgment of Slade LJ, *ante* pp. 86–89.

(F) CONVENTIONS IN THE COURTS

It is clear that courts will not enforce conventions by imposing sanctions for their breach. Recognition of the existence of a convention by a court, however, can be significant in the court's decision of the issues before it. Conventions may be used as an aid to statutory interpretation or to support judicial decisions not to review discretionary powers of the executive because of the Minister's accountability to Parliament. (see *Liversidge* v *Anderson* [1942] AC 206). In *Carltona* v *Commissioners of Works* [1943] 2 All ER 560, Lord Green MR placed considerable emphasis on the convention of ministerial responsibility in reaching his decision. He stated (at p. 563):

> In the administration of government in this country the functions which are given to ministers (and constitutionally properly given to ministers because they are constitutionally responsible) are functions so multifarious that no minister could ever personally attend to them. To take the example of the present case no doubt there

> have been thousands of requisitions in this country by individual ministries. It cannot be supposed that this regulation meant that, in each case, the minister in person should direct his mind to the matter. The duties imposed upon ministers and the powers given to ministers are normally exercised under the authority of the ministers by responsible officials of the department. Public business could not be carried on if that were not the case. Constitutionally, the decision of such an official is, of course, the decision of the minister. The minister is responsible. It is he who must answer before Parliament for anything that his officials have done under this authority, and, if for an important matter he selected an official of such junior standing that he could not be expected competently to perform the work, the minister would have to answer for that in Parliament. The whole system of departmental organisation and administration is based on the view that ministers, being responsible to Parliament, will see that important duties are committed to experienced officials. If they do not do that, Parliament is the place where complaint must be made against them.

One of the best examples of judicial consideration of conventions in a United Kingdom court is the case which follows.

Attorney-General v *Jonathan Cape Ltd*
[1976] QB 752
High Court

Between 1964 and 1970 Richard Crossman was a Cabinet minister, and he kept a political diary. Following his death in 1974, his diary for 1964–66 was edited for publication. A copy was sent to the Secretary to the Cabinet for his approval but was rejected on the ground that publication was against the public interest, in that the doctrine of collective responsibility would be harmed by the disclosure of details of Cabinet decisions, the revelation of differences between members of the Cabinet, and the disclosure of advice given by, and discussions regarding the appointment of, civil servants. When Crossman's literary executors decided to publish extracts of the diary in *The Sunday Times*, the Attorney-General sought injunctions against the publishers, literary executors and *The Sunday Times* to restrain publication of the book or extracts from it.

LORD WIDGERY CJ: . . . It has always been assumed by lawyers and, I suspect, by politicians, and the Civil Service, that Cabinet proceedings and Cabinet papers are secret, and cannot be publicly disclosed until they have passed into history. It is quite clear that no court will compel the production of Cabinet papers in the course of discovery in an action, and the Attorney-General contends that not only will the court refuse to compel the production of such matters, but it will go further and positively forbid the disclosure of such papers and proceedings if publication will be contrary to the public interest.

The basis of this contention is the confidential character of these papers and proceedings, derived from the convention of joint Cabinet responsibility whereby any policy decision reached by the Cabinet has to be supported thereafter by all members of the Cabinet whether they approve of it or not, unless they feel compelled to resign. It is contended that Cabinet decisions and papers are confidential for a period to the extent at least that they must not be referred to outside the Cabinet in such a way as to disclose the attitude of individual Ministers in the argument which preceded the decision. . . .

There is no doubt that Mr Crossman's manuscripts contain frequent references to individual opinions of Cabinet Ministers. . . . There have, as far as I know, been no previous attempts in any court to define the extent to which Cabinet proceedings should be treated as secret or confidential, and it is not surprising that different views on this subject are contained in the evidence before me. . . .

The Attorney-General contends that all Cabinet papers and discussions are prima facie confidential, and that the court should restrain any disclosure thereof if the public interest in concealment outweighs the public interest in a right to free publication. The Attorney-General further contends that, if it is shown that the public interest is involved, he has the right and duty to bring the matter before the court. In this contention he is well supported by Lord Salmon in *Reg* v *Lewes Justices, Ex parte Secretary of State for the Home Department* [1973] AC 388, 412, where Lord Salmon said:

> when it is in the public interest that confidentiality shall be safeguarded, then the party from whom the confidential document or the confidential information is being sought may lawfully refuse it. In such a case the Crown may also intervene to prevent production or disclosure of that which in the public interest ought to be protected.

I do not understand Lord Salmon to be saying, or the Attorney-General to be contending, that it is only necessary for him to evoke the public interest to obtain an order of the court. On the contrary, it must be for the court in every case to be satisfied that the public interest is involved, and that, after balancing all the factors which tell for or against publication, to decide whether suppression is necessary.

The defendants' main contention is that whatever the limits of the convention of joint Cabinet responsibility may be, there is no obligation enforceable at law to prevent the publication of Cabinet papers and proceedings, except in extreme cases where national security is involved. In other words, the defendants submit that the confidential character of Cabinet papers and discussions is based on a true convention as defined in the evidence of Professor Henry Wade, namely, an obligation founded in conscience only. Accordingly, the defendants contend that publication of these Diaries is not capable of control by any order of this court.

If the Attorney-General were restricted in his argument to the general proposition that Cabinet papers and discussion are all under the seal of secrecy at all times, he would be in difficulty. It is true that he has called evidence from eminent former holders of office to the effect that the public interest requires a continuing secrecy, and he cites a powerful passage from the late Viscount Hailsham to this effect. The extract comes from a copy of the Official Report (House of Lords) for December 21, 1932, in the course of a debate on Cabinet secrecy. Lord Hailsham said; col. 527:

> But, my Lords, I am very glad that the question has been raised because it has seemed to me that there is a tendency in some quarters at least to ignore or to forget the nature and extent of the obligations of secrecy and the limitations which rigidly hedge round the position of a Cabinet Minister. My noble friend has read to your Lordships what in fact I was proposing to read – that is, the oath which every Privy Councillor takes when he is sworn of His Majesty's Privy Council. Your Lordships will remember that one reason at least why a Cabinet Minister must of necessity be a member of the Privy Council is that it involves the taking of that oath. Having

heard that oath read your Lordships will appreciate what a complete misconception it is to suppose, as some people seem inclined to suppose, that the only obligation that rests upon a Cabinet Minister is not to disclose what are described as the Cabinet's minutes. He is sworn to keep secret all matters committed and revealed unto him or that shall be treated secretly in Council.

Lord Hailsham then goes on to point out that there are three distinct classes to which the obligation of secrecy applies. He describes them as so-called Cabinet minutes; secondly, a series of documents, memoranda, telegrams and despatches and documents circulated from one Cabinet Minister to his colleagues to bring before them a particular problem and to discuss the arguments for and against a particular course of conduct; and, thirdly, apart from those two classes of documents, he says there is the recollection of the individual Minister of what happens in the Cabinet. Then the extract from Lord Hailsham's speech in the House of Lord's report continues in these words:

I have stressed that because, as my noble and learned friend Lord Halsbury suggested and the noble Marquis, Lord Salisbury, confirmed, Cabinet conclusions did not exist until 16 years ago. The old practice is set out in a book which bears the name of the noble earl's father, Halsbury's Laws of England, with which I have had the honour to be associated in the present edition.

Then the last extract from Lord Hailsham's speech is found in col. 532, and is in these words:

It is absolutely essential in the public interest that discussions which take place between Cabinet Ministers shall take place in the full certainty of all of them that they are speaking their minds with absolute freedom to colleagues on whom they can explicitly rely, upon matters on which it is their sworn duty to express their opinions with complete frankness and to give all information, without any haunting fear that what happens may hereafter by publication create difficulties for themselves or, what is far more grave, may create complications for the King and country that they are trying to serve. For those reasons I hope that the inflexible rule which has hitherto prevailed will be maintained in its integrity, and that if there has been any relaxation or misunderstanding, of which I say nothing, the debate in this House will have done something to clarify the position and restate the old rule in all its rigour and all its inflexibility.

The defendants, however, in the present action, have also called distinguished former Cabinet Ministers who do not support this view of Lord Hailsham, and it seems to me that the degree of protection afforded to Cabinet papers and discussion cannot be determined by a single rule of thumb. Some secrets require a high standard of protection for a short time. Others require protection until a new political generation has taken over. In the present action against the literary executors, the Attorney-General asks for a perpetual injunction to restrain further publication of the Diaries in whole or in part. I am far from convinced that he has made out a case that the public interest requires such a Draconian remedy when due regard is had to other public interests, such as the freedom of speech: see Lord Denning MR in *In re X (A Minor) (Wardship: Jurisdiction)* [1975] Fam 47. . . . It seems to me . . . that the Attorney-General must first show that whatever obligation of secrecy or discretion attaches to former Cabinet Ministers, that obligation is binding in law and not merely in morals.

I have read affidavits from a large number of leading politicians, and the facts, so far as relevant, appear to be these. In 1964, 1966 and 1969 the Prime Minister (who was in each case Mr Harold Wilson) issued a confidential document to Cabinet Ministers containing guidance on certain questions of procedure. Paragraph 72 of the 1969 edition provides:

> The principle of collective responsibility and the obligation not to disclose information acquired whilst holding Ministerial office apply to former Ministers who are contemplating the publication of material based upon their recollections of the conduct of Cabinet and Cabinet committee business in which they took part.

The general understanding of Ministers while in office was that information obtained from Cabinet sources was secret and not to be disclosed to outsiders.

There is not much evidence of the understanding of Ministers as to the protection of such information after the Minister retires. It seems probable to me that those not desirous of publishing memoirs assumed that the protection went on until the incident was 30 years old, whereas those interested in memoirs would discover on inquiry at the Cabinet Office that draft memoirs were normally submitted to the Secretary of the Cabinet for his advice on their contents before publication. Manuscripts were almost always submitted to the Secretary of the Cabinet in accordance with the last-mentioned procedure. Sir Winston Churchill submitted the whole of his manuscripts concerned with the war years, and accepted the advice given by the Secretary of the Cabinet as to publication. . . .

The main framework of the defence is to be found in eight submissions from Mr Comyn. The first two have already been referred to, the allegation being that there is no power in law for the court to interfere with publication of these diaries or extracts, and that the Attorney-General's proper remedy lies in obtaining a change of the statute law.

I have already indicated some of the difficulties which face the Attorney-General when he relied simply on the public interest as a ground for his actions. That such ground is enough in extreme cases is shown by the universal agreement that publication affecting national security can be restrained in this way. It may be that in the short run (for example, over a period of weeks or months) the public interest is equally compelling to maintain joint Cabinet responsibility and the protection of advice given by civil servants, but I would not accept without close investigation that such matters must, as a matter of course, retain protection after a period of years.

However, the Attorney-General has a powerful reinforcement for his argument in the developing equitable doctrine that a man shall not profit from the wrongful publication of information received by him in confidence. This doctrine, said to have its origin in *Prince Albert* v *Strange* (1849) 1 H & T 1, has been frequently recognised as a ground for restraining the unfair use of commercial secrets transmitted in confidence. Sometimes in these cases there is a contract which may be said to have been breached by the breach of confidence, but it is clear that the doctrine applies independently of contract: see *Saltman Engineering Co. Ltd* v *Campbell Engineering Co. Ltd* (1948) 65 RPC 203. Again in *Coco* v *A. N. Clark (Engineers) Ltd* [1969] RPC 41 Megarry J, reviewing the authorities, set out the requirements necessary for an action based on breach of confidence to succeed. He said, at p. 47:

> In my judgment three elements are normally required if, apart from contract, a case of breach of confidence is to succeed. First, the information itself, in the words of Lord Greene MR . . . must 'have the necessary quality of confidence about it.' Secondly, that information must have been imparted in circumstances importing an obligation of confidence. Thirdly, there must be an unauthorised use of that information to the detriment of the party communicating it.

It is not until the decision in *Duchess of Argyll* v *Duke of Argyll* [1967] Ch 302, that the same principle was applied to domestic secrets such as those passing between husband and wife during the marriage. It was there held by Ungoed-Thomas J that the plaintiff wife could obtain an order to restrain the defendant husband from communicating such secrets, and the principle is well expressed in the headnote in these terms, at p. 304:

> A contract or obligation of confidence need not be expressed but could be implied, and a breach of contract or trust or faith could arise independently of any right of property or contract . . . and that the court, in the exercise of its equitable jurisdiction, would restrain a breach of confidence independently of any right at law.

This extension of the doctrine of confidence beyond commercial secrets has never been directly challenged, and was noted without criticism by Lord Denning MR in *Fraser* v *Evans* [1969] 1 QB 349, 361. I am sure that I ought to regard myself, sitting here, as bound by the decision of Ungoed-Thomas J.

Even so, these defendants argue that an extension of the principle of the *Argyll* case to the present dispute involves another large and unjustified leap forward, because in the present case the Attorney-General is seeking to apply the principle to public secrets made confidential in the interests of good government. I cannot see why the courts should be powerless to restrain the publication of public secrets, while enjoying the *Argyll* powers in regard to domestic secrets. Indeed, as already pointed out, the court must have power to deal with publication which threatens national security, and the difference between such a case and the present case is one of degree rather than kind. I conclude, therefore, that when a Cabinet Minister receives information in confidence the improper publication of such information can be restrained by the court, and his obligation is not merely to observe a gentleman's agreement to refrain from publication.

It is convenient next to deal with Mr Comyn's third submission, namely, that the evidence does not prove the existence of a convention as to collective responsibility, or adequately define a sphere of secrecy. I find overwhelming evidence that the doctrine of joint responsibility is generally understood and practised and equally strong evidence that it is on occasion ignored. The general effect of the evidence is that the doctrine is an established feature of the English form of government, and it follows that some matters leading up to a Cabinet decision may be regarded as confidential. Furthermore, I am persuaded that the nature of the confidence is that spoken for by the Attorney-General, namely, that since the confidence is imposed to enable the efficient conduct of the Queen's business, the confidence is owed to the Queen and cannot be released by the members of Cabinet themselves. I have been told that a resigning Minister who wishes to make a personal statement in the House, and to disclose matters which are confidential under the doctrine obtains the consent of the Queen for this purpose. Such consent is obtained through the Prime Minister. I have not been told what happened when the Cabinet disclosed divided opinions during the European Economic Community referendum. But even if there was here a breach of confidence (which I doubt) this is no ground for denying the existence of the general rule. I cannot accept the suggestion that a Minister owes no duty of confidence in respect of his own views expressed in Cabinet. It would only need one or two Ministers to describe their own views to enable experienced observers to identify the views of the others.

The other defence submissions are either variants of those dealt with, or submissions with regard to relief.

The Cabinet is at the very centre of national affairs, and must be in possession at all times of information which is secret or confidental. Secrets relating to national security may require to be preserved indefinitely. Secrets relating to new taxation proposals may be of the highest importance until Budget day, but public knowledge thereafter. To leak a Cabinet decision a day or so before it is officially announced is an accepted exercise in public relations, but to identify the Ministers who voted one way or another is objectionable because it undermines the doctrine of joint responsibility.

It is evident that there cannot be a single rule governing the publication of such a variety of matters. In these actions we are concerned with the publication of diaries at a time when 11 years have expired since the first recorded events. The Attorney-General must show (a) that such publication would be a breach of confidence; (b) that the public interest requires that the publication be restrained, and (c) that there are no other facts of the public interest contradictory of and more compelling than that relied upon. Moreover, the court, when asked to restrain such a publication, must closely examine the extent to which relief is necessary to ensure that restrictions are not imposed beyond the strict requirement of public need.

Applying those principles to the present case, what do we find? In my judgment, the Attorney-General has made out his claim that the expression of individual opinions by Cabinet Ministers in the course of Cabinet discussion are matters of confidence, the publication of which can be restrained by the court when this is clearly necessary in the public interest.

The maintenance of the doctrine of joint responsibility within the Cabinet is in the public interest, and the application of that doctrine might be prejudiced by premature disclosure of the views of individual Ministers.

There must, however, be a limit in time after which the confidential character of the information, and the duty of the court to restrain publication, will lapse. Since the conclusion of the hearing in this case I have had the opportunity to read the whole of volume one of the Diaries, and my considered view is that I cannot believe that the publication at this interval of anything in volume one would inhibit free discussion in the Cabinet of today, even though the individuals involved are the same, and the national problems have a distressing similarity with those of a decade ago. It is unnecessary to elaborate the evils which might flow if at the close of a Cabinet meeting a Minister proceeded to give the press an analysis of the voting, but we are dealing in this case with a disclosure of information nearly 10 years later.

It may, of course, be intensely difficult in a particular case, to say at what point the material loses its confidential character, on the ground that publication will no longer undermine the doctrine of joint Cabinet responsibility. It is this difficulty which prompts some to argue that Cabinet discussions should retain their confidential character for a longer and arbitrary period such as 30 years, or even for all time, but this seems to me to be excessively restrictive. The court should intervene only in the clearest of cases where the continuing confidentiality of the material can be demonstrated. In less clear cases – and this, in my view, is certainly one – reliance must be placed on the good sense and good taste of the Minister or ex-Minister concerned.

In the present case there is nothing in Mr Crossman's work to suggest that he did not support the doctrine of joint Cabinet responsibility. The question for the court is whether it is shown that publication now might damage the doctrine notwithstanding that much of the action is up to 10 years old and three general elections have been held meanwhile. So far as the Attorney-General relies in his argument on the disclosure of individual ministerial opinions, he has not satisfied me that publication would in any way inhibit free and open discussion in Cabinet hereafter.

It remains to deal with the Attorney-General's two further arguments, namely, (a) that the Diaries disclose advice given by senior civil servants who cannot be expected to advise frankly if their advice is not treated as confidential; (b) the Diaries disclose observations made by Ministers on the capacity of individual senior civil servants and their suitability for specific appointments. I can see no ground in law which entitle the court to restrain publication of these matters. A Minister is, no doubt, responsible for his department and accountable for its errors even though the individual fault is to be found in his subordinates. In these circumstances, to disclose the fault of the subordinate may amount to cowardice or bad taste, but I can find no ground for saying that either the Crown or the individual civil servant has an enforceable right to have the advice which he gives treated as confidential for all time.

For these reasons I do not think that the court should interfere with the publication of volume one of the Diaries, and I propose, therefore, to refuse the injunction sought but to grant liberty to apply in regard to material other than volume one if it is alleged that different considerations may there have to be applied.

Injunction refused.

Note

Following the decision in the case, a committee of privy councillors considered the problem of memoirs of former Cabinet ministers (Cmnd. 6386, 1976). The Committee drew a distinction between secret information relating to national security and international relations, and other confidential material about relationships between ministers or between ministers and civil servants. In the former case the minister must accept the decision of the Cabinet Secretary, while in the latter case there should be no publication within 15 years except with approval of the Cabinet Secretary but, in the event of a dispute, the final decision would lie with the former minister as to what to publish. The Committee did not consider that legislation would be appropriate.

Questions

1. What role did the convention of collective responsibility play in Lord Widgery CJ's decision? (See further on collective responsibility pp. 274–276.)

2. Do conventions, to use Dicey's words, 'secure the ultimate supremacy of the electorate as the true political sovereign of the State'?

3. Would it make for greater certainty in our constitutional arrangements, and, perhaps, an increase in the moral suasion attaching to conventions, if conventions were codified, thereby providing a clear and authoritative statement of each convention? Are there any drawbacks which would ensue from codification?

6 PARLIAMENTARY GOVERNMENT AT WORK

Note
In this chapter, which examines the operation of our parliamentary style of government, the emphasis will be upon the responsibility and accountability of the government. The most important constitutional convention is that of responsible government, the idea that the executive will be responsible for its exercise of power and be accountable to Parliament and thence to the electorate.

(A) THE ROLE OF PARLIAMENT

Philip Norton (ed.), *Parliament in the 1980s* (1985), pp. 4–6, 8

Some observers identify a variety of functions, others list only two or three. An analysis of writings on Parliament, of constitutional practice and of parliamentary behaviour would suggest three primary ones: those of providing the personnel of government, of legitimization, and of subjecting measures of public policy to scrutiny and influence. This is to identify them in rather bald terms. Each is in need of qualification and amplification.

Providing the personnel of government
This is the least problematic of the functions. By convention, ministers are drawn from and remain within Parliament. Again by convention, most ministers – including the Prime Minister and most members of the Cabinet – are drawn from the elected chamber. (No less than two but rarely more than four peers are appointed now to the Cabinet.) There is no formal prohibition on a Prime Minister appointing as a minister

someone who is neither an MP or a peer; such occasions are rare but not unknown. However, those given office are normally then elevated to the peerage or (more riskily) seek a Commons seat through the medium of a by–election. In practice, most ministers have served a parliamentary apprenticeship of several years before their appointments. Parliament provides both the personnel of government and the forum in which those seeking office can make their mark. Though there are occasional calls for non-parliamentarians (businessmen, industrialists and the like) to be brought into government, this function of Parliament arouses no serious debate or controversy.

Legitimization

Most national assemblies exist for the purpose of giving assent to measures of public policy. Indeed, this constitutes the primary purpose for which representatives of the local English communities (*communes*) were first summoned in the thirteenth century. Today, the broad rubric of legitimization encompasses different elements. The most obvious and the most significant is that of manifest legitimization. This constitutes the formal giving of assent to measures, enabling them to be designated Acts of Parliament; such Acts are accepted as having general and binding applicability by virtue of having been passed by the country's elected or part-elected national assembly (the elected chamber now having dominance within that assembly). A second element is that of latent legitimization. The government derives its primary political legitimacy from being elected through (if no longer by) the House of Commons. The collectivity of ministers that form the government enjoy enhanced legitimacy also by being drawn from and remaining in Parliament. For Parliament as an institution, this of course constitutes an essentially passive function.

There are two other sub-functions that fall under the heading of legitimization: those of tension-release and support-mobilization. By meeting and debating issues, Parliament provides an outlet, an authoritative outlet, for the expression of different views within society. Thus it plays an important part in the dissipation of tension. For example, during the Falklands crisis in 1982, Parliament provided the authoritative forum for the expression of public feelings on the issue. In Argentina, by contrast, citizens enjoyed no such body through which their views could be expressed and were forced instead to take to the streets to make their feelings known. Parliament also seeks to mobilize public support for measures which it has approved. In essence, these two sub-functions constitute a two-way process between electors and the elected, the views of citizens being channelled through Parliament (tension-release) and Parliament then mobilizing support for those measures which it has approved (support-mobilization). In practice, the extent to which Parliament is capable of fulfilling these functions has been much overlooked and, when considered by writers, has often been found wanting.

Scrutiny and influence

Parliament ceased to be a policy-making legislature in the nineteenth century. Instead it acquired the characteristics of what I have elsewhere termed a policy-influencing legislature. It ceased to be involved in the making of public policy, but it was expected to subject such policy to a process of scrutiny and influence. Scrutiny and influence are analytically separable terms, but scrutiny without any consequent sanction to effect influence is of little worth; and influence is best and most confidently attempted when derived from prior scrutiny. Hence, scrutiny and influence may be conjoined as a single function of Parliament. It is, in practice, its most debated and contentious function.

The exercise of scrutiny and influence can be seen to operate at two levels. These, in simple terms, may be characterized as being at the macro and the micro level of public policy. At the macro level, Parliament is expected to subject measures of public policy, embodied in legislative bills or in executive actions, to scrutiny and influence prior to giving assent to them. It is essentially a reactive function, exercised at a moderately late stage in the policy cycle . . . It is one which is most often carried out through the party elements in both Houses, the official Opposition or, nowadays, opposition parties seeking to exert the most sustained scrutiny of government measures. However, Parliament is but one of many influences at work in the policy cycle and, by virtue of what is usually an assured government majority at the end of the scrutinizing process, is rarely deemed to be the most important. Indeed, in some analyses, it is of no great importance at all.

At the micro level, Parliament is expected to scrutinize and respond to the effects of policy on the community. In practice, this task is exercised less through the party elements and Parliament as a collective entity, and more through Members of Parliament as Constituency representatives. Members represent territorially designated areas (constituencies) and seek to defend and pursue the interests of their constituents and groups within their constituencies. Whereas at the macro level MPs will be concerned to debate the principle of public policy, usually within the context of party ideology, at the micro level they are much more concerned with the policy's practical implications for their constituents.

In terms of the working life of Parliament, scrutiny and influence constitute its most demanding function. Seeking to subject government actions and legislative measures to scrutiny and a degree of influence occupies most of Parliament's time and energies. It is also the function that attracts the most debate and criticism. At best, effective fulfilment of the function allows Parliament to set the broad limits within which government can govern. (At the end of the day, it retains the formal sanction to deny assent to the government's legislative proposals and its request for supply.) At worst, the function may be fulfilled in the most superficial of ways, providing no effective check upon the executive.

Note

Norton does not say that the House of Commons controls the executive. Michael Ryle in *The Commons To-day* (1981) says that it is a popular misapprehension to regard the Commons as a governmental rather than a critical body. As he puts it, 'Parliament is the forum where the exercise of government is publicly displayed and is open to scrutiny and criticism.'

Questions

1. Does what Norton refers to as 'micro level' scrutiny by MPs include constituency work where the public can come to MPs' surgeries to complain about various matters? Is the redress of citizens' grievances against officialdom not a very important part of MPs' work? (See *post* pp. 362–368.)

2. What exactly is meant by legitimization? Is legitimization real if Parliament approves the actions of the executive in the manner of a rubber stamp?

(B) POLICY AND ADMINISTRATION

(i) Ministerial responsibility

C. Turpin, 'Ministerial Responsibility: Myth or Reality?' in J. Jowell & D. Oliver (eds), *The Changing Constitution* (2nd edn, 1989), pp. 55–57

When it is said that ministers are collectively and individually responsible to Parliament, what is meant by 'responsible'? It may help us find the answer if we compare the idea of ministerial responsibility to Parliament with that of *control* by Parliament of the executive. Much contemporary discussion of the relations between Parliament and government is concerned with the reassertion of parliamentary control, and by this is generally meant a power to influence the decisions of government. Control, that is to say, is exercised a priori. On the other hand, when it is said that ministers are 'responsible' or 'answerable' or 'accountable' – terms not generally distinguished in meaning – to Parliament, reference is usually being made to the obligation of ministers to respond or answer or account for actions already performed (or left unperformed): responsibility is retrospective or a posteriori. There is, of course, an overlap between the parliamentary functions of 'controlling' and 'holding responsible' ('calling to account'). Some techniques, such as parliamentary questions and scrutiny by selected committees, are directed both to control and to the assertion of responsibility. An a posteriori investigation or check may have the aim of influencing future policy-making. The notion of 'responsible government' implies both acceptance of responsibility for things done and 'responsiveness' to influence, persuasion, and pressure for modifications of policy. Activist parliamentarians of our day aim to 'redress the balance' of the constitution in favour of Parliament by strengthening both control and responsibility of the executive, without making a fine discrimination between these concepts. This is not to say that equal progress is to be expected in establishing control and in extending responsibility . . . A posteriori responsibility implies that certain obligations are owed by ministers to Parliament. What are these obligations?

It is demanded of ministers, in the first place, that they should *answer* or give account, discharging the essential 'obligation of Ministers, collectively and individually, to meet Parliament and provide information about their policies'. This includes a duty to provide financial accounts attesting to the regularity of government expenditure, as one element of a fuller 'explanatory accountability' which requires the giving of reasons and explanations for action taken, whether or not involving expenditure. That this is not a neglible aspect of responsibility was recognized by H. J. Laski: 'A Government that is compelled to explain itself under cross-examination will do its best to avoid the grounds of complaint. Nothing makes responsible government so sure.' The requirement to answer goes further: it imports an obligation to submit to scrutiny – to provide opportunities for Parliament to question, challenge, probe, and criticize. A duty to answer is something hollow if there are not apt procedures, respected by government, for such 'calling to account'.

The obligation to answer and submit to scrutiny is ancillary to what we may see as government's traditional obligation to redress grievances, which here means to take remedial action for revealed errors or defects of policy or administration, whether by compensating individuals, reversing or modifying policies or decisions, disciplining Civil Servants, or altering departmental procedures. This may be called 'amendatory accountability'; it presupposes an acknowledgement by ministers that they 'bear responsibility' to Parliament for what is shown to have gone wrong, whether or not they accept personal blame for the failure.

The obligations to answer, to submit to scrutiny, and to redress grievances may seem in practice to lack the support of any coercive rule or sanction. Undoubtedly these obligations are imperfect, resting as they do upon conventions, practices, and procedures which are liable to change and to be variously interpreted and applied, and which depend ultimately upon the political culture. But this is far from saying that the obligations in question lack substance, or that they can be flouted with impunity.

(1) Collective ministerial responsibility

Ministerial responsibility comprises both collective and individual responsibility. In his book on constitutional conventions, Marshall classifies the branches of collective ministerial responsibility as the confidence rule, the unanimity rule, and the confidentiality rule.

Confidence

G. Marshall, *Constitutional Conventions* (1984), pp. 55–56

It sometimes used to be said that a prime non-legal rule of the Constitution was that governments defeated by the House on central issues of policy were obliged to resign. But only one Prime Minister has resigned as the result of a defeat in the House in the twentieth century and that was immediately after being deprived of his majority by a General Election (Baldwin in January 1924). MacDonald was defeated on a confidence issue in 1924 and Callaghan in 1979, but neither resigned. Both fought the subsequent General Elections as leader of a government, having advised dissolution.

So the rule about a government that loses the confidence of the House seems to be that it must *either* resign *or* advise dissolution. Its right is only to advise, not to have, dissolution; since dissolution can, as we have seen, in some circumstances be refused. Resignation might therefore follow as the result of such a refusal (by the Queen), but that has not happened. As to what constitutes a loss of confidence there seems also to have been a development in doctrine. The books used to say that defeat on major legislative measures or policy proposals as well as on specifically worded confidence motions was fatal to the continuance of the government. But this no longer seems to be believed or acted on. In 1977 *The Times* propounded the view that 'there is no constitutional principle that requires a government to regard any specific policy defeat as evidence that it no longer possesses the necessary confidence of the House of Commons'. Some were greatly shocked by this doctrine and Professor Max Beloff wrote to *The Times* to say that it was inconsistent with the principles of the Constitution as hitherto understood. Sir Ivor Jennings, he pointed out, had said in *Cabinet Government* that the government must go if the House failed to approve its policy. What provoked the disagreement was that the Labour Government had just failed to carry a budget proposal about the rate of income tax and was proposing to remain in office in defiance of Sir Ivor Jennings's view of the established convention. Sir Ivor Jennings was of course dead, which is supposed to augment the authority of a textbook writer by allowing his views to be cited more freely in the course of litigation. Unfortunately there is a countervailing disadvantage in that his works may go out of print and are no longer constantly perused by Ministers, who are thereby enabled to fall into lax habits and disregard established constitutional conventions. In the 1960s and 1970s, in any event, governments seem to have been following a new rule, according to which only votes specifically stated by the Government to be matters of confidence, or votes of no confidence by the Opposition are allowed to count. Just conceivably one can imagine amongst recent Prime Ministers those who might have felt it their duty to soldier on in the general interest even in the face of such a vote.

Unanimity

House of Lords, Parl. Deb.
Vol. 239, cols. 833–34, 8 April 1878

THE MARQUESS OF SALISBURY: . . . My Lords, my noble Friend [the Earl of Derby] pointed out several measures of the Government to which in the public eye he was an assenting party. He did not, he said, in reality assent to all; one was a compromise, while to another, he was persuaded by some observations which fell from the Chancellor of the Exchequer, which appeared to be founded on a mistake. Now, my Lords, am I not defending a great Constitutional principle, when I say that, for all that passes in Cabinet, each member of it who does not resign is absolutely and irretrievably responsible, and that he has no right afterwards to say that he agreed in one case to a compromise, while in another he was persuaded by one of his Colleagues. Consider the inconvenience which will arise if such a great Constitutional law is not respected. . . . It is, I maintain, only on the principle that absolute responsibility is undertaken by every Member of a Cabinet who, after a decision is arrived at, remains a Member of it, that the joint responsibility of Ministers to Parliament can be upheld, and one of the most essential conditions of Parliamentary responsibility established.

House of Commons, H.C. Deb.
Vol. 889, Written Answers, Mr H. Wilson, col. 351, 7 April 1975

THE PRIME MINISTER: In accordance with my statement in the House on 23rd January last, those Ministers who do not agree with the Government's recommendation in favour of continued membership of the European Community are, in the unique circumstances of the referendum, now free to advocate a different view during the referendum campaign in the country.

This freedom does not extend to parliamentary proceedings and official business. Government business in Parliament will continue to be handled by all Ministers in accordance with Government policy. Ministers responsible for European aspects of Government business who themselves differ from the Government's recommendation on membership of the European Community will state the Government's position and will not be drawn into making points against the Government recommendation. Wherever necessary Questions will be transferred to other Ministers. At meetings of the Council of Ministers of the European Community and at other Community meetings, the United Kingdom position in all fields will continue to reflect Government policy.

I have asked all Ministers to make their contributions to the public campaign in terms of issues, to avoid personalising or trivialising the argument, and not to allow themselves to appear in direct confrontation, on the same platform or programme, with another Minister who takes a different view on the Government recommendation.

Note

This breach or suspension of unanimity or Cabinet solidarity was criticised as being simply a device to keep the Labour Party together. The United Kingdom's membership of the European Communities has caused problems for the Labour Party. In 1977 the point at issue was the use of proportional representation as the method of voting in the direct elections to the European Parliament. As unanimity in Cabinet could not be achieved, collective responsibility was, once again, suspended. The then Prime Minister, Mr Callaghan, answering a question in the House of Commons about collective responsibility, said 'I think the doctrine should apply except in cases where I announce that it does not.' (HC Deb, vol. 993, col. 552, 16 June 1977.)

The occasions on which it has been formally announced that unanimity in a government would be suspended have been few. Ministers have resigned because they could not agree with their colleagues on governmental policy. Mr Ian Gow resigned as a junior minister in the Treasury because he did not agree with the Anglo-Irish Agreement 1985. Mr Michael Heseltine resigned as Secretary of State for Defence in the Westland Affair because he could not accept the requirement that all ministers should clear speeches about Westland with the Cabinet Office.

Question

What purpose does Cabinet solidarity serve, and whom does it (and its suspension) benefit?

Confidentiality

The confidentiality of Cabinet proceedings is, of course, related to unanimity in that body. Disclosures of what happened in Cabinet do occur. Ministers may 'leak', i.e. brief journalists, on the basis that they do not name their source, or they may publish their memoirs. The publication of the Crossman Diaries has changed the practice, if not the convention, of confidentiality. (See *Attorney-General* v *Jonathan Cape Ltd* [1976] QB 752 and Lord Widgery CJ's judgment *ante,* at p. 263.)

Subsequently the Report of the Radcliffe Committee of Privy Councillors on Ministerial Memoirs (Cmnd 6386) was published. According to its guidelines, ministers should not disclose what happened in Cabinet until 15 years have passed where the material concerns national security; or where foreign relations would be adversely affected; or where it would reveal relationships between ministers and (a) officials, or (b) ministers' outside advisers.

(2) *Individual ministerial responsibility*

The confusion which was seen over when a government should resign when defeated in the House of Commons is also present in the issue of what should prompt the resignation of an individual minister. In 1982 Lord Carrington, the Secretary of State, and two of his junior ministers resigned from the Foreign and Commonwealth Office after Argentinian troops had invaded the Falkland Islands. Lord Carrington wrote in his letter of resignation:

> The Argentine invasion of the Falkland Islands has led to strong criticism in Parliament and in the press on the Government's policy. In my view, much of the criticism is unfounded. But I have been responsible for the conduct of that policy and I think it right that I should resign . . . [T]he invasion of the Falkland Islands has been a humiliating affront to this country.

This is an example of a classic case of a minister accepting that the faults in a Department were his responsibility and then resigning. As such it is unusual. In the following year there was a mass break-out from the Maze Prison in County Down, Northern Ireland. There was an inquiry into the circumstances of the escape by Her Majesty's Chief Inspector of Prisons (HC 203 of 1983–84), which found that the prison governor must be held accountable for a major failure in the prison's security arrangements. This report, the Hennessy Report, was debated in the House of Commons.

House of Commons, H.C. Deb.
Vol. 53, cols. 1042, 1060–61, 9 February, 1984

THE SECRETARY OF STATE FOR NORTHERN IRELAND (MR J. PRIOR): There are those who, while they accept this policy, have nevertheless suggested that the circumstances of the escape demand ministerial resignation. I take that view seriously and have given it the most careful consideration. I share hon. Members' concern about the honour of public life and the maintenance of the highest standards. I said at the time of my statement to the House on 24 October, without any pre-knowledge of what Hennessy would find:

> It would be a matter for resignation if the report of the Hennessy inquiry showed that what happened was the result of some act of policy that was my responsibility, or that I failed to implement something that I had been asked to implement, or should have implemented. In that case, I should resign. – [*Official Report,* 24 October 1983, vol. 47, c. 23–24.]

In putting the emphasis that I did on the issue of 'policy', I was not seeking to map out some new doctrine of ministerial responsibility. I was responding to the accusations made at the time that it was policy decisions, reached at the end of the hunger strike, that made the escape possible.

Since the report was published, the nature of the charges levelled at my hon. Friend and myself has changed. It is now argued in some quarters that Ministers are responsible for everything that happens in their Departments and should resign if anything goes wrong. My position has not changed, and I want to make it quite clear that if there were any evidence in the Hennessy report that Ministers were to blame for the escape, I would not hesitate to accept that blame and act accordingly, and so I know, would my hon. Friend. However, I do not accept – and I do not think it right for the House to accept – that there is any constitutional or other principle that requires ministerial resignations in the face of failure, either by others to carry out orders or procedures or by their supervisors to ensure that staff carried out those orders. Let the House be clear: the Hennessy report finds that the escape would not have succeeded if orders and procedures had been properly carried out that Sunday afternoon.

Of course, I have looked carefully at the precedents. There are those who quote the Crichel Down case. I do not believe that it is a precedent or that it establishes a firm convention. It is the only case of its sort in the past 50 years, and constitutional lawyers have concluded that the resignation was not required by convention and was exceptional.

Whatever some may wish, there is no clear rule and no established convention. Rightly, it is a matter of judgment in the light of individual circumstances. I do not intend to review the judgments made by Ministers faced with the question whether to resign following failures in their Departments. Nor do I seek to justify my decision on the ground that there are many difficulties in Northern Ireland. There are, but that adds to rather than subtracts from the argument. The question that I have asked myself is whether on Sunday afternoon, 25 September, I was to blame for those prisoners escaping. The Hennessy report is quite explicit in its conclusion that, although there may have been weaknesses in the physical security of the prison and in the prisons department, the escape could not have taken place if the procedures laid down for the running of the prison had been followed. . . .

MR J. ENOCH POWELL (Down, South): The Secretary of State, from the beginning of his speech, recognised the central issue in this debate, that of ministerial responsibility, without which the House scarcely has a real function or any real service that it can perform for the people whom it represents. We are concerned with the nature of the responsibility, the ministerial responsibility, for an event which, even in isolation from its actual context, was a major disaster.

I want to begin by eliminating from this consideration the Under-Secretary of State for Northern Ireland, the hon. Member for Chelsea (Mr Scott), because references to him in this context have shown a gross misconception. There has been argument about how long the hon. Member has been in the branch of the Northern Ireland Office concerned with the prison service, as though that were in the least degree relevant. The fact is that the entire responsibility, whether or not it is delegated to a junior Minister, rests with the Secretary of State. The Secretary of State has confirmed this to me in the past 24 hours, in another context, when I drew his attention to the reports to the fact that the Minister in charge of the environment had himself taken the decision to re-name the district of Londonderry. The right hon. Gentleman quite correctly said:

> In discharging his duties, my hon. Friend acts on my behalf. – [*Official Report*, 8 February 1984; vol. 53, c. 623.]

There is a responsibility, of a different kind, obviously, on the part of every junior Minister towards his Ministry, but the responsibility for everything that he does or says or fails to do or say rests irrevocably with the Minister – the Secretary of State – and he alone is responsible to the House.

It is, therefore, a total misconception to imagine that any of the responsibility can be devolved to a junior Minister. A junior Minister may choose, if his chief resigns, to resign in solidarity with him; he may choose himself to resign for a variety of reasons. But there is no constitutional significance in acceptance by him of a responsibility which is not his. The locus of the responsibility is beyond challenge. It lies with the Secretary of State and, through him, with the Government as a whole.

As the Secretary of State reminded us this afternoon, even before the publication of the report he drew a distinction, which I believe to be invalid, between responsibility for policy and responsibility for administration. I believe that this is a wholly fallacious view of the nature of ministerial responsibility. I shall argue presently that there is a policy element in the event that we are considering and that it cannot be understood fully except in its policy framework. But even if all considerations of policy could be eliminated, the responsibility for the administration of a Department remains irrevocably with the Minister in charge. It is impossible for him to say to the House or to the country, 'The policy was excellent and that was mine, but the execution was defective or disastrous and that has nothing to do with me.' If that were to be the accepted position, there would be no political source to which the public could complain about administration or from which it could seek redress for failings of administration.

What happened was an immense administrative disaster. It was not a disaster in a peripheral area of the responsibilities of the Northern Ireland Department. It was a disaster that occurred in an area which was quite clearly central to the Department's responsibilities. If the responsibility for administration so central to a Department can be abjured by a Minister, a great deal of our proceedings in the House is a beating of the air because we are talking to people who, in the last resort, disclaim the responsibility for the administration.

Note

Mr Powell's view is not one, it would appear, which is shared by ministers. The classic statement about the circumstances in which a minister will be responsible for the action of his officials was given in 1954 by Sir David Maxwell-Fyfe, who was Home Secretary at the time. He made his statement on the occasion of the debate of the report into the Crichel Down affair. Some land had been compulsorily acquired by the Air Ministry. It was later transferred to the Ministry of Agriculture, which then leased the land to a tenant in breach of promises made about the way in which such a disposal of the land would be carried out. The Minister for Agriculture, Sir Thomas Dugdale, resigned.

House of Commons, H.C. Deb.
Vol. 530, cols. 1285–88, 10 July 1954

THE SECRETARY OF STATE FOR THE HOME DEPARTMENT (SIR DAVID MAXWELL-FYFE): . . . There has been criticism that the principle [of Ministerial responsibility] operates so as to oblige Ministers to extend total protection to their officials and to endorse their acts, and to cause the position that civil servants cannot be called to account and are effectively responsible to no one. That is a position which I believe is quite wrong. . . . It is quite untrue that well-justified public criticism of the actions of civil servants cannot be made on a suitable occasion. The position of the civil servant is that he is wholly and directly responsible to his Minister. It is worth stating again that he holds his office 'at pleasure' and can be dismissed at any time by the Minister; and that power is none the less real because it is seldom used. The only exception relates to a small number of senior posts, like permanent secretary, deputy secretary, and principal financial officer, where, since 1920, it has been necessary for the Minister to consult the Prime Minister, as he does on appointment.

I would like to put the different categories where different considerations apply . . . [I]n the case where there is an explicit order by a Minister, the Minister must protect the civil servant who has carried out his order. Equally, where the civil servant acts properly in accordance with the policy laid down by the Minister, the Minister must protect and defend him.

I come to the third category, which is different. . . . Where an official makes a mistake or causes some delay, but not on an important issue of policy and not where a claim to individual rights is seriously involved, the Minister acknowledges the mistake and he accepts the responsibility, although he is not personally involved. He states that he will take corrective action in the Department. I agree with the right hon. Gentleman that he would not, in those circumstances, expose the official to public criticism. . . .

But when one comes to the fourth category, where action has been taken by a civil servant of which the Minister disapproves and has no prior knowledge, and the conduct of the official is reprehensible, then there is no obligation on the part of the Minister to endorse what he believes to be wrong, or to defend what are clearly shown to be errors of his officers. The Minister is not bound to defend action of which he did not know, or of which he disapproves. But, of course, he remains constitutionally responsible to Parliament for the fact that something has gone wrong, and he alone can tell Parliament what has occurred and render an account of his stewardship. The fact that a Minister has to do that does not affect his power to control and discipline his staff. One could sum it up by saying that it is part of a Minister's responsibility to Parliament to take necessary action to ensure efficiency and the proper discharge of the duties of his Department. On that, only the Minister can decide what it is right and just to do, and he alone can hear all sides, including the defence.

It has been suggested in this debate, and has been canvassed in the Press, that there is another aspect which adds to our difficulties, and that is that today the work and the tasks of Government permeate so many spheres of our national life that it is impossible for the Minister to keep track of all these matters. I believe that that is a matter which can be dealt with by the instructions which the Minister gives in his Department. He can lay down standing instructions to see that his policy is carried out. He can lay down rules by which it is ensured that matters of importance, of difficulty or of political danger are brought to his attention. Thirdly, there is the control of this House, and it is one of the duties of this House to see that that control is always put into effect.

. . . As I have said, it is a matter for the Minister to decide when civil servants are guilty of shortcomings in their official conduct. Normally, the Civil Service has no procedure equivalent to a court-martial, or anything of that kind. There have in the past been a few inquiries to establish the facts and the degree of culpability of individuals, but the decision as to the disciplinary action to be taken has been left to the Minister. . . .

Note

It has been held by some that Sir Thomas's resignation was one in which he accepted responsibility for the wrongdoing of his officials. However, the current view seems to be that the resignation occurred because Sir Thomas had lost the support of his ministerial and party colleagues. See, for example, I. F. Nicolson *The Mystery of Crichel Down* (1986) and J. A. G. Griffith 'Crichel Down: The Most Famous Farm in British Constitutional History' (1987) 1 *Contemporary Record* 35. Perhaps this explains Lord Prior's view that Crichel Down did not set a precedent for resignation.

D. Woodhouse, 'Ministerial Responsibility in the 1990s: When Do Ministers Resign?' 46 *Parliamentary Affairs* (1993), p. 277, at p. 292

The answer to the question 'when do ministers resign?' is therefore elusive, at least as it relates to departmental fault. It appears that the following conditions are required before a resignation is likely to occur. The minister must have made a grievous and foreseeable error in very high policy resulting in evident and grave consequences for a large number of people enjoying public regard and sympathy. The policy must be easily disassociated from the government as a whole. There must be no civil servant or law officer in sight to take the blame. The Prime Minister should be happy to lose the minister (but not have a reshuffle in mind) and have a replacement at hand. The parliamentary party and the tabloid press should be out for blood, with the heavy press demanding resignation. The minister must have a sense of constitutional properiety. In all other circumstances ministers can hide in the complexities outlined above and expect to survive – at least until the next Cabinet reshuffle, and frequently beyond.

Questions

1. Is Mr Powell correct in stating that the distinction between policy and administration is false and that the minister is responsible for everything done by the department?

2. Should a minister resign if he has failed to organise his departmental procedures in such a way that officials are not required to bring to his attention matters of 'importance, of difficulty or of political danger'?

(3) Ministerial responsibility and accountability

Fifth Report from the Treasury and Civil Service Select Committee HC 27 of 1993–94, paras 118–26, 132–4

118. . . . We now turn to consideration of one principle in particular which relates to the public face of Government — the principle of accountability. It is worthy of separate consideration because its precise meaning and application gave rise to greater uncertainty in the course of the inquiry than any other principle. We seek here to disentangle some of the confusion surrounding this concept and set down what we see as the basic principles of accountability.

119. Sir Robin Butler described the principle of 'accountability through Ministers to Parliament' as one of the essential characteristics of the Civil Service. It has been suggested that it is in fact the single most distinctive characteristic of the Civil Service. It has long been recognised that the requirements of accountability have a profound effect on the way the Civil Service works. A study commissioned by the Fulton Committee found that 'accountability to Parliament and the public is not a constitutional platitude; it is an integral part of the daily life of many civil servants'. The Expenditure Committee observed in 1977 that 'responsibility to Ministers and ultimately to Parliament requires much greater record-keeping than usual in organisations outside the Civil Service'. The impact of accountability on management in the Civil Service was also noted by witnesses to the Sub-Committee. It is intimately connected to the functions of the Civil Service, their methods of finance and their administrative character, and the fact that the Civil Service is involved in developing

and implementing the policies of a Government accountable to Members of Parliament who are accountable in turn to their constituents. Moreover, as our predecessors observed, Parliamentary accountability is not 'a cost which must be weighed in the balance against the benefit of effective management. It is not only important in its own right, it is also an extremely effective pressure for improvement'.

(ii) Ministerial accountability and responsibility

120. The Government's interpretation of the principles of Ministerial accountability and of responsibility has been set out in recent years in the Armstrong Memorandum and in the Memorandum of Guidance for Officials appearing before Select Committees, known after its original author as the Osmotherly Rules. The Government, and Sir Robin Butler in particular, has sought to restate the existing Government position, albeit with greater clarity of terminology than in the past. In recent pronouncements the Government has sought to draw a distinction between accountability and responsibility. According to the Government, Ministerial accountability to Parliament is a Minister's ultimate duty to account to Parliament for the work of his Department: 'the Minister in charge of a Department is the only person who may be said to be ultimately accountable for the work of his department'. In the Government's view, it means that 'in the last resort . . . Ministers can be challenged about any action of the Civil Service'. The Government contends that since civil servants act on behalf of Ministers — except in specified cases where statutes confer power or responsibility directly upon civil servants — Ministers alone are accountable to Parliament. In the view of the Government, civil servants are accountable to Ministers, and where they give evidence to Select Committees, they do so 'on behalf of Ministers'. According to the Armstrong Memorandum, even the appearance of Accounting Officers before the Committee of Public Accounts is 'without prejudice to the Minister's responsibility and accountability to Parliament in respect of the policies, actions and conduct of his Department'. Responsibility, according to the Government, has a separate meaning in this context which 'implies direct personal involvement in an action or decision, in a sense which implies personal credit or blame for that action or decision'. In the view of the Government, a Minister is *accountable* for all the actions and activities of his Department, but is not *responsible* for all the actions in the sense of being blameworthy; a civil servant is not directly accountable to Parliament for his actions, but is responsible for certain actions and can be delegated clearly defined responsibilities.

121. The Government holds that this doctrine of Ministerial accountability and of responsibility is compatible with the practice throughout the present century, including the most extreme expression of Parliament accountability — Ministerial resignations. The Government contended that 'It has never been the case that Ministers were required or expected to resign in respect of any and every mistake made by their departments, though they are clearly responsible to Parliament for ensuring that action is taken to put matters right and prevent a recurrence'. The resignation of Sir Thomas Dugdale over the Crichel Down affair in 1954 was held to be the exception that proved the rule. The notion of Ministers resigning for the mistakes of others was seen by Mr Waldegrave as 'a bad doctrine'. Mr Waldegrave suggested that in cases which might possibly entail resignation, Select Committees might inquire into whether Ministerial accountability was matched by actual Ministerial responsibility for mistakes. The Government's position was broadly consistent with that outlined by Sir David Maxwell-Fyfe in the Crichel Down debate in July 1954. He listed categories of actions or events for which, in the view of the Government, it would and would not be appropriate to hold a Minister responsible. He contended that 'a Minister is not

bound to defend action of which he did not know, or of which he disapproves', but he concluded that a Minister 'remains constitutionally responsible to Parliament for the fact that something has gone wrong, and he alone can tell Parliament what has occurred and render an account of his stewardship'. Lord Jenkins and Lord Callaghan endorsed the Government's view that Ministers should not be expected to resign for administrative failures in which they are not directly involved, the latter remarking that 'if we were to apply Thomas Dugdale's approach today we would not have the same Cabinet for three weeks running'.

122. The Government's doctrine of Ministerial accountability and responsibility appears to be open to two main objections. The first is that it is more novel than its advocates are prepared to admit, that it does not have sufficient authority and acceptance to be said to represent a 'constitutional convention'. It appears never to have been in question that Ministers are fully and clearly accountable for policy; this was described as 'axiomatic' in the original Next Steps Report. The Prime Minister in 1966, the then Mr Harold Wilson, stated that 'civil servants, however eminent, remain the confidential advisers of Ministers, who alone are answerable to Parliament *for policy*'. The use of policy alone in this context might be held to leave open the possibility that civil servants could be answerable for administrative actions. In 1986 the then Committee reaffirmed the basic, proposition that 'Ministers and not officials are responsible and accountable for policy', but questioned the wider position held by the Government.

> 'The difficulty arises not with regard to Ministerial policy or official advice but with accountability for actions by civil servants. If Crichel Down is dead and Ministers are not accountable to Parliament for some actions of their officials, then who is? Not to put too fine a point on it, who ought to resign or to be penalised if mistakes are made? If it is not Ministers, it can only be officials'.

Our predecessors were not alone in believing that there had been a time when Ministers could be held responsible for all of the actions of their officials, and that there had therefore been a change of doctrine. The Fulton Committee noted that the convention of the anonymity of civil servants 'has depended in the past on the assumption that the doctrine of Ministerial responsibility means that a Minister has full detailed knowledge and control of all the activities of his department. This assumption is no longer tenable'. In 1977 a predecessor of Sir Robin Butler as Cabinet Secretary described the concept that Ministers should resign for mistakes by officials of whom they had never heard as 'out of date'; he did not imply that such a concept had never existed. It has been held in the past that the doctrine of Ministerial accountability did not apply to all of the actions of all the officials in a Department. For example, in 1978 the then Minister for the Civil Service said that 'There are some defined exceptions to that simple structure of accountability. For instance, accounting officers are *directly accountable* to Parliament for the use made of public funds voted to their departments'.

123. A second objection to the doctrine of Ministerial accountability and of responsibility delineated by the Government is that, even if the Government's description of the doctrine were correct, it is a fundamental Victorian conception which is no longer appropriate to modern circumstances. Mr Graham Mather argued that there was in practice a shared responsibility which was not recognised in constitutional doctrine: 'Ministers do not feel either constitutionally or morally responsible for decisions which have, in all probability, involved a number of others'. Similarly Lord Callaghan referred to 'a diffusion of responsibility to the Civil Service which has created less of a sense of personal responsibility than perhaps existed forty

years ago'. Sir Brian Cubbon argued that the distinction between accountability and responsibility was untenable in practice because Ministers could not determine the extent of their own responsibilities; the scope of Ministerial accountability was in large measure determined by external pressures and events. Others believed that the growth of Ministerial responsibilities was placing the doctrine under strain. The epitome of such concepts is perhaps the sentiment, expressed by a Minister who served from 1983 to 1992, that 'No one these days resigns for anything'. Lord Jenkins believed there has been an undue reluctance to resign in recent years, which he attributed principally to 'an excessive careerisation of politics'. Lord Callaghan attributed any reluctance to resign to the diffusion of responsibility; he did not think that Ministers were less honourable than in the past. Dr Keith Dowding argued that little had changed since 1945 and that resignations reflected political weakness more than "any notion of honourable assessment of culpability". In the past, Select Committees have argued that one solution to these perceived problems is the extension of the principle of direct accountability of civil servants. In 1977 the Expenditure Committee saw a case for heads of accountable units within the Civil Service to be made publicly accountable for their actions, noting that "the introduction of publicity accountable heads would require some civil servants to be directly answerable in public to such bodies as Select Committees but this would no more infringe Ministerial accountability than the presence of Accounting Officers as respondents before such a Select Committee (the Public Accounts Committee) does now'. In 1988 the then Treasury and Civil Service Committee argued that the Chief Executive of an Executive Agency 'should give evidence [to Select Committees] on his own behalf about what he has done as the head of an agency'. We reach conclusions on the doctrine of Ministerial accountability later, but it is clear that any effective application of the doctrine depends to a considerable extent upon two elements: the honesty and integrity of Ministers and civil servants in accounting to Parliament and the public for their decisions and actions; the powers and effectiveness of Parliament, and of the Select Committees of the House of Commons in particular, in holding the Executive to account.

(iii) Honesty and integrity

124. *Questions of Procedure for Ministers* states that Ministers have 'a duty to give Parliament, including its Select Committees, and the public as full information as possible about the policies, decisions and actions of the Government, and not to deceive or mislead Parliament and the public'. There has been considerable concern recently about the adequacy of, and adherence to, this guidance. First, evidence by civil servants to the Scott Inquiry has raised questions about the framing of Ministerial answers to Parliamentary Questions and evidence to Select Committees. Second, a recent Report by the Foreign Affairs Committee on the Pergau Hydro-Electric Project found that 'Ministerial replies to certain questions were literally true, though less open and less informative than the House has a right to expect'. On 10 May 1994 the then Minister for Disabled People told the House of his 'regret that by not giving a fuller explanation' of his knowledge of the extent of his Department's involvement in amendments to the Civil Rights (Disabled Persons) Bill 'the effect of my reply was misleading'. Finally Mr Waldegrave's evidence to the Sub-Committee on 8 March 1994 stimulated a wide-ranging public discussion of Ministerial integrity and honesty. We believe this matter is relevant to this inquiry in three ways. First, it is part of the role of the Civil Service, as the Prime Minister has acknowledged, to advise Ministers so that their Parliamentary pronoucements are not misleading. Second, insofar as the Civil Service is accountable to Parliament through Ministers, the effectiveness of such

accountability depends upon the integrity of Ministerial answers. Finally, civil servants themselves are required to comply with the same standards as Ministers, and are likely in some measure to take their lead from Ministers. Any deterioration in the standards of honesty and integrity of Ministers in their dealings with Parliament would have a deleterious effect on the standards of the Civil Service.

125. Sir Robin Butler informed the Scott Inquiry that there was a category of Parliamentary answers 'where it is necessary to give an incomplete answer, but one should, in these circumstances, seek not to mislead'. Mr Waldegrave, in evidence to the Sub-Committee, vividly asserted the need, in certain circumstances, not to disclose all relevant information: 'There are plenty of cases over the years, with both Governments, where the Minister . . . will not mislead the House and will take care not to mislead the House, but may not display everything he knows about that subject . . . Much of Government activity is much more like negotiation, much more like playing poker than it is like playing chess. You do not put all the cards up all the time in the interests of the country'. The necessity for non-disclosure has been asserted in the past, even in the case of civil servants appearing before Select Committees. In 1985 the then Head of the Home Civil Service said that, taking 'an extreme case', when a decision had been made to devalue the pound, a Minister could instruct a civil servant appearing before a Select Committee not to reveal that devaluation in advance. Sir Robin Butler reaffirmed this in 1990, while emphasising that that 'would not extend to the Minister instructing the civil servants to mislead the Committee; that would be improper'. There is self-evidently a problem in determining the line between non-disclosure which is not misleading and a misleading answer or statement. The problem is more acute for Ministers than for civil servants, since a civil servant appearing before a Select Committee can refer a Committee to a Minister. Both Mr Waldegrave and Sir Robin Butler gave examples of answers which they held to be incomplete but not misleading. In such cases there was a general duty 'to make clear that you have information which you cannot disclose', although there were circumstances when even this would not be appropriate. Even in the latter circumstances, Ministers and civil servants had to 'frame their answer in a way which avoids misleading, if they possibly can'.

126. Sir Robin stressed that it was wrong for a Minister or a civil servant to lie, to mislead intentionally or to give an answer which was known to be false. The Prime Minister has made it clear in a letter to the Chairman of the Sub-Committee that, in such circumstances, a Minister would usually be expected to relinquish his office. However, Sir Robin Butler and Mr Waldegrave also contended that there were 'very rare occasions' when the wrong of lying to the House would be outweighed by the greater wrong consequent upon not lying. Three instances were adduced in support of this contention. First, Sir Stafford Cripps did not mislead Parliament over devaluation but said after the devaluation in 1949 that, if he had been asked just before devaluation whether he was gong to devalue he would have told a lie to Parliament. Second, Mr Peter Thomas gave an untrue answer about whether Mr Greville Wynne, who had just been arrested by Soviet authorities, was working for British Intelligence; this was untrue but was considered necessary to save Mr Wynne's life. Finally, both Sir Robin Butler and Mr Waldegrave alleged that, on 16 November 1967, the then Mr James (now Lord) Callaghan gave an answer which was 'false'. Mr Waldegrave did not dissent from the proposition that Lord Callaghan had lied to the House. Sir Robin Butler, who had worked in the Treasury as Secretary to the Budget Committee at the time, argued that when Lord Callaghan said in answer to a question from Mr Stanley Orme about devaluation, 'I have nothing to add to or subtract from anything I have said on previous occasions on the subject of devaluation' he was misleading the House

since his previous answers had been flat assertions that the Government was not going to devalue the pound and he therefore did have something to subtract from previous statements. He accepted that Lord Callaghan did not have an intention to mislead and was thus not 'deliberately lying to the House of Commons', but argued that he had made a 'slip', which Sir Robin Butler implied Lord Callaghan had acknowledged. In reply, Lord Callaghan vigorously contested Mr Waldegrave's implication that he had lied to the House, stating that 'none of my answers supports Mr Waldegrave's assertion that I lied to the House of Commons'. He did not admit to a false answer to Mr Orme, referring to 'one *possible* slip (which was not intended to deceive) in the reply I gave to Mr Orme'. He repudiated 'the attempt to put a construction on my replies by Sir Robin Butler and Mr Waldegrave, twenty five years after the event, that no one who was present ever did either at the time or later'. . . .

132. An effective system of Parliamentary accountability of the Executive is an essential component of a Parliamentary democracy. We believe that an effective system depends upon two vital elements: clarity about who can be held to account and held responsible when things go wrong; confidence that Parliament is able to gain the accurate information required to hold the Executive to account and to ascertain where responsibility lies. We are not convinced that the explanation of the doctrine of Ministerial accountability and its implications as presently adumbrated by the Government fully conforms to these requirements. **We find the Government's attempts to draw a sharp distinction between accountability, which cannot be delegated by Ministers, and responsibility, which can, unconvincing.** The implication of this distinction is that Ministers retain ultimate responsibility for controlling the system through which information about the allocation of responsibility on a particular matter is made available to Parliament. We believe that it is both possible and desirable to move towards a system in which responsibility and accountability are more closely aligned in clearly defined circumstances. We make particular proposals towards this end below.

133. Lord Callaghan attached importance to clarifying the circumstances in which a Minister should resign, although he noted that the influence of the Prime Minister of the day and the feelings of the Minister himself would always be important factors. Mr Waldegrave believed that such circumstances were difficult to categorise and that Ministerial resignations would continue to be decided on a case by case basis. Sir Robin Butler was critical of the 'rather foolish game of pursuing resignations', which was 'counter-productive' and debased the currency. Ministerial preparedness to resign when Ministerial responsibility for failure has been established lies at the very heart of an effective system of Parliamentary accountability and, as Mr Waldegrave acknowledged, Select Committees have an important role in determining the allocation of responsibility. In seeking to perform this function and their wider role, Select Committees might well require more information than might readily be made available in accordance with the Executive's own interpretation of the doctrine of Ministerial accountability. The recent Report by the Foreign Affairs Committee on the Pergau Hydro-Electric Project demonstrates the range of information which can be made available by the Government to a determined Select Committee. It would not be appropriate for Select Committees to seek to negotiate new rules to replace the Osmotherly Rules, because they are only to be regarded as the Government's opening negotiating position in its dealings with Select Committees. The precise implications of the doctrine of Ministerial accountability for the conduct of civil servants in relation to Select Committees is unlikely to be agreed between the Government and Select Committees. It should be borne in mind that an attempt to determine the precise level of Ministerial responsibility may sometimes involve an assessment of the extent of the

responsibility of others. We note that the structure of the Civil Service and of the Executive more generally has changed considerably since the Procedure Committee last conducted a review of the departmental Select Committees. We recommend elsewhere in this Report measures which should be taken by the Government to enhance the accountability of the Executive to Parliament. We believe that it might also be appropriate for the Procedure Committee to undertake an inquiry to consider what commensurate actions should be taken by the House of Commons in response to the changing structure of Government.

134. Effective accountability depends in considerable measure upon adherence by Ministers and civil servants to the duty set out in *Questions of Procedure for Ministers* 'to give Parliament, including its Select Committees, and the public as full information as possible about the policies, decisions and actions of the Government, and not to deceive or mislead Parliament and the public'. We are aware of considerable public cynicism about the honesty of politicians generally and in this context concern about the honesty and integrity of Ministerial statements to and answers in Parliament might seem misplaced. However, the knowledge that Ministers and civil servants may evade questions and put the best gloss on the facts but will not lie or knowingly mislead the House of Commons is one of the most powerful tools Members of Parliament have in holding the Executive to account. Not only is the requirement laid down clearly in Government guidance to Ministers, it is a requirement which the House of Commons itself expects from all its Members, departure from which standard can be treated as a contempt. We accept that the line between non-disclosure and a misleading answer is often a fine one, not least because the avoidance of misleading answers requires not only strict accuracy but also an awareness of the interpretations which could reasonably be placed upon an answer by others, but Ministers should be strengthened in their determination to remain the right side of that line by certainty about the consequences of a failure to do so. **Any Minister who has been found to have knowingly misled Parliament should resign.**

Notes

1. In the last paragraph above reference was made to *Questions of Procedure* and its requirement regarding the provision of information. Compare para. 27 with para. 1. which was amended after the publication and consideration of the Standing Committee on Standards in Public Life chaired by Lord Nolan.

2. Each Minister is responsible to Parliament for the conduct of his or her Department, and for the actions carried out by the Department in pursuit of Government policies or in the discharge of responsibilities laid upon him or her as a Minister. Ministers are accountable to Parliament in the sense that they have a duty to explain in Parliament the exercise of their powers and dutics and to give an account to Parliament of what is done by them in their capacity as Ministers or by their Departments. This includes the duty to give Parliament, including its Select Committees, and the public as full information as possible about the policies, decisions and actions of the Government, and not to deceive or mislead Parliament and the public.

3. Ministers of the Crown are expected to behave according to the highest standards of constitutional and personal conduct in the performance of their duties. In particular they must observe the following principles of Ministerial conduct: . . .

Ministers are accountable to Parliament for the policies, decisions and actions of their departments and agencies;

Ministers must not knowingly mislead Parliament and the public and should correct any inadvertent errors at the earliest opportunity. They must be as open as possible with Parliament and the public, withholding information only when disclosure would not be in the public interest, which should be decided in accordance with established Parliamentary convention, the law, and any relevant Government Code of Practice. . .

4. In the following extracts from his Inquiry into 'arms to Iraq' Sir Richard Scott discusses Government statements on defence sales policy after the ceasefire between Iran and Iraq.

Report of the Inquiry into the Export of Defence Equipment and Dual-Use Goods to Iraq and Related Prosecutions HC 115 of 1995–96, Vol 1, paras D.4.1–16, D4.52–6, D4.60, D4.63.

(I) Letters from the FCO in 1989.

D4.1 Over the period February 1989 to July 1989, a number of letters, signed mainly by Mr Waldegrave but a few by Lord Howe, were sent to MPs whose constituents had asked questions about Government policy on defence sales to Iraq. The questions had been prompted by a variety of concerns. The concerns covered specific military exports to Iraq, Iraqi atrocities against the Kurds, Iraqi human rights violations in general, British participation at the Baghdad International Military Fair (which was held from 29 April to 2 May), the British Aerospace proposal to sell Hawk Trainer Aircraft to Iraq as well as general apprehension about the sales of arms and defence equipment to the Middle East.

D4.2 A form of response to be incorporated in the letters sent to the MPs in question was settled in the FCO. The response included the following two sentences (or the gist of them):

> 'British arms supplies to both Iran and Iraq continue to be governed by the strict application of guidelines which prevent the supply of lethal equipment or equipment which would significantly enhance the capability of either side to resume hostilities. These guidelines are applied on a case by case basis.'

D4.3 Letters to MPs incorporating these sentences and signed by Mr Waldegrave numbered some seven in March 1989, five in April, twenty-three in May, one in June and two in July. Lord Howe signed two similar letters in May and two in July. In one of the April letters and in each of the May, June and July letters the formula was preceded by the statement that:

> 'The Government have not changed their policy on defence sales to Iraq or Iran.'

In one letter there was a reference to 'our firm and even-handed position over arms sales to Iran and Iraq.'

D4.4 The reference in each of these letters to the criterion that governed the supply of non-lethal defence equipment to Iraq was not accurate. Since the end of February 1989 the criterion for Iraq had been the new formulation, namely, that there would be no supply of equipment which would be of direct and significant assistance to Iraq in the conduct of offensive operations in breach of the cease-fire. The inaccuracy should have been noticed by Mr Waldegrave, who had been one of the midwives at the birth of this new formulation. Lord Howe, on the other hand, had not been informed of the junior Ministers' agreement on the new formulation.

D4.5 The statement in the letters that 'The Government have not changed their policy on defence sales to Iraq or Iran' was untrue. After the cease-fire Lord Howe had advocated, and the Prime Minister, with the concurrence of senior Ministers, had accepted, that a more liberal policy, designed to enable British exporters to take advantage of the glittering opportunities for defence-related sales to Iraq that it was believed would be available, should gradually be adopted. The discussions between the junior Ministers, which began with correspondence in November and December and with the Ministerial meeting on 21 December 1988, were for the purpose of trying to formulate a new policy which would then be brought to senior Ministers and the Prime Minister for approval. Agreement by the junior Ministers had led, by February 1989, to a new, more liberal, policy in the form of revised guideline (iii) being implemented on a trial basis. The proposed new policy, although reversed for Iran following the Rushdie affair, was continued for Iraq and finally confirmed at the 24 April 1989 Ministers' meeting and in the correspondence that followed.

D4.6 Mr Waldegrave knew, first hand, the facts that, in my opinion, rendered the 'no change in policy' statement untrue. I accept that, when he signed these letters, he did not regard the agreement he had reached with his fellow Ministers as having constituted a change in policy towards Iraq. In his evidence to the Inquiry, he strenuously and consistently asserted his belief, in the face of a volume of, to my mind, overwhelming evidence to the contrary, that policy on defence sales to Iraq had, indeed, remained unchanged. I did not receive the impression of any insincerity on his part in giving me the evidence he did. But it is clear, in my opinion, that policy on defence sales to Iraq did not remain unchanged.

D4.7 The proposition that the Government's position over 'arms sales to Iran and Iraq' was 'even-handed' had been untrue ever since the decision, taken as a consequence of the Rushdie affair, to 'return to a more strict approach to Iran.' In his letter of 28 March 1989 to Mr Clark, Mr Waldegrave had poposed that 'we should now revert to the stricter implementation of the guidelines as applied to Iran', while saying that he saw no reason to change the newly, agreed 'flexible approach for applications to export defence-related equipment to Iraq.' In his letter to Mr Waldegrave of 13 April, Lord Trefgarne, the Minister (DP), agreed with the proposal and the MOD/FCO agreement was put into effect by the MODWG at its meeting on 14 April. Mr Waldegrave's letter suggesting that an 'even-handed', position was being taken by the Government was dated 17 April. Mr Waldegrave has explained that '[his] view (and the advice of his officials) was that the policy was 'even-handed' as applied to the territorial and other ambitions of Iran and Iraq' and that 'particular steps taken in the area of exports in reaction to unforeseen events such as the Fatwah and the execution of Mr Bazoft did not detract from the even-handedness or neutrality or impartiality applied to the two states.' As to the first part of this explanation, the letter referred to the Goverment's 'even-handed position over *arms sales* to Iran and Iraq' (emphasis added); as to the second, the explanation has, in my opinion, no substance. Every government policy is bound to have some reason behind it. The unforeseen event that was the Fatwah led, inter alia, to a stricter policy on arms sales being applied to Iran than was applied to Iraq. This differential policy was already being implemented by 17 April. I could well understand that the reference in the letter to Mr Curry to the 'even-handed position' may have been an overlooked refugee from a common form sentence that would, two months earlier, have been unexceptionable. But the proposition that on 17 April, the date of the letter, it was a true statement is not, in my opinion, remotely arguable.

D4.8 Lord Howe had not been kept informed and was not aware of the detail of the manner in which the new formulation of guideline (iii) in its application to Iraq had been agreed. But he agreed, in his oral evidence to the Inquiry, that the new formulation of guideline (iii) was 'an implementation of the broad relaxation agreed in August/September [1988].' In his written and oral evidence to the Inquiry Lord Howe maintained that the 'implementation of the broad relaxation' towards Iraq and the adoption of the new criterion 'direct and significant assistance in the conduct of offensive operations in breach of the ceasefire' amounted merely to 'continuing with the original policy, subject to certain fluctuating glosses, even nuances.' Lord Howe explained the junior Ministers' agreement in this way:

> I think they were perhaps confused as to what they were doing. They said first of all 'Let's have a shot at reformulating. Let us have a trial basis.' The trial was interrupted by the Fatwah and they went back to the original basis in relation to Iran, and I think they rather forgot whether they had moved away from or applied it in a different fashion.

And, in answer to the question: 'The guidelines were reformulated were they not?', Lord Howe replied: 'Yes I think for practical purposes they were, but there was no disclosure of a reformulation. That was the last thing that people wanted to do.' He referred to the Ministers 'moving to a differential policy' and in answer to a question as to whether the 'differential policy' was no longer 'even-handed or impartial between the two countries', responded: 'It cannot be allowed to be seen like that. That is the point.' In my opinion, these answers preclude Lord Howe from maintaining his resistance to the proposition that there had been a change in policy. I do not suppose when he signed the letters in question in May and July 1989 he directed his mind to whether or not the 'no change in policy' statement was justifiable. Even if he had done so, his knowledge of the detail of what had been agreed between the junior Ministers was not such as to have necessarily alerted him to the misleading character of the 'no change in policy' statement. In the submission to him of 28 April 1989, Mr Young had said: 'We are not contemplating a major change in policy. . . . the existing guidelines on arms sales will remain in place.'

D4.9 Lord Howe, while insisting that, as I accept, he had no reason in May, June and July 1989 to have questioned the 'no change in policy' statement in the letters he had signed, firmly denied that the letters were substantially incorrect or misleading. However, he went on to say that if I considered that they were misleading, he 'would still firmly defend their contents' He said this:

> As I have explained, there were powerful foreign policy reasons why any reformulation of policy could not be announced. I regarded, and still regard, those foreign policy reasons as outweighing the public interest in full disclosure. Those were two conflicting facets of the public interest which it was my job to balance. I did so conscientiously and in good faith, seeking to ensure that public disclosure would not risk endangering British interests abroad, or obstruct the promotion or protection by the United Kingdom of those interests, or endanger the safety of British citizens abroad or at home. Any responsible Minister would have had to strive to maintain this balance and, if addressing the issues properly, would, I believe, have reached the same conclusion.

I can understand that the 'balance' to which Lord Howe referred may, in his judgment, have required that there be no public disclosure of the relaxation of restrictions on defence sales to Iraq or of the divergence between the defence sales policies being applied to Iran and Iraq respectively. I do not, however, accept that the considerations to which Lord Howe referred justified the contents of the letters. The letters need not have said that 'The Government have not changed their policy on defence sales to Iraq or Iran.' The untrue sentence could have been omitted. The letters did not need to refer to '. . . the strict application of guidelines which prevent the supply of . . . equipment which would significantly enhance the capability of either side to resume hostilities. . . .' A formulation could, and in my opinion should, have been found which would at least have avoided being misleading.

D4.10 In August 1989 a number of letters to MPs', responding to their constituents' queries about the Government's attitude to the Hawk project, were sent by Mr Waldegrave. Typical of these letters is his letter dated 10 August 1989 written to Mr Tom Sackville MP. The letter said this:

> 'Since the beginning of the conflict between Iran and Iraq, the Government has pursued a policy of impartiality as the most effective way to promote a peaceful settlement in the gulf. As a result, the Foreign Secretary announced in the House of Commons on 29 October 1985 a set of Ministerial Guidelines limiting defence sales to both Iran and Iraq. These specifically prohibit the sale of any lethal equipment or any defence-related equipment which could significantly enhance the capability of either side to prolong or exacerbate the conflict. All applications for export licences for defence equipment to Iran or Iraq continue to be rigorously scrutinised to ensure that they fall within these guidelines. These restrictions on defence sales are kept under constant review, and are applied in the light of prevailing circumstances, including the ceasefire and developments in the peace negotiations. . .'.

D4.11 Mr Waldegrave, in his written evidence to the Inquiry, contended that the passage I have cited was an accurate statement of Government policy at the time. It was not. Government policy at the time, agreed between Mr Waldegrave and his fellow Ministers, Lord Trefgarne and Mr Clark, was that the export of non-lethal defence equipment to Iraq would not be refused unless the equipment would directly assist Iraq in the conduct of offensive operations in breach of the ceasefire. Mr Waldegrave knew of this new formulation but regarded it as an interpretation of the original guideline (iii). Nonetheless, a statement in August 1989 that applications for export licences for defence equipment for Iraq 'continue to be rigorously scrutinised to *ensure* that they fall within *these* guidelines' (emphasis added), seems to me impossible to reconcile with Mr Waldegrave's statement in his letter of 28 March 1989 that 'we agreed in February to interpret the export guidelines more flexibly so as to refuse orders for non-lethal equipment only if they would be of direct and significant assistance to either side in the conduct of offensive weapons in breach of the ceasefire' and with his statement in his letter of 27 April 1989 that 'we agreed [at the 24 April meeting] that we would continue to interpret the guidelines more flexibly in respect of Iraq, as we have done in practice since the end of last year. . .'

D4.12 In addition, the natural implication from the reference in the August letters to the 'policy of impartiality' would be that that policy had continued up to the date of the letter and was continuing. This, for the reasons I have already given, was, if applied to defence sales, untrue. The constituent's letter which had prompted the letter to Mr Sackville had complained about defence sales to Iraq, and the reference to the policy of impartiality would have been naturally read accordingly. Taken overall, the terms of Mr Waldegrave's letter to Mr Sackville and his other letters in like terms were, in my opinion, apt to mislead the readers as to the nature of the policy on export sales to Iraq that was currently being pursued by the Government. Mr Waldegrave was in a position to know that that was so although I accept that he did not intend his letters to be misleading and did not so regard them.

D4.13 Mr Mark Higson, who gave evidence to the Inquiry, was, from 23 March 1989 until January 1990 when he left the FCO, the desk officer for Iraq within MED. One of his duties was to prepare drafts of the letters to be sent by FCO Ministers answering queries relating to Iraq. He was responsible for the drafts of many of the letters to MPs to which I have been referring. His drafts were approved by a second, more senior, FCO official before being placed before Mr Waldegrave for signing. Mr Higson was aware, from the papers passing across his desk, of the Ministerial correspondence relating to the new formulation for Iraq of guideline (iii). One of the letters signed by Mr Waldegrave was a letter dated 4 May 1989 to Dame Elaine Kellett-Bowman MP. In his oral evidence to the Inquiry on 15 July 1993 Mr Higson made clear that he regarded the 'no change in policy' statement contained in the letter as untrue. Mr Higson's expresed opinion of the letter corresponds with the opinion that I have formed from the documents and evidence before the Inquiry. In a letter dated 19 July 1993 to Dame Elaine, a copy of which he sent to the Inquiry, Mr Waldegrave protested that Mr Higson's criticism of the letter of 4 May 1989 was 'unfounded' and 'not correct'. In my opinion, the criticism was well founded and justified.

D4.14 The statement that '. . . the Government have pursued a policy of impartiality. . .' between Iraq and Iran is to be found, also, in letters dated 14 August 1989, 21 August 1989, 4 September 1989 and 5 September 1989, the first from Mrs Lynda Chalker, the second from Mrs Thatcher, the Prime Minister, and the other two from Mr Major, as Foreign Secretary. Each letter was a response to a query about Government policy on the proposed sale of Hawk aircraft to Iraq. Each letter followed a draft prepared by the FCO/MED. Each letter said, also, that 'Since October 1985 Government policy has prohibited the sale of any lethal equipment or any defence-related equipment which could significantly enhance the capability of either side to prolong or exacerbate the conflict' or words to that effect. In the case of Mrs Thatcher's letter, the text continued: 'That policy still applies'. These statements were not accurate.

D4.15 Mrs Chalker had taken no part in the discussions and correspondence that had led to the then current policy on defence sales to Iraq and cannot be blamed for the inaccuracies. I have already dealt with the extent to which Mrs Thatcher was in a position to have identified the inaccuracies. She had received and read the MOD paper dated 20 July 1989 on the Hawk project in which reference was made to the 'more flexible interpretation of the guidelines for Iraq (but not Iran . . .)' and so can be said to have been placed on notice that a more liberal approach to defence sales to Iraq was being adopted than had previously been the case. But the paper had been concentrating on Hawk and I do not think Mrs Thatcher can be blamed if, when signing the letter of 21 August 1989, she did not recall the implications of the reference to the Guidelines in the MOD's 20 July Hawk paper.

D4.16 Mr Major had become Foreign Secretary on 25 July 1989 and it might have been expected that, by September, he would have become aware that Government policy on the export licensing of non-lethal defence equipment to Iraq was that a more liberal criterion should be applied to Iraq than to Iran, and that the more liberal criterion for Iraq was significantly different from the original 1985 (or 1984) criterion. In his evidence to the Inquiry, Mr Major said that he believed throughout that the original Guidelines had remained in use and that he had been 'advised by those carrying out the policy at operational level that we were impartial.' As to the nature of the 'impartial' policy, Mr Major said: 'I think the Government's approach was impartial in the sense of not aiding either side in the prosecution of the war, or subsequently no doubt in the minds of officials after the war was ended, in enhancement of military capability.' However, on 25 July 1989 he received his first brief as Foreign Secretary. The brief had been prepared by Mr Stephen Lamport for the purposes of an OD Committee meeting to discuss the Hawk project. Paragraph 3 of the brief said that 'Since the ceasefire in August 1988, the Guidelines have been applied with greater flexibility for Iraq, (but since last February, with much greater rigidity for Iran . . .). Our public presentation of our policy on arms supplies to both countries has, however, stayed broadly the same. . . .' This briefing did, as it seems to me, put Mr Major on notice that Iraq was receiving more favourable treatment than Iran so far as export licensing of defence equipment was concerned, a state of affairs that, in my opinion, calls into question a continuing stance of impartiality. In his oral evidence, Mr Major disputed this conclusion. He said: 'I have no reason to believe, on the advice I received at the time, or the documentation I have subsequently seen, that there was any shift away from the intrinsic impartiality in the 1984 Guidelines, in terms of making sure that the Government was impartial in not aiding one side against the other in the prosecution of the war or the enhancement of its military capability post-war.' In any event, the briefing was directed to the Hawk project and, as with Mrs Thatcher, I do not find it very surprising that Mr Major did not advert to all the implications of the briefing on other issues. I do not doubt Mr Major's evidence that he signed the letters believing the statements they contained to be accurate, but I do not accept that they were in fact accurate. . . .

D4.52 A frank and sustained defence of the divergence between the Government's actual policy and the various Ministerial statements of policy, whether in letters or in answers to PQs, was offered by Lord Howe in his oral evidence to the Inquiry. He said:

> . . . there is nothing necessarily open to criticism in incompatibility between policy and presentation of policy . . . It [i.e. the Government] is not necessarily to be criticised for a difference between policy and public presentation of policy.

He explained:

> The fact is that, as soon as you are embarked upon the necessary policy, in competition with other nations, of enhancing a commercial position, a commercial position which is more inhibited than other nations, for reasons we have investigated, any attempt to enlarge that base is capable of being criticised by others . . . .
>
> Can this not be explained to the public in a manner the public would understand?
>
> A. Not easily, not if you visualise, as the *Independent* pointed out, the extremely emotional way in which such debates are conducted in public. . . if you look at the various reasons given by colleagues for caution in relation to the shifting nuances of policy, in the Spring of 1989, they all add up to a very good reason for not volunteering this, because the scope for misunderstanding is enormous.

And, later,

> Q. It is a sort of 'Government know best' approach, is it not?
>
> A. Yes.
>
> Q. 'We know what is good for you. You may not like it and, if you were made aware of it, you might protest, but we know what is best'?
>
> A. It is partly that, but it is partly 'if we were to lay specifically our thought processes before you, they are not just going before you; they are laid before a

worldwide range of uncomprehending or malicious commentators'. This is the point. You cannot choose a well balanced presentation to an élite Parliamentary audience.

In relation to the circumstance that, as a result of the re-formulation of guideline (iii) and the decision to apply the re-formulated guideline to Iraq but not to Iran, policy was no longer even-handed or impartial as between the two countries Lord Howe said:

'It cannot be seen like that. That is the point.'

And

Frankly the inaccuracy is intrinsic in the policy position that we are presenting. If you are saying that the Guidelines are still in place and being applied directly to Iran without any qualification, and being applied with modification to Iraq, then that is the thing you cannot disclose and you have to head back to 'The Guidelines are in place'. That is the point. The Guidelines are in place because the basic policy has not changed.

D4.53 Lord Howe was not alone in defending the variance between Government statements of policy and Government's actual policy. Mr Gore-Booth, too, defended the propriety of statements of policy that designedly gave less than the full picture. He agreed that answers to Parliamentary questions should be as forthcoming as possible, but pointed out that 'there are often cases in which you cannot be so forthcoming, for what are called reasons of foreign policy.' He agreed that answers should be accurate but said that 'half a picture can be accurate.' He defended the answers given by Ministers to PQs about policy on exports to Iraq: . . . actually I have no difficulty with [the answers] in terms of fullness. I think that some of the answers in the papers are as full as was compatible with the sensitivities to which I referred here.

D4.54 The issue was dealt with also by Sir Robin Butler. He was firm in his opinion that a public statement made by a Minister should not, save in the most exceptional case, be misleading, but, like Mr Gore-Booth, regarded it as acceptable in some circumstances for a statement to disclose only part of the full picture.

D4.55 The problem with the 'half a picture' approach is that those to whom the incomplete statement is addressed do not know unless it is apparent from the terms of the statement itself, that an undisclosed half is being withheld from them. They are almost bound, therefore, to be misled by the statement, notwithstanding that the 'half a picture' may, so far as it goes, be accurate. The proposition is not that a statement to Parliament must include each and every fact relating to the subject in order to avoid being misleading. Such a requirement would clearly be impracticable. A fair summary of the 'full picture' would often, depending on the question that had been asked and the apparent purpose of the statement, be a complete and sufficient response. The proposition is that if part of the picture is being suppressed and the audience does not know it is being suppressed, the audience will be misled into believing the half picture to be the full picture. Lord Howe's unapologetic acceptance of and support for the divergence between Government's statements of policy and Government's actual policy revealed by the public statements to which I have earlier referred was, in my opinion, more realistic than Sir Robin Butler's and Mr Gore-Booth's attempts to reconcile the giving of answers that designedly disclosed only part of the picture with the obligation to avoid giving misleading answers.

D4.56 It is, rightly, accepted that there have always been and will always be subjects in respect of which full information, or sometimes any information, cannot be made public. Current operations of the security and intelligence agencies come easily to mind as examples. Sir Robin Butler, in evidence to the Inquiry and, also, to the Treasury and Civil Service Select Committee, instanced information about imminent changes in interest rates or in exchange rates. The public interest may require information about proposed changes to be withheld from the public. The examples are cogent. It ought, nonetheless, to be recognised that the obligation of Ministers to give information about the activities of their departments and to give information and explanations for the actions and omissions of their civil servants lies at the heart of Ministerial accountability and that every decision by a Minister to withhold information from Parliament and from the public constitutes an avoidance, and sometimes an evasion, *pro tanto*, of Ministerial accountability . . .

D4.60 The reasons put forward by Lord Howe in his oral evidence to the Inquiry in justification of the withholding from Parliament and the public of knowledge, first, of the proposed relaxation of the Guidelines in favour of both Iraq and Iran, and, secondly, of the actual relaxation of the Guidelines in favour of Iraq but not of Iran, were not reasons of national security, nor did they relate to operations of the security or intelligence agencies, nor were they analogous to the reasons for not disclosing proposed changes in interest rates or exchange rates. Lord Howe's reasons were, in the main, foreign relations reasons; a fear of adverse reactions from Washington or from Riyadh at the prospect of a more favourable approach to exports to Iran; or fear of adverse reactions from Iran if it were known that Iraq was being given more favourable treatment than itself. It is not, in my opinion, in the least obvious that the foreign relations reasons identified by Lord Howe were sufficient to justify the repeated provision to Parliament and, via the letters to MPs, to members of the public, of information about Government policy that was by design incomplete and in certain respects misleading. . .

D4.63 In the circumstances, the Government statements made in 1989 and 1990 about policy on defence exports to Iraq consistently failed, in my opinion, to comply with the standard set by paragraph 27 of the Questions of Procedure for Ministers and, more important, failed to discharge the obligations imposed by the constitutional principle of Ministerial accountability.

Question

Does Sir Richard's lack of experience of government and the absence of expert assessors on the Inquiry staff, as some have contended, undermine his analysis and conclusion that there was no public interest justification for the lack of full ministerial accountability?

Note

Accountability to Parliament through ministers has been placed under further strain because of the programme of improving managerial efficiency in public administration.

Prime Minister's Efficiency Unit, *Improving Management in Government: The Next Steps* (1988), paras 19–23 and Annex A

19. **We recommend that 'agencies' should be established to carry out the executive functions of government within a policy and resources framework set by a department.** An 'agency' of this kind may be part of government and the public service, or it may be more effective outside government. We use the term

'agency' not in its technical sense but to describe any executive unit that delivers a service for government. The choice and definition of suitable agencies is primarily for Ministers and senior management in departments to decide. In some instances very large blocks of work comprising virtually a whole department will be suitable to be managed in this way. In other instances, where the scale of activity is too small for an entirely separate organisation, it may be better to have one or even several smaller agencies within departments.

20. These units, large or small, need to be given a well defined framework in which to operate, which sets out the policy, the budget, specific targets and the results to be achieved. It must also specify how politically sensitive issues are to be dealt with and the extent of the delegated authority of management. The management of the agency must be held rigorously to account by their department for the results they achieve.

21. The framework will need to be set and updated as part of a formal annual review with the responsible Minister, based on a long-term plan and an annual report. The main strategic control must lie with the Minister and Permanent Secretary. But once the policy objectives and budgets within the framework are set, the management of the agency should then have as much independence as possible in deciding how those objectives are met. A crucial element in the relationship would be a formal understanding with Ministers about the handling of sensitive issues and the lines of accountability in a crisis. The presumption must be that, provided management is operating within the strategic direction set by Ministers, it must be left as free as possible to manage within that framework. To strengthen operational effectiveness, there must be freedom to recruit, pay, grade and structure in the most effective way as the framework becomes sufficiently robust and there is confidence in the capacity of management to handle the task.

22. Once the framework had been set the head of the agency would be given personal responsibility to achieve the best possible results within it. He or she must be seen to be accountable for doing so. In due course formal accountability, before the Public Accounts Committee for example, might develop so that for significant agencies the Permanent Secretary would normally be accompanied by the head of the agency. The Permanent Secretary's role would be to justify and defend the framework; the manager would have to answer for his or her performance within that framework.

23. Placing responsibility for performance squarely on the shoulders of the manager of an agency also has implications for the way in which Ministers answer to Parliament on operational issues. Clearly Ministers have to be wholly responsible for policy, but it is unrealistic to suppose that they can actually have knowledge in depth about every operational question. The convention that they do is in part the cause of the overload we observed. We believe it is possible for Parliament, through Ministers, to regard managers as directly responsible for operational matters and that there are precedents for this and precisely defined ways in which it can be handled. If management in the Civil Service is truly to be improved this aspect cannot be ignored. In view of its importance it is considered in more detail in Annex A, where it is suggested that to achieve changes in the arrangements for formal accountability would generally require legislation and that in suitable instances this should be considered....

Annex A Accountability to Ministers and Parliament on operational matters

1. Evidence we gathered in the scrutiny suggested that when individuals had to answer personally to Parliament, as well as to Ministers, their sense of personal

responsibility was strengthened. The accountability of Permanent Secretaries to the Public Accounts Committee, as Accounting Officers, is long established. It includes direct personal accountability for financial propriety. Another instance of officials having specific functions which may require them to answer directly to Parliament (though on behalf of their Minister) is the case of principal officers, and of bodies with independent or delegated authority, answering to the Select Committee on the Parliamentary Commissioner for Administration.

2. In paragraph 23 we point out that if the concept of agencies developed in the report is to succeed, some extension of this pattern of accountability is likely to be necessary. The principal reasons are, first, that the management of an agency is unlikely in practice to be given a realistically specified framework within which there is freedom to manage if a Minister remains immediately answerable for every operational detail that may be questioned; and second, that acceptance of individual responsibility for performance cannot be expected if repeated ministerial intervention is there as a ready-made excuse.

3. The precise form of accountability for each agency would need to be established as part of drawing up the framework for agencies. Any change from present practice in accountability would, of course, have to be acceptable to Ministers and to Parliament. It is axiomatic that Ministers should remain fully and clearly accountable for policy. For agencies which are government departments or parts of departments ultimate accountability for operations must also rest with Ministers. What is needed is the establishment of a convention that heads of executive agencies would have delegated authority from their Ministers for operations of the agencies within the framework of policy directives and resource allocations prescribed by Ministers. Heads of agencies would be accountable to Ministers for the operations of their agencies, but could be called – as indeed they can now – to give evidence to Select Committees as to the manner in which their delegated authority had been used and their functions discharged within that authority. In the case of agencies established outside departments, appropriate forms of accountability to Ministers and to Parliament would need to be established according to the particular circumstances.

4. There is nothing new in the suggestion that Ministers should not be held answerable for many day-to-day decisions involving the public and public services. Apart from services delivered by local authorities, there are large numbers of central government functions carried out at arm's length from Ministers. The main categories are:

— decisions on individual cases, where these need to be protected from the risk of political influence, e.g. tax cases, social security cases;

— some management and executive functions, e.g. in Customs and Excise, Regional and District Health Authorities, Manpower Services Commission (MSC);

— quasi-judicial or regulatory functions, e.g. Office of Fair Trading, Immigration Appeals;

— nationalised industries.

5. A variety of different structures exist to cover these functions, for example:

— Customs and Excise and the Inland Revenue are non-ministerial departments with boards which have defined statutory responsibilities;

— the MSC and the other main bodies in the Employment Group (Health and Safety Executive, and ACAS) are non-departmental public bodies. The Chairman of the MSC is Accounting Officer for the MSC's expenditure;

— HMSO and some other internal service bodies (e.g. Crown Suppliers) are established as trading funds and work on a commercial basis;

— the PSA, the Procurement Executive and the NHS Management Board are agencies within departments;

— a range of quasi-judicial functions is carried out by statutory tribunals (e.g. Rent Tribunals, Industrial Tribunals).

6. Agencies outside departments generally operate within a statutory framework which lays down the constitution of the particular agency and the powers of Ministers in relation to it. In answer to Parliamentary Questions about matters within the control of the agency, Ministers often preface their reply by saying 'I am advised by the Chairman of the Board that . . .'. Most operations currently carried out within departments operate under statute. Where it is necessary to change the arrangements for formal accountability for operations currently carried out within departments, legislation (normally primary legislation) would generally be required, and in instances where this is needed it should be considered. Provided that the objective of better management is clearly explained and understood, and that an appropriate form of accountability to Ministers and to Parliament is retained, the government should be able to present such proposals in a positive light.

7. As regards the Public Accounts Committee, as explained in paragraph 22 of the report, the modification of accountability we propose should not immediately affect accountability to the PAC. This would remain, as now, with the Accounting Officer, who may still be, but need not be, the Permanent Secretary. (Of the 76 Accounting Officers appointed by the Treasury, only 18 are First Permanent Secretaries.) However, the practice might develop of the Accounting Officer being accompanied at a PAC hearing by the manager of the agency. The Accounting Officer would answer questions about the framework within which the agency operated; the manager would answer questions about operations within the framework. This would give the PAC the ability to question in detail the person who had firsthand knowledge of the particular operation. It would also in the process put a clear pressure on the agency head to be responsible for his or her agency and to strive for good value from his or her spending.

8. In the case of other Select Committees it is existing practice for officials with operational responsibility to give evidence before them. It would be normal in the future for the agency head to give evidence before a Select Committee about operational matters within his or her responsibility.

9. The powers of the Parliamentary Commissioner for Administration could continue to apply to agencies.

10. Quite apart from the issue of improving Civil Service management, there is a good case for trying to reduce the degree of ministerial overload that can arise from questions about operations, as distinct from policy. For example, Social Security Ministers receive about 15,000 letters a year from MP's, many of which are about individual cases. In the future, MPs could be asked to write about operational matters directly to the Chairman of the Board or the local office manager. Arrangements of this sort could be promulgated by a letter from the relevant Minister or the Leader of the House to all MPs. (In the past the Chancellor of the Exchequer has written to all MPs asking them to refer questions about constituents' tax to local tax offices, and the Secretary of State for Social Services has written similarly about referring social security cases to DHSS local office managers.) If an MP writes to an operational manager about matters which are essentially political, it is already normal practice for the manager to refer the letter to the Minister.

11. It would be part of the framework drawn up between the department and the agency to have specific targets for promptness in dealing with correspondence with MPs. It should be possible for MPs to get a quicker answer when dealing direct with the responsible person, because the intermediate stage of a headquarters branch calling for a report from a local manager before drafting a reply for the Minister will have been cut out.

Fifth Report from the Treasury and Civil Service Select Committee HC 27 of 1993–94, paras 163–71

163. The second main area of debate about the progress of the Next Steps programme relates to accountability and responsibility, both in terms of the means by which an account of the operations of Agencies was given to Parliament and the public and in terms of the wider allocation of responsibility. In the last Parliament our predecessors expressed concern that the practice of Ministers of asking Chief Executives to reply to Parliamentary questions on operational matters which were not then published would limit Parliamentary and public access to information on the work of Agencies. They also noted inconsistencies between Departments in the division of Parliamentary answers between Ministers and Chief Executives. Since then, the Government has accepted a recommendation from the Procedure Committee which was supported by our predecessors that all replies to Parliamentary questions from Agency Chief Executives should be published in the Official Report (Hansard). The Benefits Agency detailed the arrangements for handling Parliamentary business in its own case. The Chief Executive responded to questions about individual cases, local issues and the day-to-day operation and performance of the Agency. Ministers replied to questions relating to policy, reporting national statistics or with a policy input. They also replied to inform Members that information was not readily available and could only be obtained at disproportionate cost. The Chief Executive replied to nearly two thirds of questions. Mr Bichard believed these arrangements had 'worked well', enabling Members to receive quick and effective responses. The Next Steps Project Manager also emphasised the advantages of the new arrangements. He said that the Next Steps Team monitored the division of responsibility for answering questions. He admitted that there was a 'grey area' between policy and operations and said that in such cases the Minister should reply. Like Mr Bichard, he emphasised that Members retained the right to call Ministers to account if dissatisfied with a response from an Agency Chief Executive.

164. These arrangements have attracted criticism. Mr Gerald Kaufman has argued that they erode the rights of Members of Parliament to take up constituency cases directly with Ministers. He feared that the new practice would reduce Ministerial awareness of the problems of Members' constituents. He criticised both the quality and efficiency of replies from the Benefits Agency. Mr John Garrett echoed his concerns, stating that 'I do not want to have to write to somebody who has been parachuted into an Agency from the retail sector when I have a problem with a constituent who has been badly treated as a result of Government policy or the delivery of Government services'. Mr Robert Sheldon detected a recent trend for replies from Executive Agencies not to match the standards of Ministerial replies. Others took a different view. The General Secretary of the FDA believed that in many ways it was "the right solution" for Agency Chief Executives to answer Parliamentary questions on their responsibilities. Two academic observers considered that replies from Agency Chief Executives had 'generally been longer and more informative than Ministerial answers'.

165. In 1990 Sir Peter Kemp, the then Next Steps Project Manager, said that 'it is part of the purpose of Next Steps to try and distinguish just whose fault it is. If, in fact, the shortcoming is such that it was the fault of the lack of resources or legislation which was not within the power of the Chief Executive, the transparency of the system should enable that to be seen. If, on the other hand, it was simple bad management on the part of the Chief Executive then that should be seen too and the man should be

held to account accordingly.' Much evidence questioned whether the Next Steps Programme was providing such opportunities in practice. Our predecessors set store by the view that Agency Chief Executives who failed could be more readily dismissed than other civil servants, yet Professor Eric Caines argued that 'Nobody is sacked for making mistakes, the deal being that if Ministers are to protect Chief Executives, they for their part must shield Ministers'. He alleged that 'a compact of sorts has been struck between Ministers and Chief Executives which ensures that neither of them assumes the ultimate risk'. A Chief Executive was required to accept limited freedom and the need to keep Ministers out of political trouble in return for job security. Others suggested that the framework documents and other publicly available information on the operation of Agencies did not provide sufficient clarity for outsiders to determine the allocation of responsibility. There was a blurring of responsibilities which made it impossible to distinguish between policy and operations. Ministers might pass the buck for policy failures, and disclaim responsibility for operational activities. There was a "bureaucratic Bermuda Triangle" in which accountability disappeared. The difficulties in drawing a clear line of responsibility between policy and operations noted in the Trosa Report were observed by others. The extent to which Agency Chief Executives were bound by decisions on the level of resources on which they could not comment publicly was seen as typifying the fact that they had 'responsibility but no authority'.

166. Several solutions have been proposed to these alleged problems. In 1988 the then Treasury and Civil Service Committee recommended that the framework agreement 'should be regarded as a contract' and that a Minister should only be entitled to overrule the Chief Executive by way of a formal note. It further recommended that Chief Executives should give evidence to Select Committees on operational matters on their own behalf rather than under the instructions of Ministers. Following the Government's rejection of these recommendations, and experience of relatively helpful evidence from Chief Executives, the Committee did not advocate change in subsequent Reports, although it noted 'the profound effect' Agencies would have in practice on accountability. In evidence subsequent to his departure from the Civil Service, Sir Peter Kemp argued that the establishment of Agencies was changing the doctrine of Ministerial accountability in practice, 'creating a new sort of accountability, not a less stern accountability but in some ways a tougher accountability.' Mr Vernon Bogdanor argued that this change in practice should be mirrored by a change in theory: 'the *actual* responsibility of the Chief Executive for the work of his or her Agency should be accompanied by a direct *constitutional* responsibility for his work'. To give effect to this, Ministers should state that the Osmotherly Rules did not apply to Agency Chief Executives. The idea of giving Agency Chief Executives greater authority personally to account for their actions gained wide support, including that of Sir Peter Kemp. The original Next Steps Report envisaged that legislation might be necessary to enable Agencies to operate with sufficient independence and accountability. Several observers felt that the time had now arrived to give statutory backing to Executive Agencies, endowing their agreements with Ministers with legal force. It was suggested that this would strengthen the division of responsibility between Ministers and Chief Executives, facilitate improved public and Parliamentary scrutiny and make it more difficult to 'shift the goal posts'.

167. The Government argued that the establishment of Executive Agencies left the traditional doctrine of Ministerial accountability unimpaired while increasing 'the accountability of whole areas of Civil Service work, through greater openness and clearer lines of responsibility'. According to the Government, Agencies did not 'undermine the key constitutional principle that it is Ministers who are accountable to

Parliament for all that their Departments do'. The Government emphasised the marked growth of information about the internal operations of Government available to Parliament and the public as a result of Next Steps and argued that the creation of Agencies made accountability 'more effective' through enhanced transparency in Government. Mr Waldegrave described the previous arrangements for Ministerial replies on operational matters as 'a fiction', a view which has also been expressed by another Minister. The Government saw the new arrangements as an improvement on previous practice, because a Member of Parliament had an opportunity both to receive a reply from the responsible civil servant and to seek a reply from a Minister if he remained dissatisfied. Mr Waldegrave added that it was important that a Minister or his office scanned replies to ensure that issues were not emerging which related to policy. The Government also challenged the notion that responsibility in practice was too diffuse, Mr Waldegrave considering that it was perfectly possible under the present arrangements for an Agency Chief Executive to be dismissed if he made 'a pig's ear of managing the Agency'. With regard to the criticism that Agency Chief Exectives were unable to comment on their resource levels, Mr Michael Bichard did not believe that an Agency Chief Executive would be able to retain his credibility if he criticised the resources framework within which he was required to operate. The Government saw no case for giving statutory form to the relationship between Ministers and Chief Executives, believing the general quality of agreements reached between Departments and Agencies was 'levelling up'. The Inland Revenue's Management Plans for 1994–95 to 1996–97 include for the first time a purchase/provider contract, agreed with the Financial Secretary to the Treasury, setting out the operational targets and objectives which the Department is expected to meet in the year 1994–95 in return for the resources provided to it. The Chairman of the Board of Inland Revenue considered this to be 'an important development'; although targets were not new, the contract formalised them in a new way. It would provide a firmer basis for accountability. The Inland Revenue was 'pioneering a contract' of this kind within the British Civil Service. Mr Waldegrave commended this endeavour, which he expected other Departments to follow.

(iv) Conclusions

168. In its initial study of the Next Steps initiative the then Treasury and Civil Service Committee observed that 'it is essential that change on this scale is not only carefully considered and expertly implemented, but also carries with it the enthusiasm both of civil servants themselves, at all levels, and of those outside the Civil Service — the general public and their representatives on both sides of the Commons'. Although the Government's wider programme of reforms in the Civil Service is a matter of considerable controversy for reasons we explore elsewhere, we are struck by wide level of support for and acceptance of the Next Steps programme and the common view that it has facilitated a genuine improvement in the quality of some public services. It has been argued that, while some particular changes which have taken place might have happened without the establishment of Agencies, the overall transformation in Government would not have been brought about without Next Steps. We agree. **We believe that Next Steps Agencies represent a significant improvement in the organisation of Government and that any future Government will want to maintain them in order to implement its objectives for the delivery of services to the public.**

169. However, the success in establishing Agencies is only a means to an end. We believe that the cultural change which lies at the heart of the Next Steps programme

must be secured and reinforced. In order to achieve this, changes will be required in the framework within which Agencies are required to operate, although such changes should continue to take account of the immense diversity of Agencies in terms of size and function. Two crucial issues have been raised about Agencies during this inquiry: relations between Departments and Agencies and accountability and responsibility. These two matters are intimately connected. We consider that the delegation of freedom to manage to Executive Agencies has not been as thorough and as complete as is desirable, and that this reflects real uncertainties about the division of responsibilities between Ministers and parent Departments on the one hand and Agencies and their Chief Executives on the other, uncertainties which arise in part from difficulties in identifying and agreeing upon the dividing line between policy and operations. As a solution to these difficulties, it is necessary to base the accountability of Executive Agencies on a distinction which is more tangible: that between decisions made by the Agency and decisions made by the Minister or parent Department. To this end, **we recommend that the process of target-setting is replaced by annual performance agreements between Ministers and Agency Chief Executives.** The new performance agreements would be different in character from the current target setting process and would have the following characteristics: they would arise from a process of formal negotiation and require the active agreement of the Agency Chief Executive as well as the Minister; they would prescribe a minimum of financial controls, ideally setting a single financial target or laying down unit costs for Agency services; they would be subject to an evaluation at the end of the year to be undertaken by a body outside the Department. Where a Minister or parent Department wished to give an instruction to an Agency on a matter within the terms of the performance agreement, or to request the Agency to carry out work outside the terms of the performance agreement, this should be done in writing and with financial terms specified as appropriate. It would be for the Agency Chief Executive to determine whether such a written instruction was necessary. Although the scope for Ministerial and departmental intervention would not be subject to any enforceable restraint, we believe that this requirement, coupled with proposals below relating to accountability, would represent important restraints on unnecessary interference. We do not think that the introduction of legislation need be necessary for such annual performance agreements. They should be made under the terms of revised framework documents.

170. **We support the arrangements for Parliamentary questions on operational matters within the ambit of an Executive Agency to be referred in the first instance to Agency Chief Executives and we welcome the fact that their answers are now published in the Official Report.** The extent to which Chief Executives provide answers should, by and large, be seen as a welcome sign of the extent of their devolved responsibilities and need not of itself be a cause for concern. We nevertheless regard it as important that Ministers maintain an engagement with individual cases raised by way of Parliamentary questions. We suspect that the scope for active Ministerial involvement in individual cases raised in this manner under the previous arrangements would not be universally regarded as 'a fiction'. We believe that Ministerial intervention will sometimes be desirable, particularly in individual cases, and is a necessary part of a Minister's role. **Ministers should always respond where Members of Parliament consider the response by an Agency Chief Executive to be unsatisfactory.**

171. We do not believe that Ministerial power to intervene in the actions and decisions of Agencies justifies the retention of Ministerial accountability for the actions and decisions of Agencies for which Chief Executives are responsible. The theoretical separation of accountability and responsibility is nowhere more untenable than in the

operation of Agencies; continued adherence to the theory behind such a separation might jeopardise the durability of the delegation at the heart of Next Steps. The delegation of responsibility should be accompanied by a commensurate delegation of accountability. We recommend that Agency Chief Executives should be directly and personally accountable to Select Committees in relation to their performance agreements. Ministers should remain accountable for the framework documents and for their part in negotiating the annual performance agreement, as well as for all instructions given to Agency Chief Executives by them subsequent to the annual performance agreement. To this end, we recommend that all such instructions should be published in Agency Annual Reports, subject only to a requirement to preserve the personal confidentiality or anonymity of individual clients.

Note

Some of the problems identified by the Treasury and Civil Service Select Committee were to be found in the Prison Service. There had been a series of escapes from three prisons. Following the report by Sir John Learmont into the last of these escapes from Parkhurst, the Home Secretary Mr. M. Howard dismissed the Director-General Mr D. Lewis. The issue was raised in the House of Commons by the Shadow Home Secretary Mr. J. Straw.

House of Commons, HC Deb Vol. 264, Cols. 502–6, 516–20, 18 November 1995.

Mr JACK STRAW (Blackburn): I beg to move,

> That this House deplores the unwillingness of the Secretary of State for the Home Department to accept responsibility for serious operational failures of the Prison Service.

The Home Secretary has vested in him by section 1 of the Prison Act 1952 all powers and jurisdictions in relation to prisons and prisoners in England and Wales. He is responsible to the House for the exercise of those powers and jurisdictions. The Act makes no distinction between his responsibility for the policy of the Prison Service and the operation of that policy. We say that the right hon. and learned Gentleman is following a constitutional fiction in seeking wholly to separate the two. He says that he is responsible only for his policy towards prisons but not for operational matters, for which he is accountable but not responsible. Responsibility for the operation of the Prison Service, says the Secretary, of State, is in the hands of the Director General of the Prison Service. In return for that operational responsibility, the director general has vested in him, by the agency framework document and other documents, power over operational matters, in which the Secretary of State says emphatically that he does not interfere.

We say, however, that in practice the Secretary of State has on numerous occasions taken decisions and otherwise interfered with the operation of the Prison Service, but because of the fiction that he is not involved in it or that he is not responsible for operational matters, he has at all times had to avoid any admission that he has been so involved. That has produced two results. First, in the damning words of Her Majesty's Chief Inspector of Prisons, Judge Stephen Tumim.

> it means that the Home Secretary is not responsible for anything at all.

That means that the Home Secretary takes the credit but is free of any responsibility. In other words, he has exercised power without responsibility.

Secondly, we say that the Secretary of State has had to be so evasive as to his real involvement in operational matters that in respect of the fate of Mr. John Marriott, the former governor of Parkhurst prison, he gave explanations to the House and to the Home Affairs Select Committee which are uncorroborated and wholly at variance with other evidence that is now available. . . .

Let me deal with each of the matters in turn. First, there is the distinction that the Secretary of State draws between policy and operations. In questions on the statement on the Prison Service on Tuesday 10 January 1995, the right hon. Member for Berwick-upon-Tweed (Mr. Beith) put this to the Secretary of State when he said:

> but there is no proper control of security at the prisons. Is not that something for which he—

the Home Secretary—

> must take responsibility?"

The Secretary of State replied:

> With regard to operational policy, there has always been a division between policy matters and operational matters . . . I really do not see . . . how, whatever structure or framework is in place, one can avoid a sensible distinction between policy and operational matters. — [*Official Report*, 10 January 1995; Vol. 252, c. 39–40.]

The problem for the Secretary of State is that he is the only one who believes that in practice such a sensible distinction can be made to the point of rigidity to which he takes it, for if ministerial responsibility means anything, it must mean that his policy is judged against the operation of that policy. How else can we judge a policy? Policy is not some intellectual abstract. It can be judged only by whether it has good or bad effect.

Judge Stephen Tumim said earlier this year that the Prison Service faced a crisis of confidence. That crisis has grown worse since he spoke those words. Is it any wonder that the service is in crisis when it has no effective leadership? The Secretary of State provides none. Indeed, he does not even pretend to provide any, because he says that he is not responsible for the operation of the service. The Director General of the Prison Service, who was personally appointed by the right hon. and learned Member for Rushcliffe (Mr. Clarke), and was complimented to the hilt by the Secretary of State in the House on 10 January, has now been dismissed without notice. There is only an acting successor, Mr. Richard Tilt, who on the day of his appointment was in open disagreement with the Secretary of State, telling a meeting of prison governors that in his view the removal of Mr. Lewis was 'unnecessary'.

Virtually everyone associated with the Prison Service — the governors, the staff, all six trade unions, Judge Tumim — have palpably lost confidence in the Secretary of State. As we heard on the radio this morning, that now includes the chairman of the Association of Members of Boards of Visitors, Mr. Julian Alliss, who called on the Secretary of State to resign. . .

It is certainly the case that a great many of those with far greater knowledge of Mr. Derek Lewis's competence do not believe that he should have been summarily dismissed by the Secretary of State. That is why two non-executive directors, both with great experience outside the service, have now tendered their resignation in protest against the treatment of Derek Lewis. Mr. Geoff Keeys resigned yesterday and Mrs. Urmila Bannerjee, a senior director of British Telecom, resigned today.

For all that, the Secretary of State continues blithely to refuse to acknowledge any responsibility. . . .

The Secretary of State evaded responsibility when the Woodcock report on the Whitemoor escapes was published, claiming that it contained 'no recommendations to me' although it stated in terms:

> There exists at all levels within the Service some confusion as to the respective roles of Ministers, the Agency Headquarters and . . . Prison Governors. In particular, the Enquiry has identified the difficulty of determining what is an operational matter and what is policy, leading to confusion as to where responsibility lies.

The Secretary of State did the same on Monday, when he sought to avoid any responsibility for the matters which were the subject of the report by claiming that Learmont

> has not found that any policy decision of mine, directly or indirectly, caused the escape. — (*Official Report*, 16 October 1995; Vol. 264, c. 31.]

No such words were used anywhere in Sir John's report. Moreover, the Learmont report is replete with criticism of political involvement by Ministers in the operation of the service. Paragraph 3.83 states:

> The Director General . . . needs minimum political involvement in the day-to-day operation of the Service,

and then charts how the reverse has been the case.

The report continues:

> Any organisation which boasts one Statement of Purpose, one Vision, five Values, six Goals, seven Strategic Priorities and eight KPIs—

Key performance indicators—

> without any clear correlation between them, is producing a recipe for total confusion and exasperation amongst those undertaking a most difficult and dangerous task on behalf of the general public.

Who is responsible or the 'total confusion' identified by Learmont? Is it the Prison Service board, the director general or someone else? That 'recipe for total confusion' is contained within the framework document itself. It is here that we find the

> one Statement of Purpose, one Vision, five Values, six Goals, seven Strategic Priorities and eight KPIs, without any clear correlation between them

That document, drawn up by the former Secretary of State for the Home Department — now the Chancellor of the Exchequer — is explicitly endorsed by the current Secretary of State.

I wrote to the Secretary of State on Monday, asking him where the distinction between policy and operations was explained. His private secretary wrote back saying that the document

> explains the distinction between operations and policy.

The document, of course, does no such thing. What it does do — in Sir John Learmont's damning phrase — is to prescribe a recipe for the total confusion for which the Secretary of State is responsible. . .

THE SECRETARY OF STATE FOR THE HOME DEPARTMENT (MR. MICHAEL HOWARD): I beg to move, to leave out from 'House' to the end of the Question and to add instead thereof:

> believes that the Home Secretary is and should be accountable to this House for all matters concerning the Prison Service; believes that he is and should be accountable and responsible for all policy decisions relating to the Service; believes that the Director General of the Prison Service is and should be responsible for the day-to-day operation of the service; and utterly rejects the very serious allegations made about the Home Secretary's conduct towards the former Governor of Parkhurst, Mr. John Marriott.

What we have seen this afternoon and the whole of this week is a cheap and tawdry attempt to make petty party political capital out of the difficulties of the Prison Service. I shall deal in due course, closely and with relish, with each of the allegations put by the Labour party.

On Monday, I made a statement to the House about the independent report by General Sir John Learmont on one of the most wide-ranging reviews of prison security that has ever been conducted. The report followed two of the most serious operational failures in the history of the Prison Service. It is a devastating report, which severely criticises Parkhurst and its management. It says that the security manual of the Prison Service was disregarded at Parkhurst and that the most basic security procedures were not observed. It also makes the most trenchant criticisms of the management of the Prison Service generally and concludes with the following words:

> There is an abundance of excellent people within the Prison Service whose most fervent wish is to do a good and worthwhile job. They are yearning to be led to better things. Although much has been done to improve the corporate planning within the Service, this inquiry has starkly illustrated the need to address urgently shortcoming in leadership, operations and security.

I said on Monday that I had to be able to assure the House, and through it the people of this country, that the grave weaknesses in the service that have been disclosed would be put right. General Sir John Learmont said that responsibilities reached prisons board level and that the criticism stopped there. [HON. MEMBERS: 'That includes you'] I am not a member of the prisons board.

It was impossible for me to overlook the serious criticisms contained in that report. Of course, I took into account the lengthy submissions that the former director general put to me, which he has now made public, including his criticisms of the independent Learmont report. I had to choose between the view of the former director general and the independent views of General Learmont. I concluded that a change of leadership was required at the top of the Prison Service to address what General Learmont described as

> the shortcomings in leadership, operations and security.

So I decided that the director general's appointment should be terminated.

The material on which I made that decision is before the House — the Learmont report is a published document. The shadow Home Secretary, who has made such a fuss over all this, has complete access to that document but does not have a view on that central question . . .

MR. A. J. BEITH, (Berwick-upon-Tweed): The Home Secretary has said that he had to choose between what Mr. Lewis has said and the Learmont report. Why, therefore, does he ignore paragraph 3.83 of the report, which says:

> The Director General also needs minimum political involvement in the day-to-day operation of the Service.?

The paragraph sets out what Sir John Learmont clearly considers to be too much political involvement in the day-to-day running of the service. The right hon. and learned Gentleman cannot accept one part of the report but ignore that paragraph.

MR. HOWARD: The report goes on to indicate that it is for the director general to balance the various parts of his responsibilities and effectively to find a way of responding to reasonable ministerial requests and of dealing with operational matters. I shall refer to that function in some detail during the course of my speech, so I urge the right hon. Gentleman to restrain himself and to have a little patience.

Several hon. Members rose—

MR. HOWARD: I must make some progress, but I will give way in due course.

As to the question of accountability and my personal responsibilities as Home Secretary, my position, and that of all previous Home Secretaries, is perfectly consistent and clear. I am personally accountable to the House for all matters concerning the Prison Service. I am accountable and responsible for all policy decisions relating to the service. The director general is responsible for day-to-day operations.

That distinction between policy and operations is— . . .

MR. HOWARD: The distinction to which I referred, before I was so happily interrupted by the hon. Member is for Stratford-on-Avon, between policy and operations is nothing new. During my statement on Sir John Woodcock's inquiry on 19 December 1994, I reminded the House of what my noble Friend, Lord Prior, had said following the escape of a number of terrorist prisoners from the Maze prison in Northern Ireland. He said:

> If I had felt that ministerial responsibility was such that in this case I should have resigned, I certainly should have done so. It would be a matter for resignation if the . . . inquiry showed that what happened was the result of some act of policy that was my responsibility, or that I failed to implement something that I had been asked to implement, or should have implemented, In that case, I should resign. — [*Official Report*, 24 October 1983; Vol. 47, c. 23–4.1]

The distinction between policy and operations is also reflected in the framework document that established the Prison Service as an executive agency. It says that the Director General of the Prison Service is responsible for the day-to-day management of the Prison Service. It also says that the director general is accountable directly to me for the Prison Service's performance and operations, and that, although the Home Secretary will not normally become involved in the day-to-day management of the Prison Service, he will expect to be consulted on the handling of operational matters that could give rise to grave public or parliamentary concern. I do not imagine that any hon. Member would argue that the Parkhurst escape was not in that category.

When I received Sir John's report, I studied it very carefully. If the criticisms in it had been made of me, I should not be standing at the Dispatch Box. . .

I now turn specifically and directly to the many inconsistent and unfounded allegations that have been made this week about my conduct. Many people will think it extraordinary that, the day after the publication of such a devastating report on the security of our prisons, the Leader of the opposition chose to concentrate, not on security, not on escapes, but on allegations about the treatment of the former governor of Parkhurst.

Let me remind the House of what General Learmont said about Parkhurst under Mr. Marriott's governorship. I shall use only a few examples. Hon. Members will find many more, if they need them, in paragraphs 2.56, 2.124, 2.062, 2.07 and 2.08. General Learmont had quite a lot to say about Mr. Marriott's regime. In paragraph 2.256 he says that Mr. Marriott decided not to undertake rub-down searches. In paragraph 2.124 he says that Parkurst ignored an instruction that the duty governor should be in the prison when it was unlocked and when category A inmates were associating with others.

In paragraph 2.228 General Learmont says that there was

> a lack of visible leadership on the Wings and elsewhere at Parkhurst.

In paragraph 2.261, he pinpoints a

> multitude of security lapses and unacceptable practices

and concludes that there was

> little to commend in the way things were done.

Those are the words of a man whose independent assessment is beyond doubt.

Given those stringent and damning criticisms, I find it hard to understand how anyone could question the decision to remove Mr. Marriott from his duties at Parkhurst without delay, or to suggest that he has been used as a scapegoat. That is the man on whose behalf the Leader of the Opposition has chosen to take up the cudgels.

Questions

1. If the policy-operations distinction is difficult to maintain, does this in effect allow Ministers to decide those matters which are policy ones for which they will be responsible, and those which are operational and the responsibility of officials?

2. If the managerial logic of agencies suggest that their chief executives should be directly responsible to Parliament, is this outweighed by the constitutional logic of ministerial responsibility?

Fifth Report from the Treasury and Civil Service Select Committee HC 27 of 1993–94, paras 135–7

(vi) Non-Parliamentary accountability

135. The activities of Parliament and elections to the House of Commons are not and never have been the sole means by which the Executive is held to account. Several mechanisms of non-Parliamentary accountability were considered in the course of the Sub-Committee's inquiry. Some advocated the need to strengthen methods of non-Parliamentary accountability in response to perceived weaknesses in existing procedures and conventions. This raised questions about the extent to which the development of new procedures would be compatible with the principles of Parliamentary accountability. Some forms of holding the Executive and the Civil Service in particular to account clearly operate in support of Parliament. One such example is the work of the Comptroller and Auditor General, whose reports are normally considered by the Committee of Public Accounts. Sir Kenneth Stowe believed that

together they represented 'probably the most valuable instrument anywhere in the world for maintaining . . . standards of integrity'. The Parliamentary Commissioner for Administration represents a very important check on maladministration in the Civil Service. The Select Committee on the Parliamentary Commissioner for Administration has recently reaffirmed the value of his work while making recommendations so that the potential of that office can be further developed.

136. Aside from Parliament and its associated mechanisms, the most important form of accountability of the Government comes from the judiciary and the courts. Ministers and civil servants are subject to the law of the land in the same way as other subjects. The accountability of the Executive to the courts has been enhanced in recent years by the growth of judicial review. The Government attributed the growth of judicial review principally to changes in court procedure, most notably amendments in 1977 to the Rules of the Supreme Court, a growing propensity of the public to resort to litigation and a growth in legislation. According to the Government, 'the existence of judicial review has clearly and substantially increased the work of both lawyers and administrators, in effect to 'judicial review proof' departmental decisions, but it has also improved the quality of decision-making by making it more structured and consistent. Accordingly, judicial review is not to be seen as an irritant, but as a contribution to upholding the values of fairness, reasonableness and objectivity in the conduct of public business.' Professor Norman Lewis took a less sanguine view of the growth of judicial review. He considered that part of the explanation lay in 'increasingly confrontational politics and the lack of alternative methods for ventilating opposition' and the inadequacy of forms of redress short of resort to Judicial review. The Government did not dispute that the use of judicial review depended upon the availability of alternative mechanisms for redress against administrative action, including complaints procedures under the Citizen's Charter. It is to these that we now turn.

137. Under the Citizen's Charter which was launched in July 1991 the Government attaches a high priority to improved procedures for complaints and redress, viewing them as a necessary response to growing devolution in public services. While the Sub-Committee did not consider the operation of these procedures, it received evidence from several quarters criticising the fact that the Citizen's Charter was not justiciable and that standards laid down under it did not amount to enforceable legal rights. In the last Parliament our predecessors drew attention to the need to consider the case for strengthening administrative law in the light of the Next Steps Initiative. The case for developing a wider system of administrative law or other forms of non-Parliamentary redress was advanced in evidence to the Sub-Committee. Professor Eric Caines and others saw advantages in developing forms of accountability at local level or with client groups for central Government services. The National Consumer Council has proposed that 'charters should establish a relationship between public services and the consumer which is *as close as possible* to an explicit contractual relationship involving *enforceable* rights'. The Government was cautious about introducing legalistic structures into redress systems, and its scepticism was shared by others. It is at least open to doubt whether a civil servant can be expected to be answerable both directly to the public for the provision of a service and to Ministers and Parliament. Lord Bancroft has suggested that at present a civil servant's 'responsibilities may be *for* his clients, but they are *to* his Minister'. We are sympathetic to the idea that new forms of accountability and their constitutional implications should be the subject of further Parliamentary consideration. This matter is best examined in a Parliamentary context, since any developments in this area are likely to have implications for the role of Parliament and Members of Parliament in particular in calling the

Executive to account for its actions. We note the opinion of the Select Committee on the Parliamentary Commissioner for Administration 'that it should fall within the Committee's terms of reference to maintain an oversight of the assorted complaint and redress mechanisms in the public sector or established by statute' and we look forward to the Report arising from that Committee's current inquiry into redress.

Question
What would be the arguments for and against requiring officials to account to Ministers and to be directly answerable, perhaps even legally liable, to the public?

Fifth Report from the Treasury and Civil Service Select Committee HC 27 of 1993–94, paras 138–40

(viii) Open Government

138. Accountability depends to a considerable extent upon the accuracy, fullness and relevance of the information available to those outside the Government on its operation. Accurate information is the bedrock of accountability. Greater openness in Government is not simply an issue of accountability: up to a point, a more open administration is likely to be a more effective and efficient administration. We consider below the extent to which the policy process is an exception to this rule, but we examine here the progress which has been made towards greater openness in Government and its impact on the Civil Service. In 1986 the then Committee noted how often the subject of open government and freedom of information had arisen in the course of its inquiry into relations between Ministers and civil servants. It did not endorse a particular approach to open government, but stated that 'the evidence we have received does not suggest that the Government has made a convincing case against some form of Freedom of Information Act'. Similar issues have come to the fore during the present inquiry, not least because of a succession of initiatives by the Government since the 1992 General Election. In May 1992 the Government published for the first time a list of Cabinet Committees including their membership. The same month also saw the publication of Questions of Procedure for Ministers which we have already welcomed. Most importantly, in July 1993, the Government published an Open Government White Paper in which the Government proposed to issue a Code of Practice on Access to Government Information, to have effect from 4 April 1994, setting out the information which it would and would not make available to the public upon request. The Government announced that the Code would be independently policed by the Parliamentary Commissioner for Administration, to whom members of the public could complain about a decision under the Code of Practice through a Member of Parliament. Given the central role allocated to the Parliamentary Commissioner for Administration in supervising the Code, its operation will be considered in the first instance by the Select Committee on the Parliamentary Commissioner for Administration, and it would not be appropriate for us to comment in detail on the provisions of the Code before evidence emerges on its practical effects. There were, however, two issues raised which we consider relevant to the present inquiry.

139. First, the Government's Code of Practice states that 'there is no commitment that pre-existing documents, as distinct from information, will be made available in response to requests'. The Campaign for Freedom of Information regarded this as 'an overwhelming flaw' in the Government's proposals, which would grant undue discre-

tion to civil servants to prepare digests of information in a selective manner. It believed that this process would be more laborious than the editing of existing documents and would generate suspicion. Professor Norman Lewis expressed similar concerns. Mr Waldegrave believed that the provision of documents with some information necessarily blacked out would give rise to even greater suspicion. Digests prepared by civil servants were likely to be more succinct and relevant. Above all, the preparation of digests would be subject to independent review by the Parliamentary Commissioner for Administration who would have access to the original files and could thus monitor the integrity of such summaries.

140. Second, it was contended that the new Code was fundamentally inadequate and that the introduction of a Freedom of Information Act was both the best means of securing a truly accountable Government and would have a beneficial impact on the workings of the Civil Service and the Government more generally. Professor Norman Lewis considered such an Act to be 'essential for Parliament's traditions to be maintained . . . a weapon Parliament ought to have in its dealings with the Executive'. He considered it peculiar that the United Kingdom did not have a Freedom of Information Act when so many other democratic countries did. These views were shared by others, most notably the Campaign for Freedom of Information, who argued that a Freedom of Information Act would provide a broadly defined right of access and a more effective means of authoritative interpretation and enforcement than could be provided by the Parliamentary Commissioner for Administration. Mr Waldegrave contended that there was not a great difference of principle between the Government's proposals and a Freedom of Information Act, that the Government's Code would avoid leaving final decisions to a judge and that a system based around the Parliamentary Commssioner for Administration was compatible with the principle of Parliamentary accountability to an extent which was not true of a judge-based Freedom of Information Act. We believe that there is a greater difference between a Freedom of Information Act and a Code of Practice introduced by the Government and not subject to Parliamentary approval than Mr Waldegrave implied.

Note

Under the Code the Government has made five commitments:

(a) to give facts and analysis with major policy decisions;
(b) to open up internal guidelines about departments' dealings with the public;
(c) to give reasons with administrative decisions;
(d) to provide information under the Citizens' Charter about public services, what they cost, targets, performance, complaints and redress; and
(e) to answer requests for information.

Paragraph 4 of the Code states:

> There is no commitment that pre-existing documents, as distinct from information will be made available in response to requests. The Code does not require departments to acquire information they do not possess, to provide information which is already published, to provide material which the Government did not consider to be reliable information, or to provide information which is provided as part of an existing charged service other than through that service.

A charge may be made if the provision of the information involves additional work. If a person has a complaint then it should be raised with the department or body. If a person is not satisfied with the outcome of such an internal review then complaints may be made to the PCA through an MP.

Code of Practice on Access to Government Information
(1994) pp. 5–9

Part II

Reasons for confidentiality
The following categories of information are exempt from the commitments to provide information in this Code.

References to harm or prejudice include both actual harm or prejudice and risk or reasonable expectation of harm or prejudice. In such cases it should be considered whether any harm or prejudice arising from disclosure is outweighed by the public interest in making information available.

The exemptions will not be interpreted in a way which causes injustice to individuals.

1. Defence security and international relations

(a) Information whose disclosure would harm national security or defence.

(b) Information whose disclosure would harm the conduct of international relations or affairs.

(c) Information received in confidence from foreign governments, foreign courts or international organisations.

2. Internal discussion and advice
Information whose disclosure would harm the frankness and candour of internal discussion, including:

- proceedings of Cabinet and Cabinet committees;
- internal opinion, advice, recommendation, consultation and deliberation;
- projections and assumptions relating to internal policy analysis; analysis of alternative policy options and information relating to rejected policy options;
- confidential communications between departments, public bodies and regulatory bodies.

3. Communications with the Royal Household
Information relating to confidential communications between Ministers and Her Majesty the Queen or other Members of the Royal Household, or relating to confidential proceedings of the Privy Council.

4. Law enforcement and legal proceedings

(a) Information whose disclosure would prejudice the administration of justice, including fair trial and the enforcement or proper administration of the law.

(b) Information whose disclosure would prejudice legal proceedings or the proceedings of any tribunal, public inquiry or other formal investigation (whether actual or likely) or whose disclosure is, has been or is likely to be addressed in the context of such proceedings.

(c) Information relating to proceedings which have been completed or terminated, or relating to investigations which have or might have resulted in proceedings.

(d) Information covered by legal professional privilege.

(e) Information whose disclosure would prejudice the prevention, investigation or detection of crime, the apprehension or prosecution of offenders, or the security of any building or penal institution.

(f) Information whose disclosure would harm public safety or public order.

(g) Information whose disclosure could endanger the life or physical safety of any person, or identify the source of information or assistance given in confidence for law enforcement or security purposes.

(h) Information whose disclosure would increase the likelihood of damage to the environment, or rare or endangered species and their habitats.

5. Immigration and nationality

Information relating to immigration, nationality, consular and entry clearance cases.

6. Effective management of the economy and collection of tax

(a) Information whose disclosure would harm the ability of the Government to manage the economy, prejudice the conduct of official market operations, or could lead to improper gain or advantage.

(b) Information whose disclosure would prejudice the assessment or collection of tax, duties or National Insurance contributions, or assist tax avoidance or evasion.

7. Effective management and operations of the public service

(a) Information whose disclosure could lead to improper gain or advantage or would prejudice:

(i) the competitive position of a department or other public body or authority;

(ii) negotiations or the effective conduct of personnel management, or commercial or contractual activities;

(iii) the awarding of discretionary grants.

(b) Information whose disclosure would harm the proper and efficient conduct of the operations of a department or other public body or authority, including NHS organisations, or of any regulatory body.

8. Public employment, public appointments and honours

(a) Personnel records (relating to public appointments as well as employees of public authorities) including those relating to recruitment, promotion and security vetting.

(b) Information, opinions and assessments given in confidence in relation to public employment and public appointments made by Ministers of the Crown, by the Crown on the advice of Ministers or by statutory office holders.

(c) Information, opinions and assessments given in relation to recommendations for honours.

9. Voluminous or vexatious requests

Requests for information which are vexatious or manifestly unreasonable or are formulated in too general a manner, or which (because of the amount of information to be processed or the need to retrieve information from files not in current use) would require unreasonable diversion of resources.

10. Publication and prematurity in relation to publication

Information which is or will soon be published, or whose disclosure would be premature in relation to a planned announcement or publication.

11. Research, statistics and analysis

(a) Information relating to incomplete analysis, research or statistics, where disclosure could be misleading or deprive the holder of priority of publication or commercial value.

(b) Information held only for preparing statistics or carrying out research, or for surveillance for health and safety purposes (including food safety), and which relates to individuals, companies or products which will not be identified in reports of that research or surveillance, or in published statistics.

12. Privacy of an indivdual

Unwarranted disclosure to a third party of personal information about any person (including a deceased person) or any other disclosure which would constitute or could facilitate an unwarranted invasion of privacy.

13. Third party's commercial confidences

Information including commercial confidences, trade secrets or intellectual property whose unwarranted disclosure would harm the competitive position of a third party.

14. Information given in confidence

(a) Information held in consequence of having been supplied in confidence by a person who:

(i) gave the information under a statutory guarantee that its confidentiality would be protected; or

(ii) was not under any legal obligation, whether actual or implied, to supply it, and has not consented to its disclosure.

(b) Information whose disclosure without the consent of the supplier would prejudice the future supply of such information.

(c) Medical information provided in confidence if disclosure to the subject would harm their physical or mental health, or should only be made by a medical practitioner.

15. Statutory and other restrictions

(a) Information whose disclosure is prohibited by or under any enactment, regulation, European Community law or international agreement.

(b) Information whose release would constitute a breach of Parliamentary Privilege.

Note

In its report on Open Government the Select Committee on the Parliamentary Commissioner for Administration endorses (a) the need for open government, and (b) the Commissioner to act as the means of enforcement rather than the courts, but recommends substituting the code with a statute.

Second Report from the Select Committee on the Parliamentary Commissioner for Administration

HC 84 of 1995–96, paras 121—6

121. We have already discussed one advantage of a Freedom of Information Act, namely the publicity attending its preparation and passage through Parliament and the consequent public awareness of their access rights. Publicity alone, however, is not

enough to justify primary legislation and any shortfall in publicity could be compensated by a determined effort from Government. A more powerful reason given for a statute by those we met when we visited Australia and New Zealand was the need to change government culture from one of secrecy to one where openness is accepted and there is a willingness to allow the public to participate to a greater degree in the processes of government. It is perhaps too early to say whether the culture in the United Kingdom public service has changed. It will in any event be a process rather than a sudden event. The Committee noted that New Zealand had a directive in place prior to the Act but this was, however, later deemed to be ineffective. Indeed in the United Kingdom the so-called Croham Directive of 1976 from the then Head of the Civil Service instructed civil servants to release as much background material to policy decisions as possible. The Directive added 'that when policy studies were being undertaken in future the background material should as far as possible be written in a form which would permit it to be published separately, with the minimum of alteration, once a Ministerial decision to do so had been taken'. The Croham Directive is judged to have been ineffective — indeed the fact that renewed commitments to volunteer information had to be made under the Code suggests that the Directive was ignored. Will the Code meet the same fate? We have quoted initial assessments from a number of sources which suggest that the climate is changing and the release of more information is occurring. Central to this greater effectiveness is the existence of the Ombudsman as an independent adjudicator of appeals. It may well be too early to make a final judgement as to the effectiveness of the Code in changing Whitehall culture. We believe, if the Code scheme is refomed on the lines recommended in this Report, and putting to one side issues further discussed in the following paragraphs, that it has a good chance of furthering such cultural change.

122. The Government has made clear that it remains opposed to a single Freedom of Information Act. Mr Freeman explained why:

> First of all, I think the system we have at present, which is a Code plus a number of specific Bills which are now on the statute book . . . provides a much more flexible system. We can amend the Code and we can extend the Code far quicker than we can with legislation; we can be more responsive. Secondly, I think our procedure is cheaper and quicker in delivering action. I think to have the Ombudsman pursue individual concerns that remain after the department has considered a request which has not been immediately met provides a free, sensible and very efficient service. Thirdly, and finally, I think that to introduce the courts with a general remit to safeguard the provision of information disclosure and transparency would in some way confuse and diminish the accountability of ministers and departments to Parliament.

123. Often the argument against a Freedom of Information Act is framed in terms of the disadvantages that would spring from the involvement of the courts. There are now plenty of examples, cited above, of [Freedom of Information] FOI regimes established by statute with an Ombudsman or Commissioner rather than the court as the external appeal mechanism. There may well be recourse to the courts on a point of law or as a form of judicial review but such recourse need not be common. To introduce a statute with the Ombudsman as the final appeal process (apart from the possibility of judicial review) would seem to meet Mr Freeman's concern to avoid the court and retain the ombudsman as the form of external review.

124. As to the objection of inflexibility, some might see the case with which the Code can be amended by Governments to be a disadvantage, rather than an

advantage, of the current system. There has been no parliamentary approval or sanction given to the contents of the Code. Furthermore, such a Code is extremely vulnerable to slight amendments at the behest of departments finding the Code uncomfortable to live with. Thus the purpose of the Code might be wholly negated. But even taking Mr Freeman's point, if Parliament thought it appropriate it could legislate in such a way that later changes could be made by secondary legislation, which would preserve parliamentary approval whilst providing a fairly speedy mechanism for amendment.

125. The arguments of publicity and effect on civil service culture may not in themselves be enough to justify primary legislation. A more compelling argument, however, follows from the Government's advocacy of the advantages of the Ombudsman. The Government is, however, planning to remove from the Ombudsman's FOI jurisdiction all requests for personal information (which account for a high percentage of requests in other FOI regimes). The suggestion in the White Paper is that such requests come under the remit of the Data Protection Registrar who will thus become our version of a Privacy Commissioner. In New Zealand the Ombudsman previously had responsibility for personal information requests but they have recently been taken over by the Privacy Commissioner. In Australia the Privacy Commissioner defers on personal information matters to the Ombudsman. Other FOI regimes combine an Information and Privacy Commissioner in a single office. This Report does not attempt to explore in any detail privacy issues. How best to deal with personal information requests should be further debated. The point we would make is a simpler one. To include personal information within a privacy statute while retaining other access rights in a Code is to put the Ombudsman and open government concerns at a disadvantage. They can always be overruled by privacy considerations which have statutory authority. It is, however, difficult always to judge where privacy considerations end and public interest considerations begin.

126. The Government also proposes that environmental and health and safety information be removed from the Ombudsman's jurisdiction, being placed on a statutory footing, perhaps with a tribunal as an external appeals mechanism. It is hard to reconcile this with the advantages elsewhere cited for an Ombudsman scheme. Neither the Data Protection Registrar nor the envisaged tribunals would be as able to encourage the extension of good practice in open government, which is one of the benefits of the Ombudsman's new role. Moreover, with at least three different access regimes in place the dissemination of clear and consistent precedents for the consideration of access requests will be undermined with such complex issues as candour, harm, confidentiality, public interest being differently interpreted by different authorities. The Ombudsman and the Code would be left with the 'rump' of government information, sometimes obstructed or overruled by the impinging of statutory judgements on their own remit. This system seems complicated and effectively to cancel the very advantages for the Ombudsman's involvement which the Government advanced. We have recently seen in the Health Service a complicated complaints mechanism, established piecemeal over the years, reformed in favour of a comprehensive and unitary system. It would be unfortunate at this crucial moment to make a similar mistake, only to unravel it in a few years. It is precisely because we accept the arguments advanced by the Government for an Ombudsman supervision that we conclude that there should be a single Freedom of Information Act encompassing all access rights. This would preserve the Ombudsman's important role, maintain the consistency of open government judgements and ensure that the various considerations that inform any decision on access all carry similar statutory weight. It would also give Parliament the opportunity to approve in detail the contents of the Code. We

are convinced that on balance the advantage lies in favour of legislation. **We recommend that the Government introduce a Freedom of Information Act.**

Question

Given that law can assist in the making of cultural change, which is what the operation of freedom of information amounts to for those in government, why should the obligation to provide information be statutory, but its enforcement be pursued outside the courts?

(ii) Select Committees

An account of the genesis of the reforms of the Select Committee system can be found in Chapter 1 of G. Drewry (ed.), *The New Select Committees* (2nd edn., 1989). One of the problems which the Committees face in conducting their investigations is that of reluctant witnesses. The powers given to the Select Committees do not include compelling the attendance of a Member of either House of Parliament. It would be a matter for each House of Parliament to determine if a reluctant MP or peer should be compelled to attend a Committee which wished to speak to him or her. The Agriculture Select Committee investigated the 'salmonella in eggs' affair which had been precipitated by an answer given in a television news interview by the then junior Health minister Mrs E. Currie. The Committee wished that Mrs Currie, by then a former minister, attend them as a witness.

First Report from the Agriculture Select Committee
HC 108 of 1988–89, vol. II, pp. 182–85

Letter to Mrs Edwina Currie, MP, from the Clerk of the Committee

The Agriculture Committee is holding an inquiry into this subject, as you will know, and has asked me to invite you to give oral evidence, provisionally on Wednesday 25 January. The Committee will be taking evidence morning and afternoon that day, but has not yet taken a view when it would like you to appear. I am sure any preferences of your own could be accommodated.

I think it would be a good idea if you telephoned me after Christmas to discuss the background to this request and the lines of questioning the Committee is interested in pursuing. If you wished to submit a written memorandum, that might provide a helpful basis for questioning; but it is certainly not essential. Again, I should be happy to advise you about the content of such a memorandum.

The Committee issued the enclosed press notice this afternoon. Efforts were made to warn you in advance of its release that the invitation to give evidence would be forthcoming; but we were unable to contact you. I hope this did not cause you any inconvenience; the Committee was certainly anxious to follow the normal courtesies.

21 December 1988

Letter to the Clerk of the Committee from Mrs Edwina Currie, MP

Thank you for your letter of 21 December asking me to give evidence to the Agriculture Select Committee.

You have an impressive group of officials and others giving evidence and you will be questioning Ministers. There is nothing useful I could add to assist you in your investigation and I hope the Committee will understand that I mean no discourtesy in declining their invitation.

May I wish you the compliments of the Season.

28 December 1988

Letter to Mrs Edwina Currie, MP, from the Chairman of the Committee

The Agriculture Committee yesterday considered your letter of 28 December to the Clerk of the Committee and has asked me to write to you.

As our programme of oral evidence has only just started, it is too early to judge whether other witnesses can answer all the relevant questions. But we may come to the conclusion that the inquiry would not be complete without an examination of your own role. In that case, we shall have to ask you to reconsider your position.

More generally, there was disquiet in the Committee that a witness should decline to appear before it in this way. Committees are jealous of their right to fix their own agenda, as you know from your former exprience, and I wonder whether on reflection you would regard the precedent you were setting as a healthy one.

Perhaps you would like to reflect on this and respond in due course.

11 January 1989

Letter to the Chairman of the Committee from Mrs Edwina Currie, MP

Thank you for your letter of 11 January 1989 on behalf of your Committee.

Of course I accept that it must be for each Select Committee to determine what inquiries it wishes to undertake within its terms of reference, and to consider what evidence it needs as the basis on which to form its conclusion. It is certainly not my intention or wish to hamper the work of the Select Committee. But, as the Committee will appreciate, I am no longer a Minister in one of the relevant Departments, and I would hope that the Committee might feel that in these circumstances I could be excused from attending to give oral evidence. There are, in any case, conventions governing what can be said to Select Committees about the advice given to Ministers by officials, and I would still be bound by these conventions.

In all of these, there seems to me little that I could say to amplify the remarks I made at the time. But I hope that the Committee might, nonetheless, find it helpful to have what I do feel I can properly add by way of information about the remark I made on ITV on Saturday 3 December in which I said that 'most of the egg production in this country is now infected by salmonella'.

The first point I wish to make is that I did *not* mean and did not say, as was incorrectly reported in the Press, that most of the *eggs* in this country are infected. I intended to explain that a significant number of the egg-laying hens in many of the egg-laying flocks in the country are infected with salmonella.

The public health information, which is on the record, shows that in 1988 outbreaks of egg-related salmonellosis have occurred in many parts of England, in Wales and in Scotland, and that the number is much greater than in previous years. During 1988 there was also a substantial increase in the number of isolations of a particular type of salmonella (*s. enteritidis* PT4) both from patients, particularly those in which the infection could be traced to eggs, and from incidents in chickens (mostly in broilers), and also from the ovaries and oviducts of hens.

Much of the chicken bought in retail outlets is contaminated with salmonella, information which has been published, and in 1988 the most common type isolated was *s. enteritidis* PT4. The contents of intact hens' eggs from flocks in England and Wales and abroad have been shown to be infected with the same type of salmonella. It was data of this kind which led to public health warnings last year on 26 August, 21 November, 5 December and 14 December, and to my concern.

I hope that the Committee might feel that this deals with the points which they might wish to put to me personally and which I could properly answer. On other matters, such as the information available to the Department, the Committee might feel that they could raise these more profitably with Ministers and the Chief Medical Officer whose responsibility they still are.

25 January 1989

Letter to Mrs Edwina Currie, MP, from the Chairman of the Committee

Thank you for your letter of 25 January, which the Committee considered at its meeting this afternoon.

We thought it best to publish it this afternoon and have issued the attached press notice. Efforts were made unsuccessfully to contact you before sending it out. I hope you agree that it was better to put the letter squarely in the public domain now, rather than allow it to leak out piecemeal.

25 January 1989

Letter to the Chairman of the Committee from Mrs Edwina Currie, MP

I hope you will not mind me writing to you again, in view of Press comment and remarks made by some of the members of the Committee since I last wrote to you.

I have asked to be excused attendance at the Select Committee's current investigation as I can be of no assistance to you, not because I would withhold anything relevant, but because I have no more to tell you than you already know. The Committee has seen the research material to which I had access. My reported comments in December were based on published sources on this topic as on most of the others for which I had ministerial responsibility. I cannot convey to you any conversations which I had with officials: those must remain confidential. You are to question Ministers and no doubt they will answer you. I have nothing to add, and can be of no assistance to you.

I am quite appalled at the public speculation about any work I might write. So far I have done no more than inquire as to the rules of confidentiality and whether anyone would be willing to publish anything I might write; no contracts have been signed and no money has changed hands. No-one has bought my silence: no-one ever could. But it may be of interest to some sections of the public if I were to put down on record the work I did with others in the health of women (for example, the start of screening against breast cancer), or children (for example, my work on children in hospital, or the introduction of the triple vaccine), or preventive campaigns (for example, AIDS and drugs). I have no intention of writing any book on infection in food. The other topics appear to be of limited relevance to the Agriculture Select Committee.

Please may I be allowed to get on with the rest of my life? I am elected to care for the people of South Derbyshire and this intense interest is interfering with my ability to do that. I wish the Committee well in its endeavours and hope that it will not delay its report any further.

With very best wishes

6 February 1989

Letter to Mrs Edwina Currie, MP, from the Chairman of the Committee

Thank you for your letters of 25 January and 6 February, which the Committee considered at its meeting this afternoon.

While the letters clear up some points, they still leave questions unanswered. The Committee was of the view that you should not be excused from giving evidence; and believes it is for it, not you, to decide whether such evidence is relevant. The Committee has directed me formally to invite you to appear before it tomorrow, Wednesday 8 February 1989, and be prepared to answer questions when it has finished taking evidence from Ministers. We expect this to be about 5.00 pm.

I would be grateful if you could indicate by 2.30 pm tomorrow whether you intend to accept this invitation. If you do not do so, the Committee will have no option but to take formal steps in the House to seek to secure your attendance. I hope you will agree that it is in everyone's interest to avoid this course.

7 February 1989

Letter to the Chairman of the Committee from Mrs Edwina Currie, MP

Thank you for your further letter.

I am bound to say that I was surprised (as many colleagues will be) that your Committee should feel it is able to decide whether or not to 'excuse' me from attendance.

The rights and immunities of individual Members were established long before the rights and powers of Select Committees to compel certain witnesses.

The House was very wise not to give Departmental Select Committees the power to require individual Members to attend. This power the House reserves for itself and to exercise it would be a very serious matter for which I believe there is no precedent since 1690. In those circumstances it could well be that the House would wish to seek the advice of the Select Committee on Parliamentary Privilege before discussing any such proposition or considering any further action.

But you, Jerry, are like me a former Minister and, I hope, a friend. To spare you further embarrassment and as a personal courtesy I will come to your meeting. I repeat that there is no information I can offer the Committee over and above that which they already have.

7 February 1989

Note

It is not only MPs who may be reluctant Committee witnesses. As we have already seen, Select Committees do wish to interview officials. The Defence Select Committee, in its investigation of the Government's decision-making procedures in the Westland affair, had cause to complain about non-attendance of officials.

Fourth Report from the Defence Select Committee

HC 519 of 1985–86, paras 225–31

The attendance of named officials

225. We sought oral evidence from three officials of the Department of Trade and Industry: Mr John Michell, Under Secretary, Air Division; Mr John Mogg, Private

Secretary to the Secretary of State; and Miss Colette Bowe, Director of Information. The Permanent Secretary at the DTI, Sir Brian Hayes, informed the Clerk to the Committee that his Secretary of State, Mr Paul Channon

> ... is anxious that his Department should give all possible help to the Committee in its deliberations ... He does not however regard it as appropriate that officials you name should give evidence, and they will not therefore be accompanying me at the hearing.

226. We also sought oral evidence from Mr Bernard Ingham, Chief Press Secretary to the Prime Minister, and from Mr Charles Powell, a Private Secretary to the Prime Minister. The Secretary of the Cabinet informed the Clerk to the Committee that the No. 10 officials and the DTI officials:

> gave a full account of their role in these matters to me in the course of my recent inquiry and co-operated fully in my investigation. The Prime Minister and the Secretary of State for Trade and Industry believe that your Committee will recognise and share their view that would be neither fair nor reasonable to expect these officials to submit to a second round of detailed questioning, of the sort that would be involved in giving evidence to your Committee.
>
> With the Prime Minister's agreement, however, I am writing to you to say that, if the Committee believed that it would be helpful, I should be ready to accept an invitation to give evidence to the Committee. The basis of my evidence would of course be the comprehensive account of the matters in question which the Prime Minister gave the House of Commons on 23 and 27 January. I would hope, on the basis of my inquiry, to be able to deal as helpfully as possible with the Committee's questions, consistently with the normal conditions of confidence under which my inquiry was conducted.

227. Sir Robert Armstrong gave evidence to us on two occasions. He was not, however, prepared to name any individual official involved or to give any details of what they told him in his inquiry. As far as the actions of these officials was concerned, Sir Robert's evidence was, of course, hearsay. The evidence given by Sir Brian Hayes about the actions of the three officials in his Department was similarly hearsay; in addition, Sir Brian was under instructions from his Secretary of State not to answer on any matter covered by Sir Robert Armstrong's inquiry.

228. If a Select Committee has been given by the House the power to send for persons, papers and records, its power to secure the attendance of an individual named civil servant is unqualified. This was recognised by Sir Brian Hayes, who himself had attended a Committee as a result of such a summons in the past. Indeed, in the course of their inquiry into the handling of press and public information during the Falklands conflict our predecessor Committee required and obtained the presence of Mr Bernard Ingham before them.

229. In this context, Sir Brian Hayes drew our attention to the Memorandum of Guidance for officials giving evidence before Select Committees, This document contains instruction from the Government to its officials. It has no formal status as the Trade and Industry Committee noted in its Report on The Tin Crisis.

230. Our request to have the five officials appear before us still stands. It became clear to us during our inquiry, however, that if we were to insist on these officials appearing before us, whether in public or in private, they would be under instructions from Ministers not to answer our questions. This could have placed them in an intensely embarrassing and unfair position, particularly if we had been forced to report to the House that their refusal to answer was impeding our inquiry.

231. The explicit authority of the House would have been necessary to order or override any Ministerial instruction not to answer our questions. We considered asking for this authority, but wished to complete our inquiry, so far as was possible on the evidence before us, before reporting these circumstances to the House which we now do.

Note

In the Report which recommended the creation of the new departmental Select Committees, the position concerning the powers to send for persons and papers was considered and reforms suggested.

First Report from the Select Committee on Procedure
HC 588 of 1977–78, paras 7.5–7.9, 7.19–7.27

7.5 The power to send for persons, although generally exercisable by the House and the committees to which the power is delegated in respect of all persons presently within the jurisdiction of Parliament, is limited in certain important respects. So far as Peers are concerned the leave of the House of Lords is required and is given by that House only in so far as the Peer concerned thinks fit to attend. So far as Members of the House of Commons are concerned, their attendance before a select committee can be secured only by an Order of the House; they may be invited, but not ordered, by the committees themselves. Moreover, while the House has resolved in modern times that the refusal of a witness to answer questions put to him by a committee is a contempt, there is doubt as to whether this would apply to a Member attending voluntarily before a committee.

7.6 The power to send for papers and records is more severely limited, particularly in respect of Ministers and Government departments. The House itself can seek to obtain papers either by means of an Order, or, in the case of the Privy Council or of departments headed by a Secretary of State, by means of an Address to the Queen. However, it has been accepted, at least since the middle of the last century, that a select committee with power to send for papers and records has no power to send for papers which, if required by the House itself, would be sought by Address. Since most Government departments are now headed by a Secretary of State, the power of a committee to order the production of Government papers is in practice limited to a small number of departments including the Treasury but excluding all the principal spending departments and the Foreign and Commonwealth Office. There is no limitation on a committee's power to order the production of papers by private bodies or individuals, so long as they are relevant to its work, although attempts to do so in respect of multinational companies may be complicated by considerations of international law.

The informal use of select committee powers

7.7 In practice, the formal powers of select committees are rarely invoked. A great deal of information is obtained voluntarily from government departments and other bodies. Witnesses, including increasing numbers of civil servants, Ministers and Secretaries of State, generally attend voluntarily to give evidence before committees. As the Clerk of the House points out, 'the overwhelming majority of select committees appear to find co-operation with Government and State organisations satisfactory and seem to achieve good working relationships'.

7.8 The evidence which government departments and agencies are prepared to give, however, is limited in practice both by political considerations and by various conventions, some of which have come to be regarded as binding. There is, for instance, a long-standing practice that committees requiring evidence from a Government department usually leave it to the department to nominate their witnesses. There has also been a recent case of the Government insisting on the right to choose which Minister or Ministers should represent it before a committee. Civil Servants are presumed to attend on behalf of Ministers and under their directions, and may occasionally ask to be excused from answering questions, most often on the grounds that they involve policy matters which are the responsibility of Ministers. Moreover, the Government has expressed reluctance to provide evidence which involves, for instance, matters of national security, the affairs of private individuals or bodies, information given to them in confidence, matters which are the subject of sensitive negotiation between governments and details of future legislative proposals.

7.9 In general, select committees have preferred to use the authority derived from the House informally, rather than by invoking their formal powers, and the formal use of powers to order the attendance of witnesses and the production of papers has been very rare in modern times. The advantages of informality would seem to outweigh the disadvantages. On the credit side, committees have been able to obtain much information, particularly from the Government, which on a strict interpretation of their formal powers they would have had no unqualified right to obtain. By respecting the Government's unwillingness for certain matters to be made public, and by agreeing not to publish evidence which the Government regards as sensitive, they have frequently built up mutual trust and understanding which has paid substantial dividends in terms of their access to sensitive information and in the resulting authoritativeness and soundness of their reports and recommendations. Much the same could be said of the relations between committees and many private organisations. On the debit side, powers which have fallen into complete or partial disuse may come to be regarded as obsolete, and informal practices and conventions may come to be regarded as binding limitations. This is a particular danger if, when a committee wish to use the powers available to them, it is evident both to the committee and to the other parties involved that the opportunities for the committee to seek the support of the House for their decisions are severely limited by procedural, let alone political, obstacles. . . .

Proposed changes in the powers of select committees

7.19 We believe that the powers of committees, and the procedure for enforcing those powers, need stregthening to bring them in line with the central requirement of select committees to secure access to the information held by the Government and its agencies. Although we would expect new formal powers, and new enforcement procedures, to be used only rarely, we believe that doubts about the rights of committees to seek access to such information, either directly or through the House, could seriously undermine attempts to establish departmentally-related committees as effective agencies of the House for scrutinising departmental administration, expenditure and policies, and there is sufficient evidence to suggest that such doubts have weakened the authority of existing select committees.

7.20 The over-riding principle concerning access to government information should be that the House has power to enforce the responsibility of Ministers for the provision of information or the refusal of information. It would not, however, be appropriate for the House to seek directly or through its committees to enforce its rights to secure information from the Executive at a level below that of the ministerial head of the department concerned (normally a Cabinet Minister), since such a practice would tend to undermine rather than strengthen the accountability of Ministers to the House.

7.21 We recommend that in future select committees should be empowered by the House to order the attendance of Ministers to give evidence to them. We recognise that such orders could not be made in the case of Ministers who are Members of the House of Lords, although we have no doubt that if the House accept this recommendation Ministers in the House of Lords would recognise an obligation to conform with the spirit of the rule applied to their colleagues in the House of Commons. We do not think it necessary to extend this rule to non-Ministerial Members of the House, who are not responsible to the House for the implementation of policies approved by the House or for the expenditure of money voted by the House. On the very rare occasions when the attendance of other Members was required but resisted, the House could, as at present, be asked to order their attendance.

7.22 We further recommend that select committees should be empowered to order the production of papers and records by all Ministers, including Secretaries of State. As we have noted, the increase in modern times in the number of government departments headed by a Secretary of State has rendered almost nugatory the powers of select committees in relation to the production of government papers and records. The distinction between departments headed by Secretaries of State and those headed by other Ministers appears to have no contemporary justification. Although the enforcement of such orders against Ministers – as in the case of other committee orders – would require the authority of the House, we believe it desirable that the power of select committees to send for papers and records should be regarded as embracing all papers, from whatever source, which are required by committees in carrying out the responsibilities entrusted to them by the House.

The enforcement of select committee powers

7.23 We do not recommend any change in the principle that the enforcement of committee orders to attend or to produce papers is a matter for the House, rather than for the committees themselves. So far as private individuals or organisations are concerned, the existing contempt procedures should be adequate as a means of seeking the authority of the House for the enforcement of select committee powers, and we recommend no change in these procedures. In the case of the nationalised industries, and other public bodies whose officials are not civil servants, it is clear that contempt procedures could also be applied.

7.24 So far as Ministers and their departments are concerned, we believe that specific means should be available to select committees to seek to enforce their wishes. In theory the granting of powers to committees to order the attendance of Ministers and the production of papers by Ministers would render Ministers liable to contempt proceedings if they refused to comply. But since the argument about whether or not information should be produced would be essentially political in character we would regard recourse to contempt proceedings as inappropriate. We accordingly recommend the adoption of a procedure on the lines of that suggested to us by the Clerk of the House, which would restore to select committees, in certain specified circumstances, the right, which formerly belonged to any back-bencher, to move for an Address or an Order for a Return of papers. The procedure relates only to the production of papers, since it may be assumed that any information required in oral evidence could if necessary be provided in documentary form.

7.25 The proposed procedure, which would be available to all select committees with power to send for papers and records, would be as follows:

(i) a committee requiring the production of specific papers or records from a government department on matters falling within its terms of reference would, in the first instance, request the production of those papers and records from the departmental officials or ministers concerned; if such a request were refused, the committee would serve on the ministerial head of the department an order requiring the production of the papers within a specified period of time;

(ii) if such an order were refused, or if the papers required were not delivered within the time specified, the committee would make a Special Report to the House, informing the House of the nature of the order served on the Minister and the fact of the Minister's non-compliance; at the same time, or thereafter, the chairman of the committee concerned could table a Motion for an Address or an Order for the Return of the papers required by the committee;

(iii) if time were not provided by the Government for a debate on the committee chairman's motion by the sixth day on which the House sat after the first appearance of the motion on the Order Paper, the motion would stand as the first business at the commencement of public business on the seventh day.

7.26 We envisage that the procedure set out above would be invoked very rarely, if at all. It would stand as an ultimate weapon to be used by a committee when all attempts to persuade a department to produce the evidence required by them had failed. If in the interval before such a motion fell to be debated an acceptable understanding had not been reached between the committee and the department, the debate which ensued would be on matters of major principle of concern to Members as a whole, and possibly engaging the confidence of the House in the Government. For this reason we have not recommended any special limit upon the duration of the debate.

7.27 We would not wish our recommendations concerning enforcement to be taken to imply either that we believe that fruitful and mutually advantageous relations between select committees and the government departments and agencies with which they have to deal have broken down, or that a more formal and rigid approach should be adopted by select committees in their relations with departments. We would expect that committees would continue in certain circumstances to accept the arguments of departments and their Ministers that the provision of some information requested was undesirable and to respect the requests of departments for some evidence to be given on a confidential basis. The practice of offering facilities for 'sidelining' evidence has worked to the mutual advantage of committees and departments in the past. Our aim is not to embarrass departments and Ministers or to encourage confrontation rather than co-operation between committees and departments; nor do we believe that committees would necessarily gain the sympathy and support of the House by reliance on the exercise of formal powers. We do believe, however, that a more effective last resort should be available to committees who find their efforts to obtain the information which is necessary to their work unreasonably hampered or restricted. The duty of the Executive should be to assist the House in exercising surveillance over its work. A restatement of the powers of the investigative agencies of Parliament on the lines we have suggested should serve as a timely reminder that the House is able, if necessary, to require such assistance from the Executive and its servants.

Note

The recommended reforms were not carried out. If those powers had been available, would they have assisted the Defence Select Committee? Does reliance upon the House of Commons to enforce a Committee's powers not mean that an issue of individual ministerial responsibility becomes one of collective responsibility, that is to say confidence in the Government? If so, is it likely that back-benchers in the party of government would defy a possible three-line whip and prefer Parliament to Party?

Mrs Currie agreed to attend the Agriculture Select Committee.

First Report from the Agriculture Select Committee
HC 108 of 1988–89, vol. II, pp. 186–90

CHAIRMAN: . . . The question I had for you, which I will repeat, was: there is a feeling perhaps that at the time you made your remarks on 3 December some information was available to you, as a Minister with public health responsibilities, that you might have received in the form of a briefing or in discussion with your officials, that was perhaps not available to the general public through the medium of press announcements that your Department had made previously and so on. Is there any truth in that or would you think that was a false statement?

(Mrs Currie) I tried to set out in my letter to the Committee of 25 January [see *ante* p. 318] the background to what happened in December. I have always based everything that I have said in public as a Minister on published information. As I am sure you realise, as a former Minister, the content of any discussions that I might have had with officials, or of any papers that I might have seen other than published information, is subject to the usual convention which is that I would not discuss it now.

CHAIRMAN: We quite understand that and of course we have interviewed the appropriate officials on this matter.

MRS WINTERTON: . . . 596. So you were not specially briefed for the interview on 3 December.

(Mrs Currie) We were briefed from the summer onwards and the material on which we were briefed was either published material or subject to the rule of confidentiality.

597. Did you personally wish to qualify your remarks within the days immediately following that broadcast?

(Mrs Currie) I have set out in my letter of 25 January exactly what the background was.

598. It seems a little puzzling that the statement that you made on 3 December was somewhat qualified in the letter of 25 January. With all respect to Sir Donald Acheson, who was asked to appear on television to correct the public perception of the situation following your statement, Sir Donald does not actually have your charisma. So the message did not get over very convincingly.

(Mrs Currie) Is that a question, Chairman?

599. The question is: did you not yourself feel that it would have been better for you yourself to have cleared up any misunderstanding rather than to have left it either to your colleagues or the Chief Medical Officer?

(Mrs Currie) Sir Donald Acheson is the most distinguished public servant we have in the field for which he has been appointed. He is a man who has my complete confidence and my complete admiration, both when I was a Minister and now. I think this country is extremely fortunate to have him as its Chief Medical Officer. I am not medically qualified: I am an economist by profession. . . .

MR MORLEY: 604. After your statement on 3 December which attracted so much media interest were you advised or instructed at any time by any Ministers senior to you in the Department of Health, not to make a further statement of clarification?

(Mrs Currie) If I remember rightly, I was asked various questions and they were broadcast on the following Tuesday and I was asked questions in the House the Tuesday after that. I think that probably answers Mr Morely's question.

605. With respect, it does not quite because there was a period after the initial statement when most of the actual public fronting was Sir Donald Acheson and also Kenneth Clarke, the Secretary of State for Health. Your own statements were in a fairly low profile for a period after that until there was another statement where you made it clear you stood by what you said on 3 December. In that interim period, was any advice given to you or any instructions not to say anything to the media?

(Mrs Currie) I think I have probably answered those questions already. I must say I am fascinated at the notion that I had both charisma and a low profile at the same time. . . .

MR MACDONALD: 607. I think what Mr Morley was asking was why you did not clarify it after 3 December in the TV interview subsequently which he already referred to. Why did you not add that further clarification which has been so helpful to the Committee?

(Mrs Currie) My understanding was that I had indeed done just that.

608. No, on that TV interview on 6 December you stood by what you said on the 3 December and you did not add anything to it; you just said that you were standing by it. You must have been aware at that time of the interpretations that the media were putting upon your statement of 3 December? In your letter to us you have said that you rejected those media interpretations of your statement of 3 December. Why did you not take the opportunity of 6 December to make it clear that the media interpretation was wrong, that you had not said that most eggs were infected, that you did not intend to say that?

(Mrs Currie) What I said in my letter of 25 January was, and I quote, '. . . I did *not* mean and did not say, as was incorrectly reported in the Press, that most of the *eggs* in this country are infected'. It is a little difficult, as any Member of this House discovers, to withdraw a statement one did not make.

609. It is, on the other hand, I would have thought, fairly simple to clarify a misinterpretation or to correct a misinterpretation that has been put upon your statement. You are saying that the media put a misinterpretation upon your statement of 3 December. The media were interpreting your statement of 3 December as saying that most eggs were infected. That was a misinterpretation, according to you, of what you intended to say. Why did you not correct it then, on 6 December? Why did you not say that they had got it wrong, that they were misinterpreting your statement?

(Mrs Currie) Chairman, is this an inquiry into what I said on 6 December or an inquiry into salmonella in eggs?

MR MACDONALD: It is an inquiry into the Government's handling of the whole salmonella business. . . .

MR MARLAND: 613. Do you think that by implication, when making your statement that most of the egg production is infected with salmonella, you were indicating that in your opinion most eggs were infected with salmonella?

(Mrs Currie) My motives are as I have set out in letters to the Committee. I was at that time responsible for certain aspects of public health in this part of the country. That was what I was interested in. As I indicated to you in my letter of 25 January, we were most concerned about rising numbers of cases of infection which had been traced to certain foods. We were sufficiently concerned to have issued a number of health

warnings already and there were television programmes, there were radio programmes, articles in the press, there was a number of others who were sufficiently alarmed to make public statements. There were also large numbers of research documents being published, including one which I am sure the Committee has looked at, which was in *The Lancet* the day before and which was based on some research in Wales. That was my motive, that was my background and that was what I was referring to. . . .

619. In the interests of public health, in which you have just been expressing interest, would you agree with me that by implication your first remarks were that salmonella was prevalent in a lot of eggs, after your remarks about production? Secondly, are you aware that Sir Donald Acheson, the man for whom you had much praise earlier on, was unable in an evidence session he gave us, to back up your remark about 'most eggs'.

(Mrs Currie) I did not make any such remark and I do not have to defend such a remark.

620. When he was asked whether or not he could back up your remark, whether it was specifically stated to him or not I cannot remember, at least the implication of your remark, he was not prepared to back it up.

(Mrs Currie) I do not have to comment on that. I did not make such a remark and I do not have to comment on such remark or anybody's reaction to such a remark.

621. Thirdly, during the course of our inquiries it seems that you have grossly overstated the veterinary evidence in your original remark from the evidence that we have heard in this Committee. Would you have any comment on that?

(Mrs Currie) I am sure the Committee has taken the opportunity to see the full unedited version of the interview. That perhaps would help set the background and the context and therefore make it easier for the Committee to understand. As I understand it, it is possible for a very small proportion of eggs to be infected and yet for that to be a very large number of eggs.

622. A very small proportion is very different from the impression you actually gave in your original remark.

(Mrs Currie) I cannot account for the impression that I give. I know what motivates me in my attempts to give impressions.

Notes

1. It can be seen that a witness may answer questions but not in a very helpful fashion.

2. The Osmotherly Rules was the informal name for the Memorandum of Guidance for Officials Appearing Before Select Committees which was first published in 1988. The latest version has been given a new title.

Departmental Evidence and Response to Select Committees
Cabinet Office (1994), paras 1–2, 38–43, 45–9, 52, 60–8, 71–88, 93–100

Status of the Guidance

1. This memorandum gives guidance to officials from Departments and their Agencies who may be called upon to give evidence before, or prepare memoranda for submission to, Parliamentary Select Committees. It supersedes the 'Memorandum of Guidance for Officials Appearing before Select Committee' issued in March 1988.

2. In providing guidance, the memorandum attempts to summarise a number of long-standing conventions that have developed in the relationship between Parliament, in the form of its Select Committees, and successive Governments. As a matter of practice, Parliament has generally recognised these conventions. It is important to note, however, that this memorandum is a Government document. Although Select Committees will be familiar with its contents, it has no formal Parliamentary standing or approval, nor does it claim to have. . .

SECTION 3: ROLE OF OFFICIALS GIVING EVIDENCE TO SELECT COMMITTEES

General

38. Officials who give evidence to Select Committees do so on behalf of their Ministers and under their directions.

39. This is in accordance with the principle that it is Ministers who are directly accountable to Parliament for both their own policies and for the actions of their Departments. Officials are accountable to Ministers and are subject to their instruction; but they are not directly accountable to Parliament in the same way. This does not mean, of course, that officials may not be called upon to give an account of Government policies or indeed of their own actions or recollections of particular events.

40. This Guidance Note can therefore be seen as representing standing instructions to officials appearing before Select Committees. These instructions may be supplemented by specific Ministerial instructions on specific matters.

Summoning of named officials

41. By the same principle, it is customary for ministers to decide which official or officials should represent them. Select Committees have generally accepted this position. Should a Committee invite a named official to appear, and the Minister concerned did not wish to be represented by that official, the Minister might suggest to the Committee that another official could more appropriately do so. If a Committee insisted on a particular official appearing before them, they could issue a formal order for attendance, and request the House to enforce it. In such an event the official would have to appear before the Committee but, in all circumstances, the official would remain subject to Ministerial instruction on how to answer questions and on what information to disclose. Such an impasse is, however, unprecedented.

Agency Chief Executives

42. Where a Select Committee is investigating matters which are delegated to an Agency in its Framework Document, evidence will normally be given by the Chief Executive. Like other officials, Agency Chief Executives give evidence on behalf of the Minister to whom they are accountable and are subject to that Minister's instruction.

Position of retired officials

43. Given the above, it is extremely rare, but not unprecedented, for Committees to request evidence from officials who have retired. A Committee could, again, issue a formal order for attendance if they chose. Retired officials, would however be in a difficult and anomalous position when giving evidence on Government matters since, although they would no longer be subject to direct Ministerial instruction and therefore could not be said to represent the Minister, they would still be under a duty of confidentiality in relation to official information unless formally released from it by the relevant Minister.

SECTION 4. EVIDENCE TO SELECT COMMITTEES

4A. PROVISION OF EVIDENCE BY OFFICIALS: CENTRAL PRINCIPLES

General

45. The central principle to be followed is that it is the duty of officials to be as helpful as possible to Select Committees, and that any withholding of information should be limited to reservations that are necessary in the public interest, including the interests of good government and of safeguarding national security. Departments should therefore be as forthcoming as they can (within the limits set out in Section 4B) in providing information, whether in writing or in oral evidence, relevant to a Select Committee's field of inquiry.

Accuracy of evidence

46. Officials appearing before Select Committees are responsible for ensuring that the evidence they give is accurate. They will therefore need to be fully briefed on the main facts of the matters on which they expect to be examined. This can be a major exercise as a Committee's questions can range widely and can be expected to be testing. Should it nevertheless be discovered subsequently that the evidence unwittingly contained factual errors, these should be made known to the Committee, usually via the Clerk, at the earliest opportunity. Where appropriate, a correcting footnote will appear in the published transcript of the evidence.

Discussion of Government policy

47. Officials should as far as possible confine their evidence to questions of fact and explanation relating to government policies and actions. They should be ready to explain what those policies are; the justification and objectives of those policies as the Government sees them; the extent to which those objectives have been met; and also to explain how administrative factors may have affected both the choice of policy measures and the manner of their implementation. Any comment by officials on government policies and actions should always be consistent with the principle of civil service political impartiality. Officials should as far as possible avoid being drawn into discussion of the merits of alternative policies where this is politically contentious. If official witnesses are pressed by the Committee to go beyond these limits, they should suggest that the questioning should be referred to Ministers.

48. A Select Committee may invite specialist (as opposed to administrative) officials to comment on the professional or technical issues underlying government policies or decisions. This can require careful handling where Committees wish to take evidence from, for example, government economists or statisticians on issues which bear on controversial policy questions and which are also matters of controversy within the respective profession. Such specialists may find themselves in some difficulty if their own judgement on the professional issues has, or appears to have, implications that are critical of Government policies. It is not generally open to such witnesses to describe or comment upon the advice which they have given to Departments, or would give if asked. They should not therefore go beyond explaining the reasoning which, in the Government's judgement, supports its policy. The status of such evidence should, if necessary, be made clear to the Committee. If pressed for a professional judgement on the question the witness should, if necessary, refer to the political nature of the issue and, as above, suggest that the line of questioning be referred to Ministers.

Provision of information through memoranda

49. The Government's commitment to provide as much information as possible to Select Committees is met largely through the provision of memoranda, written replies to Committees' questions and oral evidence from Ministers and officials. It does not amount to a commitment to provide access to internal files, private correspondence, including advice given on a confidential basis or working papers. Should a Committee press to see such documents, rather than accepting written or oral evidence on the subject, Departments should consult their Ministers and Machinery of Government Division, OPSS . . .

Consulting Ministers on evidence

52. Because officials appear on behalf of their Ministers, written evidence and briefing material should be cleared with them as necessary. It may only be necessary for Ministers to be consulted if there is any doubt among officials on the detail of the policy to be explained to the Committee, or on what information should be disclosed. However, as Ministers are ultimately accountable for deciding what information is to be given and for defending those decisions as necessary, their views should be sought if a question arises of withholding information which a Committee has asked for.. .

4B. LIMITATIONS ON THE PROVISION OF INFORMATION

General

60. Although the powers of Select Committees to send for 'persons, papers and records' relating to their field of enquiry are unqualified, there are certain long-standing conventions on the provision of information which have been observed by successive administrations on grounds of public policy.

61. A classic statement of the main categories of information which should not be disclosed was contained in a letter of 9 May 1967 from the then Lord President of the Council to the Chairmen of Select Committees (the full text is reprinted as Appendix C, Annex III to the Select Committee on Procedure's First Report, Session 1977–78 HC 588–I):—

> These limitations extend to information affecting national security, which would normally be withheld from the House in the national interest; information relating to the private affairs of individuals or individual bodies, on which any information held by Ministers or their officials has been supplied on a confidential basis; and specific cases where the Minister has or may have a quasi-judicial or appellate function, for example, in relation to planning applications and appeals. It may also, for obvious reasons, be necessary for Ministers to excuse themselves from discussing matters which are, or may become, the subject of sensitive negotiation with Governments or other bodies. Further, I think it will be generally recognised that the details of legislative proposals should first be communicated to the House as a whole and that Ministers should not, therefore, be expected to give particulars of such proposals prior to the introduction of a Bill, unless the proposals have already been published in the form of a White Paper or statement to the House.

62. These principles still stand but since 1967 there have been progressive moves towards greater openness and transparency in government business and the provision of information. In a White Paper on Open Government (Cm 2290) the present Government has underlined its commitment to three key themes:

— handling information in a way that promotes informed policy making and debate, and efficient service delivery;

— providing timely and accessible information to the citizen to explain Government policies, actions and decisions; and
— restricting access to information only when there are good reasons for doing so.

63. These themes, and the reasons why confidentiality is nonetheless sometimes necessary in the public interest, are discussed in some detail in that White Paper and enunciated in the resulting **'Code of Practice on Access to Government Information'**. Although the Code of Practice was formulated principally in the context of providing fuller information to the public, the principles of openness that it enunciates should be taken to apply also to Parliament and its Select Committees. Departments may therefore find it helpful to consult both the Code and the Guidance on Interpretation issued by OPSS in amplification of some of the points in this section.

64. Information which properly carries a **protective security marking** should not be disclosed in open evidence sessions or in memoranda submitted for publication. There are, however, procedures under which Select Committees can in certain circumstances be provided with such information on a confidential basis. These procedures are described in paragraphs 92–99 below. In cases of doubt, witnesses should consult their departmental security officer.

65. Whether or not it carries a protective marking, information in certain categories should not normally be disclosed by officials to Select Committees. These categories are described in paragraphs 66 to 87 below.

Internal discussion and advice

66. Given that the essential function of Select Committees is to call Ministers to account for the decisions and actions of Government, it has generally been accepted that the internal discussion and advice which has preceded Ministerial decisions should not be disclosed. This is necessary both to preserve the principle of the **collective responsibility of Ministers** and the principle of **confidentiality between Ministers and their advisers.**

67. Witnesses may answer questions on whether or not particular decisions were referred to and approved by Ministers but should not disclose: the internal advice given to Ministers or to other officials; the details of inter-departmental exchanges on policy issues; the specific level at which particular decisions were taken, which particular Minister or official took the decision, or the manner in which a Minister consulted colleagues.

68. The application of these general rules to the special case of an Accounting Officers' responsibilities in relation to the Committee of Public Accounts is set out in the Treasury Memorandum 'The Responsibilities of an Accounting officer' . . .

Cabinet and Cabinet Committee business

71. Papers or information relating to discussions in Cabinet or Cabinet Committees, or any briefing or correspondence relating to them, are confidential and should in no circumstances be disclosed. Although the membership and terms of reference of Ministerial Cabinet Committees are now published, the agendas of their meetings remain confidential and Departments should not disclose whether a particular subject has or has not been discussed.

Advice given by the Law officers

72. There is a long standing convention that the advice which Law Officers give to Ministers is strictly confidential, as is information on whether, and if so in what circumstances, Law Officers have given such advice. It is only when Law Officers expressly authorise the disclosure of their advice, or themselves report to or advise Parliament or a Committee, that such advice may be disclosed.

Other Legal Advice

73. Advice from Treasury Solicitor's Department, or from a Department's own legal advisers, is not generally made available. There are however precedents for disclosing the substance of such advice where this is clearly relevant to a Committee's inquiry. This should only be done, however, with the express agreement of the legal adviser concerned.

Matters Sub Judice

74. Committees are subject to the same rules by which the House regulates its conduct in relation to matters awaiting the adjudication of the courts (although the bar on debating such matters may be lifted if a Committee is meeting in closed session) . If a matter already before the courts is likely to come up for discussion before a Committee at a public session, the Clerk will usually be aware of this and will draw the attention of the Chairman to the relevant rules of the House. Nonetheless, if a Department has reason to believe that such matters may arise, the Liaison Officer may wish to check with the Clerk that the Committee is also aware. It should be noted, however, that the Committee Chairman has an overriding discretion to determine what is appropriate in the hearing of evidence.

75. Officials should take care in discussing or giving written evidence on matters which may become the subject of litigation but which, at the time, do not strictly come under the rules precluding public discussion of sub judice questions. Such caution should be exercised whether or not the Crown is likely to be a party to such litigation. If such matters seem likely to be raised, officials should first consult their departmental legal advisers or the Treasury Solicitor on how to handle questions which might arise. In any case of doubt about the extent to which details may be disclosed of criminal cases, not currently sub judice, the Law Officers are available for consultation.

76. Similar considerations apply in cases where a Minister has or may have a quasi-judicial or appellate function, for example in relation to planning applications and appeals.

International relations

77. Officials should take care not to disclose information which might impair the effectiveness of the conduct of relations with other governments or international organisations, including the European Union. This includes information which has been received in confidence from other governments, foreign courts or international organisations. The Foreign and Commonwealth Office should be consulted in any cases of doubt.

Commercial and economic information

78. Officials should not disclose sensitive information of a commercial or economic nature, for example information which could affect the financial markets, without prior consultation with the Treasury. Nor should officials disclose commercially sensitive information relating to public sector operations or, without the consent of the company concerned, to private sector operations where the information has been supplied to the Government in confidence.

Personal information

79. Witnesses should not disclose personal information about any individual or body which has been supplied to government on a confidential basis, and the disclosure of which would constitute an unwarranted invasion of their privacy.

Conduct of individual officials

80. Occasionally questions from a departmentally-related Select Committee may appear to be directed to the conduct of individual officials, not just in the sense of

establishing the facts about what occurred in making decisions or implementing Government policies, but with the implication of allocating individual criticism or blame.

81. In such circumstances, and in accordance with the principles of Ministerial accountability, it is for the Minister to look into the matter and if necessary to institute a formal inquiry. Such an inquiry into the conduct and behaviour of individual officials and consideration of disciplinary action is properly carried out within a Department according to established procedures designed and agreed for the purpose, and with appropriate safeguards for the individual. It is then the Minister's responsibility to inform the Committee of what has happened, and of what has been done to put the matter right and to prevent a recurrence. Evidence to a Select Committee on this should be given not by the official or officials concerned, but by the Minister or by a senior official designated by the Minister to give such evidence on the Minister's behalf. This would include the result of any disciplinary or other departmental proceedings against individual officials.

82. Select Committees have agreed that it is not their task to act as disciplinary tribunals. Accordingly, if in the course of an inquiry a Select Committee were to discover evidence that called into question the conduct (in this sense) of individual named officials, the Committee should be asked not to pursue their own investigation into the conduct of the person concerned, but to take up the matter with the Minister.

83. If it is foreseen that a Select Committee's line of enquiry may involve questions about the conduct of named officials, it should be suggested to the Committee that it would be appropriate for a Minister or a senior official designated by the Minister to give evidence, rather than the named officials in question. If an official giving evidence to a Committee is unexpectedly asked questions which are directed at his or her individual conduct, or at the conduct of another named official, the official should indicate that he wishes to seek instructions from Ministers, and the Committee should be asked to allow time for this.

Reports commissioned by Departments

84. In many cases, reports commissioned by Departments in order to inform policy proposals or decisions will be published or otherwise made publicly available. However, requests by Committees for reports that were not intended for publication can sometimes cause difficulty. Such reports may come from a variety of sources ranging from an internal working group to an outside committee. In deciding whether to accede to requests for a particular report the primary consideration should always be the contents of the document concerned i.e. whether it contains protectively marked information or information and advice of the kinds described elsewhere in this section which should not normally be disclosed. The fact that a report is known to have been prepared does not of itself oblige a Department to disclose its contents.

85. While Committees have generally accepted that officials' advice to Ministers may remain confidential, the position may be less clear cut when such advice has been prepared by mixed committees of officials and outside experts or by outside experts alone. Where advice or reports have been commissioned on a confidential basis, and their authors and Ministers wish them to remain confidential, requests for disclosure may be declined, as appropriate, on the grounds that the Government is entitled to seek such advice in confidence.

86. In such circumstances, Departments should consider whether they can none-the-less assist the Committee by providing the report on a confidential basis, or submitting a separate memorandum which omits the non-disclosable material in the report.

Papers of a previous Administration

87. There are well established conventions which govern the withholding of policy papers of a previous Administration from an Administration of a different political complexion. These were set out in a Parliamentary answer from the Prime Minister on 24 January 1980 (*Official Report*, Columns 305–307). Since officials appear before Select Committees as representatives of their Ministers, and since Select Committees are themselves composed on a bipartisan basis, it follows that officials should not provide a Committee with evidence from papers of a previous Administration which they are not in a position to show to their present Ministers. If such evidence is sought, Ministers should be consulted. The general rule is that policy papers of a previous Administration which have not been released or published during the period of that Administration should not be released or published by a subsequent Administration. Where ministers propose to make an exception, it would be necessary to consult a representative of the previous Administration before either showing the papers to present Ministers or, with Ministers' authority, releasing information from them to a Committee.

Excessive cost

88. It may occasionally prove necessary to decline requests for information which would involve the Department in excessive cost or diversion of effort. Ministers should always be consulted on their priorities in such cases. Requests for named officials who are serving overseas to attend to give evidence should not be refused on cost grounds alone if the official is the one best placed to represent the Minister. Committees will generally be willing to arrange for such witnesses to give evidence on a mutually acceptable date. . .

Providing sensitive information in confidence

93. It is to the benefit of Committees in carrying out their task of scrutinising Government activities, and to Government in explaining its actions and policies, for sensitive information, including that carrying a protective security marking, to be provided from time to time on the basis that it will not be published and will be treated in confidence. Procedures have been developed to accommodate this.

94. When this arises, the Department should inform the Clerk that the information in question can be made available only on this basis, explaining the reasons in general terms. Such information should not be made available until the Committee has agreed to handle it appropriately, either by treating it wholly in confidence or by agreeing to publish it with a reasonable degree of *sidelining* (i.e. with the relevant passages omitted but with the location of the omissions indicated).

Handling of sensitive information in oral evidence

95. It would clearly be inappropriate for any evidence which a Department wished to be treated as confidential to be given at a public session of the Committee. If it appears likely, therefore, that subjects to be discussed at a forthcoming public session are such that the witnesses would only be able to give substantive answers in confidence, the Department should write to the Chairman or the Clerk explaining why this is so. The Committee may then agree to take that part of the Department's evidence in closed session.

96. If, despite such an approach, a Committee questions an official witness in public session on confidential matters, or if such matters are raised unexpectedly, the official should inform the Committee that the questions could only be answered on a confidential basis. The Committee may then decide to go into closed session or request a confidential memorandum. It is not for the witness to suggest that the Committee should go into closed session as this is wholly a matter for them to decide.

97. Where confidential evidence has been given in a closed session the witness should, at the end of the session, let the Clerk know which parts of the evidence these are. Pending the Committee's final decision on what they will agree to omit from the published version, the Clerk will instruct the shorthand writer not to send for printing the transcript of these passages but will send two copies of a full transcript to the Department. One copy is for retention; the other should be returned to the Clerk with those passages sidelined which contain sensitive information which, in the Department's judgment, it would not be in the public interest to publish. one copy of the full transcript is also retained in the Committee Office for Members authorised to have access to it (paragraph 100).

98. Although Committees usually respect such requests for sidelining they may occasionally challenge a particular request. Witnesses should therefore always be sure that their requests are justified — in terms of the definitions of the protective marking system or the exemptions in the Code of Practice on Access to Government Information.

Handling of sensitive information in written evidence

99. Where information is submitted to a Committee on the understanding that it will be kept confidential, this understanding should be recorded in the covering letter forwarding the evidence to the Clerk. The letter should make clear whether the whole memorandum or, as is often the case, particular annexes are to be kept confidential.

100. An agreement was reached with the Liaison Committee in 1975 on the conditions under which classified information may be disclosed to Select Committees. This agreement still stands. The key points are as follows:

(a) Information marked TOP SECRET or SECRET will be restricted to those persons (in addition to the Clerk) to whom the Department has agreed to release it. In practice this will usually mean only the members of the Select Committee or of the Sub-Committee concerned and, in the case of a Sub-Committee, the Chairman of the main Committee in addition. The disclosure of information marked RESTRICTED or CONFIDENTIAL will be similarly limited except that, where it has been disclosed to members of Sub-Committees, it may also be made available to members of the main Committee concerned.

(b) The release of TOP SECRET information under these arrangements is subject to the personal approval of the responsible Minister in each case.

(c) Protectively marked information may also be disclosed to a Committee's Specialist Advisers provided they have security clearance in accordance with arrangements agreed with the Clerk of the House.

(d) Protectively marked memoranda (and the full transcripts of oral evidence containing classified information) will be made available to those authorised to see it only during Committee or Sub-Committee meetings and on request in the Committee Office. Members may not take protectively marked documents away with them.

Question

Is the commitment to greater openness furthered or undermined by the detail of the Code of Practice on Access to Official Information and the Departmental Evidence and Response to Select Committees?

Note

Occasionally witnesses may refuse to answer questions. The Social Security Select Committee had begun a general investigation into pension funds when the death of Mr Robert Maxwell led to disclosures about malpractice concerning the management of the Mirror Group Newspapers and the Maxwell Corporation pension funds. The Committee ordered the attendance of his sons Messrs Ian and Kevin Maxwell to question them in their capacity as trustees of the pension funds. When the Maxwells appeared before the Committee on 13 January 1992, each was accompanied by Queen's Counsel. The Maxwells declined to answer questions. The Committee reported on this matter to the House of Commons.

First Special Report of the Social Security Select Committee
HC 353 of 1991–92, paras 8–21

8. During the meeting both QCs argued that the Committee should not proceed with its questions. Mr Carman, in defending his client's right to silence, introduced the concept of a person being 'on the threshold of charges.' He also said that Mr Kevin Maxwell had been 'advised by me and by others that imminently he faces the risk of a criminal prosecution' and Mr Jarvis with reference to Mr Ian Maxwell, argued that the Committee should not proceed with its questioning. There was, they said, a very real possibility of charges being made in the near future and that a public, televised Committee session could jeopardise the prospects of a fair trial. It was further argued that Mr Ian Maxwell and Mr Kevin Maxwell had a right in common law not to incriminate themselves, a possibility that might exist if they answered the Committee's questions, and also that under the terms of the House's own *sub judice* rule, the Committee should agree to postpone the meeting. Mr Jarvis did say that Mr Ian Maxwell would be prepared to answer written questions provided that no public use was made of the answers (he later added that another condition was that the answers should not be released to the Serious Fraud Office). Mr Carman said that this was something that Mr Kevin Maxwell was also prepared to consider. The Committee then went into private session to consider the points made.

9. The Committee decided that it was reasonable for the meeting to continue and for questions to be put in public. We were quite clear that the House's *sub judice* rule was **not** brought into play by any current legal proceedings. It is also the case that there is **no** right to silence in front of a Select Committee, whatever the position in common law. [See Erskine May, 21st edition, p. 680.] We also believed that, despite the legal difficulties Mr Ian Maxwell and Mr Kevin Maxwell faced, there were questions that they could answer without there being any danger of them incriminating themselves.

10. The Committee therefore proceeded to put a total of four questions to the two Mr Maxwells. The four questions were:

(i) Did you make attempts to gain copies of those documents [which the Committee had ordered them to bring to the meeting] even though you may not be in possession of the originals?

(ii) We are looking at the pension funds as they, relate to MCC and Mirror Group Newspapers, can you tell the Committee which pension trust funds you belong to and at what period?

(iii) Who owns BIM?

(iv) What advice do you have for the Committee and therefore the Government about the policy of self-investment? Do you think a rate of 5 per cent, which is what is being talked about, is sensible or not?

They each declined to answer any of these questions. The Committee saw little point in continuing in those circumstances and therefore the meeting was brought to a close.

11. Colleagues expressed two opposing points of view to us. There was the concern that either or both of the witnesses might incriminate themselves, or that the televising of the proceedings (over which the House has decided that Select Committees have no say) would prevent a fair trial taking place should Mr Carman's prediction of Mr Kevin Maxwell being on 'the threshold of charges' prove accurate. The opposing view was that the refusal of a witness to help a Committee with its inquiry, if it went unpunished, might lead to a weakening of the whole Select Committee system.

12. The Committee kept both of these considerations in its mind when making each of its relevant decisions. But against them the Committee saw an even greater threat to the Select Committee system. To opt not to undertake an inquiry into the operation of pension funds in the wake of Robert Maxwell's plundering of the pension funds he controlled would not merely be a betrayal of those citizens who have lost or may still lose their pensions. We believe it would have struck the public as an example of politicians unwilling to grapple with difficult issues which are of major importance to them.

13. Alternatively, to have undertaken an inquiry, but to have ignored the Maxwell brothers seemed to us the equivalent of suggesting to Shakespeare that he was mistaken to have included the Prince in Hamlet. As in practically all political decisions the question of balance is crucial and it is a proper balance which we have tried to maintain in all the decisions we have made.

14. The Committee decided to send a questionnaire for written answer to all those who had been trustees of the various Maxwell pension funds since 1984, the year that Robert Maxwell bought Mirror Group Newspapers. When sending out these questionnaires, we made it clear that the answers would be made public. Recipients of the questionnaire were also asked to indicate if they would be prepared to answer supplementary oral questions at a public meeting.

15. As we have already mentioned, three people declined to answer the questionnaire. These were Mr M Stoney, Mr Ian Maxwell and Mr Kevin Maxwell. Mr Ian Maxwell's and Mr Kevin Maxwell's refusals once again came *via* their solicitors. The reasons they gave for not answering the questionnaire were the same as those that had been given at the meeting on 13 January. The Committee rejected the proposals that it should meet in private and refuse to publish its Minutes of Evidence. While Members of the Committee are confident that any commitment they gave not to disclose any of the information given at that meeting would be honoured, they would not, however, be the only parties to the agreement and therefore could not guarantee that information presented to them would not be selectively leaked.

16. When the Committee changed the terms of reference of its inquiry into ownership and control of pension funds in early December it was aware that, at the very most, it would have only six months before a General Election had to be called. As events have turned out only three months were available for the Committee to complete the initial stages of its inquiry. But from the outset the Committee has attempted to take a longer term view, both of the nature and scope of its inquiry, and of the behaviour of some witnesses. Simultaneously, the Committee has always been mindful that it needed to balance a free and uninhibited inquiry against its wish to do nothing which might be used by others to claim that its activities had prevented a fair trial. The Committee was aware of course that how this balance is struck might change over time.

17. The Committee is mindful that the primary task of the Serious Fraud Office is to collect evidence on whether the law has been broken, and if so, to press charges, rather than to trace the missing funds and to secure their return. From the outset the Committee therefore was anxious, not only to play the historic role given to the House of Commons of voicing the grievance of constituents (in this instance, the grievance naturally felt by those contributors to the pension schemes run by Mr Robert Maxwell who have been defrauded) but also to open up these events to public scrutiny.

18. It is in carrying out this side of its inquiry that the refusal of the Maxwell brothers to give evidence has been most harmful to the Committee's activities. We have not been able to gain first hand information from Mr Ian and Mr Kevin Maxwell on the structure and control operated within the Maxwell 'Empire'. Nor were we able to put questions on whether any of the missing pension funds are still held by privately owned Maxwell companies, or in private Maxwell bank accounts held in countries outside the United Kingdom jurisdiction. Similarly the Committee was not able to gain first hand evidence from the Maxwell brothers on how they saw their personal role as trustees, how they carried out their responsibilities, nor to discuss with them their qualifications on being appointed to undertake such a role. Nor was the Committee able to talk to Mr Ian and Mr Kevin Maxwell about the role of those US investment banks which were involved in the alleged illegal operation to support MCC shares by routing share purchases through off-shore trusts. There were also many other matters on which Mr Ian and Mr Kevin Maxwell could have assisted the Committee.

19. Those Members who have had a chance to read our Report on the ownership of pension funds will realise that lack of time has prevented this Committee from doing any more than make a start on its inquiries into the plundering of assets from pension funds run by Mr Robert Maxwell. While the Committee cannot bind its successor, or judge whom the House may appoint to a newly constituted Social Security Committee, all the Members of the current Committee are standing for re-election and are committed after the Election to pursuing the issues raised in that Report.

20. There is no doubt that to refuse to answer questions in front of a Select Committee is a serious matter. The House of Commons expressed its view in a resolution agreed *nem con* on the 12 August 1947 'that the refusal of a witness before a Select Committee to answer any question which may be put to him is a contempt of the House and an infraction of the undoubted right of this House to conduct any inquiry which may be necessary in the public interest'.

21. **We hope our colleagues in the House support the longer term approach to our inquiry which we have adopted. Similarly, although we believe that Mr Ian Maxwell and Mr Kevin Maxwell should be brought before the House for their refusal to answer questions properly put to them by the Select Committee, this has to be a matter for our successor Committee. In political activity the question of timing is often as important as the subject itself. We therefore hope that our colleagues in the House share our view on the long term nature of the inquiries which we began in early December. We also trust that they accept that there is a need for them to find an appropriate time to consider the question of Mr Ian Maxwell and Mr Kevin Maxwell's *prima facie* contempt of the House.**

Note

The Maxwell brothers were arrested and charged with fraud on 18 June 1992. They were tried and, in early 1996, acquitted. Further charges were brought against Kevin Maxwell.

Question

Was the Committee's investigation of these particular pension funds appropriate given the inquiries conducted by the Serious Fraud Office?

Note

An assessment of the first 10 years of the working of the select committee system was carried out by the Procedure Committee.

Second Report from the Procedure Committee
HC 19 of 1989–90, paras 353–69

353. We understand the argument of those witnesses who claimed that the performance of the departmentally-related Select Committees during their first ten years could be properly assessed only on the basis of a realistic appreciation of their original aims and potential impact. But this needs to be set in the context of what had previously existed in the form of the Expenditure Committee and its Sub-Committees, which between them carried out a great deal of useful investigative scrutiny and analysis of the work of Government Departments. **In this important sense, therefore, the changes introduced in 1979 represented not so much a total break with the past as an evolutionary development, albeit a highly significant one.**

354. The introduction of the departmentally-related system of Select Committees thus left firmly in place the constitutional principles which underpin the system of government in the United Kingdom and which lie at the heart of the relationship between the Executive and the Legislature. Lord St. John of Fawsley expressed this fact succinctly when he observed: 'It has never been . . . the function of the House of Commons to govern, but it has been to check the Executive, to seek to control the Executive, in the interests of the people as a whole.' Even this cautious approach to the role of the House and its Committees carries with it certain difficulties, because of the ambiguity surrounding the notions of 'check' and 'control' in this context. In the sense of scrutinising the activities of Government these are perfectly proper functions for Select Committees. This does not, however, imply the ability either to prevent Governments from putting their policies into effect or, other than in exceptional cases, to stop Ministers doing things which they consider necessary. That would be to introduce a concept foreign to the modern British parliamentary system. For the same reason, some of the early rhetoric about a radical shift in power away from the Executive to the House was not helpful, in that it raised wholly unrealisable expectations. It thus risked devaluing in advance the genuine achievements which the departmentally-related Select Committees can now claim.

355. Chief amongst these, we are in no doubt, has been the holding of Ministers and officials to account for their policies, actions and decisions. This, in our judgment, is carried out by the departmentally-related Committees in a far more rigorous manner than is feasible on the floor of the House, where it is all but impossible to tie down an able or reasonably well-briefed Minister in a few minutes at Question Time. Moreover, the approach adopted by the existing Committees to the questioning of witnesses is significantly more systematic and comprehensive than was the case with the old Expenditure Committee. We are struck by the almost total unanimity on this point, encompassing witnesses from the Government, the House, outside observers and the Committees themselves.

356. It is no exaggeration to say that it ought to be the first duty of Ministers in a democracy to ensure that their policies are properly and fully understood, even if they do not necessarily enjoy informed *consent*. We found especially apt in this regard the phrase used by the Leader of the House, invoking the words of Balfour: 'Democracy is government by explanation'. To this, Sir Geoffrey added his own personal coda: 'Most policies which deserve to survive are capable of being explained.' Nor is this some mere abstraction; a glance at a map of the world strongly suggests that countries whose form of government has at its centre the obligation on the part of Ministers to justify themselves in detail in a parliamentary forum tend, on the whole, to be rather more congenial places to live than those where no such requirement exists.

357. **We are convinced that all these factors are sufficient on their own to justify describing the change to a system of departmentally-related Select Committees as worthwhile and as a success.** This is not to underplay the significance of some of the other positive effects of the investigative role of Select Committees, such as the discovery and publication of information; the platform they have afforded for outside organisations and individuals to express their views; and the enrichment of public debate on various issues, both by what Sir Ian Lloyd MP referred to as the provision of an 'impartial second opinion' and through the highlighting of differences between Ministers and pressure groups (and between such groups). All these have been valuable, but essentially incidental, by-products of the improved framework which the departmentally-related Committees have provided for the sustained scrutiny of Government departments.

358. Although, as most witnesses agreed, it would be misguided for the departmentally-related Committees to seek their main achievements in the degree of *direct* influence they have exerted over policy decisions, they need not, in our view, feel unduly modest on this score. Different Committees have cited cases in which it is at least reasonable to assume that their recommendations have played some part in shaping Ministerial decisions on particular issues. At the risk of invidiousness, we would repeat the examples of the Home Affairs Committee in relation to the abolition of the 'Sus' laws (on which, according to the Leader of the House at the time, Lord St. John of Fawsley, the Committee's Report 'was a very great influence'); the Foreign Affairs Committee's Report on the future of Hong Kong; and the Treasury and Civil Service Committee's recommendations on the publication of annual departmental reports. Another example was the Report by the Trade and Industry Committee on trade with ASEAN countries, which drew attention to the great damage done to British export opportunities, particularly in Malaysia, by the restrictions newly placed on access by overseas students to Higher Education in the United Kingdom. Following the Committee's Report, the Government took effective remedial action.

359. Nevertheless, welcome as these successes undoubtedly are, Select Committees are not an alternative Government, nor Royal Commissions producing detailed blueprints for the future. It is therefore much more fruitful, as many of our witnesses rightly argued, to look to more subtle and indirect signs of the impact made by departmentally-related Committees on the course of events.

360. Several different aspects of this phenomenon were quoted in evidence. There is, for instance, the long-term 'drip-drip' effect of the persistent harrying of a Department on an issue, which eventually pays off in the form of an admission of error or a change of heart (perhaps best exemplified by the Defence Committee's work on the cost of the Trident programme). Closely related to this is the vindication by events of a Committee's conclusions which had initially been rejected by a Department (a case in point is the Energy Committee's scepticism, first expressed in 1981, about the costs and viability of the nuclear power expansion programme which had recently

been announced by the Government). Then there is the intangible impact which the mere existence of the departmentally-related Committees has had on the conduct of Departments because of the permanent possibility of an enquiry or a request for evidence. We do not wish to overstate this effect; certainly, it is very difficult to quantify. But we have little doubt that it exists, judging by the weight of the evidence, some admittedly anecdotal, from witnesses with current or previous experience in Government. Fourthly, there is the role which Select Committees' recommendations can play in the process of negotiations and discussions between Departments. The Leader of the House gave as an example from his own periods as Chancellor of the Exchequer and Foreign Secretary the issue of how the Treasury controls overseas expenditure. 'The decisive input to the resolution of that problem came from the Select Committee [on Foreign Affairs]', he declared. Finally, but not the least important, there is the nourishing effect of the work of Select Committees on the quality of exchanges in the House – a fact attested to by several witnesses drawing upon their direct experience.

361. We have examined carefully the views on the role and performance of the departmentally-related Select Committees expressed by a surprisingly small number of critical witnesses, notably Professor Jones. His evidence was certainly lively and provocative, but we must say that we found his views bizarre in the extreme. His thesis that the Committees should concentrate entirely on what he described as 'administration' conjured up an image of dedicated groups of Members devoting their efforts to the counting of candle-ends and the minute scrutiny of stationery and other such matters. In many ways this is just as outdated an approach as he himself accused Lord St. John of Fawsley of having adopted when he first justified the establishment of the new Committees by reference to the need to improve the way in which the House held the Executive to account.

362. We believe that if Professor Jones's ideas were put into operation the Committees would be emasculated and shorn of any real purpose. Indeed, they would resemble little more than Sub-Committees of the PAC. We cannot imagine that it would be very easy to find Members willing to serve on bodies with such a limited remit. The only beneficiary, as far as we can see, would be the Govermment. To deny that the departmentally-related Committees have significantly raised the level of parliamentary scrutiny over the last ten years seems to us especially perverse, and contrary to all experience. As for the suggestion that the Committees have shown a centralizing tendency in their recommendations, we are at a loss to know what Professor Jones means. The example he provided in a supplementary memorandum did not, we fear, enlighten us.

363. It is not possible to set a single standard of effectiveness by which to judge all the departmentally-related Select Committees. The differences between the Departments they shadow and the varying approaches they themselves have employed in carrying out their remits make that an impractical objective. No-one claimed in their evidence either that the record was uniformly good or that it matched in every respect the original hopes and expectations. Some Committees have been consistently more effective than others; some have fluctuated in their level of performance over the past decade; similarly, some Reports might be seen as having been unduly political in a partisan sense, whilst others have, on occasion, tended to appear hypercritical. There have also been isolated cases, one quite recent, in which Committees have made strong personal attacks on Ministers for their actions without having afforded them an opportunity to present their case. We have identified specific areas in which improvement could be sought – in the examination of expenditure and on the question of overlap and duplication with the NAO and PAC, for instance. We have also dealt at

some length with the problems experienced by the Defence Committee in its relationship with the Ministry of Defence. Nevertheless, making due allowance for all these factors, **we believe we are justified in concluding that the system as a whole has proved itself a valuable and cost-effective addition to the House's ability to perform its proper function of holding Ministers to account.**

364. The reference to cost-effectiveness is deliberate. We think it right to point out that in the financial year 1988–89, total general Government expenditure was £178·2 billion and the number of staff employed by central Government in 1989 (excluding nationalized industries) was 2·3 million. By contrast, the cost of the departmentally-related Select Committee system in 1988–89 was just under £3·5 million and the total number of staff serving or supporting Select Committees and their Sub-Committees was 95. These figures should be borne in mind when assessing the worth of Select Committees, as should the evidence from Table I of the stable trend in the real costs of the departmentally-related Select Committee system during the last decade. **In our judgement, even allowing for some modest scope for further economies, most objective observers will feel that the House and the taxpayer have had a bargain.**

365. We are under no illusion that our conclusions will be popular in all quarters and especially with those who misguidedly harboured exaggerated expectations about a radical shift in power from the Government to Parliament. We may also be accused of having orchestrated a complacent chorus of approval for the departmentally-related Select Committees. **Nothing could be further from the truth**. We began with an open mind and allowed the sheer weight of the evidence to speak for itself. It happens to be the case that, with the exception of Professor Jones and three Members of the House, witnesses keen to take a basically critical or sceptical line were conspicuous by their absence.

366. We find it particularly noteworthy in this context that of the five Members who originally voted against the establishment of departmentally-related Committees in 1979 and who replied to our invitation to give evidence, three have since changed their mind and another has substantially modified his views – to the point of joining one of the Committees. We also observe with interest that the former Permanent Under Secretary at the Treasury, Sir Douglas Wass, having originally viewed the establishment of departmentally-related Select Committees 'with concern', now believes that they have had 'a number of . . . beneficial effects on policy-making'.

367. There is a theory, advanced by some, that if the Committees had really been effective, the reaction from the Government would have been more hostile and less supportive. **We do not have any time for this argument**. Rather than engage in wearisome debate about whether the Government's attitude is genuine or motivated by a cynical desire to flatter a system it privately derides as ineffectual, we prefer to take its evidence at face value. That evidence is, in any case, not free of criticism of the way in which the departmentally-related Committees have operated.

368 Our enquiry has not been, and was not intended to be, an academic exercise examining every aspect of the Select Committee system in minute detail. Rather, this Report represents our broad *political* judgement as to the adequacy and effectiveness of one crucial element in the range of tools available to assist Members of the House of Commons to carry out their principal collective task of holding Ministers and officials to account.

369. We have so far in this Report looked *back* at the way in which the departmentally-related Select Committees have operated over the last ten years. But another revealing test of their effectiveness is to imagine the consequences if they suddenly ceased to exist at some point in the future. Certain questions immediately

arise from this hypothesis. Would Ministers' and officials' lives be less comfortable? Would the House and the wider public be better informed? Would the actions of Departments be under closer scrutiny? Would Ministers and officials be more likely to give a greater emphasis to the quality of their arguments in favour of particular policies? Would the public interest be better served? These questions, and the obvious replies to them, collectively suggest another. Would any Government in the foreseeable future be prepared to abolish the system of departmentally-related Select Committees? **The fact that this last question virtually answers itself is in many ways the most eloquent testimony to the solid, unspectacular but undeniable achievements of the first decade of the new Committees.**

Questions

1. Given that the Committees' role is limited, what changes might be made which could increase their influence?

2. Is it a good idea that the Whips of the political parties play a part in choosing the members of the Committees?

3. When former ministers become Committee Chairmen, is it a case that they are gamekeepers who become poachers or vice versa?

(iii) The floor of the House of Commons

The passage of legislation, which is considered *post* at p. 368, is the activity which takes up the largest amount of time for business in the House of Commons. In the 1992–3, 1993–94 and 1994–95 sessions it accounted for 45%, 43% and 35% of time in the Commons. In the following table we can see how the rest of the time was spent.

Public Information Office, House of Commons Sessional Information Digest 1992–93, 1993–94, 1994–95, pp. 1–2

Analysis of the time of the session	**1992–93**	**1993–94**	**1994–95**
Types of Business	**Total time spent (hours:minutes)**		
1. Addresses, other than Prayers (including debate on Queen's Speech)	38:27	38:19	38:57
4. Private Business	15:20	8:06	14:49
5. Government motions			
a) European Community Documents	13:57	20:17	13:25
b) Business motions	4:36	6:28	0:00
c) General	97:18	34:50	43:44
6. Opposition motions			
a) Opposition Days	123:20	120:14	125:46
b) Opposition Motions in Government Time (No Confidence Motions)	00:00	00:00	00:00

Analysis of the time of the session Types of Business	1992–93 Total time spent (hours:minutes)	1993–94	1994–95
7. Private Members' Motions			
a) Substantive motions (Ballotted, etc)	71:58	58:38	5:04
8. Adjournment			
a) Government debates on motions for the Adjournment	163:05	79:21	140:59
b) Debates on motions for Recess adjournments (SO No. 22)	18:27	9:33	3:00
c) Last day before Recesses	27:33	20:29	14:04
d) After proceedings on Consolidated Fund Bills (SO No. 54)	49:04	27:49	8:52
e) Emergency debates (SO No. 20)	3:14	00:00	00:00
f) Daily (at end of business)	115:53	78:50	82:23
g) Wednesday morning adjournment	00:00	00:00	110:22
9. Estimates	15:57	9:51	17:15
14. a) Oral Questions	166:30	106:52	120:24
b) Private Notice Questions	11:12	3:08	4:45
c) Statements	77:41	38:27	40:11
d) Business statements	25:31	16:28	18:36
e) SO No. 20 Applications	1:03	0:07	0:17
f) Points of Order and Speaker's Rulings	23:36	9:56	11:28
g) Privilege	00:00	6:19	2:05
h) Presentation of Public Petitions	03:34	1:42	3:18
i) Miscellaneous	28:39	9:15	8:59
Daily Prayers	20:00	12:50	13:15

Notes

1. The General Election in April 1992 meant that the 1992–93 session was longer than average.

2. SO No. 20 refers to Standing Order No. 20 which is a procedure under which there is an adjournment of the House in order to discuss an urgent and important matter. It is considered *post* at p. 358.

(1) Debate

J. A. G. Griffith & M. Ryle, *Parliament: Functions, Practice and Procedures* (1989), p. 203

. . . The process of debate, as established by basic procedures . . . is the main process used for most of the House's business – but not all; it is not used in Questions or

Ministerial statements, or in select committee proceedings, for example. The process is essentially simple: a motion is made ('That this House approves . . .'); a question is proposed by the Chair in the same form; debate arises; the question is put; it is agreed to or negatived; if agreed a resolution (expressing an opinion) or an order (requiring action by the House, or a committee or individual Members or officers) results. There are all sorts of variations or modern qualifications of this basic process; amendments may be moved on which a question is again proposed and each amendment must be disposed of separately, before the main question (as amended if it has been) is put; there may be amendments to amendments; some motions may not, by standing order, be amended or others may not be debated; debate on motions or amendments may be adjourned; debate may be closured; and motions or amendments may be withdrawn. But the essentials are plain; only one motion is considered at a time and in the end all motions (and amendments) must either be agreed to, negatived, or withdrawn.

The logic of this procedure is binary. Decisions are taken in sequence, singly, and each decision on each motion and each amendment is a simple 'yes' or 'no.' With a few exceptions (for example, in the House, 100 Members must vote in the majority for a closure to be effective, and 20 or more Members can block a motion to refer a statutory instrument to a standing committee) there are no qualified majorities; there is no requirement on any question for an absolute majority; and, as we will see, there are not even any procedures for registering abstentions in a division. This binary process is mirrored in – or is a reflection of – the two-sided, confrontational nature of the House's proceedings . . . The systematic logic of these procedures protects the clarity of decision taking.

P. Norton, *The Commons in Perspective* (1981), p. 119

[G]eneral debates are nevertheless not without some uses in helping to ensure a measure of scrutiny and influence, however limited. A debate prevents a Government from remaining mute. Ministers have to explain and justify the Government's position. They may want to reveal as little as possible, but the Government cannot afford to hold back too much for fear of letting the Opposition appear to have the better argument. The involvement of Opposition spokesman and backbenchers ensures that any perceived cracks in the Government's position will be exploited. If it has failed to carry its own side privately, the Government may suffer the embarrassment of the publicly expressed dissent of some of its own supporters, dissent which provides good copy for the press. On some occasions, Ministers may even be influenced by comments made in debate. They will not necessarily approach an issue with closed minds, and will normally not wish to be totally unreceptive to the comments of the Opposition (whose co-operation they need for the efficient despatch of business) or of their own Members (whose support they need in the lobbies, and among whom morale needs to be maintained); a Minister who creates a good impression by listening attentively to views expressed by Members may enhance his own prospects of advancement. The likelihood of a Minister's being influenced may be greatest when he is at the despatch box. Though the House may be nearly empty for much of a debate, it fills up during the front-bench speeches, and this is when the atmosphere of the House becomes important. A Minister faced by a baying Opposition and silence behind him may be unnerved and realise that he is not carrying Members on either side with him, and in consequence may moderate or even, in extreme cases, reverse his position. On such an occasion, the debate-vote relationship may become important, the fear of defeat concentrating the minds of Ministers. A recent example of such a debate was that on Members' pay in 1979, when the Leader of the House, Norman St John-Stevas, received such a rough reception at the despatch box that the Cabinet realised it did not have the support of the House and changed its previous decision.

In addition, debates may act as useful channels for the expression of views held by the general interests and specific bodies represented by Members. If a Member with a known constituency interest in a certain subject rises to speak, he will invariably be listened to with greater respect than one who seeks solely to score party political points, and may even have some influence on the Minister's thinking; all MPs – Ministers and backbenchers – represent constituencies, and will normally have at least a degree of empathy for a Member seeking conscientiously to defend the interests of his constituents.

Note

Debates may be on motions proposed by the Government, the Opposition and the various committees of the House. For a motion critical of the Home Secretary see *ante* p. 303. For a House of Lords debate see *ante*, p. 200. The following extracts are taken from the debate on the report of the Commons Select Committee on Standards in Public Life which was created to make proposals carrying forward the Report of the Committee on Standards in Public Life chaired by Lord Nolan. Amongst the proposals made by the Commons Select Committee were the creation of a new Select Committee on Standards and Privileges which would oversee a new Parliamentary Commissioner for Standards, consider any breaches of a code of conduct to which the House may agree, and which have been drawn to the committee's attention by the Commissioner. The tasks of the new Commissioner would include: the maintenance of the Register of Members' Interests; to provide advice confidentially to MPs and others subject to registration on matters relating to the registration of individual interests; to advise the Committee and individual MPs on the interpretation of any code of conduct, and on issues of propriety; to monitor the operation of the register and of any code; to receive and to investigate complaints concerning the registration of the declaration of interest, and other aspects of the propriety of a Member's conduct.

House of Commons, HC Deb

Vol. 265, cols 640–4, 651–2, 6 November 1995

SIR EDWARD HEATH (Old Bexley and Sidcup): I declare all my interests as entered in the Register of Members' Interests. None of them has any connection with parliamentary affairs.

Madam Speaker was kind enough to call me in our earlier debate on these issues and I was hesitant about taking part today. However, there are one or two matters that I should like to mention. First, with the greatest respect to my right hon. Friend the Leader of the House, the whole of this affair has been appallingly handled and today has been an excellent example of that. We are squashed into a three-hour debate on an important, controversial and complicated subject. There has been little discussion of the other major issues in my right hon. Friend's speech and in his report simply because there is not enough time.

It has not been possible to interrupt some hon. Members because they can immediately say, quite rightly, 'I have only 10 minutes.' This is no way to conduct the business of the House of Commons. I do not blame the Leader of the House, because he is under tremendous pressure, above all from Opposition Front Benchers who have been screaming the whole time for rapid decisions because they want a decision on the revelation of Members' incomes.

I adhere to all the points that I made in my earlier speech and, in particular, to what I said about the appointment of a commissioner. I do not think that the House altogether recognises the problems that will face him. Any political agitator in the country will be able to write to him making allegations about Members' conduct in the ecenomic sphere, and the commissioner will be bound to investigate them. In the course of that, all the allegations will become public.

Mrs. ANN TAYLOR: No.

SIR EDWARD HEATH: Of course they can become public. The hon. Lady cannot simply think that when the commissioner starts investigating, the chap who put the allegations will not give it to the press. It will all come out and be published. If the allegations are irresponsible, there is no reason why they should be thrown to the public, and that is the problem that the commissioner will face. *[Interruption.]* The hon. Gentleman likes to indulge in justifiable allegations. We have had infinite examples of that, but perhaps he will desist for a moment.

I say to the Liberal Democrat spokesman, the hon. Member for Caithness and Sutherland (Mr. Maclennan), that the proposed bands if incomes are reviewed are absolute nonsense. What justification could there be for that? Are we to say that if an hon. Member is only mildly dishonest we should do so and so but that if he is tremendously dishonourable we should take certain other actions? The hon. Gentleman is also wrong to say that if an hon. Member had only his parliamentary income to live on and is offered £1,000 or £2,000 that is important to him. If he is a barrister earning £250,000 a year from fees, £20,000 is neither here nor there. We cannot categorise people's morality and honesty by trying to move financial barriers up and down. That is a great failure of his argument.

The argument with which I agree was about the difficulties of industry, and in some cases the professions, in dealing with the Government. In this country there is an enormous gap between them, and people in industry do not know how to deal with Government Departments. I discovered that 30 years ago in the European negotiations when I found out how close businesses in the other European Union countries were to their Governments and Ministers. Business men flew to Brussels to brief them while they were carrying on negotiations. If I mentioned that I was going to Brussels, business men would ask, "What for? Where is Brussels anyway?" That is a weakness in our structure and that is why business takes a view, "These people can help us and advise us and tell us how to do things." That is why the market has grown in such a remarkable way.

I shall now deal with the question of the public having a right to know. Of course people have a right to know about our public salaries, but we have a right to privacy. Why should people have a right to know about the financial rewards for our individual private activities? That does not stand up to any examination. It has just become a cry, "They have a right to know about us." The public have a right to know about our public position and public rewards, but not about our private activities — *[Interruption.]* The argument has gone out of the window. What is the point of publishing the private income of hon. Members?

Mr. BRYAN DAVIES (Oldham, Central and Royton): We are not proposing that.

SIR EDWARD HEATH: In that case, the hon. Gentleman disagrees with the hon. Member for Dewsbury (Mrs. Taylor), who says that it has to be punished if someone is registered at the moment.

Mrs. ANN TAYLOR: I am grateful to the right hon. Gentleman for allowing me to correct the impression that he is giving. I am not saying that everything that is registered at the moment should be declared in terms of the amount earned. At the beginning of his speech, the right hon. Gentleman said that none of his outside interests was related to parliamentary activities. In that case, none of them is covered by my amendment requiring disclosure of amounts.

SIR EDWARD HEATH: The hon. Lady is on two entirely separate points. The first is about activities related to parliamentary activities, and they are registered. She went on to say that of course those that are not related must also continue to be registered. But what is the point of registering them if they are not connected with parliamentary activities? There is no relationship at all.

On activities concerned with parliamentary activities, what is the argument for publishing the private income that a Member receives? There is no argument for it — none at all. It is just that the Labour party wants and has always wanted to publicise what Conservative Members are earning because it has always had a doctrine of envy and hatred. We know it — we have been dealing with it for a long time. The Labour party cannot produce a single valid argument for publishing those incomes connected with parliamentary activities.

Whatever Nolan may have said, he justified this House as being a very honourable House, and so it is. No justification exists for getting into the complicated arrangements that are set out here. That is why I have continually objected to these things and to the way in which they have been handled here. There has not been proper time to examine them. The Leader of the House will agree that his Select Committee has not had proper time. It has had to sit all through the summer recess. That is no way to handle the business.

This House has always been known as an honourable House and Members have been known as honourable Members. That is the way that we should behave in future and the matter should not be tied down with the machinations of Labour Members. If we want to know their real purpose, one has only to consider their handout which is released last weekend, entitled "News From Labour". What does it say? They are going to wite to 125 Members — I have not received a letter — and say, "You must tell us what your income is."

Mr. ANDREW MACKINLAY (Thurrock): Read it.

SIR EDWARD HEATH: I am not going to take up time reading out the handout — Labour Members have got copies anyhow. It says, "Unless you tell us what your income is, we shall come time and time and time again, demanding that you reveal what you are being paid."

Mr. BRYAN DAVIES: Will the right hon. Gentleman give way?

SIR EDWARD HEATH: No.

That means that the next election will be fought by Labour party agitators going to meetings and interrupting the whole time with only one question, "What is your income?" They want to fight an election not on policies but on envy, greed and dislike for the people in politics. . .

Dr. TONY WRIGHT (Cannock and Burntwood): The most devasting paragraph in the Nolan report is paragraph 58, which deals with the failure of the House over the years to put itself into some sort of order. It says that, if the House had only done that, had attended to reports such as the Strauss report and to recommendations such as those of the Salmon commission in 1976 and had dealt with the need to have an effective Register of Members' Interests and bring it up to date, it would not have brought the present situation on itself. At the end of paragraph 58 — this is the one sentence that I want to quote because it is a consummate understatement of the position in which the House finds itself — the Nolan report says:

> The overall picture is not one of an institution whose Members have been quick to recognise or respond to public concern.

That surely is the root of all that we are talking about today.

I welcome the advocacy ban because it is an attempt finally to get to grips with things that the House thought it had established almost half a century ago, in 1947. It turned out that it had not. The House failed to respond, which is why we are at this point today.

The ban as described in the motions is not effective enough without the amendment because it leaves open all the ways in which, informally, hon. Members can still make respresentations on the part of interests for which they are paid. That cannot be right. That gap must be closed to make the ban effective, but it is nevertheless important.

There are two principles in all this. One of them is prohibition. The House should say clearly, without any room for doubt, that it is not acceptable for a Member of Parliament to do certain things such as taking money from outside organisations to promote causes in this place. That is what the advocacy ban will do.

The second principle is that of transparency. People must be able to see what is going on here, how we conduct ourselves and what we are doing. The right hon. Member for Shropshire, North (Mr. Biffen) caught the essential mood of the moment when he said, "We have to take into account not what we say about these things but what people outside are saying." If hon. Members cannot recognise the country's mood now, they do not really understand what people are trying to say to them. People want to see that we are able to clean up our act. If we seem unable to do so, they will reach conclusions that will take us into ever more desperate circumstances.

I do not believe that some of the distinctions that the Select Committee on Standards in Public Life has tried to make are ultimately tenable, as the distinction between multi-client and single-client organisations was untenable: it fell away once it had begun to be scratched. The distinction between Parliament-related activities is not effective and it will begin to disintegrate when the Parliamentary Commissioner for Standards begins to consider it, which is why I tabled an amendment that I suppose stands as "the income tax return" amendment. It is not that — it does not require that — but that is what it stands as.

People want to know the answer to certain questions. First, they want to know whether Members of Parliament have other jobs and, secondly, if so, what those other jobs are for. Thirdly, they want to know how much they get paid for those other jobs and, fourthly, how much time do they devote to them. No doubt our constituents and the people of this country are awfully naive about these things, but those are precisely the questions that they are asking of us. They happen to think that they elect us to be Members of Parliament and to represent them, and that it is a job in itself. If that is not true, now is the moment for the House to tell the people of this country that it is not true.

I notice that, over the weekend, the Chancellor of the Duchy of Lancaster stumbled into that matter when he said that being a Member of Parliament was a part-time occupation. I congratulate him on the direct way in which he approaches the issue, but, if that is the House's answer to those questions, let it answer openly and not in terms of arguments about spurious distinctions that do not stand up.

Having said that, I have been prevailed upon and persuaded that Conservative Members would not understand if I were to press what is called "the income tax return" amendment — Amendment (n). They say that they are confused about all this and that their confusions will be increased if the amendment is allowed to stand. From the interventions that were made earlier, it was clear that Conservative Members were mightily confused about what was proposed. In the interests of enlightenment and the reduction of confusion, I am prepared to withdraw the amendment.

On any view, we are at a moment when the House and Parliament must take a view on whether they want to start the process of fundamental reform, of which this is only a part — indeed, it is only the beginning and, in some ways, the least significant part — or watch themselves decline ever further in public esteem.

The right hon. Member for Old Bexley and Sidcup (Sir E. Heath) said that people effectively had no right to know certain things. People do have a right to have confidence in their public institutions and, above all, in Parliament. At the moment, Parliament is getting dangerously close to eroding that confidence. What it decides today will decide whether it starts to restore it. . .

MR. DAVID WILSHIRE (Spelthorne): Even though I have no interests covered by the resolutions, I decided to become actively involved in the matter because I am fed up with being called a sleazebag. Every time that all Tory Members of Paliament are attacked, I am included, and quite frankly, it hurts. I have absolutely no doubt, however, that the overwhelming majority of Members of Parliament, whatever their political party, are decent, honourable and hard-working people. However, the public no longer think that that is true. They have reached that conclusion because of the well-publicised activities of a few hon. Members. Tonight, we have the chance to put that behind us. If it hurts us to do that, I am afraid that we have only ourselves to blame.

Because time is short, I want to confine my remarks to one issue — the disclosure of relevant outside earnings. I have come to the conclusion that we simply must disclose them. I admit that, in an ideal world, I would disagree with that and would not want to disclose such information; but we do not live in an ideal world, and we are not in an ideal House. In my judgment, the disclosure of relevant earnings has become the price that we must pay. If we do not pay that price tonight, the issue will come back, and next time the price will be higher. If we do not pay it then, the issue will come back yet again and the price will have gone up once again.

I understand the arguments of colleagues and hon. Friends — that privacy is important, and that the slippery slope beckons. My constituents and the contents of my mailbag tell me that the public do not buy those arguments. They do not believe that the Select Committee has gone far enough.

The recommendations of the Select Committee go further in respect of advocacy, and my constituents and everyone else I have spoken to are absolutely delighted about that. The Select Committee stopped short, however, of the Nolan recommendations on the giving of advice. The public will not understand that and will not be reassured by that.

Recent history has left us in the House with no choice other than not only to be above reproach but to have 150 per cent. proof that we are so. That is why we have to pay the price that some of us do not like.

I should like to mention two matters of detail covered by my amendments. The first relates to the question of disclosing bands, to which my amemdments (d) and (e) refer. I am against disclosing income in bands for two simple reasons. First, the Select Committee report requires us to draw up contracts in detail, and to submit them. If we go for bands, we shall have to Tippex out the amount in the agreement and then write another letter. I do not particularly want to do that.

Secondly, I hope that it has occurred to hon. Members that if we agree to bands and someone chooses to pay us £100 for giving advice, we will then be put in the band ranging from £1 to £1,000. You can bet your bottom dollar, Madam Speaker, that *The Sun* and the *Daily Mirror* will report that we have received £1,000, not £100, because we are in that band. I caution against bands, but I will not go to the stake for that principle.

My amendments (j) and (o) would make financial information declarable after the next general election. I must make it clear, however, that my amendments are not designed to put off the decision of principle until after the election. We shall take that decision of principle tonight, and we will then be left to implement everything barring making a declaration about amounts of money. I believe that that is the correct approach for two reasons.

First some hon. Members find a salary of £33,000 more than enough, and I respect them for that. Others come to the House, however, with certain commitments, and having made salaries well in excess of a hon. Member's salary. I respect them for that, too. There is absolutely nothing dishonourable about being in that position. If we expect those people to change the circumstances in which they find themselves, I judge that five months is not time enough for them to do so. I believe that they should be given until the date of the next general election.

Secondly, the declaration of that financial information should be put off until after the next election because of the antics of some on the Opposition Benches. I respect and agree with the official line of the Labour party that such available information is for the good of the House. Some Opposition Members, however, are already grubbing around for votes. Some of them are crowing merrily and saying, "Just you wait until the next general election, when we have the resolution. We will use it for party political purposes." I deplore such an attitude. By removing the temptation to acquire any such financial information before the next general election, my amendments enable the Labour party to prove that its members are not grubbing around for votes.

Tonight, the House faces a clear, straightforward and simple challenge: do we have what it takes to restore public confidence in the House of Commons? Are we prepared to swallow hard and pay a high price to redeem our reputation? Tonight, we do not have to decide whether we support the Government or the Labour party. Over the past few days, journalists have kept on asking me whether I intend to vote with the Labour party. One even asked me whether I planned to do the same as the hon. Member for Stratford-on-Avon (Mr. Howarth). The answer to that was simple — hell will freeze over before I join the Labour party.

Tonight, I am not voting for the Labour party; tonight no one will be voting for Labour — people will be voting for Parliament. I am not voting against my friends and my Government, but I am voting against sleaze, and I urge the House to do the same.

Note

Following an amendment proposed by Labour, the motion agreeing with the select committee's report was approved.

(2) Parliamentary Questions

Questions may be divided into those to be answered orally, or in writing. Written answers to Parliamentary Questions, or PQs, will be dealt with *post,* at p. 365.

In its report on PQs the Procedure Committee put forward the following objectives of PQs:

(a) a vehicle for individual backbenchers to raise their constituents' grievances;
(b) an opportunity for the House of Commons to probe the detailed actions of the Executive;
(c) a means of illuminating differences of policy on major issues between the various political parties or of judging the Parliamentary skills of individual MPs on both sides of the House;
(d) a combination of these or any other purposes, for example a way of enbabling the Government to disseminate information about particular policy decisions; and
(e) the obtaining of information by the House from the Government and its subsequent publication (HC 178 of 1990–91, para. 26).

PQs for oral answer must be tabled in advance by at least two days. In fact, to have any chance of being answered orally the PQ must be tabled on the first day for which PQs to a particular minister may be accepted. The Prime Minister answers PQs on Tuesdays and Thursdays, whereas question time for other ministers is determined by a rota.

There are quite detailed rules on the form and content of PQs. These rules have derived from the rulings of the Speaker and are collected in *Erskine May's Treatise on the Law, Privileges, Proceedings and Usage of Parliament* (21st edn, 1989). PQs which deal with matters under consideration by Royal Commissions, parliamentary committees, or which are *sub judice* are inadmissible. Ministers only answer PQs on matters for which they are responsible.

This can create a problem as ministers vary in their practice in answering questions which relate to nationalised industries and other public bodies. The rule in *Erskine May* is that PQs 'are restricted to those matters for which a Minister is made responsible by the statute concerned . . . and to those matters in which Ministers are known to be involved' (p. 290). The Committee recommended that the Table Office, which receives PQs, should give the benefit of the doubt to MPs when they want to ask a PQ about one of these public bodies which operates at 'arm's length' from the minister.

Where the Chief Executive of a Next Steps Executive Agency answers a PQ on an operational matter, the answer is now published in *Hansard* as would be the case with a ministerial answer.

The aim of most MPs tabling a PQ for an oral answer is to be able to pose a supplementary question for which no notice is necessary. Thus the tabled question may be quite general, or open, in nature. This is particularly so of PQs directed at the Prime Minister. A typical open PQ to the Prime Minister will inquire about the Prime Minister's engagements for that day. The Leader of Her Majesty's Opposition does not table PQs but is called by the Speaker to ask at least one supplementary, and possibly up to four supplementary, questions.

J. A. G. Griffith & M. Ryle, *Parliament: Functions, Practice and Procedures* (1989), pp. 354–55

One of the reasons for the increased number of Questions asked by Leaders of the Opposition has been the almost total adoption of 'open' Questions to the Prime Minister . . . These permit supplementaries on almost any subject of the questioner's choosing. The Leader of the Opposition is thus able to bring before the House and the public (Question hour is prime media time, and these occasions are often broadcast live on the radio) the issues of the day he thinks most relevant. Obviously these often include events where the Government looks as if it may be in trouble, or an area of policy where the Government appears to be doing badly. When the Leader of the Opposition in earlier years had to confine his supplementaries to matters relevant to the specific Question asked, he clearly was unable to pick his own topic in this way. Indeed on numerous occasions between 1970 and 1974, Mr Harold Wilson, as Leader of the Opposition, did not ask any Questions at all. . . .

It would be dangerous to draw too precise conclusions from a limited sample, but close observation of Prime Minister's Question time over the years suggests one or two significant developments. First, Leaders of the Opposition now make significantly more use of these opportunities than ever before. Second, the occasion has become much more heated politically (and also more noisy); this is no doubt a reflection of the widened political gap between the major parties, but Mrs Thatcher and Mr Kinnock, particularly, have used these occasions largely to make political points or advance broad arguments rather than to ask Questions on specific matters. Third, Mr Kinnock in particular has developed the technique of concentrating on one pre-determined area with a series of prepared questions sometimes extending over several days. The 'open question' has made this possible.

Whatever the causes – and personalities cannot be ignored – Prime Minister's Question time has become increasingly important politically and as a parliamentary occasion. Here is experienced the direct confrontation of the Prime Minister and the Leader of the Opposition in its most concentrated and highly-charged form. It is an opportunity no Leader of the Opposition can afford to neglect. It is also the occasion when the Prime Minister can be most critically tested, and various commentators or experienced observers have testified to how carefully the Prime Minister has to prepare for this ordeal. Success or failure on these occasions can greatly strengthen or seriously weaken the political standing of the two protagonists.

Note

In its report the Procedure Committee decided not to recommend any change in the balance between open and closed PQs to the Prime Minister (HC 178 of 1990–91, para. 38).

Political points are also made in PQs directed to other ministers, as this extract from Hansard shows on a day when it was the turn of ministers at the

Department of the Environment to answer questions. As will be seen, some of the issues underlying the PQ are points of local concern.

House of Commons, H. C. Deb.

Vol. 139, cols. 1008–9, 1013–15, 2 November 1988

Conduct of Local Authority Business

3. MR TONY BANKS: To ask the Secretary of State for the Environment what representations he has received in response to the publication of the White Paper on the conduct of local authority business.

THE MINISTER FOR LOCAL GOVERNMENT (MR JOHN SELWYN GUMMER): My right hon. Friend has received 65 letters from Members of Parliament, local authorities, councillors and interested organisations, commenting on the White Paper.

MR BANKS: Is the Minister aware that the White Paper is nothing more than a long essay on Government hypocrisy? How dare the Prime Minister go to Poland and start lecturing the Poles about freedom when she is dismantling local democracy? For how much longer are these attacks on local authorities going to continue? Is the Minister aware that no Government this century has sought to interfere in the affairs of local authorities as much as this Government? When will he start defending instead of destroying local democracy?

MR GUMMER: The greatest damage to local authorities and local democracy has been caused by Labour councils run not for the benefit of ratepayers or for those who are in need but for the benefit of the furtherance of extreme Left-wing Marxist ideas. Any hon. Member who can make that kind of comment after the revelations about Brent today should be ashamed of himself.

MR MCLOUGHLIN: Will my right hon. Friend, when looking at the responses that he has received on the conduct of local government business, bear in mind what happened on Cannock Chase district council when I was a member of it? The then chairman of the council lost his seat in the May election, but remained as chairman until the annual meeting. In between there was another meeting of the council, and he used his casting vote, despite not being a member of the council. Will my right hon. Friend consider whether that has any relevance to the conduct of local authority business?

MR GUMMER: The conduct of local authorities is best seen when people obey the rules and carry them out and do not try to make party political propaganda out of following the rules.

DR CUNNINGHAM: Before we have too many sanctimonious lectures about local government from the Tories, will the Minister comment on the conduct of the Conservative-controlled Westminster city council which sold cemeteries for 15p, which are now being advertised for sale at £5·5 million, and which is not charging for refuse collection from commercial organisations, which the district auditor has quite clearly said is unlawful? If the Minister has something to say about standards of conduct, why does he not look a little closer to home?

MR GUMMER: I am willing to condemn unlawful action from wherever it comes. I only hope that the hon. Gentleman will condemn his hon. Friend the Member for Livingston (Mr Cook), who is a Labour Front-Bench spokesman on the Health Service for refusing to pay taxes, which are lawfully levied, and encouraging other persons to do the same . . .

Water Meters

8. MR ATKINSON: To ask the Secretary of State for the Environment if he will make a further statement on the introduction of water meters in private homes.

THE PARLIAMENTARY UNDER-SECRETARY OF STATE FOR THE ENVIRONMENT (MR COLIN MOYNIHAN): It is for each water authority and company to decide whether to charge domestic customers by meter, taking into account all the circumstances. The metering trials which are to take place over the next three or four years are intended to help water undertakers take their decisions.

MR ATKINSON: Does my hon. Friend accept that large numbers of elderly people will be especially grateful to him and to his Department for seeking to end the unfair system of water charges based on rateable values instead of on usage? How much will consumers in the trial areas be expected to pay towards the cost of metering and does that represent the actual cost of installation?

MR MOYNIHAN: I am grateful for my hon. Friend's first comment. Under the Public Utility Transfers and Water Charges Act 1988 the cost of installing meters compulsorily will be paid for by the water authorities or the companies concerned, which will recover those charges from the generality of customers. The customer cannot be charged directly for the compulsory installation of a meter. As my hon. Friend knows, the costs of the current trial programme is being shared between the Government and the water authorities.

MR PIKE: Does the Minister accept that any move towards metering will involve large capital and ongoing revenue costs for the water authorities? Will that not mean that the water authorities will have to obtain increased income from consumers unless there is a massive saving of water because of the introduction of meters? Who, ultimately, will pay the costs involved with a metering system?

MR MOYNIHAN: It is clear that the customers, ultimately, will have to pay those costs. We are considering whether to include a condition in the privatised utility companies, terms of appointment so that they can recover the cost of installing meters through their water charges to customers.

MR BARRY FIELDS: Will my hon. Friend reconsider the trial meter areas and his Department's request that a certain number of meters be installed in homes? Does that not run contrary to the intention of the Home Office to reduce the number of people required to enter homes to read meters? The Isle of Wight is the largest meter trial area in the country, with more than 50,000 homes having meters installed and includes the homes of many elderly people. Will my hon. Friend reconsider that policy? Will he also commend the Southern water authority for its excellent consultation process on its trial area scheme?

MR MOYNIHAN: It is right that proper care and attention is taken over the vetting of anyone entering a home to install a meter for any utility purpose. I am happy to congratulate the Southern water authority on its excellent work in the Isle of Wight. It has been wise enough to set up a free hot line so that anyone can telephone directly if he or she is in the least bit concerned about the validity of the individual coming through the door to install a meter during the trial period.

MR BOYES: Does the Minister recall that during the passage of the Public Utility Transfers and Water Charges Act 1988, he gave an assurance that the views of those taking part in the meter trials would be fully taken into consideration during the consultative process? Will he prepare a report on the problems experienced during that consultative process? Is he aware that, in particular, the people of Normanton have been shabbily treated by the Yorkshire water authority and are highly dissatisfied?

Will he visit Normanton so that he can appreciate the deep opposition to the introduction of universal water metering?

MR MOYNIHAN: All schemes for approval have detailed proposals on the consultation process undertaken. They are considered in detail by my right hon. Friend before he gives approval for any of the schemes. I am aware of the strength of feeling in south Normanton and I have given an assurance to the hon. Member for Normanton (Mr O'Brien) that, once we have received the formal proposal, I shall go with him to a public meeting in the area to hear the views of local residents on its terms.

Sports Council

9. MR JESSEL: To ask the Secretary of State for the Environment when he next intends to meet the chairman of the Sports Council.

MR MOYNIHAN: I regularly meet the chairman of the Sports Council. The next occasion will be on 10 November.

MR JESSEL: When my hon. Friend meets the chairman, will he discuss the damage to the good will of the Sports Council because of its part funding of a horrible scheme to erect eight floodlight towers, 52 ft high and emitting 66,000 W in the heart of a residential area of Teddington? Richmond-upon-Thames council scheme is so unpopular that two public meetings voted against it, first by 132 to 17 and later by over 400 to 12. Will my hon. Friend invite the chairman of the Sports Council to consider instead an improved playing field for Teddington school, but without any floodlights?

MR MOYNIHAN: I am aware of the Teddington school scheme and my hon. Friend's detailed representations on the subject. He will understand that, on planning grounds, I have no locus to intervene, as my right hon. Friend the Secretary of State has already published his decision not to call in. However, I am aware that further local developments of significance to the sports initiative are now available, and I will undertake to ensure that the chairman of the Sports Council receives details of my hon. Friend's representations to the House and myself.

Note

The Procedure Committee did recommend that oral PQs to other ministers should be reasonably specific so that they will be admissible and the Speaker can allow a supplementary (HC 178 of 1990–91, para. 43).

(3) Private Notice Questions

These are questions which refer to points which are urgent matters of public importance, or which relate to the arrangement of business in the House. Application is made to the Speaker on the day on which the MP wishes to ask the question, and, if granted, it will be asked at the conclusion of the normal Question Time.

In the sessions 1992–93, 1993–94 and 1994–95, the numbers of private notice questions (excluding business questions) asked were 26, six and nine, respectively. Griffith and Ryle *Parliament: Functions, Practice and Procedures* (1989) note that private notice questions for the Opposition relate to controversial or political issues, whereas those asked by Government back-benchers are more likely to be of a local character (p. 375).

(4) *Adjournment Debates*

There are four types of adjournment debate, but only two will be covered here. These are the daily adjournment debate and the emergency adjournment debate.

Adjournment debates do not involve a division as they are a method by which an MP may raise a matter for a minister who has responsibility. There is a ballot for the daily adjournment debate. The emergency adjournment debate is a relatively rare event which deals with an urgent matter not otherwise covered in the current business of the House. The tables below give an indication of the incidence of, and topics discussed in, emergency adjournment debates.

J. A. G. Griffith & M. Ryle, *Parliament: Functions, Practice and Procedures* (1989), pp. 265, 352

Applications for emergency adjournment debates

Session	*Number of Applications (including multiple applications on the same matter)*	*Numbers granted*
1974–75	33	1
1975–76	58	3
1976–77	44	3
1977–78	38	2
1978–79(a)	66	3
1979–80(b)	89	2
1980–81	48	1
1981–82	61	2
1982–83(a)	50	2
1983–84(b)	84	3
1984–85	61	1
1985–86	87	1
1986–87(a)	48	2
1987–88(b)	88	1

(a) Unusually short session
(b) Unusually long session

Debates under Standing Order No. 20

Successful applications by Opposition front-bench

Date of debate	*Topic*	*Member moving*
January 27, 1981	Proposed purchase of *The Times*	John Smith
December 22, 1981	The GLC	Albert Booth
December 15, 1982	NATO Council meeting	Denis Healey
February 14, 1983	Dispute in the water industry	Gerald Kaufmann
October 26, 1983	Invasion of Grenada by USA	Denis Healey
May 24, 1984	Closures at British Leyland	Peter Shore
December 19, 1984	Local Authorities Capital Expenditure (England and Wales)	John Cunningham

January 27, 1986	Westland plc	Neil Kinnock
December 18, 1986	Airborne Early Warning System	Denzil Davies
February 3, 1987	Official Secrets Act: Activities of Special Branch	Gerald Kaufmann

Note

In sessions 1993–94 and 1994–95 there were three and five applications for emergency adjournment debates. Only one of these applications was granted. The subject of that emergency adjournment debate was the refit of the Trident submarines and the effect upon the Scottish economy.

(5) Early Day Motion

Public Information Office, House of Commons *Factsheet No. 30* (revd. edn 1994) pp. 1, 3–5, 10–11

. . . *'Early Day Motion'* [EDM] is a colloquial term for a notice of motion given by a Member for which no date has been fixed for debate, and it should be put on record from the outset that in the vast majority of cases, there is absolutely no prospect of these motions *ever* being debated. Their modern existence is due to Members wishing to put on record their opinion on a subject and often to canvass support from fellow Members. They do this by inviting, actively or passively, other Members to endorse the proposed motion. But it must be emphasised that no matter though 250 or 300 Members might do this, the prospects of the motions being debated remain much the same. . . .

Types of EDM and their purpose

It has sometimes been said that the EDM is the last test of parliamentary opinion, unalloyed by party discipline, which is left to Members. Certainly, EDMs are of several distinct groups and of none. Firstly, the opposition may put down an EDM *qua* opposition: many appear in the name of the Leader of the Opposition or of another opposition party to pray against Statutory Instruments. This is how the Opposition gives public notice that it may seek to secure a debate; and this type of EDM is to all intents and purposes about the only one ever debated.

Secondly, a group within a party might put down an EDM. This may express a view deviant to or beyond that of the party concerned, and Motions put down by Government backbenchers may seek to accelerate or otherwise change Government action. One of the smaller parties may put down a Motion to publicise its policy on a subject.

Another type frequently found is the all-party motion, which expresses a view across party divides, often on social issues: or one which, largely promoted by one party, can attract signatures from a section of another. All-party motions are on the increase, and a great deal of work may go into their compilation. In the nature of things it is generally only all-party motions which can obtain very large numbers of signatures . . .

Some EDMs are completely ephemeral in character – those offering congratulations to a particular football or rugby club are a case in point (it has been known for two parties to sign separate but virtually identical EDMs on this sort of thing) and others relate to purely local issues – for instance criticising the decision to close a post office or hospital, or personal matters (e.g. a deportation or similar case). . . .

Supporting EDMs

The Motion can be signed by additional Members on subsequent days. Commonly, Members do this by tearing out pages from their copy of the 'Blues' and signing below the chosen Motion or Motions. The pages are then handed to the Table Office, who cause the EDM (together with its six sponsors, but not others who have assented previously) to be reprinted in the next 'Blues' with the new names appended. Also, Members may often simply give the Table Office the relevant number and ask for their name to be added. A running total of the number of signatures to date is also printed.

In an average Session only about six or seven EDMs reach over 200 signatures, but perhaps 60 or 70 get over 100 signatures. Quite a number will attract only one or a couple of signatures . . .

Who may sign EDMs

Any Member may formulate or sign an EDM. There are – as cited above – historical examples of Ministers having done so, but no recent examples. The Official Opposition regularly promote them (for instance, prayers against Statutory Instruments and Motions of Censure – the Motion eventually approved by the House which led to the fall of the 1974–79 Labour Government started out as an EDM . . .). Similarly, a Motion put down by one or more of the smaller parties, will often be in the names of the party leader and principal spokesmen. In general, Ministers, and Whips do not sign EDMs and some Ministers have taken a dim view of their Parliamentary Private Secretaries' doing so. Neither the Speaker nor Deputy Speakers will sign such Motions. . . .

Amendments

A Member may put down an amendment or amendments to another Member's EDM, but he cannot submit an amendment if he or she has signed the Motion (which indicates his concurrence with the whole of the propositions therein). In order to do this he would have to withdraw his name from the main Motion.

Some amendments advance a view diametrically opposed to that offered by the main Motion and may advocate the replacement of the whole text from 'that' with an alternative proposition on the same subject, whilst others may seek additional or strengthening provisions.

Members 'sign' amendments in the same way as main Motions and the Notice Paper counts and records these in exactly the same way. Members can therefore solicit support for amendments; it is by no means unknown for an amendment to garner more support than the original Motion . . .

Appendix 3 Early Day Motions

(a) Some typical examples taken from Notice Papers of May 1985.

(i) EDM No. 515 of 1984–85.
An all party motion put down in the names of Conservative, Labour and Liberal Members. 96 signatures.

515 *CARE IN THE COMMUNITY*
Mr Nicholas Winterton
Mr Lewis Carter-Jones
Dr John G. Blackburn
Mr Richard Wainwright
Mr Lawrence Cunliffe
Mr Patrick Thompson

★ 96

Mr Keith Raffan Mr Paddy Ashdown Mr Clement Freud
Mr John Hunt

That this House, noting the widespread interest in the issue of care for the mentally ill and mentally handicapped in the community following the publication of the report of the Social Services Committee on this matter, calls for an early debate on the recommendations and implications of this report.

(ii) EDM No. 670 of 1984–85.
An all party EDM congratulating a football club.

670 *EVERTON FOOTBALL CLUB*
Dr John G. Blackburn
Mr David Knox
Mr Eric Cockeram
Mr Charles Irving
Mr Robert N. Wareing
Mr Sean Hughes

★ 10

That this House extends its congratulations to the Chairman, directors, management, staff and players of Everton Football Club on the brilliant performances which have resulted in the club winning the Football League Championship, together with the excellent conduct and behaviour of their supporters which have made them excellent ambassadors of the national game.

(iii) EDM No. 652 of 1984–85.
A party-based EDM of mainly Scottish interest put down by Conservatives, with amendments separately submitted by Liberal and Labour Members. 6 signatures on the motion, 2 and 41 respectively on the amendments.

652 *TRAFALGAR HOUSE*
Mrs Anna McCurley
Mr Albert McQuarrie
Mr Nicholas Fairbairn
Mr Bill Walker
Mr David Knox
Mr David Gilroy Bevan

★ 6

That this House congratulates Trafalgar House for setting up a new offshore construction group with a turnover of £400 million based at Scott Lithgow in Greenock which will secure the present jobs at that yard and create more employment for the service industries in Inverclyde District, and justifies the financial action of the Conservative Government when the yard was threatened with closure.

As Amendments to Mrs Anna McCurley's proposed Motion (Trafalgar House):

Mr Malcolm Bruce
Mr James Wallace

★ 2

Line 1, leave out from 'House' to end and add 'regrets the announcement by Trafalgar House of 600 redundancies at the Scott

Lithgow yard in Greenock; recalls the reservations expressed by Alliance honourable Members over the terms and conditions at the time of the Trafalgar House takeover; and deplores the complacency of those who praise Trafalgar House despite these redundancies, which shows how out of touch they are.'.

Dr Norman A. Godman
Mr John Maxton
Mr John Home Robertson
Mr David Marshall
Mr George Foulkes
Mr Jim Craigen

★ 41

Mr Ernie Roberts
Line 1, leave out from 'House' to end and add 'deplores the insensitivity and stupidity of the Scottish Tory Party for congratulating Trafalgar House in glowing terms on the very day that that company announced 600 redundancies at the Scott Lithgow yard in Greenock; and demands immediate and effective action to regenerate the Scottish economy in line with Labour's programme for jobs and industry.'.

Note
In sessions 1992–93, 1993–94 and 1994–95 2,595, 1,691 and 1,575 EDMs were tabled.

(iv) Correspondence

Much of the correspondence conducted by MPs is concerned with their role as the persons who attempt to remedy the grievances of their constitutents.

R. Rawlings 'Parliamentary Redress of Grievance' in C. Harlow (ed.), *Public Law and Politics* (1986), p. 120

Parliamentary Redress and Central Departments: the Grievance Chain

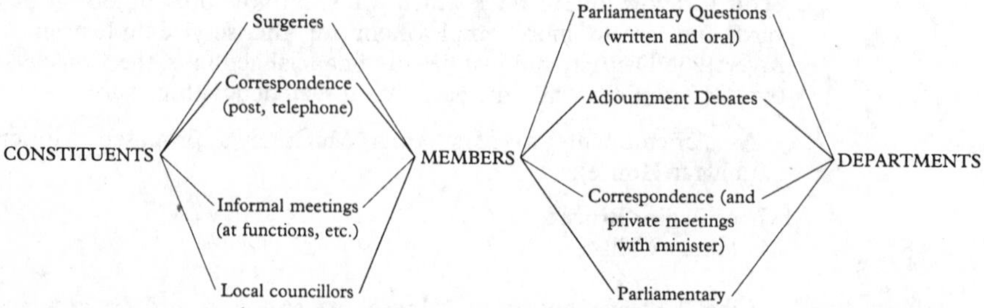

Note

Rawlings (at pp. 128–29) points out that MPs as intermediaries can act in different ways in chasing grievances on behalf of constituents. They may act as *gatekeepers,* which means that they filter out some kinds of complaint; or they may be *letterboxes,* simply passing on complaints; or they may perform the role of *advocate,* actively taking up the complaint and using whatever means they wish in order to have it resolved in the constituent's favour. An MP can, of course, act in all of these roles, depending upon expertise in the matter, availability of time, sympathy for the complainant, and party political/electoral considerations.

Some studies have attempted to gauge the amount of letters which MPs write to public authorities, including ministers, on their constituents' behalf. Ridley's conservative estimate was that public authorities receive more than half a million letters from MPs annually (F. Ridley (1984) 37 *Parliamentary Affairs* 24). Norton projected that between 156,000 and 830,000 were written to ministers by MPs each year (P. Norton (1982) 35 *Parliamentary Affairs* 60).

A. Page, 'MPs and the Redress of Grievances' [1985] *Public Law* 1, at pp. 6–9

That MPs through their intervention do succeed in getting decisions changed there is no doubt. The impression, however, is that this is a relatively infrequent outcome: '... most letters do not result in a changed decision or new course of action being pursued.' Moreover, even where a decision is changed, it is by no means clear that the same result could not have been achieved without the intervention of the MP. Indeed, the

> strict tradition is that the Member's letter does not call forth a different decision from that which would be given to any other analogous case, unless very rarely it induces a Minister to initiate a change in policy.

The only advantage of an MP's intervention which can be pointed to is that because MPs' letters are normally considered at a higher level within departments, the chances of an inappropriate routine response being made to a case are reduced.

Comment

If it is the case that MPs' intervention normally makes little difference, then it would seem legitimate to ask whether the emphasis which is placed on MPs' role in the redress of grievances is altogether justified or indeed in the best interests of their constituents. Their status in relation to many of the agencies which are the subject of complaint is uncertain, how well or badly they perform their role can normally be only guessed at, and they suffer from all of the disadvantages of being 'unspecialised, ill-equipped, amateurish and over-worked.'

In reply, a number of arguments can be put forward. Undoubtedly the strongest is that, in handling the number of cases which they do, MPs are meeting a need which is not being met by anyone else. Moreover, they are doing something which is expected of them, although, as we have seen, MPs themselves have been partly responsible for generating this expectation. Their involvement in personal cases, therefore, helps MPs to keep their constituents satisfied, a concern which although understandable does create the risk of an unspoken conspiracy between MPs and Ministers to keep aggrieved individuals happy rather than genuinely to pursue their grievances, as well as themselves informed of local problems and difficulties. It has also been argued that MPs' constituency work is an important part of the legitimation not only of MPs but also Parliament in the eyes of the electorate. On the basis of these arguments, the only question which arises is whether MPs are sufficiently well-equipped in terms of secretarial and research facilities to fulfil their constituents' expectations of them. Accepting that they are not, additional assistance might conceivably increase their effectiveness in the redress of grievances.

It is at this point that one comes back to the fact that the PCA was intended to help MPs to carry out more effectively their role in the protection of the individual against government. However, MPs are supposed to regard the PCA as of only limited value and as the least effective of the available means of pursuing their constituents' grievances. This is no doubt partly attributable to the restrictions on his jurisdiction, but MPs' views are less than disinterested. Thus, a condition of the acceptance of the PCA by MPs was the insertion of the 'MP filter' to allay their fears that the PCA might come to supplant their own role in the redress of grievances, and the fact that MPs continue to oppose removal of the filter suggests that they remain extremely jealous of their own perceived primacy in the redress of grievances.

MPs' welfare role, however, is not without its costs. It represents a substantial burden for MPs themselves and for the administration. In the view of the Fulton Committee, Parliament should 'take fully into account the cumulative cost (not only in time but in the quality of the administration) that the raising of minutiae imposes . . .' Whether MPs' insistence on their primacy in the redress of grievances is in the best interests of aggrieved individuals is also questionable. Certainly in his most recent Annual Report, the PCA questions whether it always is:

> I have often employed the familiar arguments in defence of our system, chief of which is that every Member of Parliament is an ombudsman for his constituents and that the body of Members makes a natural and valuable filter for discriminating between simple and complex cases, the worthy and the unworthy. But five years' experience has led me to doubt the validity of these arguments, at any rate in opposition to some modification of our arrangements. At present the Member may, and often does, ask the Minister for the appropriate Department to let him have, in the familiar phrase, 'an answer which I can send to my constituent' about his grievance. But on receipt of that reply, the Member has neither the time, nor the resources, nor the powers to verify by examination of departmental papers or witnesses the explanations offered, which must of necessity be composed on the basis of facts and opinions advanced by those against whom the complaint is laid. When Members do send me their files, it sometimes happens that the Minister's letter of response is the starting point of an investigation which shows that there is more to the case than the letter might be thought to suggest. [HC 322, 1983–84, para. 7.]

The PCA went on to recommend that an individual who had first asked his MP to take up his case but who was dissatisfied with the ultimate response should have the right to invite the PCA to examine the progress made. Whether this recommendation will be acted upon remains to be seen. If MPs, rather than the Government, were to oppose its implementation, their motives would be open to question, for the point which emerges from this survey is not that MPs should not act on behalf of their constituents, but that what they do should be kept firmly in perspective, and inflated claims, such as 'the primary responsibility for defending the citizen against the executive rests with the Member of Parliament,' should not be allowed to stifle the development of other forms of redress. As Mitchell observed:

The problem of finding a place in the sun for the backbench MP is essentially different from the problem of finding effective means of redress for the individual who has suffered injustice.

Note

See chapter 10 on Ombudsmen, *post,* at p. 639.

Questions

1. Is there competition between the Ombudsman and MPs in remedying citizens' grievances? Should they not work together? See Rawlings at pp. 137–41 for a proposal which seeks to use the casework of MPs as a means of external oversight, and therefore adding to the House of Commons function of scrutiny and influence.

2. Is writing a letter to a minister more effective than asking a PQ or seeking an adjournment debate, or does a MP have resort to these parliamentary procedures if a letter does not satisfactorily resolve the situation?

Parliamentary Questions for Written Answer

Public Information Office, House of Commons Sessional Information Digest 1992–93, 1993–94, 1994–95, p. 2

PARLIAMENTARY QUESTIONS

Statistics of Parliamentary Questions are available in two forms. The figures for each, which for various reasons (mainly owing to methods of counting and recording) are not exactly comparable, are as follows:

Questions appearing on the Order Paper calculated by the Journal Office

	1992–93	1993–94	1994–95
Appearing on the Order Paper for Oral Answer	7,134	4,559	4,903
Put down for priority Written Answer	23,923	14,911	20,113
Put down for non-priority Written Answer	32,627	26,140	24,881
Total	63,684	45,610	49,897

(Not more than about half of all questions put down for Oral Answer will receive such an answer – the rest are answered in writing).

Questions appearing in *Hansard* are indexed in the Parliamentary On-line Information System (POLIS)

Oral replies (including supplementaries)*	8,152	5,536	5,859
Written replies†	55,992	41,496	42,570
Total	64,144	47,027	48,429

*Number of tabled questions answered (excluding supplementaries) was 2,377 in 1990–91, 1,154 in 1991-92 and 3,143 in 1992–93.

†With POLIS, several written questions from the same Member, if answered together by the Minister may have been treated as one question.

Note

The General Election in April 1992 meant that the 1992–93 session was longer than average.

Questions for written answer are used mainly to seek information and are usually more specific than the 'open' PQ for oral answer.

House of Commons, H. C. Deb.

Vol. 139, Written Answers, cols. 557–60, 1 November 1988

WALES

Hospital Services (Privatisation)

MR DOBSON: To ask the Secretary of State for Wales if he will give the latest figures, as a percentage of services put out to tender by each district health authority, for *(a)* catering, *(b)* domestic services and *(c)* laundry; and if he will give the estimated annual savings.

MR GRIST: The information is as follows:

DHA	*Percentage by value of service for which tenders invited Per cent.*	[1]*Estimated annual savings* £
Clwyd		Not analogous with
Domestic	0·5	previous costs
Catering	Nil	Nil
Laundry	Nil	Nil
East Dyfed		
Domestic	61	107,100
Catering	52	Nil
Laundry	100	46,500
Gwent		
Domestic	37	133,600
Catering	Nil	Nil
Laundry	Nil	Nil
Gwynedd		
Domestic	88	365,000
Catering	100	Not yet known
Laundry	100	Not yet known
Mid Glamorgan		
Domestic	75	355,200
Catering	80	244,400
Laundry	100	151,500
Pembrokeshire		
Domestic	100	247,200
Catering	100	112,200
Laundry	100	10,000
Powys		
Domestic	100	68,000
Catering	100	175,000
Laundry	100	Nil

DHA	*Percentage by value of service for which tenders invited*	[1]*Estimated annual savings*
	Per cent.	*£*
South Glamorgan		
Domestic	100	Not yet known
Catering	100	Not yet known
Laundry	100	20,000
West Glamorgan		
Domestic	82	227,000
Catering	84	166,200
Laundry	100	199,600
WHCSA		
Domestic	100	18,000

[1]These figures do not include anticipated savings from contracts not yet let.

Welsh Water Authority

MR BARRY JONES: To ask the Secretary of State for Wales (1) how much land in acres is owned by the Welsh water authority in England and Wales;

(2) what types of land, urban, rural and mountain, are in Welsh water authority ownership in Wales and England;

(3) what estimate he has of the value of land in Welsh water authority ownership;

(4) how much land is in Welsh water authority ownership *(a)* with outline planning permission, *(b)* with planning permission or *(c)* currently submitted to local authorities for planning permission.

MR GRIST: These are matters for the Welsh Water Authority. I have asked the chairman to write to the hon. Gentleman.

TRANSPORT

A2 (Bexleyheath-Dartford)

MR EVENNETT: To ask the Secretary of State for Transport when he expects the carriageway restrictions on the A2 between Bexleyheath and Dartford to end; and if he will make a statement.

MR PETER BOTTOMLEY: Weather permitting, work is expected to be completed by the end of January.

MR EVENNETT: To ask the Secretary of State for Transport what representations he has received concerning delays on the A2 between Bexleyheath and Dartford.

MR PETER BOTTOMLEY: One representation has been received about delays resulting from the contract on the A2 between Bexley and Dartford.

Rail Electrification (Lichfield–Redditch)

MR HEDDLE: To ask the Secretary of State for Transport whether he has yet received British Rail's submission for the electrification of the cross-city line from Lichfield to Redditch via Birmingham New Street.

MR PORTILLO: I have not.

M1

MR GREG KNIGHT: To ask the Secretary of State for Transport whether he will reconsider the policy stated in the answer of 12 November 1987, *Official Report,* column 252, and authorise the use as an additional lane of the stretch of disused offside lane hard shoulder on the north-bound carriageway of the M1 from the junction with the M25 to its most northerly point.

MR PETER BOTTOMLEY: No. This extra lane is not long enough to be useful and safe.

MR GREG KNIGHT: To ask the Secretary of State for Transport whether, in the light of the answer of 12 November 1987 to the hon. Member for Derby, North, *Official Report,* column 252, concerning the non-construction of a stretch of additional vehicle carriageway on the north-bound side of the M1, he will explain the criteria used for deciding to construct a shorter length of carriageway on the south-bound side of the same motorway between junctions 4 and 5.

MR PETER BOTTOMLEY: The new southbound crawler lane between junctions 4 and 5 was constructed because slow-moving heavy goods vehicles on this incline were causing delays to traffic, particularly during the morning peak period.

MR GREG KNIGHT: To ask the Secretary of State for Transport what is the length of fourth lane carriageway on the south-bound side of the M1 motorway between junctions 4 and 5.

MR PETER BOTTOMLEY: The crawler lane is 1·4 km long.

MR GREG KNIGHT: To ask the Secretary of State for Transport what is the length of disused offside lane hard shoulder on the north-bound carriageway of the M1 north of the junction with the M25.

MR PETER BOTTOMLEY: Approximately 2½ miles. It has less than two miles as a continuous length.

MR GREG KNIGHT: To ask the Secretary of State for Transport how many motor vehicle accidents have been reported on the stretch of fourth lane carriageway on the south-bound side of the M1 between junctions 4 and 5 since this south lane was constructed.

MR PETER BOTTOMLEY: There have been no personal injury accidents recorded since the crawler lane was opened to traffic on 14 August 1988.

Note

Occasionally important statements by the Government are given in the form of written answer. See House of Commons Debates, Vol. 166, Written Answers, cols. 110–13, 30 January 1990 for the admission that previously the House of Commons had been misled over allegations that the Army had used 'dirty tricks' as part of the fight against terrorism in Northern Ireland.

The Procedure Committee noted the large increase in written questions since the 1960s and considered the case for rationing them. It decided not to propose this but urged (a) MPs to be sparing and selective in their designation of questions as priority, and thus to receive a quick answer; and (b) Ministers to endeavour to answer 'ordinary' written questions within a working week of their being tabled (HC 178 of 1990–91, paras 72, 75).

(C) LAW-MAKING

There are many varieties of legislation: statutes, delegated legislation, and what may be called quasi-legislation which can encompass administrative rules and guidance. Quasi-legislation can take the form, for example, of circulars from central departments, or codes of practice. The Americans refer to legislative activity carried out by administrative bodies as rule-making, and this includes what the British call delegated and quasi-legislation. It is important to realise that not all legislation will be made by Parliament. Our consideration of law-making will focus, first, on the assorted types of legislative measure and their rationale, and then on the methods for, and issues concerning, control of these legislative measures.

One of the characteristics of legislation is that it is empowering, that is it gives a public body the power to carry out tasks which the legislation also imposes upon the public body.

(i) Types of legislative measure

(1) Statute

R. Rose, 'Law as a Resource of Public Policy' (1986) 39 *Parliamentary Affairs*, pp. 297, 302–5

LAWS are a fundamental and unique resource of government. Without Acts of Parliament, force, personal preferences or momentary whim would justify the actions of government. Without laws, citizens would have no protection against arbitrary authority, no entitlements to social benefits, and no obligation to pay taxes. Without laws, civil servants would have no authority to act, or procedures to follow. Without laws, elections could not be held, for there would be no rules about who could vote, how votes should be counted, and who should be elected as MPs. In order to understand government, we must understand the uses of laws.

Until the growth of the twentieth-century welfare state, MPs viewed law as the principal resource of government. The characteristic concern of Parliament was not with public expenditure issues, but with the principles to be embodied in Acts of Parliament that involved questions of civil and political rights such as the franchise…

Once the importance of laws is recognised, the next question to address is: In what ways are laws important? The distinctive feature of law is that it is an expression of authority. It is not coercive in the sense that actions by the police may be coercive. Nor does the law consist of cash incentives to actions, as do the wages paid civil servants.

Statute laws establish parameters within which individuals and organisations may carry out their activities. Since the activities of society are heterogeneous, the parameters of laws are multiple. In order to understand the broad effect of laws, we need to understand the nature of laws as parameters; the extent of discretion that can be exercised within legal parameters; and then, whose activities have bounds set upon them by the statute book.

Parameters: more route maps than tethers. The traditional idea of laws as a set of commands and prohibitions ('Thou shalt . . .' or 'Thou shalt not . . .') presents a misleading picture of the uses of laws in the contemporary state. While there are some compelling and forbidding laws about crime, public health and safety, nine-tenths of statutes concern ways in which individuals or organisations may proceed of their own volition.

When a law sets parameters upon behaviour in society, it neither commands nor compels. Rules are promulgated which remain constant while the facts of specific circumstances vary. For example, laws governing marriage are hardly affected by characteristics of the partners of the marriage. Nor does the existence of such laws compel everyone to get married. Procedures are laid down which describe the actions that a pair of individuals should take if they want their union to be legally valid. There are few prohibitions, e.g. a minimum age, but these constrain the behaviour of a very, very small proportion of the population.

Most laws about the everyday activities of citizens are virtually unnoticed. For example, laws affecting property rights in a house; the content of foods; the conditions of driving a motor car or being a passenger on public transport; conditions of employment; or laws concerning broadcasting. This is not to say that such laws are unnecessary. Instead of involving the compulsion and prohibition of acts, most laws give guidance about ways to maintain a well ordered society.

Most contemporary laws are best conceived as a route map, laying down conditions by which one may proceed. Their relevance is contingent, taking the form of 'If . . . then' propositions. For example, 'If you want to drive a car, then you must have a driver's licence, the car must be licensed and insured, and you must drive within the traffic code'. Most laws do not tether behaviour in the sense of confining a person to act within narrowly circumscribed limits.

Scope for discretion. Both jurisprudential and sociological analyses emphasise that even the most carefully stated statute cannot control 100 per cent of behaviour. Violations of the law occur in every society. Yet violations are only a small proportion of total social activity, e.g. fraud arises in only a very small percentage of market transactions, and violent assault or murder in an infinitesimal proportion of social interactions.

The most significant limitation upon law is the existence of 'gaps' that give some latitude for discretion, i.e. choice within the parameters of the statute book. In the real world, the statute book is subject to multiple imperfections – vagueness of language, omissions, and the incapacity to anticipate every possible concatenation of events. In falling short of the perfection of an ideal-type, it is no different from administration, markets, or democracy itself. Discretion can be found in four main areas.

(a) *Judges* inevitably are faced with 'hard' cases, that is, circumstances in which lawyers dispute how the law is to be interpreted and applied to the facts of a particular case. Bell describes judges as acting as interstitial lesiglators: 'There are situations where the legal audience would recognise that there is no single clear solution to a case and that several possible solutions are at least arguable. At the same time, it must be recognised that, in presenting his decision, the judge has to justify himself within the legal materials, showing how the solution fits within existing legal prescriptions and standards. It is thus somewhat misleading to suggest that the law in such situations "runs out", as if anything at all could be used to fill the "gap".'

(b) *Executive lawmaking* occurs through the issuance of a variety of rules and regulations that can be made pursuant to Acts of Parliament; in Britain these measures can conveniently be described as Statutory Instruments. Acts of Parliament establish the parameters within which executive rule-making may be done; these are necessarily more confined than those of the Act itself. Statutory instruments typically affect procedures for putting an Act into effect, or fill out details that may be negotiated with subjects of regulation, or are likely to vary from time to time in relation to changing economic or social conditions. The limited political significance of this form of executive rulemaking is shown by the fact that less than one per cent of Statutory Instruments are deemed worthy of careful scrutiny by the parliamentary committee exercising oversight of them. The chief reason is that these regulations are likely to be agreed with affected parties in advance of their promulgation.

British membership of the European Community has created procedures authorised by Act of Parliament that enable Community laws and regulations to be put into effect by actions of the British government, without recourse to conventional procedures for a bill becoming a law. This too has led to the establishment of select committees in Parliament to monitor actions thus taken. Notwithstanding the significance of the principle, the practical political effect has been slight.

(c) *Administrative discretion* is an element in the implementation of a new Act of Parliament, and in the routine operation of many acts. The degree of discretion depends upon the extent to which laws and regulations can prescribe the parameters of action. The extent is variable: pensions officials, postal clerks and airline pilots have much less discretion than public employees who deliver services to citizens in conditions in which the services provided cannot be tightly circumscribed nor their behaviour closely monitored, for example policemen, teachers, doctors and social workers.

Lipsky argues that 'street-level' public employees are not rule-bound bureaucrats but individuals with a significant degree of discretion to decide how to treat individuals seeking their services. Just as the law sets parameters upon what officials may do, so the informal norms and routines of low-level officials may reciprocally constrain what the law can achieve. While awareness of an element of discretion is an important caution against excessive legalism, it does not justify Lipsky writing as if public policies could be carried out by ignoring or flouting the parameters of the law.

(d) *Adaptive behaviour* can be undertaken by citizens in ways that recognise the parameters of the law, but may not be what was anticipated by lawmakers. Within the parameters of any Act of Parliament citizens are free to behave in many ways. Adaptive behaviour is most familiar in tax avoidance, that is, the alteration of behaviour to lessen the legal liability to taxation. By definition, tax avoidance (e.g. working a limited number of hours a week to avoid national insurance tax, or converting income subject to a high marginal income tax rate into a capital gain subject to a lower rate) is within the law. But it is also action taken to avoid what would otherwise be undesirable consequences.

In a mixed society the role of law is not so much that of telling people what they must and must not do; it is to establish rules and regulations under which individuals and organisations can carry out their everyday affairs in ways that are orderly, predictable and recognised and accepted by all concerned. Only in a totalitarian society could the law claim to be all-powerful. A major contribution of law to public policy in a free society is that it establishes parameters within which individuals and organisations can then be free to pursue what they regard as their own wellbeing and interests. This liberal idea of the limits of laws poses problems for democratic socialists who want certain outcomes, for example, equality of educational opportunity, but do not want to use laws to prohibit private education or compel everyone to have their children educated at state schools.

Note

Legislation can be divided into public and private. Rose discussed public statutes, which are normally initiated by the government but may be introduced by MPs as a Private Member's Bill. Private legislation may confer powers or benefits on particular individuals or bodies, which may be in addition to, or in conflict with, the general law. Such measures will be promoted by the relevant individuals or bodies such as local authorities, universities or companies. A hybrid bill is one, usually initiated by the government, which is public in nature but will affect private rights. As, for example, with the Channel Tunnel, where power may be given to a minister to acquire specified land.

(2) Delegated legislation

Report of the Committee on Ministers' Powers
Cmd 4046, pp. 51–2

Necessity for Delegation

We have already expressed the view that the system of delegated legislation is both legitimate and constitutionally desirable for certain purposes, within certain limits, and under certain safeguards. We proceed to set out briefly – mostly by way of recapitulation – the reasons which have led us to this conclusion:-

(1) Pressure upon Parliamentary time is great. The more procedure and subordinate matters can be withdrawn from detailed Parliamentary discussion, the greater will be the time which Parliament can devote to the consideration of essential principles in legislation.

(2) The subject matter of modern legislation is very often of a technical nature. Apart from the broad principles involved, technical matters are difficult to include in a Bill, since they cannot be effectively discussed in Parliament. . . .

(3) If large and complex schemes of reform are to be given technical shape, it is difficult to work out the administrative machinery in time to insert in the Bill all the provisions required; it is impossible to foresee all the contingencies and local conditions for which provision must eventually be made. . . .

(4) The practice, further, is valuable because it provides for a power of constant adaptation to unknown future conditions without the necessity of amending legislation. Flexibility is essential. The method of delegated legislation permits of the rapid utilisation of experience, and enables the results of consultation with interests affected by the operation of new Acts to be translated into practice. . . .

(5) The practice, again, permits of experiment being made and thus affords an opportunity, otherwise difficult to ensure, of utilising the lessons of experience. The advantage of this in matters, for instance, like town planning, is . . . obvious. . . .

(6) In a modern State there are many occasions when there is a sudden need of legislative action. For many such needs delegated legislation is the only convenient or even possible remedy. No doubt, where there is time, on legislative issues of great magnitude, it is right that Parliament itself should either decide what the broad outlines of the legislation shall be, or at least indicate the general scope of the delegated powers which it considers are called for by the occasion.

But emergency and urgency are matters of degree; and the type of need may be of greater or less national importance. It may be not only prudent but vital for Parliament to arm the executive Government in advance with almost plenary power to meet occasions of emergency, which affect the whole nation – as in the extreme case of the Defence of the Realm Acts in the Great War, where the exigency had arisen; or in the less extreme case of the Emergency Powers Act, 1920, where the exigency had not arisen but power was conferred to meet emergencies that might arise in future. . . .

But the measure of the need should be the measure alike of the power and of its limitation. It is of the essence of constitutional Government that the normal control of Parliament should not be suspended either to a greater degree, or for a longer time, than the exigency demands. . . .

Note

Delegated legislation may take several forms – regulations, Orders in Council, rules, and orders. Parliament usually makes delegated legislation as statutory instruments, the passage of which is governed by the Statutory Instruments Act 1946. The more important pieces of delegated legislation are Orders in Council. Legislative measures which would have been passed as Acts of the Northern Ireland Parliament before it was prorogued are now passed as Orders in Council.

There is an overlap between delegated legislation and administrative rules of quasi-legislation, even though the legal form of these measures differ. The following extract suggests a classification of administrative rules based on function.

(3) Quasi-legislation

R. Baldwin & J. Houghton, 'Circular Arguments: The Status and Legitimacy of Administrative Rules' [1986] *Public Law* 239, at pp. 241–45

(1) *Procedural Rules*

Most bodies that distribute licences or money publish documents describing the procedures to be adopted. Thus, the Gaming Board and the Independent Broadcasting Authority instruct applicants for licences to follow set procedures. The Prison Rules lay down disciplinary procedures for prisoners and new police codes lay down practices to be followed in dealing with suspects and arrested persons. A principal issue is whether such rules are mandatory or directory.

(2) *Interpretative Guides*

This heading covers all official statements of departmental or agency policy, explanations of how terms or rules will be interpreted or applied, expressions of criteria to be followed, standards to be enforced or considerations to be taken into account. In Gifford's terms, this would include all 'decisional referents'' where of general applicability.

(3) *Instructions to Officials*

Although resembling interpretative guides in some respects, these instructions are principally aimed not at offering guidance to parties outside a bureaucracy but at controlling the exercise of powers within that bureaucracy. They aim not to inform citizens but to impose internal order – usually so as to facilitate planning or to encourage consistency. Strong arguments have been made for the publication of all such rules but secrecy is sustained by the desire to avoid having to justify them in public. Examples of low-visibility instructions are Prison Department Circulars, Standing Orders and Regulations and Home Office Circulars to Chief Constables.

A principal worry about secret codes is that they may conflict with published law. Thus, there was concern in 1984 when *The Observer* and the Legal Action Group exposed the operation of the Department of Health and Social Security's secret 'L' Code, a provision of which instructed legal aid assessment officers to pass on information to other officials in breach of the confidentiality provisions of section 22 of the Legal Aid Act 1974.

(4) *Prescriptive/Evidential Rules*

In some cases, regulatory bodies may want to do more than describe their policies or instruct their officials as to how to act: they may want to tell people what to do. It is of course possible to influence the behaviour of a regulated group by issuing a strong interpretative guide. ('We will only take action as provided for in the statute if conditions A, B, and C are met') or by publishing similarly formulated instructions to officials. Matters can be taken a step further, however, by prescribing courses of action on the understanding that a sanction exists at law (in primary or delegated legislation) or administratively (e.g. through non-allocation of a licence or other item of largesse). A common posture for such a 'prescriptive' rule is that of 'guide to compliance' with other legislation. Sanctions are usually indirect; thus, breach of the rule or code might not in itself lead to legal liability under a parent or associate rule.

A well-known example is the Highway Code. Breach of this is not an offence in itself but it may be taken into account in judging civil or criminal liability. Under the Health and Safety at Work Act 1974, 'approved codes of practice' may be issued by the Health and Safety Commission so as to 'provide practical guidance' in relation to the requirements of the parent Act or regulations. In the employment field, a number of codes offer 'practical guidance' but have an evidential role also. The Employment Act 1980 states that any provisions of the Secretary of State's Code of Practice on Picketing (1980) may be taken into account in proceedings before a court or tribunal. It is this code which advises that pickets should in general not exceed six at any entrance to a workplace. As has been clear from the miners' dispute of 1984, the 'guidance' offered by such a code may take a most compelling form. It may be treated by enforcement officials as if it were primary legislation.

Less contentious, perhaps, are the codes of practice on industrial relations. Power to issue these is given to the Advisory, Conciliation and Arbitration Service (ACAS), the Equal Opportunities Commission and the Commission for Racial Equality. Under the Employment Protection Act 1975, section 6, the ACAS codes again have evidential status: they are admissible in evidence and a tribunal or arbitration committee is specifically empowered to take relevant codes into account in determining issues.

Prescriptive rules may be backed up with sanctions other than the civil or criminal law such as disciplinary action. This is the case with the Codes of Practice that replace the Judges' Rules under the terms of the Police and Criminal Evidence Act. The Secretary of State issues codes on detention, treatment, questioning, identification of suspects, searches of premises, seizure and stops and searches. Failure to observe the terms of these codes may render police officers liable to disciplinary sanctions but will not give rise to criminal or civil liability or to the automatic exclusion of evidence.

(5) *Commendatory Rules*

The prescriptive model of rule involves instruction plus some variety of (often indirect) sanction. Commendation, on the other hand, has as its principal function the recommending of some course of action. Failure to adhere will not involve direct or indirect legal liability. A good example of commendations within a hierarchy of rules is provided in health and safety regulation. Primary duties are *statutory* and are set out in the Health and Safety at Work Act 1974 (see sections 2–9). These are made more specific in the Secretary of State's *regulations,* breach of which involves criminal liability and may be admissible in evidence in civil proceedings. *Codes of practice,* we have noted, offer 'practical guidance', are of evidential value and may reverse the onus of proof. *Guidance notes* constitute the lowest tier of the system. These are issued by the Health and Safety Commission and Executive: they advise on how safety objectives may be achieved, they encourage and recommend courses of action but they deal with issues beyond the area of legal sanction and lack legal force.

Commendatory rules thus do not accord with Austinian notions of threat plus sanction: they are more attuned to a facilitative role. Some rules of evidential significance might be considered commendations (e.g. the ACAS industrial relations codes) and here is the main overlap with prescriptive rules.

(6) *Voluntary Codes*

Self-regulatory codes differ from externally-imposed prescriptions in their origins and sanctions. Usually employed to stave off government regulation by upholding standards within a defined interest group, they may nevertheless carry considerable force: expulsion from the group for breach of a code may close down a business. The City Code on Takeovers and Mergers is a prime example of a voluntary code. It is issued by the Council for the Securities Industry (CSI) and offers a codification of good standards of commercial behaviour. The code has a governmental role insofar as breaches stand to be investigated by the Department of Trade.

Instances of such codes are to be found in many industries, such as advertising and housebuilding. In recent years, business self-regulation has blossomed, especially where relations with consumers are affected and deviant members of associations may be fined. Many businesses indulge in voluntary labelling, publish codes of ethics and good practice and some of these are stamped with the approval of the Office of Fair Trading. Indeed, section 124 (3) of the Fair Trading Act 1973 imposes a duty on the Director-General of Fair Trading to encourage trade associations to prepare codes of practice for guidance in promoting consumer interests and over 20 codes were approved in the period 1974–84.

The rules of domestic and professional bodies may have legal effects deriving from the law of contract, but the governmental role of many associations has led a leading text to liken such rules more to delegated legislation than to the terms of a contract.

(7) *Rules of Practice, Management or Operation*

Some rules have considerable effect without being directly normative. These are what Megarry called 'subject-and-subject' rules, 'consisting of arrangements made by administrative bodies which affect the operation of the law between one subject and another'. Thus, a new policy or enforcement practice would come under this heading.

The extra-statutory concessions made by the Commissioners for Inland Revenue are in point. Sometimes the Commissioners will act according to a stated policy, at others they will exercise discretion *ad hoc.* The courts have been uncertain in their responses. In *IRC* v *Korner* [1979] 1 All ER 679, Lord Upjohn described an unpublished concession as conducive to 'great justice between the Crown and the subject'. On the other hand, Lord Parker CJ has talked of 'the word of the Minister outweighing the law of the land' and Lord Radcliffe of 'opening the door of Parliament'. More recently in the Court of Appeal, Lawton LJ described the IRC's decision to cancel a tax advantage as 'a managerial discretion' which was reviewable only where there was an abuse of power.

(8) *Consultative Devices and Administrative Pronouncements*

There is no distinct line between legal and administrative rules or, indeed, between rules and other forms of pronouncement such as decisions. It is clear, however, that a statement may have normative effects in certain circumstances or from some perspectives and it may lack them in a different context. To adhere to rigid definitions or conceptual distinctions is therefore to fall into a trap.

Our final group is thus something of a safety-net. It covers those pronouncements which fit into none of the other groups but which have a significance that goes beyond the individual case. Principal amongst these are consultative statements. These often involve draft outlines of agency or departmental policy and invite comments. As such, they form a halfway house in the rule-making or adjudicative processes. They allow an expression of policy views without undertaking a rigid commitment.

Note

See also G. Ganz, *Quasi-Legislation: Some Recent Developments in Secondary Legislation* (1987) and R. Baldwin, *Rules and Government* (1995).

(4) Prerogative

According to Blackstone, the Royal Prerogative is 'singular and eccentrical', something which applies to rights and capacities only enjoyed by the Monarch. The *Case of Proclamations* (1611) 12 Co Rep 74 and the Bill of Rights 1689 (see *ante* p. 61) have made it clear that the prerogative cannot be used as a means to by-pass Parliament in order to change the general law of the land. Today the prerogative is restricted to the conduct of foreign affairs; the declaration of war and the disposition of the armed forces; the appointment of civil servants and ministers, Privy Councillors, judges and bishops; the conferral of peerages and honours; the dissolution of Parliament.

What is the status of the prerogative where legislation has been passed concerning an area within the scope of the prerogative?

Attorney-General v De Keyser's Royal Hotel Ltd
[1920] AC 508
House of Lords

During the First World War the Crown took possession of the respondents' hotel in order to house staff of the Royal Flying Corps. The Crown purported to do this under the authority of the Defence of the Realm Regulations. The Crown contended that compensation was not payable to the respondents because there still existed a residue of the prerogative which permitted temporary occupation of a subject's property in time of war. This residue of the prerogative was exercised under the regulations. The respondents contended that the Defence Act 1842 required that compensation should be paid.

LORD ATKINSON: . . . It is quite obvious that it would be useless and meaningless for the Legislature to impose restrictions and limitations upon, and to attach conditions to, the exercise by the Crown of the powers conferred by a statute, if the Crown were free at its pleasure to disregard these provisions, and by virtue of its prerogative do the very thing the statutes empowered it to do. One cannot in the construction of a statute attribute to the Legislature (in the absence of compelling words) an intention so absurd. It was suggested that when a statute is passed empowering the Crown to do a certain thing which it might theretofore have done by virtue of its prerogative, the prerogative is merged in the statute. I confess I do not think the word 'merged' is happily chosen. I should prefer to say that when such a statute, expressing the will and intention of the King and of the three estates of the realm, is passed, it abridges the Royal Prerogative while it is in force to this extent: that the Crown can only do the particular thing under and in accordance with the statutory provisions, and that its prerogative power to do that thing is in abeyance. Whichever mode of expression be used, the result intended to be indicated is, I think, the same – namely, that after the statute has been passed, and while it is in force, the thing it empowers the Crown to do can thenceforth only be done by and under the statute, and subject to all the limitations, restrictions and conditions by it imposed, however unrestricted the Royal Prerogative may theretofore have been.

[Lord Atkinson found that the proper construction of the regulations meant that the 1842 statute governed the occupation and that compensation under that statute was payable. Lords Dunedin, Moulton, Sumner and Parmoor delivered concurring speeches.]

Appeal dismissed.

Note

In *Studies in Constitutional Law* (1987), at p. 172, Munro argues that if a statute which overlapped with the prerogative was repealed, then the prerogative would be restored to the position it had before that statute was enacted. Thus only express statutory provision can abolish the prerogative.

(5) European Communities legislation

The legislative powers of the EC are laid down in Article 189 of the EC Treaty (see *ante* p. 115). Regulations, directives and decisions are binding, but recommendations and opinions are not. The procedural requirements specified in Article 190 (see *ante* p. 118) must be carried out otherwise the measure could be annulled under Articles 173 and 174 (see *ante* p. 111). Although Article 191 only requires publication of regulations and some directives, other directives are also published, as are many decisions.

Some legislation implementing EC measures will be passed by Parliament in the form of Orders in Council or rules and regulations. This is provided for in s. 2(2) of the European Communities Act 1972 (see *ante* p. 140).

Statutes are enacted to ratify treaty amendments, such as the SEA which was effected by the European Communities (Amendment) Act 1986).

(ii) Control

(1) Consultation

D. R. Miers and A. C. Page, *Legislation* (2nd edn, 1990), pp. 39–43

Once it has been decided that legislation is desirable, a detailed legislative proposal must be formulated. This will be undertaken within the responsible department, and the proposal will normally go through a number of drafts. Achieving a measure of coherence in government policy requires that views of other affected departments be taken into account in the preparation of proposals. For example, the Treasury must be consulted if public resources are involved, as must the Scottish, Welsh and Northern Ireland Offices if their interests are affected. Where Cabinet approval for the introduction of the measure has been obtained, consultations between the responsible department and interested departments take place on the basis of a draft memorandum. In addition, the formulation of major proposals will be supervised by the appropriate Cabinet policy committee. Where the approval of the Cabinet has not been previously obtained, it will be sought on the basis of the memorandum as revised in the light of such preliminary consultations as have taken place.

Whereas consultation within government is mandatory, consultation with outside interests takes place at the discretion of government. The extent of such consultation varies: some proposals are the subject of extensive consultation, others very little. The extent to which affected interests are consulted also varies. On major issues of party policy the government may choose not to consult affected interests (particularly those traditionally opposed to it), though even here it may do so if only to minimise disagreement. In general, however, sectional and in particular producer groups are consulted to a much greater extent than other groups. In the absence of the direct and permanent access to government enjoyed by sectional groups, cause groups' efforts are more visibly directed towards influencing the media and lobbying MPs.

How can we account for the greater likelihood of sectional group involvement in the preparation of legislation? Most commonly it is attributed to a shared pluralist conception of authority on the part of government and ouside interests. Thus, Beer attributes their greater involvement to 'the widespread acceptance of functional representation in British political culture.' Acceptance of functional representation has in turn meant that: 'It has now almost become a convention of the constitution that the interests likely to be affected by developments in public policy have, through their representative associations, a right to be consulted by policy makers,' and that governments 'are regarded as having a corresponding duty to consult before taking final decisions.' Whether these expectations as to the way in which public, including legislative, power will be examined are as widely shared today as they were 10 to 20 years ago is doubtful. But even if they are not, there remain strong incentives for government to consult. A failure to consult may make the passage of the legislation more difficult; more importantly, it may prejudice its successful implementation and thereby the attainment of the government's objectives. The brute fact is that these groups possess the capacity to 'limit, deflect and even frustrate government initiatives.' For this reason, if no other, government seeks through consultation to arrive at an understanding with them beforehand.

Commentators rightly emphasise the benefits derived from the involvement of these groups by both the groups themselves and government. For the groups, their involvement constitutes a procedural guarantee that their interests and views will be given a hearing if not reflected in the content of proposals. For government, on the other hand, the groups' expertise and advice may be crucial to the formulation of workable proposals and their acquiescence, if not active co-operation, may be equally vital to the successful implementation of proposals. These groups are thus seen as important and necessary channels of communication which parallel representation through the electoral system. Without their activity, Finer observes, party rule would be 'a rigid and ignorant tyranny,' and public administration 'a rigid and stupid bureaucracy.' Their privileged position in relation to government does, however, carry with it the danger that interests other than those immediately involved will be ignored.

The consultative process itself varies in its formality. Consultation may take place on the basis of a Green Paper published with Cabinet approval on which the views of interested parties are sought. Publication of the government's proposals in the form of a White Paper implies, instead, that the government is committed to at least the main principles of the policy outlined and the scope for consultation is correspondingly reduced. More commonly, however, consultation takes place on the basis of informal and private communications between departments and affected interests.

Consultation need not of course be confined to any single stage in the preparation of a proposal. A group's influence on a proposal cannot be determined therefore solely by reference to the extent to which it is formally consulted during its preparation. Thus it may, for example, have been the prime mover in the identification of an issue, or its views may have been canvassed and reflected in the report of a committee upon which legislation is ultimately based. Where the group has not had the opportunity of expressing its views previously, its influence will depend, in part, on the stage of the preparatory process at which it is consulted and, in particular, on whether it is consulted before the principles of the legislation have been settled.

> The most effective time for groups to operate is after a decision to legislate has been taken, but before a Bill has actually been drafted and published. Once the government has publicly committed itself to the main lines of a Bill, disagreement and opposition by interested parties can only usually be manifested by public or parliamentary campaigns, which groups are not well-fitted to undertake. Given the structure of public decision-making in Britain, in which Parliament plays a distinctly subordinate role, this line of action is usually far less likely to be successful than attempting to persuade the Minister.'

A group's influence will also depend on whether or not there is any scope for negotiation: there is a fundamental distinction between consultation involving simply an expression of views (for example, on a Green Paper or in response to specific requests) and consultation involving negotiation or actual bargaining between the parties. Whereas the views expressed in consultation of the former type may or may not be taken into account by the government, the latter implies a much greater involvement of groups in the formulation of the proposal and the effective renunciation by government of unilateral decision-making. As Hartley and Griffith point out:

> The Department will tell those whom it chooses to consult . . . what are the broad intentions of the Government, what is sought to be achieved by the Bill then being put together, and what means are proposed. On particular matters, or when asked by affected interests, the department may go into more detail, sometimes putting forward alternatives and seeking the opinion of those interested on the various merits of the alternatives. Where, as is often the case, the co-operation of the affected interests is highly desirable in order to make the Bill most effective in practice, something very like a bargain may be struck and undertakings may be given on both sides.

Note

The courts have distinguished between 'legislative' and 'administrative' activity in respect of consultation.

Bates* v *Lord Hailsham of St Marylebone
[1972] 1 WLR 1373
Chancery Division

Under s. 56 (3) of the Solicitors Act 1957, drafts of orders prescribing solicitors' remuneration in respect of non-contentious business were required to be sent to the Council of the Law Society by the Lord Chancellor. The committee which had the power to make the orders had to consider any written observations from the Council of the Law Society before making such orders.

The committee proposed an order which was sent in draft to the Law Society. The plaintiff was a member of the British Legal Association which objected to the proposed order. This body, which had some 2,900 members, wished to delay the making of the order so that there might be more consultation with the legal profession. The plaintiff sought a declaration that, if an order was made without the British Legal Association first being consulted, then this would be *ultra vires*.

MEGARRY J: . . . Mr Nicholls relied on *Reg.* v *Liverpool Corporation, Ex parte Liverpool Taxi Fleet Operators' Association* [1972] 2 QB 299; and he read me some passages from the judgments of Lord Denning MR and Roskill LJ. It cannot often happen that words uttered by a judge in his judicial capacity will, within six months, be cited against him in his personal capacity as defendant; yet that is the position here. The case was far removed from the present case. It concerned the exercise by a city council of its powers to licence hackney carriages, and a public undertaking given by the chairman of the relevant committee which the council soon proceeded to ignore. The case supports propositions relating to the duty of a body to act fairly when exercising administrative functions under a statutory power: see at pp. 307, 308 and 310. Accordingly, in deciding the policy to be applied as to the number of licences to grant, there was a duty to hear those who would be likely to be affected. It is plain that no legislation was involved: the question was one of the policy to be adopted in the exercise of a statutory power to grant licences.

In the present case, the committee in question has an entirely different function: it is legislative rather than administrative or executive. The function of the committee is to make or refuse to make a legislative instrument under delegated powers. The order, when made, will lay down the remuneration for solicitors generally; and the terms of the order will have to be considered and construed and applied in numberless cases in the future. Let me accept that in the sphere of the so-called quasi-judicial the rules of natural justice run, and that in the administrative or executive field there is a general duty of fairness. Nevertheless, these considerations do not seem to me to affect the process of legislation, whether primary or delegated. Many of those affected by delegated legislation, and affected very substantially, are never consulted in the process of enacting that legislation: and yet they have no remedy. Of course, the informal consultation of representative bodies by the legislative authority is a commonplace; but although a few statutes have specifically provided for a general process of publishing draft delegated legislation and considering objections (see, for example, the Factories Act 1961, Schedule 4), I do not know of any implied right to be consulted or make objections, or any principle upon which the courts may enjoin the legislative process at the suit of those who contend that insufficient time for consultation and consideration has been given. I accept that the fact that the order will take the form of a statutory instrument does not per se make it immune from attack, whether by injunction or otherwise; but what is important is not its form but its nature, which is plainly legislative. . . .

Order accordingly.

Note

The distinction between 'administrative' and 'legislative' is a fine one. In *R* v *Secretary of State for the Environment ex parte Brent LBC* [1982] QB 593, local authorities successfully argued that the minister was under a duty to hear their representations before exercising powers under delegated legislation to reduce their rate support grant.

In another case concerning lawyers' remuneration, representatives of the Bar argued that they had a legitimate expectation of being consulted about regulations to be made under the Legal Aid Act 1974. The point was not decided because the case was settled. See pp. 572–577 *post* on legitimate expectations.

Sometimes there is a statutory requirement to consult. Such a requirement may be derogated from, as in social security, where the minister need not consult the Social Security Advisory Committee about draft regulations if it is inexpedient to do so by reason of urgency (Social Security Administration Act 1992, s. 173(1)(a).

Where a consultation obligation is imposed in respect of legislation, what will be considered to be sufficient consultation?

R v *Secretary of State for Social Services ex parte Association of Metropolitan Authorities*

[1986] 1 WLR 1
Queen's Bench Division

Before making regulations constituting the housing benefits scheme, the minister was required, by s. 36 (1) of the Social Security and Housing Benefits Act 1982, to consult with organisations which appeared to him to be representative of the housing authorities concerned. The applicant was such an organisation whose views had been sought by the minister's officials on proposed amendments to the 1982 regulations. The consultative letter was written on 16 November 1984 and received by the applicant on 22 November. A response was requested by 30 November. The applicant complained about the shortness of time and asked for an extension so that its advisers could be consulted. On 4 December officials wrote to the applicant seeking its views on further proposed amendments. No draft of the proposals was forwarded and no mention was made of a material feature which required local authorities to investigate whether housing benefit claimants had created joint tenancies so as to gain from the housing benefit scheme. A response was requested by 12 December. The applicant answered the first letter on 7 December and sent brief comments about the second letter on 13 December. The Housing Benefits Amendment (No. 4) Order Regulations 1984 were made on 17 December and came into effect on 19 December. The applicant sought, *inter alia,* a declaration that the minister had not exercised his duty under s. 36 (1) of the Act of 1982, and an order of *certiorari* to quash the regulations because of the failure to consult.

WEBSTER J: . . . There is no general principle to be extracted from the case law as to what kind or amount of consultation is required before delegated legislation, of which consultation is a precondition, can validly be made. But in any context the essence of consultation is the communication of a genuine invitation to give advice and a genuine receipt of that advice. In my view it must go without saying that to achieve consultation sufficient information must be supplied by the consulting to the consulted party to enable it to tender helpful advice. Sufficient time must be given by the consulting to the consulted party to enable it to do that, and sufficient time must be available for such advice to be considered by the consulting party. Sufficient, in that context, does not mean ample, but at least enough to enable the relevant purpose to be fulfilled. By helpful advice, in this context, I mean sufficiently informed and considered information or advice about aspects of the form or substance of the proposals, or their implications for the consulted party, being aspects material to the implementation of the proposal as to which the Secretary of State might not be fully informed or advised and as to which the party consulted might have relevant information or advice to offer.

These propositions, as it seems to me, can partly be derived from, and are wholly consistent with, the decisions and various dicta, which I need not enumerate, in *Rollo* v *Minister of Town and Country Planning* [1948] 1 All ER 13 and *Port Louis Corporation* v *Attorney-General of Mauritius* [1965] AC 1111.

. . . In the present case, looking at the 'whole scope and purpose' of the Act of 1982, one matter which stands out is that its day-to-day administration is in the hands of local housing authorities who bear 10 per cent of the cost of the scheme. It is common ground that in them resides the direct expertise necessary to administer schemes made under the Act on a day-to-day basis. For these reasons, if for no other, I conclude that the obligation laid on the Secretary of State to consult organisations representative of those authorities is mandatory, not directory.

The last question of principle to be decided before turning to the facts is the test to be applied to the facts as I find them for the purposes of judicial review. . . . [T]o what extent is it for the Secretary of State, not the court, to judge how much consultation is necessary and how long is to be given for it? The answer to that question may qualify the word 'sufficient' in the requirements of consultation which I have set out above. . . .

[T]he first point to note is that the power to make the regulations is conferred on the Secretary of State and that his is the duty to consult. Save for those consulted, no one else is involved in the making of the regulations. Secondly, both the form or substance of new regulations and the time allowed for consulting, before making them, may well depend in whole or in part on matters of a political nature, as to the force and implications of which it would be reasonable to expect the Secretary of State, rather than the court, to be the best judge. Thirdly, issues may well be raised after the making of the regulations as to the detailed merits of one or other reason for making them, or as to the precise degree of urgency required in their making, issues which have been raised on this application. Those issues cannot be said to be wholly irrelevant to a challenge to the vires of the regulations, and Mr Beloff has not submitted that they are irrelevant; but at the same time it would seem to me to be inherently improbable that the question of the vires of the regulations should depend upon precise findings of fact on issues such as those. In my view, therefore, the court, when considering the question whether the consultation required by section 36 (1) was in substance carried out, should have regard not so much to the actual facts which preceded the making of the regulations as to the material before the Secretary of State when he made the regulations, that material including facts or information as it appeared or must have appeared to him acting in good faith, and any judgments made or opinions expressed to him before the making of the regulations about those facts which appear or could have appeared to him to be reasonable. The department's good faith is not challenged on this application.

The effect of treating as material the facts as they appeared to the Secretary of State, and not necessarily as they were, is to give a certain flexibility to the notions of sufficiency, sufficient information, sufficient time and sufficiently informed and considered information and advice in my homespun attempt to define proper consultation. Thus, it can have the effect that what would be sufficient information or time in one case might be more or less than sufficient in another, depending on the relative degrees of urgency and the nature of the proposed regulation. There is no degree of urgency, however, which absolves the Secretary of State from the obligation to consult at all.

[Upon consideration of the facts, his Lordship said that the minister's view on the urgency of the need for the amending regulations, and the nature of the proposed amendments justified requiring comments to be expressed quickly but not in so short a period which meant that the comments would be insufficiently informed or insufficiently considered. When account was also taken of the fact that the applicant had no notice of a material feature until after the regulations were made, his Lordship concluded that the minister had not discharged his duty to consult before making the regulations.]

Having decided that the provisions of section 36 (1) are mandatory and that they were not complied with before the regulations were made, I now have to consider the relief which I should give to the association. They ask me to quash the regulations. I do not think that I should do so.

I acknowledge, with respect, that in the ordinary case a decision – I emphasize the word 'decision' – made ultra vires is likely to be set aside in accordance with the dictum of Lord Diplock in *Grunwick Processing Laboratories Ltd* v *Advisory, Conciliation and Arbitration Service* [1978] AC 655, 695, where he said:

> My Lords, where a statutory authority has acted ultra vires any person who would be affected by its act if it were valid is normally entitled ex debito justiciae to have it set aside . . .

But whereas the ordinary case is that of a ministerial departmental decision, which adversely affects the rights of one person or of a class of persons, and which can be struck down without, usually, more than individual or local implications, in this case the association seeks to strike down regulations which have become part of the public law of the land. Although I have been shown and have found no authority to support the proposition, I suspect that it is not necessarily to be regarded as the normal practice, where delegated legislation is held to be ultra vires, to revoke the instrument, but that the inclination would be the other way, in the absence of special circumstances making it desirable to revoke that instrument. But in principle I treat the matter as one of pure discretion and so treating it decline to revoke the instrument for the following reasons, no particular significance being attached to the order in which I state them.

Although six organisations were and are habitually consulted in this context, only one of them has applied for revocation of the instrument and that one applies only on the ground that it was not properly consulted. It makes no formal complaint that the other organisations were not consulted. Although the association complains about the substance of the regulations, it is apparent that its principal complaint throughout is, and has been, the absence of proper consultation and it and other organisations were able to express some, albeit in a sense piecemeal, views about the proposal which apparently the department took into account before making the regulations, but without, be it noted, any effort whatsoever on the November or December amendments. The regulations have been in force for about six months and, although their implementation creates difficulties for some at least of the housing authorities who have to administer them, those authorities must by now have adapted themselves as best they can to those difficulties. If, however, the regulations were to be revoked all applicants who had been refused benefit because of the new regulations would be entitled to make fresh claims, and all authorities would be required to consider each such claim.

Finally, the Housing Benefits Amendment (No. 4) Regulations 1984 have been consolidated into the Housing Benefits Regulations 1985 (S.I. 1985 No. 677), which were made on 29 April 1985, laid before Parliament on 30 April and came into operation and indeed have come into operation for the most part, today, 21 May. Those regulations are not at present challenged. If, therefore, the Housing Benefits Amendment (No. 4) Regulations 1984 were to be revoked, and so long as the Regulations of 1985 remain valid, any person entitled to reconsideration of his claim to benefit would, if successful, at best be entitled to benefits for about six months. For all these reasons, I refuse, in the exercise of my discretion, to revoke the Housing Benefits Amendment (No. 4) Regulations 1984.

I can see no reason whatsoever, however, for refusing the association the declaration for which they ask . . .

Declaration accordingly. Application for order of certiorari refused.

Questions

1. Consultation is not generally required for legislation, although central governmental practice is usually to conduct consultation amongst interested bodies. This leaves the area of quasi-legislation produced by other public authorities and agencies. Bearing in mind that the courts seem to have regard to the distinctions between legislative, executive and administrative action, should there be a general statutory obligation imposed on all public bodies who make any measures, whether they take the form of primary, delegated or quasi-legislation?

2. What are the benefits and disadvantages of consultation, and would the benefits outweigh the disadvantages:

(a) generally;

(b) only for some types of quasi-legislation?

3. If such a general duty of consultation were required, would it be in conflict with the representative nature of our parliamentary democratic constitution?

4. For the purposes of a duty to consult, should we make a distinction between those measures which are subject to parliamentary oversight and those which are not?

Note

The Hansard Society for Parliamentary Government produced a report on the legislative process. In this they proposed guiding principles which under-pinned their recommendations for reform. The evidence which they received indicated that the current arrangements for consultation were unsatisfactory.

The Hansard Society, *Making the Law* (1993), pp. 14, 15, 139–41

. . . we have agreed five central principles which guide and govern all the recommendations we make:

- Laws are made for the benefit of the citizens of the state. All citizens directly affected should be involved as fully and openly as possible in the process by which statute law is prepared.
- Statute law should be as certain as possible and as intelligible and clear as possible, for the benefit of the citizens to whom it applies.
- Statute law must be rooted in the authority of Parliament and thoroughly exposed to open democratic scrutiny by the representatives of the people in Parliament.
- Ignorance of the law is no excuse, therefore the current statute law must be as accessible as possible to all who need to know it.
- The Government needs to be able to secure the passage of its legislation, but to get the law right and intelligible, for the benefit of citizens, is as important as to get it passed quickly.

[Recommendations on consultation]

Primary Legislation

4. The overwhelming impression from the evidence is that many of those most directly affected are deeply dissatisfied with the extent, nature, timing and conduct of consultation on bills as at present practised . . . the Government must heed this criticism and seek to meet it. . . .

5. The Government should always seek the fullest advice from those affected on the problems of implementing and enforcing proposed legislation. . . .

6. Although some bills are inevitably required in a hurry, getting a bill right should always have priority over passing it quickly, and we recommend that the Government should publicy endorse this policy. . . .

7. The Government should make every effort to get bills in a form fit for enactment, without major alteration, before they are presented to Parliament; in the Government's review of the legislative process, this should be a first and overriding objective. . . .

8. Proper consultation should play a central part in the preparation of bills, and we recommend that all Government departments should act accordingly. . . .

9. Good consultation practice requires that when a bill is being prepared, bodies with relevant experience or interests — particularly those directly affected — should be given all the relevant information and an opportunity to make their views known or to give information or advice, at each level of decision-taking. . . .

10. Consultation should be as open as possible. . . .

11. Secrecy regarding the content and results of consultations should be minimised and feed-back maximised. . . .

12. When major reviews are required of how the current law is operating and of the need for reform, we would welcome more frequent appointment of independent inquiries, including Royal Commissions. If the Government is not prepared to accept the advice of such inquiries, it would be expected to publish its reasons. . . .

13. Consultative documents should be as clear and precise as possible. They should be specific about the questions on which departments want responses, while leaving opportunity for bodies to put forward further ideas of their own on relevant points. Green Papers should set out the facts fully and, as far as possible, the options being considered. White Papers should normally be preceded by Green Papers. White

Papers should, where possible, systematically detail changes from Green Papers, indicating why these changes had been made. . . .

14. Departments should offer more consulations on draft texts, especially in so far as they relate to practical questions of the implementation and enforcement of legislation. . . .

15. The experience of the Inland Revenue in consulting on individual draft clauses of the Finance Bill should be studied by other departments and adopted in other fields. . . .

16. Where there is no great urgency for a bill, the whole bill might sometimes be published in draft in a Green Paper, as the basis for further consultation and possibly parliamentary scrutiny. . . .

17. Government departments should consult the main bodies concerned in each case and seek to agree how much time should be allowed for their responses to a consultation document. . . .

18. Consultation should not be delayed. . . .

19. Bodies invited by Government departments to respond to consultative documents on proposed legislation, and other bodies with a *bona fide* interest, should be given, free of charge, as many copies of those documents as they can show they need. . . .

20. Bodies which have contributed to consultation on proposed legislation should be supplied, free of charge, with copies of the resulting bills, Acts and statutory instruments. . . .

21. The Government should, drawing on best practice, prepare consultation guidelines which would be applicable to all Government departments when preparing legislation. . . .

22. We recommend that —

(a) the Government's guidelines on consultation should be published;

(b) each department when applying to the Future Legislation Committee for inclusion of a bill in the Government's legislative programme should submit a check-list indicating how far it has been able to comply with the guidelines, and give details of the consultations it has already carried out or proposes to conduct; and

(c) an up-dated version of the check-list and this information should be submitted with the draft bill to the Legislation Committee and published with the bill. . . .

Delegated legislation

23. There should be consultation where appropriate at the formative stage of delegated legislation, but wherever possible departments should also consult outside experts and affected bodies on drafts of the actual instruments that they propose to lay before Parliament. . . .

24. The Government's guidelines that we have recommended regarding consultation on bills, should be applied with appropriate modifications to consultation on delegated legislation. . . .

Questions

1. Does consultation operate more as a source of legitimation for, rather than control of, legislation?

2. Do the Hansard Society's proposals focus more on the workability of legislation when made, whereas the government concentrates more on the processes and politics of making legislation?

(2) Publicity

All statutes are published, as is delegated legislation governed by the Statutory Instruments Act 1946, but this does leave open the possibility of other legislative measures not being readily available or known about.

STATUTORY INSTRUMENTS ACT 1946

1.—(1) Where by this Act or any Act passed after the commencement of this Act power to make, confirm or approve orders, rules, regulations or other subordinate legislation is conferred on His Majesty in Council or on any Minister of the Crown then, if the power is expressed—

(a) in the case of a power conferred on His Majesty, to be exercisable by Order in Council;

(b) in the case of a power conferred on a Minister of the Crown, to be exercisable by statutory instrument,

any document by which that power is exercised shall be known as a 'statutory instrument' and the provisions of this Act shall apply thereto accordingly. . . .

2.—(1) Immediately after the making of any statutory instrument, it shall be sent to the King's printer of Acts of Parliament and numbered in accordance with regulations made under this Act, and except in such cases as may be provided by any Act passed after the commencement of this Act or prescribed by regulations made under this Act, copies thereof shall as soon as possible be printed and sold by the King's printer of Acts of Parliament. . . .

3.—(1) Regulations made for the purposes of this Act shall make provision for the publication by His Majesty's Stationery Office of lists showing the date upon which every statutory instrument printed and sold by the King's printer of Acts of Parliament was first issued by that office; and in any legal proceedings a copy of any list so published purporting to bear the imprint of the King's printer shall be received in evidence as a true copy, and an entry therein shall be conclusive evidence of the date on which any statutory instrument was first issued by His Majesty's Stationery Office.

(2) In any proceedings against any person for an offence consisting of a contravention of any such statutory instrument, it shall be a defence to prove that the instrument had not been issued by His Majesty's Stationery Office at the date of the alleged contravention unless it is proved that at that date reasonable steps had been taken for the purpose of bringing the purport of the instrument to the notice of the public, or of persons likely to be affected by it, or of the person charged.

(3) Save as therein otherwise expressly provided, nothing in this section shall affect any enactment or rule of law relating to the time at which any statutory instrument comes into operation. . . .

8.—(1) The Treasury may, with the concurrence of the Lord Chancellor and the Speaker of the House of Commons, by statutory instrument make regulations for the purposes of this Act, and such regulations may, in particular:— . . .

(c) provide with respect to any classes or descriptions of statutory instrument that they shall be exempt, either altogether or to such extent as may be determined by or under the regulations, from the requirement of being printed and of being sold by the King's printer of Acts of Parliament, or from either of those requirements: . . .

Note

Under the Statutory Instruments Regulations 1947, rr. 5–8 some regulations are exempted from the publication requirements of the 1946 Act. These are: local instruments and those otherwise published regularly (r. 5); temporary instruments (r. 6); schedules to rules which are too bulky and where other steps have been taken to bring them to the notice of the public (r. 7); cases in which it would be contrary to the public interest for publication to occur before the rules came into operation (r. 8). The minister making rules subject to the exceptions in rr. 6–8 must certify that the conditions are satisfied.

R* v *Sheer Metalcraft Ltd
[1954] 1 QB 586
Kingston-upon-Thames Assizes

STREATFIELD J: . . . This matter comes before the court in the form of an objection to the admissibility in evidence of a statutory instrument known as the Iron and Steel Prices Order, 1951. It appears that part and parcel of that instrument consisted of certain deposited schedules in which maximum prices for different commodities of steel were set out. The instrument is said to have been made by the Minister of Supply on February 16, 1951; laid before Parliament on February 20, 1951; and to have come into operation on February 21, 1951. It is under that statutory instrument that the present charges are made against the two defendants in this case.

The point which has been taken is that by reason of the deposited schedules not having been printed and not having been certified by the Minister as being exempt from printing, the instrument is not a valid instrument under the Statutory Instruments Act, 1946. That point was taken in *Simmonds* v *Newell* [1953] 1 WLR 826, but it was expressly left open in view of a certain admission then made by the Solicitor-General, which, however, does not apply to the present case. The point arises in this way: under regulation 55AB of the Defence (General) Regulations, 1939, as amended, a competent authority, which in this case is the Minister of Supply, may by statutory instrument provide for controlling the prices to be charged for goods of any description or the charges to be made for services of any description, and for any incidental and supplementary matters for which the competent authority thinks it expedient for the purposes of the instrument to provide. It is said in the statutory instrument here that it was made in exercise of the powers conferred upon the Minister by regulations 55AB and 98 of the Defence (General) Regulations, and other statutory authorities.

The contention is that the making of that instrument is governed by the provisions of the Statutory Instruments Act, 1946 . . .

[His Lordship read sections 1 and 2 of the Act of 1946 and regulation 7 of the Statutory Instruments Regulations, 1947, and continued:] Section 1 visualizes the making of what is called a statutory instrument by a Minister of the Crown; section 2 visualizes that after the making of a statutory instrument it shall be sent to the King's Printer to be printed, except in so far as under regulations made under the Act it may be unnecessary to have it printed. It is said here that the Minister did not certify that the printing of these very bulky deposited schedules was unnecessary within the meaning of regulation 7. It is contended, therefore, that as he did not so certify it, it became an obligation under the Act that the deposited schedules as well as the instrument itself should be printed under section 2 of the Act of 1946, and in the absence of their having been printed as part of the instrument, the instrument cannot be regarded as being validly made.

To test that matter it is necessary to examine section 3 of the Act of 1946. By subsection (1) [see *ante* p. 387] . . . There does not appear to be any definition of what is meant by 'issue,' but presumably it does mean some act by the Queen's Printer of Acts of Parliament which follows the printing of the instrument. That section, therefore, requires that the Queen's Printer shall keep lists showing the date upon which statutory instruments are printed and issued.

Subsection (2) is important and provides [see *ante* p. 387] . . . It seems to follow from the wording of this subsection that the making of an instrument is one thing and the issue of it is another. If it is made it can be contravened; if it has not been issued then that provides a defence to a person charged with its contravention. It is then upon the Crown to prove that, although it has not been issued, reasonable steps have been taken for the purpose of bringing the instrument to the notice of the public or persons likely to be affected by it.

I do not think that it can be said that to make a valid statutory instrument it is required that all of these stages should be gone through; namely, the making, the laying before Parliament, the printing and the certification of that part of it which it might be unnecessary to have printed. In my judgment the making of an instrument is complete when it is first of all made by the Minister concerned and after it has been laid before Parliament. When that has been done it then becomes a valid statutory instrument, totally made under the provisions of the Act.

The remaining provisions to which my attention has been drawn, in my view, are purely procedure for the issue of an instrument validly made – namely, that in the first instance it must be printed by the Queen's Printer unless it is certified to be unnecessary to print it; it must then be included in a list published by Her Majesty's Stationery Office showing the dates when it is issued and it may be issued by the Queen's Printer of Acts of Parliament. Those matters, in my judgment, are matters of procedure. If they were not and if they were stages in the perfection of a valid statutory instrument, I cannot see that section 3 (2) would be necessary, because if each one of those stages were necessary to make a statutory instrument valid, it would follow that there could be no infringement of an unissued instrument and therefore it would be quite unnecessary to provide a defence to a contravention of any such instrument. In my view the very fact that subsection (2) of section 3 refers to a defence that the instrument has not been issued postulates that the instrument must have been validly made in the first place otherwise it could never have been contravened.

In those circumstances I hold that this instrument was validly made and approved and that it was made by or signed on behalf of the Minister on its being laid before Parliament; that so appears on the fact of the instrument itself. In my view, the fact that the Minister failed to certify under regulation 7 does not invalidate the instrument as an instrument but lays the burden upon the Crown to prove that at the date of the alleged contraventions reasonable steps had been taken for bringing the instrument to the notice of the public or persons likely to be affected by it. I, therefore, rule that this is admissible. . . .

Verdict: Guilty on all counts.

Note

For a critical analysis of this case and s. 3 of the 1946 Act, see articles by Lanham at (1974) 37 *Modern Law Review* 510 and [1983] *Public Law* 395.

Questions

1. The publication requirements in the 1946 Act affect only statutory instruments in respect of which no exemption has been made. Should there be a general duty of publication?

2. With respect to publication of quasi-legislation:

(a) should it only be required if it is reasonable and non-disclosure would prejudice the public; and

(b) when would non-disclosure be reasonable?

(3) Parliamentary oversight

Public Information Office, House of Commons Sessional Information Digest 1992–93, 1993–94, 1994–95, pp. 1, 2

Analysis of the time of the session **Types of Business**	**Total time spent (hours:minutes)**		
	1992–93	**1993–94**	**1994–95**
2. Government Bills			
a) Second Reading debate (Bills committed to a Standing Committee)	93:58	72:35	100:15
b) Second Reading debate (Bills committed to a Committee of the Whole House)	63:00	21:59	15:36
c) Committee of the Whole House	210:59	33:21	28:53
d) Consideration (Report stage)	150:04	121:44	100:00
e) Third Reading	28:48	17:40	13:51
f) Lords Amendments	52:53	30:31	12:55
g) Allocation of Time Orders	11:00	8:40	0:00
h) Committal motion	0:59	0:00	0:00
3. Private Members' Bills			
a) Second Reading	30:59	33:47	37:27
b) Other stages	22:39	23:53	26:21
7. Private Members' Motions			
b) Motions for the introduction of Ten Minute Rule Bills	71:53	10:43	10:57
10. Money Resolutions	7:11	9:34	0:55
11. Ways and Means Resolutions (including Budget Debate)	31:37	36:04	36:56
12. Affirmative Statutory Instruments	80:03	120:49	79:39
13. Prayers against statutory instruments etc	15:55	2:11	8:00

The Hansard Society, *Making the Law* (1993), pp. 11–12

Volume of all Public General Acts, 1901–1991

Year	*No. of Acts*	*Pages*	*No. of Sections and Schedules*
1901	40	247	400
1911	58	584	701
1921	67	569	783
1931	34	375	440
1941	48	448	533
1951	66	675	803
1961	65	1048	1087
1971	81	2107	1963
1981	72	2276	2026
1991	69	2222*	1985

*Printed on A4 paper which was larger than the size previously used, so requiring fewer pages.

Volume of Public General Acts 1985–1991, showing effect of excluding consolidation Acts

Year	*No. of Acts*	*Pages*	*No. of Acts excluding cons. Acts*	*Pages excluding cons. Acts*
1985	76	3233	65	1860
1986	68	2780	64	2310
1987	57	1538*	56	1269*
1988	55	3385	49	2047
1989	46	2489	43	2399
1990	46	2391	42	1743
1991	69	2222	61	2012

*The statute book from 1987 onwards has been printed on A4 paper which is larger than the size previously used, so requiring fewer pages.

Volume of Statutory Instruments

Year	*No. of General SIs*	*Pages*
1901	156	N/A
1911	172	N/A
1921	727	N/A
1951	2335	3523
1961	2515	4524
1971	2167	6338
1981	1892	6521
1983	1966	6405
1984	2065	6062
1985	2082	6476
1986	2332	9048
1987	2279	6266*
1988	2311	6294
1989	2510	N/A
1990	2569	N/A
1991	2945	N/A

*Statutory Instruments from 1987 onwards have been printed on A4 paper which is larger than the size previously used, so requiring fewer pages.

Note

As we saw in section (b) of this chapter, one may divide the work of the House of Commons between that which takes place on the floor and that in committee. The most detailed scrutiny of a Bill or a statutory instrument will take place in committee.

The Government through its majority in the House can control the timetable for the passage of Bills. The research by Griffith & Ryle in *Parliament: Functions, Practice and Procedures* (1989) shows that the use of methods of curtailing debate on the floor and in committee has not been extensive. In the sessions of Parliament from 1974–75 until 1987–88, the largest number of Bills to have been guillotined was six in 1987–88.

There are various procedures by which statutory instruments are passed. The instrument may or may not be required to be laid before Parliament. If it is to be laid before Parliament, then there may or may not be provision for action by Parliament. The action to be taken by Parliament can be broadly divided into affirmative and negative procedures. Under the affirmative procedure Parliament must pass an affirmative resolution in order for the measure to become law or to continue as law. On the other hand, a measure will remain in force unless Parliament annuls it using the negative procedure. The negative resolution is by far the most frequently used procedure by which Parliament may supervise statutory instruments. In order to annul a statutory instrument the prayer for annulment must have been passed within 40 days of the laying of the instrument before Parliament.

The statute which enables the making of a statutory instrument will specify which procedure is to be used. Unlike the case with Bills, it is extremely rare for a statutory instrument to be amended as only a very few enabling statutes provide for amendment.

Specialist committees Parliament has created several specialist committees to examine delegated legislation and European Communities legislation. The committees dealing with delegated legislation are divided between those which deal with technical matters and those which deal with the merits. The technical committees are (i) the Joint Select Committee on Delegated Legislation; and (ii) the Commons Select Committee on Statutory Instruments, composed of the House of Commons members of the Joint Committee, which deals with instruments subject only to House of Commons oversight. The merits of an instrument may be referred to a House of Commons standing committee or be dealt with on the floor of the House.

Those committees dealing with the European Communities are, in the House of Commons, the Select Committee on European Legislation, and, in the House of Lords, the Select Committee on the European Communities. These committees consider both delegated legislation which is intended to implement EC legislation, and proposals from Brussels for future EC legislation.

The House of Commons Committee may refer matters to two European Standing Committees which were established in 1990–91. A review of their operation recommended creation of an additional committee (HC 352 of 1991–92).

J. D. Hayhurst & P. Wallington, 'The Parliamentary Scrutiny of Delegated Legislation' [1988] *Public Law* 547, at pp. 563–64

Table 3. Grounds for reporting by the Committees, 1973–83

Ground	Joint Committee	Commons Committee
Form or purport call for elucidation	343	30
Miscellaneous	124	18
Defective drafting	81	7
Unusual or unexpected use of statute	81	4
Vires	44	3
Delays in publication/laying	9	2
Unauthorised retrospective effect	7	1
Imposition of a charge	0	0
Made under legislation excluding judicial review	0	0
Totals	689	65

Table 4. Number of reported statutory instruments subsequently debated 1973–83

Forum	Joint Committee Report	Commons Committee Report
Lords and Commons Chamber	24	—
Lords and Commons Standing Committee	32	—
Lords only	23	—
Commons Chamber only	12	6
Commons standing committee only	23	9
Total Lords	79	—
Total Commons Chamber	36	6
Total Standing Committee	55	9
Not debated anywhere	526	48
Total reported	640	63

Note

Hayhurst & Wallington compute that, making allowance for instruments which might be debated in both Houses of Parliament, 129 instruments out of the 703 reported by the committees were debated, which is 18.5 per cent. None of those reported was voted down by either House.

So far as instruments subject to negative procedure are concerned, there has been an increase in the number in which no action has been taken even though a prayer for annulment has been tabled. In the session 1978–79 the number was 13 (28.3%), in 1983–84 40 (35.4%), in 1984–85 42 (46.2%), and in 1985–86 77 (69.4%) (see HC 350 of 1986–87).

A. Beith 'Prayers Unanswered: A Jaundiced View of the Parliamentary Scrutiny of Statutory Instruments' (1981) 34 *Parliamentary Affairs* 165, at pp. 170–73.

The 1977–8 Select Committee on Procedure did not neglect the question of delegated legislation, although I now regard the Committee's recommendations on the subject, for which as a member I shared responsibility, as incomplete and in some respects timid. The committee said of the present procedures that 'the system provides only vestigial control of statutory instruments – particularly in the case of negative procedure instruments – and is in need of comprehensive reform'. What, then, were these reforms to be?

Some of them concern aspects of the procedure on which this article has not concentrated. They recommend, for example, that consideration of statutory instruments – affirmative or negative – should not be completed by standing committees until the Joint Committee on Statutory Instruments has reported. The Joint Committee itself had argued for a change along these lines. In the same field – the technical aspects rather than the merits of statutory instruments – it recommended that if the joint committee drew particular attention to an instrument under a negative procedure, extra 'praying' time should be allowed, thus making it less difficult to arrange a debate or – more effectively – that such a report from the Joint Committee would make an instrument subject automatically to the affirmative instead of the negative procedure.

None of these useful recommendations on the technical aspect solve the more basic weaknesses of delegated legislation procedure, and the same can be said of a number of other recommendations in the report. . . . The more substantial recommendations are best considered separately, first in respect of affirmative and then of negative orders, since the committee approached the two types in quite different spirit. It is negative procedure which has the most deficiencies: affirmative procedure does at least guarantee an eventual vote on the floor of the House on the substance of the Order, and, at present, any 20 members can prevent the debate on it from being relegated to a committee. The main problems are insufficient time for the debates, inability to amend the Order, and the vacuity of the motion 'That the Committee have considered the Order' on which committee debates take place. The Procedure Committee recommended that in future debates should take place on a motion 'That the Committee recommend that the instrument be approved'. This would not only be open to a meaningful negative vote; it would also be open to amendment. It would not be the same thing as amending the order itself, but it would enable a Member to move, for example, that the instrument be not approved without the inclusion or deletion of whatever concerned him. The carrying of such a motion could be taken as a warning to the government not to proceed with the Order in its present form, although it would not necessarily prevent the government from carrying its original intention in the main vote on the floor of the House. It would still be an improvement.

When they came to negative procedure, the committee was much more cautious. The case against this procedure is not merely that it offers no opportunity for amendment of Orders, but that it makes it easy for the Government to avoid even a vote on the principle of the Order, either by avoiding a debate on a prayer or by sending the Order to a committee in which the only vote is meaningless and from which the matter does not return to the floor of the House. They suggest a new, fourfold procedure which emphasises and enhances the role of standing committees in considering negative instruments.

(1) If the government does not move the necessary motion to send a prayer against an Order to a committee, which at the moment it alone can do, any Member can do so if the prayer has been signed by half the voting members of the House. The requirement of half the House is in effect a wrecking limitation: in the rare case of a prayer having the support of the entire Opposition together with a large section of the governing party (which is what would be required), resistance would be on such a scale that debate would need to be on the floor of the House and the procedure would be unnecessary.

(2) A negative instrument would be considered on a motion that the committee recommend the annulment, withdrawal or approval of the motion; thus the vote would be on a matter of substance. However, the Procedure Committee did not extend to negative procedure their suggestion for affirmative procedure that the motion should be open to amendment.

(3) If a committee recommends annulment and the government does not find time for a debate on the matter in the House within seven days, any Member should have the right to insist on a one-hour debate which would also secure that a vote took place. This is the most significant improvement suggested in negative procedure, but it

has a basic flaw: it could too easily be averted by the government refusing to send the Order to a committee in the first place. At present the government has little or no reason to resist sending negative Orders to a committee, but with the possibility of a vote to annul, followed by a debate and a vote in the House, it would have far more incentive to block such reference. It can still avoid a debate in the House on the prayer unless the Opposition make a major issue of it or use up a Supply Day on it; its block can only be overruled by half the House, which means that there must be a major revolt together with massive Opposition support. The hurdle is far too high for the procedure to be of regular use.

(4) If the same hurdle – half the House – can be negotiated, even instruments which have not been annulled in committee can be the subject of a follow-up one hour debate.

The Procedure Committee also considered but ruled out making the new select committees which cover subject areas responsible for considering the merits of statutory instruments. To have done so would have been to have overburdened these committees before they had been given a chance to develop their investigatory role, and it would have imported into the select committees the party discipline associated with the government's determination to get its legislation through, thereby impairing their extremely important ability to operate on the basis of unanimous and cross-party conclusions. It recommended, however, that although it was not to be the normal pattern, select committees could have statutory instruments referred to them by the House.

None of these proposals have been implemented, despite the commendable progress which has been made in implementing the Procedure Committee's other recommendations on new select committees and, more recently, on its proposal that committees on Bills should be allowed to take evidence at their first four sittings. This may be in part due to the fact that statutory instrument procedure and its defects are not so widely understood, but it is also at least partly due to lack of confidence that the proposals represent a worthwhile improvement. Why, for instance, did the committee not take a more radical view and recommend that it should be possible to amend statutory instruments, not merely the motions which refer to them? It discussed this possibility (3.19–3.21) but came to the conclusion that it would lead to statutory instruments being used less frequently and more detail being written into bills, and that much flexibility might thereby be lost. From the point of view of parliamentary scrutiny, the proposal is attractive and the committee's reasoning seems weak. It would, however, present practical problems: amendments might need to be considered in more than one stage, as in Bills, and would have to be considered in both Houses. There might be real difficulty in deciding what the scope of amendments could be and considerably more debating time would be needed in some cases. However, even at present it is possible to amend Orders under the Census Act, and this has been done without disruptive procedural consequences. There is scope for experiment with procedure for amendment of statutory instruments, perhaps in a defined field.

At the very least, the House could bring in a strengthened version of the Procedure Committee's proposals, providing that

(1) a motion which can be amended should be the basis for discussion of all statutory instruments, affirmative or negative;

(2) the government should not be able to prevent a debate (which could be in committee) or a vote on the floor of the House on any prayer against an Order under the negative procedure. That was the intention of Parliament when the present procedures were introduced, and it has been flouted. If there has to be a threshold, it

should not be more than ten members; their support would be sufficient to secure at least a debate in committee and a subsequent vote on the floor of the House.

If these very necessary reforms were to make ministers a little more reluctant to use statutory instruments instead of putting detail in Bills, that is no cause for alarm. It is far more alarming that ministers should find it so convenient to write the law long after Parliament thinks it has done so itself, and that they should have so little difficulty in ensuring a smooth passage through Parliament for what is in effect legislation by the executive.

Notes

1. Hayhurst & Wallington also feel that, increasingly, delegated legislation is being used not only to implement details, but also to confer on ministers the power to determine major questions of policy.

2. The Hansard Society made proposals which it hoped would strike a balance between maintaining the advantages of delegated legislation but would also ensure proper scrutiny.

The Hansard Society, *Making the Law* (1993), p. 149

Annex A — Outline of Suggested Procedures for Debating Statutory Instruments in the House of Commons

1. Instruments subject to the affirmative procedure

(a) Unless the House otherwise orders on a non-debatable motion, all statutory instruments requiring affirmative resolutions should be automatically referred to standing committees for debate.

(b) Occasionally longer or more complicated instruments should go to a special standing committee which could hear evidence.

(c) Before a committee starts debating an instrument, it should be able to question Ministers on the purpose, meaning and effect of that instrument.

(d) Debate should be held on a motion moved by the Minister recommending approval of the instrument.

(e) Amendments to that motion should be permitted recommending that the instrument be not approved or that it be approved subject to amendments being made to the instrument itself.

(f) The chairman of the committee would have the power to select amendments to the motion.

(g) Subject to general time-tabling, there would be no time limit on debates.

(h) When a committee has recommended the approval of an instrument without amendment, the formal motion to approve the instrument would be put in the House without debate.

(i) When a committee recommends that an instrument be not approved, or approved subject to amendments, a Government motion in the House to approve the instrument would be debatable; debate would be time-limited.

2. Instruments subject to the negative procedure

(a) Unless the House otherwise orders on a debatable motion, all 'prayers' for the annulment of a statutory instrument subject to the negative procedure should stand referred to a standing committee.

(b) The procedures in committee for debates on 'prayers' would be as for affirmative instruments except that the Member who tabled the 'prayer' would either move a motion for annulment of the instrument concerned or a motion recommending its amendment; the Minister could move amendments to such motions.

(c) If a motion for annulment of an instrument or recommending its amendment were negatived in committee, no further proceedings would be required.

(d) If a motion for annulment of an instrument or recommending its amendment were agreed in committee, the Member who moved that motion (or another Member on his behalf) would have the right to move a formal motion in the House for the annulment of the instrument; debate would be time-limited.

C. Munro, *Studies in Constitutional Law* (1987), pp. 173–74

. . . It is true, of course, that in principle the exercise of prerogative powers by ministers is as amenable to parliamentary supervision as any other governmental actions. Thus the disposition of the armed forces is part of the prerogative power, and the government's decision to send them to the Falkland Islands to repel the Argentinian invasion was one which could be (and was) the subject of parliamentary debate, discussion and questioning, and Select Committee investigations. No doubt the supervision which members of the House of Commons are able to exercise is sporadic and imperfect, hindered by lack of knowledge, and made less effective by reason of the government's usual dominance of the House. But these are qualifications which apply equally to the supervision of statutory powers and other matters.

In practice, however, the supervision of prerogative powers does seem to be attended by greater than average difficulty. The very nature of these powers makes them less readily subject to challenge. As the authors of a study of parliamentary questions noted, 'there is a very big difference' between questioning a minister about matters for which he is statutorily responsible and about other matters: 'It is a different level of answerability, there is less opportunity to use it and even when used the results are likely to be less definite.'

In fact, it is sometimes more than just a difference of degree. When a member sought in 1955 to ascertain by way of a question in Parliament what advice the Prime Minister had given the Queen as to the dissolution of Parliament, the question was ruled out on the ground that the Prime Minister was not responsible to Parliament for that advice. 'Dissolution appears', it was remarked, 'to be one of a small number of subjects clearly within the Government's responsibility but anomalously shielded from parliamentary questioning.' The number, however, is not so small. Exercises of the personal prerogatives, where discretion still resides in the Sovereign, are shielded from questions and discussion. The advice given to the Sovereign about some wider matters has similarly been ruled out of bounds: not only the dissolution of Parliament, but also the grant of honours, the ecclesiastical patronage of the Crown, the appointment and dismissal of Privy Councillors, and the prerogative of mercy in relation to capital sentences. These are the subjects of specific rulings, but more generally ministers may simply refuse to answer questions, if there are reasons of national security, confidentiality, relations with other states, or public interest, which in their view justify a refusal. On some topics, the consistency of refusals has created a clear precedent, and from time to time governments issue a list of matters with regard to which questions will not be answered. . . . Exercises of prerogative and non-statutory powers figure prominently, although not exclusively, in the list . . . To sum up, the exercise of prerogative powers is imperfectly subject to parliamentary control. . . .

Questions

1. Is Parliamentary oversight of law-making more illusory than real, given that the Government controls the passage of primary legislation, and that the scrutiny of delegated legislation is limited and non-existent for some quasi-legislation?

2. As there is so much pressure on parliamentary time, can consultation and publicity be improved so as to control quasi-legislation?

3. Could primary legislation contain standards and guidance about the content of legislative power which it delegates, thereby facilitating judicial review?

(4) *Judicial review*

Control of law-making by the courts through judicial review has increased beyond delegated legislation and quasi-legislation. The basis of this review is the doctrine of *ultra vires*. See generally Chapters 8 and 9 on judicial review.

R* v *Secretary of State for Employment, ex parte Equal Opportunities Commission
[1994] 2 WLR 409
House of Lords

The Equal Opportunites Commission (EOC) took the view that some provisions of the Employment Protection (Consolidation) Act 1978 were not in conformity with Community Law (Art. 119 and the Equal Pay (75/117) and Equal Treatment (76/207) Directives). This view was based on the discrimination between full-time and part-time employees in relation to the periods of continuous employment which were required to qualify for rights to redundancy pay and compensation for unfair dismissal. As the great majority of full-time employees were men and the great majority of part-time employees were women, the EOC felt that this amounted to indirect discrimination against women. The chief executive of the EOC wrote to the Secretary of State asking if steps would be taken to remove this discrimination. In a letter dated 23 April 1990 the Secretary of State replied that in the Department's view redundancy pay and compensation for unfair dismissal did not constitute pay within the terms of Art. 119. The EOC obtained leave to apply for judicial review of the decision in the 23 April 1990 letter that the UK was not in breach of its Community law obligations, and sought declarations that the UK was breaching its obligations under (1) Art. 119 and Directive 75/117; and (2) Directive 76/207, by providing less favourable treatment of part-time workers (most of whom were women) than full-time workers (most of whom were men) in relation to conditions of entitlement to redundancy pay and compensation for unfair dismissal. Subsequently another applicant, Mrs Day, was joined to this application. Mrs Day, a part-time cleaner, had been made redundant by her employer, but she did not qualify under the 1978 Act's provisions for redundancy pay. She sought further declarations and *mandamus* to compel the Secretary of State to introduce legislation to amend the 1978 statute.

The major point of substantive law at issue was whether the indirect discrimination against women in the 1978 Act was based on objectively justified grounds, a test derived from the ECJ in *Bilka-Kaufhaus GmbH* v *Weber von Hartz* Case 170/84 [1986] ECR 1607.

The application was dismissed by the Divisional Court and this was affirmed by a majority in the Court of Appeal. The EOC and Mrs Day appealed to the House of Lords.

LORD KEITH OF KINKEL: . . . The next question is whether there exists any decision or justiciable issue susceptible of judicial review. The EOC's application sets out the Secretary of State's letter of 23 April 1990 as being the reviewable decision. In my opinion that letter does not constitute a decision. It does no more than state the Secretary of State's view that the threshold provisions of the Act of 1978 regarding redundancy pay and compensation for unfair dismissal are justifiable and in conformity with European Community law. The real object of the EOC's attack is these provisions themselves. The question is whether judicial review is available for the purpose of securing a declaration that certain United Kingdom primary legislation is incompatible with European Community law. It is argued for the Secretary of State that Ord. 53, r. 1(2), which gives the court power to make declarations in judicial review proceedings, is only applicable where one of the prerogative orders would be available under rule 1(1), and that if there is no decision in respect of which one of these writs might be issued a declaration cannot be made. I consider that to be too narrow an interpretation of the court's powers. It would mean that while a declaration that a statutory instrument is incompatible with European Community law could be made, since such an instrument is capable of being set aside by certiorari, no such declaration could be made as regards primary legislation. However, in the *Factortame* series of cases (*Reg.* v *Secretary of State for Transport, ex parte Factortame Ltd* [1990] 2 AC 85; *Reg.* v *Secretary of State for Transport, ex parte Factortame Ltd (No. 2)* (Case 213/89) [1991] 1 AC 603; *Reg.* v *Secretary of State for Transport, ex parte Factortame Ltd (No. 3)* (Case C 221/89) [1992] QB 680) the applicants for judicial review sought a declaration that the provisions of Part II of the Merchant Shipping Act 1988 should not apply to them on the ground that such application would be contrary to Community law, in particular articles 7 and 52 of the EEC Treaty (principle of non-discrimination on the ground of nationality and right of establishment). The applicants were companies incorporated in England which were controlled by Spanish nationals and owned fishing vessels which on account of such control were denied registration in the register of British vessels by virtue of the restrictive conditions contained in Part II of the Act of 1988. The Divisional Court (*Reg.* v *Secretary of State for Transport, ex parte Factortame Ltd* [1989] 2 CMLR 353), under article 177 of the Treaty, referred to the European Court of Justice a number of questions, including the question whether these restrictive conditions were compatible with articles 7 and 52 of the Treaty. The European Court [1992] QB 680 answered that question in the negative, and, although the final result is not reported, no doubt the Divisional Court in due course granted a declaration accordingly. The effect was that certain provisions of United Kingdom primary legislation were held to be invalid in their purported application to nationals of member states of the European Economic Community, but without any prerogative order being available to strike down the legislation in question, which of course remained valid as regards nationals of non-member states.

At no stage in the course of the litigation, which included two visits to this House, was it suggested that judicial review was not available for the purpose of obtaining an adjudication upon the validity of the legislation in so far as it affected the applicants.

The *Factortame* case is thus a precedent in favour of the EOC's recourse to judicial review for the purpose of challenging as incompatible with European Community law the relevant provisions of the Act of 1978. It also provides an answer to the third procedural point taken by the Secretary of State, which maintains that the Divisional Court had no jurisdiction to declare that the United Kingdom or the Secretary of State is in breach of obligation under Community law. There is no need for any such declaration. A declaration that the threshold provisions of the Act of 1978 are incompatible with Community law would suffice for the purposes sought to be achieved by the EOC and is capable of being granted consistently with the precedent afforded by *Factortame*. This does not involve, as contended for the Secretary of State, any attempt by the EOC to enforce the international treaty obligations of the United Kingdom. The EOC is concerned simply to obtain a ruling which reflects the primacy of European Community law enshrined in section 2 of the Act of 1972 and determines whether the relevant United Kingdom law is compatible with the Equal Pay Directive and the Equal Treatment Directive.

Similar considerations provide the answer to the Secretary of State's fourth procedural point by which it is maintained that the Divisional Court is not the appropriate forum to decide the substantive issues at stake. The issues at stake are similar in character to those which were raised in *Factortame*. The Divisional Court is the only English forum in which the EOC, having the capacity and sufficient interest to do so, is in a position to secure the result which it desires. It is said that the incompatibility issue could be tested in proceedings before the European Court of Justice instituted by the European Commission against the United Kingdom under 169 of the EEC Treaty. That may be true, but it affords no reason for concluding that the Divisional Court is an inappropriate forum for the application by the EOC designed towards a similar end and, indeed, there are grounds for the view that the Divisional Court is the more appropriate forum, since the European Court of Justice has said that it is for the national court to determine whether an indirectly discriminatory pay practice is founded on objectively justified economic grounds: see *Bilka-Kaufhaus GmbH* v *Weber von Hartz* (Case 170/84) [1987] ICR 110, 126.

I turn now to the important substantive issue in the appeal, which is whether or not the threshold provisions in the Act of 1978 have been shown to be objectively justified, the onus of doing so being one which rests on the Secretary of State. . .

The original reason for the threshold provisions of the Act of 1978 appears to have been the view that part time workers were less committed than full-time workers to the undertaking which employed them. In his letter of 23 April 1990 the Secretary of State stated that their purpose was to ensure that a fair balance was struck between the interests of employers and employees. These grounds are not now founded on as objective justification for the thresholds. It is now claimed that the thresholds have the effect that more part-time employment is available than would be the case if employers were liable for redundancy pay and compensation for unfair dismissal to employees who worked for less than eight hours a week or between eight and 16 hours a week for under five years. It is contended that if employers were under that liability they would be inclined to employ less part-time workers and more full-time workers, to the disadvantage of the former.

The bringing about of an increase in the availability of part-time work is properly to be regarded as a beneficial social policy aim and it cannot be said that it is not a necessary aim. The question is whether the threshold provisions of the Act of 1978 have been shown, by reference to objective factors, to be suitable and requisite for achieving that aim. As regards suitability for achieving the aim in question, it is to be noted that the purpose of the thresholds is said to be to reduce the costs to employers of employing part-time workers. The same result, however, would follow from a situation where the basic rate of pay for part time workers was less than the basic rate for full-time workers. No distinction in principle can properly be made between direct and indirect labour costs. While in certain circumstances an employer might be justified in paying full-time workers a higher rate than part-time workers in order to secure the more efficient use of his machinery (see *Jenkins* v *Kingsgate (Clothing Productions) Ltd* [1981] 1 WLR 1485) that would be a special and limited state of affairs. Legislation which permitted a differential of that kind nationwide would present a very different aspect and considering that the great majority of part-time workers are women would surely constitute a gross breach of the principle of equal pay and could not possibly be regarded as a suitable means of achieving an increase in part-time employment. Similar considerations apply to legislation which reduces the indirect cost of employing part-time labour. Then as to the threshold provisions being requisite to achieve the stated aim, the question is whether on the evidence before the Divisional Court they have been proved actually to result in greater availability of part-time work than would be the case without them. In my opinion that question must be answered in the negative. The evidence for the Secretary of State consisted principally of an affidavit by an official in the Department of Employment which set out the views of the Department but did not contain anything capable of being regarded as factual evidence demonstrating the correctness of these views. One of the exhibits to the affidavit was a report with draft Directives prepared by the Social Affairs Commissioner of the European Commission in 1990 (COM(90) 228 final — SYN 280 and SYN 281, Brussels, 13 August 1990; Official Journal 1990 No. C 224, pp. 4–8). This covered a wide range of employment benefits and advantages, including redundancy pay and compensation for unfair dismissal, but proposed a qualifying threshold for those benefits of eight hours of work per week. The basis for that was stated to be the elimination of disproportionate administrative costs and regard to employers' economic needs. These are not the grounds of justification relied on by the Secretary of State. The evidence put in by the EOC consisted in large measure in a report of the House of Commons Employment Committee, 'Part-Time Work,' vol. 1 in 1990 (HC 122–I, 10 January 1990) and a report of the House of Lords Select Committee on the European Communities, 'Part-Time and Temporary Employment,' in 1990 (HL Paper 7, 4 December 1990). These revealed a diversity of views upon the effect of the threshold provisions on part-time work, employers' organisations being of the opinion that their removal would reduce the amount available with trade union representatives and some employers and academics in the industrial relations field taking the opposite view. It also appeared that no other member state of the European Community, apart from the Republic of Ireland, had legislation providing for similar thresholds. The Republic of Ireland, where statute at one time provided for an 18-hour-per-week threshold, had recently introduced legislation reducing this to eight hours. In the Netherlands the proportion of the workforce in part-time employment was in 1988 29.4 per cent and in Denmark 25.5 per cent, neither country having any thresholds similar to those in the Act of 1978. In France legislation was introduced in 1982 providing for part-time workers to have the same rights as full-time, yet between 1983 and 1988 part-time work in that country increased by 36.6 per cent, compared with an increase of 26.1 per cent over the same period in the United Kingdom. While various explanations were suggested on behalf of the Secretary of State for these statistics, there is no means of ascertaining whether these explanations have any validity. The fact is, however, that the proportion of part-time employees in the national workforce is much less than the proportion of full-time employees, their weekly remuneration is necessarily much lower, and the number of them made redundant or unfairly dismissed in any year is not likely to be unduly large. The conclusion must be that no objective justification for the thresholds in the Act of 1978 has been established. . . .

In the light of the foregoing I am of the opinion that the appeal by the EOC should be allowed and that declarations should be made in the following terms: (1) that the provisions of the Employment Protection (Consolidation) Act 1978 whereby employees who work for fewer than 16 hours per week are subject to different conditions in respect of qualification for redundancy pay from those which apply to employees who work for 16 hours per week or more are incompatible with article 119 of the EEC Treaty and the Council Directive of 10 February 1975 (75/117/EEC); (2) that the provisions of the Employment Protection (Consolidation Act 1978 whereby employees who work for fewer than 16 hours per week are subject to different conditions in respect of the right to compensation for unfair dismissal from those which apply to employees who work for 16 hours per week or more are incompatible with the Council Directive of 9 February 1976 (76/207/EEC).

It remains to note that the EOC proposed that the House should grant a declaration to the effect that the Secretary of State is in breach of those provisions of the Equal Treatment Directive which require member states to introduce measures to abolish any laws contrary to the principle of equal treatment. The purpose of such a declaration was said to be to enable part-time workers who were employed otherwise than by the state or an emanation of the state, and who had been deprived of the right to obtain compensation for unfair dismissal by the restrictive thresholds in the Act of 1978, to take proceedings against the United Kingdom for compensation, founding upon the decision of the European Court of Justice in *Francovich* v *Italian Republic* (Cases C–6/90, C–9/90) [1991] ECR 1–5357. In my opinion it would be quite inappropriate to make any such declaration. If there is any individual who believes that he or she has a good claim to compensation under the *Francovich* principle, it is the Attorney-General who would be defendant in any proceedings directed to enforcing it, and the issues raised would not necessarily be identical with any of those which arise in the present appeal.

Lord Jauncey of Tullichettle dissented on the issue of the EOC's sufficient interest to seek judicial review, however, he concurred with the reasoning of his colleagues on the substance. EOC's appeal allowed, declarations made. Mrs Day's appeal dismissed.

Council of Civil Service Unions v *Minister for the Civil Service*
[1985] AC 374
House of Lords

(For the facts of this case see p. 572 *post.*)

LORD FRASER OF TULLYBELTON: . . . As *De Keyser's* case shows, the courts will inquire into whether a particular prerogative power exists or not, and, if it does exist, into its extent. But once the existence and the extent of a power are established to the satisfaction of the court, the court cannot inquire into the propriety of its exercise.

That is undoubtedly the position as laid down in the authorities to which I have briefly referred and it is plainly reasonable in relation to many of the most important prerogative powers which are concerned with control of the armed forces and with foreign policy and with other matters which are unsuitable for discussion or review in the law courts. In the present case the prerogative power involved is power to regulate the Home Civil Service, and I recognise there is no obvious reason why the mode of exercise of that power should be immune from review by the courts. Nevertheless to permit such review would run counter to the great weight of authority to which I have briefly referred. Having regard to the opinion I have reached on Mr. Alexander's second proposition, it is unnecessary to decide whether his first proposition is sound or not and I prefer to leave that question open until it arises in a case where a decision upon it is necessary. I therefore assume, without deciding, that his first proposition is correct and that all powers exercised directly under the prerogative are immune from challenge in the courts. I pass to consider his second proposition . . .

LORD SCARMAN: . . . My Lords, I would wish to add a few, very few, words on the reviewability of the exercise of the royal prerogative. Like my noble and learned friend Lord Diplock, I believe that the law relating to judicial review has now reached the stage where it can be said with confidence that, if the subject matter in respect of which prerogative power is exercised is justiciable, that is to say if it is a matter upon which the court can adjudicate, the exercise of the power is subject to review in accordance with the principles developed in respect of the review of the exercise of statutory power. Without usurping the role of legal historian, for which I claim no special qualification, I would observe that the royal prerogative has always been regarded as part of the common law, and that Sir Edward Coke had no doubt that it was subject to the common law: *Prohibitions del Roy* (1608) 12 Co Rep 63 and the *Proclamations Case* (1611) 12 Co Rep 74. In the latter case he declared, at p. 76, that 'the King hath no prerogative, but that which the law of the land allows him.' It is, of course, beyond doubt that in Coke's time and thereafter judicial review of the exercise of prerogative power was limited to inquiring into whether a particular power existed and, if it did, into its extent: *Attorney-General* v *De Keyser's Royal Hotel Ltd* [1920] AC 508. But this limitation has now gone, overwhelmed by the developing modern law of judicial review: *Reg* v *Criminal Injuries Compensation Board, Ex parte Lain* [1967] 2 QB 864 (a landmark case comparable in its generation with the *Proclamations Case,* 12 Co Rep 74) and *Reg* v *Secretary of State for Home Affairs, Ex parte Hosenball* [1977] 1 WLR 766. Just as ancient restrictions in the law relating to the prerogative writs and orders have not prevented the courts from extending the requirement of natural justice, namely the duty to act fairly, so that it is required of a purely administrative act, so also has the modern law, a vivid sketch of which my noble and learned friend Lord Diplock has included in his speech, extended the range of judicial review in respect of the exercise of prerogative power. Today, therefore, the controlling factor in determining whether the exercise of prerogative power is subject to judicial review is not its source but its subject matter. . . .

LORD DIPLOCK: . . . My Lords, that a decision of which the ultimate source of power to make it is not a statute but the common law (whether or not the common law is for this purpose given the label of 'the prerogative') may be the subject of judicial review on the ground of illegality is, I think, established by the cases cited by my noble and learned friend, Lord Roskill, and this extends to cases where the field of law to which the decision relates is national security, as the decision of this House itself in *Burmah Oil Co. Ltd* v *Lord Advocate*, 1964 SC (HL) 117 shows. While I see no *a priori* reason to rule out 'irrationality' as a ground for judicial review of a ministerial decision taken in the exercise of 'prerogative' powers, I find it difficult to envisage in any of the various fields in which the prerogative remains the only source of the relevant decision-making power a decision of a kind that would be open to attack through the judicial process upon this ground. Such decisions will generally involve the application of government policy. The reasons for the decision-maker taking one course rather than another do not normally involve questions to which, if disputed, the judicial process is adapted to provide the right answer, by which I mean that the kind of evidence that is admissible under judicial procedures and the way in which it has to be adduced tend to exclude from the attention of the court competing policy considerations which, if the executive discretion is to be wisely exercised, need to be weighed against one another – a balancing exercise which judges by their upbringing and experience are ill-qualified to perform. So I leave this as an open question to be dealt with on a case to case basis if, indeed, the case should ever arise.

As respects 'procedural propriety' I see no reason why it should not be a ground for judicial review of a decision made under powers of which the ultimate source is the prerogative. Such indeed was one of the grounds that formed the subject matter of judicial review in *Reg* v *Criminal Injuries Compensation Board, Ex parte Lain* [1967] 2 QB 864. Indeed, where the decision is one which does not alter rights or obligations enforceable in private law but only deprives a person of legitimate expectations, 'procedural impropriety' will normally provide the only ground on which the decision is open to judicial review. But in any event what procedure will satisfy the public law requirement of procedural propriety depends upon the subject matter of the decision, the executive functions of the decision-maker (if the decision is not that of an administrative tribunal) and the particular circumstances in which the decision came to be made. . . .

LORD ROSKILL: . . . My Lords, the right of the executive to do a lawful act affecting the rights of the citizen, whether adversely or beneficially, is founded upon the giving to the executive of a power enabling it to do that act. The giving of such a power usually carries with it legal sanctions to enable that power if necessary to be enforced by the courts. In most cases that power is derived from statute though in some cases, as indeed in the present case, it may still be derived from the prerogative. In yet other cases, as the decisions show, the two powers may coexist or the statutory power may by necessary implication have replaced the former prerogative power. If the executive in pursuance of the statutory power does an act affecting the rights of the citizen, it is beyond question that in principle the manner of the exercise of that power may today be challenged on one or more of the three grounds which I have mentioned earlier in this speech. If the executive instead of acting under a statutory power acts under a prerogative power and in particular a prerogative power delegated to the respondent under article 4 of the Order in Council of 1982, so as to affect the rights of the citizen, I am unable to see, subject to what I shall say later, that there is any logical reason why the fact that the source of the power is the prerogative and not statute should today deprive the citizen of that right of challenge to the manner of its exercise which he would possess were the source of the power statutory. In either case the act in question is the act of the executive. To talk of that act as the act of the sovereign savours of the archaism of past centuries. In reaching this conclusion I find myself in agreement with my noble and learned friends Lord Scarman and Lord Diplock whose speeches I have had the advantage of reading in draft since completing the preparation of this speech.

But I do not think that that right of challenge can be unqualified. It must, I think, depend upon the subject matter of the prerogative power which is exercised. Many examples were given during the argument of prerogative powers which as at present advised I do not think could properly be made the subject of judicial review. Prerogative powers such as those relating to the making of treaties, the defence of the realm, the prerogative of mercy, the grant of honours, the dissolution of Parliament and the appointment of ministers as well as others are not, I think, susceptible to judicial review because their nature and subject matter are such as not to be amenable to the judicial process. The courts are not the place wherein to determine whether a treaty should be concluded or the armed forces disposed in a particular manner or Parliament dissolved on one date rather than another.

In my view the exercise of the prerogative which enabled the oral instructions of 22 December 1983 to be given does not by reason of its subject matter fall within what for want of a better phrase I would call the 'excluded categories' some of which I have just mentioned. It follows that in principle I can see no reason why those instructions should not be the subject of judicial review. . . .

LORD BRIGHTMAN agreed with LORD FRASER on this point about the prerogative.

R v *Secretary of State for the Home Department, ex parte Fire Brigades Union*
[1995] 2 AC 513
House of Lords

The Criminal Injuries Compensation Scheme had been introduced under the prerogative. Under the Criminal Justice Act 1988, ss. 108–117, Scheds. 6 & 7 the scheme was enacted and would come into force on 'such day as the Secretary of State may . . . appoint' — s. 171(1). No day was appointed and the non-statutory scheme continued. In 1993 the Secretary of State indicated that the enacted provisions would not be brought into force and that the existing scheme would be replaced by another non-statutory scheme under which the basis for the determination of compensation awards would be changed from common law principles to a tariff fixed according to particular categories of injury. The Appropriation Act 1994 approved supply estimates which contained an amount for criminal injury compensation under the tariff scheme. The applicants, representing people likely to be the victims of violent crime, sought declarations that the Secretary of State was in breach of a duty under the 1988 Act by (1) not bringing into force the the enacted provisions, and (2) that the introduction of the tariff scheme was in breach of the duty and an abuse of prerogative power. The Divisional Court dismissed the application but the Court of Appeal allowed an appeal on the second declaration by a majority. On appeal their Lordships dismissed the cross-appeal that there was a legally enforceable duty to bring sections 108–117 into force.

LORD BROWNE-WILKINSON . . . It does not follow that, because the Secretary of State is not under any duty to bring the section into effect, he has an absolute and unfettered discretion whether or not to do so. So to hold would lead to the conclusion that both Houses of Parliament had passed the Bill through all its stages and the Act received the Royal Assent merely to confer an enabling power on the executive to decide at will whether or not to make the parliamentary provisions a part of the law. Such a conclusion, drawn from a section to which the sidenote is 'Commencement,' is not only constitutionally dangerous but flies in the face of common sense. The provisions for bringing sections into force under section 171(1) apply not only to the statutory scheme but to many other provisions. For example, the provisions of Parts I, II and III relating to extradition, documentary evidence in criminal proceedings and other evidence in criminal proceedings are made subject to the same provisions. Surely, it cannot have been the intention of Parliament to leave it in the entire discretion of the Secretary of State whether or not to effect such important changes to the criminal law. In the absence of express provisions to the contrary in the Act, the plain intention of Parliament in conferring on the Secretary of State the power to bring certain sections into force is that such power is to be exercised so as to bring those sections into force when it is appropriate and unless there is a subsequent change of circumstances which would render it inappropriate to do so.

If, as I think, that is the clear purpose for which the power in section 171(1) was conferred on the Secretary of State, two things follow. First, the Secretary of State comes under a clear duty to keep under consideration from time to time the question whether or not to bring the sections (and therefore the statutory scheme) into force. In my judgment he cannot lawfully surrender or release the power contained in section 171(1) so as to purport to exclude its future exercise either by himself or by his successors. In the course of argument, the Lord Advocate accepted that this was the correct view of the legal position. It follows that the decision of the Secretary of State to give effect to the statement in paragraph 38 of the White Paper (Cm. 2434) that 'the provisions in the Act of 1988 will not now be implemented' was unlawful. The Lord Advocate contended, correctly, that the attempt by the Secretary of State to abandon or release the power conferred on him by section 171(1), being unlawful, did not bind either the present Secretary of State or any successor in that office. It was a nullity. But, in my judgment, that does not alter the fact that the Secretary of State made the attempt to bind himself not to exercise the power conferred by section 171(1) and such attempt was an unlawful act.

There is a second consequence of the power in section 171(1) being conferred for the purpose of bringing the sections into force. As I have said, in my view the Secretary of State is entitled to decide not to bring the sections into force if events subsequently occur which render it undesirable to do so. But if the power is conferred on the Secretary of State with a view to bringing the sections into force, in my judgment the Secretary of State cannot himself procure events to take place and rely on the occurrence of those events as the ground for not bringing the statutory scheme into force. In claiming that the introduction of the new tariff scheme renders it undesirable now to bring the statutory scheme into force, the Secretary of State is, in effect, claiming that the purpose of the statutory power has been frustrated by his own act in choosing to introduce a scheme inconsistent with the statutory scheme approved by Parliament.

The lawfulness of the decision to introduce the tariff scheme

The tariff scheme, if validly introduced under the Royal Prerogative, is both inconsistent with the statutory scheme contained in sections 108 to 117 of the Act and intended to be permanent. In practice, the tariff scheme renders it now either impossible or at least more expensive to reintroduce the old scheme or the statutory enactment of it contained in the Act of 1988. The tariff scheme involves the winding-up of the old Criminal Injuries Compensation Board together with its team of those skilled in assessing compensation on the common law basis and the creation of a new body, the Criminal Injuries Compensation Authority, set up to assess compensation on the tariff basis at figures which, in some cases, will be very substantially less than under the old scheme. All this at a time when Parliament has expressed its will that there should be a scheme based on the tortious measure of damages, such will being expressed in a statute which Parliament has neither repealed nor (for reasons which have not been disclosed) been invited to repeal.

My Lords, it would be most surprising if, at the present day, prerogative powers could be validly exercised by the executive so as to frustrate the will of Parliament expressed in a statute and, to an extent, to pre-empt the decision of Parliament whether or not to continue with the statutory scheme even though the old scheme has been abandoned. It is not for the executive, as the Lord Advocate accepted, to state as it did in the White Paper (paragraph 38) that the provisions in the Act of 1988 "will accordingly be repealed when a suitable legislative opportunity occurs." It is for Parliament, not the executive, to repeal legislation. The constitutional history of this country is the history of the prerogative powers of the Crown being made subject to the overriding powers of the democratically elected legislature as the sovereign body. The prerogative powers of the Crown remain in existence to the extent that Parliament has not expressly or by implication extinguished them. But under the principle in *Attorney-General* v *De Keyser's Royal Hotel Ltd* [1920] AC 508, if Parliament has conferred on the executive statutory powers to do a particular act, that act can only thereafter be done under the statutory powers so conferred: any pre-existing prerogative power to do the same act is pro tanto excluded.

How then is it suggested that the executive has power in the present case to introduce under the prerogative power a scheme inconsistent with the statutory scheme? First, it is said that since sections 108 to 117 of the Act are not in force they confer no legal rights on the victims of crime and impose no duties on the Secretary of State. The *De Keyser* principle does not apply since it only operates to the extent that Parliament has conferred statutory powers which in fact replace pre-existing powers: unless and until the statutory provisions are brought into force, no statutory powers have been conferred and therefore the prerogative powers remain. Moreover, the abandonment of the old scheme and the introduction of the new tariff scheme does not involve any interference by the executive with private rights. The old scheme, being a scheme for ex gratia payments, conferred no legal rights on the victims of crime. The new tariff scheme, being also an ex gratia scheme, confers benefits not detriments on the victims of crime. How can it be lawful to confer benefits on the citizen, provided that Parliament has voted the necessary funds for that purpose?

In my judgment, these arguments overlook the fact that this case is concerned with public, not private, law. If this were an action in which some victim of crime were suing for the benefits to which he was entitled under the old scheme, the arguments which I have recited would have been fatal to his claim: such a victim has no legal right to any benefits. But these are proceedings for judicial review of the decisions of the Secretary of State in the discharge of his public functions. The well known passage in the speech of Lord Diplock in the G.C.H.Q. case, *Council of Civil Service Unions* v *Minister for the Civil Service* [1985] AC 374, 408–410, demonstrates two points relevant to the present case. First, an executive decision which affects the legitimate expectations of the applicant (even though it does not infringe his legal rights) is subject to judicial review. Second, judicial review is as applicable to decisions taken under prerogative powers as to decisions taken under statutory powers save to the extent that the legality of the exercise of certain prerogative powers (e.g. treaty-making) may not be justiciable.

The G.C.H.Q. case demonstrates that the argument based on the ex gratia and voluntary nature of the old scheme and the tariff scheme is erroneous. Although the victim of a crime committed immediately before the White Paper was published had no legal right to receive compensation in accordance with the old scheme, he certainly had a legitimate expectation that he would do so. Moreover, he had a legitimate expectation that, unless there were proper reasons for futher delay in bringing section 108 to 117 of the Act into force, his expectation would be converted into a statutory right. If those legitimate expectations were defeated by the composite decision of the Secretary of State to discontinue the old scheme and not to bring the statutory scheme into force and those decisions were unlawfully taken, he has locus standi in proceedings for judicial review to complain of such illegality.

Similar considerations apply when considering the legality of the minister's decisions. In his powerful dissenting judgment in the Court of Appeal Hobhouse LJ., ante, pp. 523c et seq., decided that, since the statutory provisions had not been brought into force, they had no legal significance of any kind. He held, in my judgment correctly, that the *De Keyser* principle did not apply to the present case: since the statutory provisions were not in force they could not have excluded the pre-existing prerogative powers. Therefore the prerogative powers remained. He then turned to consider whether it could be said that the Secretary of State had abused those prerogative powers and again approached the matter on the basis that since the sections were not in force they had no significance in deciding whether or not the Secretary of State had acted lawfully. I cannot agree with this last step. In public law the fact that a scheme approved by Parliament was on the statute book and would come into force as law if and when the Secretary of State so determined is in my judgment directly relevant to the question whether the Secretary of State could in the lawful exercise of prerogative powers both decide to bring in the tariff scheme and refuse properly to exercise his discretion under section 171(1) to bring the stautory provisions into force.

I turn to consider whether the Secretary of State's decisions were unlawful as being an abuse of power. In this case there are two powers under consideration: first, the statutory power conferred by section 171(1); second, the prerogative power. In order first to test the validity of the exercise of the prerogative power, I will assume that the Act of 1988, instead of conferring a discretion on the Secretary of State to bring the statutory scheme into effect, had specified that it was to come into force one year after that date of the Royal Assent. As Hobhouse LJ held, during that year the *De Keyser* principle would not apply and the prerogative powers would remain exercisable. But in my judgment it would plainly have been an improper use of the prerogative powers if, during that year, the Secretary of State had discontinued the old scheme and introduced the tariff scheme. It would have been improper because in exercising the prerogative power the Secretary of State would have had to have regard to the fact that the statutory scheme was about to come into force: to dismantle the machinery of the old scheme in the meantime would have given rise to futher disruption and expense when, on the first anniversary, the statutory scheme had to be put into operation. This hypothetical case shows that, although during the suspension of the coming into force of the statutory provisions the old prerogative powers continue to exist, the existence of such legislation basically affects the mode in which such prerogative powers can be lawfully exercised.

Does it make any difference that the statutory provisions are to come into effect, not automatically at the end of the year as in the hypothetical case I have put, but on such day as the Secretary of State specifies under a power conferred on him by Parliament for the purpose of bringing the statutory provisions into force? In my judgment it does not. The Secretary of State could only validly exercise the prerogative power to abandon the old scheme and introduce the tariff scheme if, at the same time, he could validly resolve never to bring the statutory provisions and the inconsistent statutory scheme into effect. For the reasons I have already given, he could not validly so resolve to give up his statutory duty to consider from time to time whether to bring the statutory scheme into force. His attempt to do so, being a necessary part of the composite decision which he took, was itself unlawful. By introducing the tariff scheme he debars himself from exercising the statutory power for the purpose and on the basis which Parliament intended. For these reasons, in my judgment the decision to introduce the tariff scheme at a time when the statutory provisions and his power under section 171(1) were on the statute book was unlawful and an abuse of the prerogative power. . .

LORD MUSTILL: . . . I turn to the second area of complaint, which relates to the implementation of the new scheme in a form which differs radically from that contained in Part VII of the Act. This complaint is advanced in two ways, first that the actions and statements of the Secretary of State were an abuse of the powers conferred by section 171(1), secondly, that the powers exercisable under the Royal Prerogative were limited by the presence in the background of the statutory scheme.

At first sight a negative answer to each of these averments seems inevitable, once given the premise that section 171(1) creates no duty to appoint a day. As regards the Act, in a perspective which may never yield a statutory scheme, the possibility of substituting one non-statutory scheme for another must have been just as much envisaged and tolerated as was the continuation of the existing non-statutory scheme, or indeed the termination of any scheme at all. The interval between the passing of the Act and the bringing into force of Part VII, if it ever happened, was simply a statutory blank.

So too, it would appear, as regards the argument based on the Royal Prerogative. The case does not fall within the principle of *Attorney-General* v *De Keyser's Royal Hotel* [1920] AC 508. There, in the words of Lord Dunedin, at p. 526, it was established that "if the whole ground of something which could be done by the prerogative could be done by the statute, it is the statute that rules." Thus, if in the present case Part VII had been brought into force there would have been no room left for the exercise of that aspect of the prerogative which had enabled the Secretary of State to establish and maintain the scheme. Once the superior power of Parliament has occupied the territory the prerogative must quit the field. In the present case, however, the territory is quite untouched. There is no Parliamentary dominion over compensation for criminal injuries, since Parliament has chosen to allow its control to be exercised today, or some day, or never, at the choice of the Secretary of State. Until he chooses to call the Parliamentary scheme into existence there is a legislative void, and the prerogative subsists untouched. The position is just the same as if Part VII had never been enacted, or had been repealed soon afterwards.

This is not to say that the decisions of the Secretary of State in the exercise of the prerogative power to continue, modify or abolish the scheme which his predecessor in the exercise of the same power had called into existence are immune from process. They can be called into question on the familiar grounds: *Reg* v *Criminal Injuries Compensation Board, Ex parte Lain* [1976] 2 QB 864. But no question of irrationality arises here, and the decision to inaugurate a new scheme cannot be rendered unlawful simply because of its conflict on paper with a statutory scheme which is not part of the law.

VII

My Lords, I introduced the preceding discussion with the words 'At first sight' because the applicants have a further (and to my mind altogether more formidable) argument which challenges the implicit assumption that in the absence of a duty to appoint a day the Secretary of State's dealings with the compensation scheme are entirely free from statutory restraint. Contrary to this assumption, it is said, there is no statutory void; for although Part VII is not itself in force, section 171(1) is in force and must not be ignored. The continued existence of section 171(1) means that, even if there is no present duty to appoint a day, there is a continuing duty, which will subsist until either a day is appointed or the relevant provisions are repealed, to address in a rational manner the question whether the power created by section 171(1) should be exercised. This continuing duty overshadows the exercise by the Secretary of State of his powers under the Royal Prerogative.

To some degree this argument is uncontroversial. I accept, and indeed the Lord Advocate does not dispute, that the Secretary of State cannot simply put out of his mind the subsisting discretion under section 171(1). But I part company with the argument at the next stage. One must look at the practicalities, which Parliament must be taken to have envisaged. Pending the appointment of a day it is impossible for the Secretary of State to remain completely inactive. He has no choice but to do something about compensation for criminal injuries: whether wind up the existing scheme and put nothing in its place; or keep the existing scheme in force; or modify it; or copy the statutory scheme. It seems to me inevitable, once it is acknowledged that it may be proper at any given time for the Secretary of State to say, 'It is inappropriate at present to put the statutory scheme into force' that it can be proper for him to install something different from the statutory scheme. Otherwise there would be the absurdity that the Secretary of State is obliged to do something under the Royal Prerogative which he is not obliged to do under the statute. Thus, merely to introduce a cheaper scheme cannot in itself be an abuse of the prerogative powers which subsist in the interim. If the Secretary of State had made an announcement as follows: 'I have come to the conclusion after careful study that for the reasons which I have explained the Parliamentary scheme must now be seen as too expensive, slow and top-heavy; that its priority is not sufficiently high to justify the great expense when there are other calls on the country's resources; that the scheme which I propose will do substantial justice in a more efficient way; and that accordingly I shall run the scheme for a while to see how it works and if, as I confidently expect, it is a success I will ask Parliament to agree with me and repeal the statutory scheme . . .' it is hard to see what objection could have been taken. Does not the minister's actual stance, although perhaps more likely to provoke hostility, really come to the same thing?

The applicants reply that it does not, essentially for two reasons. First, they contend that the Secretary of State has renounced the statutory duty which still dominates the prerogative in this field: not the duty, as under the argument already discussed and rejected, to bring Part VII into force, but the duty to keep under review the powers conferred by section 171(1). I would reject this argument. Perhaps the Secretary of State has laid himself open to attack more than he need have done by the tone of his announcement, but I cannot read him as having said that however much circumstances may change he will never think again; and even if he had said this his statement would have been meaningless since, leaving aside questions arising from the doctrine of 'legitimate expectation' which do not arise here, nothing that he says on one day could bind him in law, or bind his successor, not to say and do the opposite the next day.

Furthermore, even if the argument were sound it would not yield any useful relief. The most that the court could do would be to grant a declaration that the Secretary of State is now and in the future obliged to keep the power under review in a spirit of good faith: something which the Lord Advocate on his behalf has not denied. To this declaration he could respond: 'As for the present, you can see that I have not only kept the appointment of a day under review but have examined it in depth, and have come to a conclusion which, even if you do not care for it, is undeniably rational. As for the future, I will continue to keep the power under review, although I cannot at present foresee circumstances which will impel me or my successors to a different view.' Such a reply would in practice be impregnable, and for my part I would not be prepared as a matter of discretion to grant relief so empty of content.

The applicants' second contention is that the Secretary of State has frustrated the intentions of Parliament by bringing in his own inconsistent scheme and hence nullifying any realistic possibility that he will perform his continuing duty to keep the implementation of the statutory scheme under review. I do not accept this. No doubt if Part VII had been the subject of section 171(1) and hence due to come into force inevitably on a fixed date the creation of any different scheme otherwise than purely as an interim measure would have been a breach of duty. It is also possible to imagine cases where the provisions to be brought into force on an appointed day are such as to become incapable of execution if irreversible changes have been made in the meantime, and it may be that to make such changes would be an abuse of the prerogative. But this is not so here. The new scheme is not in tablets of stone. Certainly, it would be an inconvenient, time-consuming and expensive business to dismantle the scheme and return to something on the former lines. But it would be feasible to do so, just as it proved feasible to pull down the original scheme which has been firmly established over many years. Nothing is certain in politics. Who is to say that a successor in office, under the present or some future administration, with wholly different ideas on social policy and financial means and priorities, might not decide that the present Secretary of State has taken a completely wrong turning and that after all the Parliamentary scheme is best? If he did so, and made an order under section 171(1), accompanied by the necessary regulations and by executive action to wind up the new scheme, there is nothing in what the present Secretary of State has done that could stand in his way. His words have no lasting effect; he has not put an end to the statutory scheme; only Parliament can do that. So long as he and his successors in office perform in good faith the duty to keep the implementation of Part VII under review there is in my opinion no ground for the court to interfere. . . [Lords Lloyd of Berwick and Nicholls of Birkenhead gave speeches concurring with Lord Browne-Wilkinson, and Lord Keith of Kinkel concurred with Lord Mustill]

Appeal dismissed

Question

Are the majority buttressing legislative supremacy against improper executive intervention by way of the prerogative, or is their intervention improper?

Note

See I. Leigh 'The Prerogative, Legislative Power and the Democratic Deficit: the Fire Brigades Case' [1995] 3 *Web CJLI*.

The courts' general approach When the courts review delegated legislation the approach they take is to look at the purposes of the enabling statute in order to check if the delegated legislation is *intra vires* or not. The courts presume that certain things may not be done by delegated legislation without express authorisation by the enabling statute. Thus delegated legislation has been found to be *ultra vires* where it purported to:

(a) impose taxation (*Attorney-General* v *Wilts United Dairies Ltd* (1921) 37 TLR 884);
(b) deny the citizen access to the courts to determine rights and obligations (*Customs & Excise Commissioners* v *Cure & Deely Ltd* [1962] 1 QB 340);
(c) interfere with the liberty of the citizen (*Chester* v *Bateson* [1920] 1 KB 829).

Circumstances can change such a presumption, as in *Liversidge* v *Anderson* [1942] AC 206, in which a Defence of the Realm regulation was upheld which allowed a minister to order detention of persons whom he had reasonable cause to believe to be of hostile origin or associations and in need of subjection to preventive control. The fact that this case was decided during the Second World War may explain its illiberality. See the powerful dissent by Lord Atkin, at pp. 225–46.

Procedural ultra vires Delegated legislation can be challenged on the ground that specified procedures were not followed in making the legislative measure. This is part of the procedural impropriety class of judicial review (see p. 553 *post*). For an example of this ground of review, see *R* v *Secretary of State for Social Services ex parte Association of Metropolitan Authorities* [1986] 1 WLR 1, at p. 381 *ante*. An important distinction is whether the procedural requirement is mandatory or directory.

Substantive ultra vires See Chapter 8 on the illegality and irrationality grounds of review. Where irrationality or reasonableness is the ground of challenge, its chances of success would appear to be lower the more legislative in character the measure is. See *Nottinghamshire CC* v *Secretary of State for the Environment*, at p. 581 *post*. See also on the legislative/administrative distinction, *Bates* v *Lord Hailsham of St Marylebone*, at p. 379 *ante*. There also appears to be a distinction drawn between Parliamentary measures and local authority byelaws, with byelaws being less immune from challenge. There is still a presumption that byelaws passed for general welfare will be benevolently construed (see *Kruse* v *Johnson* [1898] 2 QB 91).

The grounds of judicial review which seem to be most important with respect to quasi-legislation are legitimate expectations and unreasonableness. See G. Ganz, *Quasi-Legislation; Some Recent Developments in Secondary Legislation* (1987), pp. 41–6 and R. Baldwin & J. Houghton, 'Circular Arguments: The Status and Legitimacy of Administrative Rules' [1986] *Public Law* 239.

It seems that vagueness of regulations would, in a suitable case, be a ground of review.

McEldowney v *Forde*

[1971] AC 632
House of Lords

By the Civil Authorities (Special Powers) Act (Northern Ireland) 1922, s. 1:–

> (1) The civil authority shall have power, in respect of persons, matters and things within the jurisdiction of the Government of Northern Ireland to take all such steps and issue all such orders as may be necessary for preserving the peace and maintaining order, according to and in the execution of this Act and the regulations contained in the Schedule thereto, or such regulations as may be made in accordance with the provisions of this Act (which regulations, whether contained in the said Schedule or made as aforesaid, are in this Act referred to as 'the regulations'): Provided that the ordinary course of law and avocations of life and the enjoyment of property shall be interferred with as little as may be permitted by the exigencies of the steps required to be taken under this Act.
>
> (2) For the purposes of this Act the civil authority shall be the Minister of Home Affairs for Northern Ireland. . . .
>
> (3) The Minister of Home Affairs shall have power to make regulations – (*a*) for making further provision for the preservation of the peace and maintenance of order, and (*b*) for varying or revoking any provision of the regulations, and any regulations made as aforesaid shall, subject to the provisions of this Act, have effect and be enforced in like manner as regulations contained in the Schedule to this Act. . . .'

On 22 May 1922 the Minister of Home Affairs made a regulation under the powers conferred by s. 1 (3) of the Act. This provided that:–

> 24A Any person who becomes or remains a member of an unlawful association or who does any act with a view to promoting or calculated to promote the objects of an unlawful association or seditious conspiracy shall be guilty of an offence against these regulations. . . .
>
> The following organisations shall for the purposes of this regulation be deemed to be unlawful associations:
>
> The Irish Republican Brotherhood, The Irish Republican Army, The Irish Volunteers, The Cumann na m'Ban, The Fianna na h'Eireann.

The named organisations were existing organisations of a militant type and it was conceded before the House of Lords, as it had been before the Court of Appeal in Northern Ireland, that they were in fact unlawful organisations.

On 7 March 1967 the Minister of Home Affairs made a further regulation under s. 1 (3) of the Act. After reciting that it was expedient to make further provision for the preservation of the peace and maintenance of order, this stated:

> 1. Regulation 24A of the principal regulations shall have effect as if the following organisations were added to the list of organisations which for the purpose of that regulation are deemed to be unlawful associations:

> 'The organisations at the date of this regulation or at any time thereafter describing themselves as "republican clubs" or any like organisation howsoever described.'

The appellant was charged in the magistrates' court with being a member of the Slaughtneil Republican Club contrary to regulation 24A as amended. The magistrates found that he was a member of the Club but that no evidence was given that he or the club was at any time a threat to peace, law, and order and that in so far as the police were aware there was nothing seditious in its pursuits or those of its members. The charge was dismissed but the Court of Appeal of Nothern Ireland (Lord MacDermott CJ, dissenting) held that the amended regulation was intra vires the Act of 1922 and remitted the case to the magistrates. On appeal to the House of Lords:

LORD HODSON: . . . The proscription of present and future 'republican clubs' including 'any like organisations howsoever described' is said to be something outside the scope and meaning of the Act and so incapable of being related to the prescribed purposes of the Act. Accepting that the word 'republican' is an innocent word and need not connote anything contrary to law, I cannot escape the conclusion that in its context, added to the list of admittedly unlawful organisations of a militant type, the word 'republican' is capable of fitting the description of a club which in the opinion of the Minister should be proscribed as a subversive organisation of a type akin to those previously named in the list of admittedly unlawful organisations. The context in which the word is used shows the type of club which the Minister had in mind and there is no doubt that the mischief aimed at is an association which had subversive objects. On this matter, in my opinion, the court should not substitute its judgment for that of the Minister, on the ground that the banning of 'republican clubs' is too remote. I agree that the use of the words 'any like organisation howsoever described' lends some support to the contention that the regulation is vague and for that reason invalid, but on consideration I do not accept the argument based on vagueness. It is not difficult to see why the Minister, in order to avoid subterfuge, was not anxious to restrict himself to the description 'republican' seeing that there might be similar clubs which he might seek to proscribe whatever they called themselves. If and when any case based on the words 'any like organisation' arises it will have to be decided, but I do not, by reason of the use of those words, condemn the regulation as being too vague or uncertain to be supported. I would dismiss the appeal.

LORD GUEST: . . . The final argument for the appellant related to the third category of organisations which it is said the regulation covered, namely, 'or any like organisation howsoever described.' It was submitted that this would cover any club whatever its name and whatever its objects and that such an exercise of the Minister's power was unreasonable, arbitrary and capricious. In my view this argument is not well founded. The regulation first of all embraces republican clubs eo nomine and they are caught by their very description. If they do not bear the name 'republican,' it would be a question of interpretation after evidence whether any particular club was covered by the words 'any like organisation howsoever described.' It is indeed not necessary for the purposes of this case where the organisation bore the name 'republican club' to examine this question in any great detail. But my provisional view is that the regulation would cover any organisation having similar objects to those of a republican club or of any of the named organisations or of any organisation whose objects included the absorption of Northern Ireland in the Republic of Ireland.

Having regard to all these matters I cannot say that the class of 'like organisations' is either ambiguous or arbitrary so as to invalidate the regulation. In my view this ground of attack also fails. . . . I would therefore dismiss the appeal.

LORD PEARCE: . . . Further, the 1967 regulation is too vague and ambiguous. A man may not be put in peril on an ambiguity under the criminal law. When the 1967 regulation was issued the citizen ought to have been able to know whether he could or could not remain a member of his club without being subject to a criminal prosecution. Yet I doubt if one could have said with certainty that any man or woman was safe in remaining a member of any club in Northern Ireland, however named or whatever its activities or objects.

Had the final phrase 'or any like organisation howsoever described' been absent, the regulation would have simply been an attack on the description 'republican,' however innocent the club's activities. Presumably the justification for it would have to be that the mere existence of the word republican in the name of a club was so inflammatory that its suppression was 'necessary for preserving the peace and maintaining order' and that the 'exigencies' of the need for its suppression did not permit the citizen's right in that respect to prevail. For the reasons given by the Lord Chief Justice I do not accept that such a justification could suffice. But be that as it may, the final phrase shows that this is more than an attack on nomenclature, since the club is deemed equally unlawful if it is a like organisation, whatever be the name under which it goes.

And what is the 'likeness' to a republican club which makes an organisation unlawful 'howsoever described'? Since a republican club is banned whatever may be its activities, the likeness cannot consist in its activities. And since the organisation is unlawful, howsoever described, the 'likeness' cannot consist in a likeness of nomenclature. The only possibility left seems to be that the 'likeness' may consist in the mere fact of being a club. In which case all clubs, however named, are unlawful – which is absurd.

One cannot disregard the final phrase, since that would wholly alter the meaning of the regulation. Without the final phrase it is simply an attack on nomenclature. But with the final phrase it cannot simply be an attack on nomenclature. One cannot sever the bad from the good by omitting a phrase when the omission must alter the meaning of the rest. One must take the whole sentence as it stands. And as it stands it is too vague and ambiguous to be valid.

I would therefore allow the appeal.

LORD PEARSON: . . . There is one further argument against the validity of this regulation, and it is the most formidable one. It is that the regulation is too vague, because it includes the words 'or any like organisation howsoever described.' I have had doubts on this point, but in the end I think the argument against the validity of the regulation ought not to prevail. The Minister's intention evidently was (if I may use a convenient short phrase) to ban republican clubs. He had to exclude in advance two subterfuges which might defeat his intention. First, an existing republican club might be dissolved, and a new one created. The words 'or at any time thereafter' would exclude that subterfuge as well as applying to new republican clubs generally. Secondly, a new club, having the characteristic object of a republican club, might be created with some other title such as 'New Constitution Group' or 'Society for the alteration of the Constitution.' The words 'or any like organisation however described' would exclude that subterfuge.

In construing this regulation one has to bear in mind that it authorises very drastic interference with freedom of association, freedom of speech and in some circumstances the liberty of the subject. Therefore it should be narrowly interpreted. Also it should if possible be so construed as to have sufficient certainty to be valid – ut res magis valeat quam pereat.

In my opinion the proper construction of the regulation is that the organisations to be deemed unlawful are –

(i) any organisation describing itself as a 'republican club,' whatever its actual objects may be, and

(ii) any organisation which has the characteristic object of a republican club – namely, to introduce republican government into Northern Ireland – whatever its name may be.

I would dismiss the appeal

LORD DIPLOCK: . . . But there is another reason for rejecting this construction of the regulation which I find compelling. It is not, in my view, permissible to treat the regulation as severable in the way adopted by the majority of the Court of Appeal. To do so is to treat it as striking at more than one unrelated mischief whereas the inclusion in the description of the organisations deemed to be unlawful association of the words 'any like organisation' makes it plain that it is organisations possessing a common mischievous characteristic that are intended to be proscribed.

What then is that characteristic? Even if it were legitimate to infer that the Minister had knowledge of the objects of 'republican clubs' in existence at the date of the regulation he could not have knowledge of what would be the objects of clubs to be formed in the future which would describe themselves as 'republican clubs.' The characteristic struck at, therefore, cannot be the possession *in fact* of unlawful objects by the organisations proscribed. Nor for the reasons previously indicated can the common characteristic struck at be the use of the name 'republican club.' It is conceivable that the adoption of a particular name might of itself be so inflammatory in Northern Ireland as to endanger the preservation of peace and the maintenance of order, but the regulation proscribes 'like organisations' which do not adopt this name.

But there are no other ascertainable common characteristics of the organisations described in the regulation except that they are composed of members and possess objects of some kind or other and describe themselves by some name or other. If the Minister's intention was to proscribe all clubs and associations in Northern Ireland whatever their objects and name the regulation plainly falls ouside the power delegated to him by section 1 (3) of the Special Powers Act to make regulations 'for making further provision for the preservation of the peace and the maintenance of order.' It makes unlawful conduct which cannot have the effect of endangering the preservation of the peace or the maintenance of order. But if the Minister's intention was to proscribe some narrower category of organisations the suppression of which would have the effect of preserving the peace and maintaining order he has in my view failed to disclose in the regulation what the narrower category is. A regulation whose meaning is so vague that it cannot be ascertained with reasonable certainty cannot fall within the words of delegation.

It is possible to speculate that the Minister when he made the regulation now challenged bona fide believed that the sort of club which at that date described itself as a 'republican club' was likely to have unlawful objects which would endanger the preservation of the peace and the maintenance of order and by the words that he added he may have intended to do no more than to prevent such clubs from evading the regulation by dissolving and re-forming or by changing their names. If this was his intention he signally failed to express it in the regulation, for by no process of construction can it be given this limited effect. Or he may have thought it administratively convenient to insert in the regulation a description of proscribed organisations so wide as to include also those with lawful objects in order to be sure that none with unlawful objects should be omitted, and to rely upon the administrative discretion of the Attorney-General under section 3 (2) of the Act not to enforce the regulation. But to do this, however, if administratively convenient, would be outside his delegated legislative powers.

But this is speculation not construction and your Lordships' function is limited to construing the words which the Minister has used. In my view the words used by the Minister in the regulation are either too wide to fall within the description of the regulations which he is empowered to make under section 1 (3) of the Special Powers Act or are too vague and uncertain in their meaning to be enforceable.

I would allow this appeal.

Appeal dismissed.

Note

For criticism of this case, see MacCormick (1970) 86 *Law Quarterly Review* 171.

Questions

1. Do you think that the context of the 'troubles' in Northern Ireland helps explain the decision of the majority?

2. Is it not more important in that kind of situation for the courts to examine very carefully regulations which interfere with the liberty of the citizen?

Exclusion of judicial review The exclusion of judicial review of delegated legislation has been the subject of a variety of decisions. On the one hand *Institute of Patent Agents* v *Lockwood* [1894] AC 347 indicated that it was possible, whilst *Minister of Health* v *R, ex parte Yaffe* [1931] AC 494 determined that judicial review was not excluded. See also p. 635 *post.*

Discretionary nature of judicial review See *R* v *Secretary of State for Social Services ex parte Association of Metropolitan Authorities* [1986] 1 WLR 1, at p. 381 *ante.*

See also p. 629 *post* on the discretionary nature of judicial review.

Questions

1. Is it more likely that delegated legislation which has been in existence for a little time will not be struck down by the courts than is the case with the various types of quasi-legislation and administrative action?

2. What kinds of delegated legislation might be struck down even if they had been in existence for some time?

3. Is judicial wariness in striking down delegated legislation satisfactory given the lack of real parliamentary oversight?

Partial invalidity

DPP v Hutchinson
[1990] 2 AC 783
House of Lords

The Secretary of State was empowered to make byelaws for land appropriated for military purposes under the Military Lands Act 1892, s. 14(1). The power allowed for byelaws which could prohibit intrusion onto such land but did not permit any prejudicial affect on any right in common. The Secretary of State made the RAF Greenham. Common Byelaws 1985 in respect of common land which had been appropriated for military purposes. Byelaw 2(b) provided that no person could enter or remain in the protected area without the permission of an authorised person. Protestors against nuclear weapons, who camped on the protected land, were charged and convicted of infringing byelaw 2(b). The Crown Court allowed the appeal on the basis that it was ultra vires as it prejudiced the rights of commoners. This decision was overturned by the Divisional Court on an appeal by case stated. The defendants appealed to the House of Lords.

LORD BRIDGE: My Lords, these two appeals raise important questions as to the tests to be applied in determining whether delegated legislation which on its face exceeds the power conferred upon the legislator may nevertheless be upheld and enforced by the courts in part on the basis that the legislation is divisible into good and bad parts and that the good is independent of, and untainted by, the bad.

When a legislative instrument made by a law-maker with limited powers is challenged, the only function of the court is to determine whether there has been a valid exercise of that limited legislative power in relation to the matter which is the subject of disputed enforcement. If a law-maker has validly exercised his power, the court may give effect to the law validly made. But if the court sees only an invalid law made in excess of the law-maker's power, it has no jurisdiction to modify or adapt the law to bring it within the scope of the law-maker's power. These, I believe, are the basic principles which have always to be borne in mind in deciding whether legislative provisions which on their face exceed the law-maker's power may be severed so as to be upheld and enforced in part.

The application of these principles leads naturally and logically to what has traditionally been regarded as the test of severability. It is often referred to inelegantly as the 'blue pencil' test. Taking the simplest case of a single legislative instrument containing a number of separate clauses of which one exceeds the law-maker's power, if the remaining clauses enact free-standing provisions which were intended to operate and are capable of operating independently of the offending clause, there is no reason why those clauses should not be upheld and enforced. The law-maker has validly exercised his power by making the valid clauses. The invalid clause may be disregarded as unrelated to, and having no effect upon, the operation of the valid clauses, which accordingly may be allowed to take effect without the necessity of any modification or adaptation by the court. What is involved is in truth a double test. I shall refer to the two aspects of the test as textual severability and substantial severability. A legislative instrument is textually severable if a clause, a sentence, a phrase or a single word may be disregarded, as exceeding the law-maker's power, and what remains of the text is still grammatical and coherent. A legislative instrument is substantially severable if the substance of what remains after severance is essentially unchanged in its legislative purpose, operation and effect.

The early English authorities take it for granted, I think, that if byelaws are to be upheld as good in part notwithstanding that they are bad in part, they must be both textually and substantially severable. . . .

Our attention has been drawn to a number of more recent English authorities on the severability of provisions contained in various documents of a public law character. I doubt if these throw much light on the specific problem of severance in legislative instruments. The modern authority most directly in point and that on which the Divisional Court relied is *Dunkley* v *Evans* [1981] 1 WLR 1522. The West Coast Herring (Prohibition of Fishing) Order 1978 (SI 1978 No. 930) prohibited fishing for herring in an area defined in the Schedule to the Order as within a line drawn by reference to coordinates and coastlines. The Order was made by the Minister of Agriculture, Fisheries and Food under the Sea Fish (Conservation) Act 1967. The prohibited area included a stretch of sea adjacent to the coast of Northern Ireland, representing 0.8 per cent of the total area covered by the Order, to which the enabling power in the Act of 1967 did not extend. The defendants admitted fishing in a part of the prohibited area to which the enabling power did extend but submitted that, by including the area to which the enabling power did not extend, the Minister had acted ultra vires and, since textual severance was not possible, the whole Order was invalid. The justices accepted this submission and dismissed the informations. The Divisional Court allowed the prosecutor's appeal. Delivering the judgment of the court, Ormrod LJ cited, at pp. 1524–1525, the following passage from the judgment of Cussen J in the Supreme Court of Victoria in *Olsen* v *City of Camberwell* [1926] VLR 58, 68:

> 'If the enactment, with the invalid portion omitted, is so radically or substantially different a law as to the subject matter dealt with by what remains from what it would be with the omitted portions forming part of it as to warrant a belief that the legislative body intended it as a whole only, or, in other words, to warrant a belief that if all could not be carried into effect the legislative body would not have enacted the remainder independently, then the whole must fail.'

It is to be noted that this quotation is from the judgment in a case where textual severance was possible. Following the quotation the judgment of Ormrod LJ continued:

> We respectfully agree with and adopt this statement of the law. It would be difficult to imagine a clearer example than the present case of a law which the legislative body would have enacted independently of the offending portion and which is so little affected by eliminating the invalid portion. This is clearly, therefore, an order which the court should not strive officiously to kill to any greater extent than it is compelled to do. . . . We can see no reason why the powers of the court to sever the invalid portion of a piece of subordinate legislation from the valid should be restricted to cases where the text of the legislation lends itself to judicial surgery, or textual emendation by excision. It would have been competent for the court in an action for a declaration that the provisions of the Order in this case did not apply to the area of the sea off Northern Ireland reserved by section 23 (1) of the Act of 1967, as amended, to make the declaration sought, without in any way affecting the validity of the Order in relation to the remaining 99.2 per cent of the area referred to in the Schedule to the Order. Such an order was made, in effect, by the House of Lords in *Hotel and Catering Industry Training Board* v *Automobile Proprietary Ltd*

[1969] 1 WLR 697, and by Donaldson J in *Agricultural, Horticultural and Forestry Industry Training Board* v *Aylesbury Mushrooms Ltd* [1972] 1 WLR 190. . . .

The modern English authority to which I attach most significance is *Daymond* v *Plymouth City Council* [1976] AC 609, where severability was not in issue, but where it appears to have been taken for granted without question that severance was possible. Section 30(1) of the Water Act 1973 gave power to water authorities:

> to fix, and to demand, take and recover such charges for the services performed, facilities provided or rights made available by them (including separate charges for separate services, facilities or rights or combined charges for a number of services, facilities or rights) as they think fit.

The subsection was silent as to who was liable to pay the charges. The Water Authorities (Collection of Charges) Order 1974 (SI 1974 No. 448) embodied provisions which required a rating authority to collect on behalf of a water authority a 'general services charge' (article 7(2)) referable to sewerage services 'from every person who is liable to pay the general rate in respect of a hereditament. . . .' (article 10(1)). A householder whose property was not connected to a sewer, the nearest sewer being 400 yards away from his house, refused to pay the charge and brought an action for a declaration that the Order could not properly apply to him. This House held, by a majority of three to two, that on the true construction of the enabling legislation there was no power to impose a charge for sewerage services upon occupiers of property not connected to a sewer. As I have said, the question of severability was not raised, but there is no hint in the speeches that the invalidation of the charging provision in relation to properties not connected to sewers would affect their validity in relation to properties which were so connected.

The test of textual severability has the great merit of simplicity and certainty. When it is satisfied the court can readily see whether the omission from the legislative text of so much as exceeds the law-maker's power leaves in place a valid text which is capable of operating and was evidently intended to operate independently of the invalid text. But I have reached the conclusion, though not without hesitation, that a rigid insistence that the test of textual severability must always be satisfied if a provision is to be upheld and enforced as partially valid will in some cases, of which *Dunkley* v *Evans* and *Daymond* v *Plymouth City Council* are good examples, have the unreasonable consequence of defeating subordinate legislation of which the substantial purpose and effect was clearly within the law-maker's power when, by some oversight or misapprehension of the scope of that power, the text, as written, has a range of application which exceeds that scope. It is important, however, that in all cases an appropriate test of substantial severability should be applied. When textual severance is possible, the test of substantial severability will be satisfied when the valid text is unaffected by, and independent of, the invalid. The law which the court may then uphold and enforce is the very law which the legislator has enacted, not a different law. But when the court must modify the text in order to achieve severance, this can only be done when the court is satisfied that it is effecting no change in the substantial purpose and effect of the impugned provision. Thus, in *Dunkley* v *Evans*, the legislative purpose and effect of the prohibition of fishing in the large area of the sea in relation to which the minister was authorised to legislate was unaffected by the obviously inadvertent inclusion of the small area of sea to which his power did not extend. In *Daymond* v *Plymouth City Council* the draftsman of the Order had evidently construed the enabling provision as authorising the imposition of charges for sewerage services upon occupiers of property irrespective of whether or not they were connected to sewers. In this error he was in the good company of two members of your Lordships' House. But this extension of the scope of the charging power, which, as the majority held, exceeded its proper limit, in no way affected the legislative purpose and effect of the charging power as applied to occupiers of properties which were connected to sewers.

To appreciate the full extent of the problem presented by the Greenham byelaws it is necessary to set out the full text of the prohibitions imposed by byelaw 2 which provides:

> No person shall: (a) enter or leave or attempt to enter or leave the protected area except by way of an authorised entrance or exit. (b) enter, pass through or over or remain in or over the protected area without authority or permission given by or on behalf of one of the persons mentioned in byelaw 5(1). (c) cause or permit any vehicle, animal, aircraft or thing to enter into or upon or to pass through or over or to be or remain in or upon or over the protected area without authority or permission given by or on behalf of one of the persons mentioned in byelaw 5(1). (d) remain in the protected area after having been directed to leave by any of the persons mentioned in byelaw 4. (e) make any false statement, either orally or in writing, or employ any other form of misrepresentation in order to obtain entry to any part of the protected area or to any building or premises within the protected area. (f) obstruct any constable (including a constable under the control of the Defence Council) or any other person acting in the proper exercise or execution of his duty within the protected area. (g) enter any part of the protected area which is shown by a notice as being prohibited or restricted. (h) board, attempt to board, or interfere with, or interfere with the movement or passage, of any vehicle, aircraft or other installation in the protected area. (i) distribute or display any handbill, leaflet, sign, advertisement, circular, poster, bill, notice or object within the protected area or affix the same to either side of the perimeter fences without authority or permission given by or on behalf of one of the persons mentioned in byelaw 5(1). (j) interfere with or remove from the protected area any property under the control of the Crown or the service authorities of a visiting force or, in either case, their agents or contractors. (k) wilfully damage, destroy, deface or remove any notice board or sign within the protected area. (l) wilfully damage, soil, deface or mark any wall, fence, structure, floor, pavement, or other surface within the protected area.

It is at once apparent that paragraphs (a), (b), (c), (d), (g), (j) and (l) are ultra vires as they stand. Paragraphs (e), (f), (i) and (k) appear to be valid and paragraph (h) is probably good in part and bad in part, since the exercise by a commoner of his rights may well interfere with the movement or passage of vehicles. Textual severance can achieve nothing since it is apparent that the valid provisions are merely ancillary to the invalid provisions. . . .

I think the proper test to be applied when textual severance is impossible, following in this respect the Australian authorities, is to abjure speculation as to what the maker of the law might have done if he had applied his mind to the relevant limitation on his powers and to ask whether the legislative instrument

> with the invalid portions omitted would be substantially a different law as to the subject matter dealt with by what remains from what it would be with the omitted portions forming part of it: *Rex* v *Commonwealth Court of Conciliation and Arbitration, Ex parte Whybrow & Co.* 11 CLR 1, 27.

In applying this test the purpose of the legislation can only be inferred from the text as applied to the factual situation to which its provisions relate. Considering the

Greenham byelaws as a whole it is clear that the absolute prohibition which they impose upon all unauthorised access to the protected area is no less than is required to maintain the security of an establishment operated as a military airbase and wholly enclosed by a perimeter fence. Byelaws drawn in such a way as to permit free access to all parts of the base to persons exercising rights of common and their animals would be byelaws of a totally different character. They might serve some different legislative purpose in a different factual situation, as do some other byelaws to which our attention has been drawn relating to areas used as military exercise grounds or as military firing ranges. But they would be quite incapable of serving the legislative purpose which the Greenham byelaws, as drawn, are intended to serve.

For these reasons I conclude that the invalidity of byelaw 2(b) cannot be cured by severance. It follows that the appellants were wrongly convicted and I would allow their appeals, set aside the order of the Divisional Court and restore the order of the Crown Court at Reading.

[*Lords Griffith, Goff and Oliver concurred with Lord Bridge.*)

LORD LOWRY: . . . My Lords, the accepted view in the common law jurisdictions has been that, when construing legislation the validity of which is under challenge, the first duty of the court, in obedience to the principle that a law should, whenever possible, be interpreted ut res magis valeat quam pereat, is to see whether the impugned provision can reasonably bear a construction which renders it valid. Failing that, the court's duty, subject always to any relevant statutory provision such as the Australian section 15A, is to decide whether the whole of the challenged legislation or only part of it must be held invalid and ineffective. That problem has traditionally been resolved by applying first the textual, and then the substantial, severability test. If the legislation failed the first test, it was condemned in its entirety. If it passed that test, it had to face the next hurdle. This approach, in my opinion, has a great deal in its favour.

The basic principle is that an ultra vires enactment, such as a byelaw, is void ab initio and of no effect. The so-called blue pencil test is a concession to practicality and ought not to be extended or weakened. In its traditional form it is acceptable because, once the offending words are ignored, no word or phrase needs to be given a meaning different from, or more restrictive than, its original meaning. Therefore the court has not legislated; it merely continues to apply that part of the existing legislation which is good.

It may be argued that a policy split has developed and that it is time to show common sense and bring our thinking up to date by a further application of the ut res magis valeat quam pereat principle. I am, however, chary of yielding to this temptation for a number of reasons. 1. The blue pencil test already represents a concession to the erring law-maker, the justification for which I have tried to explain. 2. When applying the blue pencil test (which actually means ignoring the offending words), the court cannot cause the text of the instrument to be altered. It will remain as the ostensible law of the land unless and until it is replaced by something else. It is too late now to think of abandoning the blue pencil method, which has much to commend it, but the disadvantage inherent in the method ought not to be enlarged. 3. It is up to the law-maker to keep within his powers and it is in the public interest that he should take care, in order that the public may be able to rely on the written word as representing the law. Further enlargement of the court's power to validate what is partially invalid will encourage the law-maker to enact what he pleases, or at least to enact what may or may not be valid, without having to fear any worse result than merely being brought back within bounds. 4. *Dunkley* v *Evans* [1981] 1 WLR, 1522 and *Thames Water Authority* v *Elmbridge Borough Council* [1983] QB, 570 are very special cases. I recall in that regard what McNeill J said in *Reg.* v *Secretary of State for Transport, Ex parte Greater London Council* [1986] QB 556, 582D. 5. To liberalise the test would, in my view, be anarchic, not progressive. It would tend in the wrong direction, unlike some developments in the law of negligence, which have promoted justice for physically or economically injured persons, or the sounder aspects of judicial review, which have promoted freedom and have afforded protection from power. 6. The current of decisions and relevant authority has flowed in favour of the traditional doctrine.

This last observation brings me back to *Daymond* v *Pymouth City Council* [1976] AC 609, the case in which, as my noble and learned friend has said, it appears to have been taken for granted that severance was possible, and the question is, what significance should be attached to that fact when reviewing the doctrine of textual severability?

One cannot gainsay the authority of the Appellate Committee or that of the individual members of your Lordships' House of whom the committee was composed. Any indication, even if given obiter, that their Lordships, having considered the point, would have held that the Water Authorities (Collection of Charges) Order 1974 was valid and effective against occupiers of property who benefited directly from the water authority's services while inoperative against the occupiers who did not so benefit, could significantly erode the received doctrine of textual severability, since the blue pencil test could not have been used. But one must consider the way in which the case proceeded in your Lordships' House and also at first instance.

The remedy which the plaintiff sought was a declaration that the Plymouth City Council were not empowered to demand from him £4.89 or any sum on behalf of the South West Water Authority by way of a charge for sewerage and sewage disposal services. He contended that the water authority had power under section 30 of the Act of 1973 only to demand charges for services performed, facilities provided or rights made available and that, if the Order of 1974 purported to confer power to demand other charges, it was *to that extent* ultra vires. The words-which I have emphasised set the stage for the argument and the decision. Phillips J. made the declaration sought. On appeal direct to this House under section 12 (1) of the Administration of Justice Act 1969 it was held, dismissing the appeal, Lord Wilberforce and Lord Diplock dissenting, that the plaintiff was entitled to the declaration made. The sole issue at each stage was whether section 30 empowered the water authority to charge occupiers of property who did not receive the benefit of the authority's services directly. No case was cited, and no argument was advanced, on the question whether the invalidity of the authority's demand against such occupiers as the plaintiff would nullify the Order of 1974 in relation to occupiers who were receiving the services, and both the initial judgment and their Lordships' speeches were entirely devoted to the complicated and strenuously contested issue concerning the scope of section 30. The minority took the view that section 30 authorised the proposed demand, and they had nothing to consider except the effect of the section on the plaintiff. And the majority, who reached the opposite conclusion, were concerned with the same point. The textual severability doctrine would have been of no help to either side.

It would therefore not be surprising if, having regard to the remedy sought and granted, the residual effect of the Order of 1974 on those who admittedly were liable for the charge was never mentioned.

I am therefore very reluctant to treat the case as an authority which by implication contradicts the established doctrine of textual severability for the purposes of the present appeal. Accordingly, I would allow this appeal on two grounds, (1) that there is no valid part of byelaw 2 (b) which can be severed from the invalid part and stand by itself and (2) that the byelaw would not in any event survive the test of substantial severability.

Appeal allowed.

Questions

1. Is the majority giving the courts a wide power to amend delegated legislation by severing invalid portions?

2. Is such a power to amend constitutional or desirable, given that Parliament can rarely amend delegated legislation?

Problems

T. Daintith, 'The Executive Power Today: Bargaining and Economic Control' in *The Changing Constitution* eds J. Jowell and D. Oliver, (2nd edn, 1989), p. 193, at pp. 197–98, 215–18

I use the term *imperium* to describe the government's use of the command of law in aid of its policy objectives, and the term *dominium* to describe the employment of the wealth of government for this purpose. The point of choosing a special terminology to mark this distinction is that different constitutional frameworks exist, as we shall see, for the deployment of these two kinds of resources.

A practical example may help to clarify the meaning of these terms, and will show incidentally the wide range of potential policy choices which government may need to consider in relation to a given problem. When oil and gas began to be discovered under the British sector of the North Sea from the early 1960s onward, government assumed that the massive investment required in rigs, platforms, barges, and other equipment would bring major opportunities for British industry. A report published in 1972 showed, however, that British industry was winning a disappointingly low share of orders, and was likely to go on doing so in the absence of government intervention: one of the reasons was that many of the major companies searching for and finding oil and gas under petroleum production licences were American and had a strong propensity to stick to their United States suppliers for all items of equipment, even down to such mundane necessities as chicken-wire. What forms might government intervention take? Using *imperium*, it could promulgate legislation (or use existing legal powers, if available) to prohibit or tax the importation or use of foreign equipment; or, more subtly, to set compulsory standards with which only British manufacturers (warned well in advance) would find it easy to conform; or to require licensees to buy British in preference to foreign goods where supplied on competitive terms. Using *dominium*, it could offer subsidies to British manufacturers of relevant equipment, or to licensees who purchased British, rather than foreign, equipment. Alternatively, *dominium* could be employed through the licence, which is in the nature of a grant to the licensee of the right to obtain for himself, against payment of a royalty, petroleum over which the State has proprietary rights. A preference in favour of British equipment could be made a term of the licence; or an undertaking to exercise such a peference, or evidence of having purchased such equipment in the past, could be made a criterion for the award of a licence. Forms of intervention other than through *imperium* or *dominium* might also be considered; government could content itself with a campaign of exhortation to licensees to buy British, or with the dissemination of information to licensees and manufacturers alike (though such measures will almost certainly involve government expenditure, and can therefore be seen as a form of *dominium*).

In the event, the government employed a variety of measures. It offered a subsidy to purchasers of British-made equipment, set up a specialized unit within the appropriate department to encourage and monitor British orders; made an informal agreement with the organization representing the main North Sea licensees, the United Kingdom Offshore Operators' Association, on tendering rules that would give British manufacturers 'full and fair opportunity' to compete for orders; and made acceptance and (where appropriate) past observance of this agreement one of the informal criteria considered by the minister in allocating petroleum licences among competing applicants . . .

During this period [1975–78], an undertaking to comply with the government's wages policy was a prerequisite for the award of almost all government contracts and of some government industrial assistance; a known breach of the policy disqualified a company from consideration for such contracts and assistance (the 'blacklist'); and compliance with the policy was secured for the future as a legally enforceable term of such contracts and assistance. By thus using its very considerable purchasing and grant-giving powers, government was able to induce compliance with its policy over a very wide area of British industry (contractors were required to procure compliance by their major subcontractors) in a way which, again, one might according to a normal model of policy implementation expect to be achieved by *imperium*-type legislation. Was it just the shock of the unexpected that caused this use of *dominium* to be branded as 'unconstitutional?'

It is noteworthy that although government had announced its intention to use contracts and assistance in this way as early as 1975, the matter did not become controversial until mid-1977. For this there may be two reasons. First, by reason of its failure to reach agreement with the TUC on a new phase of pay policy, as already noted, the government was, from mid-1977, relying almost exclusively on this instrument for the enforcement of its pay limit. Second, the pay limit adopted in this phase was extremely vague: that wage settlements should *average* 10 per cent over the year. This implied a moving target, for excessively large early settlements would mean that later ones needed to be held down well below 10 per cent if the average was to be maintained. Settlements thus had to be looked at on a case-by-case basis, and the non-award of a grant or contract, or, worse, the loss of an existing one, came to depend on criteria which might change even as the parties negotiated. Government then compounded the problem by seeking unsuccessfully to keep secret the procedures to be used by Civil Servants in assessing pay settlements. With firms being blacklisted on this basis, it is hardly surprising that by the end of 1977 the policy should have been the subject of intense controversy. What is surprising – and perhaps a measure of the economic power of government – is that in the midst of this controversy the Confederation of British Industry should have entered into negotiations on, and ultimately refrained from opposing, a new government-contract pay-clause (1) requiring from the contractor undertakings to comply with the existing pay policy and with any future policy presented to Parliament by Command Paper; (2) making the Secretary of State for Employment the sole judge of whether a pay settlement by the contractor or a subcontractor was contrary to the policy: and (3) providing for termination of the contract at the discretion of the purchasing department if the Employment Secretary so held. This clause was incorporated in government contracts let from April 1978 onwards, but was withdrawn, along with the other supporting measures, after an adverse vote on the policy by the House of Commons in December 1978.

What, if anything, was constitutionally wrong with what the government did? Can we distinguish the controversial pay policy from the uncontroversial offshore purchasing policy? It was not wrong, in my view, to use *dominium*, rather than *imperium*, as the vehicle for either policy even though government's ability to do this derived from the state of economic dependence in which many of its contractors and grant-recipients – like its North Sea licensees – found themselves. Such use was, so far as we know, fully in accord with existing constitutional law and convention. It *was* wrong, in the case of pay policy, to use *dominium* to impose a policy which Parliament would never have accepted under the form of legislation with sanctions attached. The enforcement of the pay limit in the 1977–8 phase (but not before) was both secret and arbitrary, akin to a process of enforcing a speed limit defined as '10 or more miles per hour in excess of the average speed recorded on the road and day in question' – not a likely legislative formula. The 1978 pay clause involved a delegation to the minister of rule-making power with no parliamentary control and of decision-making power with no legal control: such combinations of delegations do not appear on the peace-time statute book. These vices were absent from the offshore purchasing arrangements, which, moreover, were fully agreed with the licensees' representative body.

It is, of course, the very fact that no law or convention of our constitution appeared to prevent the use *dominium* in this arbitrary way that should cause us concern. We should not assume that this defect can be easily rectified. Practical proposals for reform can of course be made. It would be desirable to strengthen the instruments of parliamentary review of public expenditure so as to make them more sensitive to the varied ways in which expenditure – or refraining from expenditure – may promote different policy goals, and perhaps also more open to the complaints of those disadvantaged by such manipulations. A case might also be made for subjecting the use by central government of a dominant economic position to the same kinds of constraints as are imposed on private firms and some public-sector bodies by competition legislation, in particular the Fair Trading Act 1973. Useful as such improvements might be, we should not expect them to hold government back on the occasions when it feels that major political or economic gains can result from sweeping or unorthodox use of its *dominium* powers.

Whether the courts are yet equal to this task is a matter for speculation. The weak legislative structure of *dominium*, and the informality with which it may be exercised, clearly no longer inhibit judicial review as once they might have done. But judicial attitudes remain hard to predict. True it is that the actions of local authorities in a trio of recent cases: [*Wheeler* v *Leicester City Council* [1985] AC 1054; *R* v *Ealing, Hammersmith and Fulham, and Camden LBC's, ex parte Times Newspapers* [1985] 85 LGR 316; *R* v *Lewisham LBC, ex parte Shell UK Ltd* [1988] 1 All ER 938] all involved the denial of contracts or facilities, in aid of broad policies comparable to those invoked in black-listing, and were condemned by the courts with explicit reference to the impropriety of using such powers to sanction lawful behaviour. Sauce for the local authority goose may not, however, be sauce for the central government gander: *R* v *Secretary of State for the Home Department, ex parte Northumbria Police Authority* [1988] 1 All ER 556 which, while not a black-listing case, raises an important point of constitutional principle, is suffused with a much more benevolent judicial approach to central government *dominium* than was apparent in the local authority cases. None the less, the reinforcement and systematization of principles of judicial review applicable to the use of *dominium* may for the present be the best way of ensuring its constitutional rectitude while not unduly restricting governmental initiative and effectiveness in problem-solving.

Questions

1. Do you agree with Daintith that the use of *dominium* to implement the pay policy in 1975–78 was unconstitutional or inappropriate?

2. On what basis could the courts review the exercise of *dominium* powers which had been approved by Parliament?

3. Does the material in this chapter suggest that the traditional theories and methods for overseeing or controlling government cannot accommodate the new techniques and methods of government? If so, what changes should be made?

(D) STANDARDS IN PUBLIC LIFE

Note

Following the exposure by a newspaper that two MPs accepted payment for putting Parliamentary Questions, a Standing Committee on Standards in Public Life was established in October 1994. It made its first report in May 1995 which dealt with three topics: (i) Members of Parliament; (ii) The Executive: Ministers and Civil Servants; and (iii) Quangos. Topics (ii) and (iii) were within the power of the Government to deal with and the recommendations were accepted see generally the Government's response Cm 2931. Action taken in relation to (ii) included amending the first paragraph of *Questions of Procedure for Ministers,* revising the Code of Conduct for Civil Servants, applying to former ministers a regime similar to that used for civil servants, when they wish to take up business appointments on leaving office. So far as (iii) was concerned, a new Commissioner for Public Appointments was to oversee departmental arrangements for appointments to executive non-departmental public bodies and National Health Service bodies, in which merit would be the overriding principle of appointment. One of the Commissioner's tasks would be the drawing up of a code of conduct for public appointments procedures. The code and the Commissioner's guidance on it were published in April 1996.

As Parliament regulates its own affairs, the House of Commons decided upon its reaction to the Committee's report. As we saw *ante* p. 352 the House did vote for a new Select Committee on Standards and Privileges and a Parliamentary Commissioner for Standards. The extracts which follow deal with codes of conduct and Members' interests.

First Report of the Committee on Standards in Public Life
Cm 2850, pp. 14, 39, 32, 34–35

The Seven Principles of Public Life

Selflessness

Holders of public office should take decisions solely in terms of the public interest. They should not do so in order to gain financial or other material benefits for themselves, their family, or their friends.

Integrity

Holders of public office should not place themselves under any financial or other obligation to outside individuals or organisations that might influence them in the performance of their official duties.

Objectivity

In carrying out public business, including making public appointments, awarding contracts, or recommending individuals for rewards and benefits, holders of public office should make choices on merit.

Accountability

Holders of public office are accountable for their decisions and actions to the public and must submit themselves to whatever scrutiny is appropriate to their office.

Openness

Holders of public office should be as open as possible about all the decisions and actions that they take. They should give reasons for their decisions and restrict information only when the wider public interest clearly demands.

Honesty

Holders of public office have a duty to declare any private interests relating to their public duties and to take steps to resolve any conflicts arising in a way that protects the public interest.

Leadership

Holders of public office should promote and support these principles by leadership and example.

These principles apply to all aspects of public life.
The Committee has set them out here for the benefit of all who serve the public in any way.

A Draft Code of Conduct for Members of Parliament

General Principles

It is the personal responsibility of every Member of Parliament to maintain those standards of conduct which the House and the electorate are entitled to expect, to protect the good name of Parliament and to advance the public interest.

Members should observe those general principles of conduct which apply to all people in public life. [These are set out on page 14 of this report, and should be incorporated into the final code.]

The primary duty of Members is to their country and their constituents. They should undertake no actions in Parliament which conflict with that duty.

Because Members of Parliament enjoy certain privileges in law, which exist to enable them to fulfil their responsibilities to the citizens they represent, each Member has a particular personal responsibility to comply fully with all resolutions and conventions of the House relating to matters of conduct, and when in doubt to seek advice.

Financial Interests

A Member must not promote any matter in Parliament in return for payment.

A Member who has a financial interest, direct or indirect, must declare that interest in the currently approved manner when speaking in the House or in Committee, or otherwise taking part in Parliamentary proceedings, or approaching Ministers, civil servants or public bodies on a matter connected with that interest.

Where, in the pursuit of a Member's Parliamentary duties, the existence of a personal financial interest is likely to give rise to a conflict with the public interest, the member has a personal responsibility to resolve that conflict either by disposing of the interest or by standing aside from the public business in question.

In any dealings with or on behalf of an organisation with whom a financial relationship exists, a Member must always bear in mind the overriding responsibility which exists to constituents and to the national interest. This is particularly important in respect of activities which may not be a matter of public record, such as informal meetings and functions.

In fulfilling the requirements on declaration and registration of interests and remuneration, and depositing of contracts, a Member must have regard to the purpose of those requirements and must comply fully with them, both in letter and spirit.

We recommend that the House should restate the 1947 resolution which places an absolute bar on Members entering into contracts or agreements which in any way restrict their freedom to act and speak as they wish, or which require them to act in Parliament as representatives of outside bodies.

We recommend that the House should prohibit Members from entering into any agreements in connection with their role as Parliamentarians to undertake services for or on behalf of organisations which provide paid Parliamentary services to multiple clients or from maintaining any direct or active connections with firms, or parts of larger firms, which provide such Parliamentary services.

We recommend that the House should set in hand without delay a broader consideration of the merits of Parliamentary consultancies generally, taking account of the financial and political funding implications of change.

We recommend that the House should:

- **require agreements and remuneration relating to Parliamentary services to be disclosed;**
- **expand the guidance on avoiding conflicts of interest;**
- **introduce a new Code of Conduct for Members;**
- **appoint a Parliamentary Commissioner for Standards;**
- **establish a new procedure for investigating and adjudicating on complaints in this area about Members . . .**

On disclosure we recommend:

- **the Register should continue broadly in its present form, and should be published annually. However the detailed entry requirements should be improved to give a clearer description of the nature and scope of the interest declared;**
- **updating of the Register should be immediate. The current updated version should be made more widely available electronically;**
- **from the beginning of the 1995/96 session (expected in November) Members should be required to deposit in full with the Register any contracts relating to the provision of services in their capacity as Members, and such contracts should be available for public inspection;**
- **from the same time, Members should be required to declare in the Register their annual remuneration, or estimated annual remuneration, in respect of such agreements. It would be acceptable if this were done in bands: eg under £1,000; £1,000–5,000; £5,000–10,000; then in £5,000 bands. An estimate of the monetary value of benefits in kind, including support services, should also be made;**
- **Members should be reminded more frequently of their obligations to Register and disclose interests, and that Registration does not remove the need for declaration, and better guidance should be given, especially on first arrival in the House.**

71. In addition, Members with employment agreements (including Directorships and Partnerships) which are unrelated to their role as Members, and which under our proposals would not therefore have to be deposited, should be advised to ensure that those agreements do not imply that they will perform any activities related to their Parliamentary role. Such action is necessary to reduce the risk of misunderstandings.

We recommend that Members should be advised in their own interest that all employment agreements which do not have to be deposited should contain terms, or be supported by an exchange of letters, which make it clear that no activities relating to Parliament are involved.

Second Report of the Select Committee of Standards in Public Life
HC 816 of 1994–95, paras. 6–29, 35–49

6. In our First Report [HC 637 of 1994–95] we pointed to some of the possible practical difficulties associated with implementing the Nolan Committee's proposals on consultancies and disclosures in the Register, which our necessarily compressed discussions at that stage had identified.

7. As these practical issues are so important in determining our approach to the Nolan recommendations, we repeat here in full the relevant paragraphs of our First Report:

> 78. A number of key terms used in the Nolan proposals have not yet been defined — a task more difficult by Nolan's use of subtly different expressions covering apparently the same point in different recommendations. It is not clear, for example, whether 'the provision of services in their capacity as Members', 'activities in Parliament' and 'Parliamentary services' are intended to be synonymous, and their meaning is in any case not specified. Other terms which would have to be defined more closely before a workable proposal could be put to the House are 'firms' (whether, for instance, partnerships are covered) and 'agreements' (whether only a legally binding contract is included and whether only written agreements are covered).
>
> 79. Other uncertainties surround such questions as:
>
> — the extent to which the proposals are intended, and should, cover only multi-client organisations involved in activities which Nolan describes as 'lobbying' and, if so, how this is to be defined;
>
> — whether there is any logical case of exempting from the scope of any new rules firms with single clients, thus leaving a Member free to advise a number of firms individually but not to advise a firm which has them as its clients;
>
> — the effect of the proposed restrictions on bodies such as trade associations, charitable organisations and pressure groups.
>
> 80. We believe that Members who have existing agreements entered into in good faith, and in conformity with the rules as they currently exist, would be put in a wholly unreasonable position if the Nolan proposals were implemented before these practical problems had been resolved.
>
> 81. Other important factors arise. The proposal to ban any agreement 'to undertake services for or on behalf of organisations which provide paid Parliamentary services to multiple clients or to maintain any direct or active connection with firms, or parts of larger firms, which provide such Parliamentary services' is acknowledged by the Nolan report itself to raise difficult issues for those Members whose background is in the legal, accountancy or other professions, and who maintain a continuing connection with their firm or partnership. The suggestion in the Nolan report is that such a connection should not be retained 'unless arrangements can be made to separate completely the Member's interest

in the firm from that part of its work' (ie the offering of Parliamentary services). But it is far from clear what in practice might be regarded as fulfilling such a requirement.

82. Similarly, the Nolan recommendations relating to disclosure in the Register would appear, on the face of it, to entail the depositing, with an indication of the amount of payment involved, or every contract entered into by a Member undertaking in that capacity a television or radio interview, or writing an article for a newspaper or journal. We doubt that this is what Nolan intended, but it is another issue which must be clarified.

8. Our detailed consideration of these issues since our First Report was debated by the House in July has, if anything, reinforced the uncertainties we highlighted then. In particular, we have been strengthened in our original misgivings about the wisdom and practicability of seeking to distinguish between different kinds of organisations — or parts of organisations — supplying so-called 'Parliamentary services', and of attempting to reach a workable definition of lobbying companies.

9. The distinction between single and multi-client consultancies is especially difficult to understand. Public disquiet has arisen chiefly because of the perception that Members' services are 'for hire' to outside interests. In that context, the Nolan report particularly highlighted advocacy for multi-client lobbying firms. This is a cause of concern, but no more so than advocacy on behalf of lobbying companies acting for a single client. In any case it would not be difficult to devise a system whereby a multi-client organisation could operate through a series of single-client subsidiaries, thereby circumventing any prohibition directed solely at lobbying companies with multiple clients.

10. Having wrestled with this problem at great length and in exhaustive detail we have been driven to the conclusion that the Nolan Committee's attempt to regulate merely *the types* of outside bodies with which Members should be allowed to have a paid relationship will not work. The difficulties of definition, and therefore of enforcement, are simply too great. Our alternative approach, which we explain in the following paragraphs, in fact goes significantly further than the Nolan recommendations. It would address Members' relations with both single client *and* multiclient consultancies, rather than singling out the latter.

11. The main source of public anxiety, as identified by Nolan, is the notion that influence, whether real or imagined, can be bought and sold through Members. This suggests that any remedial action, rather than seeking to draw a line of legitimacy between different types of outside body with which Members should or should not be allowed to have paid relationships, ought to concentrate on defining as closely as possible those *actions* by Members which, because they give rise to suspicions about the exercise — or attempted exercise — of improper influence, need to be prohibited.

12. We note that in 1858 the House resolved:

> *That it is contrary to the usage and derogatory to the dignity of this House that any of its Members should bring forward, promote or advocate in this House any proceeding or measure in which he may have acted or been concerned for or in consideration of any pecuniary fee or reward,*

a prohibition originally directed particularly at Members who were practising barristers.

13. We propose that the rules of the House should now distinguish between paid advocacy in Parliament (unacceptable for the reasons outlined above) and paid advice (acceptable provided it is properly registered and declared). Nolan considered the idea

of separating advocacy from advice but was not persuaded finally that the difference was sufficiently clear cut to be enforceable. We believe that we have addressed the definitional problems identified by Nolan which arise from making this fundamental distinction.

14. Our Report is based on a three-pronged approach:

— a prohibition on paid advocacy in Parliament
— strict regulation governing paid advice
— transparency in all paid activities related to Parliament.

15. It is not feasible, however desirable the greater possible degree of clarity in any new rules, to provide for every conceivable eventuality in advance. Our task has been to recommend a framework to the House. It will be one of the key functions of the Parliamentary Commissioner for Standards and of the new Select Committee on Standards and Privileges to provide detailed guidance as cases of doubt arise.

III. AN EXPANDED 1947 RESOLUTION

16. We have concluded that the most sensible and fruitful course — foreshadowed in our First Report and consistent with, but going well beyond, Nolan — would be to take up and build upon the 1947 Resolution, which, amongst other things, deals with the issue of advocacy for payment. The wording of the existing Resolution reads:

That it is inconsistent with the dignity of the House, with the duty of a Member to his constituency, and with the maintenance of the privilege of freedom of speech, for any Member of the House to enter into any contractual agreement with an outside body, controlling or limiting the Member's complete independence and freedom of action in Parliament or stipulating that he shall act in any way as the representative of such outside body in regard to any matters to be transacted in Parliament; the duty of a Member being to his constituency and to the country as a whole, rather than to any particular section thereof.

17. This Resolution represents a concise and well expressed statement of basic principles. However, whilst it describes the types of agreement which Members should not enter into on the grounds that their independence would thereby be fettered, it does not indicate the specific kinds of Parliamentary action which ought not to be undertaken, for payment, on behalf of outside bodies, whether or not they form the subject of a formal arrangement.

18. **We therefore recommend that the House be asked to agree to the following addendum to the 1947 Resolution:**

and that in particular no Member of this House shall, in consideration of any remuneration, fee, payment, reward or benefit in kind, direct or indirect, which the Member or any member of his or her family has received, is receiving or expects to receive—

(i) advocate or initiate any cause of matter on behalf of any outside body or individual, or

(ii) urge any other Member of either House of Parliament, including Ministers, to do so, by means of any speech, Question, Motion, introduction of a Bill, or amendment to a Motion or Bill.

19. We repeat that, should the House agree to such a resolution, its interpretation in particular circumstances will be a matter for the Select Committee on Standards and Privileges, as advised by the Parliamentary Commissioner for Standards. Nevertheless, before deciding on its merits, the House will expect some guidance from us on its scope and intent, as we see it.

20. The specific activities included in the proposed addendum to the 1947 Resolution are those which ought to be presumed, *prima facie*, to constitute advocacy. The list should, however, be regarded as descriptive and illustrative rather than exhaustive. At the same time, we are concerned to ensure that no limitation on Members' freedom of action which we recommend interferes with their ability to inform themselves on matters of public concern, or with the performance of their paramount duty to represent the interests of their constituents and those of the public generally. The object of the prohibition contained in the Resolution is *paid* advocacy in Parliament. In their consideration of any complaint we would expect the Commissioner and the new Select Committee to have regard both to the nature and directness of the interest giving rise to any remuneration, and to how far the relevant Parliamentary activity could be regarded as conferring, or seeking to confer, a particular benefit on the interest in question.

SPECIFIC ACTIVITIES WITHIN THE HOUSE

(a) Speaking

21. No Member should take payment for speaking in the House. Such action would clearly be incompatible with the ban on paid advocacy which we have recommended. However, we recognise that speaking differs in a key respect from other forms of Parliamentary activity. The tabling of an Early Day Motion or of an amendment to a Bill, for example, is personal to the Member concerned and therefore undertaken for his own purposes of those of the cause he is espousing. A speech, by contrast, is a contribution to debate and therefore, in some sense, made for the benefit of the House as a whole; it can also be challenged or rebutted on the spot by other Members. Moreover, speaking in a debate involves participating in proceedings, as opposed, in most cases, to initiating them - a distinction to which we attach some importance [see para. 27]. For this purpose speaking includes supplementary questions (of which, by definition, no written notice is given).

22. We are not, by proposing a ban on paid advocacy in Parliament, seeking to deprive the House of well-informed contributions from Members with experience or knowledge of direct value to the subject being debated. If the ban were applied to paid advisers in all circumstances, this could lead to an undesirable position in which the Members entitled to take part in a debate would be predominantly those with less direct acquaintance with the subject before the House. We note that Nolan himself accepted that: 'There can be few cases where any damage to the public interest can result from a Member who has declared an interest speaking in the House, even in a Second Reading debate on a relevant Bill or in a Committee of the Whole House'.

23. On the other hand, it is not practicable to lay down in advance, with the precision that a Resolution of the House would require, all the circumstances in which it would or would not be proper for a Member with a paid interest to take part in a debate. It will be one of the main functions of the Code of Conduct, which the House has already decided should be drawn up, to set out a series of general principles against which particular cases can be judged. Members who, having consulted the Code, are still in doubt about their own position will be able to seek advice from the Parliamentary Commissionary on Standards or the Clerk of the House.

24. The new Committee on Standards and Privileges will be able to keep all these matters under review and will no doubt issue further guidance if it sees the need. Any significant changes would, of course, require the approval of the House. As time goes by, a body of experience and practice will be built up which will produce a clearer indication to Members as to what is likely to be thought acceptable and what is not.

But in the last resort it will be for the individual Member to judge whether to speak in any given circumstances.

25. In making that judgement Members will need to bear in mind that the absolute requirement on them not only to register but also to declare their relevant financial interests will remain unchanged. If a complaint were made in an individual case, or if advice were sought in advance, we believe that the House would expect the Parliamentary Commissioner and the Select Committee to consider any individual speech against the criterion of whether it might bring particular benefit to the organisation or individual from which the Member received payment.

26. It is important to make clear that it will not be the function of the Chair to enforce the ban on paid advocacy during speeches, either by interrupting a Member thought to be contravening it, or by declining to call him. Complaints will be a matter for the Commissioner to investigate in the first instance. The detailed procedure for the handling of complaints, and the proposed modus operandi of the Committee were set out in Appendixes 2 and 3 of our First Report.

(b) Questions, Motions, Amendments to Bills, Introduction of Bills etc

27. There is, in our view, a distinction to be drawn between initiating proceedings and merely taking part in them. The terms of our proposed addendum to the 1947 Resolution emphasise the act of initiation. In particular, the tabling of questions, motions, and amendments to bills, the introduction of bills, and the seeking of a debate on the adjournment on a Wednesday morning or at the end of the day constitute the initiation of proceedings. Any Member who is a paid Parliamentary adviser, or who receives any form of remuneration from any outside body, should not initiate proceedings of this sort if they relate specifically and directly to the affairs and interests of that body. No doubt a Member contemplating such action will wish to reflect carefully as to whether, say, the tabling of a question asking for certain statistics might be held to bring a particular benefit to a body from which he receives payment. In any case, a Member's relevant interests will now be recorded on the Order Paper under the terms of the Resolution agreed by the House on 19 July 1995.

28. The advice of the Parliamentary Commissioner, or of the other House authorities, will be available in advance to any Member who is uncertain about the precise application of the new rules in relation to any Parliamentary proceedings and who wished to seek it. If, after consulting the Commissioner, he remains in any doubt, he may feel that his proper course is to refrain from the proposed action.

(c) Voting

29. The proposed list of Parliamentary activities capable of constituting advocacy does not include voting, since that is covered by existing practice. The House's rules on voting are clear and long-established. As explained by Mr Speaker Abbot in 1811: 'This interest [that is to say an interest which disqualifies a Member from voting on a question] must be a direct pecuniary interest, and separately belonging to the persons whose votes were questioned, and not in common with the rest of His Majesty's subjects or on a matter of state policy.' We see no reason to change this practice. . .

. . .

35. Sponsorship is an issue which the Select Committee on Members' Interests has already addressed and the outcome of its deliberations is reflected in the current rules on registration, the relevant sections of which read as follows:

> Sponsorship (Category 4)
>
> 24. This part of the form is divided into two main subsections. Subsection (a) relates to sponsorship or financial support of the Member as a candidate at the

previous election: here the Member is required to register the source of any contribution to his or her election expenses in excess of 25 per cent of the total of such expenses.

25. Subsection (b) relates to other forms of sponsorship, which is interpreted to cover any regular or continuing support from companies or organisations from which the Member receives any financial or material benefit in support of his or her role as a member of Parliament. For example, it is necessary to register the provision of free or subsidised accommodation and the provision of the services of a research assistant free or at a subsidised salary rate. It is also necessary, in this subsection, to register any regular donation in excess of £500 per year made by an organisation or company to the Member's constituency party if the donation is linked directly to the Member's candidacy in the constituency or if he or she acted as an intermediary between the donor and the constituency party.

26. There is a third question in this category of the form, supplementary to subsection (b) and designed solely to elicit whether the Member benefits personally from any payment or material benefit registered in that subsection. In other words, its purpose is to distinguish clearly between benefits accruing directly to the Member and those accruing solely to the constituency party.

27. Trade union sponsorships will normally be registrable under both subsections (a) and (b), particularly if they are based on the Labour movement's 'Hastings Agreement' of 1933; but if trade union donations to a constituency party are not linked in any way to the Member's candidacy in a constituency and were not arranged or solicited by the Member, nor paid via him or her, they are exempt from registration. The same criteria for registration apply to regular donations made to a constituency party by any other organisation or company.

36. The key paragraph here is paragraph 27, which (in the case of trade union sponsorship) makes the test of registrability whether the donation to a constituency party is linked to the Member's candidacy and whether it was arranged or solicited by the Member or is paid via him or her. Since the purpose of registration is to record 'those pecuniary interests held by Members *which might reasonably be thought by others to influence their parliamentary conduct or actions*,' a Member should not be able to engage in advocacy on behalf of a sponsoring organisation, whether a trade union or a company, where the sponsorship is of a kind which already has to be registered. But no such prohibition should apply in respect of sponsorships which are not registrable under existing rules.

APPLICATION TO A MEMBER'S FAMILY

37. It is already a requirement for a Member to record in the Register of Members' Interests any shareholdings of a particular type, not only held in his name but also in that of a spouse or dependent child. Any payment to a family member which arises out of his or her own occupation or activity and which is not linked to any services provided by a Member should not be regarded as a benefit for the purposes of defining paid advocacy in Parliament on the part of that Member. As regards the proposed addendum to the 1947 Resolution, the term 'family' should be taken to include the spouse of the Member and any dependent children, as in the case of the existing rules governing the Register.

IV. EMPLOYMENT AGREEMENTS

38. We support Nolan's view that agreements relating to Parliamentary activities should be put in writing. We deal later in this Report with the question of how far such

agreements should be disclosed. We accept the Nolan recommendation that there is no need for disclosure of employment agreements unrelated to a Member's role in Parliament.

39. The present rule is that all remunerated outside employment must be included in the Register, irrespective of whether it has any bearing on a Member's actions in Parliament. We have no doubt that this discipline should continue to be observed.

40. If our recommendation that paid advocacy in Parliament should be prohibited altogether is adopted by the House, it is essential that no future agreements should require Members to take part in activities which can be described as advocacy.

41. The new requirement for employment agreements to be put in writing will apply principally to any arrangement whereby a Member may offer advice about parliamentary matters. We think it right, however, that it should also include frequent, as opposed to merely occasional, commitments outside Parliament which arise directly from membership of the House. For example, a regular, paid newspaper column or television programme would have to be the subject of a written agreement, but ad hoc current affairs or news interviews or intermittent panel appearances would not.

42. It may not always be immediately obvious whether a particular employment agreement arises directly from, or relates directly to, membership of the House. At one end of the spectrum are those Members whose outside employment pre-dates their original election, whilst at the other extreme are those who have taken up paid adviserships since entering the House. In between there will be many cases which are difficult to classify. Some Members, for example, may provide advice on Parliamentary matters incidentally as part of a much wider employment agreement covering matters wholly unrelated to the House. In these circumstances, it would be for an individual Member to decide how far it would be proper to isolate the Parliamentary services within a separate, depositable agreement; in reaching that decision he may wish to consult the Commissioner.

V. DISCLOSURE OF AGREEMENTS AND AMOUNT RECEIVED, ETC.

43. The concern which the Nolan Report as a whole sought to address was the perception — albeit stimulated by a small number of cases — that outside interests are able to buy influence in the House. We have set out our reasons for believing that the better course is to go further than Nolan suggested, and straightforwardly to ban agreements involving paid advocacy. In these cases, therefore, the question of disclosure would no longer arise.

44. As we have made clear, other agreements relating to Parliament should be put into writing and deposited with the Parliamentary Commissioner for Standards, to ensure both that they are within the rules and that the ban on advocacy is effective. Where any doubt arises, the Commissioner will of course be able to pursue the matter with the Member and, if necessary, the Select Committee.

45. Given the ban on paid advocacy, which was not envisaged by Nolan, we are not persuaded that it should be a requirement to disclose the amount of remuneration paid in respect of deposited agreements.

46. Nolan refers to the declaration of the 'financial benefits Members receive as a consequence of being elected to serve their constituents'. In practice, many of the consultancy agreements which are at present registered and which are in future likely to be deposited with the Commissioner do not arise because the individual had become a Member of the House but are a continuation of a previous occupation. Some of the consultancies, and in particular non-executive directorships, may not

arise from membership of the House at all and affairs in the House will rarely or never be relevant to them.

47. The Nolan report seemed to imply that the amount paid should be declared as an indication of how much time was being spent on outside activity rather than on the duties of a Member. But in reality any payment made will reflect not the amount of time spent in providing the advice, but the resources of the client and the quality of the advice.

48. Moreover, Nolan's reference to the 'financial benefits Members receive as a consequence of being elected' would in practice, if it were to be fairly applied, range far more widely that the Nolan Committee itself appeared to envisage. It would, for example, be hard to argue that most payments for broadcasting, newspaper articles and interviews, lecturing etc, would not be embraced.

49. In reality we judge that the real choice is between the view that compulsory disclosure of remuneration for legitimate activity is an unjustified instruction, and the view that full disclosure of all income — in effect, the publication of the tax return — should be required. Nolan concluded that 'no-one has put a convincing case' for full disclosure. We agree.

Register of Members' Interests 1996 Edition

HC 345 of 1995–96, pp. iii–v, 5, 14, 63, 66, 92, 98, 105–6, 109, 125

This edition of the Register of Members' Interests reflects certain recommendations of the First Report of the Committee on Standards in Public Life (the Nolan Committee) and subsequent decisions of the House of Commons taken in July and November 1995.

The establishment of the Register dates from a Resolution of the House of 22 May 1974. Previous editions have been prepared by the Registrar of Members' Interests. The present edition appears in my name as the first Parliamentary Commissioner for Standards, appointed by the House in November 1995. I exercise this function in agreement with the Select Committee on Standards and Privileges which has replaced the former Select Committees of Privileges and Members' Interests.

Purpose of the Register

The defining purpose of the Register is 'to provide information of any pecuniary interest or other material benefit which a Member receives which might reasonably be thought by others to influence his or her actions, speeches or votes in Parliament, or actions taken in his or her capacity as a Member of Parliament'. Members are required to keep that overall purpose in mind when registering their interests.

Form of the Register

The Nolan Committee recommended that the Register should continue broadly in its existing form but that the detailed entry requirements should be improved to give a clearer description of the nature and scope of the interests declared. To this end, I have asked many Members, particularly those who act as consultants or advisers, to indicate the nature of their services and his or her own entry' and inconsistencies of style or content in the Register are attributable largely to that fact.

Relevant Remuneration

While Members have been obliged since 1974 to register their sources of paid outside employment, there has been no requirement hitherto to disclose the amounts of remuneration obtained. Following a recommendation of the Nolan Committee, however, the House has now resolved that any Member who has an existing agreement or who proposes to enter into a new agreement *involving the provision of services in his or her capacity as a Member of Parliament* must reduce it to writing and deposit it with me. The agreements, which are available for public inspection on the same terms as the Register itself, must include the fees or benefits payable in bands of up to £1,000, up to £5,000 and thereafter in bands of £5,000, and these figures are shown in brackets after the Register entries.

Too much cannot be read into the incidence of agreements and the amounts of remuneration. The Nolan Committee considered whether full disclosure of financial matters unrelated to parliamentary business was relevant to the public interest and concluded that the case for this had not been made out. There are forms of employment (including some consultancies, directorships and partnerships) which do not involve the provision of parliamentary services and are unrelated to membership of the House. Some may be a continuation of a previous employment; others may involve skills or experience gained in other occupations or professions. Moreover, the amounts involved may be more a reflection of the resources of the client that the amount of time spent in providing advice.

Members have undoubtedly had difficulty in interpreting the new requirements and there are some apparent inconsistencies of treatment. This is not altogether surprising, given that absence of precedents. The House will now be able to judge whether the information provided matches that intended under the Resolution.

The categories of registrable interest

Subject to the requirement for the deposit of contracts and disclosure of remuneration, the Register is compiled in accordance with the revised rules of registration approved by the House of Commons on 28 June 1993. Details of the revised rules, which are summarised below, may be found in the First Report of the Select Committee on Members' Interests of Session 1991–92, as subsequently amended, in respect of membership of Lloyd's, in accordance with the Committee's Second Report of Session 1993–94.

The form supplied to Members for the registration of their interests is divided into ten sections, which are represented in this edition by the following headings:

1. Remunerated directorships

In this section Members are required to register any remunerated directorships which they may hold in public or private companies. The requirement extends to directorships which are themselves unremunerated but where the companies in question are associated with or subsidiaries of a company in which the Member holds a remunerated directorship.

2. Remunerated employment, office, profession etc.

This is the category for registering outside employment, professions and sources of remuneration not clearly covered elsewhere in the registration from. It is also the section for the registration of membership of Lloyd's of London; the requirement is to disclose the categories of insurance underwritten rather than, as previously, individual syndicate numbers.

3. Clients

In this section Members are required to disclose the names of clients (other than companies or organisations already identified in sections 1 and 2, but including clients of those companies or organisations) for whom they provide services which depend essentially upon or arise out of membership of the House; for example, sponsoring functions in the parliamentary buildings or providing advice on parliamentary or public affairs.

4. Sponsorship or financial or material support
In this section the Member is required to register the source of any contribution to his or her election expenses at the last Election which exceeded 25% of the total of such expenses. The category also covers any regular or continuing support from companies or organisations from which the Member receives any financial or material benefit in support of his or her role as a Member of Parliament. This includes any regular donation in excess of £500 per year made by an organisation or company to the Member's constituency party if the donation is linked directly to the Member's candidacy in the constituency or if the Member acted as an intermediary between the donor and the constituency party.

5. Gifts, benefits and hospitality (U.K.)
This section is for the registration of any gift or material advantage received by the Member or the Member's spouse from a United Kingdom source, which in any way relates to membership of the House. Gifts are exempt from registration if less than £125 in value. Other benefits are exempt if less than about £170 in value.

6. Overseas visits
This section covers overseas visits, made by Members or their spouses, which relate to or arise out of membership of the House, where the cost of any such visit has not been wholly borne by the Member or by United Kingdom public funds. Several categories of visit, made by Members in the normal course of their parliamentary duties, are specifically exempted from registration. These include: visits with or on behalf of a Select Committee of the House or the British-Irish Parliamentary Body; visits undertaken under the auspices of the Commonwealth Parliamentary Association, the Inter-Parliamentary Union, the British-American Parliamentary Group, the Parliamentary Assembly of the Council of Europe and equivalent recognised international parliamentary assemblies; visits arranged and paid for wholly by a Member's own political party; and visits paid for wholly by an institution of the European Union.

7. Overseas benefits and gifts
This section is subject to the same rules as section 5, but covers gifts and benefits from overseas rather than U.K. sources.

8. Land and property
The requirement in this section is to register any land or property of substantial value, other than any home used solely for the personal residential purposes of the Member or the Member's spouse.

9. Registrable shareholdings
In this section Members are required to register the name of any public or private company or other body in which, to their knowledge, they have a beneficial interest in a shareholding having a nominal (i.e. face) value: (a) greater than £25,000, or (b) greater than 1 per cent. of the issued share capital of the company or body. The letters (a) and (b) are used accordingly in the printed entries. The requirement extends to holdings in which the interest is held by or on behalf of the Member's spouse or dependent children.

10. Miscellaneous and unremunerated interests
This is a discretionary section for use by Members wishing to register interests, including unremunerated interests, which do not clearly fall within any of the specific

categories but which they consider to be relevant to the definition of the Register's purpose.

Administrative arrangements and inspection
This edition reproduces the Register of Members' Interest as it stood on 31st March 1996, the date on which the new rule for the deposit of employment agreements came into force. The printing of the Register was authorised by the Select Committee on Standards and Privileges in accordance with the general practice, established in past years, that the Register should be published and put on sale by Her Majesty's Stationery Office approximately once a year.

It is the responsibility of Members to notify changes in their registrable interests within four weeks of the change occurring; and between its annual printings the Register is periodically updated, in a looseleaf version, to take account of such amendments. The looseleaf version is open for public inspection in the Registry of Members' Interests, situated in the Committee Office of the House of Commons (Tel: 0171–219 6615). It may be inspected when the House is sitting between 11 am and 5 pm on Monday to Thursday and between 11 am and 3 pm on Friday. During parliamentary recesses, and especially during the month of August, more limited hours of inspection apply. A copy of the current looseleaf Register is also placed in the Library of the House for the use of Members.

Complaints
Any complaint of a failure to disclose interests in accordance with the rules of the House should be made to me in writing.

SIR GORDON DOWNEY, KCB
Parliamentary Commissioner for Standards . . .

ASHDOWN, RT. HON. PADDY (Yeovil):

2. Remunerated employment, office, profession, etc.

Occasional payment received for newspaper and magazine articles, television appearances, and for talks given to companies and other bodies, all the proceeds of which are use to fund the Liberal Democrat Leader's Office.

5. Gifts, benefits and hospitality (UK)

Use of car on loan from Rover PLC, exclusively for Leader's Office purposes, commencing 12 January 1994.

1994, gift of a printer for use in my office from Mr. Nazir Jessa of Watford Electronics.

6. Overseas visits

14–18 July 1995, to Bosnia, part funded by the Open Society Institute.

4–7 October 1995, to Beijing. During the course of the visit, I received hospitality from the Chinese Government, which consisted only of banquets given for me and visits under their auspices to tourist locations. The Chinese Government did not pay for my flight to Beijing or for hotel costs.

10. Miscellaneous and unremunerated interests

I own shares in Westland PLC in order to attend the AGM, whose value is less than £100.

BLAIR, RT. HON. TONY (Sedgefield):

2. Remunerated employment, office, profession, etc.

Barrister (no longer practising).

4. Sponsorship or financial or material support

A contribution of more than 25% of my election expenses at the 1992 General Election was made by the Transport and General Workers' Union. The Office of the

Leader of the Opposition receives support, in addition to public funds, from the Labour Party and its affiliates, from the Joseph Rowntree Reform Trust Ltd., and the Labour Leader's Office Fund. Any fees from broadcasting or writing are paid into the Office fund.

In 1995 the office also received support from the Lionel Cooke Memorial Fund and the Communication Managers Association.

5. Gifts, benefits and hospitality (UK)

Gift of a Fender Stratocaster guitar from the British Phonographic Industry.

6. Overseas visits

23–25 April 1993, I attended the annual Bilderberg Conference in Athens, sponsored by Bilderberg.

13–17 July 1995, I attended the Newscorp Leadership Conference in Australia as a guest.

7. Overseas benefits and gifts

Gift of a rug from Benazir Bhutto.

HATTERSLEY, RT. HON ROY (Birmingham, Sparkbrook):

2. Remunerated employment, office, profession, etc.

Journalism for *The Guardian* (£25,001–£30,000)
Journalism for *The Mail on Sunday* (£75,001–£80,000)
TV critic for *The Express*.
Occasional broadcasting and lecturing.

HESELTINE, RT. HON. MICHAEL (Henley):

8. Land and Property

Freehold house in London.

9. Registrable shareholdings

(a) Haymarket Group, principally publishing; also exhibition organisation.
The Group also owns significant property, including its own offices, principally in:
Haymarket Publishing Services Ltd.
Teddington Properties Ltd.
Ansdell Street Properties Ltd.
Thenhurst Agricultural Ltd.

(b) Kensington Freeholdings Ltd.; dormant.
Yoka Developments Ltd.; dormant.
Pridmore Ltd.; solid fuel distributors.
Cottonrose Ltd.; clothes retailer . . .

MAJOR, RT. HON. JOHN (Huntingdon):
Nil

MELLOR, RT. HON DAVID (Putney):

2. Remunerated employment, office, profession, etc.

I am an Adviser to the companies listed below. I advise British Aerospace, Racal Tacticom Ltd., Shorts and associated companies, and Vosper Thorneycroft, on export markets, primarily in the Middle East, and play no part in their domestic sales efforts. In relation to all the other companies, I am engaged in business development unrelated to my position as a Member of Parliament. It should be noted that Middle East Economic Digest, Middle East Broadcasting Centre, and Oriental Press Group are wholly or mainly active in overseas markets. Middle East Economic Digest is a business magazine circulating for the benefit of those who wish to trade with the

Middle East. MBC is the leading Arabic language satellite television channel, and Oriental Press Group is based in Hong Kong. It is not now, and never has been a contractual duty, implied or otherwise, that my services are provided in my capacity as an MP. The existence of these contracts is not dependent in any way upon my being an MP, nor does the duration of these contracts bear any relationship to any Parliamentary timetable.
Consultancy with:
RACAL Tacticom Limited; UK manufacturing company.
Middle East Economic Digest; business magazine.
Middle East Broadcasting Centre; British based satellite television company.
Abela Holdings (UK) Limited; international catering and hotel keeping.
Ernst & Young; chartered accountants.
Chelsfield PLC; a property development company.
Short Brothers PLC and associated companies; a high technology manufacturing company.
Vosper Thornycroft; shipbuilders.
British Aerospace PLC.
Oriental Press Group Ltd.; publishers of newspapers and magazines in Hong Kong.
I also receive fees from journalism, presenting or participating in radio and television programmes, and from lecturing and public speaking.
I am contracted regularly to appear upon LWT's political programme Cross Talk. My fees for this are under £5,000 per annum.
Barrister at law (not practising).
6. Overseas visits
My overseas visits are related to the business interests declared in section 2 above, and do not arise out of my membership of the House of Commons, with the exception of the following:—
11–14 February 1995, to Bahrain, as a guest of the government of Bahrain . . .

NICHOLSON, EMMA, (Torridge & West Devon):
2. Remunerated employment, office, profession, etc.
Author, occasional public speaker. (All fees go to charity.)
6. Overseas visits
23–26 July 1995, to Kuwait at the invitation of the Government of the State of Kuwait in my capacity as Chairman of the All-Party Parliamentary Group for Kuwait.
16 November 1995, to Paris at the invitation of UNESCO to participate in the 50th anniversary celebrations of the founding of the organisation, in my capacity as a Parliamentary Member of the UK Friends of UNESCO and United Nations Association.
16–22 November 1995, to Oman at the invitation of the Government of the Sultanate of Oman in my capacity as Chairman of the All-Party Parliamentary Group for Oman on the occasion of the 25th National Day celebrations.
15–16 December 1995, to Venice at the invitation of UNESCO in my capacity as UK co-Chairman of the United Nations Year for Tolerance to participate in international seminar: 'Art: Tolerance and Intolerance'
10. Miscellaneous and unremunerated interests
Parliamentary Member of the Medical Research Council.
Council Member of the Hansard Society.
Council Member of the European Movement.
Vice President of the Conservative Technology Forum.
Treasurer of the Positive European Group.

Chairman, the AMAR appeal.
Chairman, the Iraqi Humanitarian Relief Committee.
Chairman, ADAPT (Access for Disabled People to Arts Premises Today)
Chairman, Blind in Business.
Chairman, UN International Year of Tolerance (UK)
Vice Chairman of the Relatives Association
Executive Board Member of UNICEF (UK)
Trustee, the Covent Garden Cancer Research Trust
Trustee, The Little Foundation
Trustee, The Motor Neurone Disease Association
Director, Cities in Schools
Director, Shelter
Patron:
- The International Committee for a Free Iraq
- The Ecaterian Iliescu Memorial Lecture
- Orphan Aid to Romania
- The British Deaf Accord
- The National Deaf, Blind and Rubella Association
- Sauvez les Enfants (France)
- AMANA (Society to promote understanding of Islam)
- The Society for the Freedom of the City of London Municipality
- The Freedom Council
- The Berith Foundation
- The Methodist Church Home Mission Division Appeal Committee
- The Reading Industrial Therapy Organisation Ltd.
- Women into Information and Technology Foundation
- Women's Engineering Society
- Women's Business Association
- The Federal Trust for Education and Research
- The Devon Daycare Trust
- The Devon HIV/Aids Trust
- Sense South West
- Plymouth Eddystone
- Opera South West
- Wesley House, Princetown
- Plymouth Relate
- Dolphin Opera
- RHAB South West

Vice Patron, The Child Psychotherapy Trust
President:
- Hatherleigh and District Branch Save the Children
- Devon Help the Aged Committee
- The Chartered Society of Psychotherapy (Devon)
- Plymouth and West Devon Talking Cassette Newspapers
- The North West Devon Canine Association
- Okehampton Community College Appeal
- Vice-President:
- The British Tinnitus Association
- The National Association for Maternal and Child Welfare
- The Small Farmers Association
- The Duke of Edinburgh's Award (Devon)

LEPRA
Governor:
Queen's College, Taunton
The Mary Hare Grammar School, Berkshire.
Member:
The Council of Arab British Understanding
The Prince of Wales Advisory Trust on Disability
Advisory Council Justis Legal Databases, Context Ltd.
The Royal Association in Aid of Deaf People 150th Appeal Committee
Fund Raising Committee for Westminster Central Hall
Exeter University Development Committee
Royal Academy of Music Appeal Committee
Council Member Africa 95 . . .

PAISLEY, REV. IAN (North Antrim):
2. Remunerated employment, office, profession, etc.
Member of the European Parliament.
Minister of the Martyrs Memorial Free Presbyterian Church, Belfast (expenses only).
Occasional television appearances and journalism etc.: fees donated to the Church.
I receive royalties from publications.
10. Miscellaneous and unremunerated interests
Voice Newspapers Ltd. (Honorary director)
Protestant Telegraph Ltd. (Honorary director).
President, Whitefield College of the Bible (Honorary) . . .

SKINNER, DENNIS (Bolsover):
4. Sponsorship or financial or material support
A contribution of more than 25% of my election expenses at the 1992 General Election was made by the National Union of Mineworkers.

Note
It was anticipated that the Select Committee on Standards and Privileges would have produced a Code of Conduct for MPs before the end of the 1995–96 session of Parliament.

Questions
1. Will the poor public perception of MPs be changed by the banning of paid advocacy and the revised Register of Members' Interest?
2. Do you agree with the Standing Committee that MPs should be able to have outside employment?
3. Would suitable people be encouraged to seek election to the House of Commons if MPs acted more independently of their parties, and were given the same level of resources as their European and North American counterparts for their secretarial and research staff?

7 CIVIL LIBERTIES

Note

The area of civil liberties is so large that it would merit a book on its own. Consequently, treatment of this topic in this chapter will be brief and selective, seeking to highlight certain issues.

In most constitutions there are declarations of particular rights or liberties to be accorded to citizens and respected by government, such as freedom of speech, freedom of the person, freedom of conscience, freedom of movement, the right to privacy, and the right to equal treatment. These freedoms or rights usually have an entrenched or protected status so that they may not easily be restricted or overridden by temporary political majorities. The position in the United Kingdom is different, and once again owes much to Dicey.

A. V. Dicey, *An Introduction to the Study of the Law of the Constitution* (10th edn, 1969), p. 203

[W]ith us the law of the constitution, the rules which in foreign countries naturally form part of a constitutional code, are not the source but the consequence of the rights of individuals, as defined and enforced by the courts; that, in short, the principles of private law have with us been by the action of the courts and Parliament so extended as to determine the position of the Crown and of its servants; thus the constitution is the result of the ordinary law of the land.

The position in the United Kingdom was summarised as follows:

Legislation on Human Rights: A Discussion Document
(Home Office, 1976), paras. 2.01–05

Our arrangements for the protection of human rights are different from those of most other countries. The differences are related to differences in our constitutional traditions. Although our present constitution may be regarded as deriving in part from the revolution settlement of 1688–89, consolidated by the Union of 1707, we, unlike our European neighbours and many Commonwealth countries, do not owe our present system of government either to a revolution or to a struggle for independence. The United Kingdom –

(a) has an omnicompetent Parliament, with absolute power to enact any law and change any previous law; the courts in England and Wales have not, since the seventeenth century, recognised even in theory any higher legal order by reference to which Acts of Parliament could be held void; in Scotland the courts, while reserving the right to treat an Act as void for breaching a fundamental term of the Treaty of Union [see *MacCormick* v *Lord Advocate* 1953 SC 396], have made it clear that they foresee no likely circumstances in which they would do so;
(b) unlike other modern democracies, has no written constitution;
(c) unlike countries in the civil law tradition, makes no fundamental distinction, as regards rights or remedies, between 'public law' governing the actions of the State and its agents, and 'private law' regulating the relationships of private citizens with one another; nor have we a coherent system of administrative law applied by specialised tribunals or courts and with its own appropriate remedies;
(d) has not generally codified its law, and our courts adopt a relatively narrow and literal approach to the interpretation of statutes;
(e) unlike the majority of EEC countries and the United States, does not, by ratifying a treaty or convention, make it automatically part of the domestic law (nor do we normally give effect to such an international agreement by incorporating the agreement itself into our law).

In other countries the rights of the citizen are usually (though not universally) to be found enunciated in general terms in a Bill of Rights or other constitutional document. The effectiveness of such instruments varies greatly. A Bill of Rights is not an automatic guarantee of liberty; its efficacy depends on the integrity of the institutions which apply it, and ultimately on the determination of the people that it should be maintained. The United Kingdom as such has no Bill of Rights of this kind. The Bill of Rights of 1688, though more concerned with the relationship between the English Parliament and the Crown, did contain some important safeguards for personal liberty – as did the Claim of Right of 1689, its Scottish equivalent. Among the provisions common to both the Bill of Rights and the Claim of Rights are declarations that excessive bail is illegal and that it is the right of subjects to petition the Crown without incurring penalties. But the protection given by these instruments to the rights and liberties of the citizen is much narrower than the constitutional guarantees now afforded in many other democratic countries.

The effect of the United Kingdom system of law is to provide, through the development of the common law and by express statutory enactment, a diversity of specific rights with their accompanying remedies. Thus, to secure the individual's right to freedom from unlawful or arbitrary detention, our law provides specific and detailed remedies such as habeas corpus and the action for false imprisonment. The rights which have been afforded in this way are for the most part negative rights to be protected from interference from others, rather than positive rights to behave in a particular way. Those rights which have emerged in the common law can always be modified by Parliament. Parliament's role is all-pervasive – potentially, at least. It continually adapts existing rights and remedies and provides new ones, and no doubt this process would continue even if a comprehensive Bill of Rights were enacted.

The legal remedies provided for interference with the citizen's rights have in recent times been overlaid by procedures which are designed to afford not so much remedies in the strict sense of the term as facilities for obtaining independent and impartial scrutiny of action by public bodies about which an individual believes he has cause for complaint, even though the action may have been within the body's legal powers. For example, the actions of central government departments are open to scrutiny by the Parliamentary Commissioner for Administration; and complaints about the administration of the National Health Service are investigated by the Health Service Commissioners.

(A) COMMON LAW PROTECTION VERSUS LEGISLATIVE ENCROACHMENT

'Rights' and 'freedoms' are regarded negatively in the United Kingdom; they are the area of freedom which remains after legal restraints are subtracted. Thus a person is free to do anything subject to the provisions of the law. There is, however, no guarantee that the area of freedom will not be contracted by the incremental encroachment of legislation until there is no freedom remaining. In other countries rights and liberties are regarded positively; they are given a protected status which preserves them (subject to limited necessary exceptions) from encroachment.

Is Dicey's view that the common law is the best protection of liberty justified? (See Barendt, 'Dicey and Civil Liberties' [1985] *PL* 596 *ante* p. 225.) See also *Entick* v *Carrington* (1765) 19 St Tr 1030, (*ante* p. 178), where Lord Camden made it clear that Government, if it is to be free to interfere with individual rights, must be able to point to specific statutory or common law powers. The problem with this is that if these powers do not exist they can always be created by new legislation. Today the police and other officials, such as Inland Revenue Inspectors and Customs and Excise Officers, have considerable powers under various Acts to obtain warrants and enter and search premises and seize property. See, for example, Police and Criminal Evidence Act 1984, s. 8; Taxes Management Act 1970, s. 20C, inserted by Finance Act 1976; Customs and Excise Management Act 1979, s. 161; Official Secrets Act 1911, s. 9.

While some statutes may seek to limit rights, others may accord protection which did not exist at common law. For example, at common law discrimination on the grounds of race or sex was not generally prohibited. Parliament intervened by means of the Race Relations Act 1976 and the Sex Discrimination Act 1975 to prohibit discrimination in certain circumstances, such as employment, housing, education, and the provision of goods and services. This is not equivalent, however, to creating a general right to be free from discrimination. Legislative intervention by Parliament is limited as each piece of legislation represents a limited response to a perceived mischief; Parliament provides remedies against certain abuses but it stops short of providing any general declaration of particular rights.

Are the courts as prepared today to develop the common law to protect the citizen? Part of the problem is identifying what is meant by 'constitutional rights' where there is no written constitution.

(B) WHAT IS MEANT BY 'CONSTITUTIONAL RIGHTS'?

Harman v *Secretary of State for the Home Department*
[1983] AC 280
House of Lords

Harman was a solicitor, who in discovery proceedings, had obtained documents from the Home Office. These were agreed only to be used for the purpose of the proceedings. They were read out in court. A journalist present in court was shown the documents by Harman for the purposes of an article he was writing. The Home Office took proceedings against Harman alleging contempt. These were successful. In the House of Lords their Lordships could not agree on what weight freedom of speech should be given.

LORD DIPLOCK: . . . My Lords, in a case which has attracted a good deal of publicity it may assist in clearing up misconceptions if I start by saying what the case is *not* about. It is *not* about freedom of speech, freedom of the press, openness of justice or documents coming into 'the public domain'; nor, with all respect to those of your Lordships who think the contrary, does it in my opinion call for consideration of any of those human rights and fundamental freedoms which in the European Convention on Human Rights are contained in separate articles each starting with a statement in absolute terms but followed immediately by very broadly stated exceptions.

What this case *is* about is an aspect of the law of discovery of documents in civil actions in the High Court. . . .

LORD SCARMAN: . . . In framing a new rule your Lordships, in our respectful submission, must do so in a way which, first, recognises the important constitutional right to freedom of communication (though with any necessary concession to the individual citizen's right to privacy), and, secondly, is as far as possible free from anomaly. We have used the term 'freedom of communication,' but 'freedom of expression' (perhaps slightly narrower) would do equally well; the latter the United Kingdom has, by ratifying the European Convention on Human Rights, bound itself 'to secure to everyone within [its] jurisdiction': articles 1 and 10.

There must be some correlation between the right to impart information and the right to receive information. It is unnecessary to explore the relationship in all its complexities. It is sufficient for our purposes to note that the right to receive information will generally involve a right to impart it; any exception must be strictly scrutinised and powerfully justified. If (as is our view) the documents became, by production at trial, 'public property and public knowledge,' the journalist had a right to receive information about them: and the undertaking, if it applied to them after trial, at least obstructed to some degree his right. It certainly made it more inconvenient and expensive for him to exercise. . . . When the Americans made into fundamental constitutional law what they saw as the basic rights vouchsafed to them by their heritage of the common law, the very first amendment to the Constitution, inscribed in the Bill of Rights 1791, contained the following provisions: 'Congress shall make no law . . . abridging the freedom of speech, or of the press . . .'. . . . A balance has to be struck between two interests of the law – on the one hand, the protection of a litigant's private right to keep his documents to himself notwithstanding his duty to disclose them to the other side in the litigation, and, on the other, the protection of the right, which the law recognises, subject to certain exceptions, as the right of everyone, to speak freely, and to impart information and ideas, upon matters of public knowledge.

In our view, a just balance is struck if the obligation endures only so long as the documents themselves are private and confidential. Once the litigant's private right to keep his documents to himself has been overtaken by their becoming public knowledge, we can see no reason why the undertaking given when they were confidential should continue to apply to them.

Article 6 of the European Convention provides that, subject to certain defined, severely limited exceptions (which do not arise in the present case), everyone, in the determination of his civil rights and obligations or of any criminal charge against him, is entitled to a fair and public trial. . . .

[His Lordship quoted Article 10 (*post* p. 463) and continued.]

In the *Handyside case*, November 4, 1976, Publications of the European Court of Human Rights, Series A No. 24, para. 49, the European Court of Human Rights declared that freedom of expression is a basic condition, an essential foundation, of a free and democratic society and that the freedom exists not only for information and ideas which are favourably received 'but also to those that offend, shock or disturb the state or any sector of the population.'

In *The Sunday Times* v *United Kingdom* (1979) 2 EHRR 245, the court emphasised that paragraph 2 of article 10 did not establish principles in competition with the right to freedom of expression but only created 'a number of exceptions which must be narrowly interpreted' (see p. 281). The court went on to construe the exceptions permissible under paragraph 2 as limited to those which could be justified by a real pressing social need.

It can hardly be argued that there is a pressing social need to exclude the litigant and his solicitor from the right available to everyone else to treat as public knowledge documents which have been produced and made part and parcel of public legal proceedings. If English law should recognise this exclusion, it might well be inconsistent with the requirements of the European Convention.

Appeal dismissed.

Note

Pursuant to this decision Harman took her case to the European Commission on Human Rights, alleging a breach of the European Convention on Human Rights to which the United Kingdom is a signatory. A friendly settlement was arrived at on the basis that the Government would pay Harman's legal costs and make necessary amendments to English law.

In *Secretary of State for Defence* v *Guardian Newspapers* [1985] 1 AC 339, where the House of Lords had to construe s. 10 of the Contempt of Court Act 1981 (*post* p. 503), Lord Diplock repudiated any idea that this section dealt with a 'constitutional right'. This contrasts with Lord Scarman who stated:

The critical words of the section 10 of the Contempt of Court Act 1981 are:

> No court may require a person to disclose . . . the source of information contained in a publication for which he is responsible, unless it be established to the

satisfaction of the court that disclosure is necessary in the interests of justice or national security or for the prevention of disorder or crime.

'Publication' includes any speech, writing, broadcast or other communication in whatever form, which is addressed to the public at large or any section of the public: sections 19 and 2(1) of the Act of 1981. The section reflects the importance which Parliament attaches to the free flow of information to the public. Prior to its enactment, such protection as the law allowed of the sources of information of the media of public communication was a matter for the exercise of a judge's discretion as and when in the course of legal proceedings a question was put or a document was sought which appeared to threaten the confidentiality of a journalist's source of information. The section substitutes for this judicial discretion a rule of law subject only to specifically stated exceptions if established to the satisfaction of the court. And 'established,' I would observe, must mean 'proved by evidence.' This is a change in the law of profound significance. Mr Kentridge, for the appellants, described the section as introducing into the law 'a constitutional right.' There being no written constitution, his words will sound strange to some. But they may more accurately prophesy the direction in which English law has to move under the compulsions to which it is now subject than many are yet prepared to accept. The section, it is important to note in this connection, bears a striking structural resemblance to the way in which many of the articles of the European Convention for the Protection of Human Rights and Fundamental Freedoms (1953) (Cmd 8969) which formulate the fundamental rights and freedoms protected by that Convention are framed: namely, a general rule subject to carefully drawn and limited exceptions which require to be established, in case of dispute, to the satisfaction of the European Court of Human Rights.

The section provides the press and media with protection at law from disclosure of the source of their information, a protection of which they can be deprived only by a judicial finding that disclosure is necessary. The court cannot require disclosure unless satisfied that one or other of the exceptional situations specified in the section has been shown to exist. If, as in the present case, the exception relied on is necessity in the interests of national security, the necessity must be proved by evidence which satisfies the court.

(C) ADAPTING TO NEW SITUATIONS

Inevitably new situations will arise which have not been judicially considered before. If rights are best protected by the common law, as Dicey claimed, courts must be prepared to adapt to these new situations. Have they done so?

Malone v *Metropolitan Police Commissioner*
[1979] Ch 344
High Court

Malone had been prosecuted for handling stolen goods. During the trial the prosecution admitted that his telephone had been tapped on the authority of a warrant issued by the Home Secretary. Malone sought declarations *inter alia* that (1) tapping his telephone was unlawful; (2) he had a right to privacy; (3) the tapping of his telephone breached Art. 8 of the European

Convention on Human Rights which entitled everyone to 'respect for his private and family life, his home and his correspondence'; and (4) there was no effective remedy in the United Kingdom for the alleged violation of Art. 8. Sir Robert Megarry V-C refused to decide the issues relating to the European Convention on Human Rights, being of opinion that it would be better to leave these matters to the bodies set up under the Convention to decide.

SIR ROBERT MEGARRY V-C: . . . First, I do not think that any assistance is obtained from the general warrant cases, or other authorities dealing with warrants. At common law, the only power to search premises under a search warrant issued by a justice of the peace is to search for stolen goods: see *Entick* v *Carrington,* 19 St Tr 1029, 1067. However, many statutes authorise searches under search warrants for many different purposes; and there is admittedly no statute which in terms authorises the tapping of telephones, with or without a warrant. Nevertheless, any conclusion that the tapping of telephones is therefore illegal would plainly be superficial in the extreme. The reason why a search of premises which is not authorised by law is illegal is that it involves the tort of trespass to those premises: and any trespass, whether to land or goods or the person, that is made without legal authority is prima facie illegal. Telephone tapping by the Post Office, on the other hand, involves no act of trespass . . . all that is done is done within the Post Office's own domain. As Lord Camden CJ said in *Entick* v *Carrington,* 19 St Tr 1029, 1066, 'the eye cannot by the laws of England be guilty of a trespass'; and, I would add, nor can the ear.

Second, I turn to the warrant of the Home Secretary. This contrasts with search warrants in that it is issued by one of the great officers of state as such, and not by a justice of the peace acting as such. Furthermore, it does not purport to be issued under the authority of any statute or of the common law. . . .

Third, there is the right of privacy. Here the contention is that although at present no general right of privacy has been recognised by English law, there is a particular right of privacy, namely, the right to hold a telephone conversation in the privacy of one's home without molestation. This, it was said, ought to be recognised and declared to be part of English law, despite the absence of any English authority to this effect. As I have indicated, I am not unduly troubled by the absence of English authority: there has to be a first time for everything, and if the principles of English law, and not least analogies from the existing rules, together with the requirements of justice and common sense, pointed firmly to such a right existing, then I think the court should not be deterred from recognising the right.

On the other hand, it is no function of the courts to legislate in a new field. The extension of the existing laws and principles is one thing, the creation of an altogether new right is another. At times judges must, and do, legislate; but as Holmes J once said, they do so only interstitially, and with molecular rather than molar motions: see *Southern Pacific Co.* v *Jensen* (1917) 244 US 205, 221, in a dissenting judgment. Anything beyond that must be left for legislation. No new right in the law, fully-fledged with all the appropriate safeguards, can spring from the head of a judge deciding a particular case: only Parliament can create such a right. . . . Where there is some major gap in the law, no doubt a judge would be capable of framing what he considered to be a proper code to fill it; and sometimes he may be tempted. But he has to remember that his function is judicial, not legislative, and that he ought not to use his office to legislate in the guise of exercising his judicial powers.

One of the factors that must be relevant in such a case is the degree of particularity in the right that is claimed. The wider and more indefinite the right claimed, the greater the undesirability of holding that such a right exists. Wide and indefinite rights, while conferring an advantage on those who have them, may well gravely impair the position of those who are subject to the rights. To create a right for one person, you have to impose a corresponding duty on another. In the present case, the alleged right to hold a telephone conversation in the privacy of one's own home without molestation is wide and indefinite in its scope, and in any case does not seem to be very apt for covering the plaintiff's grievance. He was not 'molested' in holding his telephone conversations: he held them without 'molestation,' but without their retaining the privacy that he desired. If a man telephones from his own home, but an open window makes it possible for a near neighbour to overhear what is said, and the neighbour, remaining throughout on his own property, listens to the conversation, is he to be a tortfeasor? Is a person who overhears a telephone conversation by reason of a so-called 'crossed line' to be liable in damages? What of an operator of a private switchboard who listens in? Why is the right that is claimed confined to a man's own home, so that it would not apply to private telephone conversations from offices, call boxes or the houses of others? If they were to be included, what of the greater opportunities for deliberate overhearing that they offer? In any case, why is the telephone to be subject to this special right of privacy when there is no general right?

That is not all. Suppose that there is what for brevity I may call a right to telephonic privacy, sounding in tort. What exceptions to it, if any, would there be? Would it be a breach of the right if anyone listened to a telephone conversation in which some act of criminal violence or dishonesty was being planned? Should a listener be restrained by injunction from disclosing to the authorities a conversation that would lead to the release of someone who has been kidnapped? There are many, many questions that can, and should, be asked. . . .

I can find nothing in the authorities or contentions that have been put before me to support the plaintiff's claim based on the right of privacy. I therefore hold that the claim, so far as thus based, must fail.

Fourth, there is the right of confidentiality. . . .

It seems to me that a person who utters confidential information must accept the risk of any unknown overhearing that is inherent in the circumstances of communication. . . .

When this is applied to telephone conversations, it appears to me that the speaker is taking such risks of being overheard as are inherent in the system. . . . In addition, so much publicity in recent years has been given to instances (real or fictional) of the deliberate tapping of telephones that it is difficult to envisage telephone users who are genuinely unaware of this possibility. No doubt a person who uses a telephone to give confidential information to another may do so in such a way as to impose an obligation of confidence on that other: but I do not see how it could be said that any such obligation is imposed on those who overhear the conversation, whether by means of tapping or otherwise.

. . . The rights and liberties of a telephone subscriber are indeed important; but so also are the desires of the great bulk of the population not to be the victims of assault, theft or other crimes. The detection and prosecution of criminals, and the discovery of projected crimes, are important weapons in protecting the public. In the nature of things it will be virtually impossible to know beforehand whether any particular telephone conversation will be criminal in nature. The question is not whether there is a certainty that the conversation tapped will be iniquitous, but whether there is just cause or excuse for the tapping and for the use made of the material obtained by the tapping. . . .

Fifth, there is Mr Ross-Munro's second main head, based on the European Convention for the Protection of Human Rights and Fundamental Freedoms and the

Klass case. The first limb of this relates to the direct rights conferred by the Convention. Any such right is, as I have said, a direct right in relation to the European Commission of Human Rights and the European Court of Human Rights, and not in relation to the courts of this country; for the Convention is not law here. Article 1 of the Convention provides that the High Contracting Parties 'shall secure to everyone within their jurisdiction the rights and freedoms defined in Section I of this Convention'; and those rights and freedoms are those which are set out in articles 1 to 18 inclusive. The United Kingdom, as a High Contracting Party which ratified the Convention on March 8, 1951, has thus long been under an obligation to secure these rights and freedoms to everyone. That obligation, however, is an obligation under a treaty which is not justiciable in the courts of this country. Whether that obligation has been carried out is not for me to say. It is, I suppose, possible to contend that the de facto practice in this country sufficiently secures these rights and freedoms, without legislation for the purpose being needed. It is also plainly possible to contend that, among other things, the existing safeguards against unbridled telephone tapping, being merely administrative in nature and not imposed by law, fall far short of making any rights and freedoms 'secure' to anyone. However, as I have said, that is not for me to decide. All that I do is to hold that the Convention does not, as a matter of English law, confer any direct rights on the plaintiff that he can enforce in the English courts.

Sixth, there is the second limb of Mr Ross-Munro's contentions, based on the Convention and the *Klass* case as assisting the court to determine what English law is on a point on which authority is lacking or uncertain. Can it be said that in this case two courses are reasonably open to the court, one of which is inconsistent with the Convention and the other consonant with it? I refer, of course, to the words of Scarman LJ in the *Pan-American* case [1976] 1 Lloyd's Rep 257 that I have already quoted. I readily accept that if the question before me were one of construing a statute enacted with the purpose of giving effect to obligations imposed by the Convention, the court would readily seek to construe the legislation in a way that would effectuate the Convention rather than frustrate it. However, no relevant legislation of that sort is in existence. It seems to me that where Parliament has abstained from legislating on a point that is plainly suitable for legislation, it is indeed difficult for the court to lay down new rules of common law or equity that will carry out the Crown's treaty obligations, or to discover for the first time that such rules have always existed.

Now the West German system that came under scrutiny in the *Klass* case was laid down by statute, and it contained a number of statutory safeguards. . . . Not a single one of these safeguards is to be found as a matter of established law in England, and only a few corresponding provisions exist as a matter of administrative procedure.

It does not, of course, follow that a system with fewer or different safeguards will fail to satisfy article 8 in the eyes of the European Court of Human Rights. At the same time, it is impossible to read the judgment in the *Klass* case without its becoming abundantly clear that a system which has no legal safeguards whatever has small chance of satisfying the requirements of that court, whatever administrative provisions there may be. Broadly, the court was concerned to see whether the German legislation provided 'adequate and effective safeguards against abuse.' Though in principle it was desirable that there should be judicial control of tapping, the court was satisfied that the German system provided an adequate substitute in the independence of the board and Commission from the authorities carrying out the surveillance. Further, the provisions for the subsequent notification of the surveillance when this would not frustrate its purpose were also considered to be adequate. In England, on the other hand, the system in operation provides no such independence, and contains no provision whatever for subsequent notification. Even if the system were to be considered adequate in its conditions, it is laid down merely as a matter of administrative procedure, so that it is unenforceable in law, and as a matter of law could at any time be altered without warning or subsequent notification. Certainly in law any 'adequate and effective safeguards against abuse' are wanting. In this respect English law compares most unfavourably with West German law: this is not a subject on which it is possible to feel any pride in English law.

I therefore find it impossible to see how English law could be said to satisfy the requirements of the Convention, as interpreted in the *Klass* case, unless that law not only prohibited all telephone tapping save in suitably limited classes of case, but also laid down detailed restrictions on the exercise of the power in those limited classes. It may perhaps be that the common law is sufficiently fertile to achieve what is required by the first limb of this; possible ways of expressing such a rule may be seen in what I have already said. But I see the greatest difficulty in the common law framing the safeguards required by the second limb. Various institutions or offices would have to be brought into being to exercise various defined functions. The more complex and indefinite the subject matter, the greater the difficulty in the court doing what it is really appropriate, and only appropriate, for the legislature to do. Furthermore, I find it hard to see what there is in the present case to require the English courts to struggle with such a problem. Give full rein to the Convention, and it is clear that when the object of the surveillance is the detection of crime, the question is not whether there ought to be a general prohibition of all surveillance, but in what circumstances, and subject to what conditions and restrictions, it ought to be permitted. It is those circumstances, conditions and restrictions which are at the centre of this case; and yet it is they which are the least suitable for determination by judicial decision.

It appears to me that to decide this case in the way that Mr Ross-Munro seeks would carry me far beyond any possible function of the Convention as influencing English law that has ever been suggested; and it would be most undesirable. Any regulation of so complex a matter as telephone tapping is essentially a matter for Parliament, not the courts; and neither the Convention nor the *Klass* case can, I think, play any proper part in deciding the issue before me. Accordingly, the second limb of Mr Ross-Munro's second main contention also fails.

I would only add that, even if it was not clear before, this case seems to me to make it plain that telephone tapping is a subject which cries out for legislation. Privacy and confidentiality are, of course, subjects of considerable complexity. Yet however desirable it may be that they should at least to some extent be defined and regulated by statute, rather than being left for slow and expensive evolution in individual cases brought at the expense of litigants and the legal aid fund, the difficulty of the subject matter is liable to discourage legislative zeal. Telephone tapping lies in a much narrower compass; the difficulties in legislating on the subject ought not to prove insuperable; and the requirements of the Convention should provide a spur to action, even if belated. This, however, is not for me to decide. I can do no more than express a hope, and offer a proleptic welcome to any statute on the subject. However much the protection of the public against crime demands that in proper cases the police should have the assistance of telephone tapping, I would have thought that in any civilised system of law the claims of liberty and justice would require that telephone users should have effective and independent safeguards against possible abuses. The fact that a telephone user is suspected of crime increases rather than diminishes this requirement; suspicions, however reasonably held, may sometimes prove to be wholly unfounded. If there were effective and independent safeguards, these would not only exclude some cases of excessive zeal but also, by their mere existence, provide some degree of reassurance for those who are resentful of the police or believe themselves to be persecuted. I may perhaps add that it would be wrong to allow my decision in this case to be influenced by the consideration that if the courts were to hold that all telephone tapping was illegal, this might well offer a strong and prompt inducement to the government to persuade Parliament to legislate on the subject.

Seventh, there is Mr Ross-Munro's third main contention, based on the absence of any grant of powers to the executive to tap telephones. I have already held that if such tapping can be carried out without committing any breach of the law, it requires no authorisation by statute or common law; it can lawfully be done simply because there is nothing to make it unlawful. Now that I have held that such tapping can indeed be carried out without committing any breach of the law, the contention necessarily fails. I may also say that the statutory recognition given to the Home Secretary's warrant seems to me to point clearly to the same conclusion.

Questions

1. Was the common law able to offer protection to the citizen in the novel situation which was considered in the above case?

2. Would the decision have been different if the European Convention on Human Rights had been incorporated into the law of the United Kingdom so that it would have been justiciable in domestic courts?

(D) THE DEMANDS OF DEMOCRACY

In the absence of a constitution laying down clear principles based on certain agreed values, there is no agreement on what values judges in a democracy should be seeking to uphold. This is illustrated in the differing views articulated by judges in the following case arising out of the *Spycatcher* affair.

Attorney-General v *Guardian Newspapers Ltd (No. 1)*
[1987] 1 WLR 1248
House of Lords

The Guardian and the *Observer* newspapers both published outlines of Peter Wright's allegations contained in his book *Spycatcher*. The Attorney-General sought and obtained interlocutory injunctions from Millett J against both papers, restraining them from disclosing any information obtained by Wright in his capacity as a member of the British Security Service until a full trial of the issues took place. Sir Nicolas Browne-Wilkinson V-C discharged the injunctions but the Court of Appeal reinstated them in a modified form. On appeal before the House of Lords the injunctions were continued (Lord Bridge and Lord Oliver dissenting), although the book was, by that time, widely available internationally and copies had been imported into the United Kingdom. The majority in the House of Lords placed considerable emphasis on the duty of secrecy and confidentiality Wright owed his former employers.

LORD BRIDGE: . . . So long as any of the *Spycatcher* allegations remained undisclosed, I should have been wholeheartedly in favour of maintaining the injunctions in the interests of national security for all the reasons so cogently deployed in the affidavit of Sir Robert Armstrong. But it is perfectly obvious and elementary that, once information is freely available to the general public, it is nonsensical to talk about preventing its 'disclosure.' Whether the *Spycatcher* allegations are true or false is beside the point. What is to the point is that they are now freely available to the public or, perhaps more accurately, to any member of the public who wants to read them. I deliberately refrain from using expressions such as 'the public domain' which may have technical overtones. The fact is that the intelligence and security services of any country in the world can buy the book *Spycatcher* and read what is in it. The fact is that any citizen of this country can buy the book in America and bring it home with him or order the book from America and receive a copy by post. Some enterprising small traders have apparently found it worth their while to import copies of the book and sell them by the roadside. It remains to be seen whether the Attorney-General will institute proceedings for contempt of court against any public library which imports copies of *Spycatcher* and makes it available to borrowers. Mr Mummery had no instructions which enabled him to answer the question I asked about that.

If, as I have always thought, the interest of national security in protecting sensitive and classified information is to conceal it from those who might make improper use of it, it is manifestly now too late for the Millett injunctions to serve that interest. If the confidence of friendly countries in the ability of this country to protect its secrets has been undermined by the publication in the United States of America of *Spycatcher*, the maintenance of the Millett injunctions can do nothing to restore that confidence. So much, I believe, is obvious and incontrovertible.

I well understand the sense of indignation which all of us must feel that Mr Wright, to use the colloquialism, should have got away with it, worse still that he should make a profit from his breach of confidence. Perhaps his publishers come under the same condemnation. But the remedy for that wrong lies not in a futile injunction but in an action for an account of profits.

The legal basis for the Attorney-General's claim to enjoin the newspapers is that any third party who comes into possession of information knowing that it originated from a breach of confidence owes the same duty to the original confider as that owed by the original confidant. If this proposition is held to be of universal application, no matter how widely the original confidential information has been disseminated before reaching the third party, it would seem to me to lead to absurd and unacceptable consequences. But I am prepared to assume for present purposes that the Attorney-General is still in a position to assert a bare duty binding on the conscience of newspaper editors which is capable of surviving the publication of *Spycatcher* in America.

The key question in the case, to my mind, is whether there is any remaining interest of national security which the Millett injunctions are capable of protecting and, if so, whether it is of sufficient weight to justify the massive encroachment on freedom of speech which the continuance of the Millett injunctions in present circumstances necessarily involves. . . .

What of the other side of the coin and the encroachment on freedom of speech? Having no written constitution, we have no equivalent in our law to the First Amendment to the Constitution of the United States of America. Some think that puts freedom of speech on too lofty a pedestal. Perhaps they are right. We have not adopted as part of our law the European Convention for the Protection of Human Rights and Fundamental Freedoms to which this country is a signatory. Many think that we should. I have hitherto not been of that persuasion, in large part because I have had confidence in the capacity of the common law to safeguard the fundamental freedoms essential to a free society including the right to freedom of speech which is specifically safeguarded by article 10 of the Convention. My confidence is seriously undermined by your Lordships' decision. All the judges in the courts below in this case have been concerned not to impose any unnecessary fetter on freedom of speech. I suspect that what the Court of Appeal would have liked to achieve, and perhaps set out to achieve by their compromise solution, was to inhibit 'The Sunday Times' from continuing the serialisation of *Spycatcher*, but to leave the press at large at liberty to discuss and comment on the *Spycatcher* allegations. If there were a method of achieving these results which could be sustained in law, I can see much to be said for it on the merits. But I can see nothing whatever, either in law or on the merits, to be said for the maintenance of a total ban on discussion in the press of this country of matters of undoubted public interest and concern which the rest of the world now knows all about and can discuss freely. Still less can I approve your Lordships' decision to throw in for good measure a restriction on reporting court proceedings in Australia which the Attorney-General had never even asked for.

Freedom of speech is always the first casualty under a totalitarian regime. Such a regime cannot afford to allow the free circulation of information and ideas among its citizens. Censorship is the indispensable tool to regulate what the public may and what they may not know. The present attempt to insulate the public in this country from information which is freely available elsewhere is a significant step down that very dangerous road. The maintenance of the ban, as more and more copies of the book *Spycatcher* enter this country and circulate here, will seem more and more ridiculous. If the Government are determined to fight to maintain the ban to the end, they will face inevitable condemnation and humiliation by the European Court of Human Rights in Strasbourg. Long before that they will have been condemned at the bar of public opinion in the free world.

But there is another alternative. The Government will surely want to reappraise the whole *Spycatcher* situation in the light of the views expressed in the courts below and in this House. I dare to hope that they will bring to that reappraisal qualities of vision and of statesmanship sufficient to recognise that their wafer thin victory in this litigation has been gained at a price which no Government committed to upholding the values of a free society can afford to pay.

LORD TEMPLEMAN: . . . My Lords, this appeal involves a conflict between the right of the public to be protected by the Security Service and the right of the public to be supplied with full information by the press. This appeal therefore involves consideration of the Convention for the Protection of Human Rights and Fundamental Freedoms (1953) (Cmd. 8969) ('the Convention') to which the British Government adheres. . . .

[His Lordship quoted Article 10 of the Convention and continued.]

In *The Sunday Times* v *United Kingdom* [1979] 2 EHRR 245, a decision of 27 October 1978, the European Court of Human Rights decided by a majority of 11 to 9 that there had been a violation of the Convention by reason of the judgment of this House in *Attorney-General* v *Times Newspapers Ltd* [1974] AC 273, 327 which restrained 'The Sunday Times' from publishing:

> any article or matter which prejudges the issues of negligence, breach of contract or breach of duty or deals with the evidence relating to any of the said issues arising in any actions pending or imminent against Distillers . . . in respect of the development, distribution or use of the drug Thalidomide.

The European Court pointed out that this House applying domestic law had balanced the public interest in freedom of expression and the public interest in the due administration of justice. But the European Court [1979] 2 EHRR 245, 281, para. 65:

is faced not with a choice between two conflicting principles, but with a principle of freedom of expression that is subject to a number of exceptions which must be narrowly interpreted. . . . It is not sufficient that the interference involved belongs to that class of exceptions listed in article 10(2) which has been invoked; neither is it sufficient that the interference was imposed because its subject matter fell within a particular category or was caught by a legal rule formulated in general or absolute terms: the court has to be satisfied that the interference was necessary having regard to the facts and circumstances prevailing in the specific case before it.

The question is therefore whether the interference with freedom of expression constituted by the Millett injunctions was, on 30 July 1987 when they were continued by this House, necessary in a democratic society in the interests of national security, for protecting the reputation or rights of others, for preventing the disclosure of information received in confidence or for maintaining the authority and impartiality of the judiciary having regard to the facts and circumstances prevailing on the 30 July 1987 and in the light of the events which had happened. The continuance of the Millett injunctions appears to me to be necessary for all these purposes.

My Lords, in my opinion a democracy is entitled to take the view that a public servant who is employed in the Security Service must be restrained from making any disclosures concerning the Security Service and that similar restraints must be imposed on anybody who receives those disclosures knowing that they are confidential.

Questions

1. Which is more important to the preservation of democracy – a free press or protection of Government from criticism, merited or otherwise?

2. Is Lord Bridge's 'confidence in the capacity of the common law to safeguard the fundamental freedoms essential to a free society' misplaced?

3. Is freedom, and therefore democracy, best protected from encroachment by Government by the threat that a government which erodes freedom might be voted out of office in some future election, or would freedom be protected better by the existence of a Bill of Rights creating enforceable rights which could be asserted immediately in the courts in the face of any encroachment by Government?

(E) THE EUROPEAN CONVENTION ON HUMAN RIGHTS

This Convention has received mention in several judgments in the above cases. In 1950 member states of the Council of Europe (which included the United Kingdom) drew up the European Convention on Human Rights and Fundamental Freedoms. This was ratified by the United Kingdom in 1951 and the Convention came into force in 1953. In some states the convention has been incorporated into municipal law; in the United Kingdom it merely has the status of a treaty under international law and thus cannot be directly enforced in a United Kingdom court (cf. *Mortensen* v *Peters, ante* p. 64). The success of the Convention in protecting Human Rights is very much dependent upon the goodwill of the Government in complying with its provisions initially or in complying with the decisions of the Committee of

Ministers or Court if it has acted in contravention of the Convention. If a Government ignores their decisions there is no sanction which can be invoked. The only hope is that international diplomatic pressure will encourage compliance. The United Kingdom has breached the Convention on many occasions, but has generally complied with decisions against it by taking necessary steps to amend domestic law to comply with the Convention. The United Kingdom persists, however, in breaching Art. 13 of the Convention by not incorporating the Convention into municipal law to ensure that remedies are available before domestic courts. Taking a case to the European Court on Human Rights is a costly and lengthy process.

EUROPEAN CONVENTION FOR THE PROTECTION OF HUMAN RIGHTS AND FUNDAMENTAL FREEDOMS

Article 1
The High Contracting Parties shall secure to everyone within their jurisdiction the rights and freedoms defined in section 1 of this Convention.

SECTION I

Article 2
1. Everyone's right to life shall be protected by law. No one shall be deprived of his life intentionally save in the execution of a sentence of a court following his conviction of a crime for which this penalty is provided by law.
2. Deprivation of life shall not be regarded as inflicted in contravention of this Article when it results from the use of force which is no more than absolutely necessary:
(a) in defence of any person from unlawful violence;
(b) in order to effect a lawful arrest or to prevent the escape of a person lawfully detained;
(c) in action lawfully taken for the purpose of quelling a riot or insurrection.

Article 3
No one shall be subjected to torture or to inhuman or degrading treatment or punishment.

Article 4
1. No one shall be held in slavery or servitude.
2. No one shall be required to perform forced or compulsory labour.
3. For the purpose of this Article the term 'forced or compulsory labour' shall not include:
(a) any work required to be done in the ordinary course of detention imposed according to the provisions of Article 5 of this Convention or during conditional release from such detention;
(b) any service of a military character or, in case of conscientious objectors in countries where they are recognized, service exacted instead of compulsory military service;
(c) any service exacted in case of an emergency or calamity threatening the life or well-being of the community;
(d) any work or service which forms part of normal civic obligations.

Article 5

1. Everyone has the right to liberty and security of person.

No one shall be deprived of his liberty save in the following cases and in accordance with a procedure prescribed by law;

(a) the lawful detention of a person after conviction by a competent court;

(b) the lawful arrest or detention of a person for non-compliance with the lawful order of a court or in order to secure the fulfilment of any obligation prescribed by law;

(c) the lawful arrest or detention of a person effected for the purpose of bringing him before the competent legal authority on reasonable suspicion of having committed an offence or when it is reasonably considered necessary to prevent his committing an offence or fleeing after having done so;

(d) the detention of a minor by lawful order for the purpose of educational supervision or his lawful detention for the purpose of bringing him before the competent legal authority;

(e) the lawful detention of persons for the prevention of the spreading of infectious diseases, of persons of unsound mind, alcoholics or drug addicts, or vagrants;

(f) the lawful arrest or detention of a person to prevent his effecting an unauthorized entry into the country or of a person against whom action is being taken with a view to deportation or extradition.

2. Everyone who is arrested shall be informed promptly, in a language which he understands, of the reasons for his arrest and of any charge against him.

3. Everyone arrested or detained in accordance with the provisions of paragraph 1 (c) of this Article shall be brought promptly before a judge or other officer authorized by law to exercise judicial power and shall be entitled to trial within a reasonable time or to release pending trial. Release may be conditioned by guarantees to appear for trial.

4. Everyone who is deprived of his liberty by arrest or detention shall be entitled to take proceedings by which the lawfulness of his detention shall be decided speedily by a court and his release ordered if the detention is not lawful.

5. Everyone who has been the victim of arrest or detention in contravention of the provisions of this Article shall have an enforceable right to compensation.

Article 6

1. In the determination of his civil rights and obligations or of any criminal charge against him, everyone is entitled to a fair and public hearing within a reasonable time by an independent and impartial tribunal established by law. Judgment shall be pronounced publicly but the press and public may be excluded from all or part of the trial in the interest of morals, public order or national security in a democratic society, where the interest of juveniles or the protection of the private life of the parties so require, or to the extent strictly necessary in the opinion of the court in special circumstances where publicity would prejudice the interests of justice.

2. Everyone charged with a criminal offence shall be presumed innocent until proved guilty according to law.

3. Everyone charged with a criminal offence has the following minimum rights:

(a) to be informed promptly, in a language which he understands and in detail, of the nature and cause of the accusation against him;

(b) to have adequate time and facilities for the preparation of his defence;

(c) to defend himself in person or through legal assistance of his own choosing or, if he has not sufficient means to pay for legal assistance, to be given it free when the interests of justice so require;

(d) to examine or have examined witnesses against him and to obtain the attendance and examination of witnesses on his behalf under the same conditions as witnesses against him;

(e) to have the free assistance of an interpreter if he cannot understand or speak the language used in court.

Article 7

1. No one shall be held guilty of any criminal offence on account of any act or omission which did not constitute a criminal offence under national or international law at the time when it was committed. Nor shall a heavier penalty be imposed than the one that was applicable at the time the criminal offence was committed.

2. This Article shall not prejudice the trial and punishment of any person for any act or omission which, at the time when it was committed, was criminal according to the general principles of law recognized by civilized nations.

Article 8

1. Everyone has the right to respect for his private and family life, his home and his correspondence.

2. There shall be no interference by a public authority with the exercise of this right except such as is in accordance with the law and is necessary in a democratic society in the interests of national security, public safety or the economic well-being of the country, for the prevention of disorder or crime, for the protection of health or morals, or for the protection of the rights and freedoms of others.

Article 9

1. Everyone has the right to freedom of thought, conscience and religion; this right includes freedom to change his religion or belief, and freedom, either alone or in community with others and in public or private, to manifest his religion or belief, in worship, teaching, practice and observance.

2. Freedom to manifest one's religion or beliefs shall be subject only to such limitations as are prescribed by law and are necessary in a democratic society in the interests of public safety, for the protection of public order, health or morals, or for the protection of the rights and freedoms of others.

Article 10

1. Everyone has the right to freedom of expression. This right shall include freedom to hold opinions and to receive and impart information and ideas without interference by public authority and regardless of frontiers. This Article shall not prevent States from requiring the licensing of broadcasting, television or cinema enterprises.

2. The exercise of these freedoms, since it carries with it duties and responsibilities, may be subject to such formalities, conditions, restrictions or penalties as are prescribed by law and are necessary in a democratic society in the interests of national security, territorial integrity or public safety, for the prevention of disorder or crime, for the protection of health or morals, for the protection of the reputation or rights of others, for preventing the disclosure of information received in confidence, or for maintaining the authority and impartiality of the judiciary.

Article 11

1. Everyone has the right to freedom of peaceful assembly and to freedom of association with others, including the right to form and to join trade unions for the protection of his interests.

2. No restrictions shall be placed on the exercise of these rights other than such as are prescribed by law and are necessary in a democratic society in the interests of

national security or public safety, for the prevention of disorder or crime, for the protection of health or morals or for the protection of the rights and freedoms of others. This Article shall not prevent the imposition of lawful restrictions on the exercise of these rights by members of the armed forces, of the police or of the administration of the State.

Article 12

Men and women of marriageable age have the right to marry and to found a family, according to the national laws governing the exercise of this right.

Article 13

Everyone whose rights and freedoms as set forth in this Convention are violated shall have an effective remedy before a national authority notwithstanding that the violation has been committed by persons acting in an official capacity.

Article 14

The enjoyment of the rights and freedoms set forth in this Convention shall be secured without discrimination on any ground such as sex, race, colour, language, religion, political or other opinion, national or social origin, association with a national minority, property, birth or other status.

Article 15

1. In time of war or other public emergency threatening the life of the nation any High Contracting Party may take measures derogating from its obligations under this Convention to the extent strictly required by the exigencies of the situation, provided that such measures are not inconsistent with its other obligations under international law.
2. No derogation from Article 2, except in respect of deaths resulting from lawful acts of war, or from Articles 3, 4 (paragraph 1) and 7 shall be made under this provision.
3. Any High Contracting Party availing itself of this right of derogation shall keep the Secretary-General of the Council of Europe fully informed of the measures which it has taken and the reasons therefore. It shall also inform the Secretary-General of the Council of Europe when such measures have ceased to operate and the provisions of the Convention are again being fully executed.

Article 16

Nothing in Articles 10, 11, and 14 shall be regarded as preventing the High Contracting Parties from imposing restrictions on the political activity of aliens.

Article 17

Nothing in this Convention may be interpreted as implying for any State, group or person any right to engage in any activity or perform any act aimed at the destruction of any of the rights and freedoms set forth herein or at their limitation to a greater extent than is provided for in the Convention.

Article 18

The restrictions permitted under this Convention to the said rights and freedoms shall not be applied for any purpose other than those for which they have been prescribed.

PROTOCOL 1 – ENFORCEMENT OF CERTAIN RIGHTS AND FREEDOMS NOT INCLUDED IN SECTION I OF THE CONVENTION

Article 1

Every natural or legal person is entitled to the peaceful enjoyment of his possessions. No one shall be deprived of his possessions except in the public interest and subject to the conditions provided for by law and by the general principles of international law.

The preceding provisions shall not, however, in any way impair the right of a State to enforce such laws as it deems necessary to control the use of property in accordance with the general interest or to secure the payment of taxes or other contributions or penalties.

Article 2
No person shall be denied the right to education. In the exercise of any functions which it assumes in relation to education and to teaching, the State shall respect the right of parents to ensure such education and teaching in conformity with their own religious and philosophical convictions.

Article 3
The High Contracting Parties undertake to hold free elections at reasonable intervals by secret ballot, under conditions which will ensure the free expression of the opinion of the people in the choice of the legislature.

PROTOCOL 4 – PROTECTING CERTAIN ADDITIONAL RIGHTS

Article 1
No one shall be deprived of his liberty merely on the ground of inability to fulfil a contractual obligation.

Article 2
1. Everyone lawfully within the territory of a State shall, within that territory, have the right to liberty of movement and freedom to choose his residence.
2. Everyone shall be free to leave any country, including his own.
3. No restrictions shall be placed on the exercise of these rights other than such as are in accordance with law and are necessary in a democratic society in the interests of national security or public safety, for the maintenance of 'order public', for the prevention of crime or for the protection of the rights and freedoms of others.
4. The rights set forth in pragraph 1 may also be subject, in particular areas, to restrictions imposed in accordance with law and justified by the public interest in a democratic society.

Article 3
1. No one shall be expelled, by means either of an individual or of a collective measure, from the territory of the State of which he is a national.
2. No one shall be deprived of the right to enter the territory of the State of which he is a national.

Article 4
Collective expulsion of aliens is prohibited.

Question
As of 3 April 1995, the total number of cases in which the European Court of Human Rights had found at least one breach of the Convention by the United Kingdom was 35 (a total only exceeded by Italy with 82). At the same date 16 cases were pending before the European Court gainst the United Kingdom (again only exceeded by Italy with 22). Is this record due to a disregard of human rights by the United Kingdom, or to the lack of adequate domestic remedies which might reduce the need to resort to Europe, or to a combination of both?

The Convention in British courts

Because the Convention is not incorporated into domestic law, it will not be directly applied by courts in the United Kingdom. In *British Airways Board* v *Laker Airways Ltd* [1985] AC 58, Lord Diplock stated the general principle regarding treaties:

> The interpretation of treaties to which the United Kingdom is a party but the terms of which have not either expressly or by reference been incorporated in English domestic law by legislation is not a matter that falls within the interpretative jurisdiction of an English court of law.

In *Malone* v *MPC* (*ante* p. 452) the Convention, while noted by Megarry V-C, could not be used to protect rights which were unprotected by domestic law. But where a statute covers an issue which is also covered by the Convention the courts will endeavour to interpret it to comply with the Convention. If, however, conflict is unavoidable, domestic law will prevail. The position was reiterated by Lord Brandon of Oakbrook in *In re M. and H. (Minors)* [1988] 3 WLR 485, at p. 498:

> Although the United Kingdom is a party to the Convention, Parliament has not so far seen fit to make it part of our country's domestic law. This means that English courts are under no duty to apply its provisions directly. Further, while English courts will strive when they can to interpret statutes as conforming with the obligations of the United Kingdom under the Convention, they are nevertheless bound to give effect to statutes which are free from ambiguity in accordance with their terms, even if those statutes may be in conflict with the Convention.

See also Lord Ackner in *R* v *Secretary of State for the Home Department, ex parte Brind and Others* [1991] 2 WLR 588 (*post* p. 497). This had led to a tendency on the part of judges to pay heed to the Convention as an aid to the construction of statutes only where the statutory wording is ambiguous. An alternative approach is to construe strictly all statutes which affect basic rights on the basis of a presumption against interference with those rights. In *Raymond* v *Honey* [1983] 1 AC 1, a prisoner challenged the legality of the prison governor's actions in intercepting and retaining a letter sent by the prisoner to his solicitor relating to court proceedings. Prison rules, made by the Secretary of State under a power granted by the Prison Act 1952 to make rules 'for the regulation and mangement of prisons', gave prison governors the power to intercept outgoing mail. The House of Lords held that on a true construction of the statute the Secretary of State had no power to make rules which interfered with prisoners' fundamental human rights. Lord Wilberforce was of the opinion that the statutory power was 'quite insufficient to authorise hindrance or interference with so basic a right' as the right of access to the courts. In the extracts from the article which follows, a current Lord of Appeal in Ordinary argues cogently that the courts could legitimately develop this presumption.

Lord Browne-Wilkinson, 'The Infiltration of a Bill of Rights' [1992] *Public Law* 405–408

There is no doubt that if the words of the statute either expressly or by necessary implication authorise interference with individual freedom, they must be given their full force. Equally clearly, if the statutory words are ambigious (in the sense of being capable of bearing more than one meaning) they should be construed in favour of individual freedoms. But how are the courts to approach the construction of general words, in themselves clear, which on their face authorise almost any action including actions interfering with basic freedoms? Take for example the statutory powers in *Brind*, the power to direct the Independent Television Authority 'to refrain from broadcasting any matter.' Parliament plainly did not intend literally *any* matter. Can it really be suggested that Parliament intended to authorise, for example, a directive prohibiting broadcasts which are critical of the government for the time being in power, or of the Home Secretary himself?

There is respectable authority for the proposition that such general words, even though unambiguous, are not to be construed so as to authorise interference with individual freedom unless Parliament has made its intention so to do clear by express provision or necessary implication. In *R. and W. Paul* v *The Wheat Commission* [[1937] AC 139] a power to make regulations 'for the final determination by arbitration of disputes' was held not to authorise a regulation excluding access to the High Court. The general principle is that 'the subject cannot be deprived of his rights to resort to the courts of law of his country except by express enactment.'

In *Morris* v *Beardmore* [[1981] AC 446 at 463] Lord Scarman said, 'when for the detention, prevention or prosecution of crime Parliament confers upon a constable a power or right which curtails the rights of others, it is to be expected that Parliament intended the curtailment to extend no further than its express authorisation.' In *Raymond* v *Honey* there was no ambiguity in the statutory language, yet the general words of the statute were construed in a limited way so as not to authorise interference with basic freedoms under the common law.

In none of these cases were the statutory powers ambiguous in the strict sense. In each case the statutory provision, although wide enough on its literal meaning to authorise the act complained of, was strictly construed so as to exclude the doing of acts which curtailed individual freedom. As Lord Devlin said in *National Assistance Board* v *Leman* [[1952] 2 QB 648 at 661] 'a statute is not to be taken as effecting a fundamental alteration in the general law unless it uses words that point unmistakably to that conclusion.' This approach was echoed recently by Lord Donaldson MR in *Re O* [[1991] 2 WLR 475 at 480] where he said, 'The common law can of course be varied or overruled by statute, but it requires clear words, or even clearer implication, to achieve this result particularly where so old and fundamental a freedom is involved [as the privilege against self incrimination]. In *Wheeler* v *Leicester City Council* [[1985] AC 1054] the local authority had terminated Leicester rugby football club's right to use the authority's land because the club had refused to condemn a rugby tour of South Africa. In justifying this action, the local authority relied on the provisions of section 71 of the Race Relations Act 1976, which required them to have regard to the need to promote good race relations. In a dissenting judgment in the Court of Appeal, I held that that Act could not justify an interference with the freedom of expression of the club, I said [at p. 1065],

> These fundamental freedoms therefore are not positive rights but an immunity from interference by others. Accordingly, I do not consider that general words in an Act

> of Parliament can be taken as authorising interference with these basic immunities which are the foundation of our freedom.

The House of Lords, whilst agreeing with my conclusion, expressly did not adopt my reasoning.

More recently, I adopted the same approach in *Marcel* v *Commissioner of Police of Metropolis* [[1991] 2 WLR 1118] where the police, acting under the Police and Criminal Evidence Act 1984, had lawfully searched premises and seized documents. Police then made available seized documents to private litigants, *i.e.* the documents had been made available for non-police purposes. One of the questions was whether the police had acted unlawfully in making the document so available, the Act being silent (or obscure) as to the purposes for which seized documents could be used. Although the Court of Appeal reversed my decision, the following passage from my judgment [[1992] 2 WLR 50] was approved:

> However, there manifestly must be *some* limitation on the purposes for which seized documents can be used. Search and seizure under statutory powers constitute fundamental infringements of the individual's immunity from interference by the state with his property and privacy — fundamental human rights. Where there is a public interest which requires some impairment of those rights, Parliament legislates to permit such impairment. But, in the absence of clear words, in my judgment Parliament cannot be assumed to have legislated so as to interfere with the basic rights of the individual to a greater extent than is necessary to secure the protection of that public interest.

There are, of course, cases of high authority to the opposite effect which suggest that this presumption against interference by Parliament with fundamental human rights is only applicable where the statutory words are ambiguous. It must therefore remain an open question whether the law will be established in the terms adopted by the House of Lords in *Raymond* v *Honey* so as to require a strict construction to be applied to words which, though unambiguous, are expressed in general terms. Which way the courts will ultimately come down must be a matter of doubt depending, I believe, on the instincts of the judges who decide the question.

On the one side, it can be said that for the courts to limit, by way of construction, the clear meaning of general words of an Act of Parliament is to arrogate to the courts the right to override the intentions of Parliament expressed in the words it has used. It is not necessary to adopt a strict construction, since any attempt by the executive to use generally expressed statutory powers for alien purposes can be controlled by the courts under the doctrine restraining an abuse of powers. To require the courts, as part of the process of construction, to decide whether or not the interference with individual freedom was within the express or necessarily implied powers which Parliament intended to confer, would be to bring the courts into deciding the merits of the decision, not merely its legality. In deciding whether any particular action did or did not fall within the statutory powers, the court would have to decide whether that action was necessary for the achievement of the statutory purpose. The executive, in exercising general powers, will be left in a state of uncertainty as to their scope. These are powerful arguments against the adoption of any general presumption against interference with individual freedom.

On the other side, it can be said that a presumption in favour of individual freedom almost certainly reflects the true intention of Parliament. Although pressures on parliamentary time have led to Acts which confer powers being expressed in very general terms, Parliament must surely have intended that those wide powers were to be used to interfere with individual freedom only to the extent necessary to implement the purpose of the Act. Although the adoption of a general presumption in favour of individual freedom would certainly lead the courts closer to examining the necessity for any executive action which is impugned, that is the function which is already vested in the European Court of Human Rights. Why should not the domestic courts of this country undertake the same task?

Where the wording in a statute is similar to wording in the Convention, the decisions of the European Court of Human Rights may influence judicial interpretation. In construing the words 'torture . . . inhuman or degrading treatment' in s. 6 of the Northern Ireland (Emergency Provisions) Act 1973, McGonigal LJ in *R* v *McCormick* [1977] NI 105 looked to the jurisprudence of the European Court of Human Rights in cases arising under Art. 3 which used the same words.

Where a matter of policy falls for judicial consideration, the courts will look to conform with the Convention: see Lord Denning MR in *Schering Chemicals* v *Falkman Ltd* [1981] 2 WLR 848 (*post* p. 479). In *Derbyshire County Council* v *Times Newspapers Ltd and Others* [1992] 1 QB 770, the Court of Appeal stated that it could resort to the Convention to help resolve some uncertainty or ambiguity in municipal law. In this case the local authority was suing for libel. In defining the extent of the tort of libel, and ultimately ruling that a local authority could not sue for libel, the Court of Appeal referred to Art. 10. The Court was of opinion that 'the right to freedom of expression included freedom to impart information and ideas without interference by public authority'. If such an authority could sue for libel it would 'be able to stifle legitimate public criticism of its activities'. As individual officers could sue for libel and the authority could sue for malicious falsehood, the local authority had 'all such rights as were necessary in a democratic society'. The House of Lords [1993] 2 WLR 449 dismissed the appeal on the basis that it would be contrary to the public interest and an undesirable fetter on freedom of speech if government organs could sue for libel. Their lordships did not directly rely on the Convention but rather showed themselves to be prepared to develop the common law in a way which accorded protection to fundamental rights and was consistent with the requirements of democracy. In the article which follows a current High Court judge argues that there is still potential for the common law to develop to protect fundamental rights without the need for the Convention to be incorporated into domestic law.

Sir John Laws, 'Is the High Court the Guardian of Fundamental Constitutional Rights?' [1993] *Public Law* 60–61, 64–65, 67–71 & 76

. . . [T]he issue I will examine is this: to what extent can, and should, the common law courts themselves elaborate and make good basic rights by building on existing public law principles, so as to insist upon and secure a high degree of priority for those central rights which broadly find their place in the principal substantive provisions of the European Convention on Human Rights and Fundamental Freedoms (the ECHR)?

My thesis is that such an enterprise ought to be and can be undertaken without any heterodoxy, and that it is supported by these four propositions, three of which, at least, are self-evident: (1) none of the objections to statutory incorporation of the European Convention on Human Rights and Fundamental Freedoms (ECHR) rests on the proposition that such rights should not be enjoyed by the peoples of the United Kingdom; (2) in the community of developed democracies, we have reached the stage where it can be said that rights of this kind have become an axiom, or series of axioms, about whose desirability there can be no serious argument; (3) it has generally been the task of the judges to ascertain the principles according to which the people are to be protected from the exercise of arbitrary power; and (4) these norms or axioms ought to be developed by the distinctive process of the common law.

Of these four propositions, (1) is a proposition of fact; it is I think obviously true, and I propose to regard it as such and take no time justifying it here; (2) is a proposition of moral or (in the broadest sense) political principle; given the nature of the ideals enshrined in the ECHR, such as freedom of expression (to which in particular I shall shortly return), to deny it is by necessary implication to assert a totalitarian position in which individuals are subservient to the ends of the state. I propose to regard such a position as obviously barbarous, and therefore to assume the truth of (2); (3) is, I suppose, a proposition of legal history, and therefore, again, of fact; it is certainly an apt soubriquet to describe what the judges have been about in developing judicial review over the last 20 years or so. So I shall take this proposition as given as well. Thus the pith of what I have to say concerns the fourth. . . .

I propose to begin my task by making it clear that my argument is *not* intended to support a plea for what might be called the judicial incorporation of the ECHR. In doing so, I should like to draw what seems to me a distinction of fundamental importance, which I shall also deploy in later sections of the article. It is obvious enough, but seems to have attracted little attention in the discussions, in or out of the courts, of the impact of the ECHR on our law. It is between these two propositions: (1) the ECHR, *as a legal instrument*, is not part of the law of England; and (2) the contents of the ECHR, *as a series of propositions*, largely represent legal norms or values which are either already inherent in our law, or, so far as they are not, may be integrated into it by the judges. I am an advocate for the second proposition, not the first. . . .

[His Lordship went on to develop his argument that the ECHR is a text which may be used to inform the common law in much the same way as courts currently refer to decisions of foreign courts or academic works. His Lordship proceeded to examine the House of Lords' decision in *Derbyshire CC* v *Times Newspapers* [1993] 1 All ER 1011.]

. . . I think it no exaggeration to say that the decision of the House of Lords in the same case is a legal landmark. It points a way forward to a position in which it can no longer be fanciful to regard the superior courts in England as securing a real vindication of fundamental rights, and doing so not by means of anything approaching incorporation of the Strasbourg Convention, but by development of the common law. Lord Keith (with whom all their other Lordships agreed) said:

> It is of the highest public importance that a democratically elected governmental body, or indeed any governmental body, should be open to uninhibited public criticism. The threat of a civil action for defamation must inevitably have an inhibiting effect on freedom of speech.

After referring to authority from the United States, he continued:

> But as is shown by the decision in *Attorney-General* v *Guardian Newspapers Ltd (No. 2)* [1990] 1 AC 109 [the final appeal in the Spycatcher case] . . . there are rights

> available to private citizens which institutions of central government are not in a position to exercise unless they can show that it is in the public interest to do so.

He proceeded to hold that, as a matter of principle, neither central nor local government should be allowed to maintain a cause of action in libel:

> . . . it is contrary to the public interest that they should have it. It is contrary to the public interest because to admit such actions would place an undesirable fetter on freedom of speech.

Towards the end of his speech he said:

> The conclusion must be, in my opinion, that under the common law of England a local authority does not have the right to maintain an action of damages for defamation. That was the conclusion reached by the Court of Appeal, which did so principally by reference to Article 10 of the European Convention on Human Rights . . . My Lords, I have reached my conclusion upon the common law of England without finding any need to rely upon the European Convention.

And he called to mind Lord Goff's opinion in the final *Spycatcher* appeal 'that in the field of freedom of speech there was no difference in principle between English law on the subject and Article 10 of the Convention.'

I should also mention here another recent decision of the Court of Appeal in *Middlebrook Mushrooms Ltd* v *TGWU* [*The Times*, 18 January 1993]. It was an appeal against the grant of an interlocutory injunction in a picketing case. I need say no more about the facts. Neill LJ said, *obiter:*

> Though counsel for the appellants did not place any specific reliance on Article 10 of the ECHR, it is relevant to bear in mind that in all cases which involve a proposed restriction on the right of free speech the court is concerned when exercising its discretion to consider whether the suggested restraint is necessary.

Neill LJ evidently regarded his observation as quite uncontroversial.

Though *Derbyshire* was a private law case, it is impossible to suppose that it will not have important and, I would think, far-reaching consequences for the development of public law. It may prove to be an engine of change in the evolution of judicial review as a constitutional safeguard for substantive fundamental rights. But it cannot simply be read across; there are special problems for the ordered and rational development of public law, and in looking at the special problems which this engages in relation to public law, it is I think important to recognise the striking contrast, in the developments over the last 20 years or so, between the vigorous and increasingly sophisticated growth in *procedural* judicial review and the relatively static position occupied by *substantive* review. The doctrine of legitimate expectation has, as its parent, the old notion of natural justice; yet it stands at a considerable distance from the twin Latin tags which used to be thought to be the whole content of natural justice: *Audi alteram partem* and *Nemo judex in causa sua.* But, save for Lord Diplock's substitution of the word 'irrationality' for 'unreasonableness' *Wednesbury* [1948] 1 KB 223 has stood still; indeed some recent formulations, such as Lord Diplock's reference to logic and morals in *CCSU* [*Council of Civil Service Unions* v *Minister for the Civil Service* [1985] AC 374 at 410], and Lord Brightman's observations in *R* v *Hillingdon London Borough Council, ex parte Puhlhofer* [[1986] AC 484 at 518], suggest if anything an increasingly restrictive approach. Why is this? The reason surely consists in the judges' well-established recognition that since the merits of a decision in the public law field will ordinarily have been committed by Parliament to the decision-maker in question, they can go no further in reviewing the substance of the decision than seeing that it is one which a rational person, addressing himself to the right issues, could have arrived at. On this basis, it might be thought there was little room for conceptual development beyond the existing formulations by Lord Greene and Lord Diplock; and so far as any appeal to ECHR principles invokes in the court a more 'hands-on' approach, it is *ipso facto* liable to infringe these constitutional proprieties. And we must certainly face the fact that the pevailing view among English lawyers with expertise in the jurisprudence of the ECHR is that the 'pressing social need' test is tighter that the common law *Wednesbury* principles.

The first key to this problem, I believe, is not to lose sight of the distinction which I have already articulated. Since the task is not to incorporate the ECHR it is as much a solecism to suppose that fundamental rights may only be advanced in the common law by transporting lock, stock and barrel the Convention jurisprudence on 'pressing social need' as it is to argue for the incorporation of the ECHR text itself. That is not the way forward: and the true route is, conceptually at least, surprisingly simple, consisting as it does in a recognition of the obvious. What I have in mind is this: the greater the intrusion proposed by a body possessing public power over the citizen into an area where his fundamental rights are at stake, the greater must be the justification which the public authority must demonstrate. If this seems a proposition of child-like simplicity, see what it means for the operation in practice of substantive, as opposed to procedural, judicial review. It means that the principles by which it is conducted are neither unitary nor static; it means that the standard by which the court reviews administrative action is a variable one. It means, for example, that while the Secretary of State will largely be left to his own devices in promulgating national economic policy (as in the community charge-capping case), the court will scrutinise the merits of his decisions much more closely when they concern refugees or free speech. This would represent a conceptual shift away from *Wednesbury* unreasonabless: or, if that is too startling a description, at any rate a significant refinement of it. Irrationality is monolothic, and is for that reason an imperfect and inappropriate mechanism for the development of differential standards in judicial review.

Such an approach is, I believe, no more a usurpation of constitutional propriety than is the conventional *Wednesbury* approach itself. No one suggests, nowadays, that the courts behave improperly in requiring a Minister to bring a rational mind to bear on a question he has to decide. In doing so, the court imposes a judge-made standard on the decision-maker. To bring forward a more exacting standard where the decision-maker proposes to prohibit the citizen from expressing his opinions or communicating information in his possession is not in principle a different exercise.

In fact the courts do this already: I should refer to two well-known passages from speeches of Lord Bridge which may now be seen as all of a piece with Lord Keith's reasoning in *Derbyshire*: first, in the refugee case, *R* v *Secretary of State for the Home Department, ex parte Bugdaycay* [[1987] AC 514 at 531]:

> [the courts are entitled, within limits] to subject an administrative decision to the more rigorous examination, to ensure that it is in no way flawed, according to the gravity of the issue which the decision determines. The most fundamental of all human rights is the individual's right to life and when an administrative decision under challenge is said to be one which may put the applicant's life at risk, the basis of the decision must surely call for the most anxious scrutiny.

Secondly, in *Brind* [[1991] 1 AC 696 at 748–749]

> But I do not accept that this conclusion [*viz.* that there is no presumption that a statutory discretionary power must be exercised within ECHR limits] means that

> the courts are powerless to prevent the exercise by the executive of administrative discretions, even when conferred, as in the instant case, in terms which are on their face unlimited, in a way which infringes fundamental human rights. Most of the rights spelled out in terms in the Convention, including the right to freedom of expression, are less than absolute and must in some cases yield to the claims of competing public interests. Thus, article 10(2) of the Convention spells out and categorises the competing public interests by reference to which the right to freedom of expression may have to be curtailed. In exercising the power of judicial review we have neither the advantages nor the disadvantages of any comparable code to which we may refer or by which we are bound. But again, this surely does not mean that in deciding whether the Secretary of State, in the exercise of his discretion, could reasonably impose the restriction he has imposed on the broadcasting organisations, we are not perfectly entitled to start from the premise that any restriction of the right to freedom of expression requires to be justified and that nothing less than an important competing public interest will be sufficient to justify it. The primary judgment as to whether the particular competing public interest justifies the particular restriction imposed falls to be made by the Secretary of State to whom Parliament has entrusted the discretion. But we are entitled to exercise a secondary judgment by asking whether a reasonable Secretary of State, on the material before him, could reasonably make that primary judgment.

This latter passage involves the proposition that the court is not the primary decision-maker, however imperative may be the fundamental right in question; and there will be cases, even where the standard applied by the judges is a relatively tight one, in which there is room for differences of view within the standard. In very many instances there will be what the Convention jurisprudence calls a 'margin of appreciation' accorded to the body under review, whose primary responsibility it was to make the decision in question.

The fact is that just as the judges have evolved the *Wednesbury* doctrine, so they can refine it, and build differential principles within it. They may accord a place in our public law to the principle of proportionality, to which I shall come in a moment; and in doing so they may go further in articulating a doctrine by which substantive judicial review bears more closely on the decision-maker in some areas than in others. What I am at pains distinctly to emphasise is that in developing the law in this way they are as free to consider ECHR texts as any other legal text; that there is nothing which ought to discourage their saying so by explicit reference; and that all of this, important as it is if fundamental rights are to be safeguarded, is conceptually no different from what the courts have already done in evolving standards of administrative conduct within the four corners of conventional judicial review. The prospect of judicial examination of public decisions to test their reasonableness has none of the arresting quality of a Bateman cartoon; it is regarded as an elementary necessity, a function of the rule of law itself. But just as the citizen is entitled to expect that those having administrative power over him will bring a rational mind to bear on the subject in hand, whatever it is, so should he enjoy the assurance that where the subject-matter engages fundamental rights such as freedom of speech and person, or access to the courts, any decision adverse to him will only survive judicial scrutiny if it is found to rest on a distinct and positive justification in the public interest. . . .

My thesis at the end may be summarised thus: we may have regard to the ECHR (and, for that matter, other international texts) but not think of incorporating it. We should apply differential standards in judicial review according to the subject-matter, and to do so deploy the tool of proportionality, not the bludgeon of *Wednesbury*. A function of this is to recognise that decision-makers whose decisions affect fundamental rights must inevitably justify what they do by giving good reasons; and the judges should not construe statutes which are said to confer power to interfere with such rights any more favourably than they would view a clause said to oust their own jurisdiction. Indeed such a clause is but an example of a denial of one fundamental right. I think this is, in the end, a modest way forward, involving no sea-change in the law; but the growth of the common law has always been an incoming tide, not a storm of hurricane force; and it is better so. The tide leaves no wake of destruction when it ebbs. I propose no assertion of undue power by the judges over the elected Executive; and the only real complaint against all this would be in the mouth of someone who asserts that governmental authority, because it is there by popular vote, should possess the power to override fundamental rights without compelling good reason.

Other prominent judges, however, consider that the only way to guarantee the protection of human rights is to incorporate the Convention. One such judge is Sir Thomas Bingham, Master of the Rolls.

T. H. Bingham, 'The European Convention on Human Rights: Time to Incorporate' (1993) 109 *LQR* 390–393, 395–400

. . . [T]here is no task more central to the purpose of a moden democracy, or more central to the judicial function, than that of seeking to protect, within the law, the basic human rights of the citizen, against invasion by other citizens or by the state itself. I hope this point is too obvious to need labouring. . . .

I would suggest that the ability of English judges to protect human rights in this country and reconcile conflicting rights in the manner indicated is inhibited by the failure of successive governments over many years to incorporate into United Kingdom law the European Convention on Human Rights and Fundamental Freedoms. . . .

[Having examined the Diceyan concept of the constitution and the changes in the balance of power between the executive and legislature in this century, Sir Thomas continued.]

The elective dictatorship of the majority means that, by and large, the government of the day can get its way, even if its majority is small. If its programme or its practice involves some derogation from human rights Parliament cannot be relied on to correct this. Nor can the judges. If the derogation springs from a statute, they must faithfully apply the statute. If it is a result of administrative practice, there may well be no basis upon which they can interfere. There is no higher law, no frame of reference, to which they can properly appeal. None of this matters very much if human rights themselves are not thought to matter very much. But if the protection of its citizens' fundamental rights is genuinely seen as an important function of civil society, then it does matter. In saying this I do not suggest — and I must stress this — that the present government or any of its predecessors has acted with wilful or cynical disregard of fundamental human rights. I would adopt and apply by analogy what Samuel Johnson said about truth: 'It is more from carelessness about truth than from intentional lying that there is so much falsehood in the world.' What I do suggest is that a government intent on implementing a programme may overlook the human rights aspects of its policies and that, if a government of more sinister intent were to gain power, we should be defenceless. There would not, certainly, be much the judges could do about it. This would seem regrettable to those who, like me, would see the judges as properly playing an important part in this field. . . .

Those who share my view that the situation is unsatisfactory may well ask whether it is nonetheless inevitable, one of those inescapable blemishes which must exist in an imperfect world. I would say not. In the European Convention an instrument lies ready to hand which, if not providing an ideal solution, nonetheless offers a clear improvement on the present position. . . .

[Sir Thomas examined the history of the Convention before discussing the main arguments against incorporation.]

Constitutional experts point out, first of all, that the unwritten British constitution, unlike virtually every written constitution, has no means of entrenching, that is of giving a higher or trump-like status, to a law of this kind. Therefore, it is said, what one soverign Parliament enacts another sovereign Parliament may override: thus a government minded to undermine human rights could revoke the incorporation of the Convention and leave the citizen no better off than he is now, and perhaps worse. I would give this argument beta for ingenuity and gamma, or perhaps omega, for political nous. It is true that in theory any Act of Parliament may be repealed. Thus theoretically the legislation extending the vote to the adult population, or giving the vote to women, or allowing married women to own property in their own right, or forbidding cruel and unusual punishment, or safeguarding the independence of the judges, or providing for our adhesion to the European Community, could be revoked at the whim of a temporary parliamentary majority. But absent something approaching a revolution in our society such repeal would be unthinkable. Why? Because whatever their theoretical status constitutional measures of this kind are in practice regarded as enjoying a peculiar sanctity buttressed by overwhelming public support. If incorporated, the Convention would take its place at the head of this favoured list. There is a second reason why formal entrenchment is not necessary. Suppose the statute of incorporation were to provide that subject to any express abrogation or derogation in any later statute the rights specified in the Convention were to be fully recognised and enforced in the United Kingdom according to the tenor of the Convention. That would be good enough for the judges. They would give full effect to the Convention rights unless a later statute very explicitly and specifically told them not to. But the rights protected by the Convention are not stated in absolute terms: there are provisos to cover pressing considerations of national security and such like. Save in quite extraordinary circumstances one cannot imagine any government going to Parliament with a proposal that any human right guaranteed by the Convention be overridden. And even then (subject to any relevant derogation) the United Kingdom would in any event remain bound, in international law and also in honour, to comply with its Convention obligations. I find it hard to imagine a government going to Parliament with such a proposal. So while the argument on entrenchment has a superficial theoretical charm, it has in my opinion very little practical substance. There would be no question, as under Community law, of United Kingdom judges declaring United Kingdom statutes to be invalid. Judges would either comply with the express will of Parliament by construing all legislation in a manner consistent with the Convention. Or, in the scarcely imaginable case of an express abrogation or derogation by Parliament, the judges would give effect to that provision also.

A second and quite different argument runs roughly along the following lines. Rulings on human rights, not least rulings on the lines of demarcation between one right and another, involve sensitive judgments important to individual citizens and to society as a whole. These are not judgments which unelected English (or perhaps British) judges are fitted to make, drawn as they are from a narrow unrepresentative minority, the public-school and Oxbridge-educated, male, white, mostly protestant, mostly middle-class products of the Bar. They are judgments of an essentially political nature, properly to be made by democratically elected representatives of the people. I do not, unsurprisingly, agree with most of the criticisms which it is fashionable to direct at the composition of the modern judiciary, for reasons which could fill another lecture. Nor would I, again unsurprisingly, accept the charge sometimes made that protection of human rights cannot safely be entrusted to British judges: no one familiar with the development of the law in fields as divers as, for instance, the Rent Acts, the Factories Acts, labour law or judicial review could, I think, fairly accuse the judges of throwing their weight on the side of the big battlations against the small man or woman. But it is true that judgments on human rights do involve judgements about relations between the individual and the society of which the individual is part, and in that sense they can be described as political. If such questions are thought to be inappropriate for decision by judges, so be it. I do not agree, but I can understand the argument. What I simply do not understand is how it can be sensible to entrust the decision of these questions to an international panel of judges in Strasbourg — some of them drawn from societies markedly unlike our own — but not, in the first instance, to our own judges here. I am not suggesting that the final right of appeal to Strasbourg should be eliminated or in any way curtailed (which, indeed, is not something which most opponents of incorporation support). I am only suggesting that rights claimed under the Convention should, in the first place, be ruled upon by judges here before, if regrettably necessary, appeal is made to Strasbourg. The choice is not between judges and no judges; it is whether *all* matches in this field must be played away.

The proposition that judgments on questions of human rights are, in the sense indicated, political is relied on by opponents of incorporation to found a further argument. The argument is that if British judges were to rule on questions arising under the Convention they would ineluctably be drawn into political controversy with consequent damage to their reputation, constitutionally important as it is, for political neutrality. This argument, espoused by a number of senior and respected political figures, should not be lightly dismissed. But it should be examined. It cannot in my view withstand such examination for two main reasons. The first is that judges are already, on a regular and day to day basis, reviewing and often quashing decisions of ministers and government departments. They have been doing so on an increasing scale for 30 years. During that period ministers of both governing parties have fallen foul of court decisions, not once or twice but repeatedly. Some of these decisions have achieved great public notoriety. All judges are accustomed to making every effort to put aside their own personal viewpoints, and there is no reason to think that English judges are any less good at this than any others. Political controversy there has been, on occasion, a-plenty, but it has not by and large rubbed off on the judges. Why not? Because, I think, it is generally if not universally recognised that the judges have a job to do, which is not a political job, and their personal predilections have no more influence on the decisions than that of a boxing referee who is required to stop a fight. In a mature democracy like ours, this degree of understanding is not, surely, surprising, but it does in my view weaken this argument against incorporation.

An additional argument sometimes heard is that incorporation is unnecessary since the Convention rights are already protected by the common law. The House of Lords recently held that in the field of freedom of speech there is no difference in principle between English law and Article 10 of the Convention [*Derbyshire CC* v *Times Newspapers Ltd* [1993] 2 WLR 449]. Lord Goff of Chieveley said the same thing in one of the *Spycatcher* judgments [*Attorney-General* v *Guardian Newspapers (No. 2)* [1990] 1 AC 109 at 283–284]. But the House of Lords' earlier *Spycatcher* decision

[[1987] 1 WLR 1248] has itself been held to have violated the Convention, as of course have other of their Lordships' decisions. If in truth the common law as it stands were giving the rights of United Kingdom citizens the same protection as the Convention — across the board, not only in relation to Article 10 — one might wonder why the United Kingdom's record as a Strasbourg litigant was not more favourable. . . .

I am conscious that I have given much time to considering the arguments against incorporation and rather less to the case in favour. This is no doubt because I regard the positive case as clear and the burden as lying on the opponents to make good their grounds of opposition. But there is one argument in favour of incorporation that I would like to mention. It is not a new argument, but it is an important one, and it has recently been drawn to the House of Lords' attention by Lord Slynn of Hadley (in his legislative, and not his judicial, mode) [HL Deb. November 26, 1992 cols. 1096–1098]. The Court of Justice has now made clear that the fundamental human rights which the Convention protects are part of the law of the Community which that court is bound to secure and enforce. Community law is, of course, part of the law of the United Kingdom. As Lord Slynn put it,

> . . . every time the European Court recognises a principle set out in the convention as being part of Community law, it must be enforced in the United Kingdom courts in relation to Community law matters, but not in domestic law. So the convention becomes in part a part of our law through the back door because we have to apply the convention in respect of Community law matters as a party of Community law.

Drawing on his own experience as counsel appearing at Strasbourg, he felt it would be more satisfactory if the convention were to enter by the front door. It was he said,

> quite plain that many, although perhaps not all, of the cases could be dealt with just as well and more expeditiously by our own judges here.

(F) FREEDOM OF SPEECH AND ASSEMBLY

It is not possible to examine all aspects of civil liberties within the confines of this chapter. Freedom of speech and assembly have been chosen for limited further exposition as, in many ways, freedom of expression is the most fundamental freedom. This was highlighted by Benjamin Franklin, one of the 'Founding Fathers' of the Constitution of the United States, when he stated 'Whoever would overthrow the liberty of a nation must begin by subduing the freeness of speech'. In the United States freedom of expression is guaranteed by the First Amendment to the Constitution which provides:

> Congress shall make no law respecting an establishment of religion, or prohibiting the free exercise thereof; or abridging the freedom of speech, or of the press; or the right of the people peaceably to assemble, and to petition the Government for a redress of grievances.

The reasons for the high status accorded to freedom of speech in the United States are highlighted in the essay which follows.

N. Dorsen, 'Is there a right to stop offensive speech? The Case of the Nazis at Skokie' in *Civil Liberties in Conflict*, ed. L. Gostin (1988), pp. 122, 123–25

[F]ree speech is not absolutely protected, and should not be. But it should be inviolate unless the values on the other side are powerful and can be vindicated only by restricting speech. As Justice Cardozo once put it, the right to freedom of expression guaranteed by the First Amendment of the US Constitution is 'the matrix, the indispensable condition' of a free society. The reasons for that high status are worth recalling.

The first is that free speech permits the fulfilment of individuals by presenting their views (and therefore themselves) without legal restraint. This is a goal of the highest order. As one Supreme Court justice put it, 'the final end of the State [is] to make men free to develop their faculties.'

A second major justification of free expression stresses the concept of democratic self-government, the 'profound national commitment to the principle that debate on public issues should be uninhibited, robust, and wide open.' Indeed, a democracy cannot claim to be legitimate without freedom of speech; it cannot enjoy the consent of the governed if the governed cannot discuss and ponder matters that the government wants to exclude from public debate. Further, such debate helps to maintain 'the precarious balance between healthy cleavage and necessary consensus' by facilitating social reform. The movements on behalf of labour unions, racial minorities, and women are the most important examples of desirable social reforms advanced by the ability of people to persuade, agitate, and implore.

A third purpose of free speech is its 'checking value' against possible government corruption and excess by exposing and questioning official actions.

A fourth major purpose is to advance knowledge and reveal truth. Justice Oliver Wendell Holmes said that the 'best test of truth is the power of the thought to get itself accepted in the competition of the market.' While this may seem unduly optimistic at times, the purifying quality of speech has been evident for centuries in many spheres of human endeavour, especially the arts and sciences.

It is for these reasons that great thinkers throughout recorded history have celebrated the freedom of speech: Socrates, Milton, Locke, Jefferson, Montesquieu, and Mill. It is the keystone of our liberty. Indeed, in the course of academic discourse and courtroom combat I have rarely found a person who openly belittles the constitutional guarantee. To the contrary, everyone professes to support it. Why, then, does the First Amendment need an advocate? I suggest that the key is not whether the disputants accept the purposes of free speech but rather the *degree* to which they embrace them. Intensity of this sort cannot be measured mathematically, but it is palpable in judicial opinions, the briefs of lawyers, and articles by lawyers and journalists. I am not extolling mere emotionalism but rather laud a simple yet compelling confidence in speech values and a full sensitivity to their significance.

A key question in balancing rights concerns the burden of proof. The framers of the US Constitution made this decision, and made it wisely, in favour of free speech values. The powerful words of Justice Louis Brandeis illustrates the intensity of which I speak:

> Those who won our independence believed that freedom to think as you will and to speak as you think are means indispensable to the discovery and spread of political truth . . . that without free speech and assembly discussion would be futile; that the greatest menace to freedom is an inert people; that public discussion is a political duty; and that this should be a fundamental principle of the American government.

Without this intense commitment, the judge or scholar, after paying the obligatory homage to free expression, will nevertheless regretfully conclude that 'in *this* case' it must yield for reasons of national security, or domestic order, or government efficiency, or the other reasons that are regularly advanced to overwhelm our fragile constitutional guarantee. Indeed, the Skokie incident is a good example of a situation in which some people were willing to say 'in this case' free expression must yield. This is why it is useful to examine the case now, a decade later; its difficult facts test allegiance to free speech.

And of course there are reasons that make a full commitment to free speech seem difficult. People do say foolish and vicious things, and we may suspect that their words cause foolish and vicious acts. But to conclude that speculative harm traced to language justifies restrictions on free speech is to reverse the value judgment made by those who wrote the First Amendment to the US Constitution and lived through the turbulent times that begot it; they said by all means punish the lawless act but protect the freedom of speech.

(i) Freedom of Speech

In the United States the position may be summed up by the Duke of Wellington's rejoinder 'publish and be damned', as prior restraint of speech or publication is very difficult to achieve. By contrast, in the United Kingdom prior restraint is regularly achieved by means of interlocutory injunctions, often granted on the basis of claims that the information is confidential. Injunctions may be applied for by either the person whose interests may be affected or by the Attorney-General as guardian of the public interest. In *Attorney-General* v *Jonathan Cape Ltd* [1976] QB 752, the Attorney-General applied for injunctions against the publishers of the diaries of Richard Crossman, a former Labour Cabinet Minister, on the grounds that they contained confidential material acquired as a result of his position. Lord Widgery CJ stated the matters the Attorney-General would have to establish to succeed, as follows:

> (a) that such publication would be a breach of confidence; (b) that the public interest requires that the publication be restrained, and (c) that there are no other facets of the public interest contradictory of and more compelling than that relied upon. Moreover, the court, when asked to restrain such a publication, must closely examine the extent to which relief is necessary to ensure that restrictions are not imposed beyond the strict requirement of public need.

(For fuller excerpts from Lord Widgery CJ's judgment, see *ante* pp. 263–269.)

In the case which follows a company sought an injunction.

Schering Chemicals Ltd v *Falkman Ltd and Others*
[1981] 2 WLR 848
Court of Appeal

Between 1958 and 1967 the plaintiffs manufactured and marketed a drug, Primodos, which was used as a pregnancy test. The drug was withdrawn from the market in 1978 after suspicions arose of it causing abnormalities in new-born children. Litigation was commenced by parents of some children alleged to have been affected by the drug. Thames Television produced a documentary on Primodos, which was alleged to contain confidential material which the producer, David Elstein, who had been employed as a consultant by Falkman Ltd, had received from Schering. Falkman Ltd had been employed by Schering to run a course to train its executives in presenting the company's point of view. After a preliminary viewing of the documentary, Schering sought an interlocutory injunction to prevent the broadcasting of the film, founding its arguments on confidentiality.

LORD DENNING MR dissenting:

The remedy by injunction
The remedy sought by Schering is an injunction. They want to stop the showing of the film altogether. How far is it proper for the court to grant an injunction to restrain publication by the press and television? Such an injunction falls into a special category because it encroaches upon one of our most fundamental freedoms – the freedom of the press. . . .

Prior restraint
The freedom of the press is extolled as one of the great bulwarks of liberty. It is entrenched in the constitutions of the world. But it is often misunderstood. I will first say what it does *not* mean. It does not mean that the press is free to ruin a reputation or to break a confidence, or to pollute the course of justice or to do anything that is unlawful. I will next say what it *does* means. It means that there is to be no censorship. No restraint should be placed on the press as to what they should publish. Not by a licensing system. Nor by executive direction. Nor by court injunction. It means that the press is to be free from what Blackstone calls 'previous restraint' or what our friends in the United States – co-heirs with us of Blackstone – call 'prior restraint.' The press is not to be restrained *in advance* from publishing whatever it thinks right to publish. It can publish whatever it chooses to publish. But it does so at its own risk. It can 'publish and be damned.' Afterwards – after the publication – if the press has done anything unlawful – it can be dealt with by the courts. If it should offend – by interferring with the course of justice – it can be punished in proceedings for contempt of court. If it should damage the reputation of innocent people, by telling untruths or making unfair comment, it may be made liable in damages. But always afterwards. Never beforehand. Never by previous restraint.

Blackstone speaks
Such is the meaning of freedom of the press as enunciated by Blackstone. He put it so well in his Commentaries in the year 1765 that I would set out the passage in full (*Blackstone's Commentaries,* Book IV, 17th ed. (1830), pp. 151–152):

> In this and the other instances which we have lately considered, where blasphemous, immoral, treasonable, schismatical, seditious, or scandalous libels are punished by the English law, some with a greater, others with a less degree of severity; the *liberty of the press,* properly understood, is by no means infringed or violated. The liberty of the press is indeed essential to the nature of a free state; but this consists in laying no *previous* restraints upon publications, and not in freedom from censure for criminal matter when published. Every freeman has an undoubted right to lay what

> sentiments he pleases before the public; to forbid this, is to destroy the freedom of the press: but if he publishes what is improper, mischievous, or illegal, he must take the consequence of his own temerity. To subject the press to the restrictive power of a licenser, as was formerly done, both before and since the revolution, is to subject all freedom of sentiment to the prejudices of one man, and make him the arbitrary and infallible judge of all controverted points in learning, religion, and government. But to punish (as the law does at present) any dangerous or offensive writings, which, when published, shall on a fair and impartial trial be adjudged of a pernicious tendency, is necessary for the preservation of peace and good order, of government and religion, the only solid foundations of civil liberty. Thus the will of individuals is still left free; the abuse only of that free-will is the object of legal punishment.

That passage of Blackstone is the origin of the doctrine of 'prior restraint' which is so well known in the United States. It was quoted by Charles Evans Hughes CJ and the doctrine summarised, in the classic case in the Supreme Court of *Near* v *Minnesota* (1931) 283 US 697, 713–720.

An exception

Since Blackstone's day there has been some relaxation of this doctrine. In exceptional cases, where the intended publication is plainly unlawful and would inflict grave injury on innocent people or seriously impede the course of justice, then the court may issue a prior restraint. It may grant an interim injunction to restrain the proposed publication. The general rule – and the narrowness of the exception – is well illustrated by our practice in libel cases. On many occasions we have had cases where a plaintiff seeks an interim injunction to prevent the publication of a libel. We never grant the application when the defendant says that he intends to justify, no matter how improbable that he will succeed. We go by the ruling of this court in *Bonnard* v *Perryman* [1891] 2 Ch 269. In all but the most exceptional cases we will not grant an interim injunction to restrain the publication of a libel. Such an exceptional case was instanced by Jessel MR in *Quartz Hill Consolidated Gold Mining Co.* v *Beall* (1882) 20 ChD 501, 508; '. . . an atrocious libel wholly unjustified and inflicting the most serious injury on the plaintiff.' Except in such a case we never grant an interim injunction.

The European Convention

The same principle is contained in the European Convention for The Protection of Human Rights and Fundamental Freedoms. We are here concerned with a question of policy. What should be the policy of the law in restraining publication? On such a question, I take it that our law should conform as far as possible with the provisions of the European Convention of Human Rights. As Lord Scarman said in the *Exclusive Brethren* case, *Attorney-General* v *British Broadcasting Corporation* [1980] 3 WLR 109, 130:

> If the issue should ultimately be, as I think in this case it is, a question of legal policy, we must have regard to the country's international obligation to observe the Convention as interpreted by the Court of Human Rights.

Now we do know the views of the European Court of Human Rights on this subject. It is contained in article 10 of the Convention as interpreted in *The Sunday Times* v *United Kingdom* [1979] 2 EHRR 245, 281. The court stressed the importance of the general principle that 'everyone has the right to freedom of expression' and deliberately cut down the exceptions to it. It said that the exceptions 'must be narrowly interpreted.' The relevant exception in *The Sunday Times* case and here is that the freedom of expression may be subject to such restrictions as are 'necessary in a democratic society.' That was interpreted by the European Court of Human Rights to mean that there must be 'a social need sufficiently pressing to outweigh the public interest in freedom of expression'; see *The Sunday Times* case [1979] 2 EHRR 245, 282.

Lord Scarman's dictum
All this was well summed up by Lord Scarman in the *Exclusive Brethren* case [1980] 3 WLR 109, 138:

> . . . the prior restraint of publication, though occasionally necessary in serious cases, is a drastic interference with freedom of speech and should only be ordered where there is a substantial risk of grave injustice. I understand the test of 'pressing social need' as being exactly that.

By that one sentence Lord Scarman has brought back into English law the doctrine of prior restraint, which has been forgotten for too long. It applies not only in libel cases (as I have said) but also in all other cases where it is sought to restrain publication in the press – or on television. Such as in this case where there is an attempt to restrain publication on the ground that it would be a contempt of court or a breach of confidence. To these I now turn.

Breach of confidence
In some respects breach of confidence is different. Whilst freedom of expression is a fundamental human right, so also is the right of privacy. Everyone has the right to respect for his private life and his correspondence: article 8 of the European Convention. This includes a right to have his confidential information kept confidential. This right may in some circumstances be so important that it takes priority over the freedom of the press. An injunction may be granted restraining the newspapers from breaking the confidence. The principle is well expressed in article 10 (2) of the European Convention. It recognises that the freedom of expression may be restricted whenever a restriction is 'necessary in a democratic society, . . . for preventing the disclosure of information received in confidence . . .'

When no injunction should be granted
But there are other cases when the right of the press to inform the public – and the corresponding right of the public to be properly informed – takes priority over the right of privacy: see paragraphs 65–66 of the judgment of the European Court of Human Rights in *The Sunday Times* case [1979] 2 EHRR 245, 280–281. In such a case no injunction should be granted against the newspapers and television to prevent them from publishing the information, even though it originated in confidence: see the discussion in *Initial Services Ltd* v *Putterill* [1968] 1 QB 396.

On which side of the line did the confidential information fall in the *Granada* case [1980] 3 WLR 774? The matter never fell for decision. It was never argued out, because it was not disputed by Granada that British Steel could, if they had acted in time, have obtained from the court an injunction against publishing or reproducing any of the contents of the documents (by Lord Wilberforce at p. 821B). But Lord Salmon thought that, if the matter had been argued out, an interim injunction might have been lifted (at p. 838B-C). And I myself said, at p. 805 E-F. that, if a newspaper:

> gets hold of a trustworthy informant, who gives information of which the public ought to know, then, even though it originated in confidence, the newspaper may

well be held to act with a due sense of responsibility in publishing it. It should not be compelled to divulge its source.

Nor, may I now add, be subjected to an injunction restraining it from use of the information.

On which side of the line does the present case fall? If Thames were about to publish important private information which was highly confidential and very properly confined to Schering, I have no doubt that an injunction should be granted to prevent its publication in the film. But this information was not highly confidential. It was not confidential at all. It was not private. It was all in the public domain. Any stranger starting from scratch – and studying the old issues of 'The Sunday Times' and so forth – could have got all this information together and published it without breaking any confidence at all. Is an injunction to be granted simply because David Elstein did not start from scratch, but got the idea of doing it from the course? I am clearly of opinion that no injunction ought to be granted to prevent the publication of this information, even though it did originate in confidence. It dealt with a matter of great public interest. It contained information of which the public had a right to know. It should not be made the subject of an injunction. . . .

Conclusion

Freedom of the press is of fundamental importance in our society. It covers not only the right of the press to impart information of general interest or concern, but also the right of the public to receive it. It is not to be restricted on the ground of breach of confidence unless there is a 'pressing social need' for such restraint. In order to warrant a restraint, there must be a social need for protecting the confidence sufficiently pressing to outweigh the public interest in freedom of the press. No injunction forbidding publication should be granted except where the confidence is justifiable on moral or social grounds: *Argyll* (*Duchess*) v *Argyll* (*Duke*) [1967] Ch 302; or, I will add, on industrial grounds: the *Granada* case [1980] 3 WLR 774; and, in addition, where the *private* interest in maintaining the confidence outweighs the *public* interest in making the matter known to the public at large. . . . [I]n our present case, the *public* interest in the drug Primodos and its effects far outweighs the *private* interest of the makers in preventing discussion of it. Especially when all the information in the film is in the public domain, and where there had already been considerable coverage in newspapers and on television; and when the publication cannot in any way affect the course of justice in the pending actions. Nor affect the sales of Primodos because it has long been withdrawn from the market.

It comes back to this. Prior restraint is such a drastic interference with the freedom of the press that it should only be ordered when there is a substantial risk of grave injustice.

I stand as ever for the freedom of the press, including television, except when it is abused. I thought it was abused in the *Granada* case [1980] 3 WLR 774; but I see no abuse here. Even if there was any abuse, it was not such as to warrant the injunction of a prior restraint. I think that the judge ought to have refused the injunction on August 27, 1980. I would allow the appeal accordingly.

SHAW LJ: The obligation of confidentiality may in some circumstances be overborne. If the subject matter is something which is inimical to the public interest or threatens individual safety, a person in possession of knowledge of that subject matter cannot be obliged to conceal it although he acquired that knowledge in confidence. In some situations it may be his duty to reveal what he knows. No such consideration has existed in this case since the time that Primodos was withdrawn from the market.

Neither the public nor any individual stands in need of protection from its use at this stage in the history. There is no occasion to beat the drum again. As to any rights or liability which may have arisen from the use of Primodos in the past, these will be determined by the outcome of the pending litigation. Mr Elstein and Thames can offer no valid or effective assistance in this regard; they are without any legitimate justification for canvassing the issues in flagrant breach of an elementary duty to honour confidences acquired by Mr Elstein in the guise of a professional adviser. The law of England is indeed, as Blackstone declared, a law of liberty; but the freedoms it recognises do not include a licence for the mercenary betrayal of business confidences.

The judge added a second reason for granting the injunction against Mr Elstein, namely that 'he is the person whose conduct caused the first defendant to be in breach of contract.' Falkman would of course be palpably in breach. Mr Falk protested strongly on their behalf against Mr Elstein's proposals, but Falkman have refrained from taking steps against Mr Elstein because of the prospective burden of costs. I do not myself think that recourse to this second ground is necessary and make no comment in regard to it.

While it is true that Thames were not the direct recipients of confidential information conveyed in a fiduciary situation, it is not in controversy that they were at all times aware of the circumstances in which Mr Elstein first became possessed of it. If Mr Elstein was in breach of duty in seeking to use it at all, Thames cannot be entitled to collaborate with him by taking advantage of his repudiation of his fiduciary obligations. I agree with McNeill J when he said:

> As far as [Thames] are concerned, they should be enjoined from publishing any material that was produced consequent upon [Mr Elstein's] breach of the duty of confidentiality and [Falkman's].

The second proposition put forward on behalf of Mr Elstein and Thames was to this effect. When Mr Elstein undertook as an associate of Falkman to participate in the course for Schering, he had no intimate knowledge of the controversy and contentions which surrounded Primodos. By that time there had been numerous articles in scientific papers and journals and the first Sunday Times article had given publicity to the matter in the popular press. Mr Elstein's mind had, however, not been prompted to look in that direction. What he learned at the course came new to him. It is now said that all the information upon which the programme of the projected documentary is based could have been derived from sources available to the public before the Schering course with Executive Television Training. It is asserted also that Mr Elstein, with the assistance of a colleague at Thames, has assiduously explored and collated all those sources. The relevant facts and opinions are all to be found in what has been described as 'the public domain' or 'the public sector.' No principle of confidentiality can apply, so it is contended, to matters which have become notorious. Whatever may have been the fiduciary duty on the part of Mr Elstein not to disclose anything of a confidential nature that he had learned on the course, it had been entirely dissipated when the Primodos affair emerged into public view. What obligation of reticence can apply to what has long been an open secret? So the argument ran.

It is an argument which at best is cynical; some might regard it as specious. Even in the commercial field, ethics and good faith are not to be regarded as merely opportunist or expedient. In any case, though facts may be widely known, they are not ever-present in the minds of the public. To extend the knowledge or to revive the recollection of matters which may be detrimental or prejudicial to the interests of some person or organisation is not to be condoned because the facts are already known to some and linger in the memories of others. It is worth recalling that the London Weekend and the Granada documentaries had been shown before the Executive Television Training course for Schering was devised by Falkman. A good deal of information about Primodos was already 'in the public domain.' Schering's intention was to get what assistance could be given by Falkman to contain or to repudiate further public criticism and debate on a topic the discussion of which could only cause prejudice to Schering. Mr Elstein knew this as well as anybody. His claim that he wished to provide a debating ground in which the factors favourable to Schering could be effectively demonstrated is sheer sophistry. The importation into the programme of Professor Michael Briggs, who, from 1966 until 1969, had been Schering's research director in the United Kingdom, is said to demonstrate the even-handed treatment of the theme. I refrain from comment. Suffice it to say that Schering are naturally not eager to enter the lists and do not seek a champion for a jousting match contrived by one of their confidential advisers.

It is not the law that where confidentiality exists it is terminated or eroded by adventitious publicity. Nor is the correlative duty to preserve that confidentiality. The public interest may demand that the duty be gainsaid; but it cannot be arbitrarily cast aside. An order of a court of law may relieve the confidant of the burden of secrecy and may, after due inquiry, require him to reveal the subject matter of the confidence: but it is not to be sloughed at will for self-interest. I therefore come to the same conclusion as McNeill J on the issue of confidence.

Appeal and cross-appeal dismissed.

Questions

1. Where information is available from public sources, should it matter, in considering granting an injunction, that the defendant obtained the information through a confidential relationship with the plaintiff?

2. Which interests did the majority consider to be more important – commercial interests or the public interest?

3. If freedom of the press is one of the guarantees of freedom in our society in the absence of a Bill of Rights, is that general freedom diminished or threatened by the encroachment on press freedom which prior restraint involves?

Note

Interlocutory injunctions are granted by a judge in chambers and act to restrain the party against whom they are granted until a full trial of the issues may be held. To obtain an interlocutory injunction a party need only show that he has an arguable case and that the balance of convenience is against publishing and damages are not an adequate remedy. In *Attorney-General* v *British Broadcasting Corporation, The Times,* 18 December 1987, an interlocutory injunction was granted against the BBC to prevent it broadcasting a radio series, *My Country Right or Wrong,* on the basis of the Government's expressed fear that former security service officers might have breached confidence in the course of interviews. Owen J granted the injunction on the basis that if it proved on trial of the issue to be unnecessary, this would only have postponed broadcast of the programmes. When the High Court granted the Attorney-General discovery (i.e. it ordered the BBC to disclose the tapes of the programmes), the Government found that no breach of confidence was involved and discontinued the action. The BBC broadcast the programmes six months late.

Questions

1. If material is topical only temporarily, is there a danger that interlocutory injunctions may be used as a means to delay publication and provide a party who is likely to be embarrassed by the material with opportunity to prepare a 'damage limitation' exercise before the material is ultimately published?

2. Is the power to restrain publication by means of interlocutory injunctions and injunctions in effect a power to censor?

Note

In the litigation arising out of the publication by various newspapers of extracts from and allegations contained in Peter Wright's book *Spycatcher*, the House of Lords in *Attorney-General* v *Guardian Newspapers Ltd* [1987] 1 WLR 1248, by a three to two majority, granted interim injunctions banning any mention of Wright's allegations until proceedings against the *Guardian* and *The Sunday Times* had been completed. When a differently constituted House of Lords heard the final appeal on the trial of the issues, it decided to discharge the injunctions, as disclosure worldwide of Wright's allegations had destroyed their secrecy and no further damage could be done to the public interest. However, had Wright been resident in the United Kingdom his allegations might never have been made, as their Lordships confirmed that those employed in the Security Services owe a life-long duty of confidence to the state.

Attorney-General v *Guardian Newspapers (No. 2)*
[1988] 3 WLR 776
House of Lords

LORD GOFF: I start with the broad general principle (which I do not intend in any way to be definitive) that a duty of confidence arises when confidential information comes to the knowledge of a person (the confidant) in circumstances where he has notice, or is held to have agreed, that the information is confidential, with the effect that it would be just in all the circumstances that he should be precluded from disclosing the information to others. . . .The existence of this broad general principle reflects the fact that there is such a public interest in the maintenance of confidences, that the law will provide remedies for their protection.

I realise that, in the vast majority of cases, in particular those concerned with trade secrets, the duty of confidence will arise from a transaction or relationship between the parties – often a contract, in which event the duty may arise by reason of either an express or an implied term of that contract. . . . But it is well settled that a duty of confidence may arise in equity independently of such cases; and I have expressed the circumstances in which the duty arises in broad terms, not merely to embrace those cases where a third party receives information from a person who is under a duty of confidence in respect of it, knowing that it has been disclosed by that person to him in breach of his duty of confidence, but also to include certain situations, beloved of law teachers – where an obviously confidential document is wafted by an electric fan out of a window into a crowded street, or when an obviously confidential document, such as a private diary, is dropped in a public place, and is then picked up by a passer-by. I also have in mind the situations where secrets of importance to national security come into the possession of members of the public – a point to which I shall refer in a moment. . . .

To this broad general principle, there are three limiting principles to which I wish to refer. The first limiting principle (which is rather an expression of the scope of the duty) is highly relevant to this appeal. It is that the principle of confidentiality only applies to information to the extent that it is confidential. In particular, once it has entered what is usually called the public domain (which means no more than that the information in question is so generally accessible that, in all the circumstances, it cannot be regarded as confidential) then, as a general rule, the principle of confidentiality can have no application to it. I shall be reverting to this limiting principle at a later stage.

The second limiting principle is that the duty of confidence applies neither to useless information, nor to trivia. There is no need for me to develop this point.

The third limiting principle is of far greater importance. It is that, although the basis of the law's protection of confidence is that there is a public interest that confidences should be preserved and protected by the law, nevertheless that public interest may be outweighed by some other countervailing public interest which favours disclosure. This limitation may apply, as the learned judge pointed out, to all types of confidential information. It is this limiting principle which may require a court to carry out a balancing operation, weighing the public interest in maintaining confidence against a countervailing public interest favouring disclosure.

Embraced within this limiting principle is, of course, the so called defence of iniquity. In origin, this principle was narrowly stated, on the basis that a man cannot be made 'the confidant of a crime or a fraud': see *Gartside* v *Outram* (1857) 26 LJ Ch 113, 114, *per* Sir William Page Wood V-C. But it is now clear that the principle extends to matters of which disclosure is required in the public interest: see *Beloff* v *Pressdram Ltd* [1973] 1 All ER 241, 260, *per* Ungoed-Thomas J, and *Lion Laboratories Ltd* v *Evans* [1985] QB 526, 550, *per* Griffiths LJ. It does not however follow that the public interest will in such cases require disclosure to the media, or to the public by the media. There are cases in which a more limited disclosure is all that is required: see *Francome* v *Mirror Group Newspapers Ltd* [1984] 1 WLR 892. A classic example of a case where limited disclosure is required is a case of alleged iniquity in the Security Service. Here there are a number of avenues for proper complaint; these are set out in the judgment of Sir John Donaldson MR: see [1988] 2 WLR 805, 877–878. Like my noble and learned friend, Lord Griffiths, I find it very difficult to envisage a case of this kind in which it will be in the public interest for allegations of such iniquity to be published in the media. In any event, a mere allegation of iniquity is not of itself sufficient to justify disclosure in the public interest. Such an allegation will only do so if, following such investigations as are reasonably open to the recipient, and having regard to all the circumstances of the case, the allegation in question can reasonably be regarded as being a credible allegation from an apparently reliable source.

In cases concerned with Government secrets, as appears from the judgments of two Chief Justices – of Lord Widgery CJ in *Attorney-General* v *Jonathan Cape Ltd* [1976] QB 752, 770, and of Mason CJ (then Mason J) in *Commonwealth of Australia* v *John Fairfax & Sons Ltd*, 147 CLR 39, 51–53 – it is incumbent upon the Crown, in order to restrain disclosure of Government secrets, not only to show that the information is confidential, but also to show that it is in the public interest that it should not be published. . . . The reason for this additional requirement in cases concerned with Government secrets appears to be that, although in the case of private citizens there is a public interest that confidential information should as such be protected, in the case of Government secrets the mere fact of confidentiality does not alone support such a conclusion, because in a free society there is a continuing public interest that the workings of government should be open to scrutiny and criticism. From this it follows that, in such cases, there must be demonstrated some other public interest which requires that publication should be restrained.

Finally, I wish to observe that I can see no inconsistency between English law on this subject and article 10 of the European Convention on Human Rights. This is scarcely surprising, since we may pride ourselves on the fact that freedom of speech has existed in this country perhaps as long as, if not longer than, it has existed in any other country in the world. The only difference is that, whereas article 10 of the Convention, in accordance with its avowed purpose, proceeds to state a fundamental right and then to qualify it, we in this country (where everybody is free to do anything, subject only to the provisions of the law) proceed rather upon an assumption of freedom of speech, and turn to our law to discover the established exceptions to it. In any event I conceive it to be my duty, when I am free to do so, to interpret the law in accordance with the obligations of the Crown under this treaty. The exercise of the right to freedom of expression under article 10 may be subject to restrictions (as are prescribed by law and are necessary in a democratic society) in relation to certain prescribed matters, which include 'the interests of national security' and 'preventing the disclosure of information received in confidence.' It is established in the jurisprudence of the European Court of Human Rights that the word 'necessary' in this context implies the existence of a pressing social need, and that interference with freedom of expression should be no more than is proportionate to the legitimate aim pursued. I have no reason to believe that English law, as applied in the courts, leads to any different conclusion.

In the present case, it is possible to start with two simple propositions. First, Peter Wright, as a member of the Security Service, owed to the Crown a lifelong duty not to disclose confidential information which came into his possession in the course of his period of service with the Security Service. Second, as appears to have been common ground in these proceedings, whether or not he may have been justified in disclosing certain matters to an approriate person on the ground of iniquity, nevertheless by publishing the book as a whole he committed a clear and flagrant breach of his duty. So far as this lifelong duty of confidence is concerned, I am in respectful agreement with the observations made upon it in the speech of my noble and learned friend, Lord Griffiths, subject only to this, that I suspect that, although there may be a theoretical exception relating to trivia of the most humdrum kind, nevertheless in practice any such exception is of no importance and can be ignored. Be that as it may, these two propositions provided the starting point for the argument for the Crown so powerfully expressed by Lord Alexander on behalf of the Attorney-General. His basic submission was as follows. Although the effect of Peter Wright's breach of confidence was that the confidential information in *Spycatcher* has been widely disseminated throughout the world, nevertheless he remains to this day, and apparently for ever, under a duty of confidence in respect of that information, because he cannot by his own wrongful act destroy his own obligation of confidentiality. Anybody who has put the book in circulation knowing that the information in it derived from Peter Wright who had disclosed it in breach of confidence, must likewise have committed a breach of confidence; and since Peter Wright's duty of confidence still exists, the same must be true to this day. . . .

As I have already indicated, it is well established that a duty of confidence can only apply in respect of information which is confidential. . . .

Even so, it has been held by the learned judge, and by all members of the Court of Appeal in the present case, that Peter Wright cannot be released from his duty of confidence by his own publication of the confidential information, apparently on the basis that he cannot be allowed to profit from his own wrong. . . . [I]t is difficult to see how a confidant who publishes the relevant confidential information to the whole world can be under any further obligation not to disclose the information, simply because it was he who wrongfully destroyed its confidentiality. The information has, after all, already been so fully disclosed that it is in the public domain: how, therefore, can he thereafter be sensibly restrained from disclosing it? Is he not even to be permitted to mention in public what is now common knowledge? For his wrongful act, he may be held liable in damages, or may be required to make restitution; but . . . the confidential information, as confidential information, has ceased to exist, and with it should go, as a matter of principle, the obligation of confidence. . . . If the confidant who has wrongfully published the information so that it has entered the public domain remains under a duty of confidence, so logically must also be anybody who, deriving the information from him, publishes the information with knowledge that it was made available to him in breach of a duty of confidence. If Peter Wright is not released from his obligation of confidence neither, in my opinion, are Heinemann Publishers Pty Ltd, nor Viking Penguin Inc, nor anybody who may hereafter publish or sell the book in this country in the knowledge that it derived from Peter Wright – even booksellers who have in the past, or may hereafter, put the book on sale in their shops, would likewise be in breach of duty. If it is suggested that this is carrying the point to absurd lengths, then some principle has to be enunciated which explains why the continuing duty of confidence applies to some, but not others, who have wrongfully put the book in circulation. Such a distinction cannot however be explained by reliance upon the general statement that a man may not profit from his own wrong. . . .

[As Peter Wright was not a party to the proceedings, the question whether he owed a continuing duty of confidence did not require final decision. His Lordship continued.] Even if my provisional view on the point is wrong, and Peter Wright remains under a continuing duty of confidence, so that those who derive the information in the book from him would prima facie also be under a duty of confidence, I nevertheless take the view in the present case that to prevent the publication of the book in this country would, in the present circumstances, not be in the public interest. It seems to me to be an absurd state of affairs that copies of the book, all of course originating from Peter Wright – imported perhaps from the United States – should now be widely circulating in this country, and that at the same time other sales of the book should be restrained. To me, this simply does not make sense. I do not see why those who succeed in obtaining a copy of the book in the present circumstances should be able to read it, while others should not be able to do so simply by obtaining a copy from their local bookshop or library. In my opinion, artificially to restrict the readership of a widely accessible book in this way is unacceptable: if the information in the book is in the public domain and many people in this country are already able to read it, I do not see why anybody else in this country who wants to read it should be prevented from doing so.

Note

The decision of the House of Lords would appear to cast doubt on the correctness of the Court of Appeal's majority decision in *Schering Chemicals*

Ltd v *Falkman Ltd and Others* (see p. 479 *ante*), although their Lordships did not choose to overrule it.

Following the decision in the House of Lords, *The Observer, The Guardian* and *The Sunday Times* petitioned the European Commission on Human Rights, alleging that Art. 10 of the Convention had been breached. In *The Observer and The Guardian* v *United Kingdom* (Case 51/1990/242/313) and *The Sunday Times* v *United Kingdom (No. 2)* (Case 50/1990/241/312), *The Times,* 27 November 1991, the European Court of Human Rights ruled that the United Kingdom had breached Art. 10 in preventing the newspapers publishing the allegations contained in *Spycatcher* after it had been published in the United States, although the original interlocutory injunctions obtained before the book had been published were held to have been justified on the grounds of national security and to prevent the disclosure of confidential information. These grounds ceased to exist once the book had been published abroad, and the protection of the efficiency and reputation of MI6 was not sufficient reason in the national interest to justify continuing injunctions which thereby 'prevented newspapers from exercising their right and duty to purvey information already available on a matter of legitimate public concern'.

Questions

1. Is freedom of speech better protected by a general statement of a fundamental right, subject to limited qualifications as in Art. 10 of the European Convention on Human Rights, or by an underlying assumption on the part of judges that freedom of speech is to be respected unless established exceptions dictate otherwise?

2. Would it have been possible to obtain prior restraint in the United States in similar circumstances as those pertaining in the *Spycatcher* affair? See the following case.

New York Times v *United States*

403 US 713, 29 L Ed 2d 822
United States Supreme Court

The United States Government sought injunctions against the *New York Times* and the *Washington Post* to prevent publication of a classified study entitled 'History of US Decision-Making Process on Viet Nam Policy'. The Government argued that the First Amendment to the Constitution was not intended to make it impossible for the Executive to function or to protect the security of the United States. It claimed that its authority to protect the nation against publication of information whose disclosure would endanger national security stemmed from the constitutional power of the President over the conduct of foreign affairs and his authority as Commander-in-Chief.

MR JUSTICE BLACK: Our Government was launched in 1789 with the adoption of the Constitution. The Bill of Rights, including the First Amendment, followed in

1791. Now, for the first time in the 182 years since the founding of the Republic, the federal courts are asked to hold that the First Amendment does not mean what it says, but rather means that the Government can halt the publication of current news of vital importance to the people of this country.

In seeking injunctions against these newspapers and in its presentation to the Court, the Executive Branch seems to have forgotten the essential purpose and history of the First Amendment. When the Constitution was adopted, many people strongly opposed it because the document contained no Bill of Rights to safeguard certain basic freedoms. They especially feared that the new powers granted to a central government might be interpreted to permit the government to curtail freedom of religion, press, assembly, and speech. In response to an overwhelming public clamor, James Madison offered a series of amendments to satisfy citizens that these great liberties would remain safe and beyond the power of government to abridge. Madison proposed what later became the First Amendment in three parts, two of which are set out below, and one of which proclaimed: 'The people shall not be deprived or abridged of their right to speak, to write, or to publish their sentiments; *and the freedom of the press, as one of the great bulwarks of liberty, shall be inviolable.*' The amendments were offered to *curtail* and *restrict* the general powers granted to the Executive, Legislative, and Judicial Branches two years before in the original Constitution. The Bill of Rights changed the original Constitution into a new charter under which no branch of government could abridge the people's freedoms of press, speech, religion, and assembly. Yet the Solicitor General argues and some members of the Court appear to agree that the general powers of the Government adopted in the original Constitution should be interpreted to limit and restrict the specific and emphatic guarantees of the Bill of Rights adopted later. I can imagine no greater perversion of history. Madison and the other Framers of the First Amendment, able men that they were, wrote in language they earnestly believed could never be misunderstood: 'Congress shall make no law . . . abridging the freedom . . . of the press. . . .' Both the history and language of the First Amendment support the view that the press must be left free to publish news, whatever the source, without censorship, injunctions, or prior restraints.

In the First Amendment the Founding Fathers gave the free press the protection it must have to fulfill its essential role in our democracy. The press was to serve the governed, not the governors. The Government's power to censor the press was abolished so that the press would remain forever free to censure the Government. The press was protected so that it could bare the secrets of government and inform the people. Only a free and unrestrained press can effectively expose deception in government. And paramount among the responsibilities of a free press is the duty to prevent any part of the government from deceiving the people and sending them off to distant lands to die of foreign fevers and foreign shot and shell. In my view, far from deserving condemnation for their courageous reporting, the New York Times, the Washington Post, and other newspapers should be commended for serving the purpose that the Founding Fathers saw so clearly. In revealing the workings of government that led to the Vietnam war, the newspapers nobly did precisely that which the Founders hoped and trusted they would do.

The Government's case here is based on premises entirely different from those that guided the Framers of the First Amendment. . . . [W]e are asked to hold that despite the First Amendment's emphatic command, the Executive Branch, the Congress, and the Judiciary can make laws enjoining publication of current news and abridging freedom of the press in the name of 'national security.' The Government does not even attempt to rely on any act of Congress. Instead it makes the bold and dangerously far-reaching contention that the courts should take it upon themselves to 'make' a law abridging freedom of the press in the name of equity, presidential power, and national security, even when the representatives of the people in Congress have adhered to the command of the First Amendment and refused to make such a law. . . . To find that the President has 'inherent power' to halt the publication of news by resort to the courts would wipe out the First Amendment and destroy the fundamental liberty and security of the very people the Government hopes to make 'secure.' No one can read the history of the adoption of the First Amendment without being convinced beyond any doubt that it was injunctions like those sought here that Madison and his collaborators intended to outlaw in this Nation for all time.

The word 'security' is a broad, vague generality whose contours should not be invoked to abrogate the fundamental law embodied in the First Amendment. The guarding of military and diplomatic secrets at the expense of informed representative government provides no real security for our Republic. The Framers of the First Amendment, fully aware of both the need to defend a new nation and the abuses of the English and Colonial Governments, sought to give this new society strength and security by providing that freedom of speech, press, religion, and assembly should not be abridged. This thought was eloquently expressed in 1937 by Mr Chief Justice Hughes – great man and great Chief Justice that he was – when the Court held a man could not be punished for attending a meeting run by Communists.

> The greater the importance of safeguarding the community from incitements to the overthrow of our institutions by force and violence, the more imperative is the need to preserve inviolate the constitutional rights of free speech, free press and free assembly in order to maintain the opportunity for free political discussion, to the end that government may be responsive to the will of the people and that changes, if desired, may be obtained by peaceful means. Therein lies the security of the Republic, the very foundation of constitutional government.

MR JUSTICE DOUGLAS: Secrecy in government is fundamentally anti-democratic, perpetuating bureaucratic errors. Open debate and discussion of public issues are vital to our national health. On public questions there should be 'uninhibited, robust, and wide-open' debate.

MR JUSTICE BRENNAN: The error that has pervaded these cases from the outset was the granting of any injunctive relief whatsoever, interim or otherwise. The entire thrust of the Government's claim throughout these cases has been that publication of the material sought to be enjoined 'could,' or 'might,' or 'may' prejudice the national interest in various ways. But the First Amendment tolerates absolutely no prior judicial restraints of the press predicated upon surmise or conjecture that untoward consequences may result. Our cases, it is true, have indicated that there is a single, extremely narrow class of cases in which the First Amendment's ban on prior judicial restraint may be overridden. Our cases have thus far indicated that such cases may arise only when the Nation 'is at war,' *Schenck* v *United States*, 249 US 47, 52, 63 L Ed 470, 474, 39 S Ct 247 (1919), during which times '[n]o one would question but that a government might prevent actual obstruction to its recruiting service or the publication of the sailing dates of transports or the number and location of troops.' *Near* v *Minnesota*, 283 US 697, 716, 75 L Ed 1357, 1367, 51 S Ct 625 (1931). Even if the present world situation were assumed to be tantamount to a time of war, or if the power of presently available armaments would justify even in peacetime the suppression of information that would set in motion a nuclear holocaust, in neither of these actions has the Government presented or even alleged that publication of items from or based upon the material at issue would cause the happening of an event of that nature. '[T]he chief purpose of [the First Amendment's] guaranty [is] to prevent previous restraints upon publication.' *Near* v *Minnesota*, supra, at 713, 75 L Ed at 1366. Thus, only governmental allegation and proof that publication must inevitably, directly, and immediately cause the occurrence of an event kindred to imperiling the safety of a transport already at sea can support even the issuance of an interim restraining order. In no event may mere conclusions be sufficient: for if the Executive Branch seeks judicial aid in preventing publication, it must inevitably submit the basis upon which that aid is sought to scrutiny by the judiciary. And therefore, every restraint issued in this case, whatever its form, has violated the First Amendment – and not less so because that restraint was justified as necessary to afford the courts an opportunity to examine the claim more thoroughly. Unless and until the Government has clearly made out its case, the First Amendment commands that no injunction may issue.

Questions

1. In *Attorney-General* v *Guardian Newspapers (No. 2)* (*ante* p. 486) the House of Lords allowed for breach of a duty of confidence by members of the Security Services in three circumstances:

(a) where the information disclosed is utterly trivial;

(b) where it is already in the public domain (as it was in the case before them); and

(c) where it involves the disclosure of an iniquitous course of action which is being pursued which is clearly detrimental to the national interest, and the member has been unable to persuade any senior members of his service or any member of the establishment or the police, to do anything about it.

If any of these situations arose now, would the member involved be in breach of s. 1 of the Official Secrets Act 1989, which does not permit any defence based on 'public interest'?

2. Would a newspaper to which such a member had passed information be in breach of s. 5 of the Official Secrets Act 1989?

OFFICIAL SECRETS ACT 1989

1. Security and intelligence

(1) A person who is or has been—

(a) a member of the security and intelligence services; or

(b) a person notified that he is subject to the provisions of this subsection,

is guilty of an offence if without lawful authority he discloses any information, document or other article relating to security or intelligence which is or has been in his possession by virtue of his position as a member of any of those services or in the course of his work while the notification is or was in force.

(2) The reference in subsection (1) above to disclosing information relating to security or intelligence includes a reference to making any statement which purports to be a disclosure of such information or is intended to be taken by those to whom it is addressed as being such a disclosure.

(3) A person who is or has been a Crown servant or government contractor is guilty of an offence if without lawful authority he makes a damaging disclosure of any information, document or other article relating to security or intelligence which is or has been in his possession by virtue of his position as such but otherwise than as mentioned in subsection (1) above.

(4) For the purposes of subsection (3) above a disclosure is damaging if—

(a) it causes damage to the work of, or of any part of, the security and intelligence services; or

(b) it is of information or a document or other article which is such that its unauthorised disclosure would be likely to cause such damage or which falls within a class or description of information, documents or articles the unauthorised disclosure of which would be likely to have that effect.

(5) It is a defence for a person charged with an offence under this section to prove that at the time of the alleged offence he did not know, and had no reasonable cause to believe, that the information, document or article in question related to security or intelligence or, in the case of an offence under subsection (3), that the disclosure would be damaging within the meaning of that subsection.

. . .

(9) In this section 'security or intelligence' means the work of, or in support of, the security and intelligence services or any part of them, and references to information relating to security or intelligence include references to information held or transmitted by those services or by persons in support of, or of any part of, them.

2. Defence

(1) A person who is or has been a Crown servant or government contractor is guilty of an offence if without lawful authority he makes a damaging disclosure of any information, document or other article relating to defence which is or has been in his possession by virtue of his position as such.

(2) For the purposes of subsection (1) above a disclosure is damaging if—

(a) it damages the capacity of, or of any part of, the armed forces of the Crown to carry out their tasks or leads to loss of life or injury to members of those forces or serious damage to the equipment or installations of those forces; or

(b) otherwise than as mentioned in paragraph (a) above, it endangers the interests of the United Kingdom abroad, seriously obstructs the promotion or protection by the United Kingdom of those interests or endangers the safety of British citizens abroad; or

(c) it is of information or of a document or article which is such that its unauthorised disclosure would be likely to have any of those effects.

(3) It is a defence for a person charged with an offence under this section to prove that at the time of the alleged offence he did not know, and had no reasonable cause to believe, that the information, document or article in question related to defence or that its disclosure would be damaging within the meaning of subsection (1) above.

(4) In this section 'defence' means—

(a) the size, shape, organisation, logistics, order of battle, deployment, operations, state of readiness and training of the armed forces of the Crown;

(b) the weapons, stores or other equipment of those forces and the invention, development, production and operation of such equipment and research relating to it;

(c) defence policy and strategy and military planning and intelligence;

(d) plans and measures for the maintenance of essential supplies and services that are or would be needed in time of war.

3. International relations

(1) A person who is or has been a Crown servant or government contractor is guilty of an offence if without lawful authority he makes a damaging disclosure of—

(a) any information, document or other article relating to international relations; or

(b) any confidential information, document or other article which was obtained from a State other than the United Kingdom or an international organisation,

being information or a document or article which is or has been in his possession by virtue of his position as a Crown servant or government contractor.

(2) For the purposes of subsection (1) above a disclosure is damaging if—

(a) it endangers the interests of the United Kingdom abroad, seriously obstructs the promotion or protection by the United Kingdom of those interests or endangers the safety of British citizens abroad; or

(b) it is of information or of a document or article which is such that its unauthorised disclosure would be likely to have any of those effects.

(3) In the case of information or a document or article within subsection (1)(b) above—

(a) the fact that it is confidential, or

(b) its nature or contents,

may be sufficient to establish for the purposes of subsection (2)(b) above that the information, document or article is such that its unauthorised disclosure would be likely to have any of the effects there mentioned.

(4) It is a defence for a person charged with an offence under this section to prove that at the time of the alleged offence he did not know, and had no reasonable cause to believe, that the information, document or article in question was such as is mentioned in subsection (1) above or that its disclosure would be damaging within the meaning of that subsection.

(5) In this section 'international relations' means the relations between States, between international organisations or between one or more States and one or more such organisations and includes any matter relating to a State other than the United Kingdom or to an international organisation which is capable of affecting the relations of the United Kingdom with another State or with an international organisation.

(6) For the purposes of this section any information, document or article obtained from a State or organisation is confidential at any time while the terms on which it was obtained require it to be held in confidence or while the circumstances in which it was obtained make it reasonable for the State or organisation to expect that it would be so held.

5. Information resulting from unauthorised disclosures or entrusted in confidence

(1) Subsection (2) below applies where—

(a) any information, document or other article protected against disclosure by the foregoing provisions of this Act has come into a person's possession as a result of having been—

(i) disclosed (whether to him or another) by a Crown servant or government contractor without lawful authority; or

(ii) entrusted to him by a Crown servant or government contractor on terms requiring it to be held in confidence or in circumstances in which the Crown servant or government contractor could reasonably expect that it would be so held; or

(iii) disclosed (whether to him or another) without lawful authority by a person to whom it was entrusted as mentioned in sub-paragraph (ii) above; and

(b) the disclosure without lawful authority of the information, document or article by the person into whose possession it has come is not an offence under any of those provisions.

(2) Subject to subsections (3) and (4) below, the person into whose possession the information, document or article has come is guilty of an offence if he discloses it without lawful authority knowing, or having reasonable cause to believe, that it is protected against disclosure by the foregoing provisions of this Act and that it has come into his possession as mentioned in subsection (1) above.

(3) In the case of information or a document or article protected against disclosure by sections 1 to 3 above, a person does not commit an offence under subsection (2) above unless—

(a) the disclosure by him is damaging; and

(b) he makes it knowing, or having reasonable cause to believe, that it would be damaging;

and the question whether a disclosure is damaging shall be determined for the purposes of this subsection as it would be in relation to a disclosure of that information, document or article by a Crown servant in contravention of section 1(3), 2(1) or 3(1) above.

(4) A person does not commit an offence under subsection (2) above in respect of information or a document or other article which has come into his possession as a result of having been disclosed—

(a) as mentioned in subsection (1)(a)(i) above by a government contractor; or

(b) as mentioned in subsection (1)(a)(iii) above,

unless that disclosure was by a British citizen or took place in the United Kingdom, in any of the Channel Islands or in the Isle of Man or a colony.

(5) For the purposes of this section information or a document or article is protected against disclosure by the foregoing provisions of this Act if—

(a) it relates to security or intelligence, defence or international relations within the meaning of section 1, 2 or 3 above or is such as is mentioned in section 3(1)(b) above; or

(b) it is information or a document or article to which section 4 above applies;

and information or a document or article is protected against disclosure by sections 1 to 3 above if it falls within paragraph (a) above.

(6) A person is guilty of an offence if without lawful authority he discloses any information, document or other article which he knows, or has reasonable cause to believe, to have come into his possession as a result of a contravention of section 1 of the Official Secrets Act 1911.

Note

Sometimes freedom of the press is restricted directly by Executive action. Under s. 10 of the Broadcasting Act 1990 (previously s. 29 (3) of the Broadcasting Act 1981) and cl. 13 (4) of the BBC's Charter Licence and Agreement, the Home Secretary has power to give notice to the Independent Broadcasting Authority and the BBC to refrain from broadcasting any matter or classes of matter specified in the notice. In October 1988 the Home Secretary issued notices to the IBA and BBC requiring them to refrain from broadcasting 'any words spoken, whether in the course of an interview or discussion or otherwise, by a person who appears or is heard on the programme', where 'the person speaking the words represents or purports to represent', or 'the words support or solicit or invite support for', Sinn Fein, Provisional Sinn Fein, the Ulster Defence Association, or any proscribed terrorist organisation. (Following the announcement by the Provisional IRA in September 1994 of a cessation of violence, the broadcasting restrictions were removed.)

These notices were challenged in the High Court by a group of journalists seeking a writ of *certiorari* to quash the notices on the grounds that they were *ultra vires* and void. They claimed:

(1) that the notices breached Art. 10 of the European Convention on Human Rights;
(2) they were perverse and disproportionate to the mischief sought to be controlled;
(3) they conflicted with the duty of the BBC and IBA to be impartial in their news reporting; and
(4) there was no power to impose a blanket ban on broadcasting of all information from a particular source, as 'matter' in s. 29 (3) and cl. 13 (4) related to specific information.

R v *Secretary of State for the Home Department, ex parte Brind and Others*
[1991] 2 WLR 588
House of Lords

LORD ACKNER: . . . The applicants are neither the BBC nor the IBA. They are (with one exception) broadcast journalists who are members of the National Union of Journalists ('the NUJ'). The exception is Mr Nash, who is employed by the NUJ and who relies on broadcasting for the provision of information about current affairs. . . .

(iii) By section 29(3) of the [Broadcasting] Act 1981:

> Subject to subsection (4), the Secretary of State may at any time by notice in writing require the Authority to refrain from broadcasting any matter or classes of matter specified in the notice; and it shall be the duty of the Authority to comply with the notice.

(iv) By clause 13(4) of the licence and agreement made between the BBC and the Secretary of State on 2 April 1981:

> The Secretary of State may from time to time require the Corporation to refrain at any specified time or at all times from sending any matter or matters of any class specified in such notice . . .

The directives
The text common to both directives is as follows:

> 1. . . . to refrain from broadcasting any matter which consists of or includes — any words spoken, whether in the course of an interview or discussion or otherwise, by a person who appears or is heard on the programme in which the matter is broadcast where — (a) the person speaking the words represents or purports to represent an organisation specified in paragraph 2 below, or (b) the words support or solicit or

invite support for such an organisation, other than any matter specified in paragraph 3 below. 2. The organisations referred to in paragraph 1 above are — (a) any organisation which is for the time being a proscribed organisation for the purposes of the Prevention of Terrorism (Temporary Provisions) Act 1984 or the Northern Ireland (Emergency Provisions) Act 1978; and (b) Sinn Fein, Republican Sinn Fein and the Ulster Defence Association. 3. The matter excluded from paragraph 1 above is any words spoken — (a) in the course of proceedings in Parliament, or (b) by or in support of a candidate at a parliamentary, European parliamentary or local election pending that election. . . .

The Secretary of State's reasons for his action
The Secretary of State's decision was the subject matter of a statement made on 19 October 1988 in both Houses of Parliament and was followed by debates in both Houses. . . . The Secretary of State's reasons for taking the action complained of are set out in the Hansard reports of those debates and were before your Lordships. The four matters which influenced the Secretary of State were . . .: (1) offence had been caused to viewers and listeners by the appearance of the apologists for terrorism, particularly after a terrorist outrage; (2) such appearances had afforded terrorists undeserved publicity which was contrary to the public interest; (3) these appearances had tended to increase the standing of terrorist organisations and to create a false impression that support for terrorism is itself a legitimate political opinion; (4) broadcast statements were intended to have, and did in some cases have, the effect of intimidating some of those at whom they were directed.

The challenge
I now turn to the bases upon which it is contended that the Secretary of State exceeded his statutory powers.

1. *The directives frustrated the policy and the objects of the Act of 1981, in particular section 4(1).*
It is of course accepted by Mr Laws on behalf of the Secretary of State that the discretion given to him by section 29(3) is not an absolute or unfettered discretion. It is a discretion which is to be exercised according to law and therefore must be used only to advance the purposes for which it was conferred. It has accordingly to be used to promote the policy and objects of the Act: see *Padfield* v *Minister of Agriculture, Fisheries and Food* [1968] AC 997. It is further accepted on behalf of the Secretary of State that the powers under section 29(3) can be properly categorised as 'reserve' powers in the sense that they are to be used infrequently. In fact they have only been used once previously.

In the Divisional Court and Court of Appeal much was made of the words in section 4(1)(f), 'due impartiality.' The argument was not repeated before your Lordships. I can find nothing in paragraph 4(1)(f) to suggest that the policy and objects of section 4(1) are in any way frustrated by the Secretary of State's exercise of his reserve powers where, in the proper exercise of his discretion, he considers it appropriate to do so.

2. *The directives were unlawful on 'Wednesbury' grounds*
Save only in one respect, namely the European Convention for the Protection of Human Rights and Fundamental Freedoms (Cmd. 8969), which is the subject matter of a later heading, it is not suggested that the minister failed to call his attention to matters which he was bound to consider, nor that he included in his considerations matters which were irrelevant. In neither of those senses can it be said that the

minister acted unreasonably. The failure to mount such a challenge in this appeal is important. In a field which concerns a fundamental human right — namely that of free speech — close scrutiny must be given to the reasons provided as justification for interference with that right. . . .

There remains however the potential criticism under the *Wednesbury* grounds expressed by Lord Greene MR [1948] 1 KB 223, 230 that the conclusion was 'so unreasonable that no reasonable authority could ever have come to it.' This standard of unreasonableness, often referred to as 'the irrationality test,' has been criticised as being too high. But it has to be expressed in terms that confine the jurisdiction exercised by the judiciary to a supervisory, as opposed to an appellate, jurisdiction. Where Parliament has given to a minister or other person or body a discretion, the court's jurisdiction is limited, in the absence of a statutory right of appeal, to the supervision of the exercise of that discretionary power, so as to ensure that it has been exercised lawfully. It would be a wrongful usurpation of power by the judiciary to substitute its, the judicial view, on the merits and on that basis to quash the decision. If no reasonable minister properly directing himself would have reached the impugned decision, the minister has exceeded his powers and thus acted unlawfully and the court in the exercise of its supervisory role will quash that decision. Such a decision is correctly, though unattractively, described as a 'perverse' decision. To seek the court's intervention on the basis that the correct or objectively reasonable decision is other than the decision which the minister has made is to invite the court to adjudicate as if Parliament had provided a right of appeal against the decision — that is, to invite an abuse of power by the judiciary.

So far as the facts of this case are concerned it is only necessary to read the speeches in the Houses of Parliament, and in particular those of Mr David Alton, Lord Fitt and Lord Jakobovits, to reach the conclusion that, whether the Secretary of State was right or wrong to decide to issue the directives, there was clearly material which would justify a reasonable minister making the same decision. . . .

I entirely agree with McCowan LJ [in the Court of Appeal] when he said that he found it quite impossible to hold that the Secretary of State's political judgment that the appearance of terrorists on programmes increases their standing and lends them political legitimacy is one that no reasonable Home Secretary could hold. As he observed: 'It is, it should be noted, also the political judgment of the terrorists, or they would not be so anxious to be interviewed by the media or so against the Secretary of State's ban.'

Mr Lester has contended that in issuing these directives the Secretary of State has used a sledgehammer to crack a nut. Of course that is a picturesque way of describing the *Wednesbury* 'irrational' test. The Secretary of State has in my judgment used no sledgehammer. Quite the contrary is the case.

I agree with Lord Donaldson MR, who, when commenting on how limited the restrictions were, said in his judgment, at p. 803:

> They have no application in the circumstances mentioned in paragraph 3 (proceedings in the United Kingdom Parliament and elections) and, by allowing reported speech either verbatim or in paraphrase, in effect put those affected in no worse a position than they would be if they had access to newspaper publicity with a circulation equal to the listening and viewing audiences of the programmes concerned. Furthermore, on the applicants' own evidence, if the directives had been in force during the previous 12 months, the effect would have been minimal in terms of air time. Thus, [ITN] say that eight minutes twenty seconds (including repeats) out of 1200 hours, or 0.01 per cent., of air time would have been affected.

Furthermore, it would not have been necessary to omit these items. They could have been recast into a form which complied with the directives.

Thus the extent of the interference with the right to freedom of speech is a very modest one. On the other hand the vehemence of the criticism of the Secretary of State's decision is perhaps a clear indication of the strength of the impact of the terrorist message when he is seen or heard expressing his views.

3. The minister failed to have proper regard to the European Convention for the Protection of Human Rights and Fundamental Freedoms and in particular article 10. . . .

The Convention which is contained in an international treaty to which the United Kingdom is a party has not yet been incorporated into English domestic law. The applicants accept that it is a constitutional principle that if Parliament has legislated and the words of the statute are clear, the statute must be applied even if its application is in breach of international law. . . .

It is well settled that the Convention may be deployed for the purpose of the resolution of an ambiguity in English primary or subordinate legislation. . . .

Mr Lester contends that section 29(3) is ambiguous or uncertain. He submits that although it contains within its wording no fetter upon the extent of the discretion it gives to the Secretary of State, it is accepted that that discretion is not absolute. There is however no ambiguity in section 29(3). It is not open to two or more different constructions. The limit placed upon the discretion is simply that the power is to be used only for the purposes for which it was granted by the legislation (the so-called *Padfield* [1968] AC 997 doctrine) and that it must be exercised reasonably in the *Wednesbury* sense. No question of the construction of the words of section 29(3) arises, as would be the case if it was alleged to be ambiguous, or its meaning uncertain.

There is yet a further answer to Mr Lester's contention. He claims that the Secretary of State before issuing his directives should have considered not only the Convention (it is accepted that he in fact did so) but that he should have properly construed it and correctly taken it into consideration. It was therefore a relevant, indeed a vital, factor to which he was obliged to have proper regard pursuant to the *Wednesbury* doctrine, with the result that his failure to do so rendered his decision unlawful. The fallacy of this submission is however plain. If the Secretary of State was obliged to have proper regard to the Convention, i.e. to conform with article 10, this inevitably would result in incorporating the Convention into English domestic law by the back door. It would oblige the courts to police the operation of the Convention and to ask themselves in each case, where there was a challenge, whether the restrictions were 'necessary in a democratic society . . .' applying the principles enunciated in the decisions of the European Court of Human Rights. The treaty, not having been incorporated in English law, cannot be a source of rights and obligations and the question 'Did the Secretary of State act in breach of article 10?' does not therefore arise.

4. The Secretary of State has acted ultra vires because he has acted 'in a disproportionate manner'.

. . . Unless and until Parliament incorporates the Convention into domestic law, a course which it is well known has a strong body of support, there appears to me to be at present no basis upon which the proportionality doctrine applied by the European Court can be followed by the courts of this country.

I would accordingly dismiss this appeal with costs.

Appeal dismissed.

Note

The European Commossion on Human Rights declared inadmissible an application alleging a breach of the European Convention: *Brind and McLoughlin* v *UK Nos 18714 and 18759/91* 77-A DR 42 (1994).

Questions

1. Compare Lord Ackner's speech with the judgments in *New York Times* v *US* (*ante* p. 490). Has Lord Ackner expanded or restricted the influence of the European Convention on Human Rights? Does his speech serve to assert freedom of expression as a fundamental assumption of our constitution?

2. In the Court of Appeal Lord Donaldson MR stated that 'you have to look long and hard before you can detect any difference between the English common law and the principles set out in the Convention'. Do you agree?

Note

It is undeniable that the preceding cases display within them the continuing tension between freedom of speech and other rights and interests. There are signs, however, in several recent cases that greater importance is being attributed to freedom of speech as a fundamental legal principle of the common law. In *Derbyshire County Council* v *Times Newspapers* (see p. 469 *ante*) the House of Lords was unanimous in deciding that a democratically elected public body would not sue for libel as such an action would be contrary to the public interest and an undesirable fetter on freedom of speech. The fundamental nature of freedom of speech was emphasised in the following case.

R v Central Independent Television plc
[1994] 3 WLR 20
Court of Appeal

A television company was due to broadcast a programme about the detection and conviction of a paedophile who was the father of S, a five-year-old child. S's mother applied for an injunction from the Family Division seeking an order that the programme only be broadcast if pictures of the father were obscured. The mother feared that the identification of the father could lead to S being identified as his child with resultant psychological harm to S. Kirkwood J granted the application and the television company appealed.

HOFFMAN LJ: There are in the law reports many impressive and emphatic statements about the importance of the freedom of speech and the press. But they are often followed by a paragraph which begins with the word 'nevertheless'. The judge then goes on to explain that there are other interests which have to be balanced against press freedom. And in deciding upon the importance of press freedom in the particular case, he is likely to distinguish between what he thinks deserves publication in the public interest and things in which the public are merely interested. He may even advert to the commercial motives of the newspaper or television company compared with the damage to the public or individual interest which would be caused by publication.

The motives which impel judges to assume a power to balance freedom of speech against other interests are almost always understandable and humane on the facts of the particular case before them. Newspapers are sometimes irresponsible and their motives in a market economy cannot be expected to be unalloyed by considerations of commercial advantage. Publication may cause needless pain, distress and damage to individuals or harm to other aspects of the public interest. But a freedom which is restricted to what judges think to be responsible or in the public interest is no freedom. Freedom means the right to publish things which government and judges, however well motivated, think should not be published. It means the right to say things which 'right-thinking people' regard as dangerous or irresponsible. This freedom is subject only to clearly defined exceptions laid down by common law or statute.

Furthermore, in order to enable us to meet our international obligations under the Convention for the Protection of Human Rights and Fundamental Freedoms (1953) (Cmd. 8969), it is necessary that any exceptions should satisfy the tests laid down in article 10(2). . . .

It cannot be too strongly emphasised that outside the established exceptions, or any new ones which Parliament may enact in accordance with its obligations under the Convention, there is no question of balancing freedom of speech against other interests. It is a trump card which always wins.

This is why I respectfully think that Lord Denning MR was right in *In re X (A Minor) (Wardship: Jurisdiction)* [1975] Fam. 47 when he said that the wardship jurisdiction did not permit the courts to balance the competing interests of the child and the freedom of the press. The exceptions to freedom of speech were, he said, at p. 58F 'already staked out by the rules of law.' Section 12(1)(a) of the Administration of Justice Act 1960 prohibits the publication of information relating to a private court hearing in proceedings which concern children. It does not however apply to information which relates to the child but not to the proceedings: see *In re F (orse A.) (A Minor) (Publication of Information)* [1977] Fam. 58. It would be wrong, said Lord Denning MR in *In re X (A Minor) (Wardship: Jurisdiction)* [1975] Fam. 47, 58 to extend the law:

> so as to give the judges a power to stop publication of true matter whenever the judges — or any particular judge — thought that it was in the interests of a child to do so. . . .

In any area of human rights like freedom of speech, I respectfully doubt the wisdom of creating judge-made exceptions, particularly when they require a judicial balancing of interests. The danger about such exceptions is that judges are tempted to use them. The facts of the individual case often seem to demand exceptional treatment because the newspaper's interest in publication seems trivial and the hurt likely to be inflicted very great. The interests of the individual litigant and the public interest in the freedom of the press are not easily commensurable. It is not surprising that in this case the misery of a five year old girl weighed more heavily with Kirkwood J. than the television company's freedom to publish material which would heighten the dramatic effect of its documentary. This is what one would expect of a sensitive and humane judge exercising the wardship jurisdiction. But no freedom is without cost and in my view the judiciary should not whittle away freedom of speech with ad hoc exceptions. The principle that the press is free from both government and judicial control is more important than the particular case.

It is true that in a series of decisions commencing with *In re. C. (A Minor) (Wardship: Medical Treatment) (No. 2)* [1990] Fam 39 the courts have, without any statutory or, so far as I can see, other previous authority, assumed a power to create by injunction what is in effect a right of privacy for children. The power is said to be based on the powers of the Crown as parents patriae and the 'machinery for its exercise' is the wardship jurisdiction: see Butler-Sloss LJ in *In re M and N (Minors) (Wardship: Publication of Information* [1990] Fam. 221, 223 . . .

But this new jurisdiction is concerned only with the privacy of children and their upbringing. It does not extend, as Lord Donaldson of Lymington MR made clear in *In re M and N* at p. 231B to 'injunctive protection of children from publicity which, though inimical to their welfare, is not directed at them or those who care for them.' It therefore cannot apply to publication of the fact that the child's father has been convicted of a serious offence, however distressing it may be for the child to be identified as the daughter of such a man. If such a jurisdiction existed, it could be exercised to restrain the identification of any convicted criminal who has young children . . .

It follows that in my judgment there was in this case no jurisdiction to restrain the television company from publishing pictures of the child's father, or of the house in which he had lived and had been arrested. In fact the television company gave undertakings not to publish the pictures of the house or the mother, or to refer in any way to the fact that the father was married or had a child. In my view it was considerate and responsible of the television company to give these undertakings and I am glad that it did. But it was not obliged to do so and the judge was not entitled to impose the further condition that the father's appearance should be concealed. I therefore agreed that the appeal should be allowed.

Decision of Kirkwood J reversed.

Note

If journalists are to be effective in informing the public and calling on government and those in positions of authority to account for their actions, they need a free flow of information. In consequence journalistic sources are a valuable asset, and many sources of information would dry up if confidentiality could not be guaranteed. The Contempt of Court Act 1981 gave some recognition to this in s. 10.

CONTEMPT OF COURT ACT 1981

10. No court may require a person to disclose, nor is any person guilty of contempt of court for refusing to disclose, the source of information contained in a publication for which he is responsible, unless it be established to the satisfaction of the court that disclosure is necessary in the interests of justice or national security or for the prevention of disorder or crime.

Note

Where a journalistic claim to confidentiality is confronted by a claim by the Executive to disclosure of the source, the role of the courts in keeping the balance is quite crucial if freedom of the press is not to be detrimentally affected. See the following case.

In re An Inquiry Under the Company Securities (Insider Dealing) Act 1985
[1988] 2 WLR 33
House of Lords

Inspectors appointed under s. 177 of the Financial Services Act 1986 to investigate insider dealing allegations in respect of several take-over bids, questioned W, a financial journalist, who had written two newspaper articles disclosing that price-sensitive information had been leaked which was useful to persons wishing to speculate on the Stock Exchange. Such speculation was a form of insider dealing which is an offence under s. 2 of the Company Securities (Insider Dealing) Act 1985. W refused to give any answers which he considered might lead to the identification of the sources of the information. The inspectors then referred the matter to the High Court for its investigation with a view to punishing W for contempt under s. 178 of the Financial Services Act 1986. W claimed he had a 'reasonable excuse' within the meaning of s. 178(2) for refusing to answer questions, in that s. 10 of the Contempt of Court Act 1981 conferred immunity from disclosing the source of information unless disclosure was necessary for one of the purposes specified in the section.

LORD GRIFFITHS: Whether or not Mr Warner had a reasonable excuse for refusing to answer the inspectors' questions depends upon the true construction of section 10 of the Contempt of Court Act 1981 and a consideration of the evidence before the High Court.

. . . The genesis and purpose of this section have recently been discussed in the speeches in *Secretary of State for Defence* v *Guardian Newspapers Ltd* [1985] 1 AC 339, and in the judgment of Slade LJ in his judgment in the Court of Appeal in the present case. The effect of the section is to recognise and establish that in the interests of a free and effective press it is in the public interest that a journalist should be entitled to protect his sources unless some other overriding public interest requires him to reveal them. The section is so cast that a journalist is prima facie entitled to refuse to reveal his source and a court may make no order that has the effect of compelling him to do so unless the party seeking disclosure has established that it is necessary under one of the other four heads of public interest identified in the section.

The parties to this appeal are rightly agreed that whether or not Mr Warner has a 'reasonable excuse' to refuse to answer the inspectors' questions depends upon whether he is entitled to rely upon the public interest in protecting his source and that the test to be applied must be the same whether that question arises in judicial proceedings or in the course of an inquiry such as this. The only head of public interest upon which the inspectors rely is the prevention of crime, and so the question to be answered is whether on the material before it the court should have been satisfied that disclosure of Mr Warner's sources is 'necessary . . . for the prevention of . . . crime' within the meaning of section 10. . . .

The judge in deciding whether or not a journalist has a 'reasonable excuse' for refusing to reveal his sources is not carrying out a balancing exercise between two competing areas of public interest. The judge starts the inquiry with the presumption that the journalist's refusal to reveal his sources does provide a reasonable excuse for refusing to answer the inspectors' questions and the burden is upon the inspectors to satisfy the judge as a question of fact that identification of his sources is necessary for the prevention of crime: see *per* Lord Diplock and Lord Bridge of Harwich in *Secretary of State for Defence* v *Guardian Newspapers Ltd* [1985] 1 AC 339, 350 and 372. If the inspectors are able to discharge this burden, then, as a general rule, the judge should hold that there was no reasonable excuse for refusing to answer the inspectors' questions as to the source of the journalist's information. I say as a general rule because section 10 is not framed in language that compels a judge to order a journalist to reveal his sources and I can conceive of extreme cases in which the judge might properly refuse to do so if, for instance, the crime was of a trivial nature or, at the other end of the scale, the journalist's life might be imperilled if he revealed his source. However, it is not suggested that this is such an extreme case and Mr Warner accepts that if it has been established that the identification of his sources is necessary for the prevention of crime he has no 'reasonable excuse' for refusing to do so. I should add that even if the decision goes against him, Mr Warner says he will accept punishment rather than reveal his source, but that is not a matter which can be taken into account in deciding this appeal.

What then is meant by the words 'necessary . . . for the prevention of . . . crime' in section 10? . . .

I doubt if it is possible to go further than to say that 'necessary' has a meaning that lies somewhere between 'indispensable' on the one hand, and 'useful' or 'expedient' on the other, and to leave it to the judge to decide towards which end of the scale of meaning he will place it on the facts of any particular case. The nearest paraphrase I can suggest is 'really needed.'

The words 'prevention of . . . crime' do, however, admit of more than one construction. Hoffman J adopted a narrow construction for which Mr Warner contends. He held that: 'it must appear probable that in the absence of disclosure by the journalist further crimes are likely to be committed.' And later he said:

> The facts to which the inspectors deposed do not therefore in my judgment show a probability that only the disclosure of his sources by Mr Warner can prevent further insider dealing.

The phrase 'prevention of . . . crime' carries, to my mind, very different overtones from 'prevention of a crime' or even 'prevention of crimes.' There are frequent articles and programmes in the media on the prevention of crime. The subject on these occasions is discussed from many points of view including the social background in which crime breeds, detection, deterrence, retribution, punishment, rehabilitation and so forth. The prevention of crime in this broad sense is a matter of public and vital interest to any civilised society. Crime is endemic in society and will probably never be eradicated but its containment is essential. If crime gets the upper hand and becomes the rule rather than the exception, the collapse of society will swiftly follow. By identifying 'prevention of . . . crime' as one of the four heads of public interest to which the journalist's privilege may occasionally have to yield, I am satisfied that Parliament was using the phrase in its wider and, I think, natural meaning, rather than in the restricted sense for which the appellant contends. . . .

One of the principal objects of the inquiry is to identify the sources of the leaks and another is to establish, so far as is possible, the extent to which the leaks have led to insider dealing. It is because this type of fraud is so difficult to detect and bring home to the culprits that Parliament has given special powers to the Minister to set up this type of inquiry which is conducted by a Queen's Counsel and an accountant who have the special skills needed to investigate and expose this type of financial crime. In the light of the inspectors' report it is to be hoped that steps can be taken towards stamping out this form of insider dealing by exposing and perhaps punishing both those who leak the information and those who trade upon it, and by considering further measures that can be taken to prevent future leaks and insider trading. Mr Warner himself has recognised that the inspectors are engaged upon an investigation of a criminal nature and I have no doubt that the inquiry is being undertaken for the 'prevention of . . . crime' within the meaning of section 10 of the Act of 1981.

I turn now to consider the evidence placed before the court by the inspectors. The inspectors obviously consider that Mr Warner has no reasonable excuse for not revealing his source otherwise they would not have reported the matter to the High Court. It is, however, the duty of the High Court to satisfy itself upon evidence placed before it of the necessity that the source should be revealed, and it must not act as a rubber stamp to support the view of the inspectors. The material upon which the inspectors invite the court to act is contained in paragraphs 8 and 9 of a statement the contents of which they have sworn to be true . . .

Mr Kentridge criticised the inspectors' statement for lack of particularity. He points out that no evidence has been provided to identify any particular insider deals or to tie such deals to the bids referred to in Mr Warner's articles, or to suggest that the Crown servants involved will continue to leak information about future bids.

It is only if the narrow construction of 'prevention of . . . crime' is adopted that there is any force in these criticisms. I would agree that the evidence is not sufficient to show that the identification of the source is necessary to prevent a particular future act of insider dealing taking place. I have however rejected that narrow construction and proceeding upon the basis that the inspectors are engaged upon an inquiry the purpose of which is the prevention of crime I am satisfied that they have produced evidence sufficient to establish that it is of real importance for the purpose of their inquiry that they should know who gave Mr Warner the information in his articles. The inspectors are trying to identify the source of serious leaks from government departments which have led to insider dealing on a large scale. They have before them one who was apparently given reliable information about those leaks at the time when they occurred. Suppose Mr Warner had been prepared to tell the inspectors who gave him his information, what would have been the position of the inspectors if they had failed to ask him? The answer is that it would have been a gross dereliction of their duty because they would have neglected to obtain vital evidence that went to the heart of the matters into which they were required to inquire. Tested in this way I agree with the Court of Appeal that Mr Warner's evidence is necessary or, to use the paraphrase, really needed by the inspectors for the purpose of their inquiry the aim of which is the prevention of crime. For these reasons I would dismiss this appeal, and direct that the case be remitted to the Chancery Division of the High Court so that a judge of that division may consider the question of punishment. It would not be appropriate for the Court of Appeal to inflict punishment for that would thereby deprive Mr Warner of his right of appeal against any punishment that may be inflicted.

Question

Would compelling a journalist to disclose his sources increase or decrease the likelihood of persons giving to the journalist information which discloses wrongdoing?

Note

The authority of the above case is now uncertain in light of the recent decision of the European Court of Human Rights in the following case.

Goodwin v *United Kingdom*

Case No 16/1994/463/544

European Court of Human Rights

In November 1989 the applicant, a journalist on *The Engineer*, was given information by an informant about the financial problems facing Tetra Ltd. Tetra Ltd were contacted by Mr Goodwin for comments. Believing that the information originated from a draft of its confidential corporate plan which had gone missing earlier, Tetra Ltd applied for and obtained from the High Court an ex parte interim injunction to restrain the Publishers of *The Engineer*, Morgan-Grampian (Publisher) Ltd, from publishing Mr Goodwin's article. National newspapers and relevant journals were informed of the injunction. Tetra Ltd then sought and obtained an order from the High Court requiring Mr Goodwin to disclose his notes on the basis that this was 'necessary in the interests of justice' under s. 10 of the Contempt of Court Act 1981 so that they might identify the source, bring proceedings for the recovery of the draft plan and obtain an injunction to prevent further publication or seek damages. Appeals to the Court of Appeal and House of Lords being dismissed (see *X Ltd* v *Morgan-Grampian (Publishers) Ltd* [1991] 1 AC 1) the High Court fined Mr Goodwin £5,000 for contempt of court for refusal to disclose his source. Application was made to the European Commission alleging a violation of article 10 of the Convention. By eleven votes to six the Commission found that there had been a violation of Article 10 and having failed to secure a friendly settlement drew up a report and the case went before the European Court of Human Rights.

Summary of Judgment

A. *Article 10 of the Convention*

The applicant complained under Article 10 about the disclosure order requiring him to reveal the identity of his source and the fine imposed upon him for having refused to do so. It was undisputed that these measures constituted an interference with his right to freedom of expression.

1. *Was the interference 'prescribed by law'?*

The impugned disclosure order and fine were 'prescribed by law'. Not only did the measures have a basis in national law but the law governing the imposition of the order was moreover foreseeable for the purposes of the requirement in paragraph 2 of Article 10. On the latter point, the Court recognised that in the area under consideration it may be difficult to frame laws with absolute precision and that some flexibility might even be desirable to enable the national courts to develop the law in the light of their assessment of what measures were necessary in the interests of justice. The national courts' discretion in ordering disclosure was subjected to important limitations. The House of Lords' interpretation of the relevant law in the applicant's case did not go beyond what could be reasonably foreseen in the circumstances. Nor was there any other indication that the law in question afforded the applicant inadequate protection against arbitrariness.

2. *Did the interference pursue a legitimate aim*

The interference pursued the legitimate aim of protecting Tetra's 'rights'. It was not necessary to determine whether it was also directed towards the 'prevention of . . . crime'.

3. *Was the interference 'necessary in a democratic society'?*

(i) General principles

The Court set out a number of general principles. Protection of journalistic sources was, it noted, one of the basic conditions for press freedom, as was reflected in the laws and the professional codes of conduct in a number of Contracting States and was affirmed in several international instruments of journalistic freedoms (it cited as examples the Resolution on Journalistic Freedoms and Human Rights, adopted at the 4th European Ministerial Conference on Mass Media Policy (Prague, 7–8 December 1994) the Resolution on the Confidentiality of Journalists' Sources by the European Parliament, 18 January 1994, Official Journal of the European Communities No. C 44/34). Without such protection, sources could be deterred from assisting the press in informing the public on matters of public interest. As a result the vital public watchdog role of the press could be undermined and the ability of the press to provide accurate and reliable information could be adversely affected. Having regard to the importance of the protection of journalistic sources for press freedom in a democratic society and the potentially chilling effect an order of source disclosure had on the exercise of that freedom, such a measure could not be compatible with Article 10 of the Convention unless it was justified by an overriding requirement in the public interest. The interest of democratic society in ensuring and maintaining a free press would weigh heavily in the balance in determining whether the restriction was proportionate to the legitimate aim pursued. Limitations on the confidentiality of journalistic sources called for the most careful scrutiny by the Court.

(ii) *Court's assessment in the particular circumstances*

The justifications for the disclosure order in the present case had to be seen in the broader context of the *ex parte* interim injunction which had earlier been granted to the company. That injunction had been notified to all the national newspapers and relevant journals. The purpose of the disclosure order was to a very large extent the same as that already being achieved by the injunction, namely to prevent dissemination of the confidential information contained in the plan. There was no doubt, according to Lord Donaldson in the Court of Appeal, that the injunction was effective in stopping dissemination of the confidential information by the press. Tetra's creditors, customers, suppliers and competitors would not therefore come to learn of the information through the press. A vital component of the threat of damage to the company had thus already largely been neutralised by the injunction. This being so, in so far as the disclosure order merely served to reinforce the injunction, the additional restriction on freedom of expression which it entailed was not supported by sufficient reasons for the purposes of paragraph 2 of Article 10 of the Convention.

As to the further purposes served by the disclosure order, the Court could not find that Tetra's interests in eliminating, by proceedings against the source, the residual threat of damage through dissemination of the confidential information otherwise than by the press, in obtaining compensation and in unmasking a disloyal employee or collaborator were, even if considered cumulatively, sufficient to outweigh the vital public interest in the protection of the application journalist's source. The further purposes served by the disclosure order, when measured against the standards imposed by the Convention could not amount to an overriding requirement in the public interest.

In sum, there was not a reasonable relationship of proportionality between the legitimate aim pursued by the disclosure order and the means deployed to achieve that aim. The order requiring the applicant to reveal his source and the fine imposed upon him for having refused to do so could not be regarded as having been 'necessary in a democratic society' for the protection of Tetra's rights under English law, notwithstanding the margin of appreciation available to the national authorities.

Accordingly, the impugned measures gave rise to a violation of the applicant's right to freedom of expression under Article 10 (eleven votes to seven).

Note

The European Court of Human Rights did not find that s. 10 of the Contempt of Court Act 1981 *per se* breached the Convention but rather that the application of that section in the instant case violated Mr Goodwin's rights under article 10. Journalistic sources are not absolutely protected but greater weight will have to be given to the public interest in a democratic society in there being a free press performing an effective public watchdog role and in informing that public in an accurate and reliable way.

(ii) Freedom of assembly

An aspect of freedom of expression is the right to assemble and to march in order to express support for a particular cause. In the White Paper *Review of Public Order Law* (Cmnd 9510, 1985) the Government stated that 'the rights of peaceful protest are amongst our fundamental freedoms: they are numbered among the touchstones which distinguish a free society from a totalitarian one'. Most demonstrations, however, involve inconvenience to others and expense in policing them, particularly if violence is anticipated or occurs. This raises the question whether protest serves some social or political function which outweighs these considerations. In *Caird* (1970) 54 Cr App R 499, Sachs LJ stated:

> Any suggestion that a section of the community strongly holding one set of views is justified in banding together to disrupt the lawful activities of a section that does not hold the same views so strongly or which holds different views cannot be tolerated and must unhesitatingly be rejected by the courts. When there is wanton and vicious violence of gross degree the court is not concerned with whether it originates from gang rivalry or from political motives. It is the degree of mob violence that matters and the extent to which the public peace is being broken.

But is peaceful protest to be classed as unacceptable because it may disrupt traffic, shopping or other activities? Or is political protest part of 'normal' community life and the 'normal' political process? Is freedom to protest vital to the existence of a liberal democracy? Or should political activity be restricted to meetings, party conferences, and elections? If there is a freedom to demonstrate, should it be denied to those whose views are unpopular or obnoxious to the majority of people? Is it really a question of balance? This was the view expressed by Lord Scarman in his *Report of the Inquiry into the Red Lion Square Disorders* (1974), para. 5:

> Civilised living collapses – it is obvious – if public protest becomes violent protest or public order degenerates into the quietism imposed by successful oppression. But the problem is more complex than a choice between two extremes – one, a right to protest whenever and wherever you will and the other, a right to continuous calm upon our streets unruffled by the noise and obstructive pressure of the protesting procession. A balance has to be struck, a compromise found that will accommodate the exercise of the right to protest within a framework of public order which enables ordinary citizens, who are not protesting, to go about their business and pleasure without obstruction or inconvenience.

Questions

1. To what extent should the law seek to protect citizens from inconvenience or the expression of offensive views?

2. Is there a danger that attempting to suppress protest and demonstrations may lead to greater problems than allowing them to take place? See Lord Denning's dissenting speech in *Hubbard* v *Pitt* below.

Hubbard* v *Pitt
[1976] 1 QB 142
Court of Appeal

LORD DENNING MR: [T]he right to demonstrate and the right to protest on matters of public concern . . . are often the only means by which grievances can be brought to the knowledge of those in authority – at any rate with such impact as to gain a remedy. Our history is full of warnings against suppression of these rights. Most notable was the demonstration at St Peter's Fields, Manchester in 1819 in support of universal suffrage. The magistrates sought to stop it. At least twelve were killed and hundreds injured. Afterwards the Court of Common Council of London affirmed 'the undoubted right of English men to assemble together for the purpose of deliberating upon public grievances'.

Note

The problem which sometimes arises, however, is that certain demonstrations can be almost guaranteed to lead to disorder, commonly referred to as a breach of the peace. The response of the common law to this situation was stated in the following case.

Beatty* v *Gillbanks
(1882) 9 QBD 308
Queen's Bench Division

The magistrates of Weston-Super-Mare had found Beatty and others guilty of unlawful assembly. Beatty was a member of the Salvation Army, and he and the others marched through the streets knowing they would be opposed by members of the Skeleton Army. Notice had been served on them by the magistrates to abstain from such marches but they refused to comply and were arrested. Their convictions for riotous and tumultuous assembly were quashed by the Divisional Court.

FIELD J: Numerous instances might be mentioned of large bodies of persons assembling in much larger numbers, and marching, accompanied by banners and bands of music, through the public streets, and no one has ever doubted that such processions were perfectly lawful. Now the appellants complain that, for having so assembled as I have before stated, they have been adjudged guilty of the offence of holding an unlawful assembly, and have in consequence been ordered to find sureties to keep the peace, in the absence of any evidence of their having broken it. It was of course necessary that the justices should find that some unlawful act had been committed by the appellants in order to justify the magistrates in binding them over. The offence charged against them as 'unlawfully and tumultuously assembling with others to the disturbance of the public peace, and against the peace of the Queen,' and of course before they can be convicted upon the charge clear proof must be adduced that the specific offence charged has been committed. Now was that charge sustained? There is no doubt that the appellants did assemble together with other persons in great numbers, but that alone is insufficient. The assembly must be a 'tumultuous assembly,' and 'against the peace,' in order to render it an unlawful one. But there was nothing so far as the appellants were concerned to show that their conduct was in the least degree 'tumultuous' or 'against the peace.' All that they did was to assemble together to walk through the town, and it is admitted by the learned counsel for the respondent, that as regards the appellants themselves, there was no disturbance of the peace, and that their conduct was quiet and peaceable. But then it is argued that, as in fact their line of conduct was the same as had on previous similar occasions led to tumultuous and riotous proceedings with stone-throwing and fighting, causing a disturbance of the public peace and terror to the inhabitants of the town, and as on the present occasion like results would in all probability be produced, therefore the appellants, being well aware of the likelihood of such results again occurring, were guilty of the offence charged against them. Now, without doubt, as a general rule it must be taken that every person intends what are the natural and necessary consequences of his own acts, and if in the present case it had been their intention, or if it had been the natural and necessary consequence of their acts, to produce the disturbance of the peace which occurred, then the appellants would have been responsible for it, and the magistrates would have been right in binding them over to keep the peace. But the evidence as set forth in the case shows that, so far from that being the case, the acts and conduct of the appellants caused nothing of the kind, but, on the contrary, that the disturbance that did take place was caused entirely by the unlawful and unjustifiable interference of the Skeleton Army, a body of persons opposed to the religious views of the appellants and the Salvation Army, and that but for the opposition and molestation offered to the Salvationists by these other persons, no disturbance of any kind would have taken place. The appellants were guilty of no offence in their passing through the streets, and why should other persons interfere with or molest them? What right had they to do so? If they were doing anything unlawful it was for the magistrates and police, the appointed guardians of law and order, to interpose. The law relating to unlawful assemblies, as laid down in the books and the cases, affords no support to the view of the matter for which the learned counsel for the respondent was obliged to contend, viz., that persons acting lawfully are to be held responsible and punished merely because other persons are thereby induced to act unlawfully and create a disturbance. In 1 Russell on Crimes (4th edn. p. 387), an unlawful assembly is defined as follows: 'unlawful assembly, according to the common opinion, is a disturbance of the peace by persons barely assembling together with the intention to do a thing which, if it were executed, would make them rioters, but neither actually executing it nor making a motion towards the execution of it.' It is clear that, according to this definition of the offence, the appellants were not guilty, for it is not pretended that they had, but, on the contrary, it is admitted that they had not, any intention to create a riot, or to commit any riotous or other unlawful act. Many examples of what are unlawful assemblies are given in Hawkins' Pleas of the Crown, book 1 cap. 28, sects. 9 and 10, in all of which the necessary circumstances of terror are present in the assembly itself, either as regards the object for which it is gathered together, or in the manner of its assembling and proceeding to carry out that object. The present case, however, differs from the cases there stated; for here the only terror that existed was caused by the unlawful resistance wilfully and designedly offered to the proceedings of the Salvation Army by an unlawful organisation outside and distinct from them, called the Skeleton Army. It was suggested by that respondent's counsel that, if these Salvation processions were allowed, similar opposition would be offered to them in future, and that similar disturbances would ensue. But I cannot believe that that will be so. I hope, and I cannot but think, that when the Skeleton Army, and all other persons who are opposed to the proceedings of the Salvation Army, come to learn, as they surely will learn, that they have no possible right to interfere with or in any way obstruct the Salvation Army in their lawful and peaceable processions, they will abstain from opposing or disturbing them. It is usual happily in this country for people to respect and obey the law when once declared and understood, and I have hope and have no doubt that it will be so in the present case. But, if it should not be so, there is no doubt that the magistrates and police, both at Weston-super-Mare and everywhere else, will understand their duty and not fail to do it efficiently, or hesitate, should the necessity arise, to deal with the Skeleton Army and other disturbers of the public peace as they did in the present instance with the appellants, for no one can doubt that the authorities are only anxious to do their duty and to prevent a disturbance of the public peace. The present decision of the justices, however, amounts to this, that a man may be punished for acting lawfully if he knows that his so doing may induce another man to act unlawfully – a proposition without any authority whatever to support it. Under these circumstances, the questions put to us by the justices must be negatively answered, and the order appealed against be discharged.

Note

In *R* v *Justices of Londonderry* (1891) 28 LR Ir 440, which also arose out of a march by members of the Salvation Army, O'Brien J extended the reasoning of *Beatty* v *Gillbanks*, stating (at p. 450):

> If danger arises from the exercise of lawful rights resulting in a breach of the peace, the remedy is the presence of sufficient force to prevent that result, not the legal condemnation of those who exercise those rights.

The position now regarding demonstrations and assemblies is covered by Part II of the Public Order Act 1986, which extends and modernises the system of controls on processions and meetings.

PUBLIC ORDER ACT 1986

11. Advance notice of public processions

(1) Written notice shall be given in accordance with this section of any proposal to hold a public procession intended—

(a) to demonstrate support for or opposition to the views or actions of any person or body of persons,

(b) to publicise a cause or campaign, or

(c) to mark or commemorate an event,

unless it is not reasonably practicable to give any advance notice of the procession.

(2) Subsection (1) does not apply where the procession is one commonly or customarily held in the police area (or areas) in which it is proposed to be held or is a funeral procession organised by a funeral director acting in the normal course of his business.

(3) The notice must specify the date when it is intended to hold the procession, the time when it is intended to start it, its proposed route, and the name and address of the person (or of one of the persons) proposing to organise it.

(4) Notice must be delivered to a police station—

(a) in the police area in which it is proposed the procession will start, or

(b) where it is proposed the procession will start in Scotland and cross into England, in the first police area in England on the proposed route.

(5) If delivered not less than 6 clear days before the date when the procession is intended to be held, the notice may be delivered by post by the recorded delivery service; but section 7 of the Interpretation Act 1978 (under which a document sent by post is deemed to have been served when posted and to have been delivered in the ordinary course of post) does not apply.

(6) If not delivered in accordance with subsection (5), the notice must be delivered by hand not less than 6 clear days before the date when the procession is intended to be held or, if that is not reasonably practicable, as soon as delivery is reasonably practicable.

(7) Where a public procession is held, each of the persons organising it is guilty of an offence if—

(a) the requirements of this section as to notice have not been satisfied, or

(b) the date when it is held, the time when it starts, or its route, differs from the date, time or route specified in the notice.

(8) It is a defence for the accused to prove that he did not know of, and neither suspected nor had reason to suspect, the failure to satisfy the requirements or (as the case may be) the difference of date, time or route.

(9) To the extent that the alleged offence turns on a difference of date, time or route, it is a defence for the accused to prove that the difference arose from circumstances beyond his control or from something done with the agreement of a police officer or by his direction.

. . .

12. Imposing conditions on public processions

(1) If the senior police officer, having regard to the time or place at which and the circumstances in which any public procession is being held or is intended to be held and to its route or proposed route, reasonably believes that—

(a) it may result in serious public disorder, serious damage to property or serious disruption to the life of the community, or

(b) the purpose of the persons organising it is the intimidation of others with a view to compelling them not to do an act they have a right to do, or to do an act they have a right not to do,
he may give directions imposing on the persons organising or taking part in the procession such conditions as appear to him necessary to prevent such disorder, damage, disruption or intimidation, including conditions as to the route of the procession or prohibiting it from entering any public place specified in the directions.

(2) In subsection (1) 'the senior police officer' means—

(a) in relation to a procession being held, or to a procession intended to be held in a case where persons are assembling with a view to taking part in it, the most senior in rank of the police officers present at the scene, and

(b) in relation to a procession intended to be held in a case where paragraph (a) does not apply, the chief officer of police.

(3) A direction given by a chief officer of police by virtue of subsection (2)(b) shall be given in writing.

(4) A person who organises a public procession and knowingly fails to comply with a condition imposed under this section is guilty of an offence, but it is a defence for him to prove that the failure arose from circumstances beyond his control.

(5) A person who takes part in a public procession and knowingly fails to comply with a condition imposed under this section is guilty of an offence, but it is a defence for him to prove that the failure arose from circumstances beyond his control.

(6) A person who incites another to commit an offence under subsection (5) is guilty of an offence.

(7) A constable in uniform may arrest without warrant anyone he reasonably suspects is committing an offence under subsection (4), (5) or (6).

. . .

13. Prohibiting public processions

(1) If at any time the chief officer of police reasonably believes that, because of particular circumstances existing in any district or part of a district, the powers under section 12 will not be sufficient to prevent the holding of public processions in that district or part from resulting in serious public disorder, he shall apply to the council of the district for an order prohibiting for such period not exceeding 3 months as may be specified in the application the holding of all public processions (or of any class of public procession so specified) in the district or part concerned.

(2) On receiving such an application, a council may with the consent of the Secretary of State make an order either in the terms of the application or with such modifications as may be approved by the Secretary of State.

(3) Subsection (1) does not apply in the City of London or the metropolitan police district.

(4) If at any time the Commissioner of Police for the City of London or the Commissioner of Police of the Metropolis reasonably believes that, because of particular circumstances existing in his police area or part of it, the powers under section 12 will not be sufficient to prevent the holding of public processions in that area or part from resulting in serious public disorder, he may with the consent of the Secretary of State make an order prohibiting for such period not exceeding 3 months as may be specified in the order the holding of all public processions (or of any class of public procession so specified) in the area or part concerned.

(5) An order made under this section may be revoked or varied by a subsequent order made in the same way, that is, in accordance with subsections (1) and (2) or subsection (4), as the case may be.

(6) Any order under this section shall, if not made in writing, be recorded in writing as soon as practicable after being made.

(7) A person who organises a public procession the holding of which he knows is prohibited by virtue of an order under this section is guilty of an offence.

(8) A person who takes part in a public procession the holding of which he knows is prohibited by virtue of an order under this section is guilty of an offence.

(9) A person who incites another to commit an offence under subsection (8) is guilty of an offence.

(10) A constable in uniform may arrest without warrant anyone he reasonably suspects is committing an offence under subsection (7), (8) or (9).

. . .

14. Imposing conditions on public assemblies

(1) If the senior police officer, having regard to the time or place at which and the circumstances in which any public assembly is being held or is intended to be held, reasonably believes that—

(a) it may result in serious public disorder, serious damage to property or serious disruption to the life of the community, or

(b) the purpose of the persons organising it is the intimidation of others with a view to compelling them not to do an act they have a right to do, or to do an act they have a right not to do,

he may give directions imposing on the persons organising or taking part in the assembly such conditions as to the place at which the assembly may be (or continue to be) held, its maximum duration, or the maximum number of persons who may constitute it, as appear to him necessary to prevent such disorder, damage, disruption or intimidation.

(2) In subsection (1) 'the senior police officer' means—

(a) in relation to an assembly being held, the most senior in rank of the police officers present at the scene, and

(b) in relation to an assembly intended to be held, the chief officer of police.

(3) A direction given by a chief officer of police by virtue of subsection (2)(b) shall be given in writing.

(4) A person who organises a public assembly and knowingly fails to comply with a condition imposed under this section is guilty of an offence, but it is a defence for him to prove that the failure arose from circumstances beyond his control.

(5) A person who takes part in a public assembly and knowingly fails to comply with a condition imposed under this section is guilty of an offence, but it is a defence for him to prove that the failure arose from circumstances beyond his control.

(6) A person who incites another to commit an offence under subsection (5) is guilty of an offence.

(7) A constable in uniform may arrest without warrant anyone he reasonably suspects is committing an offence under subsection (4), (5) or (6).

. . .

14A. Prohibiting trespassory assemblies

(1) If at any time the chief officer of police reasonably believes that an assembly is intended to be held in any district at a place on land to which the public has no right of access or only a limited right of access and that the assembly—

(a) is likely to be held without the permission of the occupier of the land or to conduct itself in such a way as to exceed the limits of any permission of his or the limits of the public's right of access, and

(b) may result—

(i) in serious disruption to the life of the community, or

(ii) where the land, or a building or monument on it, is of historical, architectural, archaeological or scientific importance, in significant damage to the land, building or monument,

he may apply to the council of the district for an order prohibiting for a specified period the holding of all trespassory assemblies in the district or a part of it, as specified.

(2) On receiving such an application, a council may—

(a) in England and Wales, with the consent of the Secretary of State make an order either in the terms of the application or with such modifications as may be approved by the Secretary of State; or

(b) in Scotland, make an order in the terms of the application.

(3) Subsection (1) does not apply in the City of London or the metropolitan police district.

(4) If at any time the Commissioner of Police for the City of London or the Commissioner of Police of the Metropolis reasonably believes that an assembly is intended to be held at a place on land to which the public has no right of access or only a limited right of access in his police area and that the assembly—

(a) is likely to be held without the permission of the occupier of the land or to conduct itself in such a way as to exceed the limits of any permission of his or the limits of the public's right of access, and

(b) may result—

(i) in serious disruption to the life of the community, or

(ii) where the land, or a building or monument on it, is of historical, architectural, archaeological or scientific importance, in significant damage to the land, building or monument,

he may with the consent of the Secretary of State make an order prohibiting for a specified period the holding of all trespassory assemblies in the area or a part of it, as specified.

(5) Any order prohibiting the holding of trespassory assemblies operates to prohibit any assembly which—

(a) is held on land to which the public has no right of access or only a limited right of access, and

(b) takes place in the prohibited circumstances, that is to say, without the permission of the occupier of the land or so as to exceed the limits of any permission of his or the limits of the public's right of access.

(6) No order under this section shall prohibit the holding of assemblies for a period exceeding 4 days or in an area exceeding an area represented by a circle with a radius of 5 miles from a specified centre.

(7) An order made under this section may be revoked or varied by a subsequent order made in the same way, that is, in accordance with subsection (1) and (2) or subsection (4), as the case may be.

(8) Any order under this section shall, if not made in writing, be recorded in writing as soon as practicable after being made.

. . .

14B. Offences in connection with trespassory assemblies and arrest therefor

(1) A person who organises an assembly the holding of which he knows is prohibited by an order under section 14A is guilty of an offence.

(2) A person who takes part in an assembly which he knows is prohibited by an order under section 14A is guilty of an offence.

(3) In England and Wales, a person who incites another to commit an offence under subsection (2) is guilty of an offence.

(4) A constable in uniform may arrest without a warrant anyone he reasonably suspects to be committing an offence under this section.

(5) A person guilty of an offence under subsection (1) is liable on summary conviction to imprisonment for a term not exceeding 3 months or a fine not exceeding level 4 on the standard scale or both.

(6) A person guilty of an offence under subsection (2) is liable on summary conviction to a fine not exceeding level 3 on the standard scale.

(7) A person guilty of an offence under subsection (3) is liable on summary conviction to imprisonment for a term not exceeding 3 months or a fine not exceeding level 4 on the standard scale or both, notwithstanding section 45(3) of the Magistrates' Courts Act 1980.

. . .

14C. Stopping persons from proceeding to trespassory assemblies

(1) If a constable in uniform reasonably believes that a person is on his way to an assembly within the area to which an order under section 14A applies which the constable reasonably believes is likely to be an assembly which is prohibited by that order, he may, subject to subsection (2) below—

(a) stop that person, and
(b) direct him not to proceed in the direction of the assembly.

(2) The power conferred by subsection (1) may only be exercised within the area to which the order applies.

(3) A person who fails to comply with a direction under subsection (1) which he knows has been given to him is guilty of an offence.

(4) A constable in uniform may arrest without a warrant anyone he reasonably suspects to be committing an offence under this section.

(5) A person guilty of an offence under subsection (3) is liable on summary conviction to a fine not exceeding level 3 on the standard scale.'.

Questions

1. Does respecting freedom of speech require that we accept the right of those who wish to overthrow liberty to have freedom of speech themselves and their right to use that freedom to promote their cause?

2. Is it arguable that ss 12(1) and 13(1) of the Public Order Act 1986 provide the means whereby those who wish to overthrow liberty may subdue the freedoms of those who wish to engage in peaceful procession, by threatening disorder?

3. Does the inclusion of the phrase 'or serious disruption to the life of the community' in s. 12(1)(a), s. 14(1)(a), and 14A(1)(b) of the Public Order Act 1986, give rise to the possibility of greater limitations on the right of protest or assembly? (Cf. Art. 10 of the European Convention on Human Rights.)

4. Does the Act create a danger that the police may become politicised because of the nature of the decisions they are required to take under the Act?

(G) A BILL OF RIGHTS FOR THE UNITED KINGDOM

The argument as to whether the United Kingdom needs a Bill of Rights is a long running one. In 1977, the Standing Advisory Commission on Human

Rights in *The Protection of Human Rights by Law in Northern Ireland* (Cmnd 7009) recommended that the European Convention be incorporated into domestic law. (For a summary of some of the arguments for and against such a development, see the first edition of this book at pp. 357–358.) In 1978, the *Report of the Select Committee on a Bill of Rights* (House of Lords, HMSO) recommended that the Convention should be incorporated. In 1987, Sir Edward Gardner introduced in the House of Commons the Human Rights Bill as a private member's bill which would have incorporated the Convention. The bill was given a formal second reading without a vote but failed to complete its Commons stages due to lack of time. In 1990 the Institute for Public Policy Research, in *A British Bill of Rights* (Constitution Paper No. 1), drafted a Bill of Rights which was based on the European Convention and the United Nations International Covenant on Civil and Political Rights. In 1991, Liberty, in *A People's Charter*, published a draft Bill of Rights with a similar parentage.

Liberty, *A People's Charter*
(1991), pp. 3 – 4, 8 – 13

Liberty's concern is to defend and extend human rights within whatever political system we have. The erosion of our civil liberties – which has been particularly marked over the past 12 years (but which is by no means specific to that period) has led us to the firm belief that a Bill of Rights enforceable in law could empower individuals to challenge that erosion. However, unlike some, we do not believe that any Bill of Rights, regardless of its contents, would necessarily improve the current situation. Whether a Bill of Rights is a good thing or not would depend entirely on whom it applies to, what provisions it contains and how it is to be enforced. These are not merely questions of detail. A Bill of Rights containing open-ended limitations on our rights and enforced by unelected and unrepresentative judges could prove even worse than the arrangements we have at present.

Any Bill of Rights worthy of that title must, in our view, be drafted from the perspective of civil society rather than the state: in other words, it should act to protect the rights of the people rather than represent a compromise between these rights and the interests of the government of the day. In order to achieve that end, the rights it upholds must be based on widely recognised human rights principles embodied in a range of international and domestic conventions, charters and declarations. Any limits on rights in the Bill must reflect one principle only; the need to protect the civil liberties of others.

Even in a system based on parliamentary democracy like ours, the authority vested in the organs of the state is such that individuals and groups need protection from abuse of its power. As numerous examples throughout this report will illustrate, unaccountable decisions potentially affecting the lives of many people are taken by the government and its agents every day. In whose interests are they made? Are they an expression of arbitrary power, are they intended to further the electoral chances of the government of the day, or are they based on the need to protect our rights and freedoms or that of one group in society against another? A Bill of Rights must enable such assessments to be made and allow decisions based on the first two grounds to be quashed.

Public bodies from the Crown (a term used to describe the government of the day, including its prerogative powers) to local authorities must be duty bound to uphold the rights and freedoms in the Bill and provide an adequate remedy when they are breached. This includes a duty on the state to take measures to ensure that private organisations or individuals do not violate the rights in the Bill. All laws, past and present, must conform to the Bill and it is the responsibility of the judges to interpret them with this understanding. However, in recognition of the fact that the judiciary can through its rulings also weaken rights, or fail to protect particular groups, we accept that there needs to be democratic mechanisms through which the legislature can overturn such decisions. **In other words, the Bill must be safeguarded – or entrenched – through a combination of the judicial and democratic processes.**

The Case against a Bill of Rights

Opposition to a Bill of Rights within the UK falls under three broad headings. These can be characterised as constitutional conservatism, parliamentary supremacism and judicial scepticism.

Constitutional objections

The major constitutional objection to a Bill of Rights is that the British system will simply not accommodate an arrangement in which any one piece of legislation is supreme over all others. The Special Adviser to the 1978 House of Lords Select Committee on a Bill of Rights represented this view when he contended that such a Bill would be as vulnerable to repeal as any other, by Acts amending it by implication as much as those which did so expressly. This argument has been most famously championed by A. V. Dicey who wrote in 1885 that:

> There is no power which under the English constitution can come into rivalry with the legislative sovereignty of Parliament . . . This doctrine . . . is the very cornerstone of the constitution.

Frequently accompanying this point is the assertion that anyway we do not need a Bill of Rights: why change a flexible system which works for a more rigid one which may not? This view was articulated by Home Office Minister, Peter Lloyd, in a recent parliamentary debate on constitutional reform:

> The rights and freedom of the individual and their protection lie at the heart of our constitutional practices. Over the years they have developed pragmatically in response to society's needs and perceived problems and in keeping with the British tradition. Our system continues to allow us to adapt and change where change appears to be necessary.

Former Prime Minister, Margaret Thatcher, expressed similar sentiments in response to the demands of Charter 88 supporters:

> The Government considers that our present constitutional arrangements continue to serve us well and that the citizen in this country enjoys the greatest degree of liberty that is compatible with the rights of others and the vital interests of the state.

The human rights record of other countries with Bills of Rights and written constitutions is cited as further evidence of the validity of this argument.

Loss of parliamentary sovereignty

For some who oppose a Bill of Rights the question is not so much that parliamentary sovereignty *is* immutable but that it *should be*. John Patten, Minister of State at the Home Office, made this point when he gave the 1991 Swinton Lecture:

> Parliament is thus vital to our way of doing things, a central constitutional mechanism for protecting rights. Parliamentary sovereignty is one of the twin pillars

> of the constitution. The other was – and remains – the rule of law. The rights embodied in statute and common law are real rights because they enjoy the protection of the people themselves. People are the best defenders of rights.

According to this view the will of the people – reflected by parliamentary sovereignty – working in partnership with the judges, has provided an effective protection of our rights. A Bill of Rights, on the other hand, is time-bound, taking away from Parliament the power to legislate according to current circumstances and tying it to a set of pre-ordained values.

A variant on this theme is expressed by those on the left of the political spectrum who regard a directly-elected Parliament as one of the few means for working people to gain access to power. While strong governments dominating the legislature can threaten fundamental rights, they can also act to protect them by providing a bulwark against powerful interest groups. A Bill of Rights which rules supreme over any subsequent legislation could fatally weaken this system. Specific legislation protecting particular rights is, from this perspective, a far preferable option.

Another, similar, objection contends that supporters of a Bill of Rights fail to appreciate that such an instrument can perpetuate inequalities unless the *contents* of the Bill address the current disparity in power in society – not only between individuals and the state but between groups of people (based, for example, on race, sex or class), and between individuals and private companies.

Power to the judges

The basis for judicial scepticism, the third main objection referred to above, lies in the power that would be given to the judiciary in interpreting the broad principles enshrined in a Bill of Rights. This applies especially where the Bill is entrenched – in other words, where it is given precedence over all other laws and cannot be amended by ordinary parliamentary procedures. In these circumstances, it is the responsibility of the judges to interpret all current and future legislation in conformity with the Bill. Where the courts consider that a compatible interpretation is not possible, the legislation in question (or relevant section of it) falls, and Parliament is powerless to re-enact it short of amending the Bill itself (for which, under most models, the support of a two-thirds majority of both Houses of the legislature is required).

There are two factors to be considered here. First, there is the *principle* of transferring power from an elected body to an appointed one. Secondly, there is the *practical* objection that the past record of the judiciary does not exactly encourage confidence that this is a body to be charged with protecting fundamental rights. The unrepresentative composition of the present judiciary lends further weight to this argument. Whilst those opposed in principle to this transfer of power do not necessarily share these practical objections, those who argue for parliamentary supremacy to guarantee the interests of the less powerful groups in society do tend to back up their position with examples of how the judiciary has, in practice, restricted their rights. Indeed, many who would otherwise support a Bill of Rights oppose it solely on the grounds of the judges' record.

Cases cited in support of this objection include instances where the courts have effectively refused to review the issue at stake altogether on the ground that 'national security' is involved (the banning of trade union membership for workers at Government Communications Headquarters in 1984 and the threat of deportation of over one hundred Middle Eastern nationals during the 1990/1991 Gulf crisis are examples); the statement by Judge McGowan in the 1985 official secrets trial of former civil servant Clive Ponting that 'the policies of the state were the policies of the government then in power'; the judgment during the 1984 miners' strike that road-blocks were not unlawful because police common law powers allowed them to do whatever is necessary, including what is reasonably anticipated, to prevent breaches of the peace (*Moss* v *McLachlan*); and the jailing in 1990 of eight men for voluntary and consensual sado-masochistic sexual practices (*R* v *Williamson and others*), after the judge ruled that consent is no defence.

Also cited is the Canadian experience since the introduction of the Canadian Charter of Rights and Freedoms in 1982. Freedom of association has been interpreted by the courts as excluding the right to strike, whilst corporations have used the right to free expression to prevent restrictions on tobacco advertising. Parliament is currently free to introduce legislation to overturn such rulings; probably the most significant argument of opponents of a Bill of Rights is that under a fully entrenched model it would not be.

The Case for a Bill of Rights

The arguments in favour of a Bill of Rights can be discussed under three headings: constitutional reform, the role of the judiciary and the empowerment of civil society.

The constitutional perspective

First of all, what is and what is not possible within the British constitution has arguably been overtaken by events with the introduction of the 1972 European Communities Act. This Act effectively incorporated Community law into UK law, including the doctrine of the primacy of Community law over national law. (This is in contrast to the Convention, which, stemming from the Council of Europe, remains unincorporated and does not bind our judges in their interpretation of domestic law.) The evidence suggests that the judges have *not*, in fact, been reluctant to give priority to EC law where it has proved inconsistent with domestic legislation. This has even applied to Acts passed after 1972, effectively overturning the doctrine of implied repeal – which assumes that new legislation takes precedence over old in the face of any inconsistency between them – when it comes to EC law. . . .

This pre-eminence of EC law was brought home most forcefully in a recent decision regarding fishing rights and the Merchant Shipping Act 1988. In July 1991 the House of Lords ruled – following a judgment to the same effect by the EC Court, the European Court of Justice – that where national law contravenes EC law, British judges were bound by the terms of the 1972 Act to repeal or amend the law accordingly (*R* v *Secretary of State for Transport, ex parte Factortame Ltd and others*). In relation to EC law, therefore, parliamentary sovereignty is already a dead letter.

Far from being a defect, for many of its supporters the dent made by a Bill of Rights in parliamentary sovereignty would in fact be one of its clear advantages. Under our present constitutional arrangements, as we have seen, majority governments elected on a minority vote can dominate the legislature through a combination of party loyalty, prerogative powers and patronage (indeed one of the Houses of Parliament is not even elected). From this perspective, to extol parliamentary sovereignty is simply to extol the virtues of strong government.

Governments of whatever political persuasion, the argument continues, will to some degree sacrifice individual liberties when their own interests, including that of re-election, are at stake. The record speaks for itself: it was a Labour Government which introduced both the 1968 Immigration Act referred to above and the 1974 Prevention of Terrorism Act – whose detention procedures have been held to be in breach of the ECHR (see commentary to Article 5 of the Bill); whilst a Conservative Government introduced the 1971 Immigration Act and the 1984 Prevention of Terrorism Act, both of which built on its predecessors.

For supporters of a Bill of Rights, the inadequacy of the current constitutional arrangements for protecting fundamental rights applies particularly to minorities, not just ethnic or religious minorities but all groups who feel their rights cannot be entrusted to a system which at best reflects the 'will of the majority', and which lacks any fundamental 'ground rules' that governments cannot breach. These groups include prisoners, people with disabilities or who are mentally ill, gays and lesbians, and those whose lifestyles or tastes differ from the perceived norm. Capital punishment, which opinion polls suggest continues to receive popular support, is frequently cited as an example of a policy affecting a fundamental right which should not be left to the vagaries of majority rule. Nor should fundamental rights be relegated to the status of the mundane or everyday. If they are to be treated with the reverence necessary to ensure their survival, they must be harder to repeal and amend than, say, laws governing dog registration.

Finally, advocates of a Bill of Rights can point to the record of successive UK governments when judged by the rulings of the European Court of Human Rights which seems to give the lie to the claim that the flexibility characterising our present constitutional arrangements effectively safeguards our rights. . . . [T]he UK has the worst record for violations of the Convention of any state which has ratified it. In the period since individuals have been able to lodge complaints with the European Commission (January 1966 to June 1990), 37 cases against the UK government were heard by the European Court involving at least one violation in 27 of these. (This does not include the cases found against the UK not referred to the European Court; 30 cases have been decided by the Committee of Ministers of which 20 involved at least one violation.) Next in the league is Belgium with 20 cases heard by the European Court, involving at least one violation in 14 of these.

The Government's usual response to such statistics is to claim that the UK granted the right of individual petition earlier than many other countries. However, Belgium granted the right of individual petition a decade earlier than Britain; in fact ten countries did so before the UK. Of course the fact that the UK is one of only seven members of the Council of Europe not to have incorporated the Convention into domestic law (out of the 23 states which have ratified it) would partly account for the large number of cases going to the European Court.

Furthermore, the UK is the only EC country not to have *explicit* rights – to freedom of conscience, religion, assembly and speech – enshrined in its laws. It is also the *only* member state of the EC or Council of Europe without either a written constitution or an enforceable Bill of Rights. In fact the UK is one of very few modern democracies not to have either one or the other. Virtually every former British colony was bequeathed some kind of rights charter or written constitution on independence, including Hong Kong – whose Bill of Rights, based on the UN Covenant, came into force in 1991. As illustrations cited throughout this report demonstrate, the contention that Britain's human rights record is so uniquely good that it does not need a Bill of Rights is one of the easier points for supporters of a Bill of Rights to refute.

But what about the judges?

The issue over which there is most contention amongst supporters of a Bill of Rights concerns the question of the transfer of law-making powers from the legislature to the judiciary. For some of those who favour a Bill of Rights in the context of broader constitutional change, this shift would help separate powers between the three arms of the state (the executive, legislature and judiciary), a particularly desirable development given the current domination of the executive.

It is further pointed out that judges already make laws, not only through common law but in the unaccountable and often controversial way in which they interpret statute law . . . . A Bill of Rights, it is argued, would at least provide the courts with a set of principles with which to make these judgments insofar as they affect human rights: judgments for which the courts themselves could be held accountable (to the Supreme Court that we are proposing in Chapter Three should be established).

In essence, therefore, the very existence of a Bill of Rights would influence the judges who would be bound to consider human rights jurisprudence in relevant rulings. And judicial reform could in time address the unrepresentative nature of the current judiciary (see Chapter Three below for our own proposals).

Finally, it is argued that judicial review in the High Court challenging the decisions of public authorities might give some indication of how judges would deal with a Bill of Rights, and suggests that the courts *can* be an effective means of challenging abuse of power by the state in certain circumstances. Judicial review allows the High Court to overturn the decision of a government minister, local authority, tribunal, lower court or other public body if, for example, it is made by taking into account irrelevant matters or not taking into account relevant matters; it is based on an incorrect interpretation of the law; it is so unreasonable that no reasonable person could have come to that decision; or was made in a way that is contrary to natural justice (by not giving a person affected the right to make representations).

Although there is no mandatory right to judicial review, its use has increased considerably over the last 20 years, in particular when no right of appeal has been provided; for example, in immigration and asylum cases. A number of deportations have been prevented as a result of judicial review. This procedure also overturned a recent decision by Barnet Council banning political groups from taking part in a community festival, and declared as unlawful the use by tax officials of search warrants with insufficient details. . . .

Other proponents of a Bill of Rights are, however, more equivocal about giving judges the last word in human rights cases. What if the elderly white men who dominate the judiciary decide that the right to life outlaws abortions? What if they declare that freedom from discrimination makes positive action policies for minorities unlawful? Should one generation set down a human rights programme in tablets of stone to bind future generations? Surely there has to be an effective mechanism for review and revision which involves the democratic process rather than the courts? These are the kinds of questions asked by those who doubt the value of fully entrenched Bills of Rights relying exclusively on the judges for their enforcement.

There is thus a debate within a debate amongst supporters of a Bill of Rights. The entrenched school argues that the only way to guarantee the protection of fundamental rights, in the face of political expediency, is to allow the courts to overturn any legislation which threatens to infringe them. On the other hand, the unentrenched school argues that Parliament must retain the last word to guard against judicial decisions which weaken rights. What both schools acknowledge is that for a Bill of Rights to be more than a declaratory statement it must involve procedures enabling individuals to enforce their rights and freedoms through the courts.

A Bill of Rights as a source of empowerment

The opportunity for individuals to take the state to court for infringing their rights, or for failing to provide adequate protection against such infringements by other individuals or private corporations, is one of the main advantages of a Bill of Rights. And whilst Bills of Rights traditionally put a premium on individual rights over all others, a number of the rights they guarantee (such as the right to demonstrate and to join trade unions) in practice operate only in collective circumstances, increasing their impact.

The avenues currently open to individuals to challenge the decisions of public bodies are, from this perspective, clearly inadequate. Habeas corpus, the procedure for challenging unlawful detention, does not involve a judgment on the merits of the detention, only whether the imprisoning authority had the jurisdiction to carry it out. Judicial review, discussed above, provides a useful remedy for disputing the decisions of public bodies in many situations. Actions, however, must be taken within a three-month time limit and the judge has the discretion not to proceed with the review even if the decision being challenged was unlawful. As with habeas corpus, it is difficult to use judicial review to question the merits of a decision. Under a Bill of Rights, judicial review in relation to the rights it upholds would be automatic, and remedies for any breaches mandatory. **From the empowerment perspective, the greatest value of a Bill of Rights is therefore the chance it offers to enhance the rights of those who are most vulnerable to abuse of power by the state.**

For this reason the *contents* of a Bill of Rights is crucial. Its construction needs to take account of already existing power inequalities lest powerful bodies (like large private companies) safeguard their rights through the Bill at the expense of ordinary individuals. Similarly, any limitations on rights under the Bill need to be tightly worded to avoid giving judges the discretion to interpret them in the interests of the state. And the method of enforcing the Bill must address the issue of *how* to protect the rights it upholds from judicial rulings – as well as legislation – which weaken them (these issues are elaborated further in the discussion on Liberty's Bill below).

For these reasons, advocates of a Bill of Rights from the empowerment perspective tend to qualify their support for incorporating the European Convention, particularly with regard to the range of limitations on rights it contains.

Nevertheless, the changes brought about by successful cases taken under the ECHR (some of which, as explained in Appendix I, have been resolved by a 'friendly settlement' or a ruling from the Committee of Ministers) are cited as evidence of what *might* have been achieved had a Bill of Rights been in force or the Convention incorporated at the time. How many more human rights gains might there have been, it is asked, if complainants could have taken the government to court in the UK without the expense or staying power required to see a case through to Europe? Moreover, a glance at the cases in Appendix II indicates that it is not the powerful and the privileged who have benefited from the Convention, nor just isolated individuals, but *groups* of people such as mental hospital patients, prisoners, gay men and children. It has also been pointed out that the small advances in freedom of information or privacy over the last decade – which benefit everyone – have also been due largely to cases taken to Europe.

Finally, what makes a Bill of Rights particularly significant for the less powerful groups in society is that it can provide protection – through the application of its broad principles – against events which cannot necessarily be predicted when specific legislation guaranteeing individual rights is drafted. Such legislation might prove inadequate in the light of a future event and anyway can simply be repealed by subsequent Acts. To continue with the examples referred to above, both the 1968 Immigration Act and the 1974 Prevention of Terrorism Act were passed by Parliament during periods of mounting national panic following a largely media-induced immigration scare in the first case, and the Birmingham pub bombings in the second. If there had been a Bill of Rights in force at the time, the question as to whether such legislation did or did not breach fundamental rights enshrined in the Bill would at the very least have been publicly aired in Parliament and/or a domestic court. At most, depending both on the contents of the Bill and on the enforcement procedure adopted, the offending legislation could have been overturned by the courts as being in breach of a fundamental right.

From this point of view, Bills of Rights empower individuals and groups not only by providing rights and remedies in a direct sense, but by imbuing laws which protect human rights with a greater significance than that accorded to all other legislation. With a Bill of Rights, people would know what their rights are because they would be written down. They would learn about them in schools. Officials and drafters of legislation would become more conscious of rights than they are at present, more fearful of the consequences of breaching them. Debates and disputes would develop about the nature of fundamental rights and where the dividing line should lie when they conflict. Developments such as these would give rise to a rights consciousness which in turn would act as a popular bulwark against attempts to dilute or erode fundamental rights and freedoms.

8 JUDICIAL REVIEW: THE GROUNDS

(A) INTRODUCTION

(i) The role of judicial review in the constitution

In some countries, for example in the United States of America, the judges are permitted to review legislation in order to establish whether it complies with the terms of the constitution. In the United Kingdom, the absence of a written constitution with the status of a higher law and the doctrine of parliamentary supremacy prevent the judges from exercising this role. They may, however, review the manner in which public authorities exercise the powers which have been conferred upon them by the legislature.

This power of judicial review may be defined as the jurisdiction of the superior courts (the High Court, the Court of Appeal and the House of Lords) to review the acts, decisions and omissions of public authorities in order to establish whether they have exceeded or abused their powers. The courts have developed a number of principles in order to establish whether there has been an excess or abuse of power. For example, a public authority must direct itself properly on the law, it must not use its powers for improper purposes, and it must not act in breach of the rules of natural justice.

What is the justification for permitting such judicial control? One theory, discussed in the following extract, is that the courts are simply giving effect to the intentions of Parliament.

P. Cane, *An Introduction to Administrative Law* (1992), pp. 340-43

A great many of the powers and duties of governmental agencies, whether they are part of central or of local government, are laid down by statute. It follows from the first proposition about Parliamentary supremacy that courts are bound to apply statutes according to their terms. Traditional theory also says, although this does not follow from the first proposition, that ambiguities in the language of statutes should be resolved, and gaps in them filled, by reference to the intention of the legislature. Thus, it is often said that the enforcement of statutory duties and the control of the exercise of statutory powers by the courts is ultimately justifiable in terms of the doctrine of Parliamentary supremacy: even though Parliament has not expressly authorised the courts to supervise governmental activity, it cannot have intended breaches of duty by governmental agencies to go unremedied (even if no remedy is provided in the statute tself), nor can it have intended to give administrative agencies the freedom to exceed or abuse their powers, or to act unreasonably. It is the task of the courts to interpret and enforce the provisions of statutes which impose duties and confer powers on administrative agencies. In so doing they are giving effect to the will of Parliament.

There are two main weaknesses in this theory of the basis of judicial control of the exercise of statutory functions. The first is relevant to statutory interpretation generally: it is unrealistic to treat the process of interpreting statutes, resolving ambiguities, and filling gaps, as always being a matter of discerning and giving effect to the intentions of Parliament. Even assuming that we can make some sense of the notion of intention when applied to a multi-member body following simple majoritarian voting procedures, there will be many cases in which Parliament did not think about the question relevant to resolving the ambiguity or filling the gap. In such cases the courts must act creatively in deciding what the statute means. The weakness of the intention theory of statutory interpretation is made very clear by the recent development of the notion of 'purposive interpretation'. Especially (but not only) in the context of interpreting statutes passed to give effect to EC law, the courts are now willing to go beyond interpreting the words actually used in statutes and to *insert* (or 'imply') into legislative provisions words or phrases needed to give effect to what the court perceives to be the true purpose or aim of the provision in question. It makes little sense to describe this process in terms of giving effect to what Parliament actually intended all along.

A second weakness of this justification of judicial control of governmental action is that it is at variance with the actual conduct of the courts. The principles which form the basis of judicial review — the doctrine of *ultra vires* and the rules of natural justice — are common law principles created and developed *by the courts* as means of controlling administrative activities. The courts have shown themselves prepared to go a very long way to preserve their jurisdiction to supervise administrative action by applying these principles. Perhaps the most striking modern example of this is the case of *Anisminic Ltd* v *Foreign Compensation Commission* [[1969] 2 AC 147]. The main question in this case was whether a section in the Foreign Compensation Act purporting to oust the jurisdiction of the court to review 'determinations' of the Commission, was effective to that end. The House of Lords held that the word 'determination' must be read so as to exclude *ultra vires* determinations; it then went on to extend considerably the notion of *ultra vires* as it applied to decisions on questions of law, the final result being to reduce the application of the ouster clause almost to vanishing point, despite the fact that Parliament had arguably intended it to have wide effect. More recent cases suggest that the courts are now more willing to give effect to statutory ousters of judicial review than they were 25 years ago, but this change in judicial attitude also serves to illustrate the important role which the courts play in determining the availability of judicial review as a means of controlling government action.

A second example is provided by the attitude of the courts to the exclusion by statute of the rules of natural justice. In the face of legislative silence on the question of whether an applicant before an administrative body is entitled to the protection of these procedural rules, two approaches are possible. It could be said that the rules of natural justice will apply only if there is evidence of a legislative intention that they should; alternatively, it could be argued that silence should be construed as an invitation to the courts to apply common law procedural standards of natural justice. On the whole the courts, especially in recent years, have tended to the latter view, thus asserting the independent validity of the rules of natural justice.

A third example is provided by cases, which we examined earlier, concerning powers given to a Minister, for example, 'to act as he sees fit'. Such phraseology appears to give the Minister unfettered discretion, but the courts tend to hold that such powers must be exercised reasonably in the light of the aims and purposes of the legislation conferring the power and of the relevant facts. In reality, the terms of the legislation may give very little guidance as to the way Parliament wished the power to be exercised, even assuming that it did not intend, as the phrase itself indicates, to leave the Minister free to exercise his or her own best judgment. In effect, the courts are imposing their own standards of reasonable conduct on the Minister, irrespective of the question of legislative intent.

Even more importantly, the idea that the courts are enforcing the intention of the legislature when they control governmental action does not justify judicial control of the exercise of *non-statutory* powers and functions. As we have seen, in the *GCHQ* case the House of Lords rejected the proposition that the common law (prerogative) powers of central government are immune from judicial review in favour of the proposition that the exercise of a common law power can be challenged provided only that the power or the circumstances of its exercise do not raise non-justiciable issues of policy. We have also seen that the courts have extended the scope of judicial review to embrace the exercise, for public purposes, of *de facto* power which has no identifiable legal source whether in common law or statute. Whatever the criteria which the courts will apply in reviewing the exercise of non-statutory powers, they cannot, by definition, be derived from a power-conferring statute.

How is this independent attitude of the courts to be justified? Two lines of argument suggest themselves. First, despite the second proposition of parliamentary supremacy stated above, there are certain features of our constitutional and political arrangements which are so basic to our system of government that it is not seriously thought that they could ever be subject to the whim of Parliament — for example, the right to vote in free elections. Parliament could, of course, pass legislation inimical to this right, but attempts to enforce it, whether in the courts or outside would, no doubt, precipitate a crisis. Similarly, the rights to apply to the courts for judicial review of the exercise of public powers and to receive a fair hearing before administrative bodies are of such fundamental importance in a democratic society, that it is vital that some independent body has the power to protect these rights from any but the most limited statutory abridgement. A second line of argument which might support the refusal of the courts to be too subservient to Parliament is this: a vital underpinning assumption of Parliamentary supremacy is that Parliament is the most democratic governmental institution in our system. But the political reality is that when the party in government has a comfortable majority in the House of Commons, the House is almost as much under the control of the government as is the administration. The implications of this line of argument will be considered more later.

The autonomy of judicial review has an important implication which ought to be made explicit, namely that in controlling government activity the courts are asserting and exercising, in their own right and in their own name, a power to limit and define the powers of other governmental agencies. Parliament allocates decision-making powers to governmental agencies by virtue of its unlimited legislative power. The courts, by virtue of their inherent (i.e. self-conferred) common law power of judicial review of administrative action, decide the legal limits of those allocations of power. In so doing they can not only castigate governmental agencies for abuses or excesses of power but, equally importantly, they can legitimise controversial exercises of power by holding them to have been lawful. The courts, in short, perform an indirect power-allocation function. Once this is realized, it can be seen how important it is to understand the nature of this function and the justification for it, since it is clear that the courts are not detached umpires in the governmental process but that they play an integral part in deciding how it will operate.

Note

Anisminic Ltd v *Foreign Compensation Commission* [1969] 2 AC 147 is considered further, *post* at pp. 535 and 635 and the rules of natural justice are explained, *post* at p. 553.

Question

In considering whether there is a justification for judicial review do you think it matters whether or not Parliament is truly democratic?

Notes

1. Cane refers to the view that the independent attitude of the courts may be justified because a vital underpinning of the assumption of parliamentary supremacy – that Parliament is the most democratic governmental institution in our system – is not borne out in practice. In considering the implications of this argument later in the chapter, he states, at p. 345, 'although judicial and parliamentary control of government activity are directed to different ends, it can be argued that the popularity and importance of judicial review is likely to bear an inverse relationship to the strength of parliamentary and other non-legal means of controling government.' (See *ante* chapter 6 for a discussion of the mechanisms of political accountability.)

The links between judicial review and democracy are also explored by T. S. R. Allan in 'Legislative Supremacy and the Rule of Law' (1985) 44 *Cambridge Law Journal,* 111–43 at 129–33. In this extract Allan argues that judicial review is not inconsistent with the legislative supremacy of Parliament because the courts will give effect to the clear and unambiguous words of statutes. He also argues that judicial review functions to protect the democratic principle of the political sovereignty of the people. Unless prevented from doing so by the clear and unambiguous words of statutes, the courts in judicial review proceedings will give effect to common standards of morality and the natural expectations of the citizen. Allan thus differs from Cane in that he claims that ultimately judicial review poses no threat to the doctrine of parliamentary supremacy. Further, while Cane raises the possibility that judicial review may be more justifiable because of the inadequacies of other means of scrutinising the Executive, he does not claim, as Allan does, that judicial review actually promotes democracy because it gives effect to common standards of morality and the natural expectations of the citizen.

2. Cane's discussion is concerned with judicial review of statutory powers, but we shall see below that the courts have reviewed the exercise of powers conferred by the royal prerogative (see *CCSU* v *Minister for the Civil Service* [1985] AC 374). Recently, it has been clearly established that, in certain circumstances, the courts may review the exercise of powers which are not conferred by either statute or the royal prerogative but which depend on the consent of those who are subject to them (see *R* v *Panel on Take-overs and Mergers, ex parte Datafin Plc* [1987] QB 815 at *post* p. 621). Can any of the justifications which have been put forward for judicial review of statutory powers be used to justify judicial review of powers derived from other sources?

(ii) The distinction between review and appeal

The courts have been concerned to emphasise that, in judicial review proceedings, they are exercising a supervisory, not an appellate, jurisdiction. Where statute provides for an appeal and the grounds of appeal are not restricted by the statute itself, the court is generally required to decide whether the decision under appeal was right or wrong. If it decides that the decision was wrong, the court hearing the appeal is generally permitted to substitute its decision for that of the authority which first determined the matter in question. What is the position in judicial review proceedings?

Chief Constable of the North Wales Police v _Evans_
[1982] 1 WLR 1155
House of Lords

The Chief Constable of North Wales decided that Evans, a probationer constable in the force, should be required to resign or, if he refused, be discharged from the force. Evans resigned but subsequently challenged the decision on the ground that it was taken in breach of natural justice because he was not told of the allegations which had led to the decision and had not been given an opportunity to offer any explanation. The House of Lords agreed with the decision of the Court of Appeal that there had been a breach of natural justice, but in the light of comments made in the Court of Appeal, felt it necessary to make some general comments on the scope of judicial review.

LORD HAILSHAM: The first observation I wish to make is by way of criticism of some remarks of Lord Denning MR which seem to me to be capable of an erroneous construction of the purpose and the remedy by way of judicial review under RSC Ord 53. This remedy, vastly increased in extent, and rendered, over a long period in recent years, of infinitely more convenient access than that provided by the old prerogative writs and actions for a declaration, is intended to protect the individual against the abuse of power by a wide range of authorities, judicial, quasi-judicial, and, as would originally have been thought when I first practised at the Bar, administrative. It is not intended to take away from those authorities the powers and discretions properly vested in them by law and to substitute the courts as the bodies making the decisions. It is intended to see that the relevant authorities use their powers in a proper manner.

Since the range of authorities, and the circumstances of the use of their power, are almost infinitely various, it is of course unwise to lay down rules for the application of the remedy which appear to be of universal validity in every type of case. But it is important to remember in every case that the purpose of the remedies is to ensure that the individual is given fair treatment by the authority to which he has been subjected and that it is no part of that purpose to substitute the opinion of the judiciary or of individual judges for that of the authority constituted by law to decide the matters in question. The function of the court is to see the lawful authority is not abused by unfair treatment and not to attempt itself the task entrusted to that authority by the law. There are passages in the judgment of Lord Denning MR (and perhaps in the other judgments of the Court of Appeal) in the instant case and quoted by my noble and learned friend which might be read as giving the courts carte blanche to review the decision of the authority on the basis of what the courts themselves consider fair and reasonable on the merits. I am not sure whether the Master of the Rolls really intended his remarks to be construed in such a way as to permit the courts to examine, as for instance in the present case, the reasoning of the subordinate body with a view to substituting its own opinion. If so, I do not think this is a correct statement of principle. The purpose of judicial review is to ensure that the individual receives fair treatment, and not to ensure that the authority, after according fair treatment, reaches on a matter which it is authorised by law to decide for itself a conclusion which is correct in the eyes of the court. . . .

LORD BRIGHTMAN: . . . I turn secondly to the proper purpose of the remedy of judicial review, what it is and what it is not. In my opinion the law was correctly stated in the speech of Lord Evershed [in *Ridge* v *Baldwin* [1964] AC 40], at p. 96. His was a dissenting judgment but the dissent was not concerned with this point. Lord Evershed referred to 'a danger of usurpation of power on the part of the courts . . . under the pretext of having regard to the principles of natural justice.' He added:

> I do observe again that it is not the decision as such which is liable to review; it is only the circumstances in which the decision was reached, and particularly in such a case as the present the need for giving the party dismissed an opportunity for putting his case.

Judicial review is concerned, not with the decision, but with the decision-making process. Unless that restriction on the power of the court is observed, the court will in my view, under the guise of preventing the abuse of power, be itself guilty of usurping power. . . .

Questions

1. What, then, are the differences between appeal and review?

2. This case concerned the principles of natural justice. The other grounds for judicial review are summarised *post*, at pp. 534–535. Do you think they could all be said to be concerned not with 'the decision but with the decision-making process'? Do you think their Lordships intended their remarks to apply to all the grounds for judicial review?

(iii) The use of judicial review

Recent research has been conducted into the use of judicial review. The table set out below indicates the principal areas in which judicial review was sought over the period 1987–1989 and the first quarter of 1991.

M. Sunkin, L. Bridges, G. Mészáros,
***Judicial Review in Perspective*, (1993) p. 4**

Table 1.1

Applications for Leave to Seek Judicial Review by Subject Areas, 1987–1989 and 1st quarter of 1991

	1987		1988		1989		1991 (Jan-Mar)	
	No	**%**	**No**	**%**	**No**	**%**	**No**	**%**
Criminal:	214	14.2	164	13.4	219	14.2	71	15.6
Civil:								
Immigration	671	44.4	356	29.1	430	27.7	103	22.7
Housing	141	9.3	161	13.2	232	15.0	108	23.8
Planning	59	3.9	84	6.9	132	8.5	17	3.7
Family	42	2.8	44	3.6	26	1.7	7	1.5
Discipline	36	2.3	27	2.2	18	1.2	6	1.3
Tax	29	1.9	17	1.4	41	2.6	6	1.3
Education	27	1.8	24	2.0	46	3.0	27	5.9
Legal Process	25	1.7	43	3.5	36	2.3	20	4.4
Lcl. Govt. Affairs	25	1.7	37	3.0	38	2.5	17	3.7
Prisoners	17	1.1	25	2.0	16	1.0	5	1.1
Health	17	1.1	24	2.0	34	2.2	3	0.7
Environment	15	1.0	11	0.9	21	1.4	3	0.7
Employment	15	1.0	16	1.3	18	1.2	2	0.4
Rates	14	0.9	9	0.7	13	0.8	2	0.4
Agriculture	12	0.8	7	0.6	7	0.5	—	—
Transport	12	0.8	7	0.6	14	0.9	—	—
Legal aid	10	0.7	20	1.6	32	2.1	5	1.1
Coroners	10	0.7	9	0.7	15	1.0	3	0.7
Benefits	10	0.7	15	1.2	29	1.9	4	0.9
Trade	9	0.5	7	0.4	19	1.2	4	0.9
Compensation	6	0.4	6	0.8	11	0.9	9	2.0
Travellers	6	0.4	4	0.8	16	1.0	3	0.6
Other	90	6.0	107	8.7	123	7.9	29	6.4

Notes

1. The statistics relate solely to applications for judicial review. As the researchers subsequently show there is a steady reduction in the cases dealt with at the various stages of the judicial review process, culminating in a hearing.

2. Even in the relatively short period covered by the table it is clear that there are rises and falls both within the dominant areas of immigration and housing, and in other areas, e.g., the rise in education and the erratic pattern in tax.

3. The researchers note that judicial review 'has been used more often as a weapon to limit the autonomy of local government rather than as a constraint on the power of the central state' (p. 101).

Question
What factors might explain the urges in applications for judicial review?

(B) THE GROUNDS FOR JUDICIAL REVIEW

This chapter is concerned with the grounds for judicial review. The extracts which are included do, however, contain a number of references to the remedies which are available where there is a breach of the principles of judicial review. Before reading the cases, students should acquaint themselves with the following terms.

Subject to certain qualifications, which will be examined in further detail in chapter 9, the normal method of seeking review is through making an application for judicial review. In the application for judicial review the court may grant one or more of the following remedies:

The prerogative orders

(1) Certiorari: this remedy quashes an unlawful decision of a public authority.

(2) Prohibition: this remedy prohibits an unlawful act which a public authority is proposing to perform.

(3) Mandamus: this remedy compels a public authority to perform a public duty.

Prerogative orders may not be granted against the Crown, although they may be granted against individual ministers of the Crown. They may not be used to challenge delegated legislation.

Injunctions Injunctions may be prohibitory (restraining unlawful action) or mandatory (compelling the performance of a duty). Many applications are for interlocutory or interim injunctions. Interlocutory injunctions continue until the trial of the action or further order of the court. Interim injunctions continue until a fixed date or further order. In an emergency an injunction may be granted *ex parte,* without hearing the defendant. Note, however, that s. 21 of the Crown Proceedings Act 1947 prevents the grant of injunctions against the Crown. So far as ministers of the Crown are concerned, injunctions can be granted against them, both in matters of European Community law (see *R* v *Secretary of State for Transport, ex parte Factortame (No. 2)* [1990] 1 AC 603) and in domestic law (see *R* v *M* [1994] 1 AC 377, *ante* p. 214).

Declarations Declarations are a very flexible remedy. They may, for instance, simply state the parties' rights, set out the true construction of a statute, or state that an administrative act is invalid.

Damages Damages may be awarded in an application for judicial review provided the applicant has claimed one or more of the remedies specified above. Damages are not available simply because one of the principles of judicial review has been breached. The applicant must show, in addition, that the authority has breached a right of his for which damages are available (e.g. that the authority has committed a tort or breach of contract).

Various attempts have been made to find a general principle underlying the grounds for judicial review. The traditional approach is to say that the courts may review action which is *ultra vires* – outside the power of – the authority whose action is being challenged.

It is clear, however, that this very general principle tells us very little about the particular grounds for challenge. (An analysis of the problems in using the *ultra vires* principle as the basis for judicial review may be found in D. Oliver, 'Is the *Ultra Vires* Rule the Basis for Judicial Review' [1987] *Public Law,* 543–69.) The following extract provides further detail.

Council of Civil Service Unions v *Minister for the Civil Service*
[1985] AC 374
House of Lords

The facts are stated *post,* at p. 572.

LORD DIPLOCK: . . . Judicial review has I think developed to a state today when, without reiterating any analysis of the steps by which the development has come about, one can conveniently classify under three heads the grounds on which administrative action is subject to control by judicial review. The first ground I would call 'illegality', the second 'irrationality' and the third 'procedural impropriety'. That is not to say that further development on a case by case basis may not in course of time add further grounds. I have in mind particularly the possible adoption in the future of the principle of 'proportionality' which is recognised in the administrative law of several of our fellow members of the European Economic Community; but to dispose of the instant case the three already well-established heads that I have mentioned will suffice.

By illegality as a ground for judicial review I mean that the decision-maker must understand correctly the law that regulates his decision-making power and must give effect to it. Whether he has or not is par excellence a justifiable question to be decided in the event of dispute, by those persons, the judges, by whom the judicial power of the state is exercisable.

By irrationality I mean what can by now be succinctly referred to as '*Wednesbury* unreasonableness' (see *Associated Provincial Picture Houses Ltd* v *Wednesbury Corp* [1948] 1 KB 223). It applies to a decision which is so outrageous in its defiance of logic or accepted moral standards that no sensible person who had applied his mind to the question to be decided could have arrived at it. Whether a decision falls within the category is a question that judges by their training and experience should be well-equipped to answer, or else there would be something badly wrong with our judicial system. To justify the court's exercise of this role, resort I think today is no longer needed to Viscount Radcliffe's ingenious explanation in *Edwards* v *Bairstow* [1956] AC 14 of irrationality as a ground for a court's reversal of a decision by ascribing it to an inferred though identifiable mistake of law by the decision-maker. 'Irrationality' by now can stand on its own feet as an accepted ground on which a decision may be attacked by judicial review.

I have described the third head as 'procedural impropriety' rather than failure to observe basic rules of natural justice or failure to act with procedural fairness towards the person who will be affected by the decision. This is because susceptibility to judicial review under this head covers also failure by an administrative tribunal to observe procedural rules that are expressly laid down in the legislative instrument by which its jurisdiction is conferred, even where such failure does not involve any denial of natural justice.

Notes

1. Lord Diplock's threefold classification of the grounds for judicial review has been cited in many subsequent cases. The classification will be followed in this chapter, where each of the three categories will be examined in more detail. The chapter will conclude with a look at substantive legitimate expectations a potential new ground of review.

2. For advocacy of recognising proportionality in domestic law see Jowell and Lester 'Proportionality: Neither Novel Nor Dangerous' in Jowell and Oliver (eds) *New Directions in Judicial Review* (1988). See Boyron 'Proportionality in English Administrative Law: A Faulty Translation?' (1992) 12 *Oxford Journal of Legal Studies* 237. For an interesting proposal as to how to operate proportionality see Craig *Administrative Law* (1994) pp. 414–418.

(i) Illegality

Lord Diplock used this phrase to cover a number of different grounds which are frequently treated separately. The most important are:

(1) An authority must not exceed its jurisdiction by purporting to exercise powers which it does not possess.
(2) An authority must direct itself properly on the law.
(3) An authority must not use its power for an improper purpose.
(4) An authority must take into account all relevant considerations and disregard all irrelevant considerations.
(5) An authority to which the exercise of a discretion has been entrusted cannot delegate the exercise of its discretion to another unless clearly authorised to do so.
(6) An authority must not fetter its discretion.
(7) Finally, an authority acts unlawfully if it fails to fulfil a statutory duty.

It should be noted that this list is not exhaustive and that the grounds clearly overlap to some extent. Consider the following cases.

Anisminic* v *Foreign Compensation Commission
[1969] 2 AC 147
House of Lords

Anisminic Ltd owned property in Egypt which was sequestrated in 1956 by the Egyptian government. In 1957 Anisminic sold the property, for substantially less than its real value, to TEDO, an Egyptian organisation.

Under a treaty, the United Arab Republic paid to the United Kingdom £27.5 million as compensation for property confiscated in Egypt in 1956. Responsibility for distributing the compensation money was vested in the Foreign Compensation Commission (FCC). Anisminic Ltd submitted a claim for compensation to the FCC.

Article 4 of the Foreign Compensation (Egypt) (Determination and Registration of Claims) Order 1962 provided that the Commission shall treat a claim as established if satisfied of the following matters:

(a) the applicant is the person referred to in the relevant part of Annex E of the Order as 'the owner of the property or is the successor in title of such a person';

(b) the person referred to in the relevant part of Annex E 'and any person who became successor in title of such person on or before February 28, 1959, were British nationals on October 31, 1956, and February 28, 1959.'

The Commission's provisional determination was that Anisminic Ltd had failed to establish its claim because TEDO, its successor in title, was not a British national.

Anisminic Ltd sought a declaration that the Commission had misconstrued the Order.

LORD REID: It has sometimes been said that it is only where a tribunal acts without jurisdiction that its decision is a nullity. But in such cases the word 'jurisdiction' has been used in a very wide sense, and I have come to the conclusion that it is better not to use the term except in the narrow and original sense of the tribunal being entitled to enter on the inquiry in question. But there are many cases where, although the tribunal had jurisdiction to enter on the inquiry, it has done or failed to do something in the course of inquiry which is of such nature that its decision is a nullity. It may have given its decision in bad faith. It may have a made decision which it had no power to make. It may have failed in the course of the inquiry to comply with the requirements of natural justice. It may in perfect good faith have misconstrued the provisions giving it power to act so that it failed to deal with the question remitted to it and decided some question which was not remitted to it. It may have refused to take into account something which it was required to take into account. Or it may have based its decision on some matter which, under the provisions setting it up, it had no right to take into account. I do not intend this list to be exhaustive. But if it decides a question remitted to it for decision without committing any of these errors it is as much entitled to decide that question wrongly as it is to decide it rightly. I understand that some confusion has been caused by my having said in *Reg* v *Governor of Brixton, Ex parte Armah* [1968] AC 192, 234 that if a tribunal has jurisdiction to go right it has jurisdiction to go wrong. So it has, if one uses 'jurisdiction' in the narrow original sense. If it is entitled to enter on the inquiry and does not do any of those things which I have mentioned in the course of the proceedings, then its decision is equally valid whether it is right or wrong subject only to the power of the court in certain circumstances to correct an error of law. I think that, if these views are correct, the only case cited which was plainly wrongly decided is *Davies* v *Price* [1958] 1 WLR 434. But in a number of other cases some of the grounds of judgment are questionable.

I can now turn to the provisions of the Order under which the commission acted, and to the way in which the commission reached their decision. It was said in the Court of Appeal that publication of their reasons was unnecessary and perhaps undesirable. Whether or not they could have been required to publish their reasons, I dissent emphatically from the view that publication may have been undesirable. In my view, the commission acted with complete propriety, as one would expect looking to its membership.

The meaning of the important parts of this Order is extremely difficult to discover, and, in my view, a main cause of this is the deplorable modern drafting practice of compressing to the point of obscurity provisions which would not be difficult to understand if written out at rather greater length. . . .

The main difficulty in this case springs from the fact that the draftsman did not state separately what conditions have to be satisfied (1) where the applicant is the original owner and (2) where the applicant claims as the successor in title of the original owner. It is clear that where the applicant is the original owner he must prove that he was a British national on the dates stated. And it is equally clear that where the applicant claims as being the original owner's successor in title he must prove that both he and the original owner were British nationals on those dates, subject to later provisions in the article about persons who had died or had been born within the relevant period. What is left in obscurity is whether the provisions with regard to successors in title have any application at all in cases where the applicant is himself the original owner. If this provision had been split up as it should have been, and the conditions, to be satisfied where the original owner is the applicant had been set out, there could have been no such obscurity.

This is the crucial question in this case. It appears from the commission's reasons that they construed this provision as requiring them to inquire, when the applicant is himself the original owner, whether he had a successor in title. So they made that inquiry in this case and held that TEDO was the applicant's successor in title. As TEDO was not a British national they rejected the appellants' claim. But if, on a true construction of the Order, a claimant who is an original owner does not have to prove anything about successors in title, then the commission made an inquiry which the Order did not empower them to make, and they based their decision on a matter which they had no right to take into account. If one uses the word 'jurisdiction' in its wider sense, they went beyond their jurisdiction in considering this matter. It was argued that the whole matter of construing the Order was something remitted to the commission for their decision. I cannot accept that argument. I find nothing in the Order to support it. The Order requires the commission to consider whether they are satisfied with regard to the prescribed matters. That is all they have to do. It cannot be for the commission to determine the limits of its powers. Of course if one party submits to a tribunal that its powers are wider than in fact they are, then the tribunal must deal with that submission. But if they reach a wrong conclusion as to the width of their powers, the court must be able to correct that – not because the tribunal has made an error of law, but because as a result of making an error of law they have dealt with and based their decision on a matter with which, on a true construction of their powers, they had no right to deal. If they base their decision on some matter which is not prescribed for their adjudication, they are doing something which they have no right to do and, if the view which I expressed earlier is right, their decision is a nullity. So the question is whether on a true construction of the Order the applicants did or did not have to prove anything with regard to successors in title. If the commission were entitled to enter on the inquiry whether the applicants had a successor in title, then their decision as to whether TEDO was their successor in title would I think be unassailable whether it was right or wrong: it would be a decision on a matter remitted to them for their decision. The question I have to consider is not whether they made a wrong decision but whether they inquired into and decided a matter which they had no right to consider.

I have great difficulty in seeing how in the circumstances there could be a successor in title of a person who is still in existence. This provision is dealing with the period before the Order was made when the original owner had no title to anything: he had nothing but a hope that some day somehow he might get some compensation. The rest of the article makes it clear that the phrase (though inaccurate) must apply to a person who can be regarded as having inherited in some way the hope which a deceased original owner had that he would get some compensation. But 'successor in title' must I think mean some person who could come forward and make a claim in his own right. There can only be a successor in title where the title of its original possessor has passed to another person, his successor, so that the original possessor of the title can no longer make a claim, but his successor can make the claim which the original possessor of the title could have made if his title had not passed to his successor. The 'successor' of a deceased person can do that. But how could any 'successor' do this while the original owner is still in existence? One can imagine the improbable case of the original owner agreeing with someone that, for a consideration immediately paid to him, he would pay over to the other party any compensation which he might ultimately receive. But that would not create a 'successor in title' in any true sense. And I can think of no other way in which the original owner could transfer inter vivos his expectation of receiving compensation. If there were anything in the rest of the Order to indicate that such a case was intended to be covered, we might have to attribute to the phrase 'successor in title' some unusual and inaccurate meaning which would cover it. But there is nothing of that kind. In themselves the words 'successor in title' are, in my opinion, inappropriate in the circumstances of this Order to denote any person while the original owner is still in existence, and I think it most improbable that they were ever intended to denote any such person. There is no necessity to stretch them to cover any such person. I would therefore hold that the words 'and any person who became successor in title to such person' in article 4(1)(b)(ii) have no application to a case where the applicant is the original owner. It follows that the commission rejected the appellants' claim on a ground which they had no right to take into account and that their decision was a nullity. I would allow this appeal.

LORD PEARCE: Lack of jurisdiction may arise in various ways. There may be an absence of those formalities or things which are conditions precedent to the tribunal having any jurisdiction to embark on an inquiry. Or the tribunal may at the end make an order that it has no jurisdiction to make. Or in the intervening stage, while engaged on a proper inquiry, the tribunal may depart from the rules of natural justice; or it may ask itself the wrong questions; or it may take into account matters which it was not directed to take into account. Thereby it would step outside its jurisdiction. It would turn its inquiry into something not directed by Parliament and fail to make the inquiry which Parliament did direct. Any of these things would cause its purported decision to be a nullity. . . .

LORD WILBERFORCE: In every case, whatever the character of a tribunal, however wide the range of questions remitted to it, however great the permissible margin of mistakes, the essential point remains that the tribunal has a derived authority, derived, that is, from statute: at some point, and to be found from a consideration of the legislation, the field within which it operates is marked out and limited. There is always an area, narrow or wide, which is the tribunal's area; a residual area, wide or narrow, in which the legislature has previously expressed its will and into which the tribunal may not enter. Equally, though this is not something that arises in the present case, there are certain fundamental assumptions, which without explicit restatement in every case, necessarily underlie the remission of power to decide such as (I do not attempt more than a general reference, since the strength and shade of these matters will depend upon the nature of the tribunal and the kind of question it has to decide) the requirement that a decision must be made in accordance with principles of natural justice and good faith. The principle that failure to fulfil these assumptions may be equivalent to a departure from the remitted area must be taken to follow from the decision of this House in *Ridge* v *Baldwin* [1964] AC 40. Although, in theory perhaps, it may be possible for Parliament to set up a tribunal which has full and autonomous powers to fix its own area of operation, that has, so far, not been done in this country. The question, what is the tribunal's proper area, is one which it has always been permissible to ask and to answer, and it must follow that examination of its extent is not precluded by a clause conferring conclusiveness, finality, or unquestionability upon its decisions. These clauses in their nature can only relate to decisions given within the field of operation entrusted to the tribunal. They may, according to the width and emphasis of their formulation, help to ascertain the extent of that field, to narrow it or to enlarge it, but unless one is to deny the statutory origin of the tribunal and of its powers, they cannot preclude examination of that extent. . . .

The extent of the interpretatory power conferred upon the tribunal may sometimes be difficult to ascertain and argument may be possible whether this or that question of construction has been left to the tribunal, that is, is within the tribunal's field, or whether, because it pertains to the delimitation of the tribunal's area by the legislature, it is reserved for decision by the courts. Sometimes it will be possible to form a conclusion from the form and subject-matter of the legislation. In one case it may be seen that the legislature, while stating general objectives, is prepared to concede a wide area to the authority it establishes: this will often be the case where the decision involves a degree of policy-making rather than fact-finding, especially if the authority is a department of government or the Minister at its head. I think that we have reached a stage in our administrative law when we can view this question quite objectively, without any necessary predisposition towards one that questions of law, or questions of construction, are necessarily for the courts. In the kind of case I have mentioned there is no need to make this assumption. In another type of case it may be apparent that Parliament is itself directly and closely concerned with the definition and delimitation of certain matters of comparative detail and has marked by its language the intention that these shall accurately be observed. . . . The present case, by contrast, as examination of the relevant Order in Council will show, is clearly of the latter category. . . .

Lord Pearce and Lord Wilberforce also agreed with Lord Reid's interpretation of the Order. Lord Morris and Lord Pearson dissented.

Question

On what ground or grounds did the court grant judicial review?

Notes

1. The Foreign Compensation Act 1950 purported to oust the jurisdiction of the courts to question any determination of the Commission. This aspect of the case is considered *post* at p. 635.

2. Since *Anisminic*, there has been considerable dispute as to whether all errors of law take a public authority outside its jurisdiction. In *Re Racal Communications Ltd* [1981] AC 374 Lord Diplock stated, at p. 383:

> The break-through made by *Anisminic* [1969] 2 AC 147 was that, as respects administrative tribunals and authorities, the old distinction between errors of law that went to jurisdiction and errors of law that did not, was for practical purposes abolished. Any error of law that could be shown to have been made by them in the course of reaching their decision on matters of fact or of administrative policy would result in their having asked themselves the wrong question with the result that the decision they reached would be a nullity. . . .
>
> But there is no similar presumption that where a decision-making power is conferred by statute upon a court of law, Parliament did not intend to confer upon it power to decide questions of law as well as questions of fact. Whether it did or did not and, in the case of inferior courts, what limits are imposed on the kinds of questions of law they are empowered to decide, depends upon the construction of the statute unencumbered by any such presumption. In the case of inferior courts where the decision of the court is made final and conclusive by the statute, this may involve the survival of those subtle distinctions formerly drawn between errors of law which go to jurisdiction and errors of law which do not that did so much to confuse English administrative law before *Anisminic* [1969] 2 AC 147; but upon any application for judicial review of a decision of an inferior court in a matter which involves, as so many do, interrelated questions of law, fact and degree the superior court conducting the review should not be astute to hold that Parliament did not intend the inferior court to have jurisdiction to decide for itself the meaning of the ordinary words used in the statute to define the question which it has to decide.

In *O'Reilly* v *Mackman* [1983] 2 AC 237, at p. 278, Lord Diplock referred to the *Anisminic* case as liberating English public law 'from the fetters that the courts had theretofore imposed upon themselves so far as determinations of inferior courts and statutory tribunals were concerned by drawing esoteric distinctions between errors of law committed by such tribunals that went to their jurisdiction, and errors of law committed by them within their jurisdiction'.

There is division of opinion on the point as to whether inferior courts, but not administrative tribunals, may be immune from judicial review for errors of law within jurisdiction. In *R* v *Lord President of the Privy Council, ex parte Page* [1993] AC 682 (a case concerning the jurisdiction of a university visitor), the majority of Lords Keith, Griffiths and Brown-Wilkinson affirmed Lord Diplock's dicta in *Re Racal Communications* on inferior courts.

Question

What light is thrown on judicial thinking on the boundaries and basis of judicial review by:

(a) the erosion of the difference between jurisdictional errors and errors of law within jurisdiction; and

(b) the exception to this for inferior courts and visitors but not administrative tribunals, even those staffed by lawyers?

Wheeler v *Leicester City Council*
[1985] AC 1054
House of Lords

Leicester Football Club had a licence to use a recreation ground administered by the local council. Under s. 10 of the Open Spaces Act the council held and administered the recreation ground in trust to allow, and with a view to, its enjoyment by the public as an open space. Section 76 of the Public Health (Amendment) Act 1907 gave the council power to set apart pitches for the purpose of playing football. Section 56 of the Public Health Act 1925 gave the council power to permit the exclusive use by any club of such a pitch, subject to such charges and conditions as the local authority thought fit.

In April 1984 three members of the club were invited to join the English rugby football team selected to tour South Africa. The council supported a Commonwealth Agreement to withhold support for and discourage sporting links with South Africa. It put four questions to the club and indicated that only an affirmative answer to each of them would be acceptable:

(a) Does the Leicester Football Club support the Government opposition to the tour?

(b) Does the Leicester Football Club agree that the tour is an insult to a large proportion of the Leicester population?

(c) Will the Leicester Football Club press the Rugby Football Union to call off the tour?

(d) Will the Leicester Football Club press the players to pull out of the tour?

The club stated that, while it agreed with the council in condemning apartheid in South Africa, it was not unlawful for members to participate in the tour, nor was it contrary to the rules of the Rugby Football Union or the club. The club's role was purely advisory and it had asked the members to consider the memorandum to the Rugby Football Union prepared by the anti-apartheid movement. The three members subsequently took part in the tour. In August 1984 the council passed a resolution banning the club and its members from using the recreation ground for 12 months. The club applied for an order of *certiorari* to quash the decision. The judge refused the application and his decision was upheld by the Court of Appeal.

ACKNER LJ: . . . [Counsel], for the council, has submitted, and I entirely accept, that in exercising their discretion the council are entitled to take into account the effect that such an exercise would have on the performance of their other statutory functions. He gave us instances where the use of the pitch might potentially contravene the council's policies under the Town and Country Planning Acts, or interfere with their obligations under the Housing Acts, or contravene the Public Health Acts. In all such cases obviously the council, in considering how to exercise its discretion in relation to the recreation ground, would be entitled to and indeed be under a duty to have regard to their other statutory functions and duties.

The statutory function which [counsel] submits the council were fully entitled to take into account in exercising their discretionary powers in relation to this recreation ground, is to be found in section 71 of the Race Relations Act 1976. . . . The relevant words of the section read as follows:

> . . . it shall be the duty of every local authority to make appropriate arrangements with a view to securing that their various functions are carried out with due regard to the need . . . (b) to promote . . . good relations, between different persons of different racial groups.

[Counsel] for the club accepts that a local authority are, vis-à-vis race relations, in a very special position. It is the local authority that provides many of the social services, they are a substantial employer of labour and are thus capable of setting an example in regard to race relations conduct and policies which is likely to be followed. Notwithstanding this concession, [counsel] submits that this section is what he describes as an 'inward-looking' section, directed to requiring that the local authority themselves maintain the standards laid down by the Act, that is to say their codes of practice in regard to their own internal behaviour so as to comply with the requirements of the Act. It is a section whose function is limited to ensuring that the local authority put their own house in order.

I consider this to be too narrow a construction. To my mind the section is imposing an obligation on the local authority, when they consider discharging any of their functions which might have a race relations content, to do so in such a manner as would tend to promote good relations between persons of different racial groups. Accordingly, in my judgment, the council were fully entitled when exercising their discretionary powers in relation to this recreation ground to have regard to the purposes expressed in section 71. . . .

If I am right so far, this leaves only one final question to consider. Can it be said in the circumstances of this case that no reasonable local authority could properly conclude that temporarily banning from the use of their recreational ground an important local rugger club, which declined to condemn a South African tour and declined actively to discourage its members from participating therein, could promote good relations between persons of different racial groups? (see the well-known Wednesbury test: *Associated Provincial Picture Houses Ltd* v *Wednesbury Corp* [1948] 1 KB 223).

Ackner LJ decided that the answer to this question was no (for reasons which are outlined *post* at p. 580.). Sir George Waller also dismissed the club's appeal, but Browne-Wilkinson LJ dissented. The club then appealed to the House of Lords.

LORD TEMPLEMAN: . . . My Lords, the laws of this country are not like the laws of Nazi Germany. A private individual or a private organisation cannot be obliged to display zeal in the pursuit of an object sought by a public authority and cannot be obliged to publish views dictated by a public authority.

The club having committed no wrong, the council could not use their statutory powers in the management of their property or any other statutory powers in order to punish the club. There is no doubt that the council intended to punish and have punished the club. When the club were presented by the council with four questions it was made clear that the club's response would only be acceptable if, in effect, all four questions were answered in the affirmative. When the club committee made their dignified and responsible response to these questions, a response which the council find unsatisfactory to the council, the council commissioned a report on possible sanctions that might be taken against the club. That report suggested that delaying tactics could be used to hold up the grant of a lease then being negotiated by the club. It suggested that land could be excluded from the lease as it was 'thought that this could embarrass the club because it had apparently granted sub-leases . . .' It was suggested that the council's consent, which had already been given for advertisements by the club's sponsors, could be withdrawn although according to the report 'the actual effect of this measure on the club is difficult to assess.' It was suggested that 'a further course is to insist upon strict observance of the tenant's covenants in the lease. However, the city estate's surveyor, having inspected the premises, is of the opinion that the tenant's covenants are all being complied with.' Finally, it was suggested that 'the council could terminate the club's use of the recreation ground.' This might cause some financial loss to the council and might 'form the basis of a legal challenge to the council's decision. The club may contend that the council has taken an unreasonable action against the club in response to personal decisions of members of its team over which it had no control.' Notwithstanding this warning, the council accepted the last suggestion and terminated the club's use of the recreation ground. In my opinion, this use by the council of its statutory powers was a misuse of power. The council could not properly seek to use its statutory powers of management or any other statutory powers for the purposes of punishing the club when the club had done no wrong.

In *Congreve* v *Home Office* [1976] 1 QB 629 the Home Secretary had a statutory power to revoke television licences. In exercise of that statutory power he revoked the television licences of individuals who had lawfully surrendered an existing licence and taken out a new licence before an increase in the licence fee was due to take effect. Lord Denning MR said at p. 651:

> If the licence is to be revoked – and his money forfeited – the Minister would have to give good reasons to justify it. Of course, if the licensee had done anything wrong – if he had given a cheque for £12 which was dishonoured, or if he had broken the conditions of the licence – the Minister could revoke it. But when the licensee has done nothing wrong at all, I do not think the Minister can lawfully revoke the licence, at any rate, not without offering him his money back, and not even then except for good cause. If he should revoke it without giving reasons, or for no good reason, the courts can set aside the revocation and restore the licence. It would be a misuse of the power conferred on him by Parliament: and these courts have the authority – and I would add the duty – to correct a misuse of power by a Minister or his department, no matter how much he may resent it or warn us of the consequences if we do.

Similar considerations apply, in my opinion, to the present case. Of course this does not mean that the council is bound to allow its property to be used by a racist organisation or by any organisation which, by its actions or its words, infringes the letter or the spirit of the Race Relations Act 1976. But the attitude of the club and of the committee of the club was a perfectly proper attitude, caught as they were in a political controversy which was not of their making.

For these reasons and the reasons given by my noble and learned friend Lord Roskill I would allow this appeal.

Lord Roskill decided that the council had made a decision which was so unreasonable that no reasonable authority could have come to it (on this aspect of the case see post p. 578). The other Law Lords agreed with both Lord Templeman and Lord Roskill.

Questions

1. On which ground(s) for judicial review did each of the judges base his decision ?

2. How did (a) Ackner LJ and (b) Lord Templeman decide which purposes the council was/was not entitled to pursue ? Did they find assistance in the statutes under which the council managed the recreation ground or in the Race Relations Act 1976 ? What other matters did they refer to in determining this issue?

3. How did they decide which purposes the club had pursued ?

4. Would it have made any difference to the decision of Lord Templeman if the club had espoused racist views in its reply to the council's request ?

5. Does this case provide support for Allan's view that in judicial review proceedings the judges are furthering the political sovereignty of the people by giving effect to common standards of morality or the natural expectations of citizens?

Note

Lord Templeman based his decision on the ground that the council had acted for an improper purpose. Difficulties may arise when an authority acts for more than one purpose, some of which are lawful and others unlawful. The courts have not always been consistent in deciding how to deal with this conflict. Consider the approach adopted in the following extract.

R* v *ILEA ex parte Westminster City Council
[1986] 1 WLR 28
High Court

The Inner London Education Authority (ILEA) determined the rates for education spending precepted on rating authorities in Inner London, including Westminster City Council. ILEA was opposed to the Government's policies, announced in 1983, of limiting the amount of rates levied by local authorities, a process known as rate-capping. By s. 142(2) of the Local Government Act 1972 ILEA was empowered to incur expenditure on arranging for the publication within their area of information on matters relating to local government. In July 1983 an education sub-committee of ILEA agreed to retain an advertising agency, referred to in the extract below as AMV, at a cost of £651,000, to mount a media and poster campaign to 'gain awareness of the authority's views of the needs of the education service and to alter the basis of the public debate about the effect of . . . Government actions.' Westminster City Council sought a declaration that the decision of the sub-committee was *ultra vires* because ILEA sought to persuade the public to support ILEA's views on rate-capping. ILEA accepted that the decision was made with the dual purpose of informing and persuading.

GLIDEWELL LJ: . . .

Two purposes

This brings me to what I regard as being the most difficult point in the case, namely, if a local authority resolves to expend its ratepayers' money in order to achieve two purposes, one of which it is authorised to achieve by statute but for the other of which it has no authority, is that decision invalid?

I was referred to the following authorities.

(i) *Westminster Corp* v *London and North Western Rly Co* [1905] AC 426. Westminster City Council had power to provide public lavatories under the Public Health (London) Act 1891, section 44. They constructed public lavatories underground, under the centre of the south end of Whitehall. The lavatories were approached from each side of the street by a subway, which could also be used as a pedestrian subway for people who wished to cross the street and not to use the lavatories. The London and North Western Railway Co., who owned the land at the east end of the subway, challenged the construction of the lavatories and subway, alleging that the main purpose of the Corporation was to construct a pedestrian subway which did not fall within the power of the Act. The Court of Appeal found for the railway company. By a majority, the House of Lords allowed the appeal, but did so on the facts, i.e., by holding that the Court of Appeal had drawn a wrong inference from the affidavits and documents before the court. In his speech, the Earl of Halsbury LC said at p. 428:

> I quite agree that if the power to make one kind of building was fraudulently used for the purpose of making another kind of building, the power given by the legislature for one purpose could not be used for another.

Lord Macnagthen said at p. 433:

> I entirely agree with Joyce J at first instance that the primary object of the council was the construction of the conveniences with the requisite and proper means of approach thereto and exit therefrom.

This suggests that a test for answering the question is, if the authorised purpose is the primary purpose, the resolution is within the power.

(ii) . . . . [is omitted]

(iii) More recently in *Hanks* v *Minister of Housing and Local Government* [1963] 1 QB 999, Megaw J did have to deal with a case in which it was alleged that a compulsory purchase order had been made for two purposes, one of which did not fall within the empowering Act. . . . [He stated] at [1963] 1 QB 999 at 1020–1021:

> I confess that I think confusion can arise from the multiplicity of words which have been used in this case as suggested criteria for the testing of the validity of the exercise of a statutory power. The words have included 'objects', 'purposes', 'motives', 'motivation', 'reasons', 'grounds' and 'considerations'. In the end, it seems to me, the simplest and clearest way to state the matter is by reference to 'considerations'. A 'consideration', I apprehend, is something which one takes into account as a factor in arriving at a decision. I am prepared to assume, for the

> purposes of the case, that, if it be shown that an authority exercising a power has taken into account as a relevant factor something which it could not properly take into account in deciding whether or not to exercise the power, then the exercise of the power, normally at least, is bad. Similarly, if the authority fails to take into account as a relevant factor something which is relevant, and which is or ought to be known to it, and which it ought to have taken into account, the exercise of that power is normally bad. I say 'normally', because I can conceive that there may be cases where the factor wrongly taken into account, or omitted, is insignificant, or where the wrong taking-into-account, or omission, actually operated in favour of the person who later claims to be aggrieved by the decision.

. . . I have considered also the views of the learned authors of the textbooks on this. Professor Wade in his book *Administrative Law* 5th edn (1982) under the heading Duality of Purpose says at p. 388:

> Sometimes an act may serve two or more purposes, some authorised and some not, and it may be a question whether the public authority may kill two birds with one stone. The general rule is that its action will be unlawful provided the permitted purpose is the true and dominant purpose behind the act, even though some secondary or incidental advantage may be gained for some purpose which is outside the authority's powers.

Professor Evans, in *de Smith's Judicial Review of Administrative Action* 4th edn (1980) p. 329, comforts me by describing the general problem of plurality of purpose as 'a legal porcupine which bristles with difficulties as soon as it is touched.' He distils from the decisions of the courts five different tests on which reliance has been placed at one time or another, including, at pp. 330–332:

> (1) What was the *true purpose* for which the power was exercised? If the actor has in truth used his power for the purposes for which it was conferred, it is immaterial that he was thus enabled to achieve a subsidiary object . . . (5) Was any of the purposes pursued an unauthorised purpose? If so, and if the unauthorised purpose has materially influenced the actor's conduct, the power has been invalidly exercised because irrelevant considerations have been taken into account.

These two tests, and Professor Evans's comment on them, seem to me to achieve much the same result and to be similar to that put forward by Megaw J in *Hanks* v *Minister of Housing and Local Government* [1963] 1 QB 999 in the first paragraph of the passage I have quoted from his judgment. That is the part that includes the sentence: 'In the end, it seems to me, the simplest and clearest way to state the matter is by reference to considerations.' I gratefully adopt the guidance of Megaw J and the two tests I have referred to from *de Smith's Judicial Review of Administrative Action*.

It thus becomes a question of fact for me to decide, on the material before me, whether, in reaching its decision of 23 July 1984, the staff and general sub-committee of ILEA was pursuing an unauthorised purpose, namely that of persuasion, which has materially influenced the making of its decision. I have already said that I find that one of the sub-committee's purposes was the giving of information. But I also find that it had the purpose of seeking to persuade members of the public to a view identical with that of the authority itself, and indeed I believe that this was a, if not the, major purpose of the decision. In reaching this decision of fact, I have taken into account in particular the material to which I have referred above in AMV's 'presentation' of 18 July 1984, the passages I have quoted from the report of the Education Officer to the sub-committee, particularly the reference to changing 'the basis of public debate', and the various documents which have been published by AMV since 23 July with the approval of ILEA. I accept that some of the documents do inform, but in my view some of them contain little or no information and are designed only to persuade. This is true in particular, in my view, of the poster slogan 'Education Cuts Never Heal' (skilful though I think it is) and it is also true of the advertisement 'What do you get if you subtract £75 million from London's education budget?'

Adopting the test referred to above, I thus hold that ILEA's sub-committee did, when making its decision of 23 July 1984, take into account an irrelevant consideration, and thus that decision was not validly reached.

Questions

1. On which of the grounds for judicial review did the court base its decision?

2. Glidewell LJ quoted part of a passage from de Smith. Do you agree with his comment that the two tests set out in this passage achieve much the same result? On the facts of *Westminster Corporation* v *London and North Western Railway Co* [1905] AC 426, might it have been possible to say that, although the construction of a subway was not a primary object, the desire to provide such a subway was a material influence on the council's decision?

Note

In *R* v *Greenwich London Borough Council, ex parte Lovelace* [1991] 3 All ER 511, Staughton LJ in the Court of Appeal stated that, in cases of 'mixed motives', the question was whether the improper motive had exercised a 'substantial influence' on the decision.

Although *R* v *ILEA, ex parte Westminster City Council* was argued on the basis that the authority had acted for an improper purpose, Glidewell LJ stated that he felt the case was best approached on the basis of whether the authority had been materially influenced by an irrelevant consideration. This ground for judicial review is dealt with in more detail in the following extract.

Padfield v *Minister for Agriculture, Fisheries and Food*
[1968] AC 997
House of Lords

The Agricultural Marketing Act 1958 regulated the marketing of various agricultural products, including milk. Section 19(3) provided: 'A committee of investigation shall . . . (b) be charged with the duty, if the Minister in any case so directs, of considering and reporting to the Minister . . . any complaint made to the Minister as to the operation of any scheme which, in the opinion of the Minister, could not be considered by a consumers' committee . . .'. The south-eastern dairy farmers complained to the Minister about the operation of a scheme involving the fixing of price differentials by the Milk Marketing Board, but the Minister refused to refer the complaint to a committee of investigation. They accordingly applied for an order of mandamus.

The Divisional Court made an order against the Minister which was set aside by the Court of Appeal.

LORD REID: . . . The question at issue in this appeal is the nature and extent of the Minister's duty under section 19(3)(b) of the Act of 1958 in deciding whether to refer to the committee of investigation a complaint as to the operation of any scheme made by persons adversely affected by the scheme. The respondent contends that his only duty is to consider a complaint fairly and that he is given an unfettered discretion with regard to every complaint either to refer it or not to refer it to the committee as he may think fit. The appellants contend that it is his duty to refer every genuine and substantial complaint, or alternatively that his discretion is not unfettered and that in this case he failed to exercise his discretion according to law because his refusal was caused or influenced by his having misdirected himself in law or by his having taken into account extraneous or irrelevant considerations.

In my view, the appellants' first contention goes too far. There are a number of reasons which would justify the Minister in refusing to refer a complaint. For example, he might consider it more suitable for arbitration, or he might consider that in an earlier case the committee of investigation had already rejected a substantially similar complaint or he might think the complaint to be frivolous or vexatious. So he must have at least some measure of discretion. But is it unfettered?

It is implicit in the argument for the Minister that there are only two possible interpretations of this provision - either he must refer every complaint or he has an unfettered discretion to refuse to refer in any case. I do not think that is right. Parliament must have conferred the discretion with the intention that it should be used to promote the policy and objects of the Act; the policy and objects of the Act must be determined by construing the Act as a whole and construction is always a matter of law for the court. In a matter of this kind it is not possible to draw a hard and fast line, but if the Minister, by reason of his having misconstrued the Act or for any other reason, so uses his discretion so as to thwart or run counter to the policy and objects of the Act, then our law would be very defective if persons aggrieved were not entitled to the protection of the court. So it is first necessary to construe the Act. . . .

The approval of Parliament shows that this scheme was thought to be in the public interest, and in so far as it necessarily involved detriment to some persons, it must have been thought to be in the public interest that they should suffer it. But in sections 19 and 20 Parliament drew a line. They provide machinery for investigating and determining whether the scheme is operating or the board is acting in a manner contrary to the public interest.

The effect of these sections is that if, but only if, the Minister and the committee of investigation concur in the view that something is being done contrary to the public interest the Minister can step in. Section 20 enables the Minister to take the initiative. Section 19 deals with complaints by individuals who are aggrieved. I need not deal with the provisions which apply to consumers. We are concerned with other persons who may be distributors or producers. If the Minister directs that a complaint by any of them shall be referred to the committee of investigation, that committee will make a report which must be published. If they report that any provision of this scheme or any act or omission of the Board is contrary to interests of the complainers *and* is not in the public interest, then the Minister is empowered to take action but not otherwise. He may disagree with the view of the committee as to public interest, and, if he thinks that there are other public interests which outweigh the public interest that justice should be done to the complainers, he would be not only entitled but bound to refuse to take action. Whether he takes action or not, he may be criticised and held accountable in Parliament but the court cannot interfere.

I must now examine the Minister's reasons for refusing to refer the appellant's complaint to the committee. I have already set out the letters of March 23 and May 3, 1965. I think it is right also to refer to a letter sent from the Ministry on May 1 1964, because in his affidavit the Minister says he has read this letter and there is no indication that he disagrees with any part of it.

[Lord Reid read the letter and continued.] The first reason which the Minister gave in his letter of March 23, 1965, was that this complaint was unsuitable for investigation because it raised wide issues. Here it appears to me that the Minister has clearly misdirected himself. Section 19(6) contemplates the raising of issues so wide that it may be necessary for the Minister to amend a scheme or even to revoke it. Narrower issues may be suitable for arbitration but section 19 affords the only method of investigating wide issues. In my view it is plainly the intention of the Act that even the widest issues should be investigated if the complaint is genuine and substantial, as this complaint certainly is.

Then it is said that the issue should be 'resolved through the arrangements available to producers and the board within the framework of the scheme itself.' This re-states in a condensed form the reasons given in paragraph 4 of the letter of May 1, 1964, where it is said ' the Minister owes no duty to producers in any particular region,' and reference is made to the 'status of the Milk Marketing Scheme as an instrument for the self-government of the industry,' and to the Minister 'assuming an inappropriate degree of responsibility.' But as I have already pointed out, the Act imposes on the Minister a responsibility whenever there is a relevant and substantial complaint that the board are acting in a manner inconsistent with the public interest, and that has been relevantly alleged in this case. I can find nothing in the Act to limit this responsibility or to justify the statement that the Minister owes no duty to producers in a particular region. The Minister is, I think, correct in saying that the board is an instrument of the self-government of the industry. So long as it does not act contrary to the public interest the Minister cannot interefere. But if it does act contrary to what both the committee of investigation and the Minister hold to be the public interest the Minister has a duty to act. And if a complaint relevantly alleges that the board has so acted, as this complaint does, then it appears to me that the Act does impose a duty on the Minister to have it investigated. If he does not do that he is rendering nugatory a safeguard provided by the Act and depriving complainers of a remedy which I am satisfied that Parliament intended them to have. . . .

The House of Lord by a majority allowed the appeal and granted an order of mandamus (Lord Morris of Borth-y-Gest dissenting).

Note

The aftermath of this case provides a good illustration of the point that success in a judicial review application does not require that the authority whose actions have been challenged must reach a decision which is favourable to the applicant. After this case the Minister submitted a complaint for investigation to the investigative committee. The Minister then rejected the committee's advice. Commenting on this Carol Harlow stated that 'The remedy had proved illusory; the same decision could be reached with only nominal deference to the court, and the waste of time and money entailed is a deterrent to future complainants' (C. Harlow, 'Administrative Reaction to Judicial Review' [1976] *Public Law* 116). Do you agree?

Questions

1. How did the House of Lords decide which considerations were relevant and which were irrelevant?

2. How did the House of Lords decide which considerations had been taken into account?

3. Are there any circumstances in which the taking into account of an irrelevant consideration will not render the decision unlawful. Does *R* v *Inner London Education Authority* (*ante,* p. 544) suggest an answer? (See also *R* v *BBC ex parte Owen* [1985] 2 All ER 522.)

Note

It will be clear that the court is required to address some difficult issues in deciding upon the legality of an authority's decisions. For example, how do the courts decide what considerations were taken into account? How do they decide whether an irrelevant consideration has had only an insignificant or insubstantial influence on a decision?

Two points in particular should be noted. First, the burden of proof in an application for judicial review generally falls on the applicant. Hence, for example, the onus was on the complainants in *Padfield* to prove that irrelevant consideration(s) were taken into account.

Secondly, there is no general requirement that the authority should give reasons for its decision. In the course of argument in *Padfield* it was submitted that the Minister may properly refuse to act on a complaint without giving any reasons, and that in such a case a complainant would have no remedy and the decision could not be questioned. Lord Pearce stated at pp. 1053–4:

> I do not regard a Minister's failure or refusal to give any reasons as a sufficient exclusion of the court's surveillance. If all the prima facie reasons seem to point in favour of his taking a certain course to carry out the intention of Parliament in respect of a power which it has been given to him in that regard, and he gives no reason whatever for taking a contrary course, the court may infer that he has no good reason and that he is not using the power given by Parliament to carry out its intentions. In the present case, however, the Minister has given reasons which show that he was not exercising his discretion in accordance with the intentions of the Act.

(See also the comments of Lord Reid, at pp. 1032(G)–1033(A) and Lord Upjohn, at pp. 1061(G)–62(A).)

After citing this passage in the recent case of *Lonrho plc* v *Secretary of State* [1989] 2 All ER 609, at p. 620, Lord Keith, with whom the other Law Lords agreed, stated:

> The absence of reasons for a decision where there is no duty to give them cannot of itself provide any support for the suggested irrationality of the decision. The only significance of the absence of reasons is that if all other known facts and circumstances appear to point overwhelmingly in favour of

a different decision, the decision-maker who has given no reasons cannot complain if the court draws the inference that he had no rational reason for his decision.

To what extent does this statement differ from that of Lord Pearce in *Padfield*?

While there is no general duty to provide reasons authorities are sometimes obliged by statute to provide them (see, in particular, s. 10 of the Tribunal and Inquiries Act 1992, *post* at p. 710). It has also been recently accepted that natural justice could, in exceptional cases, require the provision of reasons (see *R* v *Civil Service Appeal Board, ex parte Cunningham* [1991] 4 All ER 310, discussed at [1991] *Public Law*, pp. 340–46). In *Doody* v *Secretary of State for the Home Department* [1993] 3 All ER 92 the House of Lords held that the Secretary of State was obliged to give reasons to prisoners when he proposed to depart from the periods recommended by the judiciary for the purposes of retribution and deterrence. Yet in *R* v *Higher Education Funding Council, ex parte Institute of Dental Surgery* [1994] 1 All ER 651, although the council's reasons for refusing to give reasons for its decision to lower the institute's research rating were not well grounded, this was not a case in which the law might require reasons. Examples of situations in which reasons might be required include (a) personal liberty, and (b) where a decision appears aberrant. (See Craig (1994) 53 *CLJ* 282).

British Oxygen Co. Ltd v Minister of Technology
[1971] AC 610
House of Lords

British Oxygen Co. Ltd used metal cylinders to store pressurised gases which it manufactured. It applied for a grant in respect of the cylinders under s. 1(1) of the Industrial Development Act 1966, which provided that the Board of Trade 'may make to any person carrying on a business in Great Britain a grant towards approved capital expenditure incurred by that person in providing new machinery or plant.' The Board had a policy of denying grants for any item of plant costing less than £25 and, in pursuance of that policy, rejected British Oxygen's application as the gas cylinders cost just under £20 each. British Oxygen sought declarations that (inter alia) the cylinders were eligible for grant.

LORD REID: Section 1 of the Act provides that the Board of Trade 'may' make grants. It was not argued that 'may' in this context means 'shall', and it seems to me clear the the Board were intended to have a discretion. But how were the Board intended to operate that discretion? Does the Act read as a whole indicate any policy which the Board is to follow or even give any guidance to the Board? If it does then the Board must exercise its discretion in accordance with such policy or guidance (*Padfield* v *Minister of Agriculture, Fisheries and Food* [1986] AC 997). One generally expects to find that Parliament has given some indication as to how public money is to be distributed. In this Act Parliament has clearly laid down the conditions for eligibility for grants and it has clearly given to the Board a discretion so that the Board is not bound to pay to every person who is eligible to receive such a grant. But I can find nothing to guide the Board as to the circumstances in which they should pay or the circumstances in which they should not pay grants to such persons. . . .

There are two general grounds on which the exercise of an unqualified discretion can be attacked. It must not be exercised in bad faith, and it must not be so unreasonably exercised as to show that there cannot have been any real or genuine exercise of the discretion. But, apart from that, if the Minister thinks that policy or good administration requires the operation of some limiting rule, I find nothing to stop him.

It was argued on the authority of *Rex* v *Port of London Authority ex parte Kynoch* [1919] 1 KB 176 that the Minister is not entitled to make a rule for himself as to how he will in future exercise his discretion. In that case Kynoch owned land adjoining the Thames and wished to construct a deep water wharf. For this they had to get the permission of the authority. Permission was refused on the ground that Parliament had charged the authority with the duty of providing such facilities. It appeared that before reaching their decision the authority had fully considered the case on its merits and in relation to the public interest. So their decision was upheld.

Bankes LJ said at p. 184:

> There are on the one hand cases where a tribunal in the honest exercise of its discretion has adopted a policy, and, without refusing to hear an applicant, intimates to him what its policy is, and that after hearing him it will in accordance with its policy decide against him, unless there is something exceptional in his case. I think counsel for the applicants would admit that, if the policy has been adopted for reasons which the tribunal may legitimately entertain, no objection could be taken to such a course. On the other hand there are cases where a tribunal has passed a rule, or come to a determination, not to hear any application of a particular character by whomsoever made. There is a wide distinction to be drawn between these two classes.

I see nothing wrong with that. But the circumstances in which discretions are exercised vary enormously and that passage cannot be applied literally in every case. The general rule is that anyone who has to exercise a statutory discretion must not 'shut his ears to an application'(to adapt from Bankes LJ on p. 183). I do not think there is any great difference between a policy and a rule. There may be cases where an officer or authority ought to listen to a substantial argument reasonably presented urging a change of policy. What the authority must not do is to refuse to listen at all. But a ministry or large authority may have had to deal already with a multitude of similar applications and then they will almost certainly have evolved a policy so precise that it could well be called a rule. There can be no objection to that, provided the authority is always willing to listen to anyone with something new to say – of course I do not mean to say that there need be an oral hearing. In the present case the respondent's officers have carefully considered all that the appellants have had to say and I have no doubt that they will continue to do so . . . .

VISCOUNT DILHORNE: [T]he distinction between a policy decision and a rule may not be easy to draw. In this case it was not challenged that it was within the power of the Board to adopt a policy not to make a grant in respect of such an item. The policy might equally well be described as a rule. It was both reasonable and right that the Board should make known to those interested the policy it was going to follow. By doing so fruitless applications involving expense and expenditure of time might be avoided. The Board says that it has not refused to consider any application. It considered the appellants'. In these circumstances it is not necessary to decide in this case whether, if it had refused to consider an application on the ground that it related to an item costing less than £25, it would have acted wrongly.

I must confess that I feel some doubt whether the words used by Bankes LJ in the passage cited above [see p. 413 *supra*] are really applicable to a case of this kind. It seems somewhat pointless and a waste of time that the Board should have to consider applications which are bound as a result of its policy decision to fail. Representations could of course be made that the policy should be changed . . .

Lord Morris of Borth-y-gest, Lord Wilberforce and Lord Diplock agreed with Lord Reid.

Questions

1. On which ground(s) was the decision of the House of Lords based?

2. Under the Children Act 1989 local authorities have a duty to safeguard and promote the welfare of children within their area who are in need 'by providing a range and level of services appropriate to those children's needs' (s. 17). The services may include giving assistance in kind or, in exceptional circumstances, in cash. Assume that a local authority has made certain policies to govern the provision of such assistance. An applicant for assistance in cash is told that her application will be refused under the general policies operated by the council (of which she is aware) unless she wishes to make representations that the policies should be altered and the authority is prepared to accept the representations. Would the applicant be able to challenge this decision? (See *Attorney-General ex relator Tilley* v *Wandsworth LBC* [1981] 1 WLR 854.)

Note

The application of a policy may result in breaches of the duty to be fair (see *post*, p. 558). For example, in *R* v *Secretary of State for the Environment, ex parte Brent LBC* [1982] QB 593 the Secretary of State failed to consider any of the representations made to him to change his policy on reducing the rate support grant to certain authorities. The Divisional Court held that he had both unlawfully fettered his discretion and failed to discharge the duty of fairness.

(ii) Procedural impropriety

In *CCSU* v *Minister for the Civil Service* (*ante*, p. 534) Lord Diplock used this phrase specifically to include both a breach of express statutory procedural requirements and the common law rules of natural justice. Express statutory requirements include, for example, a requirement to give notice or to consult certain persons before a decision is made. Whether or not a breach of a statutory requirement will render the resulting decision invalid depends on a number of circumstances, including the importance of the provision which has been disregarded in the light of the objects of the statute, whether there was total or only partial breach of the requirement, and whether or not the breach caused any prejudice (see, for example, *Coney* v *Choyce* [1975] 1 All

ER 979: *Bradbury* v *London Borough of Enfield* [1967] 3 All ER 434: *London and Clydeside Estates Ltd* v *Aberdeen DC* [1979] 2 All ER 876). This section will focus on the common law rules of natural justice.

Council of Civil Service Unions v *Minister for the Civil Service*
[1985] AC 374
House of Lords

The facts are set out *post,* at p. 572.

LORD ROSKILL: . . . the use of this phrase [natural justice] is no doubt hallowed by time and much judicial repetition, but it is a phrase often widely misunderstood and therefore as often misused. The phrase perhaps might now be allowed to find a permanent resting place and be better replaced by speaking of a duty to act fairly. But the latter phrase must not in its turn be misunderstood or misused. It is not for the courts to determine whether a particular policy or particular decisions taken in fulfilment of that policy are fair. They are only concerned with the manner in which those decision have been taken and the extent of the duty to act fairly will vary greatly from case to case as indeed the decided cases since 1950 consistently show. Many features will come into play including the nature of the decision and the relationship of those involved on either side before the decision was taken.

Note

The use of the phrase 'duty to act fairly' rather than 'natural justice' is frequently traced to the decision in *Re HK* [1967] 2 QB 617 where it was held that, although immigration officers were not obliged to hold a hearing before determining an immigrant's status, they were obliged to act fairly. Since then there has been a difference of opinion on the correct use of the two phrases. In *McInnes* v *Onslow Fane* [1978] 1 WLR 1520 Megarry V-C stated that 'the further the situation is away from anything that resembles a judicial or quasi-judicial decision, and the further the question is removed from what may reasonably be called a justiciable question, the more appropriate it is to reject an expression which includes the word justice and to use instead terms such as "fairness" or "the duty to act fairly".' Other judges have used the phrases interchangeably. What did Lord Roskill state on this point and why?

A related difficulty is whether there is any difference between the content of natural justice and the content of the duty to be fair. On one view, which appears to be that of both Lord Roskill and Megarry V-C, there is no difference: the content of natural justice and the content of the duty to be fair are both flexible and depend on all the circumstances of the case. Another view, however, is that the duty to be fair might include requirements which were not part of the traditional concept of natural justice, for example a duty to act on evidence (see *R* v *Deputy Industrial Injuries Commissioner ex parte Moore* [1965] 1 QB 456).

In the notes and questions which follow, reference will be made to the duty to be fair. The cases cited will, however, contain references to both concepts for the reasons explained above.

What then is required of the duty to be fair? As Lord Fraser indicated in *CCSU* v *Minister for the Civil Service*, the requirements of fairness depend on all the circumstances of the case. In an earlier case, *Russell* v *Duke of Norfolk* [1949] 1 All ER 109, in which the term natural justice was used, Tucker LJ stated, at p. 118:

> . . . There are, in my view, no words which are of universal application to every kind of inquiry and every kind of domestic tribunal. The requirements of natural justice must depend on the circumstances of the case, the nature of the inquiry, the rules under which the tribunal is acting, the subject matter which is being dealt with and so forth. Accordingly, I do not derive much assistance from the definitions of natural justice which have been from time to time used . . .

The requirements of the duty to be fair are generally divided into two general principles, the rule against bias and the right to a fair hearing.

(1) The rule against bias

A distinction is normally drawn between direct pecuniary interests and other interests. Where a decision-maker has a direct pecuniary interest in the outcome of a decision, he ought not to partake in it. In respect of all other interests (e.g. family relationship), the courts have formulated a test for bias. There has been disagreement as to the precise nature of the test which has now been resolved.

R* v *Gough
[1993] AC 646
House of Lords

Following conviction and sentence of the appellant at trial, a member of the jury realised that she lived next door to the brother of the appellant. On appeal against conviction the Court of Appeal rejected the contention that there had been a serious irregularity at the trial. The test for this is whether there was a real danger that the appellant might not have had a fair trial. On appeal to the House of Lords.

LORD GOFF of CHIEVELY: . . . The argument before the Appellate Committee was presented on the basis that there were two rival, alternative tests for bias to be found in the authorities, and that the result in the present case depended on the choice made by your Lordships' House between them. The first test, favoured by Mr Hytner for the appellant, was whether a reasonable and fair minded person sitting in the court and knowing all the relevant facts would have had a reasonable suspicion that a fair trial by the defendant was not possible. The second test, favoured by Mr Leveson for the Crown, was whether there was a real likelihood of bias. I shall for convenience refer to these two tests respectively as the reasonable suspicion test, and the real likelihood test. It was recognised by Mr Hytner before the Appellate Committee, as before the Court of Appeal, that if the real likelihood test is to be preferred, the appeal must fail.

. . .

I wish to draw attention to the fact that there are certain cases in which it has been considered that the circumstances are such that they must inevitably shake public confidence in the integrity of the administration of justice if the decision is to be allowed to stand. Such cases attract the full force of Lord Hewart CJ's requirement that justice must not only be done but must manifestly be seen to be done. These cases arise where a person sitting in a judicial capacity has a pecuniary interest in the outcome of the proceedings. In such a case, as Blackburn J said in *Reg* v *Rand* (1886) LR 1 QB 230, 232: 'any direct pecuniary interest, however small, in the subject of inquiry, does disqualify a person from acting as a judge in the matter.' The principle is expressed in the maxim that nobody may be judge in his own cause (nemo judex in sua causa). Perhaps the most famous case in which the principle was applied is *Dimes* v *Proprietors of Grand Junction Canal* (1852) 3 HLCas 759, in which decrees affirmed by Lord Cottenham LC in favour of a canal company in which he was a substantial shareholder were set aside by this House, which then proceeded to consider the matter on its merits, and in fact itself affirmed the decrees. Lord Campbell said, at p. 793:

> No one can suppose that Lord Cottenham could be, in the remotest degree, influenced by the interest that he had in this concern; but, my Lords, it is of the last importance that the maxim that no man is to be a judge in his own cause should be held sacred.

In such a case, therefore, not only is it irrelevant that there was in fact no bias on the part of the tribunal, but there is no question of investigating, from an objective point of view, whether there was any real likelihood of bias, or any reasonable suspicion of bias, on the facts of the particular case. The nature of the interest is such that public confidence in the administration of justice requires that the decision should not stand.

I turn next to the broader question of bias on the part of a member of the relevant tribunal. Here it is necessary first to put on one side the very rare case where actual bias is shown to exist. Of course, if actual bias is proved, that is an end of the case; the person concerned must be disqualified. But it is not necessary that actual bias should be proved; and in practice the inquiry is directed to the question whether there was such a degree of possibility of bias on the part of the tribunal that the court will not allow the decision to stand.

I think it possible, and desirable, that the same test should be applicable in all cases of apparent bias, whether concerned with justices or members of other inferior tribunals, or with jurors, or with arbitrators. Likewise I consider that, in cases concerned with jurors, the same test should be applied by a judge to whose attention the possibility of bias on the part of a juror has been drawn in the course of a trial, and by the Court of Appeal when it considers such a question on appeal. Furthermore, I think it unnecessary, in formulating the appropriate test, to require that the court should look at the matter through the eyes of a reasonable man, because the court in cases such as these personifies the reasonable man; and in any event the court has first to ascertain the relevant circumstances from the available evidence, knowledge of which would not necessarily be available to an observer in court at the relevant time. Finally, for the avoidance of doubt, I prefer to state the test in terms of real danger rather than real likelihood, to ensure that the court is thinking in terms of possibility rather than probability of bias. Accordingly, having ascertained the relevant circumstances, the court should ask itself whether, having regard to those circumstances, there was a real danger of bias on the part of the relevant member of the tribunal in question, in the sense that he might unfairly regard (or have unfairly regarded) with favour, or disfavour, the case of a party to the issue under consideration by him; though, in a case concerned with bias on the part of a justices' clerk, the court should go on to consider whether the clerk has been invited to give the justices advice and, if so, whether it should infer that there was a real danger of the clerk's bias having infected the views of the justices adversely to the applicant.

It follows from what I have said that the Court of Appeal applied the correct test in the present case. On that test, it was accepted by Mr Hytner that there was no ground for disturbing the jury's verdict. I would therefore dismiss the appeal.

Their Lordships unanimously dismissed the appeal.

R v *Secretary of State for the Environment, ex parte Kirkstall Valley Campaign Ltd*

(1996) 146 NLJ 478
Divisional Court

The applicants challenged the planning permission granted by the Leeds Development Corporation (LDC). The permission related to development on a rugby ground owned by the Headingley Football Club. The chairman of the LDC owned land to which the rugby club was considering moving if it could sell its ground for a significant amount. Such a sum would be paid if the land had the benefit of planning permission for commercial development. One of the members, and one of the officers of the LDC were Vice-Presidents of the rugby club, and another one of its members acted in a professional capacity for the club.

SEDLEY J:. . . This application for judicial review raises questions of some importance about the obligation of members of a statutory corporation to abstain from participation in the corporation's proceedings when matters arise in which they have a pecuniary or personal interest . . .

Mr Hobson's governing proposition [was] that the law on apparent bias is not to be found in unitary form in the decision of the House of Lords in *R* v *Gough* [1993] 2 All ER 724 as developed in *R* v *Inner West London Coroner, ex p Dallaglio* [1994] 4 All ER 129 [*sic*, 139 is correct] [but] Mr Ryan has advanced a radical alternative: that non-judicial bodies such as an urban development corporation are governed by a different set of principles, to be found in a succession of cases beginning with the decision of Glidewell J in *R* v *Sevenoaks District Council, ex p Terry* [1985] 3 All ER 226 . . . [In] Gough . . . Lord Goff went beyond the classic formulation of Lord Hewart CJ in *R* v *Sussex Justices, ex p McCarthy* [1924] 1 KB 256 that justice should not only be done, but should manifestly and undoubtedly be seen to be done and . . . held that the single appropriate test was whether on the evidence there had been 'a real danger of bias' . . . *Ex p Terry* is not, in my judgment, a case on the disqualification through personal interest of a member of a decision-making body; nor does it support the proposition that such a ground of challenge is unavailable in local government law . . . The surrender by a decision-making body of its judgment, which would have been another way of putting the ground of challenge in *Ex p Terry*, while it can legitimately be described as a form of bias, is jurisprudentially a different thing from a disqualifying interest held by a participant in the process . . . in *Gough* the House of Lords has assimilated the test of appearance of bias to the now unitary test of a real danger of bias, in part by assimilating the hypothetical observer to the court hearing the challenge, and correspondingly by assimilating the maxim that justice must be seen to be done to the court's duty to identify any real danger of unjust bias. It is by these criteria in the context of the respondent's statutory function, and not be a prior characterisation of that function, that the facts . . . would today fall to be tested . . . The line of authority relied upon by Mr Ryan represents, in my view, a different although equally important principle: that the decision of a body, albeit composed of disinterested individuals, will be struck down if its outcome has been predetermined whether by the adoption of an inflexible policy or by the effective surrender of the body's independent judgment . . .

I hold, therefore, that the principle that a person is disqualified from participation in a decision if there is a real danger that he or she will be influenced by a pecuniary or personal interest in the outcome is of general application in public law and is not limited to judicial or quasi-judicial bodies or proceedings. How then will the principle apply to a body exercising town and country planning powers? In the case of [both] an elected body [and] an [appointed] urban development corporation, where predetermination of issues or forfeiture of judgment is alleged the court will be concerned to distinguish, within the statutory framework, legitimate prior stances or experience from illegitimate ones. But such issues will be governed by the separate line of authority on predetermination. So far as concerns apparent bias, there can be little if any difference between an elected and an appointed planning authority. In both cases . . . unless it is too remote or insignificant to matter, the interest must be declared and the member concerned must not participate in the decision . . . The *Gough* test of bias will be uniformly applied: what will differ from case to case is the significance of the interest and its degree of proximity or remoteness to the issue to be decided and whether, if it is not so insignificant or remote as to be discounted, the disqualified member has violated his disqualification by participating in the decision.

The law makes a distinction between pecuniary and other personal interests. On authority, a 'direct' pecuniary or proprietary interest, however small, is conclusively presumed to create a real danger of bias: see *Gough* . . . what should a member of a body do or refrain from doing when a conflict of interest arises? Where the issue arises in a lis inter partes . . . if either party objects to the continued participation of the person declaring an interest, the objection is ordinarily conclusive; and even in the absence of objection it may be wise in some cases for the decision-maker to stand down . . . Where, however, the body is taking a decision in which all those interested are not before it and able to waive the objection . . . then the disqualification operates without the possibility of waiver . . . The applicable principle is not a matter of form but of substance: it is that an individual with a personal, pecuniary or proprietary interest in the subject matter of the decision is disqualified from participating in it . . . Participation can manifestly be more than voting or discussion . . . Similarly it is not necessary for a disqualified member to cast a vote which is counted in order to be guilty of participation . . . It is thus distinctly possible that the mere declaration of a disqualifying interest, followed by abstention on discussion or voting, will not be enough to negate participation in the decision . . .

[His Lordship held on the facts that the impugned decision was not vitiated by bias.]

(2) Right to a fair hearing

Ridge* v *Baldwin
[1964] AC 40
House of Lords

Following his arrest and charge for conspiracy to obstruct the course of justice, Ridge, the Chief Constable of Brighton, was suspended from duty.

At his trial Ridge was acquitted but the judge was critical of his leadership of the force. A further charge of corrruption was brought against Ridge and the judge repeated these comments when directing Ridge's acquittal.

Under the Municipal Corporations Act 1882, s. 191(4) a watch committee could dismiss 'any borough constable whom they think negligent in the discharge of his duty, or otherwise unfit for the same'. After Ridge's acquittals the watch committee met and decided that Ridge should be dismissed. Ridge was not asked to attend the meeting, but at the request of his solicitor the watch committee reconvened some days later and decided not to change its original decision. Before this second meeting Ridge gave notice of appeal against the original decision to the Home Secretary under the Police (Appeals) Act 1927. He also stated, however, that this was without prejudice to his right to argue that the procedure adopted by the committee was in breach of the relevant statutory provisions and of the rules of natural justice. The Home Secretary dismissed his appeal and Ridge appealed to the courts, seeking a declaration that the purported dismissal was *ultra vires.* Ridge, whose case failed before Streatfield J and the Court of Appeal, appealed to the House of Lords. The following extract deals with his claim that there was a breach of natural justice.

LORD REID: The appellant's case is that in proceeding under the Act of 1882 the watch committee were bound to observe what are commonly called the principles of natural justice. Before attempting to reach any decision they were bound to inform him of the grounds on which they proposed to act and give him a fair opportunity of being heard in his own defence. The authorities on the applicability of the principles of natural justice are in some confusion, and so I find it necessary to examine this matter in some detail. The principle audi alteram partem goes back many centuries in our law and appears in a multitude of judgments of judges of the highest authority. In modern times opinions have sometimes been expressed to the effect that natural justice is so vague as to be almost meaningless. But I would regard these as tainted by the perennial fallacy that because something cannot be cut and dried or nicely weighed and measured therefore it does not exist . . . It appears to me that one reason why the authorities on natural justice have been found difficult to reconcile is that insufficient attention has been paid to the great difference between various kinds of cases in which it has been sought to apply the principle. What a minister ought to do in considering objections to a scheme may be very different from what a watch committee ought to do in considering whether to dismiss a chief constable. So I shall deal first with cases of dismissal. These appear to fall into three classes: dismissal of a servant by his master, dismissal from an office held during pleasure, and dismissal from an office where there must be something against a man to warrant his dismissal.

[Lord Reid then went on to consider the three different cases and concluded that, in the case of the third category (into which Ridge fell), there was an unbroken line of authority to the effect that an officer cannot lawfully be dismissed without first telling him what is alleged against him and hearing his defence or explanation.]

Stopping there, I would think that authority was wholly in favour of the appellant, but the respondent's argument was mainly based on what has been said in a number of fairly recent cases dealing with different subject-matter. Those cases deal with decisions by ministers, officials and bodies of various kinds which adversely affected property rights or privileges of persons who had no opportunity or no proper opportunity of presenting their cases before the decisions were given. And it is necessary to examine those cases for another reason. The question which was or ought to have been considered by the watch committee on March 7, 1958, was not a simple question whether or not the appellant should be dismissed. There were three possible courses open to the watch committee – reinstating the appellant as chief constable, dismissing him, or requiring him to resign. The difference between the latter two is that dismissal involved forfeiture of pension rights, whereas requiring him to resign did not. Indeed, it is now clear that the appellant's real interest in this appeal is to try to save his pension rights. . . .

I would start an examination of the authorities dealing with property rights and privileges with *Cooper* v *Wandsworth Board of Works* (1863) 14 CBNS 180. Where an owner had failed to give proper notice to the Board they had under an Act of 1855 authority to demolish any building he had erected and recover the cost from him. This action was brought against the board because they had used that power without giving the owner an opportunity of being heard. The board maintained that their discretion to order demolition was not a judicial discretion and that any appeal should have been to the Metropolitan Board of Works. But the Court decided unanimously in favour of the owner . . .

[Lord Reid examined a number of other authorities and continued.] . . . It appears to me that if the present case had arisen thirty of forty years ago the court would have had no difficulty in deciding this issue in favour of the appellant on these authorities which I have cited. So far as I am aware none of these authorities has ever been disapproved or even doubted. Yet the Court of Appeal have decided this issue against the appellant on more recent authorities which apparently justify that result. How has this come about?

At least three things appear to have contributed. In the first place there have been many cases where it has been sought to apply the principles of natural justice to the wider duties imposed on Ministers and other organs of government by modern legislation. For reasons which I shall attempt to state, it has been held that those principles have a limited application in such cases and those limitations have tended to be reflected in other decisions on matters to which in principle they do not appear to me to apply. Secondly, again for reasons which I shall attempt to state, those principles have been held to have a limited application in cases arising out of war-time legislation; and again such limitations have tended to be reflected in other cases. And, thirdly, there has, I think, been a misunderstanding of the judgment of Atkin LJ in *Rex* v *Electricity Commissioners ex parte London Electricity Joint Committee Co.* [1924] 1 KB 171.

In cases of the kind I have been dealing with the Board of Works or the Governor of the club committee was dealing with a single isolated case. It was not deciding, like a judge in a lawsuit, what were the rights of the person before it. But it was deciding how he should be treated – something analogous to a judge's duty in imposing a penalty. No doubt policy would play some part in the decision – but so it might when a judge is imposing a sentence. So it was easy to say that such a body is performing a quasi-judicial task in considering and deciding such a matter, and to require it to observe the essentials of all proceedings of a judicial character – the principles of natural justice.

Sometimes the functions of a minister or department may also be of that character, and then the rules of natural justice can apply in much the same way. But more often their functions are of a very different character. If a minister is considering whether to make such a scheme for, say, an important new road, his primary concern will not be with the damage which its construction will do to the rights of individual owners of land. He will have to consider all manner of questions of public interest and, it may be, a number of alternative schemes. He cannot be prevented from attaching more importance to the fulfilment of his policy than to the fate of individual objectors, and it would be quite wrong for the courts to say that the minister should or could act in the same kind of way as a board of works deciding whether a house should be pulled down. And there is another important difference. As explained in *Local Government Board* v *Arlidge* [1915] AC 120 a minister cannot do everything himself. His officers will have to gather and sift all the facts, including objections by individuals, and no individual can complain if the ordinary accepted methods of carrying on public business do not give him as good protection as would be given by the principles of natural justice in a different kind of case.

[Lord Reid continued to discuss cases decided under the Defence Regulations made in war-time and concluded that the fact that the rules of natural justice were not applied should not be regarded as of any great weight in cases arising under the 1882 Act because it was a reasonable inference in the former case that it was Parliament's intention to exclude the application of the rules of natural justice.] . . .

The matter has been further complicated by what I believe to be a misunderstanding of a much-quoted passage in the judgment of Atkin LJ in *Rex* v *Electricity Commissioners, ex parte London Electricity Joint Committee Co.* [1925] 1 KB 171. He said '. . . the operation of the writs [of prohibition and certiorari] has extended to control the proceedings of bodies which do not claim to be, and would not be recognised as courts of justice. Wherever any body of persons having legal authority to determine questions affecting the rights of subjects, and having the duty to act judicially, act in excess of their legal authority, they are subject to the controlling jurisdiction of the King's Bench Division exercised in these writs.'

A gloss was put on this by Lord Hewart CJ in *Rex* v *Legislative Committee of the Church Assembly, ex parte Haynes-Smith* [1928] 1 KB 411. . . . Lord Hewart said, having quoted the passage from Atkin LJ's judgment: '. . . It is to be observed that in the last sentence which I have quoted . . . the word is not "or", but "and". In order that a body may satisfy the required test it is not enough that it should have legal authority to determine questions affecting the rights of subjects; there must be superadded to that characteristic the further characteristic that the body has the duty to act judicially. The duty to act judicially is an ingredient which, if the test is to be satisfied, must be present. As these writs in the earlier days were issued only to bodies which without any harshness of construction could be called, and naturally would be called courts, so also today these writs do not issue except to bodies which act or are under a duty to act in a judicial capacity.'

. . . If Lord Hewart meant that it is never enough that a body simply has a duty to determine what the rights of an individual should be, but that there must always be something more to impose on it a duty to act judicially before it can be found to observe the principles of natural justice, then that appears to me impossible to reconcile with the earlier authorities . . .

There is not a word in Atkin LJ's judgment to suggest disapproval of the earlier line of authority which I have cited. On the contrary, he goes further than those authorities. I have already stated my view that it is more difficult for the courts to control an exercise of power on a large scale where the treatment to be meted out to a particular individual is only one of many matters to be considered. This was a case of that kind, and, if Atkin LJ was prepared to infer a judicial element from the nature of the power in this case, he could hardly disapprove such an inference when the power relates solely to the treatment of a particular individual.

I would sum up my opinion in this way. Between 1882 and the making of police regulations in 1920, section 191(4) had to be applied to every kind of case. The respondents' contention is that, even where there was a doubtful question whether a constable was guilty of a particular act of misconduct, the watch committee were under no obligation to hear his defence before dismissing him. In my judgment it is abundantly clear from the authorities I have quoted that at that time the courts would have rejected any such contention. In later cases dealing with different subject-matter opinions have been expressed in wide terms so as to appear to conflict with those earlier authorities. But learned judges who expressed those opinions generally had no power to overrule those authorities, and in any event it is a salutary rule that a judge is not to be assumed to have intended to overrule or disapprove of an authority which has not been cited to him and which he does not even mention. So I would hold that the power of dismissal in the Act of 1882 could not then have been exercised and cannot now be exercised until the watch committee have informed the constable of the grounds on which they propose to proceed and given him a proper opportunity to present his case in defence. . . .

Lord Reid decided that this failure was not made good by the reconvening of the watch committee because this did not provide for a full rehearing and granted a declaration that the dismissal was unlawful. Lord Morris, Lord Hodson and Lord Devlin delivered judgments in favour of allowing the appeal. Lord Evershed delivered a speech in favour of dismissing the appeal.

Notes

1. The significance of *Ridge* v *Baldwin* is that it helped to free the rules of natural justice from strict limitations which had been imposed in earlier decisions, in particular from the requirement that the decision-making body must be under a duty to act judicially. The decision in the case may be compared with that in *Nakkuda Ali* v *Jayaratne* [1951] AC 66 which was disapproved in *Ridge* v *Baldwin.*

2. The application of the rules of natural justice to cases involving dismissal from employment has been extended since *Ridge* v *Baldwin.* (See the discussion in Craig, *Administrative Law* (3rd edn, 1994), pp. 318–9; H. W. R. Wade, *Administrative Law* (7th edn, 1994), pp. 557–60.)

3. The requirements of a fair hearing depend on all the circumstances. They may include:

(a) the right to notice, but restrictions may be placed on this where the public interest so requires (see, for example, *R* v *Gaming Board of Great Britain, ex parte Benaim and Khaida* [1970] 2 QB 417);

(b) the right to make representations, whether in writing or orally; oral hearings are not required in all circumstances where the rules of natural justice apply (see, for example, *Lloyd* v *McMahon* [1987] 1 All ER 1118);

(c) where an oral hearing is held –

(i) the right to comment on any evidence presented,

(ii) where evidence is given orally by witnesses, the right to put questions to those witnesses (see, for example, *R* v *Deputy Industrial Injuries Commissioner ex parte Moore* [1965] 1 QB 456);

(d) legal representation (see *post,* at pp. 571–572).

In order to understand the flexibility of the principles, consider the following cases.

R v *Board of Visitors of Hull Prison, ex parte St Germain (No. 2)*
[1979] 1 WLR 1401
Divisional Court

Following a riot in Hull Prison in 1976, numerous charges of breaches of the Prison Rules 1964 were heard by the prison's board of visitors. During the hearing reference was made to a number of statements by prison officers, who were not available to give evidence, to support the evidence given by a witness. Seven of the prisoners who were found guilty of offences against prison discipline sought an order of *certiorari* on the grounds that the proceedings before the prison's board of visitors breached the rules of natural justice. The following extracts relate to the prisoners' complaint that hearsay evidence was taken into account.

GEOFFREY LANE LJ: [W]e now turn to the suggestion that hearsay evidence is not permissible in a hearing before a board of visitors. It is of course common ground that the board of visitors must base their decisions on evidence. But must such evidence be restricted to that which would be admissible in a criminal court of law? Viscount Simon LC in *General Medical Council* v *Spackman* [1943] AC 627, 634, considered there was no such restriction. That was also clearly the view of the Privy Council in the *Ceylon University* v *Fernando* [1960] 1 WLR 223, 234. The matter was dealt with in more detail by Diplock LJ in *Reg.* v *Deputy Industrial Injuries Commissioner ex parte Moore* [1965] 1 QB 456, 488:

> These techncial rules of evidence, however, form no part of the rules of natural justice. The requirement that a person exercising quasi-judicial functions must base his decision on evidence means no more than it must be based upon material which tends logically to show the existence or non-existence of facts relevant to the issue to be determined, or to show the likelihood or unlikelihood of the occurence of some future event the occurrence of which would be relevant. It means that he must not spin a coin or consult an astrologer, but he may take into account any material which, as a matter of reason, has some probative value in the sense mentioned above. If it is capable of having any probative value, the weight to be attached to it is a matter for the person to whom Parliament has entrusted the responsibility of deciding the issue. The supervisory jurisdiction of the High Court does not entitle it to usurp this responsibility and to substitute its own view for his.

However, it is clear that the entitlement of the board to admit hearsay evidence is subject to the overriding obligation to provide the accused with a fair hearing. Depending upon the facts of the particular case and the nature of the hearsay evidence provided to the board, the obligation to give the accused a fair chance to exculpate himself, or a fair opportunity to controvert the charge – to quote the phrases used in the passages cited above – or a proper or full opportunity of presenting his case – to quote the language of section 47 or rule 49 – may oblige the board not only to inform the accused of the hearsay evidence but also to give the accused a sufficient opportunity to deal with that evidence. Again, depending upon the nature of that evidence and the particular circumstances of the case, a sufficient opportunity to deal with the hearsay evidence may well involve the cross-examination of the witness whose evidence is initially before the board in the form of hearsay.

We again take by way of example the case in which the defence is an alibi. The prisoner contends that he was not the man identified on the roof. He, the prisoner, was at the material time elsewhere. In short the prisoner has been mistakenly identifed. The evidence of identification given by way of hearsay may be of the 'fleeting glance' type as exemplified by the well-known case of *Reg* v *Turnbull* [1977] QB 224. The prisoner may well wish to elicit by way of questions all manner of detail, e.g. the poorness of the light, the state of the confusion, the brevity of the observation, the absence of any contemporaneous record, etc., all designed to show the unreliability of the witness. To deprive him of the opportunity of cross-examination would be tantamount to depriving him of a fair hearing.

We appreciate that there may well be occasions when the burden of calling the witness whose hearsay evidence is readily available may impose a near impossible burden upon the board. However, it has not been suggested that hearsay evidence should be resorted to in the total absence of any first-hand evidence. In the instant cases hearsay evidence was only resorted to to supplement the first-hand evidence and this is the usual practice. Accordingly where a prisoner desires to dispute the hearsay evidence and for this purpose to question the witness, and where there are insuperable or very grave difficulties in arranging for his attendance, the board should refuse to admit that evidence, or, if it has already come to their notice, should expressly dismiss it from their consideration. . . .

The findings of guilt which were based on hearsay evidence were quashed by orders of certiorari.

R* v *Commissioner for Racial Equality, ex parte Cottrell & Rothon
[1980] 1 WLR 1580
Court of Appeal

The Commission for Racial Equality received a complaint that a firm of estate agents, Messrs Cottrell & Rothon, was committing acts of unlawful discrimination in the course of its business as an estate agent. Under s. 48 of the Race Relations Act 1976, the Commission nominated two of its members to conduct an investigation. When the Commission were minded to issue a non-discrimination notice, they notified the firm under s. 58(5) of the Act of their intention, and gave the firm an opportunity to make written and oral representations to the nominated commissioners. The firm took the opportunity to make both oral and written representations. At the hearing before the commissioners, no witnesses were available to give evidence to sustain the complaint or be cross-examined on behalf of the firm. The Commission decided to issue the notice. The firm applied for an order of *certiorari* on the ground, inter alia, that witnesses ought to have been available for cross-examination.

LORD LANE CJ: Of course there is a wealth of authority on what are and what are not the rules of natural justice. The rules have been described in various ways, as an 'unruly horse,' I think, in one decision, and there is no doubt that what may be the rules of natural justice in one case may well not be the rules of natural justice in another. As has frequently been said, and there is no harm in repeating it, all that the rules of natural justice mean is that the proceedings must be conducted in a way which is fair to the firm in this case, fair in all the circumstances. All the circumstances include a number of different considerations: first of all, the penalties, if any. There are no penalties under the Race Relations Act in the form of fines or imprisonment or anything like that, but what [counsel for the firm] has drawn to our attention, quite correctly, is that under the terms of the Estate Agents Act 1979 (and no one has been able to discover whether that has come into operation yet or not) there is no doubt that a person on whom a non-discriminatory notice has been served may, if he is an estate agent, suffer, if certain procedural steps are taken, grave disadvantages because it is open, under a number of safeguards into which I do not propose to go, for the Director General of Fair Trading to take steps to see that a person against whom this action had been taken under the Race Relations Act 1976 does not practise in business as an estate agent. Of course it is a very long call from saying that a person who has this non-discriminatory notice served on him is necessarily going to suffer in his business by the action of the Director General of Fair Trading. Many procedures have to be gone through before that can take place, but there is a danger there, and that is one of the matters which is a circumstance to be taken into account.

The next matter, and possibly the most important matter, is the nature of the provisions of the Race Relations Act 1976 itself. I have read sufficient of the contents of section 58 of that Act to indicate that there is no mention in that section, or indeed in any other section, of any right to cross-examine any of the witnesses. That perhaps is a surprising omission if it was the intention of Parliament to allow a person in the position of the firm in this case the full panoply of legal rights which would take place at a judicial hearing.

It seems to me that there are degrees of judicial hearing, and those degrees run from the borders of pure administration to the borders of the full hearing of a criminal cause or matter in the Crown Court. It does not profit one to try to pigeon-hole the particular set of circumstances either into the administrative pigeon-hole or into the judicial pigeon-hole. Each case will inevitably differ, and one must ask oneself what is the basic nature of the proceeding which was going on here. It seems to me that, basically, this was an investigation being carried out by the commission. It is true that in the course of the investigation the commission may form a view, but it does not seem to me that is a proceeding which requires, in the name of fairness, any right in the firm in this case to be able to cross-examine witnesses whom the commission have seen and from whom they have taken statements. . . .

[Counsel for the firms] sought to derive assistance from some of the passages of the decision of this court in *Reg* v *Hull Prison Board of Visitors ex parte St Germain (No. 2)* [1979] QB 425, but it seems to me that the decision there was based on facts widely differing from those in the present case. That was truly a judicial proceeding carried out by the prison visitors and the complaint there was that there had been no opportunity to cross-examine prison officers in hotly disputed questions of identity. Speaking for myself, I derive little assistance from any dicta in that case.

. . . It seems to me for the reasons I have endeavoured to set out that in this case there was no breach of the rules of fairness in that cross-examination was not permitted or that the witnesses did not attend. . . .

Woolf J agreed with Lord Lane LJ.

R* v *Army Board of the Defence Council, ex parte Anderson
[1991] 3 WLR 42
Divisional Court

In this case the court had to scrutinise the procedures adopted by the Army Board in deciding upon complaints of racial discrimination by soldiers under the Race Relations Act 1976. (Complaints of racial discrimination in employment are normally dealt with by industrial tribunals but special procedures apply to complaints by soldiers.) The applicant was a former soldier who alleged that he had been subjected to forms of racial abuse which caused him to go absent without leave. The papers relating to the complaint were seen separately by two members of the Army Board who reached individual conclusions that, although there was some truth in the applicant's claim, there was no basis for making an apology to him or awarding him compensation. The applicant's requests for disclosure of documents relating to investigations into his complaints were refused, as was his request for an oral hearing. He applied for judicial review of the Board's decision.

TAYLOR LJ: . . .

Procedural requirements

What procedural requirements are necessary to achieve fairness when the Army Board considers a complaint of this kind? In addressing this issue, counsel made much of the distinction between judicial and administrative functions. Were it necessary to decide in those terms the functions of the Army Board when considering a race discrimination complaint, I would characterise it as judicial rather than administrative. The board is required to adjudicate on an alleged breach of a soldier's rights under the 1976 Act and, if it be proved, to take any necessary steps by way of redress. It is accepted that the board has the power, inter alia, to award compensation. A body required to consider and adjudicate upon an alleged breach of statutory rights and to grant redress when necessary seems to me to be exercising an essentially judicial function. It matters not that the body has other functions which are non-judicial: see *R v Secretary of State for the Home Dept, ex p Tarrant* [1985] QB 251, 268.

However, to label the board's function either 'judicial' or 'administrative' for the purpose of determining the appropriate procedural regime is to adopt too inflexible an approach. . . .

What, then, are the criteria by which to decide the requirements of fairness in any given proceeding? Authoritative guidance as to this was given by Lord Bridge in *Lloyd v McMahon* [1987] AC 625, 702. He said:

> My Lords, the so-called rules of natural justice are not engraved on tablets of stone. To use the phrase which better expresses the underlying concept, what the requirements of fairness demand when any body, domestic, administrative or judicial, has to make a decision which will affect the rights of individuals depends on the character of the decision-making body, the kind of decision it has to make and the statutory or other framework in which it operates. In particular, it is well established that when a statute has conferred on any body the power to make decisions affecting individuals, the courts will not only require the procedure prescribed by the statute to be followed, but will readily imply so much and no more to be introduced by way of additional procedural safeguards as will ensure the attainment of fairness.

Applying these principles to the present case, the character of the Army Board and its role in this context have already been described. It is pertinent, however, to note that its decision is final apart from the possibility of judicial review. There is no appeal from its findings. The kind of decision it has to make has also been described. [Mr Sedley, counsel for the applicant] argues from that and from the statutory framework that all the procedural features to be found in a court trial are required – full discovery of documents, an oral hearing and cross-examination. As to the statutory framework, he points out that complaints of racial discrimination under Pt III of the 1976 Act relating to goods and services go before the county court with all the incidents of court procedure. Most civilian complaints of racial discrimination contrary to s. 4 of the 1976 Act go to an industrial tribunal under s. 54(1). There they are subject to rules requiring the procedures Mr Sedley claims here. Thus, if Mr Anderson had been seeking entry to the army, and had been turned down on allegedly racial grounds, his case could have been presented to the industrial tribunal under s. 4(1)(c), and he would have enjoyed all the procedures claimed here. Why should he be worse off simply because he is actually in the army and s. 54(2) requires his complaint to be considered by a different body?

Against this, [Mr Pannick, counsel for the Army Board] contends that Parliament has expressly provided that a soldier's complaint shall not go before an industrial tribunal but shall instead be subject to the army procedures pursuant to s. 181 of the 1955 Act. Parliament must, he submits, have been aware of the procedures normally followed in regard to other complaints under that section. Moreover, had Parliament wished to impose a more rigid and rigorous procedure, still in an army context, it could have directed that complaints of racial discrimination should be subject to s. 135 (board of inquiry), s. 137 (regimental inquiry) or even ss. 92 to 3 (court-martial). Process under each of those sections would have afforded the complainant the procedural formalities contended for here.

I should say that the existence of those forms of inquiry and their procedure undercuts [the] suggestion that exigencies of the service would make oral hearings impracticable.

In my judgment, there is force in Mr Pannick's argument. Since Parliament has deliberately excluded soldiers' complaints from industrial tribunals and thus from the procedures laid down for such tribunals, it cannot be axiomatic that by analogy all those procedures must be made available by the Army Board. Had Parliament wished to impose those detailed procedures on the Army Board, it could have done so.

However, Mr Pannick went on to contend that the Army Board's duty of fairness required no more than that it should act bona fide, not capriciously or in a biased manner, and that it should afford the complainant a chance to respond to the basic points put against him. In my judgment, this does not go far enough. The Army Board as the forum of last resort, dealing with an individual's fundamental statutory rights, must by its procedures achieve a high standard of fairness. I would list the principles as follows.

(1) There must be a proper hearing of the complaint in the sense that the board must consider, as a single adjudicating body, all the relevant evidence and contentions before reaching its conclusions. This means, in my view, that the members of the board must meet. It is unsatisfactory that the members should consider the papers and reach their individual conclusions in isolation and, perhaps as here, having received the concluded views of another member. Since there are ten members of the Army Board and any two can exercise the board's powers to consider a complaint of this kind, there should be no difficulty in achieving a meeting for the purpose.

(2) The hearing does not necessarily have to be an oral hearing in all cases. There is ample authority that decision-making bodies other than courts and bodies whose procedures are laid down by statute are masters of their own procedure. Provided that they achieve the degree of fairness appropriate to their task it is for them to decide how they will proceed and there is no rule that fairness always requires an oral hearing: see *Local Government Board* v *Arlidge* [1915] AC 120, 132–133, *Selvarajan* v *Race Relations*

Board [1975] 1 WLR 1686, 1694 and *R* v *Immigration Appeal Tribunal, ex p Jones* [1988] 1 WLR 477, 481. Whether an oral hearing is necessary will depend upon the subject matter and circumstances of the particular case and upon the nature of the decision to be made. It will also depend upon whether there are substantial issues of fact which cannot be satisfactorily resolved on the available written evidence. This does not mean that, whenever there is a conflict of evidence in the statements taken, an oral hearing must be held to resolve it. Sometimes such a conflict can be resolved merely by the inherent unlikelihood of one version or the other. Sometimes the conflict is not central to the issue for determination and would not justify an oral hearing. Even when such a hearing is necessary, it may only require one or two witnesses to be called and cross-examined.

Mr Sedley submits that, whatever the position regarding other complaints under s. 181, an oral hearing should be obligatory where the complaint is of race discrimination. He submits that experience shows proof of discrimination to be elusive. Discriminatory motivation can be innocent and subconscious. Without cross-examination at an oral hearing it may not emerge. I recognise the difficulties of proving discrimination in many cases, but I do not accept that a general rule requiring oral hearings must be applied by the Army Board to all complaints of discrimination. In the present case, for example, the direct and crude nature of the alleged racial abuse hardly raises any specially subtle possibility of subconscious motivation. Either the racial attacks, oral and physical, took place or they did not. Whether, when the Army Board sees all the statements and transcripts, it considers it necessary to hold an oral hearing to decide that issue or whether it can resolve it on the written material will be for it to decide in its discretion. What it cannot do, at the other extreme from Mr Sedley's submission, is to have an inflexible policy not to hold oral hearings. The findings of the two members in this case suggest that is what they did. . . .

[T]he board fettered its discretion and failed to consider the request for an oral hearing in the present case on its own merits.

(3) The opportunity to have the evidence tested by cross-examination is again within the Army Board's discretion. The decision whether to allow it will usually be inseparable from the decision whether to have an oral hearing. The object of the latter will usually be to enable witnesses to be tested in cross-examination, although it would be possible to have an oral hearing simply to hear submissions.

(4) Whether oral or not, there must be what amounts to a hearing of any complaint under the 1976 Act. This means that the Army Board must have such a complaint investigated, consider all the material gathered in the investigation, give the complainant an opportunity to respond to it and consider his response.

But what is the board obliged to disclose to the complainant to obtain his response? Is it sufficient to indicate the gist of any material adverse to his case or should he be shown all the material seen by the board?

Mr Pannick submits that there is no obligation to show all to the complainant. He relies upon three authorities, *R* v *Secretary of State, ex p Mughal* [1974] QB 313, *R* v *Secretary of State, ex p Santillo* [1981] QB 778 and *R* v *Monopolies and Mergers Commission, ex p Matthew Brown plc* [1987] 1 WLR 1235. However, in each of those cases, the function of the decision-making body was towards the administrative end of the spectrum. Because of the nature of the Army Board's function pursuant to the 1976 Act, already analysed above, I consider that a soldier complainant under that Act should be shown all the material seen by the board, apart from any documents for which public interest immunity can properly be claimed. The board is not simply making an administrative decision requiring it to consult interested parties and hear their representations. It has a duty to adjudicate on a specific complaint of breach of a statutory right. Except where public interest immunity is established, I see no reason why on such an adjudication the board should consider material withheld from the complainant.

In the present case it is true that Mr Anderson was shown a summary of the SIB report, though not the report itself. He also received the commanding officer's letter of 20 July which summarised points made against him, but he did not see the statements of other soldiers. Nor was he shown the information obtained individually by each of the board members. Thus, the response he made to the commanding officer's letter was hampered by a lack of full information. . . .

The Divisional Court granted an order of certiorari to quash the Board's decision.

Notes

1. A commentary on the use of judicial review in the context of racial discrimination in the public sector may be found at [1991] *Public Law*, at pp. 317–25.

2. *Ex parte St Germain (No. 2)* and *ex parte Cottrell and Rothon* have been used by H.F. Rawlings to illustrate a particular criticism of the rules of natural justice.

H. F. Rawlings 'Judicial Review and the Control of Government' (1986) 64 *Public Administration*, 135–145 at 140–41

. . . It has long been the concern of many academic administrative lawyers that our system of judicial review is for various reasons not adequate to ensure protection of the citizen against government excess. . . . In contrast, the adequacy of our administrative law principles from the point of view of the civil or public servant has rarely been considered. I suggest that the principles which have been developed by the courts over the last twenty years are quite simply not sufficiently precise to offer any meaningful guidance to administrators in their day-to-day decision-making, even if those administrators are aware of the existence of administrative law. . . .

What, then, are those principles? In essence there are two (I leave out of account here the question of illegality, which is not germane to the present discussion). First, there is the obligation to observe the rules of natural justice. Here we may return to *Ridge* v *Baldwin* [1964] AC 40. That case establishes that in a far wider category of situations than had previously been thought true, a public authority had, in exercising statutory functions, to observe the natural justice requirement. But what is that requirement? It must be remembered that the content of the natural justice rule derives from the court proceedings paradigm – judges must be unbiased, and parties must be given an opportunity to present their cases. How might these rules be applied in the infinite variety of administrative practices to which *Ridge* v *Baldwin* now extends them?

Two possibilities were open to the courts, given this new activist approach to the applicability of natural justice. [W]e might characterise these as the 'formal activist' and the 'informal activist' approaches. Under the former, the courts could seek, by firm application of the rules, to force the administrative process into a more judicial mould, to follow the formal procedures of the courts so far as possible. Under the latter, the courts could permit administrators a greater degree of latitude in their procedures and allow the applicability of the rules of natural justice in particular circumstances to be determined by the realities of administration, while all the time insisting that compliance with the rules was necessary. As is now well-known, the courts adopted the latter approach – natural justice was to be flexibly applied, to fit the circumstances of the case. In the result, observation of the rules of natural justice came to mean that the procedure required of the administrator had to be, in all the circumstances of the case, 'fair' (see, for example *Re HK* [1967] 2 QB 617 and *R* v *Commission for Racial Equality ex parte Cottrell and Rothon* [1980] 1 WLR 1580).

Now it may be that this was an inevitable result, although potentially pregnant with danger for the individual citizen asserting a right to be heard. It seems to me, however, that in their understandable desire to avoid over-judicialising administrative procedures, the courts have thrown out the baby with the bath-water. Flexible natural justice, or 'fairness', has come to have no fixed or settled content that an administrator should know must be observed in exercising decision-making powers. All he knows . . . is that he must be 'fair' – and what 'fairness' requires in the particular circumstances he can only ultimately find out when the court, on judicial review, tells him that he has, or has not, been fair. Is this an adequate administrative law principle, from the point of view of the administrator?

The point may briefly be illustrated by considering a specific issue in natural justice. It is sometimes said that, before any administrative decision is taken, a party who is likely to be affected by it shall have the right to hear what evidence against his interests has been given by someone else, and shall have the opportunity to question that person on the assertions contained therein . . . Decided cases, tell us, to take just two examples, that in the context of prison disciplinary proceedings, 'fairness' requires that such cross-examination is permitted (*R* v *Hull Prison Visitors ex parte St Germain (No. 2)* [1979] 1 WLR 1401), whereas in the context of issuance of a non-discrimination notice against a private estate agency under the Race Relations Act, 'fairness' does not require that such cross-examination is permitted (*R* v *CRE ex parte Cottrell and Rothon* [1980] 1 WLR 1580).

Now these results can be defended, because as Lord Lane CJ says in the *Cottrell and Rothon case,* there are 'degrees of judicial hearing, and those degrees run from the borders of pure administration to the borders of a full hearing of a criminal cause or matter'. The precise requirements of fairness depend upon how far along that continuum is the particular administrative process to be placed – the closer to 'pure administration' it is, the less onerous will be the procedural requirements imposed on administrators. This, as I have said, is defensible as a matter of theory, but I suggest that as guidance to administrative practice it is hopelessly imprecise from the point of view of those who want to know what procedural requirements the law lays down for them to observe.

Questions

1. What distinctions did Lord Lane CJ draw between the circumstances in *ex parte St Germain* and those in *ex parte Cottrell and Rothon*? Do you consider that the distinctions justify the different decisions reached in each case?

2. Cane, in the extract at pp. 526–529 *ante,* has suggested that there are two possible approaches which the court might adopt in the face of legislative silence on the precise content of the rules of natural justice. 'It could be said that the rules of natural justice will apply only if there is evidence of a legislative intention that they should; alternatively it could be argued that silence should be construed as an invitation by the courts to apply common law procedural standards of natural justice.' Which approach did the courts adopt in *ex parte St Germain*, *ex parte Cottrell and Rothon* and *ex parte Anderson*?

3. Write a paragraph to guide public administrators on the circumstances in which public authorities should be willing (a) to permit oral hearings and (b) to permit the cross-examination of witnesses.
4. Is there any solution to the problems identified by Rawlings?
5. Can there be a breach of the rules of natural justice where an applicant has been deprived of an opportunity to present his case, not through the fault of the decision-making body, but through the fault of his own advisers? (See *Al-Mehdawi* v *Secretary of State for the Home Department* [1990] AC 876, noted at [1990] *Public Law*, pp. 467–75.)

Note
One problem which has been discussed in a number of recent cases is that of legal representation. In *R* v *Board of Visitors of HM Prison, The Maze, ex parte Hone* [1988] 2 WLR 177 the House of Lords rejected the argument that a prisoner facing a disciplinary charge before a prison board of visitors had a right to legal representation. The House of Lords did, however, approve the decision in *R* v *Secretary of State for the Home Department, ex parte Tarrant* [1985] QB 251 that a board of visitors still has a discretion to allow legal representation and that in certain circumstances it would be wrong not to allow it. Webster J specified a number of points which are to be taken into account, including the seriousness of the charge and potential penalty, whether points of law are likely to arise, the particular prisoner's ability to present his case and the need for reasonable speed in reaching a decision.

The rules governing hearings before the prison board of visitors did not state that legal representation was prohibited. What is the position where the rules governing a particular hearing *do* prohibit legal representation? In *Enderby Town Football Club Ltd* v *Football Association Ltd* [1971] Ch 591 Lord Denning MR stated at p. 607:

> Seeing that the courts can inquire into the validity of the rule, I turn to the next question: Is it lawful for a body to stipulate in its rules that its domestic tribunal shall not permit legal representation? Such a stipulation is, I think, clearly valid so long as it is construed as directory and not imperative: for that leaves it open to the tribunal to permit legal representation in an exceptional case when the justice of the case so requires. But I have some doubt whether it is legitimate to make a rule which is so imperative in its terms as to exclude legal representation altogether, without giving the tribunal any discretion to admit it, even when the justice of the case so requires.

Lord Denning has repeated this view on other occasions (see e.g. *Edwards* v *SOGAT* [1971] Ch 354). In *Enderby Town* itself, however, Cairns LJ took a contrary view.

In *Maynard* v *Osmond* [1977] QB 240 Lord Denning was a member of the Court of Appeal which was required to consider the validity of police discipline regulations prohibiting legal representation. The regulations were made under statutory powers. It was held unanimously that the regulations were not *ultra vires,* and in particular that they were not in breach of natural justice. In this case Lord Denning stated, obiter, that it is permissible for a domestic tribunal to adopt a rule forbidding legal representation, and Orr LJ endorsed the view of Cairns LJ in *Enderby Town.*

The two principles so far discussed have been concerned with procedural fairness. In recent years the courts have begun to develop a principle of fairness which may require public authorities to reach a particular decision rather than simply to follow a fair procedure. The concept of legitimate expectation, which is explained in *CCSU* v *Minister for the Civil Service,* has been important in the development of this principle.

Council of the Civil Service Unions v *Minister for the Civil Service*
[1985] AC 374
House of Lords

Government Communications Headquarters, a branch of the civil service, is responsible for the security of the United Kingdom military and official communications and the provision of signals intelligence for the Government. Since the formation of GCHQ in 1947, all the staff had been permitted to belong to trade unions. There was an established practice of consultation between the management and the civil service unions at GCHQ. Following incidents of industrial action at GCHQ the Minister for the Civil Service, the Prime Minister, issued an oral instruction to the effect that the terms and conditions of civil servants at GCHQ should be revised to exclude membership of any trade union other than a departmental staff association approved by the Minister. The instruction was issued under art. 4 of the Civil Service Order in Council 1982 'to give instructions . . . for controlling the conduct of the Service, and providing for the . . . conditions of service', the Order itself having been made under the royal prerogative. The union applied for judicial review, seeking a declaration that the Minister had acted unfairly in removing their fundamental right to belong to a trade union without consultation. The Court of Appeal allowed the Minister's appeal against the judge's decision that the Minister had acted unlawfully. The appellants appealed to the House of Lords. Having held that the courts could review the exercise of a power delegated to the decision-maker under the royal prerogative, Lord Fraser went on to consider whether there was a duty to consult the unions.

LORD FRASER:

The duty to consult
[Counsel for the appellants] submitted that the Minister had a duty to consult the CCSU, on behalf of employees at GCHQ, before giving the instruction on 22 December 1983 for making an important change in their conditions of service. His main reason for so submitting was that the employees had a legitimate, or reasonable,

expectation that there would be such prior consultation before any important change was made in their conditions.

It is clear that the employees did not have a legal right to prior consultation. The Order in Council confers no such right and article 4 makes no reference at all to consultation . . . But even where a person claiming some benefit or privilege has no legal right to it, as a matter of private law, he may have a legitimate expectation of receiving the benefit or privilege, and, if so, the courts will protect his expectation by judicial review as a matter of public law. This subject has been fully explained by Lord Diplock, in *O'Reilly* v *Mackman* [1983] 2 AC 237 and I need not repeat what he has so recently said. Legitimate, or reasonable, expectation may arise either from an express promise given on behalf of a public authority or from the existence of a regular practice which the claimant can reasonably expect to continue. Examples of the former type of expectation are *Reg* v *Liverpool Corporation, ex parte Liverpool Taxi Fleet Operators Association* [1972] 2 QB 299 and *A-G of Hong Kong* v *Ng Yuen Shiu* [1983] 2 AC 629. (I agree with Lord Diplock's view, expressed in the speech in this appeal, that 'legitimate' is to be preferred to the word 'reasonable' in this context. I was responsible for using the word 'reasonable' for the reason explained in *Ng Yuen Shiu,* but it was intended only to be exegetical of 'legitimate'.) An example of the latter is *Reg* v *Hull Prison Board of Visitors ex p St Germain* [1979] 1 All ER 701, [1979] QB 425, approved by this House in *O'Reilly* v *Mackman* [1982] 3 All ER 1124 at 1126, [1983] 2 AC 237 at 274. The submission on behalf of the appellants is that the present case is of the latter type. The test of that is whether the practice of prior consultation of the staff on significant changes in their conditions of service was so well established by 1983 that it would be unfair or inconsistent with good administration for the Government to depart from the practice in this case. Legitimate expectations such as are now under consideration will always relate to a benefit or privilege to which the claimant has no right in private law, and it may even be to one which conflicts with his private law rights. In the present case the evidence shows that, ever since GCHQ began in 1947, prior consultation has been the invariable rule when conditions of service were to be significantly altered. Accordingly in my opinion if there had been no question of national security involved, the appellants would have had a legitimate expectation that the Minister would consult them before issuing the instruction of 22 December 1983.

Note

A majority of their Lordships held that the exercise of prerogative powers could be challenged in judicial review proceedings provided that the subject matter was justiciable. (On the issue of justiciability, see *post,* p. 626.) Lord Fraser and Lord Brightman left open the question whether a direct exercise of the prerogative powers could be subject to judicial review, but they did accept that powers which had been delegated to decision-makers by an Order in Council made under prerogative powers were subject to judicial review. All their Lordships agreed that, had issues of national security not been involved, the unions would have been entitled to consultation. (On the issues of national security which arose in this case see *post,* at p. 626.)

Since this case there have been a number of decisions in which the courts have explored the meaning of legitimate expectation. Read the extract from one such case, *R* v *Secretary of State for the Home Department ex parte Khan* [1984] 1 WLR 1337 below, paying particular attention to the cases discussed therein.

R v *Secretary of State for the Home Department ex parte Khan*
[1984] 1 WLR 1337
Court of Appeal

The applicant and his wife wished to adopt a relative's child who lived with its natural mother in Pakistan. A Home Office circular gave guidance to persons in the United Kingdom who wished to adopt a child from abroad. It stated that, although the immigration rules did not permit a foreign child to enter the United Kingdom for the purposes of adoption, the Secretary of State would in exceptional circumstances exercise a discretion to allow a child to enter the United Kingdom for adoption if certain specified criteria were met. The circular stated that, when an application was referred to the Secretary of State he would make certain inquiries within the Department of Health and Social Security whether there were any reasons why the adoption order was likely to be refused. The applicant and his wife obtained a copy of the Home Office circular and applied for an entrance clearance certificate for the child. The application, together with the entry clearance officer's report on the child, was referred to the Secretary of State. Although there was nothing in the report to indicate that the criteria set out in the circular had not been met, the Secretary of State did not make any inquiries within the Department of Health and Social Security or apply the criteria set out in the circular. Instead he applied the criteria for deciding whether to admit for settlement children who were already adopted by persons settled in the United Kingdom and refused leave to enter. The applicant applied for an order of *certiorari* which was refused. On appeal to the Court of Appeal the appeal was allowed.

PARKER LJ: . . . The applicant relies on three authorities on the basis of which he contends that the refusal of entry clearance should be quashed. The first of these cases is *Reg* v *Liverpool Corporation ex parte Liverpool Fleet Operators' Association* [1972] 2 QB 299. In that case the corporation had statutory powers to license such numbers of Hackney carriages or coaches as they thought fit. The corporation gave public and private undertakings that no licences in addition to the existing number (300) would be issued until proposed legislation had been enacted and come into force. Notwithstanding the undertakings, which were given on 4 and 11 August 1971, the corporation in December resolved to increase the number of licences to 350 from 1 January 1972, to 400 from 1 July 1972 and thereafter without limits. The proposed legislation was expected to be in force in early 1973. The Court of Appeal prohibited the corporation from acting on the resolution to increase the number of licences without first hearing any representations which might be made by interested persons and any other matters relevant thereto including the undertaking of 11 August.

The form of the order was the result of the decision that the undertaking was binding so long as the performance of it was compatible with the corporation's public duty. Lord Denning MR said at p. 308:

> they ought not to depart from it [the undertaking] except after the most serious consideration and hearing what the other party has to say: and then only if they are satisfied that the over-riding public interest requires it. The public interest may be better served by honouring the undertaking than by breaking it . . . they broke their undertaking without any sufficient cause or excuse.

Reference may also be made to the judgment of Roskill LJ, where he said at p. 311:

> it seems to me, therefore, that now to allow the council to resile from that undertaking without notice to and representations from the applicants is to condone unfairness in a case where the duty was to act fairly. . . .

In that case there was a specific undertaking whereas here there is not; the corporation had a statutory power, whereas here the power of the Secretary of State is a common law power; and the matter complained of was a positive act, whereas here the complaint is a refusal to act. There can, however, be no doubt that the Secretary of State has a duty to exercise his common law discretion fairly. Furthermore, just as in the case stated, the corporation was held not to be entitled to resile from an undertaking and change its policy without giving a fair hearing so in principle, the Secretary of State, if he undertakes to allow in persons if certain conditions are satisfied, should not in my view be entitled to refuse to do so without affording interested persons a hearing and then only if the overriding public interest demands it.

[His Lordship then discussed *O'Reilly* v *Mackman* [1983] 2 AC 237 which was the second of the authorities relied upon by the applicant. He agreed with the submission of counsel for the applicants that *O'Reilly* provided authority for the proposition that the applicant's legitimate expectation gave him locus standi to challenge the Secretary of State's decision. (Both the decision in *O'Reilly* and the law on *locus standi* are discussed further post, at pp. 421 and 429.) His Lordship continued] . . .

But to have a sufficient interest to afford a locus standi to challenge is a long way from being entitled to succeed in such challenge.

The applicant, however, contends on the basis of the third authority on which he relies, coupled with his first which I have already considered, he is so entitled. That authority is a Privy Council case, *Attorney-General of Hong Kong* v *Ng Yuen Shiu* [1983] 2 AC 629 . . . The advice of their Lordships was delivered by Lord Fraser . . . For some years prior to 23 October 1980 the government of Hong Kong had adopted a policy under which illegal immigrants from China were not repatriated if they had managed to reach the urban areas without being arrested. This was known as the 'reached base' policy. On 23 October 1980 the government announced that this policy would be discontinued forthwith and at the same time issued a new ordinance which, inter alia, gave the Director of Immigration power to make orders in respect of illegal immigrants. There was no contrary provision for a hearing or inquiry before a removal order was made. Subsequent to the change of policy there were a series of television announcements stating that all illegal immigrants from China would be liable to be repatriated. Mr Ng like many others in the colony, although they had entered illegally from Macau, were of Chinese origin. They were accordingly worried and on 28 October 1980 a group, not including Mr Ng, went to Government House and submitted a petition.

There there were read out a series of questions and answers prepared in the office of the Secretary for Security which dealt with the position of such persons and the action they should take. One of such questions, with its answer, was at p. 635:

> Q. Will we be given identity cards? A. Those illegal immigrants from Macau will be treated in accordance with procedures for illegal immigrants from anywhere other than China. They will be interviewed in due course. No guarantee can be given that you may not subsequently be removed. Each case will be treated on its merits.

Although Mr Ng was not present he did see a television programme on the subject on the evening of the same day.

On 31 October a removal order was made against him. This he challenged and eventually on 13 May 1981 the Court of Appeal of Hong Kong made an order of prohibition prohibiting the Director of Immigration from executing the removal order before an opportunity had been given to Mr Ng of putting all the circumstances of the case before the director. The Attorney-General of Hong Kong appealed to the Privy Council.

The High Court and the Court of Appeal in Hong Kong had both held that Mr Ng had no general right to a fair hearing before a removal order was made against him and the Judicial Committee assumed without deciding that they had rightly so decided. It was concerned only with the narrow question whether what had been said outside Government House entitled Mr Ng to such a hearing.

It is necessary to cite four passages from Lord Fraser of Tullybelton's judgment:

(1) '. . . "legitimate expectations" in this context are capable of including expectations which go beyond legal rights, *provided they have some reasonable basis*. . . .' (p. 636 E-F)

(2) 'The expectations may be based on some statement or undertaking by, or on behalf of, the public authority which has the duty of making the decision, if the authority has, through its officers, acted *in a way that would make it unfair or inconsistent with good administration for him to be denied such an inquiry*.' (637 C-D).

(3) 'Their Lordships see no reason why the principle should not be applicable when the person who will be affected by the decision is an alien, just as much as when he is a British subject. The justification for it is primarily that, *when a public authority has promised to follow a certain procedure, it is in the interest of good administration that it should act fairly and should implement its promise, so long as implementation does not interfere with its statutory duty*. The principle is also justified by the further consideration that, when the promise was made, *the authority must have considered that it would be assisted in discharging its duty fairly* by any representations from interested parties and as a general rule that is correct. In the opinion of their Lordships the principle that a public authority is bound by its undertakings as to the procedure it will follow, provided they do not conflict with its duty, is applicable to the undertaking given by the government of Hong Kong to the applicant, along with other illegal immigrants from Macau, in the announcement made outside Government House on 28 October 1980, that each case would be considered on its merits. The only ground on which it was argued before the Board that the undertaking had not been implemented was that the respondent had not been given an opportunity to put his case for an exercise of discretion, which the director undoubtedly possesses, in his favour before a decision was reached.' (638 E-H)

(4) 'Their Lordships consider that this is a very narrow case on its facts, but they are not disposed to differ from the view expressed by both the courts below, to the effect that the government's promise to the applicant has not been implemented. Accordingly the appeal ought to be dismissed . . . The appropriate remedy is . . . an order of certiorari to quash the removal order made by the director . . . That order of certiorari is of course entirely without prejudice to the making of a fresh removal order by the Director of Immigration after a fair inquiry has been held at which the applicant has been given an opportunity to make such representations as he may see fit as to why he should not be removed.' (p. 639 E-F). . . .

That case is, of course, not binding on this court but it is of high persuasive authority. In my view it correctly sets out the law of England and should be applied.

I have no doubt that the Home Office letter afforded the applicant a reasonable expectation that the procedures it set out, which were just as certain in their terms as the question and answer in Mr Ng's case, would be followed; that if the result of the implementation of those procedures satisfied the Secretary of State of the four matters mentioned a temporary entry clearance certificate would be granted and that the ultimate fate of the child would then be decided by the adoption court of this country. I have equally no doubt that it was considered by the department at the time the letter was sent out that if those procedures were fully implemented they would be sufficient to safeguard the public interest. The letter can mean nothing else. This is not surprising. The adoption court will apply the law of this country and will thus protect all the interests which the law of this country considers should be protected. The letter can mean nothing else. The Secretary of State is, of course, at liberty to change the policy but in my view, vis-à-vis the recipient of such a letter, a new policy can only be implemented after such recipient has been given a full and serious consideration whether there is some overriding public interest which justifies a departure from the procedures stated in the letter. . . .

I refer to the policy of refusing entry save where the natural parents are incapable of looking after the child as a new policy for, without specific evidence, which is not present, that such policy existed at the time, I am not prepared to assume that the Home Office would have issued a letter in the terms which they did or have failed both to mention that the sponsors would be required to satisfy the Home Secretary on the point and to have instructed officers to make inquiries as to the position.

. . . I would allow the appeal and quash the refusal of entry clearance. This will leave the Secretary of State free either to proceed on the basis of the letter or, if he considers it desirable to operate the new policy, to afford the applicant a full opportunity to make representations why, in his case, it should not be followed.

Dunn LJ delivered a judgment in which he agreed with Parker LJ. Watkins LJ dissented.

Questions

1. Read again the decision in *British Oxygen Co. Ltd* v *Minister of Technology* [1971] AC 610 (at p. 551 *ante*). If the Department of Trade and Industry had originally stated that it would look favourably on applications for grants for items under £25 each and, before considering the application by British Oxygen, altered its policy to one of denying such grants, would the Company have had a stronger case?

2. What was Mr Khan's legitimate expectation?

3. How did the court state it would protect Mr Khan's legitimate expectation?

Note

The concept of legitimate expectation has been discussed by a number of writers (see, for example, C. Forsyth, 'The Provenance and Protection of Legitimate Expectations' 47 (1988) CLJ, 238–260; B. Hadfield, 'Judicial Review and the Concept of Legitimate Expectation' (1988) 39 *Northern Ireland Legal Quarterly,* 103–119; Ganz, in *Public Law and Politics,* ed. Harlow ch. 8; P. Craig, 'Legitimate Expectations: A Conceptual Analysis', (1992) 108 *Law Quarterly Review* 79). They have highlighted the different ways in which the concept is used by the courts. Predominantly, the legitimate expectation has related to fair procedures. See *post* (p. 589) for discussion of substantive legitimate expectations.

(iii) *Irrationality*

Prior to the decision in *CCSU* v *Minister for the Civil Service* this ground was often expressed in the principle that an authority must not reach a decision which is so unreasonable that no reasonable body could have come to it. After *CCSU* the use of the term 'irrationality' has become more common, but in *R* v *Devon CC ex parte G* [1988] 3 WLR 49, at p. 51, the Master of the Rolls stated that he preferred the older test because the term 'irrationality' could be widely misunderstood as casting doubt on the mental capacity of the decision-maker. Subsequent cases have used both terms.

Wheeler v Leicester City Council
[1985] AC 1054
House of Lords

The facts are set out at p. 541, *ante*.

LORD ROSKILL: It is important to emphasise that there was nothing illegal in the action of the three members in joining the tour. The government policy recorded in the well-known Gleneagles agreement has never been given the force of law at the instance of any government, whatever its political complexion, and a person who acts otherwise than in accordance with the principles of that agreement, commits no offence even though he may by his action earn the moral disapprobation of large numbers of his fellow citizens. That the club condemns apartheid, as does the council, admits of no doubt. But the council's actions against the club were not taken, as already pointed out, because the club took no action against its three members. They were taken, according to Mr Soulsby, because the club failed to condemn the tour and to discourage its members from playing. The same point was put more succinctly by Mr Sullivan QC, who appeared for the council – 'The club failed to align themselves whole-heartedly with the council on a controversial issue.' The club did not condemn the tour. They did not give specific affirmative answers to the first two questions. Thus, so the argument ran, the council, legitimately bitterly hostile to the policy of apartheid, were justified in exercising their statutory discretion to determine by whom the recreation ground should be used so as to exclude those, such as the club, who would not support the council's policy on the council's terms. The club had, however, circulated to those involved the powerfully reasoned and impressive memorandum which had been sent to the RFU [the Rugby Football Union] on 12 March 1984 by the anti-apartheid movement. Of the club's own opposition to apartheid as expressed in its memorandum which was given to Mr Soulsby, there is no doubt. But the club recognised that those views, like those of the council, however passionately held by some, were by no means universally held, especially by those who sincerely believed that the evils of apartheid were enhanced rather than diminished by a total prohibition of all sporting links with South Africa.

The council's main defence rested on section 71 of the Race Relations Act 1976. That section appears as the first section in Part X of the Act under the cross-heading 'Supplemental.' For ease of reference I will set out the section in full:

> Without prejudice to their obligation to comply with any other provision of this Act, it shall be the duty of every local authority to make appropriate arrangements with a view to securing that their various functions are carried out with due regard to the

need – (a) to eliminate unlawful racial discrimination; and (b) to promote equality of opportunity, and good relations, between persons of different racial groups.

My Lords, it was strenuously argued on behalf of the club that this section should be given what was called a 'narrow' construction. It was suggested that the section was only concerned with the actions of the council as regards its own internal behaviour and was what was described as 'inward looking.' The section had no relevance to the general exercise by the council or indeed of any local authority of their statutory functions, as for example in relation to the control of open spaces or in determining who should be entitled to use a recreation ground and on what terms. It was said that the section was expressed in terms of a 'duty.' But it did not impose any duty so as to compel the exercise by a local authority of other statutory functions in order to achieve the objectives of the Act of 1976.

My Lords, in respectful agreement with the courts below, I unhesitatingly reject this argument. I think the whole purpose of the section is to see that in employment, and in Part III, education, local authorities must in relation to 'their various functions' make 'appropriate arrangements' to secure that those functions are carried out 'with due regard to the need' mentioned in the section.

It follows that I do not doubt that the council were fully entitled in exercising their statutory discretion under, for example, the Open Spaces Act 1906 and the various Public Health Acts, which are all referred to in the judgments below, to pay regard to what they thought to be in the best interests of race relations.

The only question is, therefore, whether the action of the council of which the club complains is susceptible of attack by way of judicial review. It was forcibly argued by Mr Sullivan QC for the council, that once it was accepted, as I do accept, that section 71 bears the construction for which the council contended, the matter became one of political judgment only, and that by interfering the courts would be trespassing across that line which divides a proper exercise of a statutory discretion based on a political judgment, in relation to which the courts will not interfere, from an improper exercise of such a discretion in relation to which the courts will interfere.

[Lord Roskill referred to the judgment in *Council for the Civil Service Unions* v *Minister for the Civil Service* (*ante* at p. 534) and continued.]

To my mind the crucial question is whether the conduct of the council in trying by their four questions, whether taken individually or collectively, to force acceptance by the club of their own policy (however proper that policy may be) on their own terms, as for example, by forcing them to lend their considerable prestige to a public condemnation of the tour, can be said either to be so 'unreasonable' as to give rise to '*Wednesbury* unreasonableness' (*Associated Provincial Picture Houses Ltd* v *Wednesbury Corporation* [1948] 1 KB 223) or to be so fundamental a breach of the duty to act fairly which rests upon every local authority in matters of this kind and thus to justify interference by the courts.

I do not doubt for one moment the great importance which the council attach to the presence in its midst of a 25 per cent population of persons who are either Asian or of Afro-Caribbean origin. Nor do I doubt for one moment the sincerity of the view expressed in Mr Soulsby's affidavit regarding the need for the council to distance itself from bodies who hold important positions and who do not actively discourage sporting contacts with South Africa. Persuasion, even powerful persuasion, is always a permissible way of seeking to obtain an objective. But in a field where other views can equally legitimately be held, persuasion, however powerful, must not be allowed to cross that line where it moves into the field of illegitimate pressure coupled with the threat of sanctions. The four questions, coupled with the insistence that only affirmative answers to all four would be acceptable, are suggestive of more than powerful persuasion. The second question is to my mind open to particular criticism. What, in the context, is meant by the 'club?' The committee? 90 playing members? 4,300 non-playing members? It by no means follows that the committee would all have agreed on an affirmative answer to the question and still less that a majority of their members, playing or non-playing, would have done so. Nor would any of these groups of members necessarily have known whether 'the large proportion,' whatever that phrase may mean in the context, of the Leicester population would have regarded the tour as 'an insult' to them.

None of the learned judges in the court below have felt able to hold that the action of the club was unreasonable or perverse in the *Wednesbury* sense. They do not appear to have been invited to consider whether those actions, even if not unreasonable on *Wednesbury* principles, were assailable on the grounds of procedural impropriety or unfairness by the council in the manner in which, in the light of the facts I have outlined, they took their decision to suspend for 12 months the use by the club of the Welford Road recreation ground.

I greatly hesitate to differ from four learned judges on the *Wednesbury* issue but for myself I would have been disposed respectfully to do this and to say that the actions of the council were unreasonable in the *Wednesbury* sense. But even if I am wrong in this view, I am clearly of the opinion that the manner in which the council took that decision was in all the circumstances of the case unfair within the third of the principles stated in *Council for the Civil Service Unions* v *Minister for the Civil Service* [1985] AC 374. The council formulated those four questions in the manner of which I have spoken and indicated that only such affirmative answers would be acceptable. They received reasoned and reasonable answers which went a long way in support of the policy which the council had accepted and desired to see accepted. The views expressed in these reasoned and reasonable answers were lawful views and the views which, as the evidence shows, many people sincerely hold and believe to be correct. If the club had adopted a different and hostile attitude, different considerations might well have arisen. But the club did not adopt any such attitude. . . .

I would therefore allow the appeal.

Note

The judgment of Lord Roskill may be compared to that of Ackner LJ in the Court of Appeal in *Wheeler*. Having decided that the council were lawfully entitled to take into account the purposes expressed in s. 71 of the Race Relations Act 1976, Ackner LJ continued:

> If I am right so far, this leaves only one final question to consider. Can it be said in the circumstances of the case that no reasonable local authority could properly conclude that temporarily banning from the use of its recreation grounds an important local rugger club, which declined to condemn a South African tour and declined actively to discourage its members from participating therein, could promote good relations between persons of different racial groups? (The well-known *Wednesbury* test: see *Associated Provincial Picture Houses Ltd* v *Wednesbury Corp.* [1947] 2 All ER 680, [1948] 1 KB 223). Forbes J was at pains to point out, as I certainly would wish also to do, that courts are not concerned with the merits of the two rival views, no doubt equally honestly held, as to the value of severing

sporting links with South Africa. I am fully prepared to accept that, even amongst those who feel strongly that sporting links should be severed, there may be some who could take the view that the club acted wholly reasonably in the action it took and should not have been expected to go further. But to accept the mere existence of such a school of thought does not establish that the council's decision was perverse and this is what the club is obliged to do to succeed under this head. Nor is the club's case advanced by emphasising that the council were imposing a sanction against members of the club for refusing publicly to endorse the reasonable views of the council and thereby interfering with the club's freedom of speech. The view which the council held as to the importance of severing sporting links with South Africa had clearly been fully considered by the council well before the events of 1984, and in view of the make-up of the population of the city it was a view which understandably was very strongly supported. It represented no more than that clearly recorded in the Gleneagles Agreement. In my judgment it would be quite wrong to categorise as perverse the council's decision to give an outward and visible manifestation of their disapproval of the club's failure, indeed refusal, 'to take every practical step to discourage' the tour, and in particular the participation of its members.

I would accordingly dismiss this appeal.

Questions

1. On the question of whether the council had acted in a way in which no reasonable council could have acted, do you find the reasoning of Lord Roskill or that of Ackner LJ more convincing?

2. Does Lord Roskill explain which of the particular aspects of Lord Diplock's third category, procedural impropriety, he considered to have been breached?

Nottinghamshire CC v *Secretary of State for the Environment*

[1986] 1 AC 240

House of Lords

In 1984 the Secretary of State issued a report containing the guidance for expenditure by local authorities for 1985/86. The guidance was based on the 1984/85 budgets of local authorities and an amount known as 'grant-related expenditure' (GRE). Grant-related expenditure is the notional expenditure which an authority might incur if all authorities provided the same standard of service with the same degree of efficiency at a level consistent with the Government's aggregate spending plans for local authorities. The guidance for 1985/86 stated that authorities which had budgeted to spend at or below the GRE expenditure in 1984/85 could budget in 1985/86 for the 1984/85 GRE plus 3.75 per cent. Those which had budgeted at above their GRE for 1984/85 could budget for the figure in the 1984/85 guidance plus 3.75 per cent. Under the scheme established by the Local Government Planning and Land Act 1980, if a local authority's expenditure exceeded that set in the guidance to it, the Secretary of State was empowered to reduce the amount of the rate support grant made by central government to the authority.

The report was laid before the House of Commons pursuant to s. 60 of the Act, and was approved by an affirmative resolution of the House. Nottinghamshire CC and the City of Bradford MC applied for an order of *certiorari* to quash the decision of the Secretary of State contained in the report and for declarations that the expenditure guidance contained in the report was invalid. They based their application on two grounds. First, the Secretary of State's guidance did not comply with the requirement in s. 59(11A) of the 1980 Act that 'any guidance issued . . . be framed by reference to principles applicable to all local authorities . . .' because it differentiated between authorities budgeting to spend above or below the GRE. Second, they argued that the decision of the Secretary was unreasonable because the guidance was disproportionately disadvantageous to a small group of public authorities whose 1984/85 guidance was below GRE and who were budgeting to spend above GRE.

At first instance, the application was dismissed but the Court of Appeal allowed the authority's appeal. On appeal to the House of Lords the first ground was rejected; it was held that, on the true construction of the Act, while there had to be one set of principles applicable to all local authorities, it was permissible for those principles to identify and reflect differences between local authorities, including their past expenditure records. The following extracts deal with the second ground.

LORD SCARMAN: . . . Their second submission is that, even if the guidance complies with the words of the statute, it offends a principle of public law in that the burden which the guidance imposes on some authorities, including Nottingham and Bradford, is so disproportionately disadvantageous when compared with its effect upon others that it is a perversely unreasonable exercise of the power conferred by the statute upon the Secretary of State. The respondents rely on what has become known to lawyers as the 'Wednesbury principles' – by which is meant the judgment of Lord Greene MR in *Associated Provincial Picture House Ltd* v *Wednesbury Corporation* [1948] 1 KB 223, 229. . . .

The submission raises an important question as to the limits of judicial review. We are in the field of public financial administration and we are being asked to review the exercise by the Secretary of State of an administrative discretion which inevitably requires a political judgment on his part and which cannot lead to action by him against a local authority unless that action is first approved by the House of Commons.

. . . My Lords, I think the courts below were absolutely right to decline the invitation to intervene. I can understand that there may well be a justiciable issue as to the true construction of the words of the statute and that, if the Secretary of State has issued guidance which fails to comply with the requirement of subsection (11 A) of section 59 of the Act of 1980 the guidance can be quashed. But I cannot accept that it is constitutionally appropriate, save in very exceptionable circumstances, for the courts to intervene on the ground of 'unreasonableness' to quash guidance framed by the Secretary of State and by necessary implication approved by the House of Commons, the guidance being concerned with the limits of public expenditure by local authorities and the incidence of the tax burden as between taxpayers and ratepayers. Unless and until a statute provides otherwise, or it is established that the Secretary of State has abused his power, these are matters of political judgment for him and for the House of Commons. They are not for the judges or your Lordships' House in its judicial capacity.

For myself, I refuse in this case to examine the detail of the guidance or its consequences. My reasons are these. Such an examination by a court would be justified only if a prima facie case were to be shown for holding that the Secretary of State has acted in bad faith, or for an improper motive, or that the consequences of his guidance were so absurd that he must have taken leave of his senses. The evidence comes nowhere near establishing any of these propositions. Nobody in the case has ever suggested bad faith on the part of the Secretary of State. Nobody suggests, nor could it be suggested in the light of the evidence as to the matters he considered before reaching his decision, that he had acted for an improper motive. Nobody now suggests that the Secretary of State failed to consult local authorities in the manner required by statute. It is plain that the timetable, to which the Secretary of State in the preparation of the guidance was required by statute and compelled by circumstances to adhere, involved him necessarily in framing guidance on the basis of the past spending record of authorities. It is recognised that the Secretary of State and his advisers were well aware that there would be inequalities in the distribution of the burden between local authorities but believed the guidance upon which he decided would by discouraging the high spending and encouraging the low spending be the best course of action in the circumstances. And as my noble and learned friend, Lord Bridge of Harwich, demonstrates, it was guidance which complied with the terms of the statute. This view of the language of the statute has inevitably a significant bearing upon the conclusion of 'unreasonableness' in the *Wednesbury* sense. If, as your Lordships are holding, the guidance was based on principles applicable to all authorities, the principles would have to be either a pattern of perversity or an absurdity of such proportions that the guidance could not have been framed by a bona fide exercise of political judgment on the part of the Secretary of State. And it would be necessary to find as a fact that the House of Commons had been misled: for their approval was necessary and was obtained to the action that he proposed to take to implement the guidance.

. . . The present case raises in acute form the constitutional problem of the separation of powers between Parliament, the executive, and the courts. In this case, Parliament has enacted that an executive power is not to be exercised save with the consent and approval of one of its Houses. It is true that the framing of the guidance is for the Secretary of State alone after consultation with local authorities; but he cannot act on the guidance so as to discriminate between local authorities without reporting to, and obtaining the approval of, the House of Commons. That House has, therefore, a role and responsibility not only at the legislative stage when the Act was passed but in the action to be taken by the Secretary of State in the exercise of the power conferred upon him by the legislation.

To sum it up, the levels of public expenditure and the incidence and distribution of taxation are matters for Parliament and, within Parliament, especially for the House of Commons. If Parliament legislates, the courts have their interpretative role: they must, if called upon to do so, construe the statute. If a minister exercises a power conferred on him by the legislation, the courts can investigate whether he has abused his power. But if, as in this case, effect cannot be given to the Secretary of State's determination without the consent of the House of Commons and the House of Commons has consented, it is not open to the courts to intervene unless the minister and the House must have misconstrued the statute or the minister has – to put it bluntly – deceived the House. The courts can properly rule that a minister has acted unlawfully if he has erred in law as to the limits of his power even when his action has the approval of the House of Commons, itself acting not legislatively but within the limits set by a statute. But, if a statute, as in this case, requires the House of Commons to approve a minister's decision before he can lawfully enforce it, and if the action proposed complies with the terms of the statute (as your Lordships, I understand, are convinced that it does in the present case), it is not for the judges to say that the action has such unreasonable consequences that the guidance upon which the action is based and on which the House of Commons had notice was perverse and must be set aside. For that is a question of policy for the minister and the Commons, unless there has been bad faith or misconduct by the minister. Where Parliament has legislated that the action to be taken by the Secretary of State must, before it is taken, be approved by the House of Commons, it is no part of the judge's role to declare that the action proposed is unfair, unless it constitutes an abuse of power in the sense which I have explained; for Parliament has enacted that one of its Houses is responsible. Judicial review is a great weapon in the hands of the judges: but the judges must observe the constitutional limits set by our parliamentary system upon their exercise of this beneficent power. . . .

Lord Bridge and Lord Templeman delivered judgments in which they agreed with Lord Scarman. Lord Roskill and Lord Griffiths agreed with Lord Scarman.

Note

Lord Scarman's judgment was discussed and followed by the House of Lords in *R* v *Secretary of State for the Environment, ex parte Hammersmith and Fulham LBC* [1990] 3 All ER 589, a case which also involved a dispute between central and local government over finances. The House of Lords held that the Secretary of State had acted lawfully in setting a maximum amount for the budgets of a number of authorities under the Local Government Finance Act 1988.

Questions

1. Do you interpret Lord Scarman's judgment as stating that judicial review of a decision of this nature on the ground of unreasonableness is excluded?
2. Would judicial review be available on any other grounds, for example that the Minister had acted for an improper purpose or on the basis of irrelevant considerations?
3. Which constitutional theory did his Lordship rely on in this case?
4. Commenting on this decision in (1986) 45 CLJ (169–173), Colin Reid sees it, at p. 171:

> . . . as an affirmation of our traditional constitutional theory. There may be no formal separation of powers in this country, but the basic notions of our constitution, such as parliamentary sovereignty, the rule of law and responsibility of the Executive to Parliament, do create a fundamental distribution of powers and functions between the various elements of the state. It is to Parliament that one must look to control the executive on matters of policy and principle, *a fortiori* in cases where it has been enacted that the

> Executive must seek parliamentary approval for the exercise of the powers conferred on it. . . .
>
> The question must be asked, though, how well this structure serves us in the political realities of today. Can we rely on Parliament to provide an adequate check on the powers of the executive?

If the answer is no, can judicial review provide a solution? Note that Reid's view is that it cannot; 'the way to achieve greater control over the Executive must lie in far-reaching reforms to our constitutional structure, rather than to a continued extension, or rather distortion, of judicial review to embrace issues and arguments not suited to judicial resolution.' Compare this with the view expressed by Cane (*ante*, at pp. 526–9).

Note

The *Nottinghamshire* and *Hammersmith & Fulham* cases have been described as being super-*Wednesbury* because their approach imposes a higher threshold. The appropriate standard of *Wednesbury* review was at issue in the next case.

R v *Ministry of Defence, ex parte Smith*

[1996] 2 WLR 305

Divisional Court and Court of Appeal

> The four applicants had been serving member of the armed forces until they had been administratively discharged because they had a homosexual orientation contrary to the Ministry's policy. The applicants' grounds of challenge in their application for judicial review claimed that the policy was irrational; contrary to Art. 8 of the European Convention on Human Rights and contrary to Art. 2 of the Equal Treatment Directive (76/207/EEC).
>
> Counsel for the Ministry had argued that the higher threshold (super-*Wednesbury* approach) was the correct basis on which to review the policy.

SIMON BROWN LJ:. . . Nor am I persuaded that any test more favourable to the executive than the conventional *Wednesbury* approach should be adopted in the present context. It is difficult to imagine an area of decision-making further removed than this from that — national economic policy — under consideration in *Reg* v *Secretary of State for the Environment, ex parte Hammersmith and Fulham London Borough Council* [1991] 1 AC 521. Whilst I understand Mr. Richards's argument that the policy presently impugned should properly be debated and considered on its merits in Parliament, I cannot accept that it depends essentially on political judgment. In the *Hammersmith and Fulham* case, moreover, there was no human rights dimension to the case; here it is prominent, and in my judgment a powerful countervailing weight when considering both the level at which the irrationality test should be fixed and the intensity of review appropriate.

(3) I approach the case, therefore, on the conventional *Wednesbury* basis adapted to a human rights context and ask: can the Secretary of State show an important

competing public interest which he could reasonably judge sufficient to justify the restriction? The primary judgment is for him. Only if his purported justification outrageously defies logic or accepted moral standards can the court, exercising its secondary judgment, properly strike it down.

There can be no doubting the importance of the competing public interest advanced by the Secretary of State as justifying this policy: the delivery of an operationally efficient and effective fighting force. The real question becomes: is it reasonable for the Secretary of State to take the view that allowing homosexuals into the forces would imperil that interest? Is that, in short, a coherent view, right or wrong? I have already said enough to indicate my own opinion that it is a wrong view, a view that rests too firmly upon the supposition of prejudice in others and which insufficiently recognises the damage to human rights inflicted. But can it properly be stigmatised as irrational? We live in changing times. That was expressly recognised both by the select committee in its April 1991 report and by the Prime Minister in July 1991. It is only recently that many of the other armed forces who do now admit homosexuals came to adopt their present policies. Mr Richards submits that the full impact of these changes abroad is not yet apparent; their wisdom has still to be demonstrated. When exactly can this policy be said to have become irrational?

I do not pretend to have found this an easy case. On the contrary I recall none harder. The protection of human rights is, Mr Pannick submits, a matter with which the courts are particularly concerned and for which they have an undoubted responsibility. So they do. But they owe a duty too to remain within their constitutional bounds and not trespass beyond them. Only if it were plain beyond sensible argument that no conceivable damage could be done to the armed services as a fighting unit would it be appropriate for this court now to remove the issue entirely from the hands both of the miliary and of the government. If the Convention for the Protection of Human Rights and Fundamental Freedoms were part of our law and we were accordingly entitled to ask whether the policy answers a pressing social need and whether the restriction on human rights involved can be shown proportionate to its benefits, then clearly the primary judgment (subject only to a limited 'margin of appreciation') would be for us and not others: the constitutional balance would shift. But that is not the position. In exercising merely a secondary judgment, this court is bound, even though adjudicating in a human rights context, to act with some reticence. Our approach must reflect, not overlook where responsibility ultimately lies for the defence of the realm and recognise too that Parliament is exercising a continuing supervision over this area of prerogative power.

With all these considerations in mind, I have come finally to the conclusion that, my own view of the evidence notwithstanding, the minister's stance cannot properly be held unlawful. His suggested justification for the ban may to many seem unconvincing; to say, however, that it is outrageous in its defiance of logic is another thing. There is, I conclude, still room for two views. Similarly it is difficult to regard the policy as wholly incompatible with 'accepted moral standards.' There is no present uniformity of outlook on this issue: not everyone would condemn the ban on moral grounds, morally neutral though the ministry avow their own stance to be.

It follows from all this that I for my part would refuse these applications albeit with hesitation and regret. I conclude that the decision upon the future of this policy must still properly rest with others, notably the government and Parliament. But I make no secret of this: that my greatest concern in leaving the matter in this way is lest the policy's human rights dimension becomes depreciated once the court's doors are closed. There is little in the papers before us to instil confidence that the fundamental human rights of these applicants and others like them will be fully and faithfully recognised elsewhere.

[*The application was refused with none of the grounds finding favour with the court. On appeal to the Court of Appeal.*]

SIR THOMAS BINGHAM MR: . . . Mr. David Pannick, who represented three of the applicants, and whose arguments were adopted by the fourth, submitted that the court should adopt the following approach to the issue of irrationality:

> The court may not interfere with the exercise of an administrative discretion on substantive grounds save where the court is satisfied that the decision is unreasonable in the sense that it is beyond the range of responses open to a reasonable decision-maker. But in judging whether the decision-maker has exceeded this margin of appreciation the human rights context is important. The more substantial the interference with human rights, the more the court will require by way of justification before it is satisfied that the decision is reasonable in the sense outlined above.

This submission is in my judgment an accurate distillation of the principles laid down by the House of Lords in *Reg* v *Secretary of State for the Home Department, ex parte Bugdaycay* [1987] AC 514 and *Reg* v *Secretary of State for the Home Department, ex parte Brind* [1991] 1 AC 696. In the first of these cases Lord Bridge of Harwich said [1987] AC 514, 531:

> I approach the question raised by the challenge to the Secretary of State's decision on the basis of the law stated earlier in this opinion, viz. that the resolution of any issue of fact and the exercise of any discretion in relation to an application for asylum as a refugee lie exclusively within the jurisdiction of the Secretary of State subject only to the court's power of review. The limitations on the scope of that power are well known and need not be restated here. Within those limitations the court must, I think, be entitled to subject an administrative decision to the more rigorous examination, to ensure that it is in no way flawed, according to the gravity of the issue which the decision determines. The most fundamental of all human rights is the individual's right to life and when an administrative decision under challenge is said to be one which may put the applicant's life at risk, the basis of the decision must surely call for the most anxious scrutiny.

Lord Templeman, at p. 537H, spoke to similar effect. In the second case, having concluded that it was not open to an English court to apply the European Convention on Human Rights, Lord Bridge said [1991] 1 AC 696, 748–749:

> But I do not accept that this conclusion means that the courts are powerless to prevent the exercise by the executive of administrative discretions, even when conferred, as in the instant case, in terms which are on their face unlimited, in a way which infringes fundamental human rights. Most of the rights spelled out in terms in the Convention, including the right to freedom of expression, are less than absolute and must in some cases yield to the claims of competing public interests. Thus, article 10(2) of the Convention spells out and categorises the competing public interests by reference to which the right to freedom of expression may have to be curtailed. In exercising the power of judicial review we have neither the advantages nor the disadvantages of any comparable code to which we may refer or by which we are bound. But again, this surely does not mean that in deciding whether the Secretary of State, in the exercise of his discretion, could reasonably impose the restriction he has imposed on the broadcasting organisations, we are not perfectly entitled to start from the premise that any restriction of the right to

> freedom of expression requires to be justified and that nothing less than an important competing public interest will be sufficient to justify it. The primary judgment as to whether the particular competing public interest justifies the particular restriction imposed falls to be made by the Secretary of State to whom Parliament has entrusted the discretion. But we are entitled to exercise a secondary judgment by asking whether a reasonable Secretary of State, on the material before him, could reasonably make that primary judgment.

Again, Lord Templeman spoke to similar effect, at p. 751:

> It seems to me that the courts cannot escape from asking themselves whether a reasonable Secretary of State, on the material before him, could reasonably conclude that the interference with freedom of expression which he determined to impose was justifiable.

It is important to note that, in considering whether English law satisfies the requirement in article 13 of the European Convention that there should be a national remedy to enforce the substance of the Convention rights and freedoms, the European Court of Human Rights has held that it does, attaching very considerable weight to the power of the English courts to review administrative decisions by way of judicial review: see *Vilvarajah* v *United Kingdom* (1991) 14 EHRR 248, 291, 292.

It was argued for the ministry in reliance on *Reg* v *Secretary of State for the Environment, ex parte Nottinghamshire County Council* [1986] AC 240 and *Reg* v *Secretary of State for the Environment, ex parte Hammersmith and Fulham London Borough Council* [1991] 1 AC 521 that a test more exacting than *Wednesbury (Associated Provincial Picture Houses Ltd.* v *Wednesbury Corporation* [1948] 1 KB 233) was appropriate in this case. The Divisional Court rejected this argument and so do I. The greater the policy content of a decision, and the more remote the subject matter of a decision from ordinary judicial experience, the more hesitant the court must necessarily be in holding a decision to be irrational. That is good law and, like most good law, common sense. Where decisions of a policy-laden, esoteric or security-based nature are in issue even greater caution than normal must be shown in applying the test, but the test itself is sufficiently flexible to cover all situations.

The present cases do not affect the lives or liberty of those involved. But they do concern innate qualities of a very personal kind and the decisions of which the applicants complain have had a profound effect on their careers and prospects. The applicants' rights as human beings are very much in issue. It is now accepted that this issue is justiciable. This does not of course mean that the court is thrust into the position of the primary decision-maker. It is not the constitutional role of the court to regulate the conditions of service in the armed forces of the Crown, not has it the expertise to do so. But it has the constitutional role and duty of ensuring that the rights of citizens are not abused by the unlawful exercise of executive power. While the court must properly defer to the expertise of responsible decision-makers, it must not shrink from its fundamental duty to 'do right to all manner of people . . .'

None of the grounds of appeal found favour with the court, although, they all agreed with the formulation of the test for irrationality in a human rights context proposed by counsel for the appellants.

Note

Simon Brown LJ said, in a case involving a successful challenge to the action of public authorities in banning export shipments of livestock through sea ports and airports because of the fear of the consequences which might be carried out by animal rights protestors, that where issues involved were the rule of law or fundamental rights then 'the courts will adopt a more interventionist role' (*R* v *Coventry City Council, ex parte Phoenix Aviation* [1995] 3 All ER 37, 62).

Question
Does Simon Brown LJ think that there is a lower threshold for *Wednesbury* review for fundamental rights (and the rule of law), and is that the implication of the test adopted by the Court of Appeal in *ex parte Smith*?

Note
Jowell and Lester argue in 'Beyond *Wednesbury:* Substantive Principles of Administrative Law' [1987] *Public Law,* 368 that irrationality is unsatisfactory as a ground for review for three reasons:

(a) It is inadequate: 'the incantation of the word "unreasonable" simply does not provide sufficient justification for judicial intervention. Intellectual honesty requires a further and better explanation as to why the act is unreasonable.'
(b) It is unrealistic: it seeks to prevent review except in cases where the official has behaved absurdly, but 'in practice the courts are willing to impugn decisions that are far from absurd and indeed often coldly rational.'
(c) It is tautologous: this is because an unreasonable decision is defined as one which no reasonable authority could take. Hence, the authors invite us to imagine a law providing for the demolition of unfit houses and then defining unfit in the sense that no fit house could be so.

Question
Do you agree that such criticisms are justified, in the light of the cases discussed in this section? For the authors' suggestions for reform, see further Jowell and Lester.

(iv) Substantive legitimate expectations

R v *Ministry of Agriculture, Fisheries and Food, ex parte Hamble Fisheries*
[1995] 2 All ER 714
Divisional Court

The applicants had purchased The Nellie, a beam trawler in 1987, with a view to taking advantage of the Ministry's policy which permitted transfer of pressure stock licences from one vessel to another. Pressure stocks were fish species which would not be sustainable given unrestricted fishing within the applicable EC quota. The applicant obtained the transfer of miscellaneous species licences to The Nellie enabling it to fish for any non-pressure stock in any sea area. In 1990 the Ministry decided to permit capacity aggregation, which is the transfer of similar licences from existing vessels to a larger one, provided that total capacity of the fleet was not increased. The applicant bought two more vessels which had beam trawler licences with the intention of transferring them to the larger Nellie. In March 1992 the Ministry announced a moratorium on the transfer and aggregation of pressure stock licences on the beam trawlers which were fishing in the North Sea, or off the West Coast of Scotland. In the new North Sea beam trawl policy, owners of any vessel with any licence other than a miscellaneous species licence, which had a track record of using the beam trawl method in the North Sea between 12 March 1992 and 11 March 1992 would be eligible for a North Sea beam trawl licence equivalent to their current one. There were also two 'pipeline' exceptions to this policy. First, if on 12 March 1992 a valid application was being considered for transfer of a pressure stock licence, then this would be eligible if the owners satisfied the Ministry that they had a genuine intention to fish for sole and/or plaice in the North Sea by beam trawl. Secondly, if anyone had entered into a binding contract, before the date of the announcement, to purchase, build or convert a vessel to fish for sole and/or plaice by beam trawl, then the vessel is eligible for the licence if all of the following conditions are met: (a) the Ministry is satisfied about intention; (b) at least one of the licences comes from an eligible vessel, and (c) a licence has been applied for, or permission granted to make a late application (by 11 June 1992). The applicant was informed by letter, that the Nellie would not qualify for a North Sea beam trawl licence because it currently had a miscellaneous licence and had no track record of beam trawling in the North Sea. The grounds of challenge to this decision were that the applicant had a legitimate expectation that (i) any change in the policy would not frustrate the completion of licence aggregation for the Nellie, thus enabling it to trawl for pressure stocks in the North Sea, and (ii) there should have been proper 'pipeline' provisions in the new policy of licensing by track record for fishermen who had entered irrevocably into agreements to obtain beam trawl licences and had demonstrated a real and genuine intent to do so. The Ministry contented that it was not reasonable to expect that possession of 'hip-pocket' licences (i.e. licence entitlements which could be used by way of aggregation) would insulate these people from the effects of a change in the licensing policy, since any limitation would handicap the Ministry's performance of its duty to monitor and control the intensity of fishing.

SEDLEY J: . . .

(c) *Legitimate expectation*

The first question under this head, posed by Mr Paines, is whether there can in law be a legitimate expectation of anything more than a procedural benefit or protection. There is no doubt that the expectation to which Mr Green lays claim is of a substantive benefit or advantage, not merely a procedural one. Mr Paines relies upon a passage in the decision of Laws J in *R* v *Secretary of State for Transport, ex p Richmond upon Thames London BC* [1994] 1 All ER 577 at 594–596, [1994] 1 WLR 74 at 92–94. The respect to which this passage is entitled is not diminished by the fact that it is obiter, the decision having turned upon an unrelated point. But I regret to say that I disagree with significant elements of Laws J's reasoning, although not with its starting and finishing points. The subject matter was a submission of Mr Richard Gordon QC that the applicant local authority had acquired a legitimate expectation that policy would not be shifted in any circumstances beyond a certain point. Laws J's conclusion that neither precedent not principle could carry Mr Gordon that far is one with which I would entirely agree. But, in order to develop his submission, Mr Gordon had contended that the law now recognised not only procedural but substantive legitimate expectations. Laws J said, 'This is an antithesis which is liable to cause confusion' . . . (see [1994] 1 All ER 577 at 595, [1994] 1 WLR 74 at 92). This too I would respectfully indorse, as I would Laws J's conclusion of principle ([1994] 1 All ER 577 at 595, [1994] 1 WLR 74 at 93):

> I consider that the putative distinction between procedural and substantive rights in this context has little (if any) utility: the question is always whether the discipline of fairness, imposed by the common law, ought to prevent the public authority respondent from acting as it proposes.

But it is for precisely this reason that I would not accept Laws J's further proposition that neither precedent nor principle goes further than the enforcement of legitimate *procedural* expectations. *R* v *Secretary of State for the Home Dept, ex p Ruddock* [1987] 2 All ER 518, [1987] 1 WLR 1482, which it was the privilege of Laws J and myself to argue at the Bar before Taylor J, was precisely a case of legitimate expectation of a substantive benefit, namely that individuals not falling within the government's publicised criteria for telephone surveillance would not have their telephones tapped by the security services. Taylor J held ([1987] 2 All ER 518 at 531, [1987] 1 WLR 1482 at 1497):

> '. . . I conclude that the doctrine of legitimate expectation in essence imposes a duty to act fairly. Whilst most of the cases are concerned . . . with a right to be heard, I do not think the doctrine is so confined . . . Of course, [a promise or undertaking given by a minister as to how he will proceed] must not conflict with his statutory duty . . . the Secretary of State . . . cannot fetter his discretion. By declaring a policy he does not preclude any possible need to change it.'

In so deciding, Taylor J founded upon the speech of Lord Scarman in *Findlay* v *Secretary of State for the Home Dept* [1984] 3 All ER 801, [1985] AC 318 in which the possibility of a substantive legitimate expectation was recognised.

In my respectful view, principle as well as precedent points to these conclusions. As Laws J points out in the passage I have cited, the real question is one of fairness in public administration. It is difficult to see why it is any less unfair to frustrate a legitimate expectation that something will or will not be done by the decision-maker than it is to frustrate a legitimate expectation that the applicant will be listened to before the decision maker decides whether to take a particular step. Such a doctrine does not risk fettering a public body in the discharge of public duties because no individual can legitimately expect the discharge of public duties to stand still or be distorted because of that individual's peculiar position. As I hope to show in what follows, legitimacy is itself a relative concept, to be gauged proportionately to the legal and policy implications of the expectation. This, no doubt, is why it has proved easier to establish a legitimate expectation that an applicant will be listened to than that a particular outcome will be arrived at by the decision-maker. But the same principle of fairness in my judgment governs both situations . . .

I turn therefore, to the question which has been most heavily fought over in these proceedings: did the applicant have a legitimate expectation that an exception would be made for fishermen in its position? It has been debated before me almost entirely in terms of the jurisprudence of the Court of Justice of the European Communities. Neither counsel submits that there is any material difference between this body of law and the domestic law of England and Wales. (Since some of the leading cases in the Court of Justice concern legitimate expectations of substantive benefits or protections in the face of policy shifts, they furnish further support for the view that I have expressed above on this topic.) . . .

Professor Schwarze summarises the case law of the Court of Justice as follows [*European Administrative Law*, 1992, pp. 1134–1135]:

> For the principle of the protection of legitimate expectations to be applicable, an objective basis must exist for this principle in the shape of an expectation which is worthy of protection. Because of the broad freedom of action enjoyed by the legislature, the mere existence of a legal rule is not normally a suitable basis for a legitimate expectation which must be taken into account. Adequate grounds for a solid expectation can be provided on the one hand by the fact of having entered into certain obligations towards the authorities, or on the other hand by a course of conduct on the part of the authorities giving rise to specific expectations — which in certain circumstances may arise out of a commitment entered into by the authorities.

From its terms it can be seen that this is not an exhaustive formulation, but it seems to me an excellent account of the body of law relied upon by Mr Green under this head, including *Deuka* v *Einfuhr-und Vorratsstelle für Getreide und Futtermittel* Case 78/74 [1975] ECR 421.

So far as concerns the respondent's objection that it is unreasonable to expect them to judge whether licences have been acquired otherwise than for a speculative purpose, Mr Green points cogently to the fact that at two points of the policy itself the respondent has assumed exactly this task, for both exceptions are predicated on proof of a genuine intention to beam trawl specifically for sole or plaice in the North Sea. Certainly it is harder to judge whether a licence has been acquired for a speculative purpose, but I would not think such a problem insuperable. What matters, therefore, in the common law both of the European Community and of Britain, is whether (in Professor Schwarze's words) the applicant can demonstrate 'an expectation which is worthy of protection' (p 1134) . . .

What then is the legal alchemy which gives an expectation sufficient legitimacy to secure enforcement in public law? Where the expectation has been raised by a public promise made by government 'it is in the interest of good administration that it should act fairly and should implement its promise, so long as implementation does not interfere with its statutory duty,' (see *A-G of Hong Kong* v *Ng Yuen Shiu* [1983] 2 All ER 346 at 351, [1983] 2 AC 629 at 638 per Lord Fraser).

But where the expectation is based upon practice, the issue is more elusive. A promise is, precisely, a representation about future conduct, making it relatively straightforward to decide whether the promisor should be held to it. Practices may, but do not necessarily, have the same character. Where the material practice is generated by a policy which is itself liable to change, the practice cannot be logically expected to survive a policy change, and policy change may not be able to be withheld consistently with the statutory duties or powers under which the policy has been brought into existence.

Mr Green has relied prominently in this regard upon the decision of Popplewell J in *R* v *Ministry of Agriculture Fisheries and Food, ex p Cox* [1993] 2 CMLR 917. The applicant was the beneficiary of a grazing licence to which was attached a milk quota registered in her name with the respondent. Because she did not take up occupation of the land the respondent in 1988 considered revoking her entry but decided not to do so. Three years later it changed its mind and gave the applicant notice of its intention. In judicial review proceedings Popplewell J held that although in law actual occupation was required, so that there should truly have been no registration in the first place, the respondent had forfeited its power to remove the applicant from the register when it declined to do so in 1988. The judge accepted that the ministry had had the power, and by parity of reasoning the duty, to make the change in 1988, but held (at 930):

> It was always open to (the licensor) at the end of the grazing licence to seek alteration of the register and thereafter if they were dissatisfied by the decision of 11 July 1988 to challenge that decision. I am wholly unpersuaded either that the minister had the power to vary his decision of 11 July 1988 or if he had the power it was a proper exercise of that power.

The decision, therefore, seems to me not to lie in the field of legitimate expectation but in that of finality of decision-making. Undoubtedly it raises the question whether finality can save an unlawful decision, but that is not the question in the present case.

Let me then turn to what it is that gives an expectation legitimacy. In *Council of Civil Service Unions* v *Minister for Civil Service* [1984] 3 All ER 835 at 949, [1985] AC 374 at 408 Lord Diplock tabulated existing pathways to judicial review (an analysis described by Lord Scarman in *Nottinghamshire CC* v *Secretary of State for the Environment* [1986] 1 All ER 199 at 203, [1986] AC 204 at 249 as 'valuable, and already "classical", but certainly not exhaustive . . .'). In relation to his second class of protected interest, which included benefits or advantages which the applicant can legitimately expect to be permitted to continue to enjoy, Lord Diplock added the following parenthetic comment ([1984] 3 All ER 935 at 949, [1985] AC 374 at 408):

> I prefer to continue to call the kind of expectation that qualifies a decision for inclusion in class (b) a 'legitimate expectation' rather than a 'reasonable expectation', in order thereby to indicate that it has consequences to which effect will be given in public law, whereas an expectation or hope that some benefit or advantage would continue to be enjoyed, although it might well be entertained by a 'reasonable' man, would not necessarily have such consequences.

Lord Diplock instanced the decision of their Lordships in *Findlay* v *Secretary of State for the Home Dept* [1984] 3 All ER 801, [1985] AC 318 as an example of an expectation of the latter kind. *Findlay's* case concerned the legitimacy of a sudden change of policy by the Home Secretary which resulted in the loss by a number of life sentence prisoners of an expectation of early release on parole. Of two of them Lord Scarman, with whom the other members of the House concurred, said ([1984] 3 All ER 801 at 830, [1985] AC 318 at 338):

> They had good reason under the practice which prevailed before the adoption of the new policy to expect release much earlier than became likely after its adoption. The doctrine of a legitimate expectation has an important place in the developing law of judicial review . . . It is said that the refusal to except them from the new policy was

> an unlawful act on the part of the Secretary of State in that his decision frustrated their expectation. But what was their *legitimate* expectation? Given the substance and purpose of the legislative provisions governing parole, the most that a convicted prisoner can legitimately expect is that his case will be examined individually in the light of whatever policy the Secretary of State sees fit to adopt, provided always that the adopted policy is a lawful exercise of the discretion conferred upon him by the statute. Any other view would entail the conclusion that the unfettered discretion conferred by the statute on the minister can in some cases be restricted so as to hamper, or even prevent, changes of policy. Bearing in mind the complexity of the issues which the Secretary of State has to consider and the importance of the public interest in the administration of parole, I cannot think that Parliament intended the discretion to be restricted in this way. (Lord Scarman's emphasis.)

The importance of an unfettered power to change policy was stressed by Lord Diplock in *Hughes* v *Dept of Health and Social Security* [1985] AC 776 at 788. The case concerned the compulsory retirement of civil servants before the age of 65, to which it had previously been departmental policy to allow them to continue:

> But this remains the case only so long as the departmental circular announcing that administrative policy to the employees affected by it remains in force. Administrative policies may change with changing circumstances, including changes in the political complexion of governments. The liberty to make such changes is something that is inherent in our constitutional form of government. When a change in administrative policy takes place and is communicated in a departmental circular ... any reasonable expectations that may have been aroused ... by any previous circular are destroyed . . .

These passages might be thought to suggest that no expectation, however reasonable, can survive a change in policy. But it is also well established that 'it is a misuse of power for (a public body) to act unfairly or unjustly towards the private citizen when there is no overriding public interest to warrant it.' (See *HTV Ltd* v *Price Commission* [1976] ICR 170 at 185 per Lord Denning MR, cited with approval by Lord Templeman in *Preston* v *IRC* [1985] 2 All ER 327 at 340, [1985] AC 835 at 865.)

In a recent article 'Making legitimate use of legitimate expectation' (1994) 144 NLJ 1215 at 1215 Rabinder Singh puts the consequent law neatly in this proposition:

> Legitimate expectation cannot be used to defeat a duty which public law imposes on a body nor to extend the power of a public body beyond what legislation has prescribed but it can be used to ensure that an act which is *intra vires* is performed if the public body has given rise to a legitimate expectation that it will be.

Thus it is the obligation to exercise powers fairly which permits expectations to be counterposed to policy change, not necessarily in order to thwart it but — as in the present case — in order to seek a proper exception to the policy within the *British Oxygen* principle.

These considerations, I think, bring one closer to some conceptual understanding of what makes an expectation legitimate. Legitimacy in this sense is not an absolute. It is a function of expectations induced by government and of policy considerations which militate against their fulfilment. The balance must in the first instance be for the policy-maker to strike; but if the outcome is challenged by way of judicial review, I do not consider that the court's criterion is the bare rationality of the policy-maker's conclusion. While policy is for the policy-maker alone, the fairness of his or her decision not to accommodate reasonable expectations which the policy will thwart remains the court's concern (as of course does the lawfulness of the policy). To postulate this is not to place the judge in the seat of the minister. As the foregoing citations explain, it is the court's task to recognise the constitutional importance of ministerial freedom to formulate and to reformulate policy; but it is equally the court's duty to protect the interests of those individuals whose expectation of different treatment has a legitimacy which in fairness outtops the policy choice which threatens to frustrate it.

Thus in *R* v *Secretary of State for the Home Dept, ex p Khan* [1985] 1 All ER 40 at 46, [1984] 1 WLR 1337 at 1344 it was held that the Home Secretary might not resile from conditions on which he had stated that entry to the United Kingdom would be permitted 'without affording interested persons a hearing and then only if the overriding public interest demands it.' In other words, not only must the individual be given the procedural opportunity to argue why the policy change should not affect him, but the administration was subject to the substantive requirement that there must be an overriding public interest if the change were to override the individual's prior expectation. This is as near as public law is able to approach to estoppel, for as Lord Greene MR pointed out in *Ministry of Agriculture and Fisheries* v *Hunkin* (1948, unreported) but cited in *Ministry of Agriculture and Fisheries* v *Matthews* [1949] 2 All ER 724 at 729, [1950] 1 KB 148 at 153–154 estoppel against government would mean that the donee of a statutory power could be bound by an ultra vires representation with the dual effect of unlawfully extending the statutory power and destroying the ultra vires doctrine by permitting public bodies arbitrarily to extend their powers. But this prohibited area does not impinge upon the present area of debate, which concerns an intra vires policy of which the applicant had hoped to take advantage but has been frustrated by its supersession by a new, also intra vires, policy. Here too expectation, although reasonable, may have to yield to policy change:

> The. applicants are understandably aggrieved that, after leading them on, the government should then strike them a mortal blow by totally banning their products . . . However, a minister cannot fetter a discretion given him under statute. Providing he acts within his statutory powers, rationally and fairly, he is entitled to change his policy.' (See *R* v *Secretary of State for Health, ex p US Tobacco International Inc* [1992] 1 All ER 212 at 222, [1992] QB 353 at 368–369 per Taylor LJ.)

It was not because of any legitimate expectation of continued benefit but because of the want of fairness in arriving at the policy without giving the applicants a change to have their say, that the decision in question was struck down. The *US Tobacco* case thus illustrates two important aspects of this developing branch of the law: first, that legitimate expectation is now in effect a term of art, reserved for expectations which are not only reasonable but which will be sustained by the court in the face of changes of policy; secondly, that whether this point has been reached is determined by the court, whether on grounds of rationality, of legality or of fairness, of all of which the court, not the decision-maker, is the arbiter.

The notion that the legitimacy of an expectation depends ultimately on the weight it carries in the face of the need for the policy change which threatens to frustrate it is explored perceptively by P P Craig in his article 'Legitimate expectations: A conceptual analysis' (1992) 108 LQR 79 and in his *Administrative Law* (3rd edn, 1994) ch 18, p 652. It seems to me the approach which both best explains the current state of the law and offers a principle by which the courts may balance the two countervailing propositions advances in Wade and Forsyth *Administrative Law* (7th edn, 1994) pp 419–420:

> . . . the courts now expect government departments to honour their statements of policy or intention of else to treat the citizen with the fullest personal consideration ... But those demands cannot be pressed to the point where they obstruct changes of policy which a government should be at liberty to make within its discretionary powers . . .

In my judgment, the real distinction between the pipe-line case and the applicant's case is that genuineness of intention, though a necessary condition in all three, is not a sufficient condition. The cases of pending applications and binding contracts which were exempted represent narrow categories capable of being further narrowed by proof of genuine intention. The applicant's category, even if subjected to a similar test of genuine intent, is an open-ended category. Applying to it the principles which I have sought to describe above, first of all it cannot be said, and Mr Green has not sought to say, that it was illogical to distinguish it from the two pipe-line categories. In other words, the rationality of the policy and its limited exemptions is not an issue. Was it then fair? This, as I have held, while initially a question for the minister is ultimately a question for the court. But, in answering the question, the minister's policy objectives and reasoning form as important an element of the forensic exercise as do the potency and reasonableness of the applicant's expectations. The latter were, I have no doubt, entirely genuine; but at 11 March 1992 they were a long way from fulfilment, to the extent that much was still in the realms of hope or planning. Although the applicant had embarked upon a process of investment, the investment was not going to be thrown away, even though it would diminish in value if its purpose was frustrated by a change in policy. Once it is accepted that nobody has a legitimate expectation that policy will not change, it is more accurate to describe the applicant's anticipation of being permitted nevertheless to see to an end the process of acquisition and aggregation of North Sea beam trawling licences for the Nellie as, objectively, a hope rather than an expectation.

The minister, for his part, together with his counterparts for the rest of the United Kingdom, had to give effect to the United Kingdom's share in preserving pressure stocks in the North Sea from extinction. He was in my view entitled to draw a line as tightly around the existing fleet as could fairly be done. That he considered the position of fishermen who were incipiently dependent on North Sea beam trawling is shown by the two pipe-line provisions added to the policy; but it was in my judgment not unfair, in the light of the government's legitimate policy imperatives and objectives, to exclude from the policy's transitional provisions enterprises in the position of the applicant, notwithstanding that the latter had embarked upon the acquisition of transferable licence entitlements in the anticipation, and with the genuine intention, of being able in due course to aggregate them on to a vessel for the purpose of beam trawling for pressure stock in area IV. Fairness did not, in my judgment, require the perceived need for a swift limitation of North Sea beam trawling for pressure stock to be sacrificed in favour of a class whose expectations, however reasonable and however genuine, might well have eventually subverted the policy. The means adopted bore a fair proportion to the end in view, both in respect of what was included in, and of what was excluded from, the pipe-line provisions.

This application accordingly fails.

Question

What is the constitutional basis for substantive legitimate expectations as a ground of judicial review?

Notes

1. Himsworth in his comment upon this case, [1996] PL 46, asks if the courts when deciding if an expectation is legitimate are not, in effect, second-guessing the minister when changing a policy.

2. Himsworth also points out that Sedley J, while not needing to refer EC law on legitimate expectations, did so mentioning concerns of a drift between principles of national law and EC law. As Sedley J incorporated notions of proportionality in his reasoning, Himsworth wonders if the foundations are being laid for the recognition of proportionality as a ground of review in domestic law.

9 THE AVAILABILITY OF JUDICIAL REVIEW

Note
The previous chapter considered the grounds for judicial review. There are, however, a number of other questions which must be addressed in order to determine the availability of judicial review and, hence, its significance in the constitution. What is the nature of the procedure which must be followed in order to seek judicial review? Who can apply for judicial review? Against whom and in respect of what matters may judicial review be sought? It must also be remembered that the remedies available in judicial review proceedings are discretionary. Hence, an understanding of the availability of judicial review requires an examination of the nature of the courts' discretion and the manner in which it is exercised. Finally, the approach of the courts to legislative attempts to exclude judicial review must be considered.

(A) THE APPLICATION FOR JUDICIAL REVIEW

In 1969 the Law Commission was asked to 'review the existing remedies for the judicial control of administrative acts or omissions with a view to evolving a simpler and more effective procedure.' At that time litigants seeking to challenge administrative acts or omissions had a choice of two procedures. They could begin an action by writ or originating summons seeking an injunction, declaration and, if appropriate, damages. This is the normal way of commencing an action to establish a breach of a private law right, but the courts also allowed it to be used to challenge the decisions of public authorities on the ground that they had acted beyond their powers. Alternatively, litigants could use a special procedure to seek one or more of the prerogative orders, *certiorari,* prohibition or mandamus. The difficulties surrounding the old prerogative order procedure are set out in the judgment of Lord Diplock in *O'Reilly* v *Mackman* (*post,* at p. 602).

The result of the review was the Report on Remedies in Administrative Law (Law Com. No. 73, Cmnd 6407) which made a number of recommendations. It was assumed that implementation of the recommendations would require legislation, but the bulk of the changes contained in the proposals were in fact made by an amendment in 1977 to Ord. 53 of the Rules of the Supreme Court (SI 1977 No. 1955). Some of these provisions were themselves amended in 1980 by SI 1980 No. 2000. A number of provisions relevant to the application for judicial review were subsequently enacted in the Supreme Court Act 1981. The relevant provisions of the Supreme Court Act 1981 and the Rules are set out below. Certain parts of Ord. 53 which are substantially similar to provisions in the Act are omitted.

SUPREME COURT ACT 1981

31.—(1) An application to the High Court for one or more of the following forms of relief, namely—

(a) an order of mandamus, prohibition or certiorari;

(b) a declaration or injunction under subsection (2); . . .

shall be made in accordance with rules of court by a procedure to be known as an application for judicial review.

(2) A declaration may be made or an injunction granted under this subsection in any case where an application for judicial review, seeking that relief, has been made and the High Court considers that, having regard to—

(a) the nature of the matters in respect of which relief may be granted by orders of mandamus, prohibition or certiorari;

(b) the nature of the persons and bodies against whom relief may be granted by such orders; and

(c) all the circumstances of the case,

it would be just and convenient for the declaration to be made or the injunction to be granted, as the case may be.

(3) No application for judicial review shall be made unless the leave of the High Court has been obtained in accordance with rules of court; and the court shall not grant leave to make such an application unless it considers that the applicant has a sufficient interest in the matter to which the application relates.

(4) On an application for judicial review the High Court may award damages to the applicant if—

(a) he has joined with his application a claim for damages arising from any matter to which the application relates; and

(b) the court is satisfied that, if the claim had been made in an action begun by the applicant at the time of making his application, he would have been awarded damages.

(5) If, on an application for judicial review seeking an order of certiorari, the High Court quashes the decision to which the application relates, the High Court may remit the matter to the court, tribunal or authority concerned, with a direction to reconsider it and reach a decision in accordance with the findings of the High Court.

(6) Where the High Court considers that there has been undue delay in making an application for judicial review, the court may refuse to grant—

(a) leave for the making of the application; or
(b) any relief sought on the application,

if it considers that the granting of the relief sought would be likely to cause substantial hardship to, or substantially prejudice the rights of, any person or would be detrimental to good administration.

(7) Subsection (6) is without prejudice to any enactment or rule of court which has the effect of limiting the time within which an application for judicial review may be made.

Rules of the Supreme Court

Order 53

APPLICATIONS FOR JUDICIAL REVIEW

1. Cases appropriate for application for judicial review

(1) An application for—
(a) an order of mandamus, prohibition or certiorari . . .

shall be made by way of an application for judicial review in accordance with the provisions of this Order.

(2) An application for a declaration or an injunction . . . may be made by way of an application for judicial review, and on such an application the Court may grant the declaration or injunction claimed if it considers that, having regard to—

(a) the nature of the matters in respect of which relief may be granted by way of an order of mandamus, prohibition or certiorari,

(b) the nature of the persons and bodies against whom relief may be granted by way of such an order, and

(c) all the circumstances of the case,

it would be just and convenient for the declaration or injunction to be granted on an application for judicial review.

2. Joinder of claims for relief

On an application for judicial review any relief mentioned in rule 1 (1) or (2) may be claimed as an alternative or in addition to any other relief so mentioned if it arises out of or relates to or is connected with the same matter.

3. Grant of leave to apply for judicial review

. . .

(2) An application for leave must be made *ex parte* to a judge by filing in the Crown Office—

(a) a notice in Form No. 86A containing a statement of
(i) the name and description of the applicant,
(ii) the relief sought and the grounds upon which it is sought,
(iii) the name and address of the applicant's solicitors (if any), and
(iv) the applicant's address for service; and

(b) an affidavit which verifies the facts relied on.

(3) The judge may determine the application without a hearing, unless a hearing is requested in the notice of application, and need not sit in open court; in any case, the Crown Office shall serve a copy of the judge's order on the applicant.

(4) Where the application for leave is refused by the judge, or is granted on terms, the applicant may renew it by applying—

(a) in any criminal cause or matter, to a Divisional Court of the Queen's Bench Division;

(b) in any other case, to a single judge sitting in open court or, if the Court so directs, to a Divisional Court of the Queen's Bench Division;

Provided that no application for leave may be renewed in any non-criminal cause or matter in which the judge has refused leave under paragraph (3) after a hearing. . . .

(10) Where leave to apply for judicial review is granted, then—

(a) if the relief sought is an order of prohibition or certiorari and the Court so directs, the grant shall operate as a stay of the proceedings to which the application relates until the determination of the application or until the Court otherwise orders;

(b) if any other relief is sought, the Court may at any time grant in the proceedings such interim relief as could be granted in an action begun by writ.

4. Delay in applying for relief

(1) An application for leave to apply for judicial review shall be made promptly and in any event within three months from the date when grounds for the application first arose unless the Court considers that there is good reason for extending the period within which the application shall be made.

(2) Where the relief sought is an order of certiorari in respect of any judgment, order, conviction or other proceedings, the date when grounds for the application first arose shall be taken to be the date of that judgment, order, conviction or proceeding.

(3) The preceding paragraphs are without prejudice to any statutory provision which has the effect of limiting the time within which an application for judicial review may be made.

5. Mode of applying for judicial review

(1) In any criminal cause or matter, where leave has been granted to make an application for judicial review, the application shall be made by originating motion to a Divisional Court of the Queen's Bench Division.

(2) In any other such cause or matter, the application shall be made by originating motion to a judge sitting in open court, unless the Court directs that it shall be made—

(a) by originating summons to a judge in chambers; or

(b) by originating motion to a Divisional Court of the Queen's Bench Division. . . .

(7) If on the hearing of the motion or summons the Court is of opinion that any person who ought, whether under this rule or otherwise, to have been served has not been served, the Court may adjourn the hearing on such terms (if any) as it may direct in order that the notice or summons may be served on that person.

8. Application for discovery, interrogatories, cross-examination, etc.

(1) Unless the Court otherwise directs, any interlocutory application in proceedings on an application for judicial review may be made to any judge or a master of the Queen's Bench Division, notwithstanding that the application for judicial review has been made by motion and is to be heard by a Divisional Court. . . .

(3) This rule is without prejudice to any statutory provision or rule of law restricting the making of an order against the Crown.

9. Hearing of application for judicial review

(1) On the hearing of any motion or summons under rule 5, any person who desires to be heard in opposition to the motion or summons, and appears to the Court to be a proper person to be heard, shall be heard, notwithstanding that he has not been served with notice of the motion or the summons. . . .

(5) Where the relief sought is a declaration, an injunction or damages and the Court considers that it should not be granted on an application for judicial review but might have been granted if it had been sought in an action begun by writ by the applicant at the time of making his application, the Court may, instead of refusing the application, order the proceedings to continue as if they had been begun by writ . . .

(B) THE EXCLUSIVITY PRINCIPLE

As stated above, prior to the introduction of the revised Ord. 53, the courts frequently permitted litigants to commence an action by way of writ or originating summons (hereinafter referred to as the ordinary procedure) for a declaration or injunction as an alternative to using the special procedure for obtaining orders of *certiorari,* mandamus, and prohibition. Would the courts continue to offer litigants this choice following the introduction of the reformed procedure in 1977 ?

O'Reilly v *Mackman*
[1983] 2 AC 237
House of Lords

A number of prisoners at Hull Prison wished to challenge decisions reached by the prison's board of visitors on the ground that they were in breach of the rules of natural justice. They did not make use of Ord. 53, but instead began proceedings by writ or originating summmons, asking for a declaration that the findings and subsequent penalties were null and void. The application was refused by the judge at first instance but the Court of Appeal allowed an appeal by the board. On appeal to the House of Lords:

LORD DIPLOCK: . . . All that is at issue in the instant appeal is the procedure by which such relief ought to be sought. Put in a single sentence the question for your Lordships is: whether in 1980 after RSC Ord. 53 in its new form, adopted in 1977, had come into operation it was an abuse of the process of the court to apply for such declarations by using the procedure laid down in the Rules for proceedings begun by writ or by originating summons instead of using the procedure laid down by Ord. 53 for an application for judicial review of the awards of forfeiture of remission of sentence made against them by the board which the appellants are seeking to impugn?

In their respective actions, the appellants claim only declaratory relief. It is conceded on their behalf that, for reasons into which the concession makes it unnecessary to enter, no claim for damages would lie against the members of the board of visitors by whom the awards were made. The only claim was for a form of relief which it lies within the discretion of the court to grant or withhold. So the first thing to note is that the relief sought in the action is discretionary only.

It is not, and it could not be, contended that the decision of the board awarding him forfeiture of remission had infringed or threatened to infringe any right of the appellant derived from private law, whether a common law right or one created by statute. Under the Prison Rules remission of sentence is not a matter of right but of indulgence. So far as private law is concerned all that each appellant had was a legitimate expectation, based upon his knowledge of what is the general practice, that he would be granted the maximum remission permitted by rule 5(2) of the Prison

Rules, of one third of his sentence if by that time no disciplinary award of forfeiture of remission had been made against him. So the second thing to be noted is that none of the appellants had any remedy in private law.

In public law, as distinguished from private law, however, such legitimate expectation gave to each appellant a sufficient interest to challenge the legality of the adverse disciplinary award made against him by the board on the ground that in one way or another the board in reaching its decision had acted outwith the powers conferred upon it by the legislation under which it was acting; and such grounds would include the board's failure to observe the rules of natural justice: which means no more than to act fairly towards him in carrying out their decision-making process, and I prefer so to put it.

[Lord Diplock went on to outline the disadvantages of the procedure for applying for prerogative orders prior to 1977. These were:

(1) the absence of any provision for discovery;
(2) the absence of any express provision for cross-examination.

His Lordship continued to outline, on the other hand, the protections which the procedure for applying for prerogative orders afforded to public bodies:

(1) the requirement to obtain leave;
(2) the time-limits on the grant of certiorari.

His Lordship continued]

. . . I accept that having regard to disadvantages . . . [of the prerogative order procedure], it could not be regarded as an abuse of the process of the court, before the amendments made to Order 53 in 1977, to proceed against the authority by an action for a declaration of nullity of the impugned decision with an injunction to prevent the authority from acting on it, instead of applying for an order of certiorari; and this despite the fact that, by adopting this course, the plaintiff evaded the safeguards imposed in the public interest against groundless, unmeritorious or tardy attacks upon the validity of decisions made by public authorities in the field of public law.

Those disadvantages, which formerly might have resulted in an applicant's being unable to obtain justice in an application for certiorari under Order 53, have all been removed by the new Order introduced in 1977. . . .

[Lord Diplock discussed the provisions of the new Order which allow for interlocutory applications for discovery and cross-examination. He also discussed the provisions which permit claims for damages and applications for declarations and injunctions to be included in applications under the Order.

His Lordship continued.]

So Order 53 since 1977 has provided a procedure by which every type of remedy for infringement of the rights of individuals that are entitled to protection in public law can be obtained in one and the same proceeding by way of an application for judicial review, and whichever remedy is found to be the most appropriate in the light of what has emerged upon the hearing of the application, can be granted to him. If what should emerge is that his complaint is not of an infringement of any of his rights that are entitled to protection in public law, but may be an infringement of his rights in private law and thus not a proper subject for judicial review, the court has power under rule 9(5), instead of refusing the application, to order the proceedings to continue as if they had begun by writ. There is no such converse power under the RSC to permit an action begun by writ to continue as if it were an application for judicial review; and I respectfully disagree with that part of the judgment of Lord Denning MR which suggests that such a power may exist; nor do I see the need to amend the rules in order to create one.

My Lords, Order 53 does not expressly provide that procedure by application for judicial review shall be the exclusive procedure available by which the remedy of a declaration or injunction may be obtained for infringement of rights that are entitled to protection under public law; nor does section 31 of the Supreme Court Act 1981. There is great variation between individual cases that fall within Order 53 and the Rules Committee and subsequently the legislature were, I think, for this reason content to rely upon the express and the inherent power of the High Court, exercised upon a case to case basis, to prevent abuse of its process whatever might be the form taken by that abuse. Accordingly, I do not think that your Lordships would be wise to use this as an occasion to lay down categories of cases in which it would necessarily always be an abuse to seek in an action begun by writ or originating summons a remedy against infringement of rights of the individual that are entitled to protection in public law. . . .

Now that those disadvantages to applicants have been removed and all remedies for infringements of rights protected by public law can be obtained upon an application for judicial review, as can also remedies for infringements of rights under private law if such infringements should also be involved, it would in my view as a general rule be contrary to public policy and, as such an abuse of the process of the court, to permit a person seeking to establish that a decision of a public authority infringed rights to which he was entitled to protection under public law to proceed by way of an ordinary action and by this means to evade the provisions of Order 53 for the protection of such authorities.

My Lords, I have described this as a general rule; for though it may normally be appropriate to apply it by the summary process of striking out the action, there may be exceptions, particularly where the invalidity of the decision arises as a collateral issue in a claim for infringement of a right of the plaintiff arising under private law, or where none of the parties objects to the adoption of the procedure by writ or originating summons. Whether there should be other exceptions should, in my view, at this stage in the development of procedural public law, be left to be decided on a case to case basis — a process that your Lordships will be continuing in the next case in which judgment is to be delivered today [*Cocks* v *Thanet District Council* [1983] 2 AC 286].

In the instant cases where the only relief sought is a declaration of nullity of the decisions of a statutory tribunal, the Board of Visitors of Hull Prison, as in any other case in which a similar declaration of nullity in public law is the only relief claimed, I have no hesitation, in agreement with the Court of Appeal, in holding that to allow the actions to proceed would be an abuse of the process of the court. They are blatant attempts to avoid the protections for the defendants for which Order 53 provides.

The other Law Lords agreed with Lord Diplock.

Question

The Law Commission's Report on Administrative Law Remedies, Law Com. No. 73, Cmnd 6407, stated in para. 34 that 'we are clearly of the opinion that the new procedure we envisage in respect of applications to the Divisional Court should not be exclusive in the sense that it would become the only way by which issues relating to the acts or omissions of public authorities should come before the courts'.

The *JUSTICE-All Souls Report on Administrative Law* (1988) criticises the decision in *O'Reilly* v *Mackman* on the ground 'that it has all the appearance of judicial legislation without the benefit of the consultation and debating process normally associated with legislation' (para. 6.19).
Do you agree?

Notes
The procedural safeguards referred to in *O'Reilly* v *Mackman* require some further explanation.
1. *Leave* (see Supreme Court Act 1981, s. 31(3); RSC Ord. 53, r. 3, *ante* at pp. 600–1) The requirement that an applicant for judicial review must obtain leave has been criticised. The *JUSTICE-All Souls Report* recommended that it should be abolished for several reasons:

(a) Leave is not required in private law proceedings. A particular category of litigants, namely those seeking judicial review, should not be subjected to an impediment which is not placed before litigants generally.
(b) The administration can be protected from 'groundless, unmeritorious or tardy harassment' by the procedure which allows parties to apply to strike out a case. Pleadings may be struck out under the rules of court (Ord. 18, r. 19) if they disclose no reasonable cause of action, if they are scandalous, frivolous, or vexatious, or if they otherwise constitute an abuse of the process of the court, and the action may be dismissed.
(c) Issues of standing are no longer conclusively determined at the stage of the application for leave (see *IRC* v *National Federation of Self-Employed and Small Businesses Ltd* [1982] AC 617, *post* at p. 615).

2. A. P. Le Sueur & M. Sunkin [1992] *Public Law* 102 argue that the leave stage is flawed but recognise that their desire to have it abolished is unlikely to be achieved. The Law Commission in their report *Administrative Law: Judicial Review and Statutory Appeals* (Law Com No 226 HC 669 of 1993-94) were persuaded that there should continue to be a filtering requirement. They recommended that the application for leave should be renamed the preliminary consideration, and should be determined on paper unless it includes a claim for interim relief, or the Crown Office, or the judge thinks that a hearing is desirable in the interests of justice. As the purpose of the filter is to protect public bodies from unmeritorious applications, leave would be granted if the application discloses a serious issue which ought to be determined. The Law Commission also recommended that cases should only proceed to a substantive hearing if the applicant has been or would be adversely affected, or the court considers that it is in the public interest for an applicant to make the application. This broad discretion was preferred to a listing in the rules of the factors to be taken account of in public interest cases.
3. *Time-limits* Problems have arisen as to the relationship between the provisions in the Supreme Court Act 1981, s. 31(6) and the RSC Ord. 53, r. 4 (see *ante* at pp. 516–18). The House of Lords dealt with time-limits in *R* v *Dairy Produce Quota Tribunal, ex parte Caswell* [1990] 2 AC 738.

(a) At the stage of the application for leave the court considers whether the application has been made promptly. The fact that an application has been made within three months does not necessarily mean that it has been made promptly.

(b) If the application has not been made promptly or within three months the court will have to consider whether there is good reason for the delay.
(c) Where there is a finding of promptness at the leave stage, this does not preclude a finding of undue delay at the substantive hearing.
(d) Whenever there is a failure to act promptly or within three months there is undue delay, and the court may either refuse to grant leave for the making of the application or, at the hearing, refuse to grant relief if it considers that the granting of the relief sought would be likely to cause substantial hardship to, or substantially prejudice the rights of, any person or would be detrimental to good administration.

4. The *JUSTICE-All Souls Report* (1988), criticises the three-month period as too short, and recommends that Ord. 53, r. 4 be removed, thus leaving the question of delay to be dealt with by reference to the statutory test in s. 31(6) of the 1981 Act (see paras 6.28–6.31). The Law Commission concluded that certainty was desirable and recommended the continuance of the three month time limit. A case could move to a substantive hearing if the reason for the delay in making the leave application was the pursuit of an alternative remedy.
5. *Discovery and cross-examination* (RSC Ord. 53, r. 8, *ante* at p. 601) Commenting on the statement of Lord Diplock in *O'Reilly* v *Mackman* that leave for discovery and cross-examination in judicial review should be allowed 'whenever the justice of the particular case so requires', the *JUSTICE-All Souls Report* observes that 'there has been little change in old attitudes' [para. 6.32].

Question
Do the criticisms made of the procedural safeguards in the Ord. 53 procedure undermine the basis of the decision in *O'Reilly* v *Mackman*?

Note
Lord Diplock mentioned that there may be certain exceptions to the general exclusivity principle. The courts have been required to consider the scope of the exclusivity rule, and the exceptions to it, in a number of cases.

Wandsworth London Borough Council v *Winder*
[1985] AC 461
House of Lords

Mr Winder, the respondent, was a tenant of a council flat in Wandsworth. In March 1981, the appellants, Wandsworth Borough Council, gave notice to the respondent, as they were required to do under s. 40 of the Housing Act 1980, that from April 1981 his rent would be increased from £12.06 to £16.56 a week. The respondent regarded the increase as unreasonable and paid only £12.06, plus an amount which he considered to be reasonable. When the appellants increased the rent in the following year he adopted the same stance. The appellants then took proceedings against the respondent in Wandsworth County Court claiming arrears of rent, and also claiming possession of the premises on the ground that the rent lawfully due had not been paid. The respondent defended the action on the ground that the appellants' decisions to make the increases, and the increases themselves, were so unreasonable that no local authority could have come to them and were therefore *ultra vires*. He also counterclaimed for a declaration that the notices of increase were *ultra vires* and void and of no effect, and for a declaration that the rent payable under the tenancy was £12.06 per week. The Court of Appeal allowed Mr Winder's appeal from the decision of the judge at first instance that the relevant paragraphs of his defence and the counter-claim should be struck out. The council appealed to the House of Lords.

LORD FRASER: The respondent seeks to show in the course of his defence in these proceedings that the appellant's decisions to increase the rent were such as no reasonable man could consider justifiable. But your Lordships are not concerned in this appeal to decide whether that contention is right or wrong. The only issue at this stage is whether the respondent is entitled to put forward the contention as a defence in the present proceedings. The appellants say that he is not because the only procedure by which their decision could have been challenged was by judicial review under RSC Ord. 53. The respondent was refused leave to apply for judicial review out of time and (say the appellants) he has lost the opportunity to challenge the decisions. The appellants rely on the decisions of this House in *O'Reilly* v *Mackman* [1983] 2 AC 237 and *Cocks* v *Thanet District Council* [1983] 2 AC 286. The respondent accepts that judicial review would have been an appropriate procedure for the purpose, but he maintains that it is not the only procedure open to him, and that he was entitled to wait until he was sued by the appellants and then to defend the proceedings, as he has done.

In order to deal with these contentions, it is necessary to consider what was decided by the House of Lords in those two cases. The question raised in *O'Reilly* was not the same as that in the present case, although of course, the circumstances were different. . . .

There are two important differences between the facts in *O'Reilly* and those in the present case. First, the plaintiffs in *O'Reilly* had not suffered any infringement of their rights in private law; their complaint was that they had been ordered to forfeit part of their remission of sentence but they had no right in private law to such a remission, which was granted only as a matter of indulgence. Consequently, even if the board of visitors had acted contrary to the rules of natural justice when making the award, the members of the board would not have been liable in damages to the prisoners. In the present case what the respondent complains of is the infringement of a contractual right in private law. Secondly, in *O'Reilly* the prisoners had initiated the proceedings, and Lord Diplock, throughout in his speech, treated the question only as one affecting a claim for infringing a right of the plaintiff while in the present case the respondent is the defendant. The decision in *O'Reilly* is therefore not directly in point in the present case, but the appellants rely particularly on a passage in the speech of Lord Diplock, with whose speech the other members of the Appellate Committee agreed . . .

[His Lordship read from the judgment of Lord Diplock; the relevant paragraph, *ante* at p. 604 above, beginning 'Now that . . .']

The last paragraph in that quotation shows that Lord Diplock was careful to emphasise that the general rule which he had stated in the previous paragraph might well be subject to exceptions. The question for your Lordships is whether the instant appeal is an exception to the general rule. It might be possible to treat this case as falling within one of the exceptions suggested by Lord Diplock, if the question of the invalidity of the appellants' decision had arisen as a collateral issue in a claim by the respondent (as defendant) for infringement of his right arising under private law to occupy the flat. But I do not consider that the question of invalidity is truly collateral to the issue between the parties. Although it is not mentioned in the appellant's statement of claim, it is the whole basis of the respondent's defence and it is the central issue which has to be decided. The case does not fall within any of the exceptions specifically suggested in *O'Reilly* v *Mackman* [1983] 2 AC 237. Immediately after the decision in *O'Reilly,* the House applied the general rule in the case of *Cocks* [1983] 2 AC 286. The proceedings in *O'Reilly* had begun before the Supreme Court Act 1981 (especially section 31) had been passed. The proceedings in *Cocks* were begun after that Act was passed, but for the present purpose nothing turns on that distinction. *Cocks* was an action by a homeless person claiming that the local housing authority had a duty to provide permanent accommodation for him. The council resolved that the plaintiff had become homeless 'intentionally' in the sense of the Housing (Homeless Persons) Act 1977. Consequently the plaintiff had no right in private law to be provided with permanent housing accommodation by the authority. The plaintiff raised an action in the county court claiming, inter alia, a declaration that the council were in breach of their duty to him in not having provided him with permanent accommodation. In order to proceed in his action he had to show as a condition precedent that the council's decision was invalid. This House held that the plaintiff was not entitled to impugn the council's decision in public law otherwise than by judicial review, notwithstanding that the effect of the decision was to prevent him from 'establishing a necessary condition precedent to the statutory private law right which he [was seeking] to enforce': see *per* my noble and learned friend Lord Bridge of Harwich at p. 294E. The essential difference between that case and the present is that the impugned decision of the local authority did not deprive the plaintiff of a pre-existing private law right; it prevented him from establishing a new private law right. There is also the same distinction as in *O'Reilly* [1983] 2 AC 237, namely, that the party complaining of the decision was the plaintiff.

Although neither *O'Reilly* nor *Cocks* [1983] 2 AC 286 is an authority which directly applies to the facts of the instant appeal, it is said on behalf of the appellants that the principle underlying those decisions applies here, and that, if the respondent is successful, he will be evading that principle. My Lords, I cannot agree. The principle underlying those decisions, as Lord Diplock explained in *O'Reilly* [1983] 2 AC 237, 284, is that there is a 'need, in the interests of good administration and of third parties who may be indirectly affected by the decision, for speedy certainty as to whether it has the effect of a decision that is valid in public law.' The main argument urged on behalf of the appellants was that this is a typical case where there is a need for speedy certainty in the public interest. I accept, of course, that the decision in the appeal will indirectly affect many of the appellants' tenants, and perhaps most if not all of their ratepayers because if the appellants' impugned decisions are held to be invalid, the basis of their financial administration since 1981 will be upset. That would be highly inconvenient from the point of view of the appellants, and of their rate-payers, and it would be a great advantage to them if persons who seek to challenge their decisions were limited to doing so by procedure under Order 53. . . . It may well be that such protection to public authorities tends to promote good administration. But there may be other ways of obtaining speedy decisions; for example in some cases it may be possible for a public authority itself to initiate proceedings for judicial review. In any event the arguments for protecting public authorities against unmeritorious or dilatory challenges to their decisions have to be set against the arguments for preserving the ordinary rights of citizens to defend themselves against unfounded claims.

It would in my opinion be a very strange use of language to describe the respondent's behaviour in relation to this litigation as an abuse or misuse by him of the process of the court. He did not select the procedure to be adopted. He is merely seeking to defend proceedings brought against him by the appellants. In so doing he is seeking only to exercise the ordinary right of any individual to defend an action against him on the ground that he is not liable for the whole sum claimed by the plaintiff. Moreover he puts forward his defence as a matter of right whereas in an application for judicial review, success would require an exercise of the court's discretion in his favour. Apart from the provisions of Order 53 and section 31 of the Supreme Court Act 1981, he would certainly be entitled to defend the action on the ground that the plaintiff's claim arises from a resolution which (on his view) is invalid: see for example *Cannock Chase District Council* v *Kelly* [1978] 1 WLR 1, which was decided in July 1977, a few months before Order 53 came into force (as it did in December 1977). I find it impossible to accept that the right to challenge the decision by a local authority in the course of defending an action for non-payment can have been swept away by Order 53, which was directed to introducing a procedural reform. As my noble and learned friend Lord Scarman said in *Reg* v *Inland Revenue Commissioners, ex parte Federation of Self-Employed and Small Businesses Ltd* [1982] AC 617, 647g 'The new RSC Ord 53 is a procedural reform of great importance in the field of public law but it does not — indeed, cannot — either extend or diminish the substantive law. Its function is limited to ensuring "ubi jus, ibi remedium".' Lord Wilberforce spoke to the same effect at p. 631A. Nor, in my opinion, did section 31 of the Supreme Court Act 1981 which refers only to 'an application for judicial review' have the effect of limiting the rights of a defendant sub silentio. I would adopt the words of Viscount Simonds in *Pyx Granite Co. Ltd* v *Ministry of Housing and Local Government* [1960] AC 260, 286 as follows:

> It is a principle not by any means to be whittled down that the subject's recourse to Her Majesty's courts for the determination of his rights is not to be excluded except by clear words.

The argument of the appellants in the present case would be directly in conflict with that observation.

If the public interest requires that persons should not be entitled to defend actions brought against them by the public authority where the defence rests on a challenge to a decision by the public authority, then it is for Parliament to change the law.

I would dismiss the appeal.

The other Law Lords agreed with Lord Fraser.

Note

It was subsequently held that the rent increases were in fact valid and an appeal to the Court of Appeal was dismissed (see *London Borough of Wandsworth* v *Winder (No. 2)* (1987) 19 HLR 204; (1988) 20 HLR 400.

Roy v *Kensington and Chelsea FPC*
[1991] 2 WLR 239
House of Lords

The Kensington and Chelsea and Westminster Family Practitioner Committee (FPC) was responsible, under the National Health Service (General Medical and Pharmaceutical Services) Regulations 1974, for making payments to general practitioners undertaking National Health Service work within its area. Dr Roy was on the list of doctors undertaking National Health Service work within the FPC's area. The FPC decided to use its powers under the Regulations to reduce Dr Roy's basic practice allowance by 20 per cent on the basis that he was not devoting a substantial amount of time to general practice under the National Health Service. Dr Roy issued a writ claiming the full amount of the basic practice allowance. In the same writ he also claimed repayment of sums due to him in relation to the employment of ancillary staff. The FPC argued that the inclusion of the claim relating to the basic practice allowance was an abuse of the process of the court. The judge decided that, as the committee's decision was clearly a public law decision, it could only be challenged by judicial review. His decision was reversed by the Court of Appeal and the FPC appealed to the House of Lords. (In the meantime Dr Roy proceeded with his claim in relation to the employment of ancillary staff and obtained an order for repayment.)

LORD BRIDGE OF HARWICH: My Lords, the circumstances from which this appeal arises are fully set out in the speech of my learned and noble friend, Lord Lowry, in which he has also undertaken a comprehensive review of the relevant authorities. Agreeing, as I do, with the conclusion he reaches, I shall state my own reasons briefly.

The decisions of this House in *O'Reilly* v *Mackman* [1983] 2 AC 237 and *Cocks* v *Thanet District Council* [1983] 2 AC 286, have been the subject of much academic criticism. Although I appreciate the cogency of some of the arguments advanced in support of that criticism, I have not been persuaded that the essential principle embodied in the decisions requires to be significantly modified, let alone overturned. But if it is important, as I believe, to maintain the principle, it is certainly no less important that its application should be confined within proper limits. It is appropriate that an issue which depends exclusively on the existence of a purely public law right should be determined in judicial review proceedings and not otherwise. But where a litigant asserts his entitlement to a subsisting right in private law, whether by way of claim or defence, the circumstance that the existence and extent of the private right asserted may incidentally involve the examination of a public law issue cannot prevent the litigant from seeking to establish his right by action commenced by writ or originating summons, any more than it can prevent him from setting up his private law right in proceedings brought against him. I think this proposition necessarily follows from the decisions of this House in *Davy* v *Spelthorne Borough Council* [1984] AC 262 and *Wandsworth London Borough Council* v *Winder* [1985] AC 461. In the latter case Robert Goff LJ in the Court of Appeal, commenting on a passage from the speech of Lord Fraser of Tullybelton in the former case, said, at p. 480:

> I read this passage in Lord Fraser of Tullybelton's speech as expressing the opinion that the principle in *O'Reilly* v *Mackman* should not be extended to require a litigant to proceed by way of judicial review in circumstances where his claim for damages for negligence might in consequence be adversely affected. I can for my part see no reason why the same consideration should not apply in respect of any private law right which a litigant seeks to invoke, whether by way of action or by way of defence. For my part, I find it difficult to conceive of a case where a citizen's invocation of the ordinary procedure of the courts in order to enforce his private law rights, or his reliance on his private law rights by way of defence in an action brought against him, could, as such, amount to an abuse of the process of the court.

I entirely agree with this. . . .

I do not think the issue in the appeal turns on whether the doctor provides services pursuant to a contract with the family practitioner committee. I doubt if he does and am content to assume that there is no contract. Nevertheless, the terms which govern the obligations of the doctor on the one hand, as to the services he is to provide, and of the family practitioner committee on the other hand, as to the payments which it is required to make to the doctor, are all prescribed in the relevant legislation and it seems to me that the statutory terms are just as effective as they would be if they were contractual to confer upon the doctor an enforceable right in private law to receive the remuneration to which the terms entitle him. It must follow, in my view, that in any case of dispute the doctor is entitled to claim and recover in an action commenced by writ the amount of remuneration which he is able to prove as being due to him. Whatever remuneration he is entitled to under the statement is remuneration he has duly earned by the services he has rendered. The circumstance that the quantum of that remuneration, in the case of a particular dispute, is affected by the discretionary decision made by the committee cannot deny the doctor his private law right of recovery or subject him to the constraints which the necessity to seek judicial review would impose upon that right.

LORD LOWRY: [Lord Lowry reviewed a number of authorities including *Wandsworth Borough Council* v *Winder* [1985] AC 461 and *Cocks* v *Thanet DC* [1983] 2 AC 286 and continued.] . . .

[T]he actual or possible absence of a contract is not decisive against Dr Roy. He has in my opinion a bundle of rights which should be regarded as his individual private law rights against the committee, arising from the statute and regulations and including the very important private law right to be paid for the work that he has done. As Judge White put it [1989] 1 Med LR 10, 12:

> The rights and duties are no less real or effective for the individual practitioner. Private law rights flow from the statutory provisions and are enforceable, as such, in the courts but no contractual relations come into existence.

The judge, however, held that, *even if the doctor's rights to full payments under the scheme were contractually based*, the committee's duty was a public law duty and could be challenged only on judicial review. Mr Collins admitted that, if the doctor had a *contractual* right, he could . . . vindicate it by action. But, my Lords, I go further: if Dr Roy has any kind of *private law right*, even though not contractual, he can sue for its alleged breach.

In this case it has been suggested that Dr Roy could have gone by judicial review, because there is no issue of fact, but that would not always hold good in a similar type of case. . . . In any event, a successful application by judicial review could not lead directly, as it would in an action, to an order for payment of the full basic practice allowance. Other proceedings would be needed.

An important point is that the court clearly has *jurisdiction* to entertain the doctor's action. Furthermore, even if one accepts the full rigour of *O'Reilly* v *Mackman*, there is ample room to hold that this case comes within the exceptions allowed for by Lord Diplock. It is concerned with a private law right, it involves a question which *could* in some circumstances give rise to a dispute of fact and one object of the plaintiff is to obtain an order for the payment (not by way of damages) of an ascertained or ascertainable sum of money. If it is wrong to allow such a claim to be litigated by action, what is to be said of other disputed claims for remuneration? I think it is right to consider the whole spectrum of claims which a doctor might make against the committee. The existence of any dispute as to entitlement means that he will be alleging a breach of his private law rights through a failure by the committee to perform their public duty. If the committee's argument prevails, the doctor must in all these cases go by judicial review, even when the facts are not clear. I scarcely think that this can be the right answer. . . .

The judgments [in the Court of Appeal] to which I have referred effectively dispose of an argument pressed by the committee that Dr Roy had no right to be paid a basic practice allowance until the committee had carried out their public duty of forming an opinion under paragraph 12.1(b) [of the National Health Service Regulations 1974] with the supposed consequence that, until that had happened, the doctor had *no private law right* which he could enforce. The answer is that Dr Roy had a right to a fair and legally correct consideration of his claim. Failing that, his private law right has been infringed and he can sue the committee.

Mr Collins [counsel for the FPC] sought to equate the committee's task under paragraph 12.1(b) with the council's duty in phase 1 of *Cocks* v *Thanet District Council* and the committee's duty to pay with the council's duty in phase 2. For an answer to that argument I refer to the judgments in the Court of Appeal and would also point out that Mr Cocks was simply a homeless member of the public in phase 1, whereas Dr Roy had already an established relationship with the committee when his claim . . . fell to be considered.

Dr Roy's printed case contained detailed arguments in favour of a contract between him and the committee, but before your Lordships Mr Lightman simply argued that the doctor had a private law right, whether contractual or statutory. With regard to *O'Reilly* v *Mackman* [1983] 2 AC 237 he argued in the alternative. The 'broad approach' was that the rule in *O'Reilly* v *Mackman* did not apply generally against bringing actions to vindicate private rights in all circumstances in which those actions involved a challenge to a public law act or decision, but that it merely required the aggrieved person to proceed by judicial review only when private law rights were not at stake. The 'narrow approach' assumed that the rule applied generally to *all* proceedings in which public law acts or decisions were challenged, subject to some exceptions when private law rights were involved. There was no need in *O'Reilly* v *Mackman* to choose between these approaches, but it seems clear that Lord Diplock considered himself to be stating a general rule with exceptions. For my part, I much prefer the broad approach, which is both traditionally orthodox and consistent with the *Pyx Granite* principle [1960] AC 260, 286, as applied in *Davy* v *Spelthorne Borough Council* [1984] AC 262, 274 and in *Wandsworth London Borough Council* v *Winder* [1985] AC 461, 510. It would also, if adopted, have the practical merit of getting rid of a procedural minefield. I shall, however, be content for the purpose of this appeal to adopt the narrow approach, which avoids the need to discuss the proper scope of the rule, a point which has not been argued before your Lordships and has hitherto been seriously discussed only by the academic writers.

Whichever approach one adopts, the arguments for excluding the present case from the ambit of the rule or, in the alternative, making an exception of it are similar and to my mind convincing.

(1) Dr Roy has either a contractual or a statutory private law right to his remuneration in accordance with his statutory terms of service.

(2) Although he seeks to enforce performance of a public law duty . . . his private law rights dominate the proceedings.

(3) The type of claim and other claims for remuneration (although not this particular claim) may involve disputed issues of fact.

(4) The order sought (for the payment of money due) could not be granted on judicial review.

(5) The claim is joined with another claim which is fit to be brought in an action (and has already been successfully prosecuted).

(6) When individual rights are claimed, there should not be a need for leave or a special time limit, nor should the relief be discretionary.

(7) The action should be allowed to proceed unless it is plainly an abuse of process.

(8) The cases I have cited show that the rule in *O'Reilly* v *Mackman* [1983] 2 AC 237, assuming it to be a rule of general application, is subject to many exceptions based on the nature of the claim and on the undesirability of erecting procedural barriers.

My Lords, I have already disclaimed the intention of discussing the scope of the rule in *O'Reilly* v *Mackman* but, even if I treat it as a general rule, there are many indications in favour of a liberal attitude towards the exceptions contemplated but not spelt out by Lord Diplock. For example: (1) the Law Commission, when recommending the new judicial review procedure, contemplated the continued coexistence of judicial review proceedings and actions for a declaration with regard to public law issues. *Associated Provincial Picture Houses Ltd* v *Wednesbury Corporation* [1948] 1 KB 223 is a famous prototype of the latter.

(2) This House has expressly approved actions for a declaration of nullity as alternative to applications for certiorari to quash, where private law rights were concerned: *Wandsworth London Borough Council* v *Winder* [1985] 461, 477 *per* Robert Goff LJ.

(3):

> "The principle remains intact that public authorities and public servants are, unless clearly exempted, answerable in the ordinary courts for wrongs done to individuals. But by an extension of remedies and a flexible procedure it can be said that something resembling a system of public law is being developed. Before the expression 'public law' can be used to deny a subject a right of action in the court of his choice it must be related to a positive prescription of law, by statute or by statutory rules. We have not yet reached the point at which mere characterisation of a claim as a claim in public law is sufficient to exclude it from consideration by the ordinary courts: to permit this would be to create a dual system of law with the rigidity and procedural hardship for plaintiffs which it was the purpose of the recent reforms to remove": *Davy* v *Spelthorne Borough Council* [1984] AC 262, 276, *per* Lord Wilberforce.

In conclusion, my Lords, it seems to me that, unless the procedure adopted by the moving party is ill suited to dispose of the question at issue, there is much to be said in favour of the proposition that a court having jurisdiction ought to let a case be heard rather than entertain a debate concerning the form of the proceedings.

For the reasons already given I would dismiss this appeal.

The other Law Lords agreed with Lord Bridge and Lord Lowry.

Questions

1. Has the House of Lords retreated from the decision in *O'Reilly* v *Mackman*?

2. Why are the safeguards to public authorities less important in cases where private rights are involved?

3. Are defendants always entitled to challenge decisions in proceedings brought against them by public authorities? For example, if Mr Cocks (see the references to *Cocks* v *Thanet DC* in the extracts from *Wandsworth Borough Council* v *Winder* above) had squatted in council property, would he have been able to challenge the decision not to provide him with permanent accommodation in proceedings for possession brought against him by the local authority? See on this point *Avon County Council* v *Buscott* [1988] 2 WLR 788.

Note

The Law Commission in its 1994 report supported the development of the 'broad' approach in *Roy* so that Ord 53 is to be used only if a challenge is solely on public law grounds and the litigant does not seek to enforce or defend a completely constituted private law right.

The Law Commission also recommend that it ought to be easier to transfer into, or out of, Ord 53.

(C) WHO MAY APPLY FOR JUDICIAL REVIEW?

The principles of *locus standi* or standing determine *who* is entitled to bring a particular dispute before the courts. They can thus be distinguished from the principles which determine whether a particular matter is suitable for adjudication in the courts (see the section on justiciability at p. 626), whether a particular matter is one of public law (see p. 620), and what proceedings may be used to challenge the decision (see p. 602).

There are many people who may consider that they are affected or have an interest in an administrative decision. Consider, for example, the range of persons who might be said to have an interest in a decision to close a school because of falling numbers. The list will obviously include persons whose children will have to start a new school, but it could also include a number of others, for example persons who are opposed in principle to the closure of small schools and persons who are concerned about the financial implications of the closure for the local education authority. The principles of *locus standi* have the function of determining which interests merit access to the courts.

What arguments might be put forward in favour of the courts' power to select the interests which merit access to the courts? Cane, in *An Introduction to Administrative Law* (1992), at pp. 58-59, suggests a number of possible functions.

An Introduction to Administrative Law

What is the function of standing rules? In general terms it is to restrict access to judicial review. But why restrict access? One suggested reason is to protect public bodies from vexatious litigants with no real interest in the outcome of the case but just a desire to make things difficult for the government. But it is highly doubtful that many such litigants exist in real life, and if they do, the requirement of leave to apply for judicial review should be adequate to deal with them. Others have been suggested: to prevent the conduct of government business being unduly hampered and delayed by 'excessive' litigation; to reduce the risk that civil servants will behave in over-cautious and unhelpful ways in dealing with citizens for fear of being sued if things go wrong; to ration scarce judicial resources; to ensure that the argument on the merits is presented in the best possible way, by a person with a real interest in presenting it (but quality of presentation and personal interest do not always go together); to ensure that people do not meddle paternalistically in the affairs of others (query: can representative applicants be accused of this?); to ensure that the applicant has a personal interest not just an ideological concern in the outcome (but, query, may not a genuine concern for the interests of others be neither purely personal nor purely ideological?).

What, then, are the principles of *locus standi* in judicial review proceedings?

Inland Revenue Commissioners v *National Federation of Self-Employed and Small Businesses Ltd (NFSESB)*
[1982] AC 617
House of Lords

The NFSESB sought an order of mandamus requiring the Inland Revenue Commissioners to assess and collect arrears of income tax due by a number of workers in the printing industry, known as the Fleet Street Casuals. This group had for some years been engaged in practices which deprived the Revenue of tax due in respect of their casual earnings. The Inland Revenue, on becoming aware of this, made an arrangement under which the workers were required to register in respect of their casual employment, so that in future tax could be collected in the normal way. Arrears of tax from 1977–78 were to be paid and current investigations to proceed, but investigations in respect of earlier years were not to take place. The House of Lords considered whether the Federation had locus standi. At that time the relevant rule was r. 3(5) of the Rules of the Supreme Court. Section 31(3) of the Supreme Court Act 1981 (*ante* at p. 599) and r. 3(7) now repeat the provisions that used to be contained in this rule.

LORD WILBERFORCE: . . . There may be simple cases in which it can be seen at the earliest stage that the person applying for judicial review has no interest at all or no sufficient interest to support the application: then it would be quite correct at the threshold to refuse him leave to apply. The right to do so is an important safeguard against the courts being flooded and public bodies being harassed by irresponsible applications. But in other cases this will not be so. In these it will be necessary to consider the powers or the duties in law of those against whom the relief is asked, the position of the applicant in relation to those powers or duties, and to the breach of those said to have been committed. In other words, the question of sufficient interest cannot, in such cases, be considered in the abstract, or as an isolated point: it must be taken together with legal and factual context. The rule requires sufficient interest in the matter to which the application relates. This, in the present case, necessarily involves the whole question of the duties of the Inland Revenue and the breaches for failure of those duties of which the respondents complain. . . .

[After examining the relevant statutory provisions, his Lordship continued.]

From this summary analysis it is clear that the Inland Revenue Commissioners are not immune from the process of judicial review. They are an administrative body with statutory duties, which the courts, in principle, can supervise . . . It must follow from these cases and from principle that a taxpayer would not be excluded from seeking judicial review if he could show that the revenue had either failed in its statutory duty toward him or had been guilty of some action which was an abuse of their powers or outside their powers altogether. Such a collateral attack — as contrasted with a direct appeal on law to the courts — would no doubt be rare, but the possibility certainly exists.

The position of other taxpayers — other than the taxpayers whose assessment is in question — and their right to challenge the revenue's assessment or non-assessment of that taxpayer, must be judged according to whether, consistently with the legislation, they can be considered as having sufficient interest to complain of what has been done or omitted. I proceed therefore to examine the revenue's duties in that light.

These duties are expressed in very general terms and it is necessary to take account also of the framework of the income tax legislation. This established that the commissioners must assess each individual taxpayer in relation to his circumstances. Such assessments and all information regarding a taxpayer's affairs are strictly confidential. There is no list or record of assessments which can be inspected by other taxpayers nor is there any common fund of the produce of income tax in which income taxpayers as a whole can be said to have any interest. The produce of income tax, together with that of other inland revenue taxes, is paid into the consolidated fund which is at the disposal of Parliament for any purposes that Parliament thinks fit.

The position of taxpayers is therefore very different from that of ratepayers. As explained in *Arsenal Football Club Ltd* v *Ende* [1979] AC 1, the amount of rates assessed upon ratepayers is ascertainable by the public through the valuation list. The produce of rates goes into a common fund applicable for the benefit of the ratepayers. Thus any ratepayer has an interest, direct and sufficient, in the rates levied upon other ratepayers; for this reason his right as a 'person aggrieved' to challenge assessments upon them has long been recognised and is so now in section 69 of the General Rate Act 1967. This right was given effect to in the *Arsenal* case.

The structure of the legislation relating to income tax, on the other hand, makes clear that no corresponding right is intended to be conferred upon taxpayers. Not only is there no express or implied provision in the legislation upon which such a right could be claimed, but to allow it would be subversive of the whole system, which involves that the commissioners' duties are to the Crown, and that matters relating to income tax are between the commissioners and the taxpayer concerned. No other person is given any right to make proposals about the tax payable by any individual: he cannot even inquire as to such tax. The total confidentiality of assessments and of negotiations between individuals and the revenue is a vital element in the working of the system. As a matter of general principle I would hold that one taxpayer has no sufficient interest in asking the court to investigate the tax affairs of another taxpayer or to complain that the latter has been under-assessed or over-assessed: indeed, there is a strong public interest that he should not. And this principle applies equally to groups of taxpayers: an aggregate of individuals each of whom has no interest cannot of itself have an interest.

That a case can never arise in which the acts or abstentions of the revenue can be brought before the court I am certainly not prepared to assert, nor that, in a case of sufficient gravity, the court might not be able to hold that another taxpayer or other taxpayers could challenge them. Whether this situation has been reached or not must depend upon an examination, upon evidence, of what breach of duty or illegality is alleged. Upon this, and relating it to the position of the complainant, the court has to make its decision. . . .

[After considering the evidence his Lordship decided that the Federation had no sufficient interest.]

LORD DIPLOCK: For my part I should prefer to allow the appeal and dismiss the Federation's application under RSC Ord. 53, not upon the specific ground of no sufficient interest but upon the more general ground that it has not been shown that in the matter of which complaint was made, the treatment of the tax liabilities of the Fleet Street casuals, the board did anything that was *ultra vires* or unlawful. They acted in the bona fide exercise of the wide managerial discretion which is conferred on them by statute. . . .

[His Lordship nonetheless went on to consider the question of *locus standi.*]

The procedure under the new Order 53 involves two stages: (1) the application for leave to apply for judicial review, and (2) if leave is granted, the hearing of the application itself. The former, or 'threshold' stage is regulated by rule 3. The application for leave to apply for judicial review is made ex parte, but may be adjourned for the persons or bodies against whom relief is sought to be represented. This did not happen in the instant case. Rule 3(5) specifically requires the court to consider at this stage whether 'it considers that the applicant has a sufficient interest in the matter to which the application relates.' So this is a 'threshold' question in the sense that the court must direct its mind to it and form a prima facie view about it upon the material that is available at the first stage. The prima facie view so formed, if favourable to the applicant, may alter on further consideration in the light of further evidence that may be before the court at the second stage, the hearing of the application for judicial review itself.

The need for leave to start proceedings for remedies in public law is not new. It applied previously to applications for prerogative orders, though not to civil actions for injunctions or declarations. Its purpose is to prevent the time of the court being wasted by busybodies with misguided or trivial complaints of administrative error, and to remove the uncertainty in which public officers and authorities might be left as to whether they could safely proceed with administrative action while proceedings for judicial review of it were actually pending even though misconceived. . . .

My Lords, at the threshold stage, for the Federation to make out a prima facie case of reasonable suspicion that the board in showing a discriminatory leniency to a substantial class of taxpayers had done so for ulterior reasons extraneous to good management, and thereby deprived the national exchequer of considerable sums of money, constituted what was in my view reason enough for the Divisional Court to consider that the Federation or, for that matter, any taxpayer, had a sufficient interest to apply to have the question whether the board was acting *ultra vires* reviewed by the court. The whole purpose of requiring that leave should first be obtained to make the application for judicial review would be defeated if the court were to go into the matter in any depth at that stage. If, on a quick perusal of the material then available, the court thinks that it discloses what might on further consideration turn out to be an arguable case in favour of granting to the applicant the relief claimed, it ought, in the exercise of a judicial discretion, to give him leave to apply for that relief. The discretion that the court is exercising at this stage is not the same as that which it is called upon to exercise when all the evidence is in and the matter has been fully argued at the hearing of the application . . .

The analyses to which, on the invitation of the Lord Advocate, the relevant legislation has been subjected by some of your Lordships, and particularly the requirement of confidentiality which would be broken if one taxpayer could complain that another taxpayer was being treated by the revenue more favourably than himself, mean that occasions will be very rare on which an individual taxpayer (or pressure group of taxpayers) will be able to show a sufficient interest to justify an application for judicial review of the way in which the revenue has dealt with the tax affairs of any taxpayer other than the applicant himself.

Rare though they may be, however, if, in the instant case, what at the threshold stage was suspicion only had been proved at the hearing of the application for judicial review to be true in fact (instead of being utterly destroyed), I would have held that this was a matter in which the federation had a sufficient interest in obtaining an appropriate order, whether by way of declaration or mandamus, to require performance by the board of statutory duties which for reasons shown to be *ultra vires* it was failing to perform.

It would, in my view, be a grave lacuna in our system of public law if a pressure group, like the Federation, or even a single public-spirited taxpayer, were prevented by outdated technical rules of *locus standi* from bringing the matter to the attention of the court to vindicate the rule of law and get the unlawful conduct stopped. The Attorney-General, although he occasionally applies for prerogative orders against public authorities that do not form part of central government, in practice never does so against government departments. It is not, in my view, a sufficient answer to say that judicial review of the actions of officers or departments of central government is unnecessary because they are accountable to Parliament for the way in which they carry out their functions. They are accountable to Parliament for what they do so far as regards efficiency and policy, and of that Parlaiment is the only judge; they are responsible to a court of justice for the lawfulness of what they do, and of that the court is the only judge.

Lord Fraser and Lord Roskill delivered judgments in which they agreed with Lord Wilberforce. Lord Scarman delivered a judgment which agreed in general with that of Lord Diplock.

Note

Lord Diplock refers in his judgment to the role of the Attorney-General. The Attorney-General has a discretion to institute legal proceedings in the public interest. He may do so on his own initiative or upon the request of an individual or organisation. Where the Attorney-General institutes litigation at the request of an individual or organisation, this is known as a relator action. The Attorney-General's decision whether to bring a relator action cannot be challenged (see *Gouriet* v *Union of Post Office Workers* [1978] AC 435).

Questions

1. What are the differences, if any, between the approaches of Lord Diplock and Lord Wilberforce ?

2. Do the judgments suggest what their Lordships perceived to be the justification for standing rules (see Cane, *ante* at p. 615)?
3. Do the judgments suggest that the function of judicial review is:

(a) to protect the individual who is specially affected by the decision;
(b) to protect the public interest in rooting out administrative illegality?

Notes
1. In *R* v *The Attorney-General, ex parte ICI plc* [1987] 1 CMLR 72 the applicant, ICI, was held to have standing to question the validity of the Inland Revenue's assessment of the tax payable by one of its competitors. The fact that ICI was challenging the assessment of a competitor was held to distinguish the application from that of the NFSESB in the *National Federation* case. Furthermore, the issue of confidentiality did not arise because the Revenue had already agreed voluntarily to disclose the basis of its assessment.
2. The Law Commission in its 1994 report favoured the broadly liberal approach of the courts on sufficient interest. They were concerned about the effect of *R* v *Secretary of State for the Environment, ex parte Rose Theatre Trust* [1990] 1 QB 504 on challenges brought by people who were concerned about, but not directly affected by, the administrative action. The Law Commission recommended that public interest applications be treated as having sufficient interest. Subsequently the courts have taken this approach. in *R* v *HM Inspector of Pollution, ex parte Greenpeace Ltd (No. 2)* [1994] 4 All ER 329 Otton J declined to follow *Rose Theatre Trust.* Greenpeace, an environmental pressure group, not only had a genuine interest in the issues involved (disposal of radioactive waste) but it had some 2,500 supporters in the area where the plant was situated and it if was not permitted to seek judicial review, then those who Greenpeace represents, who would have sufficient interest e.g. neighbours, would not be able to command the expertise which Greenpeace has. A less well informed challenge would not render the court the assistance which it needs in order to do justice between the parties. In *R* v *Secretary of State for Foreign Affairs, ex parte World Development Movement Ltd* [1995] 1 WLR 386 the applicant pressure group was regarded as having sufficient interest to challenge the decision by the Foreign Secretary to make a payment of aid under the Overseas Development and Co-operation Act 1980 to the Malaysian Government towards the construction of the Pergau dam and hydro-electric scheme. This was despite the fact that, unlike Greenpeace, it was unlikely that any of the applicant's individual members had a direct interest in the issue. The significant factors listed by Rose LJ were that the issue was important; it involved the vindication of the rule of law; there appeared to be no other responsible challenger; the nature of the breach of duty against which relief was sought, and the prominent role of these applications in giving advice, guidance and assistance with regard to aid.
3. The above rules apply where the challenge is made under the application for judicial review. What is the position where the challenge is made in an

action begun by writ or originating summons, as is sometimes still permitted? In *Barrs* v *Bethell* [1982] Ch 294 Warner J stated, at p. 313:

> To my mind the crucial difference between an action [begun by writ] and an application for judicial review is that the former can be brought as of right whereas the latter requires the leave of the court. It appears to me, with respect, illogical to say that, because a person has a 'sufficient interest' to apply for a declaration or an injunction in proceedings for judicial review, he has a sufficient right to apply for the same relief in an action brought, without leave, in his own name. Nor do I think that the substantial difference between the two kinds of proceedings can be disregarded on the ground that at the end of they day the court has a discretion as to the relief to be given. . . . [I]n *Reg* v *Inland Revenue Commissioners, ex parte National Federation of Self-Employed and Small Businesses Ltd* [1982] AC 617, 630, Lord Wilberforce observed that the right for the court to refuse a person, at the threshold, leave to apply for judicial review '. . . is an important safeguard against the courts being flooded and public bodies harassed by irresponsible applications.' The Court's discretion as to the relief to be given does not afford a prospective defendant the same kind of protection. It does not protect him from the burden of being subjected to litigation or from the risk of having to bear all or part of the costs of it – because the plaintiff may not be good for them and because, in any case, only party and party costs will normally be recoverable from him.

Warner J concluded that a plaintiff seeking a declaration or injunction in such circumstances will only have standing if he can show that a private law right has been infringed or that he has suffered 'special damage' as a result of an infringement of a right in public law. This is the normal test of standing in private law proceedings.

(D) AGAINST WHOM AND IN RESPECT OF WHAT ACTIVITIES MAY JUDICIAL REVIEW BE SOUGHT?

O'Reilly v *Mackman* concerned a case in which the litigants attempted to use the procedure by way of writ instead of the application for judicial review. Conversely, there have been a number of cases in which the courts have held that litigants are not entitled to use the procedure for judicial review because their cases do not raise issues of 'public law'.

In *R* v *BBC ex parte Lavelle* [1983] 1 WLR 23, the applicant sought to challenge a decision of a disciplinary board within the BBC suspending her from her employment. Woolf LJ considered that the scope of Ord. 53 was not necessarily confined to that of the old prerogative orders but depended solely on the criteria set out in Ord. 53, r. 1(2) (*ante,* at p. 600). He did, however, hold that Ord. 53 could not be used to challenge the decisions of purely private or domestic tribunals such as the disciplinary body within the BBC which derived its power solely from the contract between Miss Lavelle and the BBC.

In the case which follows, the applicants sought to use judicial review to challenge the decision of an unincorporated association which exercised no statutory or prerogative powers.

R* v *Panel on Take-overs and Mergers, ex parte Datafin plc
[1987] QB 815
Court of Appeal

The Take-over Panel is an unincorporated association which represents a wide range of institutional bodies operating in the financial market, for example, the Stock Exchange. It has a regulatory function concerning take-overs and mergers. In this role it makes, administers and enforces a code of conduct known as the City Code.

The applicants, Datafin Plc, were involved in a competitive take-over and complained to the Panel that their rivals, Norton Opax plc, had breached the City Code. The Panel dismissed the complaint and Datafin unsuccessfully sought leave in the High Court to apply for judicial review, seeking *certiorari*, prohibition, *mandamus* and an injunction. Leave was granted on appeal by the Court of Appeal. The Court of Appeal considered three main issues:

(a) the susceptibility of the Panel's decisions to judicial review;
(b) the manner in which any jurisdiction was to be exercised; and
(c) whether, if there was jurisdiction, relief should be granted in the present case.

The following extracts are concerned only with the first question.

SIR JOHN DONALDSON MR: The Panel on Take-overs and Mergers is a truly remarkable body. Perched on the 20th floor of the Stock Exchange building in the City of London, both literally and metaphorically it oversees and regulates a very important part of the United Kingdom financial market. Yet it performs this function without any visible means of legal support. . . . 'Self-regulation' is an emotive term. It is also ambiguous. An individual who voluntarily regulates his life in accordance with stated principles, because he believes that this is morally right and also, perhaps, in his own long-term interests, or a group of individuals who do so, are practising self-regulation. But it can mean something quite different. It can connote a system whereby a group of people, acting in concert, use their collective power to force themselves and others to comply with a code of conduct of their own devising. This is not necessarily morally wrong or contrary to the public interest, unlawful or even undesirable. But it is very different.

The panel is a self-regulating body in the latter sense. Lacking any authority de jure, it exercises immense power de facto by devising, promulgating, amending and interpreting the City Code on Take-overs and Mergers, by waiving or modifying the application of the code in particular circumstances, by investigating and reporting on alleged breaches of the code and by the application or threat of sanctions. The sanctions are no less effective because they are applied indirectly and lack a legally enforceable base . . .

The unspoken assumption, which I do not doubt is a reality, is that the Department of Trade and Industry or, as the case may be, the Stock Exchange or other appropriate body would in fact exercise statutory or contractual powers to penalise the transgressors . . .

The principal issue in this appeal, and the only issue which may matter in the long term is whether this remarkable body is above the law. Its respectability is beyond question. So is its bona fides. I do not doubt for one moment that it is intended to and does operate in the public interest and that the enormously wide discretion which it arrogates to itself is necessary if it is to function efficiently and effectively. Whilst not wishing to become involved in the political controversy on the relative merits of self-regulation and governmental or statutory regulation, I am content to assume for the purposes of this appeal that self-regulation is preferable in the public interest. But that said, what is to happen if the panel goes off the rails? Suppose, perish the thought, that it were to use its powers in a way which was manifestly unfair. What then? [Counsel for the panel] submits that the panel would lose the support of public opinion in the financial markets and would be unable to operate. Further or alternatively, Parliament could and would intervene. Maybe, but how long would that take and who in the meantime could or would come to the assistance of those who were being oppressed by such conduct? . . .

The jurisdictional issue

. . . The picture which emerges is clear. As an act of government it was decided that, in relation to take-overs, there should be a central self-regulatory body which would be supported and sustained by a periphery of statutory powers and penalties wherever non-statutory powers and penalties were insufficient or non-existent or where EEC requirements called for statutory provisions. . . .

The issue is whether the historic supervisory jurisdiction of the Queen's courts extends to such a body discharging such functions, including some which are quasi-judicial in their nature, as part of such a system. [Counsel] for the panel, submits that it does not. He says that this jurisdiction only extends to bodies whose power is derived from legislation or the exercise of the prerogative. [Counsel for the applicants] submits that this is too narrow a view and that regard has to be had not only to the source of the body's power, but also to whether it operates as an integral part of a system which has a public law character, is supported by public law in that public law sanctions are applied if its edicts are ignored and performs what might be described as public law functions.

[After discussing a number of cases, *R* v *Criminal Injuries Compensation Board ex parte Lain* [1967] 2 QB 864, *O'Reilly* v *Mackman* [1983] 2 AC 237, *Council for the Civil Service Unions* v *Minister for the Civil Service* [1985] AC 374 and *Gillick* v *West Norfolk and Wisbech Area Health Authority* [1986] AC 112, the Master of Rolls continued] . . .

In all the reports it is possible to find enumerations of factors giving rise to the jurisdiction, but it is a fatal error to regard the presence of all those factors as essential or as being exclusive of other factors. Possibly the only essential elements are what can be described as a public element, which can take many different forms, and the exclusion from the jurisdiction of bodies whose sole source of power is a consensual submission to its jurisdiction.

In fact, given its novelty, the panel fits surprisingly well into the format which this court had in mind in the *Criminal Injuries Compensation Board* case. It is without doubt performing a public duty and an important one. This is clear from the expressed willingness of the Secretary of State for Trade and Industry to limit legislation in the field of take-overs and mergers and to use the panel as the centrepiece of his regulation of that market. The rights of citizens are indirectly affected by its decisions, some, but by no means all of whom, may in a technical sense be said to have assented to this situation, e.g. the members of the Stock Exchange. At least in its determination of whether there has been a breach of the code it has a duty to act judicially and it asserts that its raison d'être is to do equity between one shareholder and another. Its source of power is only partly based upon moral persuasion and the assent of institutions and their members, the bottom line being the statutory powers exercised by the Department of Trade and Industry and the Bank of England. In this context I should be very disappointed if the courts could not recognise the realities of executive power and allowed their vision to be clouded by the subtlety and sometimes the complexity of the way in which it can be exerted.

Given that it is really unthinkable that, in the absence of legislation such as affects trade unions, the panel should go on its way cocooned from the attention of the courts in defence of the citizenry, we sought to investigate whether it could conveniently be controlled by established forms of private law, e.g. torts such as actionable combinations in restraint of trade, and, to this end, pressed [counsel for the applicants] to draft a writ. Suffice it to say that the result was wholly unconvincing and, not surprisingly, [counsel for the panel] did not admit that it would be in the least effective. . . .

LLOYD LJ: . . . I add only a few words on the important question whether the Panel on Take-overs and Mergers is a body which is subject to judicial review. In my judgment it is. . . .

On this part of the case counsel for the panel has advanced arguments on two levels. On the level of pure policy he submits that it is undesirable for decisions or rulings of the panel to be reviewable. The intervention of the court would at best impede, at worst frustrate, the purposes for which the panel exists. Secondly, on a more technical level, he submits that to hold that the panel is subject to the supervisory jurisdiction of the High Court would be to extend that jurisdiction further than it has ever been extended before.

On the policy level, I find myself unpersuaded. Counsel for the panel made much of the word 'self-regulating'. No doubt self-regulation has many advantages. But I was unable to see why the mere fact that a body is self-regulating makes it less appropriate for judicial review. The committee of an ordinary club affords an obvious example. But the reason why a club is not subject to judicial review is not just because it is self-regulating. The panel wields enormous power. It has a giant's strength. The fact that is is self-regulating, which means, presumably, that it is not subject to regulation by others, and in particular the Department of Trade and Industry, makes it not less but more appropriate that it should be subject to judicial review by the courts. . . .

So long as there is a possibility, however remote, of the panel abusing its great powers, then it would be wrong for the courts to abdicate responsibility. The courts must remain ready, willing and able to hear a legitimate complaint in this as in any other field of our national life. I am not persuaded that this particular field is one in which the courts do not belong, or from which they should retire, on grounds of policy. And if the courts are to remain in the field, then it is clearly better, as a matter of policy, that legal proceedings should remain in the realm of public law rather than private law, not only because they are quicker, but also because the requirement of leave under Ord. 53 will exclude claims which are clearly unmeritorious.

So I turn to [counsel for the panel's] more technical argument . . .

[After referring to Lord Diplock's speech in *Council of Civil Service Unions* v *Minister for the Civil Service* [1985] AC 374 Lloyd LJ continued.]

I do not agree that the source of the power is the sole test whether a body is subject to judicial review, nor do I so read Lord Diplock's speech. Of course the source of power will often, perhaps usually, be decisive. If the source of power is a statute, or subordinate legislation under a statute, then clearly the body in question will be subject to judicial review. If, at the other end of the scale, the source of power is contractual, as in the case of private arbitration, then clearly the arbitrator is not subject to judicial review: see *R* v *National Joint Council for the Craft of Dental Technicians (Disputes Committee), ex parte Neate* [1953] 1 QB 704.

But in between these extremes there is an area in which it is helpful to look not just at the source of the power but at the nature of the power. If the body in question is exercising public law functions, or if the exercise of its functions have public law consequences, then that may, as counsel for the applicants submitted, be sufficient to bring the body within the reach of judicial review. . . .

But suppose I am wrong: suppose that the courts are indeed confined to looking at the source of the power, as [counsel for the panel] submits. Then I would accept the submission of counsel for the applicants that the source of the power in the present case is indeed governmental, at least in part. [Counsel for the panel] argued that, so far from the source of the power being governmental, this is a case where the government has deliberately abstained from exercising power. I do not take that view. I agree with [counsel for the applicants] when he says there has been an implied devolution of power. Power exercised behind the scenes is power nonetheless. The express powers conferred on inferior tribunals were of critical importance in the early days when the sole or main ground for intervention by the courts was that the inferior tribunal had exceeded its powers. But those days are long since past. Having regard to the way in which the panel came to be established, the fact that the Governor of the Bank of England appoints both the chairman and the deputy chairman, and the other matters to which Sir John Donaldson MR has referred, I am persuaded that the panel was established under the authority of the government, to use the language of Diplock LJ in *Lain's* case. If in addition to looking at the source of the power we are entitled to look at the nature of the power, as I believe we are, then the case is all the stronger. . . .

NICHOLLS LJ: . . .

Jurisdiction

I take as my starting point *Reg* v *Criminal Injuries Compensation Board, ex parte Lain* [1967] 2 QB 864, 882, where Lord Parker CJ noted that the only constant limits on the ancient remedy of certiorari were that the tribunal in question was performing a public duty. He contrasted private or domestic tribunals whose authority is derived solely from the agreement of the parties concerned. . . .

In my view, and quite apart from any other factors which point in the same direction, given the leading and continuing role played by the Bank of England in the affairs of the panel, the statutory source of the powers and duties of the Council of the Stock Exchange, the wide-ranging nature and importance of the matters covered by the code, and the public law consequences of non-compliance, the panel is performing a public duty in prescribing and operating the code (including ruling on complaints).

Questions

1. Is it correct to say, after *Datafin,* that the only criterion for deciding whether an authority is subject to judicial review is whether it performs a public function?

2. Would judicial review be available to challenge the decisions of the following:

(a) the Advertising Standards Authority (see *R* v *Advertising Standards Authority Limited, ex parte The Insurance Service* (1989) 133 SJ 1545);

(b) the National Greyhound Racing Club (see *Law* v *National Greyhound Racing Club* [1983] 1 WLR 1302, but note that this case was decided before *ex parte Datafin*. Do you think it would be decided any differently after *ex parte Datafin*?);

(c) the Jockey Club (see *R* v *Disciplinary Committee of the Jockey Club, ex parte Aga Khan* [1993] 1 WLR 909);

(d) the Association of the British Pharmaceutical Industry (see *R* v *Code of Practice Committee of the Association of the British Pharmaceutical Industry, The Times*, 7 November 1990);

(e) a university (see *Page* v *Hull University Visitor* [1993] AC 682).

Note

There have been a number of cases in which the courts considered whether the decisions of statutory bodies to dismiss an employee/employees could be challenged under Ord. 53. In *R* v *East Berkshire Health Authority ex parte Walsh* [1985] QB 152 the Court of Appeal held that this question depended on whether the employment had sufficient 'statutory underpinning'. The health authority was required by statute to contract with its employees on terms which included the conditions agreed by the Whitley Council for the Health Service and approved by the Secretary of State. The Court of Appeal decided that this did not provide a sufficient statutory underpinning. On the other hand, in *R* v *Secretary of State for the Home Department ex parte Benwell* [1985] QB 152 Hodgson J granted judicial review of a decision to dismiss a prison officer. Benwell was not in a contractual relationship with his employers and Hodgson J considered that, because his employment was governed by a code of discipline issued under statutory authority, there was sufficient statutory underpinning to provide a public law element. See also *Roy* v *Kensington and Chelsea FPC ante* at p. 610. Ordinary civil servants have now been held to have contracts of employment (*R* v *Lord Chancellor's Department, ex parte Nangle* [1992] 1 All ER 897.)

For further discussion of the distinction between public law and private law, see J. Beatson, "'Public' and 'Private' in English Administrative Law" (1987) 103 LQR, 34–65.

Although the courts might decide that the application for judicial review (under Ord. 53) is not available because the dispute does not raise issues of public law, this does not mean that the principles of judicial review are irrelevant. The rules of natural justice are frequently applied to bodies (such as sporting clubs) which could not be challenged under the application for judicial review procedure (see, for example, *R* v *BBC, ex parte Lavelle* [1983] 1 WLR 23). In such cases the judges may describe their role as one of exercising judicial review. This means that it is important to bear in mind that there may be a distinction between the scope of judicial review at the substantive level (that is, the scope of the principles of judicial review) and the scope of judicial review at the procedural level (the scope of the application for judicial review).

(E) JUSTICIABILITY

Even if a matter raises an issue of public law, the courts may nonetheless refuse to review it on the grounds that the matter is not justiciable. This generally means that the courts consider judicial procedures are unsuitable to control the exercise of discretion. This may be for a variety of reasons, for example because of lack of expertise on the part of the court or because of the constitutional inappropriateness of judicial intervention.

Council of Civil Service Unions v *Minister for the Civil Service*
[1985] AC 374
House of Lords

The facts of this case are at p. 572 *ante*. In it, the court accepted that prerogative powers were subject to judicial review. The question of whether public powers are subject to judicial review was not therefore to be established on the basis of whether the source of the powers was statute or the prerogative (see further *R* v *Panel on Take-overs and Mergers*). Review of the exercise of powers might, however, be denied if the subject matter of the dispute raised issues which were not justiciable.

LORD FRASER OF TULLYBELTON: . . . The respondent's case is that she deliberately made the decision without prior consultation because prior consultation 'would involve a real risk that it would occasion the very kind of disruption [at GCHQ] which was a threat to national security and which it was intended to avoid.'. . .

The question is one of evidence. The decision on whether the requirements of national security outweigh the duty of fairness in any particular case is for the Government and not for the courts; the Government alone has access to the necessary information, and in any event the judicial process is unsuitable for reaching decisions on national security. But if the decision is successfully challenged, on the ground that it has been reached by a process which is unfair, then the Government is under an obligation to produce evidence that the decision was in fact based on grounds of national security. . . .

[After considering *The Zamora* [1916] 2 AC 77 and the speeches of Lord Reid and Viscount Radcliffe in *Chandler* v *Director of Public Prosecutions* [1964] AC 763 his Lordship concluded that] . . . The affidavit [of Sir Robert Armstrong], read as a whole, does in my opinion undoubtedly constitute evidence that the Minister did indeed consider that prior consultation would have involved a risk of precipitating disruption at GCHQ. I am accordingly of opinion that the respondent has shown that her decision was one which not only could reasonably have been based, but was in fact based, on considerations of national security, which outweighed what would otherwise have been the reasonable expectation on the part of the appellants for prior consultation. . . .

LORD SCARMAN: My Lords, I would dismiss this appeal for one reason only. I am satisfied that the respondent has made out a case on the ground of national security. Notwithstanding the criticisms which can be made of the evidence and despite the fact that the point was not raised, or, if it was, was not clearly made before the case reached the Court of Appeal, I have no doubt that the respondent refused to consult the unions before issuing her instruction of the 22 December 1983 because she feared that, if she did, union-organised disruption of the monitoring services of GCHQ could well result. I am further satisfied that the fear was one which a reasonable minister in the circumstances in which she found herself could reasonably entertain. I am also satisfied that a reasonable minister could reasonably consider such disruption to constitute a threat to national security. I would, therefore, deny relief to the appellants upon their application for judicial review of the instruction, the effect of which was that staff at GCHQ would no longer be permitted to belong to a national trade union.

The point of principle in the appeal is as to the duty of the court when in proceedings properly brought before it a question arises as to what is required in the interest of national security. The question may arise in ordinary litigation between private persons as to their private rights and obligations: and it can arise, as in this case, in proceedings for judicial review of a decision by a public authority. The question can take one of several forms. It may be a question of fact which Parliament has left to the court to determine: see for an example section 10 of the Contempt of Court Act 1981. It may arise for consideration as a factor in the exercise of an executive discretionary power. But, however it arises, it is a matter to be considered by the court in the circumstances and context of the case. Though there are limits dictated by law and common sense which the court must observe in dealing with the question, the court does not abdicate its judicial function. If the question arises as a matter of fact, the court requires evidence to be given. If it arises as a factor to be considered in reviewing the exercise of a discretionary power, evidence is also needed so that the court may determine whether it should intervene to correct excess or abuse of the power. . . .

[Lord Scarman after discussing *The Zamora, Chandler* v *Director of Public Prosecutions* and *Secretary of State for Defence* v *Guardian Newspapers Ltd* [1985] AC 339, continued.]

My Lords, I conclude, therefore, that where a question as to the interests of national security arises in judicial proceedings the court has to act on evidence. In some cases a judge or jury is required by law to be satisfied that the interest is proved to exist: in others, the interest is a factor to be considered in the review of the exercise of an executive discretionary power. Once the factual basis is established by evidence so that the court is satisfied that the interest of national security is a relevant factor to be considered in the determination of the case, the court will accept the opinion of the Crown or its responsible officer as to what is required to meet it, unless it is possible to show that the opinion was one which no reasonable minister advising the Crown could in the circumstances reasonably have held. There is no abdication of the judicial function, but there is a common sense limitation recognised by the judges as to what is justiciable: and the limitation is entirely consistent with the general development of the modern case law of judicial review. . . .

LORD ROSKILL: My Lords, the conflict between private rights and the rights of the state is not novel either in our political history or in our courts. Historically, at least since 1688, the courts have sought to present a barrier to inordinate claims by the executive. But they have also been obliged to recognise that in some fields that barrier must be lowered and that on occasions, albeit with reluctance, the courts must accept that the claims of executive power must take precedence over those of the individual. One such field is that of national security. The courts have long shown themselves sensitive to the assertion by the executive that considerations of national security must preclude judicial investigation of a particular individual grievance. But even in that field the courts will not act on a mere assertion that questions of national security are involved. Evidence is required that the decision under challenge was in fact founded on those grounds. That that principle exists is I think beyond doubt. In a famous passage in *The Zamora* [1916] 2 AC 77, 107 Lord Parker of Waddington, delivering the opinion of the Judicial Committee, said:

> Those who are responsible for the national security must be the sole judges of what the national security requires. It would be obviously undesirable that such matters should be the subject of evidence in a court of law or otherwise discussed in public.

The Judicial Committee were there asserting what I have already sought to say, namely that some matters, of which national security is one, are not amenable to the judicial process. . . .

Lord Diplock and Lord Brightman delivered judgments in favour of dismissing the appeals.

Question

What differences, if any, are there between the speeches of Lord Fraser and Lord Roskill on the one hand, and Lord Scarman on the other?

Notes

1. In *R* v *Secretary of State for the Home Department, ex parte Ruddock* [1987] 1 WLR 1482, at p. 1490 it was said that 'credible evidence' was required in support of a plea of national security before judicial investigation of a factual issue (in this case whether a warrant had been issued to tap Mrs Ruddock's telephone) is precluded. Taylor J rejected the argument that the court should decline jurisdiction because a Minister states that to do so would be detrimental to national security. He did, however, accept that in an extreme case where there was 'cogent', 'very strong and specific' evidence of potential damage to national security flowing from the trial of the issues a court might have to decline to try factual issues.

2. In other cases the courts have held that certain decisions cannot be challenged on particular grounds (see *Nottinghamshire CC* v *Secretary of State for the Environment* [1986] AC 240, *ante* at p. 581).

3. In *R* v *Secretary of State for the Home Department, ex parte Bentley* [1994] QB 349 the exercise of the prerogative of mercy was successfully challenged, albeit on a narrow ground. The court held the Minister approached the question of a posthumous pardon on the wrong basis that a grant of a free pardon required moral and technical innocence, rather than considering whether, in all the circumstances, the appropriate punishment had been suffered.

The challenge to the Treaty on European Union was not successful (*R* v *Secretary of State for Foreign and Commonwealth Affairs, ex parte Rees-Mogg* [1994] QB 552).

Question

Consider whether you think each of the following issues is justiciable and why/why not? Then read the cases cited to establish the views of the courts. What reasons did the courts give?

(a) A British citizen residing in Spain applied for a British passport. The application was refused, and he was told that the reason for this was that a warrant for his arrest had been issued in the United Kingdom and the Secretary of State would not issue a passport in such circumstances (see *R* v *Secretary of State for Foreign and Commonwealth Affairs ex parte Everett* [1989] 2 WLR 224).

(b) The Attorney-General has power to stop or institute prosecutions and to issue directions to the Director of Public Prosecutions to take over the conduct of prosecutions. He may also give, or refuse to give, consent to the institution of relator actions (actions brought at the instance of a relator by the Attorney-General to restrain infringements of public rights). (See *Gouriet* v *UPOW* [1978] AC 435.)

(F) JUDICIAL REVIEW AS A DISCRETIONARY REMEDY

Note

It is important to remember that judicial review is a discretionary remedy. Hence, the effective scope of the principles of judicial review will depend on how the court chooses to exercise its discretion.

There are a number of factors which are relevant to the exercise of the court's discretion: the availability of alternative remedies and the question whether the applicant has suffered injustice have been particularly important in recent years.

(i) The availability of alternative remedies

R* v *Chief Constable of the Merseyside Police, ex parte Calveley and others

[1986] 2 WLR 144
Court of Appeal

In 1981, following complaints by persons who were arrested, an investigating officer was appointed to inquire into the conduct of five police officers who were the subjects of complaints. In 1983 the officers were interviewed by the investigating officer and issued with notices under regulation 7 of the Police (Discipline) Regulations, which provides that the investigating officer must 'as soon as is practicable' inform the member subject to investigation of, *inter alia,* his right to make a written or oral statement concerning the matter to the investigating officer. In 1984 the officers were found guilty of disciplinary offences by the Chief Constable of Merseyside, and were either dismissed from the force or required to retire. They appealed to the Secretary of State as they were entitled to do under the statutory scheme governing their dismissal, and sought an order of *certiorari* on the grounds that there had been a breach of regulation 7. The Court of Appeal held that the applicants had been prejudiced by the delay in issuing the regulation 7 notices and went on to consider the argument that judicial review was not available because the applicants had an alternative remedy by appeal to the Home Secretary.

SIR JOHN DONALDSON MR: [Counsel] for the Chief Constable, submits that the application for judicial review was rightly dismissed, not upon the ground that it was premature, but because judicial review is not an available remedy when another avenue of appeal is open. In this context he referred to *Reg* v *Epping and Harlow General Commissioners, ex parte Goldstraw* [1983] 3 All ER 257 where, with the agreement of Purchas LJ, I said, at p. 262:

> it is a cardinal principle that, save in the most exceptionable circumstances, [the judicial review] jurisdiction will not be exercised where other remedies were available and have not been used.

This, like other judicial pronouncements on the interrelationship between remedies by way of judicial review on the one hand and appeal procedures on the other, is not to be regarded or construed as a statute. It does not support the proposition that judicial review is not available where there is an alternative remedy by way of appeal. It asserts simply that the court, in the exercise of its discretion, will very rarely make this remedy available in these circumstances.

In other cases courts have asserted the existence of this discretion, albeit with varying emphasis on the reluctance to grant judicial review. Thus in *Reg* v *Paddington Valuation Officer, ex parte Peachey Property Corporation Ltd* [1966] 1 QB 380, 400, Lord Denning MR, with the agreement of Danckwerts and Salmon LJJ, held that certiorari and mandamus were available where the alternative statutory remedy was 'nowhere near so convenient, beneficial and effectual.' In *Reg* v *Hillingdon London Borough Council, ex parte Royco Homes Ltd* [1974] QB 720, 728 Lord Widgery CJ said: ' it has always been a principle that certiorari will go only where there is no other equally effective and convenient remedy.' In *Ex parte Waldron* [1985] 3 WLR 1090, 1108, Glidewell LJ, after referring to this passage, said:

> Whether the alternative statutory remedy will resolve the question at issue fully and directly; whether the statutory procedure would be quicker, or slower, than procedure by way of judicial review; whether the matter depends on some particular or technical knowledge which is more readily available to the alternative appellate body; these are amongst the matters which a court should take into account when deciding whether to grant relief by judicial review when an alternative remedy is available.

Finally, this approach is, I think, consistent with *Reg* v *Inland Revenue Commissioners, ex parte Preston* [1985] AC 835. . . .

The statutory scheme for police discipline contained in the Police (Discipline) Regulations 1977 and the Police (Appeals) Rules 1977 (SI 1977 No. 759) contemplates a right of appeal to the Secretary of State from a determination by the Chief Constable. . . . However, it is not speedy and, even if there had been no application for judicial review, it is not certain that the appeal would have been determined much before the present time. The application for judicial review in fact caused the appeal to be stayed and, on the most optimistic view, it could not be determined in less than five to six months from now.

Mr Livesey submits that the applicants' complaint of delay in serving the regulation 7 notices and of consequential prejudice should be determined by the appeal procedure provided by Parliament. The appeal tribunal would have a specialised expertise rendering it better able than a court to assess the prejudice. Furthermore, the applicants would be able to raise new points and call fresh evidence directed to the disciplinary charges themselves.

I acknowledge the specialised expertise of such a tribunal, but I think Mr Livesey's submission overlooks the fact that a police officer's submission to police disciplinary procedures is not unconditional. He agrees and is bound by these procedures taking them as a whole. Just as his right of appeal is constrained by the requirement that he give prompt notice of appeal, so he is not to be put in peril in respect of disciplinary, as contrasted with criminal, proceedings unless there is substantial compliance with the police disciplinary regulations. That has not occurred in this case. Whether in all the circumstances the Chief Constable, and the Secretary of State on appeal, is to be regarded as being without jurisdiction to hear and determine the charges which are not processed in accordance with the statutory scheme or whether, in natural justice, the Chief Constable and the Secretary of State would, if they directed themselves correctly in law, be bound to rule in favour of the applicants on the preliminary point, is perhaps only of academic interest. The substance of the matter is that, against the background of the requirement of regulation 7 that the applicants be informed of the complaint and given an opportunity to reply within days rather than weeks, the applicants had no formal notice of the complaints for well over two years. This is so serious a departure from the police disciplinary procedure that, in my judgment, the court should, in the exercise of its discretion, grant judicial review and set aside the determination of the Chief Constable.

I would allow the appeal accordingly.

May LJ delivered a judgment in favour of allowing the appeal, in which he agreed with the dictum in Reg v *Epping and Harlow General Commissioner, ex parte Goldstraw [1983] All ER 257, referred to in the judgment of Lord Donaldson MR. Glidewell LJ agreed with the reasoning of the Master of the Rolls.*

R v ***Secretary of State for the Home Department, ex parte Swati***
[1986] 1 WLR 477
Court of Appeal

Mr Swati, a citizen of Pakistan, sought leave to enter and remain in the United Kingdom for one week in order to visit places of interest. He was refused leave to enter and, rather than return to Pakistan, he remained in Ashford Remand Centre and sought to challenge the decision of the immigration authorities by making an application for judicial review, seeking orders of certiorari and mandamus. The Divisional Court refused an application for leave to apply for judicial review. This decision was upheld on appeal to the Court of Appeal when it was decided that the applicant had failed to show that he had an arguable case for the purposes of applying for judicial review.

SIR JOHN DONALDSON MR: . . . However, the matter does not stop there, because it is well established that in giving or refusing leave to apply for judicial review, account must be taken of the alternative remedies available to the applicant. This aspect was considered by this court very recently in *Reg* v *Chief Constable of the Merseyside Police, ex parte Calveley* [1986] 2 WLR 144 and it was held that the jurisdiction would not be exercised where there was an alternative remedy by way of appeal, save in exceptional circumstances. By definition, exceptional circumstances defy definition, but where Parliament provides an appeal procedure, judicial review will have no place, unless the applicant can distinguish his case from the type of case for which the appeal procedure was provided.

The applicant may have no basis for complaint at being refused leave to enter. He may have cause to complain that the immigration officer erred in her assessment of the evidence – that her credulity threshold was too high. He may have cause to complain that she misunderstood and therefore misapplied the criteria for granting leave to enter. We simply have no idea which is the case. All these matters will be open on a statutory appeal, but only the latter could form the basis for judicial review, since as Lord Brightman pointed out in *Chief Constable of the North Wales Police* v *Evans* [1982] 1 WLR 1155, 1174G, judicial review is not so much concerned with the merits of the decision as with the way in which it was reached. In a word, the applicant's case is wholly indistinguishable from the general run of cases where someone arrives in the United Kingdom and is dissatisfied because he is denied leave to enter. Accordingly, in my judgment, he should not be allowed to pursue it by way of judicial review.

Stephen Brown LJ and Parker LJ delivered judgments in favour of dismissing the appeal.

Questions

1. In *ex parte Swati* did the court consider all the factors which were stated to be relevant in *ex parte Calveley?*

2. Parker LJ stated at p. 490:

> It is impossible and would be legally wrong to define what are exceptional circumstances and what are not. Each case will depend on its own facts. It is of course clear that some circumstances are not even arguably sufficient, and that others equally plainly are . . . An example of the former would be the mere fact that the appeal procedure is only available on leaving the country.

Do you agree with this assessment of the relevance of the fact that the statutory appeals procedure could only be invoked from outside the country (s. 13(3) of the Immigration Act 1971)?

3. Do you think the ground on which judicial review was sought was an important factor in the decisions in *ex parte Calveley* and *ex parte Swati?*

Note

The effect of *ex parte Swati* on the number of applications in judicial review proceedings is considered by Sunkin in (1987) 50 *Modern Law Review* 432–67 at pp. 444–7. See generally N. Collar (1991) 10 CLQ 138 and C. Lewis [1992] CLJ 138.

(ii) Needs of good administration

R* v *Monopolies and Mergers Commission, ex parte Argyll Group plc
[1986] 1 WLR 763
Court of Appeal

Argyll Group plc and Guinness plc were rivals in a bid to take over another company, Distillers. The Secretary of State for Trade and Industry referred the Guinness proposal to the Monopolies and Mergers Commission for inquiry and report. One week later the Chairman of the Monopolies and Mergers Commission sought and obtained the consent of the Secretary of State for Trade and Industry to the withdrawal of the reference on the ground that the proposal to make the arrangements had been abandoned. Argyll sought judicial review of this decision, seeking an order of *certiorari*. The Court of Appeal accepted that the Chairman of the Commission did not have the power to act alone in the matter. The following extracts relate to the court's discretion whether to grant a remedy.

SIR JOHN DONALDSON MR:

Discretion

The judge accepted that the chairman derives authority to act as he did from paragraph 10 of schedule 3 to the Act, read with section 75(5). He did not, therefore, have to consider the issue of discretion. As I respectfully disagree with the judge on this aspect, I do, therefore, have to consider how discretion should be exercised.

We are sitting as a public law court concerned to review an administrative decision, albeit one which has to be reached by the application of judicial or quasi-judicial principles. We have to approach our duties with a proper awareness of the needs of public administration. I cannot catalogue them all, but, in the present context, would draw attention to a few which are relevant.

Good public administration is concerned with substance rather than form. Difficult although the decision upon the fact of abandonment may or my not have been, I have little doubt that the commission, or a group of members charged with the conduct of the reference, would have reached and would now reach the same conclusion as did their experienced chairman.

Good public administration is concerned with speed of decision, particularly in the financial field. The decision to lay aside the reference was reached on 20 February 1986. If relief is granted, it must be some days before a new decision is reached.

Good public administration requires a proper consideration of the public interest. In this context, the Secretary of State is the guardian of the public interest. He consented to the reference being laid aside, although he need not have done so if he considered it to be in the public interest that the original proposals be further investigated. He could have made a further reference of the new proposals, if such they be, but has not done so.

Good public administration requires a proper consideration of the legitimate interests of individual citizens, however rich and powerful they may be and whether they are natural or juridical persons. But in judging the relevance of an interest, however legitimate, regard has to be had to the purpose of the administrative process concerned. Argyll has a strong and legitimate interest in putting Guinness in baulk, but that is not the purpose of the administrative process under the Fair Trading Act 1973. To that extent their interest is not therefore of any great, or possibly any, weight.

Lastly good public administration requires decisiveness and finality unless there are compelling reasons to the contrary. The financial public has been entitled to rely upon the finality of the announced decision to set aside the reference and upon the consequence that, subject to any further reference, Guinness were back in the ring, from 20 February until at least 25 February when leave to apply for judicial review was granted, and possibly longer in the light of the judge's decision. This is a very long time in terms of a volatile market and account must be taken of the probability that deals have been done in reliance upon the validity of the decisions now impugned.

Taking account of all these factors, I do not consider that this is a case in which judicial review should be granted. Accordingly, I would dismiss the appeal.

Dillon LJ and Neill LJ delivered judgments in favour of dismissing the appeal.

Note

R v *Panel on Take-overs and Mergers, ex parte Datafin plc* [1987] QB 815 also illustrates the use of discretion in the grant of remedies. Sir John Donaldson MR stated (at p. 841) that the court would decide what order, if any, needed to be made, bearing in mind 'the likely outcome of the proceedings which will depend partly upon the facts as they appear from the information available to the court, but also in part upon the public administrative purpose which the panel is designed to serve'.

Questions

1. Commenting on the factors referred to by Sir John Donaldson, S. Lee writes in (1987) 103 LQR 166–8, at 167 that:

> If these are only a few of the possible reasons for judicial restraint, then their discretion is indeed very wide. There are obvious dangers to good public administration, let alone to aggrieved citizens, in such broad judicial discretion. Firstly, there is the danger that administrators will come to believe that they can get away with a breach of the principles of administrative action. Secondly, the prospect of winning the argument on abuse of administrative discretion but failing to secure a remedy through the exercise of judicial discretion may well act as a disincentive to bring applications for judicial review.

Do you agree that decisions such as *R* v *Monopolies and Mergers Commission* carry such risks ?

2. Contrast the approach adopted in this case to arguments based on the interests of good administration with *O'Reilly* v *Mackman* (*ante* at p. 602) and *Wandsworth Borough Council* v *Winder* (*ante* at p. 606).

Note

The relevance of the argument that a fair hearing would make no difference has been considered by the courts in recent years. There are, in fact, a number of contrasting cases. Of these, *Glynn* v *Keele University* [1971] 1 WLR 487 provides an example of a case which accepts, as in *R* v *Monopolies and*

Mergers Commission, ex parte Argyll Group plc, that a remedy may be denied where a fair hearing 'would make no difference'. In that case the plaintiff had been fined and excluded from residence on a university campus for a particular period. Pennycuick V-C found that there had been a breach of the rules of natural justice, but he refused to grant an injunction since he thought that the plaintiff had only lost a chance to make a plea in mitigation, and this was not a sufficient reason to set aside a decision which he believed to be perfectly proper. In contrast Megarry J in *John* v *Rees* [1970] Ch 345, at 402 stated:

> It may be that there are some who would decry the importance which the courts attach to the observance of the rules of natural justice. 'When something is obvious,' they may say, 'why force everybody to go through the tiresome waste of time involved in framing charges and giving an opportunity to be heard? The result is obvious from the start.' Those who take this view do not, I think, do themselves justice. As everybody who has anything to do with the law well knows, the path of the law is strewn with open and shut cases which, somehow, were not; of unanswerable charges which, in the event, were completely answered; of inexplicable conduct which was fully explained; of fixed and unalterable determinations that, by discussion, suffered a change. Nor are those with any knowledge of human nature who pause to think for a moment likely to underestimate the feelings of resentment of those who find that a decision against them has been made without their being afforded any opportunity to influence the course of events.

(G) EXCLUSION OF JUDICIAL REVIEW

The legislature has sometimes attempted to protect public authorities from judicial review by inserting clauses which appear to be intended to exclude the jurisdiction of the court. For example, in *Anisminic Ltd* v *Foreign Compensation Commission* [1969] 2 AC 147, Anisminic Ltd wished to challenge a decision of the Foreign Compensation Commission that it was not entitled to compensation in respect of the sequestration of property which it had owned in Egypt, and accordingly applied for a declaration (see *ante* at p. 535). The legislation, however, provided that any determination by the Commission of an application 'shall not be called in question in any court of law' (Foreign Compensation Act 1950, s. 4(4)). The House of Lords considered the effect of this clause.

Anisminic Ltd v *Foreign Compensation Commission*
[1969] 2 AC 147
House of Lords

LORD REID: . . . The next argument was that, by reason of the provisions of section 4(4) of the 1950 Act, the courts are precluded from considering whether the respondent's determination was a nullity, and therefore it must be treated as valid whether or not inquiry would disclose that it was a nullity . . .

The respondent maintains that these are plain words only capable of having one meaning. Here is a determination which is apparently valid: there is nothing on the face of the document to cast any doubt on its validity. If it is a nullity, that could only be established by raising some kind of proceedings in court. But that would be calling the determination in question, and that is expressly prohibited by statute. The appellants maintain that this is not the meaning of the words of this provision. They say that 'determination' means a real determination and does not include an apparent or purported determination which in the eyes of the law has no existence because it is a nullity. Or, putting it another way, if you seek to show that a determination is a nullity you are not questioning the purported determination – you are maintaining that it does not exist as a determination. It is one thing to question a determination which does not exist: it is quite another to say that there is nothing to be questioned.

Let me illustrate the matter by supposing a simple case. A statute provides that a certain order may be made by a person who holds a specified qualification or appointment, and it contains a provision similar to section 4(4), that such an order made by such a person shall not be questioned in any court of law. A person aggrieved by an order alleges that it is a forgery or that the person who made the order did not hold that qualification or appointment. Does such a provision require the court to treat that order as a valid order? It is a well-established principle that a provision ousting the ordinary jurisdiction of the court must be construed strictly - meaning, I think, that, if such provision is reasonably capable of having two meanings, that meaning shall be taken which preserves the ordinary jurisdiction of the court.

Statutory provisions which seek to limit the ordinary jurisdiction of the court have a long history. No case has been cited in which any other form of words limiting the jurisdiction of the court has been held to protect a nullity. If the draftsman or Parliament had intended to introduce a new kind of ouster clause so as to prevent any inquiry as to whether the document relied on was a forgery, I would have expected to find something much more specific than the bald statement that a determination shall not be called in question in any court of law. Undoubtedly such a provision protects every determination which is not a nullity. But I do not think that it is necessary or even reasonable to construe the word 'determination' as including everything which purports to be a determination but which is in fact no determination at all. . . .

The other Law Lords delivered speeches in which they agreed that the ouster clause would not protect a decision from challenge if the FCC had acted outside its jurisdiction. A majority of their Lordships also held that Anisminic Ltd was entitled to the declaration which it sought because the FCC had made an error of law which took it outside its jurisdiction (ante at p. 465).

Note

After the decision in *Anisminic* the Foreign Compensation Act 1969 was passed. Section 3 provided that a person aggrieved by a determination of the Commission on any question of law had a right to require the Commission to state and sign a case for the Court of Appeal. It was provided, however, that there was to be no appeal to the House of Lords from a decision of the Court of Appeal. Section 3(9) stated that, except as provided by the section and in respect of claims that the Commission had breached the rules of natural justice, no determination by the Commission on any claim under the Foreign

Compensation Act 1950 shall be called in question in any court of law. Determination was defined as including a purported determination.

Question
If these provisions had been in force at the time of the decision in *Anisminic,* do you think House of Lords would have granted the declaration sought?

Note
The Tribunals and Inquiries Act 1992, s. 12(1) (formerly s. 11 of the Tribunal and Inquiries Act 1958) now provides that, as respects England and Wales:

> any provision in an Act passed before 1 August 1958 that any order or determination shall not be called in question in any court, or any provision in such an Act which by similar words excludes any of the powers of the High Court, shall not have effect so as to prevent the removal of the proceedings into the High Court by order of certiorari or to prejudice the powers of the High Court to make orders of mandamus.

(Section 11 of the 1958 Act expressly excluded orders or determinations of the Foreign Compensation Commission from this general provision; in *Anisminic,* however, Lord Pearce specifically stated that s. 11 had no bearing on the issue which the court was required to consider.)

Question
Why do you think this provision was confined to Acts passed before 1 August 1958?

Notes
1. *Anisminic* concerned an absolute ouster clause. Partial or limited ouster clauses sometimes appear in certain statutory provisions. For example, in planning law persons aggrieved by a compulsory purchase order are permitted to appeal to the High Court on certain grounds within six weeks of publication of the order. Apart from this it is provided that a compulsory purchase order 'shall not . . . be questioned in any legal proceedings whatsoever' (see Acquisition of Land Act 1981, ss. 23–25). The courts have upheld the validity of the partial or limited ouster clauses which attempt to protect decisions from challenge after the expiry of a time-limit (see *R* v *Secretary of State for the Environment, ex parte Ostler* [1977] QB 122).
2. Where a legislative provision stipulates that the issuing of a certificate 'shall be conclusive evidence' that the conditions for the issue of the certificate had been satisfied, it seems that this can exclude review of the decision to issue the certificate — *R* v *Registrar of Companies, ex parte Central Bank of India* [1986] QB 1114.
3. An example of a recent ouster clause is the Security Services Act 1989, s. 5(4) 'decisions of the Tribunal . . . (including any decisions as to their

jurisdiction) shall not be subject to appeal or liable to be questioned in any court'.

Questions

1. Do you think that the decision in *Anisminic* reflected the intention of Parliament?

2. Cane, in the extracts set out *ante* at p. 526, uses this case to support a particular argument which he wishes to make. What was the argument, and do you agree that the decision in *Anisminic* supports it?

10 OMBUDSMEN

(A) INTRODUCTION

In 1961 an influential report by the JUSTICE organisation recommended that an impartial officer, to be known as a Parliamentary Commissioner, should be established and report on complaints of maladministration in central government. It argued that:

> there appears to be a continuous flow of relatively minor complaints, not sufficient in themselves to attract public interest but nevertheless of great importance to the individuals concerned, which give rise to feelings of frustration and resentment because of the inadequacy of the existing means of seeking redress. (JUSTICE, *The Citizen and the Administration* (1961), para. 76.)

The report outlined the weaknesses in the parliamentary question procedure and in adjournment debates as mechanisms for the investigation of complaints (on parliamentary questions and adjournment debates, see *ante* at pp. 344–368). The report envisaged that the Parliamentary Commissioner would be independent of the Executive and responsible only to Parliament. He would conduct investigations informally, in order to ensure that there would be no serious interference with the working of a department, and have access to departmental files. A Select Committee would be established to consider the annual reports of the Parliamentary Commissioner and any special reports which he might issue on particular issues. On the controversial question of whether the establishment of a Parliamentary Commissioner would have any implications for the doctrine of ministerial responsibility, the Report stated, at para. 155:

> . . . It is a principle of such fundamental importance in our constitution that we think it would be wrong to make any proposal which might seem to qualify it and therefore we have suggested that a Minister should have the power to veto any proposed investigation by the Parliamentary Commissioner against his Department. We would expect, however, that as so often has happened in our constitutional history, a convention would grow up that the Minister would not exercise his power of veto unreasonably.

The report was also careful to stress that 'any additional procedure should not disturb the basic position of Parliament as a channel for complaint against the Executive and should not even appear to interfere with the relations between individual members and their constituents' (para. 156). With this in mind it recommended that, during an initial testing period, complaints should only be considered on reference from a Member of either House of Parliament. It did, however, anticipate that, after a period of about five years, the Commissioner should be empowered to receive complaints direct from the public. 'The ultimate object', according to the report, 'should be to establish a channel by which the investigation of administrative grievances should take place initially outside the political sphere. Parliament would, however, always be able to take up grievances in the last resort if the Commissioner's investigation failed to procure justice' (para. 157).

Following the publication of *The Citizen and the Administration,* the Conservative Lord Chancellor, Lord Dilhorne, argued that 'a Parliamentary Commissioner would seriously interfere with the prompt and efficient dispatch of public business' (HL Deb., vol. 244, cols. 384-5). Subsequently, however, a new Government accepted, with certain modifications, the introduction of the Parliamentary Commissioner as a development and reinforcement of 'our existing constitutional arrangements for the protection of the individual' (see *The Parliamentary Commissioner for Administration,* Cmnd 2767 (1965)). On the introduction of the ombudsman system in the United Kingdom, see further, Stacey, *The British Ombudsman.*

The office of the Parliamentary Commissioner for Administration (PCA) was thus created in 1967. Since then there has been a proliferation of ombudsmen in the United Kingdom. In 1969 the offices of PCA for Northern Ireland and the Commissioner for Complaints for Northern Ireland were established; both offices are held by the same person. The offices of Health Service Commissioners of England, Wales, and Scotland were created by legislation in 1972 and 1973; all three posts are presently held by the person who is the PCA. In 1974 Local Commissioners were established to deal with maladministration in local government in England and Wales. The office of Local Ombudsman for Scotland was established in 1975; the work of the Scottish Local Ombudsman has been studied by J. Logie and P. Watchman, *The Local Ombudsman* (1990).

There are now ombudsmen in the private sector, for example the banking ombudsman and the insurance ombudsman. The office of legal services ombudsman was created by the Courts and Legal Services Act 1990, following the Government's recommendations in *Legal Services: A Framework for the Future* (Cm. 740 (1989), paras 10.13–10.27).

This chapter focuses on the Parliamentary Commissioner and the Local Commissioners. The Parliamentary Commissioner will be referred to in the notes and questions as either the PCA or the Ombudsman. The Local Commissioners will be referred to as either Local Commissioners or the Local Ombudsmen.

The main legislative provisions governing the Parliamentary Commissioner for Administration are contained in the Parliamentary Commissioner Act 1967. The provisions governing the Local Commissioners are set out in the Local Government Act 1974. Both pieces of legislation have been amended on a number of occasions.

The following extracts from the reports of the PCA and the Local Commissioners provide some indication of the work which they carry out.

Parliamentary Commissioner for Administration
Annual Report for 1995
HC of 1995–96

Department of Social Security

10. The Department of Social Security (DSS), with its Agencies, again accounted for the largest proportion of my workload in 1995. Of the 1,706 new complaints which were referred to me this year, 834 related to social security matters. DSS cases also accounted for some 45 per cent of those on which I reported in 1995.

Child Support Agency

11. I refer in the Introduction, paragraphs 8 and 9, to the issues surrounding the Child Support Agency (CSA), and to my second special report.

. . . *Child Support Agency*

8. Last year's report described the growing number of complaints against the Child Support Agency which had been referred to me. I explained why I had felt obliged to take the unprecedented step of declining to investigate fresh individual complaints except where they concerned aspects of the Agency's work I had not previously looked into or actual financial loss to the complainant was involved; and that in January 1995 I laid before Parliament under section 10(4) of the Parliamentary Commissioner Act a special report including a selection of cases on which I had reported in 1994. The Select Committee took evidence from the Permanent Secretary of the department, from the Chief Executive of the Agency and from the Parliamentary Under-Secretary of State, Department of Social Security. The Select Committee's report was published in March 1995. In May the Government replied to that report, indicating that various measures had been introduced to improve the quality of CSA's work.

9. In 1995 complaints against CSA accounted for one-quarter of those referred to me — although many related to the actions of the Agency before those changes, together with legislative changes, were introduced, or before they could be expected to have brought about an improvement. I continued to decline to investigate most individual examples of familiar kinds of maladministration considering it preferable to deploy my resources in investigating novel aspects, monitoring the effectiveness of the measures introduced with a view to improving the service and looking into those cases

where there appeared to have been actual financial loss. Even so, I accepted for investigation in 1995 105 complaints against CSA. I published shortly before this report a further special report including a selection of cases I have investigated in 1995 and describing my present view of the Agency's more recent performance as seen through my consideration of complaints.

. . . *Income Support and housing costs*

15. In last year's report I commented on the growing proportion of cases involving IS referred to me which related to difficulties and delays in establishing the correct amount of loan interest allowable for claimants' housing costs. That remained a significant source of complaint in 1995. In May they failed to hand over to their respective building societies sums paid to them (including in one case an arrears payment of over £7,000) in respect of housing costs. In the light of all the evidence I did not find made out their complaints that DSS had been responsible for the repossession of their homes.

. . . 18. The eight remaining cases involving housing costs all exhibited laxity in varying degrees in the general standard of service provided by DSS. It is not surprising that the complainants in those cases should have sought to draw to my attention the considerable worry and distress that such errors can cause. What was particularly interesting in some cases, however, was the difference between the complainant's perception of the consequences of the poor service which they had received from DSS, and the actual outcome revealed by my investigations. In four of the cases, where the complaint was that the mishandling of the claim had caused arrears in mortgage repayments, I found that the complainants had in fact benefited in real terms from departmental errors and had been overpaid benefit which they would not be required to repay. The sums involved ranged from £651 to over £3,000.

19. Another of the cases showed that a 'stitch in time' by DSS could have saved both the complainant and the department a good deal of time and effort. Where DSS pay mortgage interest direct to building societies, that is normally done at four-weekly intervals. DSS have an agreement with the Council of Mortgage Lenders that accounts will be adjusted where necessary to ensure that customers are not disadvantaged where a building society normally operates on the basis of calender month accounts. In the investigated case that arrangement did not appear to be working and the account was falling into arrears even though DSS were making the required payments. DSS offered to take up the matter with the building society, but were then very slow to honour that undertaking. Not only did they fail for almost two years to take any positive action to resolve what should have been a relatively simple matter, but they mistakenly made deductions from the complainant's benefit to meet those arrears (although, fortunately, that additional error was quickly rectified).

National Insurance Contributions

20. In my 1992 report I referred to the work of the Contributions Agency (CA) and cited two cases where contributors had not been told of the procedure for resolving disputes over liability for National Insurance contributions (NICs). The correct procedure in such cases, once it becomes clear that there is a dispute which cannot be resolved, is for the department to notify the contributor of his or her right to have the matter referred to the Secretary of State for formal determination. I was therefore concerned that, in a further case investigated in 1995, CA had again failed to tell a man about that despite repeated requests from him. That was all the more disturbing since the Chief Executive of CA had assured me that a previous, similar error had been an isolated occurrence. I therefore sought the department's assurance that staff

would be reminded of the proper procedures to be followed in such cases. I was told that guidance had been issued in the light of the previous case, but that — as a result of my later investigation — further guidance would be issued immediately to reinforce the point. The guidance was issued in March 1995. I very much hope that that will have put matters right once and for all but, given the difficulties which have persisted, my staff will continue to keep a close eye on this area.

21. In a second case a man who had been assessed as liable for class 1 NICs as an employed earner received a demand from CA which appeared to be seeking class 2 and class 4 contributions also for the same period. The Agency stated that that was not the intention but the complainant said that that would be the effect, as his accounts included earnings from previous tax years. In order to resolve matters the complainant asked to see the legal authority on which CA were basing their demands, but the Agency appeared unable to provide him with a copy of the regulations concerned and took far too long to settle his case. The complainant eventually secured a refund of overpaid contributions (which was used to offset remaining liabilities) and, as a result of my intervention, was also awarded an *ex gratia* payment equivalent to the loss of interest on the overpayment.

. . .

Tax matters

50. Inland Revenue cases still made up a substantial part of my workload in 1995. I received 160 complaints, an increase of 19 per cent on the number put to me in 1994. However, because of the big increase in CSA cases, the Revenue cases as a percentage of the complaints accepted for investigation reduced from 19 per cent in 1994, to 14.2 per cent in 1995. 35 investigations against the Revenue were completed of which six were against the Valuation Officer Agency (VOA). I completed four investigations against Customs and Excise.

Inland Revenue

51. During 1995 I observed a greater willingness on the part of the Revenue to accept responsibility for maladministration and offer redress at the first stage of my investigation when I put the complaint to them. I commend that trend and I await the changes to their Code of Practice on Mistakes which are under consideration by the Revenue as a result of the Government's acceptance in March 1995 of the recommendations of the Select Committee (see my Introduction, paragraph 2). The influence of the revised Code of Practice may be seen in 1996.

52. During 1995 the Revenue produced a complaints handbook for issue to their staff as a guide to dealing with and avoiding giving rise to complaints. I welcome the introduction of the handbook which sets out clearly the approach which Revenue staff should adopt in order to obviate complaints and, if they are made, to deal with them sympathetically and with understanding. The handbook says that Revenue staff should identify what has gone wrong, put it right quickly and efficiently, apologise and consider whether financial redress is appropriate and what lessons can be learned. The handbook demonstrates a change in attitude. It stresses how important it is that Revenue staff look at a complaint from the point of view of the complainant and adopt a positive attitude towards complaints. I agree with the comment in the handbook that, if the new approach to complaints is adopted, it will save time in the long run by reducing the number of complaints which have to be dealt with at more senior levels, including through referrals to me.

53. The handbook says that the Revenue should not attempt to put a mistake right without telling the taxpayer what is being done. For example, if a taxpayer receives a revised notice of coding unexpectedly he or she may well be justifiably aggrieved at not

being told what is happening. In one case I investigated which related to ancient events a taxpayer completed his tax return for 1987/88 and included on a separate sheet of paper a computation of capital gains for the year 1986/87. That computation was overlooked and not until 1991 was an assessment issued. I criticised the Revenue for the way in which they issued that assessment without any explanation or apology for the delay.

54. At the end of the year I had all but concluded my investigation of a case which has already resulted in various procedural changes. That case is expected to be the subject of a special report later in 1996, but I see it as appropriate to mention the changes here. The new procedures affect the Revenue's Special Compliance Office (SCO) which deals with investigations and they will be incorporated into a new SCO manual. A central registry for complaints against the SCO offices has been introduced, and SCO's policy on unannounced visits has been reviewed. As a result new internal guidance on visits to taxpayers' private residences, and guidelines to be followed when making other unannounced calls, have been brought into use. (That guidance applies only to SCOs, and not to similar visits by other Revenue staff, although it seems to be that the guidance merits wider application). Training for new SCO staff is being improved with attention being focused on basic procedures, including preliminary reviews of all the papers held by the Revenue, and the need to seek specialist advice within the Revenue as appropriate. General guidance to staff on the need for confidentiality has been revised and updated.

55. The Revenue consider any expression of dissatisfaction to be a complaint to be handled in accordance with the procedures set out in their handbook. When something has gone wrong, Revenue staff need to take extra care in their subsequent contacts with the taxpayer. A case which would probably not have reached me if that practice had been applied concerned a taxpayer who was seeking loss relief for a conversion of part of his property to provide self-contained holiday lettings. He was relying on the loss relief to make a go of the venture. The Inspector dealing with the application for loss relief dismissed it without giving any explanation. Ten months after the claim had been made the taxpayer asked his accountants to write to the District Inspector to try to get the question of the loss relief determined, because the delay was significantly affecting his business plans. The District Inspector apologised for the delay and said that the Inspector would be giving the matter priority. Several months passed without any progress being made. A meeting with the accountants did not resolve the matter and the Inspector told the taxpayer that all other similar claims to the tax office had been withdrawn — none had been successful. The Inspector continued to ask for information which the accountants had already sent her and, when the taxpayer said that he was going to complain to me, the Inspector said that that would delay matters further. After referring the case to head office for advice and over two years after the original application, the loss relief claim was formally rejected and the taxpayer appealed to the Special Commissioners of Income Tax. The taxpayer also complained to me about the excessive delay which had made it difficult to plan his business and had cost him extra accountancy fees. Unusually, I carried on my investigation concurrently with the taxpayer's appeal to the Special Commissioners because I did not see any conflict between the maladministration which I was asked to investigate and the issues before the Special Commissioners concerning loss relief. I criticised the Revenue for their delays and inappropriate and piecemeal enquiries. I criticised the Inspector for her attempt to deter a complaint to me and for saying that no similar claims had succeeded in her area. That conveyed the impression that whatever efforts the taxpayer and his accountants made to reach agreement they were bound to be futile.

. . .

Lord Chancellor's Department

84. I reported on nine complaints involving the Lord Chancellor's Department (LCD) and its Executive Agencies, the Court Service (established on 3 April 1995) and the Public Trust Office. The extension of my Office's jurisdiction brought about by the Courts and Legal Services Act 1990 has been shown to be fully justified, as the following account reveals. Six complaints were about mishandling of cases at county court. Errors in three of those cases led to incorrect entries in the Register of County Court Judgments and showed that administrative mistakes can be costly to departments. In the first case the plaintiff in an action obtained a judgment against the complainant on the ground that he had not replied to a summons. His defence had arrived within the time allowed at the county court but had been misdirected to the Crown Court. The court then issued a warrant of execution even though the complainant had applied for judgment to be set aside and they later failed to send a fully pleaded defence to the plaintiff. The man complained that the court's errors had caused him additional legal costs, that inclusion on the Register had damaged his private credit and business interests and that the issue of a warrant had caused distress LCD initially rejected his claim for compensation but after my intervention agreed to make an *ex gratia* payment of £35,000 for legal costs, loss of value of a house when he was unable to obtain a mortgage for a new one and distress. In the second investigation I found that the transfer of a man's case between three courts was mishandled because of a failure by staff to comply with requests from solicitors. Further errors increased confusion about where the case was to proceed. The man's action was successful but an entry was recorded against him on the Register because the court sent notification of the judgment on the wrong form. The man discovered the court's error when he was refused credit. In trying to correct their mistake the court sent him two further incorrect forms. LCD agreed to make an *ex gratia* payment of £1,000 and introduced new procedures. In the third case, which also involved a complaint against the Data Protection Registrar, I found no evidence that a court had sent notification of cancellation of a debt to the Register of County Court Judgments even though a man had paid the debt in full two days after judgment was awarded against him. That omission caused his son to be refused a credit card. LCD paid £500 each to the man and three members of his family but I criticised them for taking nine months to settle his claim. LCD improved their procedures for dealing with *ex gratia* claims.

85. Two further cases concerned complaints that court staff had failed to follow instructions properly. The first involved a series of errors at two courts. Staff at the first court persisted in corresponding with solicitors although the complainant was acting for himself. They transferred his case to the wrong court. The case was then struck out when the complainant failed to attend a hearing because staff at the second court had not told him its date. After my investigation LCD agreed to increase an earlier offer of compensation to the complainant by £196 for additional costs incurred because of the short-comings. In the other case I found no evidence that a court had received a letter sent by a Court Welfare Officer saying that she could not attend a hearing; even if the letter had been received it was unlikely to have reached the case file because it did not include a case reference or any indication of the type of case concerned. I therefore found no fault on the part of LCD on the basis of which I might ask them to make an *ex gratia* payment for a wasted court attendance but I welcomed improvements to their procedures to help identify correspondence about civil cases where the case number is not given. The sixth report involving a county court concerned information in a LCD leaflet about the conduct of small claim cases. I found that the leaflet and a form for requesting judgment were unclear and

misleading. The Court Service agreed to amend both at the earliest opportunity and to improve their guidance.

86. A man complained that the IAA, a tribunal administered by LCD, mishandled his wife's appeal against a refusal of entry clearance. The appeal hearing was adjourned twice, first because the Adjudicator had not received the case files IAA had sent to his home address, and secondly when the Adjudicator decided there was not enough time to hear the complainant's case or that of his solicitors' other client. On both occasions the complainant incurred costs for the attendance at the hearing of his solicitors and counsel.

I found no evidence that errors by LCD staff caused either adjournment, but I considered that the procedure for sending files could be improved. I welcomed LCD's decision to reconsider their procedures and to make an *ex gratia* payment of £625 to the complainant to cover the wasted costs of the first hearing date and another payment to his solicitors' other client.

87. A complaint was made against the Public Trust Office, an agency of LCD, about maladministration in their handling of a woman's affairs during their time as her receiver, and subsequently about their alleged bias against the complainant, one of her sons. I did not uphold the complaint about bias but found some shortcomings in the handling of the woman's affairs which led to a full reimbursement to the son for the cost of some household repairs.

Commission for Racial Equality

88. My Annual Report for 1994 described a complaint against the Commission for Racial Equality (CRE) that they had failed to monitor the activities of a private solicitor whom they had assigned to assist with a complaint. An investigation in 1995 concerned a similar complaint. The complainant lived and worked in the North of England but CRE appointed a solicitor in London to represent him at a hearing. The complainant, who was in dispute with his employer, had to take time off work at short notice to attend meetings in London. The solicitor's firm closed down before he had made significant progress. I found that CRE had failed to monitor the solicitor's work with sufficient thoroughness. CRE have changed their arrangements to ensure that lawyers are more easily accessible to complainants and have decided to discontinue the practice of employing outside solicitors. They have also introduced a system whereby complaints relating to poor service are investigated and addressed. As a result of the poor service that the complainant had received and the extra expense he had been put to, the Chairman agreed to my suggestion and offered the complainant an *ex gratia* payment of £300.

National Rivers Authority

89. I reported on four cases concerning NRA. One concerned NRA charges for navigation licences and two related to fishing licences. The fourth case, concerning the designation wrongly of a millrace as main river has been reported at paragraph 72. In the first case mentioned above the complainant considered NRA's navigation charges to be excessive, suggested that he pay only a proportion of the annual fee to reflect the seasonal use he made of the river and also complained that NRA had mishandled a consultation exercise into a review of navigation charges. I found no evidence of maladministration in the way NRA had reviewed navigation charges and considered that it was not unreasonable for NRA to give priority to other work over consideration of the possibility of changing their licensing arrangements. Another complainant objected to NRA's refusal to issue him with a licence to fish for salmon and migratory trout when he had held such a licence for the previous three seasons. I did not criticise

NRA's decision because they were acting consistently with their decisions in other cases where licence holders had not used their licences and had offered no explanation. However I did criticise NRA insofar as they had not warned the complainant of the possible consequences of not using his licence. I had previously investigated a similar complaint in another NRA region and I found further fault with NRA in that they had not circulated my report to all NRA regions. That was not done until after I had begun my investigation into the later complaint. I had further reason to criticise NRA over the third complaint. That concerned NRA's decision to make the observance of draft bylaws a condition of eel fishing licences. NRA had been aware since 1988 that the use of fyke nets to catch eels was an offence unless authorised by a bylaw. Although work had started on the necessary bylaws other work took priority and in the 1993 season NRA decided to issue licences on condition that fishermen complied with draft bylaws. The complainant objected to that condition and felt that he had no choice by to remove his nets from the water. I criticised NRA for the delay in finalising the bylaws and found unacceptable their imposition of such condition in licences, in advance of a final decision on the bylaws. NRA had also not responded properly to the complainant's concerns and as a result he had incurred losses of £550. The Chief Executive of NRA agreed to make a payment to the complainant but my staff had to contact NRA again, some weeks later, having heard from the complainant that he had not received the promised payment; it was then made.

. . .

Channel Tunnel Rail Link

109. Three Members of Parliament for constituencies in Kent referred to me at the end of 1992 and early in 1993 five complaints about the DOT's handling of the proposal to build a new high-speed rail link between London and the Channel Tunnel. I treated them as 'specimen' complaints and extended my investigation to the wider implications of the proposals to establish the Channel Tunnel Rail Link project for those persons living along the various routes proposed. The project had attracted a very high level of Parliamentary and public interest.

110. On 8 February 1995 I laid a report before Parliament under section 10(3) of the Parliamentary Commissioner Act. Under that subsection I may lay a special report where it appears to me that injustice has been caused to a person in consequence of maladministration and that the injustice has not been, and will not be, remedied. My findings appear in paragraphs 40 to 46 of that special report entitled 'The Channel Tunnel Rail Link and Blight: Investigation of Complaints against the Department of Transport' and I record a summary of them here.

111. I did not consider that the railway companies concerned (that is British Rail (BR) and their successors Union Railways) were acting as DOT's agents; DOT could not therefore be held responsible for their administrative actions, or for the operation of their compensation schemes.

112. I concluded however that DOT had acted maladministratively and in a way that had resulted in unremedied injustice. The maladministration lay in their not having considered the effects of the policy on those affected by it; and became more evident when the problems caused to individuals through the implementation of the policy became apparent but no action was taken to consider a remedy.

113. Widespread blight had occurred after BR had announced four possible routes in July 1988; thereafter there was an obvious danger that unusually high levels of anxiety and uncertainty would continue in relation to the project which was rarely far from the news. That difficulty was exacerbated because of the exceptional nature of the CTRL project. It will be the first major railway to be built in Britain for over a

century. Those affected were unable to assess the likely impact upon themselves, there being no directly comparable development. The speeds at which the trains are likely to travel exceed those previously possible in this country. Large scale property purchases had begun at a much earlier stage and were more extensive than would be the case in a typical road scheme. One of the effects of the geographical extent of BR's compensation schemes was to introduce what is termed 'snowballing' blight. DOT's policy on the establishment on the link had two key components: a new line would be needed at some point; its construction would have to be financed largely by the private sector. As early as February 1989 DOT had been advised by BR that, as matters then stood, the project was not commercially viable. The perceived solution was to seek private sector involvement but, even when that was done, no genuine way forward was found because the necessary funding was not forthcoming. The Secretary of State made a statement to the House of Commons on 14 June 1990 saying that BR and the consortium which was their joint venture partner had agreed that there was not a basis on which the project might be taken forward in the private sector at that stage. Their request for Government financial support was rejected. He asked BR to complete their studies into alternative routes, and meantime safeguard the preferred route through Kent between the North Downs and the Channel Tunnel. That statement left open the possibility that the preferred route might alter as a result of BR's further studies; so, even though broad agreement on the route through Kent was identified, even that route could not be regarded as settled. The statement was silent as to there being at that time no firm prospect that the line would be built because there was no finance in place or in prospect to fund its construction. The decision to keep the project in play and to await BR's further studies without any reasonable prospect of the necessary private funding was a policy decision which DOT were entitled to take, and I made no comment on it. I commented on the *effect* of that policy approach. It was to prolong the uncertainty and associated blight for a period of unknown duration with no certainty that the position would be resolved. At that point I perceived DOT's maladministration began.

114. It was apparent that some householders had suffered during that prolonged period who were not catered for by the existing compensation schemes; and, since their plight was in consequence of the policy approach adopted, DOT had a responsibility in my view to consider whether some redress should be available to such persons. The existing compensation schemes addressed the effects of the possible physical proximity of the route proposed. In my view, the delay in arriving at definitive decisions on the route caused problems which the existing compensation schemes were not designed to solve. Safeguarding of the route through Kent was introduced in September 1990 but that did not remove blight; nor was it likely to since BR were studying other route options. It certainly did not resolve the problems of some of those whose complaints I subsequently investigated. I found nothing in the department's papers to suggest that DOT gave any thought to whether anything else might be done and, if so, what. The Secretary of State acknowledged the problem in a minute of 25 July 1991 to the Prime Minister. Action was taken four months later when the Ove Arup route was adopted. Adopting a significantly different route caused further uncertainty and prolonged blight. I saw no evidence that DOT even then addressed the question whether some form of redress should be considered for persons for whom it was not otherwise available, nor that they did so in the period that followed. The position changed only when DOT formally announced a change of policy in December 1993 — that a public subsidy would be paid towards the project enabling the announcement soon afterwards of a final route, save for some adjustments. Once those adjustments had been made in April 1994 the project was once more in a

position where it could be taken forward and from that point, therefore, there was a prospect that uncertainty and blight arising from it might begin to reduce. I regarded the period between June 1990 and April 1994 as the one associated with the maladministration I had identified. I recognised that it was not maladministrative of DOT not to have devised a scheme to cater for all those affected, in the relevant period, by generalised blight. Nevertheless it was and remains my view that some provision should have been considered for cases of exceptional or extreme hardship.

115. The maladministration I found, in summary, was this. The effect of DOT's policy was to keep the project alive when it could not be funded. That increased uncertainty and blight in the period from June 1990. The position was not the same as that pertaining when a road scheme is introduced — the project raised exceptional difficulties and exceptional measures were called for. Persons not covered by the compensation schemes may have suffered as a result of the delay in settling the route. DOT had a responsibility to consider the position of such persons suffering exceptional or extreme hardship and to provide for redress where appropriate. They undertook no such consideration. That merited my criticism. I emphasised that I was proposing a scheme to address a limited number of cases of extreme or exceptional hardship and I did not suggest that all those whose complaints I had investigated would have merited a remedy.

116. I sent my report, as is my usual practice, to the Permanent Secretary of DOT, inviting him to comment on its factual content and to offer a remedy. The Permanent Secretary did not share my view, and offered no remedy and I included his comments as an Appendix to my special report. I was not persuaded by those comments to alter my findings.

117. The Select Committee subsequently took evidence from the Permanent Secretary and from the then Secretary of State. They set out their conclusions in their own Report 'The Channel Tunnel Rail Link and Exceptional Hardship' published on 19 July 1995. They considered the three propositions in my report to which DOT had taken exception; whether the project had generated exceptional uncertainty, whether the project itself was exceptional, and whether DOT should have considered compensation for some cases of exceptional suffering. They reached the view that DOT's arguments against the exceptional nature of the project relied too heavily on hindsight and ignored the extent of public anxiety; and, recognising that I had repeatedly and specifically disclaimed any intention to question the policy not to compensate for generalised blight, that cases of maladministration would be very few in number and capable of being met by *ex gratia* payments. Their conclusions were that DOT should have considered whether any *ex gratia* payments were due when the Channel Tunnel Rail Link project entered the period of uncertainty caused by problems of funding between June 1990 and April 1994; that it was desirable to grant redress to those affected to an extreme and exceptional degree by generalised blight, in line with the principle that maladministration includes a 'failure to mitigate the effects of rigid adherence to the letter of the law where that produces manifestly inequitable treatment'; and that it should be possible to distinguish a small number of cases of exceptional hardship. They recommended that DOT should reconsider their response to my findings, accept my conclusion that maladministration had occurred and consider arrangements to determine whether there were householders who merited compensation on the grounds of exceptional hardship.

118. The Select Committee fully supported the description of one form of maladministration which I had set out in my Annual Report for 1993 and which the Government have subsequently endorsed by its inclusion in evidence by a Treasury Minister to the Select Committee and by putting it into their leaflet 'The Ombudsman

in Your Files': 'failure to mitigate the effects of rigid adherence to the law where that produces manifestly inequitable treatment'. That category of maladministration, the Select Committee said, 'implies an expectation that when an individual citizen is faced with extraordinary hardship as a result of strict application of law or policy, the Executive must be prepared to look again and consider whether help can be given'.

119. On 1 November the present Secretary of State gave the Select Committee the Government's formal response; it was published the next day. The Government maintained the view that there was nothing 'exceptional' about the planning and funding of the rail link project; that the project was never kept alive 'in limbo' as suggested by me; and that they could not accept that officials should have considered and proposed to Ministers that something should have been done for cases of exceptional hardship when there was a clear Government policy, endorsed by Parliament during the period of alleged 'maladministration', that there should be no remedy for generalised blight. They also did not accept the Select Committee's interpretation of the principle set out in paragraph 118. Despite those views, the Government were prepared to consider afresh whether a scheme might be formulated to implement the Select Committee's recommendation that redress should be granted to those affected to an extreme and exceptional degree by generalised blight from the Channel Tunnel Rail Link during the period June 1990 and April 1994 and how it might operate. They did so 'out of respect for the PCA Select Committee and the Office of the Parliamentary Commissioner, and without admission of fault or liability'. The Government undertook to consult the Select Committee as the proposals were developed. I have recorded above in my Introduction (paragraph 7) my welcome for the decision.

Commission for Local Administration in England, Local Government Ombudsman Annual Report 1994/95, pp. 20–25

Housing

The council failed to deal properly with a housing transfer application made on the grounds of racial harassment. The complainant was a white woman whose husband was Turkish and a Moslem. She and her husband reported racial harassment in the form of broken windows, attempted break-ins, racist graffiti chalked outside their home, an offensive and threatening note, banging on the door, excrement smeared on the door and through the letterbox, and lighted materials pushed through the letterbox. The transfer application was not recorded on the computer for six months and was not treated as a racial harassment case until nearly a year after that. These errors led to an unnecessary delay in rehousing the family. To remedy the injustice the council paid the complainant £600 in compensation, including £100 for the time and trouble she had taken in pursuing her complaint.

The council failed to deal properly with the problem of nuisance a young family were suffering from their neighbour's dog. Officers assumed without sufficient enquiry that the dog was not of a dangerous breed and that the family's safety was not threatened. No approach was made to the owner to ask him to control his dog. The first complaint was made in December 1991, but in February 1993 the dog was still causing a nuisance. To remedy the injustice the council paid the complainant £500 in compensation and £250 to recognise his time, trouble and legal expenses in pursuing his complaint.

The council failed to consider the complainant's application for housing properly. His name was recorded on the computer system as requiring a type of property which did not exist in the area of his choice; as a result, when a suitable property became available, his name did not appear on the print-out of possible tenants. The flat was allocated to a man who had been on the waiting list for only four months compared to the complainant's six-and-a-half years. The Ombudsman recommended that the council remedy the injustice by allocating the complainant the first available two-bedroom flat in his chosen area and paying him as compensation the sum of £10 a month from the date of the allocation of the flat he should have been offered to the date on which he is given a tenancy, plus £150 for his time and trouble in pursuing his complaint.

The council delayed in dealing with the complainant's claim for compensation for damage caused to his home by flooding from the council's property next door. Three years after the flooding occurred, and despite continual chasing by the complainant, no decision had been made on his claim against the council. There was a catalogue of administrative failings by the council. The Ombudsman recommended that the council remedy the injustice by ensuring that the council's insurers had all the information they needed to determine the claim. The Ombudsman thought the insurers' ability to assess the merits of the claim may have been hindered by the delays caused by the council. If this resulted in the insurers refusing to accept liability, or not settling the claim in full, the council should settle the claim by making an appropriate payment to the complainant. It should also pay him an additional 10 per cent per annum *pro rata* from January 1992 to the date of any payment being made, and £250 for the anxiety and uncertainty caused, and for his time and trouble in pursuing the complaint.

The council failed to deal properly with the homelessness application of a woman who had left her council home because she was in fear of domestic violence. Proper enquiries were not made and there was inadequate consideration of whether or not the woman was 'vulnerable' under the terms of the Housing Act 1985. The Ombudsman recommended that the council remedy the injustice by paying the complainant £250 in compensation (she had already been made an offer of accommodation). The council should also examine the reasons why the complainant's vulnerability was not considered properly and ensure that staff dealing with homelessness have accurate and up-to-date guidance on the council's policies and legal responsibilities.

The council failed to make direct payments of housing benefit to a landlord even though it was aware that his tenants had rent arrears in excess of eight weeks. The tenants then absconded with over £4,239 which should have been paid to him. To remedy the injustice the council paid the complainant the same amount that had been paid direct to his tenants plus interest from July 1991, and £250 for his time and trouble in pursuing his complaint.

The council gave a couple incorrect advice about their eligibility for a grant to renovate their home. The couple were told they were too young to be eligible, but this was not the case. Their home was unfit at the time and they should therefore have received financial assistance from the council to help remedy the dampness and disrepair. The Ombudsman recommended that the council remedy the injustice by: establishing what works would have qualified for grant aid at the outset; assessing what grant would have been available had an application been made before any work was done; and paying an amount equivalent to the grant which would have been approved for the works which had already been carried out, and any additional works which would have been eligible.

The council failed for six years to take action to secure and make safe a privately-owned derelict house adjoining the complainant's home. Rubbish accumulated on the property and there were problems with vandals and vermin. The council failed to identify and serve notices on the owner of the property, failed to take remedial action in default, and failed as mortgagee to take possession of the property. The Ombudsman recommended that the council remedy the injustice by immediately taking steps to take the derelict house into its possession and to manage its disposal in such a way as to safeguard the amenity of the complainant. To compensate the complainant for the distress caused the council should pay her £1,500, together with a further £5 for each week the house remained derelict.

Planning

The council failed to deal properly with an application from the complainant's neighbour to carry out the administrative work of a small business from his home. The impact on the complainant's amenity of the neighbour's use of a new garden room as an office was not fully assessed, and councillors were not fully appraised of the details of the scheme. To remedy the injustice caused the council paid the complainant £600 to compensate him for his share of the cost of a new fence between his property and that of his neighbour.

The council failed to act effectively and in good time to remedy a breach of planning control in respect of regular car boot sales on land near the complainants' homes. Residents suffered detrimental effects from the proximity to their homes of the car boot sales, and from a temporary blight on house sales. To remedy the injustice the council did all it could to control the car boot sales. The council also paid £1,000 to each of the five complainants who were most affected by their proximity to the car boot sales; three other complainants received £750 each and one received £500 since they were less affected. The complainants also received between £250 and £50 for their time and trouble in pursuing their complaints.

The complainants lived next to a new residential development on sloping ground. The council granted detailed planning permission for the development without checking the relative levels of the complainants' homes and the proposed new dwellings. The ground floor levels of the new houses were raised above the existing contours of the land; as a result, the complainants' homes were overlooked to a greater degree than they should have been. The Ombudsman recommended that the council remedy the injustice by inviting the district valuer to calculate the current values of the complainants' houses and what the values would have been if the houses had been at the level assumed by the council when it granted planning permission. The council should pay the complainants any difference in these values, together with £250 for their time and trouble in pursuing their complaints.

Education

The council delayed unreasonably in issuing a draft statement of special educational needs for one of the complainant's twin sons; there was also an unreasonable delay in dealing with the assessment of the other twin's needs. The complainant withdrew the boys from school in June 1991 and the council failed to secure their full-time attendance at school between that date and November 1992. To remedy the injustice to the complainant the council paid her £250. To remedy the injustice to her children, the council paid her £1,000 to be used for their sole benefit. The council also reviewed its policies and procedures concerning these matters.

The council refused to hear an appeal against its decision not to admit a boy to a particular school on the grounds that it would be a repeat of an appeal made in the previous academic year. Both the council and the Ombudsman sought clarification of the guidance given by the Department for Education in its circular 11/88. The guidance indicated that an appeal in a different academic year should be treated as a new appeal. The council's failure to review its policy in the light of the advice from the

Department for Education, and its failure to publicise its policy, was also maladministration.

To remedy the injustice the council offered to hear the appeal and paid the complainant £350 for her distress and her time and trouble in pursuing her complaint. The council also reviewed its policy and practice on admission appeals.

The council failed to consider properly the safety of a child's walking route to school. A blanket judgement was made that the road was safe because it was more than five-and-a-half metres wide, but the Ombudsman considered that the specific circumstances of walking with a pushchair along a main road on the way to school were not properly taken into account. To remedy the injustice the council provided free transport and paid the complainant £750 in compensation. The council has also reviewed its policy and practice.

Social services

There were failures in some aspects of the way the council dealt with community care provision for a man with symptomatic HIV-positive infection. There was a delay in the installation of facilities to enable him to use his bath, delay in sending him a copy of his assessment and community care plan, and a limit was improperly placed on the number of hours of home help provision available to him, whereas the correct procedure should have been for an assessment to be based on need. To remedy the injustice the council paid the complainant £300. It has also ensured that assessments for home help are carried out according to an individual's needs.

Highways

The complainant bought her home from the district council in 1987. A pre-purchase search showed that the route of a public footpath ran through the house. The district council undertook to apply for a Diversion Order and the complainant went ahead with the purchase on the understanding that the footpath would be diverted. The district council delayed applying to the county council for the diversion and failed to warn the woman unequivocally that there was no certainty that the application would succeed. The county council delayed its initial consideration of the application for five months and then placed it in abeyance without reference to either the complainant or the district council. No further action was taken by the county council between 1989 and 1992. The Ombudsman recommended that the councils, acting in concert, should remedy the injustice by doing everything reasonably practicable to divert or extinguish the footpath. If this proved impossible, the councils should purchase the complainant's house at a price approved by the district valuer. Each council should also pay the complainant £250 in recognition of the distress, time and trouble their faults had caused.

Land

The complainant enquired about purchasing a piece of land at the rear of her home. She was wrongly told that the council did not own the land. A councillor, after making enquiries of officers of the council, advised her that she could acquire ownership of the land by erecting a fence and making a claim of 'adverse possession'. She and her neighbours acted on this advice. The council then discovered that it owned the freehold of the land which it had leased to a local farmer who took down the fence. To remedy the injustice the council paid the complainant compensation of £250 to cover her abortive costs and her time and trouble in pursuing the matter.

Environmental health

The council's dog warden collected a stray dog and placed it in kennels. The owners were informed that there was a fee of £35 payable for retrieving the dog, but were not advised that daily charges would accumulate and that these would be payable even if the dog was not collected. As they felt they could not immediately afford the £35 they delayed collecting the dog, but had they known of the accumulating charges they would somehow have raised the £35 and collected the dog without delay. To remedy the injustice the council wrote off the sum of £76 — which represented the difference between the fee for collecting the dog and the actual sum the complainants were being asked to pay. The council also wrote off the complainants' court costs and paid them £50 to reflect their time and trouble in pursuing the case with the council and with the Ombudsman.

Commercial
The council failed to deal properly with the complainant's application for a mooring licence. The Ombudsman found multiple administrative defects by the council, including: approving drying moorings when the application was for deep-water moorings; demanding the payment of fees, for which no correct bill had been sent, two days before the Christmas holiday under threat of removal of existing moorings if payment was not received within 14 days; unreasonable delay in addressing concerns about a licence condition that the moorings should carry riding lights; failure to reply to letters; delays in replying to other letters, loss of the complainant's cheque and destruction of the signed licence agreements he had returned to the council. To remedy the injustice the council paid the complainant £500 in compensation.

Community charge
The council sent the complainants amended demands for community charge payments showing additional amounts outstanding with no explanation. Despite writing to the council to query the bills, the couple were served with court summonses for non-payment. The name of a non-existing person had been wrongly added to the council's records for the couple's home and this had affected the amount charged. The Ombudsman recommended that the council remedy the injustice by paying the couple £100, plus £250 for their time and trouble in making their complaint. The council should also carry out a review of its procedures.

Drainage
The council failed to advise the National Rivers Authority that it had sold a sewage treatment works to the complainants. It also failed to forward to the complainants information from the National Rivers Authority about the quality of effluent from the works, even though as owners the data was intended for them. To remedy the injustice the council paid the complainants £500 for the worry and uncertainty they had experienced, together with £250 for their time and trouble in making their complaint.

(B) ACCESS TO THE OMBUDSMAN

PARLIAMENTARY COMMISSIONER ACT 1967

5.—(1) Subject to the provisions of this section, the Commissioner may investigate any action taken by or on behalf of a government department or other authority to which this Act applies, being action taken in the exercise of administrative functions of that department or authority, in any case where—

(a) a written complaint is duly made to a member of the House of Commons by a member of the public who claims to have sustained injustice in consequence of maladministration in connection with the action so taken; and

(b) the complaint is referred to the Commissioner, with the consent of the person who made it, by a member of that House with a request to conduct an investigation thereon.

6.—(3) A complaint shall not be entertained under this Act unless it is made to a member of the House of Commons not later than twelve months from the day on which the person aggrieved first had notice of the matters alleged in the complaint; but the Commissioner may conduct an investigation pursuant to a complaint not made within that period if he considers that there are special circumstances which make it proper to do so.

LOCAL GOVERNMENT ACT 1974

26.—(2) A complaint shall not be entertained under this Part of this Act unless it is made in writing to the Local Commissioner specifying the action alleged to constitute maladministration or —

(a) it is made in writing to a member of the authority, or of any other authority concerned, specifying the action alleged to constitute maladministration, and

(b) it is referred to the Local Commissioner, with the consent of the person aggrieved, or of a person acting on his behalf, by that member, or by any other person who is a member of any authority concerned, with a request to investigate the complaint.

(3) If the Local Commissioner is satisfied that any member of any authority concerned has been requested to refer the complaint to a Local Commisioner and has not done so, the Local Commissioner may, if he thinks fit, dispense with the requirements in subsection (2)(b) above.

(4) A complaint shall not be entertained unless it was made to the Local Commissioner or a member of any authority concerned within twelve months from the day on which the person aggrieved first had notice of the matters alleged in the complaint, but a Local Commissioner may conduct an investigation pursuant to a complaint not made within that period if he considers that it is reasonable to do so.

(5) Before proceeding to investigate a complaint, a Local Commissioner shall satisfy himself that the complaint has been brought, by or on behalf of the person aggrieved, to the notice of the authority to which the complaint relates and that that authority has been afforded a reasonable opportunity to investigate, and reply to, the complaint.

Note

The tables on the next page set out the number of complaints made to the Parliamentary Commissioner and the Local Commissioners.

Number of complaints made to the Parliamentary Commissioner

Year	Number of complaints	Number of MPs referring complaints
1984	837	386
1985	759	373
1986	719	387
1987	677	379
1988	701*	359*
1989	677	361
1990	704	371
1991	801	432
1992	945	460
1993	986	429
1994	1,332	501
1995	1,706	506

* During this year the PCA received several hundred complaints from investors who were affected by the collapse of Barlow Clowes. The PCA decided to treat these complaints as a single investigation. If he had treated each complaint separately, then the total number would have been increased by several hundred, and the number of MPs who referred complaints would have been increased to 424.

Number of complaints made to the local commissioners

Year	Number of complaints
1983/84	3,034
1984/85	3,389
1985/86	3,502
1986/87	4,059
1987/88	4,229
1988/89	7,055
1989/90	8,733
1990/91	9,169
1991/92	12,123
1992/93	13,307
1993/94	14,253
1994/95	15,525

Question

The number of complaints to the Local Commissioners has grown rapidly in recent years. Why has there been no comparable growth in the number of complaints made to the Parliamentary Commissioner? The notes which follow may provide some assistance in answering this question (see further G. Drewry and C. Harlow, 'A "Cutting Edge"? The Parliamentary Commissioner and MPs' [1990] 53 MLR, 745).

Note

Both the PCA and the Local Commissioners have attracted criticism on the ground that the public is insufficiently aware of their existence. In his 1988 Annual Report, the PCA devoted a separate paragraph to publicity.

> As in previous years, I continued to provide to the media press notices on each occasion (usually quarterly) that I published a selection of my investigation reports. I also took such opportunities as arose for the giving of press, radio and television interviews as well as undertaking (as did members of my staff) speaking engagements to various public and private audiences about the work of the office. The Central Office of Information continued to provide me with valuable help in this connection – not least in ensuring the availability in Citizens Advice Bureaux and Public Libraries up and down the country of our booklet 'Can the Parliamentary Ombudsman help you?' One subject which attracted considerable publicity during the second half of the year was the referral to me by numerous Members of complaints (and my acceptance of them in November, for investigation) against the Department of Trade and Industry about the Barlow Clowes affair . . .

Question

Can you think of any other ways of publicising the work of the ombudsmen?

Notes

1. As the PCA points out in this extract, it is sometimes the case that a particular complaint generates greater public awareness of the institution of the Ombudsman. In 1988 the PCA accepted that he had jurisdiction to investigate complaints into the Department of Trade's handling of investigations into the investment group Barlow Clowes. The Department of Trade and Industry had allowed Barlow Clowes to operate without a licence for ten years and later issued it with a licence when it had concerns about the operation of the group. When the company was wound up in 1988, 18,000 investors were affected, many of whom complained to the Ombudsman in the hope that he would recommend compensation for them. The publication of the Ombudsman's report in December 1989 made headline news (see, for example, *The Times* and *The Independent* on 20 December 1989). He found that there were five areas in which there had been significant maladministration by the Department, and that the complainants had sustained injustice in consequence of maladministration. Although the Government stated that it did not accept the findings of maladministration it stated that it would offer substantial compensation to the investors. The Ombudsman concluded that it could not be said that the Government's proposals would not constitute a fair remedy for the injustice which had been suffered. The Ombudsman, who was then Sir Anthony Barrowclough, is reported to have said that the case was the most complicated he had had to deal with by 'a very, very long chalk' (*Financial Times,* 20 December 1989). Further details may be found in *First Report of the Parliamentary Commissioner for Administration of Session 1989–90, The Barlow Clowes Affair.* The issues arising from the Ombudsman's investigations are discussed by R. Gregory and G. Drewry, 'Barlow Clowes and the Ombudsman' [1991] *Public Law,* at pp. 192–215 and pp. 408–43.

2. The Select Committee on the PCA in its 1993 report on *The Powers, Work and Jurisdiction of the Ombudsman* (HC 33 of 1993–94) recommended that instead of speculation about the level of public awareness of the Ombudsman there should be a survey on this topic as part of a general programme of research into the work and effectiveness of the Ombudsman system. The committee also thought that the publication of a newsletter summarising cases of interest might aid the publicity of the work of the PCA amongst the public and MPs. The committee urged continuous appraisal of methods of publicity and an exploration of all those ways that might foster increased accessibility.
3. There is no provision for direct access to the PCA. The requirement that complaints to the PCA should be filtered through MPs has provoked considerable discussion.

First Report from the Select Committee on the Parliamentary Commissioner For Administration
HC 33 of 1993–94, paras 53–77

The History of the Debate
We do not want to create any new institution which would erode the functions of Members of Parliament . . . nor to replace remedies which the British Constitution already provides. Our proposal is to develop those remedies still further. We shall give Members of Parliament a better instrument which they can use to protect the citizen, namely the services of a Parliamentary Commissioner for Administration (Government White Paper 'Parliamentary Commissioner for Administration' 1965, para. 4)

54. When the proposals for a United Kingdom Ombudsman were first put forward by the Government in its 1965 White Paper, it was clear that his Office would be a 'further expression of Parliamentary control'. Parliament was to remain the place where the grievances of the citizen could be ventilated. The MP filter was designed to allay the fears of those who thought that the Ombudsman system would detract from the traditional constitutional role of Parliament in its scrutiny of the Executive. The original report from Justice which had proposed the Ombudsman system had suggested that a MP filter be established on a trial basis for a limited period, perhaps five years. The Government, however, had built in the MP filter 'as a permanent part of the structure of the Bill' on grounds of constitutional principle.

55. In 1977 Justice published 'Our Fettered Ombudsman' in which they argued for the removal of the MP filter — 'We see the true function of the Commissioner as that of helping the citizen obtain redress against administrative injustice, and consider that direct access is essential if he is to perform that task as effectively as possible'. In 1978 this Select Committee considered the proposal in a Report entitled 'Parliamentary Conmmissioner for Administration (Review of Access and Jurisdiction)'. The Committee concluded 'that the principle on which the 1965 White Paper was founded — that the primary responsibility for defending the citizen against the executive rests with the Member of Parliament — is still valid, and [the Committee] would be reluctant to endorse any change which might weaken it'. This opinion has been repeated by the Committee in later reports, most recently in Session 1990–91.

The Benefits of the MP Filter

56. In its 1978 Report the Committee concluded that the filter worked to the advantage of:

(a) the complainant, because his problem can often be resolved quickly through the intervention of a Member;
(b) the Member, because he is kept in touch with the problems which his constituents are facing in their daily contact with the machinery of the State; and
(c) the Commissioner, because he is normally asked to investigate only complaints that the Member has been, or knows that he will be, unable to resolve himself.

57. In our current inquiry, Mr Waldegrave, speaking 'as an MP', told us that he considered that 'the filter is rather a good thing because I believe that to divorce the House and constituency MPs from this work would be a pity . . . conscientious MPs actually settle a lot of cases which would otherwise waste the Ombudsman's time'. This was also the view of the Cabinet Office. The Centre for Ombudsman Studies emphasised the advantages of the current system, in particular as 'an effective means of "screening out" complaints which MPs are able to resolve by their own efforts'.

58. The filter remains popular with Members themselves. Of the 333 Members who responded to the Committee's Questionnaire, 128 (38.4 per cent) were in favour of direct access to the Commissioner and 193 (58.0 per cent) were against direct access. It is clear that many Members value their role as champions of their constituents' complaints and are unwilling to see this constitutional function in any way by-passed or diminished. There is a clear majority amongst those who responded to the Questionnaire against direct access and in favour of the current MP filter.

59. We consider the advantages of the MP filter to be the same as when they were so ably summarised by our predecessor Committee in 1978. Constituents have their complaints resolved speedily and effectively. Members remain in contact with the problems and concerns of their constituents. The Ombudsman is spared needless work. We note that no witness has attempted to deny these benefits. Any argument against the MP filter must therefore demonstrate that its disadvantages outweigh any advantage.

The Disadvantages of the MP Filter and Proposals for Change

60. Perhaps the most significant witness to mention disadvantages to the MP filter was the Ombudsman himself. In his memorandum to the Committee he asked whether it was time 'to introduce a provision whereby complaints to PCA need not be channelled through a Member? PCA was clearly intended at his inception to be a Parliamentary body. Since then many other Ombudsmen including the HSC have been created to whom the public have direct access. Has the time come similarly to allow direct access to the PCA?'

61. In oral evidence Mr Reid answered his own question. Having pointed out that only in Sri Lanka and France were there similar stipulations for access to the Ombudsman, he continued:

> It has seemed to me for some time that it is potentially disadvantageous for complainants to have to approach the Parliamentary Commissioner . . . through a Member of Parliament whether because they misapprehend that a Member of a different colour from their own political persuasion will not help them or because not all complainants are administratively capable, and there is the sheer mechanical labour for Members and their secretaries of transmitting material to me, especially when I have to refer back to get further and better particulars of what is adumbrated in the initial complaint . . . there is some advantage to the public wanting to complain to cut out the middle man.

62. Justice repeated their opposition to the filter and argued instead for direct access as an alternative route to the Parliamentary Ombudsman, with the proviso that

the complainant first approach the internal complaints mechanism of the body concerned. They also considered that the Parliamentary Ombudsman's 'lack of visibility to members of the public to be partly due to the restriction which exists on access'. The National Consumer Council phrased their opposition to the Member filter trenchantly —

> . . . it is extremely difficult for consumers to gain access to the Parliamentary Ombudsman. Complainants must know of the existence of the Office. Secondly, they must know the process for persuading the MP to refer the complaint — a letter to an MP requesting that he or she refers the complaint to the Ombudsman. Thirdly, they must persuade the MP that the complaint should be investigated by the Parliamentary Ombudsman . . . The limited information which is available indicates that, from the consumer's perspective, the MP filter operates inequitably. A complainant's chance of having a grievance dealt with by the Parliamentary Ombudsman seems to depend on the approach of individual MPs.

The 'Compromise Proposal'

63. An alternative has in the past been proposed as a compromise between the current MP filter and its abolition in favour of direct access. In 1984 the then Parliamentary Ombudsman, Sir Cecil Clothier, suggested that the citizen might have a right of appeal to the Ombudsman if he remained dissatisfied with the response elicited by the MP from the Department. The National Consumer Council mentioned this as a second and less favoured option to the complete abolition of the filter.

64. The Centre for Ombudsman Studies also proposed as an alternative to the complete abolition of the filter the granting to the Ombudsman discretion to investigate a complaint when complainants are unwilling to involve a Member or where Members and constituents disagree about questions of jurisdiction or outcome of case.

Summary of Objections to the MP Filter

65. Objections to the MP filter can be summarised as follows:

(a) The public should have direct access to the Commissioner as a matter of right.

(b) The filter is an anomaly, almost unknown in other Ombudsman systems. No such requirement exists, for instance, in the case of the Health Service Commissioner.

(c) Individuals with complaints may be unwilling to approach an MP, while desiring the Ombudsman's assistance.

(d) The filter means that the likelihood of individuals' cases being referred to the Commissioner will largely depend on the views and practice of the particular constituency MP. Some look with more favour on the Office of the Commissioner than others.

(e) The filter acts as an obstacle to the Commissioner effectively promoting his services.

(f) The filter creates an unnecessary bureaucratic barrier between the complainant and the Commissioner involving considerable paperwork for MPs and their offices.

The Unheard Complaint

> . . . in the absence of a reliable crystal ball predictions about the consequences of removing the MP filter amount to little more than guesswork.

66. The central thesis of all arguments against the MP filter is that it is denying the public access to the Commissioner and the opportunity for him to investigate appropriate complaints. Various statistical arguments are adduced to support this

contention. One is a comparison of the number of complaints received by the Parliamentary Ombudsman with the number received by foreign Ombudsmen. In Australia in 1991–92, for instance, the Commonwealth Ombudsman received 17,153 oral and written complaints. This compares with the United Kingdom's Parliamentary Ombudsman receiving 945 complaints in 1992. It is, however, difficult to compare Ombudsman systems in this regard. Jurisdictions vary widely as does the role of Members of Parliament. The greater number of complaints can in certain circumstances, for instance, be attributed to the fact that the Ombudsman 'is often the aggrieved person's first and only port of call outside of the organisation concerned'.

67. A second statistical argument used to support the theory of a mass of unheard complaints is the experience of the Local Government Ombudsman after the introduction of direct access in May 1988. Until then members of the public had to approach the Local Government Ombudsman through the 'Councillor Filter'. Since May 1988 the public had the choice of either approaching the Local Government Ombudsman directly or through a Councillor. The memorandum from Dr David Yardley, Chairman of the Commission for Local Administration in England, charts the subsequent growth in the number of complaints:

> The average annual increase each year between the time the Commission was established in 1974 and the financial year 1988–89 had been 9 per cent. In 1988–89 the increase was 44 per cent, and this high level continued in 1989–90 when the increase was 24 per cent. In 1990–91 the increase returned to a more usual figure of 5 per cent . . . In the first year following the introduction of direct access 72 per cent of complaints were sent direct to the Local Government Ombudsman, and this figure had increased to 92 per cent by the end of 1992–93.

68. These statistics were referred to by Mr Reid in discussing the possible effect of the introduction of direct access on his Office. He made clear that additional resources would have to be made available to the Parliamentary Commissioner if direct access were introduced to deal with a comparable increase in the number of complaints received.

69. Mr Waldegrave cast doubt on the relevance of the Local Government Ombudsman comparison, 'I have a suspicion that the suppression in relation to the Local Government Ombudsman was much more to do with the fact that people felt it was no good going to that chap [a Councillor] to follow a complaint because he had just voted through the very thing that they were objecting to'.

70. In both instances the statistical argument is difficult to prove and must be considered with caution. We agree with the Centre for Ombudsman Studies when they warn that **any projection as to the effect of the MP filter on the work of the Parliamentary Commissioner or on the number of unheard complaints must remain speculative.**

71. It is difficult to quantify the number of complaints never heard because the complainants do not approach an MP. We do, however, have more information on how Members use the MP filter. The numbers of MPs referring cases in the last five years are as follows:

1988	359
1989	361
1990	371
1991	432
1992	460

We are pleased to note the recent increase in the number of Members referring cases to the Ombudsman. This suggests that the efforts of the Ombudsman to publicise his work among Members are bearing fruit. It may also relate to the growing awareness of the Ombudsman among new MPs during the course of a Parliament.

72. Mr Reid pointed out that 'if an individual Hon Member decides not to use my services he is in effect denying potential redress to his constituents'. It is undoubtedly the case that the operation of the filter depends to a great degree on the activity of the Member. Although it is possible for a complaint to be referred from a Member other than the constituency MP, the results of the Questionnaire suggest that this rarely happens and that many Members would be extremely reluctant to refer a non-constituency complaint. Moreover, a majority of MPs rarely if ever suggest to the complainant a reference to the Ombudsman and in our survey 45 per cent of Members reported that they seldom or never referred complaints to the Ombudsman. Yet the exercise of individual discretion by the Member on whether or not to refer a complaint is precisely the function of the filter. There could be various reasons for differing usage of the Ombudsman among Members. Access depends on the 'filtering' role of Members and it is clear that some Members are more active in this role than others. Some Members might refer complaints even in instances where they are aware the Ombudsman cannot investigate. Others might steadfastly refuse to do so. Some Members might always resolve complaints to the satisfaction of their constituents. Others might come across more intractable cases. Although the evidence suggests that the use of the filter is variable, it does not necessarily suggest significant numbers of those who approach their MP are dissatisfied or denied appropriate redress. It does suggest, however, that those who stress the importance of retaining the filter need also to give attention to the way in which the filter is working and how its operation may be improved.

Direct Access

73. We have seen that many propose the introduction of direct access as a means of ensuring that 'unheard complaints' reach the Ombudsman. Concern was expressed by the Centre for Ombudsman Studies and by some Members at the effect this would have on the workload of the Ombudsman's office. The Centre warned that 'if a system of direct access were to result in a high ratio of "inappropriate" to "appropriate" cases reaching the PCA, with very large numbers of the former type of complaint occupying the attention of the Office, amending the 1967 Act in this sense might prove to be one of those legislative changes, not unknown in recent years, which quickly comes to be a matter of considerable regret'.

74. We believe that the abolition of the MP filter would result not only in unheard complaints being heard for the first time but in some complaints reaching the Ombudsman's office which would previously have been more appropriately resolved by a Member. The effect of this will be either to increase unnecessarily the resources allocated to the Ombudsman's office or to cause a decline in the thoroughness of the Ombudsman's investigations as his office struggles to cope with the increased volume of work. Yet we do believe that access should be improved if the potential of the office is to be further developed. We have weighed carefully the substantial volume of evidence, including that from the Ombudsman himself, suggesting that this now requires a move to direct access. If we reject this conclusion, it is because there is more to be done in enhancing access through the present indirect route. 'Going to your MP' is an established part of the British political culture as far as citizens with grievances are concerned. If the work of the Ombudsman is fully explained and publicised among Members of Parliament and the public, the MP filter could also be a 'gateway', an invaluable opportunity for further development of the Ombudsman's role.

75. The most important issue in deciding the fate of the MP filter remains a constitutional one. Will direct access undermine the constitutional role of Members in

taking up the grievances of their constituents? Should the Parliamentary Ombudsman remain an 'instrument' of MPs or should access to his services now be seen as a right of the citizen? It is clear that the majority of Members appreciate the filter. We continue to believe that the Member of Parliament has an irreplaceable role in pursuing complaints of the public against the Executive, notwithstanding the development within public bodies of an array of direct access complaint and redress mechanisms for the citizen. We note that since the introduction of direct access in the case of the Local Government Ombudsman the proportion of cases referred by Councillors has declined from 28 per cent in the first year of direct access to 8 per cent by the end of 1992–93. Moreover only approximately 5 per cent of cases are referred by MPs to the Health Service Ombudsman where direct access applies. Direct access, it appears, may well result in fewer MPs being involved in the Ombudsman's work.

76. The work of the Parliamentary Ombudsman, acting at the behest of MPs and reporting to them the details of his investigations, has a vital role in equipping the Member for the tasks of Parliament. The knowledge of the details of and problems in administration has an important part in any effective scrutiny of the Executive. The publication of anonymised reports can never be a genuine substitute for direct involvement in the case which the Member has referred. Direct access will result in the denial to Members of expertise in the problems facing their constituents as they come into contact with the Executive. This is to impoverish parliamentary, and thus political, life. **We recommend that the MP filter be retained but coupled with concerted attention to the means whereby access to the Ombudsman can be strengthened and enlarged.**

77. We consider that the retention of the MP filter in its current form is preferable to the 'compromise proposal' of a right of appeal from MPs to the Ombudsman in certain circumstances. This amounts to an attempt to retain the 'filtering' advantages of the Member while denying him the power of veto over a further reference to the Ombudsman should the complainant remain dissatisfied. We consider that this merely places the Ombudsman in the invidious position of acting as a court of appeal against the decisions of Members.

Note

For MPs' views on the question of direct access, see G. Drewry and C. Harlow, 'A "Cutting Edge"? The Parliamentary Commissioner and MPs' [1990] 53 MLR 745, at pp. 758–61.

Questions

1. Apart from discontinuing the MP filter, by what other means can access to the PCA be strengthened and enlarged?

2. Which of the points referred to by JUSTICE are not met by the half-way house procedure? (Note that the consent of the complainant is required before the Ombudsman passes a complaint on to a MP.)

3. Do MPs filter out the correct complaints (see *post* at p. 668)?

Note

There is now provision for direct access to the Local Commissioners (see *ante* at pp. 655). This change was urged in a number of reports, including the *Report of the Inquiry into the Conduct of Local Authority Business* (Cmnd 9767 1986), generally known as the *Widdicombe Report,* pp. 218–19, and the

JUSTICE-All Souls Review on Administrative Law, p. 113. Prior to this amendment, the Local Commissioners had jurisdiction to consider complaints directly from members of the public only if a member of the local authority against whom the complaint was made had been asked to refer the complaint to the relevant Local Commissioner and had refused. In its *Annual Report for 1988/89* the Commission for Local Administration in England welcomed this change but observed at p. 4 that '[T]here is a price to pay. The number of complaints to the Ombudsmen has risen by 44 per cent and this has made exceptional demands on all the Commission's staff.' (See also the table at p. 656 *ante*). In another paragraph the increase is attributed in part to growing awareness of the Ombudsmen's role. Of the 13,307 complaints received during the year ending 31 March 1993, 92 per cent were sent direct to the Local Ombudsmen and 8 per cent were referred by members. In the year ending 31 March 1988, on the other hand, only 42 per cent were sent direct. (Under the procedures then in operation such complaints would have been sent by the Local Ombudsmen to the civic head of the authority which was the subject of the complaint. He would be asked to settle the complaint locally or send it back to the Ombudsman as a properly referred complaint.)

Questions

1. What inferences, if any, may be drawn from these statistics?

2. What is the justification for permitting direct access to the Local Commissioners but not to the PCA?

(C) JURISDICTION OF THE OMBUDSMAN

PARLIAMENTARY COMMISSIONER ACT 1967

4.—(1) Subject to the provisions of this section and to the notes contained in Schedule 2 to this Act, this Act applies to the government departments, corporations and unincorporated bodies listed in that Schedule; and references in this Act to an authority to which this Act applies are references to any such corporation or body.

(2) Her Majesty may by Order in Council amend Schedule 2 to this Act by the alteration of any entry or note, the removal of any entry or note or the insertion of any additional entry or note.

(3) An Order in Council may only insert an entry if—

(a) it relates—

(i) to a government department; or

(ii) to a corporation or body whose functions are exercised on behalf of the Crown; or

(b) it relates to a corporation or body—

(i) which is established by virtue of Her Majesty's prerogative or by an Act of Parliament or an Order in Council or order made under an Act of Parliament or which is established in any other way by a Minister of the Crown in his capacity as a Minister or by a government department;

(ii) at least half of whose revenues derive directly from money provided by Parliament, a levy authorised by an enactment, a fee or charge of any other description so authorised or more than one of those sources; and

(iii) which is wholly or partly constituted by appointment made by Her Majesty or a Minister of the Crown or government department.

(4) No entry shall be made in respect of a corporation or body whose sole activity is, or whose main activities are, included among the activities specified in subsection (5) below.

(5) The activities mentioned in subsection (4) above are—

(a) the provision of education, or the provision of training otherwise than under the Industrial Training Act 1982;

(b) the development of curricula, the conduct of examinations or the validation of educational courses;

(c) the control of entry to any profession or the regulation of the conduct of members of any profession;

(d) the investigation of complaints by members of the public regarding the actions of any person or body, or the supervision or review of such investigations or of steps taken following them.

(6) No entry shall be made in respect of a corporation or body operating in an exclusively or predominantly commercial manner or a corporation carrying on under national ownership an industry or undertaking or part of an industry or undertaking.

(7) Any statutory instrument made by virtue of this section shall be subject to annulment in pursuance of a resolution of either House of Parliament.

5.—(2) Except as hereinafter provided, the Commisioner shall not conduct an investigation under this Act in respect of any of the following matters, that is to say—

(a) any action in respect of which the person aggrieved has or had a right of appeal, reference or review to or before a tribunal constituted by or under any enactment or by virtue of Her Majesty's prerogative;

(b) any action in respect of which the person aggrieved has or had a remedy by way of proceedings in any court of law:

Provided that the Commissioner may conduct an investigation notwithstanding that the person aggrieved has or had such a right or remedy if satisfied that in the particular circumstances it is not reasonable to expect him to resort or have resorted to it.

(3) Without prejudice to subsection (2) of this section, the Commissioner shall not conduct an investigation under this Act in respect of any such action or matter as is described in Schedule 3 to this Act.

(4) Her Majesty may by Order in Council amend the said Schedule 3 so as to exclude from the provisions of that Schedule such actions or matters as may be described in the Order; and any statutory instrument made by virtue of this subsection shall be subject to annulment in pursuance of a resolution of either House of Parliament.

(5) In determining whether to initiate, continue or discontinue an investigation under this Act, the Commissioner shall, subject to the foregoing provisions of this section, act in accordance with his own discretion; and any question whether a complaint is duly made under this Act shall be determined by the Commissioner.

(6) For the purposes of this section, the administrative functions exercisable by any person appointed by the Lord Chancellor as a member of the administrative staff of any court or tribunal shall be taken to be administrative functions of the Lord Chancellor's Department or, in Northern Ireland, of the Northern Ireland Court Service.

SCHEDULE 3

MATTERS NOT SUBJECT TO INVESTIGATION

1. Action taken in matters certified by a Secretary of State or other Minister of the Crown to affect relations or dealings between the Government of the United Kingdom

and any other Government or any international organisation of States or Governments.

2. Action taken, in any country or territory outside the United Kingdom, by or on behalf of any officer representing or acting under the authority of Her Majesty in respect of the United Kingdom, or any other officer of the Government of the United Kingdom other than action which is taken by an officer (not being an honorary consular officer) in the exercise of a consular function on behalf of the Government of the United Kingdom and which is so taken in relation to a citizen of the United Kingdom and Colonies who has the right of abode in the United Kingdom.

3. Action taken in connection with the administration of the government of any country or territory outside the United Kingdom which forms part of Her Majesty's dominions or in which Her Majesty has jurisdiction.

4. Action taken by the Secretary of State under the Extradition Act 1870 or the Fugitive Offenders Act 1881.

5. Action taken by or with the authority of the Secretary of State for the purposes of investigating crime or of protecting the security of the State, including action so taken with respect to passports.

6. The commencement or conduct of civil or criminal proceedings before any court of law in the United Kingdom, of proceedings at any place under the Naval Discipline Act 1957, the Army Act 1955 or the Air Force Act 1955, or of proceedings before any international court or tribunal.

6A. Action taken by any person appointed by the Lord Chancellor as a member of the administrative staff of any court or tribunal, so far as that action is taken at the direction, or on the authority (whether express or implied) of any person acting in a judicial capacity or in his capacity as a member of the tribunal.

7. Any exercise of the prerogative of mercy or of the power of a Secretary of State to make a reference in respect of any person to the Court of Appeal, the High Court of Justiciary or the Courts-Martial Appeal Court.

8. Action taken on behalf of the Minister of Health or the Secretary of State by a Regional Health Authority, an Area Health Authority, a District Health Authority, a special health authority except the Rampton Hospital Review Board, the Rampton Hospital Board, the Broadmoor Hospital Board or the Moss Side and Park Lane Hospital Boards, a Family Practitioner Committee, a Health Board or the Common Services Agency for the Scottish Health Service or by the Public Health Laboratory Service Board.

9. Action taken in matters relating to contractual or other commercial transactions, whether within the United Kingdom or elsewhere, being transactions of a government department or authority to which this Act applies or of any such authority or body as is mentioned in paragraph (a) or (b) of subsection (1) of section 6 of this Act and not being transactions for or relating to—

(a) the acquisition of land compulsorily or in circumstances in which it could be acquired compulsorily;

(b) the disposal as surplus of land acquired compulsorily or in such circumstances as aforesaid.

10. (1) Action taken in respect of appointments or removals, pay, discipline, superannuation or other personnel matters, in relation to—

(a) service in any of the armed forces of the Crown, including reserve and auxiliary and cadet forces;

(b) service in any office or employment under the Crown or under any authority to which this Act applies; or

(c) service in any office or employment, or under any contract for services, in respect of which power to take action, or to determine or approve the action to be taken, in such matters is vested in Her Majesty, any Minister of the Crown or any such authority as aforesaid.

11. The grant of honours, awards or privileges within the gift of the Crown, including the grant of Royal Charters.

LOCAL GOVERNMENT ACT 1974

25.—(1) This Part of this Act applies to the following authorities —

(a) any local authority,

. . .

(ca) any other police authority, except the Secretary of state;

. . .

(d) any water authority within the meaning of the Water Act 1973.

(2) Her Majesty may by Order in Council provide that this Part of this Act shall also apply, subject to any modifications or exceptions specified in the Order, to any authority specified in the Order, being an authority which is established by or under an Act of Parliament, and which has power to levy a rate, or to issue a precept.

26.—(6) A Local Commissioner shall not conduct an investigation under this Part of this Act in respect of any of the following matters, that is to say:

(a) any action in respect of which the person aggrieved has or had a right of appeal, reference or review to or before a tribunal constituted by or under any enactment;

(b) any action in respect of which the person aggrieved has or had a right of appeal to a Minister of the Crown; or

(c) any action in respect of which the person aggrieved has or had a remedy by way of proceedings in any court of law:

Provided that a Local Commissioner may conduct an investigation notwithstanding the existence of such a right or remedy if satisfied that in the particular circumstances it is not reasonable to expect the person aggrieved to resort or have resorted to it.

(7) A Local Commissioner shall not conduct an investigation in respect of any action which in his opinion affects all or most of the inhabitants of the . . . area of the authority concerned.

(8) Without prejudice to the preceding provisions of this section, a Local Commissioner shall not conduct an investigation under this Part of this Act in respect of any such action or matter as is described in Schedule 5 to this Act.

(9) Her Majesty may by Order in Council amend the said Schedule 5 so as to add to or exclude from the provisions of that Schedule . . . such actions or matters as may be described in the Order;

[Schedule 5 contains a number of exclusions, including in particular: legal proceedings; investigation or prevention of crime, contractual or commercial transactions (but excluding the acquisition or disposal of land and certain statutory functions other than the procurement of goods and services); personnel matters, and educational matters.]

(10) In determining whether to initiate, continue or discontinue an investigation, a Local Commissioner shall, subject to the preceding provisions of this section, act at discretion; and any questions whether a complaint is duly made under this Part of this Act shall be determined by the Local Commissioner.

Notes

1. In 1987 the jurisdiction of the PCA was expanded to include a number of non-departmental bodies. These include the Arts Council, the Red Deer Commission, and the Sports Council. It was originally stated in the House of

Commons that the criteria for inclusion in this list were that the bodies should:

(a) be subject to some degree of ministerial accountability to Parliament because they are dependent for their financing and continuing existence on Government policy; and

(b) have 'executive or administrative functions that directly affect individual citizens or groups of citizens' (see HC Deb., vol. 112 (6th Series), col. 1081). See now s. 4(3) of the 1967 Act (*ante* at p. 664).

2. The PCA, and his Northern Ireland counterpart, have had their jurisdiction widened by the addition of the responsibility of investigating complaints of breaches of the Code of Practice on Access to Government Information. This has been brought about on the basis that all departments, agencies and other bodies within the jurisdiction of the PCA (listed in Sch. 2 of the 1967 Act) are subject to the Code and failure to comply with it will amount to maladministration and injustice, which could be delay, an unreasonable charge for the provision of information, a failure to provide information or the provision of incomplete information. For details of the Code see *ante* at p. 311.

Parliamentary Commissioner for Administration Annual Report for 1995 HC of 1995–96, pp. 57–8

Rejections

4. During the year I rejected as not appropriate for investigation 1,226 cases — 79 per cent of those screened during the year, a proportion which is broadly in line with that in previous years. They included some complaints against CSA which, had I not been investigating other such complaints, I would have investigated. They also included 110 cases where enquiries at the screening stage obviated the need for a full investigation. (Three further cases were discontinued during investigation). Diagram 4 below gives a summary of the main reasons why cases were rejected by reference to the Parliamentary Commissioner Act 1967. Table 2 at the end of the chapter gives numbers of rejected complaints by Department or body concerned.

Diagram 4: Cases rejected and investigations discontinued

Parliamentary Commissioner Act 1967		No of Cases	%
Section 5(1)	Complaint did not concern administrative actions	535	43.25
Section 5(2)(a)	Right to appeal to tribunals	311	25
Section 4(1)	Authority outside scope	105	8.5
Section 5(5)	Ombudsman's discretion[1]	71	6
Schedule 3(10)	Public service personnel matters	44	4
	Others[2]	160	13
	Discontinued investigations	3	0.25
	TOTAL cases rejected and investigations discontinued	**1229**	**100**

[1] For example, no evidence of fault leading to unremedied injustice; no reasonable prospects of a worthwhile outcome to an investigation.

[2] For example: legal remedy in a court of law; complaint by a public body; contractual and other commercial transactions; time barred; court proceedings; grant of honours and awards.

(i) Contractual and commercial matters

Fourth Report from the Select Committee on the Parliamentary Commissioner for Administration

HC 593 of 1979–80, paras 3, 8

Contractual and Commercial matters

3. In its observations the Government said that it believed that the Parliamentary Commissioner system should operate in the field of the relations between the executive and those whom it governs, and that it would not be in the general interest to extend it to commercial transactions. It did not consider that the commercial activities of Government Departments should be open to examination while other contracting parties were free from such investigation. In the area of assistance to industry, the Government acknowledged that the dividing line between transactions that were within jurisdiction and those which were not was a difficult one, but it took the view that the use of statutory powers involving a wide measure of commercial discretion should not be subject to review by the Commissioner. . . .

8. We do not accept the Government's contention that only those activities which are unique to the function of government should be subject to review by the Parliamentary Commissioner; rather we believe that in principle all areas of Government administration should be investigable by him unless in particular cases a compelling argument can be made out for their exclusion. Accordingly, the claim that the government's commercial activities should be exempt from examination because private contractors are exempt is in our view beside the point. The Government has a duty to administer its purchasing policies fairly and equitably, and if those policies are the subject of complaint then the complaints should be investigated; this is particularly important if any future Government were again to use the award of contracts as a political weapon. Section 12(3) of the Act would prevent the Commissioner from questioning a *bona fide* commercial decision to purchase goods and services from one firm rather than another, or the legitimate exercise of a Department's discretion to give selective assistance to one firm or one industry rather than another, but if decisions of this kind are taken with maladministration then it is right that they should be reviewed. It was suggested in evidence that the Commissioner would not be able to decide whether maladministration had been committed, but we note the Commissioner's view that that is the kind of judgment that he and his officers are making 'every day of the week.' In any case, a belief that the Commissioner might have difficulty in making such a decision may be thought to be poor ground for refusing him the right to try. It is true that any commercial maladministration by a Department can be investigated by the Exchequer and Audit Department and censured by the Public Accounts Committee, but neither of these bodies is primarily concerned, as the Parliamentary Commissioner is, with any injustice a complainant might have suffered as a result. We are satisfied that sections 5 and 12(3) of the Parliamentary Commissioner Act are sufficient on their own and that the further exemption from investigation conferred by paragraph 9 of Schedule 3 is not justified.

(ii) Public service personnel matters

Fourth Report from the Select Committee on the Parliamentary Commissioner for Administration

HC 593 of 1979–80, paras 9, 11, 15

Public Service personnel matters

9. In 1978 the Select Committee again recommended that complaints about public service personnel matters, except complaints from serving civil servants and

members of the armed forces about discipline, establishment questions and terms of service, should be investigable by the Parliamentary Commissioner. The Government rejected their recommendation, as it had a similar recommendation by the Select Committee in 1977, on the ground that there was no evidence that grievance machinery available to intending, present or former Crown servants was inferior to that available to workers generally. The government also noted that the Parliamentary Commissioner had not been established to deal with relations between the State as employer and its employees. . . .

11. The Commissioner told us that in his view the remedies for grievances about personnel matters which the Government had described to the Select Committee in 1977 were quite illusory . . .

15. As we have said earlier in this Report, we do not accept the view that the role of the Parliamentary Commissioner should be restricted to those activities which are unique to the function of government, and so we reject the contention that because not every employee can call upon the Commissioner to enquire into grievances about personnel matters the State's employees should not be able to do so. We accept, as the Commissioner does and as the Committee did in 1978, that the exclusion of complaints from serving public employees about matters of discipline, promotion, rates of pay and terms of service is justified, but we do not consider than any evidence has been produced to show that bringing within jurisdiction other purely administrative acts of Government Departments in their capacity as employers would cause harm to anyone: experience in Northern Ireland bears this out. There has always been evidence of a demand for the Commissioner's services in this area, and the arguments that if they were available a great number of extra complaints might have to be investigated comes perilously close to saying that one ought not to have an Ombudsman at all lest people should complain to him.

Notes

1. In its observations on the *Fourth Report* the Government stated that it believed its view on the exclusion of contractual and commercial matters remained sound (see Cmnd 8274 (1981)).

With regard to the exclusion of public service personnel matters, the Government stated that it remained unpersuaded of the merits of allowing the Parliamentary Commissioner to investigate complaints about recruitment to the Home Civil Service and the Diplomatic Corps and about superannuation. With regard to recruitment, the Government reiterated its view that it is already subject to rigorous scrutiny by an independent body, the Civil Service Commissioners, and further that it would be wrong to give applicants for jobs in the Civil Service a channel for the investigation of complaints which was not open to other employees.

With regard to superannuation, the Government considered that public service pensioners already had the advantage that their grievances might be raised in either House of Parliament, and that further preferential treatment would be inequitable. The Government also restated its view that the Commissioner was not established to investigate relations between the state as employer and its employees.

2. In his *Annual Report for 1988* the Parliamentary Commissioner for Administration stated, at p. 1:

. . . I have, naturally, to recognise that Parliament, by the terms of the Parliamentary Commissioner Act, has explicitly excluded from the Parliamentary Commissioner's jurisdiction certain defined categories of administrative action taken by government departments and public bodies. Perhaps the most notable of these excluded areas are action taken in public service personnel matters and 'action taken in matters relating to contractual or other commercial transactions.' In both cases the reasoning was, no doubt, that the Parliamentary Commissioner's proper concern was with complaints *qua* citizen, and not with complaints *qua* employee, or *qua* supplier of goods or services to a department or public body. The wording of the second of the exclusions I have mentioned has however been the cause of some concern and difficulty. That is because the dealings of departments and public bodies with citizens, *qua* citizens, can in some instances take on the appearance – and perhaps the reality – of 'contractual . . . transactions.' Indeed that is particularly so in the case of many of the non-departmental public bodies recently brought within jurisdiction, whose functions will often include the giving of aid or assistance on terms which may well have a contractual flavour. Yet if transactions of that kind are to be regarded as excluded from the Parliamentary Commissioner's scrutiny, I entertain some doubt as to whether it would really reflect Parliament's intentions. This, it seems to me, is an area in which clarification may be needed.

3. In its 1993 report the Select Committee indicated that it would return to the topic of personnel matters following the report of the Treasury and Civil Select Committee's inquiry into the Role of the Civil Service.

4. There are similar exclusions relating to the jurisdiction of the Local Commissioners (see Local Government Act 1974, schedule 5). The *Widdicombe Report* urged that there should be a review of the exclusions. It specifically stated that it did not consider that there was a case for the retention of the exclusion of contractual and commercial matters and the appointment of staff.

Question

On the basis of the extracts from the *Fourth Report of the Select Committee on the Parliamentary Commissioner for Administration,* what are the differences between the Government's view on the proper functions of the PCA and that of the Select Committee?

(iii) Authorities outside scope

Note

The number of authorities coming within the PCA's jurisdiction was increased in 1987 (see *ante* at p. 667). Section 110 of the Courts and Legal Services Act 1990 makes it clear that certain aspects of court and tribunal administration fall within the jurisdiction of the Ombudsman; his jurisdiction does not, however, extend to any action taken at the direction of, or on the authority of, any person acting in a judicial capacity or in his capacity as a member of a tribunal (see s. 5(6) and sch. 3, para. 6A of the Parliamentary Commissioner Act 1967, *ante* at pp. 665–666).

(iv) Rights of appeal to a tribunal or remedies in a court

Note

Section 5(2) of the Parliamentary Commissioner Act 1967 (*ante* p. 665) refers to both a right of appeal to tribunals and to the jurisdiction of the courts. Yet the reports of the PCA commonly refer to complaints being refused only because there is a right of appeal to a tribunal. It is, however, clear that cases come before the PCA in which there is a possibility of a successful legal challenge in the courts (see e.g. *Congreve* v *Home Office* [1976] QB 629, *post* at p. 673 and the decision of the PCA to conduct an investigation in the Barlow Clowes case: on the latter case see further R. Gregory and G. Drewry, 'Barlow Clowes and the Ombudsman – Part II' [1991] *Public Law*, 408, at p. 422). This suggests that the PCA tends to exercise his discretion to accept such complaints. Can you think of any reasons why this might be so?

In *Parliamentary Commissioner for Administration: Annual Report for 1980* (HC 148 of 1980–81), the then PCA explained his approach:

> As a matter of practice, where there appears on the face of things to have been a substantial legal wrong for which, if proved, there is a substantial legal remedy, I expect the citizen to seek it in the courts and I tell him so. But where there is doubt about the availability of a legal remedy or where the process of law seems too cumbersome, slow and expensive for the objective to be gained, I exercise my discretion to investigate the complaint myself. For example, I may receive a complaint that a particular tax ffice has been dilatory and inattentive in issuing an amended assessment of liability to tax. The taxpayer may say that he is worried and anxious about how he stands and that it affects his business. But would it be reasonable for him to take the Inland Revenue to court to obtain an injunction commanding them forthwith to perform their statutory duty, a theoretically available remedy? Surely not. This approach derives validity from the fact that very few people whose complaints have been investigated by my Office have later gone to seek a legal remedy in the courts. So the boundary is reasonably clear and well-observed.

The Local Ombudsmen are reported as considering that it is unreasonable to expect the average person aggrieved to resort to High Court proceedings for review, having regard to their cost and to the limited availability of legal aid. They must, however, comply with the terms of the legislation. In *R* v *Local Commissioner for Administration, ex parte Croydon London Borough Council* [1989] 1 All ER 1033 the Commissioner was criticised for having failed to appreciate, if not at the outset of his investigation, then as it continued, that the complainant might have had a remedy by way of judicial review. The court held that the Commissioner had not properly considered how he should exercise his discretion under ss. 26(6) and 26(10) of the Local Government Act 1974. Woolf LJ considered that s. 26(6) is directed to the stage where a Commissioner is deciding whether or not to conduct an investigation. He added that if, during an investigation, a Commissioner satisfies himself that the complainant has a legal remedy, then the Commissioner should consider whether to discontinue it using his discretion under s. 26(10).

One of the cases in which both the powers of the PCA and the courts were invoked concerned television licences. In 1975 some people obtained a new TV licence during the currency of an old one. Subsequently, the licence fee was increased. The people with overlapping licences were asked to pay the difference in fees, in which case their new licence would be made to run for 12 months from the expiry of the old licence. The Home Office stated that otherwise it would revoke the new licence, thereby leaving the old licence to be renewed from the time it expired at the new rate. Later the Home Office introduced a concession: if the holder of the licence so wished, the new licence would only be revoked after the holder had held it for the proportion of the year which the fee he had paid would entitle him to at the new rate.

The PCA investigated the matter and laid a special report before Parliament under s. 10(4) of the 1967 Act. The Home Office had been advised that it was lawfully entitled to revoke the licence. The PCA concluded that to act on this advice could not *per se* constitute maladministration, but that the Home Office had acted with both inefficiency and lack of foresight. No remedy was, however, recommended. One of the holders of an overlapping licence, Mr Congreve, succeeded in having the Home Office's action declared unlawful by the courts (see *Congreve* v *Home Office* [1976] QB 629).

(D) MEANING OF INJUSTICE IN CONSEQUENCE OF MALADMINISTRATION

PARLIAMENTARY COMMISSIONER ACT 1967

10.—(3) If, after conducting an investigation under this Act, it appears to the Commissioner that injustice has been caused to the person aggrieved in consequence of maladministration and that the injustice has not been, or will not be, remedied, he may, if he thinks fit, lay before each House of Parliament a special report upon the case.

[See also s. 5(1) *ante,* at p. 654]

12.—(3) It is hereby declared that nothing in this Act authorises or requires the Commissioner to question the merits of a decision taken without maladministration by a government department or other authority in the exercise of a discretion vested in that department or authority. . . .

LOCAL GOVERNMENT ACT 1974

26.—(1) Subject to the provisions of this Part of this Act where a written complaint is made by or on behalf of a member of the public who claims to have sustained injustice in consequence of maladministration in connection with action taken by or on behalf of an authority to which this Part of this Act applies, being action taken in the exercise of administrative functions of that authority, a Local Commissioner may investigate that complaint.

34.—(3) It is hereby declared that nothing in this Part of this Act authorises or requires a Local Commissioner to question the merits of a decision taken without maladministration by an authority in the exercise of a discretion vested in that authority.

Debate on the Second Reading of the Parliamentary Commissioner Bill House of Commons, House of Commons Debates, vol. 734 (18 October 1966), col. 51

MR CROSSMAN: We might have made an attempt . . . to define, by catalogue, all of the qualities which make up maladministration by a civil servant. It would be a wonderful exercise – bias, neglect, inattention, delay, incompetence, inaptitude, perversity, turpitude, arbitrariness and so on. It would be a long and interesting list.

R v *Local Commissioner, ex parte Eastleigh Borough Council*
[1988] 3 WLR 116
Court of Appeal

Eastleigh Borough Council challenged an adverse report of the Local Commissioner on the basis that it sought to challenge a decision taken without maladministration by an authority in the exercise of a discretion vested in the authority. Nolan J held that the ombudsman had indeed exceeded its jurisdiction, but that it would be wrong to make a declaration to that effect. The authority appealed to the Court of Appeal and the Local Commissioner cross-appealed. There were three main issues in the appeal:

(a) Had the Commissioner acted contrary to law in concluding that the council had been guilty of maladministration?

(b) Had the Commissioner acted contrary to law in concluding that such maladministration, if it had occurred, had caused injustice to the complainant?

(c) If the Commissioner had acted contrary to law in one or both of these respects, should the court grant a remedy?

LORD DONALDSON OF LYMINGTON MR: This appeal is about drains and an ombudsman. Most of the time the drains served six houses in Hampshire. However, on occasion they backed up to the discomfiture of the householders. The ombudsman was, to give him his proper title, a Local Commissioner of the Commission for Local Administration in England whose territory included the borough of Eastleigh. On the complaint of one of the householders, he investigated and concluded that the continued existence of the defect in the drains was caused by maladministration upon the part of the Eastleigh Borough Council. The council was not amused and sought judicial review of the ombudsman's report.

Nolan J held that the council had cause for complaint on two grounds. First, the ombudsman had acted contrary to section 34(3) of the Local Government Act 1974, in that he had questioned 'a decision taken without maladministration by an authority in the exercise of a discretion vested in that authority.' Second, the ombudsman had acted contrary to section 26(1) of the Act in that he had made a report on a complaint when it had not been established that the complainant had suffered injustice in consequence of the maladministration which was the subject of that complaint. However the judge refused to quash the report or to grant the council a declaration that the ombudsman had exceeded his jurisdiction. The council now appeals against this refusal and the ombudsman cross-appeals against the finding that he exceeded his powers.

Although this might be dismissed as a storm in a sewer, in fact it raises issues of some importance concerning the relationship between the courts and the local ombudsmen. But before considering those issues, I must say a word about the facts. These I take from the ombudsman's report, because for the purposes of judicial review proceedings he, and he alone, is the tribunal of fact.

The six houses were built in 1977 within the area of the Eastleigh Borough Council. It was accordingly the function of that council to enforce the Building Regulations 1976 (SI 1976 No. 1676): see section 4(3) of the Public Health Act 1961. It was for the council to decide on the scale of resources which it could make available to carry out this function. In doing so it had to strike a balance between the claims of efficiency and thrift, being answerable for that balance to the electorate through the ballot box rather than to the courts: *per* Lord Wilberforce in *Anns* v *Merton London Borough Council* [1978] AC 728, 754.

The ombudsman has found that the building control staff processed, on average, 210 applications per officer, which was 50 per cent higher per officer than in the remainder of Hampshire. This placed considerable demands on the staff and was achieved by limiting inspection to four of the more important of the nine stages requiring statutory notice of inspection to be submitted by builders. These four stages were the excavations for foundations, the oversite concrete, the damp proof course and the drains. The reason for limiting the inspections to these four stages was that the council had always been 'lean on members of staff' and it was thought appropriate to concentrate resources on inspections at the 'critical stages' of building work, on the basis that defects at these stages were likely to prove the most difficult to correct at a later date. The council operated a 'demand' system for inspection, meaning thereby that the council did not indulge in random inspections, but only inspected when notified that the appropriate stages had been reached. This was the policy of the council. It is now necessary to look at the practice.

It is now known that the problem experienced by the householders stemmed from the fact that the sewer over part of its length had a very shallow gradient of 1 in 140 and that there were undulations in it such that in places it was flat or had a reverse fall. The relevant code of practice called for a minimum gradient of 1 in 80 and the plans showed a gradient of 1 in 27 in one section and 1 in 70 in another. A gradient of 1 in 140 would not have been approved. . . .

The ombudsman's conclusions are stated in paragraphs 30 and 31 of his report:

> 30. In my view good administration dictates that the council should carry out an inspection under the Building Regulations in respect of all stage inspections for which they have received notice from the owner or builder as the case may be. Where inspections have not been made at a particular stage I consider that special attention should be given on the final inspection to remedy the omission. In the case of drains it is a relatively easy matter to carry out a full test, such as a ball test or its equivalent, at the final inspection stage and I consider that a council have a duty to

ensure that this is done because a final inspection should mean that, so far as the council are concerned, they have with reasonable diligence and expenditure of officer time found no defect under the Building Regulations. I am satisfied that in this case the private foul sewer in question was not fully or thoroughly inspected. The defects in piping discovered as a result of the soil and vent pipe test should have alerted officers to the possibility of other defects in the pipe work.

31. I find, therefore, that the complainant has sustained injustice as a result of the council's maladministration. However, I cannot say, categorically, whether had the council carried out the final inspection in accordance with the dictates of good administration the trouble at the centre of this complaint would not have arisen. Equally, I have taken account of the argument that with synthetic piping of the sort employed in this case soil compaction can cause undulation at a later date. I have also considered the fact that the original fault was the builder's and that that (and the council's fault) occurred some years ago. On the other hand the final inspection was, in my view, incomplete and the council could have become aware of the problem at an early stage because of the difficulties experienced by the owner of house 3. Having considered these factors I feel on balance it would be inequitable to ask the council to defray the whole cost of the necessary remedial work. Accordingly, upon the residents' agreement to pay a proportion of the reasonable cost, I consider that the council themselves should take the action which the Assistant Director of Technical Services commended to the residents (see paragraph 29, above).

The action referred to in paragraph 29 consisted of exposing that part of the sewer which lay between two manholes and adjusting the pipe work to eliminate the undulation.

The ombudsman's cross-appeal

Section 34(3)

This subsection is in the following terms:

> It is hereby declared that nothing in this Part of this Act authorises or requires a Local Commissioner to question the merits of a decision taken without maladministration by an authority in the exercise of a discretion vested in that authority.

'Maladministration' is not defined in the Act, but its meaning was considered in *Reg* v *Local Commissioner for Administration for the North and East Area of England, Ex parte Bradford Metropolitan City Council* [1979] QB 287. All three judges (Lord Denning MR, at p. 311, Eveleigh LJ, at p. 314, and Sir David Cairns, at p. 319) expressed themselves differently, but in substance each was saying the same thing, namely, that administration and maladministration in the context of the work of a local authority is concerned with the *manner* in which decisions by the authority are reached and the *manner* in which they are or are not implemented. Administration and maladministration have nothing to do with the nature, quality or reasonableness of the decision itself.

The key to this part of the cross-appeal lies in identifying the policy decision of the council in relation to the inspection of drains. This was, as I have stated, to inspect at four of the more important of nine stages of construction. I did not condescend to the nature of the inspections. These houses were built in 1977 and that was the policy in that year. In 1980 and 1984 the policy was modified, so that not all houses were inspected, but that is immaterial for present purposes. That being the 1977 policy of the council, it was for its building control officers to implement that policy as a matter of administration.

Nolan J read paragraph 30 of the ombudsman's report, which I have set out in full, as questioning the merits of that policy. I do not so read it. I can best illustrate my understanding of that paragraph by adding words which render explicit what, in my judgment, is implicit [the words in square brackets are the words added by Sir John Donaldson MR to the report of the ombudsman]:

> In my view good administration dictates that the council should carry out an inspection under the Building Regulations in respect of all stage inspections for which they have received notice from the owner or builder as the case may be. [However I recognise that, on the authority of *Anns'* case [1978] AC 728 to which I have referred at length earlier in this report, it was open to the council in the exercise of their discretion and taking account of the competing claims of efficiency and thrift to decide to inspect on fewer occasions. This the council has done and I accept its decisions. That said] Where inspections have not been made at a particular stage I consider that special attention should be given on the final inspection to remedying the omission. [In saying this I am not calling for an expenditure of time and effort which would nullify the council's discretionary decision on the resources to be devoted to building regulation inspections.] In the case of drains it is a relatively easy matter to carry out a full test, such as a ball test or its equivalent, at the final inspection stage . . . [The choice of test must be a matter for the council's officers and I would not criticise them for not using the ball test, if they had used some equivalent test. However an air pressure test, such as the council's officers used, is not such an equivalent, because it only reveals whether or not the sewer is watertight. It tells the inspector nothing about its gradient or its ability to self-clear and efficiently carry away matter discharged into it as required by regulation N10.] I consider that [this is of considerable importance and that] a council have a duty to ensure that this is done because a final inspection [if the council decide to make one, as this council did] should mean that, so far as the council are concerned, they have with reasonable diligence and expenditure of officer time found no defect under the Building Regulations. I am satisfied that in this case the private foul sewer in question was not fully or thoroughly inspected [in terms of the council's own 1977 policy. Even if in other circumstances a lesser inspection might have been justified in terms of that policy] the defects in piping discovered as a result of the soil and vent pipe tests should have alerted officers to the possibility of other defects in the pipe work.

So read, and I do so read it, paragraph 30 loyally accepts the council's discretionary decision on the inspection of drains. It simply criticises the way in which that decision was implemented. I do not, therefore, think that this complaint by the council is made out.

Section 26(1)
This subsection is in the following terms:

> Subject to the provisions of this Part of this Act where a written complaint is made by or on behalf of a member of the public who claims to have sustained injustice in consequence of maladministration in connection with action taken by or on behalf of an authority to which this Part of this Act applies, being action taken in the exercise of administrative functions of that authority, a Local Commissioner may investigate that complaint.

Clearly this subsection does not prevent the ombudsman from investigating a complaint of maladministration which prima facie may have led the complainant to sustain consequential injustice (see the *Bradford Council* case [1979] QB 287), but it does mean that he cannot report adversely upon an authority unless his investigation reveals not only maladministration, but injustice to the complainant sustained as a consequence of that maladministration.

The mischief at which this subsection is directed is not difficult to detect. Every local authority has living within its boundaries a small cadre of citizens who would like nothing better than to spend their spare time complaining of maladministration. The subsection limits the extent to which they can involve the ombudsman by requiring, as a condition precedent to his involvement, that the complainant shall personally have been adversely affected by the alleged maladministration. If he was not so affected, he did not himself suffer injustice. If he was, he did. . . .

Like Nolan J, I am loath to criticise a busy Local Commissioner on merely semantic grounds, but I think that he laid himself open to criticism by finding maladministration in paragraph 30 and then proceeding, without any explanation, to his conclusion of consequential injustice. The words 'I find, therefore . . .' without further ado might suggest that, having found maladministration, injustice to the complainant followed as a matter of course.

This is not the case and I do not understand the ombudsman to be suggesting that it was. The facts, as found by him, were that the inspection by the council's officers was designed to detect defects in the drains, it was inadequate and it failed to detect the defects which in fact caused substantial inconvenience to the complainant. If the matter had stopped there, his finding of a causal connection would have been clear and not open to attack. It is his reference in paragraph 31 to the fact that he could not affirm categorically that a proper inspection would have revealed the defects and to the argument that the synthetic piping soil compaction can cause undulation at a later date which has cast doubt on his finding. This point has given me some concern, but in the end I have come to the conclusion that the ombudsman was intending to say that, whilst there could be no absolute certainty that a proper inspection would have revealed the defects and it was a possibility that the undulation occurred after the date of the inspection, on the balance of probabilities he was satisfied that the defects were present at the time of the inspection, that a proper inspection would have revealed them and that he was therefore satisfied that the complainant had suffered injustice in consequence of the maladministration.

An ombudsman's report is neither a statute nor a judgment. It is a report to the council and to the ratepayers of the area. It has to be written in everyday language and convey a message. This report has been subjected to a microscopic and somewhat legalistic analysis which it was not intended to undergo. Valid criticisms have been made, particularly of paragraph 31, but in my judgment they go to form rather than substance and, notwithstanding occasional dicta to the contrary, judicial review is concerned with substance. I would therefore allow the ombudsman's cross-appeal.

The council's appeal

As Parker and Taylor LJJ are minded to dismiss the ombudsman's appeal, it is necessary to consider the council's appeal. I would allow it.

Nolan J considered that there was no need for any declaration that the ombudsman had exceeded his remit by contravening the limits upon his jurisdiction set by section 34(3). He said that this was a free country and that there was nothing to prevent the council responding to the report with equal publicity. He concluded by saying that, since Parliament had not thought it necessary to create a right of appeal against the findings in the Local Commissioner's report, and in the absence of impropriety, it seemed to him that the courts ought not to provide the equivalent of such a right by judicial review.

I have to say that I profoundly disagree with this approach. Let me start with the fact that Parliament has not created a right of appeal against the findings in a Local Commissioner's report. It is this very fact, coupled with the public law character of the ombudsman's office and powers, which is the foundation of the right to relief by way of judicial review.

Next there is the suggestion that the council should issue a statement disputing the right of the ombudsman to make his findings and that this would provide the council with an adequate remedy. Such an action would wholly undermine the system of ombudsman's reports and would, in effect, provide for an appeal to the media against his findings. The Parliamentary intention was that reports by ombudsmen should be loyally accepted by the local authorities concerned. This is clear from section 30(4) and (5), which require the local authority to make the report available for inspection by the public and to advertise this fact, from section 31(1), which requires the local authority to notify the ombudsman of the action which it has taken and proposes to take in the light of his report and from section 31(2), which entitles the ombudsman to make a further report if the local authority's response is not satisfactory.

Whilst I am very far from encouraging councils to seek judicial review of an ombudsman's report, which, bearing in mind the nature of his office and duties and the qualification of those who hold that office, is inherently unlikely to succeed, in the absence of a succesful application for judicial review and the giving of relief by the court, local authorities should not dispute an ombudsman's report and should carry out their statutory duties in relation to it.

If Nolan J thought that the publication of his judgment in favour of the council was itself an adquate remedy, he did not say so, and, in any event, I think that he would have been mistaken, because this by itself does not relieve the council of its obligations to respond to the report in accordance with section 31(1) and, assuming that the report should never have been made, it is wrong that the council should be expected to respond.

I would grant a declaration in terms which reflect the decision of this court on the ombudsman's appeal against the decision of Nolan J.

PARKER LJ: The only question of difficulty arises on the cross-appeal of the ombudsman. If the cross-appeal is dismissed, I agree that the appeal must be allowed for the reasons given by Lord Donaldson of Lymington MR. On that matter I have nothing to add. I turn therefore to the cross-appeal.

The first question thereby raised is whether, as Nolan J held, the ombudsman has in his report acted contrary to section 34(3) of the Local Government Act 1974, the terms of which have been set out by Lord Donaldson MR. I do not therefore repeat them. Whether he has or not depends upon the interpretation of paragraph 30 of his report, read of course in its context. This context includes amongst other things an early paragraph in which the ombudsman specifically refers to and quotes the relevant passage from the speech of Lord Wilberforce in *Anns* v *Merton London Borough Council* [1978] AC 728. It must therefore be taken that he correctly directed himself as to the law. Accordingly I approach paragraph 30 on the basis that it is inherently unlikely that, having so directed himself, he would in the vital paragraph have intended to act contrary to his own direction. I also approach the paragraph on the basis that it should not be interpreted to lead to such a result if on a fair reading such a result can be avoided.

Before turning to the paragraph itself I should mention two further matters. The first is that the terms of section 34(3) do not preclude the ombudsman from questioning the merits of all discretionary policy decisions, but only those taken without maladministration. He can therefore examine or investigate a decision, as Eveleigh LJ said in *Reg.* v *Local Commissioner for Administration for the North and East Area of England, Ex parte Bradford Metropolitan City Council* [1979] QB 287, 316–317:

> If the commissioner carries out his investigation and in the course of it comes personally to the conclusion that a decision was wrongly taken, but is unable to point to any maladministration other than the decision itself, he is prevented by section 34(3) from questioning the decision.

The second matter to which attention may be usefully directed is that section 26(1) of the Act of 1974, which provides for complaints to a Local Commissioner, specifies that the complaint must be made by a member of the public

> who claims to have sustained injustice in consequence of maladministration in connection with action taken by or on behalf of an authority . . . *being action taken in the exercise of administrative functions* of that authority . . . (My emphasis.)

It appears to me to be plain from the report that the council had failed to carry out their own policy, and indeed it was made plain by Mr Sullivan on their behalf that, had the report so found, the council would have had no objection. The objection taken is that the report goes further than this and questions the merits of the policy decision to inspect only 'at the four more important of the nine stages requiring statutory notice of inspection to be submitted by builders.' The council's case depends entirely upon the wording of paragraph 30, and particularly the opening words thereof:

> In my view good administration dictates that the council should carry out an inspection under the Building Regulations in respect of all stage inspections for which they have received notice from the owner or builder as the case may be.

This, it is submitted, clearly questions the merits of the decision to inspect at the four more important stages only and, there being no suggestion of any maladministration in arriving at that decision, clearly exceeds the powers of the ombudsman.

I can see no answer to that submission, but it does not follow that the conclusion reached is vitiated. On a fair reading of the whole of paragraph 30 it appears to me that the ombudsman is not concluding that there was maladministration because there was no inspection at all nine stages, but merely that the inspections of the sewer which were called for by the policy of inspecting at the four most important stages were not fully or thoroughly carried out. This conclusion was not dependent upon the view expressed in the opening sentence and indeed it could not have been because the policy did call for drain inspections, indeed two drain inspections. The policy was silent as to the nature of such inspections, but, since the regulations (see regulation N10(1)(e)) call for a drain or private sewer to be 'so designed and constructed, of such size and . . . laid at such a gradient as to ensure that it is self-cleansing and efficiently carries away the maximum volume of matter which may be discharged into it,' it appears to me that inspections which were not directed at all to checking whether the private sewer was so designed, constructed and laid were rightly found to constitute maladministration by the council in its administrative funtions.

I conclude therefore that the ombudsman's conclusion in paragraph 30 was valid, but if the council felt it necessary to seek some declaratory relief with regard to the opening words of the paragraph I would be prepared to consider granting it.

I turn to the second question raised on the cross-appeal, namely, whether the conclusion that the complainant had suffered injustice as a result of the maladministration can be sustained. This depends upon paragraph 31 of the report. Had the ombudsman stopped at the first sentence, I should have had no doubt that the decision was sustainable. It seems to me abundantly clear that the complainant had suffered injustice if the failure to inspect properly led to the subsequent expenditure and the ombudsman could in my view easily have determined that it had. It is submitted however that, having stated his conclusion in the opening sentence, he proceeds to negate it and that the paragraph read as a whole really amounts to this: 'I cannot say whether the failure to inspect led to the expenditure, but as the council were at fault it would be fair that they should contribute to the cost of remedial measures.' For the ombudsman it is submitted that this is not so and that on a fair reading the paragraph says no more than: 'I cannot be absolutely sure, but on the balance of probabilities I conclude . . .'

I regret to say that, unlike Lord Donaldson MR I cannot accept this construction. It appears to me that to do so involves applying legal concepts of differing standards of proof in order to uphold a paragraph which, like its predecessor, must be broadly considered. I have, despite its opening words, been able, by a broad reading and the correctness of the ombudsman's directions to himself on the law, to uphold the conclusion in paragraph 30. In the case of paragraph 31 I am unable to do so.

I would therefore dismiss the cross-appeal and allow the appeal.

TAYLOR LJ: I agree that the council's appeal must be allowed if the ombudsman's cross-appeal fails. The council should not be denied a remedy if the ombudsman's finding was ultra vires or otherwise unlawful. I agree that for the reasons given by Lord Donaldson MR, Nolan J's grounds for refusing a declaration cannot be sustained.

The crucial issue therefore is whether the ombudsman's findings in both paragraphs 30 and 31 of his report can be upheld and his cross-appeal thus allowed. I agree with Nolan J that both paragraphs contain findings which cannot be justified.

As to paragraph 30, the conclusion adverse to the council is contained in the penultimate sentence. Its rationale is said to be that, in terms of the council's own 1977 policy, the foul sewer was not fully or thoroughly inspected because no gradient test was applied such as the ball test or its equivalent. It is accepted to be a matter for the council's discretion whether, with their available resources, they could and should have inspected at all stages or only at the four most important stages. But in my judgment, it was equally a matter for the council's discretion as to what tests they could and should carry out having regard to those resources. The ombudsman's finding in paragraph 30 is that at the final inspection, if not before, the council:

> have a duty to insure that [a gradient test] is done because a final inspection should mean that, so far as the council are concerned, they have with reasonable diligence and expenditure of officer time found no defect under the Building Regulations.

This begs the question whether 'reasonable diligence and expenditure of officer time' permits and requires a gradient test to be made of every drain and sewer. It was not the policy of this council that they did. That is a matter of discretion for the council. I do not accept Mr Beloff's suggestion that what precedes the penultimate sentence in paragraph 30 should be regarded as obiter dicta. The paragraph is headed 'Conclusions' and should be read as a whole. It culminates in, and is explanatory of, the finding. In my judgment its tenor shows the ombudsman to be trespassing into the field of discretion by laying down what policy as to inspections the dictates of good administration require, and what tests the council ought to ensure are carried out. That is quite different from finding that a test specifically required by the council's policy has not been carried out or has been carried out inefficiently. I therefore agree with Nolan J that the ombudsman was in breach of section 34(3) of the Local Government Act 1974 in his conclusion that maladministration was established.

As to paragraph 31, I agree with Parker LJ. Only by straining the language used by the ombudsman and attributing to him speculatively considerations as to the burden of proof, could one render his finding on causation sound. I do not think such straining and speculation is justified.

Accordingly I conclude that in respect of both paragraphs 30 and 31 of the report, Nolan J reached the correct conclusions. I would therefore dismiss the cross-appeal and allow the council's appeal.

Questions

1. How did each of the three judges answer the questions raised in the appeal?

2. Is there any difference between the interpretation placed on s. 34(3) by Lord Donaldson MR and that by Parker LJ?

3. What advice would you give to Commissioners on the drawing up of their reports after this case?

Notes

1. Croydon Council also succeeded in obtaining judicial review of the decision of another Local Commissioner criticising the operation of the council's education appeals policy (see *R* v *Local Commissioner for Administration ex parte Croydon London Borough Council* [1989] 1 All ER 1033; see also M. Jones, 'The Local Ombudsmen and Judicial Review' (1988) *Public Law* 608–22).

2. The *JUSTICE-All Souls Report on Administrative Law* (1988), at pp. 133–4, noted that the Commission for Local Administration in England stated that the word 'maladministration' is disliked by councillors and officials and means little to many complainants. It recommended that, in addition to the Commissioners' powers to make a finding of maladministration, the Commissioners should be able to report in terms critical of the local authority, but falling short of making a finding of maladministration against it, and it should then be obligatory for the local authority to consider such a report with a view to taking any necessary remedial action.

Questions

1. The *JUSTICE-All Souls Report* was not, however, in favour of removing the term 'maladministration'. 'In our view' it stated 'a spade should be called a spade'. In the light of the evidence of the Commission for Local Administration, do you think a spade would be called a spade if its own proposal was implemented.

2. If this proposal was implemented, what meaning could be given to s. 34(3) of the 1974 Act?

Notes

1. In its *Second Report for the Session 1967–68* (HC 350) the Select Committee encouraged the PCA to investigate complaints relating to 'bad decisions' and 'bad rules'. In respect of the 'bad decision' the Select Committee (at para. 14) stated that if the PCA

> finds a decision which, judged by its effect upon the aggrieved person, appears to him to be thoroughly bad in quality, he might infer from the quality of the decision itself that there had been an element of maladministration in the taking of it and ask for its review.

In respect of the 'bad rule', where an administrative rule, despite being applied properly, has caused hardship and injustice, the PCA was urged

> . . . to enquire whether, given the effect of the rule in the case under his investigation, the Department had taken any action to review the rule. If found defective and revised, what action had been taken to remedy the hardship sustained by the complainant? If not revised, whether there had been due consideration by the Department of the grounds for maintaining the rule?

The PCA accepted these suggestions, but it has been argued that they have had little impact on the number of cases in which he has been willing to find maladministration. In relation to the 'bad rule', Gregory in 'The Select Committee on the PCA 1967–80' [1982] *Public Law* 49–88, at p. 69 points out that 'only an extraordinarily inept department might be expected to conduct its review of a rule [so] that the Commissioner would find defects in the process subsequently described to him.'

2. A number of the cases considered by the PCA and Local Commissioners have involved allegations that authorities have failed to give proper advice; for a discussion of the Parliamentary Commissioner's approach to such cases, see A. Mowbray, 'A Right to Official Advice: The Parliamentary Commissioner's Perspective' [1990] *Public Law*, 68–69.

3. In *Our Fettered Ombudsman* (1977), ch. VII, JUSTICE suggested that, following the New Zealand model, the jurisdiction of the PCA should be extended to allow him to investigate any action which is 'unreasonable, unjust or oppressive . . . instead of maladministration'. The PCA responded to this suggestion in his *Annual Report for 1977* (HC 157 of 1977–78) by stating that he believed he already had power to investigate complaints that actions by Government Departments are unjust or oppressive. He continued:

> 21. What the Act certainly does exclude from my jurisdiction are complaints about discretionary decisions taken 'without maladministration'. I believe this to be right. It is no part of my function to substitute my judgment for that of a Minister or one of his officials if I see no evidence of 'maladministration' either in the way the decision was taken or in the nature of the decision itself.
>
> 22. I believe therefore that the difficulty which has been detected in the limitation of my investigation powers to cases of 'maladministration' is more theoretical than practical. But if there is thought to be some semantic difficulty

which confuses members of the public or members of parliament than I should see no objection to seeing my powers redefined in the sort of language suggested by JUSTICE. I think that in practice it would make very little difference.

Subsequently JUSTICE adopted the view that the definition of maladministration was not a source of much difficulty, bearing in mind the approach which the Commissioner took to his jurisdiction (see the reference to this in the *Fourth Report from the Select Committee,* HC 615 of 1977–78). More recently the *JUSTICE-All Souls Report on Administrative Law* (1988) did not recommend any change in the definition (see pp. 92–3 and 133–4).

Question

In the light of the decision in *ex parte Eastleigh Borough Council* (*ante* at p. 674), do you think the PCA was correct in the extract from the Annual Report for 1977?

Note

Sir Cecil Clothier, who was PCA from 1979 to 1985, stated that he did not wish to be dragged into a review of political decision-making; and he suggested that a complaint is political if it has been debated in Parliament or where a very large proportion of the population are affected as well as the person making the complaint (see Clothier (1984) 81 *Law Society's Gazette* 3108–9). On this ground he refused to investigate complaints relating to the Inland Revenue's agreement concerning Fleet Street casual workers who evaded their tax arrangements. This agreement subsequently gave rise to *Inland Revenue Commissioners* v *National Federation of Self-Employed and Small Businesses* [1982] AC 617 (see *ante* at p. 615).

Section 26(7) of the Local Government Act 1974 specifically provides that a local commissioner shall not conduct an investigation in respect of any action which in his opinion affects all or most of the inhabitants in the area of the authority concerned.

(E) CONDUCT OF INVESTIGATION

PARLIAMENTARY COMMISSIONER ACT 1967

7.—(1) Where the Commissioner proposes to conduct an investigation pursuant to a complaint under this Act, he shall afford to the principal officer of the department or authority concerned, and to any other person who is alleged in the complaint to have taken or authorised the action complained of, an opportunity to comment on any allegations contained in the complaint.

(2) Every such investigation shall be conducted in private, but except as aforesaid the procedure for conducting an investigation shall be such as the Commissioner considers appropriate in the circumstances of the case; and without prejudice to the generality of the foregoing provision the Commissioner may obtain information from such persons and in such manner, and make such inquiries, as he thinks fit, and may determine whether any person may be represented, by counsel or solicitor or otherwise, in the investigation.

(3) The Commissioner may, if he thinks fit, pay to the person by whom the complaint was made and to any other person who attends or furnishes information for the purposes of an investigation under this Act—

(a) sums in respect of expenses properly incurred by them;

(b) allowances by way of compensation for the loss of their time,

in accordance with such scales and subject to such conditions as may be determined by the Treasury.

(4) The conduct of an investigation under this Act shall not affect any action taken by the department or authority concerned, or any power or duty of that department or authority to take further action with respect to any matters subject to the investigation.

8.—(1) For the purposes of an investigation under this Act the Commissioner may require any Minister, officer or member of the department or authority concerned or any other person who in his opinion is able to furnish information or produce documents relevant to the investigation to furnish any such information or produce any such document.

(2) For the purposes of any such investigation the Commissioner shall have the same powers as the Court in respect of the attendance and examination of witnesses (including the administration of oaths or affirmations and the examination of witnesses abroad) and in respect of the production of documents.

(3) No obligation to maintain secrecy or other restriction upon the disclosure of information obtained by or furnished to persons in Her Majesty's service, whether imposed by any enactment or by any rule of law, shall apply to the disclosure of information for the purposes of an investigation under this Act; and the Crown shall not be entitled in relation to any such investigation to any such privilege in respect of the production of documents or the giving of evidence as is allowed by law in legal proceedings.

(4) No person shall be required or authorised by virtue of this Act to furnish any information or answer any question relating to proceedings of the Cabinet or of any committee of the Cabinet or to produce so much of any document as relates to such proceedings; and for the purposes of this subsection a certificate issued by the Secretary of the Cabinet with the approval of the Prime Minister and certifying that any information, question, document or part of a document so relates shall be conclusive.

(5) Subject to subsection (3) of this section, no person shall be compelled for the purposes of any investigation under this Act to give any evidence or produce any document which he could not be compelled to give or produce in [civil] proceedings before the Court.

9.—(1) If any person without lawful excuse obstructs the Commissioner or any officer of the Commissioner in the performance of his functions under this Act, or is guilty of any act or omission in relation to an investigation under this Act which, if that investigation were a proceeding in the Court, would constitute contempt of court, the Commissioner may certify the offence to the Court . . .

Note

Similar provisions regarding the conduct of investigations by the Local Commissioners are set out in the Local Government Act 1974, ss. 26(5), 28–29.

Parliamentary Commissioner for Administration Annual Report for 1992

HC 569 of 1992–93, pp. 5–7

Screening of complaints

16. All complaints which are referred to my Office go through a relatively rapid initial sift or screen so that I may determine whether or not they are candidates for full investigation. Where I conclude not, I give the referring Member, and so the complainant, a full statement of my reasons for my conclusion. That, however, does not stop many complainants from coming back for a second or even a third try. In other cases, I ask the complainant, through the Member, to provide further evidence before I can decide whether to accept the complaint for a full investigation, since my powers to require a department's papers come into play only after I have decided to begin an investigation on the basis of the initial evidence put to me by the complainant. That quirk in my jurisdiction is not always readily understood by those amazed that I cannot intervene at pleasure.

17. The screening process is relatively rapid but it must still be done with care and thoroughness if justice is to be done to the complainant. It can involve, for example, my screening officers mastering the details of thick files sent in by complainants about disputed planning or taxation cases, then tracking down and searching through complex and detailed legislation relevant to the complaint, or in trying to make sense of sad and sometimes disjointed life histories of disappointed benefit claimants whose grievances, especially in pensioner cases, can extend back over many years. In suitable cases screening officers will make informal enquiries of departments or agencies to check that letters have been answered, concerns have been addressed or sums due to complainants have been paid. That enables me often, when I reply to the referring Member, to let the Member know that the cause of a complaint has been removed even though I will not be going on to conduct a formal investigation. Whatever the complaint, all the papers sent to me will have been read with care and the background thoroughly researched before I reach my decision whether to put it formally to the department or body complained against and to begin a full investigation using the formidable powers which the Act gives me.

18. As part of their background research my screening officers seek to keep track of changes in the machinery of government to ensure that I am up to date with changes affecting the roles of departments and agencies over whom I have jurisdiction. Given the size and complexity of government that is not easy. The growth in the number of agencies, the changes to their titles and their roles leads to understandable confusion at times among members of the public as to the precise body with whom they have dealings. Many complaints are presented to me on the basis that the complainant does not know whether or not they are directed against a department or body which is within my jurisdiction or against someone acting on behalf of such a body — a difficulty with which I sympathise and which, with the adoption of market testing and contracting out, is likely to increase. In 1992, for example, I received complaints against bodies where, at first sight, the complaint appeared to have little to do with me, but which on further enquiry turned out to be within my jurisdiction; and I had complaints which the complainant and the Member confidently thought were within my jurisdiction but which I had to tell the Member were not. Time-consuming though such cases can be, I had far rather that Members should ask me if doubtful cases are for me than risk a person with a grievance against a body which might be within my jurisdiction being turned away, without the complaint being put to me. Where it seems likely that a complaint referred to me does not fall to me but comes within the responsibilities of another Ombudsman, I try to let the referring Member

know accordingly, though I am careful not to raise the complainant's hopes when I do so.

19. Later I refer to jurisdictional changes in 1992 which have affected or seem likely to affect my relationship with specific departments. Significant machinery of government changes are by no means unusual after an election, when responsibilities change and new departments or offices (the Department of National Heritage and the Office of Public Service and Science, for example) are set up, while others (the Department of Energy in 1992) are abolished. Such well publicised changes are only the visible tip of the iceberg. Less visibly smaller, but still significant, changes frequently occur. New Urban Development Corporations may be set up. Old Residuary Bodies are abolished. New tribunals are created; old ones vanish. New bodies may be established reflecting European-wide legislation. It is, I consider, unfortunate that, because of the way in which the Parliamentary Commissioner Act 1967 was drafted, it is only where such new bodies are specifically brought within my jurisdiction that I can consider complaints against them. I have drawn this problem, too, to the attention of the Select Committee and expressed the hope that, for the future, some way will be found of bringing such new bodies automatically within my jurisdiction unless, in the legislation establishing them, they are specifically excluded from it; in other words that a form of opting out, not opting in, should apply.

20. Not all the complaints which I turn away after the screening stage are turned away because the body complained against is outside my jurisdiction, though that was largely true of the well publicised complaints from the Maxwell pensioners which were referred to me during 1992. I had to explain that the Securities and Investments Board, the Investment Management Regulations Organisation and the Occupational Pensions Board were not within my jurisdiction, though the Select Committee have recommended in the past that the last named should be. Sometimes I turn away complaints because, given the issues involved, I conclude that there are or have been available to the complainants other more appropriate avenues through which to seek redress. The legislation under which I operate enjoins me, save where I feel that special circumstances apply, to leave to tribunals those issues for which tribunals have been set up and to leave to the courts those issues which may be tried by them. In 1992 therefore I declined to take up one widely publicised complaint which had been referred to me by several Members that the Charity Commissioners were at fault in allowing a University College to dispose of valuable paintings which were said to be subject to trusts. That was after I had established that the Charity Commissioners' decision could have been challenged in the courts. I also did not take up a complaint that alleged shortcomings by the Department of Transport had contributed to the Lockerbie disaster, once I had established the scope of the enquiry which had already been carried out by the Sheriff Principal under the Fatal Accidents and Sudden Death Inquiry (Scotland) Act 1976. I also advised that a complaint against the Scottish Office over their alleged shortcomings in connection with the construction of the Skye Bridge crossing was taken outside my jurisdiction by an appeal which had been lodged in the Court of Session.

Parliamentary Commissioner for Administration Annual Report for 1993

HC 290 of 1993–94, pp. 7–9

. . .

Screening of Complaints

20. In my Annual Report for 1992 [see *ante* p. 686] I explained in some detail the process known as screening which every complaint referred to me undergoes to see if it

is one which I can, and should, investigate. I shall not repeat that description though, in a sense, every case which I do not take through to a full investigation can be called a fast-track case. In view of the Select Committee's recommendation, referred to in my Introduction (paragraph 2), that I should deal directly with complainants when requesting further information, while keeping the referring Member fully informed, I now explain the way in which such requests are handled. Where I decide that I need more information before I can determine whether a complaint merits a full investigation my officials will make contact with the complainant concerned, by letter or by telephone, to explain what information I shall need and to invite them to send it direct to me. (It will remain open to complainants to send it through the referring Member if they prefer.) At the same time I will let the referring Member know what is happening. Once the information requested is to hand and I am in a position to decide whether the complaint requires a full investigation or not I shall let the referring Member know what I decide. The legislation requires that. My staff will also let the complainant know I am doing so. It is then up to the Member to let the complainant know in whatever way he or she chooses the decision I have reached. Where that decision is to proceed to a full investigation of the complaint, I shall normally expect to deal direct with the complainant thereafter, having informed the Member that that is what I shall be doing. My final report will, as now, be addressed to the Member with a copy for the complainant.

. . .

Time taken for investigations

15. In 1993 the average time taken to complete a full investigation and to report on it to the Member of the House of Commons who had referred the complaint to me was 13 months and 16 days compared with the corresponding time of 12 months and 13 days for 1992. That meant that average case throughput times worsened by 8.8%. That is a disappointing reversal of the trend I have achieved in earlier years and which has seen average case throughput times fall from 15 months and 4 days in 1989 to 12 months and 13 days in 1992. Even so it does not compare unfavourably with the time taken for full investigations by some other Ombudsmen and with the time before judicial review decisions are obtained in the English courts. Put simply, the continuing sharp rise in incoming work, which, until this last year, has not been matched by growth in the resources available to me, has taken its toll. Cases have had to queue at times before full investigations can be started; the result is that average case throughput times have lengthened. By June 1993 I was able to deploy two further investigation units and that has helped. It takes time for the benefits that additional resources bring to be reflected in the statistics of average case throughput time. The extra capacity my office has now obtained will not be truly reflected in the time taken to complete investigations for some time yet. I share in full the objectives of the Select Committee who have recommended that every effort should be made to bring average case throughput times down to nine months. With my staff I am considering further measures to achieve this goal without sacrificing the standards of accuracy and thoroughness for which this Office has a reputation to maintain. My staff and I are finding that cases referred for investigation are, if anything, becoming more complex; but there is also a more cheerful side to the story (see paragraph 18).

16. Another indication of the cumulative effect of the extra work in recent years is the growth in the number of cases which have been in the Office for a year or more. At the end of 1993, out of a current workload of 333 investigations on hand, that figure stood at 101 cases, compared with 42 cases out of the 260 investigations on hand at the end of 1992. Again I am considering ways of keeping such cases to a minimum.

17. In recent reports I have referred to my concern about the time it can take some departments, in certain cases, to provide information and, in particular, to confirm the

accuracy of the facts contained in the report which I intend to make to the referring Member. Sometimes, too, there is a reluctance to accept the need for redress for the complainant and others in similar circumstances which I suggest as a result of my investigations. I see no reason for that final stage to take longer than the six weeks maximum to which I referred in my last Annual Report. During 1993 there were 22 cases which took longer than that; 8 of them took more than three months, Some cases are extremely complex but such delays in agreeing recompense after my investigation has been completed and my recommendation made are unfair to justified complainants.

Fast-track cases

18. The statistics in paragraphs 15 to 17 do not, however, tell the whole story. Once I intervene it is often the case that departments take a fresh look at complaints which they have earlier rejected. My intervention brings the matters complained of right to the top of the organisation concerned, sometimes for the first time. In that case, either straightaway or during the course of my investigation, they may offer a remedy. In such cases I normally complete my investigation to ensure (i) that the remedy offered is sufficient, (ii) that there are no systems defects which need to be put right and (iii) that there are no other identifiable persons, in a similar position to the complainant's, who, because their complaints have not been referred, may be left with their grievances unresolved and in ignorance of the redress they might achieve. Points such as these add to the length of time which some investigations take, although the individual complainants may have had redress much more promptly. The Select Committee have recommended that I should include information about such cases in my Annual Report. For 1993 my staff have carried out a retrospective analysis of the investigations completed during that year to assemble this information. For 1994 and in future it will be recorded through the year. In 1993 a total of 107 investigations out of the 208 completed produced financial or other tangible redress for the individual concerned. That redress was achieved on *average* 8 months and 17 days after the complaint was referred to me. In some cases the original redress was augmented later. In 16 cases the redress was achieved within two months of the start of my investigation.

19. There is another category of fast-track cases. It is made up of those cases where, as a result of an informal enquiry made by my staff, I establish that a complainant's grievance either has very lately been, or will very shortly be, remedied. I do not then normally conduct a formal investigation at all. Those cases have not featured in my statistics of investigated cases, being paradoxically classified under the heading 'rejected at Parliamentary Commissioner's discretion'. 13 cases of this kind were included in 1993 in the 53 cases rejected under that heading. (The other 40 cases included instances where I had investigated similar complaints before and/or I was satisfied that my intervention could not benefit the complainant.) What happened in practice in those 13 cases was that my officials, through their enquiries and actions, ensured that the complainants' grievances had been or were about to be satisfactorily resolved before finally recommending to me that I need take no further action. The end result was that another 13 complainants' grievances had been suitably redressed.

Notes

1. The nature of the investigations of the PCA is discussed further in the extracts *post* pp. 704–705.

2. The Northern Ireland PCA and Commissioner for Complaints appear to have been using a fast-track procedure for longer than the PCA. In evidence to the Select Committee both the PCA and the Northern Ireland PCA pointed out that the use of the fast-track has to be considered carefully, as 'wider administrative issues' might be raised by a case and these should not escape formal investigation. The Select Committee noted that the smaller jurisdiction in Northern Ireland lent itself to informal approaches (HC 33 of 1993–94, paras. 17–18).

3. The reports of the Commission for Local Administration place more emphasis on pursuing the possibility of a settlement which arises in the course of an investigation. The Commission for Local Administration explicitly states as one of its objectives 'to encourage authorities to develop and publicise their own procedures for the fair local settlement of complaints'. The reasons for this emphasis on settlement may be partially explained by considering the consequences of findings of maladministration by the PCA and Local Commissioners (see section (F) below).

K. Thompson considered the adavantages and disadvantages of local settlement in 'Conciliation or Arbitration?' [1991] *Local Government Studies* 15–26 at p. 25.

> While settlements can save time and expense, provide an acceptable solution to all parties, and indicate a willingness on the part of authorities to seek out and remedy shortcomings, they may also be used to 'buy off' complainants. This can mean the avoidance of unwelcome publicity and indeed promised remedial action may not be implemented.

Question

Are there any differences in the attitudes of the various Ombudsmen to informal resolution of complaints; if so what factors might account for them; and are the possible problems associated with fast-tracks/local settlements worse than the problem of the time taken to conduct formal investigations?

(F) OUTCOME OF INVESTIGATIONS AND REMEDIES

PARLIAMENTARY COMMISSIONER ACT 1967

10.—(1) In any case where the Commissioner conducts an investigation under this Act or decides not to conduct such an investigation, he shall send to the member of the House of Commons by whom the request for investigation was made (or if he is no longer a member of that House, to such member of that House as the Commissioner thinks appropriate) a report of the results of the investigation or, as the case may be, a statement of his reasons for not conducting an investigation.

(2) In any case where the Commissioner conducts an investigation under this Act, he shall also send a report of the results of the investigation to the principal officer of the department or authority concerned and to any other person who is alleged in the relevant complaint to have taken or authorised the action complained of.

(3) [see *ante* at p. 673]

(4) The Commissioner shall annually lay before each House of Parliament a general report on the performance of his functions under this Act and may from time

to time lay before each House of Parliament such other reports with respect to those functions as he thinks fit.

11.—(2) Information obtained by the Commissioner or his officers in the course of or for the purposes of an investigation under this Act shall not be disclosed except—

(a) for the purposes of the investigation and of any report to be made thereon under this Act;

(b) for the purposes of any proceedings for an offence under the Official Secrets Acts 1911 to 1939 alleged to have been committed in respect of information obtained by the Commissioner or any of his officers by virtue of this Act or for an offence of perjury alleged to have been committed in the course of an investigation under this Act or for the purposes of an inquiry with a view to the taking of such proceedings; or

(c) for the purposes of any proceedings under section 9 of this Act;

and the Commissioner and his officers shall not be called upon to give evidence in any proceedings (other than such proceedings as aforesaid) of matters coming to his or their knowledge in the course of an investigation under this Act.

(3) A Minister of the Crown may give notice in writing to the Commissioner, with respect to any document or information specified in the notice, or any class of documents or information so specified, that in the opinion of the Minister the disclosure of that document or information, or of documents or information of that class, would be prejudicial to the safety of the State or otherwise contrary to the public interest; and where such a notice is given nothing in this Act shall be construed as authorising or requiring the Commissioner or any officer of the Commissioner to communicate to any person or for any purpose any document or information specified in the notice, or any document or information of a class so specified.

Note

On the rather different provisions governing the Local Commissioners, see *post* at pp. 693–694.

Parliamentary Commissioner for Administration
Annual Report for 1995
HC of 1995–96, p. 58

Diagram 5: Outcomes of investigations

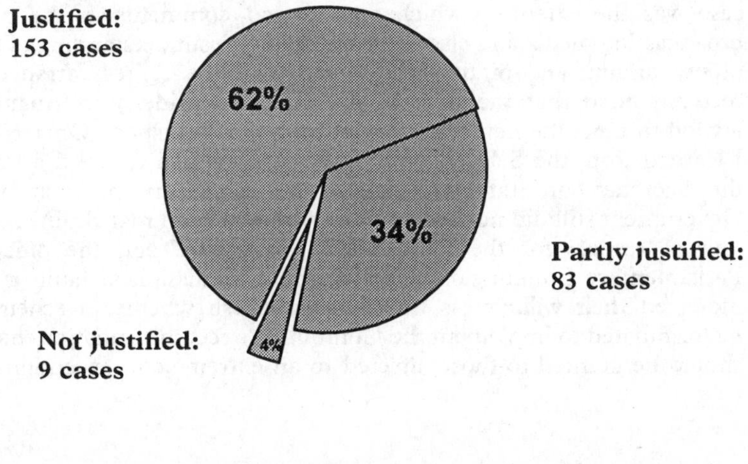

Notes

1. The Parliamentary Commissioner for Administration is normally able to report that there had been full compliance with his recommendations. The evidence suggests that in general the PCA has normally had little difficulty in securing compliance with his recommendations. He reported on one difficult case in the 1995 Annual Report

Channel Tunnel Rail Link

7. On 8 February 1995 I laid before Parliament my report 'The Channel Tunnel Rail Link and Blight: Investigation of complaints against the Department of Transport'. Paragraphs 109-119 in Chapter I of this report describe the case and its consideration by the Select Committee in more detail. I record here its highly unusual features. It was the largest single investigation I had undertaken in my time as Parliamentary Commissioner. I laid the report before Parliament under the Parliamentary Commissioner Act 1967, section 10(3), which applies when it appears to me that injustice has been caused to a person in consequence of maladministration and that the injustice has not been, and will not be, remedied. It was only the second time in the 28 years since my office was established that the power in that subsection had been used. I had shown my report in draft to the Permanent Secretary (in accordance with my usual procedure) but — unusually — he did not accept that his department had been maladministrative or, therefore, that any remedy for injustice was due. I published as an Appendix to my report the comments of the Permanent Secretary. The then Secretary of State and he gave evidence to the Select Committee on 23 May and 1 March respectively. On 19 July the Select Committee issued their report in which they concluded that the department had acted maladministratively in failing to consider whether any *ex gratia* payments were due when the Channel Tunnel Rail Link project entered the period of uncertainty caused by problems of funding between June 1990 and April 1994; that it was desirable to grant redress to those affected to an extreme and exceptional degree; and that it should be possible to distinguish a small number of cases of exceptional hardship. (I may add that a further unusual feature of the case was the extent to which reports and comments in the press and broadcasting media and elsewhere showed a misunderstanding of the basis of my finding and of the limited scope of the redress arrangements I recommended that the department should consider.) In August I was invited to meet the new Secretary of State for Transport. On 1 November I learned from the Select Committee that they had received a reply from the Secretary of State, and it was published on the next day. The Government still did not accept that there had been maladministration but 'out of respect for the PCA Select Committee and the office of the Parliamentary Commissioner, and without admission of fault or liability' indicated their willingness 'to consider afresh whether a scheme might be formulated to implement the Committee's recommendation that redress should be granted to those affected to an extreme and exceptional degree

by generalised blight from CTRL during the period between June 1990 and April 1994 and how it might operate'. I welcome that decision and I hope for speedy progress.

2. The Local Commissioners, on the other hand, have frequently reported difficulties in securing compliance. In the Annual Report for 1992–93, the Commission for Local Administration in England stated that there had been an unsatisfactory outcome in 201 of 3,548 reports issued since 1974. What explanations might there be for this distinction? Note, however, that, as explained in point 2 below, the powers of the Local Commissioners to secure compliance have recently been increased.

3. Gregory, in 'The Select Committee on the PCA 1967–80' [1982] *Public Law,* 49–88, at p. 49 comments on the role of the Select Committee in ensuring that there is compliance with the recommendations of the Parliamentary Commissioner. Until recently, the main sanction available to Local Commissioners has been to issue further reports. It was not until 1988 that local authorities were placed under a statutory obligation to consider such further reports. Each of the Commissions was also obliged to issue an annual report, together with the reports of the relevant Local Commissioners, to its 'representative body'. The 1974 legislation had provided for the establishment of a representative body for each of England and Wales. Their main tasks were to consider, comment and pass on to the local authorities any general conclusions reached by the Ombudsmen about the operation of their powers, and to consider and comment on their annual estimates of expenditure. The existence of the representative bodies was not, however, perceived to be of great assistance to the Local Commissioners. The *Widdcombe Report* concluded at p. 223, that the representative body in England

> has tended to take a negative view of proposals from the Commission for modifications to their procedures. We also consider it anomalous in principle that a body which represents those who are the subject of investigation should play a major part in dictating the budget of the investigators. There is no parallel here with the position of the Parliamentary ombudsman who is accountable not to the Government but to the Commons Select Committee.

The report concluded that the Government should consider the abolition of the representative bodies and that the cost of the Ombudsmen's services should be a charge against central government funds.

Following the report the Government stated that it intended to introduce measures to increase compliance by local authorities. The Local Government and Housing Act 1989, ss. 26 and 28, consequently amended the Local Government Act 1974 to provide that authorities must notify the Local Ombudsman of the action which they propose to take within three months from the date of an adverse report (Local Government Act 1974, s. 31(2), as amended). Similar time-limits apply in respect of the consideration of a further report (s. 31(2)–(2)(c)). If an authority proposes not to accept the recommendation of the Ombudsman in a further report, the report must generally be considered by the authority as a whole (s. 31(A)(1)). If, in considering the report, the authority take into account a report by a person or body with an interest in the Local Ombudsman's report, they must also take into account a report by a person or body without an interest in the report (s. 31(A)(4)). No member of the council is entitled to vote on any question with respect to a report or a further report in which he is named and criticised (s. 31(A)(5)). If the authority do not satisfy the Local Ombudsman with respect to a further report, he may require the authority to publish a statement, in a form agreed between the local authority and the Ombudsman, consisting of the details of the action recommended by the Local Ombudsman, such supporting material as he may require, and, if the authority so require, a statement of the reasons for non-compliance with the Local Ombudsman's recommendations. The statement must be published in two editions of a local newspaper within a fortnight, the first publication to be as soon as possible. If the authority do not arrange for publication, the Local Ombudsman may do so at their expense (s. 31(2)(D)–(H)).

The 1989 Act also provided for the abolition of the representative bodies. Each Commission is now under a duty to submit its annual reports and the reports of each of the relevant local commissioners to such persons as appear to the Commission to represent authorities in England or Wales (as the case may be) or, where there are no such persons, to the authorities themselves. Responsibility for the publication of reports rests with each Commission, which must give the persons or authorities to whom the report was submitted an opportunity to comment upon it.

Question

M. Jones, in 'The Local Ombudsmen and Judicial Review' [1988] *Public Law,* 608–22, commenting on the proposals which are now enshrined in the amendments introduced by the Local Government and Housing Act 1989, states at p. 622 that: 'The reform now proposed is so modest that it is difficult to see how it can effect any significant or lasting change in the behaviour of local authorities.' Do you agree with this statement?

Note

In the Annual Report for 1994–95, it is reported that, together all of the Local Commissioners used the power to require publication of a statement on 9 occasions.

Prior to the amendments in 1989 there was considerable discussion of the implementation of the recommendations of the Local Ombudsmen. The Select Committee of the PCA itself suggested that the 'best method of providing support for local ombudsmen's reports would be for our remit to be extended to allow the possibility of our calling recalcitrant local authorities to account' (see the *Third Report of the Select Committee on the PCA* HC 448 of 1985–86, para. 31). Proposals have also been made to make the recommendations of the Ombudsmen enforceable in court.

JUSTICE-All Souls Report on Administrative Law (1988) paras 5.84–5.97

Appraisal of the Select Committee's recommendation

5.84 The proposal of the Select Committee on the PCA . . . that it should supervise compliance by local authorities with the recommendations of the Local Ombudsman deserves serious consideration. In its favour it may be said that supervision by the Select Committee would afford the opportunity for regular oversight rather than the episodic review which might result from a system of *ad hoc* court enforcement . . .

5.85 There are, however, counter-arguments. In the first place there is the inevitable encroachment on the independence of local government. The spectre of political contests being fought between local councillors and a Parliamentary Committee over local issues is an unattractive one. The ultimate consequence of continued defiance by a local authority would presumably be that it would be in contempt of Parliament and subject to punishment accordingly. Unlike ministers, who are in contention with the Select Committee, councillors cannot take part in debate and defend themselves on the floor of the House of Commons.

5.86 Our own conclusion on this matter is that the implementation of the Select Committee's proposal is likely to be so hazardous that it should only be adopted if there is no better answer to hand. Accordingly we turn to consider the strength of the arguments against the court enforcement route.

The arguments against court enforcement

5.87 The Representative Body for England has argued that if the Northern Ireland enforcement model was to be imported here every investigation by a Local Ombudsman would start off as one likely to end up in the courts. The investigation would virtually be on a judicial basis, the system would be lengthened, more costly, and to the detriment of the complainant because of the longer time taken in arriving at a decision . . .

5.88 At the Edinburgh Conference the arguments against judicial enforcement were forcefully put . . . [Criticisms were made] of the way in which the ombudsman system sometimes works. The troublesome cases tended to be those in which the ombudsman's findings of maladministration were felt by the authorities concerned to be wrong. Sometimes the ombudsmen were thought to be entering into the forbidden area of policy and into the merits of the particular decision under investigation rather than confining themselves (as they should) to the steps by which the decision was reached. [Criticisms were also made] of the inquisitorial methods followed by the Commissioners if these were to form the procedural prelude to a recommendation which could be judicially enforced. Thus, he said that the local authority did not usually see the full terms of the complaint and was put in the position of having to answer specific questions while ignorant of the case made against it. There was no provision between the two sides, or confrontation between the two sides, no evidence on oath, and no opportunity for testing by cross-examination. Finally, it was contended that there would be no objection to making maladministration which caused injustice justiciable by the courts. What was objectionable was to bring within the ambit of the court's powers only those cases where an opinion on the issue of maladministration had already been formed by an ombudsman on facts found by him.

Our proposal on enforcement in relation to further reports made by the local ombudsmen

5.89 While recognizing the force of the above objections, we have concluded that enforcement through the courts does offer the best solution to what has become a major problem. We have recounted the continuing history detailed above of failures by a minority of local authorities to comply with the recommendations contained in further reports made by Local Ombudsmen. The combined total of further reports issued in England, Wales and Scotland was at 31 March 1986 issued in England, Wales and Scotland was at 31 March 1986 160, of which 120 ended in failure. We have taken into account the other evidence which we have recounted . . . of lack of co-operation and the lukewarm support of the local authorities associations. As we have shown, the Local Commissioners are treated contemptuously by some local authorities and the public are repeatedly being made aware of their inability to achieve results. Thus, the impotence of the Local Ombudsmen formed the theme of three articles published in *The Times* on successive days . . . under the titles 'Investigators without enforcement power', 'Case still drags on after three years', and 'Injustices that go unresolved'. The second article detailed a current case where the complainant, having failed to receive the remedy recommended in two reports by the ombudsman, lodged a new complaint alleging maladministration by the council in not implementing the first two reports.

5.90 We think that the time has now come to add teeth to the ombudsman scheme by making it possible for successful complainants to apply to the country court or, in Scotland, the sheriff court for appropriate relief. The time has passed for saying 'One day it may be necessary to consider enforcement powers.' The hour has come. As regards the objection which we have set out above . . . we think that the fears on the ground of delay and formalism are exaggerated. The system has worked well in Northern Ireland and we think it should now be tried in England, Wales and Scotland. If . . . the ombudsmen stray outside their statutory jurisdiction, the powers of the courts can be invoked to restrain them.

5.91 As the system of first reports and further reports is already well established we would not propose any change in that. The 'mischief' at which we are striking is failure or refusal to comply with further reports. The conditions precedent to the application to the court would be:

(a) a first report containing a finding in favour of the person aggrieved that he had suffered injustice in the consequence of maladministration;

(b) a further report (following on the authority's failure or refusal to implement the first report) containing a recommendation as to the action which it would be appropriate for the authority to take to remedy or compensate for the injustice;

(c) a certificate from the Local Ombudsman issued to the complainant to the effect that the local authority had a reasonable time within which to comply with his further report and that no action to his satisfaction had been taken by the local authority, and further certifying that the case was, in his opinion, an appropriate one for application to the court for relief.

5.92 We propose a certificate as in (c) above because, in the first place, the authority must have some time within which to comply with the further report and we feel that it would be wrong to allow legal proceedings to be launched prematurely. What is a reasonable time will vary with the circumstances. . . . Secondly, we think that it is important that the Local Ombudsman should officially record his view that there has been no compliance or that the purported compliance does not satisfy him. As we have seen, some local authorities go through the motions of redressing a grievance but fail to provide the remedy that the Local Ombudsman regards as adequate. Finally, we have a special reason for requiring the Local Ombudsman to certify that in his opinion the case is an appropriate one for an application to the court. A study of the annual reports of the Local Commissioners shows that in some cases where a further report has been ignored the only recommendation made was that the authority should make a written apology. Other cases have involved a recommendation for the payment of a trifling sum of money or for a local authority to take action in relation to some highly personal matter (such as altering the precise language of an entry in a Book of Remembrance at a council crematorium). The system might be brought into ridicule if the coercive power of the court were to be invoked in such cases or others of a sensitive nature where a Local Commissioner would judge that more harm than good would be done by permitting the complainant to go to court. In the ordinary case, however, where there was a recommendation for a substantial payment or for the taking of action that could appropriately be enforced by injunction there would be no difficulty in obtaining the certificate. Nevertheless, we think that it is too facile simply to suggest that all recommendations which have not been complied with should be enforceable in the courts.

5.93 We propose that the court itself should have the same discretion as regards the relief to be granted as is conferred upon the county court in Northern Ireland when dealing with cases where the Commissioner for Complaints has found maladministration causing injustice . . . . The effect would be that the court has both a discretion as to the type of relief which should be granted and a discretion to withhold relief altogether.

5.94 We also consider that while section 7 of the Northern Ireland Act [the Commissioner for Complaints Act (Northern Ireland) 1969] provides a valuable precedent to which reference may be made, it would be inadvisable to follow its provisions literally. We are particularly concerned about section 7(8) which makes the Commissioner's report available as evidence in the legal proceedings. The report is not made conclusive evidence; the subsection goes no further than to state that the report 'shall, unless the contrary is proved, be accepted as evidence of the facts stated therein.' This raises the possibility that the defendant authority in any legal proceedings might try to reopen the whole matter investigated by the Local Commissioner and seek to establish that the facts found in his report were wrong and that his conclusions on maladministration and resulting injustice were also ill-founded. As we have shown, recalcitrant authorities not infrequently adopt the line that the ombudsman's report is mistaken, that there has been no maladministration and that the complainant is in any event not entitled to a remedy. Such local authorities, which are already undermining the voluntary system, based (as it is supposed to be) on the willing acceptance of the umpire's verdict, would not hesitate to use the law courts as the forum for seeking to demolish or gravely impugn ombudsmen's reports.

5.95 We are also concerned about the disadvantageous position of the complainant (plaintiff) in the litigation. He would be trying to uphold the Commissioner's report but he would be at a financial disadvantage in taking on the local authority in what might become protracted litigation. Furthermore, he might well be unable to give strict proof of all the material facts in the report. Sources of information which were available to the Local Ombudsman in preparing his report might not be available to him as a private litigant . . .

5.96 These considerations make it necessary, in our view, to entrench and protect the findings of fact made by the Local Ombudsman in his report and further report and his conclusions that there has been maladministration causing injustice to the person aggrieved (the plaintiff) . . . .

5.97 The statutory protection for the reports and findings of Local Ombudsmen which we advocate would not, of course, preclude a local authority from showing that in a particular instance the ombudsman had stepped outside his jurisdiction. On ordinary principles the protection would not avail the ombudsman in such circumstances.

Note
Where the Commissioner for Complaints in Northern Ireland makes a finding that an individual has sustained injustice in consequence of maladministration, the individual may apply to the county court, and the court may award 'such damages as the court may think just in all the circumstances to compensate' the applicant for loss or injury suffered on account of (a) expenses reasonably incurred, and (b) lost opportunity of acquiring benefit (Commissioner for Complaints Act (Northern Ireland) 1969, s. 7(2)). If it appears to the court that justice can only be done by ordering that body to take or refrain from taking some action, then the court may, if satisfied that in all the circumstances it is reasonable so to do, grant a mandatory or other injunction (s. 7(3)). In addition, where maladministration coupled with injustice has been found, and it appears to the Commissioner for Complaints that the body concerned has previously engaged in conduct of the same kind and is likely to continue to engage in future in conduct of the type which he has condemned, he may request the Attorney-General to apply to the High Court for appropriate relief, such as an injunction to restrain the continuation of the maladministration (s. 7(5)). From 1978–88 there were on average three applications each year to the county court by successful complainants. The Attorney-General has, however, never been asked to make an application (see the *JUSTICE-All Souls Report on Administrative Law* (1988), pp. 123–5 for a discussion of the role of the Commissioner for Complaints in Northern Ireland and White (1994) 45 NILQ 395 on the Northern Ireland enforcement provision).

Questions
1. Do you consider it is necessary to introduce further reforms relating to the enforcement of the recommendations of either the PCA or the Local Commissioners?
2. Do you agree with the *JUSTICE-All Souls Report's* rejection of the reasoning of the Select Committee (see further C. Himsworth, 'Parliamentary Teeth for Local Ombudsmen' [1986] *Public Law* 546–50)?
3. In Lewis et al., *Complaints Procedures in Local Government* (1988), the view was expressed, at p. 39, that court enforcement was not a good solution:

> We became convinced that enforcement would imperil that relationship [the relationship between the commissioners and the local authorities] and make local authorities 'minimalist' in their response and particularly defensive. Anything which might be enforced by a court would be hard fought over and agreed with maximum reluctance. Currently some of the Ombudsmen find that the lack of firm recommendations, at least at the preliminary stage, allows them to see what the local authority will offer. Again, some of them appear to adopt the practice of telephoning a chief executive and asking what kind of recommendation the authority would best respond to, and what in particular might be acceptable to the elected member. We strongly believe that such co-operation would be placed in jeopardy by . . . [court enforcement].

If the recent reforms do not go far enough and court enforcement is not desirable, what other solutions might there be?

A complainant's unhappiness with an investigation may not be about the response of the authority complained against but with the way in which the PCA has conducted the investigation.

R v *Parliamentary Commissioner for Administration, ex parte Dyer*
[1994] 1 All ER 375
Divisional Court, Queen's Bench Division

The applicant had complained to the PCA through an MP about the handling of claims for certain benefits by the Department of Social Security. The PCA found injustice caused by maladaminstration and recommended an ex gratia payment and an apology. The applicant was dissatisfied with the PCA's report and sought judicial review of the PCA's decision not to re-open the investigation on the grounds that (i) the PCA had only investigated some of her complaints; (ii) that while he had given the Department the opportunity to comment upon the report in draft, he had not given the applicant that opportunity; (iii) that he had decided not to re-open the investigation after being informed of the failure to consider a number of the applicant's complaints; and (iv) he had wrongly considered himself precluded from re-opening the investigation. The PCA contended that, as the Parliamentary Commissioner Act 1967, s. 5 provided that the PCA initiated investigations on reference by, and reported back to, an MP, and because he was subject to oversight by a select committee that the court had no jurisdiction to review his exercise of discretion under the 1967 Act as he was answerable solely to Parliament about the discharge of his responsibilities. Alternatively the court could only review the PCA for exceptional cases of abuse of power.

SIMON BROWN LJ: . . . As to his wider proposition — that this court has literally no right to review the PCA's exercise of his discretion under the 1967 Act (not even, to give the classic illustration, if he refused to investigate complaints by red-headed complainants) — Mr Richards submits that the legislation is enacted in such terms as to indicate an intention that the PCA should be answerable to Parliament alone for the way he performs his functions. The PCA is, he suggests, an officer of the House of Commons, and, the argument runs, the parliamentary control provided for by the statute displaces any supervisory control by the courts. Mr Richards relies in particular on these considerations: first, the stipulation under s. 5 that a complaint must be referred to the PCA by a member of Parliament before even his powers of investigation are engaged; second, the requirement under s. 10(1) to report back to the member of Parliament (and, in certain circumstances, to each House of Parliament — see s. 10(3)); third, the requirement under s. 10(4) annually to lay a general report before Parliament; fourth, the provision under s. 1(3) of the Act for the PCA's removal from office only in the event of addresses from both Houses of Parliament. Mr Richards points also to the PCA being always answerable to the select committee.

Despite these considerations I, for my part, would unhesitatingly reject this argument. Many in government are answerable to Parliament and yet answerable also to the supervisory jurisdiction of this court. I see nothing about the PCA's role or the statutory framework within which he operates so singular as to take him wholly outside the purview of judicial review.

I turn next, therefore, to Mr Richards's alternative and narrower submission that, by analogy with the two House of Lords cases already mentioned, the courts should regard their powers as restricted with regard to reviewing the PCA's exercise of the discretions conferred upon him by this legislation.

I need cite one passage only from the speeches in those two cases, this from Lord Bridge's speech in *Hammersmith and Fulham London BC* v *Secretary of State for the Environment* [1990] 3 All ER 589 at 637, [1991] 1 AC 521 at 597:

> The restriction which the *Nottinghamshire* case [1986] 1 All ER 199, [1986] AC 240 imposes on the scope of judicial review operates only when the court has first determined that the ministerial action in question does not contravene the requirements of the statute, whether express or implied, and only then declares that, since the statute has conferred a power on the Secretary of State which involves the formulation and the implementation of national economic policy and which can only take effect with the approval of the House of Commons, it is not open to challenge on the grounds of irrationality short of the extremes of bad faith, improper motive or manifest absurdity. Both the constitutional propriety and the good sense of this restriction seem to me to be clear enough. The formulation and the implementation of national economic policy are matters depending essentially on political judgment. The decisions which shape them are for politicians to take and it is in the political forum of the House of Commons that they are properly to be debated and approved or disapproved on their merits. If the decisions have been taken in good faith within the four corners of the Act, the merits of the policy underlying the decisions are not susceptible to review by the courts and the courts would be exceeding their proper function if they presumed to condemn the policy as unreasonable.

Mr Richards concedes that the analogy between the position considered there and that arising here is not a very close one. He submits, however, that the underlying rationale for restricting the scope of judicial review in those cases applies also here. Although, as counsel recognises, the PCA's functions are manifestly not political, nevertheless, he submits, the provisions here for parliamentary control afford this case a comparable dimension.

This submission too I would reject. There seems to me no parallel whatever between, on the one hand, decisions regarding the formulation and implementation of national economic policy — decisions 'depending essentially on political judgment . . . for politicians to take . . . in the political forum of the House of Commons' — and, on the other hand, decisions of the PCA regarding the matters appropriate for investigation and the proper manner of their investigation.

All that said, however, and despite my rejection of both Mr Richards's submissions on the question of jurisdiction, it does not follow that this court will readily be persuaded to interfere with the exercise of the PCA's discretion. Quite the contrary. The intended width of these discretions is made strikingly clear by the legislature: under s. 5(5), when determining whether to initiate, continue or discontinue an investigation, the commissioner shall 'act in accordance with his own discretion'; under s. 7(2), 'the procedure for conducting an investigation shall be such as the commissioner considers appropriate in the circumstances of the case'. Bearing in mind too that the exercise of these particular discretions inevitably involves a high degree of subjective judgment, it follows that it will always be difficult to mount an effective challenge on what may be called the conventional ground of *Wednesbury* unreasonableness (see *Associated Provincial Picture Houses Ltd* v *Wednesbury Corp* [1947] 2 All ER 680, [1948] 1 KB 223).

Recognising this, indeed, one may pause to wonder whether in reality the end result is much different from that arrived at by the House of Lords in the two cases referred to, where the decisions in question were held 'not open to challenge on the grounds of irrationality short of the extremes of bad faith, improper motive or manifest absurdity'. True, in the present case 'manifest absurdity' does not have to be shown; but inevitably it will be almost as difficult to demonstrate that the PCA has exercised one or other of his discretions unreasonably in the public law sense.

Before passing from this part of the case I should mention briefly two authorities with regard to the exercise of the courts' review jurisdiction over local commissioners' reports — *R* v *Comr for Local Administration, ex p Eastleigh BC* [1988] 3 All ER 151, [1988] QB 855, and *R* v *Comr for Local Administration, ex p Croydon London BC* [1989] 1 All ER 1033. Only in *Ex p Eastleigh BC* [1988] 3 All ER 151 at 157–158, [1988] QB 855 at 866 was the jurisdictional issue raised, Lord Donaldson MR stating:

> Let me start with the fact that Parliament has not created a right of appeal against the findings in an ombudsman's report. It is this very fact, coupled with the public law character of the ombudsman's office and powers which is the foundation of the right to relief by way of judicial review.

Mr Richards accepts that the scheme, and indeed language, of the Local Government Act 1974, which created local commissioners, is very similar to that of the 1967 Act (on which it was clearly based), but he draws our attention to certain particular differences which he suggests are possibly material, and he submits that merely because local commissioners have been held reviewable by the courts it does not follow that Parliament intended the PCA's powers under the original legislation to be reviewable. For my part I find it unnecessary to consider this submission in any depth. For this reason: both these local commissioner cases appear to have been concerned not with reviewing the exercise of the local commissioner's discretion but rather with the examination of his powers; what was being alleged was that he had contravened the requirements of the statute. There can surely be no possible question but that the court's supervisory jurisdiction exists for this purpose and, indeed, Mr Richards has not submitted to the contrary. To my mind, therefore, these local commissioner cases do not advance the argument one way or the other with respect to the court's jurisdiction to review the exercise of the PCA's discretionary powers. But of course it follows from my already expressed conclusion upon that point that I would regard the exercise of the local commisioner's discretion as reviewable too. Again, however, only with inevitable difficulty. As Lord Donaldson MR said in *Ex p Eastleigh BC* [1988] 3 All ER 151 at 158, [1988] QB 855 at 867:

> . . . I am very far from encouraging councils to seek judicial review of an ombudsman's report, which, bearing in mind the nature of his office and duties and the qualifications of those who hold that office, is inherently unlikely to succeed . . .

Both those cases were, of course, concerned with judicial review applications by local authorities against whom the local commissioner had reported adversely. Certainly no greater encouragement should be afforded to those whose complaints the commissioner has investigated; their prospects of success are clearly no higher.

Recognising the full width of our jurisdiction but with those considerations in mind I turn to Miss Dyer's grounds of challenge.

As to her contention that the PCA investigated some only of her original grounds of complaint, that is undoubtedly the case. But is she entitled to criticise the PCA for taking that course? More particularly, was the PCA acting outside the proper ambit of his discretion under s. 5(5) of the 1967 Act in doing so?

The following two passages in his report are relevant: first from para 14:

> In her letter of complaint [Miss Dyer] gave examples of what she considered maladministration by the local and regional offices. I decided to investigate six main aspects — (i) an inaccurate letter, (ii) an unnecessary appeal, (iii) the withdrawal of her benefit without a decision, (iv) the failure to issue decisions, (v) inaccurate information and (vi) unanswered correspondence.

And from para. 17:

> The papers supplied to me by both Miss Dyer and the DSS contained much correspondence, minutes, notes of interviews and notes of telephone conversations. I have not found it either necessary or expedient to set them all out in detail in my report; but they have all been scrutinised and taken into account in reaching these findings. It is clear that Miss Dyer received a very poor service from the local office. There were problems in the handling of her correspondence, which was often unanswered, in making, or purporting to make, decisions on her claims and in the general relationship between the local office and Miss Dyer. I do not propose to address each and every shortcoming in the local office's conduct of the case but the following are my findings on the six main elements of her complaint.

He then set out his findings in some considerable detail.

In my judgment, the PCA was entitled in the exercise of his discretion to limit the scope of his investigation, to be selective as to just which of Miss Dyer's many detailed complaints he addressed, to identify certain broad categories of complaint (the six main aspects as he called them) and investigate only those. Inevitably such an approach carried the risk that some of the problems which Miss Dyer complained of having experienced with the local office would continue, and that indeed is what Miss Dyer says has occurred. But no investigation should be expected to solve all problems for all time and it cannot in my judgment be said that the approach adopted here by the PCA was not one properly open to him,

Turning to Miss Dyer's complaint that the draft report was sent to the department for comment on the facts but not to her, the respondent's evidence indicates that this is a practice which has existed for 25 years, and is known to and acquiesced in by the select committee. The reasons for it are explained as follows. First, that it is the department rather than the complainant who may subsequently be called upon to justify its actions before the select committee and, if it is shown the draft report and does not point out any inaccuracy, it will then be unable to dispute the facts stated in it. Second, the practice affords the department an opportunity to give notice in writing to the PCA, as expressly provided for by s. 11(3) of the 1967 Act, of any document or information the disclosure of which, in the opinion of the relevant minister, would be prejudicial to the safety of the state or otherwise contrary to the public interest. Third, sight of the draft report gives the department the opportunity to propose the remedy it is prepared to offer in the light of any findings of maladministration and injustice contained in it. The commissioner can then include in his final report what that proposed remedy is and indicate whether he finds that it satisfactorily meets the need.

Miss Dyer recognises, I think, that the same reasons do not exist for sending the draft report to her. Indeed, having regard to s. 11(3), it could not be sent to her unless and until it had already been cleared by the department. Therefore, to graft on to the existing practice a need to show the draft report to complainants too would introduce a further stage into the process. Does natural justice require this? I do not think so. As Lord Bridge said in *Lloyd* v *McMahon* [1987] 1 All ER 1118 at 1161, [1987] AC 625 at 702:

> My Lords, the so-called rules of natural justice are not engraved on tablets of stone. To use the phrase which better expresses the underlying concept, what the requirements of fairness demand when any body, domestic, administrative or judicial, has to make a decision which will affect the rights of individuals depends on the character of the decision-making body, the kind of decision it has to make and the statutory or other framework in which it operates.

Assuming, as I do, and indeed as Mr Richards concedes, that the PCA makes a decision which will affect the rights of Miss Dyer, it should nevertheless be borne in mind that it is the department and not her who is being investigated and who is liable to face public criticism for its acts. I cannot conclude that fairness here demanded that she too be shown the draft report. Rather it seems to me that the PCA, in determining the procedure for conducting his investigation as provided for by s. 7(2), was amply entitled to consider it appropriate to follow his long-established practice.

I come finally to Miss Dyer's complaint about the PCA's refusal to reopen this investigation. This I can deal with altogether more shortly. It seems to me that the PCA is clearly correct in his view that, once his report had been sent to Mr Hattersley and the DSS (as required by s. 10(1) and (2)), he was functus officio and unable to reopen the investigation without a further referral under s. 5(1). Section 5(5), as already indicated, confers a wide discretion indeed; it does not, however, purport to empower the PCA to reopen an investigation once his report is submitted. It would seem to me unfair to the department and outside the scheme of this legislation to suppose that the PCA could do as Miss Dyer wished.

That apart, however, it is plain that even if the PCA had had the power to reopen his investigation he would inevitably have refused to do so: he had long since decided not to investigate Miss Dyer's further complaints and I have already held that he was entitled to limit his investigations in that way.

It follows that, in my judgment, none of Miss Dyer's grounds of challenge can be made good and this application accordingly fails.

Application refused

Questions

1. Why does it appear that the PCA fares better in judicial review proceedings than the Local Commissioners?

2. If the Department or body complained against can check the facts in a draft report for accuracy, why is this denied to an complainant?

3. Is the PCA subject to less oversight than the bodies he supervises, and if so, what are the reasons for this?

(G) REFORM OF THE INSTITUTION OF THE OMBUDSMAN

The preceding sections have raised questions about the desirability of reform of the institution of the ombudsman. Occasionally more wide-ranging reforms have been suggested.

C. Harlow, 'Ombudsmen in Search of a Role' (1978) 41 MLR 446, 450–453

[Sir Idwal Pugh, a former Parliamentary Commissioner for Administration] sees his office:

> as having two functions. One is the statutory one of investigating individual complaints and, where appropriate, recommending remedies for individual injustices sustained through maladministration. The other is to draw attention to lessons which should be learned from such individual cases and applied to improving administrative practices generally.

. . . [T]he advocates of reform direct their attention to those barriers which seem to hinder the PCA from processing the maximum number of 'small claims.' It is argued, for example, that if the 'MP filter' were removed, more 'suits' could be 'filed'; and that if the PCA possessed powers of command, he could, like a court, enforce his 'judgments'.

These are fallacious arguments, because PCA procedure is not really appropriate to handle a large number of 'small claims.' . . . [T]he PCA prefers investigatory to adversarial procedures. But although he makes visits to departments and on occasion interviews claimants, the emphasis is always on the case-file . . . Investigation procedure is thorough but costly . . . it is time consuming . . .

Obviously the PCA cannot abandon the investigation of individual complaints if only because, without complaints, grave administrative deficiencies would rarely come to light. But the arguments for removal of the 'MP filter' should be rigorously examined. The new compromise according to which the PCA forwards complaints received directly from the public to the constituency MP may be the ideal solution. It remedies the problem that not all complaints returned for resubmission through the proper channels will be resubmitted. Yet it allows the MP to settle the trivial administrative muddles, resubmitting only the hard nuts. Even then the PCA probably needs to develop a subsidiary procedure for the very small cases to run alongside his 'Rolls-Royce method'. . . .

When we turn to the second Ombudsman function, which may appropriately be termed the 'Parliamentary Commissioner' role we find the PCA is uniquely well placed to undertake the task, and that his procedures are entirely appropriate. . . . Furthermore, no other institution exists which can perform exactly this function. Parliamentary questions are a blunt instrument. The classic doctrine of Ministerial Responsibility may actually shelter more administrative blunders than it exposes. The efficacy of court orders is limited by the absence of supervisory powers. The PCA on the other hand, has available to him all the information on which the disputed decision was based. He has behind him the considerable authority of a Parliamentary Select Committee. He may issue special reports, if necessary, successively. It is submitted, therefore, that his *primary* role should be that of an independent and unattached investigator, with a mandate to identify maladministration, recommend improved procedures and negotiate their implementation. Changes in his jurisdiction and procedures should be made only if they facilitate the execution of this task.

If this is right, the individual complaint is primarily a mechanism which draws attention to more general administrative deficiencies . . .

There are two deductions to be drawn. First, the PCA should not allow himself to be tempted into areas outside the mainstream of the administrative process which he is technically ill-equipped to handle . . . Secondly, the essential question with regard to access is whether the PCA should be given power to intervene of his own initiative. It is submitted that he should.

Question
Did this conception of the proper role of the ombudsman institution play any part at all in the discussions which preceded the establishment of the first Ombudsman, the PCA, in 1967?

Note
The Select Committee of the PCA, in its reports (HC 615 of 1977–78 and HC 33 of 1993–94), recommended that if, on the basis of previous complaints, the PCA believed that a particular office was working inefficiently, he should be able, subject to the Committee's approval, to mount a systematic investigation with a view to making recommendations for putting things right.

Question
Does this recommendation meet the suggestion of Harlow?

The Government's response to the suggestion of the Select Committee is outlined below.

Fourth Report from the Select Committee on the Parliamentary Commissioner for Administration (Review of Access and Jurisdiction) of Session 1977–78: Observations by the Government
Cmnd 7499 (1977), paras 17–19

(k) The Commissioner should draw Parliament's attention to any unforeseen injustices resulting from the legislation

17. The Government believe that where the Commissioner finds a complaint to relate to the content of legislation rather than to maladministration, he is already free to do so. However, as the Select Committee make clear, it is important to avoid any suggestion that the Commissioner might act as a constitutional court attempting to over-ride Parliament's decisions. It is for Parliament to consider whether legislation requires amendment, and it is open to Parliament, if it so wishes, to take note of any relevant findings of the Commissioner based on his investigation of complaints from members of the public which he has investigated.

(l) The Commissioner should be able [subject to the approval of the Select Committee] to carry out inspections of branches or establishments of bodies within his jurisdiction

18. The Government note the Select Committee's rejection of investigation by the Commissioner of direct evidence of possible maladministration; but that the Committee suggest he should be able to extend the scope of his enquiries ' if, for example on the basis of complaints which he had investigated and upheld, the Commissioner had reason to believe that a particular branch or establishment . . . was not dealing efficiently with its business.' The Committee think that the Commissioner should be able, subject to their approval, 'to carry out a systematic investigation of all aspects of the work of the branch or establishment in question, with a view to identifying the cause of the problem and making recommendations for putting it right'.

19. This would represent a significant change in the nature of the Commissioner's role which the Government believe would be both unnecessary and undesirable. It

would place a heavy burden on the Commissioner if he were required in effect to 'audit' the administrative competence of government departments and would distract him and his staff from their central purpose of investigating individual complaints. However, where the Commissioner investigates a series of complaints relating to a particular area of administration, he is, as a result of his normal investigations, able to form a clear view of the procedures in force there and to make any recommendations which he sees fit in consequence. Any lessons to be drawn from investigation by the Commissioner are already studied by departments and acted upon. In the nature of the present system of access to the Commissioner, the complaints which he investigates tend to be substantial ones. Section 10(2) of the Act provides that in all cases the Commissioner shall send a report of the results of his investigation to the Principal Officer of the department concerned. The department is thus in a position to consider whether the act of maladministration was an isolated one, or whether it discloses wider deficiencies. The Government believe that it should be for Ministers and their departments to decide what action is necessary to prevent further maladministration by a particular branch or establishment, and to be answerable, as may be necessary, to Parliament for the adequacy of the action which has been taken to this end.

Notes

1. The *JUSTICE-All Souls Report on Administrative Law* expressed its support for the limited extension of jurisdiction of the powers of the PCA favoured by the Select Committee in 1978 (paras 5.10–5.15, pp. 90–2)

2. The *Widdicombe Report,* which was concerned only with local government, considered that the Local Ombudsmen should have power to act on their own initiative where there was reason to suppose that injustice had occurred (p. 222). The *JUSTICE-All Souls Report on Administrative Law* favoured allowing the Local Ombudsmen to conduct a systematic investigation of the work of a department or part of it where, on the basis of individual complaints, the Commissioner has reason to believe a department is not being run properly and either the local authority consents or the Secretary of State gives his approval (see paras 5.105–5.106).

Questions

1. In reaching its conclusion the *Widdicombe Report* referred to research undertaken by JUSTICE in 1976–77 which showed a very strong middle-class bias among complainants to the Local Ombudsmen, with over 70 per cent of complaints being made by non-manual households. It considered that 'a power to take the initiative in an investigation could help towards redressing this imbalance.' Do you think it could, and if so why?

2. Does the Government's response suggest any particular view of the role of the PCA ?

Note

Although the Ombudsmen's role (both that of the PCA and the Local Ombudsmen) is thus at present primarily directed to the redress of individual grievances, their recommendations do, in certain circumstances, have a more wide-ranging effect. For example, a finding in one case may lead the authority concerned to review its policies and procedures. In addition there is some evidence that the very existence of the Ombudsmen has led some authorities to review their existing procedures for dealing with complaints and, generally, to take steps to avoid maladministration. As a result of amendments introduced by the Local Government and Housing Act 1989, Local Commissioners have power (following consultation) to issue advice and guidance about good administrative practice either to particular local authorities or all authorities (see Local Government Act 1974, s. 23(12)(A)–(B)). The Commission for Local Administration has now produced three sets of Guidance on Good Practice: Devising a Complaints System (February 1992), Good Administrative Practice (August 1993) and Council Housing Repairs (August 1993). Various commentators had urged that the Ombudsmen were well placed to produce guidance, especially on good administrative practice: *JUSTICE-All Souls* (1988), Lewis *et al.*, *Complaints procedures in Local Government*, (1988) and C. Crawford 'Complaints, Codes and Ombudsmen in Local Government' [1988] *Public Law*, 246.

The PCA, as P. Birkinshaw and N. Lewis (*When Citizens Complain* 1993, p. 123) note, has not been as active as the Local Commissioners with regard to the function of improving administration. In its 1993 report, the Select Committee on the PCA recommended that:

(a) the PCA should produce occasional publications on good administration;
(b) the government should introduce legislation to grant the Ombudsman the power to conduct audits of the operation of administrative procedures of bodies within his jurisdiction;
(c) epitomes of PCA reports which would point out matters of concern and good practice should be circulated amongst departments by the Office of Public Service and Science (OPSS);
(d) the OPSS should produce a booklet on the work of the Ombudsman for distribution amongst civil servants (HC 33 of 1993-94 paras. 33–40).

Questions

1. Would the nature of the institution of the Ombudsmen alter if they took on a greater role in administrative audit?

2. If so, would this alteration have an impact on the ability of the PCA or the Local Commissioners to perform their present functions? (See further, C. Crawford, 'Complaints, Codes and Ombudsmen in Local Government' (1988) *Public Law*, 246–67.)

11 STATUTORY TRIBUNALS

(A) INTRODUCTION: THE RATIONALE FOR TRIBUNALS

Concern about the growth of tribunals and their functions and procedures prompted the formation of the Committee on Administrative Tribunals and Inquiries in 1955. The Committee reported in 1957, and several of its recommendations are discussed below. The Committee also dealt with inquiries, but this topic is not covered in this chapter.

The Report led to important reforms in the Tribunal and Inquiries Act 1958. The major provisions of this Act were subsequently re-enacted first in the Tribunals and Inquiries Act 1971 and then, with minor amendments, in the Tribunals and Inquiries Act 1992, which is set out below. In addition, there are many specific legislative provisions governing the procedure at particular tribunals (see, for example, the Social Security (Adjudication) Regulations 1986). Reference to the Act will be required throughout this chapter.

TRIBUNALS AND INQUIRIES ACT 1992

1.—(1) There shall continue to be a council entitled the Council on Tribunals . . . —

(a) to keep under review the constitution and working of the tribunals specified in Schedule 1 . . . and from time to time, to report on their constitution and working;

(b) to consider and report on such particular matters as may be referred to the Council under this Act with respect to tribunals other than the ordinary courts of law, whether or not specified in Schedule 1 to this Act, or any such tribunal;

. . .

2.—(1) Subject to subsection (3) of this section the Council shall consist of not more than fifteen nor less then ten members appointed by the Lord Chancellor and the Lord Advocate, and one of the members shall be so appointed to be chairman of the Council.

. . .

3.—(1) Persons appointed under section 2 of this Act shall hold and vacate office under the terms of the instruments under which they are appointed but may resign office by notice in writing to the Minister or Ministers by whom they were appointed; and any such person who ceases to hold office shall be eligible for re-appointment.

. . .

4.—(1) Subject to the provisions of this section, any report by, or reference to, the Council shall be made to or, as the case may be by, the Lord Chancellor and the Lord Advocate.

. . .

5.—(1) Subject to section 6 but without prejudice to the generality of section 1(1)(a) of this Act, the Council may make to the appropriate Minister general recommendations as to the making of appointments to membership of any tribunals mentioned in Schedule 1 to this Act or of panels constituted for the purposes of any such tribunals; and (without prejudice to any statutory provisions having effect with respect to such appointments) the appropriate Minister shall have regard to recommendations under this section.

(2) In this section 'the appropriate Minister', in relation to appointments of any description, means the Minister making the appointments or, if they are not made by a Minister, the Minister in charge of the government department concerned with the tribunals in question.

. . .

6.—(1) The chairman, or any person appointed to act as chairman, of any of the tribunals to which this subsection applies shall (without prejudice to any statutory provisions as to qualifications) be selected by the appropriate authority from a panel of persons appointed by the Lord Chancellor. . . .

(6) In this section 'the appropriate authority' means the Minister who apart from this Act would be empowered to appoint or select the chairman, person to act as chairman, members or member of the tribunal in question. . . .

7.—(1) Subject to subsection (2) of this section, no power of a Minister other than the Lord Chancellor, to terminate a person's membership of any such tribunal as is specified in Schedule 1, or of a panel constituted for the purposes of any such tribunal, shall be exercisable except with the consent of:

(a) the Lord Chancellor, the Lord President of the Court of Session and the Lord Chief Justice of Northern Ireland, if the tribunal sits in all parts of the United Kingdom;

(b) the Lord Chancellor and the Lord President of the Court of Session, if the tribunal sits in all parts of Great Britain;

(c) the Lord Chancellor and the Lord Chief Justice of Northern Ireland, if the tribunal sits both in England and Wales and in Northern Ireland;

(d) the Lord Chancellor, if the tribunal does not sit outside England and Wales;

(e) the Lord President of the Court of Session, if the tribunal sits only in Scotland;

(f) the Lord Chief Justice of Northern Ireland, if the tribunal sits only in Northern Ireland.

8.—(1) The power of a Minister . . . to make, approve, confirm or concur in procedural rules for any tribunal specified in Schedule 1 shall be exercisable only after consultation with the Council.

. . .

(4) In this section 'procedural rules' includes any statutory provision relating to the procedure of the tribunal in question.
. . .

10.—(1) Subject to the provisions of this section, where:
(a) any tribunal specified in Schedule 1 to this Act gives any decision; . . .
it shall be the duty of the tribunal or Minister to furnish a statement, either written or oral, of the reasons for the decision if requested, on or before the giving or notification of the decision, to state the reasons.
(2) The statement referred to in subsection (1) may be refused, or the specification of the reasons restricted, on grounds of national security.
(3) . . .
(4) Subsection (1) does not apply to any decision taken by a Minister after the holding by him or on his behalf of an inquiry or hearing which is a statutory inquiry by virtue only of an order made under section 16(2) unless the order contains a direction that this section is to apply in relation to any inquiry or hearing to which the order applies.
(6) Any statement of the reasons for a decision referred to in paragraph (a) or (b) of subsection (1), whether given in pursuance of that subsection or of any other statutory provision, shall be taken to form part of the decision and accordingly to be incorporated in the record.
(7) If, after consultation with the Council, it appears to the Lord Chancellor and the Lord Advocate that it is expedient that—
(a) decisions of any particular tribunal or any description of such decisions, or
(b) any description of decisions of a Minister
should be excluded from the operation of subsection (1) of this section on the ground that the subject-matter of such decisions, or the circumstances in which they are made, make the giving of reasons unnecessary or impracticable, the Lord Chancellor and the Lord Advocate may by order direct that subsection (1) of this section shall not apply to such decisions.

11.—(1) Subject to subsection (2), if any party to proceedings before any tribunal specified in paragraph 8, 15(a) or (d), 16, 18, 24, 26, 31, 33(b), 37, 44 or 45 of Schedule 1 is dissatisfied in point of law with a decision of the tribunal he may, according as rules of court may provide, either appeal from the tribunal to the High Court or require the tribunal to state and sign a case for the opinion of the High Court.
(2) Subsection (1) shall not apply in relation to proceedings before industrial tribunals which arise under or by virtue of any of the enactments mentioned in section 136(1) of the Employment Protection (Consolidation) Act 1978.

Note
H. W. R. Wade's *Administrative Law* (7th edn) (1994) contains further details of the rights of appeal (see pp. 956–63).

All the textbooks covering the topic of tribunals comment on the proliferation of tribunals during the twentieth century and the great variety of types of tribunals (see e.g. Wade and Bradley, *Constitutional and Administrative Law* (1992), chapter 28, De Smith and Brazier, *Constitutional and Administrative Law* (1994), chapter 31). This variety makes it difficult to provide a generic account of the characteristics of tribunals. It is, however, generally accepted that many statutory tribunals are a mechanism for resolving disputes which arise in the operation of particular governmental schemes. Why are such tribunals established?

Report of the Committee on Administrative Tribunals and Enquiries
Cmnd 218 (1957), paras 20–22, 26–27, 29–32

20. It is noteworthy that Parliament, having decided that the decisions with which we are concerned should not be remitted to the ordinary courts, should also have decided that they should not be left to be reached in the normal course of administration. Parliament has considered it essential to lay down special procedures for them.

Good administration

21. This must have been to promote good administration. Administration must not only be efficient in the sense that the objectives of policy are securely attained without delay. It must also satisfy the general body of citizens that it is proceeding with reasonable regard to the balance between the public interest which it promotes and the private interest which it disturbs. Parliament has, we infer, intended in relation to the subject-matter of our terms of reference that the further decisions or, as they may rightly be termed in this context, adjudications must be acceptable as having been properly made.

22. It is natural that Parliament should have taken this view of what constitutes good administration. In this country government rests fundamentally upon the consent of the governed. The general acceptability of these adjudications is one of the vital elements in sustaining that consent. . . .

26. At this stage another question naturally arises. On what principle has it been decided that some adjudications should be made by tribunals and some by Ministers? If from a study of the history of the subject we could discover such a principle, we should have a criterion which would be a guide for any future allocation of these decisions between tribunals and Ministers.

27. The search for this principle has usually involved the application of one or both notions, each with its antithesis. Both notions are famous and have long histories. They are the notion of what is judicial, its antithesis being what is administrative, and the notion of what is according to the rule of law, its antithesis being what is arbitrary.

. . .

29. The rule of law stands for the view that decisions should be made by the application of known principles or laws. In general such decisions will be predictable, and the citizen will know where he is. On the other hand there is what is arbitrary. A decision may be without principle, without any rules. It is therefore unpredictable, the antithesis of a decision taken in accordance with the rule of law.

30. Nothing that we say diminishes the importance of these pairs of antitheses. But it must be confessed that neither pair yields a valid principle on which one can decide whether the duty of making a certain decision should be laid upon a tribunal or upon a Minister or whether the existing allocation of decisions between tribunals and Ministers is appropriate. But even if there is no such principle and we cannot explain all the facts, we can at least start with them. An empirical approach may be the most useful.

31. Starting with the facts, we observe that the methods of adjudication by tribunals are in general not the same as those of adjudication by Ministers. All or

nearly all tribunals apply rules. No ministerial decision of the kind denoted by the second part of our terms of reference is reached in this way. Many matters remitted to tribunals and Ministers appear to have, as it were, a natural affinity with one or other method of adjudication. Sometimes the policy of the legislation can be embodied in a system of detailed regulations. Particular decisions cannot, single case by single case, alter the Minister's policy. Where this is so, it is natural to entrust the decisions to a tribunal, if not to the courts. On the other hand it is sometimes desirable to preserve flexibility of decision in the pursuance of public policy. Then a wise expediency is the proper basis of right adjudication, and the decision must be left with a Minister.

32. But in other instances there seems to be no such natural affinity. For example, there seems to be no natural affinity which makes it clearly appropriate for appeals in goods vehicles cases to be decided by the Transport Tribunal when appeals in a number of road passenger cases are decided by the Minister.

Note

The authors of the report have candidly confessed that the principles they cite do not yield an explanation for why a particular decision should be laid upon a tribunal rather than upon a Minister. Other factors which may come into play are explored by Keith Hendry in the following article.

K. H. Hendry, 'The Tasks of Tribunals: Some Thoughts' (1982) 1 *Civil Justice Quarterly*, 253, 256–259

Tribunals as components of administration schemes

A peremptory glance at the governmental picture in a modern welfare state such as the United Kingdom, will show a multiplicity of tribunals each operating within the bounds of a confined jurisdiction and each directed toward disposing of claims and arguments arising out of a particular stautory scheme. So, for example, Supplementary Benefits Appeal Tribunals constituted under Schedule 4 of the Supplementary Benefits Act 1976 deal with the many disputes that arise from the grant or withholding of supplementary benefit; similarly under section 40 of the Finance Act 1972 (as amended) Value Added Tax Tribunals hear disagreements between tax officials and those liable to pay VAT. Many more examples could be given.

Parliament's enactment of various schemes and the inclusion within these schemes of specialist tribunals recognises firstly the social need for that scheme and secondly a social need for having machinery to dispose of disputes arising under that scheme. It is insufficiently stressed that as such tribunals have a task as essential parts of the machinery of administrative government.

So we see in particular the Council on Tribunals stressing that 'tribunals are bodies set up to *adjudicate* between the State and the individual . . .' with little mention of a tribunal's role in the administrative field. This is not to belittle their role as adjudicatory machinery, but at the same time their responsibilities to their schemes will be vitally important to administration. To take an example: under section 3 of the Mental Health Act 1959, 14 Mental Health Review Tribunals are constituted. They disposed of 696 cases in 1978. The gravity of these tribunals should not be underestimated – they are empowered to determine whether a patient shall be compulsorily detained, and so lose his personal liberty. As such they are vital to the administration of a particular social necessity recognised by legislation.

The Franks Report expressly recognises this factor, albeit in a somewhat guarded way. Having noted that 'Parliament' decided that certain decisions should not be dealt with by the ordinary courts, nor in the normal course of administration, the Report sees tribunals existing so as to 'promote good administration,' that is 'efficient in the sense that the objectives of policy are securely attained without delay,' but at the same time 'with reasonable regard to the balance between the public interest . . . and the private interest' '. . . adjudications must be acceptable as having been properly made.' Already we can see the emergence of the Franks bias, carried on today by its offspring, the Council on Tribunals, namely that what was important was the *correctness* of administration to the detriment of *administration* itself. Had more attention been paid to this task of tribunals one might have seen a greater recognition of its central importance and a consequent appreciation of tribunals as instruments of government. Having devised special procedures as essential elements of administration it can be inferred that tribunals have two further linked, but not quite so obvious, tasks. These are to avoid Ministerial Responsibility and to ease the workload of Governmental Departments.

Under the United Kingdom constitution, a Minister is primarily responsible to Parliament for his and his department's activities. Ultimately he is responsible to public opinion. Under a new legislative scheme it is a matter of choice as to whether decisions will be left to the Minister personally or to his Department. In both cases he remains responsible. However, if a dispute is to be decided outside the Department, for present purposes by a tribunal, the Minister will be able to disclaim responsibility for it. Furthermore, it will not be possible to bring political pressure to bear in order to affect that decision. The creation of a tribunal may therefore have as one of its purposes the evasion of Ministerial responsibility and the easing of Departmental workloads. So under section 12 of the Immigration Act 1971, one sees a two-tier appeal system; at first instance, adjudicators, and above them Immigration Tribunals. The volume of work done by these tribunals indicates the extent to which particularly the Home Office's workload is eased, and how a very politically sensitive decision is hived off to tribunals.

The decision to retain a decision within Departmental/Ministerial hands or to turn it over to a tribunal will, of course, be motivated by a number of factors: a 1980 Council on Tribunals Special Report felt that 'Parliament's' selection of subjects to be referred to tribunals does not form a regular pattern although basic guidelines and various factors included the nature of the decision, historical accidents, Departmental preferences and political consideration. The last-mentioned consideration could operate in both ways – one could give a matter which is potentially sensitive to a tribunal to desensitise it (the system of Immigration Tribunals is an example), or alternatively retain it for that reason within Departmental/Ministerial hands. Other factors would include the likely number of disputes, national interest, the level of discretion involved and so on, but one is forced to agree with the Council on Tribunals that there is no application of a set of coherent principles.

It seems, therefore, that the use of tribunals is a convenient means for affording Ministers immunity from responsibility to Parliament and public opinion for certain kinds of decision. It might even be argued that it is an aspect of 'good administration' for Departments to be denied and/or relieved of certain kinds of decisions which could expose them to pressures of many kinds – not least political.

The Franks Committee stressed that tribunals were not to be seen as 'appendages of Government Departments' . . . 'Parliament has deliberately provided for a decision outside and independent of the Department concerned' . . . 'the intention of Parliament to provide for the independence of tribunals is clear and unmistakable.' With respect, there seems to be a rather large degree of unadulterated constitutional fiction here. John Griffith argues strongly that it is completely wrong to refer to some theoretic notion of Parliamentary intention; tribunals he says are instituted in reality by the Government of the day and in effect it is the relevant Department which will make the rules. The Council on Tribunals expressly cited Departmental preferences as one of the factors relevant to the creation of a tribunal. In their Annual Report for 1975–76 the Council states specifically that the detailed arrangements for tribunals remains the responsibility of Departments. To say, therefore, that tribunals are created to ensure that decisions should be made independently of Departments is simply not valid. Griffith suggests that Departments simply do not want to be bothered with the sorts of decisions tribunals will make: the policy is settled; it only has to be administered and disputes sorted out.

I introduce all this merely to stress the important role of tribunals as rudimentary but nevertheless vital components of administration. Writers today still insist on taking issue with the term '*administrative* tribunals' as giving too much emphasis to the administrative associations that tribunals have: ever since Franks the 'machinery for adjudication' theme has been predominant. In particular the Council of Tribunals has seen its most important contribution as being 'our constant effort to translate the general ideals of the Franks Committee into workable codes of principle and practice . . .' As I have suggested it is my view that the Franks Report seriously underplayed the task of tribunals to be instruments of their respective administrative schemes. Be that as it may the Council on Tribunals continues the ideals of Franks with some zeal despite the fact that the Tribunals and Enquiries Act simply asks that they keep under review the constitution and working of Schedule 1 tribunals, report thereon and consider and report on matters as may be referred to them in respect of any tribunals other than courts of law. Is there not here some leeway for a more expansive notion of what tribunals are supposed to be doing?

Notes

1. On the role of the Council on Tribunals, see *post* at p. 717.

2. A recent and controversial example of apparent governmental disenchantment with a tribunal arose in the field of social security. Until 1986 there was an appeal from all claims concerning supplementary benefit, a means-tested benefit available to unemployed persons on low incomes. Such appeals were made to Supplementary Benefit Appeal Tribunals until 1984, when tribunals concerned with social security benefits were re-organised, and thereafter to Social Security Appeal Tribunals (SSATs). In 1986 changes were made under which supplementary benefit was replaced by income support, and a Social Fund was established to consider claims for specific items, such as furniture and clothing. Prior to this such claims had been made under the Single Payments regulations and appeals concerning single payments were dealt with by SSATs. The amended scheme did not, however, provide for any appeal from the Social Fund to an independent tribunal.

The reasoning of the Government was explained in the White Paper on *The Reform of Social Security* (1985) (Cmnd 9518), paras 2.107–2.112.

The Reform of Social Security

Cmnd 9518 (1985), paras 2.107–2.112

How the social fund will be run

2.107 The fund will be run from DHSS local offices by a group of specialist officers. Special expertise will be needed, based on specific training in relevant skills, such as interviewing, counselling, and knowledge of help available from other sources. Decision-making will rest more on casework, liaison with other bodies and discussion with claimants. There will need to be clear links with the work of social service and health professionals who may also be involved in helping the same person. The views of outside professionals may have a part to play in helping officers reach judgments on individual cases.

2.108 Such expertise is to an extent already possessed by special case officers who since 1980 have had a remit to help claimants whose cases present special difficulty. Special case officers' concerns include: claimants with difficulties in adjusting to major changes in their circumstances (such as marital breakdown or discharge after a long stay in hospital); cases where there are doubts about claimants' ability to care for themselves or their children; those who have problems in managing essential living expenses; and others whose characteristics may create tension in dealing with staff. The Government believe it is right to develop existing good practice in this area and to expand the responsibilities of special case officers.

2.109 Specialist staff will exercise their judgment in reaching decisions on individual cases. The basis of deciding social fund payments is rather different from traditional benefit decision-making. There is widespread recognition that the present adjudication arrangements for handling special needs have not worked satisfactorily. There is also widespread agreement that, in handling the special difficulties of a minority of claimants, the scheme needs a degree of flexibility that is only possible with discretion.

2.110 The Government recognise that people who have asked for help with particular pressures should have an effective means of questioning the outcome. In all organisations, management has the first responsibility to see that services are well handled. This basic principle applies just as much to the administration of benefits as it does to other areas. It is however clear that the present appeal arrangements in special needs areas can have a sledgehammer effect. The full weight of legal consideration can be brought to bear on matters which may involve small sums of money for particular items with considerable delays between initial decision and formal review. We do not believe that the present system of appeals has best served the claimant's prime interest of a quick and effective reconsideration of decisions. The result is too slow, too cumbersome, and too inflexible.

2.111 The first safeguard for claimants under the new arrangements will be a professional approach to the administration of the social fund. That is the reason for using specialist officers. Reviews which turn on judgment in difficult individual circumstances are best handled as near to the point of decision as possible. The further the review gets from the initial judgment both in terms of formality and time, the less equipped the reviewing authority is to judge whether the outcome is sensible. The Government therefore intend to provide for review by management as near as possible to where responsibility for the original decision rests. Just as social service and health care decisions are best taken locally by those directly responsible, so should the social fund be seen as an important responsibility of those administering it in local offices. The arrangements proposed by the Government involve judgment – local people are best placed to make that judgment.

2.112 The fund will work successfully only if there is a clear limit to its role; that is, if it concentrates on the special needs of a limited number of claimants. The fund will have a fixed annual budget. Some form of budgeting is the reality in most areas of social provision. The Government do not consider that this specialist part of the new arrangements should be any different.

Note

In the absence of a right of appeal, judicial review proceedings have been used to challenge the operation of the Social Fund (see *R* v *Secretary of State for Social Services, ex parte Stitt, The Times*, 5 July 1990).

Question

Does either the Franks Report or Hendry's article provide an explanation for these developments?

Notes

1. The removal of the right of appeal was criticised by the Council on Tribunals (see *post* at p. 726 for its role and subsequent developments).

2. The Franks Report referred to the natural affinity between, on the one hand, cases where the policy of legislation can be set out in detailed regulations and adjudication by tribunals and, on the other hand, cases where it is necessary to preserve flexibility in the pursuance of policy and ministerial decision-making. There are, however, tribunals which operate largely for the purposes of developing and applying policy (see, for example, the Independent Television Commission and the Monopolies and Mergers Commission). This has led some commentators to draw a distinction between court-substitute and policy-oriented tribunals (on this distinction see further, B. Abel-Smith and R. Stevens, *In Search of Justice*, pp. 20–21 and J. A. Farmer, *Tribunals and Government*, chapter 8).

3. The preceding extracts from the Franks Report have been concerned with the choice between providing an appeal to a Minister and providing an appeal to a tribunal. Assuming, then, that a decision has been made to establish a form of adjudication independently of the Department, what explains the decision to establish a tribunal rather than provide a statutory right of appeal to the courts?

Report of the Committee on Administrative Tribunals and Enquiries
Cmnd 218 (1957), paras 38–39

The choice between tribunals and courts of law

38. We agree with the Donoughmore Committee that tribunals have certain characteristics which often give them advantages over the courts. These are cheapness, accessibility, freedom from technicality, expedition and expert knowledge of their particular subject . . . But as a matter of general principle we are firmly of the opinion that a decision should be entrusted to a court rather than to a tribunal in the absence of special considerations which make a tribunal more suitable.

39. Moreover, if all decisions arising from new legislation were automatically vested in the ordinary courts the judiciary would by now have been grossly overburdened . . . We agree with the Permanent Secretary to the Lord Chancellor that any wholesale transfer to the courts of the work of tribunals would be undesirable.

Note

The Donoughmore Committee produced a *Report on Ministers' Powers*, Cmd 4060 in 1932 which concerned delegated legislation and tribunals and inquiries.

Questions
1. Are the two paragraphs consistent with each other? Is the objective of not overburdening the judiciary a special consideration in favour of establishing a tribunal?
2. What do these passages indicate about the Franks Committee's view on the desirable qualities of tribunals and, in particular, how those qualities should differ from those of the courts. See further *post* at p. 729.

Note
In De Smith and Brazier, *Constitutional and Administrative Law* (7th edn. 1994), the point is made, at p. 656, that:

> The climate of opinion has now changed. No longer must exceptional circumstances be present to justify the establishment of a special tribunal to determine controversies arising under regulatory or welfare legislation. We have fifty different *types* of these tribunals and some 2,000 tribunals altogether. If, for instance, the question of how disputes about the entitlement of dismissed workers to redundancy payments from their employers ought to be decided under a new Act, there is an *expectation* that the deciding body will be a special tribunal.

(B) THE GENERAL ORGANISATION OF TRIBUNALS

In recent years there has been concern about the proliferation of tribunals and the difficulties which this raises with regard to their supervision. This concern has focused attention both on the role of the Council on Tribunals and on the development of 'presidential systems'.

(i) Council on Tribunals

Tribunals and Inquiries Act 1992, ss. 1–5 (*ante* at pp. 708–709).

Note
In 1980 the Council on Tribunals reviewed its work and made certain recommendations for improvements.

The Functions of the Council on Tribunals
Cmnd 7805 (1980), paras 2.4–2.8, 5.4–5.5, 6.3, 6.7–6.10, 6.14, 7.3, 7.5, 7.7, 7.9–7.10, 7.17–7.19, 9.1–9.2, 9.5–9.8, 9.10

The Franks Committee and subsequent legislation
2.4 The Committee recommended that the two Councils on Tribunals, one for England and Wales and the other for Scotland, should be set up to supervise tribunal and inquiry procedures. The report stressed the importance of continuous supervision: the supervising bodies would be consulted whenever it was proposed to establish

a new type of tribunal, and would also keep under review the constitution and working of existing tribunals. The Council for England and Wales would be appointed by and report to the Lord Chancellor . . .

2.5 As proposed by the Franks Committee, the Council on Tribunals would have had important executive powers as well as advisory ones. For example, they would have been empowered to appoint the members (as distinct from the chairmen) of tribunals; to review the remuneration of tribunal appointments; to give advice on the basis of which the duties and conduct of tribunal clerks would be regulated; and to formulate procedural rules for tribunals, in the light of the general principles enunciated by the Committee.

2.6 The main powers which were in fact conferred on us and on the Scottish Committee of the Council by the Tribunals and Inquiries Act of 1958 were subsequently embodied in the Act of 1971. They may be paraphrased as follows:

(a) to keep under review the constitution and working of the tribunals specified in Schedule 1 to the Act;

(b) to consider and report on particular matters referred to the Council by the Lord Chancellor and the Lord Advocate with respect to any tribunal other than an ordinary court of law, whether or not specified in Schedule 1; and

(c) to consider and report on such matters as may be so referred, or as the Council may consider to be of special importance, with respect to administrative procedures which may involve the holding by or on behalf of a Minister of a statutory inquiry.

2.7 Our powers are thus consultative and advisory, not executive; and in certain respects they are more limited than the Franks Committee recommended. We have no function with regard to the remuneration or conditions of service of tribunal chairmen, members of staff: and no power to make appointments or to formulate rules.

2.8 However, we must be consulted by the appropriate rule-making authority before procedural rules are made for any tribunal specified in Schedule 1 to the 1971 Act and on procedural rules made by the Lord Chancellor in connection with statutory inquiries. We must be consulted before any scheduled tribunal can be exempted from the requirement under section 12 of the Act to give reasons for its decision upon request. (Note this requirement is now in section 10 of the Tribunals and Inquiries Act 1992.) The same situation applies to Ministerial decisions taken after a statutory inquiry. We may make general recommendations to appropriate Ministers about tribunal membership. We are required to make an Annual Report to the Lord Chancellor and the Lord Advocate, which must be laid by them before Parliament with such comments, if any, as they think fit. . . .

Some problems

5.4 Under the heading of matters requiring statutory attention, our committee considered the lack of clarity as to the extent of our general jurisdiction in relation to tribunals; our lack of a specific power to investigate complaints; and the absence of any requirement that we be consulted on proposed primary legislation affecting tribunals or inquiries, and of any power to require our views [expressed in response to statutorily prescribed consultation] to be made public.

5.5. The last mentioned point is of particular importance. From time to time we have been consulted by a Minister and our views have not been accepted. Ministers are, of course, fully entitled to disregard our recommendations, but a statement in Parliament or in regulations that action has been taken after consultation with us is then – although strictly correct – misleading because it gives the impression that we agreed with the course adopted . . .

[The Council went on to recommend that a Minister be required to inform Parliament of the extent to which the Council's recommendations have been given effect and the reasons why any of them has not been accepted.]

Some features of the Council's work

6.3. Our most important contribution over the years has, we believe, been our constant effort to translate the general ideals of the Franks Committee into workable codes of principles and practice, accepted and followed by all those responsible for setting up administrative tribunals, devising their manner of operation and, indeed, serving upon them as chairmen and members. . . .

6.7 The points with which we are particularly concerned at the formative stage are all directed to improving the ability of citizens to challenge administrative decisions affecting their interests. For example, we are vigilant in seeking to ensure that people are given a hearing as of right in suitable cases, and are not denied one if they request it; that rights of appeal are granted wherever appropriate and not eroded where they already exist; and that parties to tribunal proceedings are treated equitably, neither side being given an unfair advantage. . . . .

6.8 In relation to the constitution of tribunals we have (following a recommendation of the Franks Committee) advocated that chairmen should, in most cases, be legally qualified: and we have lost no opportunity of recommending the 'presidential' system of organisation under which a particular class of tribunal has a national president or chairman and, where the number of tribunals in that class justifies it, regional chairmen as well . . .

6.9 Some of the safeguards which we are anxious to secure are best embodied in primary legislation or procedural rules. This applies, for example, to provisions governing time-limits within which rights of appeal must be exercised and various procedural steps taken. Another example is the giving of properly reasoned decisions by tribunals. In relation to this matter we are fortified by a statutory provision, but it is also necessary for us to monitor the observance of this practice so far as we are able to do so. For instance, we found it necessary to issue detailed advice to Supplementary Benefit Appeal Tribunals as to how they should interpret and implement the duty to give reasons which is placed on them by the relevant rules. This advice is repeated in the official guide to the procedure of tribunals.

6.10 Our interest is not, however, limited to matters which figure in Acts of Parliament or procedural rules. For example, we are particularly concerned that tribunals should be able to cope effectively with the volume of business coming before them, and the appearance of a substantial back-log of cases awaiting decision has caused us to intervene on several occasions. We take constant interest in the fitness and accessibility of the premises in which tribunal hearings are held, and make representations if premises appear to be unsuitable – for example, because of their lack of provision for disabled people, or because of their location in relation to the offices of the responsible Government department.

[The report continued to stress the role of the Council in providing proper training and in ensuring the independence of clerks.]

6.14 In all our work in connection with tribunals we have to bear in mind that they do not represent a single homogeneous group but vary widely in their constitution, membership, functions and organisation. . . .

Complaints

7.3 We have no statutory jurisdiction in relation to complaints, but during the Parliamentary proceedings which led to the enactment of the Tribunals and Inquiries

Act 1958 it was indicated by a Government spokesman that we would be able to deal with complaints. In our early years the handling of complaints – in the absence of any other machinery for dealing with them - bulked quite large in our work. For some years our Annual Report provided details of the more important investigations which we carried out. . . .

7.5 We can usefully consider complaints drawing attention to some procedural difficulty which points to the need for an amendment of rules or an alteration of administrative practice. Even in relation to complaints of this type, however, we are conscious that we can very rarely give any direct satisfaction to an individual who has complained. . . .

7.7 The Parliamentary Commissioner cannot consider the substance of any matter which has been referred to a tribunal or public inquiry, but he can investigate a department's administrative handling of its own procedures before and after a tribunal or inquiry hearing. He can also investigate the way in which public local inquiries are conducted. In relation to tribunals, the actual proceedings and decisions are outside the jurisdiction of the Parliamentary Commissioner. . . .

7.9 Where a complaint is in substance an attempted appeal on the merits or a protest against an adverse decision, we are convinced that we should not attempt to deal with it. Such complaints can properly be entertained only by the tribunal or court (if any) empowered to deal with appeals from the particular tribunal concerned, or to carry out a judicial review. Substantial cases of procedural error can also be challenged in court proceedings, and it is clearly desirable that if such a remedy exists it should be used.

7.10 This leaves us with the problem of deciding how best to deal with the residual body of complaints arising from the hearings of tribunals. We see no difficulty in continuing to handle those representations which can be satisfactorily answered without carrying out an investigation. The main difficulty for us lies in those cases where there is a suggestion of procedural deficiencies but conflicting accounts are given of the same events, because we have no means of getting at the truth by interviewing people or calling for files and other papers. After making whatever inquiries are possible in the circumstances we frequently have to say that there is a conflict of evidence which cannot be resolved. Inevitably, time is taken up by these inquiries, and this may increase the disappointment felt by some complainants with the results of our investigations.

7.17 To give us a wide statutory power for the handling of complaints would almost inevitably have certain consequences. The work-load would increase, with heavier pressure on the members; and there would be repercussions on staffing and accommodation. Although unlikely, it is also possible that our present relationship with Government Departments might be endangered, and the chairmen and members of tribunals and inspectors at statutory inquiries might become less co-operative than they now are. In the long run, the balance of our work might be significantly changed, with the focus shifting to our role as ombudsman for tribunals and inquiries, in priority over our existing functions. This in our view would be undesirable.

7.18 On balance, therefore, although we propose that we should be given specific responsibility for complaints in relation to our field of work, it is important that the extent of our jurisdiction be clearly defined. The power could be on the following lines:

(a) a member of the public alleging a procedural irregularity in a hearing before a tribunal or statutory inquiry would be entitled to make a formal complaint to us;

(b) we would then have to consider whether the complaint *prima facie* raised a substantial point of principle relating to procedure;

(c) if we came to that conclusion, we would be empowered to obtain papers and other information from the relevant tribunal or inquiry and from the Government department concerned, to question the complainant and any other person involved, and to submit a report to the complainant, the department and, at our discretion, to anyone else . . .

(d) if we decided that the complaint did not *prima facie* raise a substantial point of principle we would refer the matter without comment to the department concerned, who would be required to report to us the outcome of their own inquiries.

7.19 In addition to this action on complaints from members of the public, we would be empowered at our discretion to conduct an investigation into an alleged procedural irregularity referred to us by the department concerned. We would not, however, at any time investigate a complaint relating to the merits of a decision or recommendation; or concerning the conduct of chairmen or members; or which fell within the competence of the Parliamentary Commissioners; or which could reasonably form the basis of an appeal or some other proceeding in a court of law. An investigation which we had undertaken would be discontinued if, it any stage, it appeared that one of these grounds of exclusion applied. And we would not, unless the circumstances were wholly exceptional, seek to intervene during the currency of tribunal or inquiry proceedings.

What is needed – a general perspective

9.1 The purpose of this chapter is to discuss briefly the more general aspects of the Council's responsibility for keeping under review the constitution and working of bodies in the field of administrative adjudication. We have already emphasised the importance of specific knowledge of the functions of different classes of tribunals and types of inquiries. But there is another dimension to our work, which involves taking a 'bird's eye view' of the territory falling within our jurisdiction. In this connection we believe the Council are in a unique position. With the changes recommended in this report we should be able to make a continued contribution – indeed, a more positive and constructive one – to the development of an effective and well planned system.

9.2 The case for a statutory advisory body with this kind of general oversight appears to us to be even stronger now that at the time of the Franks Committee. Since then the tendency for issues arising out of legislative schemes to be referred to tribunals has continued unabated, in a largely piecemeal manner. Not only has there been considerable growth in the number of tribunals, they are operating increasingly in difficult and sensitive areas – for example, immigration, compulsory detention under the mental health legislation, misuse of drugs, equal pay, redundancy, unfair dismissal from employment, and supplementary benefits.

. . .

9.5 Since we were set up, significant changes have also taken place in the general constitutional and administrative climate. There is, for example, a movement towards greater formalism in procedures for settling disputes. The process started with reforms following the Franks Report which, in general, made tribunals more like courts. It had to be demonstrated that tribunals were not adjuncts of Government departments and that in their decision-making they followed a judicial process. Since then the trend towards judicialisation has gathered momentum with the result that tribunals are becoming more formal, expensive and procedurally complex. Consequently they tend to become more difficult for an ordinary citizen to comprehend and cope with on his own. There is, we believe, an urgent need to keep the whole of this movement under the closest scrutiny. We believe that we are in a position to play a key role in the achievement of a right balance.

9.6 There is also a constant need, as was emphasised in discussion with our Committee, for an independent body able to offer advice to Government on what kinds of dispute are appropriate or inappropriate for adjudication by tribunals. We believe we can exercise this function, and can develop criteria indicating the kinds of decision which, if disputed, should be subject to review by processes external to the departments concerned; the most appropriate form of review; the degree of formality required, according to the type of decision; and whether a proposed tribunal should come under our supervision.

9.7 While we have always emphasised the basic elements of good practice common to all tribunals, we accept that there should be differences in their constitution and detailed procedures according to the complexity of their jurisdictions. The need to review the appropriateness of several classes of tribunals for the work they have to do seems to us to be overdue. Simplification is desirable wherever this is compatible with justice. Moreover, we think there is a case for transferring adjudication of some issues to the courts. . . .

9.8 Finally, we draw attention to particular problems running across the whole field which need co-ordination rather than piecemeal approach: for example, a much wider system for recruitment of tribunal members, including more women; arrangements for training of both chairmen and members; the presidential system; conferences and seminars; the publication of explanatory leaflets; and the clarification and simplification of official forms. . . .

9.10 . . . At present we are perhaps in a better position than any other official body to appreciate the wider implications of the particular matters referred to us, and to consider the important issues relating to the system as a whole to which they give rise. We therefore recommend strongly that the statutory power of the Council to act as a *general* advisory body in the field of administrative adjudication be placed beyond doubt.

Notes

1. One of the main advantages of tribunals is reputed to be their speed (see *post* at p. 734). It is therefore unsurprising that the Council on Tribunals has concerned itself with the problem of delays. See, for example, the following extract which shows concern about another aspect of the Child Support Arrangements which has been criticised by the PCA see *ante* p. 641.

Annual Report of the Council on Tribunals for 1994/95

HC 64 of 1994–95, paras. 1.35—50

1.35 **Here we record our continuing concern about delays in the hearing of appeals brought before the Child Support Appeal Tribunals. The delays are caused by the time taken by the Child Support Agency to provide submissions for consideration by the tribunals. The administrative problems of the Agency are well publicised. Its work is not our direct concern, but when visiting the tribunals we have seen examples of errors and delays by the Agency. Its continued problems inevitably affect the submission of appeals to the tribunals and make it more difficult for the tribunals themselves to dispose of appeals without adjournments or reference back to the Agency. The measures being taken to effect improvements within the appeal system which we describe in the following paragraphs are welcome, but cannot of**

themselves go to the root of the problems encountered by the Agency's clients before their cases reach the appeal stage.

1.36 We recorded last year our concern about the delays which were developing in the hearing of child support appeals. These delays arise chiefly out of the time taken for appeal submissions to reach the Child Support Appeal Tribunals (CSATs). The submissions are prepared by Child Support Officers (CSOs) within the Child Support Agency (CSA) and we reported that arrangements were being made for the preparation of submissions to be handled within a CSA central office.

1.37 We understand that this change has had an impact upon the output of submissions but it is clear from reports on monitoring that the quality of the work carried out at the initial decision making stage, on review, and in the preparation of the appeal submissions leaves much to be desired. The CSATs are revising 50–60% of all decisions which go before them on appeal. The introduction of new procedures, which we describe below, should alleviate some of the problems at present encountered by allowing an element of discretion to be exercised by the CSA, and the CSATs, in departing, in certain cases, from the fixed formula used for calculating maintenance assessments. Nevertheless, we expect that it will be some time before this system has settled down. We also expect that the new arrangements will need to be accompanied by training for the CSA staff and, indeed, for the CSATs. Moreover the measures themselves will almost certainly bring with them an increase in work for the CSATs, which could well increase the pressure overall on the appeal system.

Delays and the quality of appeal submissions

1.38 There is some evidence that the output of submissions to the CSATs, at least so far as quantity is concerned, is improving. The Chief Executive of the CSA, in a memorandum submitted to the House of Commons Social Security Committee on 16th March 1995, said that more cases were being cleared to the CSATs each month that were cleared in the whole of 1993–94, and there was hope that the current backlog would be cleared by the Summer 1995. The ITS statistics for June 1995 show that the number of appeals that were then awaiting a submission was 2,661, (compared with 2,686 as at September 1994).The number of cases actually listed during June 1995 was 445 (an improvement on the 122 listed in September 1994). On the other hand, ITS statistics also show that, in June 1995, the CSO's decision of 383 cases out of 519 cleared was revised, which is a clear indication of the scale of the problem. In September 1994, the number of appeals cleared was 148, and 84 of the CSOs decisions were revised. The clearance rate of the cases listed by the CSATs has increased since last year. In June 1995, an average of 2.42 cases were listed for each hearing (2.11 cases cleared), compared with 1.8 cases in September 1994 (1.6 cases cleared).

1.39 We discussed the difficulties faced by the CSOs and the CSATs with the President of the Independent Tribunal Service (ITS), Judge Bassingthwaighte, who took office in October 1994, and with Mr Ernie Hazelwood, the Chief Child Support Officer, who took office in March 1994.

Discussion with the President of the Independent Tribunal Service

1.40 The President, who came to talk to us in April 1995, said that there were significant problems with appeal submissions for the CSATs. These were gradually being addressed following the advent of the specialised unit set up by the CSA. However, the system was so complex that, even with advanced training, mistakes were bound to occur. Often the CSOs did not understand the problem 'on the ground'. He considered that greater effort should be concentrated on the first stage of the decision making process, indicating that it was too soon to question whether the statutory review required before a case can proceed to appeal contributed to delay overall. We mention the issue of statutory reviews at paragraph 2.145 below.

1.41 We also discussed with the President the implications for the appeal system of draft provisions in the Child Support Bill (see paragraph 1.45 below). The changes include a provision whereby an appeal could be lapsed at the review stage if the CSO's decision at that stage would be likely to satisfy the appellant. We expressed our concern that the CSO needed to be satisfied, before making such a decision, that all the issues arising in the appeal had been covered, in particular when a third party was involved. The President felt that many CSOs would not feel confident enough to deal with the new departure application cases. We also mentioned our views about the provision for a CSAT chairman to sit alone, in particular where, in cases of complexity, three heads might be better than one. The President envisaged that, in such circumstances, and where there were far wider issues, it would be appropriate to bring in the wing members to sit with the CSAT chairman. He considered that the CSAT's work would increase as a result of the new legislation.

First Report of the Chief Child Support Officer

1.42 We were very interested in the first Report produced by the Chief Child Support Officer (CCSO) on the performance of the CSOs. The overall standard was reported as being poor, with evidence of staggering errors. This suggested to us that there might be an issue about the extent to which making improvements to the system could result, not in simplification, but more complexity. The typical errors found in appeal submissions included insufficiency of argument, incomplete documentation, and support for a incorrect review decision. The CCSO, whose staff were working closely with the CSA to effect improvement, considered that the numbers of submissions examined during the year were too small to draw any conclusions but that this area of work would receive more attention during 1994/95. We will report further on this aspect of work next year.

Discussion with the CCSO

1.43 We had a helpful discussion on these matters with the CCSO in February 1995, and expressed concern that the proposed changes would have little effect if not accompanied by additional resources. Although not a matter for him, he understood that extra resources were to be made available to meet the new demands. He told us that there was at that stage within the CSA, a massive backlog of work and a turnover of staff with people still being trained but, in time, the CCSO considered that the staff should be extremely good. The CCSO pointed out that, apart from having to work within a complicated formula, the CSA staff had encountered several other changes since the creation of the Agency including amendments to the regulations. There would be further changes flowing from the new Bill including the departure directions, the work on which he understood might be concentrated in one office. He agreed that there were arithmetical problems which contributed to the high comment rate during the monitoring of decisions and reviews. A changed system of grading comments would enable a check to be made on whether the final assessment was accurate, and would highlight the significance of errors.

1.44 The CCSO confirmed that his staff were providing quarterly reports on performance to the CSA, attending quarterly meetings with senior staff, and working closely with the CSA to provide guidance. There was commitment to improvement on the part of the Chief Executive and the CSOs were keen to do a good job. The CCSO has our support in his efforts to achieve higher standards. We hope that the measures to which we refer below and the efforts of the CCSO's staff will lead to an improvement in the standards attained by the CSOs. The quality of their work has a high impact on the workload of the CSATs.

Child Support Act 1995

1.45 During the year, we considered the proposals for change to the child support system, some of which we refer to in the preceding paragraphs. The changes were first outlined in the White Paper 'Improving Child Support' and have been implemented by the Child Support Act 1995.

1.46 It was clear to us that the new measures would impact upon the CSAT's workload and we have urged the need for the ITS to be adequately resourced as a consequence. The new provisions include the introduction of a right to apply for a departure from a maintenance assessment where, for instance, there has been a previous 'clean-break' settlement between the parents of the child, and the amount allowed in the formula does not reflect adequately the effect of the capital transfer. The CSATs will be able to substitute their decision for that of the Secretary of State. We welcomed this provision, which introduced an element of discretion for the Secretary of State and the CSATs that had not previously been enjoyed, although we anticipated the possibility of it leading to more appeals, and more delay before cases are ready to be heard by the CSATs.

1.47 We were also surprised to note the insertion of a provision to enable a CSAT to consist of a chairman sitting alone. So far as we are aware, this is the first time where such a proposal has been made for tribunals within the ITS jurisdiction. The draft legislation gave no indication about the circumstances where a chairman could sit alone. We were concerned about the introduction of such a measure where the overall effect of the new provisions might make appeals more complicated, for instance, because of the terms of a previous divorce settlement, or because of the need to give consideration to the welfare of a child affected by the decision. There were other factors, such as the possible inconsistency of approach which might develop across the country with chairmen opting to exercise their discretion differently in relation to similar types of cases, and the absence of a requirement for the parties to consent to the chairman sitting alone. Furthermore, the parties might feel that they were not getting full measure without an appearance before a tribunal of three persons, and there was a risk of the loss of informed experience of absent members.

1.48 In their response to our observations, the Department said that no decisions had been taken as to when it might be appropriate for tribunals to be differently constituted, or whether certain types of case would be better heard by a chairman sitting alone. The intention was to provide as much flexibility as possible for the ITS. They believed that this approach, novel in social security matters, was justified by the very different jurisdiction which would be exercised by the CSATs in this area. On the question of the possible inconsistency in the approach to departure applications, the Department agreed that as far as possible, where discretion was to be exercised, there was a need for a consistent approach, whether the initial decision was taken by the Secretary of State, a full tribunal, or a chairman sitting alone. The area would be explored further with the ITS as would our suggestion about the question of obtaining consent to the hearing of an appeal by a chairman sitting alone. We shall give further attention to these issues when consulted upon the amending regulations.

1.49 The Act includes a provision which will enable an appeal to be lapsed if the decision reached by a CSO following a review of the decision under appeal is the same as that which would have been reached had every ground of the appeal succeeded. We welcomed this measure which should help to alleviate the unnecessary listing of cases which are, in effect, agreed. However, we considered that the CSO should first ensure the agreement of the appellant to the case being so resolved since a lapsed appeal would be, in effect, a withdrawn appeal. We put this to the Department of Social Security who informed us that such an approach had been considered. However, they anticipated that, in the majority of cases, the appellant would be content with the outcome. If he remained dissatisfied the appellant could exercise his right of appeal against that decision. We remained concerned. It seemed to us that where an appeal was allowed to lapse the appellant might not know that the appeal could be reinstated. We considered that this process would equate to a review, which did not make clear that there was a right not to accept the decision. We also considered that, in such cases, the non-appealing party would not have the opportunity to put forward his or her own views. The Department have since confirmed to us that both parties to an appeal will be advised that the appeal will lapse, and will be informed at that stage that they have a fresh right of appeal to a CSAT against the new decision. We welcome this confirmation.

1.50 We take this opportunity of recording our appreciation to the Department for notifying us at an early date about the proposed legislation and helpfully thereafter sending to us draft prints of the Bill. We were kept closely advised about policy and given detailed explanations about the intention behind several of the draft provisions. We were glad to have the opportunity of submitting our advice in good time.

2. The Council on Tribunals took the unusual step of issuing a special report in January 1986 in which it criticised the Government's decision not to provide an independent appeal from decisions relating to the new Social Fund (Cmnd 9722) (see *ante* p. 714). It considered that very good reasons were needed before a right of appeal which had existed for more than 50 years was abolished. The Council pressed for the restoration of such an appeal. The Government made no formal response to this, but, at the Report stage of the Social Security Bill in the Commons, it substituted a review of the decisions of the local Social Fund inspectors outside the local office management hierarchy. In the House of Lords a right of appeal from a Social Fund decision to a Social Security Appeal Tribunal was inserted. This was, however, removed in the Commons. The Social Security Act 1986 provided for a Social Fund Commissioner who is responsible for appointing Social Fund inspectors and checking their work, and who will report annually to the House of Commons (s. 35) (see now s. 65 of the Social Security Administration Act 1992). There is, however, no right of appeal to a SSAT from decisions of the Social Fund inspectors except with regard to payments for funerals and maternity.

3. The Government considered that the changes suggested by the Council in its 1980 report were largely unnecessary. It did, however, accept that its role in relation to consultation on procedural rules should be re-stated and made clearer. The Council drafted guidelines which provided that the optimum period of consultation should be two months for routine matters and four months for matters raising major issues of principle. The minimum periods were expressed to be four weeks and six weeks respectively (see the *Annual Report of the Council on Tribunals for 1986/87,* p. 53).

4. In its *Annual Report for 1990–91,* the Council on Tribunals devoted a special section to the publication of its Report on Model Rules of Procedure for Tribunals.

The Annual Report of the Council on Tribunals 1990/91
HC 97 of 1990–91, Part II, paras 2.4, 2.5

2.4 The compilation of model rules is designed to provide a comprehensive collection of rules for the use of Departments and tribunals engaged in drafting or amending rules for tribunals. The compilation is, however, not a code. It is a store from which Departments and tribunals may select and adopt what they need. In making their selection from the various provisions, we would expect Departments and tribunals to give careful consideration to what is necessary or useful for the purposes of the particular tribunal and not simply adopt the rule because it happens to be included in the Report. Moreover, we would expect them to modify or adapt the rules if the models do not fit the particular needs or circumstances of the tribunal and to add to the rules in the Report specialised rules required for particular tribunals' needs. Such amendments or additions are necessary because the function and jurisdiction of existing Tribunals is so varied that it is not possible to provide models to deal with all aspects of their respective procedures, let alone to anticipate the future.

2.5 As will be clear from the foregoing, we expect the primary users of the rules to be Departments and tribunals and we hope, and indeed expect, that close consideration will be given to them when rules of procedure for new tribunals come to be drafted, and when rules of existing tribunals come to be revised. By this means, we believe that, over what will no doubt be a substantial period of time, a certain degree of harmonisation of tribunal procedures will be effected. Such a harmonisation will be of great benefit to the tribunal system as a whole and will lead to increased clarity and ease of usage. But from the inception of the project it has been clear to us that, because of the variety of the functions and jurisdictions of tribunals, there are limitations on the extent to which we could provide simple, common form, procedural rules which would enable lay people appearing before tribunals to conduct their own cases – the end in view recommended by the Royal Commission in 1979. In our view, that aim is more properly met by explanatory guides issued by tribunals, while the rules themselves are directed primarily towards the tribunals and those who administer them. Nonetheless, we have tried to ensure that, so far as possible, the Report uses plain and uncluttered language, which, if adopted for the future, should help the parties to prepare their cases more effectively.

Questions

1. Yardley, commenting on the Council on Tribunals' special report in 1980, writes that:

> The main message coming from this report is nowhere directly expressed. But it is implicit from the comparatively minor nature of the recommendations that the Council is in fact working well, and that its achievements in the field of tribunals and inquiries have been substantial. It is a paradox that a body with a statutory constitution, but with no powers actually to achieve anything directly, should be so valuable. But it is submitted that this paradox is nonetheless true. (D. C. M. Yardley, 'The Functions of the Council on Tribunals' (1980) *Journal of Social Welfare Law,* 265.)

Do you agree?

2. Harlow and Rawlings, in *Law and Administration* (1984) draw a distinction between fire-fighting institutions, which are concerned with the redress of individual grievances, and fire watching institutions, which are more concerned with the general oversight of the administration. How would you classify the Council on Tribunals? Would this classification alter if the proposals in the special report in 1980 had all been accepted?

(ii) The presidential system

The Social Security Appeal Tribunals are organised on a presidential basis. This system is also used in the Pensions Appeal Tribunals and the Lands Tribunal. In such systems there is generally a full-time officer responsible for the overall administration and practice of a particular class of tribunals. What might the advantages of a presidential system be?

Annual Report of the Council on Tribunals for 1982/83
HC 129 of 1983–84, paras 2.15–2.16

Tribunal constitution – presidential system

2.15 We have frequently recommended the presidential system of organisation under which a particular class of tribunal has a national president or chairman and, where the number of tribunals in that class justifies it, regional chairmen as well. We have made a further study of the presidential system this year. We see as its advantages:—

(a) there is an obvious independence from the Government departments responsible either for decisions appealable to the tribunal or for its financing;

(b) a president can be responsible for the administrative arrangements, instead of a Government department having that role;

(c) he can appoint or advise on the appointment of tribunal chairmen, members, clerks and other staff;

(d) he can monitor the performance of tribunals, arrange for necessary training, and encourage consistency;

(e) co-ordination and communication between tribunals of the same type are facilitated and a sense of corporate identity and team spirit is fostered;

(f) the tribunal has a spokesman and a focal point for relationships and communication with other bodies; and

(g) a president may make interlocutory decisions and may give guidance about the allocation of cases and about other matters of practice and procedure.

In our view a presidential system ought to be established for a particular type of tribunal when a significant number of cases is dealt with every year and there is also an appreciable number of tribunals within the system, whether or not they sit in many locations or already have a regional organisation.

2.16 We favour the introduction of regional chairmen for certain types of tribunals where both the appointment of a national president is justified and the number of tribunals would make administration easier through regional centres. The appointment of regional chairmen also helps to spread the workload and responsibility, while keeping a central focus. However, we accept that in those types of tribunal which handle a comparatively small number of cases a looser structure of quasi-autonomous regional chairmen without a national president would be acceptable. In such circumstances we would expect the regional chairmen to meet reasonably frequently to plan and co-ordinate their work in relation to administration, training and the other matters which would otherwise be the responsibility of a president. One of the senior regional chairmen could act as a focal point and take responsibility for organising the regional chairmen's activities.

Questions

1. Does the presidential system contribute to the realisation of the aims of the Franks Committee (see *post* at pp. 729–731)?

2. Can you think of any disadvantages?

(C) THE CHARACTERISTICS OF TRIBUNALS

Report of the Committee on Administrative Tribunals and Enquiries

Cmnd 218 (1957), paras 40–42, 62-64, 71–72, 76–77, 90

[See also paras 38–39, *ante* at pp. 716]

40. Tribunals are not ordinary courts, but neither are they appendages of Government Departments. Much of the official evidence, including that of the Joint Permanent Secretary to the Treasury, appeared to reflect the view that tribunals should properly be regarded as part of the machinery of administration, for which the Government must retain a close and continuing responsibility. Thus, for example, tribunals in the social services field would be regarded as adjuncts to the administration of the services themselves. We do not accept this view. We consider that tribunals should be regarded as machinery provided by Parliament for adjudication rather than as part of the machinery for administration. The essential point is that in all these cases Parliament has deliberately provided for a decision outside and independent of the Department concerned, either at first instance (for example in the case of Rent Tribunals and the Licensing Authorities for Public Service and Goods Vehicles) or on appeal from a decision of a Minister or of an official in a special statutory position (for example a valuation officer or an insurance officer). Although the relevant statutes do not in all cases expressly enact that tribunals are to consist entirely of persons outside the Government service, the use of the term 'tribunal' in legislation undoubtedly bears this connotation, and the intention of Parliament to provide for the independence of tribunals is clear and unmistakeable.

The application of the principle of openness, fairness and impartiality

41. We have already expressed our belief, in Part 1, that Parliament in deciding that certain decisions should be reached only after a special procedure must have intended that they should manifest three basic characteristics: openness, fairness and impartiality. The choice of a tribunal rather than a Minister as the deciding authority is itself a considerable step towards the realisation of these objectives, particularly the third. But in some cases the statutory provisions and the regulations thereunder fall short of what is required to secure these objectives. . .

42. In the field of tribunals openness appears to us to require the publicity of proceedings and knowledge of the essential reasoning underlying the decisions; fairness to require the adoption of a clear procedure which enables parties to know their rights, to present their case fully and to know the case which they have to meet; and impartiality to require the freedom of tribunals from the influence, real or apparent, of Departments concerned with the subject-matter of their decisions.

Codes of procedure

62. Most of the evidence we have received concerning tribunals has placed great emphasis upon procedure, not only at the hearing itself but also before and after it. There has been general agreement on the broad essentials which the procedure, in this wider sense, should contain, for example provision for notice of the right to apply to a tribunal, notice of the case which the applicant has to meet, a reasoned decision by the tribunal and notice of any further right of appeal.

63. We agree that procedure is of the greatest importance and that it should be clearly laid down in a statute or statutory instrument. Because of the great variety of the purposes for which tribunals are established, however, we do not think it would be appropriate to rely upon either a single code or a small number of codes. We think that there is a case for greater procedural differentiation and prefer that the detailed procedure for each type of tribunal should be designed to meet the particular circumstances. . . .

Informality of atmosphere

64. There has been considerable emphasis, in much of the evidence we have received, upon the importance of preserving informality of atmosphere in hearings before tribunals, though it is generally conceded that in some tribunals, for example the Lands Tribunal, informality is not an over-riding necessity. We endorse this view, but we are convinced that an attempt which has been made to secure informality in the general run of tribunals has in some instances been at the expense of an orderly procedure. Informality without rules of procedure may be positively inimical to right adjudication, since the proceedings may well assume an unordered character which makes it difficult, if not impossible, for the tribunal properly to sift the facts and weigh the evidence. It should be remembered that by their very nature tribunals may be less skilled in adjudication than courts of law. None of our witnesses would seek to make tribunals in all respects like courts of law, but there is a wide measure of agreement that in many instances their procedure could be made more orderly without impairing the desired informality of atmosphere. The object to be aimed at in most tribunals is the combination of a formal procedure with an informal atmosphere. We see no reason why this cannot be achieved. On the one hand it means a manifestly sympathetic attitude on the part of the tribunal and the absence of the trappings of a court, but on the other hand such prescription of procedure as makes the proceedings clear and orderly.

Knowledge of the case to be met

71. The second most important requirement before the hearing is that citizens should know in good time the case which they will have to meet . . .

72. We do not suggest that the procedure should be formalised to the extent of requiring documents in the nature of legal pleadings. What is needed is that the citizen should receive in good time beforehand a document setting out the main points of the opposing case. It should not be necessary and indeed in view of the type of person frequently appearing before tribunals it would in many cases be positively undesirable, to require the parties to adhere rigidly at the hearing to the case previously set out, provided always that the interests of another party are not prejudiced by such flexibility.

Public hearings

76. We have already said that we regard openness as one of the three essential features of the satisfactory working of tribunals. Openness includes the promulgation of reasoned decisions, but its most important constituent is that the proceedings

should be in public. The consensus of opinion in the evidence received is that hearings before tribunals should take place in public except in special circumstances.

77. We are in no doubt that if adjudicating bodies, whether courts or tribunals, are to inspire that confidence in the administration of justice which is a condition of civil liberty they should, in general, sit in public. But just as on occasion the courts are prepared to try certain types of case wholly or partly *in camera* so, in the wide field covered by tribunals, there are occasions on which we think that justice may be better done, and the interests of the citizen better served, by privacy.

[The Committee went on to outline three types of case: where considerations of public security are involved, where intimate personal or financial circumstances have to be disclosed and where there are preliminary hearings involving professional capacity and reputation.]

Evidence

90. Tribunals are so varied that it is impossible to lay down any general guidance on the requirement of evidence at hearings. In the more formal tribunals, for example, the Lands Tribunal, there seems no good reason why some of the rules of evidence as in courts of law should not apply. In the majority of tribunals, however, we think it would be a mistake to introduce the strict rules of evidence of the courts. The presence of a legally qualified chairman should enable the tribunal to attach the proper weight to such matters as hearsay and written evidence.

Note

The Committee made a number of other more specific recommendations. For those relating to appointment, legal representation, appeals and the Council on Tribunals see, respectively, *post* at pp. 737–749 and *ante* pp. 717–718.

Other recommendations included the following:

(a) All tribunals should have power to administer the oath. The Franks Committee considered, however, that only those tribunals which are most akin to courts of law, for example, the Lands Tribunal, should be required to hear evidence on oath (para. 91).

(b) Applicants should have the right to apply to the tribunal for the issue of a subpoena requiring the attendance of a witness (para. 92).

(c) Unsuccessful applicants should not be required to pay costs, and both successful and unsuccessful applicants should be entitled to a reasonable allowance in respect of expenses (paras 94–97).

(d) Tribunals should give a statement of reasons in order to fulfil the requirements of fairness and to enable applicants to decide whether to exercise any right of appeal (para. 98).

(e) All final appellate tribunals should publish selected decisions. The Committee considered this would be of help, not only in satisfying the public that decisions were reasonably consistent, but also as a guide to appellants and their advisers (para. 102).

Question

Which of the provisions of the Tribunals and Inquiries Act 1992 seek to implement the recommendations in the report? (See *ante* at pp. 708–710.)

Note

As the Franks Committee recognised, the implementation of many of its objectives could not be achieved by general provisions in an Act, but only in the detailed provisions governing particular tribunals. For the role of the Council on Tribunals in this context, see *ante* at pp. 719 and 727.

Question

Are the Franks Committee's recommendations on the characteristics of tribunals consistent with its statement of the reasons for adjudication by tribunals rather than by the courts (*ante* at p. 716)? Consider the following extract, which also discusses the relevant provisions of the Tribunals and Inquiries Act and the role of the Council on Tribunals.

K. H. Hendry, 'The Tasks of Tribunals: Some Thoughts'
(1982) 1 *Civil Justice Quarterly*, 253, 255–256, 259–266

. . . [T]ribunals are seen as providing a form of 'administrative justice' as opposed to 'judicial justice.' To the English administrative lawyer this simply asks the average tribunal to be simpler, quicker, cheaper, more accessible, more expert and more flexible than the ordinary courts. As important as these characteristics are I hope to suggest that a concept of 'administrative justice' ought to go further than this. Linked to all these qualities a tribunal should have, is the need contemporaneously to act 'justly.' The Franks Committee, and using the ensuing Report as their basis, the Council on Tribunals, equated the task to act justly with a task to act judicially. One is forced to ask whether acting administratively justly and acting 'judicially' are in fact co-terminous?

Furthermore, since tribunals are meant to provide a system of administrative justice outside the normal courts we can infer that one of the tasks of tribunals is to lighten the regular courts' case-load, or to put it negatively, to avoid judicial justice in these matters. In keeping with classic constitutional principles, however, the ordinary courts were still to have powers of review and appeal; despite the fact that a rudimentary system of administrative justice was identifiable it was to go so far and no further – ultimately judicial justice would be paramount. This built-in paradox bears some examination, as does a further issue, namely the tension which must bear in on bodies that inhabit the twilight world of being theoretically divorced from the ordinary judicial hierarchy and at the same time independent of the administration.

It will have been gathered that tribunals could be classified as machinery for adjudication or for administration. The writer's view is that they are probably machinery for both – there seems to be no reason why the two functions cannot exist within one body. To fully understand this it is essential that a cogent concept of 'administrative justice' is developed and not to stop there: questions must be asked about the role and meaning of 'administrative law' and furthermore, about the nature of 'public law.' To some of these matters I now turn in greater detail . . .

The task of tribunals to provide 'administrative justice'

Writing in 1958 William A. Robson expressed the view that the Franks Report and, by implication, ensuing legislation have the effect of importing administrative justice into the general system of adjudication; in short there had been a reception of administrative justice.

There can be no doubt that an overriding purpose of the creation of specialised administrative tribunals was to institute a means of dealing with disputes outside the normal court hierarchies, but can this be described as 'administrative justice'? In England, the concept, if there is one, is rather woolly; it seems to mean no more and no less than those alternative means of dispute-settlement provided by statute under various administrative schemes. These alternative means, by and large tribunals, have certain advantages over the normal courts and they are preferable in certain circumstances; in essence, they do the same job (they resolve disputes) – thus the one is 'judicial justice,' if you like, and the other is 'administrative justice.'

The tendency is to leave it at that, to ask no more and to look no further. The Franks Committee was not asked to look at 'administrative justice' as a whole but only to consider and make recommendations in respect of the constitution and working of tribunals. The Committee could not, therefore, look at Departmental/Ministerial decisions in disputes between the citizen and public authorities. As Franks put it, in these circumstances the citizen was 'less protected against unfair or wrong decision.' The impact of Franks was to see tribunals as a rather specialised part of the machinery of justice. In consequence, and in accordance with traditional constitutional principle, tribunals were not to be severed from the regular courts who would, on the contrary, supervise their activities. Furthermore the Franks Committee favoured the view that all decisions of tribunals should be subject to review by the courts on points of law.

Classic systems of administrative justice provide a fully fledged hierarchy of administrative courts, equal in status to 'ordinary courts,' staffed by specialised judges, within a separate and self-contained structure. Common law 'ad-hocery' spawned tribunals devoid of any real concept of administrative justice, devoid also of the context of administrative justice, namely public law. Shocked eventually at the sight of 'tribunal proliferation,' reform did not attempt a uniform structure but concentrated rather on 'minimum standards' (fairness, openness, impartiality, etc.). The guardians of the system were, of course, to be the regular courts – any notion of the evolution of two distinct systems of law was deprecated, despite the fact that if one looked closely enough it was clear that two systems in fact existed. Would not tribunals have stood a better chance of fulfilling their essential tasks had the approach been different?

Despite the palpable lack of any principled, theoretical approach, it was felt by some that a form of 'administrative justice' existed in the system of tribunals. Tribunals, it was said, were possessed of certain characteristics, or at least, *should* be possessed of these characteristics, which when compared to 'judicial justice' made them, in certain circumstances, preferable. These characteristics are well known and self-explanatory, but a few words on each is not out of place for the simple reason that it is possible to argue that one of the major tasks of tribunals as a whole is to maintain these features which make them preferable to the ordinary courts.

(i) *Simplicity and informality*

It is argued that tribunals can adopt more informal methods, making it easier for the inexperienced to present their cases. Courts, on the other hand, adhere to the adversarial system (a judge sitting on high, observing the contest, ensuring that the rules are obeyed, assessing the performance, and giving judgment according to the evidence before him). This is, apparently, true of some tribunals, notably if they have to deal with a *lis inter partes,* but very often the issues before tribunals are essentially non-combative, such as: is X entitled to supplementary benefit? or, is Y well enough to be released from a mental hospital? Wraith and Hutchesson found that this factor very often went hand in hand with an informal atmosphere in many tribunals; the appellant was greeted by name, invited to sit down, the procedures casually explained and the surroundings were conspicuously devoid of the grandeur of judicial proceedings.

Through simplicity and informality it would seem that there has been a fairly large measure of success in making tribunals acceptable to the average man in the street. Indeed, there is a suggestion that the relatively more informal atmosphere of county court proceedings is in large measure due to the success it has had in tribunal operations.

On the other hand, there would appear to be a number of factors which, due to the view of tribunals in the United Kingdom, would detract from the simplicity and informality of tribunals; in particular the need and stress laid on the necessity for a legal chairman and quasi-legal procedures before, during and after hearings could well be counter-productive in this area. In this respect, the Tribunals and Inquiries Act requires consultation with the Council on Tribunals for the making, approving, confirming or concurring in Schedule 1, Tribunals' rules of procedure.

(ii) *Speed*

The delays occasioned by redress through the ordinary courts are notorious. Thus it has been stressed that an overriding advantage of specialised tribunals is their alacrity. It would be easy to take this for granted. The situation as a whole is undoubtedly better than in the courts, but the expedition of tribunals will vary from one to another. In 1973 it was found that Supplementary Benefit Appeal Tribunals matters were determined within two to four weeks, an appeal to a national insurance local tribunal took three to five weeks, and rent assessment committees dealt with their matters in two to three months. It can only be said that in this respect one cannot generalise; it is probably true that most tribunals provide reasonably speedy resolution of disputes, but some important Tribunals are not immune from delay. In this respect the work of the council of Tribunals has been valuable; they have highlighted delays and suggested improvements. Generally they have shown concern that tribunals should be able to cope effectively with the volume of business coming before them. More specifically, the council has highlighted delays in Immigration Appeals and also for National Insurance Commissioners. Furthermore, it should be noted that the whole purpose of speedy administrative justice can be obliterated by appeal/review by the ordinary courts – a subject returned to below.

(iii) *Cheapness*

Use of the normal courts is often an expensive way of resolving a dispute. Tribunals, on the other hand, are meant to be cheaper. This is undoubtedly so: the cost of officials and building comes out of public funds and in neither case is as expensive or grandiose as the courts with their well-paid officials. Similarly, the proceedings being flexible and informal, will normally not require expensive involvement of lawyers and officials in gathering evidence, presenting cases, and so on. It is probably this characteristic which most sharply distinguishes tribunals from the ordinary courts of law. The Franks Committee recognised that if tribunals were to be made truly accessible 'the citizen must be able to have recourse to them without running the risk of being out of pocket' and thus proposed that as a general principle a successful applicant should be given a reasonable allowance in respect of expenses and that an unsuccessful applicant should not only never have to pay any costs but should be entitled to the same reasonable allowance as the successful applicant. The proposal was largely accepted by the Government of the day, but even today a fairly wide spectrum of practice with regard to costs still operates. The attitude of the Council of Tribunals is to deal with this problem in an ad hoc, tribunal by tribunal, way; in particular they have consistently advocated that legal aid should be available in all tribunals in which legal representation is permitted.

(iv) *Accessibility*
The whole system fails if recourse to a tribunal is in any way difficult. Wraith and Hutchesson noted tartly that with regard to publicity, this was not one of the most conspicuous features of tribunals except in so far as it was conspicuous by its absence; this relates to publicity to potential applicants and to the publicity of actual proceedings – the two go hand in hand. There is the added difficulty here of the extreme complexity of some of the statutory schemes involved, and the likely difficulty the layman will have firstly with dealing with what he considers to be faceless, uninterested bureacracy in attempting to make a claim and generally the paperwork involved. In the latter respect the council on Tribunals has stresed that the wording of official forms and leaflets should be as clear and simple as possible, but the problem still remains. The Franks Committee itself stressed that the citizen should be both aware and understand his right to apply to a tribunal.

There is a further danger of a larger kind here: the system of tribunals as is known resists uniformity and simplicity – under new social legislation the line of least resistance will be to create a new tribunal rather than to reorganise in a systematic way. The result is naturally a maze of different jurisdictions which, for the citizen, is not only inconvenient but also perplexing. At the time of the Franks Report there was, it was felt, little scope for fundamental reorganisation or amalgamation. Subsequently there has been piecemeal rationalisation but the attractiveness of a complete system of tribunals increases when one considers the in-built, day to day, difficulties of accessibility.

(v) *Expertise*
The courts are, in the main, fundamentally generalist. An advantage, characteristic and task of a specialised tribunal on the other hand is its expertness. This is achieved by ensuring that the composition of the body consisted of persons who have special skills, knowledge or expertise of the matter in hand. Ideally, therefore, tribunals are the embodiment of expert adjudication.

It should be noted that expertise is a somewhat elastic notion and will vary from tribunal to tribunal; further the Franks Committee clearly felt that the term should include legal expertise, generally in the chairman. This will to some extent guarantee the objectivity of proceedings and perhaps the proper sifting of facts, but as regards the expertness of non-legal members the range of skills and knowledge will vary from tribunal to tribunal. More will be said about the composition of tribunals later.

(vi) *Flexibility*
The avowed flexibility of tribunals exists not only in the informal procedures they adopt, their more or less ready accessibility and speed, but more importantly in that they to some extent avoid the rigidity of precedent to be found in the regular courts. Tribunals, more often than not have been created because the change required had to be rapid and effective; a tribunal was unlikely, as Jackson says, to 'achieve the futility of saying that a conclusion is ridiculous and yet necessary because of the system of precedent'.

Yet it must be borne in mind that because of the present supervision of tribunals by the ordinary courts, all tribunals are, in principle, bound to follow precedents set by decisions of the ordinary courts. Similarly where there is an appellate tribunal it binds lower tribunals in its system. But the more important element is the arbitrary intrusion of the regular courts' 'law' into the so-called flexibility of tribunal activities. Writers have noted that some tribunals pay great devotion to judicial precedent.

The question has to be asked whether allowing the generalist normal courts to, in effect, dictate to specialists on 'questions of law,' which to a skilful lawyer could cover almost any aspect of an administrative scheme, ensures the flexible ascertainment of the objectives of an administrative scheme. Indeed, it has been strongly argued that the intrusion of the ordinary courts into what should be administrative adjudication is clearly harmful.

The characteristics of tribunals listed above are well known. It is recognised though that quick, simple, informal, cheap and flexible adjudication runs the risk of being arbitrary – the wise man under a palm tree could adjudicate in exactly this way. Thus an overriding task of tribunals was to be intrinsically *just* in their adjudications. As we have seen the Franks Report explicitly saw tribunals as 'machinery for adjudication' that is as essential components of the machinery of justice. Therefore (said Franks) the activities of tribunals had to be marked by 'openness, impartiality and fairness.' Recognising that secrecy would destroy confidence they stressed the publicity of proceedings and knowledge of the essential reasoning underlying decisions; similarly oppression could result from a party not being able to state his case, therefore they suggested procedures which would enable parties to know their rights, present their cases and know the case against them; finally, parties had to be satisfied that the body adjudicating had an open mind and in this respect the Report stressed especially the freedom of tribunals from Government Departments most concerned with the subject-matter.

In more detail, the Franks Report's recommendations suggest that a task to act 'justly' is not in essence different from a duty to act 'judicially.' One finds suggestions for public hearings, privilege for witnesses, legal representation, legal aid, the power to administer the oath, the power to subpoena witnesses and documents, the right to cross-examine directly, the publication of decisions and their circulation amongst tribunals and so on. Many of these separate ideas have been taken up and developed by the Council on Tribunals.

Now there are quite clearly safeguards of a fundamentally legal kind and their value is not in dispute. However, there would appear to be some tension between these clearly 'judicial' procedures and the essential worth of tribunals as cheap, flexible and fast dispensers of administrative justice. As stated, the Franks Committee was not concerned with a coherent concept of administrative justice, but it is suggested that a task to be 'just' is somewhat wider than the simple adoption of quasi-legal procedures. Franks expressly avoided any involvement in the policy behind particular administrative schemes – indeed many of the complaints the Council on Tribunals receive seem to relate to a rather wider concept of justice than simple 'judicialised procedures' – but their power to deal with general complaints are not very well defined. In the light of the terms of reference of the Franks Committee, namely to 'review the constitution and working of tribunals,' it would have been difficult to review the multiplicity of policies involved, but it seems a pity not to have at least mentioned that the operation of tribunals ought, at the end of the day, to promote the objectives of the scheme for which they were constituted, and to perhaps suggest ways in which this could be achieved. Within this context it is of some worth to make the following ancillary comments:

(a) *Tribunals' independence from Government Departments*

It has been argued that Departments and Ministers, and not 'Parliament,' will have been largely responsible for the drafting of the rules relating to the constitution, functions and operation of tribunals. To some extent the statements of the Council on Tribunals and the Franks stress on independence from Departments, however, is impossible if taken literally. What is possible, and indeed desirable, is that a Department should not attempt to influence a decision: of this there is no evidence.

What one cannot evade, it is suggested, is that tribunals are part of administrative schemes and to these schemes they have some responsibility. The Franks attempt at, and the Council of Tribunals stress on, the independence of tribunals, one cannot help but feel, is a rather charming attempt to approximate tribunals to ordinary courts of law. . . .

(c) *Procedure*

Finally in this regard, a word about tribunal procedures: as stated the impact of Franks was to apply 'judicial' principles to them. On the other hand the Report rejected the idea of a single code of procedure since flexibility would be jeopardised if this took place. However, each statutory tribunal had to have a definite procedure specified by statute or statutory instrument. Informality was to be retained but within an orderly procedure. The Council on Tribunals has a consultative role with regard to the making of Schedule 1 tribunals' rules of procedure and as we have seen this is largely handled by their Legal Committee. We have already seen that the vast majority of procedural recommendations by Franks have been followed and persisted in by the Council on Tribunals; of these we will undoubtedly approve for they guarantee a very basic procedural justice. One is left wondering, however, whether the Franks Committee was 'asked to look at already open, fair and impartial administrative procedures and asked to see if they could be made more so?'

Questions

1. What aspects of (a) the Franks Report, (b) the Tribunals and Inquiries Act, and (c) the work of the Council on Tribunals does Hendry consider promote the characteristics which make adjudication by tribunals preferable to adjudication by the courts?

2. Conversely, what aspects does he consider have the potential to undermine such characteristics?

3. Is there any indication in the extract of the changes which Hendry considers desirable?

Three particular issues concerning the desirable characteristics of tribunals have stimulated much debate: the method of appointment and qualifications of members, legal representation and legal aid, and rights of appeal.

(i) Appointment

See the Tribunal and Inquiries Act 1992, ss. 5 and 6 (*ante* at p. 709).

The Franks Committee had originally recommended that the Council on Tribunals should appoint the members of tribunals but this was not implemented. For the present role of the Council on Tribunals see s. 5 of the 1992 Act.

There are many different systems in operation for appointment of members. It is most common for tribunal members to be appointed by the relevant Minister, but there are other methods in operation, for example members of Social Security Appeal Tribunals are appointed from a panel drawn up by the President of the Social Security Appeal Tribunals.

The Franks Report had recommended, at para. 55, that chairmen of tribunals should ordinarily have legal qualifications, but that the appointment of persons without legal qualifications should not be ruled out when they are particularly suitable. The Council on Tribunals has in fact recommended that all chairmen of tribunals should normally be legally qualified, stating that its experience showed that proceedings did not tend to become more formal with a legally qualified chairman (*Annual Report for 1959*, para. 290).

Questions

1. In what ways, if at all, did the recommendations of the Franks Committee on appointment and membership seek to achieve what it perceived to be the desirable characteristics of tribunals, i.e. openness, fairness, and impartiality? Do you think that the fact that the recommendations were not wholly implemented has had any impact on the chances of achieving such objectives? Is this a cause for concern?

2. Does the method of appointment adopted for SSATs have any advantages as compared to appointment by Ministers or the Council on Tribunals (see further on the presidential system, *ante* at pp. 728–729)?

Note

Some of the issues raised by question 1 are addressed in the following extract.

K. H. Hendry, 'The Tasks of Tribunals: Some Thoughts'
(1982) 1 *Civil Justice Quarterly*, 253, 265–266

(b) *Method of appointment*

Linked to the issue of independence is the way in which members of tribunals are appointed. The Franks Committee, consistent with their conception of tribunals, felt that the to-be-created Council on Tribunals should appoint thereby reinforcing Tribunal independence. This was one of the few recommendations rejected by Parliament as such a situation, it was felt, would conflict with the responsibility of Ministers to Parliament. The inevitable compromise was that generally Ministers would continue to appoint but after consulation with the Council. The Tribunals and Inquiries Act specifies that the Council may make general recommendations in this regard and that the appropriate Minister 'shall have regard to these recommendations.' On the face of it this might appear a somewhat sinister rejection of an important recommendation but this is so only if our conception of tribunals is as only machinery of justice; seen as machinery for administration too, appointment by Ministers is unsurprising.

Furthermore Franks felt chairmen should, ordinarily, have legal qualifications which (they said) would guarantee objectivity and the proper sifting and finding of facts. The Council on Tribunals, as previously indicated, has been the most consistent advocate of this particular cause. The question is: are the undoubted qualities of lawyers, the only qualities required of the chairmen of tribunals? A legal qualification is no real guarantee of total understanding of a statutory scheme, or insight into the objectives of empowering legislation. Furthermore, the impact of lawyers (cold, inhuman, unsympathetic?) on individual applicants may well be counter-productive.

Similarly the impact on other members of the tribunal may be of an overbearing, aloof and superior individual. To some extent, this is a stereo-type lawyer but the essential point is this: a balance has to be struck between a variety of considerations in the appointment of chairmen; the focus on legal qualifications appears both conventional and superficial and may, in addition, be a barrier to informal justice. It is interesting to note here that there is no general legal requirement in the Tribunals and Inquiries Act for legally qualified chairmen. The Council on Tribunals has found that with regard to Supplementary Benefit Appeal Tribunals, where there has been a consistent campaign for legally qualified chairmen on the part of the Council on Tribunals, the role of members other than chairmen in coming to a decision has been minimal and that very often these members feel left out. One wonders whether the stress on legally qualified chairmen has contributed to this.

(ii) Legal representation and legal aid

The Franks Committee recommended that legal representation should be permitted except in exceptional circumstances. It further recommended that, in order to provide effective access to tribunals, legal aid should be extended at once to the more formal tribunals (such as the Lands Tribunal) and that further extensions of the legal aid scheme in the courts should be accompanied by an extension to all tribunals.

There have been a number of changes to the legal aid scheme since the publication of the Franks Report. The current position is that *legal advice and assistance* not extending to cover representation before the tribunal itself is available under 'the green form scheme'. In addition, in relation to proceedings before mental health review tribunals and in disciplinary hearings before the boards of visitors, legal representation is available under this scheme. *Legal aid,* which is the normal method of providing public funds to cover representation in proceedings, is only available in relation to the Commons Commissioners, the Lands Tribunal, and the Employment Appeal Tribunal. In its 24th Report the Lord Chancellor's Advisory Committee considered the arguments for and against an extension of legal aid for representation before tribunals.

Recommendations of the Lord Chancellor's Advisory Committee on Legal Aid

1973–74 (Twenty-fourth Report) HC 20 of 1974–75, paras 33, 35–41

Assistance and representation by lay organisations

33. A large body of assistance in tribunal cases is provided by lay organisations. In particular, there are the services of trades unions, ex-service organisations, Citizens' Advice Bureaux and other bodies. There are many types of case which are too complex for a lay client to handle but in which these organisations have built up their own skills and expertise. At the same time, most of these organisations would recognise that there are some cases where a lawyer is essential. There is a wide spectrum of need on the part of tribunal applicants, ranging from moral support and encouragement at one extreme to experienced legal advocacy on difficult issues of law on the other . . .

Legal aid for representation

35. Whatever arrangements are made for lay representation and assistance, there remains the question whether legal aid should be extended to cover representation by a solicitor or, where necessary, counsel in tribunal matters. We set out the arguments on either side.

36. *The arguments for extension*
The basic arguments for extending legal aid to tribunals are that many of those appearing before them are at a disadvantage in that they lack confidence and skill to make the best of their case, and because they find it hard to deal with the complex issues which can arise to a greater or lesser extent in all tribunals. This point was repeatedly made in evidence to us and in our view there can be no doubt of its validity. A more difficult question is to determine the form which the assistance should take and the machinery for selecting those cases where legally aided representation is needed.

37. *The arguments against extension*
The arguments which we received against extending legal aid fell broadly into two categories. The first comprised ones which suggested that legal aid was unnecessary, the second were ones maintaining that it would be positively undesirable. We need not take up much time in considering the first, since, once it is assumed that there will be effective selection machinery, few of the arguments appeared to us to raise any issues of difficulty . . . The only argument in this category which appeared to us to be of consequence was the suggestions that tribunals can be relied on to look after applicants' interests and to see that relevant facts are brought out. We know that many tribunal chairmen are experienced and conscientious in acting in this way but we do not consider that it is a satisfactory substitute for effective representation, particularly in cases where the other side is represented.

38. The arguments suggesting that it would be undesirable to extend legal aid to tribunals seemed to raise more serious issues of principle. The first, which was put forward by a number of witnesses, was that legal aid would lead to proceedings being formalised and the benefits of informality being lost . . . We agree there is a danger that some informality may be lost if, through the introduction of legal aid, representation by legally qualified persons becomes more common in tribunals, but we do not consider it would justify a refusal to extend legal aid. This would amount, in effect, to saying that representation is permissible provided it is restricted to those who are able to afford it. In our view, if legal aid has the effect suggested, the Government will have to consider whether the advantages of informality outweigh those of representation. If they do, the right course, we suggest, will be to ban legal representation altogether; what cannot be justifiable is to restrict its benefits to those wealthy enough to afford it for themselves.

39. Another objection put forward is that legal aid would lead to proceedings being lengthened and would cause delay. We think there is force in this. We have received evidence that solicitors and counsel find it difficult, because of their other commitments, to match the need for expedition to which many tribunals attach importance. Moreover, some of them tend to conduct the preliminary stage of proceedings before a tribunal in the same way as before a court. They are likely, for example, to seek further and better particulars and to take other interlocutory steps which are not well suited for the type of work with which tribunals normally deal. Here again, if the effect of extending legal aid is to introduce unacceptable delays in the bringing on of tribunal proceedings, the Government will have to consider alterations in the procedure of the tribunals affected. It may be, however, that as

solicitors become more accustomed to tribunal work, they will cease to take steps which are rarely suited to the type of case dealt with by tribunals.

40. The other main objection is that members of the legal profession are inexpert in tribunal work and are too hard-pressed to be able to deal with it. We think that the first part of this objection may often be valid; the work of some tribunals tends to be specialised and to need considerable expertise. . . . If your Lordship decides to extend legal aid to tribunals this is an aspect of the matter which we will need to keep under careful review.

41. Having taken all the evidence into account, we are satisfied that legal aid should be extended to all statutory tribunals at present within the supervision of the Council on Tribunals in which representation is permitted . . . We do not suggest any order of priority as between different tribunals since we consider that such an approach would be unsound. . .

Notes

1. While adhering to its view that legal aid ought to be available in all tribunals, the Advisory Committee has subsequently agreed to establishing priorities as between different tribunals. In its 27th Annual Report (1976–77) it indicated that industrial tribunals were among the most pressing candidates for some form of legal aid (para. 73), and in the 30th (1979–80) and 31st (1980–81) Annual Reports it identified Mental Health Review Tribunals as the tribunals for which an extension of legal aid was urgent. (Assistance by way of representation before Mental Health Review Tribunals is now available under the legal aid and advice scheme.) More recently, in its 33rd Annual Report, the Advisory Committee stated that priority should be given to bail applications to the Immigration Appellate Authorities, the Social Security Commissioners, and the Industrial Tribunals. The 35th Annual Report added Vaccine Damages Tribunals to the list of priorities.

2. The Government recently conducted a major review of the legal aid scheme, which eventually led to the enactment of the Legal Aid Act 1988. The White Paper which preceded the legislation stated:

> 30. The Government's policy on extensions of legal aid and assistance by way of representation to further tribunals was set out in its response to the Royal Commission on Legal Services. Extensions of assistance by way of representation and legal aid are made where it is shown to be necessary and resources allow . . .
>
> It is not clear that publicly funded representation is necessary for all tribunal proceedings. Another approach might be to simplify tribunal procedure wherever possible in order to render legal representation unnecessary. The Lord Chancellor's Department has recently commissioned research into the effectiveness of representation at tribunals. Against this background, the Government does not intend that there should be any general extension of publicly funded representation.

3. The effectiveness of representation at tribunals was the subject of a research paper by Hazel Genn and Yvette Genn. The report and the Council on Tribunals' response to it are discussed in the following extract.

Annual Report of the Council on Tribunals 1989/90

HC 64 of 1989–90, paras 1.35–1.50

Representation at tribunals - a strategy for the future

1.35 The evidence of the Genn Report on the Effectiveness of Representation at Tribunals has reinforced our long-held view that further measures are needed to aid such representation. We examine the implications of the Report and address the action which we believe should now be taken.

1.36 In our Annual Report for 1987/88 we set out at length our settled view that publicly funded advice and, where appropriate, representation should be available to those of modest means who appear before tribunals. We recorded our concern that the Legal Aid Act 1988 had made no explicit extension of legal aid for representation in this area, and expressed the view that it was unlikely that the Lord Chancellor's Department would reach decisions on publicly funded representation for tribunals until research being undertaken on their behalf by Hazel and Yvette Genn of London University was completed. That report has once again focused interest on this area, and we believe the importance of the issues raised justifies its reconsideration in depth.

The Genn Report

1.37 The research Report by Hazel and Yvette Genn entitled 'The Effectiveness of Representation at Tribunals' was published by the Department in July 1989. The broad objectives of the research had been to establish the effect of representation on the outcome of tribunal hearings and to analyse the contribution of representation to both pre-hearing processes and hearings themselves. It became evident to us, on a preliminary consideration, that the Report contained a great deal of important material and deserved the most careful consideration. The Report made out a strong case for extra funding of representation, and of lay agencies in particular, and before reaching any final assessment on it we took the opportunity to discuss both the research methodology and the Report's findings with Hazel Genn. Our views, which we record below, have been passed to the Lord Chancellor's Department and to the Legal Aid Board.

1.38 In our view there is nothing in the Report which would lead us to modify our long-held views on the need for extra funding of advice and representation. To the contrary, the evidence in the Report has added weight to those views, and demonstrated the need for a coherent strategy to be devised which will ensure that appropriate levels of advice, assistance and representation are made available where and when they are needed. We draw attention to a number of factors emerging both from the Report and from our discussion with Hazel Genn which, in our view, would have an important bearing on the shaping of the strategy required.

Type of representation

1.39 The Report provides incontrovertible evidence not only of the importance of representation at tribunals, but also of the need to ensure that the formality and complexity of certain tribunals is taken into account when deciding what level of representation should be appropriate. While it demonstrates the significant role of advice agencies in the tribunal field, and the effectiveness of specialist lay representation in some tribunals, it also emphasises that there are certain tribunals where the complexity of the law and the adversarial nature of the proceedings make skilled legal representation necessary. Such representation is also preferable to specialist lay representation in those cases before other tribunals which raise difficult legal issues.

1.40 These findings, in our view, support the case for extra funding of advice agencies in particular, and for a selective extension of legal aid. In this connection, we note that the Report reached no firm conclusions on the desirability of extending legal aid to tribunals. Instead, it put forward the idea of a 'government tribunal representation service', on the model of the United Kingdom Immigration Advisory Service. In our view, such a substantial body could present major difficulties in terms of its independence and funding; thus we are not yet persuaded that this is the most appropriate way forward. Our present view is that the means must be found to provide extra funding for advice agencies and to provide legal aid where and when it is needed. We agree with the Legal Aid Advisory Committee that 'questions relating to the extension of legal aid should be considered separately in relation to each tribunal'. We have therefore urged the Department to take steps at an early stage to identify those tribunals which would be appropriate to an extension of legal aid, preferably on the criteria we have previously advocated, and have offered our advice to assist in the process of identification.

1.41 We emphasise, however, that funding of this nature must be provided in a way which will take account of the qualitative issues addressed in the Report, and ensure that the substantial regional and geographical differences in the availability and scope of legal services are overcome.

Quality of representation

1.42 The evidence in the Report demonstrated that the chances of success at tribunal hearings were significantly affected by the fact of representation and by the quality of representatives coming before tribunals. We have noted in this connection the consistency of views expressed by tribunals concerning the contribution of good representation to hearings, and the general view that the quality of representation varies over a wide range. . . . These considerations raise important qualitative issues concerned with standards of performance and training to which we believe greater weight must be given in future.

Regional differences

1.43 We note with concern the significant regional differences in the provision and scope of legal services in the tribunal field which the Report revealed. We believe it is important to devise a scheme which will ensure that the respective roles of advice agencies, law centres, and private solicitors in the provision of advice and representation at tribunals are properly coordinated. There is no comprehensive overview of the provision of these services throughout the country . . . .

Relationship between advice and representation

1.44 We also note the emphasis which the Report placed on the value of good pre-hearing advice, on the effect that advice has on the way in which cases are ultimately decided, and on the relationship between advice and representation. In our view, the evidence demonstrates clearly that the components of advice and assistance on the one hand, and representation on the other, cannot be viewed as distinct alternatives, but must be regarded as complementary elements . . . .

The way forward

1.45 At paragraphs 2.60–2.75 of our Annual Report for 1987/88, we referred in some detail to the missed opportunities in the 1987 White Paper on Legal Aid and, later, in the Legal Aid Bill itself, to provide for publicly funded advice and representation for those of modest means appearing before tribunals. In the light of the evidence in the Genn Report, and the factors to which we had drawn the Department's attention, we have repeated our call for such provision to be made without delay, and for a coherent scheme to be devised which would ensure that appropriate levels of advice, assistance and representation are made available where and when they are needed. However, a general call for extra funding of this nature would not, of itself, be as persuasive as it might unless it recognises the need to ensure that the qualitative issues raised in the Report are properly addressed. We have therefore surveyed recent developments in order to suggest the way in which the strategy we advocate might best be carried forward.

1.46 The Efficiency Scrutiny of Legal Aid in 1986 recommended the making of more coordinated provision for tribunal representation by advice agencies, stating that a trained lay advocate should be competent to conduct cases, and that representation by a lawyer would rarely be necessary. The Government's response in the 1987 White Paper decided that power to enter into contracts for the exclusive provision of legal advice should be determined by a new Legal Aid Board. Before such provision was made, the Government would have to be satisfied that all areas of the country would be provided for in all types of work. It repeated the familiar formula that legal aid would be extended to tribunals when it was shown to be necessary and when resources allowed it.

1.47 As we recorded in our Annual Report for 1987/88 (paragraph 2.74), the Legal Aid Act made no explicit extension of legal aid for representation at tribunals. The Lord Chancellor explained in the second reading debate that the Legal Aid Board would have power to make contracts and grants to law centres. The powers would allow (the seven) law centres funded by the Board to undertake representation and to meet the cost from grants they received. If, at some stage in the future, publicly funded representation were to be extended to more tribunals, it might well be more convenient for the same agency that gave advice to provide representation. But there were at that stage no plans to extend legal aid to tribunals.

. . .

1.49 In the light of these developments and the proposals made by the Board, we have advised the Department that questions about the extension of legal aid to tribunals, and the funding of advice agencies and law centres, as recommended by the Genn Report, would in our view be wholly appropriate for consideration by the Legal Aid Board, as part of a wider consideration of legal aid in general. Many of the issues addressed in the Report – on the balance between specialist lay representation and the need for legal representation, on the need to ensure adequate geographical coverage, particularly in the rural areas, and on the need to ensure that the qualitative issues in the Report are properly addressed – are matters which the Board have been actively considering . . . .

1.50 We have therefore urged the Lord Chancellor's Department, in conjunction with the Legal Aid Board, to develop a scheme, in the context of a wider consideration by the Board of legal aid in general, for the provision of advice, assistance and representation at tribunals. If additional funding is shown to be necessary for that purpose, appropriate provision should be made for it. We have offered to provide further advice to the Department on any aspects of such a scheme as it is developed.

Note

Unsurprisingly the Legal Aid Act 1988 made no provision for further provision of public funds for representation before tribunals. The *JUSTICE-All Souls Report on Administrative Law* (1988) has endorsed the views of the Lord Chancellor's Advisory Committee (see pp. 249–51).

The Government has proposed more changes to Legal Aid.

Annual Report of the Council on Tribunals for 1994/95
HC 64 of 1995–96, paras. 1.14–22, 1.26–34

Green Paper: Legal Aid — Targeting Need

1.14 **The most recent statement of our support for publicly-funded advice, assistance and representation at tribunals can be found in our Annual Report for 1989/90 which recorded our reaction to the Genn Report on the 'Effectiveness of Representation at Tribunals'. We describe this year our response to certain connected proposals contained in the recent Green Paper entitled 'Legal Aid — Targeting Need'.**

The Green Paper

1.15 This consultation paper, which was published by the Lord Chancellor's Department in May 1995, described the role which legal aid would play in the Government's overall strategy for improving access to justice, and proposed radical changes to the way in which legal aid should in future be delivered. We had no legitimate basis for offering comments on the general framework under which it was proposed that publicly-funded legal services should in future be delivered, since much of this fell outside our remit. However, we took a close interest in that part of the Green Paper which put forward proposals for public-funding of work in the area of social welfare law, and invited views on whether this should include the funding of representation at those tribunals whose jurisdiction covers that category of work.

The main proposals

1.16 In summary, the Government's proposals envisaged that legal aid services should in future be delivered through the means of block contracts granted to suppliers of those services, to be paid for from an overall national and predetermined budget allocated to the main areas of business, eg. criminal, family and civil non-family work. Contracts would be awarded, possibly by the Regional Area Offices of the Legal Aid Board, to a supplier for the provision of legal services to clients for an agreed period and cost. The contracts would cover the type of services to be provided, the quality, volume and price. One result would be the end of the present arrangements whereby a person is entitled to legal aid merely by satisfying certain financial and merits criteria. In future legal aid, in all its forms, would be dependent upon the contract holder agreeing to take on the case having regard to his legal obligations with the Legal Aid Board. He would be contractually obliged to discourage poor or hopeless cases.

1.17 The proposals described how the national, pre-determined legal aid budgets, including that for civil non-family work, would be distributed among and within the Areas for England and Wales. It was from the civil non-family work budget that any funding of tribunal representation in social welfare law cases would come. The principal aim would be to allocate funds to the Area Offices in a way which took proper account of local needs. The Area Offices would allocate their budgets through the award of block contracts, the type, number and distribution of which would be determined by local needs. Area Offices would be advised on these matters by a network of Regional Committees modelled on the lines of the North Western Legal Services Committee. The Legal Aid Board, through its Area Offices would be required to ensure through block contracts that there was a comprehensive range of publicly-funded legal services that were easily accessible. There would be a diversity of suppliers and a diversity of services contracted for. We noticed here that the means being proposed for identifying local need broadly reflected the approach we had previously suggested in our 1989/90 Annual Report.

Social welfare law cases

1.18 As we have said, the proposals of most interest to us were those concerned with the provision of publicly-funded legal services in the area of social welfare law, in which context the Government sought views of whether legal aid should be more widely extended to tribunal representation. The term 'social welfare law' was defined for the purposes of the Paper as covering housing, employment, immigration, debt and welfare benefits. The contracts to be awarded in social welfare cases would be available to solicitors in private practice, to voluntary advice agencies which employ or use solicitors, and to non-solicitor advice agencies. They would cover work in three stages: (i) fact finding and initial diagnosis, (ii) advice and assistance, and (iii) representation or some other means of resolving disputes. Contracts awarded to non-solicitor agencies would be limited to the first two stages, that is, up to the giving of advice and assistance. Where the problem subsequently gave rise to court proceedings, the matter would be passed to a solicitor to handle the court work and to provide any necessary representation before the court.

1.19 However, the contracts to non-solicitor agencies might also permit representation before certain tribunals to be carried out by the agency concerned as part of the advice and assistance given at stage (ii). Contracts to solicitors, or to agencies employing or using them, would allow tribunal representation on the same basis. In this respect, the proposals were not dissimilar to the arrangements currently in place for funding representation at Mental Health Review Tribunals under the Green Form (Assistance By Way Of Representation) Scheme. However, representation would only be permitted if certain grant criteria were satisfied.

Our response

1.20 Our response covered a range of questions posed by the Green Paper about whether legal aid should be provided for tribunal representation and the mechanisms for achieving this. Our views and comments on each of those questions are summarised below.

Should legal aid be available for representation in non-court based proceedings including tribunals?

The case for tribunal representation

1.21 We were firmly of the view that it should. We welcomed the recognition given in the Paper to the importance of the research in this area conducted by Hazel and Yvette Genn, and reminded the Government of the main findings of the Genn Report, as recorded in detail in our 1989/90 Annual Report, and of their direct relevance to the issue in question. We emphasised that, in our extensive experience of the working of tribunals, the findings of that research remained wholly valid not solely in relation to the tribunals which were the subject of the research but across a broad range of other tribunals which fell within our supervisory jurisdiction. In support of that view, we explained that, in the course of our many visits to tribunal hearings across a wide spectrum of jurisdictions, we continue to come across major deficiencies in the provision of effective advice and representation, leading to examples of unmeritorious cases clogging the lists, of unnecessary and wasteful adjournments or delays because parties are poorly prepared or ill-equipped for the hearing and, most disturbingly apparent, of prejudice to the outcome through the absence of effective representation.

1.22 We therefore concluded in response to this first proposition that, if the major shortcomings identified by the Genn Report, and subsequently reinforced from our own experiences, were to be rectified, publicly-funded advice and, where appropriate, representation must be made available to those of modest means who appear before tribunals.

Could a pilot scheme address whether legal aid improved access to justice, efficiency and effectiveness, and did not lead to more elaborate and costly processes?

A pilot scheme

1.26 These are important issues on which we have commented in the past, and we believe it is right that they should be addressed. We therefore strongly supported the suggestion of a pilot scheme to test the effect of extending legal aid to tribunals under the proposed system of block contracts. We believe that we can make an effective contribution to any pilot study which is undertaken. Over the years we have developed a practical understanding of the shortcomings which give rise to problems in the area of tribunal representation, and we have substantial experience of the procedures and working of the seventy or so tribunal systems which fall within our supervision. We therefore suggested that the Government should consult us at an early stage on the pilot scheme, including the most effective means by which it might be carried forward. We offered to give advice on such matters and to assist those whose task it will be to carry the pilot project forward.

What areas of the law should be covered by the term 'social welfare'?

Too narrow a definition

1.27 The definition of 'social welfare law' suggested in the Green Paper clearly embraced the limited range of tribunals for whom we have previously regarded legal aid as a priority (see our Annual Report for 1987/88). But there have been considerable changes and developments since we last assessed priorities and, upon further examination, we were in no doubt that the Green Paper definition was too narrow. However, we did not dissent from the idea that, for all immediate and practical purposes, the pilot scheme should be applied to all 'social welfare' tribunals, and we provided the Government with a list of tribunals under our supervision which fall within the subject headings suggested in the Paper: namely, housing, employment, immigration, debt and welfare benefits.

1.28 However, our experience shows that there are many other areas of the law (for example, in the area of education and National Health Service appeals, as well as appeals concerning taxation in its various forms) where tribunal representation is of equal importance. Accordingly, we advised the Government that, if the pilot scheme proves successful in establishing the mechanism by which legal aid can be provided for tribunal representation, we will wish to return to the question whether or not representation under the new Scheme should be available across a much wider range of tribunals. We believe here that the pilot scheme will be important in testing whether the means can be established for ensuring that legal aid is available only in restricted cases, on the strict criteria we advocate below. Indeed, the individual tribunal systems involved in the pilot study will have a crucial role to play in advising whether the criteria operate in a way which includes the right type of case and excludes others.

What criteria should be satisfied before legal aid would be granted for representation before a tribunal?

Support for those outside the Scheme

1.29 In line with our previous views, we had no objection in principle to the proposal that legal aid for tribunal representation should be subject to a simple means test but free to those who qualify. However, we urged the Government to continue the current arrangements whereby legal aid for representation before Mental Health Review Tribunals is provided free and without a means test. We also expressed strong support for the view that those bodies which currently assist advice agencies with grants should see block contracts for legal aid work as an addition to, rather than a substitute for, the services provided by those agencies. It is vitally important, in our view, that the voluntary advice sector should continue to be in a position to assist those who fall outside the new Scheme. We therefore made clear that this must apply equally to the central funding given to such bodies as the Citizens Advice Bureaux and, in the area of immigration work, to the Refugee Legal Centre and the Immigration Appeals Advisory Service.

The criteria for eligibility

1.30 As to the criteria which might be adopted, we suggested that legal aid for tribunal representation might be appropriate in the following circumstances:

- where a significant point of law arises
- where the evidence is likely to be so complex or specialised that the average layman could reasonably wish for expert help in assembling and evaluation the evidence and in its testing and interpretation
- where a test case arises, or
- where deprivation of liberty or the ability of an individual to follow his or her occupation is at stake.

1.31 In our view, the application of such criteria would significantly curtail the number of cases in which a supplier of legal services is entitled to consider whether to provide tribunal representation. It is in that light that we emphasised to the Government that, once the results of the pilot scheme are known, we will want to review whether there is scope for extending the Scheme beyond the narrow definition of 'social welfare law' currently envisaged.

How could the Government ensure that relative informality in tribunals was retained, and that tribunals did not become lawyer dominated, if legal aid were available for professional representation?

Maintaining informality

1.32 Our own experience, which is supported by the findings of the Genn Report, is that specialist lay representatives from the voluntary advice sector already play a significant and effective role in the area of tribunal representation. But the evidence also shows that the formality and complexity of certain tribunals, including the industrial tribunals, favours lawyer rather than expert lay representation in certain difficult and complex cases. Tribunals will always strive to conduct their proceedings in an informal manner, but the complexity or the adversarial nature of certain cases may sometimes require a more formal approach. Accordingly, we pointed out that the ability to maintain informality in the conduct of proceedings must be a matter for the tribunals themselves, and is largely dependent on effective chairmanship and training, as well as the procedural rules governing their working. In this connection, we suggested that a principal task for the Legal Aid Board, perhaps as part of the pilot project, will be to look at the question of effective training of both legal and lay representatives to ensure proper standards of performance in this area.

Should those who have access to assistance at present, for example, through a trade union or pressure group, be eligible for legal aid?

Freedom of choice

1.33 Finally, although the Green Paper gave no indication of the Government's specific concerns in this area, we made clear our view that if an individual qualifies for legal aid he should be entitled to it in the normal way, irrespective of whether he is a member of a trade union or pressure group. There must be freedom of choice for the individual concerned to use a firm of solicitors or any other contracted supplier, or to use the legal services made available to him as a member of an organisation. Indeed, we could see no reason why the legal departments of such organisations should not be permitted to apply for a contract in line with other voluntary agencies.

Conclusion

1.34 **We broadly welcome the proposals in the Green Paper for testing whether the means can be established for extending legal aid to cover tribunal representation. In our view considerable thought will need to be given to the nature of the pilot project, and how it is to be carried out, if the proposals are to have any chance of success. We wait to learn whether the Government will consult us about the project and whether we will be called upon to assist those whose task it will be to take the project forward. We are not persuaded that legal aid for tribunal representation would be limited to social welfare law cases, and will review the scope for extending it further once the results of the pilot project are known.**

Note

The Government's White Paper on Legal Aid was due to be published when this book was *at press.*

H. Genn 'Tribunal Review of Administrative Decision-Making' in G. Richardson & H. Genn, (eds) *Administrative Law and Government Action* (1994), pp 284–6

This chapter has attempted to show that there are considerable limits to the effectiveness of tribunals as a check on administrative decision-making and that these limitations stem at least in part from the design of tribunals and the low levels of representation at tribunals. In order for tribunals to act as an *effective* means of review they must be capable of conducting an accurate and fair review of administrative decisions. This requires time, expertise, and full information. It also requires that those who appear before tribunals are capable of understanding the relevance of regulations and the basis of their entitlement, and can provide relevant information and evidence of facts, largely without the benefit of advice or representation.

Given the weakness of first-line administrative decision-making, tribunals theoretically represent an important means of minimizing administrative injustice. However, evidence collected from recipients of adverse administrative decisions, although not conclusive, suggests that even when a relatively straightforward mechanism exists for review of decisions the opportunity is not taken because those affected may assume that the original decision was 'correct' or that it is unlikely to be changed. Thus, even if tribunal hearings provided perfect conditions for effective review of administrative decisions, they could only every afford a partial corrective to poor decision-making and administrative injustice. In practice, however, from the perspective of tribunal applicants, the conditions that operate in many tribunals are far from perfect. Despite their conventional characterization as informal, accessible, and non-technical, frequently tribunals are not particularly quick, there is considerable variation in the degrees of informality, and the issues dealt with are highly complex in terms of both the regulations to be applied and the factual situations of applicants. This study of tribunal processes and decision-making has highlighted the complexity of many areas of law with which tribunals must deal and the impact of this complexity on decision-making. Although tribunal procedures are generally more flexible and straightforward than court hearings, the nature of tribunal adjudication means that those who appear before tribunals without representation are often at a disadvantage. The short-comings of tribunals as effective checks on administrative decisions are the result of misdescription of procedures as informal and misconceptions about simple decision-making and the scope for unrepresented applicants to prepare, present, and advocate convincing cases.

The analysis of factors influencing the outcome of tribunal hearings suggests that increased advice and representation for applicants, and improved training and monitoring of tribunals, would be likely to increase the rate at which cases reviewed at tribunal hearings were allowed. This may not, of course, be the desired objective. It has been argued that tribunals were never intended to act as 'effective review mechanisms' and that their primary role is to provide a cloak of legitimacy for unpopular social regulation. If, however, there is a genuine intention that tribunals should provide a check on administrative decision-making, rather than merely providing a forum in which disappointed and disgruntled applicants can let off steam, their deficiencies must be addressed. It is not sufficient to assume or to assert that tribunals operate well. In order to achieve their theoretical objectives and to attain the qualities claimed for tribunals, consideration must be given to their procedures and to standards of tribunal adjudication. Finally, and most importantly, explicit attention must be paid to the means by which a balance can be struck between the conflicting demands of procedural simplicity and legal precision, in order to achieve substantive justice.

Question

Are tribunals more a substitute for courts than an alternative to courts, and if so, what are the implications for the system of tribunals and their users?

(iii) Rights of appeal

See the Tribunals and Inquiries Act 1992, s. 11 (at p. 710 *ante*).

There is great diversity in the systems of appeals from tribunals. In some contexts, for example social security, employment, and immigration, there is a special appellate tribunal. In the case of social security and employment there is a further right of appeal to the Court of Appeal. (Despite repeated recommendations to the contrary from the Council on Tribunals there is still no right of appeal from the decisions of the Immigration Appeal Tribunal.) In others there is an appeal from a tribunal on a point of law to the High Court under s. 11 of the Tribunals and Inquiries Act 1992. Where there is no appeal procedure the only way to challenge a decision is to seek judicial review (see, for example, the Betting Levy Appeal Tribunal).

The Franks Committee recommended that there should be a general right of appeal on matters of fact, law or merits from the decision of a tribunal to an appellate tribunal except where the tribunal of first instance is so exceptionally strong and well qualified that an appellate tribunal would be no better qualified to review its decision (para. 105). It also recommended that, with some exceptions, there should be a general appeal on a point of law to the courts.

In the extract below Hendry challenges the view that rights of appeal and judicial review are advantageous in the system of tribunals.

K. H. Hendry, 'The Tasks of Tribunals: Some Thoughts'
(1982) 1 *Civil Justice Quarterly*, 253, 266–268

Tribunals and the Courts

One more task of tribunals needs mention and in many ways it brings the gist of the above into focus: that task is to lighten the load of the ordinary courts. To put it negatively and perhaps more accurately, a purpose of the creation of Tribunals was expressly to avoid 'judicial justice.' The 1970/71 Holdsworth Club Presidential Address by Lord Hailsham expressed the view that the 'public' (*sic*) felt that many new questions were simply not for decision by the ordinary courts. The reason, says Lord Hailsham, was an inherent distrust of trial by judge alone as a method of deciding questions of fact or mixed question of fact and law. As a purely theoretical proposition in constitutional law, Hailsham condemned the proliferation of ad hoc tribunals as unhealthy; why could many of these cases, he asks, not be referred to the existing network of county courts? We return thus once again to the question of how we should view tribunals. Are they machinery of adjudication as Franks said they were? Are they machinery for administration? The answer is probably in shades of grey rather than black or white; they are machinery of adjudication within administration. The effect of Franks and the continuing work of the Council on Tribunals has been to hide the hybrid nature of tribunals; accordingly administrative lawyers have evaluated the performance and role of tribunals with normal judicial processes in mind.

Related to this and of the utmost importance are the powers of review and appeal that the ordinary courts have over the activities of tribunals. The real task of tribunals as presently constituted is to provide, cheap, informal, expert and speedy administrative justice. It must, therefore, be asked whether in the quest for judicialisation of administrative justice, the leap, by means of review or appeal, to judicial justice will, in certain cases, totally defeat the acknowledged virtues of adjudication by tribunals. This is a problem to be seen in terms of finality: the Tribunals and Inquiries Act provides that if a party before certain Schedule 1 Tribunals is dissatisfied with the outcome, he may appeal to the High Court, or require the tribunal to state a case for resolution by the High Court. Furthermore the Act seeks to preserve the venerable orders of certiorari and mandamus as methods of review. What is clearly implicit is the assumption that ordinary courts and legal profession are able to deal satisfactorily with the subject-matter involved. The most recent example of this perhaps misplaced trust is the Social Security Act 1980 which gives a right of appeal, with leave, on a question of law from a National Insurance Commissioner direct to the Court of Appeal which, with respect, is not unlike fitting a penny-farthing with an overhead camshaft and twin exhausts! What is glaringly ignored in all of this is that tribunals were set up to infuse certain decisions with policy factors which the courts by definition are ill-equipped to deal with.

It could, of course, be argued that review and appeal by the courts is a potentially important way of introducing order into administrative systems dominated by ad-hocery. Experience, unfortunately, has in many instances demonstrated the opposite. As Prosser has argued, the relationship between the courts and administration is a very complex one and that the intrusion of purely legal principles in administrative schemes could create chaos. Moreover, the 'test-case strategy' may be of little effect particularly where administrative pratices, irrespective of the legal norms laid down by the courts, have basic governmental support. Prosser feels that whether or not a case has an effect will depend more upon traditional political forces at play in society and that the application of norms of judicial review are a relatively subordinate part of that process.

Furthermore, it is pre-eminently clear that the advantages of tribunals could be destroyed by the expense, complexity, lack of expertise and delay of the normal judicial process. Proposals for a more self-contained system of administrative justice such as Professor Robson's proposal for an Administrative Appeal Tribunal with a wide jurisdiction, not only to hear appeal from tribunals but also cases where a public authority prima facie appears to have acted in an unduly harsh, unjust or improper manner – or even Sir Carlton Allen's proposal for an Administrative Division of the High Court – have been given short shrift, primarily by the Franks Committee and ever since.

Question

Social security appeals are now heard by social security appeal tribunals, and there is an appeal therefrom to the social security commissioners and a further appeal to the Court of Appeal. Presumably this organisational change would not alter Hendry's criticism that the right of appeal to the Court of Appeal is rather like fitting a penny-farthing with an overhead camshaft and twin exhausts. What alternatives might there be to this?

(D) A GENERAL ADMINISTRATIVE TRIBUNAL

As has already been noted, concern has been expressed about the proliferation of tribunals. The Council on Tribunals has objected where the establishment of a new tribunal seemed in its view to be unnecessary and recommended the amalgamation of existing tribunals (e.g. the formation of social security appeal tribunals from national insurance local tribunals and supplementary benefit appeal tribunals). The presidential system has also been advocated as a means of achieving rationalisation. More sweeping reforms have from time to time been suggested, such as the formation of a general administrative appeals tribunal. This proposal was considered by the *JUSTICE-All Souls Report on Administrative Law* (1988). The background to the discussion includes the formation in Australia of the Administrative Appeals Tribunal (AAT), which has express power to review the merits of certain specified statutory decisions.

> 9.77 We have considered whether there should be a single appeal tribunal similar to the AAT in place of the multitude of tribunals which exist at present. . . . The most serious objection remains the problem of scale. For this reason we think it would not be sensible to dispense with the network of specialized tribunals and to replace them with a single administrative appeal tribunal. We do not consider that the adoption of such a system here would be either practicable, having regard to the much larger volume of business undertaken by tribunals in this country compared

with that of the AAT, or productive when the gain is balanced against the disruption that such a change would cause initially. In our view effort should be directed towards the improvement of existing institutions in this field rather than their wholesale replacement. Improvement of the United Kingdom system is more likely to be achieved by the amalgamation, where appropriate, of existing tribunals as discussed in paragraph 9.72, and the extension of their jurisdiction.

9.78. But there remains the area of administrative decision-making from which there is no appeal on the merits. We think the first task is to ascertain the extent of this problem. We recommend that this inquiry should be one of the first tasks to be undertaken by the Administrative Review Commission, the establishment of which we recommended in chapter 4. We envisage that when the extent of the problem is ascertained, it can then be decided whether to provide an appeal on the merits in this area by further specialised tribunals or whether one general appeal tribunal would be better.

Note

The reference to the Administrative Review Commission is explained by the fact that the *JUSTICE-All Souls Report* also recommended the establishment of an Administrative Review Commission, which would be independent of government and have the tasks of commenting on pending legislation, proposing reforms, and drawing attention to deficiencies in the law pertaining to the administration. It considered that the Council on Tribunals should remain in existence alongside this new body to perform its specialist role in relation to the day-to-day operation of tribunals under its surveillance. See also Birkinshaw and Lewis *When Citizens Complain* (1993) for similar reform proposals.

Questions

1. Do you agree with the *JUSTICE-All Souls Report's* rejection of the proposal for a single administrative appeal tribunal? Would it none the less be beneficial to have a single appeal tribunal to hear all appeals from the different specialised tribunals?

2. If the proposal for an Administrative Review Commission was implemented, do you think the tasks of the Council on Tribunals would change? Would such change be in the direction favoured by the Council on Tribunals in its report (see *ante* at p. 717)?

INDEX